TEACHER'S EDITION

GRADE 11

Program Consultants:

Kylene Beers

Martha Hougen

Elena Izquierdo

Carol Jago

Erik Palmer

Robert E. Probst

Front Cover Photo Credits: (outer ring): © Magdalena Kowalik/Shutterstock, (bottom inset): ©Joseph Sohm-Visions of America/Digital Vision/Getty Images, (inner ring): ©Creative Travel Projects/Shutterstock, (c) ©Carrie Garcia/Houghton Mifflin Harcourt, (c overlay): ©Eyewire/Getty Images, (bc overlay): ©elenamiv/Shutterstock

Back Cover Photo Credits: (Units 1-6): ©Diana Ong/Getty Images; ©Roy Scott/Getty Images; ©CliquePhoto/Moment/Getty Images; © Sherry Lachelle Photography; ©Library of Congress/Corbis/VCG via Getty Images; ©Veronika By/Shutterstock

Printed in the U.S.A.

ISBN 978-1-328-47489-6

2 3 4 5 6 7 8 9 10 0690 27 26 25 24 23 22 21 20 19

4500752975   B C D E F G

Teacher's Edition Table of Contents

Program Consultants T2

Into Literature Overview T4

Data-Driven Differentiation and Assessment T14

Foster a Learning Culture T18

Build a Culture of Professional Growth T20

Annotated Student Edition Table of Contents T22

HMH *Into Literature* Dashboard T40

HMH *Into Literature* Studios T42

Featured Essays
    Notice & Note T44
    Reading and Writing Across Genres T58

Unit 1 1

Unit 2 94

Unit 3 204

Unit 4 324

Unit 5 452

Unit 6 568

Student Resources R1

into Literature

PROGRAM CONSULTANTS

Kylene Beers

Nationally known lecturer and author on reading and literacy; coauthor with Robert Probst of *Disrupting Thinking, Notice & Note: Strategies for Close Reading,* and *Reading Nonfiction;* former president of the National Council of Teachers of English. Dr. Beers is the author of *When Kids Can't Read: What Teachers Can Do* and coeditor of *Adolescent Literacy: Turning Promise into Practice,* as well as articles in the *Journal of Adolescent and Adult Literacy.* Former editor of *Voices from the Middle,* she is the 2001 recipient of NCTE's Richard W. Halle Award, given for outstanding contributions to middle school literacy. She recently served as Senior Reading Researcher at the Comer School Development Program at Yale University as well as Senior Reading Advisor to Secondary Schools for the Reading and Writing Project at Teachers College.

Martha Hougen

National consultant, presenter, researcher, and author. Areas of expertise include differentiating instruction for students with learning difficulties, including those with learning disabilities and dyslexia; and teacher and leader preparation improvement. Dr. Hougen has taught at the middle school through graduate levels. In addition to peer-reviewed articles, curricular documents, and presentations, Dr. Hougen has published two college textbooks: *The Fundamentals of Literacy Instruction and Assessment Pre-K–6* (2012) and *The Fundamentals of Literacy Instruction and Assessment 6–12* (2014). Dr. Hougen has supported Educator Preparation Program reforms while working at the Meadows Center for Preventing Educational Risk at The University of Texas at Austin and at the CEEDAR Center, University of Florida.

Elena Izquierdo

Nationally recognized teacher educator and advocate for English language learners. Dr. Izquierdo is a linguist by training, with a Ph.D. in Applied Linguistics and Bilingual Education from Georgetown University. She has served on various state and national boards working to close the achievement gaps for bilingual students and English language learners. Dr. Izquierdo is a member of the Hispanic Leadership Council, which supports Hispanic students and educators at both the state and federal levels. She served as Vice President on the Executive Board of the National Association of Bilingual Education and as Publications and Professional Development Chair.

Carol Jago

Teacher of English with 32 years of experience at Santa Monica High School in California; author and nationally known lecturer; former president of the National Council of Teachers of English. Ms. Jago currently serves as Associate Director of the California Reading and Literature Project at UCLA. With expertise in standards assessment and secondary education, Ms. Jago is the author of numerous books on education, including *With Rigor for All* and *Papers, Papers, Papers*, and is active with the California Association of Teachers of English, editing its scholarly journal *California English* since 1996. Ms. Jago also served on the planning committee for the 2009 NAEP Reading Framework and the 2011 NAEP Writing Framework.

Erik Palmer

Veteran teacher and education consultant based in Denver, Colorado. Author of *Well Spoken: Teaching Speaking to All Students* and *Digitally Speaking: How to Improve Student Presentations with Technology*. His areas of focus include improving oral communication, promoting technology in classroom presentations, and updating instruction through the use of digital tools. He holds a bachelor's degree from Oberlin College and a master's degree in curriculum and instruction from the University of Colorado.

Robert E. Probst

Nationally respected authority on the teaching of literature; Professor Emeritus of English Education at Georgia State University. Dr. Probst's publications include numerous articles in *English Journal* and *Voices from the Middle*, as well as professional texts including (as coeditor) *Adolescent Literacy: Turning Promise into Practice* and (as coauthor with Kylene Beers) *Disrupting Thinking, Notice & Note: Strategies for Close Reading,* and *Reading Nonfiction*. He regularly speaks at national and international conventions including those of the International Literacy Association, the National Council of Teachers of English, the Association for Supervision and Curriculum Development, and the National Association of Secondary School Principals. He has served NCTE in various leadership roles, including the Conference on English Leadership Board of Directors, the Commission on Reading, and column editor of the NCTE journal *Voices from the Middle*. He is also the 2004 recipient of the CEL Exemplary Leadership Award.

Lead and Learn

Students who communicate...

- **Listen** actively
  - **Present** effectively
    - **Expand** vocabulary
      - **Question** appropriately
        - **Engage** constructively

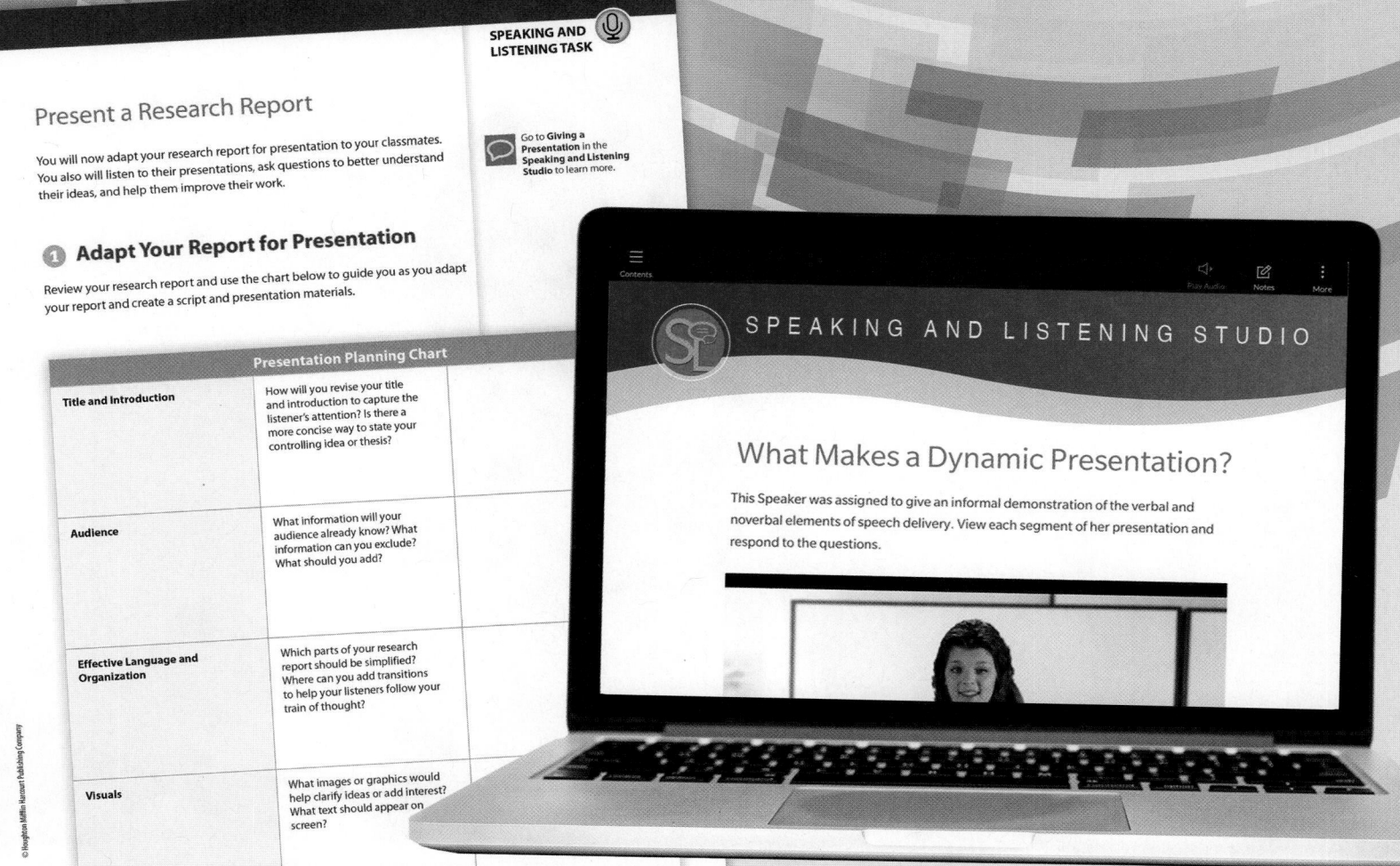

Present a Research Report

You will now adapt your research report for presentation to your classmates. You also will listen to their presentations, ask questions to better understand their ideas, and help them improve their work.

SPEAKING AND LISTENING TASK

Go to **Giving a Presentation** in the **Speaking and Listening Studio** to learn more.

1 Adapt Your Report for Presentation

Review your research report and use the chart below to guide you as you adapt your report and create a script and presentation materials.

Presentation Planning Chart

Title and Introduction	How will you revise your title and introduction to capture the listener's attention? Is there a more concise way to state your controlling idea or thesis?
Audience	What information will your audience already know? What information can you exclude? What should you add?
Effective Language and Organization	Which parts of your research report should be simplified? Where can you add transitions to help your listeners follow your train of thought?
Visuals	What images or graphics would help clarify ideas or add interest? What text should appear on screen?

Present a Research Report 201

SPEAKING AND LISTENING STUDIO

What Makes a Dynamic Presentation?

This Speaker was assigned to give an informal demonstration of the verbal and noverbal elements of speech delivery. View each segment of her presentation and respond to the questions.

Question and Respond

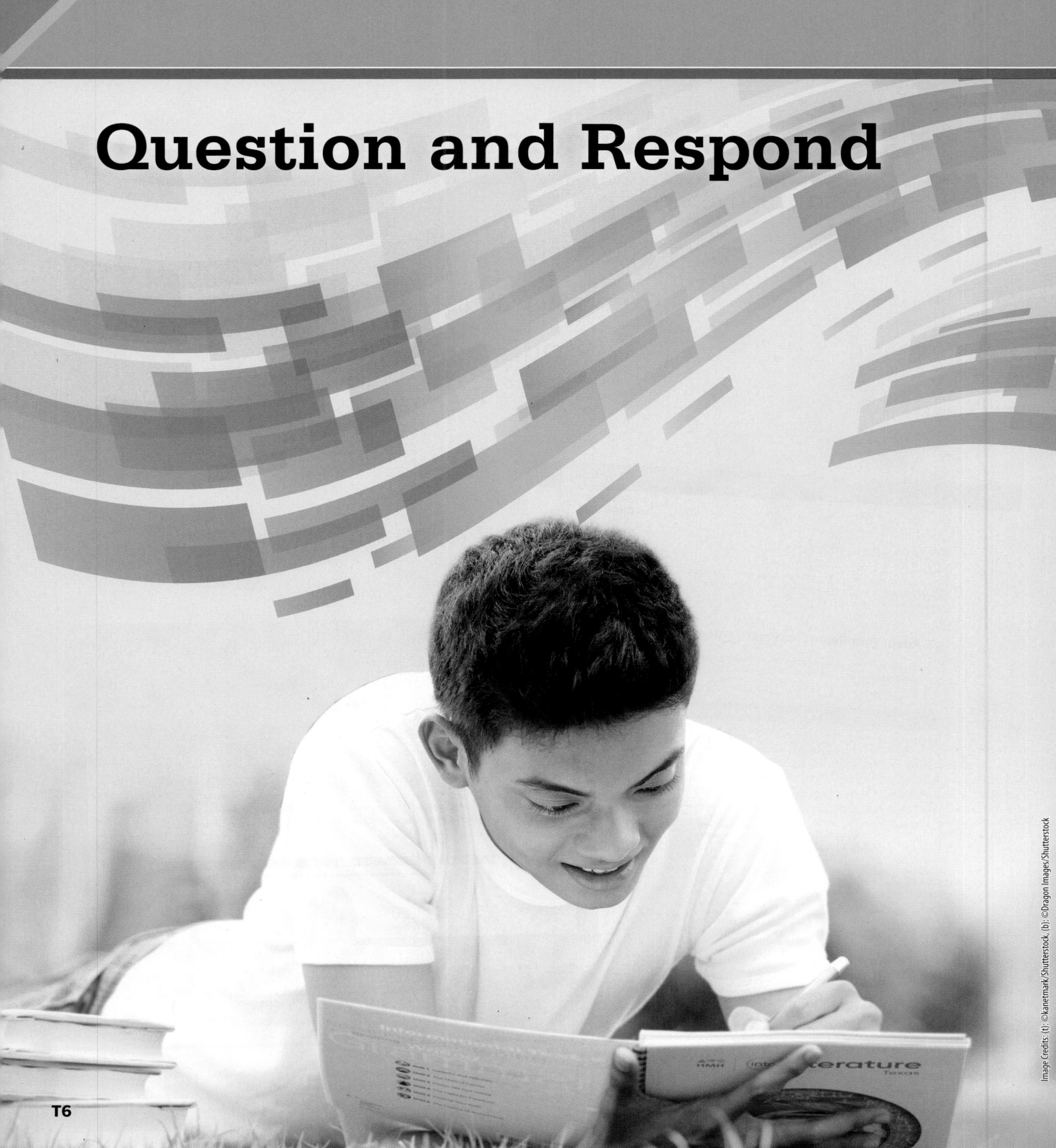

Students who read…

- **Acquire** fluency
- **Choose** independently
- **Monitor** understanding
- **Annotate** and use evidence
- **Write** and discuss within and across texts

ANNOTATION MODEL

As you read, note how the author compares Hamilton and Jefferson and uses time order words to tell you the sequence of events. In the model, you can see one reader's notes about Chernow's article.

On March 21, 1790, Thomas Jefferson belatedly arrived in New York City to assume his duties as the first Secretary of State after a five-year ministerial stint in Paris. Tall and lanky, with a freckled complexion and auburn hair, Jefferson, 46, was taken aback by the adulation being heaped upon the new Treasury Secretary, Alexander Hamilton, who had streaked to prominence in his absence. Few people knew that Jefferson had authored the Declaration of Independence, ... Instead, the Virginian was eclipsed by the 35-year-old wunderkind from the Caribbean. . . .

author includes time references to events he will describe

compares age, accomplishments, background

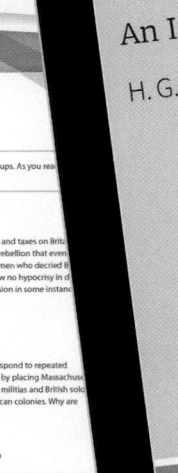

HMH DIGITAL LIBRARY

The Time Machine
An Invention

H. G. Wells

UNIT 2

BUILDING A DEMOCRACY
THE REVOLUTIONARY PERIOD

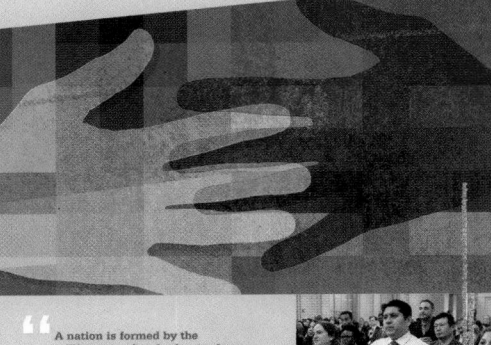

> A nation is formed by the willingness of each of us to share the responsibility for upholding the common good.
>
> —Barbara Jordan

Discuss the **Essential Questions** with your whole class or in small groups. As you read a Democracy, consider how the selections explore these questions.

? ESSENTIAL QUESTION:
What does oppression look like?

Between 1763 and 1775 Parliament imposed a number of regulations and taxes on Britain American colonies. The colonists reacted with pamphlets and acts of rebellion that even led to a declaration of independence and war. Ironically, many of the men who decided fi oppression were themselves slaveholders. Even those who weren't saw no hypocrisy in d women the same rights as men. Why might someone identify oppression in some instanc yet be blind to it in others?

? ESSENTIAL QUESTION:
How do we gain our freedom?

It is often necessary to fight to gain freedom. When Britain failed to respond to repeated requests from the colonists, their protests escalated. Britain retaliated by placing Massachuse under the direct control of a military governor. Clashes between local militias and British sol became a war for independence that involved all 13 of Britain's American colonies. Why are people motivated to risk everything for freedom?

? ESSENTIAL QUESTION:
How can we share power and build alliances?

After gaining independence from England, the 13 former colonies had to come up with a plan for the future. They knew that they stood a better chance if they could work together, but how? Their first attempt at unification failed because the states did not want to relinquish any authority to a central government. The Constitution, however, provided a balance of power between federal and state governments. How does sharing power make partners stronger?

? ESSENTIAL QUESTION:
How do we transform our lives?

Americans had to make the transition from colonists to citizens of a new nation, one that was an experiment in democracy founded on Enlightenment ideals. Generation after generation, Americans have reinvented themselves as they confronted new opportunities and challenges. For more than two centuries, people from many lands have arrived with new customs and ideas. How does this experience change their lives and the lives of those they encounter?

Connect
Reading and Writing

ANALYZE & APPLY

GENRE:
Short Story

A SOLDIER FOR THE CROWN

Short story by **Charles Johnson**

? ESSENTIAL QUESTION:

How do we gain our freedom?

130 Unit 2

ANALYZE & APPLY

GENRE:
History Writing

THOMAS JEFFERSON: THE BEST OF ENEMIES

History Writing by **Ron Chernow**

? ESSENTIAL QUESTION:

How can we share power and build alliances?

Students who explore genre...

- **Analyze** features

- **Understand** effects of authors' choices

- **Emulate** craft

- **Use** mentor texts

- **Synthesize** ideas

**GENRE ELEMENTS:
HISTORY WRITING**

- presents information about historical events or persons

- includes facts, dates, and information, presented in chronological order

- may employ literary devices to emphasize details and increase engagement

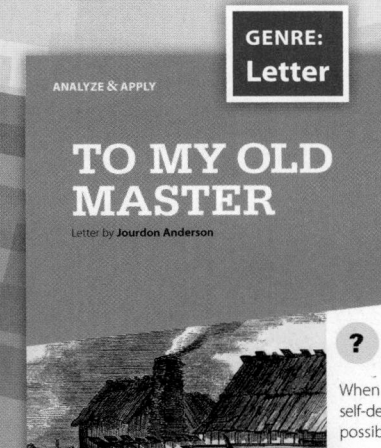

ANALYZE & APPLY

**GENRE:
Letter**

TO MY OLD MASTER

Letter by **Jourdon Anderson**

? ESSENTIAL QUESTION:

When is self-determination possible?

WRITING STUDIO

Ways to Organize Reasons and Evidence

Every argument must include reasons and evidence to support a claim. There are several effective ways you can organize that support. Check out some of those ways here.

Read the following techniques that will help you achieve cohesion, or coherence, in your writing.

Order of Importance

Least to most important

Claim: Homewood must switch from a volunteer fire department to a full-time fire department

Craft and Communicate

Students who compose...

- **Inform,** argue, and connect
- **Create** in a literary genre
- **Imitate** mentor texts
- **Apply** conventions
- **Use** process and partners

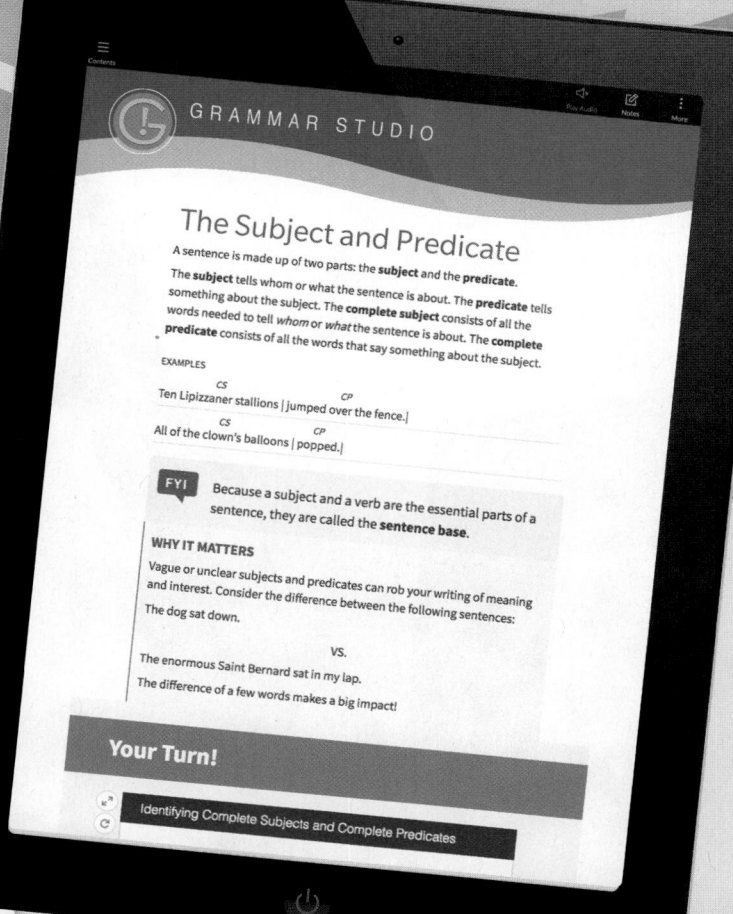

WRITING TASK

Write a Literary Analysis

Go to the **Writing Studio** for help writing a literary analysis.

In this unit, you have read works about early explorations in America. Andrés Reséndez based his article "A Desperate Trek Across America" on Álvar Núñez Cabeza de Vaca's *La relación,* a first-hand account of the ill-fated Spanish expedition to Florida beginning in 1528. Although Reséndez's narrative article on Cabeza de Vaca's account is not a formal analysis, he uses several techniques which you can apply to the literary analysis you are going to create for your next writing task.

As you write your literary analysis, you can use the notes from your [...] after reading the texts in this unit.

FOUNDATIONS AND ENCOUNTERS

This is the conte[...] for your literary analysis.

How might th[...] Essential Ques[...] relate to other[...] literary select[...] you have read[...]

Think about[...] selections an[...] possible con[...] to the theme[...] you make yo[...] choice.

Review the[...] you write an[...] when you f[...] any needed[...]

84   Unit 1

WRITING TASK

A DESPERATE TREK ACROSS AMERICA

Use the Mentor Text

Making a Claim or Thesis Statement
A literary analysis will always contain a claim or thesis statement, usually near the beginning of your essay. The following paragraph from Reséndez's article "A Desperate Trek Across America" contains a thesis statement. Reséndez had already described the adventurers' plight and their initial attempt at survival. They have eaten their horses and used their firearms to build rafts. In the passage below, notice how Reséndez contrasts their previous sense of confidence with their current state.

> Like past conquistadors, Cabeza de Vaca and his men had relied on their breastplates, horses, and lethal weapons to keep the Indians at bay. Such overwhelming technological advantages meant they often did not even bother to negotiate. . . . By sacrificing the very tools of their supremacy, they would now have to face the New World fully exposed to its perils and hold on only by their wits.

The last sentence expresses the overall perspective of his article— it is similar to a thesis.

The rest of the author's article shows their struggle to survive only by their wits.

Apply What You've Learned After you've chosen the selection, the topic, and the point you want to make, begin your analysis with a clear thesis statement or claim. Tell your reader which selection you are writing about and what claim you are making. What interesting insight will you be conveying to your reader?

Offering Details and Evidence from the Text
When you analyze a literary selection, it is important to offer specific details and evidence from the text in order to support your thesis. Like Reséndez, you can use direct quotations to strengthen your thesis.

> Fifty men crowded aboard each craft, the fifth commanded by Cabeza de Vaca. "And so greatly can necessity prevail," he observed, "that it made us risk going in this manner and placing ourselves in a sea so treacherous, and without any one of us who went having any knowledge of the art of navigation."

Notice that Reséndez directly quotes Cabeza de Vaca to support his idea that the Spaniards were surviving on their wits alone.

Apply What You've Learned When you are giving reasons for your claim, be sure to offer details that will help convince your reader of your point. Try to cite direct evidence from the text whenever you make a main point. Use multiple pieces of evidence when possible.

Write a Literary Analysis   87

GRAMMAR STUDIO

Contents

The Subject and Predicate
A sentence is made up of two parts: the **subject** and the **predicate**. The **subject** tells whom or what the sentence is about. The **predicate** tells something about the subject. The **complete subject** consists of all the words needed to tell *whom* or *what* the sentence is about. The **complete predicate** consists of all the words that say something about the subject.

EXAMPLES

CS   CP
Ten Lipizzaner stallions | jumped over the fence. |

CS   CP
All of the clown's balloons | popped. |

FYI Because a subject and a verb are the essential parts of a sentence, they are called the **sentence base**.

WHY IT MATTERS

Vague or unclear subjects and predicates can rob your writing of meaning and interest. Consider the difference between the following sentences:

The dog sat down.

VS.

The enormous Saint Bernard sat in my lap.

The difference of a few words makes a big impact!

Your Turn!

Identifying Complete Subjects and Complete Predicates

Explore and Research

Image Credit: (t) ©kcanetmark/Shutterstock; (b) ©Tyler Olson/Shutterstock

Students who inquire...

- **Generate** questions
- **Plan** and revise
- **Synthesize** information
- **Cite** sources
- **Deliver** results

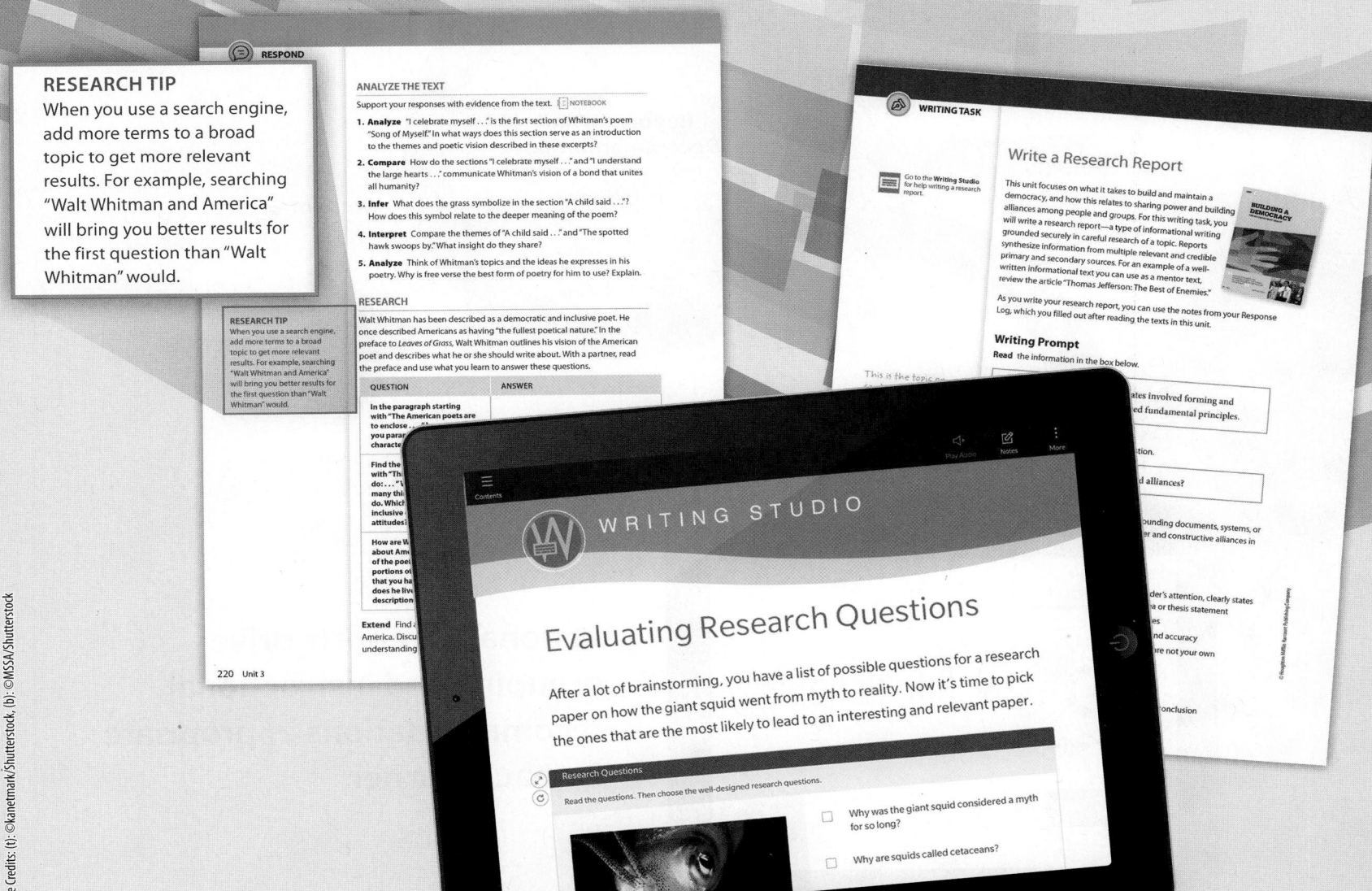

RESEARCH TIP

When you use a search engine, add more terms to a broad topic to get more relevant results. For example, searching "Walt Whitman and America" will bring you better results for the first question than "Walt Whitman" would.

Maximize Growth through Data-Driven Differentiation and Assessment

Ongoing assessment and data reporting provide critical feedback loops to teachers and students, so that each experience encourages self-assessment and reflection, and drives positive learning outcomes for all students.

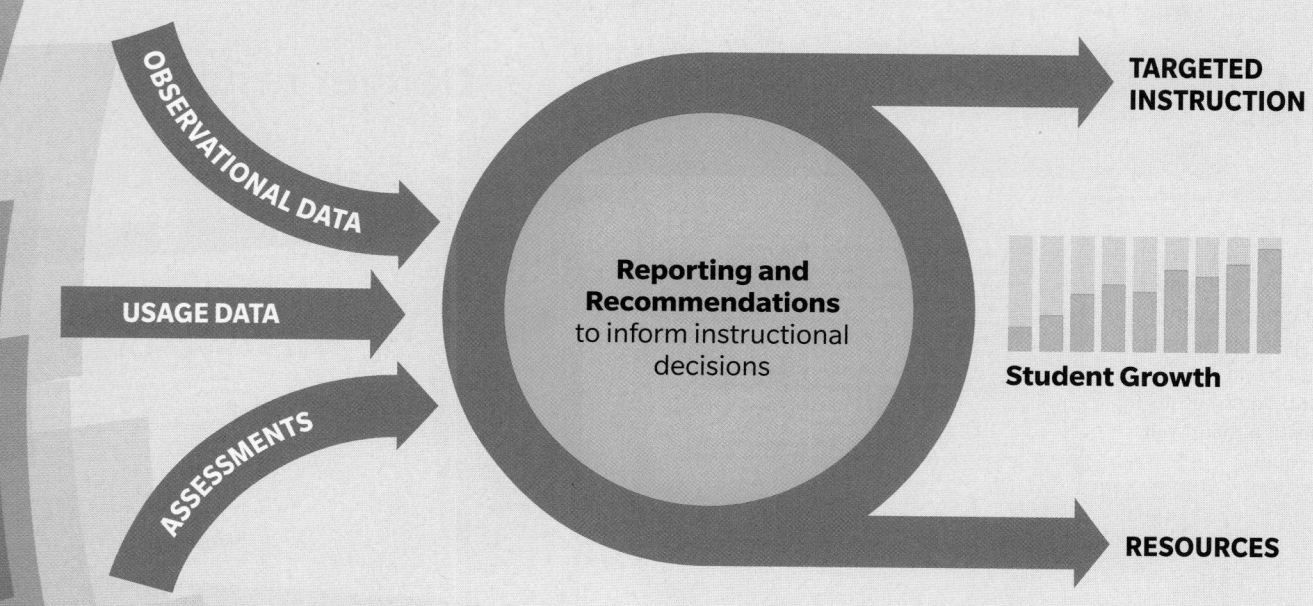

OBSERVATIONAL DATA

USAGE DATA

ASSESSMENTS

Reporting and Recommendations
to inform instructional decisions

TARGETED INSTRUCTION

Student Growth

RESOURCES

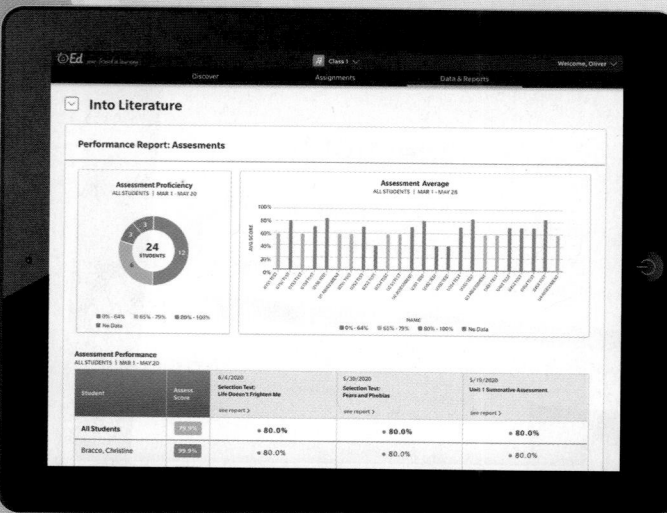

Actionable reports drive grouping and instructional recommendations appropriate for each learner.

Program Assessments

Adaptive Growth Measure

3 times per year

Adaptive Growth Measure allows teachers to gain an understanding of where students are on the learning continuum and identify students in need of intervention or enrichment.

Unit Assessments

6 times per year

Unit Assessments identify mastery of skills covered during the course of the unit across all literacy strands.

Ongoing Feedback from Daily Classroom Activities

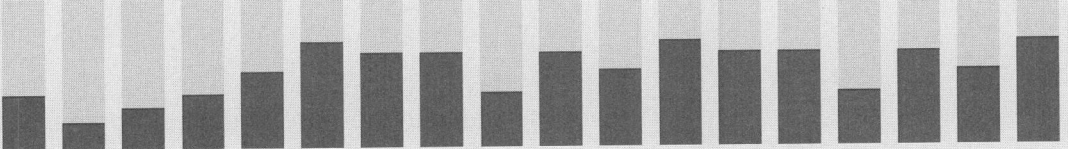

Formative Assessment data is collected across a variety of student activities to help teachers make informed instructional decisions based on data.

- Check Your Understanding
- Selection Tests
- Writing Tasks
- Independent Reading

- Usage Data
- Online Essay Scoring
- Teacher Observations
- Research Projects

Assessments

HMH Into Literature *has a comprehensive suite of assessments to help you determine what students already know and how they are progressing through the program lessons.*

Diagnostic Assessment for Reading

is an informal, criterion-referenced assessment designed to diagnose the specific reading comprehension skills that need attention.

Skills-based Diagnostic Assessments will help you quickly

gauge a student's mastery of common, grade-level appropriate skills.

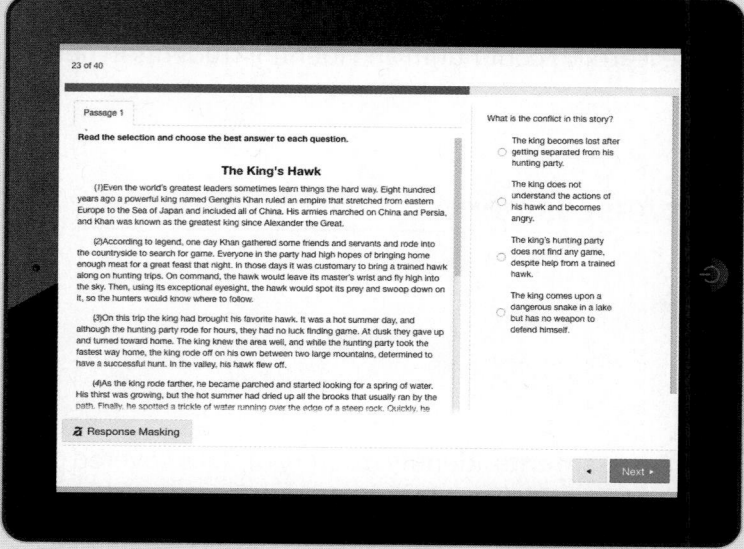

Every selection in the *Into Literature* program has a corresponding **Selection Test,** focusing on the skills taught in each lesson.

• Analyze & Apply

• Collaborate & Compare, and

• Independent Reading

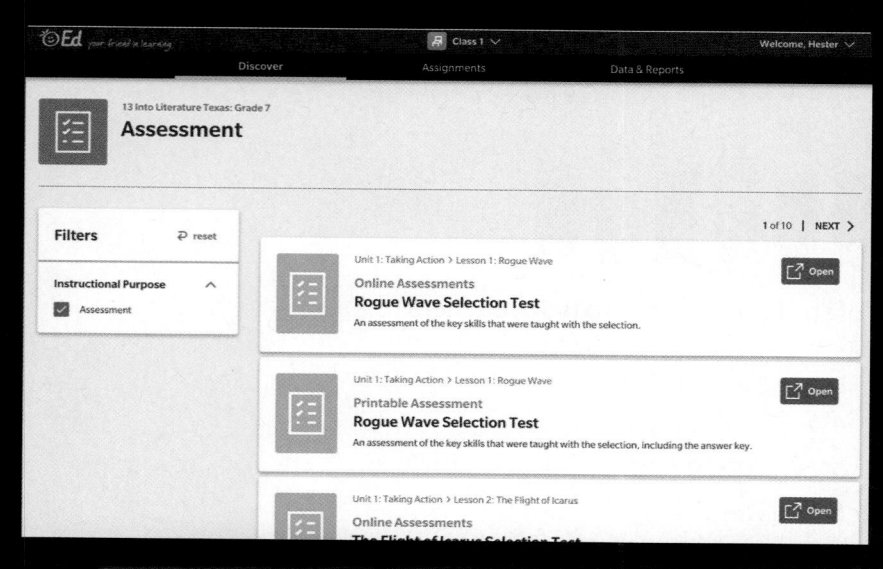

A **Unit Test** assesses mastery of the skills taught in the entire Unit using new readings aligned with the Unit topic.

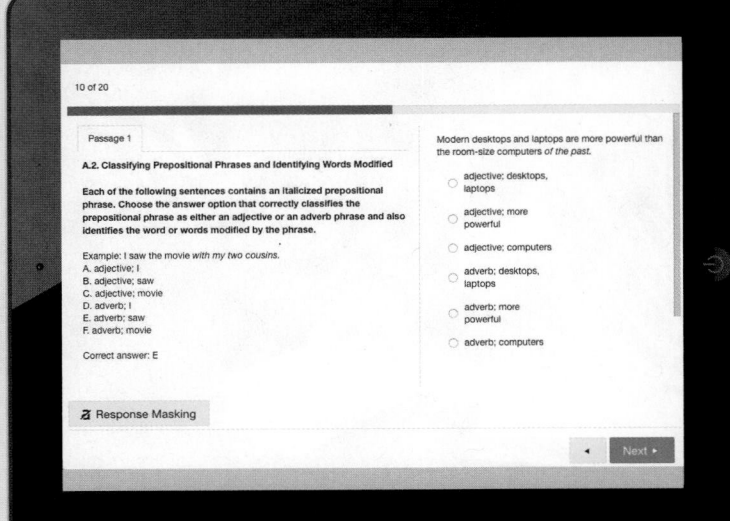

The **Diagnostic Screening Test** for Grammar, Usage, and Mechanics provides an assessment of strengths and weaknesses in the conventions of written English.

Each Module in the Grammar Studio has a **Diagnostic Assessment** and a **Summative Assessment,** for before and after instruction.

Foster a Learning Culture

As you encourage a culture of responsibility and collaboration, essential for students' success in the world of work, you will find learning activities that are social, active, and student owned.

COLLABORATE & COMPARE lessons are designed to support individual accountability as well as team aptitude. These lessons require students to read and annotate texts and compare their response in a collaborative project.

PEER REVIEW is a critical part of students' creative process. Tools such as Checklists for writing and listening and speaking tasks and the Revision Guide with questions, tips, and techniques offer practical support for peer interaction.

LEARNING MINDSET notes and strategies in your Teacher's Edition are designed to help students acquire the attitude of perseverance needed to successfully negotiate learning obstacles. Other resources such as ongoing formative assessments, peer evaluation, and Reflect on the Unit questions encourage students to monitor their progress and develop metacognitive ability.

RESILIENCE

SETTING GOALS

GRIT

WONDER

LEARNING MINDSET

Persistence Remind students that challenging moments are when growth and learning occur. Encourage students not to give up when they find something challenging. Explain that making an effort is a crucial part of increasing knowledge, intelligence, and ability. Being persistent in the face of challenges requires great effort, because these are moments that can have big pay-offs in terms of intellectual and academic growth. Model positive self-talk to students, such as "I know I can do this if I keep at it." Ask volunteers to offer other examples of positive self-talk that can help students be persistent.

PROBLEM SOLVING

CURIOSITY

SEEKING CHALLENGES

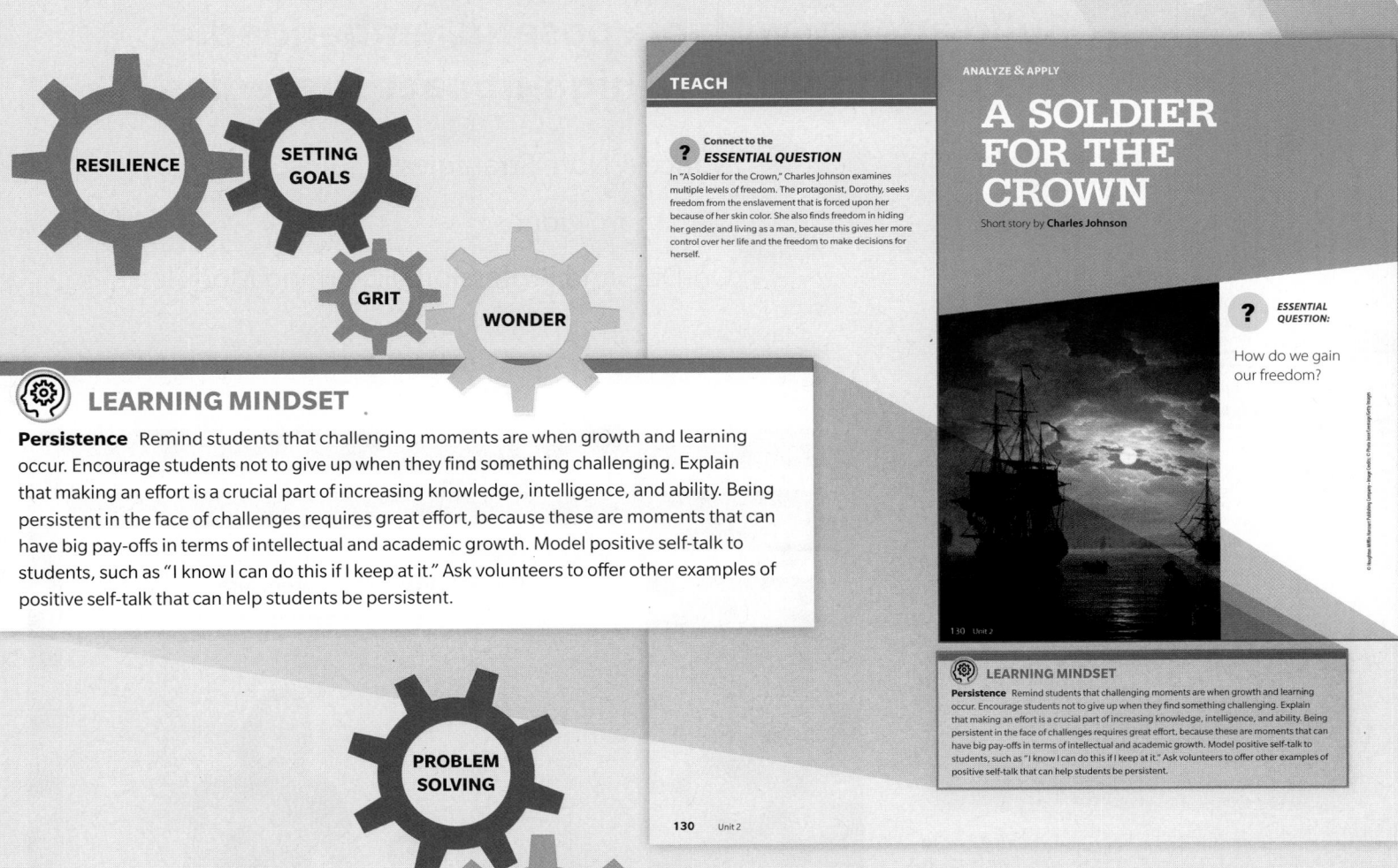

Build a Culture of Professional Growth

Embedded and on-going Professional Learning empowers you to develop high-impact learning experiences that provide all students with opportunities for reading and writing success.

Build agency with purposeful, embedded teacher support and high-impact strategies

- Notice & Note Strategies for Close Reading
- Classroom Videos
- On-Demand Professional Learning Modules

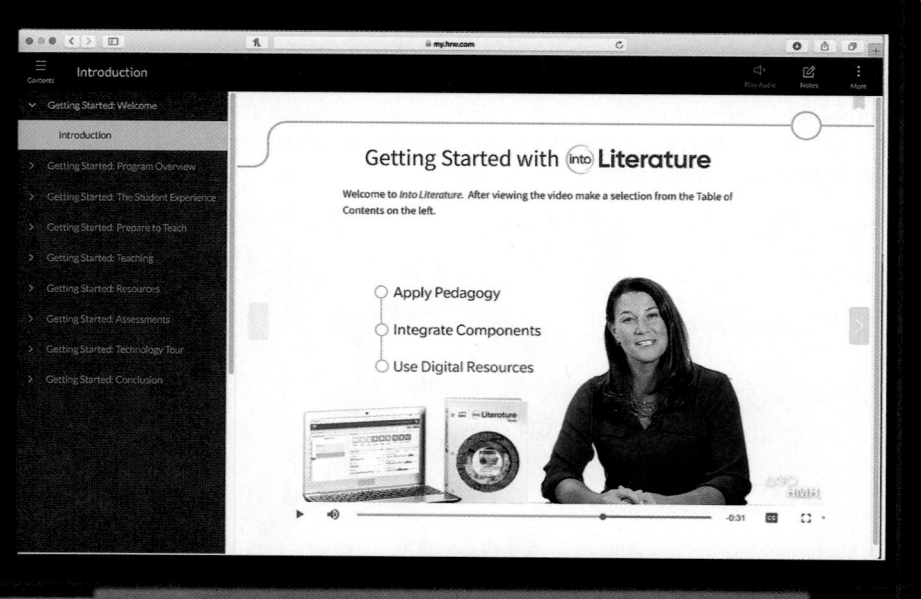

Grow Your Practice with Personalized Blended Professional Learning

- **Getting Started Course and Professional Learning Guide:** Learn the program components, pedagogy, and digital resources to successfully teach with *Into Literature*.

- **Follow-Up:** Choose from relevant instructional topics to create a personalized in-person or online Follow-Up experience to deepen program mastery and enhance teaching practices.

- **Coaching and Modeling:** Experience just-in-time support to ensure continuous professional learning that is student-centered and grounded in data.

- **askHMH:** Get on-demand access to program experts who will answer questions and provide personalized conferencing and digital demonstrations to support implementation.

- **Technical Services:** Plan, prepare, implement, and operate technology with ease.

HMH | into **Literature**

PROFESSIONAL LEARNING GUIDE

Research and Program Overview

The Student Experience

Teaching and Planning

Assessment

First Steps for Success

Annotated Student Edition Table of Contents

UNIT ①

Instructional Overview and Resources 1A

UNIT ①

FOUNDATIONS AND ENCOUNTERS

PAGE 1

Topical Focus

Each unit reflects a topic linking selections, Essential Questions, a quotation, and unit tasks for analysis, discussion, synthesis, and response.

Essential Questions

Posing thought-provoking ideas for discussion and reflection as students read, the Essential Questions stimulate analysis and synthesis, leading to a richer understanding of the unit's texts.

? **ESSENTIAL QUESTIONS**

- Why are we bound to certain places?
- What motivates people to explore the unknown?
- What does it mean to be a stranger in a strange land?
- What happens when cultures collide?

Early American Literature   2

ANALYZE & APPLY

MYTH
The World on the Turtle's Back   6
by Iroquois storytellers

SHORT STORY
Balboa 20
by Sabina Murray

ARTICLE   **MENTOR TEXT**
A Desperate Trek Across America 34
by Andrés Reséndez

POEM
Here Follow Some Verses Upon the Burning of Our House, July 10th, 1666 46
by Anne Bradstreet

COLLABORATE & COMPARE

COMPARE AUTHOR'S PURPOSE

HISTORICAL NARRATIVE
from **Of Plymouth Plantation** 54
by William Bradford

HISTORY WRITING
from **Coming of Age in the Dawnland** *from* **1491** 66
by Charles C. Mann

T22

INDEPENDENT READING 82
These selections can be accessed through the digital edition.

MEMOIR
from **The Way to Rainy Mountain**
by N. Scott Momaday

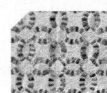
POEM
To My Dear and Loving Husband
by Anne Bradstreet

HISTORICAL NARRATIVE
from **La relación**
by Álvar Núñez Cabeza de Vaca

HISTORICAL NARRATIVE
from **The General History of Virginia**
by John Smith

POEM
New Orleans
by Joy Harjo

Suggested Novel Connection

NOVEL
The Namesake
by Jhumpa Lahiri

Additional Connections

- **The Lost Horizon**
  by James Hilton (novel)

- **Barrio Boy**
  by Ernesto Galarza (novel)

Unit **Tasks**
- Write a Literary Analysis 84
- Participate in a Panel Discussion 91

Reflect on the Unit 93

Key Learning Objectives
In abbreviated form, each unit's main instructional goals are listed for planning and quick reference.

Key Learning Objectives
- Analyze folk literature
- Make inferences
- Analyze thematic development
- Analyze plot structure
- Analyze and evaluate evidence
- Analyze informational texts
- Analyze voice
- Paraphrase
- Analyze allusions
- Analyze language
- Evaluate author's purpose
- Compare author's purpose

 Visit the Interactive Student Edition for:
- Unit and Selection Videos
- Media Selections
- Selection Audio Recordings
- Enhanced Digital Instruction

Contents   FM7

Annotated Student Edition Table of Contents

UNIT (2)

Instructional Overview and Resources 94A

UNIT (2)

BUILDING A DEMOCRACY
PAGE 94

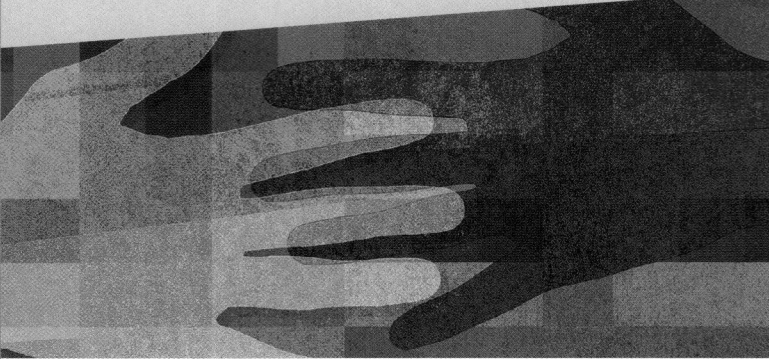

? **ESSENTIAL QUESTIONS**

- What does oppression look like?
- How do we gain our freedom?
- How can we share power and build alliances?
- How do we transform our lives?

The Revolutionary Period 96

ANALYZE & APPLY

PUBLIC DOCUMENT
The Declaration of Independence 100
by Thomas Jefferson

HISTORY WRITING   MENTOR TEXT
Thomas Jefferson: The Best of Enemies 112
by Ron Chernow

VIDEO
American Experience: Alexander Hamilton 126
by PBS

SHORT STORY
A Soldier for the Crown 130
by Charles Johnson

AUTOBIOGRAPHY
from **The Autobiography** 142
by Benjamin Franklin

COLLABORATE & COMPARE

COMPARE
THEMES

POEM
On Being Brought from Africa to America 156
by Phillis Wheatley

POEM
Sympathy 162
by Paul Laurence Dunbar

Analyze & Apply

This section of the Table of Contents groups a variety of selections for analysis, annotation, and application of the Notice & Note protocol, as well as standards instruction.

Collaborate & Compare

This section of the Table of Contents provides a comparative analysis of two selections linked by topic but different in genre, craft, or focus. Standards instruction and annotation are also applied.

FM8   Grade 11

COMPARE VOICE AND TONE

LETTER
Letter to John Adams 168
by Abigail Adams

ESSAY
from **Lean In** 178
by Sheryl Sandberg

INDEPENDENT READING 192
These selections can be accessed through the digital edition.

SPEECH
Speech to the Virginia Convention
by Patrick Henry

PUBLIC DOCUMENT
from **The United States Constitution:**
The Bill of Rights

APHORISMS
from **Poor Richard's Almanack**
by Benjamin Franklin

HISTORY WRITING
Abigail Adams' Last Act of Defiance
by Woody Holton

POEM
Democracy
by Langston Hughes

Suggested Nonfiction Connection

NONFICTION
1776
by David McCullough

Unit ② Tasks
• Write a Research Report 194
• Present a Research Report 201

Reflect on the Unit 203

Online Ed

Independent Reading
Interactive digital texts linked to the unit topic and in a wide range of genres and Lexile levels provide additional resources for students' independent reading, expanding student choice and experience.

Additional Connections

• **I, Juan de Pareja**
by Elizabeth Borton de Treviño
(novel)

• **Common Sense**
by Thomas Paine (pamplet)

Key Learning Objectives

• Analyze argumentative texts
• Analyze text structure
• Analyze informational texts
• Determine author's purpose
• Analyze effectiveness of digital texts
• Analyze literary elements
• Analyze and evaluate plot
• Monitor comprehension
• Evaluate print and graphic features
• Analyze speaker
• Analyze and compare themes
• Compare voice and tone

Online Ed **Visit the Interactive Student Edition for:**

• Unit and Selection Videos
• Media Selections
• Selection Audio Recordings
• Enhanced Digital Instruction

Annotated Student Edition Table of Contents

UNIT (3)

**Instructional Overview
and Resources** 204A

UNIT (3)

THE INDIVIDUAL AND SOCIETY
PAGE 204

? ***ESSENTIAL QUESTIONS***

- In what ways do we seek to remain true to ourselves?
- How do we relate to the world around us?
- What do we secretly fear?
- When should we stop and reflect on our lives?

Literature of the American Renaissance 206

ANALYZE & APPLY

POEM
***from* Song of Myself** 210
by Walt Whitman

ESSAY
My Friend Walt Whitman 222
by Mary Oliver

Poems by Emily Dickinson

POEMS
The Soul selects her own Society 232
Because I could not stop for Death 237
Much Madness is divinest Sense 238
Tell all the Truth but tell it slant 239

POEM
In the Season of Change 242
by Teresa Palomo Acosta

COLLABORATE & COMPARE

COMPARE
MAIN IDEAS

ESSAY
***from* Walden** 250
by Henry David Thoreau

INFORMATIONAL TEXT   MENTOR TEXT
***from* Last Child in the Woods** 258
by Richard Louv

Mentor Text

This selection exemplifies genre characteristics and craft choices that will be used in end-of-unit writing tasks as models for students.

© Houghton Mifflin Harcourt Publishing Company • Image Credits: ©Cliquephoto/Moment/Getty Images; ©John Morrison/Alamy; ©Roy Botterell/Getty Images; ©Lynne Furrer/Shutterstock; ©Gabriel Negron/Alamy; ©OJO Images/Getty Images

COMPARE THEMES

SHORT STORY
The Minister's Black Veil 268
by Nathaniel Hawthorne

SHORT STORY
The Pit and the Pendulum 290
by Edgar Allan Poe

Online
Ed
INDEPENDENT READING 314
These selections can be accessed through the digital edition.

ESSAYS
from **Nature**
from **Self-Reliance**
by Ralph Waldo Emerson

ARTICLE
The Pointlessness of Unplugging
by Casey N. Cep

POEM
The Raven
by Edgar Allan Poe

POEM
Pastoral
by Jennifer Chang

Suggested Novel Connection

NOVEL
Fahrenheit 451
by Ray Bradbury

Unit ③ **Task**
• Write an Explanatory Essay 316

Reflect on the Unit 323

Additional Connections

• **The Scarlet Letter**
by Nathaniel Hawthorne (novel)

• **The Last of the Mohicans**
by James Fenimore Cooper (novel)

Key Learning Objectives
• Analyze poetry
• Analyze theme and structure
• Analyze essays
• Analyze development of key ideas
• Analyze figurative language
• Analyze sound devices
• Summarize
• Analyze author's craft
• Compare main ideas
• Analyze literary elements
• Analyze structure
• Analyze mood
• Compare themes

Online
Ed
Visit the Interactive Student Edition for:
• Unit and Selection Videos
• Media Selections
• Selection Audio Recordings
• Enhanced Digital Instruction

Contents **FM11**

Annotated Student Edition Table of Contents

UNIT 4

**Instructional Overview
and Resources** 324A

UNIT 4

THE QUEST FOR FREEDOM
PAGE 324

? ***ESSENTIAL
QUESTIONS***

- When is self-determination
  possible?
- What divides us as human
  beings?
- How do we face defeat?
- What is the price of progress?

The Civil War and Its Aftermath 326

ANALYZE & APPLY

SPEECH
Second Inaugural Address 330
by Abraham Lincoln

LETTER
To My Old Master 340
by Jourdon Anderson

IMAGE COLLECTION
Civil War Photographs 350

SHORT STORY
An Occurrence at Owl Creek Bridge 360
by Ambrose Bierce

HISTORY WRITING
Building the Transcontinental Railroad 378
by Iris Chang

COLLABORATE & COMPARE

COMPARE
ARGUMENTS

ARGUMENT   MENTOR TEXT
Declaration of Sentiments 396
by Elizabeth Cady Stanton

ARGUMENT
Speech to the American Equal Rights Association 404
by Sojourner Truth

Variety of Genres
Each unit is comprised of different kinds of
texts or genres. Essential characteristics of
each genre are identified and illustrated.
Students then apply those characteristics
to their own writing.

COMPARE WRITER'S VOICE

POEM
Runagate Runagate 414
by Robert Hayden

AUTOBIOGRAPHY
from **Incidents in the Life of a Slave Girl** 424
by Harriet Jacobs

INDEPENDENT READING 440
These selections can be accessed through the digital edition.

LETTER
Letter to Sarah Ballou
by Sullivan Ballou

DIARY
from **A Diary from Dixie**
by Mary Chesnut

SPEECH
from **What to the Slave Is the Fourth of July?**
by Frederick Douglass

SPIRITUALS
**Go Down, Moses; Follow the Drinking Gourd;
Swing Low, Sweet Chariot**

POEM
Imagine the Angels of Bread
by Martín Espada

Suggested Novel Connection

NOVEL
Uncle Tom's Cabin
by Harriet Beecher Stowe

Additional Connections

- **Their Eyes Were Watching God**
  by Zora Neale Hurston

- **The Piano Lesson**
  August Wilson (play)

Tasks

Each unit concludes with one or two culminating tasks that demonstrate essential understandings, synthesizing ideas and text references in oral and written responses.

Unit **Tasks**
• Write an Argument 442
• Debate an Issue 449

Reflect on the Unit 451

Key Learning Objectives

- Analyze author's purpose
- Analyze letters
- Analyze tone
- Make connections
- Analyze media effectiveness
- Analyze literary elements
- Analyze structure
- Analyze informational texts
- Analyze and evaluate arguments
- Analyze speaker and voice
- Analyze sound devices
- Analyze language
- Compare writer's voice

 Visit the Interactive Student Edition for:

- Unit and Selection Videos
- Media Selections
- Selection Audio Recordings
- Enhanced Digital Instruction

Contents **FM13**

Annotated Student Edition Table of Contents

UNIT **5**

**Instructional Overview
and Resources** 452A

UNIT **5**

AMERICA TRANSFORMED
PAGE 452

? ***ESSENTIAL
QUESTIONS***

- To what degree do we control our lives?
- Why do humans cause harm?
- What are the consequences of change?
- What makes a place unique?

An Age of Realism 454

ANALYZE & APPLY

SHORT STORY
To Build a Fire 458
by Jack London

ESSAY
The Lowest Animal 482
by Mark Twain

ARTICLE
**Why Everyone Must Get Ready For the Fourth
Industrial Revolution** 496
by Bernard Marr

SHORT STORY   MENTOR TEXT
The Story of an Hour 506
by Kate Chopin

POEM
Chicago 518
by Carl Sandburg

COLLABORATE & COMPARE

COMPARE
AUTHOR'S
PURPOSE

NOVEL
from **The Jungle** 526
by Upton Sinclair

INVESTIGATIVE JOURNALISM
Food Product Design *from* **Fast Food Nation** 538
by Eric Schlosser

INDEPENDENT READING 558
These selections can be accessed through the digital edition.

SHORT STORY
The Men in the Storm
by Stephen Crane

SHORT STORY
A Journey
by Edith Wharton

SHORT STORY
A Wagner Matinee
by Willa Cather

ARTICLE
Evidence that Robots Are Winning the Race for American Jobs
by Claire Cain Miller

ARTICLE
Healthy Eaters, Strong Minds: What School Gardens Teach Kids
by Paige Pfleger

Suggested Nonfiction Connection •

NONFICTION
Into Thin Air
by Jon Krakauer

 Unit 5 Task
• Write a Short Story 560

Reflect on the Unit 567

Suggested Connection
One extended text is recommended for its topical and thematic connection to other texts in the unit.

Additional Connections

• **And the Earth Did Not Devour Him**
by Tomás Rivera

• **As I Lay Dying**
by William Faulkner (novel)

Key Learning Objectives

• Analyze character
• Analyze setting
• Analyze author's purpose
• Analyze tone
• Evaluate graphic features
• Evaluate counterarguments
• Analyze point of view
• Make and confirm predictions
• Synthesize information
• Compare author's purpose

Visit the Interactive Student Edition for:

• Unit and Selection Videos
• Media Selections
• Selection Audio Recordings
• Enhanced Digital Instruction

Contents   FM15

Annotated Student Edition Table of Contents

UNIT 6

**Instructional Overview
and Resources** 568A

UNIT 6

CONTEMPORARY VOICES AND VISIONS

PAGE 568

 ? **ESSENTIAL QUESTIONS**

- How do we deal with rejection or isolation?
- For whom is the American Dream relevant?
- When should personal integrity come before civic duty?
- What would we do if there were no limits?

Modern and Contemporary Literature 570

ANALYZE & APPLY

SHORT STORY
A Rose for Emily 574
by William Faulkner

POEM
Mending Wall 592
by Robert Frost

DRAMA
Modern American Drama 600
The Crucible 602
by Arthur Miller

PRODUCTION IMAGES
The Crucible 716

OPEN LETTER
My Dungeon Shook: Letter to My Nephew 726
by James Baldwin

SPEECH

Speech on the Vietnam War, 1967 738
by Martin Luther King Jr.

SHORT STORY

Ambush 760
by Tim O'Brien

POEM

The Universe as Primal Scream 772
by Tracy K. Smith

COLLABORATE & COMPARE

ESSAY   MENTOR TEXT

How It Feels to Be Colored Me 780
by Zora Neale Hurston

COMPARE
IDEAS
ACROSS
GENRES

HISTORY WRITING

from **The Warmth of Other Suns** 792
by Isabel Wilkerson

POEM

Poetry 806
by Marianne Moore

COMPARE
THEMES

POEM

The Latin Deli: An Ars Poetica 812
by Judith Ortiz Cofer

© Houghton Mifflin Harcourt Publishing Company • Image Credits: ©Bettmann/Getty Images; ©World History Archive/Alamy; ©SzB/Getty Images; ©NASA Images/Shutterstock; ©PhotoQuest/Getty Images; ©Corbis Historical/Getty Images; ©Sergey Nivens/Shutterstock; ©Dorothy Alexander/Alamy

Cultural Diversity
Each unit includes a rich array of selections that represent multicultural authors and experiences.

UNIT

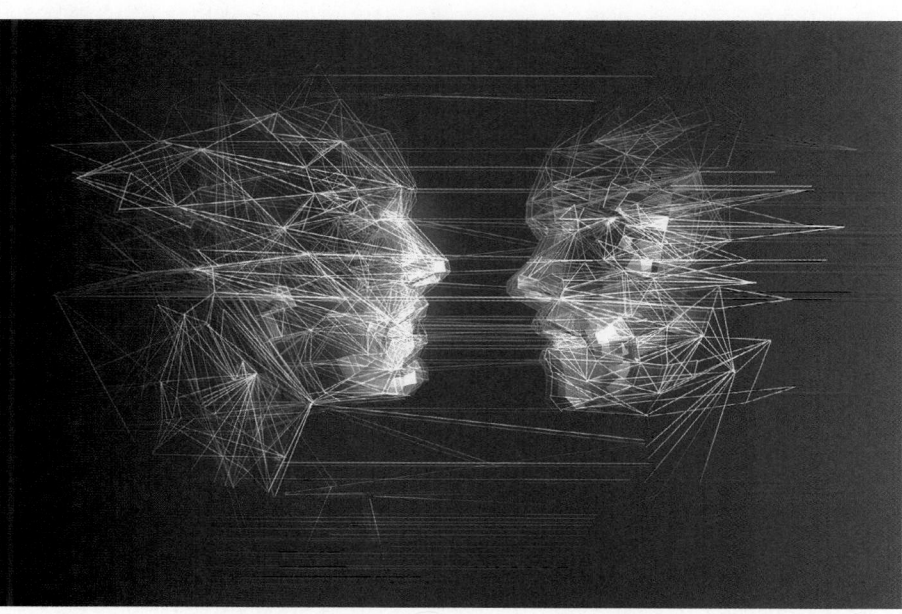

Online Ed   **INDEPENDENT READING** 820

These selections can be accessed through the digital edition.

Poems of the Harlem Renaissance

POEMS

The Weary Blues
by Langston Hughes

Song of the Son
by Jean Toomer

From the Dark Tower
by Countee Cullen

A Black Man Talks of Reaping
by Arna Bontemps

ESSAY

Martin Luther King Jr.: He Showed Us the Way
by César Chávez

ESSAY

Mother Tongue
by Amy Tan

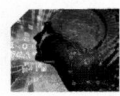

SHORT STORY

Reality Check
by David Brin

ARTICLE

YouTube Stars Stress Out, Just Like the Rest of Us
by Neda Ulaby

Suggested Novel Connection

NOVEL

The Great Gatsby
by F. Scott Fitzgerald

Unit 6 **Task**
• Write a Personal Essay 822

Reflect on the Unit 829

Additional Connections

- **The Fire Next Time**
  by James Baldwin (nonfiction)

- **The Bluest Eye**
  by Toni Morrison (novel)

Reflection
Students may pause and reflect on their process and understanding of the selections and the themes in each unit.

Key Learning Objectives
- Make and confirm predictions
- Analyze author's message
- Analyze dramatic elements
- Analyze and evaluate arguments
- Analyze and evaluate rhetorical devices
- Analyze poetry
- Determine theme
- Analyze development of ideas
- Analyze poetry
- Analyze point of view

 Online Ed **Visit the Interactive Student Edition for:**

- Unit and Selection Videos
- Media Selections
- Selection Audio Recordings
- Enhanced Digital Instruction

Contents FM19

SELECTIONS BY GENRE

FICTION

NOVEL

from **The Jungle**
Upton Sinclair 526

ORAL TRADITION

The World on the Turtle's Back
Iroquois storytellers
MYTH 6

SHORT STORY

Ambush
Tim O'Brien 760

Balboa
Sabina Murray 20

A Journey
Edith Wharton . . . . Online

The Men in the Storm
Stephen Crane . . . . Online

The Minister's Black Veil
Nathaniel Hawthorne 268

An Occurrence at Owl Creek Bridge
Ambrose Bierce 360

The Pit and the Pendulum
Edgar Allan Poe 290

Reality Check
David Brin . . . . Online

A Rose for Emily
William Faulkner 574

A Soldier for the Crown
Charles Johnson 130

The Story of an Hour
Kate Chopin 506

To Build a Fire
Jack London 458

A Wagner Matinee
Willa Cather . . . . Online

NONFICTION

ARGUMENT

Declaration of Sentiments
Elizabeth Cady Stanton 396

Martin Luther King Jr.: He Showed Us the Way
César Chávez
ESSAY . . . . Online

AUTOBIOGRAPHY/MEMOIR/DIARY

from **The Autobiography**
Benjamin Franklin 142

from **A Diary from Dixie**
Mary Chesnut . . . . Online

from **Incidents in the Life of a Slave Girl**
Harriet Jacobs 424

from **The Way to Rainy Mountain**
N. Scott Momaday . . . . Online

INFORMATIONAL TEXT

Abigail Adams' Last Act of Defiance
Woody Holton
HISTORY WRITING . . . . Online

Building the Transcontinental Railroad
Iris Chang
HISTORY WRITING 378

from **Coming of Age in the Dawnland** *from* **1491**
Charles C. Mann
HISTORY WRITING 66

A Desperate Trek Across America
Andrés Reséndez
ARTICLE 34

Evidence that Robots Are Winning the Race for American Jobs
Claire Cain Miller
ARTICLE . . . . Online

Food Product Design *from* **Fast Food Nation**
Eric Schlosser
INVESTIGATIVE JOURNALISM 538

from **The General History of Virginia**
John Smith
HISTORICAL NARRATIVE . . . . Online

Healthy Eaters, Strong Minds: What School Gardens Teach Kids
Paige Pfleger
ARTICLE . . . . Online

from **La relación**
Álvar Núñez Cabeza de Vaca
HISTORICAL NARRATIVE . . . . Online

from **Last Child in the Woods**
Richard Louv 258

from **Lean In**
Sheryl Sandberg
ESSAY 178

from **Of Plymouth Plantation**
William Bradford
HISTORICAL NARRATIVE 54

The Pointlessness of Unplugging
Casey N. Cep
ARTICLE . . . . Online

Thomas Jefferson: The Best of Enemies
Ron Chernow
HISTORY WRITING 112

from **The Warmth of Other Suns**
Isabel Wilkerson
HISTORY WRITING 792

Why Everyone Must Get Ready For the Fourth Industrial Revolution
Bernard Marr
ARTICLE 496

YouTube Stars Stress Out, Just Like the Rest of Us
Neda Ulaby
ARTICLE . . . . Online

LETTER/APHORISM

Letter to John Adams
Abigail Adams 168

Letter to Sarah Ballou
Sullivan Ballou . . . . Online

from **Poor Richard's Almanack**
Benjamin Franklin
APHORISMS . . . . Online

To My Old Master
Jourdon Anderson 340

NARRATIVE NONFICTION

How It Feels to Be Colored Me
Zora Neale Hurston 780

The Lowest Animal
Mark Twain 482

Mother Tongue
Amy Tan . . . . Online

© Houghton Mifflin Harcourt Publishing Company

SELECTIONS BY GENRE

My Dungeon Shook: Letter to My Nephew
James Baldwin 726

My Friend Walt Whitman
Mary Oliver 222

from **Nature**
Ralph Waldo Emerson . . . . Online

from **Self-Reliance**
Ralph Waldo Emerson . . . . Online

from **Walden**
Henry David Thoreau 250

PUBLIC DOCUMENT

The Declaration of Independence
Thomas Jefferson 100

from **The United States Constitution: The Bill of Rights** . . . . Online

SPEECH

Second Inaugural Address
Abraham Lincoln
ARGUMENT 330

Speech on the Vietnam War, 1967
Martin Luther King Jr.
ARGUMENT 738

Speech to the American Equal Rights Association
Sojourner Truth
ARGUMENT 404

Speech to the Virginia Convention
Patrick Henry . . . . Online

from **What to the Slave Is the Fourth of July?**
Frederick Douglass . . . . Online

POETRY

Because I could not stop for Death
Emily Dickinson 237

A Black Man Talks of Reaping
Arna Bontemps
HARLEM RENAISSANCE . . . . Online

Chicago
Carl Sandburg 518

Democracy
Langston Hughes . . . . Online

From the Dark Tower
Countee Cullen
HARLEM RENAISSANCE . . . . Online

Go Down, Moses; Follow the Drinking Gourd; Swing Low, Sweet Chariot
SPIRITUALS . . . . Online

Here Follow Some Verses Upon the Burning of Our House, July 10th, 1666
Anne Bradstreet 46

Imagine the Angels of Bread
Martín Espada . . . . Online

In the Season of Change
Teresa Palomo Acosta 242

The Latin Deli: An Ars Poetica
Judith Ortiz Cofer 812

Mending Wall
Robert Frost 592

Much Madness Is divinest Sense
Emily Dickinson 238

New Orleans
Joy Harjo .... Online

On Being Brought from Africa to America
Phillis Wheatley 156

Pastoral
Jennifer Chang .... Online

Poetry
Marianne Moore 806

The Raven
Edgar Allan Poe .... Online

Runagate Runagate
Robert Hayden 414

from **Song of Myself**
Walt Whitman 210

Song of the Son
Jean Toomer
HARLEM RENAISSANCE .... Online

The Soul selects her own Society
Emily Dickinson 232

Sympathy
Paul Laurence Dunbar 162

Tell all the Truth but tell it slant
Emily Dickinson 239

To My Dear and Loving Husband
Anne Bradstreet .... Online

The Universe as Primal Scream
Tracy K. Smith 772

The Weary Blues
Langston Hughes
HARLEM RENAISSANCE .... Online

DRAMA

The Crucible
Arthur Miller 602

MEDIA STUDY

American Experience: Alexander Hamilton
PBS
VIDEO 126

Civil War Photographs
IMAGE COLLECTION 350

The Crucible
PRODUCTION IMAGES 716

© Houghton Mifflin Harcourt Publishing Company

HMH
Into Literature Dashboard

Easy to use and personalized for your learning.

Monitor your progress in the course.

Review your assignments and check your progress.

Quickly access content and search program resources.

Explore Online to Experience the Power of HMH *Into Literature*

All in One Place

Readings and assignments are supported by a variety of resources to bring literature to life and give you the tools you need to succeed.

Supporting 21st-Century Skills

Whether you're working alone or collaborating with others, it takes effort to analyze the complex texts and competing ideas that bombard us in this fast-paced world. What will help you succeed? Staying engaged and organized. The digital tools in this program will help you take charge of your learning.

FM24   Grade 11

Ignite Your Investigation

You learn best when you're engaged. The **Stream to Start** videos at the beginning of every unit are designed to spark your interest before you read. Get curious and start reading!

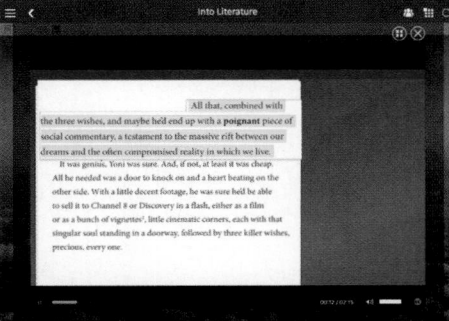

Learn How to Close Read

Close reading effectively is all about examining the details. See how it's done by watching the **Close Read Screencasts** in your eBook. Hear modeled conversations on targeted passages.

Personalized Annotations

My Notes encourages you to take notes as you read and allows you to mark the text in your own customized way. You can easily access annotations to review later as you prepare for exams.

Interactive Graphic Organizers

Graphic organizers help you process, summarize, and keep track of your learning and prepare for end-of-unit writing tasks. **Word Networks** help you learn academic vocabulary, and **Response Logs** help you explore and deepen your understanding of the **Essential Questions** in each unit.

No Wi-Fi? No problem!

With HMH *Into Literature,* you always have access: download when you're online and access what you need when you're offline. Work offline and then upload when you're back online.

Communicate "Raise a Hand" to ask or answer questions without having to be in the same room as your teacher.

Collaborate Collaborate with your teacher via chat and work with a classmate to improve your writing.

FM25

HMH
Into Literature
STUDIOS

All the help you need to be successful in your literature class is one click away with the Studios. These digital-only lessons are here to tap into the skills that you already use and help you sharpen those skills for the future.

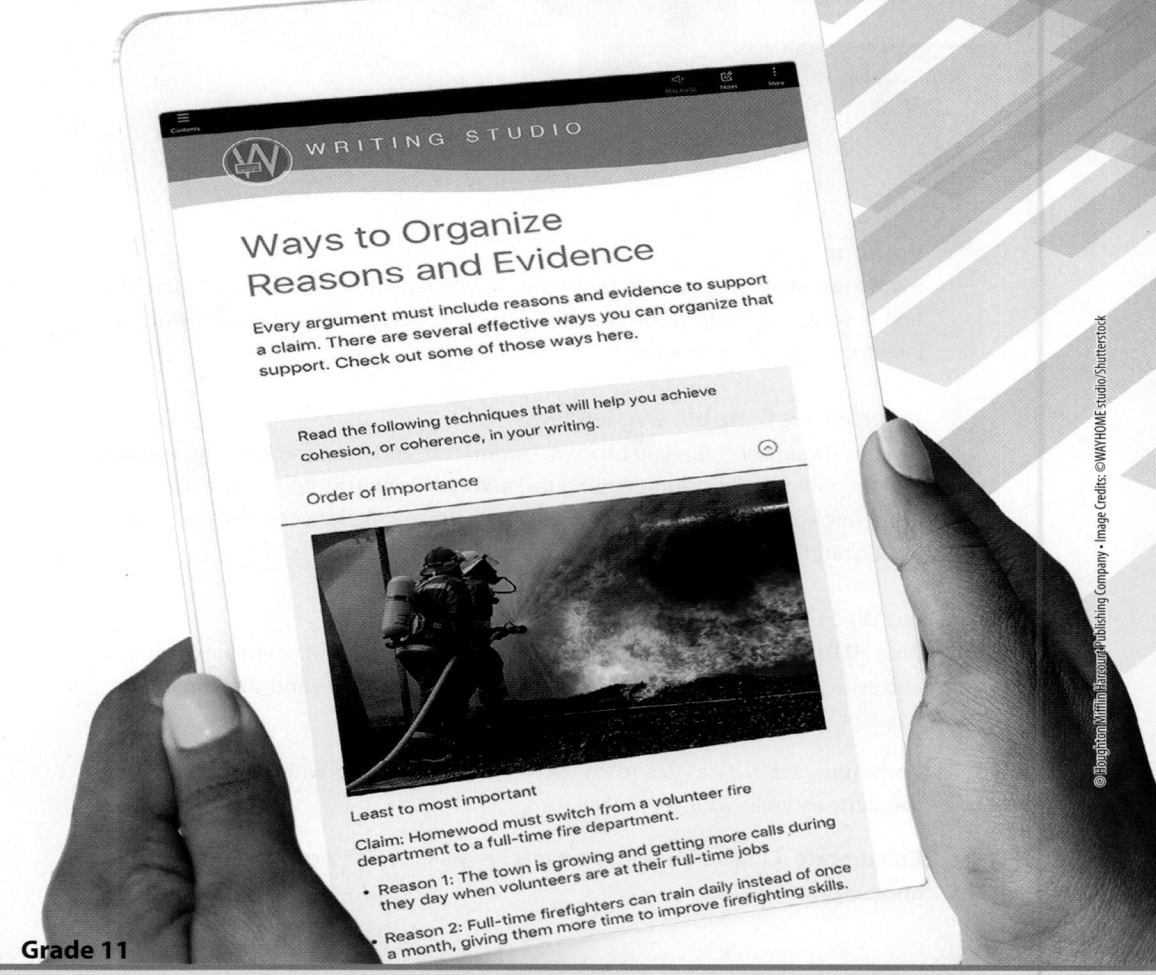

Easy-to-find resources, organized in five separate STUDIOS. On demand and on ED!

Look for links in each lesson to take you to the appropriate Studio.

READING STUDIO

Go beyond the book with the Reading Studio. With over 100 full-length downloadable titles to choose from, find the right story to continue your journey.

WRITING STUDIO

Being able to write clearly and effectively is a skill that will help you throughout life. The Writing Studio will help you become an expert communicator—in print or online.

SPEAKING & LISTENING STUDIO

Communication is more than just writing. The Speaking & Listening Studio will help you become an effective speaker and a focused listener.

GRAMMAR STUDIO

Go beyond traditional worksheets with the Grammar Studio. These engaging, interactive lessons will sharpen your grammar skills.

VOCABULARY STUDIO

Learn the skills you need to expand your vocabulary. The interactive lessons in the Vocabulary Studio will grow your vocabulary to improve your reading.

FM27

ESSAY ON
Notice & Note

Dr. Kylene Beers and Dr. Robert E. Probst

In reading, as in almost everything else, paying attention is most important.

You wouldn't stand in the batter's box, facing a hard-throwing pitcher, with your mind wandering to what you may have for dinner that evening. The prospect of a fastball coming toward you at 80 miles an hour tends to focus the mind.

And you wouldn't attempt to sing a difficult song in front of a large crowd with your thoughts on what dress you're going to wear to the dance this coming weekend. The need to hit the high note, without cracking, in front of 500 people evokes concentration.

Paying attention is essential.

It's the same with reading. Of course, if you don't concentrate while reading, you won't suffer the pain of being knocked down by the fastball or the embarrassment of failing to hit the notes in front of the crowd, but you'll miss what the text offers. If you don't pay attention, there is barely any purpose in picking up the text at all.

But there is a purpose in reading. And that purpose, that point, is to enable us to change. The change may be slight, or it might be dramatic. We might, at one extreme, simply get a little more information that we need:

- Where is tonight's game?
- What time is band practice?
- What pages do we need to read for homework?

Reading for that sort of information doesn't dramatically change who we are, but it does change us slightly. Or, at least, it **might** change us slightly. Obviously, it is **we**, the readers, who must do the changing. The text doesn't do it for us. When we read that tonight's game is away, instead of at home, we have to change our plans to let us get to the other school. We have to take in the information and do something with it. If we don't, if we show up at the home field despite what we have read, the reading will have been pointless, a waste of time. And the evening will be wasted, as well. We have to pay attention to the book — what's on the page, and to our heads — what we thought before we read and what we now think. And we have to take it to heart — that is to say, we have to act on what we now know and think.

Other reading, however, might enable us to change more significantly. We might change our thinking about an important problem, or we might change our attitude about an important issue. We can't tell you which text will do that for you or how you might grow and change as a result of reading it. That's much too individual. It's hard to predict unless you know the reader well and know some of the texts that might matter to him or her:

- Some of us might read about child labor in foreign countries and change our minds about what we will buy and what we will boycott.

- You might read *To Kill a Mockingbird*, and change your thinking about race relations.

- You might read about climate change and wonder what you can do to help preserve the earth.

We can't know exactly what book will be powerful for which reader. But we can safely predict that if you don't notice what the text offers, think about it, and take what matters to you into your head and heart, then the reading probably won't mean much to you.

We're going to urge you to pay attention to three elements as you read:

- **The Book.** Or whatever text you have in your hand, whether it is a book, an article, a poem, or something else. We are going to urge you to listen carefully to what it tells you, and we're going to give you some strategies that we hope will make that easy for you to do.

- **Your Head.** We're going to ask you also to pay attention to your own thoughts. If it's an article you're reading, then keep in mind what you thought about the topic before you began, and then think seriously about how you might have changed your thinking as a result of what you've read. If it's a story or a poem or a movie, then think about what thoughts or feelings it brought to mind and how they might have shaped your reaction to the text.

- **Your Heart.** Finally, we encourage you to ask yourself what you want to carry away from the reading. What matters to you? How might you change your thinking? How might you have shifted your attitudes about something, even if only slightly? What do you take to heart?

It all begins with noticing.

But there's a lot in a book to notice, so it might help to keep in mind just a few things that you will probably see in almost any text (unless it is very short). We call these elements "signposts" because they serve readers just as signposts or street signs serve drivers — they alert them to something significant. The careless driver, who doesn't pay attention and misses a stop sign or a hairpin-curve sign, is likely to end up in trouble. The lazy reader, who doesn't notice the signposts, won't end up in trouble — he just isn't likely to know what's going on in the text.

FM29

THE FICTION SIGNPOSTS

We want to share 6 signposts that help you when reading fiction.

▶ CONTRASTS AND CONTRADICTIONS

Without a contrast or a contradiction, everything is just the same, just the usual, just what you would have expected. Boring.

But when some event occurs that contrasts vividly with what you would have expected, then you are likely — if you're paying attention — to notice it.

When a friend's behavior suddenly changes and contrasts with what you would expect, you will notice it and ask yourself why. Similarly, when a character in a story does something drastically different from what he has usually done, you should pause and wonder why. Or, when a writer gives you an idea that contradicts the thoughts you have always held, again you might slow down and ask yourself, "Is she right or am I? Should I accept those thoughts or reject them? Is the answer somewhere in between what I have read and what I used to think?" Keep in mind the general question "Why is the character doing or saying that?" and it will lead you to other questions you might ask about the moment of contrast and contradiction, that moment when you bump into something unexpected.

> In Nathaniel Hawthorne's **"The Minister's Black Veil,"** a student has noted **CONTRASTS AND CONTRADICTIONS** and asked this question: Why would the characters act this way?

After a brief interval, forth came good Mr. Hooper also, in the rear of his flock. Turning his veiled face from one group to another, he paid due reverence to the hoary heads, saluted the middle-aged with kind dignity, as their friend and spiritual guide, greeted the young with mingled authority and love, and laid his hands on the little children's heads to bless them. Such was always his custom on the Sabbath day. <u>Strange and bewildered looks repaid him for his courtesy. None, as on former occasions, aspired to the honor of walking by their pastor's side. Old Squire Saunders</u>, doubtless by an accidental lapse of memory, <u>neglected to invite Mr. Hooper to his table, where the good clergyman had been wont to bless the food almost every Sunday since his settlement.</u> He returned, therefore, to the parsonage, and at the moment of closing the door, was observed to look back upon the people, all of whom had their eyes fixed upon the minister. <u>A sad smile gleamed faintly from beneath the black veil</u>, and flickered about his mouth, glimmering as he disappeared.

Members of the congregation seem confused, and none of them walk with Mr. Hooper after the church service ends.

Even Squire Saunders breaks with his long tradition of inviting Mr. Hooper to dinner.

They're staying away from him.

Perhaps they're embarrassed or even frightened by Mr. Hooper's behavior, leading him to feel sad and lonely.

▶ AHA MOMENT

Sometimes too many days go by without one of those moments when you suddenly understand something. But when you have such a moment you recognize that it's important and you stop and think about it. One day you might suddenly say to yourself "I'm echoing everything my friends say, but I don't really believe any of it." That's an important moment that may lead to a change in what you do, or at least to some hard thinking about the choices you have made. You've had an insight — an Aha — and you have to ask yourself what it means.

In the same way, the character in the story will almost always come to some insight into his situation, some "Aha" moment in which he realizes, perhaps suddenly, something about himself, his situation, or his life. When you come to such a moment, ask yourself "How will this change things?" Because it almost always will. Aha Moments are usually indicated with phrases such as "I knew," "I understood," "He figured it out," "She slowly realized," or "She nodded, knowing what she had to do . . ."

> **In Jack London's "To Build a Fire," a student has noted an AHA MOMENT and asked this question: How might this change things?**

<u>Fifty degrees below zero stood for a bite of frost that hurt and that must be guarded against by the use of mittens, earflaps, warm moccasins, and thick socks.</u> Fifty degrees below zero was to him just precisely fifty degrees below zero. <u>That there should be anything more to it than that was a thought that never entered his head.</u>

As he turned to go on, <u>he spat speculatively</u>. <u>There was a sharp, explosive crackle that startled him.</u> He spat again. And again, in the air, before it could fall to the snow, the spittle crackled. <u>He knew that at fifty below, spittle crackled on the snow, but this spittle had crackled in the air.</u> Undoubtedly <u>it was colder than fifty below—how much colder he did not know.</u>

The man understands how to survive when it's fifty degrees below zero, but he has never imagined what might happen if it were colder.

He has an Aha Moment when he spits and realizes that it's much, much colder than he'd expected.

He might be realizing that he's in trouble—that he needs to act quickly in order to survive.

FM31

TOUGH QUESTIONS

"Do you want pizza or spaghetti for dinner?" really isn't a tough question, even if you can't make up your mind. Your answer isn't going to change much of anything, and tomorrow you probably won't even remember that you made a choice. You aren't going to think about it for very long or very hard, and no one will ever write a book about the choice between pizza and spaghetti. If they do, we won't read it.

A tough question is one we struggle with, one that might change the course of our lives — one, at least, that will have some serious consequences for us. "Should I play football, as the coach wants me to, or should I join the band, as I want to?" "Should I follow the crowd, as everyone is pressing me to do, or should I respect my own thoughts and let the crowd condemn me for it?" These are tough questions, and how we might answer them will shape the days to come.

Often a story, even an entire book, is built around the tough question. If we ask ourselves "What does this make me wonder about?," we will probably be led into exploring the same issue the character or the writer is exploring. The writer probably wanted to see what would happen if his character answered the question in a certain way. If you notice the tough question, and ask yourself about it, you will probably be looking at the main issue of the book.

In Kate Chopin's **"The Story of an Hour,"** a student has noted a **TOUGH QUESTION** and asked: What does this question make me wonder about?

She was young, with a fair, calm face, whose lines bespoke repression and even a certain strength. But now there was a dull stare in her eyes, whose gaze was fixed away off yonder on one of those patches of blue sky. <u>It was not a glance of reflection, but rather indicated a suspension of intelligent thought.</u>

<u>There was something coming to her and she was waiting for it, fearfully.</u> <u>What was it?</u> She did not know; it was too subtle and elusive to name. But she felt it, creeping out of the sky, reaching toward her through the sounds, the scents, the color that filled the air.

In response to news of her husband's death, Mrs. Mallard feels something "coming to her," but she has no idea what it is. She asks a Tough Question, "What was it?"

I wonder if she's going to realize something about herself or about what life will be like now that she's alone.

© Houghton Mifflin Harcourt Publishing Company

WORDS OF THE WISER

You may think that you have heard too many of these in your own life.

You probably think there is always someone around who wants to offer you advice, teach you how things are, and tell you what to do and how to think. Sometimes these wise words are right, truly wise, and sometimes they are wrong. But they are almost always an effort to guide you, or the character, to teach something about living in the world.

In a story, we usually hear Words of the Wiser in a quiet moment, when two characters are in a serious conversation about a problem or a decision. Usually the one who is — or thinks she is — wiser, will offer a serious lesson about life. The story will be about the character struggling along, unwilling to learn that lesson until the end; or about the character accepting the lesson and following it to whatever adventures it leads; or perhaps, in rare cases, about the words of the wiser not being wise after all.

In any case, when you notice Words of the Wiser in the story you should ask the same question you are likely to ask in your own life — "What is the lesson, and how will it affect the character (or me)?"

> In Tim O'Brien's "**Ambush**," a student has noted **WORDS OF THE WISER** and asked this question: What is the life lesson, and how might it affect the character?

He fell on his back. His rubber sandals had been blown off. He lay at the center of the trail, his right leg beneath him, his one eye shut, his other eye a huge star-shaped hole.

For me, it was not a matter of live or die. I was in no real peril. Almost certainly the young man would have passed me by. And it will always be that way.

Later, I remember Kiowa tried to tell me that the man would've died anyway. He told me that it was a good kill, that I was a soldier and this was a war, that I should shape up and stop staring and ask myself what the dead man would've done if things were reversed.

The narrator feels guilty for killing an enemy soldier who posed no threat. Kiowa counsels him with Words of the Wiser, trying to help him understand the reality of warfare.

The narrator might accept his own role in the conflict, and he may begin acting without any sense of guilt or regret.

AGAIN AND AGAIN

One teacher I had always called on the second or third person to raise a hand, or perhaps on some student who was looking out the window — never on the first hand in the sky.

It happened again and again. Until, of course, I got clever and decided to shoot my hand up quickly even though I didn't have the foggiest notion what the answer was. That must have been the day that the teacher recognized the

FM33

lesson of Again and Again, and realized that he had established a pattern. Or perhaps he had been planning the switch all along. In any case, it was the day I shot my hand up first that he decided to change his routine. At my expense. . . .

Something that happens over and over, again and again, establishes a pattern. If we pay attention, we'll notice that pattern and ask ourselves, "Why does this happen over and over, again and again?" In our lives, the again and again moment probably teaches us something about our friends, or our teachers, or, perhaps, about the way the world works. And sometimes it alerts us to something that is likely to change.

In any case, whenever we notice something happening again and again, we should take note of it, and ask ourselves "Why does this keep happening repeatedly?" Our answer may be that it teaches us some consistent pattern that we can rely on. Or it may be that it is setting up expectations that we can predict will suddenly not be met. It may be leading us into a surprising Contrast and Contradiction. That, after all is what my teacher did to me. If I had thought more carefully about the Again and Again, and asked myself why he was always avoiding the first hand that waved, I might have guessed that he was preparing a trick and that one day he would call on that first hand.

In Robert Frost's **"Mending Wall,"** a student has noted an instance of **AGAIN AND AGAIN** and asked this question: Why might the author bring this up again and again?

My apple trees will never get across
And eat the cones under his pines, I tell him.
He only says, "Good fences make good neighbors."
Spring is the mischief in me, and I wonder
If I could put a notion in his head:
"*Why* do they make good neighbors? Isn't it
Where there are cows? But here there are no cows.
Before I built a wall I'd ask to know
What I was walling in or walling out,
And to whom I was like to give offence.
Something there is that doesn't love a wall,
That wants it down." I could say "Elves" to him,
But it's not elves exactly, and I'd rather
He said it for himself. I see him there
Bringing a stone grasped firmly by the top
In each hand, like an old-stone savage armed.
He moves in darkness as it seems to me,
Not of woods only and the shade of trees.
He will not go behind his father's saying,
And he likes having thought of it so well
He says again, "Good fences make good neighbors."

The speaker's neighbor says that "good fences make good neighbors" again and again, and the speaker wonders if that's true.

I think Frost may be repeating the words to emphasize the idea that people, like the speaker's neighbor, sometimes rely on old sayings and beliefs to guide their actions, even when those sayings and beliefs don't make sense anymore.

► MEMORY MOMENT

Sometimes, in a reflective moment, a memory will surprise you. You won't have been trying to remember that day, or that person, or that event. It will just pop up like an almost forgotten old friend who knocks at your door and surprises you.

But something called that memory up at that moment. Something that was happening right now reached into your distant past and pulled that memory into your thoughts. Figuring out why that happened will probably tell you something important. It may explain why you are feeling the way you are feeling. It may even explain why you are acting as you are at the moment.

In a story, the Memory Moment is an author's creation. She has decided to reach back into the past for something that she thinks you, as a reader, need to know. It's easy to skip over these moments. After all, you want to go forwards, not backwards, and the Memory Moment steps back into the past. But it's probably important to ask yourself "Why is this moment important?" Because you can assume that if the writer is any good at all, she thinks you should notice it and take note of it.

> In Ambrose Bierce's **"An Occurrence at Owl Creek Bridge"** a student has noted a **MEMORY MOMENT** and asked this question: Why might this memory be important?

One evening while Farquhar and his wife were sitting on a rustic bench near the entrance to his grounds, a gray-clad soldier rode up to the gate and asked for a drink of water. Mrs. Farquhar was only too happy to serve him with her own white hands. While she was fetching the water her husband approached the dusty horseman and inquired eagerly for news from the front.

"The Yanks are repairing the railroads," said the man, "and are getting ready for another advance. They have reached the Owl Creek bridge, put it in order and built a stockade on the north bank. The commandant has issued an order, which is posted everywhere, declaring that any civilian caught interfering with the railroad, its bridges, tunnels or trains will be summarily hanged. I saw the order."

This section of the story describes events in the past, events that might form a Memory Moment for Peyton Farquhar.

I think the exchange with the soldier reveals a lot about Farquhar's motivations. It also explains events described previously in the story: Farquhar had been caught trying to stop Northern soldiers from using the railroads during their advance.

© Houghton Mifflin Harcourt Publishing Company

FM35

NONFICTION SIGNPOSTS

Nonfiction has text clues as well. Just as in fiction, they invite you to stop and think about what's happening. These clues will help you focus on author's purpose — a critical issue to keep in mind when reading nonfiction. More importantly, these signposts will help you as you keep in mind what we call the Three Big Questions. These questions ought to guide all the reading we do, but especially the nonfiction reading. As you read, just keep asking yourself:

- What surprised me?
- What did the author think I already knew?
- What changed, challenged, or confirmed my thinking?

That first one will keep you thinking about the text. Just look for those parts that make you think, "Really!?!" and put an exclamation point there. The second one will be helpful when the language is tough, or the author is writing about something you don't know much about. Mark those points with a question mark and decide if you need more information. That final question, well, that question is why we read. Reading ought to change us. It ought to challenge our thinking. And sometimes it will confirm it. When you find those parts, just put a "C" in the margin. When you review your notes, you will decide if your thinking was changed, challenged, or confirmed.

As you're looking at what surprised you, or thinking about what is challenging you, or perhaps even as you find a part where it seems the author thinks you know something that you don't, you might discover that one of the following signposts appears right at that moment. So, these signposts help you think about the Three Big Questions. We have found five useful signposts for nonfiction.

CONTRASTS AND CONTRADICTIONS

The world is full of contrasts and contradictions — if it weren't, it would be a pretty dull place to live.

This is the same Contrast and Contradiction that you are familiar with from fiction. It's that moment when you encounter something you didn't expect, something that surprises you. It may be a fact that you find startling, a perspective that you had never heard before, or perhaps an argument that is new to you. We should welcome those moments, even though they may be disconcerting. They give us the opportunity to change our minds about things, to sharpen our thinking. The last person we want to become is that reader who reads only to confirm what he has already decided. That reader is committed to not learning, not growing, and standing absolutely still intellectually.

> In Iris Chang's **"Building the Transcontinental Railroad,"** a student has noted a **CONTRAST AND CONTRADICTION** and asked this question: What is the difference, and why does it matter?

As the railroad neared completion, the Chinese encountered the Irish workers of the Union Pacific for the first time. When the two companies came within a hundred feet of each other, the Union Pacific Irish taunted the Chinese with catcalls and threw clods of dirt. When the Chinese ignored them, the Irish swung their picks at them, and to the astonishment of the whites, the Chinese fought back. The level of antagonism continued to rise. Several Chinese were wounded by blasting powder the whites had secretly planted near their side. Several days later, a mysterious explosion killed several Irish workers. The presumption was that the Chinese had retaliated in kind. At that point, the behavior of white workers toward the Chinese immediately improved.

Initially, the author contrasts the behavior of each group toward the other: Chinese workers ignored the taunts of their Irish competitors.

That contrast, when those same workers respond to violence with violence, helps draw attention to how much abuse Chinese workers were willing to take before taking action to defend themselves.

EXTREME AND ABSOLUTE LANGUAGE

We are all guilty of overstatement all the time.

Well, that's an overstatement. We aren't all guilty, and those of us who are probably aren't guilty all of the time. When we hear "all," or "none," or "always," or "never," we can be absolutely certain — let's make that "almost certain" — that we are hearing absolute language. All it takes is one exception to make the claim false.

But we do tend to exaggerate and occasionally overstate our claims. Absolute language is easy to spot, and it's often harmless over-statement. Extreme language approaches absolute language but usually stops short. Much of the time, it's harmless, too. When you tell your buddy you're starving,

FM37

you probably aren't. Or when you say you just heard the funniest joke in the world, even though that's probably not true, your comment causes no real harm.

Sometimes, however, an extreme statement is potentially dangerous. If, for example, someone in authority were to say something like, "I am 100% certain that the airline crash was caused by terrorists," and we had not yet even found the black box that would explain the cause of the accident, then gullible listeners might believe and form opinions based on that statement, even though the phrase "100% certain" shows us clearly that it is an extreme statement. After all, no one ever claims to be 100% certain unless he isn't. So the question becomes, "How certain is he?" 80%? 40%? 20%?

When we spot absolute or extreme language, we should ask ourselves "Why did the author say it this way?" Sometimes the answer will be revealing.

In Thomas Jefferson's "**The Declaration of Independence,**" a student has noted instances of **EXTREME AND ABSOLUTE LANGUAGE** and asked this question: Why did the author use this language?

Prudence, indeed, will dictate that governments long established should not be changed for light and transient causes; and, accordingly, all experience hath shown that mankind are more disposed to suffer, while evils are sufferable, than to right themselves by abolishing the forms to which they are accustomed. But, when a long train of abuses and usurpations, pursuing invariably the same object, evinces a design to reduce them under absolute despotism, it is their right, it is their duty, to throw off such government, and to provide new guards for their future security. Such has been the patient sufferance of these colonies; and such is now the necessity that constrains them to alter their former systems of government. The history of the present King of Great Britain is a history of repeated injuries and usurpations, all having, in direct object, the establishment of an absolute tyranny over these States.

Wow! Jefferson uses both absolute and extreme language throughout the text.

Not only does his language draw attention to the colonists' suffering, but it also stresses the idea that the government has had only one goal, to establish tyrannical power over the states.

His use of language creates a clear sense that the colonists' decision is just.

NUMBERS AND STATS

"If I've told you once, I've told you a million times. . . ."

Those are numbers — 1 (once) and 1,000,000 — though we prefer to see that as Extreme and Absolute Language. Still, it allows us to make the point, which is that numbers are used to make a point. In this case, they reveal that the speaker is annoyed at how often he has to repeat himself for you to get the message. You barely have to ask the anchor question "Why did the writer or speaker use those numbers or amounts?"

But that's the question you should ask when numbers or stats or amounts appear in something you are reading. Writers include them because they think those numbers, which look like hard, objective, indisputable data, will be persuasive. The questions are, "What are they trying to persuade you to think or believe?" And, "Are the numbers reliable?"

When a writer tells you, for instance, that 97–98% of scientists who have studied the issue think that humans are affecting the environment in damaging ways, we probably want to ask what those figures tell us, both about the situation and the writer's purpose. Our answer will probably be that the writer believes the scientists have reached a consensus that we are endangering the planet. The writer might have said "most of the scientists agree," but "most" is vague. It could mean anything from slightly more than half to almost all. But "97–98%" is much more precise. And it's very close to 100%, so it should be persuasive. Numbers and stats help us visualize what the author is trying to show; it's up to you to decide if there's more you need to know.

> In Ron Chernow's "Thomas Jefferson: The Best of Enemies," a student has noted **NUMBERS AND STATS** and asked this question: Why did the author use these numbers or amounts?

Hamilton—brilliant, brash and charming—had the self-reliant reflexes of someone who had always had to live by his wits. His overwhelming intelligence petrified Jefferson and his followers. As an orator, Hamilton could speak extemporaneously for hours on end. As a writer, he could crank out 5,000- or 10,000-word memos overnight. Jefferson never underrated his foe's copious talents. At one point, a worried Jefferson confided to his comrade James Madison that Hamilton was a one-man army, "a host within himself."

Not only could Hamilton speak off-the-cuff for hours, but he could also write incredibly long memos in a single night.

The author includes these Numbers and Stats to help illustrate and explain why Jefferson and his allies were "petrified" by the single-handed power and abilities of Hamilton.

QUOTED WORDS

American writer Ambrose Bierce said that quotation is "The act of repeating erroneously the words of another." When writers use quotations they are probably doing one of two things. They may be giving you an individual example so that you can see what some person thought or felt about a certain situation, event, or idea. In that case, the writer is probably trying to help you see the human impact of what otherwise might be an abstract idea, difficult to imagine. A writer might, for instance, tell you about the massive damage Hurricane Harvey brought to the coast of Texas. A description of the widespread destruction will give you a picture of what happened; but the quoted words of someone who heard the hundred-mile-an-hour winds for hours when the storm came ashore or whose house was flooded by the rising waters will give you a feel for the impact of the storm on a real person.

Writers also use quoted words to lend authority to a claim they are making. Quoting the authority adds some credibility to the situation. The

FM39

Houston meteorologist who has studied the data and reports, "Harvey dumped more water in a shorter period of time on Houston than any other storm in Houston's history" ought to be believed more than the guy on the street corner who announces, "This is the worst storm ever."

In Abraham Lincoln's **Second Inaugural Address**, a student has noted **QUOTED WORDS** and asked this question: Why was this person or text quoted or cited, and what did this add?

The Almighty has his own purposes. "Woe unto the world because of offences! for it must needs be that offences come; but woe to that man by whom the offence cometh." If we shall suppose that American slavery is one of those offences which, in the providence of God, must needs come, but which, having continued through his appointed time, he now wills to remove, and that he gives to both North and South this terrible war, as the woe due to those by whom the offence came, shall we discern therein any departure from those divine attributes which the believers in a living God always ascribe to him?

Lincoln uses Quoted Words from the Bible to suggest that the nation's suffering during the Civil War is the result of divine punishment—a punishment that resulted from the nation's failure to end slavery when it was time for it to end.

▶ WORD GAPS

Unless we read such simple texts that we know everything there is to know about the subject, we will almost inevitably stumble into the gap between the writer's vocabulary and ours. Although that's occasionally frustrating, we might see it as an opportunity to sharpen our understanding. We might either learn a new word or learn how a word we already know might be used in a new way.

If we are in a hurry (and reading in a hurry is probably a bad idea because it doesn't give us time to think), then when we encounter a new word our first question might be, "Can I get by without knowing this word?" If you can, maybe you should make what sense you can of the sentence and move on. When we do that we lose the opportunity to learn something, but occasionally we just don't have the time. At the very least, you might jot down the word on the blank pages at the back of the book as a reminder to look it up later, so that the opportunity won't be completely lost.

A better way to approach the problem of the unknown word, however, might be to strategically ask several questions. Obviously the first step is to see if the word is at least partially explained by the context. For instance, if you read "hard, objective, indisputable data," and you don't know what "indisputable" means, you can easily figure out that it is something close to "hard" or "objective." Perhaps it means "definite," "not arguable," or something similar. Close enough. If you can get that far you can probably go on without

© Houghton Mifflin Harcourt Publishing Company

losing much. You may want to ask someone later what the word "indisputable" means, or look it up in the dictionary, but at the moment you will be able to read on.

If that easy fix doesn't work, however, you might start with "Do I know this word from somewhere else?" If you do, then you have a place to begin. What the word meant in the context with which you are familiar might be a clue to what it means in this new context. For instance, you know what it means when someone says, "I'm depositing my paycheck in the bank." But then you hear your friend say, "You can bank on me." You know your friend isn't becoming a financial lending institution. But, if you'll give yourself a moment to think about what you know about banks, then you might be able to figure out that this means you can count on your friend.

Sometimes, the word is a technical word, a term used primarily by experts in the field, and if you don't know the language of that field, you'll simply need to look it up.

In Charles C. Mann's **"Coming of Age in the Dawnland,"** a student has noted a **WORD GAP** and asked this question: Can I find clues in the sentence to help me understand the word?

Armed conflict was frequent but brief and mild by European standards. The *casus belli* was usually the desire to avenge an insult or gain status, not the wish for conquest. Most battles consisted of lightning guerrilla raids by ad hoc companies in the forest: flash of black-and-yellow-striped bows behind trees, hiss and whip of stone-tipped arrows through the air, eruption of angry cries. Attackers slipped away as soon as retribution had been exacted. Losers quickly conceded their loss of status.

I don't know the phrase "casus belli," but the author lists two common reasons for "armed conflict" and war among Native American groups, so I can guess that "casus belli" probably means "reasons or causes for war."

The essay by program consultant Carol Jago is an accessible explanation of **genre** and its importance. Genre has an elevated role in the new standards—both in reading and writing.

Ask students to read the first and second paragraphs and then to write their own definition of genre in the margin of their book.

If your students need an analogy to better understand **genre**, explain that genre refers to different categories or kinds of texts we read. This is similar to vehicles that we use for transportation. Vehicles transport people and goods but may be trucks, vans, sedans or sports cars—different categories for vehicles—different genres for texts.

Ask students to turn to a partner and provide examples of their favorite genre.

READING AND WRITING ACROSS GENRES

by Carol Jago

Reading is a first-class ticket around the world. Not only can you explore other lands and cultures, but you can also travel to the past and future. That journey is sometimes a wild ride. Other books can feel like comfort food, enveloping you in an imaginative landscape full of friends and good times. Making time for reading is making time for life.

Genre

One of the first things readers do when we pick up something to read is notice its genre. You might not think of it exactly in those terms, but consider how you approach a word problem in math class compared to how you read a science fiction story. Readers go to different kinds of text for different purposes. When you need to know how to do or make something, you want a reliable, trusted source of information. When you're in the mood to spend some time in a world of fantasy, you happily suspend your normal disbelief in dragons.

In every unit of *Into Literature,* you'll find a diverse mix of genres all connected by a common theme, allowing you to explore a topic from many different angles.

Writer's Craft

Learning how writers use genre to inform, to explain, to entertain, or to surprise readers will help you better understand—as well as enjoy—your reading. Imitating how professional writers employ the tools of their craft—descriptive language, repetition, sensory images, sentence structure, and a variety of other features—will give you many ideas for making your own writing more lively.

Into Literature provides you with the tools you need to understand the elements of all the critical genres and advice on how to learn from professional texts to improve your own writing in those genres.

**GENRE ELEMENTS:
SHORT STORY**

- is a work of short fiction that centers on a single idea and can be read in one sitting
- usually includes one main conflict that involves the characters and keeps moving
- includes the basic ele of fiction—plot, chara setting, and theme
- may be based on real and historical events

**GENRE ELEMENTS:
INFORMATIONAL TEXT**

- provides factual information
- includes evidence to support ideas
- contains text features
- includes many forms, such as news articles and essays

**GENRE ELEMENTS:
LITERARY NONFICTION**

- shares factual information, ideas, or experiences
- develops a key insight about the topic that goes beyond the facts
- uses literary techn as figurative langu narration
- reflects a persona involvement in th

GENRE ELEMENTS: POETRY

- may use figurative language, including personification
- often includes imagery that appeals to the five senses
- expresses a theme, or a "big idea" message about life

Reading with Independence

Finding a good book can sometimes be a challenge. Like every other reader, you have probably experienced "book desert" when nothing you pick up seems to have what you are looking for (not that it's easy to explain exactly what you are looking for, but whatever it is, "this" isn't it). If you find yourself in this kind of reading funk, bored by everything you pick up, give yourself permission to range more widely, exploring graphic novels, contemporary biographies, books of poetry, historical fiction. And remember that long doesn't necessarily mean boring. My favorite kind of book is one that I never want to end.

Moby-Dick
Or, The Whale
Herman Melville

The Last of
the Mohicans
Or a Narrative of 1757
James Fenimore Cooper

Take control over your own reading with *Into Literature's* Reader's Choice selections and the HMH Digital Library. And don't forget: your teacher, librarian, and friends can offer you many more suggestions.

SHORT STORY

Reality Check
David Brin

Explore the ways humans may continue to evolve when all concrete possibilities have been exhausted.

POEM

Democracy
Langston Hughes

How does a poet express his passionate plea for freedom?

ESSAY

**Martin Luther King Jr.:
He Showed Us the Way**
César Chávez

Find out why César Chávez believes that King's form of protest is the only way to achieve meaningful change.

FM43

Direct students to read the paragraph under the heading "Writer's Craft." Ask students to write their own definition of *writer's craft* in the margin of *Into Literature*. Discuss, asking students to cite examples.

Encourage students to find the Genre Elements feature with each selection in *Into Literature*.

Call students' attention to the **Reader's Choice** selections listed at the end of each unit and show students how to find the **HMH Digital Library** in the **Reading Studio**.

TEACHER'S EDITION

GRADE 11

Program Consultants:

Kylene Beers

Martha Hougen

Elena Izquierdo

Carol Jago

Erik Palmer

Robert E. Probst

UNIT (1)

Instructional Overview and Resources

	Instructional Focus	Online **Ⓔⓓ** **Resources**
 **Unit Introduction Foundations and Encounters**	**Unit 1 Essential Question** **Unit 1 Academic Vocabulary**	**Stream to Start:** Foundations and Encounters **Unit 1 Response Log**

ANALYZE & APPLY

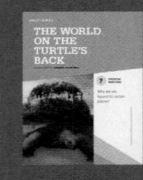 **"The World on the Turtle's Back"** Myth by Iroquois storytellers **Lexile 850L**	**Reading** • Analyze Folk Literature • Make Inferences **Writing:** Write a Myth **Speaking and Listening:** Present a Myth **Vocabulary:** Multiple-Meaning Words **Language Conventions:** Reflexive Pronouns	🔊 **Audio** **Reading Studio:** Notice & Note **Writing Studio:** Writing Narratives **Speaking and Listening Studio:** Giving a Presentation **Vocabulary Studio:** Multiple-Meaning Words **Grammar Studio:** Pronouns
 **"Balboa"** Short Story by Sabina Murray **Lexile 920L**	**Reading** • Analyze Thematic Development • Analyze Plot Structure **Writing:** Write a Dramatic Monologue **Speaking and Listening:** Present a Dramatic Monologue **Vocabulary:** Context Clues **Language Conventions:** Verb Tenses	🔊 **Audio** **Reading Studio:** Notice & Note **Writing Studio:** Writing Narratives **Speaking and Listening Studio:** Giving a Presentation **Vocabulary Studio:** Context Clues **Grammar Studio:** Verb Tense
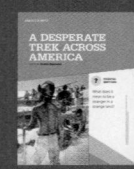 **MENTOR TEXT** **"A Desperate Trek Across America"** Article by Andrés Reséndez **Lexile 1230L**	**Reading** • Analyze Informational Texts • Analyze and Evaluate Evidence **Writing:** Write an Analytic Response **Speaking and Listening:** Present a Response **Vocabulary:** Foreign Words in English **Language Conventions:** Infinitives and Infinitive Phrases	🔊 **Audio** **Reading Studio:** Notice & Note **Writing Studio:** Using Textual Evidence **Speaking and Listening Studio:** Giving a Presentation **Vocabulary Studio:** Understanding Word Origins **Grammar Studio:** Infinitives and Infinitive Phrases
 **"Here Follow Some Verses Upon the Burning of Our House, July 10th, 1666"** Poem by Anne Bradstreet **Lexile N/A**	**Reading** • Analyze Voice • Paraphrase • Analyze Allusions **Writing:** Write a Poem **Speaking and Listening:** Discuss a Poem	🔊 **Audio** **Reading Studio:** Notice & Note **Speaking and Listening Studio:** Participating in Collaborative Discussions

SUGGESTED PACING: 30 DAYS

Unit Introduction — 1

The World on the Turtle's Back — 2 3 4 5 6

Balboa — 7 8 9

A Desperate Trek Across America — 10 11 12 13 14

Here Follow Some Verses Upon the Burning of Our House, July 10th, 1666 — 15 16

English Learner Support		Differentiated Instruction	Online Ed Assessment
• Building Background Knowledge		**When Students Struggle** • Take Notes	
• Text X-Ray • Language Conventions • Understand Idioms • Analyze Social Context • Analyze Folk Literature • Define Words	• Respond to Questions • Oral Assessment • Vocabulary Strategy	**When Students Struggle** • Sequence Events • Reteaching **To Challenge Students** • Compare Miraculous Birth Stories	**Selection Test**
• Text X-Ray • Learning Strategies • Understand Contrasts • Understand Plot Devices • Explain Text • Oral Assessment	• Vocabulary Strategy • Language Conventions	**When Students Struggle** • Analyze Plot • Analyze Character • Reteaching: Determining Themes **To Challenge Students** • Explore the Issue	**Selection Test**
• Text X-Ray • Use Cognates • Shared Responding • Use Prior Knowledge • Oral Assessment	• Vocabulary Strategy • Language Conventions	**When Students Struggle** • Understand Evidence	**Selection Test**
• Text X-Ray • Understand Archaic Language • Oral Assessment		**When Students Struggle** • Understand Poetry • Reteaching: Allusions	**Selection Test**

from **Of Plymouth Plantation/**
Coming of Age in the Dawnland *from* **1491**

**Independent
Reading**

End of Unit

| 17 | 18 | 19 | 20 | 21 | 22 | 23 | 24 | 25 | 26 | 27 | 28 | 29 | 30 |

UNIT 1 Continued

	Instructional Focus	Online  Ed Resources

COLLABORATE & COMPARE

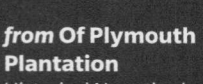

from Of Plymouth Plantation
Historical Narrative by William Bradford
Lexile 1440L

Reading
• Evaluate Author's Purpose
• Analyze Language

Writing: Write an Informational Text

Speaking and Listening: Hold a Group Discussion

Vocabulary: Archaic Vocabulary

Language Conventions: Active and Passive Voice

🔊 **Audio**

Reading Studio: Notice & Note

Close Read Screencast: Modeled Discussion

Writing Studio: Writing Informative Texts

Speaking and Listening Studio: Participating in Collaborative Discussions

Grammar Studio: Active and Passive Voice

Coming of Age in the Dawnland from 1491
History Writing by Charles C. Mann
Lexile 1290L

Reading
• Evaluate Author's Purpose
• Analyze Language

Writing: Write an Argument

Speaking and Listening: Share and Debate

Vocabulary: Specialized Vocabulary

Language Conventions: Dependent (or Subordinate) Clauses

🔊 **Audio**

Reading Studio: Notice & Note

Writing Studio: Writing Arguments

Speaking and Listening Studio: Analyzing and Evaluating Presentations

Vocabulary Studio: Specialized Vocabulary

Grammar Studio: Kinds of Clauses

Collaborate and Compare

Reading: Compare Author's Purpose

Speaking and Listening: Collaborate and Present

Speaking and Listening Studio: Giving a Presentation

Online Ed INDEPENDENT READING

The Independent Reading selections are only available in the eBook.

 Go to the Reading Studio for more information on NOTICE & NOTE.

 *from* The Way to Rainy Mountain
Memoir by N. Scott Momaday
Lexile 1000L

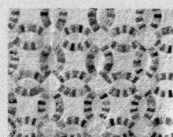 "To My Dear and Loving Husband"
Poem by Anne Bradstreet
Lexile N/A

END OF UNIT

Writing Task: Write a Literary Analysis

Speaking and Listening Task: Participate in a Panel Discussion

Reflect on the Unit

Writing: Write a Literary Analysis

Language Conventions: Active and Passive Voice

Speaking and Listening: Participate in a Panel Discussion

Unit 1 Response Log

Mentor Text: "A Desperate Trek Across America"

Writing Studio: Writing Informative Texts

Speaking and Listening Studio: Participating in Collaborative Discussions

Grammar Studio: Active Voice and Passive Voice

English Learner Support	Differentiated Instruction	Online Ed Assessment
• Text X-Ray • Use Cognates • Use Contextual Support • Demonstrate Comprehension • Language Conventions • Oral Assessment • Vocabulary Strategy	**When Students Struggle** • Use Graphic Organizers **To Challenge Students** • Challenge Central Ideas	**Selection Test**
• Text X-Ray • Use Cognates • Demonstrate Comprehension • Provide Contextual Support • Oral Assessment • Vocabulary Strategy • Language Conventions	**When Students Struggle** • Reteaching: Determine the Meaning of Words and Phrases	**Selection Test**
• Ask Questions	**To Challenge Students** • Compare Sources	
from La relación Historical Narrative by Álvar Núñez Cabeza de Vaca **Lexile 1010L**	*from* The General History of Virginia Historical Narrative by John Smith **Lexile 1680L**	"New Orleans" Poem by Joy Harjo	**Selection Tests**
• Language X-Ray • Understand Academic Language • Write a Group Analysis • Use the Mentor Text • Use Transitional Words • Passive Voice • Revise the Essay	**When Students Struggle** • Develop a Draft • Practice Presentations **To Challenge Students** • Voice and Tone	**Unit Test**

DISCUSS THE QUOTATION

Tell students that this quotation is from an essay written in 1782 by French immigrant Michel-Guillaume Jean de Crèvecoeur. His essay, titled "What Is an American?", uses the idea of a melting pot to describe the American population. The quotation expresses the ideal that America is a place where people of different backgrounds can come together and form a unified nation. This ideal is one of the foundations upon which America was established.

Ask students to think about how their school or community reflects Crèvecoeur's idea of a melting pot. Have them support their ideas with examples.

■ English Learner Support

Learn New Expressions Make sure students understand that the phrase *melted into a new race* means "combined into one nationality from many." **ALL LEVELS**

FOUNDATIONS AND ENCOUNTERS

EARLY AMERICAN LITERATURE

> " [In America] individuals of all nations are melted into a new race . . . whose labors . . . will one day cause great changes in the world. "
>
> —Michel-Guillaume Jean de Crèvecoeur

 LEARNING MINDSET

Growth Mindset Explain that students who believe they can learn and improve their skills are more successful than students who believe they're "just not good at" certain subjects. But in order to grow their brain, students must be willing to put forth effort and accept challenges, even if it means making mistakes. This is called having a *growth mindset*. Tell students it is essential to embrace this kind of mindset so they can break out of their comfort zones and reach their full potential.

Discuss the **Essential Questions** with your whole class or in small groups. As you read Foundations and Encounters, consider how the selections explore these questions.

? *ESSENTIAL QUESTION:*

Why are we bound to certain places?

For thousands of years, Native Americans regarded themselves as caretakers, not owners, of the land. The Europeans who began arriving in North America, however, saw things differently. They laid claim to the land and aggressively defended it from Native Americans—and from one another. In the end, the British claim overpowered all others. Yet the question remains: What connects people to the places they live, work, and fight to preserve?

? *ESSENTIAL QUESTION:*

What motivates people to explore the unknown?

America's early explorers traveled for many reasons: to gain glory for themselves or for their countries, to find gold or other riches, to discover new routes for travel and trade. Yet none of these motivators alone seems like enough to make the uncertainties of exploration—unknown destinations, unknown rewards, unknown dangers—worth the risk. What is it that causes people to seek out the unknown?

? *ESSENTIAL QUESTION:*

What does it mean to be a stranger in a strange land?

The first European settlers in America found a land completely foreign to anything they had known in their home countries. For many of them, America was an experiment in hope. However, they first had to make sense of the challenging environment and unfamiliar people with whom they shared it as they forged a new life for themselves. How do our surroundings affect the way we live and view the world?

? *ESSENTIAL QUESTION:*

What happens when cultures collide?

About five hundred years ago, European explorers and Native Americans encountered each other for the first time. In 1620 the first English Puritans landed at Plymouth, Massachusetts. At first, the two cultures were mutually dependent, interacting peacefully and engaging in trade; but as many more Europeans arrived, tensions and conflicts arose. What opportunities present themselves when people from very different cultures meet and engage with each other for the first time? What is lost when those cultures come into conflict?

Connect to the

ESSENTIAL QUESTIONS

Read aloud the Essential Questions and the paragraphs that follow them. Open the discussion of each idea by having students respond to the questions that conclude each paragraph.

? *ESSENTIAL QUESTION*

Why are we bound to certain places?

Challenge students to think about the differences between being a "caretaker" and an "owner." How does the Native American view explain why they felt connected to the land?

? *ESSENTIAL QUESTION*

What motivates people to explore the unknown?

Encourage students to suggest additional motivators—both internal and external—that would cause people to "seek out the unknown" despite the various risks of doing so. Extend the discussion by asking what character traits modern-day explorers are likely to share with early explorers.

? *ESSENTIAL QUESTION*

What does it mean to be a stranger in a strange land?

The early settlers were coming to live in a new and unexplored continent. Ask students to discuss the kinds of changes the colonists would have had to make in adapting to their new environment.

? *ESSENTIAL QUESTION*

What happens when cultures collide?

Have students discuss some of the "tensions and conflicts" that developed between the European settlers and the Native Americans.

EARLY AMERICAN LITERATURE

This essay provides students with a historical context for the Unit 1 selections. It presents a brief overview of early European contact with the native peoples living in North America, the first English settlers, Native American oral literature, and precolonial literature.

Tell students that much of what we know about Native American societies comes from the observations of Europeans, who recorded their experiences in America in diaries, letters, and reports back home, beginning with the journals of Christopher Columbus.

English Settlers By 1733, English colonies stretched all along the Atlantic coast. The first English colonists thought of themselves as English subjects, even though they did not have representation in the British Parliament. Once rooted in North American soil, the colonies became increasingly self-reliant and practiced local self-rule. However, they still supported England economically by exporting raw materials to the homeland and importing British manufactured goods. In return, Britain protected its territories.

COLLABORATIVE DISCUSSION

Ask groups to share key ideas from their discussions with the class. Have students support their responses with prior knowledge, reasons, or details from the essay.

EARLY AMERICAN LITERATURE

People have been living in the Americas for at least tens of thousands of years, adapting to its diverse environments. Millions of Native Americans lived on the land, in small villages and in large cities, such as the Aztec capital of Tenochtitlán, the site of present-day Mexico City. When Europeans arrived in 1492, there were many Native American cultures in North America with strongly differing customs and about 300 different languages.

Christopher Columbus's voyage to the Caribbean in 1492 marked the beginning of contact between Europeans and Native Americans. Spain, Portugal, England, France, and the Netherlands all staked claims in the Americas. At first, Native Americans were helpful to the Europeans, but it soon became clear that the newcomers intended to take control of the land. However, firearms were not the most dangerous weapons the Europeans brought with them; they also brought new diseases that killed millions.

In the early 1500s Spain conquered the great Aztec and Inca Empires and claimed Mexico, most of South America, and large portions of what is now the United States. The first French settlements in New France were founded in the early 1600s by fur traders along the St. Lawrence River. Eventually, French holdings included the Great Lakes region and most of the land along the Mississippi River, which was named Louisiana.

English Settlers The English were eager to have a colony in the New World and to prevent the northward expansion of the Spanish colony in Florida. A private trading company, the Virginia Company of London, established the first permanent English settlement at Jamestown, Virginia, in 1607. In 1619 the first Africans were brought to Virginia as enslaved persons to work for white slaveholders.

The original settlers of New England were Pilgrims, Protestant reformers who wanted to separate from the Church of England. Among them was William Bradford, who helped organize the voyage of the *Mayflower*, bringing nearly a hundred people to Massachusetts in 1620. Another group who settled in New England were the Puritans, who wanted to "purify" the Church of England. The Puritans' religious beliefs influenced all aspects of their lives, and the values of hard work, thrift, and responsibility led to thriving settlements and financial success.

COLLABORATIVE DISCUSSION
In a small group, review the timeline and discuss which literary or historical events had the most impact and why.

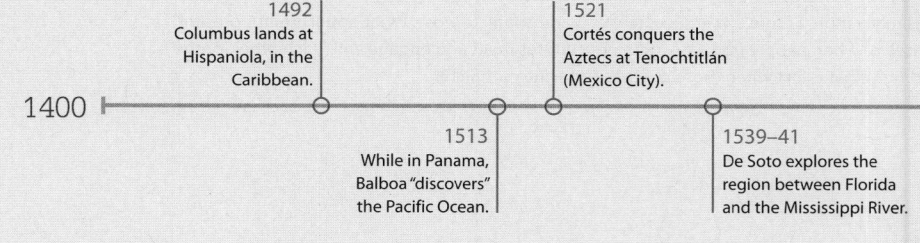

1400

1492 Columbus lands at Hispaniola, in the Caribbean.

1513 While in Panama, Balboa "discovers" the Pacific Ocean.

1521 Cortés conquers the Aztecs at Tenochtitlán (Mexico City).

1539–41 De Soto explores the region between Florida and the Mississippi River.

 ENGLISH LEARNER SUPPORT

Build Background Knowledge To aid comprehension of the essay, provide students with the following definitions.

diverse: differing from one another

environment: the totality of the natural world

aspect: a way in which something can be viewed by the mind

culture: the arts, beliefs, customs, and institutions of a particular group

reverence: a feeling of awe and respect

potential: the ability for growth or future success

desolate: deserted or barren **ALL LEVELS**

Native American Oral Traditions Few of the Native American cultures had a written language, but all possessed strong oral cultures and a rich tradition of storytelling. Creation stories—ways to explain how the universe and humans came into being—can be found in every Native American culture. Other forms include legendary histories tracing the migration of peoples or the deeds of cultural heroes, trickster tales, lyrics, chants, songs, healing ceremonies, and dream visions.

Tragically, much of this literature did not survive after so many Native Americans died from European diseases. The surviving works, however, show that diverse Native American groups explored common themes in their spoken literature, including a reverence for nature and the worship of many gods. Contemporary Native American writers, such as Joy Harjo, often incorporate elements of these traditional tales in their writing.

Pre-Colonial Literature While Native American literature offers us a glimpse into the ways and values of America's indigenous peoples, much of our understanding of pre-colonial America comes from the first-person accounts of its early explorers, settlers, and colonists. One of the founders of Jamestown, John Smith, wrote about conflicts with Native Americans, but he also described the "New World" as a paradise with great economic

Native American Oral Traditions Point out to students that one of the main differences between oral and written literature is that literature of oral traditions usually does not have a single, identifiable author. Stories would be handed down by members from one generation to the next, and each storyteller might add variations that in turn would be passed down to the next generation. As one Native American holy woman pointed out, "When you write things down you don't have to remember them. But for us it is different. . . . [All] that we are, all that we have ever been, all the great names of our heroes and their songs and deeds are alive within each of us . . . living in our blood." Ask students to consider why preservation through oral tradition is more vulnerable to loss than preservation through written works.

Pre-Colonial Literature Remind students that religion was the most influential cultural force of the period. The Puritans believed that writing should be useful, a tool to help readers understand the Bible and guide them in their daily lives. For this reason, logic, clarity, and order were more prized in writing than beauty or adornment. One Puritan compared adorned writing to stained-glass windows: "The paint upon the glass may feed the fancy, but the room is not well lighted by it." Using a familiar, down-to-earth metaphor such as this to make a deeper point is a common feature of Puritan writing. The direct, powerful, plain language of much of American literature owes a debt to the Puritans.

RESEARCH
What about this historical period interests you? Choose a topic, event, or person to learn more about. Then, add your own entry to the timeline.

RESEARCH

Encourage students to learn more about their chosen topic by searching for primary sources from the historical period. Have students choose excerpts from one of their sources to present to the class.

1607
First permanent English settlement is founded in Jamestown, Virginia.

1676
English settlers defeat Native Americans in King Philip's War.

1620
Mayflower Pilgrims found Plymouth colony in Massachusetts.

1700

1682
France claims the Mississippi River valley and names it *Louisiana*.

Foundations and Encounters   3

WHEN STUDENTS STRUGGLE . . .

Take Notes Students may experience difficulty learning the facts, events, and issues presented in the historical background essays that begin each unit. Encourage students to use the side margins in their write-in text to take notes. They can refer to their notes if they have questions about the historical setting for selections in each unit.

✏️ CHECK YOUR UNDERSTANDING

Have students answer the questions independently.

Answers:

1. *B*
2. *F*
3. *C*

If students answer any question incorrectly, have them reread the text to confirm their understanding.

potential. William Bradford, governor of Plymouth Plantation, described North America as "a hideous and desolate wilderness, full of wild beasts and wild men." Bradford and other colonial writers were motivated by their beliefs about their role in God's plan. Their writings included historical narratives, sermons, and poems written in a generally plain style.

Anne Bradstreet was one of the first poets in the American colonies. A volume of her poetry was published in England in 1650 as The Tenth Muse. Some of her best work is on personal themes, such as childbirth and the death of a grandchild.

CHECK YOUR UNDERSTANDING

Choose the best answer to each question.

1 What was North America like before the arrival of Europeans?

A It was an empty continent with abundant resources.

B It was a diverse land with more than 300 well-developed cultures with strongly differing customs.

C North America was a land recently settled by Native American groups that shared a single culture.

D North America was a continent ravaged by disease and warfare.

2 Which statement is an accurate description of Native American literature?

F It was a rich oral tradition focusing on creation stories and a reverence for nature.

G It was written in pictographs similar to Egyptian hieroglyphics.

H It contained many of the same myths and folktales that appear in European cultures.

J It had no literature because Native Americans did not have a written language.

3 We get most of our information about pre-colonial America from —

A modern-day scholars of the historical period

B elaborate written records from ancient civilizations

C first-person accounts of early explorers, settlers, and colonists

D Native American creation myths

ACADEMIC VOCABULARY

Academic Vocabulary words are words you use when you discuss and write about texts. In this unit, you will learn the following five words:

☑ adapt ❏ coherent ❏ device ❏ displace ❏ dynamic

Study the Word Network to learn more about the word **adapt.**

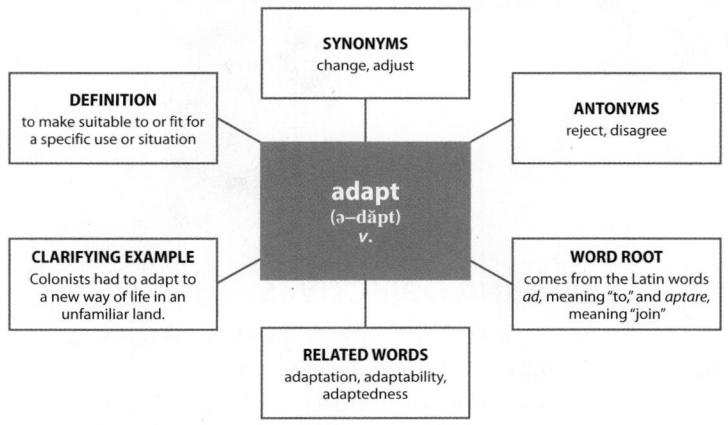

SYNONYMS
change, adjust

DEFINITION
to make suitable to or fit for a specific use or situation

ANTONYMS
reject, disagree

adapt
(ə–dăpt)
v.

CLARIFYING EXAMPLE
Colonists had to adapt to a new way of life in an unfamiliar land.

WORD ROOT
comes from the Latin words *ad,* meaning "to," and *aptare,* meaning "join"

RELATED WORDS
adaptation, adaptability, adaptedness

Write and Discuss Discuss your completed Word Network with a partner, making sure to talk through all of the boxes until you both understand the word, its synonyms, antonyms, and related forms. Then, fill out a Word Network for the remaining four words. Use a dictionary or online resource to help you complete the activity.

 Go online to access the Word Networks.

RESPOND TO THE ESSENTIAL QUESTIONS

In this unit, you will explore four different **Essential Questions** about early American literature and related texts. As you read each selection, you will gather your ideas about one of these questions and write about it in the **Response Log that appears on page R1**. At the end of the unit, you will have the opportunity to write a **literary analysis** related to one of the Essential Questions. Filling out the Response Log after you read each text will help you prepare for this writing task.

 You can also go online to access the Response Log.

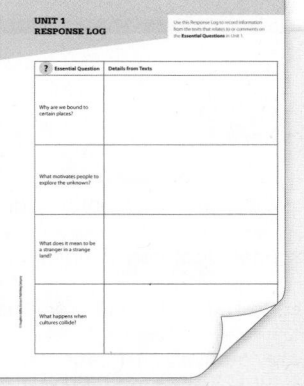

ACADEMIC VOCABULARY

Have students complete Word Networks for the remaining four vocabulary words. Encourage them to include all the categories shown in the completed network if possible, but point out that some words do not have clear synonyms or antonyms.

adapt (ə-dăpt´) *v.* to make something suitable for a particular situation; to adjust to an environment (Spanish cognate: *adaptar*)

coherent (kō-hîr´ənt) *adj.* holding together in an orderly, logical, or consistent way (Spanish cognate: *coherente*)

device (dĭ-vīs´) *n.* something made for a specific purpose; a literary technique used to achieve a certain effect

displace (dĭs-plās´) *v.* to move or force from one place or position to another (Spanish cognate: *desplazar*)

dynamic (dī-năm´ĭk) *adj.* characterized by change, movement, or activity (Spanish cognate: *dinámico*)

RESPOND TO THE ESSENTIAL QUESTIONS

Direct students to the Unit 1 Response Log. Explain that students will use it to record ideas and details from the selections that help answer one of the Essential Questions. When they work on the Writing Task at the end of the unit, their Response Logs will help them think about what they have read and make connections between the texts.

THE WORLD ON THE TURTLE'S BACK

Myth by Iroquois storytellers

GENRE ELEMENTS
CREATION MYTH

Creation myths are stories told within cultural groups that explain how the world or some natural wonder came to be or how it works. Characters in these stories often possess qualities that commonly exist in human nature— called **archetypes** —and are often repeated in literary works. Some cultures believe the myth is merely symbolic of some profound truth, while others believe the story is literal; however, the stories usually convey a message about the customs and values of the culture.

LEARNING OBJECTIVES

- Identify the elements and message of a myth.
- Conduct research and compare myths.
- Write a myth about an aspect of nature or a human characteristic.
- Present a myth orally.
- Use strategies to understand multiple-meaning words.
- Use reflexive pronouns in writing.
- **Language** Discuss with a partner the question that the myth answers.

TEXT COMPLEXITY

Quantitative Measures	The World on the Turtle's Back	Lexile: 850L
Qualitative Measures	**Ideas Presented** Multiple levels; use of symbolism; some ambiguity; greater demand for inference.	
	Structures Used Clear, chronological, conventional.	
	Language Used Mostly explicit; some figurative or allusive language; some unconventional language.	
	Knowledge Required More complexity in theme; experiences may be less familiar to many; cultural or historical references may make heavier demands.	

RESOURCES

- Unit 1 Response Log
- Selection Audio
- Reading Studio: Notice & Note
- Level Up Tutorial: Reading for Details; Myths, Legends, and Tales
- Writing Studio: Writing Narratives
- Speaking and Listening Studio: Giving a Presentation
- Vocabulary Studio: Multiple-Meaning Words
- Grammar Studio: Module 2, Lesson 2: Using Pronouns
- "The World on the Turtle's Back" Selection Test

SUMMARIES

English

In this Iroquoian creation myth, a curious woman who is with child falls from her home in the sky when she attempts to eat the roots of a sacred tree. Plummeting to her death, she is saved by the creatures of the air and the sea, who build the world on the back of a turtle. The woman bears a daughter who grows up and conceives twins from two arrows placed on her belly by a mysterious man as she sleeps. The new mother dies giving birth to twin boys. They quarrel, but their opposite natures bring balance to the world.

Spanish

En este mito creacionista iroqués, una curiosa mujer embarazada secae de su casa en el cielo al tratar de comer las raíces de un árbol sagrado. Mientras cae en picada, las criaturas del aire y el agua, quienes construyen el mundo en el caparazón de una tortuga, la salvan. La mujer tiene una hija, quien crece y concibe gemelos luego de que un hombre misterioso pone dos flechas en su vientre mientras duerme. La nueva madre muere cuando da a luz a los gemelos, quienes pelean; sin embargo, sus naturalezas opuestas traen equilibrio al mundo.

SMALL-GROUP OPTIONS

Have students work in small groups and pairs to read and discuss the selection.

Activating Academic Vocabulary

- Draw students' attention to the academic vocabulary words found on Student Edition page 5.
- During instruction and class discussion, model the appropriate use of each word.
- Challenge students to use the academic vocabulary words in oral discussions, written responses, and assessments.

Three Before Me

- After students have finished composing their myths on Student Edition page 17, ask them to review and revise the text.
- Have each student ask three other students to edit his or her text.
- Have each student evaluate the editing suggestions made by their three peers and make appropriate revisions before writing the final draft to be turned in.

Text X-Ray: English Learner Support
for "The World on the Turtle's Back"

Use the Text X-Ray and the supports and scaffolds in the Teacher's Edition to help guide students at different proficiency levels through the selection.

INTRODUCE THE SELECTION
DISCUSS IROQUOIS BELIEFS

In this lesson, students will need to be able to discuss Iroquois beliefs. Read paragraph 3 aloud to the students and point out the description of the Great Tree.

Explain to students that the Iroquois believed that nature (for example, the Great Tree) was sacred, or holy, and should not be damaged in any way. Some cultures believe other things are sacred, such as clothing, food, animals, ceremonies, or music. Have volunteers share examples of things that are sacred in their cultures or a culture with which they are familiar. Supply the following sentence frames:

- The Great Tree reminds me of _____.
- In my culture, many people believe that _____ is sacred.

CULTURAL REFERENCES

The following words or phrases may be unfamiliar to students:

- *center of the universe* (paragraph 3): the middle point that everything else in space moves around; something that is very important
- *broke her fall* (paragraph 7): softened someone's landing when he or she fell
- *rituals* (paragraph 13): ceremonies that are always performed in the same way
- *carnivorous* (paragraph 24): meat-eating

LISTENING

Understand Characters

Draw students' attention to the words in the passage that describe the twins and how they relate to each other. As you read the passage aloud, have the students jot down other words or phrases they hear that tell what the twins are like.

Have students listen as you read paragraphs 20–24 aloud. Use the following supports with students at varying proficiency levels:

- Explain to students that the selection is a creation myth. It tells how things came to be. Repeat sentences that describe how items were created. Ask what each of the sentences describes. Students can use this sentence frame: *This part tells how ___ came to be.* **SUBSTANTIAL**
- Have students work in pairs to describe what the myth explains, using the details they noted. Ask: *What do the brothers create? How do their creations help explain their world?* **MODERATE**
- After you read the passage aloud, have the students work in pairs to share their ideas about a question the myth answers. Encourage partners to refer to their notes for evidence that supports their conclusion. **LIGHT**

SPEAKING

Discuss Character Traits

Have students discuss the characters in the story and how they relate to each other. Circulate around the room to assess their use of new vocabulary and provide support as needed.

Use the following supports with students at varying proficiency levels:

- Explain that someone with "creative powers" can make things or have new ideas. Display and read the following sentence aloud: *"The twins had creative powers."* Have the students practice repeating the sentence back to you and then practice saying it to a partner. **SUBSTANTIAL**

- To help students describe the characters in the story, display the following sentence frame: *I know (name a character) is (describe a character), because the passage says (read a quote from the passage).* **MODERATE**

- Have students work with a partner to choose other characters in the story besides the twins, identify words and phrases from the text that describe those characters, and discuss what those characters are like with each other. **LIGHT**

READING

Understand Characters by Analyzing Text

Tell the students that storytellers help readers understand the characters in the story by describing them and by explaining what the characters do or the choices they make.

Work with the students to reread paragraphs 2, 4, and 5. Use the following supports with students at varying proficiency levels:

- Remind the students that the woman in the story was "curious," meaning that she wanted to learn more about something. Read details about the woman aloud and ask students to raise their hands when they hear clues that show her curiosity. **SUBSTANTIAL**

- Guide students to identify a choice one of the characters made and explain how that choice helped them understand the character better. Provide the following sentence frame: *When _____ made the choice to _____, I understood that the character was _____.* **MODERATE**

- Have students identify one of the characters in the story, describe what the character is like, and share two pieces of evidence from the text that support the students' claim. **LIGHT**

WRITING

Write a Myth

Work with students to read the writing assignment on Student Edition page 17.

Use the following supports with students at varying proficiency levels:

- Have students draw a picture or a series of pictures that tell their story. Have students label the pictures using newly acquired vocabulary. Ask students to write one or two sentences that tell the story. Allow them to use words from their native language if they do not know the English words that represent their ideas. **SUBSTANTIAL**

- Have students think of a question they would like to answer, such as "Why are there floods?" Have students list the characters in their story and write one sentence about each one using the following sentence frame: _____ is _____ because he or she _____. **MODERATE**

- Remind students that they can tell their readers more about the characters by explaining the choices the characters make when they are faced with a problem or conflict. Have them create a conflict and explain how the characters respond. **LIGHT**

THE WORLD ON THE TURTLE'S BACK

Myth by **Iroquois storytellers**

? **ESSENTIAL QUESTION:**

Why are we bound to certain places?

? Connect to the

ESSENTIAL QUESTION

Why are we bound to certain places?

"The World on the Turtle's Back" is an Iroquois creation myth that tells how opposite natures brought balance to the world. The myth helps readers understand how people are bound to nature and to their place in it.

6   Unit 1

QUICK START

Think about creation myths you have heard or read. Do they tell how something began or how something in nature works? Did you believe in the myth? Discuss with a partner.

ANALYZE FOLK LITERATURE

You may already be familiar with **folk literature,** which includes folk tales, myths, fables, and legends passed orally from one generation to the next. A **creation myth** is a traditional folk story with supernatural elements that describes how the universe, Earth, and life began, or explains the workings of the natural world.

Folk literature often include **archetypes,** or characters, situations, or actions that represent universal examples of human nature. For example, the twins in this myth represent two archetypal characters: the hero and the villain. Note other elements that may represent universal examples as you read.

Using the following strategies as you read will help you understand and appreciate the myth's message:

- Read the myth aloud, or imagine a storyteller's voice as you read silently.
- Note mysteries of nature and details about creation that the myth explains.
- Keep track of the ways in which the elements of a creation myth are used. What does this tell you about the genre?

MAKE INFERENCES

This myth articulates the religious beliefs, social customs, and values of the Iroquois culture. However, these beliefs and customs are not directly stated. It is up to you to **infer** them based on the details in the text. The characters' behavior and the way conflicts are resolved suggest the social values and customs that the storytellers wish to convey. As you read, use a chart to note your observations and inferences about what the Iroquois value.

DETAILS ABOUT STORY EVENTS	SOCIAL VALUES AND CUSTOMS	OTHER CULTURAL DETAILS

QUICK START

Have students read the Quick Start questions and invite them to discuss different accounts of creation with a partner. Ask students to consider why writers at different points in history might use existing explanations of the creation of the universe to create their own myths. Point out that creation myths also reflect a culture's physical environment. Ask students what kinds of questions a creation myth is likely, or unlikely, to answer.

ANALYZE FOLK LITERATURE

Review the elements of a myth with students. Then, discuss how myths and folk literature share important messages about life, human nature, or the world. Some creation myths, unlike many types of folk literature, were oral traditions, which means storytellers passed down the myths from generation to generation. Explain that one important characteristic of folk literature is the archetype. Review the common archetypal characters: hero, villain, mentor, everyman/everywoman, and innocent. Provide examples from well-known books or movies. For example, Gandalf in *The Lord of the Rings* is a mentor who provided knowledge and assistance. Harry Potter is a hero, while Lord Voldemort is the villain. Ask students to provide other examples of archetypal characters.

MAKE INFERENCES

Point out that the myth reveals information about the social practices and values of the Iroquois. For example, in paragraph 27, we learn that the Iroquois played lacrosse. They also held ceremonies to prepare for the New Year. Students should use the chart to record similar observations. To help students identify social values and customs, have students ask themselves how the people behaved, what they thought, and what was important to them.

TEACH

CRITICAL VOCABULARY

Encourage students to read all the sentences before deciding which word best completes each one. Remind them to look for context clues that match the precise meaning of each word.

Answers:

1. *pliable*

2. *frantically*

3. *delicacies*

4. *vanquish*

■ English Learner Support

Use Cognates Tell students that one of the Critical Vocabulary words has a Spanish cognate: *delicacy/ delicadeza.* **ALL LEVELS**

LANGUAGE CONVENTIONS

Review the information about reflexive pronouns. Then, ask students to name several reflexive pronouns (e.g., *myself, herself, yourself*). To help students remember the function of this type of pronoun, point out that a reflexive pronoun *reflects back* upon a sentence's subject or an earlier noun or pronoun.

ANNOTATION MODEL

Remind students of the annotation ideas, such as using a chart to record notes about this myth. Tell students they can underline or circle parts of the story or use their own system for marking up the selection in their write-in text. They may want to color-code their annotations, using a different color for details about story events, social values and customs, and other cultural details.

 **GET READY**

CRITICAL VOCABULARY

delicacies	frantically	vanquish	pliable

To see how many Critical Vocabulary words you already know, use them to complete the sentences.

1. Some plastics are hard, while others are as _____ as rubber.

2. The coach _____ ran onto the field to help his injured player.

3. The menu included many _____, such as truffles and caviar.

4. Ultimately, our forces will _____ the enemy.

LANGUAGE CONVENTIONS

Reflexive Pronouns In this lesson you will learn about reflexive pronouns. They are formed by adding *-self* or *-selves* to certain personal pronouns. A reflexive pronoun follows a verb or preposition and reflects back on an earlier noun or pronoun.

> He wouldn't get any of the roots for her, so she set out to do it **herself.**

The reflexive pronoun *herself* refers back to the pronoun *she.* As you read "The World on the Turtle's Back," note the use of reflexive pronouns.

ANNOTATION MODEL   **NOTICE & NOTE**

As you read, record your notes and observations about the kinds of information you find in this creation myth. You may also mark the details in the text that suggests the social values of the Iroquois. In the model, you can see one reader's notes about "The World on the Turtle's Back."

In the beginning there was no world, no land, no creatures of the kind that are around us now, and there were no men. But there was a great ocean which occupied space as far as anyone could see. Above the ocean was a great void of air. And in the air there lived the birds of the sea; in the ocean lived the fish and the creatures of the deep. Far above this unpeopled world, there was a Sky-World. Here lived gods who were like people—like Iroquois.

> The opening words suggest that this is a story of creation.
>
> Gods are supernatural beings, so this is a myth.
>
> Gods appear in human form.

EL ENGLISH LEARNER SUPPORT

Language Conventions Help students choose correct reflexive pronouns such as *himself* and *themselves.* Provide a sentence frame such as *He fed ___self.* Read the sentence frame aloud and draw or act out the action being described. Then, ask students to fill in the blank with either *him* or *his.* Point out that the word *him* (not *his*) would be used in the sentence *He fed him,* so *him* belongs in the blank. **ALL LEVELS**

BACKGROUND

"The World on the Turtle's Back" is an Iroquois (ĭr´ə-kwoi´) creation myth filled with conflict and compelling characters. In 1828, Iroquois author David Cusick was the first to write the story down. Today, more than 25 written versions exist.

The term **Iroquois** *refers to six Native American groups that share a culture. Most of them reside in what is now New York state. They call themselves Haudenosaunee, meaning "People of the Longhouse," after the longhouses in which they lived. Between 1570 and 1600, they formed the Iroquois League and managed to remain free from European rule.*

THE WORLD ON THE TURTLE'S BACK

Myth by Iroquois storytellers

SETTING A PURPOSE

As you read, pay attention to the details of this Iroquois creation myth. Note similarities and differences between this account and other tales of creation you are familiar with.

1   In the beginning there was no world, no land, no creatures of the kind that are around us now, and there were no men. But there was a great ocean which occupied space as far as anyone could see. Above the ocean was a great void of air. And in the air there lived the birds of the sea; in the ocean lived the fish and the creatures of the deep. Far above this unpeopled world, there was a Sky-World. Here lived gods who were like people—like Iroquois.

2   In the Sky-World there was a man who had a wife, and the wife was expecting a child. The woman became hungry for all kinds of strange **delicacies**, as women do when they are with child. She kept her husband busy almost to distraction finding delicious things for her to eat.

3   In the middle of the Sky-World there grew a Great Tree which was not like any of the trees that we know. It was tremendous; it had grown there forever. It had enormous roots

Notice & Note

Use the side margins to notice and note signposts in the text.

delicacy
(dĕl´ĭ-kə-sē) *n.* something pleasing and appealing, especially a choice food.

BACKGROUND

The Iroquois passed down myths such as "The World on the Turtle's Back" from one generation to the next through oral tradition, telling it in elaborate performances. Explain to students that, in the words of Native American literature scholars Larry Evers and Paul Pavich, such stories "remind the people of who and what they are, why they are in this particular place, and how they should continue to live here."

SETTING A PURPOSE

Direct students to use the Setting a Purpose prompt to focus their reading.

For **speaking** and **reading support** for students at varying proficiency levels, see the **Text X-Ray** on page 6D.

CRITICAL VOCABULARY

delicacy: The woman in the story is pregnant. Sometimes women crave certain special foods during their pregnancies.

ASK STUDENTS what the woman did to satisfy her cravings for delicacies. (*She kept her husband busy finding delicious things for her to eat.*)

EL ENGLISH LEARNER SUPPORT

Respond to Questions   Paragraphs 1–3 introduce the mythical setting and the woman who is a key character. Paragraph 3 also describes the sacred Great Tree. Ensure that students focus on and understand key story events and concepts by having them find the answers to these questions:

- What is the setting of this myth?
- Who lives in the Sky-World?
- What two characters are introduced?
- What is special about the Great Tree?   **MODERATE**

ANALYZE FOLK LITERATURE

Remind students that **archetypes** are characters, situations, or actions that represent universal examples of human nature. Common archetypal characters include hero, villain, mentor, innocent, and everyman/everywoman. (**Answer:** *Answers will vary. Students should cite details both from this myth and from the creation accounts they've heard or read. Some students may recognize similarities between the beginning of this myth and the biblical story of Adam and Eve, who tasted the fruit of the tree of knowledge in the Garden of Eden. Eve encouraged Adam to taste the fruit; the woman in this myth encouraged her husband to get some bark from the sacred tree.*)

(EL) ENGLISH LEARNER SUPPORT

Understand Idioms Tell students that the term *fed up with* at the end of paragraph 5 is an idiom — an expression that means something different from the literal meaning of the words. *Fed up with* means "wearied or tired of" (to the point of losing patience or control). Ask students to use this idiom to explain in their own words why the husband was tired or weary.
MODERATE

CRITICAL VOCABULARY

frantically: Whether the wife slipped or was pushed, she was not expecting to fall from the Sky-World. She reacted frantically, or in a panicked way.

ASK STUDENTS how the word *grabbed* helps them understand the meaning of *frantically*. (*Grabbed means "to grasp suddenly" and reinforces the idea that the wife was surprised and frantically trying to keep from falling.*)

 **NOTICE & NOTE**

ANALYZE FOLK LITERATURE

Annotate: In the first four paragraphs, mark words and phrases that indicate that this is a creation myth.

Evaluate: Explain whether the man and his wife are archetypal characters. In your response, consider details in the text, as well as other accounts of creation you've heard or read.

frantically
(frăn´tĭ-kəl-lē) *adv.* excitedly, with strong emotion or frustration.

that spread out from the floor of the Sky-World. <u>And on its branches there were many different kinds of leaves and different kinds of fruits and flowers.</u> The tree was not supposed to be marked or mutilated by any of the beings who dwelt in the Sky-World. It was a <u>sacred tree</u> that stood at the center of the universe.

4   The woman decided that she wanted some bark from one of the roots of the <u>Great Tree</u>—perhaps as a food or as a medicine, we don't know. She told her husband this. He didn't like the idea. <u>He knew it was wrong. But she insisted,</u> and he gave in. So he dug a hole among the roots of this great sky tree, and he bared some of its roots. But the floor of the Sky-World wasn't very thick, and he broke a hole through it. He was terrified, for he had never expected to find <u>empty space underneath the world.</u>

5   But his wife was filled with curiosity. He wouldn't get any of the roots for her, so she set out to do it herself. She bent over and she looked down, and she saw the ocean far below. She leaned down and stuck her head through the hole and looked all around. No one knows just what happened next. Some say she slipped. Some say that her husband, fed up with all the demands she had made on him, pushed her.

6   So she fell through the hole. As she fell, she **frantically** grabbed at its edges, but her hands slipped. However, between her fingers there clung bits of things that were growing on the floor of the Sky-World and bits of the root tips of the Great Tree. And so she began to fall toward the great ocean far below.

7   <u>The birds of the sea saw the woman falling, and they immediately consulted with each other as to what they could do to help her.</u> Flying wingtip to wingtip they made a great feathery raft in the sky to support her, and thus <u>they broke her fall.</u> But of course it was not possible for them to carry the woman very long. <u>Some of the other birds of the sky flew down to the surface of the ocean and called up the ocean creatures to see what they could do to help. The great sea turtle came and agreed to receive her on his back. The birds placed her gently on the shell of the turtle, and now the turtle floated about on the huge ocean with the woman safely on his back.</u>

8   The beings up in the Sky-World paid no attention to this. They knew what was happening, but they chose to ignore it.

9   When the woman recovered from her shock and terror, she looked around her. All that she could see were the birds and the sea creatures and the sky and the ocean.

10   And the woman said to herself that she would die. <u>But the creatures of the sea came to her and said that they would try to help her and asked her what they could do.</u> She told them that if they could find some soil, she could plant the roots stuck between her fingers, and from them plants would grow. <u>The sea animals said</u>

perhaps there was dirt at the bottom of the ocean, but no one had ever been down there so they could not be sure.

11   If there was dirt at the bottom of the ocean, it was far, far below the surface in the cold deeps. But the animals said they would try to get some. One by one the diving birds and animals tried and failed. They went to the limits of their endurance, but they could not get to the bottom of the ocean. Finally, the muskrat said he would try. He dived and disappeared. All the creatures waited, holding their breath, but he did not return. After a long time, his little body floated up to the surface of the ocean, a tiny crumb of earth clutched in his paw. He seemed to be dead. They pulled him up on the turtle's back and they sang and prayed over him and breathed air into his mouth, and finally, he stirred. Thus it was the muskrat, the Earth-Diver, who brought from the bottom of the ocean the soil from which the earth was to grow.

12   The woman took the tiny clod of dirt and placed it on the middle of the great sea turtle's back. Then the woman began to walk in a circle around it, moving in the direction that the sun goes. The earth began to grow. When the earth was big enough, she planted the roots she had clutched between her fingers when she fell from the Sky-World. Thus the plants grew on the earth.

13   To keep the earth growing, the woman walked as the sun goes, moving in the direction that the people still move in the dance rituals. She gathered roots and plants to eat and built herself a little hut. After a while, the woman's time came, and she was delivered of a daughter. The woman and her daughter kept walking in a circle around the earth, so that the earth and plants would continue to grow. They lived on the plants and roots they gathered. The girl grew up with her mother, cut off forever from the Sky-World above, knowing only the birds and the creatures of the sea, seeing no other beings like herself.

14   One day, when the girl had grown to womanhood, a man appeared. No one knows for sure who this man was. He had something to do with the gods above. Perhaps he was the West Wind. As the girl looked at him, she was filled with terror, and amazement, and warmth, and she fainted dead away. As she lay on the ground, the man reached into his quiver, and he took out two arrows, one sharp and one blunt, and he laid them across the body of the girl, and quietly went away.

15   When the girl awoke from her faint, she and her mother continued to walk around the earth. After a while, they knew that the girl was to bear a child. They did not know it, but the girl was to bear twins.

16   Within the girl's body, the twins began to argue and quarrel with one another. There could be no peace between them. As the time approached for them to be born, the twins fought about their birth.

NOTICE & NOTE

MAKE INFERENCES
Annotate: Reread paragraphs 7–11 and mark the phrases that describe the roles "all the creatures" play in this myth.

Infer: What do these passages suggest about the Iroquois' attitude toward animals?

LANGUAGE CONVENTIONS
Annotate: A reflexive pronoun reflects back on a noun or pronoun. Mark the reflexive pronouns in paragraph 13.

Identify: Identify the word each pronoun reflects back on.

The World on the Turtle's Back   11

MAKE INFERENCES

Remind students that the way **characters** act and respond to each other reveals important information about them. In creation myths, the way characters behave can also reveal important social values. Discuss how the creatures' actions and reactions reveal the Iroquois' positive feelings toward animals. (***Possible answer:*** *The animals play a significant role in the myth, helping and supporting the woman. They are depicted as wise and resourceful, suggesting that the Iroquois had a respectful, even reverential, attitude toward animals.*)

■ English Learner Support

Analyze Social Context   To model analyzing the Iroquois' attitude toward animals, read paragraphs 7 and 10 aloud. Think aloud to help students understand what these actions reveal about the Iroquois: "I see that the birds and animals tried several times to help the woman. They didn't give up. Finally the muskrat said he would help. That they wanted to help the woman shows that the Iroquois believed animals were wise and resourceful. This shows they respected animals."

Use descriptive words to discuss how the other creatures responded to the woman's situation. **MODERATE**

LANGUAGE CONVENTIONS

Remind students that a reflexive pronoun follows a verb or preposition and reflects back on an earlier noun or pronoun. Tell students the same reflexive pronoun is used twice in paragraph 13—and in each instance it reflects back onto a different person. (***Answer:*** *The first instance of "herself" reflects back onto the pronoun "She" [the woman]. The second instance of "herself" reflects back onto the phrase "The girl."*)

WHEN STUDENTS STRUGGLE . . .

Sequence Events   Have students use a graphic organizer to create a timeline of events from paragraphs 12–15 of the story. Students should record a detail about a story event from paragraph 12 in the first "bubble," from paragraph 13 in the second, and so on.

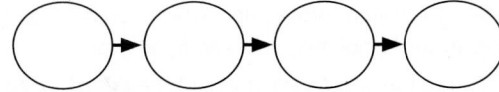

 For additional support, go to the **Reading Studio** and assign the following **LEVEL UP** **Level Up Tutorial: Reading for Details.**

ANALYZE FOLK LITERATURE

Remind students that a character's words and actions reveal his or her personality and motivations. Have students look for key words and actions that give clues about the twins' feelings for each other as well as their respective personalities. (**Answer:** *Students may think that one brother will end up killing the other as in the biblical story of Cain and Abel.*)

■ English Learner Support

Analyze Folk Literature Stress that the conflict between the twins takes many forms, which are signified in the words used in this part of the story. For example, call attention to the word *argue* in paragraph 16. Have students identify other words in paragraphs 16–18 that are specifically related to hostility or aggression (examples include *quarrel, fought, kill, murdering,* and *conflict*). **MODERATE**

For **listening support** for students at varying proficiency levels, see the **Text X-Ray** on page 6C.

 **NOTICE & NOTE**

ANALYZE FOLK LITERATURE

Annotate: Mark the phrases in paragraphs 16–18 that describe the twins' relationship.

Predict: Based on the details in these paragraphs, how do you think the twins' conflict will be resolved? Why?

The right-handed twin wanted to be born in the normal way, as all children are born. But the left-handed twin said no. He said he saw light in another direction, and said he would be born that way. The right-handed twin beseeched him not to, saying that he would kill their mother. But the left-handed twin was stubborn. He went in the direction where he saw light. But he could not be born through his mother's mouth or her nose. He was born through her left armpit, and killed her. And meanwhile, the right-handed twin was born in the normal way, as all children are born.

17   The twins met in the world outside, and the right-handed twin accused his brother of murdering their mother. But the grandmother told them to stop their quarreling. They buried their mother. And from her grave grew the plants which the people still use. From her head grew the corn, the beans, and the squash—"our supporters, the three sisters."[1] And from her heart grew the sacred tobacco, which the people still use in the ceremonies and by whose upward-floating smoke they send thanks. The women call her "our mother," and they dance and sing in the rituals so that the corn, the beans, and the squash may grow to feed the people.

18   But the conflict of the twins did not end at the grave of their mother. And, strangely enough, the grandmother favored the left-handed twin.

19   The right-handed twin was angry, and he grew more angry as he thought how his brother had killed their mother. The right-handed twin was the one who did everything just as he should. He said what he meant, and he meant what he said. He always told the truth, and he always tried to accomplish what seemed to be right and reasonable. The left-handed twin never said what he meant or meant what he said. He always lied, and he always did things backward. You could never tell what he was trying to do because he always made it look as if he were doing the opposite. He was the devious one.

20   These two brothers, as they grew up, represented two ways of the world which are in all people. The Indians did not call these the right and the wrong. They called them the straight mind and the crooked mind, the upright man and the devious man, the right and the left.

21   The twins had creative powers. They took clay and modeled it into animals, and they gave these animals life. And in this they contended with one another. The right-handed twin made the deer, and the left-handed twin made the mountain lion which kills the deer. But the right-handed twin knew there would always be more deer than mountain lions. And he made another animal. He made the ground squirrel. The left-handed twin saw that the mountain lion

---

[1] **the three sisters:** Corn, beans, and squash—the Iroquois' staple food crops—were grown together. The bean vines climbed and were supported by the corn stalks, while squash, which spread across the ground and kept weeds from growing, was planted around the bean plants.

12   Unit 1

© Houghton Mifflin Harcourt Publishing Company

APPLYING ACADEMIC VOCABULARY

☑ **adapt**   ☐ **coherent**   ☐ **device**   ☑ **displace**   ☐ **dynamic**

Write and Discuss Have students turn to a partner to discuss the following questions. Guide students to include the Academic Vocabulary words *adapt* and *displace* in their responses. Ask volunteers to share their responses with the class.

- After the woman fell from the Sky-World, how did she **adapt** to life on Earth?
- Did the right-handed twin **displace** his brother as his grandmother's favorite? How do you know?

could not get to the ground squirrel, who digs a hole, so he made the weasel. And although the weasel can go into the ground squirrel's hole and kill him, there are lots of ground squirrels and not so many weasels. Next the right-handed twin decided he would make an animal that the weasel could not kill, so he made the porcupine. But the left-handed twin made the bear, who flips the porcupine over on his back and tears out his belly.

22   And the right-handed twin made berries and fruits of other kinds for his creatures to live on. The left-handed twin made briars and poison ivy, and the poisonous plants like the baneberry and the dogberry, and the suicide root with which people kill themselves when they go out of their minds. And the left-handed twin made medicines, for good and for evil, for doctoring and for witchcraft.

23   And finally, the right-handed twin made man. The people do not know just how much the left-handed twin had to do with making man. Man was made of clay, like pottery, and baked in the fire. . . .

24   The world the twins made was a balanced and orderly world, and this was good. The plant-eating animals created by the right-handed twin would eat up all the vegetation if their number was not kept down by the meat-eating animals, which the left-handed twin created. But if these carnivorous animals ate too many other animals, then they would starve, for they would run out of meat. So the right- and the left-handed twins built balance into the world.

25   As the twins became men full grown, they still contested with one another. No one had won, and no one had lost. And they knew that the conflict was becoming sharper and sharper, and one of them would have to **vanquish** the other.

26   And so they came to the duel. They started with gambling. They took a wooden bowl, and in it they put wild plum pits. One side of the pits was burned black, and by tossing the pits in the bowl and betting on how these would fall, they gambled against one another, as the people still do in the New Year's rites.[2] All through the morning they gambled at this game, and all through the afternoon, and the sun went down. And when the sun went down, the game was done, and neither one had won.

27   So they went on to battle one another at the lacrosse[3] game. And they contested all day, and the sun went down, and the game was done. And neither had won.

28   And now they battled with clubs, and they fought all day, and the sun went down, and the fight was done. But neither had won.

---

[2] **New Year's rites:** Various ceremonies to get ready for the New Year. They often included community confession of sins, the replenishing of hearths in the homes, sacred dances, as well as the gambling ritual.

[3] **lacrosse:** a game of Native American origin wherein participants on two teams use long-handled sticks with webbed pouches to maneuver a ball into the opposing team's goal.

MAKE INFERENCES
Annotate: Mark phrases in paragraphs 19–23 that describe each twin's character and behavior.

Infer: Which twin is characterized as being more admirable? What does this characterization tell you about Iroquois values?

vanquish
(văng´kwĭsh) *v.* to defeat in a contest or conflict.

 MAKE INFERENCES

Remind students that they can infer social values of Iroquois culture from these characters' words, actions, and interactions. (**Answer:** *The right-handed twin is characterized as admirable. He is truthful and direct, while the left-handed twin is untruthful and devious. This characterization suggests the Iroquois valued honesty and straightforwardness.*)

EL ENGLISH LEARNER SUPPORT

Define Words   Have students look at the word *doctoring* at the end of paragraph 22. Many students will be familiar with the noun *doctor,* but *doctoring* or *to doctor* might be unfamiliar. Ask students to offer definitions of the word *doctor* (someone who helps people who are sick). Ask how the meaning of the word *doctor* can help them guess the meaning of *doctoring* (helping people who are sick). Remind students to use clues from the text to help them determine a word's meaning. **ALL LEVELS**

TO CHALLENGE STUDENTS . . .

Compare Miraculous Birth Stories   In the Iroquois myth, the twins demonstrated their special powers soon after their birth. This is a particular feature of the text structure of Miraculous Birth stories. Have students think about other creation myths they have read or are familiar with. Have students discuss the similarities and differences among the stories, thinking particularly about the traits of the characters and their roles, how/why they were created, and what they tell us about these cultures' values. Then, ask students to speculate about how the differences they see in these views might affect these cultures in their real-life interactions with one another.

CRITICAL VOCABULARY

vanquish: The twins were continually fighting with each other; eventually, there could be only one winner.

ASK STUDENTS to discuss why one twin would have to be vanquished. What might the conflict between the twins represent symbolically? (***Possible answer:*** *In a battle, only one person can win. The conflict might represent the struggle between good and evil in the world.*)

ANALYZE FOLK LITERATURE

Tell students that the transformation of a character—such as the grandmother—is a common element of mythology and is often used to explain natural phenomena. (**Answer:** *The left-handed son rules the night. The right-handed son made the grandmother the moon when he killed her so she could still watch "over the realm of her favorite grandson," which was the left-handed son.*)

CRITICAL VOCABULARY

pliable: One name for the right-handed twin is *Sapling*. A sapling is *pliable* in that it might bend in the wind without breaking.

ASK STUDENTS if they think the characterization of the right-handed twin as *pliable* is meant as a compliment or an insult. (*In this context, pliable seems to mean "able to adjust readily to different conditions"; the other surrounding words are positive, so it is meant as a compliment.*)

 NOTICE & NOTE

29 And they went from one duel to another to see which one would succumb. Each one knew in his deepest mind that there was something, somewhere, that would vanquish the other. But what was it? Where to find it?

30 Each knew somewhere in his mind what it was that was his own weak point. They talked about this as they contested in these duels, day after day, and somehow the deep mind of each entered into the other. And the deep mind of the right-handed twin lied to his brother, and the deep mind of the left-handed twin told the truth.

31 On the last day of the duel, as they stood, they at last knew how the right-handed twin was to kill his brother. Each selected his weapon. The left-handed twin chose a mere stick that would do him no good. But the right-handed twin picked out the deer antler, and with one touch he destroyed his brother. And the left-handed twin died, but he died and he didn't die. The right-handed twin picked up the body and cast it off the edge of the earth. And some place below the world, the left-handed twin still lives and reigns.

32 When the sun rises from the east and travels in a huge arc along the sky dome, which rests like a great upside-down cup on the saucer of the earth, the people are in the daylight realm of the right-handed twin. But when the sun slips down in the west at nightfall and the dome lifts to let it escape at the western rim, the people are again in <u>the domain of the left-handed twin—the fearful realm of night.</u>

33 Having <u>killed his brother,</u> the right-handed twin returned home to his grandmother. And she met him in anger. She threw the food out of the cabin onto the ground and said that he was a murderer, for he had killed his brother. He grew angry and told her she had always helped his brother, who had killed their mother. <u>In his anger, he grabbed her by the throat and cut her head off. Her body he threw into the ocean, and her head, into the sky. There, "Our Grandmother, the Moon" still keeps watch at night over the realm of her favorite grandson.</u>

34 The right-handed twin has many names. One of them is Sapling. It means smooth, young, green and fresh and innocent, straightforward, straight-growing, soft and **pliable**, teachable and trainable. These are the old ways of describing him. But since he has gone away, he has other names. He is called "He Holds Up the Skies," "Master of Life," and "Great Creator."

35 The left-handed twin also has many names. One of them is Flint. He is called the devious one, the one covered with boils. Old Warty. He is stubborn. He is thought of as being dark in color.

ANALYZE FOLK LITERATURE
Annotate: Mark the phrases in paragraphs 32–33 that tell what happened to the left-handed twin and the grandmother.

Analyze: How does this myth explain the fact that the moon is visible mainly at night?

pliable
(plī´ə-bəl) *adj.* easily bent or shaped; easily influenced, persuaded, or controlled.

IMPROVE READING FLUENCY

Targeted Passage Use the lyrical language in paragraphs 34–38 to promote readers' interest. Have students work in small groups, with different individuals reading one each of the five paragraphs aloud. Remind them to be expressive and to use punctuation as a guide for pauses and other emphasis. Encourage students to share their thoughts on how a fluent reader keeps listeners interested and engaged.

Go to the **Reading Studio** for additional support in developing fluency.

36   These two beings rule the world and keep an eye on the affairs of men. The right-handed twin, the Master of Life, lives in the Sky-World. He is content with the world he helped to create and with his favorite creatures, the humans. The scent of sacred tobacco rising from the earth comes gloriously to his nostrils.

37   In the world below lives the left-handed twin. He knows the world of men, and he finds contentment in it. He hears the sounds of warfare and torture, and he finds them good.

38   In the daytime, the people have rituals which honor the right-handed twin. Through the daytime rituals, they thank the Master of Life. In the nighttime, the people dance and sing for the left-handed twin.

MAKE INFERENCES

Annotate: Reread paragraphs 36–38. Circle information that tells you about the right-handed twin. Underline information that tells you about the left-handed twin.

Infer: Based on the information contained in these paragraphs, what can you infer about Iroquois customs and values?

 MAKE INFERENCES

Point out to students that paragraphs 36–38 summarize the twins' shared role in ruling the world. Have them compare the information about the twins and then think about what the contrast reveals. (**Answer:** *The Iroquois performed rituals, danced, and sang in honor of both the right-handed twin and the left-handed twin. The Iroquois also sometimes engaged in warfare.*)

CHECK YOUR UNDERSTANDING

Answer these questions before moving on to the **Analyze the Text** section on the following page.

1 How does the turtle help the woman who fell from the sky?

  A He brings soil from the ocean floor.

  B He carries the woman on his back.

  C He breaks the woman's fall.

  D He makes the earth grow.

2 What happened when the twins' mother is buried?

  F A sacred tree grew from her head.

  G Man was created from her ribs.

  H The plants that people still use grew.

  J She became the light in the sky.

3 What happens to the left-handed twin?

  A He kills his brother and mother.

  B He kills his grandmother.

  C He becomes the Master of Life.

  D He becomes ruler of the underworld.

CHECK YOUR UNDERSTANDING

Have students answer the questions independently.

Answers:

  1. *B*

  2. *H*

  3. *D*

If students answer any questions incorrectly, have them reread the text to confirm their understanding. Then, they may proceed to ANALYZE THE TEXT on page 16.

EL **ENGLISH LEARNER SUPPORT**

Oral Assessment Use the following sentences to assess students' comprehension and speaking skills.

  1. The _____ carries the woman on his back. (*turtle*)

  2. After the mother of the twins is buried, _____ grow from her head and heart. (*plants*)

  3. The left-handed twin becomes ruler of _____. (*the underworld*)

  SUBSTANTIAL/MODERATE

ANALYZE THE TEXT

Possible answers:

1. **DOK 2:** *The story shows that the Iroquois value of helping others, doing everything that one can to be helpful, and discussing problems to find a solution.*

2. **DOK 4:** *The right-handed twin would be considered the hero because he made all things that were good or helpful. He also created humans, which would make him a hero to everyone. The left-handed twin created all things that were bad or deadly. The Iroquois called the right-handed twin "the straight mind" and called the left-handed twin "the crooked mind."*

3. **DOK 4:** *The right-handed twin killed his brother and casted his body out of that world and into another. The resolution suggests that the Iroquois believed there was a place for both of the brothers and that they continued to act as a balance to each other.*

4. **DOK 3:** *The right-handed twin was the "Great Creator" and lived in the Sky-World, while the left-handed twin lived in the world below and found the sounds of warfare and torture good. The myth explains why humans have both good and evil impulses.*

5. **DOK 4:** *Nature is extremely important to the Iroquois' way of life because they were hunters and gatherers. They believed important crops grew from the woman who gave birth to the creators of the world. They believed the twins created animals, plants, and humans. They believed all gods were important and they honored all gods because the gods created different things.*

RESEARCH

Remind students that they should confirm any information they find by checking multiple websites and assessing the credibility of each.

Extend Answers will vary depending on the creation myths students examine. Students may note, for example, differences regarding attitudes toward nature; views of their gods; beliefs about good and evil; and important foods, games, and rituals.

💬 **RESPOND**

ANALYZE THE TEXT

Support your responses with evidence from the text. 📝 NOTEBOOK

1. **Infer** What Iroquois values are revealed by the creatures' actions toward the woman who fell?

2. **Analyze** What characteristics and behaviors suggest that the right-handed twin is an archetypal hero? What characteristics and behaviors suggest the left-handed twin is an archetypal villain? Cite text evidence in your response.

3. **Analyze** How is the conflict between the twins resolved? What does the resolution suggest about the Iroquois' view of both twins?

4. **Draw Conclusions** What elements of the world and human nature does this creation myth explain? Cite text evidence in your response.

5. **Connect** Folk literature often conveys information about a people's culture. From this myth, what do you learn about the Iroquois' attitude toward nature and their view of their gods?

RESEARCH TIP
You might want to begin your research by learning more about creation myths in general. There are websites or books that include creation myths. Find at least two reliable sources about another culture's creation myth for the information you use.

RESEARCH

Almost every culture has an explanation of how the world was created. Research creation myths from a variety of cultures around the world, including other Native American groups. Choose one creation myth to compare with "The World on the Turtle's Back." Write the name of the myth and the culture it comes from in the first column of the chart. Then record two similarities and two differences between the myth you chose and "The World on the Turtle's Back."

CREATION MYTH	SIMILARITIES	DIFFERENCES
Answers will vary.		

Extend Think about what you have learned about creation myths from this activity. Did they have many of the characteristics you learned about in this lesson? What do the two myths you compared tell you about the values of their respective cultures? How do those values compare with the values of modern American culture?

WHEN STUDENTS STRUGGLE . . .

Reteaching Students may struggle with the concept of archetypes and why it is important to recognize them when reading folk literature, particularly creation myths. Write the five most common archetypal characters on the board: mentor, hero, villain, innocent, and everyman/everywoman. Review each type and then ask students which archetypal characters the twins, man, woman, and grandmother represent. Ask students questions to help them explain the archetypes.

 For additional support, go to the **Reading Studio** and assign the following LEVELUP **Level Up Tutorial: Myths, Legends, and Tales.**

CREATE AND PRESENT

Write a Myth A myth is a traditional story that explains how some aspect of human nature or the natural world came to be. Work with a partner to write a myth.

- ❏ Decide on an aspect of nature or a human characteristic that you want to write about. Start by asking yourself a question, such as "Why do giraffes have long necks?"

- ❏ Create a cast of characters and give them appropriate names. Keep in mind that your characters may be gods, humans, or animals, and may be able to act in exceptional ways.

- ❏ Develop a conflict and resolution that will allow you to provide the answer to your question.

- ❏ As you describe the events in your myth, use vivid imagery that will help paint a mental picture for readers or listeners.

Present a Myth Prepare to present your myth orally with your partner, either before a small group or the whole class.

- ❏ Decide how you will divide your myth for presentation. Will each of you read alternate paragraphs, or will one person read the narration and the other read the dialogue?

- ❏ Practice reading the myth together before you make your presentation.

- ❏ Be prepared to answer other students' questions about your myth and its meaning.

RESPOND TO THE ESSENTIAL QUESTION

 Why are we bound to certain places?

Gather Information Review your annotations and notes on "The World on the Turtle's Back." Then add relevant information to your Response Log. As you determine which information to include, think about:

- the role of folk literature in a culture
- the view of humanity expressed by the myth
- Iroquois beliefs and rituals that are revealed through the story

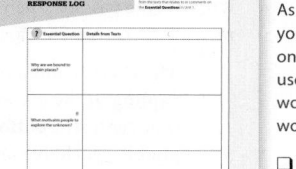

 RESPOND

Go to **Writing Narratives** in the **Writing Studio** for help.

Go to **Giving a Presentation: Delivering Your Presentation** in the **Speaking and Listening Studio** for help.

ACADEMIC VOCABULARY

As you write and discuss what you learned from "The World on the Turtle's Back," be sure to use the Academic Vocabulary words. Check off each of the words that you use.

- ❏ **adapt**
- ❏ **coherent**
- ❏ **device**
- ❏ **displace**
- ❏ **dynamic**

© Houghton Mifflin Harcourt Publishing Company

CREATE AND PRESENT

Write a Myth Remind students to use the elements of myths that they have examined in this section. Ancient myths were created by people who were well acquainted with the natural world and with human nature. Students should research the natural phenomenon they have chosen to write about and weave facts about it into their myth. Students may find it helpful to plan the myth's entire plot in a graphic organizer before writing. Encourage them to close the myth with a reference to the element of the natural world or human behavior it resolves.

Present a Myth Have students anticipate some of the questions their classmates might ask them about their myth and its meaning and rehearse answers.

For **writing support** for students at varying proficiency levels, see the **Text X-Ray** on page 6D.

RESPOND TO THE ESSENTIAL QUESTION

Allow time for students to add details from "The World on the Turtle's Back" to their Unit 1 Response Logs.

CRITICAL VOCABULARY

Answers:

Answers will vary but should demonstrate an understanding of the Critical Vocabulary terms.

VOCABULARY STRATEGY:
Multiple-Meaning Words

Answers:

sapling

1. *Definition 1: a youth*

2. *Definition 2: a young tree*

green

1. *Definition 1: lacking in training or experience*

2. *Definition 2: the color of grass*

 RESPOND

WORD BANK
delicacies
frantically
vanquish
pliable

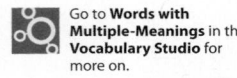 Go to **Words with Multiple-Meanings** in the **Vocabulary Studio** for more on.

CRITICAL VOCABULARY

Practice and Apply Answer each question with a complete sentence to show that you understand the meaning of each Critical Vocabulary word.

1. How would you respond if you were offered a variety of **delicacies?**

2. How would you feel if you were searching **frantically** for something?

3. What might someone do to **vanquish** an enemy?

4. Would someone who is **pliable** stand firm or be willing to compromise?

VOCABULARY STRATEGY:
Multiple-Meaning Words

Many words have more than one meaning. For example, when the word *delicacies* is used in "The World on the Turtle's Back," it means "a pleasing or appealing food choice," as in this sentence from the myth:

> The woman became hungry for all kinds of strange delicacies, as women do when they are with child.

The word *delicacy* can also mean "fineness in appearance or construction," "frailty of bodily heath," "sensitivity to the feelings of others," or "sensitivity to small changes." When you come across a familiar word used in an unfamiliar way, follow these steps to determine its meaning:

- Look at the word's context to determine its part of speech and infer the correct meaning.
- Consult a print or digital dictionary to look up all the meanings of the word.
- Compare your preliminary determination of the word's meaning to the dictionary definitions to verify the meaning of the word in context.

Practice and Apply Each of the underlined words in the following passage has multiple meanings. For each word, write the definition of the word as it is used in the passage. Then write a definition of the word using a different meaning. Use a print or digital resource to validate your responses.

> The right-handed twin has many names. One of them is <u>Sapling</u>. It means smooth, young, <u>green</u> and fresh and innocent, straightforward, straight-growing, soft and pliable, teachable and trainable.

Sapling

1. Definition 1: _____

2. Definition 2: _____

green

1. Definition 1: _____

2. Definition 2: _____

 ENGLISH LEARNER SUPPORT

Vocabulary Strategy Model how to determine the meaning of simpler multiple-meaning words, such as *park* or *bark*. Provide sentences using the terms in different ways:

- I like going to the **park** with my friends.
- Please **park** the car in the garage.
- The old tree's **bark** was peeling off.
- My dogs **bark** when they see squirrels.

Review each example, pointing out the context clues that help you determine the word's meaning. Then model looking up the word in the dictionary to confirm the definition.
ALL LEVELS

LANGUAGE CONVENTIONS:
Reflexive Pronouns

Reflexive pronouns are used as direct objects or indirect objects. Reflexive pronouns are used when the subject and object are the same, so they reflect on the subject of the sentence. The following words are reflexive pronouns: *myself, yourself, herself, himself, itself, ourselves, yourselves,* and *themselves.*

Reflexive pronouns can be used to provide emphasis—that the subject did something alone and not with the help of someone else. For example, *Leslie did the experiment by <u>herself</u>.* This sentence stresses that no one helped Leslie.

Reflexive pronouns are also used to avoid awkwardness. For example, it would be awkward to repeat the subject: *Brian made Brian a salad.* Using a reflexive pronoun eliminates the repetition: *Brian made himself a salad.*

Reflexive pronouns are used in the following ways in "The World on the Turtle's Back":

• As an indirect object to tell whom the woman said something to.

And the woman said to <u>herself</u> that she would die.

• As a direct object to tell whom the woman built the hut for.

She gathered roots and plants to eat and built <u>herself</u> a little hut.

Practice and Apply Write your own sentences using reflexive pronouns. Use the examples from "The World on the Turtle's Back" as models. When you have finished, share your sentences with a partner.

! Go to **Pronouns** in the **Grammar Studio** for help.

LANGUAGE CONVENTIONS:
Reflexive Pronouns

Review the information about reflexive pronouns with students. Explain that reflexive pronouns cannot be removed from a sentence without changing the meaning (*I scored the winning basket by myself*), and they may act as direct or indirect objects (*She allowed herself a cookie after dinner*).

Point out that reflexive pronouns are often misused, particularly in compound subjects or compound objects in a sentence. For example, show students the following sentence:

Bailey and myself will conduct the meeting.

The use of *myself* is incorrect here. How do we know? Remove *Bailey* from the sentence to see if what remains is grammatical:

Myself will conduct the meeting.

Myself does not work in this sentence, but the subject pronoun *I* does work. A reflexive pronoun can never be the subject of a sentence.

Practice and Apply Have partners discuss whether reflexive pronouns are used correctly and effectively in their sentences. *(Students' sentences will vary.)*

EL **ENGLISH LEARNER SUPPORT**

Language Conventions Use the following supports with students at varying proficiency levels:

• Have students find two sentences in the selection that use reflexive pronouns and underline the reflexive pronoun. **SUBSTANTIAL**

• Have students write two sentences using reflexive pronouns. Then have them meet with a partner to compare sentences. Students can underline the reflexive pronouns in their partners' sentences. **MODERATE**

• Show students the sentences below and ask them to identify problems (if any) with the reflexive pronouns. Have them meet with a partner to compare answers.

The twins blamed themself for the messy kitchen. (themselves)

Miguel made breakfast for himself this morning.

Hanna asked if Rob and herself could go to the movies. (Rob and her)

LIGHT

BALBOA
Short Story by Sabina Murray

GENRE ELEMENTS
SHORT STORY

A **short story** is a brief piece of fiction in which the author explores insights about life or human nature through a theme. To develop the theme, authors use literary elements such as character, plot, and setting. Sometimes authors use narrative techniques such as flashback or flash forward, allowing the events of the story to unfold out of order. These literary devices, or techniques, create suspense and keep readers interested.

LEARNING OBJECTIVES

- Analyze the relationship between theme, characters, plot, and setting.
- Research European explorers of the 1400s and 1500s.
- Plan and compose a dramatic monologue.
- Present a dramatic monologue.
- Analyze context to learn the meanings of unfamiliar words.
- Evaluate how authors use verb tenses.
- **Language** Discuss with a partner the characters in the text using lesson vocabulary.

TEXT COMPLEXITY

Quantitative Measures	**Balboa**	Lexile: 920L
Qualitative Measures	**Ideas Presented** Multiple levels, use of symbolism, irony, satire. Some ambiguity. Greater demand for inference.	
	Structures Used More complex; multiple perspectives. More deviation from chronological or sequential order.	
	Language Used Meanings are implied, but support is offered. More figurative or ironic language. More inference is demanded.	
	Knowledge Required More complexity in theme. Experiences may be less familiar to many. Cultural or historical references may make heavier demands.	

RESOURCES

- Unit 1 Response Log
- 🔊 Selection Audio
- 📖 Reading Studio: Notice & Note
- LEVELUP Level Up Tutorials: Plot Stages; Character Traits; Theme
- ▬ Writing Studio: Writing Narratives
- 💬 Speaking and Listening Studio: Giving a Presentation
- ⚬ Vocabulary Studio: Context Clues
- ❗ Grammar Studio: Module 8: Lesson 5: Verb Tense
- ☑ "Balboa" Selection Test

SUMMARIES

English

This selection tells the story of a Spanish explorer and conquistador, Vasco Núñez de Balboa, as he climbs a mountain and becomes the first European to see the Pacific Ocean and claim it for Spain. On his journey, Balboa reflects upon the events that led him to this moment and considers how he will be remembered to future generations.

Spanish

Esta selección cuenta la historia del explorador y conquistador español, Vasco Núñez de Balboa, mientras escala una montaña y se convierte en el primer europeo en ver el océano Pacífico y reclamarlo para España. En su viaje, Balboa reflexiona sobre los sucesos que lo llevaron a este momento y considera cómo será recordado por futuras generaciones.

 ## SMALL-GROUP OPTIONS

Have students work in small groups and pairs to read and discuss the selection.

Think-Pair-Share

- Ask, "What is a character trait that describes Balboa, and what might this suggest about the stories theme?"
- Allow time for students to think independently and take notes.
- Have students collaborate to discuss the question and prepare a response.
- Allow time for students to share their responses and contribute to a class discussion.

Three-Minute Review

- Reread paragraph 30 with the class and discuss the ending.
- Ask students to consider another way Balboa's story could have ended. Give them three minutes to write an alternate ending.
- Organize students into small groups, and have them share their alternate endings.
- Ask, "How does knowing what happened to Balboa affect your understanding of him? Did Balboa see justice, or would another conclusion have been more just? Do people usually get what they deserve?"

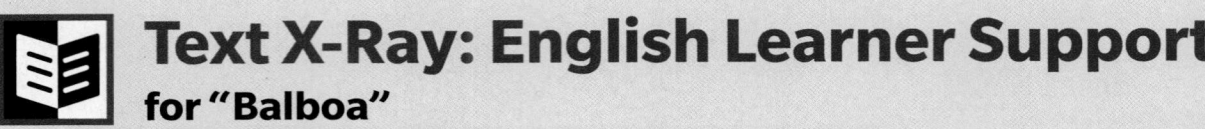

Text X-Ray: English Learner Support
for "Balboa"

Use the Text X-Ray and the supports and scaffolds in the Teacher's Edition to help guide students at different proficiency levels through the selection.

INTRODUCE THE SELECTION
DISCUSS MOSES AND THE ISRAELITES

In this lesson, students will need to understand references to Moses and the Israelites in paragraphs 1 and 7. Explain that the Israelites were enslaved Hebrews in Egypt, described in religious texts. Moses was an Israelite who escaped from Egypt; he is an important figure in Christianity, Judaism, and Islam. Religious texts say God spoke to Moses from a burning bush on a mountain called Mount Horeb. He told Moses to help free the Israelites from slavery. Following God's instructions, Moses led the Israelites out of Egypt.

Explain that authors sometimes use an **allusion** to refer to something indirectly in order to make a point. Discuss why a writer might use these allusions:

- He was a real Scrooge and spent as little as possible on gifts. (*Scrooge was a miserly character in Charles Dickens'* A Christmas Carol.)
- After the house fire, her neighbor became her fairy godmother. (*In the fairy tale, Cinderella's fairy godmother gave her things she needed.*)

CULTURAL REFERENCES

The following words or phrases may be unfamiliar to students:

- *as if they are the Israelites and Balboa alone is off to speak with God* (paragraph 1): as if Balboa were Moses, talking to God about helping his people become free
- *civilized* (paragraph 4): behaving according to well-organized rules or laws
- *virgin mountain air* (paragraph 9): air that is unchanged from its natural condition
- *outcropping of rock* (paragraph 12): part of a rock formation that can be seen above the surface of the land
- *smallpox and syphilis* (paragraph 18): new and often fatal diseases brought by Europeans

LISTENING

Pronunciation and Spelling

Say the word *allusion* several times, and ask the students to repeat after you. Then, help students to recognize pronunciation and spelling patterns in similar words.

Use the following supports with students at varying proficiency levels:

- Make a knocking gesture as you say each syllable in the word *allusion*. Say *allusion* again, and open your fist as you stress the second syllable. Have students repeat after you other words that follow this pattern (e.g., explOsion, tempTAtion, conFUsion). **SUBSTANTIAL**
- Say the word *allusion*. Ask students what sound they hear at the end of the word. Then say *decision, condition, location*. Point out that these words end in the suffix -*sion* or -*tion*. Explain that the syllable before the suffix is stressed. Invite volunteers to say other words that end in this sound. Listeners should repeat the word and the ending sound. **MODERATE**
- Display and say *allusion* and *allude*. Explain that many verbs ending in a /d/ or /s/ sound are root words for nouns ending in -*sion*. Say *conclude/conclusion, expand/expansion*, and *express/expression*. Have students repeat them. **LIGHT**

SPEAKING

Understand Characters

Display a K-W-L graphic organizer. Tell students it can help them use questions and text details to understand the main character in the story. Guide them to list what they know and want to know about Balboa.

Use the following supports with students at varying proficiency levels:

- Ask students what they know about Balboa, and write their ideas in the first column. *(Spanish, explorer)* Then help students form questions about what they want to know. For example: *What did he _____? When did he ____?* Write their questions in the second column. **SUBSTANTIAL**

- Organize the students into pairs to complete the first two columns. Provide the following sentences to guide their discussions: *I know Balboa (was, had, liked, did, thought) _____. I want to know (whether, who, when, why, how) Balboa _____.* **MODERATE**

- Have pairs of students complete the first two columns. As they fill in the second column, have them pose questions to each other using *Who, What, When, Where, Why,* and *How*? **LIGHT**

READING

Read for More Information

Continue to display the K-W-L graphic organizer as students read and locate evidence in the text to help them complete the third column.

Use the following supports with students at varying proficiency levels:

- Read aloud text details that relate to students' questions. Ask, *Does this help us answer the question?* As students say yes or no, add key words to the third column of the organizer. **SUBSTANTIAL**

- Have student pairs locate answers to their questions in the text. Provide the paragraph numbers that contain the answers. Have students complete the third column. **MODERATE**

- Have partners find answers to their questions and fill in the third column. If the text does not explicitly state answers, ask them to make inferences based on the text. **LIGHT**

WRITING

Write a Dramatic Monologue

Explain that a dramatic monologue is a lyric poem (like a song) in which one speaker expresses deep feelings, as if speaking to himself or herself.

Ask students to think about how Balboa felt when he was standing on the mountain and saw the Pacific Ocean for the first time. Use the following supports with students at varying proficiency levels:

- Ask students to identify some words that describe feelings, or emotions (e.g., *proud, peaceful, angry*). Guide them to imagine how they would feel if they were Balboa. Provide the following sentence frame to help them describe Balboa's emotions: *I feel _____ because _____.* **SUBSTANTIAL**

- Help students write slightly more complex sentences from Balboa's perspective using these frames: *I feel _____ because _____, so I will _____. I want _____ so I can _____, but I must _____.* **MODERATE**

- Ask: *What were Balboa's reasons for climbing the mountain? What did being the first to see the Pacific Ocean mean to him?* Have students consider their answers to these questions and create a personal word bank to consult as they compose their dramatic monologues. **LIGHT**

Connect to the
ESSENTIAL QUESTION

"Balboa" takes the reader on a journey of discovery through the jungles of Central America. The story delves into Vasco Núñez de Balboa's thought process and begins to unravel what motivates people to explore the unknown.

BALBOA

Short Story by **Sabina Murray**

? *ESSENTIAL QUESTION:*

What motivates people to explore the unknown?

QUICK START

Is your image of yourself different from the image you want others to see? How so? Does this ever cause conflict with others—or within yourself? Take a few minutes to write your thoughts on these questions.

ANALYZE THEMATIC DEVELOPMENT

Writers of fiction often use their works to communicate insights about life or human nature called **themes.** Most of these themes are not stated; readers must infer them by looking closely at other elements of the work, such as characters, plot, and setting. To identify and trace the development of the themes in "Balboa," ask yourself these questions:

- **Character** How does the main character change or fail to change? What qualities does the main character possess? How do these qualities determine his or her reaction to the conflict? What message does the author convey through how the character's traits influence his or her reactions?

- **Plot** What is the major conflict in the story? How does this conflict lead to other problems? How is the conflict resolved? Is there a lesson to be learned from the way the conflict is resolved?

- **Setting** How does the setting contribute to the problem or challenge a character faces? What qualities does the character reveal as he or she interacts with the setting? What theme might emerge from the way the character solves the problem?

ANALYZE PLOT STRUCTURE

The structure of a story is its organization. Many stories are organized chronologically, following a tale from its beginning to its end. Sometimes, however, authors decide to present the sequence of events out of order to add interest or suspense. They may also seek to achieve a more subtle effect, such as providing information on characters or setting that may be important to the plot. To analyze the structure of "Balboa," look at how the author uses the narrative techniques described in the chart.

FLASHBACK	FLASH FORWARD
A flashback is a scene that interrupts the action to describe events that took place earlier in time. Flashbacks add important background information to help readers gain a new perspective on characters and their motives, understand the causes of events, or see the author's message more clearly. You will see the protagonist in "Balboa" recall significant past events several times.	Flash forward interrupts the narrative to give readers a look at what will happen after the events in the main plot take place. A flash forward may change readers' outlook on events and characters in the story, affect the mood that is created, or illuminate the meaning of the work. In "Balboa," the author chooses to conclude her story with a flash forward focusing on the end of the protagonist's life.

GENRE ELEMENTS: SHORT STORY

- expresses a theme, or insight about life or human nature
- contains literary elements such as character, plot, and setting that develop the theme
- may use narrative techniques such as flashbacks or flash forwards to build interest and suspense

---

QUICK START

Have students read the Quick Start questions, and tell them to make a simple version of the popular 3-panel meme "How the World Sees Me, How I See Myself, & How I Really Am." Remind students that a meme is a cultural practice or idea. Explain that memes are designed to share ideas about behavior, social concepts, and so forth. Discuss with students that memes like this are mostly for humorous value, but there is often a grain of truth in them. Tell students that their memes can be visual or word based. Ask volunteers to share their memes and to explain them, if necessary.

ANALYZE THEMATIC DEVELOPMENT

Review the terms and questions with students. Then, draw a triangle on the board. At each corner of the triangle, write one of the following: *character*, *plot*, and *setting*. Discuss with students how these elements of the story interact with each other to convey theme. For example, what might the characters' interactions with the setting reveal about them? How might the setting affect the events and conflicts of the plot? In this way, have students discuss interactions between paired items. Talk about how these interactions allow an author to develop theme in a more complex way than if the author were limited to only one of the three elements. It may be helpful to illustrate this using a story that students have recently read or are familiar with.

ANALYZE PLOT STRUCTURE

Review the definitions of *flashback* and *flash forward* with students. Tell them that recognizing flashbacks or flash forwards will help them better understand the characters, conflicts, and theme. Ask students for examples of flashbacks they have seen in other media, such as movies, television shows, cartoons, or graphic novels. Discuss the more widely seen examples and what the flashbacks accomplished. Did they add to the understanding of the plot, or were they simply an amusement or a distraction? Would students have included the flashback if they were the author? Why or why not?

CRITICAL VOCABULARY

Encourage students to read all the sentences before deciding which word best completes each one. Remind them to look for context clues that match the precise meaning of each word.

Possible Answers:

1. *spotless*
2. *sticks out*
3. *replaces the leader*
4. *hostile*
5. *point of view*
6. *food and clothing*
7. *gives up*

■ English Learner Support

Use Cognates Tell students that one of the Critical Vocabulary words has a Spanish cognate: *distinction/distinción*. **ALL LEVELS**

LANGUAGE CONVENTIONS

Review the information about verb tense with students. Point out that they use different verb tenses in their daily speech. Have them think about which verb tenses they have used in the last 24 hours. Ask students when they are most likely to use the three different verb tenses. (*Past tense: to tell a story. Present tense: to discuss what is happening now or to tell a story in a more interesting way. Future tense: to discuss what is happening later*)

Ask if any students have told a story about themselves recently using the present tense. Discuss why they chose this tense instead of the more common past tense. Draw students' attention to the narrative value of using the present tense in this situation. (*Using the present tense can lend immediacy and energy to a story.*)

 ANNOTATION MODEL

Remind students of the narrative elements that develop theme in Analyze Thematic Development on page 21: *character*, *plot*, and *setting*. As they read, they should look for these three elements in the text and make notes about each.

CRITICAL VOCABULARY

pristine   supplant   protrude   provision   discord   distinction   cede

To see how many Critical Vocabulary words you already know, work with a partner to complete the following sentence stems.

1. If a landscape is **pristine,** it looks . . .
2. When a seedling **protrudes** from the soil, it . . .
3. If someone **supplants** a leader, he or she . . .
4. When there is **discord** between siblings, the mood in a family is . . .
5. The **distinction** between a blog and an online news source is . . .
6. For a camping trip, I need the following **provisions**: . . .
7. If a knight in a story **cedes** victory to his opponent, he . . .

LANGUAGE CONVENTIONS

Verb Tenses The tense of a verb indicates the time of the action or state of being. An action or state of being can occur in the present, the past, or the future. Short stories are usually told in **past tense** (Sam walked to the store) or **present tense** (Sam walks to the store). However, if the author wants to use plot structures other than chronological order, such as flashback or flash forward, other verb tenses may be used. As you read "Balboa," look for ways the author moves the story around in time by changing the verb tense.

ANNOTATION MODEL   **NOTICE & NOTE**

As you read, note details about plot, character, and setting that develop the theme. You may also note any information that seems important to you. In the model, you can see one reader's notes about "Balboa."

> Vasco Núñez de Balboa ascends the mountain alone. His one thousand Indians and two hundred Spaniards wait at the foot of the mountain, as if they are the Israelites and Balboa alone is off to speak with God. Balboa knows that from this peak he will be able to see the western water, what he has already decided to name the South Sea. He takes a musket with him. The Spaniards have been warned that if they follow, he will use it, because discovery is a tricky matter and he wants no competition. The day is September 25, 1513.

The word "alone" is repeated; Balboa thinks he is exceptional.

Details paint Balboa as ambitious and arrogant.

Ambition and power are key ideas; probably related to the theme.

BACKGROUND

Vasco Núñez de Balboa (1475–1519) was a Spanish explorer and conquistador who first came to the Americas in 1500 as part of a voyage exploring the coast of present-day Colombia. He is most remembered for being the first European to view the Pacific Ocean in 1513. This event and other facts of Balboa's life form the basis of **Sabina Murray's** *story, published in her book* Tales of the New World *(2011). Murray lives in western Massachusetts, where she is on the Creative Writing faculty at the University of Massachusetts Amherst.*

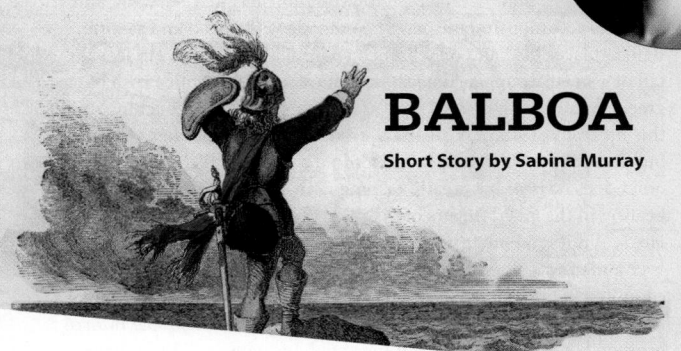

BALBOA

Short Story by Sabina Murray

SETTING A PURPOSE

As you read, pay special attention to Balboa's character traits and any problems he faces. Consider how the author's characterization of Balboa develops the author's message, or theme. Write down any questions you generate during reading.

1   Vasco Núñez de Balboa ascends the mountain alone. His one thousand Indians and two hundred Spaniards wait at the foot of the mountain, as if they are the Israelites and Balboa alone is off to speak with God. Balboa knows that from this peak he will be able to see the western water, what he has already decided to name the South Sea. He takes a musket with him. The Spaniards have been warned that <u>if they follow, he will use it,</u> because discovery is a tricky matter and <u>he wants no competition.</u> The day is September 25, 1513.

2   Balboa ascends slowly. His musket is heavy and he would have gladly left it down below, but <u>he doesn't trust his countrymen any more than he trusts the sullen Indians.</u> So he bears the weight. But the musket is nothing. He is dragging the mantle[1] of civilization up the **pristine** slopes, over the mud, over

---

[1] **mantle:** a cloak or robe worn by royalty.

Notice & Note

Use the side margins to notice and note signposts in the text.

ANALYZE THEMATIC DEVELOPMENT
Annotate: Mark phrases in paragraphs 1 and 2 that describe Balboa.

Infer: Based on the phrases you marked, what is a character trait that describes Balboa? What might this trait suggest about the story's theme?

pristine
(prĭsˊtēnˊ) *adj.* pure or unspoiled.

Balboa   23

BACKGROUND

Have students read the background information about Vasco Núñez de Balboa. Tell students that Balboa was born in Spain to a poor but noble family. He sailed to the Americas to seek fortune and fame. This story sheds light on his motivations, as well as on different aspects of colonization.

SETTING A PURPOSE

Direct students to use the Setting a Purpose prompt to focus their reading.

ANALYZE THEMATIC DEVELOPMENT

Explain to students that a **theme** is the key message or insight of a work. Since fiction writers don't explicitly state their themes but instead weave them out of smaller details, readers must infer the theme. To make inferences, students must analyze clues about characters and events and make connections. (**Answer:** *Self-importance or arrogance; the theme may involve Balboa's image of himself or the nature of colonialism.*)

For **listening support** for students at varying proficiency levels, see the **Text X-Ray** on page 20C.

EL ENGLISH LEARNER SUPPORT

Learning Strategies Play the audio for paragraph 1 and have students follow along using the text. Ask what Balboa does. Students can identify phrases in the text that describe his actions. As they answer, summarize Balboa's actions: *He goes to the top of a mountain carrying a musket, or gun. He warns others not to follow him because he wants to discover the water himself.* Ask students to describe Balboa based on his actions. Guide them by providing words to describe character traits and asking which words best describe Balboa. **ALL LEVELS**

CRITICAL VOCABULARY

pristine: The mountain's natural beauty has not been disturbed by outsiders.

ASK STUDENTS how European explorers might affect the pristine setting. (*Explorers might destroy the landscape through deforestation or mining. This would ruin the beauty and destroy habitat for animals, among other effects.*)

CONTRASTS AND CONTRADICTIONS

To understand how an author is developing **character**, the reader must look closely at a character's speech, thoughts, and actions. In this story, Balboa seems to see himself differently than the reader sees him. Contrasts like this are a signal to the reader of something meaningful. (**Answer:** *The narrator says that Balboa would like to think of himself as a lion, compares himself to other famous explorers, and wants his name to be remembered as Balboa the Valiant, Balboa the Fearsome, and Balboa the Brave.*)

■ English Learner Support

Understand Contrasts Help students locate Balboa's names for himself—*Balboa the Lion, Balboa the Valiant,* and so on. Explain that *valiant* means "brave or heroic." Ask if students agree with these names for Balboa. Guide their thinking by pointing out details from the text that describe Balboa's actions or feelings. For each detail, ask whether it shows that Balboa was brave or valiant.

SUBSTANTIAL/MODERATE

 For **speaking support** for students at varying proficiency levels, see the **Text X-Ray** on page 20D.

 NOTICE & NOTE

the leaves that cast as much shade as a parasol[2] but with none of the charm.

3   Balboa is that divining line[3] between the modern and the primitive. As he moves, the shadow of Spain moves with him.

4   Balboa steps cautiously into a muddy stream and watches with fascination as his boot sinks and sinks. He will have to find another way. Upstream he sees an outcropping of rock. Maybe he can cross there. He tells himself that there is no hurry, but years of staying just ahead of trouble have left him anxiety-ridden. He would like to think of himself as a lion. Balboa the Lion! But no, he is more of a rat, and all of his accomplishments have been made with speed and stealth. Balboa places his hand on a branch and pulls himself up. He sees the tail of a snake disappearing just past his reach. The subtle crush of greenery confirms his discovery and he shrinks back, crouching. In this moment of stillness, he looks around. He sees no other serpents, but that does not mean they are not there. Only in this momentary quiet does he hear his breath, rasping with effort. He hears his heart beating in the arced fingers of his ribs as if it is an Indian's drum. He does not remember what it is to be civilized, or if he ever was. If ever a man was alone, it is he. But even in this painful solitude, he cannot help but laugh. Along with Cristóbal Colón, backed by Isabel I herself, along with Vespucci the scholar, along with the noble Pizarro brothers[4] on their way to claim Inca gold, his name will live—Balboa. Balboa! Balboa the Valiant. Balboa the Fearsome. Balboa the Brave.

5   Balboa the gambling pig farmer, who, in an effort to escape his debt, has found himself at the very edge of the world.

6   Balboa stops to drink from the stream. The water is cold, fresh, and tastes like dirt, which is a relief after what he has been drinking—water so green that the very act of ingesting it seems unnatural, as though it is as alive as he, and sure enough, given a few hours, it will get you back, eager to find its way out. He has been climbing since early morning and it is now noon. The sun shines in the sky unblinking, white-hot. Balboa wonders if it's the same sun that shines in Spain. The sun seemed so much smaller there. Even in Hispaniola,[5] the sun was Spanish. Even as he prodded his pigs in the heat, there was Spain all around, men with dice, men training roosters, pitting their dogs against each other. But here…then he hears a twig snap and the sound of something brushing up against the bushes. Balboa stands.

CONTRASTS AND CONTRADICTIONS

Notice & Note: Mark details in paragraph 4 that suggest a discrepancy between who Balboa is and how he would like to be perceived.

Analyze: How would Balboa like to be viewed by others? Cite text evidence in your response.

---

[2] **parasol:** light umbrella.

[3] **divining line:** point of separation between ideas.

[4] **Cristóbal Colón . . . Pizarro brothers:** Cristóbal Colón is the Spanish name for Christopher Columbus. Isabel I was queen of Castile (Spain) from 1474 until 1504. Amerigo Vespucci (1451–1512) was an Italian explorer and cartographer. Francisco, Gonzalo, Juan, and Hernándo Pizarro were Spanish conquistadors in Peru.

[5] **Hispaniola:** site of Columbus's first colony; the island containing modern Haiti and the Dominican Republic.

WHEN STUDENTS STRUGGLE . . .

Analyze Plot Point out that this page is establishing the plot of the story. Emphasize that a sense of the plot helps anticipate later events. Ask what students know about the plot so far. (*Balboa is climbing a mountain to be the first Spaniard to view the Pacific Ocean.*) As Balboa climbs, he thinks of other explorers and his own past. These interjections will likely continue.

For additional support, go to the **Reading Studio** and assign the following **Level Up Tutorial: Plot Stages.**

7   "I give you this one chance to turn back," he says, raising his musket as he turns. And then he freezes. It is not one of the Spaniards hoping to share the glory. Instead, he finds himself face-to-face with a great spotted cat. On this mountain, he's thought he might find his god, the god of Moses, sitting in the cloud cover near the peaks, running his fingers through his beard. But no. Instead he finds himself face-to-face with a jaguar, the god of the Indians. He knows why these primitives have chosen it for their deity. It is hard to fear one's maker when he looks like one's grandfather, but this great cat can make a people fear god. He hears the growling of the cat and the grating, high-pitched thunder sounds like nothing he has ever heard. The cat twitches its nose and two great incisors show at the corners of its mouth. Balboa raises his musket, ignites the flint,[6] and nothing happens. He tries again and the weapon explodes, shattering the silence, sending up a big puff of stinking smoke. The cat is gone for now, but Balboa knows he hasn't even injured it.

8   And now it will be tailing him silently.

9   There is nothing he can do about it. He should have brought an Indian with him. The Indians have all seen the South Sea before, so why did he leave them at the foot of the mountain? They have no more interest in claiming the South Sea than they do rowing off to Europe in their dug-out canoes[7] and claiming Spain. But Balboa's hindsight is always good, and no amount of swearing—which he does freely, spilling Spanish profanity into the virgin mountain air—is going to set things straight.

10   He is already in trouble. His kingdom in Darién on the east coast of the New World is under threat, and not from the Indians, whom he manages well, but from Spain. Balboa had organized the rebellion, supplanted the governor—all of this done with great efficiency and intelligence. What stupidity made him send the governor, Martín Fernández de Enciso, back to Spain? Enciso swore that he would have Balboa's head on a platter. He was yelling from the deck of the ship as it set sail. Why didn't he kill Enciso? Better yet, why didn't he turn Enciso over to some Indian tribe that would be glad to have the Spaniard, glad to have his blood on their hands? How could Balboa be so stupid? Soon the caravels[8] would arrive and his days as governor (king, he tells the Indians) of Darién will be over. Unless, Balboa thinks, unless he brings glory by being the first to claim this great ocean for Spain. Then the king will see him as the greatest of his subjects, not a troublemaking peasant, a keeper of pigs.

11   Unless that jaguar gets him first.

12   Balboa looks nervously around. The only sound is the trickle and splash of the stream that he is following, which the Indians tell

---

[6] **flint:** stone used to create a spark.
[7] **dug-out canoes:** narrow boats made by hollowing out tree trunks.
[8] **caravels:** small sailing ships with two or three masts.

supplant
(sə-plănt´) v. to take the place of.

LANGUAGE CONVENTIONS
Annotate: In paragraph 10, mark verbs that are in the past tense.

Analyze: How do these verbs signal a transition in the plot structure?

© Houghton Mifflin Harcourt Publishing Company

✎ LANGUAGE CONVENTIONS

Tell students that authors may include **flashbacks** to offer insight about a character or plot. Flashbacks are often signaled by a shift in verb tense. (**Answer:** *The past-tense verbs indicate that there is a flashback.*)

■ English Learner Support

Understand Plot Devices   Draw students' attention to the first three lines of paragraph 10. Explain that in this paragraph the author is going to launch into a flashback—a memory or piece of history that is relevant to the story.

ASK STUDENTS how the verb tense in the first line is different from the verb tense in the third line. (*The first line has a present-tense verb, while the third line begins the use of past-tense verbs.*) **MODERATE**

TO CHALLENGE STUDENTS . . .

Explore the Issue   Balboa is not only concerned about his fame and fortune—he is also concerned about his fate. He guesses that if he can "claim this great ocean for Spain" it will help him overcome his troubles with Spanish authorities. Encourage students to share their ideas concerning why explorers such as Balboa might have had problems with authorities in their homelands. Could their desire for fame and power conflict with the needs of these authorities? In what ways might the explorers' discoveries strengthen the authorities' power?

CRITICAL VOCABULARY

supplant: Balboa organized a rebellion and successfully overthrew the government headed by Enciso. Afterward, however, he regrets not having killed Enciso.

ASK STUDENTS why Balboa was unhappy that he had supplanted Enciso but had chosen to let him live. (*The governor was still alive and wanted revenge because Balboa had kicked him out of office. This might cause problems for Balboa when he returns from his trip.*)

him leads to a large outcropping of rock from which he will see the new ocean. Insects swoop malevolently[9] around his head. A yellow and red parrot watches him cautiously from a branch, first looking from one side of its jeweled head, then the other. Where is the jaguar? Balboa imagines his body being dragged into a tree, his boots swinging from the limbs as the great cat tears his heart from his ribs. He hears a crushing of vegetation and ducks low. He readies his musket again. "Please God, let the damned thing fire." He breathes harshly, genuflecting,[10] musket steady.

13 The leaves quiver, then part. There is no jaguar.

14 "Leoncico!" he cries out. Leoncico is his dog, who has tracked him up the slope. Leoncico patters over, wagging his tail, his great wrinkled head bearded with drool. Leoncico is a monster of a dog. His head is the size of a man's, and his body has the look of a lion—shoulders and hipbones **protruding** and muscle pulling and shifting beneath the glossy skin—which is where he gets his name. "Leoncico" means little lion.

15 "Good dog," says Balboa. "Good dog. Good dog."

16 He has never been so grateful for the company, not even when he was hidden on board Enciso's ship bound for San Sebastian, escaping his creditors, wrapped in a sail. No one wondered why the dog had come on board. Maybe the dog had been attracted by the smell of **provisions**, the great barrels of salted meat. The soldiers fed him, gave him water. Balboa worried that Leoncico would give him away, but the dog had somehow known to be quiet. He had slept beside Balboa, and even in Balboa's thirst and hunger, the great beast's panting and panting, warm through the sailcloth, had given him comfort. When Enciso's crew finally discovered Balboa—one of the sails was torn and needed to be replaced—they did not punish him. They laughed.

17 "The Indians massacre everyone. You are better off in a debtors' prison," they said.

18 Balboa became a member of the crew. When the boat shipwrecked off the coast of San Sebastian (they were rescued by Francisco Pizarro), Enciso had been at a loss as to where to go, and Balboa convinced him to try Darién to the north. Once established there, Enciso had shown himself to be a weak man. How could Balboa not act? Enciso did not understand the Indians as Balboa did. He could see that the Indians were battle-hardened warriors. The Spaniards had not been there long enough to call these armies into existence. Balboa's strength had been to recognize this **discord**. He divided the great tribes, supported one against the other. His reputation spread. His muskets blasted away the faces of the greatest warriors. Balboa's soldiers spread smallpox and syphilis. His Spanish

protrude
(prō-trōōd´) *v.* to stick out or bulge.

provision
(prə-vĭzh´ən) *n.* food supply.

discord
(dĭs´kôrd) *n.* disagreement or conflict.

---
[9] **malevolently:** with evil intent.
[10] **genuflecting:** bending one knee to the ground.

26   Unit 1

© Houghton Mifflin Harcourt Publishing Company

CRITICAL VOCABULARY

protrude: Balboa's dog is huge, with a head as big as a man's. He is named Leoncico because his body has the look and build of a lion.

ASK STUDENTS what Leoncico's muscles and his protruding shoulders and hip bones have to do with his name. *(Leoncico, whose name means "little lion," has muscles and protruding bones that remind people of the build of a lion.)*

provision: Due to the lack of refrigeration during Balboa's time, ships kept barrels of salted meat because it wouldn't spoil during their voyages.

ASK STUDENTS why Leoncico may have been drawn to the barrels of provisions on Enciso's ship. *(The barrels contained the ship's supply of meat.)*

discord: Balboa realizes that on the battlefield the Spaniards would be no match for the Indians.

ASK STUDENTS to explain why recognizing the Indians' discord benefited Balboa. *(By recognizing the disagreement among the tribes, Balboa is able to turn them against each other. As a result, he directs their attention away from the Spaniards who are taking over their land and encourages conflict between Indian groups.)*

APPLYING ACADEMIC VOCABULARY

❏ **adapt**   ☑ **coherent**   ☑ **device**   ❏ **displace**   ❏ **dynamic**

Write and Discuss Have students turn to a partner to discuss the following questions. Guide students to include the Academic Vocabulary words *coherent* and *device* in their responses. Ask volunteers to share their responses with the class.

- Balboa has many thoughts as he climbs the mountain. Is his stream of thought **coherent**?

- How does the author use flashbacks as a plot **device**?

war dogs, great mastiffs and wolfhounds, tore children limb from limb. The blood from his great war machine made the rivers flow red and his name, Balboa, moved quickly, apace[11] with these rivers of blood.

19   Balboa is loved by no one and feared by all. He has invented an unequaled terror. The Indians think of him as a god. They make no **distinction** between good and evil. They have seen his soldiers tear babies from their mothers, toss them still screaming to feed the dogs. They have seen the great dogs pursue the escaping Indians, who must hear nothing but a great panting, the jangle of the dogs' armor, and then, who knows? Do they feel the hot breath on their cheek? Are they still awake when the beasts unravel their stomachs and spill them onto the hot earth? Balboa's dogs have been his most effective weapon because for them, one does not need to carry ammunition, as for the muskets; one does not need to carry food, as for the soldiers. For the dogs, there is fresh meat everywhere. He knows his cruelty will be recorded along with whatever he discovers. This does not bother him, even though one monk, Dominican—strange fish— cursed him back in Darién. He was a young monk, tormented by epileptic[12] fits. He approached Balboa in the town square in his bare feet, unarmed, waving his shrunken fist.

20   "Your dogs," screamed the monk, "are demons."

21   As if understanding, Leoncico had lunged at the monk. Leoncico is not a demon. He is the half of Balboa with teeth, the half that eats. Balboa has the mind and appetite. Together, they make one. It is as if the great beast can hear his thoughts, as if their hearts and lungs circulate the same blood and air. What did the monk understand of that? What did he understand of anything? He said that he was in the New World to bring the Indians to God. So the monk converts the Indians, and Balboa sends them on to God. They work together, which is what Balboa told the monk. But the monk did not find it funny.

22   How dare he find fault with Balboa? Is not Spain as full of torments as the New World? The Spaniards are brought down by smallpox at alarming rates in Seville, in Madrid. Every summer the rich take to the mountains to escape the plague, and in the fall, when they return, aren't their own countrymen lying in the streets feeding the packs of mongrels? Half of all the Spanish babies die. It is not uncommon to see a peasant woman leave her screaming infant on the side of the road, so why come here and beg relief for these savages? Why not go to France, where, one soldier tells Balboa, they butcher the Huguenots[13] and sell their limbs for food in the street? Why rant

---

[11] **apace:** fast enough to keep up with something.
[12] **epileptic:** caused by epilepsy, a neurological disorder.
[13] **Huguenots:** French Protestants who were persecuted for their faith in the 16th and 17th centuries.

(left margin, rotated) © Houghton Mifflin Harcourt Publishing Company

distinction
(dĭ-stĭngk´shən) *n.* difference in quality.

ANALYZE PLOT STRUCTURE
Annotate: Mark the transition to the flashback in paragraph 19.

Analyze: Analyze the conflict between Balboa and the monk in the flashback. What does this reveal about Balboa's character?

ANALYZE PLOT STRUCTURE

Explain to students that literary elements, such as structure and theme, do not function independently but rather work hand in hand. Authors may use flashbacks to help readers identify **conflict,** the key problem in a plot, and thus, the theme. (***Answer:*** *The monk is horrified by Balboa's violence and lust for power. Balboa cynically justifies his methods by comparing the "New World" to Spain. The exchange reveals that Balboa will say and think anything in order to get what he wants. The exchange reveals his values.*)

ENGLISH LEARNER SUPPORT

Explain Text Have students examine the first five sentences in paragraph 21. Then, read aloud the fifth sentence: "Together, they make one." Instruct students to use what they learn in the rest of the paragraph to write a brief explanation of this sentence. Tell them to use at least one new vocabulary word in their explanation and to write complete sentences and use correct grammar. **SUBSTANTIAL**

For **reading support** for students at varying proficiency levels, see the **Text X-Ray** on page 20D.

IMPROVE READING FLUENCY

Targeted Passage Point out to students that paragraph 21 is a particularly dramatic paragraph. It contains vivid imagery, violence, and even humor. Have multiple students perform a dramatic reading of the paragraph. As the paragraph is repeated, readings should improve each time, with stresses occurring on the colorful and impactful parts of the paragraph.

Go to the **Reading Studio** for additional support in developing fluency.

CRITICAL VOCABULARY

distinction: The Indians do not consider whether Balboa is good or evil.

ASK STUDENTS to explain, based on the Indians' lack of distinction between good and evil, how the Indians might decide that someone is a god. (*They seem to perceive power as a godlike quality, so powerful beings are regarded as gods.*)

 ANALYZE PLOT STRUCTURE

Remind students that **foreshadowing** is a writer's use of hints about what will happen in the story. It creates suspense and prepares the reader for what is to come. Sometimes foreshadowing is very subtle; for example, a character may come across a symbol that might indicate something will happen later. Sometimes the foreshadowing is very direct, as is the case in paragraph 24. (**Answer:** *The monk's curse foreshadows Balboa's death. The foreshadowing connects to the end of the story, which tells Balboa's fate.*)

over the impaling of the Indians when Spaniards—noblemen among them—have suffered the same fate in the name of God? In fact, the Inquisition[14] has been the great educator when it comes to subduing the Indian population.

23   Why take him to task when the world is a violent place?

24   "May your most evil act be visited on you," said the monk. "I curse you."

25   The monk died shortly after that. His threats and bravery were more the result of a deadly fever than the words of a divine message. Did the curse worry Balboa? Perhaps a little. He occasionally revisits a particularly spectacular feat of bloodshed—the time Leoncico tore a chieftain's head from his shoulders—with a pang of concern. But Balboa is a busy man with little time for reflection. When the monk delivered his curse, Balboa was already preparing his troops for the great march to the west. His name had reached Spain, and the king felt his authority threatened.

26   He is the great Balboa.

27   But here, on the slope of the mountain, his name does not seem worth that much. He has to relieve himself and is terrified that some creature—jaguar, snake, spider—will take advantage of his great heaving bareness.

28   "Leoncico," he calls. "At attention."

29   Not that this command means anything to the dog. Leoncico knows "attack," and that is all he needs to know. Leoncico looks up, wags his tail, and lies down, his face smiling into the heat. Balboa climbs onto a boulder. Here, he is exposed to everything, but if that jaguar is still tracking him, he can at least see it coming. He sets his

ANALYZE PLOT STRUCTURE

Annotate: Mark an example of foreshadowing in paragraph 24.

Analyze: What does this example foreshadow? To what part of the story does it connect?

---

[14]**the Inquisition:** an investigation by the Roman Catholic Church to identify and punish heretics.

WHEN STUDENTS STRUGGLE . . .

Analyze Character   Discuss how character traits may be inferred from a character's own thoughts, words, and actions, as well as from those of other characters. Have students list one of Balboa's thoughts or statements that reflect his character and one from another character about Balboa. (*Balboa: thought himself brave; Others: Enciso swore he would have Balboa's head.*)

 For additional support, go to the **Reading Studio** and assign the following **LEVEL UP** **Level Up Tutorial: Character Traits.**

musket down and listens. Nothing. He loosens his belt and is about to lower his pants when he sees it—the flattened glimmer, a shield, the horizon. He fixes his belt and straightens himself. He stares out at the startling bare intrusion, this beautiful nothing beyond the green tangle of trees, the *Mar del Sur*, the glory of Balboa, his gift to Spain.

30   Balboa, having accomplished his goal, luxuriates in this moment of peaceful ignorance. He does not know that his days are numbered, that even after he returns to Darién with his knowledge of the South Sea, even after he has **ceded** the governorship to Pedro Arias Dávila, even after he is promised Dávila's daughter, he has not bought his safety. Dávila will see that as long as Balboa lives he must sleep with one eye open. With the blessing of Spain, Dávila will bring Balboa to trial for treason, and on January 21, 1519, Balboa's head will be severed from his shoulders. His eyes will stay open, his mouth will be slack, and his great head will roll in the dust for everyone—Indians, Spaniards, and dogs—to see.

NOTICE & NOTE

cede
(sēd) *v.* to yield or give away.

ANALYZE THEMATIC DEVELOPMENT
Annotate: Mark details in paragraph 30 that tell you what happens to Balboa.

Analyze: How does the knowledge of what happens affect your understanding of Balboa?

CHECK YOUR UNDERSTANDING

Answer these questions before moving on to the **Analyze the Text** section.

1 What surprises Balboa when he drinks from the mountain stream?

   A A jaguar

   B An Indian

   C A thunderstorm

   D A Spaniard hoping to share in his glory

2 Why does Martín Fernández de Enciso dislike Balboa?

   F Balboa called him "weak."

   G Balboa led a rebellion against him.

   H Balboa stole money and property from him.

   J Balboa gave the governorship to Pedro Arias Dávila.

3 What eventually happens to Balboa?

   A Balboa kills Pedro Arias Dávila.

   B Balboa is killed by a wild animal.

   C Balboa goes to jail for a violent crime.

   D Pedro Arias Dávila executes Balboa for treason.

Balboa   29

ANALYZE THEMATIC DEVELOPMENT

Explain to students that the author is providing the reader with a glimpse into Balboa's future—facts that Balboa himself has no way of knowing. (**Answer:** *Through this knowledge, the reader learns how Balboa's plan to achieve power and glory backfired and that he dies as violently as he killed. This ending refines the reader's understanding of the theme, suggesting that arrogance and lust for power do not pay.*)

CHECK YOUR UNDERSTANDING

Have students answer the questions independently.

Answers:

   1. *A*

   2. *G*

   3. *D*

If they answer any questions incorrectly, have them reread the text to confirm their understanding. Then they may proceed to ANALYZE THE TEXT on page 30.

ENGLISH LEARNER SUPPORT

Oral Assessment Use the following questions to assess students' comprehension and speaking skills.

   1. As Balboa is drinking from the stream, what suprises him? (*a jaguar*)

   2. Why does Enciso dislike Balboa? (*because Balboa led a rebellion and had him sent to Spain*)

   3. What happens to Balboa in the end? (*Balboa is tried and killed by the governor for treason.*)

   MODERATE

CRITICAL VOCABULARY

cede: In the end, Balboa loses his position as governor of Darién.

ASK STUDENTS if the text suggests that Balboa was on bad terms with Dávila when he ceded the governorship. (*Balboa must have been on good terms with Dávila when he yielded office because he had plans to marry the new governor's daughter.*)

ANALYZE THE TEXT

Possible answers:

1. **DOK 4:** *It suggests that the civilization Balboa is bringing contains great cruelty and barbarity—and that the pristine slopes will soon be drenched in blood. In fact, the "mantle of civilization" is polluting the slopes.*

2. **DOK 2:** *In the flashback, Balboa reveals that he ended up in Darién because he was fleeing from his creditors. This suggests that power is often in the hands of the strongest individual, not the best.*

3. **DOK 4:** *The dogs are used as a symbol of the savagery of the Spanish. "Balboa's war dogs" refers literally to animal soldiers and figuratively to vicious, brutal human soldiers.*

4. **DOK 4:** *Balboa's abuse of power leads to his death. He turns people against each other for his own benefit, which in the end fosters mistrust in Dávila. Balboa's lust for power corrupts him, and, in the end, he loses all power. Dávila has Balboa put to death and his severed head paraded before the people he terrorized.*

5. **DOK 4:** *The writer makes it clear that Balboa understands he is from a modest background. However, because of his arrogance, he wants to be regarded as a king or other powerful figure. This difference shows that Balboa is perhaps delusional, or, at the very least, bent on acquiring as much power and regard as possible, no matter the cost.*

RESEARCH

Draw students attention to the Research Tip. Point out that a writer often reveals a positive or negative opinion by presenting only one way of looking at an event or issue. Encourage students to look for words with intensely positive or negative connotations.

Extend Balboa was born into the lower ranks of Spanish nobility and, like similar young men, saw exploration as a way to make his fortune. After joining an expedition to explore the coast of present-day Colombia, he settled in what is now Haiti. He was unsuccessful as a farmer and escaped his creditors by joining another expedition to a colony in present-day Colombia. Balboa led the colonists to a safer location in the Isthmus of Panama and gained favor in the eyes of the Spanish king. Eventually, political conflicts with the king's local representative led to a charge of treason, a guilty verdict, and a death sentence.

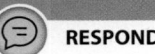 **RESPOND**

ANALYZE THE TEXT

Support your responses with evidence from the text. NOTEBOOK

1. **Analyze** The narrator says that Balboa is "dragging the mantle of civilization up the pristine slopes, over the mud, over the leaves" (paragraph 2). What does this image suggest about Balboa and the "civilization" that he is bringing with him to the setting of the New World?

2. **Interpret** After Leoncico surprises Balboa on the mountain, the action of the story is interrupted by a flashback. What do readers learn about Balboa from this flashback? What theme does it suggest about the nature of power?

3. **Analyze** Note the references to, and images of, dogs throughout the story. What message does the author convey through these references?

4. **Analyze** What is revealed by the flash forward at the end of the story? How does this revelation affect the overall meaning of the work?

5. **Notice & Note** Think about the difference between how Balboa regards himself and how he would like to be regarded. Why does the writer include this information about Balboa? How does this affect your understanding of his character?

RESEARCH

RESEARCH TIP
Even credible resources can have bias. When you read a source, make sure to differentiate between the factual information and the source's interpretation of the facts.

Balboa, from Spain, was just one of many European explorers who sailed during the late 1400s and early 1500s. With a partner, research other explorers of this time from the countries listed in the chart. Summarize why they are remembered.

COUNTRY	EXPLORER	NOTABLE ACHIEVEMENT
France	Jacques Cartier Jacques Marquette	Answers will vary based on students' research findings.
Spain	Francisco Pizarro Juan Ponce de León	
Portugal	Vasco da Gama Pedro Álvares Cabral	

Extend Find another source that mentions Vasco de Balboa. Find three facts about this explorer that were not reflected in the short story. Discuss with your partner whether the facts align with the depiction of Balboa in the story.

WHEN STUDENTS STRUGGLE . . .

Reteaching: Determining Themes Review the terms *theme, structure, character, plot,* and *conflict*. Remind students to infer an implied theme by analyzing details. Making connections about characters, plot, and conflict will help them infer the theme.

Ask students what Balboa says and does that suggest his motivation. (*He wants to be the first to see the Pacific Ocean in order to "claim" it for Spain so the king will realize his importance.*)

 For additional support, go to the **Reading Studio** and assign the following LEVEL UP **Level Up Tutorial: Theme.**

CREATE AND PRESENT

Write a Dramatic Monologue Murray's portrayal of Balboa creates a dynamic character whom readers can visualize and almost hear. Write a dramatic monologue from the point of view of this fictional Balboa, expressing what he might have said aloud as he stood on the boulder surveying the Pacific Ocean.

❏ Draw upon the text for details about the path Balboa followed to "the edge of the world." Reveal his motives and feelings upon reaching his goal.

❏ Include his reflections on what his accomplishment really means, incorporating your ideas about the story's theme.

❏ As you compose your monologue, try using end rhymes. Decide on a rhyme scheme, and consult a rhyming dictionary for help.

Present a Dramatic Monologue Present your monologue to a small group.

❏ Mark your monologue with notes indicating where you intend to slow down, speak forcefully or quietly, and pause.

❏ Practice several times before presenting to an audience.

❏ Remember to speak clearly at an appropriate volume, using eye contact to connect with your audience.

 Go to **Writing Narratives** in the **Writing Studio** for help with using narrative techniques in writing.

 Go to **Giving a Presentation** in the **Speaking and Listening Studio** for help with presenting to others.

RESPOND TO THE ESSENTIAL QUESTION

 What motivates people to explore the unknown?

Gather Information Review your annotations and notes on "Balboa." Then, add relevant information to your Response Log. As you determine which information to include, think about:

- Balboa's character traits
- experiences that influenced Balboa's willingness to explore
- Balboa's motivations for exploring

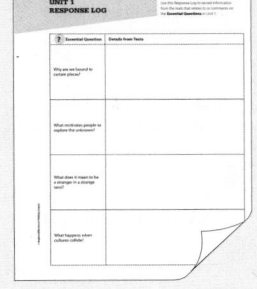

ACADEMIC VOCABULARY

As you write and discuss what you learned from "Balboa," be sure to use the Academic Vocabulary words. Check off each of the words that you use.

❏ **adapt**

❏ **coherent**

❏ **device**

❏ **displace**

❏ **dynamic**

CREATE AND PRESENT

Write a Dramatic Monologue Have students scan the selection for clues to Balboa's personality and motives. Suggest that they create a list of his traits. Monologues should include details from the story about his journey, his motives, and his feelings. His views on his accomplishments and their significance should also be included.

Present a Dramatic Monologue Presentations should reflect an understanding of the needs of the audience. Speakers should be able to maintain eye contact, adjust their rate of speaking, and use pitch and volume to stress different parts of their monologues. Presentations should also show evidence of practice.

For **writing support** for students at varying proficiency levels, see the **Text X-Ray** on page 20D.

RESPOND TO THE ESSENTIAL QUESTION

Allow time for students to add details from "Balboa" to their Unit 1 Response Logs.

CRITICAL VOCABULARY

Answers:

1. No, because yielding to him would not cause disagreement. Other answers may be possible.

2. No, because both had unspoiled reputations, it would be difficult to see a difference in them.

3. If young children replaced their parents in the task of grocery shopping, their food supply would likely be less healthy.

4. No, if many weeds were sticking out of a lawn, it would not look unspoiled.

VOCABULARY STRATEGY:
Context Clues

Answers:

Possible words, context clues, and definitions are below. Original sentences should reflect an understanding of the words' definitions.

Word	Context Clues	Dictionary Definition
stealth	Balboa compares himself to a rat. (paragraph 4)	the act of proceeding secretly
ingesting	He says he has been drinking the water. (paragraph 6)	swallowing or gulping down
incisors	They are described as showing at the corners of the jaguar's mouth. (paragraph 7)	front teeth designed for cutting
mastiffs	The word appears in a phrase set off after the term "war dogs." (paragraph 18)	a type of large dog, sometimes used as guard dogs

WORD BANK
pristine
supplant
protrude
provision
discord
distinction
cede

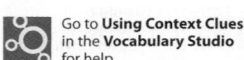 Go to **Using Context Clues** in the **Vocabulary Studio** for help.

CRITICAL VOCABULARY

Practice and Apply Answer each question, referring to the meaning of each Critical Vocabulary word in your response.

1. If you **ceded** a toy to your younger brother, would there be **discord?**

2. If both candidates had **pristine** reputations and equal leadership experience, would it be easy to make a **distinction** between them?

3. If children in a family **supplanted** their parents in control of the grocery shopping, how would the family's **provisions** be different?

4. If the lawn has weeds **protruding** from it, is it in **pristine** condition?

VOCABULARY STRATEGY:
Context Clues

The context of a word is the words, phrases, and sentences around it. Looking at the context of an unfamiliar word can help you define it.

> Balboa had organized the rebellion, supplanted the governor—all of this done with great efficiency and intelligence.

In this sentence, the word *rebellion* helps you understand that *supplanted* means "to overthrow or replace."

Key words can signal a relationship between the unknown word and others that help define it.

KEY WORDS	CONTEXT CLUES
such as, like, for example, including	The unknown word is followed by examples that illustrate its meaning: *We packed <u>provisions</u>, such as <u>fruit and water</u>.*
unlike, but, in contrast, although, on the other hand	The unknown word is contrasted with a more familiar word or phrase: *The tablecloth was <u>pristine</u> before dinner, <u>but it was covered with stains</u> afterward.*
also, similar to, as, like, as if	The unknown word is compared to a more familiar word or phrase: *The wad of gum <u>protruding</u> from his cheek made him look <u>as if he had the mumps</u>.*
or, that is, which is, in other words	The unknown word is preceded or followed by a restatement of its meaning: *The <u>distinction</u>, or <u>difference</u>, between the identical twins was slight.*

Practice and Apply With a partner, choose three unfamiliar words from the story. Then, to demonstrate your understanding, use context clues to define the unfamiliar words, verify the meanings of the words using a print or digital dictionary, and write original sentences using the words correctly.

© Houghton Mifflin Harcourt Publishing Company

ENGLISH LEARNER SUPPORT

Vocabulary Strategy Some sounds in English do not appear in other languages and therefore may pose challenges for English learners. For example, the short vowel sound *i*, as in *sit*, may be unknown or confusing to speakers of Spanish, Vietnamese, Hmong, Cantonese, Haitian Creole, and Korean. Making sure students can produce and perceive this sound will help them with language acquisition.

Several of the Critical Vocabulary terms contain a short *i* sound. These include *pristine*, *provision*, *discord*, and *distinction*. As a class, repeat these words, focusing on the *i* sound.
ALL LEVELS

LANGUAGE CONVENTIONS:
Verb Tenses

Verb tense indicates the time of the action or state of being. An action or state of being can occur in the present, the past, or the future.

VERB TENSES		
TENSE	**USE**	**EXAMPLE**
Present	describe action that is happening at the present time, occurs regularly, or is constant	Balboa stops to take a drink.
Past	describe action that began and ended in the past	Balboa stopped to take a drink.
Future	describe action that will occur	Balboa will stop to take a drink.
Present Perfect	describe action that was completed at an indefinite past time or began in the past and still continues	Balboa has stopped to take a drink.
Past Perfect	describe action in the past that came before another action in the past	Balboa had stopped to take a drink.
Future Perfect	describe action in the future that will be completed before another action in the future	Balboa will have stopped to take a drink.

For the most part, "Balboa" uses present-tense verbs to tell the story. Note the present-tense verbs in this passage from the story:

> Balboa <u>ascends</u> slowly. His musket <u>is</u> heavy and he would have gladly left it down below, but he <u>doesn't trust</u> his countrymen any more than he <u>trusts</u> the sullen Indians.

The story also uses past and future tenses to move the story around in time, allowing the author to use flashback to delve into Balboa's memories and flash forward to show how the story ends.

Practice and Apply Identify the verb and its tense in each sentence.

SENTENCE FROM "BALBOA"	VERB	TENSE
But here . . . then he hears a twig snap and the sound of something brushing up against the bushes.	*hears*	*present*
The sun seemed so much smaller there.	*seemed*	*past*
Dávila will see that as long as Balboa lives he must sleep with one eye open.	*will see* *lives* *must sleep*	*future* *present* *present*

Then, choose a passage in "Balboa" and rewrite it in a different tense. Share this with a partner and discuss how it affects the narrative and the mood or tone.

 Go to **Tense** in the **Grammar Studio** for help.

© Houghton Mifflin Harcourt Publishing Company

LANGUAGE CONVENTIONS:
Verb Tenses

Review the information about verb tense with students. Remind students that tense generally remains consistent throughout a single sentence, although there are exceptions to this rule.

Practice and Apply

Sentence #1: Verb: "hears," Tense: present (The present participle "brushing up" is used as an adjective.)

Sentence #2: Verb: "seemed," Tense: past

Sentence #3: Verb: "will see," Tense: future; Verb: "lives," Tense: present; Modal verb: "must sleep," Tense: present

Students' rewritten passages should include verbs that have had a change in tense from the original. Encourage students to discuss the different ways the change in verb tense affects the text. Is it more engaging or less? Does it make the action clearer or less clear?

EL ENGLISH LEARNER SUPPORT

Language Conventions Use the following supports with students at varying proficiency levels.

Have students find three present-tense and three past-tense verbs on page 24 of the story. **SUBSTANTIAL**

Have students find where the verb tense shifts from present tense to past tense, indicating a flashback. Then, have students write a sentence using both present and past tense verbs. **MODERATE**

MENTOR TEXT

A DESPERATE TREK ACROSS AMERICA

Article by Andrés Reséndez

This informational text serves as a **mentor text,** a model for students to follow when they come to the Unit 1 Writing Task: Write a Literary Analysis.

GENRE ELEMENTS
INFORMATIONAL TEXT

Informational texts are nonfiction, and their purpose is to give facts or details about the natural or social world. They are focused on a single topic. An **article** is a shorter informational text that focuses on a narrower topic. Authors assert a clear thesis and give strong supporting evidence. Supporting evidence may include information from primary sources, such as letters, diaries, or autobiographies, which are accounts given by people who experienced events. Articles may also contain the author's point of view about the topic.

LEARNING OBJECTIVES

- Analyze informational texts and evaluate information.
- Research the conquest of the Aztec empire.
- Write a response analyzing the author's view of Cabeza de Vaca.
- Present a response to a group of classmates.
- Determine the meaning of foreign words in English.
- Analyze how writers use infinitives.
- **Language** Express opinions about the text.

TEXT COMPLEXITY

Quantitative Measures	A Desperate Trek Across America	Lexile: 1230L
Qualitative Measures	**Ideas Presented** Simple, single meaning. Literal, explicit, and direct.	
	Structures Used Clear, chronological, conventional.	
	Language Used Mostly explicit, some figurative or allusive language. Some dialect or other unconventional language.	
	Knowledge Required More complexity in theme. Experiences may be less familiar to many. Cultural or historical references may make heavier demands.	

RESOURCES

- Unit 1 Response Log
- Selection Audio
- Reading Studio: Notice & Note
- Level Up Tutorial: Evidence
- Writing Studio: Using Textual Evidence
- Speaking and Listening Studio: Giving a Presentation
- Vocabulary Studio: Understanding Word Origins
- Grammar Studio: Module 3: Lesson 5: Infinitives and Infinitive Phrases
- "A Desperate Trek Across America"

SUMMARIES

English

Andrés Reséndez gives an account of a group of 250 Spanish conquistadors stranded on the coast of Florida in 1528. The men, led by Álvar Núñez Cabeza de Vaca, endured starvation, disease, exposure, and enslavement. After many years, only four men survived. They lived among Native Americans who believed the four men possessed healing powers. Eventually, Cabeza de Vaca returned to Spain and advocated for the humane colonization of the New World.

Spanish

Andrés Reséndez describe a un grupo de 250 conquistadores españoles varados en la costa de la Florida en 1528. Los hombres, al mando de Álvar Núñez Cabeza de Vaca, soportaron atrocidades como la inanición, enfermedades, exposición y esclavitud. Luego de muchos años, solo cuatro hombres sobrevivieron. Vivían entre indígenas americanos quienes creían que los cuatro hombres poseían poderes curativos dados por Dios. Finalmente, Cabeza de Vaca regresó a España y abogó por una colonización humanitaria del Nuevo Mundo.

SMALL-GROUP OPTIONS

Have students work in small groups and pairs to read and discuss the selection.

Two-Column Notes

- Have students fold a piece of paper into thirds vertically.
- On the left third of the page, have them label the heading *Characteristics of Informational Texts*.
- Underneath the heading, have the students list *clear thesis, strong supporting evidence, relevant examples, commentary, summary,* and *conclusion*. Briefly review the meaning of these words.
- As the students read the selection, ask them to make notes on the right two-thirds of the page citing textual evidence that corresponds with each term on the left.
- When students have finished reading and taking notes, organize them into small groups to compare notes and analyze the article for characteristics of informational texts.

Jigsaw with Experts

- Divide the selection into parts and assign parts to students.
- Have students individually read and take notes on their section. Then group students with the same section, and have them discuss their section. They should consolidate their notes and reread to clarify ideas. Students will become "experts" on their sections.
- Then form new groups consisting of one student for each section of text.
- Have students discuss their respective sections. Encourage students to ask the "experts" questions.

Text X-Ray: English Learner Support
for "A Desperate Trek Across America"

Use the Text X-Ray and the supports and scaffolds in the Teacher's Edition to help guide students at different proficiency levels through the selection.

INTRODUCE THE SELECTION
DISCUSS GEOGRAPHICAL TERMS

Draw the students' attention to paragraph 1 in the selection that provides the following setting: "Florida panhandle, Fall 1528."

Display a map of the United States. To demonstrate what students should look for on the map, display a pan (or a photo of one) and point to the handle. Ask: *If this is the handle of a pan, where is the Florida panhandle?* Then, ask students to identify other states that have a "panhandle." See how many they can identify before you point them out. (There are nine states and ten panhandles: Alaska, Florida, Nebraska, Idaho, Maryland, West Virginia (eastern), West Virginia (northern), Oklahoma, Texas, and Connecticut.)

Students should be able to identify the Florida panhandle, discuss what a panhandle is, and how it got its name. (*It is a narrow piece of land that sticks out from a larger piece of land, such as a state, just like the handle of a pan.*)

CULTURAL REFERENCES

The following words or phrases may be unfamiliar to students:

- *technological advantages* (paragraph 4): The Spanish in 1528 used technology (things invented by using science or engineering), such as breastplates, weapons, and horses, that the Native Americans did not have.
- *mortifications of the flesh* (paragraph 10): In early Catholicism, brought to the Americas by the Spanish, mortification (suffering pain or discomfort) to the body was thought to bring a period of darkness so that one could be spiritually reborn.
- *nursed that fire* (paragraph 11): kept the fire going by feeding it
- *lobbying* (paragraph 16): asking for something you want

LISTENING

Understand the Author's Point of View

Explain that readers can understand what authors think by examining the author's words and the quotes they choose from primary sources.

Have students listen as you read paragraphs 13–15. If appropriate, have them make annotations or notes as they follow along.

- Explain that the paragraphs describe two groups of people from Spain: the explorers and the posse, or group, of Spanish slavers. Read words and phrases used to describe each group, such as *walking barefoot and clad in skins* and *went about dressed and on horses and with lances*. Explain the meaning of each word or phrase, and ask students to identify which group is being described. **SUBSTANTIAL**
- Have students refer to the text or their notes and ask questions about meanings they do not understand. Provide sentence frames and model their use. *I don't understand what _____ means. Will you explain? I am confused by _____. Will you clarify, please? What does the author mean by _____?* **MODERATE**
- Have students close their books and work in pairs to list evidence from what they heard that helps them understand how the author views Cabeza de Vaca. **LIGHT**

SPEAKING

Express Opinions

The author added his opinions to the article. Adding opinions is a feature of many informational texts. Oral rehearsal helps writers experiment with the best words to use to convey their messages.

Ask students to think about and express their own opinions of Cabeza de Vaca and the events recounted in the article.

- Remind students that an opinion is what they believe or think. Provide sentence frames: *I think that he _____. I believe that _____.* Help students complete the sentence frames. If necessary, allow students to respond in their own language and then translate it. **SUBSTANTIAL**

- Organize the students into pairs. Ask them to tell each other their opinion of Cabeza de Vaca. Provide the following sentence frames: *I think _____ because _____. I believe he changed because _____.* **MODERATE**

- Pair students and have them discuss their opinions of Cabeza de Vaca. Students should ask and answer questions to elicit opinions and reasons. **LIGHT**

READING

Evaluate Author's Opinions

Readers often return to the text to check their initial understanding and evaluate the author's opinions.

Use the following supports with students at varying proficiency levels.

- Read paragraph 3 with students. Work with them to determine the author's opinion of Cabeza de Vaca's choice to make the trade. Point out words and phrases such as *desperate gamble* to help students identify the author's opinion. Discuss whether students agree with this opinion. **SUBSTANTIAL**

- Have students read paragraph 3 and identify the author's opinion of the trade. Have them underline text evidence that supports the opinion. Provide sentence frames: *The author thinks that _____. I agree because _____.* **MODERATE**

- Have students return to the selection to find two of the author's opinions. Pair students and have them state whether or not they agree with those opinions. Students should give reasons for their opinions. **LIGHT**

WRITING

Write an Analytic Response

Read the prompt on Student Edition page 43. Explain that *to analyze* means to study something closely and carefully.

Work with students to read the description of the assignment on page 43 entitled *Write an Analytic Response*.

- Explain that an *admirable* person does good things and is worthy of respect. Provide the following sentence frame and help students complete it: *Cabeza de Vaca was/was not admirable because _____.* Then write a paragraph as a class. Have students copy the paragraph in their notebooks.

- Have students work in pairs and return to the text to determine their opinion of Cabeza de Vaca and find evidence to support it. Provide sentence frames to help students write their essays: *Cabeza de Vaca was/was not admirable because _____. The detail _____ shows that he was/was not admirable.*

- Have students work individually to draft an essay that expresses their opinion and uses text evidence to support it. Then have students exchange papers with a partner and do a peer review. Reviewers should note if the opinion is clearly stated and the text evidence supports that opinion. Encourage reviewers to suggest ways to combine sentences to add variety.

? **Connect to the**
ESSENTIAL QUESTION

"A Desperate Trek Across America" explores how people can adapt to new and challenging situations in order to survive. The article emphasizes how wits, or intelligence, may be the best resource a person has in order to adjust to unfamiliar circumstances.

MENTOR TEXT

At the end of the unit, students will be asked to write a literary analysis. "A Desperate Trek Across America" provides a model for how a writer can support a claim, or thesis, with supporting evidence, including direct quotations from a primary source.

A DESPERATE TREK ACROSS AMERICA

Article by **Andrés Reséndez**

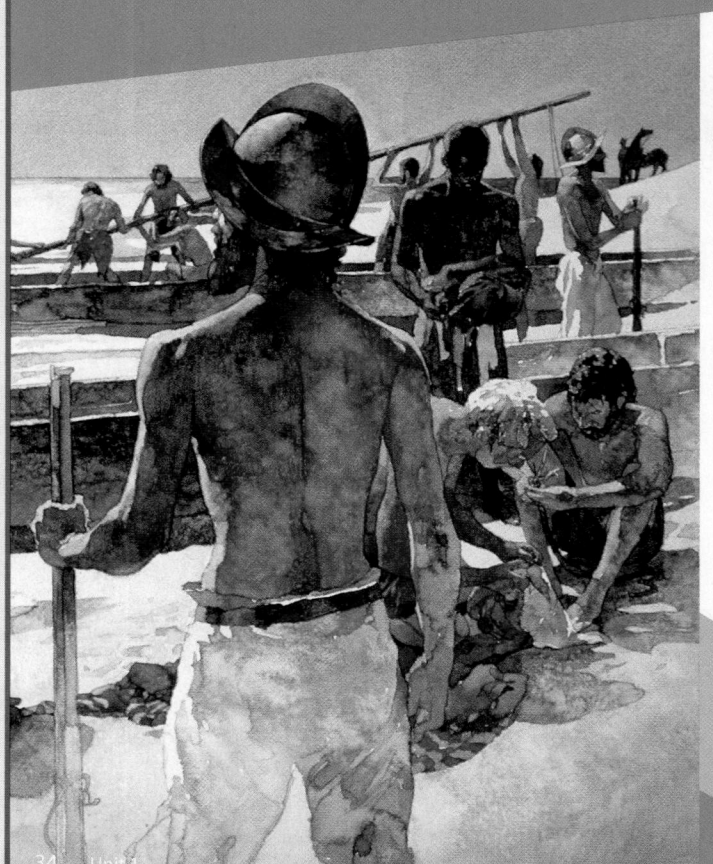

? ***ESSENTIAL QUESTION:***

What does it mean to be a stranger in a strange land?

© Houghton Mifflin Harcourt Publishing Company • Image Credits: © Cabeza de Vaca, 1994 (w/c on paper), Harlin, Greg (b.1957)/Private Collection/Wood Ronsaville Harlin, Inc. USA/Bridgeman Images

34　Unit 1

 LEARNING MINDSET

Setting Goals　Tell students that setting goals is an important part of having a learning mindset. Explain that setting goals can help to identify and quantify growth. Encourage students to set a goal for reading informational texts outside of class, for example, reading one news article per day. Consider having students summarize the article in class in order to keep track of their goals.

QUICK START

Most people have experienced failure. But sometimes failure can have unintended benefits. Think of a time when you or someone you know unexpectedly benefited from failure. Discuss your ideas with a partner.

ANALYZE INFORMATIONAL TEXTS

"A Desperate Trek Across America" is an **informational text** that chronicles the efforts of Spanish explorers of North America to recover from disaster. Informational texts may be written for a number of purposes, including:

- to explain or describe a situation or process
- to analyze a situation by explaining causes and effects
- to narrate a sequence of events

Though informational texts are factual, they may also include the author's commentary, including judgments, opinions, or conclusions. The evidence and examples included in the text and the way the text is structured support the author's purpose for writing. As you read, think about the kinds of details the author includes and what they suggest about his purpose.

**GENRE ELEMENTS:
INFORMATIONAL TEXT**

- includes articles, essays, and reference materials
- provides factual information but can include author's commentary, such as judgments, opinions, or conclusions
- may include primary source material for a particular purpose.

DETAILS	PURPOSE
What details does the author include about the explorers' situation at the beginning of the text?	• The narrative starts in the fall of 1528 • The explorers were Spanish, stranded in Florida • Out of 250 stranded men, 50 had died from disease, injury, and starvation.
What details does the author include about their efforts to address their problem?	• Every third day, the stranded men killed a horse to avoid starving. • The men traded weapons for shoddy vessels.

ANALYZE AND EVALUATE EVIDENCE

Authors of informational texts that describe historical events may integrate primary source material—the accounts of people who experienced the event—into their writing. In the text you are going to read, the author includes first-hand quotations from Spanish explorers alongside his descriptions and commentary. As you read, think about what these quotations add to the text, how they support the main idea, and how they influence your understanding of events. The primary source material may also provide insight into the writer's purpose.

A Desperate Trek Across America   35

QUICK START

After students have read the Quick Start prompt, have them share their thoughts on failure with a partner. Remind them that the purpose of the activity is to find the unexpected rewards that can come from failure, and that sometimes these benefits may not be obvious at first. Point out that people often benefit from failure because it leads to growth and self-realization.

ANALYZE INFORMATIONAL TEXTS

Help students understand the characteristics that are common to informational texts, so that they can recognize and analyze works in this genre. Explain that these characteristics include a strong text structure; factual information from primary and/or secondary sources; detailed descriptions of people, places, or things; and a sequence of events. Further point out that in some informational texts, such as this one, the author seeks to convey a clear purpose, or message. You may choose to discuss the difference between an unbiased journalistic piece, which is mainly a description of an event, and an opinion piece, in which the writer's own opinions are stated.

ANALYZE AND EVALUATE EVIDENCE

Remind students that primary source material offers readers insight into the perspectives and values of individuals and historical periods. Tell them to pay special attention to the firsthand quotations in the text, especially as they relate to the author's purpose or to the Essential Question. Ask students to put themselves in Cabeza de Vaca's shoes and, as he said, imagine for themselves *"what could happen in a land so strange."*

CRITICAL VOCABULARY

Point out to students that some of these words have their origins in the Spanish language (*conquistador* and *flotilla*). Ask them to identify other words from foreign languages that are routinely used when speaking or writing in English.

Answers:

1. *conquistador*
2. *posse*
3. *flotilla*
4. *expedition*
5. *interminable*
6. *unimpeded*
7. *straits*

■ English Learner Support

Use Cognates Spanish speakers will recognize many of these words, especially *flotilla* (fleet) and *conquistador* (conqueror). Spanish cognates include *impede/impedir; expedition/expedición;* and *interminable/interminable.*
ALL LEVELS

LANGUAGE CONVENTIONS

Remind students that an **infinitive** uses *to* plus the verb. An **infinitive phrase** is an infinitive plus any modifiers. Have students come up with more examples of infinitive phrases. For example, model: *"I am teaching my students to learn complicated grammar structures."* Have students use the infinitive *to take* and create another sentence with an infinitive phrase.

ANNOTATION MODEL

Remind students of annotation ideas, such as underlining or circling the text, or they may want to use their own system for marking up the selection in their write-in text. They might want to color-code their annotations by using highlighters. Their notes in the margin should identify various types of evidence and examples, including direct quotations, historical facts, sequence of events, and observational details.

 **GET READY**

CRITICAL VOCABULARY

straits	conquistador	flotilla	posse
expedition	interminable	unimpeded	

To see how many Critical Vocabulary words you know, choose the word that is closest in meaning to each numbered phrase.

1. a Spanish warrior _____

2. an armed band _____

3. a fleet of water vessels _____

4. an arduous journey _____

5. long and drawn out _____

6. not disrupted _____

7. a position of difficulty _____

LANGUAGE CONVENTIONS

Infinitives and Infinitive Phrases An **infinitive** is a verb in its stem form that is used in a sentence as a noun, adjective, or adverb. An **infinitive phrase** is an infinitive plus any modifiers or complements added to the base infinitive.

Infinitive: to take

Infinitive phrase: ordering the captains to take their ships

As you read, notice the writer's use of infinitives and infinitive phrases to describe actions and express ideas.

ANNOTATION MODEL
 NOTICE & NOTE

As you read, notice the details that describe the explorers' situation as well as the author's commentary about what is happening. Note quotations from primary sources and what they add to your understanding. In the model, you can see one reader's notes about "A Desperate Trek Across America."

The 250 <u>starving</u> Spanish adventurers dubbed the shallow estuary near their campsite the "Bay of Horses," because <u>every third day they killed yet another draft animal</u>, roasted it, and consumed the flesh. <u>Fifty men had already died of disease, injury, and starvation.</u> What was worse, after having walked the length of Florida without finding gold, those still alive had <u>lost contact</u> with their ships. They were <u>stranded in an alien continent.</u>

details about explorers' condition

"What was worse" gives author's view.

BACKGROUND

From a base in Cuba, conquistadors enriched themselves and the Spanish crown by conquering the Aztec empire. Their success prompted Spain to seek wealth elsewhere in the Americas. In 1527, Álvar Núñez Cabeza de Vaca was second in command of a massive expedition to Florida that included five ships and 600 men. The effort ended disastrously. Two ships sank in a hurricane, and a third of the men perished or deserted. After reaching Florida in the spring of 1528, the party of about 300 men marched overland and raided the Native American settlements they encountered. **Andrés Reséndez's** *historical account begins at this point.*

A DESPERATE TREK ACROSS AMERICA
Article by Andrés Reséndez

Left margin, rotated: © Houghton Mifflin Harcourt Publishing Company • Image Credits: © Cabeza de Vaca, 1994 (w/c on paper), Harlin, Greg (b. 1957)/Private Collection/Wood Ronsaville Harlin, Inc. USA/Bridgeman Images

SETTING A PURPOSE

As you read, pay attention to the details that convey the explorers' situation and the efforts they undertook to save themselves.

Florida panhandle, Fall 1528

1   The 250 starving Spanish adventurers dubbed the shallow estuary near their campsite the "Bay of Horses," because every third day they killed yet another draft animal, roasted it, and consumed the flesh. Fifty men had already died of disease, injury, and starvation. What was worse, after having walked the length of Florida without finding gold, those still alive had lost contact with their ships. They were stranded in an alien continent.

2   "We were in such **straits** that anything that had some semblance of a solution seemed good to us," wrote Álvar Núñez Cabeza de Vaca, the **expedition's** royal treasurer, in one of the most harrowing[1] survival stories ever told. "I refrain here from telling this at greater length because each one can imagine for himself what could happen in a land so strange."

_____
[1] **harrowing:** referring to an experience that is extremely distressing.

Notice & Note

Use the side margins to notice and note signposts in the text.

straits
(strāts) *adj.* a position of difficulty, distress, or extreme need.

expedition
(ĕk´spĭ-dĭsh´ən) *n.* a journey, especially a difficult or hazardous one, undertaken after extensive planning and with a definite objective in mind.

WHEN STUDENTS STRUGGLE . . .

Understand Evidence Some students might find it hard to distinguish between factual information and the author's own personal opinions. Have students isolate the facts, such as dates, numbers, names, and locations and quotations from Cabeza de Vaca himself. Have them read the text and make a note of any details that are strictly factual or quotations. Tell them to summarize the narrative using just their notes. After they read the text again, they should be better able to identify the author's commentary.

   For additional support, go to the **Reading Studio** and assign the following **Level Up Tutorial: Evidence.**

BACKGROUND

Help students understand a bit more about the European expansion into the Americas by discussing the conquistadors. Students may already guess that *conquistador* is the Spanish word for *conqueror*, which describes these Spanish men who came to the New World during the 16th century. Point out to students that the word itself assumes a European view of events, in that the Spanish generally saw themselves as imposing their will over the Native Americans through sheer force. Challenge students to think about this historical period from the Native Americans' point of view. This will prepare them for Cabeza de Vaca's own empathetic conclusions at the end of the text.

SETTING A PURPOSE

Direct students to use the Setting a Purpose prompt to focus their reading.

CRITICAL VOCABULARY

straits: Paragraph 1 of the text details the difficult circumstances in which the conquistadors found themselves. In a quotation, Cabeza de Vaca encapsulates the distress caused by disease, injury, starvation, and isolation by using the phrase "such straits."

ASK STUDENTS what mental or emotional conditions accompany dire straits. (*When people say they are in dire straits, they are feeling desperate, hopeless, and often on the edge of death.*)

expedition: In the Background note, the text mentions the purpose of this expedition was to explore Florida and seek any riches for the Spanish Crown.

ASK STUDENTS to recall the details of the expedition. How many men were left when the expedition launched their improvised rafts? (*After being stranded, 250 men fit into 5 makeshift vessels.*)

TEACH

 ANALYZE AND EVALUATE EVIDENCE

Remind students that primary source material—in this case a direct quotation—is used in informational texts to support and enhance descriptive passages. Have students read paragraph 6 without the quotation to see if it changes their understanding of the text. (**Answer:** *The quote emphasizes the desperation of the explorers to survive. The conquistadors produced rafts, made from dead horse parts and tattered clothing, not only because they were merely inventive but because they needed to survive. Humans are capable of great feats when their survival is at stake.*)

For **reading support** for students at varying proficiency levels, see the **Text X-Ray** on page 34D.

CRITICAL VOCABULARY

conquistador: The text explains how conquistadors were able to overwhelm the Native Americans through superior weaponry. These soldier-explorers didn't bother with negotiations; instead, they bullied their way through the New World.

ASK STUDENTS if the advanced weaponry of today also means that aggressors, like conquistadors, do not try to negotiate. (*This may be true to an extent, but such clear arms advantages may not have the exact same effect today. Countries around the world use negotiating tactics, as well as military force, to advance their agendas.*)

interminable: Viewing a coastline from sea can give a false impression about how the actual land is laid out inland. Florida's coast along the Gulf is tricky to navigate on foot.

ASK STUDENTS if they have ever been separated from a group. Did they feel rising panic? How did their anxieties affect their sense of time and make the period it took to find the group seem interminable? (*Many people, when separated from parents or a group, experience stress about time passing and confusion about where they are or where they should go.*)

 **NOTICE & NOTE**

conquistador
(kŏng-kē´stə-dôr, kŏn-kwĭs´tə-dôr) *n.* a 16th-century Spanish soldier-explorer who took part in the defeat of the Indian civilizations of Mexico, Central America, or Peru.

interminable
(ĭn-tûr´mə-nə-bəl) *adj.* seemingly endless.

ANALYZE AND EVALUATE EVIDENCE

Annotate: Mark the words and phrases in paragraph 6 that come from a primary source.

Infer: What does the information that is included add to your understanding of the explorers' situation?

3   Indeed, Cabeza de Vaca and the other leaders of the ill-fated venture had agreed to a desperate gamble: to trade their most effective weapons against the Indians—horses and firearms—for five makeshift vessels that might or might not be capable of carrying them to safety. Eating the horses gave them time to build the rafts. To make nails and saws, they threw their crossbows,[2] along with stirrups and spurs, into an improvised forge.

4   Like past **conquistadors**, Cabeza de Vaca and his men had relied on their breastplates,[3] horses, and lethal weapons to keep the Indians at bay. Such overwhelming technological advantages meant they often did not even bother to negotiate, instead simply imposing their will. By sacrificing the very tools of their supremacy, they would now have to face the New World fully exposed to its perils and hold on only by their wits.

5   The expedition had unraveled with frightening speed. Just months earlier, the hopeful adventurers had embarked from Cuba in four ships and a brigantine[4] and made landfall near present day Tampa Bay, intending to take possession of Florida in the name of His Most Catholic Majesty.[5] Caught up in the excitement and rush to explore, the commander rashly divided the expedition, ordering the captains to take their ships on an exploration of the coast, while the men and the horses were put ashore. They agreed to meet just a few miles north of the debarkation point. But the **interminable** and confusing coast of Florida prevented the two parties from making contact.

6   With their jury-rigged[6] saws they cut down trees, dragged them to the beach, lashed them together with the tails and manes of their dead horses, and fashioned sails from their tattered shirts. After five or six weeks, they slaughtered their last horse, then dragged the 15-ton rafts into the water. Fifty men crowded aboard each craft, the fifth commanded by Cabeza de Vaca. "And so greatly can necessity prevail," he observed, "that it made us risk going in this manner and placing ourselves in a sea so treacherous, and without any one of us who went having any knowledge of the art of navigation." The rafts floated only a few inches above the waterline; the waves would wash over the men as they traveled.

7   Little did the men on the rafts know that they were embarking on an eight-year adventure that would ultimately take their few survivors across the entire continent. After several weeks, storms separated

---

[2] **crossbows:** weapons made by fixing a bow crosswise on a wooden base and including grooves on that base to guide the flight of the arrow.
[3] **breastplates:** pieces of armor covering the chest.
[4] **brigantine:** a two-masted sailing ship with square sails on the forward mast and a large mainsail positioned from the front to the back of the ship.
[5] **His Most Catholic Majesty:** honorary title of the king of Spain granted by Pope Alexander VI in 1494.
[6] **jury-rigged:** assembled for temporary use in an improvised way.

 ENGLISH LEARNER SUPPORT

Shared Responding Have students work in groups of four to read paragraph 4. Ask each student to identify a word in the text that is important to the main idea. Have all students share their words and state why they chose them. Then have the group work together to create a sentence that summarizes the main idea of the paragraph. **MODERATE**

the **flotilla**. Tormented by extreme hunger and drenched by the splashing of the waves, they were on the brink of death. "The people began to faint in such a manner that when the sun set," Cabeza de Vaca would recall, "all those who came in my raft were fallen on top of one another in it, so close to death that few were conscious." Only the helmsman and Cabeza de Vaca took turns steering the raft: "Two hours into the night, the helmsman told me that I should take charge of the raft, because he was in such condition that he thought he would die that very night." Near dawn, Cabeza de Vaca heard the surf, and later that day they landed.

8   While most of the men survived the harrowing month long passage across the Gulf, eventually washing up on the coast of what is now Texas, many more perished of exposure and hunger that winter, some even resorting to cannibalism. Fewer still withstood enslavement at the hands of the natives in the vicinity of Galveston Bay. Ultimately, only four—Cabeza de Vaca, two other Spaniards in commanding positions, and an African slave named Estebanico— would escape their Indian masters after six years of toil. As slaves, Cabeza de Vaca and his companions were forced to cope with native North America on its own terms, bridging two worlds that had remained apart for 12,000 years or more. They lived by their wits, coming to terms with half a dozen native languages and making sense of societies that other Europeans could not even begin to fathom.

9   Incredibly, the four castaways used this knowledge to refashion themselves into medicine men. As Cabeza de Vaca would explain it: "we made the sign of the cross over them and blew on them and recited a Pater Noster[7] and an Ave Maria;[8] and then we prayed as best we could to God Our Lord to give them health and inspire them to give us good treatment." In one instance he revived a man who appeared to be dead. At the Indians' insistence, all four survivors performed curing ceremonies. And thus many natives came to believe that these four strange-looking beings were able to manipulate the power of nature.

10   This real or imagined gifts of healing enabled the four survivors to move **unimpeded**, their reputation preceding them wherever they went. Nor were their actions a mere charade to win food and respect. They believed that their curative abilities went somehow much deeper: they came to see their incredible suffering odyssey as a test to which God had subjected them before revealing the true purpose of their existence. They viewed their sufferings as mortifications of the flesh, their beatings and extreme hunger akin to those of flagellants[9]

---

[7] **Pater Noster:** a Latin phrase meaning "Our Father" that refers to the Lord's Prayer.
[8] **Ave Maria:** a Latin phrase meaning "Hail Mary" that refers to a Roman Catholic prayer.
[9] **flagellants:** members of a Christian religious sect who publicly beat themselves with whips as an act of religious devotion and discipline.

NOTICE & NOTE

flotilla
(flō-tĭl´ə) *n.* a fleet of small water craft.

LANGUAGE CONVENTIONS
Annotate: Mark the infinitive phrase in the last sentence of paragraph 8.

Analyze: How does this phrase suggest that the explorers are exceptional? Explain.

unimpeded
(ən-im-pē´-dəd) *adj.* not delayed or obstructed in its progress.

LANGUAGE CONVENTIONS

Review the three possible ways in which an infinitive can be used in a sentence (noun, adjective, or adverb). Explain that in this example, the infinitive is used as a noun. More specifically, it is the direct object for the verb *begin*. (**Answer:** *The Native American cultures were so foreign to the explorers, there was no way for them to interpret these new customs according to their own beliefs and experiences. They had to completely rethink the way people approach life.*)

CRITICAL VOCABULARY

flotilla: The term *flotilla* is a diminutive version of the Spanish word *flota*, or "fleet." In Spanish, a diminutive version of a word can indicate youth or small size.

ASK STUDENTS why the author chose the word *flotilla*, rather than a more common word or phrase, such as *fleet*, or group of rafts. (*By using the Spanish word* flotilla, *the author helps reinforce the nationality of the explorers.*)

unimpeded: By taking on the identity of "healers," the explorers were able to move through Native American societies with some ease. Their captors, who respected their perceived skills, gave them a measure of freedom and allowed them to move unimpeded.

ASK STUDENTS how much freedom the explorers truly had in their time with the Native Americans. (*Although they could move unimpeded through society, the explorers were still captives.*)

IMPROVE READING FLUENCY

Targeted Passage   Have students work in pairs and read the Background paragraphs, as well as paragraphs 1 and 2 to each other. If possible, pair a Spanish student with a native English speaker. As they take turns reading to each other, tell them to note the transitions between Spanish words and names, such as *conquistador* and *Álvar Núñez Cabeza de Vaca*, and the rest of the English text. Tell students to make sure their pace of reading remains constant and does not speed up for familiar words.

Go to the **Reading Studio** for additional support in developing fluency.

QUOTED WORDS

Remind students that quoted words are used in informational texts to support an author's purpose. Ask students what point the author is trying to make about Cabeza de Vaca by using this quote. (**Answer:** *The quote shows that Cabeza de Vaca sees himself as helped by God. It also helps show the difficult circumstances he survived.*)

ENGLISH LEARNER SUPPORT

Use Prior Knowledge Draw students' attention to the words *aflame* and *nursed* in paragraph 11. Ask if these words remind them of other words they know. Guide them to understand the relationship between *flame* (a synonym for *fire*) and *aflame* (a synonym for *on fire*). Guide them to understand the relationship between the noun *nurse* (a person who cares for others, especially when they are sick) and the verb *nursed* (which means "cared for" or "restored to health").

ALL LEVELS

For **listening support** for students at varying proficiency levels, see the **Text X-Ray** on page 34C.

CRITICAL VOCABULARY

posse: The word *posse* comes from a Latin word, and was originally meant to describe a group of men whose purpose was to uphold the law. Today, the word is more associated with Western movies and groups of men acting to enforce the law, or acting outside of the law. Here, the author uses it to indicate a group of slavers who are looking to kidnap and enslave Native Americans.

ASK STUDENTS what comes to mind when they read the word *posse*. (*Students might think of a group of angry people seeking revenge, or they might think of a slang use of the word meaning a group of friends or allies.*)

 NOTICE & NOTE

QUOTED WORDS

Notice & Note: Mark details in paragraph 11 that tell what Cabeza de Vaca does to survive the cold night.

Infer: What does the quotation tell you about Cabeza de Vaca?

posse
(pŏs´ē) *n.* a group of civilians temporarily authorized by officials to assist in pursuing fugitives.

who inflicted torment upon themselves or of monks who fasted nigh unto death.

11 Once, alone and unable to find his party's camp, Cabeza de Vaca wandered in the woods naked in dread of the approaching chill of night. "But it pleased God that I found a tree aflame, and warmed by its fire I endured the cold that night." For five days he nursed that fire, before finally finding his companions.

12 The four wanderers were no longer mere castaways; they had become explorers once again. Yet theirs was a most peculiar expedition. Four naked and unarmed outsiders were led by hundreds, even thousands, of Indians. They were fed, protected, and passed off as though prized possessions from one indigenous group to the next. They became the first outsiders to behold what would become the American Southwest and northern Mexico, the first non-natives to describe this enormous land and its peoples.

13 By the time the four reemerged from the continental interior and reached the Pacific Coast, they had been so utterly transformed by the experience that fellow Europeans could hardly recognize them. A **posse** of Spanish slavers[10] operating in what is now northwestern Mexico spotted potential prey: 13 Indians walking barefoot and clad in skins. On closer inspection, some of the details did not seem quite right. One was a black man. Could he be an Indian or an African emerging from the heart of the continent? Another member of the party appeared to be a haggard white man with hair hanging down to his waist and a beard reaching to his chest.

14 When Cabeza de Vaca addressed them in perfect Spanish, the slavers were "so astonished," he wrote, "that they neither talked to me nor managed to ask me anything," but bent themselves on rounding up the Indian escort. But Cabeza de Vaca and his companions would not allow it. No longer did the castaways view their companions as mere chattels,[11] the rightful prize of Christian conquest.

15 Perhaps no one understood their transformation more than the Indians themselves, who were unable to believe that Cabeza de Vaca

---

[10]**slaver:** one who catches people to enslave them.
[11]**chattels:** enslaved persons.

APPLYING ACADEMIC VOCABULARY

☑ **adapt**   ❏ **coherent**   ❏ **device**   ❏ **displace**   ☑ **dynamic**

Write and Discuss Have students turn to a partner to discuss the following questions. Guide students to include the Academic Vocabulary words *adapt* and *dynamic* in their responses. Ask volunteers to share their responses with the class.

- How did Cabeza de Vaca **adapt** to a new way of life in a foreign land?
- In what ways can the survivors' journey be considered **dynamic**?

and his three companions belonged to the same race as the slavers. The Indians had observed, he later wrote, that "we cured the sick, and they [the Spanish slavers] killed those who were well; that we came naked and barefoot, and they went about dressed and on horses and with lances; and that we did not covet anything but rather, everything they gave us we later returned and remained with nothing, and that the others had no other objective but to steal everything they found and did not give anything to anyone."

16   Cabeza de Vaca went back to Spain, attached himself to the court of Charles V, and was able to present his ideas of a humane colonization of the New World. After years of lobbying, he was dispatched to South America, where he attempted to carry out his plans, alas with little success. He spent the last years of his life in his native Andalusia,[12] reminiscing about his adventures in another world.

---

[12] **Andalusia:** southernmost region of Spain.

ANALYZE INFORMATIONAL TEXTS

Annotate: Mark what happens to Cabeza de Vaca in paragraph 16.

Analyze: As a conclusion, what do these examples add to your impression of Cabeza de Vaca?

CHECK YOUR UNDERSTANDING

Answer these questions before moving on to the **Analyze the Text** section.

1 Why do the Spanish adventurers call the estuary near their campsite the "Bay of Horses"?

  A There are several herds of horses nearby.

  B The surrounding land is shaped like a horse's head.

  C They are killing, roasting, and eating their horses.

  D The expedition's leader raises and sells horses.

2 Why is the trip by raft so difficult for the Spaniards?

  F They face constant storms while traveling the Gulf.

  G They do not know how to navigate, and grow weaker.

  H They are frequently attacked by Native Americans.

  J They have to travel by night for safety.

3 What does Cabeza de Vaca do after returning to Spain the first time?

  A He pushes for better treatment of Native Americans.

  B He retires and vows never to return to North America again.

  C He writes a report glorifying his achievements.

  D He argues that Spain should abandon efforts to colonize the Americas.

CHECK YOUR UNDERSTANDING

Have students answer the questions independently.

Answers:

  1. C

  2. G

  3. A

If they answer any questions incorrectly, have them reread the text to confirm their understanding. Then they may proceed to ANALYZE THE TEXT on page 42.

EL ENGLISH LEARNER SUPPORT

Oral Assessment Use the following questions to assess students' comprehension and speaking skills.

  1. How did the "Bay of Horses" get its name? (*The explorers were stranded in a Florida bay, starving, and were able to survive by eating their horses.*)

  2. Why was traveling by raft difficult? (*None of the survivors knew how to navigate in the open seas. They were also weak from starvation.*)

  3. What does Cabeza de Vaca do after he goes back to Spain? (*He tries to get Spanish leaders to treat Native Americans better.*)
  SUBSTANTIAL/MODERATE

ANALYZE THE TEXT

Possible answers:

1. **DOK 2:** *The author uses these terms to depict the lack of resources available to the explorers. Adjectives, such as "makeshift" and "jury-rigged," let the reader know that the stranded men were desperate and willing to try anything to survive.*

2. **DOK 3:** *In order to survive, Cabeza de Vaca and his men had to immerse themselves in and adapt to Native American culture. The explorers had to learn "half a dozen native languages," were forced to "make sense of societies," and adapted their Christianity to "refashion themselves into medicine men."*

3. **DOK 3:** *The survivors transformed themselves into medicine men by reciting Christian prayers, such as the Pater Noster and Ave Maria, which the Native Americans believed to have healing powers. The survivors used this perceived power as a means to become valuable assets. This mash-up of cultural beliefs shows the ingenuity and resourcefulness of the men.*

4. **DOK 4:** *Cabeza de Vaca and the other men developed an appreciation for Native American values that often ran contrary to their European roots. Paragraph 1 of the text states that the explorers were on a journey to find gold. By the end of the text, the survivors state that they "did not covet anything" and any possessions they were given were "later returned." Further, upon returning to Spain, Cabeza de Vaca advocated a "humane colonization of the New World," rather than one led by brute force.*

5. **DOK 4:** *The use of firsthand quotations allows readers to judge Cabeza de Vaca for themselves. Several quotations point to Cabeza de Vaca's strong faith: "we prayed as best we could to God Our Lord"; "it pleased God that I found a tree aflame."*

RESEARCH

Encourage students to find information from reliable sources, such as text encyclopedias or websites from established academic institutions. Explain that Cortés made contact with the Aztec empire in the early 16th century.

Extend Cabeza de Vaca treated native peoples with respect and integrated himself into Native American tribes, while Cortés only sought to conquer them and left destruction in his wake.

 RESPOND

ANALYZE THE TEXT

Support your responses with evidence from the text. 📓 NOTEBOOK

1. **Interpret** The author includes descriptions of "makeshift vessels" manufactured using "jury-rigged" tools. How do these descriptions affect your perception of the situation?

2. **Cite Evidence** In what ways were Cabeza de Vaca and the other survivors "forced to cope with native North America on its own terms"? Cite text evidence in your response.

3. **Draw Conclusions** What is the author's purpose for including information on the survivors' transformation into medicine men?

4. **Analyze** The author concludes that Cabeza de Vaca and the others "had been so utterly transformed" by their experience. What examples and evidence support this conclusion?

5. **Notice & Note** How do the first-hand quotations from Cabeza de Vaca affect your understanding of him? Cite evidence in your response.

RESEARCH

RESEARCH TIP
Consider using a history textbook to look for answers to the questions. You could check the table of contents or index to see if the conquest of the Aztec empire is covered in the book.

The author writes that the Spaniards benefited greatly from having a technological advantage in carrying out their conquests of Native American empires. With a partner, research the conquest of the Aztec empire to answer these questions.

QUESTION	ANSWER
What technological advantages did Cortés and his men have over the Aztecs?	*They had steel swords, guns, armor, and horses, all of which the Aztecs lacked.*
What role did non-Aztec people play in the conflict between the Spaniards and Aztecs?	*Many non-Aztec peoples who resented Aztec rule allied with the Spaniards, which strengthened them.*
What role did natural causes play in the Spaniards' ability to defeat and rule over Native American peoples who outnumbered them?	*Diseases from Europe killed many thousands of Native Americans, which weakened their society.*

Extend Based on the answers to the questions, compare and contrast Cortés's interactions with Native Americans to those of Cabeza de Vaca. Discuss your thoughts with a partner.

 LEARNING MINDSET

Belonging Remind students that everyone in the classroom is part of a learning community. A strong learning community benefits all students. Working with different partners helps to strengthen this community. When students help or challenge each other, they learn more about the topic and they also develop overall thinking and learning skills. Remind students that all members of the community have something valuable to contribute, including asking questions and giving answers, support, or encouragement.

CREATE AND PRESENT

Write an Analytic Response Write a response in which you analyze the author's view of Cabeza de Vaca.

❏ Ask yourself whether the writer finds Cabeza de Vaca admirable. Develop a thesis that states your ideas about the writer's view of Cabeza de Vaca.

❏ Determine what text evidence you can use to support your thesis.

❏ Add original commentary to enhance your ideas.

❏ Include at least one quotation from Cabeza de Vaca in your response.

Present a Response Prepare to present your response to a small group of classmates.

❏ Practice reading your response. Speak loudly enough to be heard, use appropriate vocabulary, pronounce all words clearly, and place emphasis on the most important points.

❏ Present your response to the group. When you are done, ask your listeners if they have any questions and respond to them.

❏ Listen to others in the group make their presentations and ask clarifying questions of them.

RESPOND TO THE ESSENTIAL QUESTION

 What does it mean to be a stranger in a strange land?

Gather Information Review your annotations and notes on "A Desperate Trek Across America." Then add relevant information to your Response Log. As you determine which information to include, think about:

• the situations and experiences the Spaniards encountered
• what they thought about Native American culture and society
• the information and sources the author used in the article

 RESPOND

 Go to **Using Textual Evidence** in the **Writing Studio** for help.

 Go to **Giving a Presentation: Delivering Your Presentation** in the **Speaking and Listening Studio** for help.

UNIT 1
RESPONSE LOG

Essential Question	Details from Texts
Why are we bound to certain places?	
What motivates people to explore the unknown?	
What does it mean to be a stranger in a strange land?	
What happens when cultures collide?	

ACADEMIC VOCABULARY
As you write and discuss what you learned from "A Desperate Trek Across America," be sure to use the Academic Vocabulary words. Check off each of the words that you use.

❏ adapt
❏ coherent
❏ device
❏ displace
❏ dynamic

CREATE AND PRESENT

Write an Analytic Response After reading "A Desperate Trek Across America," students should be able to describe the author's view in a concise thesis statement. Have them start with this thesis and support it with the evidence they detailed in their Notice & Note answers. Remind students that they should not just paraphrase the author but also use direct quotations from the article.

📖 For **writing support** for students at varying proficiency levels, see the **Text X-Ray** on page 34D.

Present a Response Divide the class into several small groups. Have students compare their analyses on the author's views after they have all presented their responses to their small groups. Encourage students to give each other feedback about whether supporting evidence used in their responses was strong enough to prove the thesis.

📖 For **speaking support** for students at varying proficiency levels, see the **Text X-Ray** on page 34D.

RESPOND TO THE ESSENTIAL QUESTION

Allow time for students to add details from "A Desperate Trek Across America" to their Unit 1 Response Logs.

CRITICAL VOCABULARY

Answers:

1. *mountain climbers; because they engage in extensive planning for a hazardous journey*

2. *barriers; because a person who is unimpeded does not face any obstacles in his or her path*

3. *boring lecture; because something that is uninteresting can seem endless*

4. *hurricane victim; because a hurricane victim is in need of essential services, such as fresh water, shelter, and food*

5. *chief of police; because a posse is meant to uphold the law*

6. *navy; because a flotilla consists of ships, not land vehicles*

7. *king of Spain; because the United States never used the conquistadors*

VOCABULARY STRATEGY:
Foreign Words in English

Answers:

conquistador; Spanish; Cabeza de Vaca was a conquistador, sent to the Americas to conquer the native peoples.

posse; Latin; The sheriff gathered a posse to search for the bank robber, who fled to the countryside.

flotilla; Spanish; The commander was in charge of the flotilla, which consisted of 10 ships.

RESPOND

WORD BANK
straits
expedition
conquistador
interminable
flotilla
unimpeded
posse

CRITICAL VOCABULARY

Practice and Apply Circle the letter of the best answer to each question. Then, explain your response.

1. Who is mostly likely to undertake an **expedition?**
   a. football players   b. mountain climbers

2. What is someone who is **unimpeded** not likely to face?
   a. barriers   b. success

3. Which event is a person most likely to perceive as **interminable?**
   a. boring lecture   b. exciting movie

4. Which of these individuals is in dire **straits?**
   a. first responder   b. hurricane victim

5. Who might look to a **posse** for help?
   a. chief of police   b. criminal

6. Which branch of the armed forces would dispatch a **flotilla?**
   a. army   b. navy

7. Who relied on **conquistadors?**
   a. king of Spain   b. president of United States

Go to **Understanding Word Origins** in the **Vocabulary Studio** for more.

VOCABULARY STRATEGY: Foreign Words in English

Many **foreign words and phrases** have come into the English language and kept their original spelling. Some words appear similar to English words or phrases, but to be sure of the meanings, use a dictionary. For example, the word *conquistador* is a form of a Spanish word that means "to conquer." Notice that *conquistador* begins with the same letters as the English word *conquer.* Thinking of clues like this can help you remember the meanings of foreign words and phrases.

Practice and Apply Demonstrate your knowledge of foreign words in English by completing the chart. First, note the language that each word comes from. Then, use each word correctly in a sentence.

FOREIGN WORD	LANGUAGE	SENTENCE
conquistador	Spanish	
posse		
flotilla		

EL ### ENGLISH LEARNER SUPPORT

Vocabulary Strategy Review the "Foreign Words in English" chart on page 44 with students. Choose a student's sentence for each word and read it aloud, emphasizing the pronunciation in English (flō-tǐl´ə). Explain to students that foreign words are often pronounced differently in English than in their original language. Highlight *flotilla* as an example. Have students write the sentences that were read aloud and practice reading them aloud to a partner, correcting each other if necessary. **ALL LEVELS**

LANGUAGE CONVENTIONS: Infinitives and Infinitive Phrases

Authors use **infinitives** and **infinitive phrases** to meet several functions in their writing. Infinitives can be used as nouns, adverbs, or adjectives. An infinitive is the base form of the verb. It is usually, but not always, signaled by the word *to*. An infinitive phrase opens with the infinitive but includes additional modifiers. Those modifiers can be just one word, as in "She hoped to finish **quickly**," or it could include multiple words, such as, "She hoped to finish **her chores quickly so she could read her book.**"

- In this example from "A Desperate Trek Across America," an infinitive phrase is used as a noun. It functions in the sentence as a direct object.

> They agreed <u>to meet</u> just a few miles north of the debarkation point.

- In this example from the selection, an infinitive phrase is used as an adjective. It modifies the direct object *time*.

> Eating the horses gave them time <u>to build the rafts.</u>

- In this example from the selection, an infinitive phrase is used as an adverb modifying the verb *threw*.

> <u>To make nails and saws,</u> they threw their crossbows, along with stirrups and spurs, into an improvised forge.

It is generally not desirable to split an infinitive by placing an adverb between the *to* and the base verb form. Thus, "to wait excitedly" is preferred over "to excitedly wait."

Practice and Apply Write three of your own sentences about Cabeza de Vaca's experience using the examples as models. Use a mix of simple infinitives and infinitive phrases. Write one example of each type of function—noun, adjective, and adverb. When you have finished, share your sentences with a partner and compare your use of infinitives and infinitive phrases.

> ! Go to **Infinitives and Infinitive Phrases** in the **Grammar Studio** for help.

LANGUAGE CONVENTIONS:
Infinitives and Infinitive Phrases

Remind students how infinitives can be easily recognized and the three main ways in which they are typically used. Tell students that although an infinitive is the base form of a verb, it is not a verb itself. This means that it cannot be altered by adding -*s*, -*ing*, -*ed*, etc. Infinitives can often be used to simplify writing.

To explore the effect of using infinitives in writing or speaking, you can rewrite the example sentences without using the infinitives. Point out to students how the impact of the sentence changes when the infinitive is gone.

- "They agreed to meet just a few miles north of the debarkation point." (They agreed on a meeting point just a few miles north of the debarkation point.)
- "Eating the horses gave them time to build the rafts." (Eating the horses gave them time in which they built rafts.)
- "To make nails and saws, they threw their crossbows, along with stirrups and spurs, into an improvised forge." (They made nails and saws by throwing their crossbows, stirrups, and spurs into an improvised forge.)

Practice and Apply As an alternative to having students write three sentences, have them look through their responses from page 43 and circle the infinitives they used. Challenge them to identify if the infinitives were used as nouns, adverbs, or adjectives.

(EL) ENGLISH LEARNER SUPPORT

Language Conventions Point out to Spanish speakers that infinitives in the Spanish language are often preceded by a preposition. This tendency often carries over to English; some students may make transfer errors such as "They went <u>for</u> to see the movie." Have students fill in the sentence blanks, correctly using the infinitive form of the given word. Challenge them to identify if the infinitives are used as nouns, adverbs, or adjectives.

- survive; The Spanish explorers used their wits _____.
- appreciate; After living with the Indians for years, Cabeza de Vaca grew _____ their way of life.
- lead; Inspired by his time with the Indians, Cabeza de Vaca lobbied Charles V _____ a humane approach to colonization of the New World. **MODERATE/LIGHT**

HERE FOLLOW SOME VERSES UPON THE BURNING OF OUR HOUSE, JULY 10TH, 1666

Poem by Anne Bradstreet

GENRE ELEMENTS
POETRY

Poetry is language arranged in lines. Poems are used to recreate emotions and experiences for the audience. Poems are often arranged into small groups of lines called **stanzas** that are equal or variable in length and size. Other common features of poems are the use of **meter** (i.e., patterns of syllabic stress), **rhyme** (i.e., similar sounds at the end of words), sounds of words, and **figurative** (i.e., not literal) **language.** In poetry, meaning is conveyed using **form,** or the way the words are arranged on the page, and **content.**

LEARNING OBJECTIVES

- Analyze how a poet accomplishes purpose through voice.
- Paraphrase difficult passages to clarify meaning.
- Analyze biblical allusion in words, phrases, passages, and literary works.
- Locate sources to find answers to questions.
- **Language** Use high-frequency words to tell personal experiences.

TEXT COMPLEXITY

Quantitative Measures	Here Follow Some Verses Upon the Burning of Our House, July 10th, 1666	Lexile: N/A
Qualitative Measures	**Ideas Presented** Multiple levels, subtle implied meanings and purpose; abstract, difficult ideas; use of symbolism, irony, satire.	
	Structures Used More complex; narrow or perhaps multiple perspectives; more deviation from chronological or sequential order.	
	Language Used Implied meanings; illusive, figurative, or ironic language, perhaps archaic or formal; complex sentence structures.	
	Knowledge Required Explores complex ideas; refers to texts or ideas that may be beyond students' experiences; may require specialized knowledge.	

RESOURCES

- Unit 1 Response Log
- Selection Audio
- Reading Studio: Notice & Note
- Level Up Tutorial: Elements of Poetry; Figurative Language
- Speaking and Listening Studio: Participating in Collaborative Discussions
- "Here Follow Some Verses Upon the Burning of Our House, July 10th, 1666" Selection Test

SUMMARIES

English

After her beloved home is destroyed in a fire, the poem's speaker grieves over her devastating loss but recognizes that true wealth and her true home are in heaven.

Spanish

Luego de que un incendio destruyera su querido hogar, la voz narrativa lamenta la devastadora pérdida, pero reconoce que la verdadera riqueza y su verdadero hogar están en el cielo.

SMALL-GROUP OPTIONS

Have students work in small groups and pairs to read and discuss the selection.

Think-Pair-Share

- After students have read and analyzed "Here Follow Some Verses Upon the Burning of Our House," pose this question: *How does the fire change the speaker's perspective about life?*
- Have students think about the question individually and take notes.
- Then, have pairs discuss their ideas about the question. Encourage them to use evidence from the poem to support their ideas.
- Finally, ask pairs to share their responses with the class.

Learning Circles

- To deepen students' understanding of the selection, arrange them into groups of three or four.
- Have each member of the group select a task that will help him or her better understand the poem. For example, find the meaning of unfamiliar vocabulary, identify interesting language, or prepare questions about the text.
- Read the poem aloud to the class. Then have students perform their tasks.
- Have each group member report back what he or she learned and respond to others by asking questions and commenting on others' experiences.

Text X-Ray: English Learner Support
for "Here Follow Some Verses Upon the Burning of Our House, July 10th, 1666"

Use the Text X-Ray and the supports and scaffolds in the Teacher's Edition to help guide students at different proficiency levels through the selection.

INTRODUCE THE SELECTION
DISCUSS *DISTRESS* AND *HOPE*

In line 9, the speaker asks for God's help in her distress. Model the pronunciation of *distress,* making sure to emphasize the *str-* consonant cluster, and have students repeat the word after you. Guide students to use context clues to determine what this word means (e.g., worry, sorry, pain). Ask the students to show on their faces how distress looks and feels.

In line 54, the speaker expresses a feeling of hope. Ask students to explain what *hope* means (e.g., optimism, expecting something good). Ask the students to show on their faces how hope looks and feels. Have one or two students share a story about a time when their distress turned to hope.

Ask: *What gives you comfort when you feel distress?*

CULTURAL REFERENCES

The following words may be unfamiliar to students:

- *His; Architect* (line 14; 44): Many believe that using the uppercase when referring to God shows reverence. If a word is capitalized, that is a clue that the writer is referring to God. When Bradstreet refers to God as an architect, or building designer, she suggests that God created a future home for her in heaven.

- *e'er* (line 31): a contraction of *ever* used in *archaic,* or old, forms of English

- *thy* (lines 29–30, 38–39): an archaic way of saying *your*

- *thou* (line 35): an archaic way of saying *you*

LISTENING

Recognize Feeling Words

Tell students that poetry is often used to express emotion or stir emotions in the audience. Identifying feeling words will help them better understand the poet's ideas and message.

Read aloud the first two stanzas of the poem. Use the following supports with students at varying proficiency levels:

- Read feeling words in a way that expresses the feeling to provide the students a clue about the word's meaning. Have students share the words they recognized and confirm whether they are feeling words (e.g., *sorrow, fearful*). **SUBSTANTIAL**

- Ask students to identify words that express feelings or emotions. Then read the stanzas again. Ask students questions to confirm understanding. *What does the speaker wake up to? How does she feel? What does she discover?* **MODERATE**

- Ask students to identify words that express feelings and emotions and explain what kinds of feelings or emotions these words express. Then read aloud the rest of the poem and have students identify and explain additional feeling words. **LIGHT**

SPEAKING

Share Personal Experiences

Explain that poetry is often used to share personal experiences. Help students begin thinking of an experience or personal object they could write about.

Ask students to think about a personal experience they are willing to share that evoked strong emotions. Use the following supports with students at varying proficiency levels:

- Have students identify or draw an object that is important to them (e.g., a photo, a gift). Have students tell a partner about the object, recount how they acquired it, and explain why they value it, using words from the word wall to convey meaning. **SUBSTANTIAL**
- Have students share an important personal experience with a partner. Provide the following sentence frames: *When _____, I felt_____. This experience reminded me that _____, because_____.* **MODERATE**
- Have students share a personal experience with a partner. Remind them to describe what happened and how they felt about what happened. **LIGHT**

READING

Identify Author's Message

Remind students that a poet's message, or theme, is what he or she wants to share about life. Readers can determine the message by looking for key details and ideas.

Use the following supports with students at varying proficiency levels:

- Help students read the last three stanzas of the poem. Ask yes/no questions to help students understand the theme. *Does the speaker watch her house burn?* (Yes.) *Does she feel that she should not care about losing her things?* (Yes.) *Does she want people to understand that the things we own aren't important?* (Yes.) **SUBSTANTIAL**
- Group students and have them read the last three stanzas of the poem. Have students identify important details and determine the theme. Provide sentence frames: *The speaker is thinking about _____. She realizes that _____. She wants people to understand that _____.* **MODERATE**
- Pair students and have them read the last three stanzas of the poem. Students should underline important details and then discuss those details and how they help them determine the theme. **LIGHT**

WRITING

Write a Poem

Read aloud the prompt on Student Edition page 53. Remind students that a poem expresses thoughts or feelings about an event or object.

Use the following supports with students at varying proficiency levels:

- Work with students to brainstorm an idea for their poems. Choose one idea and create a word web that describes or tells about the idea. Students can fill in the web with words or drawings. Use details in the web to write a poem on the board. Have students copy the poem in their notebooks. **SUBSTANTIAL**
- As a class, discuss some ideas for a poem. Then pair students and have them write a poem together. Students should include words and phrases that describe the idea or express emotions. Have partners share their poem with another pair. **MODERATE**
- Have students work with a partner to write a poem. They should include sensory details and memories or feelings. Circulate the room and help students include an allusion. **LIGHT**

Connect to the
ESSENTIAL QUESTION

We often base at least part of our identity on places—towns, countries, schools, neighborhoods. The most fundamental of these connections is often family or home. In "Here Follow Some Verses Upon the Burning of Our House, July 10th, 1666," the writer mourns the loss of the place where so much of her life was focused, after losing her house to a fire. She struggles to identify where her "real" home lies, finally finding comfort in her belief that she has another home in heaven.

HERE FOLLOW SOME VERSES UPON THE BURNING OF OUR HOUSE, JULY 10th, 1666

Poem by **Anne Bradstreet**

ESSENTIAL QUESTION:

Why are we bound to certain places?

QUICK START

Have you ever thought about what you value most? Some people especially prize a particular possession. Others may value an idea or feeling instead of a possession. What do you value most? Freewrite your ideas.

ANALYZE VOICE

"Here Follow Some Verses Upon the Burning of Our House, July 10th, 1666" relates the speaker's feelings about losing a home and belongings. Over the course of the poem a distinctive voice emerges. **Voice** refers to the poet's unique use of language that enables a reader to perceive the writer's feelings, attitudes, and personality. To determine a writer's voice, think about:

- **Diction:** What words did the writer choose? What images stand out?
- **Tone:** What is the writer's attitude on the subject?
- **Structure:** How long are lines and stanzas? How does this impact meaning?

To keep track of how the voice changes, look for words and phrases that indicate a shift in the tone of the poem, such as words that suggest a contrast. Think about how the voice can help you identify the poet's purpose for writing. What feelings and beliefs is the poet sharing?

PARAPHRASE

When you **paraphrase** a text, you restate it in your own words, making sure to maintain the meaning and order of the writer's ideas. To paraphrase a poem, you restate each line or sentence in clear and simple prose. Paraphrasing can be especially helpful when you want to clarify the meaning of a difficult section of the poem. For example, when Bradstreet uses **inverted syntax,** or sentence structure in which the expected order of words is reversed, paraphrasing the passage can ensure that you understand it.

A sample paraphrase of the first stanza of Bradstreet's poem appears below. As you read, remember to paraphrase when it can help you comprehend the poem.

POEM	PARAPHRASE
In silent night when rest I took For sorrow near I did not look I wakened was with thund'ring noise And piteous shrieks of dreadful voice. That fearful sound of "Fire!" and "Fire!" Let no man know is my desire.	In the silence of night, I was sleeping and did not expect something bad to happen. I awoke to a loud noise and a voice pitifully shrieking "Fire!" I pray that no person ever hears such a frightening sound. Bradstreet conveys her fear by contrasting the silence and peace of sleep with the terror of waking to cries of "Fire!"

GENRE ELEMENTS: POETRY

- uses diction, tone, and structure to create a distinctive voice
- often uses figurative language and allusions to deepen meaning
- may be written to express a writer's feelings or beliefs

QUICK START

Have students read the Quick Start activity and create a graphic organizer to record their ideas. To get students started, you might want to discuss the intangible things one values, such as love and freedom. Point out that most possessions can be replaced, while the more valuable things often cannot be replaced. Without saying any choice is wrong, guide students toward thinking about what they value. If students are stuck, give a few more suggestions, such as health, friends, and, for some, faith.

ANALYZE VOICE

Discuss with students how words can help express emotions, and relate that, in this poem, a shift in word choice helps express a shift in how the writer is dealing with the loss of her home. To get students started, you may wish to point out phrases such as "My sorrowing eyes" in line 22, which contrasts with "There's wealth enough" in line 51.

As students consider the author's purpose, encourage them to think about two different purposes: What the author's purpose was for herself (*encouraging herself in a difficult situation*) and what message the author might want to give the reader (*given her faith, the message would be that there is a life beyond this one*).

PARAPHRASE

Explain to students that sometimes paraphrasing is the easiest way to understand a difficult passage or poem. Tell them that to paraphrase a line or stanza in a poem, they should determine its main idea and replace difficult words with easier ones. Remind students to read the footnotes because they can help clarify meaning.

Review the sample with students. Point out how the paraphrase replaces some of the difficult words and phrases with simpler ones, such as "rest I took" with "sleeping," "sorrow" with "something bad," and "thund'ring" with "loud." Then, read aloud the last sentence and explain that the paraphrase also includes a statement that explains what Bradstreet is trying to convey in these lines.

ANALYZE ALLUSIONS

To let students know that allusions are not limited to Puritan poetry, mention such familiar allusions as the book and story titles *East of Eden, The Sun Also Rises, Stranger in a Strange Land,* and "By the Waters of Babylon" and sayings such as "salt of the earth" and "feet of clay"—all from the Bible. In this poem, the allusions help confirm the idea from the Bible that this life has less value than the next. Point out that the allusions are identified in the footnotes so students can read what each allusion means. Ask students to consider how much longer the poem would have to be if all these things had to be explained in detail within the poem.

 ## ANNOTATION MODEL

Remind students that they can benefit from annotating the text as they read, identifying important points and making notes in the margins. Point out in this sample that words are circled and underlined to identify emotions in the poem. Explain that this system of notetaking is just a suggestion and that students can use it as a guideline or create their own systems. For example, they may want to color-code their annotations using highlighters. Their notes in the margin may include questions about ideas that are unclear or topics they want to learn more about.

 **GET READY**

ANALYZE ALLUSIONS

An **allusion** is a direct or indirect reference to a person, place, event, or literary work that the poet believes the reader will know. By calling to mind other ideas, stories, or insights, allusions shape the reader's perceptions of events and expand the meaning of the work. Writers frequently make allusions to stories in the Bible because ideas and stories such as the Garden of Eden or David and Goliath are widely known. Bradstreet's Puritan readers would know the Bible well, so they would recognize the allusions in her poems.

In this poem, the phrase "all's vanity" alludes to the book of Ecclesiastes in the Bible, which describes how what we value is meaningless and will vanish. There are also references to the Book of Job, in which a man suffers many losses but stays faithful to God, and to the creation story in the Book of Genesis. By comparing the events in the poem to biblical stories, Bradstreet gives her readers insight into the nature of her loss and recovery. As you read, note how the allusions contribute to the meaning of the poem.

DETAIL FROM POEM	ALLUSION	MEANING
all's vanity	The book of Ecclesiastes	What we value is meaningless and will vanish.

ANNOTATION MODEL

NOTICE & NOTE

As you read, notice words and phrases that develop the voice of the poem. Note when the writer includes allusions and what they add to the poem's meaning. This model shows one reader's notes on the first lines of Bradstreet's poem.

In silent night when rest I took,
For sorrow near I did not look,
I wakened was with thund'ring noise
And piteous shrieks of dreadful voice.
That fearful sound of "Fire!" and "Fire!"
Let no man know is my desire.

The word "sorrow" suggests that what follows will be sad.

Words such as "piteous shrieks," "dreadful voice," and "fearful" all convey emotions of horror.

BACKGROUND

Anne Bradstreet *(1612–1672) was one of the first poets in the American colonies and the first woman in the colonies to gain recognition for her work. She had given up a life of wealth in England to follow her father and husband to the wild, unsettled colonies of New England. Much of her poetry focuses on her internal struggle between desiring the pleasures of the world and focusing on the promise of heaven. On the date referenced in the title of this poem, Bradstreet's home was destroyed by a fire.*

HERE FOLLOW SOME VERSES UPON THE BURNING OF OUR HOUSE, JULY 10th, 1666

Poem by Anne Bradstreet

SETTING A PURPOSE

As you read, note the details that show how Bradstreet's focus shifts from what she has lost to what she believes is more important.

In silent night when rest I took
For sorrow near I did not look
I wakened was with thund'ring noise
And piteous shrieks of dreadful voice.
5 That fearful sound of "Fire!" and "Fire!"
Let no man know is my desire.

I, starting up, the light did spy,
And to my God my heart did cry
To strengthen me in my distress
10 And not to leave me succorless.[1]
Then, coming out, beheld a space
The flame consume my dwelling place.

---

[1] **succorless** (sŭk´ər-lĭs): without help or relief.

Notice & Note

Use the side margins to notice and note signposts in the text.

ANALYZE VOICE
Annotate: Mark words that suggest a contrast in lines 1–6.

Analyze: What is happening in these lines? How does the diction convey the urgency of the situation?

Upon the Burning of Our House 49

BACKGROUND

Anne Dudley Bradstreet was born in England and raised on an estate, which her father managed for the Earl of Lincoln. With access to the earl's library, she received a good education. In 1628, at the age of 16, she married Simon Bradstreet, and two years later the young couple sailed for Massachusetts. Nothing in Anne Bradstreet's past prepared her for the harsh living conditions of colonial America. Her religious faith helped her endure the hardships, as did writing poetry. Bradstreet's poetry focused primarily on the realities of her life: her husband, her eight children, and her house. In 1650 her brother-in-law had some of her verses published in London, England. It was the first book of poetry ever published by an American colonist.

SETTING A PURPOSE

Direct students to use the Setting a Purpose prompt to focus their reading.

ANALYZE VOICE

Remind students that *poetic voice* refers to the poet's use of language to share feelings and attitudes. (***Possible answer:*** *There is a disturbance at night thought to be a fire. The contrasting image shows that the fire is dangerous and startling.*)

For **listening support** for students at varying proficiency levels, see the **Text X-Ray** on page 46C.

WHEN STUDENTS STRUGGLE . . .

Understand Poetry Read the first stanza aloud to students, with careful phrasing and intonation. For example, when reading the first line, pause between "In silent night" and "when rest I took." Help students translate the line into plainer language. For example, guide them to translate the first line as "I was sleeping, during a silent night." Guide students through the first stanza. Then, have pairs work to do the same exercise with the remaining stanzas.

 For additional support, go to the **Reading Studio** and assign the following **Level Up Tutorial: Elements of Poetry.**

TEACH

ANALYZE ALLUSIONS

Point out that this instruction refers to the allusion in the top stanza on this page, not to the whole poem. Tell students to read the footnote first if they need help determining the allusion. (**Possible answer:** *It underscores how much she has lost. It reminds her that others have lost their belongings and not lost their faith.*)

PARAPHRASE

Remind students that to paraphrase a poem they need to determine the main idea of the lines and simplify the language. Because these lines have an inverted sentence structure, the paraphrase should be written in the expected order (subject-verb-object) so that it is easier to understand. (**Possible answer** *for lines 27–28: My favorite possessions lie in ashes, and I will never see them again.*)

(EL) ENGLISH LEARNER SUPPORT

Understand Archaic Language The use of a slightly older form of English may require additional support. To help English language learners, you may want to note the current spelling of some of the words: *didst/did, e'er/ever, oft/often, 'gin/begin.* Explain that some words have accents, so that the poem can maintain its meter (for example, "furnishéd"—pronounced "furnish-ed"). Then, discuss any other words that might be standing in the way of comprehension. **ALL LEVELS**

NOTICE & NOTE

ANALYZE ALLUSIONS

Annotate: Mark the words in lines 13–18 that match the allusion identified in the footnote.

Draw Conclusions: Why do you think the poet includes an allusion to the story of Job?

PARAPHRASE

Annotate: Recall that **inverted syntax** refers to sentence structure in which the expected order of words is reversed. Mark an example of inverted syntax in lines 25–30.

Paraphrase: Create a paraphrase of the example of inverted syntax you marked.

    And when I could no longer look,
    I blest His name that gave and took,[2]
15 That laid my goods now in the dust:
    Yea, so it was, and so 'twas just.
    It was His own, it was not mine,
    Far be it that I should repine;[3]

    He might of all justly bereft,
20 But yet sufficient for us left.
    When by the ruins oft I past,
    My sorrowing eyes aside did cast,
    And here and there the places spy
    Where oft I sat and long did lie:

25 Here stood that trunk and there that chest,
    There lay that store I counted best.
    My pleasant things in ashes lie,
    And them behold no more shall I.
    Under thy roof no guest shall sit,
30 Nor at thy table eat a bit.

    No pleasant tale shall e'er be told,
    Nor things recounted done of old.
    No candle e'er shall shine in thee,
    Nor bridegroom's voice e'er heard shall be.
35 In silence ever shalt thou lie;
    Adieu, Adieu, all's vanity.[4]

    Then straight I 'gin my heart to chide,[5]
    And did thy wealth on earth abide?
    Didst fix thy hope on mold'ring[6] dust?
40 The arm of flesh didst make thy trust?
    Raise up thy thoughts above the sky
    That dunghill mists away may fly.

    Thou hast an house on high erect,
    Framed by that mighty Architect,
45 With glory richly furnishéd,[7]
    Stands permanent though this be fled.

---

[2] **1 . . . took:** an allusion to Job 1:21 in the Bible—"The Lord gave, and the Lord hath taken away; blessed be the name of the Lord."

[3] **repine:** to complain or fret; to long for something.

[4] **all's vanity:** an allusion to Ecclesiastes 1:2 in the Bible—"All is vanity," meaning that all is temporary and meaningless.

[5] **chide:** to scold mildly so as to correct or improve.

[6] **mold'ring:** crumbling, disintegrating, decaying.

[7] **Thou . . . furnishéd:** an allusion to John 14:2–3 in the Bible, where Jesus assures his disciples that, even if they have nothing in this life, there are mansions prepared for them in heaven.

It's purchaséd and paid for too
By Him who hath enough to do.

A price so vast as is unknown
50 Yet by His gift is made thine own;
There's wealth enough, I need no more,
Farewell, my pelf,[8] farewell my store.
The world no longer let me love,
My hope and treasure lies above.[9]

---

[8] **pelf:** wealth or riches, especially when dishonestly acquired.
[9] **treasure . . . above:** an allusion to Matthew 13:44–46, which relates how heavenly
treasures are safe from thieves and destruction.

ANALYZE VOICE

Annotate: Mark words in the final stanzas that suggest a change in voice.

Compare: How does the poet's choice of words differ at the end of the poem from that of the beginning?

CHECK YOUR UNDERSTANDING

Answer these questions before moving on to the **Analyze the Text** section on the following page.

1 What is the speaker's first response to hearing the "fearful sound" of fire?

A She looked for water.

B She prayed for strength.

C She gathered her belongings.

D She started to scream.

2 The lines *When by the ruins oft I past, / My sorrowing eyes aside did cast* emphasize that the speaker —

F is struggling to let go of her home

G is glad her house burned down

H is watching the house be rebuilt

J no longer wants to have a house

3 What conclusion helps the poet overcome her sorrow?

A Her family is still around her.

B She has started to build anew.

C She knows heaven will be her home.

D She replaces sorrow with anger.

TEACH

ANALYZE VOICE

Encourage students to look at their responses to the question on page 49. What was the emotion there, and what is the emotion here? How do the words communicate that change? (**Possible answer:** *The poem began with words expressing fear and defeat, but now they express hope and even triumph.*)

For **reading support** for students at varying proficiency levels, see the **Text X-Ray** on page 46D.

CHECK YOUR UNDERSTANDING

Have students answer the questions independently.

Answers:

1. *B*

2. *F*

3. *C*

If they answer any questions incorrectly, have them reread the text to confirm their understanding. Then they may proceed to ANALYZE THE TEXT on page 52.

 ENGLISH LEARNER SUPPORT

Oral Assessment Use the following fill-in sentences to assess students' comprehension and speaking skills.

1. The first thing the speaker does during the fire is to _____. (*pray; "And to my God my heart did cry/To strengthen me in my distress"*)

2. Seeing the ruins of her house makes the speaker feel _____. (*sad; she is talking about how sad she is to no longer live there*)

3. The speaker feels better when she thinks of _____. (*God or heaven; she believes that heaven is her real home*) **SUBSTANTIAL/MODERATE**

ANALYZE THE TEXT

Possible answers:

1. **DOK 3:** *Lines 10–20 and 49–54 reveal a strong faith in God; lines 25–34 suggest a happy and sociable daily life. The voice changes from alarmed and sorrowful to accepting.*

2. **DOK 2:** *Bradstreet's "mighty Architect" is a metaphor for God, who both built and paid for her future "house on high," or her place in heaven.*

3. **DOK 2:** *More than her house, Bradstreet valued her faith in God. This faith helped her accept her loss and recognize that material possessions are relatively unimportant.*

4. **DOK 4:** *In line 15, Bradstreet says her goods are "now in the dust." Then, in line 39, she describes her belongings as "mold'ring dust." This underscores the reality that everything is temporary in line 36.*

5. **DOK 2:** *God is entitled to take everything away but he will meet our needs.*

RESEARCH

Make sure students read and apply the Research Tip. Also remind them that they should confirm any information they find by checking multiple websites and assessing the credibility of each one.

Extend If students have trouble discussing the allusions in the poem they select, be prepared to share a resource that could help them identify the allusions, or guide them to a version of the poem that has footnotes.

ANALYZE THE TEXT

Support your responses with evidence from the text. **NOTEBOOK**

1. **Draw Conclusions** Use details from the poem to explain what you learn about the speaker's feelings and beliefs. How does the voice change over the course of the poem?

2. **Interpret** A **metaphor** is a direct comparison of two unlike things that does not use the word *like* or *as*. In lines 43–48, Bradstreet uses a metaphor to make a comparison to something she holds dear. What two things does she compare, and what do they stand for?

3. **Infer** What does the speaker value more than the house? How did this help her accept the loss of her house by fire?

4. **Analyze** A popular verse from the Book of Genesis is "Dust thou art and unto dust shalt thou return." Where in the poem can you find allusions to this verse? How do these allusions relate to the allusion in line 36?

5. **Paraphrase** How would you paraphrase lines 19–20 of the poem: "He might of all justly bereft, / But yet sufficient for us left"?

RESEARCH TIP
In addition to online encyclopedias, information on Anne Bradstreet can also be found on sites about literature and poetry.

RESEARCH

Time and place can have a direct impact on a poet's style, the content of the work, and his or her worldview. Research Anne Bradstreet's life and the time period in which she lived. Use what you learn to answer these questions.

QUESTION	ANSWER
What was Anne Bradstreet's life like before she moved to New England?	*Possible answer: She had lived comfortably on an earl's estate in England.*
How did Bradstreet's Puritan beliefs help her cope with her loss?	*Possible answer: Her beliefs gave her something to focus on instead of her loss. Her belief in heaven made it easier to accept the loss of her home.*
What impact did the Puritan era have on the style and language of the poem?	*Possible answer: Like many older poems, it rhymes. The language is not modern.*

Connect Read another well-known poem that contains allusions to biblical stories, such as "Nothing Gold Can Stay" by Robert Frost. With a partner, discuss what the allusion adds to the poem and whether the use of allusion was similar to or different from Bradstreet's allusions. In which poem is the writer's beliefs more evident?

© Houghton Mifflin Harcourt Publishing Company

WHEN STUDENTS STRUGGLE . . .

Reteaching: Allusions Students may struggle with the concept of allusions. Remind them that allusions can refer to something in another work of literature or to events or persons in history, art, religion, or some other aspect of culture. Explain that in order for allusions to be effective, they must refer to someone or something with which the reader is familiar. Ask students why biblical allusions were an appropriate choice for Bradstreet's readers. (***Answer:*** *Bradstreet's Puritan readers would have been well-acquainted with the Bible.*)

 For additional support, go to the **Reading Studio** and assign the following **Level Up Tutorial: Figurative Language.**

CREATE AND DISCUSS

Write a Poem Write a poem that expresses your thoughts about what matters to you most. Review your notes on the Quick Start activity before you begin.

❑ Decide if you want the speaker to be yourself or someone else.

❑ Choose examples of memories or feelings you associate with what you have chosen. Use language that evokes those emotions.

❑ Include an allusion to something you have read or heard, such as a book or song.

Discuss a Poem Every reader has a unique response to a poem. They may also have a different view of the effectiveness of literary elements. In a small group, discuss your response to "Here Follow Some Verses Upon the Burning of Our House."

❑ Think about the events of the poem and how the speaker reacts to them.

❑ Talk about how the time period and the poet's beliefs influence her response to losing her house.

❑ Discuss how the literary elements in the poem influence your reaction.

❑ Make sure everyone gets a chance to participate in the discussion.

 Go to **Participating in Collaborative Discussions** in the **Speaking and Listening Studio** for help.

RESPOND TO THE ESSENTIAL QUESTION

? Why are we bound to certain places?

Gather Information Review your annotations and notes on "Here Follow Some Verses Upon the Burning of Our House." Then, add relevant information to your Response Log. As you determine what information to include, think about:

• the details the poet includes to describe her house and belongings
• the way the poet reveals her feelings and beliefs
• how the voice changes over the course of the poem

UNIT 1 RESPONSE LOG

Essential Question	Details from Texts
Why are we bound to certain places?	
What motivates people to explore the unknown?	
What does it mean to be a stranger in a strange land?	
What happens when cultures collide?	

ACADEMIC VOCABULARY

As you write and discuss what you learned from the poem, be sure to use the Academic Vocabulary words. Check off each of the words that you use.

❑ **adapt**
❑ **coherent**
❑ **device**
❑ **displace**
❑ **dynamic**

CREATE AND DISCUSS

Write a Poem Assure students that they do not have to write in the same style as Anne Bradstreet. You may also want to take some time to brainstorm ideas for allusions, such as movies, TV shows, books read in class, sporting figures, or any other source that will add to the meaning of the poem. Tell students to pick something that seems natural to them, just as alluding to the Bible was completely natural for Bradstreet.

Discuss a Poem Remind students to think about what they want to say and state it as clearly as possible but also listen carefully to what others have to say. They can ask questions to clarify meaning, to make sure they really know what someone else thinks. You may also want to discuss why people have different reactions to the poem or believe they would react differently to loss.

For **writing support** for students at varying proficiency levels, see the **Text X-Ray** on page 46D.

RESPOND TO THE ESSENTIAL QUESTION

Allow time for students to add details from "Here Follow Some Verses Upon the Burning of Our House, July 10th, 1666" to their Unit 1 Response Logs.

from OF PLYMOUTH PLANTATION

Historical Narrative by William Bradford

GENRE ELEMENTS
HISTORICAL NARRATIVE

Remind students that a **historical narrative** tells a true story about real people and events that happened in the past, told in the order in which they happened. If the person giving the account was at the scene when the events happened, the narrative is a **primary source.** In this selection, students will evaluate the text's message, tone, and use of language to identify the author's purpose for writing the narrative.

LEARNING OBJECTIVES

- Evaluate the text to determine the author's purpose and analyze the author's use of language.
- Conduct research about Native American farming.
- Write an informational text about colonists and Native Americans confronting challenges.
- Discuss the relationship between Native Americans and colonists.
- Use strategies to define archaic vocabulary.
- Use active and passive voice effectively.
- **Language** Describe events experienced by the Native Americans and colonists using time-order words.

TEXT COMPLEXITY

Quantitative Measures	*Of Plymouth Plantation*	Lexile: 1440L
Qualitative Measures	**Ideas Presented** Mostly explicit, but moves to some implied meaning.	
	Structures Used Clear, chronological, conventional.	
	Language Used Complex sentence structures with use of archaic and formal language.	
	Knowledge Required Cultural and historical references may make heavier demands.	

Online **Ed**

RESOURCES

- Unit 1 Response Log
-  Selection Audio
- Close Read Screencast: Modeled Discussion
- Reading Studio: Notice & Note
- Level Up Tutorial: Chronological Order
- Writing Studio: Writing Informative Texts
- Speaking and Listening Studio: Participate in a Collaborative Discussion
- Grammar Studio: Module 8: Lesson 7: Active Voice and Passive Voice
- ✓ *Of Plymouth Plantation*/"Coming of Age in the Dawnland" Selection Test

SUMMARIES

English

Before the Pilgrims came ashore, they wrote the Mayflower Compact to form a government and choose a governor. In the first few months, half of the group died of diseases. Native Americans were wary, but a chief called Samoset, who had learned English from fishers, came and helped the settlers. He brought five others, including Squanto, and they made a peace agreement. Squanto served as interpreter and taught the settlers how to survive in the new land. At their first harvest, the Pilgrims and Native Americans had a feast, which was the first Thanksgiving.

Spanish

Antes de que los peregrinos desembarcaran, escribieron el Pacto de Mayflower para formar un gobierno y elegir un gobernador. Durante los primeros meses, la mitad del grupo murió debido a enfermedades. Los indígenas americanos eran cautelosos, pero Samoset, un jefe que había aprendido inglés de los pescadores, ayudó a los colonizadores. Llevó a otros cinco con él, incluyendo a Squanto, e hicieron un acuerdo de paz. Squanto sirvió de interprete y les enseñó a los colonizadores cómo sobrevivir en la tierra nueva. Durante su primera cosecha, los peregrinos y los indígenas americanos tuvieron un banquete, que fue el primer día de Acción de Gracias.

SMALL-GROUP OPTIONS

Have students work in small groups and pairs to read and discuss the selection.

Reciprocal Teaching

- Have students read "The Mayflower Compact" section of the text (paragraphs 2–6).
- After reading, ask students to write three to five questions about the section, using these stems: *What is the _____? Why did the _____? What happened after _____? How did the _____? Why was the _____?*
- Form teams of three students.
- Each student offers two questions for group discussion.
- The group reaches consensus on the answers and finds supporting text evidence.

Think-Pair-Share

- After students have read the section "Indian Relations" (paragraphs 8–10), pose this question: *Why did relations between the Native Americans and colonists improve?*
- Have students think about the question individually, making notes.
- Organize students into pairs, and have partners listen, discuss, and formulate a shared response to the question.
- Finally, have pairs share their responses with the class.

Text X-Ray: English Learner Support
for Of Plymouth Plantation

Use the Text X-Ray and the supports and scaffolds in the Teacher's Edition to help guide students at different proficiency levels through the selection.

INTRODUCE THE SELECTION
DISCUSS HARDSHIPS AND CONVENIENCES

In this lesson, students will need to be able to discuss the hardships the colonists experienced. Provide the following explanations:

- A *hardship* is something that causes great suffering or difficulty.
- A *convenience* is something that increases comfort or fulfills needs.

Ask students to discuss hardships they have experienced, as well as conveniences they enjoy. Provide sentence frames, such as: *I faced a hardship when I_____. _____ is a modern convenience that makes my life easier.*

Explain to students that because the events in the narrative took place hundreds of years ago, before the existence of certain modern conveniences, the colonists faced many hardships.

CULTURAL REFERENCES

The following words or phrases may be unfamiliar to students:

- *make use of* (paragraph 1): to use for a purpose
- *common store* (paragraph 5): supplies or goods shared by all of the people in a group
- *of 100 and odd persons, scarce fifty remained* (paragraph 7): out of more than 100 people, only 50 people survived
- *spared no pains* (paragraph 7): did all that they could
- *skulking* (paragraph 8): moving around quietly to avoid being noticed
- *made way for* (paragraph 9): to clear a path for

LISTENING

Understand Main Ideas

Direct students to the six terms of the treaty in paragraph 9. Review that the treaty terms were written to confront the challenge of making peace between the Native Americans and the colonists.

Have students listen as you read aloud the six terms of the treaty in paragraph 9. Use the following supports with students at varying proficiency levels:

- Read aloud each item of the treaty in simplified language (for example, *Squanto and his tribe should not injure or hurt the settlers*). Have students listen and repeat each item after you. **SUBSTANTIAL**
- As students listen to the items in the treaty, have them write down key words and phrases. Then, ask them to compare the words and phrases they noted with a partner. **MODERATE**
- Have students note important words and phrases as they listen to you read the items in the treaty. Ask students to work in pairs to discuss the main idea of the treaty. **LIGHT**

SPEAKING

Use Time-Order Words

Review a list of time-order words and demonstrate how they can be used to describe a familiar event. Have students use time-order words to describe events from the text.

Use the following supports with students at varying proficiency levels:

- Use time-order words to describe events in the text. Have students repeat each sentence, then practice saying it aloud to a partner. Direct students to emphasize time-order words. For example: *First*, the colonists chose a leader. *Then*, they came ashore. *Later*, colonists died. **SUBSTANTIAL**
- Provide sentence frames and have students supply the time-order words. For example: ____, *the colonists chose a leader.* ____, *they came ashore.* ____, *many colonists died.* **MODERATE**
- Have partners take turns describing events in the text using time-order words. Direct them to begin at paragraph 2 and continue until the end of the selection. **LIGHT**

READING

Distinguish Central Idea and Supporting Details

Explain that the central idea is the most important point the author wants to make. Supporting details help readers understand the central idea.

Work with students to reread paragraph 7. Use the following supports with students at varying proficiency levels:

- Explain that the central idea of this paragraph is that many colonists died and healthy colonists took care of the sick. Ask: *What is one supporting detail?* Accept single words or phrases. **SUBSTANTIAL**
- Have pairs read the third sentence of the paragraph. Have them locate and circle words and phrases that show colonists caring for others. **MODERATE**
- Have students write the central idea of the paragraph. Then, have them list as many supporting details as they can. Have pairs exchange papers and check each other's work. **LIGHT**

WRITING

Write an Informational Text

Work with students to help them understand the different sections of the informational text they are asked to write on page 63 of the Student Edition.

Use the following supports with students at varying proficiency levels:

- Create a two-column chart with the heads *Native Americans* and *Colonists*. Help students list verbs from the text in the appropriate column, based on who took the action. Have students copy it. **SUBSTANTIAL**
- Provide sentence frames for students to help write their informational texts. For example: *After the colonists came to North America, they* ____. *At first, the Native Americans and the colonists* ____. *One challenge the Native Americans and colonists faced was* ____. **MODERATE**
- Provide a transition word bank for students to refer to as they write—for example, *in contrast, however, similarly, furthermore*. Direct students to look for places in their writing where a transition word could make ideas flow more smoothly.

TEACH

Connect to the
ESSENTIAL QUESTION

In the excerpt from *Of Plymouth Plantation,* settlers brought their culture from Britain, only to find a very different culture already established in North America. Bradford's writing shows what happened when these cultures collided and how each changed as a result.

COMPARE AUTHOR'S PURPOSE

Point out that primary sources and secondary sources provide different perspectives for the reader. Ask students to discuss the difference between a diary and a biography. Which provides a more personal perspective? How might each be biased? What kinds of facts might appear in each?

COLLABORATE & COMPARE

HISTORICAL NARRATIVE

from

OF PLYMOUTH PLANTATION

by **William Bradford**
pages 57–61

COMPARE AUTHOR'S PURPOSE

As you read, note how each text describes encounters between British settlers and Native Americans. *Of Plymouth Plantation* is a primary source, or a first-hand account. "Coming of Age in the Dawnland" is a secondary source, an account written after events took place, and it includes information from other sources. Notice how each text presents information about each culture and how groups built relationships with each other. After reading both selections, you will collaborate with a group on a final project.

? ESSENTIAL QUESTION:

What happens when cultures collide?

HISTORY WRITING

COMING OF AGE IN THE DAWNLAND

by **Charles C. Mann**
pages 69–75

LEARNING MINDSET

Growth Mindset   Remind students that their goal isn't to be seen as "smart" or to get the right answers, but to make progress on learning. Mistakes can be a sign of progress because they offer opportunities to find new approaches and ways to improve. Have students set a goal for the selection related to what they want to learn from the reading.

from **Of Plymouth Plantation**

QUICK START

Think about what you know about the challenges faced by colonists and Native Americans when they encountered each other. With a partner, share one fact you know about their encounters. Then, share one question you have about the challenges faced by each group.

ANALYZE AUTHOR'S PURPOSE

The **author's purpose** is the reason he or she writes a particular text. This purpose might be to inform, to entertain, to express beliefs or feelings, or to persuade. Some texts seek to achieve more than one of these purposes. To analyze and then evaluate an author's purpose, consider the following.

- A text's **genre** provides clues to the author's overall purpose. *Of Plymouth Plantation* is a historical narrative, a text that tells about real events that happened in the past.

- A text's intended **audience,** or the people intended to read the text, helps suggest the author's reason for writing. *Of Plymouth Plantation,* for example, was intended to be read by future generations.

- A work's **tone,** the author's attitude toward the subject, provides clues about purpose. As you read, note Bradford's vivid descriptions and what they reveal about his feelings about events and people.

- The text's overall **message,** or its central idea, suggests the author's purpose for writing. Note clues about Bradford's message as you read.

ANALYZE LANGUAGE

Diction and rhetorical devices are elements of language that help authors shape the perceptions of readers. **Diction** is the writer's choice of words and it may be formal or informal, technical or common, or abstract or concrete. **Rhetorical devices** are techniques a writer uses to communicate ideas and convince readers of their truth. Repetition and allusions are two examples of rhetorical devices, among others.

RHETORICAL DEVICE	DEFINITION
repetition	repeating a word, phrase, or idea
allusion	references to something the author expects will be familiar to readers; for example, references to the Bible for Bradford's audience

As you read *Of Plymouth Plantation,* notice Bradford's diction and his use of repetition and allusion to convey the events he describes. Also, consider how his use of language supports his purpose for writing.

GENRE ELEMENTS: HISTORICAL NARRATIVE

- tells a true story about events that happened in the past
- is a narrative text that relates events in chronological order, or the order in which they happened
- may be considered a **primary source** if the author observed the events personally

QUICK START

Have students read the Quick Start activity and consider their fact and question individually before sharing them with a partner. Have students write their questions on slips of paper or index cards. After reading, revisit these, read each one aloud, and see if it was answered in the reading.

ANALYZE AUTHOR'S PURPOSE

Help students understand the terms *genre, audience, tone,* and *message,* expanding on the information given as needed. Discuss why considering the audience is essential to understanding an author's purpose. For example, a speech to a group of young children would include different information and words than a speech to a group of adults. Who an author expects will be reading a text determines not only what is written but how it is written.

ANALYZE LANGUAGE

Remind students that authors have an intention behind every word choice, and this intention is related to that author's purpose. Capable writers are extremely careful to choose just the right words to convey meaning in a way that will successfully communicate it to readers.

Focus on repetition and allusion. Note that **repetition** is often used to emphasize important ideas or details. **Allusion** is used to add significance by pulling meaning from another text that readers are likely to already know. An allusion allows the author to reference and draw a parallel to another event or story without summarizing or explaining. Readers are expected to be familiar with the references. This can pose challenges if the text is very old or from a different culture or context.

TEACH

CRITICAL VOCABULARY

Encourage students to read all the sentences before deciding which word best completes each one. Remind them to look for context clues that suggest the meaning of the best word to answer each question.

Answers:

1. *calamity*
2. *patent*
3. *divers, sundry*
4. *clave*

■ English Learner Support

Use Cognates Tell students that these Critical Vocabulary words have Spanish cognates: *divers/diverso, calamity/ calamidad, patent/patente.* **ALL LEVELS**

LANGUAGE CONVENTIONS

Review the information about active and passive voice. Remind students that the subject of a sentence is often a noun. *Liam* is the subject of the first example sentence, and *letter* is the subject of the second example sentence.

Read aloud the example sentences, emphasizing *mailed* and *was mailed* to show the difference. Discuss what information is in the first sentence that is not mentioned in the second. Point out that using the passive voice in the second sentence emphasizes the letter, not the person mailing it.

ANNOTATION MODEL

Remind students of the ideas in Analyze Author's Purpose and Analyze Language on page 55, which suggest noticing descriptions that affect tone as well as allusions and repeated words and phrases. Point out that they may follow the method of marking the text shown in the Annotation Model, or use their own system for marking up the selection in their write-in text. They may want to color-code their annotations by using highlighters. Their notes in the margin may include questions about ideas that are unclear or topics they want to learn more about.

 **GET READY**

CRITICAL VOCABULARY

patent	clave	calamity	sundry	divers

Use the Critical Vocabulary words to answer the following questions.

1. Which word might be used in a description of a hurricane?
2. What might you display to prove that you own something?
3. Which two Critical Vocabulary words are synonyms for the word *various*?
4. Which word describes an action you might take toward someone next to you if you were startled?

LANGUAGE CONVENTIONS

Active and Passive Voice The voice of a verb tells whether its subject performs or receives the action expressed by the verb.

- If the subject performs the action, the verb is in the **active voice:** *Liam mailed the letter.*

- If the subject receives the action, the verb is in the **passive voice:** *The letter was mailed.*

As you read the excerpt from *Of Plymouth Plantation,* think about when and why Bradford uses active and passive voice and how each use affects your perception of the event or events he describes.

ANNOTATION MODEL

NOTICE & NOTE

As you read, note details that suggest the author's purpose. Here are one reader's notes about *Of Plymouth Plantation.*

> The rest of this (history) (if God give me life and opportunity) I shall, for brevity's sake, handle by way of annals, noting only the heads of principal things, and passages as they fell (in order of time) and may seem to be profitable to know or to make use of. And this may be as the Second Book.
>
> ### Chapter XI
>
> *The Remainder of Anno 1620*
> *[The Mayflower Compact]*
>   I shall a little return back, and begin with a combination made by them before they came ashore; being the first foundation of their government in this place.

"History" and "in order of time" tell me that this is a fact-based account told in chronological order.

Bradford believes this record, including the "first foundation of their government," may be "profitable" to his readers. He thinks others might learn from the experiences he will relate.

© Houghton Mifflin Harcourt Publishing Company

WHEN STUDENTS STRUGGLE . . .

Use Graphic Organizers Tell students that creating a graphic organizer can sometimes help them to understand the sequence of events in a text. Provide a sequence graphic organizer for students. As they read the selection, have them work either independently or in pairs to create a timeline of the events. After they have finished reading, have them summarize the events using the graphic organizer.

 For additional support, go to the **Reading Studio** and assign the following **LEVEL UP** **Level Up Tutorial: Chronological Order.**

BACKGROUND

*Born in England in 1590, **William Bradford** became involved in the Protestant Reformation while still a boy. He joined the Puritans, reformers who wanted to purify the Church of England and eventually separated from it. With other Puritans, he migrated to Holland in search of religious freedom. He helped organize the journey on the Mayflower in 1620 that brought about 100 people—half of them his fellow "Pilgrims"—to the New World. His* History of Plymouth Plantation, 1620–1647, *describes this journey and provides a glimpse of the settlers' life in what became New England.*

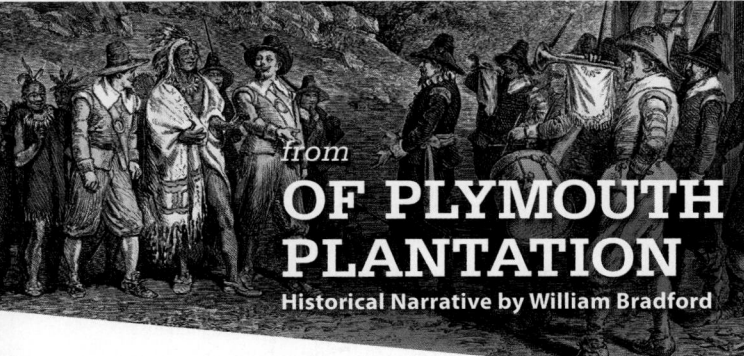

from

OF PLYMOUTH PLANTATION

Historical Narrative by William Bradford

PREPARE TO COMPARE

As you read, pay attention to how the relationship between the colonists and Native Americans changed over time. Note details that help you understand how individuals were able to negotiate a peaceful relationship between the two groups. Identifying these details will help you compare this text with "Coming of Age in the Dawnland."

The Second Book

1   The rest of this history (if God give me life and opportunity) I shall, for brevity's sake, handle by way of annals, noting only the heads of principal things, and passages as they fell in order of time, and may seem to be profitable to know or to make use of. And this may be as the Second Book.

Chapter XI

The Remainder of Anno 1620
[The Mayflower Compact]

2   I shall a little return back, and begin with a combination made by them before they came ashore; being the first foundation of their government in this place. Occasioned partly by the

Notice & Note

Use the side margins to notice and note signposts in the text.

BACKGROUND

Point out that while Bradford never published his **narrative**, he did intend for it to be read by future generations, noting in his account that he wrote it so "that their children may see with what difficulties their fathers wrestled in going through these things in their first beginnings, and how God brought them along not withstanding all their weaknesses and infirmities."

PREPARE TO COMPARE

Direct students to use the Prepare to Compare prompt to focus their reading.

 For **speaking support** or students at varying proficiency levels, see the **Text X-Ray** on page 54D.

CLOSE READ SCREENCAST

Modeled Discussion   In their eBooks, have students view the Close Read Screencast, in which readers discuss and annotate paragraph 2, background for the Mayflower Compact.

As a class, view and discuss the video. Then have students pair up to do an independent close read of paragraph 7. Students can record their answers on the Close Read Practice PDF.

Close Read Practice PDF

ANALYZE AUTHOR'S PURPOSE

Draw attention to the indentation of paragraph 4, showing that it is a quoted section of text, and have students identify its source from the heading of the section (The Mayflower Compact). Ask what students can tell about the tone of the paragraph based on its source, and whether the author would want to use formal or informal language. (**Answer:** *The author's formal tone is due to the legal nature of the Mayflower Compact. Bradford wants to remind readers that the Mayflower Compact is set out in legal, formal language because the purpose of the settlement is to be both a religious and nationalistic community.*)

CRITICAL VOCABULARY

patent: Before leaving England, the Pilgrims received legal permission—in the form of a patent—from the king to settle in the "Northern Parts of Virginia" (now the Hudson Bay area).

ASK STUDENTS to explain why settlers would need a patent from the king to form a colony in Virginia. (*Previous English explorers had claimed Virginia for the king. In England, the king was considered Virginia's legal owner.*)

NOTICE & NOTE

patent
(păt′nt) *n.* an official document granting ownership.

ANALYZE AUTHOR'S PURPOSE

Annotate: Mark three phrases in paragraph 4 that suggest a formal tone.

Infer: What can you infer about the author's purpose based on his tone thus far? Cite text evidence in your response.

---

discontented and mutinous[1] speeches that some of the strangers amongst them had let fall from them in the ship: That when they came ashore they would use their own liberty, for none had power to command them, the **patent** they had being for Virginia and not for New England, which belonged to another government, with which the Virginia Company had nothing to do. And partly that such an act by them done, this their condition considered, might be as firm as any patent, and in some respects more sure.

The form was as followeth:
In the Name of God, Amen.

3   We whose names are underwritten, the loyal subjects of our dread Sovereign Lord King James, by the Grace of God of Great Britain, France, and Ireland King, Defender of the Faith, etc.

4   Having undertaken, for the Glory of God and advancement of the Christian Faith and Honour of our King and Country, a Voyage to plant the First Colony in the Northern Parts of Virginia, do by these presents solemnly and mutually in the presence of God and one of another, Covenant and Combine ourselves together into a Civil Body Politic, for our better ordering and preservation and furtherance of the ends aforesaid; and by virtue hereof to enact, constitute and frame such just and equal Laws, Ordinances, Acts, Constitutions and Offices, from time to time, as shall be thought most meet and convenient for the general good of the Colony, unto which we promise all due submission and obedience. In witness whereof we have hereunder subscribed our names at Cape Cod, the 11th of November, in the year of the reign of our Sovereign Lord King James, of England, France and Ireland the eighteenth, and of Scotland the fifty-fourth. Anno Domini 1620.

5   After this they chose, or rather confirmed, Mr. John Carver (a man godly and well approved amongst them) their Governor for that year. And after they had provided a place for their goods, or common store (which were long in unlading for want of boats, foulness of the winter weather and sickness of divers) and begun some small cottages for their habitation; as time would admit, they met and consulted of laws and orders, both for their civil and military government as the necessity of their condition did require, still adding thereunto as urgent occasion in several times, and as cases did require.

6   In these hard and difficult beginnings they found some discontents and murmurings arise amongst some, and mutinous speeches and carriages in other; but they were soon quelled and overcome by the wisdom, patience, and just and equal carriage

---

[1] **mutinous:** rebellious.

58   Unit 1

ENGLISH LEARNER SUPPORT

Use Contextual Support   Explain to students that archaic English sometimes uses words that are unfamiliar to modern English speakers. Other times, words may be used differently than they are now used. For example, the words *dread, meet,* and *want* are used on this page. But they are not used in the way modern readers use them. Have students give examples of how they use these words in everyday language (for example, *I dread taking the test; I will meet you for lunch; I want a million dollars*). Then, discuss how these words are used in this document, using context to guide understanding of the meaning of these words as used.
MODERATE/LIGHT

of things, by the Governor and better part, which **clave** faithfully together in the main.

[The Starving Time]

7   But that which was most sad and lamentable was, that in two or three months' time half of their company died, especially in January and February, being the depth of winter, and wanting houses and other comforts; being infected with the scurvy[2] and other diseases which this long voyage and their inaccommodate condition had brought upon them. So as there died some times two or three of a day in the foresaid time, that of 100 and odd persons, scarce fifty remained. And of these, in the time of most distress, there was but six or seven sound persons who to their great commendations, be it spoken, spared no pains night nor day, but with abundance of toil and hazard of their own health, fetched them wood, made them fires, dressed them meat, made their beds, washed their loathsome[3] clothes, clothed and unclothed them. In a word, did all the homely and necessary offices for them which dainty and queasy stomachs cannot endure to hear named; and all this willingly and cheerfully, without any grudging in the least, showing herein their true love unto their friends and brethren; a rare example and worthy to be remembered. Two of these seven were Mr. William Brewster, their reverend Elder, and Myles Standish, their Captain and military commander, unto whom myself and many others were much beholden in our low and sick condition. And yet the Lord so upheld these persons as in this general **calamity** they were not at all infected either with sickness or lameness. . . .

[Indian Relations]

8   All this while the Indians came skulking about them, and would sometimes show themselves aloof off, but when any approached near them, they would run away; and once they stole away their tools where they had been at work and were gone to dinner. But about the 16th of March, a certain Indian came boldly amongst them and spoke to them in broken English, which they could well understand but marveled at it. At length they understood by discourse with him, that he was not of these parts, but belonged to the eastern parts where some English ships came to fish, with whom he was acquainted and could name **sundry** of them by their names, amongst whom he had got his language. He became profitable to them in acquainting them with many things concerning the state of the country in the east parts where he lived, which was afterwards profitable unto them; as also of the people here, of their names, number and strength, of their situation and distance from this place, and who was chief amongst

---

[2] **scurvy:** a disease caused by a lack of vitamin C in the diet.
[3] **loathsome:** offensive or disgusting.

© Houghton Mifflin Harcourt Publishing Company

clave
(klăv) *v.* past tense of *cleave*: to cling; to adhere

calamity
(kə-lăm´ĭ-tē) *n.* an event that brings terrible loss or lasting distress.

ANALYZE LANGUAGE
Annotate: Mark words in paragraph 8 that describe the interaction between colonists and Native Americans.

Evaluate: How does Bradford's diction reflect a change in tone? What does this change reveal about his attitude toward the Native Americans?

sundry
(sŭn´drē) *adj.* various or assorted.

Of Plymouth Plantation   59

 ANALYZE LANGUAGE

Remind students that word choice is the tool authors use to convey tone, or the author's attitude, toward the subject. As Bradford describes the interactions with Native Americans, his word choice reflects his changing tone. Have students look for vivid adjectives and strong verbs that convey tone. (***Answer:*** *Bradford shows how the colonists went from thinking about the Native Americans as sneaky and nefarious to marveling at how one came boldly and spoke to them. The tone goes from distrustful to pleasantly surprised.*)

■ **English Learner Support**

Demonstrate Comprehension Before students answer the Analyze Language question, have them circle adjectives and action verbs in paragraph 8. Then, have them identify the circled words as positive, negative, or neutral, and note where they occur in the paragraph.
SUBSTANTIAL/MODERATE

For **reading support** for students at varying proficiency levels, see the **Text X-Ray** on page 54D.

CRITICAL VOCABULARY

clave: Although there were divisions, the Governor and majority of the people clung, or clave, together.

ASK STUDENTS to suggest why it was important that the entire settlement clave together as a unified group. (*It may have been important for their safety and for keeping peace in a small settlement where everyone needed to work together to survive.*)

calamity: The hunger and sickness of the first winter was a time of terrible distress, or calamity, that had been completely unexpected.

ASK STUDENTS why they think Bradford gave such a detailed description of the calamity. (*He is recording it for history, so details are important; he wanted to show how miraculous it was that seven were able to stay healthy and care for the others.*)

sundry: Samoset had become friendly with various, or sundry, English-speaking men from English ships.

ASK STUDENTS why Bradford did not name these "sundry" men, when he provides great detail about Samoset and the other Native Americans. (*Bradford's purpose is focused on the settlers and their important interactions, not the actions and interactions of other Englishmen.*)

TO CHALLENGE STUDENTS . . .

Challenge Central Ideas Direct students to the first lines of "The Starving Time." Ask students to read this passage and discuss what happened to the Pilgrims during their first winter on Cape Cod. How many settlers died? (*approximately 50 people*) What caused these deaths? (*exposure to cold temperatures, lack of housing, scurvy and other diseases*) Challenge students to work in a small group to discuss how these details fit into the central idea that the colonists had found a promised land.

TEACH

LANGUAGE CONVENTIONS

Remind students that verbs have either an active voice or a passive voice. If the subject performs the action, the verb is in the **active voice.** If the subject receives the action, the verb is in the **passive voice.** One way to find examples of passive voice is to look for "be" verbs: *am, is, are, was, were.* (**Answer:** *It places emphasis on the act of stealing, not on who might do the stealing.*)

For **listening support** for students at varying proficiency levels, see the **Text X-Ray** on page 54C.

■ **English Learner Support**

Language Conventions Display and read aloud examples of simple sentences in the active and passive voice, such as *Squanto helped the settlers* and *The settlers were helped by Squanto.* Help students identify the subject and verb of each sentence. Then, guide them to identify whether the subject of each sentence is performing the action being described. **SUBSTANTIAL/MODERATE**

CRITICAL VOCABULARY

divers: Squanto had not been taken away all alone, but with divers, or several, others.

ASK STUDENTS what they can infer about the divers "others" that were taken with Squanto. *(They were other Native Americans who were being kidnapped as part of the slave trade.)*

 **NOTICE & NOTE**

them. His name was Samoset. He told them also of another Indian whose name was Squanto, a native of this place, who had been in England and could speak better English than himself.

9   Being, after some time of entertainment and gifts dismissed, a while after he came again, and five more with him, and they brought again all the tools that were stolen away before, and made way for the coming of their great Sachem,[4] called Massasoit. Who, about four or five days after, came with the chief of his friends and other attendance, with the aforesaid Squanto. With whom, after friendly entertainment and some gifts given him, they made a peace with him (which hath now continued this 24 years) in these terms:

1. That neither he nor any of his should injure or do hurt to any of their people.
2. That if any of his did hurt to any of theirs, he should send the offender, that they might punish him.
3. That if anything were taken away from any of theirs, he should cause it to be restored; and they should do the like to his.
4. If any did unjustly war against him, they would aid him; if any did war against them, he should aid them.
5. He should send to his neighbours confederates[5] to certify them of this, that they might not wrong them, but might be likewise comprised in the conditions of peace.
6. That when their men came to them, they should leave their bows and arrows behind them.

10   After these things he returned to his place called Sowams, some 40 miles from this place, but Squanto continued with them and was their interpreter and was a special instrument sent of God for their good beyond their expectation. He directed them how to set their corn, where to take fish, and to procure other commodities, and was also their pilot to bring them to unknown places for their profit, and never left them till he died. He was a native of this place, and scarce any left alive besides himself. He was carried away with **divers** others by one Hunt, a master of a ship, who thought to sell them for slaves in Spain. But he got away for England and was entertained by a merchant in London, and employed to Newfoundland and other parts, and lastly brought hither into these parts by one Mr. Dermer, a gentleman employed by Sir Ferdinando Gorges and others for discovery and other designs in these parts. . . .

[First Thanksgiving]

11 They began now to gather in the small harvest they had, and to fit up their houses and dwellings against winter, being all well recovered in health and strength and had all things in good plenty. For as

---
[4] **Sachem:** chief.
[5] **confederates:** allies; persons who share a common purpose.

LANGUAGE CONVENTIONS
Annotate: Circle the passive-voice verb in item 3 of the list, and underline the active verbs.

Respond: What is the effect of using the passive voice in this item?

divers
(dī´vərz) *adj.* various; several.

© Houghton Mifflin Harcourt Publishing Company

APPLYING ACADEMIC VOCABULARY

☑ **adapt**   ❏ **coherent**   ❏ **device**   ❏ **displace**   ☑ **dynamic**

Write and Discuss Have students turn to a partner to discuss the following questions. Direct students to include the academic vocabulary words *adapt* and *dynamic* in their responses. Invite volunteers to share their responses with the class.

• How did the Native Americans help the English settlers **adapt** to their new home?
• How would you describe the **dynamic** between Squanto and the settlers?

some were thus employed in affairs abroad, others were exercised in fishing, about cod and bass and other fish, of which they took good (store) of which every family had their portion. All the summer there was no want; and now began to come in store of fowl, as winter approached, of which this place did abound when they came first (but afterward decreased by degrees). And besides waterfowl there was great (store) of wild turkeys, of which they took many, besides venison, etc. Besides they had about a peck a meal a week to a person, or now since harvest, Indian corn to that proportion. Which made many afterwards write so largely of their plenty here to their friends in England, which were not feigned but true reports.[6]

_____

[6] **reports:** Although the specific day of the Plymouth colonists' first Thanksgiving is not known, it occurred in the fall of 1621. For three days, Massasoit and almost a hundred of his men joined the Pilgrims for feasts and games.

ANALYZE LANGUAGE
Annotate: Mark two examples of repetition in the final paragraph of the excerpt.

Analyze: What does this repetition emphasize in the description?

CHECK YOUR UNDERSTANDING

Answer these questions before moving on to the **Analyze the Text** section on the following page.

1 Why did the colonists decide to create the *Mayflower Compact*?

   A King James required them to sign such a document.

   B Some of them were speaking out against King James.

   C Their original patent did not extend to establishing a colony in New England.

   D They were facing extreme hardship and starvation and wanted to elect a new leader.

2 Why were Squanto and Samoset able to help make peace between the colonists and the Native Americans?

   F They spoke English and could help the two groups communicate.

   G They showed the colonists what foods to eat to avoid scurvy.

   H They brought the colonists food during the winter so they would not starve.

   J They planned a three-day festival where both groups could share abundant food.

3 How did Squanto help the colonists prepare for the winter?

   A He showed them how to build fires and cook food.

   B He showed them how to sew warmer clothing.

   C He showed them how to make their homes sturdier.

   D He showed them how to grow and find food to store.

 ANALYZE LANGUAGE

Remind students that repetition emphasizes important ideas and details. Discuss the relationship between the two repeated words (*store* and *plenty*) and the ideas they express. (**Answer:** *The repetition emphasizes the abundance of food they have and that they will have enough food stored up for winter, so that people will not starve as before.*)

CHECK YOUR UNDERSTANDING

Have students answer the questions independently.

Answers:

   1. *C*

   2. *F*

   3. *D*

If they answer any questions incorrectly, have them reread the text to confirm their understanding. Then they may proceed to ANALYZE THE TEXT on page 62.

 ENGLISH LEARNER SUPPORT

Oral Assessment Use the following fill-in statements to assess students' comprehension and speaking skills.

   1. The Mayflower Compact listed the _____. (*the rules they needed for establishing a new colony in New England*)

   2. Squanto and Samoset helped the colonists _____ with other Native Americans. (*talk*)

   3. Samoset taught the colonists how to _____ food. (*grow, keep*)
   SUBSTANTIAL/LIGHT

ANALYZE THE TEXT

Possible answers:

1. **DOK 4:** *The compact says the Pilgrims—who traveled for God, king, and country to establish a colony in the "Northern Parts of Virginia"—promised to create and obey a local government. Its diction and imagery suggest formality, legality, and authority.*

2. **DOK 4:** *Pilgrims and Native Americans should not hurt each other or steal property. If they do, they will be punished. The two groups will defend each other in times of "unjust" war. When Native Americans visit the Pilgrims, they must come unarmed. Except for the last item, the treaty seems fair.*

3. **DOK 4:** *The Pilgrims believed they were on a journey that would advance "the Christian Faith and Honour of our King and Country" and that God would provide for them even through hardships. Evidence of this can be found in paragraphs 3 and 4 and at the end of paragraph 7.*

4. **DOK 3:** *In paragraph 4, the language of the Mayflower Compact says the mission is "for the Glory of God." In paragraph 10, Bradford says "Squanto . . . was a special instrument sent of God for their good." Both references support Bradford's idea that the Pilgrims' voyage was a mission from God.*

5. **DOK 4:** *Bradford's central idea was that the Pilgrims endured great hardship, but by God's providence they survived and thrived. His purpose was to educate future settlers about the realities of their sufferings and reassure them that God would provide.*

RESEARCH

Emphasize that all facts should be verified in a second source. You may want to suggest students focus on Native American groups in your own area. Have students share their research to see if there are practices or crops several groups had in common.

Extend Students may wish to use a Venn diagram or another graphic organizer to compare and contrast the groups they researched.

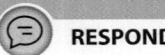 **RESPOND**

ANALYZE THE TEXT

Support your responses with evidence from the text. 📓 NOTEBOOK

1. **Analyze** What does the Mayflower Compact explicitly say? What does it suggest through its careful diction, or word choice, and tone?

2. **Evaluate** Paraphrase the terms of the treaty between Massasoit and the Pilgrims (paragraph 9). Then, evaluate the treaty. Is it equally fair to both sides? Explain.

3. **Analyze** Which beliefs most contributed to the colonists' willingness to face hardships together? What passages best reveal those beliefs?

4. **Cite Evidence** Locate and analyze two examples of Bradford's use of biblical allusions or references to God's intervention in events. What purpose might these devices serve in his account?

5. **Synthesize** What is the central idea of the excerpt from *Of Plymouth Plantation*? How does this reflect Bradford's purpose in writing it?

RESEARCH

RESEARCH TIP
To make sure your information is accurate, confirm all facts with at least two credible sources.

Find out more about Native American farming. Do some research on two Native American groups and their agricultural practices. Record your findings in the chart below.

NATIVE AMERICAN GROUP	MAIN CROPS	IMPORTANT FARMING METHODS AND TOOLS
Wampanoag	corn, beans, squash	planted all three crops together
Pawnee	corn, beans, squash	planted in floodplains

Extend Compare and contrast the groups you researched. How were their farming practices and crops similar? How were they different?

 LEARNING MINDSET

Belonging Emphasize to students that every one of them is a valuable member of the learning community and has something to offer. This means it is important and valuable for everyone to participate in discussions. As more people participate, the entire community has a greater chance of learning something new or gaining new insight into the topic.

CREATE AND DISCUSS

Write an Informational Text Bradford's account describes how the Native Americans helped the colonists adapt to life in New England. Write a three- or four-paragraph informational text that explains how the colonists and Native Americans confronted challenges together.

❏ Include an introduction with a thesis on how Native Americans helped the colonists adapt.

❏ Support your thesis with relevant supporting details.

❏ Use verbs in both active and passive voice.

❏ Sum up your ideas in a conclusion.

Hold a Group Discussion With a small group, discuss how the relationship between Native Americans and colonists developed over time and what factors caused changes to occur.

❏ Review the selection with your group to identify the specific events that sparked change.

❏ Then, discuss how each event caused a positive or negative change.

❏ Finally, end your discussion by summarizing your group's main ideas.

 Go to **Writing Informative Texts** in the **Writing Studio** for help.

Go to **Participating in Collaborative Discussions** in the **Speaking and Listening Studio** for help with having a group discussion.

RESPOND TO THE ESSENTIAL QUESTION

? What happens when cultures collide?

Gather Information Review your annotations and notes on the excerpt from *Of Plymouth Plantation*. Then, add relevant details to your Response Log. As you determine which information to include, think about:

• how the colonists initially viewed the Native Americans

• how and why this view changed

• particular actions that helped change the relationship between the two groups

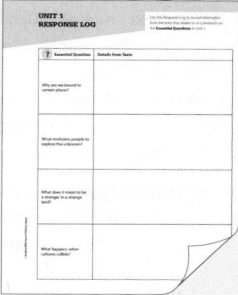

ACADEMIC VOCABULARY

As you write and discuss what you learned from the historical account, be sure to use the Academic Vocabulary words. Check off each of the words that you use.

❏ adapt

❏ coherent

❏ device

❏ displace

❏ dynamic

CREATE AND DISCUSS

Write an Informational Text Review the basic structure of an informational text with students: an introduction that engages readers' attention and states the thesis, or controlling idea of the text; one or more paragraphs that are the body of the text and that expand on and support the thesis; a conclusion that follows logically from the body and sums up the thesis and its support in a satisfying way.

For **writing support** for students at varying proficiency levels, see the **Text X-Ray** on page 54D.

Hold a Group Discussion Tell groups to have one or more members take notes on the discussion, capturing the changes group members mention and classifying each as a positive or negative change. After groups discuss, have one person from each group use the notes to summarize the main ideas of the group in the class discussion.

RESPOND TO THE ESSENTIAL QUESTION

Allow time for students to add details from the excerpt from *Of Plymouth Plantation* to their Unit 1 Response Logs.

CRITICAL VOCABULARY

Answers:

1. *difficult;* divers *means "numerous"*

2. *officially;* the patent granted ownership of the land

3. *different;* sundry *means "various"*

4. *bad;* calamity *means "a distressing event"*

5. *support them;* clave *means "cling"*

VOCABULARY STRATEGY:

Archaic Vocabulary

Answers:

aforesaid: *spoken of earlier*

thereunto: *to that, this, or it*

inaccommodate: *not preferable*

 RESPOND

WORD BANK
patent
clave
calamity
sundry
divers

CRITICAL VOCABULARY

Practice and Apply Mark the italicized alternative that best relates to the Critical Vocabulary word in each sentence. Then, explain your choice.

1. If you and your friends have **divers** opinions about what to eat, is it *easy* or *difficult* to choose a restaurant?

2. Did the *Mayflower* passengers' **patent** *officially* or *unofficially* suggest that they would live in Virginia?

3. Would **sundry** pairs of shoes be *identical* or *different* from each other?

4. If you experienced a **calamity,** would the result be *good* or *bad*?

5. If you **clave** to someone's principles, did you *support* or *oppose* them?

VOCABULARY STRATEGY:
Archaic Vocabulary

Of Plymouth Plantation contains many examples of **archaic vocabulary**—words that are no longer commonly used. The Critical Vocabulary word *divers*, for example, was common until the end of the 17th century but has now been almost completely replaced by *diverse*. English usage and vocabulary have changed a great deal over time.

Here are some strategies to help you understand archaic vocabulary:
- Notice if the word is similar to a current, familiar word, and try substituting the current word to make a meaningful sentence.
- Use context clues as much as possible when reading a selection that contains archaic vocabulary. Don't stop at every unfamiliar word, but read on to see if you can discover hints about the word's meaning.
- Look up archaic words in a dictionary. Many dictionaries include notes for archaic words or for archaic meanings of familiar words; this information is often at the end of an entry and is labeled with the word *archaic* or *obsolete*.

Practice and Apply Use the strategies above to determine the meaning of the following archaic vocabulary from *Of Plymouth Plantation*. Identify each strategy you used, and explain how it helped you find the word's meaning.

WORD	MEANING	NOTES ON STRATEGY
aforesaid (paragraph 4)		
thereunto (paragraph 5)		
inaccommodate (paragraph 7)		

EL ## ENGLISH LEARNER SUPPORT

Vocabulary Strategy Give students additional practice in determining the meanings of archaic words from the selection. Write the following words from the selection on the board: *followeth, whereof, habitation*. Have pairs of students find the words on page 58, then apply the three strategies listed on page 64 (look for a similar modern word; use context; use a dictionary). Have them share their ideas with the group. **ALL LEVELS**

LANGUAGE CONVENTIONS:
Active and Passive Voice

The **voice** of a verb tells whether its subject performs or receives the verb's action. If the subject *performs* the action, the verb is in the **active voice.** If the subject *receives* the action, the verb is in the **passive voice.** In Bradford's writing, the colonists or the Native Americans are most often subjects who perform the action. Sometimes, however, the subject of a sentence or clause receives the action.

Consider this example from the narrative, which contains several active voice verbs in succession, emphasizing the praiseworthy work the "six or seven" did when a terrible illness struck:

> . . . there was but six or seven sound persons who to their great commendations, be it spoken, <u>spared</u> no pains night nor day, but with abundance of toil and hazard of their own health, <u>fetched</u> them wood, <u>made</u> them fires, <u>dressed</u> them meat, <u>made</u> their beds, <u>washed</u> their loathsome clothes, <u>clothed</u> <u>and unclothed</u> them.

Now consider this example, which contains both active voice and passive voice:

> He <u>was carried</u> away with divers others by one Hunt, a master of a ship, who thought to sell them for slaves in Spain. But he <u>got away</u> for England and <u>was entertained</u> by a merchant in London. . . .

This example describes how Squanto managed to learn English through a sequence of events in which he sometimes takes action ("got away") and sometimes has actions done to or for him ("was carried," "was entertained"). Note how the sentence shows a contrast between the way the slaver and the merchant treated Squanto—he was carried away by one but entertained by another. How his fortunes changed!

Practice and Apply Return to the informational text you wrote in response to this selection's Create and Present. First, identify any examples of passive voice and rewrite those sentences in the active voice. Then, choose two examples of active voice and rewrite those sentences in the passive voice. Finally, compare the emphasis and clarity created by the use of each voice. Write your original and revised sentences below.

ORIGINAL SENTENCE	REVISED SENTENCE

> ! Go to **Active Voice and Passive Voice** in the **Grammar Studio** for help.

LANGUAGE CONVENTIONS:
Active and Passive Voice

Review the information about active and passive voice verbs with students. Explain that passive voice is sometimes frowned upon because it is wordier and less focused, and often unnecessary. However, passive voice works very well when the writer wants to emphasize who or what received the action.

Point out that in the second example, the focus of the passage is on Squanto—what he did as well as what happened to him. Passive voice verbs keep the focus on Squanto rather than equally on the slaver and the merchant, who are not as important in the story. Writers may also use passive voice if the person or group performing the action is unknown or should remain mysterious.

Generally, students should strive to use active voice in their own writing, unless there is a good reason to use the passive voice.

Practice and Apply Have partners compare their active and passive voice sentences, stating reasons for their opinions. *(Sentences will vary.)*

ENGLISH LEARNER SUPPORT

Language Conventions Note that some students may be used to different rules for using passive voice. Use the following supports with students at varying proficiency levels:

• Have students convert simple passive sentences *(such as "The letter was sent by Jim.")* to active voice. **SUBSTANTIAL**

• Have students each write one sentence in passive voice. Have them switch with a partner and revise their sentences to be in active voice. **MODERATE**

• Have students work with partners to identify examples of active and passive voice sentences in a textbook or on a website. Have them share their examples. **LIGHT**

COMING OF AGE IN THE DAWNLAND

History Writing by Charles C. Mann

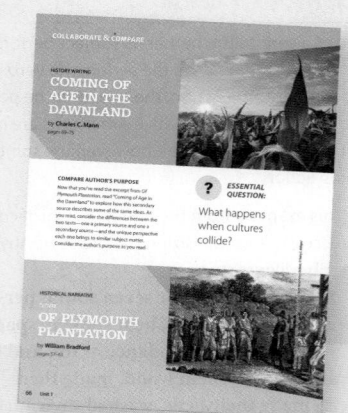

GENRE ELEMENTS
HISTORY WRITING

Remind students that **history writing** is nonfiction that informs readers about true events and people from a particular time in history. Facts, dates, and quotations from primary sources help verify and support the main ideas. If the author of history writing did not experience the events directly, the writing is called a **secondary source**. In this selection, students will identify the author's purpose for writing and determine literal and nonliteral meanings of important words and phrases.

LEARNING OBJECTIVES

- Evaluate author's purpose.
- Determine the meaning of words and phrases.
- Conduct research about Native American alliances.
- Evaluate how successfully the author achieves his purpose by writing a brief argument.
- Discuss claims and supportive evidence for arguments.
- Use strategies to define specialized vocabulary.
- Identify dependent clauses and subordinating conjunctions.
- **Language** Discuss details on a map and photographs.

TEXT COMPLEXITY

Quantitative Measures	Coming of Age in the Dawnland	Lexile: 1290L
Qualitative Measures	**Ideas Presented** Multiple levels, greater demand for inference.	
	Structures Used More complex organization of main ideas and details, but mostly explicit.	
	Language Used Complex sentence structures with unfamiliar, academic and domain-specific words.	
	Knowledge Required Cultural and historical references may make heavier demands.	

Online **Ed**

RESOURCES

- Unit 1 Response Log
- Selection Audio
- Reading Studio: Notice & Note
- Level Up Tutorial: Connotations and Denotations
- Writing Studio: Writing Arguments
- Speaking and Listening Studio: Analyzing and Evaluating Presentations
- Vocabulary Studio: Specialized Vocabulary
- Grammar Studio: Module 4: Lesson 1: Kinds of Clauses
- *Of Plymouth Plantation*/ "Coming of Age in the Dawnland" Selection Test

SUMMARIES

English

In this selection, science journalist Charles C. Mann reviews and synthesizes the work of recent scholars who have studied early Native American societies. Mann draws parallels between the daily lives of settlers and Native American people and discusses how the European settlers viewed Native American customs and practices.

Spanish

En esta selección, el periodista científico Charles C. Mann critica y sintetiza el trabajo de los eruditos recientes, quienes estudian las sociedades primitivas de indígenas americanos. Mann establece un paralelo entre los conquistadores y los indígenas americanos. Y discute cómo los conquistadores europeos veían las costumbres de los indígenas americanos.

SMALL-GROUP OPTIONS

Have students work in small groups and pairs to read and discuss the selection.

Three-Minute Review

- As you read the text, pause after every two or three paragraphs.
- Direct students to reread the paragraphs and write clarifying questions. Set a timer for three minutes.
- After three minutes, ask: *What did you notice as you reread the text?*
- Invite volunteers to share clarifying questions.
- Guide small groups to discuss and answer the questions.

Send a Problem

- After reading paragraphs 5 and 6, pose this question: *How would you describe Tisquantum's home?*
- Call on a student to respond. Wait up to 11 seconds.
- If the student has no response, he or she must call on another student by name to answer the same question.
- Have students continue asking each other for assistance as needed. Monitor responses and ask more questions as appropriate.

Text X-Ray: English Learner Support
for "Coming of Age in the Dawnland"

Use the Text X-Ray and the supports and scaffolds in the Teacher's Edition to help guide students at different proficiency levels through the selection.

INTRODUCE THE SELECTION
DISCUSS SETTLEMENTS AND DAILY LIFE

In this selection, students will need to be able to understand settlements, daily life, and coming of age in the Massachusett Alliance (later known as New England). Explain that a settlement is a sparsely populated area where different groups live. Review settlements on the map on page 70.

Explain to students that life for Native Americans was different from life for Europeans. Native Americans ate heartier food and lived in houses that were drier, warmer, and sounder than European homes. Native American children did not begin working at a young age, but were free to explore and play. During adolescence, they would "come of age," which meant they would do certain things to prove that they were adults. For example, boys were expected to spend the winter alone in the forest. Have volunteers share ideas about daily life or family values in their cultures. Supply sentence frames: *We value _____ in my culture. We think that family is _____. We do _____ most days. We eat _____ and live in _____.*

CULTURAL REFERENCES

The following words or phrases may be unfamiliar to students:

- *at the heart of* (paragraph 1): the most important part
- *jigsawed* (paragraph 4): cut or separated into pieces
- *sparing the rod* (paragraph 7): not punishing or disciplining, usually a child
- *chatterboxes* (paragraph 8): people who talk too much

LISTENING

Identify Claims and Supporting Evidence

Review with students that a claim is an opinion and supporting evidence are facts. Remind students that authors of history writing may make claims that tell their opinion based on factual evidence.

Have students listen as you reread paragraph 8. Help students identify the claim Mann makes about Dawnland education, and the evidence he uses to support it.

- Reread the final three sentences from paragraph 8. Ask yes/no questions, such as *Did Native American boys spend a winter alone in the forest? Did they bring tools with them?* **SUBSTANTIAL**
- After listening to the paragraph, have students repeat the sentence that names Mann's claim and identify one phrase or example that gives evidence to support the claim. **MODERATE**
- After students listen to the paragraph, have them restate Mann's claim and one piece of supporting evidence in their own words. **LIGHT**

SPEAKING

Use Graphic Features

Have students create a word bank based on the map and photos in the text to use in a discussion of Native Americans' daily life. Words may include *settlement, alliance, wetu* (home), *domed, platform beds, stew, crushed,* and *maize* (corn).

Use the following supports with students at varying proficiency levels:

- Have students repeat the words from the word bank as they point to related elements on the map and in photographs. Use the words in simple sentences and have students repeat them. For example: *There were many* settlements. *Native Americans lived in* wetus. **SUBSTANTIAL**

- Have partners use the words from the word bank in simple sentences related to the daily life of Native Americans and point to the related graphic feature. **MODERATE**

- Have partners ask each other questions about the daily life of Native Americans using the word bank, map, and photographs. For example: *Why did the Patuxet people sleep on platform beds? (to stay dry) What types of things did they eat? (stew and crushed maize)* **LIGHT**

READING

Understand Author's Purpose

Tell students that an author's purpose for writing a text may not be stated directly. Guide students to identify words and tone that show Mann's attitude toward his subject.

Work with students to reread paragraph 6.

- Point to the text and ask questions to help students identify tone and the purpose of imagery. For example: *Does "cheerful thud" convey a happy or sad tone? (happy) What is the purpose of describing a bed "piled with mats and furs"? (to show the home was comfortable)* **SUBSTANTIAL**

- Have pairs identify words that show tone and imagery. Provide sentence frames, such as: *The phrase shows a _____ tone. The image of _____ appeals to my sense of _____.* **MODERATE**

- Have students ask each other *"Have you ever?"* questions about the imagery in the paragraph. For example: *Have you ever heard a cheerful thud? What made the sound? How did it make you feel? Have you ever jumped into a pile of furs or soft blankets? How did it feel?* **LIGHT**

WRITING

Write an Argument

Work with students to complete the writing assignment on Student Edition page 77. Students will evaluate how successfully Mann achieved his purpose for writing about Native American societies.

Use the following supports with students of varying proficiency levels:

- Read paragraph 6 aloud to students. Have them write words from the paragraph that describe the diet of the Patuxet people. **SUBSTANTIAL**

- Help pairs of students create an outline for their argument. Direct them to reread the checklist on page 77 of the Student Edition. Remind them to create one item on their outline for each of the first three items on the checklist. **MODERATE**

- Have pairs of students exchange first drafts of their arguments. Guide them to locate any dependent clauses in each other's work and check for accuracy. If there are no dependent clauses, have them mark a place in the draft where one would make the writing more effective. **LIGHT**

? Connect to the
ESSENTIAL QUESTION

In "Coming of Age in the Dawnland," the author takes a broad look at what happened when European and Native American cultures collided, challenging some preconceived ideas that readers may have.

COMPARE AUTHOR'S PURPOSE

While Bradford was one of the settlers whom he writes about, Mann is a journalist writing hundreds of years later than the events he describes. Ask students to consider how this perspective can work together with primary documents to give readers a more informed understanding of a time period. What can a secondary source written many years later provide that a single primary source cannot?

HISTORY WRITING

COMING OF AGE IN THE DAWNLAND

by **Charles C. Mann**
pages 69–75

COMPARE AUTHOR'S PURPOSE

Now that you've read the excerpt from *Of Plymouth Plantation,* read "Coming of Age in the Dawnland" to explore how this secondary source describes some of the same ideas. As you read, consider the differences between the two texts—one a primary source and one a secondary source—and the unique perspective each one brings to similar subject matter. Consider the author's purpose as you read.

 ESSENTIAL QUESTION:

What happens when cultures collide?

HISTORICAL NARRATIVE

from

OF PLYMOUTH PLANTATION

by **William Bradford**
pages 57–61

Coming of Age in the Dawnland

QUICK START

Pretend you have landed on an unfamiliar island and are approached by an inhabitant. What might happen? What might you do? Think of a few scenarios for your first interaction, and discuss them with your group.

EVALUATE AUTHOR'S PURPOSE

The **author's purpose** is the reason he or she writes a particular text, and this purpose generally is not stated. Instead, readers must **infer** the purpose, or draw a logical conclusion about it, based on text evidence. The purpose might be to inform, to entertain, or to persuade readers to agree with the author.

No matter the purpose, effective writing must have an appealing style. Style elements include **word choice, tone** (the writer's attitude about the topic), and **imagery** (words that appeal to a reader's senses). Use these points to analyze and evaluate "Coming of Age in the Dawnland":

- Think about what the text says. What ideas does the author state directly, and what facts and examples does he include?

- Analyze the author's style. What words and images do you find especially powerful? What tone does the writing convey? What does the text's use of graphics or illustrations suggest?

- Evaluate the text. How well do the elements support Mann's purpose?

ANALYZE LANGUAGE

To understand a sophisticated text like "Coming of Age in the Dawnland," you must analyze the meanings of words and phrases as the author uses them. These meanings may be literal or nonliteral. The chart provides examples.

TECHNICAL TERMS	FIGURATIVE LANGUAGE	CONNOTATIONS
Mann draws on evidence from social scientists, and some of the language he uses comes from specialized fields of study. Examples are *casus belli* and *tripartite alliance*. Mann also uses some Native American words when no accurate translation is available. He defines some terms in the text; others you must look up in a dictionary.	Words are often used in an imaginative way to make comparisons. A **simile,** for example, compares things using the word *like* or *as*. Mann says an Indian not admitting a loss in a fight was "like failing to resign after losing a major piece in a chess tournament." This simile helps readers grasp an unfamiliar topic by comparing it to a familiar one.	To convey subtle shades of meaning, authors choose words with particular **connotations,** or associated feelings. For example, describing bedtime for a Native American family, Mann uses the words *firelight* and *lullaby*. These words have pleasant connotations that help readers connect with the lives of the people.

GENRE ELEMENTS: HISTORY WRITING

- is a type of nonfiction writing meant to inform readers about a historical person, time, or event
- relies on facts, dates, and verifiable details to support the main ideas
- incorporates quotations from and references to experts and scholars
- uses primary sources to provide authenticity
- may use graphic features, such as maps and photographs

QUICK START

Have students read the Quick Start note and its two questions. Give students a few minutes to think about the scenario, and then hold a class discussion in which they share their ideas. Ask students how expectations held by those of different cultures meeting for the first time might affect their views of one another.

EVALUATE AUTHOR'S PURPOSE

Revisit what students have already learned about an author's purpose by reading the excerpt from *Of Plymouth Plantation*. Review how audience and genre affect purpose and how that purpose affects the author's tone (attitude) and diction (such as formal or informal word choice). Tell students to use these concepts learned in the previous selection to help them analyze this text.

Point out the introduction of the term *imagery*. Discuss how authors use imagery to convey ideas by helping the reader visualize settings, people, and events. Strong imagery is especially useful when the settings an author writes about are unfamiliar—such as the historical settings of both Bradford's and Mann's texts.

ANALYZE LANGUAGE

Have students read the information about how Mann uses technical terms, figurative language, and words with strong connotations to help readers learn more about people who lived a long time ago. Point out that some informational texts can be dry. To add interest to his text, Mann uses Native American words, imagery, similes, and words with connotations to make events that occurred in the past come alive for modern readers.

TEACH

CRITICAL VOCABULARY

Encourage students to read all the sentences before deciding which word best completes each one. Remind them to look for context clues that suggest the meaning of the best word to complete the sentence.

Answers:

1. *project*
2. *defection*
3. *settlement*
4. *regimen*
5. *stoically*

■ English Learner Support

Use Cognates Tell students that several of the Critical Vocabulary words have Spanish cognates: *project/proyecto, defect/defecto, regimen/régimen. Defecto* means "defect," or "imperfection," which is different from the meaning of the vocabulary word *defect/defection*. **ALL LEVELS**

LANGUAGE CONVENTIONS

Review with students the information about clauses. Explain that the word "As" in the example sentence is the clue that this clause is a dependent clause. Other common words that signal dependent clauses are *while, because, since, after, although, though, unless, until,* and *before.* Students can look for these words as they read.

ANNOTATION MODEL

Remind students of the ideas included in the Evaluate Author's Purpose and Analyze Language sections on page 67. As they read, students should notice word choice, imagery, technical terms, and figurative language that convey meaning and author's purpose. Point out that students may follow the method of marking the text shown in the Annotation Model or use their own system for marking up the selection in their write-in text. They may want to color-code their annotations by using highlighters. Their notes in the margin may include questions about ideas that are unclear or topics they want to learn more about.

CRITICAL VOCABULARY

| project | settlement | regimen | defection | stoically |

To preview the Critical Vocabulary words, complete the sentences.

1. To _____ is to communicate or put forth an impression or message.

2. When a community experiences _____, it loses members.

3. A _____ is a small community in an area without a large population.

4. A daily _____ is a routine of behavior performed every day.

5. If you endure something _____, you do not show emotion.

LANGUAGE CONVENTIONS

Clauses All clauses contain a subject and a verb. An **independent clause** can stand on its own. However, a **dependent clause** (often called a **subordinate clause**) cannot stand alone as a sentence; it depends on, or is subordinate to, an independent clause. Consider the sentence:

As Tisquantum's later history made clear, he regarded himself first and foremost as a citizen of Patuxet, a shoreline settlement halfway between what is now Boston and the beginning of Cape Cod.

"As Tisquantum's later history made clear" is a dependent clause; it cannot stand on its own. As you read, look for ways Mann uses dependent clauses to add detail, interest, and variety.

ANNOTATION MODEL

NOTICE & NOTE

Here are one reader's notes about the author's purpose and language in "Coming of Age in the Dawnland."

Consider Tisquantum, the ⟨friendly Indian⟩ of the textbook. More than likely Tisquantum was not the name he was given at birth. In that part of the Northeast, *tisquantum* referred to rage, especially the rage of *manitou,* the world-suffusing spiritual power at the heart of coastal Indians' religious beliefs. When Tisquantum approached the Pilgrims and identified himself by that sobriquet, it was as if he had stuck out his hand and said, Hello, I'm the Wrath of God. No one would lightly adopt such a name in contemporary Western society. Neither would anyone in seventeenth-century indigenous society. Tisquantum was trying to project something.

The words "friendly Indian" are in quotation marks. Mann wants to call attention to the way Tisquantum is frequently described to students.

Mann explains that the name Tisquantum was chosen to make an impression, even if the Pilgrims didn't understand. Mann's purpose is to dispel myths about Tisquantum and provide a more accurate portrayal.

68   Unit 1

© Houghton Mifflin Harcourt Publishing Company

BACKGROUND

In his 2005 book, 1491: New Revelations of the Americas Before Columbus, *science journalist* **Charles C. Mann** *reviews and synthesizes the work of recent scholars who have studied early Native American societies. Christopher Columbus's voyage to the Caribbean in 1492 marked the beginning of contact between native people in the Americas and Europeans. By 1620 Native Americans in coastal New England had been trading on a limited basis with Europeans for about a hundred years. The man named Tisquantum in this excerpt from Mann's book is the person whom William Bradford called Squanto.*

COMING OF AGE IN THE DAWNLAND

History Writing by Charles C. Mann

PREPARE TO COMPARE

As you read, look for ways Mann draws parallels between the daily lives of settlers and Native American people. Notice how the European settlers viewed Native American customs and practices. Think back to Bradford's account in the excerpt from Of Plymouth Plantation, *and look for similar ideas in this text.*

1   Consider Tisquantum, the "friendly Indian" of the textbook. More than likely Tisquantum was not the name he was given at birth. In that part of the Northeast, *tisquantum* referred to rage, especially the rage of *manitou*, the world-suffusing spiritual power at the heart of coastal Indians' religious beliefs. When Tisquantum approached the Pilgrims and identified himself by that sobriquet,[1] it was as if he had stuck out his hand and said, Hello, I'm the Wrath of God. No one would lightly adopt such a name in contemporary Western society. Neither would anyone in seventeenth-century indigenous society. Tisquantum was trying to **project** something.

---
[1] **sobriquet** (sō´brĭ-kā´): nickname.

Notice & Note

Use the side margins to notice and note signposts in the text.

project
(prə-jĕkt´) *v.* to communicate or put forth.

© Houghton Mifflin Harcourt Publishing Company • Image Credits: © Verity E. Milligan/Getty Images; © Phillippe MATSAS/Agence Opale/Alamy

IMPROVE READING FLUENCY

Targeted Passage   Have students work with partners to read the opening paragraphs of the excerpt. First, use paragraph 1 to model how to read informational text. Have students follow along in their books as you read the text with appropriate phrasing and emphasis. Then have partners take turns reading aloud paragraphs 2 and 3. Encourage students to provide feedback to their partners on accuracy, rate, and expression. Remind students that when they are reading aloud for an audience they should read to make the meaning of the text clear and pace their reading so the audience has time to understand difficult concepts.

 Go to the **Reading Studio** for additional support in developing fluency.

BACKGROUND

Have students read the background information. Point out that Mann's article includes information about Native American life before the arrival of the Pilgrims. Suggest that students keep Bradford's descriptions of Native Americans in mind as they read this excerpt. How do the two descriptions vary?

PREPARE TO COMPARE

Direct students to use the Prepare to Compare prompt to focus their reading.

CRITICAL VOCABULARY

project: Mann explains that Tisquantum is trying to make an impression on the Pilgrims by projecting a certain image.

ASK STUDENTS what kind of impression Tisquantum is trying to make. *(The meaning of his name indicates he's trying to project an image of anger and power.)* How well does his attempt to project an image succeed, based on the Pilgrims' interpretation of his actions? *(It fails because he is known as the "friendly Indian.")*

EVALUATE AUTHOR'S PURPOSE

Point out the date on the map to students. This indicates that the map shows locations that were in place in 1600, before the area was called "New England." (**Answer:** *The author wants to help readers connect locations mentioned in the text to their locations on a map and show where they are relative to each other; the author wants to help readers visualize the area he is describing and see where it corresponds to today's locations.*)

For **speaking support** for students at varying proficiency levels, see the **Text X-Ray** on page 66D.

EVALUATE AUTHOR'S PURPOSE

Read aloud paragraph 2, placing a dramatic pause after the first sentence and using expression to emphasize the "true" and "it is true." Point out that the author writes as if he is refuting an argument or arguing with someone about the claim made in the first sentence. Discuss what this shows about Mann's expectations of his audience. (**Answer:** *The author wants to grab readers' interest; he wants to challenge readers' expectations.*)

 **NOTICE & NOTE**

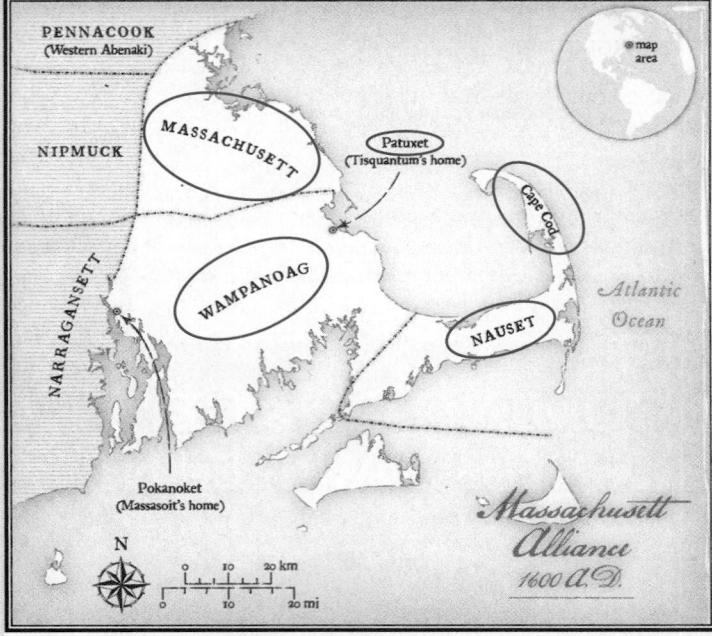

MASSACHUSETT ALLIANCE, 1600 A.D.

EVALUATE AUTHOR'S PURPOSE

Annotate: Mark places on the map that correspond to places mentioned in the text.

Infer: What can you infer about the author's purpose for including this map?

EVALUATE AUTHOR'S PURPOSE

Annotate: Mark words and phrases in paragraph 2 that indicate the author is presenting new or surprising information.

Infer: What can you infer about the author's purpose?

settlement
(sĕt´l-mənt) *n.* a small community in a sparsely populated area.

2   Tisquantum was not an Indian. True, he belonged to that category of people whose ancestors had inhabited the Western Hemisphere for thousands of years. And it is true that I refer to him as an Indian, because the label is useful shorthand; so would his descendants, and for much the same reason. But "Indian" was not a category that Tisquantum himself would have recognized, any more than the inhabitants of the same area today would call themselves "Western Hemisphereans." Still less would Tisquantum have claimed to belong to "Norumbega," the label by which most Europeans then referred to New England. ("New England" was coined only in 1616.) As Tisquantum's later history made clear, he regarded himself first and foremost as a citizen of Patuxet, a shoreline **settlement** halfway between what is now Boston and the beginning of Cape Cod.

3   Patuxet was one of the dozen or so settlements in what is now eastern Massachusetts and Rhode Island that comprised[2] the Wampanoag confederation. In turn, the Wampanoag were part of a tripartite alliance with two other confederations: the Nauset, which comprised some thirty groups on Cape Cod; and the Massachusett, several dozen villages clustered around Massachusetts Bay. All of these people spoke variants of Massachusett, a member of the

---

[2] **comprised:** made up of.

CRITICAL VOCABULARY

settlement: Tisquantum considered himself part of one of the small communities, or settlements, along the coast.

ASK STUDENTS how these small settlements were bound together. (*The settlements were bound together because they were in a similar area, by being part of the Wampanoag confederation, and by being part of the tripartite alliance.*)

Algonquian language family, the biggest in eastern North America at the time. (Massachusett thus was the name both of a language and of one of the groups that spoke it.) In Massachusett, the name for the New England shore was the Dawnland, the place where the sun rose. The inhabitants of the Dawnland were the People of the First Light. . . .

4   Tucked into the great sweep of Cape Cod Bay, Patuxet sat on a low rise above a small harbor, jigsawed by sandbars and shallow enough that children could walk from the beach hundreds of yards into the water before the waves went above their heads. To the west, maize hills marched across the sandy hillocks[3] in parallel rows. Beyond the fields, a mile or more away from the sea, rose a forest of oak, chestnut, and hickory, open and park-like, the underbrush kept down by expert annual burning. "Pleasant of air and prospect," as one English visitor described the area, Patuxet had "much plenty both of fish and fowl every day in the year." Runs of spawning Atlantic salmon, shortnose sturgeon, striped bass, and American shad annually filled the harbor. But the most important fish harvest came in late spring, when the herring-like alewives swarmed the fast, shallow stream that cut through the village. So numerous were the fish, and so driven, that when mischievous boys walled off the stream with stones the alewives would leap the barrier—silver bodies gleaming in the sun—and proceed upstream.

5   Tisquantum's childhood *wetu* (home) was formed from arched poles lashed together into a dome that was covered in winter by tightly woven rush mats and in summer by thin sheets of chestnut bark. A fire burned constantly in the center, the smoke venting through a hole in the center of the roof. English visitors did not find this arrangement peculiar; chimneys were just coming into use in Britain, and most homes there, including those of the wealthy, were still heated by fires beneath central roof holes. Nor did the English regard the Dawnland *wetu* as primitive; its multiple layers of mats, which trapped insulating layers of air, were "warmer than our English houses," sighed the colonist William Wood. The *wetu* was less leaky than the typical English wattle-and-daub house, too. Wood did not conceal his admiration for the way Indian mats "deny entrance to any drop of rain, though it come both fierce and long."

6   Around the edge of the house were low beds, sometimes wide enough for a whole family to sprawl on them together; usually raised about a foot from the floor, platform-style; and always piled with mats and furs. Going to sleep in the firelight, young Tisquantum would have stared up at the diddering[4] shadows of the hemp bags and bark boxes hanging from the rafters. Voices would skirl[5] up in the darkness: one person singing a lullaby, then another person,

---

[3] **hillocks:** small hills.
[4] **diddering:** trembling.
[5] **skirl:** make a high-pitched sound, like bagpipes.

ANALYZE LANGUAGE

Annotate: Mark words with positive connotations in the first five lines of paragraph 4.

Evaluate: What feeling about Patuxet do these words create?

EVALUATE AUTHOR'S PURPOSE

Annotate: Mark examples in paragraph 5 that describe English reactions to Patuxet homes.

Evaluate: What can you infer about the author's purpose for including these descriptions? How effective are the descriptions?

 ANALYZE LANGUAGE

Have students focus on visualizing Patuxet as they read paragraph 4. Then, identify words that were especially visual or vivid. What is the overall impression Mann gives about this location? (***Answer:*** *Patuxet seems like a safe, comforting, beautiful place.*)

 EVALUATE AUTHOR'S PURPOSE

Point out to students that the English reactions described may challenge readers' preconceived ideas about how English settlers reacted to Native Americans, or which group had the more comfortable lifestyle. (***Answer:*** *The author wants to show readers, who may have envisioned the English settlers as disparaging or acting superior to Native Americans, that the settlers were, in fact, envious and admiring of many aspects of Native American lifestyles and skills.*)

 For **reading support** for students at varying proficiency levels, see the **Text X-Ray** on page 66D.

EL **ENGLISH LEARNER SUPPORT**

Demonstrate Comprehension Point out to students that in paragraph 6, Mann uses the conditional forms of verbs. Conditional forms of verbs indicate a hypothetical, or imagined, situation. Have students underline verb forms that include the word *would* (*would have stared, would skirl, would be,* and *would hear*). Mann does not know for certain that Tisquantum woke to "cheerful thuds." Rather, he speculates that this is likely.

EL **ENGLISH LEARNER SUPPORT**

Provide Contextual Support Point out to students that Mann's use of very specific nouns enlivens his writing. However, this means that some of the vocabulary he uses may be unfamiliar. Use the following supports with students at varying proficiency levels:

• Read aloud paragraph 4. Point out the words *salmon, shortnose sturgeon, striped bass, American shad,* and *herring -like alewives*. Show pictures of some of the fish. Explain that Mann uses specific names to help the reader understand how many types of fish were available. Repeat the activity for *oak, chestnut,* and *hickory*. **SUBSTANTIAL/MODERATE**

• Have partners read paragraph 4 and underline the specific nouns that Mann uses to describe the trees and fish. Provide students with online access or dictionaries to look up the words. Have students write a brief description of each fish or tree. Have students discuss why Mann used specific names. (*It shows how plentiful the fish were and how many types of trees there were.*) **LIGHT**

EVALUATE AUTHOR'S PURPOSE

Point out to students that just as the Europeans admired the homes of the Dawnland people, they found much to admire about their food as well. Note that 2,500 calories a day is close to the recommended calorie intake of an average adult man, so this was an adequate and healthy diet. (**Answer:** *The author wants to show that, in many ways, Dawnland was superior to Europe, to counteract the idea that Europeans were more civilized.*)

ANALYZE LANGUAGE

Explain to students that although the goal of the Dawnland education was to produce good characteristics, the methods may seem harsh. Discuss which actions were meant to produce each virtue. (**Answer:** *The author first describes the difficult training most boys had to go through, and then shows how Tisquantum's training was even harsher. Spending an entire winter alone does not seem nearly as bad as spending an entire winter alone, and also running through brambles and throwing up blood.*)

For **listening support** for students at varying proficiency levels, see the **Text X-Ray** on page 66C.

The exterior of a *wetu*

EVALUATE AUTHOR'S PURPOSE
Annotate: Mark a comparison in paragraph 6 of the diets of Patuxet and European citizens.

Infer: What can you infer about the author's purpose in including this comparison?

until everyone was asleep. In the morning, when he woke, big, egg-shaped pots of corn-and-bean mash would be on the fire, simmering with meat, vegetables, or dried fish to make a slow-cooked dinner stew. Outside the *wetu* he would hear the cheerful thuds of the large mortars and pestles[6] in which women crushed dried maize into *nokake*, a flour-like powder "so sweet, toothsome, and hearty," colonist Gookin wrote, "that an Indian will travel many days with no other but this meal." Although Europeans bemoaned the lack of salt in Indian cuisine, they thought it nourishing. According to one modern reconstruction, Dawnland diets at the time averaged about 2,500 calories a day, better than those usual in famine-racked Europe.

7   Pilgrim writers universally reported that Wampanoag families were close and loving—more so than English families, some thought. Europeans in those days tended to view children as moving straight from infancy to adulthood around the age of seven, and often thereupon sent them out to work. Indian parents, by contrast, regarded the years before puberty as a time of playful development, and kept their offspring close by until marriage. (Jarringly, to the contemporary eye, some Pilgrims interpreted this as sparing the rod.) Boys like Tisquantum explored the countryside, swam in the ponds at the south end of the harbor, and played a kind of soccer with a small leather ball; in the summer and fall they camped out in huts in the fields, weeding the maize and chasing away birds. Archery practice began at age two. By adolescence boys would make a game of shooting at each other and dodging the arrows.

ANALYZE LANGUAGE
Annotate: Mark words and images in paragraphs 8–9 that have negative connotations.

Analyze: How do these words support the idea that "Tisquantum's regimen was probably tougher than that of his friends"?

8   The primary goal of Dawnland education was molding character. Men and women were expected to be brave, hardy, honest, and uncomplaining. Chatterboxes and gossips were frowned upon. "He that speaks seldom and opportunely, being as good as his word, is the only man they love," Wood explained. Character formation began early, with family games of tossing naked children into the

---

[6] **mortars and pestles:** bowl-shaped containers and blunt tools for grinding and crushing.

APPLYING ACADEMIC VOCABULARY

❏ adapt   ❏ coherent   ☑ device   ❏ displace   ☑ dynamic

Write and Discuss Have students turn to a partner to discuss the following questions. Guide students to include the Academic Vocabulary words *device* and *dynamic* in their responses. Ask volunteers to share their responses with the class.

- What **devices** did Native American boys use to survive their winters alone in the forest?
- What evidence shows that the Native Americans' culture and lifestyle were **dynamic**?

The interior of a *wetu*

snow. (They were pulled out quickly and placed next to the fire, in a practice reminiscent of Scandinavian saunas.) When Indian boys came of age, they spent an entire winter alone in the forest, equipped only with a bow, a hatchet, and a knife. These methods worked, the awed Wood reported. "Beat them, whip them, pinch them, punch them, if [the Indians] resolve not to flinch for it, they will not."

9   Tisquantum's **regimen** was probably tougher than that of his friends, according to Salisbury, the Smith College historian, for it seems that he was selected to become a *pniese*, a kind of counselor-bodyguard to the sachem. To master the art of ignoring pain, future *pniese* had to subject themselves to such miserable experiences as running barelegged through brambles. And they fasted often, to learn self-discipline. After spending their winter in the woods, *pniese* candidates came back to an additional test: drinking bitter gentian juice until they vomited, repeating this bulimic process over and over until, near fainting, they threw up blood.

10   Patuxet, like its neighboring settlements, was governed by a sachem, who upheld the law, negotiated treaties, controlled foreign contacts, collected tribute, declared war, provided for widows and orphans, and allocated farmland when there were disputes over it. (Dawnlanders lived in a loose scatter, but they knew which family could use which land—"very exact and punctuall," Roger Williams, founder of Rhode Island colony, called Indian care for property lines.) Most of the time, the Patuxet sachem owed fealty[7] to the great sachem in the Wampanoag village to the southwest, and through him to the sachems of the allied confederations of the Nauset in Cape Cod and the Massachusett around Boston. Meanwhile, the Wampanoag were rivals and enemies of the Narragansett and Pequots to the west and the many groups of Abenaki to the north. As a practical matter, sachems had to gain the consent of their people, who could easily move away and join another sachemship. Analogously, the great

---

[7] **fealty:** obedient loyalty.

regimen
(rĕj´ə-mən) *n.* a system or organized routine of behavior.

LANGUAGE CONVENTIONS
Annotate: Subordinate clauses add details and cannot stand alone as sentences. Underline one subordinate clause in paragraph 10 and circle its subordinating conjunction.

Analyze: Explain the relationship between the subordinate clause and the independent clause. Why do you think Mann used a subordinate clause in this sentence?

Coming of Age in the Dawnland   73

✎ LANGUAGE CONVENTIONS

Remind students that the words *unless, until,* and *when* are common subordinating conjunctions. (**Answer:** *The subordinating conjunction "when" in the first sentence of paragraph 10 connects to a subordinate clause that adds more details about when farmland was allocated.*)

CRITICAL VOCABULARY

regimen: Mann describes the regimen, or program of education and training, that Tisquantum may have followed to become a *pniese*.

ASK STUDENTS to describe the training regimen of an elite athlete. (*Elite athletes must spend time practicing their own sport, as well as doing general physical and strength training. They may also have to follow a special diet to have adequate nutrition.*)

WORD GAPS

Remind students that **Word Gaps** are unfamiliar words in a text. Students should look for clues in the passage to help them figure out the meaning. (**Answer:** *The writer mentions "armed conflict" and explains the reason why the conflict took place, thus suggesting that "casus belli" means "cause for war.")*

CRITICAL VOCABULARY

defection: Mann discusses why and how the most important sachems had to retain the loyalty of lesser sachems and smaller communities to avoid defections.

ASK STUDENTS to explain how members' defections would damage an alliance. (*If some members defected, the alliance would have fewer members and become weaker.*)

stoically: Mann discusses the kinds of behavior the Native Americans valued, especially to endure pain and hardship stoically—without complaint or showing emotion.

ASK STUDENTS to explain why the Indians might admire someone who endured torture stoically. (*Students may say that Indians themselves generally acted stoically by not showing emotion so they would admire this quality in other peoples.*)

NOTICE & NOTE

defection
(dē-fĕkt´shŭn) *n.* the abandonment of one social or political group in favor of another.

WORD GAPS

Notice & Note: Mark the foreign phrase the author uses in the second sentence of paragraph 12.

Analyze: What clues in the sentence help you figure out the meaning of the phrase? Explain.

stoically
(stō´ĭk-lē) *adv.* without showing emotion or feeling.

---

sachems had to please or bully the lesser, lest by the **defection** of small communities they lose stature.

11   Sixteenth-century New England housed 100,000 people or more, a figure that was slowly increasing. Most of those people lived in shoreline communities, where rising numbers were beginning to change agriculture from an option to a necessity. These bigger settlements required more centralized administration; natural resources like good land and spawning streams, though not scarce, now needed to be managed. In consequence, boundaries between groups were becoming more formal. Sachems, given more power and more to defend, pushed against each other harder. Political tensions were constant. Coastal and riverine New England, according to the archaeologist and ethnohistorian Peter Thomas, was "an ever-changing collage of personalities, alliances, plots, raids and encounters which involved every Indian [settlement]."

12   Armed conflict was frequent but brief and mild by European standards. The *casus belli*[8] was usually the desire to avenge an insult or gain status, not the wish for conquest. Most battles consisted of lightning guerrilla raids by ad hoc companies in the forest: flash of black-and-yellow-striped bows behind trees, hiss and whip of stone-tipped arrows through the air, eruption of angry cries. Attackers slipped away as soon as retribution had been exacted. Losers quickly conceded their loss of status. Doing otherwise would have been like failing to resign after losing a major piece in a chess tournament—a social irritant, a waste of time and resources. Women and children were rarely killed, though they were sometimes abducted and forced to join the winning group. Captured men were often tortured (they were admired, though not necessarily spared, if they endured the pain **stoically**). Now and then, as a sign of victory, slain foes were scalped,

---

[8] *casus belli* (kä´səs bĕl´ī): Latin: cause for war.

Ground maize used to make *nokake*

much as British skirmishes with the Irish sometimes finished with a parade of Irish heads on pikes. In especially large clashes, adversaries might meet in the open, as in European battlefields, though the results, Roger Williams noted, were "farre less bloudy, and devouring then the cruell Warres of Europe." Nevertheless, by Tisquantum's time defensive palisades[9] were increasingly common, especially in the river valleys.

13   Inside the settlement was a world of <u>warmth, family, and familiar</u> custom. But the world outside, as Thomas put it, was "<u>a maze of confusing actions and individuals fighting to maintain an existence in the shadow of change.</u>"

14   And that was before the Europeans showed up.

_____
[9] **defensive palisades:** fortified walls of tall stakes.

NOTICE & NOTE

ANALYZE LANGUAGE
Annotate: Mark words in paragraph 13 that describe the contrast between life inside and outside the settlement.

Predict: Given this contrast, what is suggested by the final sentence of the selection?

CHECK YOUR UNDERSTANDING

Answer these questions before moving on to the **Analyze the Text** section on the following page.

1 Why does Mann begin the selection with a discussion of Tisquantum?

A It serves to introduce the topic of Wampanoag culture at Patuxet.

B It gives important details about the way the Wampanoag lived at Patuxet.

C It suggests a reason that the Pilgrims continually failed to understand Wampanoag culture.

D It provides background information on why the Pilgrims traveled from Europe and encountered Wampanoag culture.

2 Why was Patuxet called the Dawnland?

F The Pilgrims called the New England shoreline the Dawnland.

G The Pilgrims called their own settlement in New England the Dawnland.

H In the language of the Wampanoag, the New England shoreline was called the Dawnland.

J In the language of the Wampanoag, the Pilgrim settlement in New England was called the Dawnland.

3 How does Mann characterize life at Patuxet?

A Difficult and harsh

B Peaceful and civilized

C Unorganized and chaotic

D Primitive and violent

ANALYZE LANGUAGE

Have students look for words that have negative and positive connotations and explain how these connotations help make the contrast between inside and outside the settlement sharper. (**Answer:** *Europeans will increase the external threats to the warmth and familiarity of the settlement.*)

✐ CHECK YOUR UNDERSTANDING

Have students answer the questions independently.

Answers:

1. *A*

2. *H*

3. *B*

If they answer any questions incorrectly, have them reread the text to confirm their understanding. Then they may proceed to ANALYZE THE TEXT on page 76.

 ## ENGLISH LEARNER SUPPORT

Oral Assessment   Use the following questions to assess students' comprehension and speaking skills.

1. Mann begins the article talking about Tisquantum. Why? What is his purpose? (*The article is about Native Americans living at Patuxet and that is where Tisquantum lived. Describing Tisquantum immediately gets the reader interested in the article.*)

2. Why was Patuxet called the Dawnland? (*It was a New England shoreline settlement, the place where the sun rose. The people who lived there were called People of the First Light.*)

3. What was life like at Patuxet? (*peaceful, pleasant, with enough food to eat all year long*) **MODERATE/LIGHT**

ANALYZE THE TEXT

Possible answers:

1. **DOK 4:** *This imagery creates an impression of a happy, quiet, and prosperous community.*

2. **DOK 4:** *The text says "one English visitor" described the area as "Pleasant of air and prospect" and having "much plenty both of fish and fowl every day in the year." These and other examples reveal the Europeans' admiration for Native Americans and their lifestyles.*

3. **DOK 3:** *The central idea about Native American societies in the Dawnland in this excerpt is that they were highly developed, sophisticated civilizations—especially compared to contemporary European communities.*

4. **DOK 4:** *Mann's purpose for writing this text is to give readers a more complex view of Indian life in New England before European settlement. Mann explains the Indians' lifestyle, shows ways in which they were like modern Americans, and compares their achievements favorably with those of Europeans at the same time.*

5. **DOK 4:** *He might want to use this comparison to make the Indians' lifestyle seem more familiar and understandable to readers.*

RESEARCH

Emphasize that students should look for unbiased sources for this initial research. You may want to break students into small groups and assign each group one Native American group to research and then share facts in a class discussion.

Extend Students should give specific reasons why they believe a source to be biased or unbiased. Have students present their sources and evaluations to the class and see if there is a consensus about which are biased and which are more objective.

⊜ RESPOND

ANALYZE THE TEXT

Support your responses with evidence from the text. 📓 NOTEBOOK

1. **Analyze** Note sensory details Mann uses in paragraph 4 to describe life in Patuxet at the end of the 16th century. What is the purpose of these details? What impression of the community does this use of imagery create?

2. **Synthesize** Review instances in which Mann cites evidence from European primary sources from the 17th century. What does word choice and tone in the sources reveal about the opinions of these Europeans?

3. **Draw Conclusions** What central idea about Native American societies in the Dawnland is communicated in this excerpt? Explain.

4. **Evaluate** What do you think was Mann's overall purpose for writing this text? Did he successfully achieve that purpose? Cite reasons and evidence in your answer.

5. **Notice & Note** In paragraph 6, Mann describes *nokake* as "a flour-like powder." What purpose might he want to achieve by comparing a Native American food with one that is commonly known today?

RESEARCH TIP

Avoid biased sources during most research. These sources present one viewpoint and include websites designed to promote products, opinion sites or publications, and other sites that present the agendas of specific groups.

Rely instead on objective sources, such as those maintained by educational institutions, museums, government offices, and scientific organizations.

RESEARCH

The selection mentions three confederations that were part of an alliance of Native American groups in the New England area. Research these groups and compare their first interactions with Europeans by completing the chart.

	FIRST CONTACT WITH EUROPEAN COLONISTS
Wampanoag	*in 1500s; with people on fishing and trading boats*
Nauset	*first contacts shortly after Columbus due to coastal location; unfriendly with de Champlain in 1605*
Massachusett	*mid-1500s; in 1617, outbreak of disease from Europeans with high mortality rate.*

Extend Evaluate the sources you used for your research. List the source in the chart and state whether the source seems biased or objective. Then give reasons for each evaluation. Consider why it is important to use objective sources in your research and writing.

SOURCE	BIASED/OBJECTIVE	REASONS
Students' responses will vary based on the sources used.		

WHEN STUDENTS STRUGGLE . . .

Reteaching: Determine the Meaning of Words and Phrases Remind students that some words can have positive or negative connotations, or the feelings associated with them. For example, the word *skinny* has a negative connotation, while the word *petite* has a positive connotaion. Point out the word *primitive* in paragraph 5 of the selection. Ask: *What connotation does it have? (negative) Why do you think Mann uses this word? (People often have the misconception that Native Americans were primitive. He is using the word

to show that the English did not believe this.)* Then, point out the word *fierce* in paragraph 5. Ask students similar question about the word. Then, have students scan the article and look for other words with positive or negative connotations.

 For additional support, go to the **Reading Studio** and assign the following 📖 LEVEL **Level Up Tutorial: Connotations and Denotations.**

CREATE AND DEBATE

Write an Argument This selection presents Mann's view of Native American societies in New England. Evaluate how successfully he achieves his purpose by writing a brief argument.

- ❏ Write a statement that summarizes Mann's purpose for writing.
- ❏ Decide whether he succeeded or failed in achieving that purpose. How well do his word choices, tone, and content support his purpose? Your position on that question will form the claim of your argument.
- ❏ If you think Mann achieved his purpose, cite evidence that supports this claim. If you think he failed, provide reasons for this opinion.
- ❏ Incorporate appropriate dependent clauses to make your writing more specific, interesting, and varied.

Share and Debate Use your reasons and evidence to debate a partner with a different point of view.

- ❏ Share your argument's claim, reasons, and supporting evidence.
- ❏ Listen as your partner explains his or her argument.
- ❏ Compose and present counterarguments based on your partner's claims and supporting evidence.

 Go to **Writing Arguments** in the **Writing Studio** for help.

Go to **Analyzing and Evaluating Presentations** in the **Speaking and Listening Studio** for help.

RESPOND TO THE ESSENTIAL QUESTION

? What happens when cultures collide?

Gather Information Review your annotations and notes on "Coming of Age in the Dawnland." Then add relevant details to your Response Log. As you determine which information to include, think about:

- Mann's descriptions of life at the time
- ideas that Mann conveys about Native American societies
- memorable phrases Mann uses to describe situations

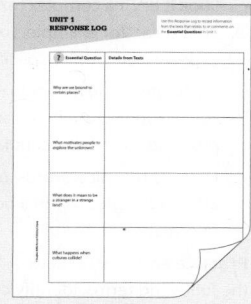

ACADEMIC VOCABULARY
As you write and discuss what you learned from the selection "Coming of Age in the Dawnland," be sure to use the Academic Vocabulary words. Check off each of the words that you use.

- ❏ **adapt**
- ❏ **coherent**
- ❏ **device**
- ❏ **displace**
- ❏ **dynamic**

CREATE AND DEBATE

Write an Argument Remind students that before they evaluate Mann's success in achieving his purpose, they need to have a clear idea of what that purpose is. Have them review their annotations and notes about the author's purpose. These notes may provide text evidence for students' positions.

For **writing support** for students at varying proficiency levels, see the **Text X-Ray** on page 66D.

Share and Debate If time permits, hold a class discussion in which students share their opinions and reasons, including their counterarguments.

RESPOND TO THE ESSENTIAL QUESTION

Allow time for students to add details from "Coming of Age in the Dawnland" to their Unit 1 Response Logs.

APPLY

CRITICAL VOCABULARY

Answers:

1. A Native American who acted stoically during torture hoped to project an image of bravery and indifference to pain.

2. A sachem might be concerned about the defection of a small settlement because of the loss of loyalty of its residents.

3. Young Indians had to endure their training regimen stoically because the program of learning to be an adult included many difficult tasks, and the community valued those who could endure difficulties in silence.

VOCABULARY STRATEGY:
Specialized Vocabulary

Answers:

tripartite alliance *Context clues: "part of"; "two other confederations"; meaning: an alliance, or agreement to work together, formed between three groups*

sachem *Context clues: "governed by a sachem, who upheld the law, negotiated treaties, controlled foreign contacts, collected tribute, declared war, provided for widows and orphans, and allocated farmland"; meaning: a leader or governor*

ad hoc *Context clues: "lightning guerrilla raids"; "as soon as retribution had been exacted"; meaning: informal and for a particular purpose*

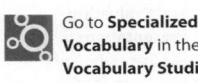 **RESPOND**

WORD BANK
project
settlement
regimen
defection
stoically

 Go to **Specialized Vocabulary** in the **Vocabulary Studio** for help.

CRITICAL VOCABULARY

Practice and Apply Use complete sentences to answer each question, showing that you understand the meaning of each Critical Vocabulary word.

1. When a Native American acted **stoically** during torture, what image did she or he hope to **project?**

2. Why would a *sachem* be concerned about the **defection** of a small **settlement?**

3. Why did young Indians have to endure their training **regimen stoically?**

VOCABULARY STRATEGY:
Specialized Vocabulary

Mann's writing contains language from a variety of sources. For example, he cites an archaeologist and ethnohistorian, recounts observations from Pilgrim writers, uses foreign words and phrases, and even uses some Native American words when there is no accurate or exact English translation. Many of the words he uses are examples of **specialized vocabulary,** or words specific to a particular topic. The Critical Vocabulary word *settlement*, for example, is used in a specialized sense, "a small community in a sparsely populated area." This is an example of a specialized meaning for a word with which you might already be familiar.

The following strategies can help you determine the meaning of specialized vocabulary.

- Look it up. If a complex text is about a specialized topic with which you are unfamiliar (for example, *volcanology*, the study of volcanoes), you should expect to encounter specialized vocabulary that you will need to look up.

- Try to guess the meaning. Use context clues, including the word's part of speech and its use in the sentence, to help determine the meaning. Very often, specialized vocabulary will be defined in the text for readers.

- For very technical words, use a specialized reference work, such as an atlas or the glossary in a book on a specialized topic, to get more specific information.

Practice and Apply Review "Coming of Age in the Dawnland" to find the following terms. Identify context clues for each word's meaning. Then complete the chart.

WORD	CONTEXT CLUES	MEANING
tripartite alliance		
sachem		
ad hoc		

EL ENGLISH LEARNER SUPPORT

Vocabulary Strategy Give students additional practice in determining the meanings of specialized words by writing the following words on the board: *alliance, wetu, indigenous, descendants, confederation,* and *treaties.* Use the following supports with students at varying proficiency levels:

- Have students repeat the words. Then, work with students to find the meaning of each word. Write the definition on the board, and help students use the word in a sentence. For example: *The wetu kept rain out. Treaties helped keep peace.* **SUBSTANTIAL**

- Have pairs find the words in the text and use context clues to determine each word's meaning. Then, have them use online or print dictionaries to confirm their understanding of the word. **MODERATE**

- Have students determine the meaning of each word. Then, pair students and have partners discuss their findings. Ask students why they think Mann used specialized vocabulary. How does the vocabulary help them understand the main ideas? **LIGHT**

LANGUAGE CONVENTIONS: Dependent (or Subordinate) Clauses

All **clauses** contain a subject and a verb. A **dependent** or **subordinate clause** depends on, or is subordinate to, an independent clause and cannot stand alone. Using dependent clauses skillfully allows Charles Mann to vary the **syntax,** or arrangement of words, of his sentences.

Consider these examples from "Coming of Age in the Dawnland."

> And it is true that I refer to him as an Indian, <u>because the label is useful shorthand</u> . . .

> <u>Although Europeans bemoaned the lack of salt in Indian cuisine,</u> they thought it nourishing.

In each of these complex sentences, the dependent clause begins with a **subordinating conjunction** (*because* and *although*). The conjunction reveals a relationship between the two clauses. The word *because* indicates a cause-and-effect relationship between two factors. *Although* indicates a concession or exception to the point that Mann makes. Using subordinating conjunctions allows Mann to make nuanced and detailed arguments appropriate to his topic. It also allows him to create a varied rhythm in his prose, making his text more engaging and easier to read.

This chart shows some common subordinating conjunctions and the relationships they signal.

TYPE OF RELATIONSHIP	SUBORDINATING CONJUNCTIONS
Causal (i.e., making something happen)	because, since
Concession/Contrast	although, as, as much as, than, though, while
Place	where, wherever
Purpose	in order that, so that, that
Time	after, as, as long as, as soon as, before, since, until, when, whenever, while

Practice and Apply Look back at the argument you wrote in response to this selection's Create and Debate. Revise your argument by crafting complex sentences to replace some of your simple sentences. Use appropriate subordinating conjunctions to show the relationships between ideas. Vary the placement of dependent clauses at the beginning, the middle, and the end of sentences to create varied sentence structure and a smooth, flowing rhythm.

RESPOND

Go to **Kinds of Clauses** in the **Grammar Studio** for help.

LANGUAGE CONVENTIONS: Dependent (or Subordinate) Clauses

Review with students the information about dependent clauses. Make sure students can identify the subject and verb of a clause. Write several different types of sentences on the board and have volunteers identify the subject and verb of each clause. Point out how some sentences have more than one subject and verb.

Review the chart of subordinating conjunctions with students, and have volunteers offer sentences that use each conjunction listed. Write examples on the board, underlining the subordinating conjunction.

Practice and Apply Have partners compare their revised arguments and check to make sure that subordinating conjunctions are used correctly. *(Revisions will vary.)*

 ENGLISH LEARNER SUPPORT

Language Conventions Note that students with Arabic language background have been taught to favor coordinating conjunctions over subordinating conjunctions. Review coordination and subordination. Use the following supports with students at varying proficiency levels:

- Have students make a word wall for the coordinating conjunctions using the acronym FANBOYS: *for, and, nor, but, or, yet,* and *so.* Then, review the list of subordinating conjunctions on page 79. Have students copy the list into their notebooks. **SUBSTANTIAL**

- Have students write one sentence using a coordinating conjunction and one using a subordinating conjunction. Ask them to switch with a partner. Have partners circle and identify the conjunctions. **MODERATE**

- Have students work with partners to identify examples of coordinating conjunctions and subordinating conjunctions in a fictional or informational text. Have them share and explain their examples. **LIGHT**

COMPARE AUTHOR'S PURPOSE

Before students begin, have them revisit their notes about author's purpose, audience, genre, and tone from the two selections. This will allow them to come prepared to their small group discussion.

ANALYZE THE TEXTS

Possible answers:

1. **DOK 2:** *In Of Plymouth Plantation, Squanto is portrayed as an individual who was sent by God to help the colonists survive and live in their new home. In "Coming of Age in the Dawnland," Tisquantum is portrayed as a representative of a culture and way of life—an individual and a culture that have been misunderstood or flattened over time.*

2. **DOK 2:** *In both texts, the colonists were surprised by the extensive knowledge and skills Native Americans had. In Of Plymouth Plantation, the Pilgrims are amazed that some Native Americans speak English, and by the important farming skills they learned from Squanto. In "Coming of Age in the Dawnland," the colonists are struck by how advanced and healthy the Native Americans are. For example, they have watertight homes, ample food, organized government structures, and effective parenting methods.*

3. **DOK 2:** *A main idea in Of Plymouth Plantation is that God provided for the colonists through severe hardships. This is related to Bradford's purpose of supporting the idea that God was in favor of colonizing New England. A main idea of "Coming of Age in the Dawnland" is that Native Americans had an advanced and peaceful society when the first colonists from Europe arrived. This main idea is related to the purpose of challenging readers' preconceived ideas about these first encounters.*

4. **DOK 4:** *Of Plymouth Plantation uses the eyewitness account effectively to describe the terrible suffering and amazing recovery of the Plymouth Colony. Bradford's use of descriptive details, specific details about individuals and their actions, and emotional language conveys an authentic view of the colony's first years. "Coming of Age in the Dawnland" uses both primary documents and secondary sources to present a thorough look at the meeting of these two cultures. The use of a variety of sources advances the author's purpose of presenting an objective and credible perspective.*

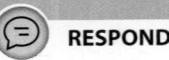

RESPOND

Collaborate & Compare

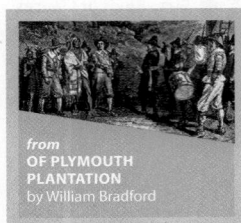

from
OF PLYMOUTH PLANTATION
by William Bradford

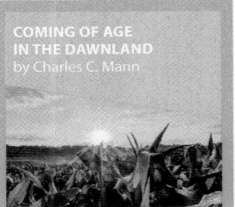

COMING OF AGE IN THE DAWNLAND
by Charles C. Mann

COMPARE AUTHOR'S PURPOSE

Compare Genres Comparing two different genres, or types of writing, on the same topic can help you better understand the topic. William Bradford wrote *Of Plymouth Plantation* from his own personal experience. As an eyewitness account, it is a **primary source** about a crucial time in American history. Charles C. Mann wrote *1491: New Revelations of the Americas Before Columbus* in 2005. As a **secondary source,** it draws on a broad range of sources, both primary sources and other secondary sources, to give a wider perspective of events in the past. Using primary sources, such as diaries, in historical writing helps readers visualize and understand the events and people.

To compare the two authors' purposes, consider each text's audience and tone. How did each author envision the audience? How did each feel about his subject matter? Then, consider the events described in each text. Why did the author choose to include these particular events?

In a small group, complete the chart with the audience, tone, and main events of each text. You will use these to identify and compare the authors' purposes.

	OF PLYMOUTH PLANTATION	"COMING OF AGE IN THE DAWNLAND"
Audience	*other settlers, future historians*	*students of North American history*
Tone	*formal at times; lofty; personal; grateful*	*objective and formal*
Main Events	*Compact; starving time; Native Americans help; feast*	*Native American life before/with settlers*
Author's Purpose	*show that God provided; set down a history*	*counter preconceived ideas; to inform*

ANALYZE THE TEXTS

Discuss these questions in your group.

1. **Contrast** How is the historical figure Tisquantum, or Squanto, portrayed in each text?

2. **Compare** How were the European colonists surprised by the Native Americans they encountered in each text?

3. **Infer** How do the main ideas of each selection reflect the author's purpose?

4. **Evaluate** How effectively does each author use the characteristics of its genre—primary versus secondary sources—to support his purpose?

ENGLISH LEARNER SUPPORT

Ask Questions Use questions to have small groups synthesize and compare the selections: In Mann's text, what do Europeans think of Native Americans? In *Of Plymouth Plantation,* how do the colonists feel about the Native Americans? *(In Mann's text, Europeans do not think the Native American way of life is primitive. They admire the wetus and appreciate the hearty food. The Europeans in* Of Plymouth Plantation *think the Native Americans are fair and good people.* How does "Coming of Age in the Dawnland" help you learn why Squanto knew English in *Of Plymouth Plantation*? *(Squanto was a native of the area where English ships came to fish. This area must have been the Dawnland, where the Massachusett Alliance settlements were.)*
MODERATE/LIGHT

COLLABORATE AND PRESENT

Now, your group can collaborate on a project that compares and evaluates benefits and drawbacks of primary and secondary sources. Follow these steps:

1. **Analyze the Selections** With your group, review the selections. Analyze the effectiveness of their elements: their purposes, main ideas, use of evidence, and use of language and tone. Then, determine how effectively each text supports its author's purpose.

	ELEMENTS	EFFECTIVENESS
Primary Source: *Of Plymouth Plantation*	*provides personal observations, in a formal tone, to describe settlers' experiences*	*effectively uses specific details to give an eyewitness account of the settlers' lives*
Secondary Source: "Coming of Age in the Dawnland"	*uses several sources and an objective tone to give an overview of a period of history*	*effectively uses sources and descriptive imagery to show how Europeans reacted to Native Americans*

2. **Compare Types of Sources** Use your analysis to consider the benefits and drawbacks of primary and secondary sources for learning about history. Record the benefits and drawbacks of each.

	BENEFITS	DRAWBACKS
Primary Source	*up close and personal; written by people who witnessed events first hand*	*may be biased; only one person's perspective*
Secondary Source	*uses many sources; represents broad range of knowledge; can be objective*	*distanced from actual events; some context may be lost*

3. **Present Your Ideas** Work together to present your ideas about the two types of sources. Your presentation should include:

   • definitions and characteristics of primary and secondary sources
   • a comparison of each author's purpose and a claim about how effectively each text met that purpose
   • a statement about the benefits and drawbacks of each type of source for learning about history
   • evidence from the texts to support your ideas
   • relevant images and text to clarify your points and add interest

Go to **Giving a Presentation** in the **Speaking and Listening Studio** for help.

COLLABORATE AND PRESENT

Explain that the culmination of the small group's work together will be a presentation. Review the requirements of step 3 (Present Your Ideas) before students begin, to help direct their discussion.

1. **Analyze the Selections** Remind students to use the annotations and notes from their reading to help them analyze the effectiveness of each author's text. They must first identify the purpose of the text, main ideas, use of evidence, and use of language and tone. Then, students decide if the key qualities effectively support the author's purpose.

2. **Compare Types of Sources** Discuss the differences between primary and secondary sources, including the way the author's proximity to events influences his account of those events. Remind students that each type of source offers different benefits for readers.

3. **Present Your Ideas** Before groups present their presentations, have them rehearse the presentation to work out the technical and personnel details. Students should divide up responsibilities and run through the presentation several times before giving it to the entire class.

TO CHALLENGE STUDENTS . . .

Compare Sources Challenge students to find another primary source text that was written during the European settlement of America. Have them search online or at the library, or provide suggestions, such as the writings of John Winthrop and John Smith. Ask them to analyze the purpose and effectiveness of their chosen primary source, as they have done for *Of Plymouth Plantation* and "Coming of Age in the Dawnland." Then have them discuss whether this primary source gives them any additional insights into the benefits and drawbacks of primary sources. Encourage them to include these insights in their presentation.

INDEPENDENT READING

READER'S CHOICE

Setting a Purpose Have students review their Unit 1 Response Log and think about what they've already learned about people exploring the unknown and experiencing new places with different cultures. As they choose their Independent Reading selections, encourage them to consider what more they want to know.

NOTICE NOTE

Explain that some selections may contain multiple signposts; others may contain only one. And the same type of signpost can occur many times in the same text.

 LEARNING MINDSET

Setting Goals Tell students that setting goals is an important part of having a learning mindset. Encourage students to set a goal for reading self-selected texts outside of class,—for example, reading for a set time or number of pages a day. Consider setting up a class progress report for students to track their goals.

 INDEPENDENT READING

 ESSENTIAL QUESTIONS

Review the four Essential Questions for this unit on page 1.

Reader's Choice

Setting a Purpose Select one or more of these options from your eBook to continue your exploration of the Essential Questions.

- Read the descriptions to see which text grabs your interest.
- Think about which genres you would like to learn more about.

Notice Note

In this unit, you practiced noticing and noting the signposts and asking big questions about nonfiction. As you read independently, these signposts and others will aid your understanding. Below are the anchor questions to ask when you read literature and nonfiction.

Reading Literature: Stories, Poems, and Plays	
Signpost	**Anchor Question**
Contrasts and Contradictions	Why did the character act that way?
Aha Moment	How might this change things?
Tough Questions	What does this make me wonder about?
Words of the Wiser	What's the lesson for the character?
Again and Again	Why might the author keep bringing this up?
Memory Moment	Why is this memory important?

Reading Nonfiction: Essays, Articles, and Arguments	
Signpost	**Anchor Question(s)**
Big Questions	What surprised me? What did the author think I already knew? What challenged, changed, or confirmed what I already knew?
Contrasts and Contradictions	What is the difference, and why does it matter?
Extreme or Absolute Language	Why did the author use this language?
Numbers and Stats	Why did the author use these numbers or amounts?
Quoted Words	Why was this person quoted or cited, and what did this add?
Word Gaps	Do I know this word from someplace else? Does it seem like technical talk for this topic? Do clues in the sentence help me understand the word?

 ENGLISH LEARNER SUPPORT

Develop Fluency Select a passage from a text that matches students' reading abilities. Read the passage aloud while students follow along silently.

- Echo read the passage by reading aloud one sentence and then having students repeat the sentence back to you. Then have the students read the passage silently several times. Check their comprehension by asking yes/no questions about the passage. **SUBSTANTIAL**
- Have students read and then reread the passage silently. Ask students to time their reading and keep track of their improvements. **MODERATE**

- Allow more fluent readers to select their own texts. Set a specific time for students to read silently (for example, 30 minutes). Check their comprehension by having them write a summary of what they've read. **LIGHT**

 Go to the **Reading Studio** for additional support in developing fluency.

You can preview these texts in Unit 1 of your eBook.

Then, check off the text or texts that you select to read on your own.

MEMOIR

from **The Way to Rainy Mountain**
N. Scott Momaday

A man visits the grave of his grandmother to reflect on his Native American heritage and connect to his homeland.

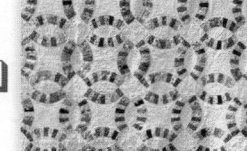

POEM

To My Dear and Loving Husband
Anne Bradstreet

A wife speaks eloquently of love and marriage.

HISTORICAL NARRATIVE

from **La relación**
Álvar Núñez Cabeza de Vaca

How do Native Americans respond to shipwrecked Spanish explorers who are starving and near death?

HISTORICAL NARRATIVE

from **The General History of Virginia**
John Smith

What is the fate of Jamestown when colonist John Smith is taken prisoner by Powhatan?

POEM

New Orleans
Joy Harjo

See how a writer resurrects Creek Indian culture in a town where her Creek ancestors were exploited.

Collaborate and Share With a partner, discuss what you learned from at least one of your independent readings.

- Give a brief synopsis or summary of the text.
- Describe any signposts that you noticed in the text and explain what they revealed to you.
- Describe what you most enjoyed or found most challenging about the text. Give specific examples.
- Decide if you would recommend the text to others. Why or why not?

 Go to the **Reading Studio** for more resources on **Notice & Note.**

MATCHING STUDENTS TO TEXTS

Use the following information to guide students in choosing their texts.

from **The Way to Rainy Mountain**   **Lexile: 1000L**
   Genre: memoir
   Overall Rating: Accessible

To My Dear and Loving Husband
   Genre: poem
   Overall Rating: Accessible

from **La relación**   **Lexile: 1010L**
   Genre: historical narrative
   Overall Rating: Accessible

from **The General History of Virginia**   **Lexile: 1680L**
   Genre: historical narrative
   Overall Rating: Challenging

New Orleans
   Genre: poem
   Overall Rating: Accessible

Collaborate and Share To assess how well students read the selections, walk around the room and listen to their conversations. Encourage students to be focused and specific in their comments.

 Online

Ed **for Assessment**

- Independent Reading Selection Tests

 Encourage students to visit the **Reading Studio** to download a handy bookmark of **NOTICE & NOTE** signposts.

WHEN STUDENTS STRUGGLE . . .

Keep a Reading Log As students read their selected texts, have them keep a reading log for each selection to note signposts and their thoughts about them. Use their logs to assess how well they are noticing and reflecting on elements of their texts.

Reading Log for (title)		
Location	**Signpost I Noticed**	**My Notes about it**

UNIT ① Tasks

- **WRITE A LITERARY ANALYSIS**
- **PARTICIPATE IN A PANEL DISCUSSION**

MENTOR TEXT

A DESPERATE TREK ACROSS AMERICA
Article by Andrés Reséndez

LEARNING OBJECTIVES

Writing Task

- Write a literary analysis of how a selection connects with the idea of strangers in a strange land.
- Use strategies and graphic organizers to plan and organize information.
- Use the Mentor Text as a model for writing a claim and supporting evidence.
- Form a clear thesis statement and support it with reasons in a logical order.
- Revise drafts incorporating feedback from peers.
- Edit draft to incorporate the active voice.
- Use a rubric to evaluate writing.
- Publish writing to share with an audience.
- **Language** Ask questions that begin with *who, what, where, when, why,* and *how.*

Speaking Task

- Present a literary analysis to an audience.
- Adapt a literary analysis for a presentation.
- Practice with a partner to appropriately use verbal and nonverbal techniques.
- Provide and consider advice for improvement.
- Listen actively to a panel discussion.
- **Language** Ask for clarification using the sentence stem: *Why did you ____?*

Assign the Writing Task in *Ed*.

Online

RESOURCES

- Unit 1 Response Log
- Writing Studio: Writing Informative Texts
- Listening and Speaking Studio: Giving a Presentation
- Grammar Studio: Module 8 Lesson 7: Active Voice and Passive Voice

Language X-Ray: English Learner Support

Use the instruction below and the supports and scaffolds in the Teacher's Edition to help you guide students at different proficiency levels.

INTRODUCE THE WRITING TASK

Explain that a literary analysis is a type of writing that examines and evaluates a work of literature. Point out that the word *analysis* is the same as *análisis* in Spanish, which means a "close examination." Make sure students understand that they will be closely examining and writing their opinion about a piece of literature, and then supporting or proving their opinion with quotations and details from that text.

Remind students that they will be evaluating the text for the way it connects to the idea of being a stranger in a strange land. Provide a sentence frame. For example: *[Selection] uses the example of _____ to connect with the idea of a stranger in a strange land.* Brainstorm a list of words related to the topic. Then have students use their completed sentence frame and the words to write a clear claim for their analysis.

WRITING

Ask Questions to Add Details

Tell students that one way they can increase specificity and detail in their writing is to ask and answer questions that begin with *Who, What, Where, When, Why*, and *How*.

Use the following supports with students at varying proficiency levels:

- Provide a sample of a literary analysis and help students underline answers to the questions you ask. For example: *Who is this analysis discussing? What did they do?* Help students use the underlined words to write answers to your questions. **SUBSTANTIAL**
- Have partners exchange drafts and ask each other simple questions. For example: *Who is the stranger being discussed?* Have each writer revise the draft to add specific details. **MODERATE**
- Have partners exchange drafts and ask questions about how it connects with the idea of being a stranger in a strange land. Have students revise the draft to add more details. **LIGHT**

SPEAKING

Ask for Clarification

Provide a sentence frame for students to use as they ask their peers for clarification after the panel discussion on Student Edition page 92. For example: *Why did you _____?*

Use the following supports with students at varying proficiency levels:

- Provide a word bank of terms students can use to ask for clarification, such as *thesis, claim, quotation, detail*. Show students how to use the words to formulate questions. For example: *Why did you make this claim?* Have students repeat the questions. **SUBSTANTIAL**
- Have partners write words they can use to ask questions about presentations, such as *thesis, claim, anecdote, quotation, detail, example, restatement, stranger in a strange land*. Have students use the words and sentence frame to orally state questions. **MODERATE**
- Have students ask for clarification of the presentations after the discussion. Direct students to ask at least one *Why did you _____?* question about each presentation. **LIGHT**

WRITING

WRITE A LITERARY ANALYSIS

Introduce students to the Writing Task by reading the introductory paragraph with them. Remind students to refer to the notes they recorded in the Unit 1 Response Log as they plan and draft their literary analysis essays. The Response Log should contain ideas about early American literature and the exploration and settlement of what is now the United States. Drawing on these different perspectives will make their own writing more interesting and well informed.

 For **writing support** for students at varying proficiency levels, see the **Language X-Ray** on page 84B.

USE THE MENTOR TEXT

Point out that students' essays will be similar in tone to "A Desperate Trek Across America," but that this text is not a literary analysis. Reséndez does, however, illustrate what it means to be a stranger in a strange land. He makes a claim with evidence on which students can model their literary analysis.

WRITING PROMPT

Review the prompt with students. Encourage them to ask questions about any part of the assignment that is unclear. Make sure they understand that the purpose of their literary analysis essay is to make a claim about a text they choose, give reasons and evidence to support the claim, and include quotations from the text they are analyzing.

Write a Literary Analysis

 Go to the **Writing Studio** for help writing a literary analysis.

In this unit, you have read works about early explorations in America. Andrés Reséndez based his article "A Desperate Trek Across America" on Álvar Núñez Cabeza de Vaca's *La relación*, a first-hand account of the ill-fated Spanish expedition to Florida beginning in 1528. Although Reséndez's narrative article on Cabeza de Vaca's account is not a formal analysis, he uses several techniques which you can apply to the literary analysis you are going to create for your next writing task.

As you write your literary analysis, you can use the notes from your Response Log, which you filled out after reading the texts in this unit.

Writing Prompt

Read the information in the box below.

> Reséndez creatively presented a historical narrative that explores the theme of meeting challenges in strange surroundings. Use this theme as a starting point to make your own connections with the literary selection of your choice.

This is the context for your literary analysis.

Think carefully about the following question.

> What does it mean to be a stranger in a strange land?

How might this Essential Question relate to other literary selections you have read?

Write a literary analysis explaining how your chosen selection connects with the idea of being a stranger in a strange land or unfamiliar surroundings.

Think about several selections and their possible connections to the theme before you make your final choice.

Be sure to—

❑ make a clear thesis statement or claim
❑ give reasons for your claim in a logical order
❑ support your claim with details and evidence from the text
❑ quote passages from the text
❑ end your analysis with a strong conclusion

Review these points as you write and again when you finish. Make any needed changes.

LEARNING MINDSET

Belonging Remind students that everyone in the classroom is part of a learning community. Everyone belongs, and everyone has something to contribute. When students team up with classmates for a peer review of their drafts, encourage them to take advantage of the different perspectives and suggestions each person can offer that might help them improve their writing.

① Plan

Plan your analysis carefully before you start to write. First, note the genre—literary analysis. Then, you need to settle on a particular topic which is reflected in the selection you choose and its Essential Question. For example, if you choose to analyze *La relación,* your topic might be about survival in a strange land. Next, gather ideas for the claim you will make in your thesis statement. What does the author of the literary text seem to convey about your topic? As you consider how you may support your claim, use any background reading or class discussions for ideas. Use the table below to help in your planning.

Literary Analysis Planning Table	
Genre	Literary analysis
Selection	
Possible topics	
Ideas for the thesis statement	
Ideas from background reading	
Ideas from class discussion	

Background Reading Review the notes you have taken in your Response Log that relate to the question, "What does it mean to be a stranger in a strange land?" Texts in this unit provide background reading that will help you formulate the thesis and evidence you will use in your literary analysis.

Go to **Writing Informative Texts: Developing a Topic** for help planning your literary analysis.

Notice & Note

From Reading to Writing

As you plan your literary analysis, apply what you've learned about signposts to your own writing. Remember that writers use common features, called signposts, to help convey their message to readers.

Think how you can incorporate **Quoted Words** into your literary analysis.

Go to the **Reading Studio** for more resources on **Notice & Note**.

Use the notes from your Response Log as you plan your literary analysis.

UNIT 1 RESPONSE LOG

---

① PLAN

Allow time for students to review the reading selections in Unit 1, including the Independent Reading selections, to select a piece to analyze. Once they have made their selection, have them complete the Literary Analysis Planning Table.

■ English Learner Support

Understand Academic Language Make sure students understand words and phrases used in the charts, such as *genre, topic,* and *claim.* Provide sentence frames and have students complete the frames with the correct word: *The ___ is the type of writing you will do. (genre) The ___ is the subject of the essay, or what the essay will be about. (topic) A ___ is the writer's position on an issue or problem. (claim)* Have students copy the sentences into their notebooks. Then work with students to fill in the blank sections of the chart, providing text that they can copy into their charts as needed.

NOTICE & NOTE

From Reading to Writing Remind students that they can use **Quoted Words** from the text they are analyzing as a way to support their claim. They can also quote scholars who have reviewed or analyzed the text. Remind students to format direct quotations correctly and to give credit to the source.

Background Reading As students plan their literary analyses, remind them to refer to the notes they took in the Response Log. They may also review the selections to find additional ideas to help them form a claim or find evidence.

TO CHALLENGE STUDENTS . . .

Voice and Tone Remind students that a writer's voice is the unique ways he or she uses word choice, sentence structure, and tone to express his or her personality or vision. Tone is the writer's attitude toward the subject. Have students begin thinking of ways they can make their voice "heard" by varying their sentence structure and using concrete nouns and figurative or persuasive language. Have students add a row to the chart so they can jot down words, figurative or persuasive language, or phrases they can include. When students begin drafting, they should establish a tone that helps persuade their readers.

Organize Your Ideas Have students work independently to outline their literary analyses. Encourage them to reread the selection they have chosen to analyze. As they do so, have them look for evidence that they can use to support their opinions. They may wish to underline passages they will want to quote in their essays.

Tell students to clearly state their claim or thesis statement. This is the point they wish to make in their analysis. Tell them that they should provide context or background information that will help their readers understand their position. Remind them that they must provide strong, logical reasons to support their claim. Remind students that a reason tells why their claim is valid. Each reason should be fully supported with relevant evidence. Evidence provides specific examples that illustrate each reason.

2 DEVELOP A DRAFT

Remind students to follow their graphic organizers as they draft their essays. Point out that they can still make changes if needed. To help students develop their first draft, review the following tips:

- The first sentence must grab the reader's attention, and the first paragraph must tell what the writer thinks and why the reader should care.

- To keep the reader interested, the body should begin with the strongest reasons, backed with supporting evidence. The body contains a logical progression of reasons and supporting evidence.

- Make sure that the connections between reasons and the central claim or thesis statement are clear.

- Organize evidence so that the topic of the essay will develop into a unified whole.

- Use appropriate transitions, varied syntax, and precise language to maintain a formal style.

- Provide a concluding statement that follows from the evidence presented.

■ English Learner Support

Write a Group Analysis Pair or group students of mixed proficiencies and have them work together to write a literary analysis essay. Or simplify the task by having them write an informative essay about the topic of being a stranger in a strange land. **ALL LEVELS**

Go to **Writing Informative Texts: Organizing Ideas** for more help.

Organize Your Ideas After you have gathered ideas from your planning activities, you need to organize them in a way that will help you draft your literary analysis. Choose your selection and topic. Next, you need to decide what claim you will make about the selection. Write your claim in a clear thesis statement. List reasons for your claim. Then, find specific evidence in the text that supports your opinion. Use the chart below to assist your organization.

Organizational Plan	
Genre	Literary analysis
Selection	
Topic	
Claim/Thesis Statement	
Reasons	1. 2. 3.
Evidence	

2 Develop a Draft

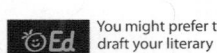 You might prefer to draft your literary analysis online.

Once you have completed your planning activities, you will be ready to begin drafting your literary analysis. Refer to your Graphic Organizer, your planning chart, and any notes you took as you studied the texts in this unit as a kind of map for you to follow as you write. Using an online writing application makes it easier to make changes or move sentences around later when you are ready to revise your first draft.

WHEN STUDENTS STRUGGLE . . .

Develop a Draft Students may struggle writing a claim and organizing their reasons and evidence. You may want to provide a sentence frame to help them get started with their claim: *I believe that ___ because ___.* Then have students review their reasons and think about which is the strongest and why it supports the claim. Remind students that this is not their final draft. The importance of writing a draft is to get ideas on a page. They can reorganize as needed in the next step. After students have finished their drafts, have them review the claim and revise it to make it more precise.

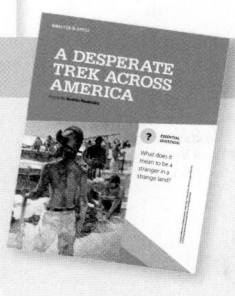

Use the Mentor Text

Making a Claim or Thesis Statement

A literary analysis will always contain a claim or thesis statement, usually near the beginning of your essay. The following paragraph from Reséndez's article "A Desperate Trek Across America" contains a thesis statement. Reséndez had already described the adventurers' plight and their initial attempt at survival. They have eaten their horses and used their firearms to build rafts. In the passage below, notice how Reséndez contrasts their previous sense of confidence with their current state.

> Like past conquistadors, Cabeza de Vaca and his men had relied on their breastplates, horses, and lethal weapons to keep the Indians at bay. Such overwhelming technological advantages meant they often did not even bother to negotiate. . . . <u>By sacrificing the very tools of their supremacy, they would now have to face the New World fully exposed to its perils and hold on only by their wits.</u>

The last sentence expresses the overall perspective of his article—it is similar to a thesis.

The rest of the author's article shows their struggle to survive only by their wits.

Apply What You've Learned After you've chosen the selection, the topic, and the point you want to make, begin your analysis with a clear thesis statement or claim. Tell your reader which selection you are writing about and what claim you are making. What interesting insight will you be conveying to your reader?

Offering Details and Evidence from the Text

When you analyze a literary selection, it is important to offer specific details and evidence from the text in order to support your thesis. Like Reséndez, you can use direct quotations to strengthen your thesis.

> Fifty men crowded aboard each craft, the fifth commanded by Cabeza de Vaca. "And so greatly can necessity prevail," he observed, "that it made us risk going in this manner and placing ourselves in a sea so treacherous, and without any one of us who went having any knowledge of the art of navigation."

Notice that Reséndez directly quotes Cabeza de Vaca to support his idea that the Spaniards were surviving on their wits alone.

Apply What You've Learned When you are giving reasons for your claim, be sure to offer details that will help convince your reader of your point. Try to cite direct evidence from the text whenever you make a main point. Use multiple pieces of evidence when possible.

Write a Literary Analysis   87

WHY THIS MENTOR TEXT?

"A Desperate Trek Across America" is an example of historical narrative writing, whereas literary analysis is a form of argumentative writing. Both genres make use of claims or thesis statements, reasons, and evidence. Use the instruction below to help students use the mentor text as a model for writing a claim or thesis statement and backing it up with evidence.

USE THE MENTOR TEXT

Making a Claim or Thesis Statement Tell students that the claim or thesis statement of a literary analysis is typically in the first paragraph and often at the end of the paragraph. Point out, however, that this narrative begins with a dramatic scene in the first paragraph, which ends with the sentence, "They were stranded in an alien continent." The thesis statement underlined here comes at the end of paragraph 4 of the Mentor Text and expands on that idea. It is followed by a paragraph explaining how these conquistadors ended up in that situation. Discuss the author's possible reasons for starting the article in the way he does. Then discuss how students can begin their essays and why they might start with this information.

Offering Details and Evidence from the Text Tell students that including direct quotations is a good way of providing evidence. The quotation on this page is from paragraph 6 of the Mentor Text. Have students locate other direct quotations in the essay. *(Other direct quotations appear in paragraphs 2, 7, 9, 11, and 14. The name the Spanish explorers gave their campsite in paragraph 1 is also enclosed in quotation marks.)* As they locate each one, ask them to discuss how it contributes to the author's narrative. What other specific details does Reséndez provide? Discuss how students can use their examples to help them incorporate quotations into their analyses.

 ## ENGLISH LEARNER SUPPORT

Use the Mentor Text Use the following supports with students at varying proficiency levels.

- Review the underlined claim. Ask yes/no questions to help students understand the author's claim: *Did the men give away all of their weapons and horses? (yes) Did the men negotiate, or talk to try to make a deal? (yes) Was giving away their tools a good idea? (no)* **SUBSTANTIAL/MODERATE**

- Have a volunteer read aloud the second passage. Ask students to restate the main idea of the passage and identify the evidence the author uses. Then have student pairs discuss what evidence they can use to support their claims. **LIGHT**

WRITING

3 REVISE

Have students answer each question in the Revision Guide to determine how they can improve their drafts. Tell students that this step in the writing process gives them a chance to take a critical look at what they have written to see if they have included all of the necessary elements of a literary analysis and have organized their ideas in a logical manner. Remind students that at this stage, they can move ideas, revise the claim, or add evidence if necessary.

With a Partner When students have completed drafts of their essays, have them exchange their papers with a partner and use the questions in the Revision Guide to evaluate the drafts and provide constructive feedback on at least three of the items. At this point in the writing process, tell students to focus on these major points, not on picky details such as commas. They will edit for grammar, usage, and spelling in the next stage. The purpose of feedback at the Revise stage is to help students determine if their readers will understand their ideas. Have students use their reviewers' feedback to add relevant facts, details, examples, or quotations that further develop their main points.

 WRITING TASK

Go to **Writing Informative Texts: Precise Language and Vocabulary** for help revising your analysis.

3 Revise

On Your Own Once you have written your draft, you'll want to go back and look for ways to improve your literary analysis. As you reread and revise, think about whether you have achieved your purpose. The Revision Guide will help you focus on specific elements to make your writing stronger.

Revision Guide		
Ask Yourself	**Tips**	**Revision Techniques**
1. Did I state my thesis, or claim, clearly and in an interesting way?	**Highlight** your thesis statement.	If necessary, add a sentence or two to clarify your thesis. **Add** an interesting example or related quotation to hook your reader.
2. Do I have enough reasons to support my thesis?	**List** your reasons.	**Read** your thesis statement aloud, followed by your reasons. Does your argument make sense so far? **Add** another reason if you can.
3. Are my thoughts logically organized?	**Outline** your main ideas and check for the most logical order.	**Reorder** ideas, if needed, so that each idea flows easily to the next one.
4. Did I include sufficient evidence from the text?	**Underline** any specific quotations or examples you used.	**Add** more details from the text to strengthen your claim.
5. Did I prove my point by the end of the analysis?	**Review** the main points and ideas of your analysis.	**Fill** in any noticeable gaps with more relevant details.
6. Is my conclusion strong?	**Highlight** your conclusion.	**Add** a statement that summarizes your ideas.

ACADEMIC VOCABULARY
As you conduct your **peer review**, be sure to use these words.

- ☐ adapt
- ☐ coherent
- ☐ device
- ☐ displace
- ☐ dynamic

With a Partner Once you and your partner have worked through the Revision Guide on your own, exchange analyses and evaluate each other's draft in a **peer review.** Focus on providing revision suggestions for at least three of the items mentioned in the chart. Explain why you think your partner's draft should be revised and make your specific suggestions.

When receiving feedback from your partner, listen attentively and ask questions to make sure you fully understand the revision suggestions.

ENGLISH LEARNER SUPPORT

Use Transitional Words Write the following transitions on the board: *first, second, then, after, later,* and *finally*. Explain that writers use transitional words to connect ideas and improve clarity and flow. Have students identify the transition in this passage:

"After five or six weeks, they slaughtered their last horse, then dragged the 15-ton rafts into the water. Fifty men crowded aboard each craft, the fifth commanded by Cabeza de Vaca." *(After, then)*

Then, have students work with a partner to take turns reading each other's drafts. Students should note where they can use transitions to connect ideas or improve clarity and flow. Have students revise their drafts based on the feedback. **MODERATE**

4 Edit

Once you have written and revised your literary analysis, it is time to edit for some of the finer details. Read through your draft carefully to ensure proper use of standard English conventions. Look for ways to improve your word choice and be sure to correct all spelling and grammatical errors.

Language Conventions

Active and Passive Voice As you edit, try to liven up your writing with verbs in the active voice as much as possible. Remember, a verb is in the **active voice** when its subject is performing the action. If the subject is the receiver of the action, the verb is in the **passive voice.** Notice that the verb in the following sentence is in the active voice because the subject is performing the action: *Cabeza de Vaca* **heard** *the surf.* The verb in this next sentence, however, is in the passive voice because the subject is being acted upon: *Four naked and unarmed outsiders* **were led** *by hundreds . . . of Indians.*

Note Reséndez's use of active and passive voice verbs in the chart. Notice how his frequent use of the active voice makes his narrative vibrant. When he uses the passive voice, he emphasizes what is happening to de Vaca and his men.

Active Voice	Passive Voice
• every third day they killed yet another draft animal	• Cabeza de Vaca and his companions were forced to cope
• they threw their crossbows	• They were fed, protected, and passed off
• they cut down trees, dragged them to the beach, lashed them together	• they had been . . . transformed by the experience

As you edit your literary analysis, find any verbs in the passive voice. Unless you need to emphasize the receiver of an action, or unless the doer is unknown, try to change the passive voice to active.

5 Publish

Finalize your literary analysis and choose a way to share it with your audience. Consider these options:

• Save your analysis as a writing sample to include with your college application.

• Research various literary journals and their guidelines for submission. Choose at least one to which you will submit your paper.

Go to **Active and Passive Voice** in the **Grammar Studio** to learn more.

---

4 EDIT

Suggest that students read their drafts aloud to assess how clearly and smoothly they have presented their ideas. Remind students to be on the lookout for errors in spelling, punctuation, and grammar as well as smooth transitions. Encourage them to combine short sentences and vary sentence structure to make their writing more interesting.

LANGUAGE CONVENTIONS

Active and Passive Voice Review the information about active and passive voice with students. Discuss the examples in the chart, asking students to identify the verb or verbs in each one. Then have students return to their literary analysis to see how often they have used the passive voice. Have them see if it would be better to rewrite those sentences in the active voice. Finally, have them choose two examples of the active voice and rewrite those sentences in the passive voice so that they can compare the strength and clarity of writing in each voice.

■ English Learner Support

Passive Voice Passive voice in Cantonese and Vietnamese does not require helping verbs. For example, students may write *The food done*. Help students understand that in English, helping verbs are required when writing in the passive voice—for example, *The food is done*. Remind students to use the active voice whenever possible, but if they do use the passive voice, a helping verb is necessary.

5 PUBLISH

In addition to print literary journals, there are many literary websites on the Internet that provide a viable alternative for publishing. Encourage students to read their classmates' published essays and to write comments about them. The authors can then respond to the comments.

 ENGLISH LEARNER SUPPORT

Revise the Essay Use the following supports with students at varying proficiency levels.

• Review the questions in the Revision Guide on page 88 to ensure students understand how to use the questions to revise their essays. Point out how the bolded words show what they should do as they read and revise. Suggest simplified ways to ask the questions as needed. Then have students work in pairs to revise their essays based on the questions in the chart. **MODERATE**

• Have students read the questions silently, noting the revisions they need to make. Then have them work with a partner to discuss their findings. Have students work individually to make the revisions they discussed. **LIGHT**

USE THE SCORING GUIDE

Allow students time to read the scoring guide and to ask questions about any words, phrases, or ideas that are unclear. Then have partners exchange final drafts of their literary analyses. Ask them to score their partner's analysis using the scoring guide. Each student should write a paragraph explaining the reasons for the score he or she awarded in each category.

 WRITING TASK

Use the scoring guide to evaluate your literary analysis.

Writing Task Scoring Guide: Literary Analysis

	Organization/Progression	Development of Ideas	Use of Language and Conventions
4	• The structure is clearly organized and appropriate. • The analysis includes a strong thesis statement; all ideas are related to the thesis. • Ideas are in logical order and connected with meaningful transitions.	• The development of ideas is effective, with credible and compelling analysis. • The analysis includes sufficient, relevant textual evidence. • The analysis contains thoughtful and engaging content; it demonstrates thorough understanding of the text.	• Word choice is precise and appropriate. • Sentences are strong and varied. • Command of spelling, punctuation, grammar, and usage conventions is strong.
3	• The structure is, for the most part, organized and appropriate. • The analysis includes a clear thesis statement; most ideas are related to the thesis, with only minor lapses in unity or focus. • Ideas are generally in logical order and connected with sufficient transitions.	• The development of ideas is fairly sound, with largely convincing analysis. • The analysis includes sufficient, relevant textual evidence, though at times this needs to be more complete. • The analysis provides thoughtful content; it demonstrates good understanding of the text.	• For the most part, word choice is clear and specific. • Sentences are reasonably varied. • Command of spelling, punctuation, grammar, and usage conventions is adequate.
2	• The structure is evident but is not always appropriate or clear. • The thesis statement is weak or unclear; some irrelevant information affects unity and focus. • Ideas are not always in logical order or connected with sufficient transitions.	• The development of ideas is minimal, with superficial analysis. • The analysis includes textual evidence which is sometimes irrelevant or inaccurate, or underdeveloped ideas. • The analysis reflects little thoughtfulness; it demonstrates limited understanding of the text.	• Word choice is general or imprecise. • Sentences are sometimes awkward. • Command of spelling, punctuation, grammar, and usage conventions is less than adequate.
1	• The structure is inappropriate to the purpose. • The thesis statement is missing, unclear, or illogical; the analysis contains irrelevant information. • The analysis demonstrates a weak progression of ideas; it includes repetition and wordiness, or lacks sufficient transitions.	• The development of ideas is weak, with ineffective analysis. • The analysis includes little if any relevant textual evidence; overall, there is vague development. • The analysis provides a vague or confused response to the text; it demonstrates lack of understanding of the text.	• Word choice is vague or limited. • Sentences are simplistic and awkward. • The writing shows little or no command of spelling, punctuation, grammar, and usage conventions.

Participate in a Panel Discussion

 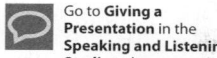

You will now adapt your literary analysis for presentation to your classmates. You also will listen to their presentations, ask questions to better understand their ideas, and help them improve their work.

Go to **Giving a Presentation** in the **Speaking and Listening Studio** to learn more.

1 Adapt Your Essay for Presentation

In the chart below, record specific ideas for your presentation, which you will use as part of a panel discussion.

Presentation Planning Chart		
Introduction	Begin with an interesting quotation or anecdote from the literary selection. State your **thesis** and the **title** and **author** of your selection. Clarify its connection to the question: What does it mean to be a stranger in a strange land?	
Major Points	Write main ideas on note cards to aid your memory. Make sure you present them in a logical order.	
Cite Evidence	Include quotations and details from the text to support your claim.	
Hold the Attention of Your Audience	Consider using a visual aid. Charts, photos, or short video clips make effective and memorable presentations. Prepare a handout outlining important ideas.	
Conclusion	Close your presentation with a strong restatement of your thesis and a memorable quote, illustration, or example from your literary selection.	

SPEAKING AND LISTENING

PARTICIPATE IN A PANEL DISCUSSION

Introduce students to the Speaking and Listening Task by discussing what makes reading an essay different from hearing someone speak about the same topic. Point out that readers can adjust their reading rate when the text presents difficult or complicated information. Readers can also reread passages they did not understand the first time. Listeners cannot adjust the reading rate or reread; however, they can ask questions after a presentation to clarify information or get additional information. Have students consider what they can do to make sure everyone in the audience understands the information they are presenting to their classmates.

1 ADAPT YOUR ESSAY FOR PRESENTATION

Have students review the ideas they recorded in the Presentation Planning Chart. Tell them they will need to reorganize their material to make their literary analysis essays clear to listeners, focusing on the most important points they analyzed in their essays. Then work with the class to list some general principles for presenting information orally. (*Examples: a simplified thesis statement, limited number of main points, accurate and well-chosen details, logical structure, and smooth transitions*) Discuss verbal and nonverbal techniques—such as eye contact, gestures, change in volume, and change in tone—to help students improve their presentations. Encourage students to use visuals, such as slides with titles or important bullet points, to help listeners follow the presentation.

② PRACTICE WITH A PARTNER

Review the information and tips with the class, ensuring that all the terms and ideas are clear. Remind students that the purpose of practicing their presentations is to gain useful feedback from their peers. Emphasize that it is common to feel nervous, so everyone should be as supportive and helpful as possible.

③ HOLD A PANEL DISCUSSION

Set aside time for all students to give their presentations. When everyone has finished, ask students to share their thoughts on how their classmates' feedback helped them improve their performance.

 For **speaking support** for students at varying proficiency levels, see the **Language X-Ray** on page 84B.

 **SPEAKING AND LISTENING TASK**

② Practice with a Partner

Once you've prepared your materials, practice with a partner to improve the following elements of your presentation:

❏ **Voice** Enunciate your words clearly and speak slowly and loudly enough so that everyone can hear you. Use your voice to show enthusiasm and emphasis.

❏ **Eye Contact** Try to let your eyes rest on each member of the audience at least once.

❏ **Facial Expression** Smile, frown, or raise an eyebrow to show your feelings or to emphasize points.

❏ **Gestures** Use natural gestures—shrugs, nods, or shakes of your head—to add meaning and interest to your presentation.

Provide and Consider Advice for Improvement

As you and your partner practice, take notes and provide helpful advice to each other. Consider ways to revise your presentation to make sure your points are clear and logically sequenced.

③ Hold a Panel Discussion

- Create panels of four or five people.
- The panelists will remain seated in front of the class to make their presentations.
- Choose one person from the class to be the moderator. He or she can open with a comment on the Essential Question that ties the discussion together.
- The moderator will introduce all of the speakers on the panel and then each panelist will present his or her analysis in turn.
- After all the members of the panel have made presentations, the moderator will recognize those audience members who wish to ask questions and the panelists will respond.
- If necessary, remind participants that discourse should be meaningful and respectful throughout the discussion.
- To conclude, the moderator can summarize the discussion.
- To evaluate the experience, audience members can engage in an informal follow-up discussion. Compare the panelists' analyses with the mentor text. How well did Reséndez show what it was like for the explorers and how they adapted to a strange land? How well did each panelist present his or her analysis?

As you work to improve your presentations, be sure to follow discussion rules:

❏ **Listen closely to each other.**
❏ **Don't interrupt.**
❏ **Stay on topic.**
❏ **Ask only helpful, relevant questions.**
❏ **Provide only clear, thoughtful, and direct answers.**

WHEN STUDENTS STRUGGLE . . .

Practice Presentations Tell students one way to practice a presentation is to record it and then watch the recording to note ways the presentation can be improved. Students can also practice in front of a mirror or in front of trusted friends or family members. Remind students to practice verbal and nonverbal techniques. For example, they can raise their voice to emphasize an important point, pause after important ideas, and speak clearly. Also note that they should maintain eye contact with the audience, stand up straight, avoid nervous movements, and use expressive body language, such as moving hands for emphasis.

Reflect on the Unit

By completing your literary analysis, you have created a writing product that pulls together and expresses your thoughts about the reading you have done in this unit. Now is a good time to reflect on what you have learned.

Reflect on the Essential Questions

• Review the four Essential Questions. How have your answers to these questions changed in response to the texts you read in this unit?

• What are some examples from the texts you read that show what it means to be a stranger in a strange land?

Reflect on Your Reading

• Which selections were the most interesting or surprising to you?

• From which selection did you learn the most about what it means to be a stranger in a strange land?

Reflect on the Writing Task

• What difficulties did you encounter while working on your literary analysis? How might you avoid them next time?

• What part of the literary analysis was the easiest and hardest to write? Why?

• What improvements did you make to your literary analysis as you were revising?

UNIT 1 SELECTIONS
• "The World on the Turtle's Back"
• "Balboa"
• "A Desperate Trek Across America"
• "Here Follow Some Verses Upon the Burning of Our House, July 10th, 1666"
• from *Of Plymouth Plantation*
• "Coming of Age in the Dawnland"

 LEARNING MINDSET

Self-Reflection Explain to students that an important part of developing a learning mindset is the ability to recognize strengths and weaknesses. As students reflect on the unit, encourage them to ask themselves these questions: *Did I ask questions if I needed help? Did I review my work for possible errors? Am I proud of the work I turned in?*

REFLECT ON THE UNIT

Have students reflect on the questions independently and write some notes in response to each one. Then have students meet with partners or in small groups to discuss their reflections. Circulate during these discussions to identify the questions that are generating the liveliest conversations. Wrap up with a whole-class discussion focused on these questions.

UNIT (2)

Instructional Overview and Resources

	Instructional Focus	Online  **Resources**
 **Unit Introduction** **Building a Democracy**	**Unit 2 Essential Question** **Unit 2 Academic Vocabulary**	**Stream to Start:** Building a Democracy **Unit 2 Response Log**

ANALYZE & APPLY

 **The Declaration of Independence** Public Document by Thomas Jefferson **Lexile 1320L**	**Reading** • Analyze Argumentative Texts • Analyze Text Structure **Writing:** Write an Argument **Speaking and Listening:** Present an Argument **Vocabulary:** Domain-Specific Words **Language Conventions:** Parallel Structure	🔊 **Audio** **Reading Studio:** Notice & Note **Close Read Screencast:** Modeled Discussion **Writing Studio:** Writing Arguments **Speaking and Listening Studio:** Giving a Presentation **Vocabulary Studio:** Specialized Vocabulary
MENTOR TEXT "Thomas Jefferson: The Best of Enemies" History Writing by Ron Chernow **Lexile 1340L**	**Reading** • Analyze Informational Texts • Analyze Structure **Writing:** Write an Essay **Speaking and Listening:** Present an Essay **Vocabulary:** Use Print and Digital Resources **Language Conventions:** Hyphenation	🔊 **Audio** **Reading Studio:** Notice & Note **Writing Studio:** Writing Informative Texts **Speaking and Listening Studio:** Giving a Presentation **Vocabulary Studio:** Using Reference Sources
 *American Experience:* **"Alexander Hamilton"** Video by PBS **Lexile N/A**	**Reading** • Determine Author's Purpose • Analyze Effectiveness of Digital Text **Writing:** Write an Essay **Speaking and Listening:** Present Your Ideas	🔊 **Audio** **Reading Studio:** Notice & Note **Writing Studio:** Writing Informative Texts **Speaking and Listening Studio:** Using Media in a Presentation
 **"A Soldier for the Crown"** Short Story by Charles Johnson **Lexile 1250L**	**Reading** • Analyze and Evaluate Plot • Analyze Literary Elements **Writing:** Write an Argumentative Essay **Speaking and Listening:** Have a Debate **Vocabulary:** Prefixes and Suffixes **Language Conventions:** Subject-Verb Agreement	🔊 **Audio** **Reading Studio:** Notice & Note **Writing Studio:** Writing Arguments **Vocabulary Studio:** Analyzing Word Structure **Grammar Studio:** Subject-Verb Agreement

SUGGESTED PACING: **30 DAYS**	Unit Introduction	The Declaration of Independence	Thomas Jefferson: The Best of Enemies	American Experience: Alexander Hamilton	A Soldier for the Crown
	1	2 3 4	5 6 7 8	9 10 11	12 13 14

English Learner Support	Differentiated Instruction	Online Ed Assessment
• Learn New Expressions • Build Background Knowledge	**When Students Struggle** • Create a Timeline	
• Text X-Ray • Use Cognates • Understand Text Structure • Use Synonyms • Oral Assessment • Sound Transfer • Language Convention	**When Students Struggle** • Categorize Supporting Details • Evidence	**Selection Test**
• Text X-Ray • Use Cognates • Compare and Contrast • Acquire Vocabulary • Identify Verb Tenses • Use Hyphens • Oral Assessment • Vocabulary Strategy • Language Conventions	**When Students Struggle** • Understand Structure **To Challenge Students** • Organize Ideas	**Selection Test**
• Text X-Ray • Acquire Vocabulary • Practice Content-Area Vocabulary • Oral Assessment	**When Students Struggle** • Organize Information	**Selection Test**
• Text X-Ray • Use Cognates • Practice Subject-Verb Agreement • Understand Sentence Fragments • Acquire Vocabulary • Analyze Details • Oral Assessment • Work with Prefixes and Suffixes • Practice Subject-Verb Agreement	**When Students Struggle** • Analyze Story Elements	**Selection Test**

from The Autobiography

On Being Brought from Africa to America/Sympathy

Letter to John Adams/*from* Lean In

Independent Reading

End of Unit

15 ⟩ 16 ⟩ 17 ⟩ 18 ⟩ 19 ⟩ 20 ⟩ 21 ⟩ 22 ⟩ 23 ⟩ 24 ⟩ 25 ⟩ 26 ⟩ 27 ⟩ 28 ⟩ 29 ⟩ 30 ⟩

UNIT 2 Continued

	Instructional Focus	Online  Resources

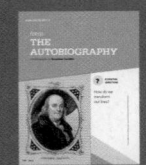

from *The Autobiography*
Autobiography by Benjamin Franklin
Lexile 1390L

Reading
• Monitor Comprehension
• Evaluate Print and Graphic Features

Writing: Write an Essay

Speaking and Listening: Discuss Autobiographies

Vocabulary: Latin Roots

Language Conventions: Standard English

 Audio

Reading Studio: Notice & Note

Writing Studio: Developing a Topic

Speaking and Listening Studio: Participating in Collaborative Discussions

Vocabulary Studio: Understanding Word Origins

Grammar Studio: Sentence Structure

COLLABORATE & COMPARE

"On Being Brought from Africa to America"
Poem by Phillis Wheatley
Lexile N/A

"Sympathy"
Poem by Paul Laurence Dunbar
Lexile N/A

Reading
• Analyze Speaker
• Analyze Theme
• Analyze Sound Devices and Voice

Writing: Write a Prose Adaptation

Speaking and Listening: Present a Theme Board

Audio

Reading Studio: Notice & Note

Writing Studio: Writing Narratives

Speaking and Listening Studio: Participating in a Collaborative Discussion

---

Collaborate and Compare

Reading: Compare Themes

Speaking and Listening Studio: Giving a Presentation

"Letter to John Adams"
Letter by Abigail Adams
Lexile 1180L

Reading
• Analyze Author's Purpose
• Analyze Language: Voice and Tone

Writing: Write a Letter

Speaking and Listening: Discuss with a Small Group

Vocabulary: Evaluating Nuances in Meaning

Language Conventions: Formal English

Audio

Reading Studio: Notice & Note

Writing Studio: Informative Texts

Speaking and Listening Studio: Participating in Collaborative Discussions

Vocabulary Studio: Denotation and Connotation

---

from **"Lean In"**
Essay by Sheryl Sandberg
Lexile 1000L

Reading
• Analyze Author's Purpose
• Analyze Language: Voice and Tone

Writing: Write an Essay

Speaking and Listening: Hold a Debate

Vocabulary: Analyze Meanings of Idioms

Language Conventions: Contested Usage

Audio

Reading Studio: Notice & Note

Writing Studio: Writing Narratives

Speaking and Listening Studio: Analyzing and Evaluating Presentations

Vocabulary Studio: Idioms, Slang, and Figurative Language

Collaborate and Compare

Reading: Compare Voice and Tone

Speaking and Listening Studio: Giving a Presentation

English Learner Support	Differentiated Instruction	Online Ed Assessment
• Text X-Ray • Use Cognates • Retelling • Acquire New Vocabulary • Language Conventions • Oral Assessment • Spanish Word Families • Connect Verbs	**When Students Struggle** • Evaluate Graphic Features • Reteaching: Evaluate Graphic Features **To Challenge Students** • Write Creatively	**Selection Test**
• Text X-Ray • Practice Vowel Sounds • Identify Thematic Elements • Interpret Poetry • Identify Contrasts • Oral Assessment • Identify Alliteration	**When Students Struggle** • Analyze Poetry • Reinforce Meaning	**Selection Test**
	When Students Struggle • Identify Themes	
• Text X-Ray • Use Cognates • Learn New Expressions • Analyze Ideas • Oral Assessment • Vocabulary Strategy • Language Conventions	**When Students Struggle** • Evaluate Author's Purpose • Reteaching: Analyze Voice and Tone **To Challenge Students** • Imitate Style	**Selection Test**
• Text X-Ray • Use Cognates • Make Verbs and Nouns from Adjectives • Oral Assessment • Understand Idioms • Language Conventions	**When Students Struggle** • Reteaching: Understand Purpose **To Challenge Students** • Understand Tone	**Selection Test**
• Ask Questions	**When Students Struggle** • Outline Ideas	

UNIT 2 Continued

Instructional Focus

Online **Resources**

INDEPENDENT READING

The Independent Reading selections are only available in the eBook.

Go to the Reading Studio for more information on NOTICE & NOTE.

"Speech to the Virginia Convention"
Speech by Patrick Henry
Lexile 990L

from *The United States Constitution: Preamble and Bill of Rights*
Public Document
Lexile 1580L

END OF UNIT

Writing Task: Write a Research Report

Speaking and Listening Task: Present a Research Report

Reflect on the Unit

Writing: Write a Research Report

Language Conventions: Dashes

Speaking and Listening: Present a Research Report

Unit 2 Response Log

Mentor Text: "Thomas Jefferson: The Best of Enemies"

Writing Studio: Writing Informative Texts

Speaking and Listening Studio: Giving a Presentation

Grammar Studio: Punctuation

English Learner Support	Differentiated Instruction	 Assessment

 from *Poor Richard's Almanack* Aphorisms by Benjamin Franklin **Lexile 520L**

 "Abigail Adams' Last Act of Defiance" History Writing by Woody Holton **Lexile 1250L**

 "Democracy" Poem by Langston Hughes

Selection Tests

- Language X-Ray
- Acquire Academic Language
- Write a Group Report
- Use Punctuation
- Build Academic Language Proficiency

When Students Struggle
- Cite Sources
- Proofread for Parenthetical Documentation
- Prepare and Practice

To Challenge Students
- Use Sources

Unit Test

DISCUSS THE QUOTATION

Tell students that Barbara Jordan was a pioneering legislator from Texas and a leader of the civil rights movement. She was the first African American woman elected to the Texas Senate, and the first woman elected by Texas to serve in the U.S. House of Representatives. She fought for voting rights for all citizens, including language minorities. She believed all citizens had the right to participate in our democracy and the responsibility to do so.

Ask students to read the quotation. Discuss the importance of sharing the responsibilities of democracy and what those responsibilities are. Have them support their answers with examples. Voting, being informed citizens, advocating for one's beliefs, and volunteering can all be discussed.

■ English Learner Support

Learn New Expressions Read aloud the quotation. Explain that the expression "upholding the common good" means making sure everyone is taken care of. Help students restate the quotation in simpler language. For example, "A nation is formed when people are willing to make sure everyone is taken care of." **MODERATE**

BUILDING A DEMOCRACY
THE REVOLUTIONARY PERIOD

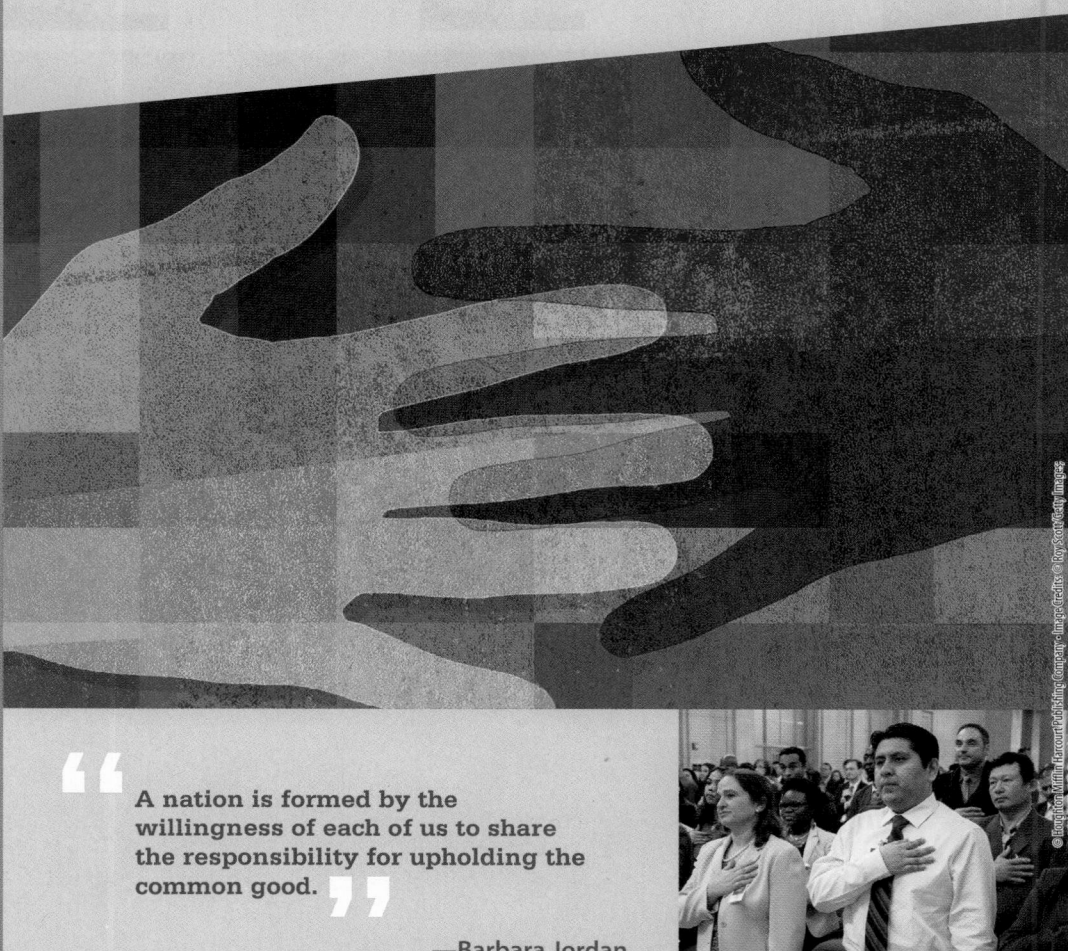

> " A nation is formed by the willingness of each of us to share the responsibility for upholding the common good. "
>
> —Barbara Jordan

94   Unit 2

LEARNING MINDSET

Curiosity Discuss the value of curiosity with your students and how it leads to learning. Curiosity can motivate learners to challenge themselves to learn new information and skills. Encourage students to think about what "Building a Democracy" means and how the pictures on the page relate to that. Then, ask students to share what they are curious about learning in this unit.

Discuss the **Essential Questions** with your whole class or in small groups. As you read Building a Democracy, consider how the selections explore these questions.

? ESSENTIAL QUESTION:
What does oppression look like?

Between 1763 and 1775 Parliament imposed a number of regulations and taxes on Britain's American colonies. The colonists reacted with pamphlets and acts of rebellion that eventually led to a declaration of independence and war. Ironically, many of the men who decried British oppression were themselves slaveholders. Even those who weren't saw no hypocrisy in denying women the same rights as men. Why might someone identify oppression in some instances and yet be blind to it in others?

? ESSENTIAL QUESTION:
How do we gain our freedom?

It is often necessary to fight to gain freedom. When Britain failed to respond to repeated requests from the colonists, their protests escalated. Britain retaliated by placing Massachusetts under the direct control of a military governor. Clashes between local militias and British soldiers became a war for independence that involved all 13 of Britain's American colonies. Why are people motivated to risk everything for freedom?

? ESSENTIAL QUESTION:
How can we share power and build alliances?

After gaining independence from England, the 13 former colonies had to come up with a plan for the future. They knew that they stood a better chance if they could work together, but how? Their first attempt at unification failed because the states did not want to relinquish any authority to a central government. The Constitution, however, provided a balance of power between federal and state governments. How does sharing power make partners stronger?

? ESSENTIAL QUESTION:
How do we transform our lives?

Americans had to make the transition from colonists to citizens of a new nation, one that was an experiment in democracy founded on Enlightenment ideals. Generation after generation, Americans have reinvented themselves as they confronted new opportunities and challenges. For more than two centuries, people from many lands have arrived with new customs and ideas. How does this experience change their lives and the lives of those they encounter?

© Houghton Mifflin Harcourt Publishing Company

Building a Democracy   95

Connect to the
ESSENTIAL QUESTIONS

Read aloud the Essential Questions and the paragraphs that follow them. Open the discussion of each idea by having students respond to the questions that conclude each paragraph.

? ESSENTIAL QUESTION:
What does oppression look like?

Discuss how different people view oppression in the same situation. Is it possible to see one kind of oppression and not another? Is it easier for the person being oppressed to see it while the person oppressing others cannot? Why or why not?

? ESSENTIAL QUESTION:
How do we gain our freedom?

Explain the meaning of *freedom* with students. What freedoms do they have that people in other countries may not? Are there any freedoms they don't have that they wish they did? What would they be willing to sacrifice to keep the freedoms they have or to gain others?

? ESSENTIAL QUESTION:
How can we share power and build alliances?

Encourage students to think about how the images on page 94 relate to this question. How can people with different goals and desires work together? What is power, and what does it take to share it? Ask students to give examples of sharing power from their own lives or from the world.

? ESSENTIAL QUESTION:
How do we transform our lives?

Discuss how the images on page 94 relate to this question. Does being open to new ideas help people transform their lives? Ask students to talk about times they transformed their lives. What did it take for them to be able to do it?

THE REVOLUTIONARY PERIOD

This essay provides students with a historical context for the Unit 2 selections. It presents a brief overview of the major political and social events of the time period the selections represent. The essay also provides an idea of the topics and themes prevalent in the culture of the time, which impacts the literature created during that period.

The Seven Years' War The French and Indian War in North America turned out to be one of the earliest conflicts in the global war between the British and the French colonial empires, pulling in many of their colonies and allies. The Seven Years' War was truly one of the first global conflicts, and in some ways it presaged the world wars of the 20th century.

Ideas of the Age Inspired by the ideas of the Enlightenment, people began to revolt against authoritarian governments headed by monarchs who claimed to have been chosen by God to lead. Instead, they attempted to use reason to set up new systems of democratic government that would be mutually agreed upon and designed to protect people's rights to gain knowledge, enjoy freedom, and experience happiness.

COLLABORATIVE DISCUSSION

Point out to students that after settling in North America for 250 years (since Christopher Columbus landed here in 1492), it took less than 20 years for the colonists to free themselves from European rule. Discuss how historical trends can simmer beneath the surface for long periods of time before finally coming to a head. What do they see simmering beneath the surface in the world today?

THE REVOLUTIONARY PERIOD

By the 1750s the colonies in North America had already begun to bind themselves together into a confederation. Even then, the colonists still thought of themselves as British subjects, despite a lack of representation in Parliament. The British government, in turn, protected the colonies from Native American and other European threats. After American colonial forces under George Washington tried unsuccessfully to drive the French from the Ohio River valley, Britain sent reinforcements, whom colonists helped support. By the time the French and Indian War ended in 1763, Britain controlled all the land east of the Mississippi River. But when the British tried to recover the costs of the war by taxing the colonists, they rebelled.

As the colonists moved toward independence, they drew on Enlightenment ideals, which questioned previously accepted truths about strongly centralized governments. People began to question traditional authority, eventually leading the colonists to break from Britain's control and embrace democracy. American colonial writers such as Benjamin Franklin, Thomas Paine, and Thomas Jefferson adapted the ideals of the European Enlightenment to their own circumstances. In time, this new philosophy combined with a wave of religious enthusiasm called the Great Awakening. Preachers such as Jonathan Edwards called upon colonists to rededicate themselves to the original Puritan vision of sinless living, hard work, thrift, and responsibility, thus rekindling in the geographically and culturally diverse colonists a desire to be religious and ethical role models for all.

As the colonists began to question their relationship with Great Britain, many gifted minds turned to political writing. Between 1763 and 1783, about two thousand inexpensive pamphlets were published, reaching thousands of people and stirring debate and action. *Common Sense* by Thomas Paine was a key pamphlet that helped move the colonists to revolution. Paine's Enlightenment ideas were combined with the Puritan belief that America was destined to be a model of freedom to the world. Thomas Jefferson also wrote pamphlets, but his great contribution to American government, literature, and the cause of freedom throughout the world is the Declaration of Independence, in which he eloquently articulated the natural law that would govern America. This natural law is

COLLABORATIVE DISCUSSION
In a small group, review the timeline and discuss which literary or historical events had the most impact.

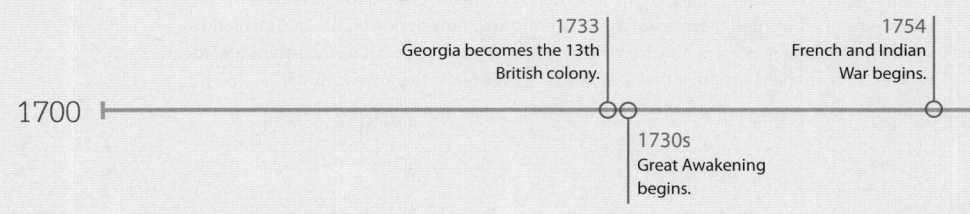

1733
Georgia becomes the 13th British colony.

1754
French and Indian War begins.

1700

1730s
Great Awakening begins.

96   Unit 2

© Houghton Mifflin Harcourt Publishing Company

 ## ENGLISH LEARNER SUPPORT

Build Background Knowledge Remind students that the American colonies were originally part of Britain. The colonists fought a war, the American Revolution, to become an independent country—the United States. To help students understand the essay, provide them with these definitions. Have students write the definitions in their notebooks.

- *original Puritan vision:* sinless living, hard work, thrift, responsibility
- *thrift:* spend very little money; not wasting money or resources

- *pamphlets:* short texts given out to spread information or ideas
- *stirring:* start; encourage
- *articulated:* said; expressed; explained
- *govern:* in charge; set laws; control
- *framework:* a system that organizes
- *enslavement:* the action of making a person a slave

ALL LEVELS

the idea that people are born with rights and freedoms and that it is the function of government to protect those freedoms.

Jefferson's Declaration marked the beginning of the colonies' independence, but it was the adoption of the Constitution of the United States of America in 1788 that created the lasting framework for an independent government and cemented the historical and literary legacies of its founders. Ideological debates over the scope and nature of federal power raged throughout the republic's early years. For example, in 1803 President Thomas Jefferson stirred controversy by purchasing the vast Louisiana Territory west of the Mississippi River from France, thus doubling the size of the United States. Jefferson, who normally favored a limited federal government, took this bold step even though the Constitution gave him no explicit authority to do so.

During the second half of the 18th century, the religious grip of the Puritans on New England began to relax as a new Yankee secular society emerged. In the early Colonial period, Puritan literary achievements were great, although they decried fiction and drama. As the Puritans saw their spiritual world view challenged by the political views of Enlightenment thinkers, even poetry sometimes examined political and social themes. Among the finest is the work of former slave Phillis Wheatley. In her poems and letters, Wheatley wrote of the "natural rights" of African Americans and pointed out the discrepancy between the colonists' "cry for freedom" and their enslavement of fellow human beings.

RESEARCH
What about this historical period interests you? Choose a topic, event, or person to learn more about. Then, add your own entry to the timeline.

The Declaration of Independence Thomas Jefferson drew on different sources when crafting the Declaration of Independence. Many of the individual colonies had already drafted their own statements of independence, including his home colony of Virginia. The pamphlets of Thomas Paine and others also served as inspiration, as did the writings of philosopher John Locke who believed that good governments must rule only by the consent of the people. Decades earlier, a Christian pastor from Massachusetts, John Wise, had fought against taxation without representation and declared all men equal. In the end, Jefferson only had 17 days to write the Declaration of Independence, and Congress made many changes to its final form before it was signed.

Puritans in America The Puritans had dominated much of religious and cultural life in the two centuries before the American Revolution, and many of their beliefs and practices remain influential today. The Puritans believed that all citizens should be educated to read and write in order to understand the Bible and the laws of the land. One of the most renowned works of literature produced during the colonies' first few centuries was *The Pilgrim's Progress*, written by the Puritan John Bunyan. Some of the Puritans' strict rules about personal behavior, such as not practicing other religions, celebrating Christmas, and forbidding gambling, dancing, and the going to the theater, began to relax as the Age of Independence began, while other of their rules took much longer to come to an end.

RESEARCH

To learn more about their chosen topic, encourage students to search for primary sources from the historical period. Have students choose excerpts from a source to present to the class.

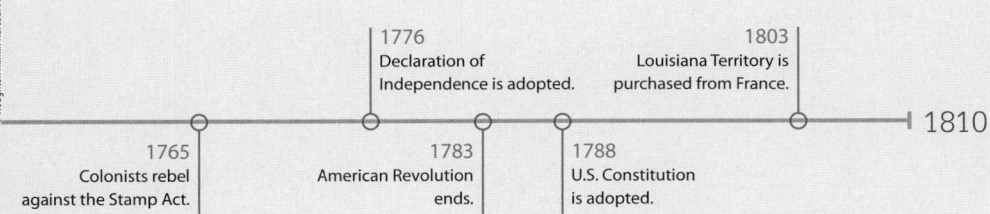

| 1776 | 1803 |
| Declaration of Independence is adopted. | Louisiana Territory is purchased from France. |

1810

| 1765 | 1783 | 1788 |
| Colonists rebel against the Stamp Act. | American Revolution ends. | U.S. Constitution is adopted. |

Building a Democracy   97

© Houghton Mifflin Harcourt Publishing Company • Image Credits: © larry1235/Shutterstock

WHEN STUDENTS STRUGGLE...

Create a Timeline If students have difficulty understanding the events in the essay, have them refer to the timeline and answer questions, such as *Was the Declaration of Independence adopted before or after the American Revolution ended? Why is that order of events significant?*

Created Equal? Even at the time of the American Revolution, there were many voices calling out for the rights of women and African Americans. Abigail Adams and Phyllis Wheatley were two of the more prominent women speaking out. Even Thomas Jefferson, though a slave owner himself, included language in his original draft of the Declaration of Independence calling for the ending of slavery. Congress removed this language so as not to alienate supporters of slavery. In fact, slavery was outlawed by the British long before it became illegal in the United States. The fight for freedom contained contradictions and paradoxes. To this day, whenever people claim to be fighting for freedom, two important questions to ask are: whose freedom, and the freedom to do what?

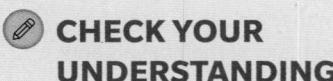 **CHECK YOUR UNDERSTANDING**

Have students answer the questions independently.

Answers:

1. *B*

2. *H*

3. *A*

If students answer any question incorrectly, have them reread the text to confirm their understanding.

Another voice calling for the rights of all citizens was Abigail Adams, whose husband John became the nation's second president. In letters written while the couple was apart, Adams encouraged her husband to include the rights of women in the nation's founding documents. Wheatley, Adams, and other women writers joined the Puritans and patriots who came before them to give us an understanding of the dreams and values that shaped our nation. All contributed their voices and ideals to building the metaphorical "city upon a hill" that Puritan preacher John Winthrop first envisioned as a beacon to all in 1630.

CHECK YOUR UNDERSTANDING

Choose the best answer to each question.

1 Why did the American colonists rebel against Britain?

  A They didn't want to defend territory Britain had captured from the French.

  B They didn't want to pay the costs of the French and Indian War.

  C Britain tried to outlaw slavery in the colonies.

  D Britain tried to keep Jefferson from buying the Louisiana Territory.

2 What type of publication became the major means of spreading political ideas?

  F Books

  G Almanacs

  H Pamphlets

  J Newspapers

3 What kind of writing did the Puritans disapprove of?

  A Drama

  B Poetry

  C Sermons

  D Letters

ACADEMIC VOCABULARY

Academic Vocabulary words are words you use when you discuss and write about texts. In this unit, you will learn the following five words:

☑ contrary   ☐ founder   ☐ ideological   ☐ publication   ☐ revolution

Study the Word Network to learn more about the word **contrary.**

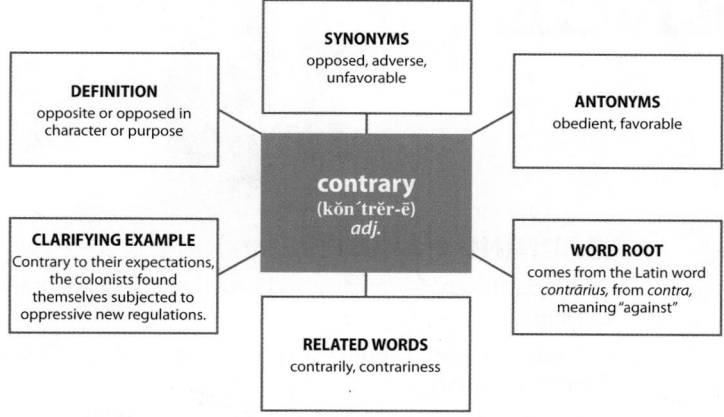

DEFINITION
opposite or opposed in character or purpose

SYNONYMS
opposed, adverse, unfavorable

ANTONYMS
obedient, favorable

contrary
(kŏn´trĕr-ē)
adj.

CLARIFYING EXAMPLE
Contrary to their expectations, the colonists found themselves subjected to oppressive new regulations.

WORD ROOT
comes from the Latin word *contrārius,* from *contra,* meaning "against"

RELATED WORDS
contrarily, contrariness

Write and Discuss Discuss your completed Word Network with a partner, making sure to talk through all of the boxes until you both understand the word, its synonyms, antonyms, and related forms. Then, fill out a Word Network for the remaining four words. Use a dictionary or online resource to help you complete the activity.

    Go online to access the Word Networks.

RESPOND TO THE ESSENTIAL QUESTIONS

In this unit, you will explore four different **Essential Questions** about 18th-century literature and other related texts. As you read each selection, you will gather your ideas about one of these questions and write about it in the **Response Log** that appears on page R2. At the end of the unit, you will have the opportunity to write a **research report** related to one of the Essential Questions. Filling out the Response Log after you read each text will help you prepare for this writing task.

    You can also go online to access the Response Log.

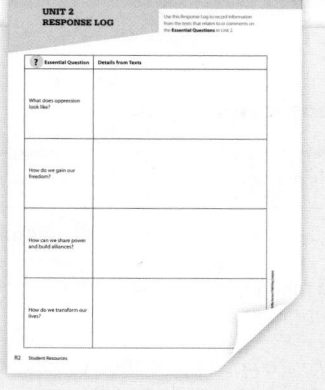

UNIT 2
RESPONSE LOG

© Houghton Mifflin Harcourt Publishing Company

ACADEMIC VOCABULARY

Have students complete Word Networks for the remaining four vocabulary words. Encourage them to include all the categories shown in the completed Word Network if possible, but point out that some words may not have clear synonyms or antonyms.

contrary (kŏn´trĕr-ē) *adj.* opposite or opposed in character or purpose. (Spanish cognate: *contrario*)

founder (foun´dər) *n.* someone who sets up, establishes, or provides the basis for something. (Spanish cognate: *fundador*)

ideological (ī-dē-ə-lŏj´ĭ-kəl) *adj.* based on ideas, beliefs, or doctrines. (Spanish cognate: *idealógico*)

publication (pŭb-lĭ-kā´shən) *n.* the act of making public in printed or electronic form; the product of this act. (Spanish cognate: *publicación*)

revolution (rĕv-ə-loō´shən) *n. the overthrow and replacement of a government, often through violent means.* (Spanish cognate: *revolución*)

RESPOND TO THE ESSENTIAL QUESTIONS

Direct students to the Unit 2 Response Log. Explain that students will use it to record ideas and details from the selections that help answer one of the Essential Questions. When they work on the Writing Task at the end of the unit, each Response Log will help them think about what they have read and make connections between the texts.

THE DECLARATION OF INDEPENDENCE

Public Document by Thomas Jefferson

GENRE ELEMENTS
PUBLIC DOCUMENTS

Explain to students that public documents are widely available, and are meant to reach (and usually influence) a large audience. Public documents typically do not involve elements of storytelling such as climax, character, and plot, but instead deal with the communication of a message.

LEARNING OBJECTIVES

- Analyze the characteristics and structure of argumentative writing.
- Conduct research about laws passed by Great Britain prior to the Declaration.
- Write an essay explaining how effective you think Jefferson's argument was.
- Present Jefferson's ideas like a lawyer in a court case.
- Use semantic maps to analyze vocabulary words.
- Discuss *parallelism* as a tool in Jefferson's argument.
- **Language** Discuss a text using the key term *reason*.

TEXT COMPLEXITY

Quantitative Measures	The Declaration of Independence	Lexile: 1320L
Qualitative Measures	**Ideas Presented** Much is explicit but moves to some implied meaning; requires some inferential reasoning.	
	Structures Used Primarily explicit; may vary from a simple chronological order; largely conventional.	
	Language Used Implied meanings; allusive, figurative, or ironic language, perhaps archaic or formal; complex sentence structure.	
	Knowledge Required More complexity in theme; experiences may be less familiar to many. Cultural or historical references may make heavier demands.	

Online Ed

RESOURCES

- Unit 2 Response Log
- Selection Audio
- Cold Read Screencast: Modeled Discussion
- Reading Studio: Notice & Note
- Level Up Tutorial: Taking Notes and Outlining
- Writing Studio: Writing Arguments
- Speaking and Listening Studio: Giving a Presentation
-  Vocabulary Studio: Specialized Vocabulary
- The Declaration of Independence Selection Test

SUMMARIES

English

The Declaration of Independence was the document that unified the thirteen American colonies against the Kingdom of Great Britain, forming the United States of America. It was originally drafted by Thomas Jefferson, and was ratified with no dissenting votes on July 4th, which is now known as Independence Day. The Declaration both lists the colonial grievances against Great Britain and details Jefferson's idea of basic human rights.

Spanish

La Declaración de Independencia fue el documento que unificó las trece colonias americanas en contra del reino de Gran Bretaña, formando los Estados Unidos. Thomas Jefferson redactó la declaración original y la ratificaron, sin votos en contra, el 4 de Julio, día que se conoce como el Día de la Independencia. La declaración enumera las quejas formales en contra de Gran Bretaña y detalla las ideas de Jefferson sobre los derechos humanos básicos.

 ## SMALL-GROUP OPTIONS

Have students work in small groups and pairs to read and discuss the selection.

Activating Academic Vocabulary

- Provide a list of academic vocabulary words, such as *contrary, founder, ideological, publication,* and *revolution.*
- Read a section of the text (20 lines or so), and show students how the academic vocabulary words can inform their discussion of the section.
- Have students read a different section in pairs, and use their academic vocabulary words to discuss the new section.

Three-Minute Review

- Pause at any time during reading, lecture, or discussion.
- Set a timer for three minutes.
- Direct students to work independently to reread material, review class notes, and write clarifying questions.
- Solicit clarifying questions from students. Then, hold a brief discussion and clarification.

Text X-Ray: English Learner Support
for the Declaration of Independence

Use the Text X-Ray and the supports and scaffolds in the Teacher's Edition to help guide students at different proficiency levels through the selection.

INTRODUCE THE SELECTION
DISCUSS ARGUMENTATIVE TEXTS

Explain that the Declaration of Independence is an argumentative text. It was written to present reasons why the areas of North America colonized by Britain wanted to be independent, or free, from British rule. This document marks the start of the new country known as the United States. The language choices present an argument for independence. The Declaration also uses arguments about natural rights—the ideas that people are born with certain rights that cannot be taken away.

Provide these definitions of the elements of argumentative texts: thesis—central idea; evidence—facts, examples, and quotations that support the thesis; appeal—request for help; call to action—request for the audience to do something. Have students discuss with a partner these questions: What do you think the thesis of this document will be? What kind of evidence would support a declaration of independence? Ask volunteers to share their ideas with the class.

CULTURAL REFERENCES

The following words or phrases may be unfamiliar to students:

- *candid world* (paragraph 2): honest people
- *erected* (paragraph 12): put into place
- *imposing* (paragraph 19): to force something to occur
- *tyrant* (paragraph 30): someone who rules over people in an oppressive way
- *native justice* (paragraph 31): the belief that people are born with a desire for equality
- *independent states* (paragraph 33): states working alone but in tandem with a centralized government

LISTENING

Identify an Argument

Remind students that an argument is writing that expresses a position on an issue or problem and supports it with reasons and evidence. As students listen to a rereading of the text, have them focus on what arguments Jefferson makes and why he makes them.

Use the following support with students at varying proficiency levels:

- Read aloud the last two sentences of paragraph 2. Ask yes/no questions to assess students' understanding of Jefferson's argument. For example: *Does Jefferson argue that the King has been unfair to the colonists?* (Yes) **SUBSTANTIAL**
- Read aloud the last two sentences of paragraph 2. Ask: *What is Jefferson's argument?* (The King has been unjust and has harmed the colonists.) *Why does Jefferson give facts?* (to prove his argument) **MODERATE**
- Read aloud paragraphs 2–5. After reading the text, ask students to identify Jefferson's argument. Then, ask students what reasons Jefferson gives to support his argument. (*The King refused to grant just laws, stopped the colonists from passing their own laws, and passed laws without representation.*) **LIGHT**

PLAN

SPEAKING

Identify Key Points

Focusing in on the core argument will help students understand the text. Restating or paraphrasing the key ideas will help students understand the text and acquire and reinforce vocabulary.

Use the following supports with students at varying proficiency levels:

- Echo read paragraph 13. Ask students what the king kept in the colonies. Provide sentence frames: *The King kept _____ in the colonies. Colonists did not _____ with this.* **SUBSTANTIAL**
- Read aloud the beginning of paragraph 2, through ". . . of happiness." Have students identify the key ideas by completing these frames orally: *One key idea is that everyone has _____.* (rights) *Another key idea is that three important rights are _____, _____, and _____.* (life, liberty, happiness) **MODERATE**
- Call on students to read aloud the first half of paragraph 2. Then, ask guiding questions about the key ideas such as: *Can you explain the word* Creator? *What is one key idea?* (Jefferson thinks everyone has the right to life, liberty, and pursuit of happiness.) **LIGHT**

READING

Use Context to Determine Meaning

Remind students that it is important to understand each word in an argument. When readers come across unfamiliar words, they use the context or ask for help to determine the meaning.

Use the following supports with students at varying proficiency levels:

- Work with students to read aloud paragraphs 12 and 13. Have students circle and read familiar words. Have students underline unfamiliar words and ask for help. **SUBSTANTIAL**
- Read aloud from paragraph 33, from "these United Colonies . . . British crown." Have students read along silently. Have students underline unfamiliar words. Work with students to find context clues to help them determine the meaning of unfamiliar words. **MODERATE**
- Have student pairs read paragraph 30. Have students note any unfamiliar words and use the context to determine the meaning. Have students use a dictionary to confirm the meaning. **LIGHT**

WRITING

Write an Argument

Read the Create and Present prompt on Student Edition p. 109. Tell students that they will write an essay to evaluate if Jefferson's argument was effective, or successful.

Use the following supports with students at varying proficiency levels:

- Summarize Jefferson's argument. Have students agree on an opinion statement (effective/not effective). Work with students to find one detail to support the opinion. Use the opinion and detail to draft a paragraph on the board. Have students copy it into their notebooks. **SUBSTANTIAL**
- Summarize Jefferson's argument. Have pairs of students review the text to look for examples and work together to draft their essays. Provide sentence frames to help them get started: *I think Jefferson's argument is effective/not effective because _____. An important detail he gives is _____.* **MODERATE**
- Have a volunteer summarize Jefferson's argument. Then, have partners work together to write a draft giving an opinion about the effectiveness of Jefferson's writing. **LIGHT**

? Connect to the
ESSENTIAL QUESTION

The Declaration of Independence was written by men who knew that signing it would be seen as an act of treason by England. To gain their freedom, the founders wrote a declaration to assert their freedom and ultimately went to war.

THE DECLARATION OF INDEPENDENCE

Public Document by **Thomas Jefferson**

? *ESSENTIAL QUESTION:*

How do we gain our freedom?

100   Unit 2

© Houghton Mifflin Harcourt Publishing Company • Image Credits: © John Parrot/Stocktrek Images/Getty Images

QUICK START

The Declaration of Independence represented the views of American patriots on what constituted good government and oppressive government. What are your ideas about good government and bad government?

ANALYZE ARGUMENTATIVE TEXTS

Thomas Jefferson wrote this text to justify to the British the colonies' move toward independence. It is an **argumentative text** with the following characteristics:

- a clear, arguable **thesis,** or central idea

- **reasons** and **evidence** that support the thesis

- logical and emotional **appeals** to the audience

- a convincing **conclusion** that sums up the important ideas

- a **call to action** that encourages the audience to do something

As you read, identify the thesis, types of support, appeals, conclusion, and call to action in the Declaration of Independence.

ANALYZE TEXT STRUCTURE

The power of the Declaration of Independence comes not just from *what* it says, but also from *how* Jefferson says it. Jefferson's style is reflected in the **structure** of the work. The Declaration can be divided into four sections: a preamble, or forward, that announces the reason for the document; a declaration of people's fundamental rights; the presentation of evidence and responses to **counterarguments,** or claims against Jefferson's proposal; and a conclusion that states the desired action. Jefferson also uses **syntax**—the arrangement of words to express and emphasize ideas. The structure and syntax convey a determined tone and reflect the purpose of his argument.

Use the chart to record key ideas in each section of the text.

GENRE ELEMENTS: PUBLIC DOCUMENT

- provides information of public interest or concern

- may include attempts at persuasion using sophisticated language

- includes government documents, speeches, signs, and rules and regulations

PREAMBLE	DECLARATION OF RIGHTS	EVIDENCE	CONCLUSION/CALL TO ACTION

TEACH

QUICK START

After students have read the Quick Start question, have them share their thoughts on government with a partner. Encourage students to give reasons for their opinions and to listen to their partner's opinions with an open mind, as this can be a contentious topic.

ANALYZE ARGUMENTATIVE TEXTS

Remind students that the Declaration of Independence was a bold action and the leaders of the revolution were putting their life on the line. With that in mind, encourage students to think about why each of the characteristics of argumentative texts would have been important for the Declaration of Independence. For instance, if Jefferson had not provided clear evidence to support his thesis, what would have happened? Review the characteristics of an argumentative text. Remind students that reasons explain why the thesis is valid. Evidence can include facts, quotations, examples, statistics, or personal experiences, among other things. Emotional appeals may include language with strong connotations such as appeals to fear, pity, or vanity.

ANALYZE TEXT STRUCTURE

Tell students that text structure is a main way writers of argumentative texts can create tone for their readers and reflect the author's purpose. Often, timing and buildup can be the main difference between a powerful call to action and one that leaves people uncertain. Encourage students to look for places where the text structure intensifies the text or makes it more persuasive.

TEACH

CRITICAL VOCABULARY

Point out to students that all these words are derived from Latin words.

Answers:

1. *established*

2. *abdicated*

3. *invested*

4. *affected*

■ English Learner Support

Use Cognates Tell students that all of the Critical Vocabulary words have Spanish cognates: *establish/ establecer; invest/invertir; affect/afectar; abdicate/abdicar.*
ALL LEVELS

LANGUAGE CONVENTIONS

Remind students that parallelism emphasizes the ideas in the writing. The repeated construction emphasizes ideas of equal importance. As students read, encourage them to ask themselves why Jefferson uses parallelism and what he is trying to achieve with it in each instance.

✏ ANNOTATION MODEL

Remind students of the annotation ideas such as underlining important details and circling words that signal how the text is organized. Point out that they may follow this suggestion or use their own system for marking up the selection in their write-in text. They may want to color-code their annotations by using highlighters. Their notes in the margin may include questions about ideas that are unclear or topics they want to learn more about.

 **GET READY**

CRITICAL VOCABULARY

established	affected	invested	abdicated

To see how many Critical Vocabulary words you already know, use them to complete the sentences.

1. The U.S. Constitution _____ our current form of government.

2. Due to ill health, the king _____ the throne and was succeeded by his oldest child.

3. In a republican government, elected officials are _____ with the authority of office by voters.

4. Representatives of people who would be most _____ by the new law testified about its provisions to the congressional committee.

LANGUAGE CONVENTIONS

Parallel Structure Parallelism, or parallel structure, is the use of similar grammatical constructions to express ideas that are closely related or equal in importance. Constructions may include phrases, clauses, or sentences. Parallel structures are an important element in a writer's syntax. Consider this example from the Declaration of Independence:

> . . . laying its foundation on such principles, and organizing its powers in such form . . .

Jefferson uses two phrases with parallel structure. The use of parallel phrases makes it clear that the two actions are of equal importance.

ANNOTATION MODEL   NOTICE & NOTE

As you read, notice how Jefferson presents his ideas. Mark words or phrases that reveal key ideas, present evidence, or move the argument forward. In the model, you can see one reader's notes about the Declaration of Independence.

> When, in the course of human events, it becomes necessary for one people to dissolve the political bands which have connected them with another, and to assume, among the powers of the earth, the separate and equal station to which the laws of nature and of nature's God entitle them, a decent respect to the opinions of mankind requires that they should declare the causes which impel them to the separation.

Jefferson states up front what he thinks must happen.

Jefferson will offer reasons for the action he proposes.

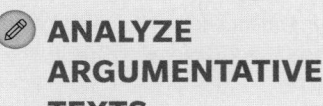

BACKGROUND

Thomas Jefferson *(1743–1826) was one of the most accomplished of our nation's founders. He was minister to France after the American Revolution and the third president of the United States. However, more important than his titles was his vision of liberty and self-government, eloquently expressed in the Declaration of Independence. Drafted by Jefferson, the Declaration was debated by the Second Continental Congress and adopted July 4, 1776. The Declaration begins with an assertion of the Enlightenment ideas of "self-evident" truths of liberty and human rights.*

THE DECLARATION OF INDEPENDENCE
Public Document by Thomas Jefferson

SETTING A PURPOSE

As you read, pay attention to the evidence Jefferson uses to support the idea of American independence.

1 When, in the course of human events, it becomes necessary for one people to dissolve the political bands which have connected them with another, and to assume, among the powers of the earth, the separate and equal station to which the laws of nature and of nature's God entitle them, a decent respect to the opinions of mankind requires that they should declare the causes which impel them to the separation.

2 We hold these truths to be self-evident:—That all men are created equal; that they are endowed by their Creator with certain unalienable rights; that among these are life, liberty, and the pursuit of happiness. That, to secure these rights, governments are instituted among men, deriving their just powers from the consent of the governed; that, whenever any form of government becomes destructive of these ends, it is the right of the people to alter or to abolish it, and to institute a new government, laying its foundation on such principles, and organizing its powers in such form, as to them shall seem most likely to effect their safety

Notice & Note

Use the side margins to notice and note signposts in the text.

ANALYZE ARGUMENTATIVE TEXTS

Annotate: Mark words in paragraph 2 that state Jefferson's thesis.

Cite Evidence: What details in paragraph 2 present justification for his thesis? Explain.

BACKGROUND

Have students read the information about the Second Continental Congress, Jefferson's decision to draft the Declaration of Independence, and the other foundational documents from the time of the Revolutionary War. The original purpose of the Second Continental Congress was to negotiate for the rights of the colonies with Britain, but its members gradually came to believe that the colonies would have to become an independent nation. The Second Continental Congress made the New England military forces that had already been fighting the British an official army and named George Washington its commander-in-chief. It also issued and borrowed money, formed a postal service, and created a navy.

SETTING A PURPOSE

Direct students to use the Setting a Purpose prompt to focus their reading.

ANALYZE ARGUMENTATIVE TEXTS

The first sentence of paragraph 2 is perhaps the most famous line of the Declaration of Independence. However, this line is not the thesis. Tell students that to find the thesis, they should think about what Thomas Jefferson is claiming and what he wants readers to know. Encourage them to ask themselves what Thomas Jefferson particularly wants readers to know. (**Answer:** *Governments exist to secure people's rights to life, liberty, and the pursuit of happiness.*)

CLOSE READ SCREENCAST

Modeled Discussion In their eBooks, have students view the Close Read Screencast in which readers discuss and annotate paragraph 2, Jefferson's recommendations about if and when to consider rejecting an established government.

As a class, view and discuss the video. Then have students pair up to do an independent close read of paragraph 31. Students can record their answers on the Close Read Practice PDF.

 Close Read Practice PDF

TEACH

ANALYZE TEXT STRUCTURE

Tell students that Jefferson varies the rhythm and content of the words that follow them. Discuss with students how the addition of clauses keeps the reader interested by varying the rhythm and adding information about the king's actions. (**Answer:** *They emphasize how many things the king has done to take away the rights of the colonists.*)

■ English Learner Support

Understand Text Structure Point out the phrase *He has* in paragraph 3. Then, read aloud paragraphs 3–6, emphasizing the repeated phrase. Because students are taught to vary sentence structure, students may not understand this use of repetition. Explain that Jefferson repeats the phrase to emphasize how many things the king has done. This structure strengthens his argument. Read aloud paragraphs 7–15, or have a volunteer read them. Then, ask students to explain in their own words why this repetition helped them understand Jefferson's argument. (*I can easily keep track of the argument because he starts each paragraph with the same phrase. I can just concentrate on what the King has done.*) **MODERATE**

For **listening support** for students at varying proficiency levels, see the **Text X-Ray** on page 100C.

CRITICAL VOCABULARY

establish: Jefferson warns against changing an existing government and establishing a new one without good reason.

ASK STUDENTS to explain the advantage of maintaining an established government. (*An established government ensures stability and order.*)

104 Unit 2

 **NOTICE & NOTE**

establish
(ĭ-stăb´lĭsh) *v.* to formally set up; institute.

ANALYZE TEXT STRUCTURE
Annotate: Circle the repeated phrase in paragraphs 3–10. Underline the phrases in paragraphs 6 and 7 that give reasons for the King's behavior.

Draw Conclusions: How do the examples of Jefferson's syntax strengthen his argument?

and happiness. Prudence, indeed, will dictate that governments long **established** should not be changed for light and transient causes; and, accordingly, all experience hath shown that mankind are more disposed to suffer, while evils are sufferable, than to right themselves by abolishing the forms to which they are accustomed. But, when a long train of abuses and usurpations, pursuing invariably the same object, evinces a design to reduce them under absolute despotism,[1] it is their right, it is their duty, to throw off such government, and to provide new guards for their future security. Such has been the patient sufferance of these colonies; and such is now the necessity that constrains them to alter their former systems of government. The history of the present King of Great Britain[2] is a history of repeated injuries and usurpations, all having, in direct object, the establishment of an absolute tyranny over these States. To prove this, let facts be submitted to a candid world.

3 He has refused his assent to laws[3] the most wholesome and necessary for the public good.

4 He has forbidden his Governors to pass laws of immediate and pressing importance, unless suspended in their operation till his assent should be obtained; and, when so suspended, he has utterly neglected to attend to them.

5 He has refused to pass other laws for the accommodation of large districts of people, unless these people would relinquish the right of representation in the legislature—a right inestimable to them, and formidable to tyrants only.

6 He has called together legislative bodies at places unusual, uncomfortable, and distant from the depository of their public records, for the sole purpose of fatiguing them into compliance with his measure.

7 He has dissolved representative houses repeatedly, for opposing, with manly firmness, his invasions on the rights of the people.

8 He has refused, for a long time after such dissolutions, to cause others to be elected; whereby the legislative powers, incapable of annihilation, have returned to the people at large for their exercise; the State remaining, in the meantime, exposed to all dangers of invasion from without, and convulsions within.

9 He has endeavored to prevent the population[4] of these States; for that purpose obstructing the laws for the naturalization of foreigners; refusing to pass others to encourage their migration hither, and raising the conditions of new appropriations of lands.

---

[1] **despotism** (dĕs´pə-tĭz əm): government by a ruler with unlimited power.
[2] **the present King of Great Britain:** George III, who reigned from 1760 to 1820.
[3] **refused his assent to laws:** Laws passed in the colonial legislative assemblies needed the king's approval; sometimes it took years for laws to be approved or rejected.
[4] **to prevent the population:** to keep the population from growing.

104 Unit 2

 ENGLISH LEARNER SUPPORT

Use Synonyms Explain that a synonym is a word with a meaning similar to that of another word. Tell students that when they come across unfamiliar words, they can use a thesaurus to find synonyms that they are more familiar with. Substituting synonyms can help them better understand the text. Read aloud paragraph 2. Point out the following words and their synonyms: *prudence—wisdom; abolish—end; usurpations—wrongful actions; evinces—shows; design—plan; invariably—always; security—safety; candid—honest.* Have students work in pairs to find the words in the paragraph and then read each sentence once using the synonym and once as written. **MODERATE**

10   He has obstructed the administration of justice, by refusing his assent to laws for establishing judiciary powers.

11   He has made judges dependent on his will alone for the tenure of their offices,[5] and the amount and payment of their salaries.

12   He has erected a multitude of new offices, and sent hither swarms of officers to harass our people and eat out their substance.[6]

13   He has kept among us, in times of peace, standing armies, without the consent of our legislatures.

14   He has **affected** to render the military independent of, and superior to, the civil power.

15   He has combined with others to subject us to a jurisdiction foreign to our constitutions,[7] and unacknowledged by our laws; giving his assent to their acts of pretended legislation:

16   For quartering large bodies of armed troops among us;

17   For protecting them, by a mock trial, from punishment for any murders which they should commit on the inhabitants of these States;

18   For cutting off our trade with all parts of the world;

19   For imposing taxes on us without our consent;

20   For depriving us, in many cases, of the benefits of trial by jury;

21   For transporting us beyond the seas, to be tried for pretended offenses;

22   For abolishing the free system of English laws in a neighboring province,[8] establishing there an arbitrary government, and enlarging its boundaries, so as to render it at once an example and fit instrument for introducing the same absolute rule into these colonies;

23   For taking away our charters, abolishing our most valuable laws, and altering, fundamentally, the forms of our governments;

24   For suspending our own legislatures, and declaring themselves **invested** with power to legislate for us in all cases whatsoever.

25   He has **abdicated** government here, by declaring us out of his protection, and waging war against us.

26   He has plundered our seas, ravaged our coasts, burnt our towns,[9] and destroyed the lives of our people.

27   He is at this time transporting large armies of foreign mercenaries to complete the works of death, desolation, and tyranny, already begun with circumstances of cruelty and perfidy scarcely paralleled in the most barbarous ages, and totally unworthy the head of a civilized nation.

---

[5] **the tenure of their offices:** their job security.

[6] **eat out their substance:** use up their resources.

[7] **subject us . . . our constitutions:** Parliament had passed the Declaratory Act in 1766, stating that the king and Parliament could make laws for the colonies.

[8] **a neighboring province:** the province of Quebec, which at the time extended south to the Ohio River and west to the Mississippi.

[9] **plundered . . . our towns:** American seaports such as Norfolk, Virginia, had already been shelled.

affect
(ə-fĕkt´) *v.* to cause or influence.

LANGUAGE CONVENTIONS
Annotate: Mark examples of parallelism that Jefferson uses in paragraphs 16–24.

Analyze: How does this structure strengthen Jefferson's argument against the king?

invest
(ĭn-vĕst´) *v.* to grant or endow.

abdicate
(ăb´dĭ-kāt) *v.* to relinquish or cede responsibility for.

The Declaration of Independence   105

WHEN STUDENTS STRUGGLE...

Categorize Supporting Details Explain to students that when a text contains many supporting details, they can help themselves understand and remember the details by jotting them down in an organized way. Have students group different ways the king frustrated the colonists by using a four-column chart with the headings *Military Actions, Administrative Actions, Legal Actions,* and *Economic Actions.*

 For additional support, go to the **Reading Studio** and assign the following [LEVEL UP] **Level Up Tutorial: Taking Notes and Outlining**.

LANGUAGE CONVENTIONS

Invite a volunteer to read this section aloud so that students can hear the aural effect. (**Answer:** *It emphasizes how many offensive things he has done to the colonists.*)

For **speaking and reading support** for students at varying proficiency levels, see the **Text X-Ray** on page 100D.

CRITICAL VOCABULARY

affect: Because of King George's actions and decisions, British soldiers were not accountable to the colonies. He affected the soldiers to be above the government.

ASK STUDENTS how it would affect the colonists to have the military be superior to the civil authorities. (*They cannot defend themselves against military injustice and overreach.*)

invest: King George invested, or granted, Quebec with the rights to govern parts of the colonies.

ASK STUDENTS to explain why Jefferson rejects the idea that Quebec was invested by Great Britain with the power to legislate for the colonies. (*Quebec can't be invested with this power because Great Britain cannot grant something it does not rightfully have.*)

abdicate: Jefferson argues that the king should abdicate, or give up, his right to govern the colonies.

ASK STUDENTS how King George abdicated his role as king. (*by being a despotic king who did things including increasing the military's power, deporting colonists, and destroying their land*)

The Declaration of Independence   **105**

NOTICE & NOTE

J·O·I·N, or D·I·E.

✎ ANALYZE TEXT STRUCTURE

Tell students that anticipating and answering a **counterargument**—an argument, based on a counterclaim, that opposes another argument—is an advanced strategy in argumentative texts. (**Answer:** *The colonists have patiently and repeatedly petitioned for help. They have not been rash.*)

ANALYZE TEXT STRUCTURE
Annotate: Mark the sentence in paragraph 30 that describes the response of the colonists to the king's actions.

Infer: How does Jefferson use the colonists' actions to rebut the counterargument that declaring independence is a rash decision?

28   He has constrained our fellow citizens, taken captive on the high seas, to bear arms against their country, to become the executioners of their friends and brethren, or to fall themselves by their hands.

29   He has excited domestic insurrection amongst us,[10] and has endeavored to bring on the inhabitants of our frontiers the merciless Indian savages, whose known rule of warfare is an undistinguished destruction of all ages, sexes, and conditions.

30   In every stage of these oppressions we have petitioned for redress,[11] in the most humble terms; our repeated petitions have been answered only by repeated injury. A prince whose character is thus marked by every act which may define a tyrant is unfit to be the ruler of a free people.

31   Nor have we been wanting in our attentions to our British brethren. We have warned them, from time to time, of attempts by their legislature to extend an unwarrantable jurisdiction over us. We have reminded them of the circumstances of our emigration and settlement here. We have appealed to their native justice and magnanimity; and we have conjured them, by the ties of our common kindred, to disavow these usurpations, which would inevitably interrupt our connections and correspondence.

32   They, too, have been deaf to the voice of justice and of consanguinity.[12] We must, therefore, acquiesce in the necessity which denounces our separation; and hold them, as we hold the rest of mankind, enemies in war, in peace friends.

33   We, Therefore, the Representatives of the United States of America, in General Congress assembled, appealing to the Supreme Judge of the world for the rectitude[13] of our intentions, do, in the name and by the authority of the good people of these colonies,

---

[10] **excited . . . amongst us:** Lord Dunmore, the royal governor of Virginia, had encouraged slaves to rise up and rebel against their masters.
[11] **redress:** the correction of a wrong; compensation.
[12] **deaf to . . . consanguinity:** The British have ignored pleas based on their common ancestry with the colonists.
[13] **rectitude:** morally correct behavior or thinking.

APPLYING ACADEMIC VOCABULARY

☐ **contrary**   ☐ **founder**   ☑ **ideological**   ☐ **publication**   ☑ **revolution**

Write and Discuss Have students turn to a partner to discuss the following questions. Direct students to include the academic vocabulary words *ideological* and *revolution* in their responses. Ask volunteers to share their responses with the class.

- Which of Jefferson's reasons for **revolution** is most persuasive to you?
- Do you think Jefferson's **ideological** reasons are still persuasive today? Why or why not?

solemnly publish and declare, that these United Colonies are, and of right ought to be, Free and Independent States; that they are absolved from all allegiance to the British crown, and that all political connection between them and the state of Great Britain is, and ought to be, totally dissolved; and that, as free and independent states, they have full power to levy war, conclude peace, contract alliances, establish commerce, and to do all other acts and things which independent states may of right do. And, for the support of this declaration, with a firm reliance on the protection of Divine Providence, we mutually pledge to each other our lives, our fortunes, and our sacred honor.

ANALYZE ARGUMENTATIVE TEXTS

Annotate: Mark the call to action in paragraph 33.

Analyze: How does Jefferson's use of "ought" in this call to action relate to his thesis?

CHECK YOUR UNDERSTANDING

Answer these questions before moving on to the **Analyze the Text** section on the following page.

1 On what did Jefferson base his belief that all men are created equal?

A Their rights as British citizens

B The will of the British king

C The laws of nature and God

D Traditions of the colonies

2 What is Jefferson's main argument against remaining connected to Great Britain?

F The colonies are ready to be on their own.

G The British king has been an unjust tyrant.

H The colonists no longer wish to obey British law.

J Other countries expect this of the colonists.

3 What is the conclusion of Jefferson's argument?

A The colonists must separate from Britain.

B The colonists should give Britain another chance.

C Britain had always been good to the colonists.

D Britain should overthrow its king.

The Declaration of Independence   107

ANALYZE ARGUMENTATIVE TEXTS

Remind students that a call to action does not always have to be direct. A call to action can also be text which implies action, as in this case. When Jefferson says that the colonies are free and should be free, he is implying that the colonists should, and even must, take steps to achieve their freedom. (**Answer:** *Jefferson says that citizens ought to throw off bad government.*)

CHECK YOUR UNDERSTANDING

Have students answer the questions independently.

Answers:

1. *C*

2. *G*

3. *A*

If they answer any questions incorrectly, have them reread the text to confirm their understanding. Then, they may proceed to ANALYZE THE TEXT on page 108.

ⓔ ENGLISH LEARNER SUPPORT

Oral Assessment Use the following questions to assess students' comprehension and speaking skills.

1. Jefferson believed that all men are created _____. *(equal)*

2. Did the King of England treat the colonists fairly? *(No.)*

3. Jefferson says the colonists should be free from _____. *(from Britain's rule)*
SUBSTANTIAL

APPLY

ANALYZE THE TEXT

Possible answers:

1. **DOK 4:** *The use of the phrase "to secure these rights" directly connects the purpose of government to the unalienable rights identified in the first sentence. The use of two short phrases together "it is their right, it is their duty" adds emphasis to what follows.*

2. **DOK 4:** *Jefferson's list of self-evident truths—all are created equal, all have unalienable rights, governments should secure those rights—support his thesis that people have a right to overturn a government that doesn't respect their rights.*

3. **DOK 4:** *The list of complaints emphasizes the grievances and the effects of the King's actions on the colonies. It supports the claim that the colonies are justified in eradicating tyranny.*

4. **DOK 4:** *The repetition of the word "all" and the use of "totally dissolved" contribute to the power and persuasiveness of the document. These words help create a tone that is direct, confident, and determined.*

5. **DOK 3:** *Jefferson begins with his purpose, provides evidence in support of this purpose (ways the King has mistreated the colonists, unfair laws the King has imposed on the colonies, ways the colonists have tried to solve problems with England without success), and concludes that the United States now considers itself a free nation. Jefferson's call to action includes a reference to reliance on God and a pledge of everyone's lives, fortunes, and honor.*

RESEARCH

Remind students that websites that are not peer reviewed are not reliable sources for research. Many good sources besides ones ending in .gov will end in .edu.

Extend Tell students that, in addition to the documents suggested, they may also consider looking up information on the British point of view at the time of the colonial issue.

 **RESPOND**

ANALYZE THE TEXT

Support your responses with evidence from the text. 📑 NOTEBOOK

1. **Analyze** How does the syntax in paragraph 2 add to the persuasiveness of Jefferson's argument? Cite at least two examples in your response.

2. **Analyze** A **logical appeal** is a method of argument based on evidence and reasons. Choose an example of a logical appeal in the Declaration and explain how it supports the thesis.

3. **Evaluate** Jefferson's list of complaints makes up the largest part of his structure. How does this structure contribute to his argument? How does it support his thesis?

4. **Evaluate** In the final paragraph, what tone is created by Jefferson's use of the word *all* several times, as well as the phrase *totally dissolved?*

5. **Draw Conclusions** How does the structure of Jefferson's argument support his purpose? Consider elements such as evidence and a call to action in your response.

RESEARCH

RESEARCH TIP
When researching information about the United States, its history, its government, and its founders, websites that end in .gov are often very useful. Also, a search of "acts leading to American Revolution" will turn up lists of laws to which colonists objected.

The colonists' differences with Great Britain had grown over a long period of time. Research the laws Britain passed in the years before the Declaration of Independence and the colonists' responses. Then, complete the chart.

QUESTION	ANSWER
What did the Stamp Act do?	*The Stamp Act of 1765 required American colonist to pay a tax on every piece of printed paper they used.*
What was required by the Quartering Act?	*The Quartering Act of 1765 required the colonies to provide barracks for British soldiers.*
What did the laws the colonists called the Intolerable Acts do?	*The Intolerable Acts were passed in retaliation for the Boston Tea Party. They became a rallying cry and helped unite the colonies, resulting in the First Continental Congress convening in 1774.*

Extend Research another document about colonial relations with Great Britain written at the time, such as Thomas Paine's *Common Sense.* Compare its ideas to those presented in the Declaration of Independence and discuss what the second text adds to your understanding of the historical period.

WHEN STUDENTS STRUGGLE...

Evidence Encourage students to use an outline as a way to analyze an argumentative text. Have them revisit the chart on p. 101. For each section, have them write whether the section is mostly a thesis or evidence for a thesis. If the section is a thesis, have them state the thesis. If the section is evidence, have them evaluate whether the evidence is persuasive or not and state reasons why.

 For additional support, go to the **Reading Studio** and assign the following 𝐋𝐄𝐕𝐄𝐋 **Level Up Tutorial: Evidence.**

CREATE AND PRESENT

Write an Argument Write an essay in which you evaluate the effectiveness of Jefferson's argument. Review your notes before you begin.

❏ Decide if you think Jefferson successfully supported his thesis, and then defend or challenge his claims.

❏ Carefully choose details and examples from the text that support your opinion.

❏ Outline your points in a logical structure with smooth transitions.

❏ Cite supporting examples and passages accurately.

❏ Add rhetorical devices such as repetition and parallelism to strengthen your argument.

Present an Argument Imagine you are trying to convince an audience to adopt Jefferson's ideas. Prepare a script of an argument that you will present to the class.

❏ Practice your presentation, reading it over a few times so you are comfortable presenting it.

❏ Use eye contact with your audience to engage their attention.

❏ Use facial expressions and appropriate gestures to emphasize key points.

 Go to **Writing Arguments** in the **Writing Studio** for help.

Go to **Giving a Presentation** in the **Speaking and Listening Studio** for help.

RESPOND TO THE ESSENTIAL QUESTION

 How do we gain our freedom?

Gather Information Review your annotations and notes on the Declaration of Independence. Then, add relevant information to your Response Log. As you determine which information to include, think about:

• how Jefferson defines freedom
• why he saw freedom as important
• what the last paragraph suggests about the cost of freedom

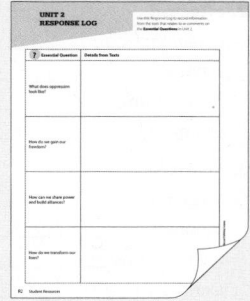

ACADEMIC VOCABULARY
As you write and discuss what you learned from the document, be sure to use the Academic Vocabulary words. Check off each of the words that you use.

❏ **contrary**
❏ **founder**
❏ **ideological**
❏ **publication**
❏ **revolution**

CREATE AND PRESENT

Write an Argument Encourage students to test the success of defense or challenge by thinking of the other point of view. Just as Jefferson anticipated counterarguments, what can they do to answer those who disagree?

 For **writing support** for students at varying proficiency levels, see the **Text X-Ray** on page 100D.

Present an Argument Have students think about who their audience would have been back in Jefferson's time. What would the concerns of Jefferson's contemporaries be? Have them do research to better address their argument to their audience.

RESPOND TO THE ESSENTIAL QUESTION

Allow time for students to add details from the Declaration of Independence to their Unit 2 Response Logs.

CRITICAL VOCABULARY

Possible answers:

1. *meaning: to have formally set up*
   synonyms: instituted, created, founded
   related forms: An establishment is the act of establishing something formally or a place of business and its structures and staff.
   example: The president established a commission to study the problem.

2. *meaning: to cause or influence*
   synonyms: involved, changed
   related forms: An affectation is a behavior that has been adopted and is contrary to a person's fundamental character.
   example: The powerful hurricane affected a wide area.

3. *meaning: to have granted or endowed*
   synonyms: provided, empowered
   related forms: An investiture is the act or formal ceremony of conferring the authority and symbols of a high office.
   example: The board of directors invested the new university president with the powers of the office.

4. *meaning: to relinquish or cede responsibility for*
   synonyms: renounced, resigned, stepped down from
   related forms: An abdication is the act of abdicating.
   example: The people were shocked when the king abdicated.

RESPOND

WORD BANK
established
affected
invested
abdicated

CRITICAL VOCABULARY

One way to explore a new word is to use a semantic map, which identifies the definition of the term, related words, examples of the word in use, and synonyms of the word. Study the web below, which provides a semantic map for the word *instituted* from paragraph 2 of the Declaration of Independence.

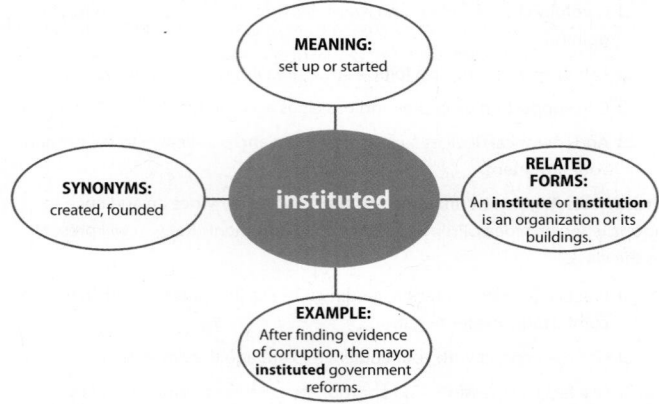

MEANING:
set up or started

SYNONYMS:
created, founded

instituted

RELATED FORMS:
An **institute** or **institution** is an organization or its buildings.

EXAMPLE:
After finding evidence of corruption, the mayor **instituted** government reforms.

Practice and Apply Fill in the blanks to create a semantic map for each Critical Vocabulary word. Use print or online references to check your work.

1. established
   meaning: _____
   synonyms: _____
   related forms: _____
   example: _____

2. affected
   meaning: _____
   synonyms: _____
   related forms: _____
   example: _____

3. invested
   meaning: _____
   synonyms: _____
   related forms: _____
   example: _____

4. abdicated
   meaning: _____
   synonyms: _____
   related forms: _____
   example: _____

 ENGLISH LEARNER SUPPORT

Sound Transfer Note that short *e* as in the first sound in *established* may be a difficult sound for speakers of Spanish, Hmong, Cantonese, Haitian Creole, and Korean, as the sound either does not exist in the language, does exist but is pronounced somewhat differently, or is likely to be confused with another sound. Be sure to pronounce such words for students while they can see the letters. Then, have them repeat chorally.   **SUBSTANTIAL/MODERATE**

VOCABULARY STRATEGY:
Domain-Specific Words

In the Declaration of Independence, Jefferson uses the Critical Vocabulary word *abdicated*. This word is more common in works of political science than in other writing. The field of political science, the study of government, has **domain-specific words** that identify types of government or government functions or describe the way a government acts. Context clues, knowledge of Greek and Latin roots, and a dictionary or other reference work can help establish the meaning of a word. Dictionaries also show related forms of the word, such as *legislative*, *legislature*, and *legislate*.

Practice and Apply Work with a partner to investigate the meaning, **etymology** (word origin), and related forms of these domain-specific words. Use a dictionary or other reference work to help you.

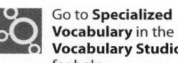 Go to **Specialized Vocabulary** in the **Vocabulary Studio** for help.

1. sovereign
2. despotism
3. tyranny
4. govern
5. oligarchy
6. republic
7. democracy
8. legislative
9. executive
10. judicial

LANGUAGE CONVENTIONS:
Parallel Structure

Jefferson makes frequent use of the rhetorical device of parallelism in the Declaration of Independence. **Parallelism** is the use of similar grammatical constructions to express ideas that are closely related or equal in importance. It helps emphasize important ideas.

The chart shows examples of parallel structure from the Declaration of Independence. Try reading each passage aloud. Note how the parallelism creates rhythm and helps emphasize similarities among related ideas.

STRUCTURE	EXAMPLE
Parallel phrases	He has plundered our seas, ravaged our coasts, burnt our towns, and destroyed the lives of our people.
Parallel clauses or sentences	We have warned them, from time to time, of attempts by their legislature to extend an unwarrantable jurisdiction over us. We have reminded them of the circumstances of our emigration and settlement here. We have appealed to their native justice and magnanimity; and we have conjured them, by the ties of our common kindred, to disavow these usurpations, which would inevitably interrupt our connections and correspondence.

Practice and Apply Review the essay you wrote for your Create and Present activity in which you evaluated Jefferson's ideas. Incorporate parallel structure into your essay by grouping related ideas together using parallel construction.

 ENGLISH LEARNER SUPPORT

Language Conventions Use the following supports with students at varying proficiency levels: Past tense verbs are a backbone of many of Jefferson's parallel structures. Have students find past tense verbs in the text and copy them. **SUBSTANTIAL**

Engage students to find some past tense verbs in parallel verb structures, and change their tenses, keeping the parallel structure. **MODERATE**

Challenge students to write their own parallel clauses with a past tense verb in each one. **LIGHT**

VOCABULARY STRATEGY:
Domain-Specific Words

Possible answers:

1. *meaning: a supreme ruler, especially a monarch; synonyms: ruler, monarch; related forms: sovereignty*

2. *meaning: the exercise of absolute power, especially in a cruel and oppressive way; synonyms: dictatorship, tyranny; related forms: despot*

3. *meaning: cruel and oppressive government or rule; synonyms: oppression, dictatorship; related forms: tyrant*

4. *meaning: exercise sovereign authority over; synonyms: rule, oversee; related forms: government, governance*

5. *meaning: small group of people having control of a country, organization, or institution; synonyms: government by a few; related forms: oligarch*

6. *meaning: a state in which supreme power is held by the people and their elected representatives; synonyms: representative government; related forms: republican*

7. *meaning: a system of government by the whole population or all the eligible members of a state; synonyms: elective government; related forms: democrat, democratic*

8. *meaning: having the power to make laws; synonyms: law-making, governmental; related forms: legislature, legislate, legal*

9. *meaning: having the power to put plans, actions, or laws into effect; synonyms: administrative, decision-making; related forms: execute, executor*

10. *meaning: of, by, or appropriate to a court or judge; synonyms: legal; related forms: judge*

LANGUAGE CONVENTIONS:
Parallel Structure

Review parallel structure with students. Have them find another instance of parallelism in the Declaration besides the examples given. Illustrate the use of parallelism by having them rewrite their examples in a non-parallel structure. Discuss which they find stronger and why. Have the class state how the various kinds of parallel structures are different and similar. Encourage students to realize that parallel phrases are simpler than parallel sentences and less subtle. This means their rhythm is more obvious and pronounced, and the equal ideas are more directly compared.

Practice and Apply Students should revise the essay they wrote and incorporate parallel structure.

THOMAS JEFFERSON: THE BEST OF ENEMIES

History Writing by Ron Chernow

This writing serves as a **mentor text**, a model for students to follow when they come to the Unit 2 Writing Task: Write a Research Report.

GENRE ELEMENTS
HISTORY WRITING

Tell students that **history writing** presents the reader with information about historical events or people. History writing always includes relevant facts and dates, while also offering further historical context and explaining the lasting significance of the events or people being highlighted. The information in the writing can come from a variety of sources, including primary sources that are directly connected to what took place.

LEARNING OBJECTIVES

- Analyze the structure and purpose of informative texts.
- Research the *Federalist Papers* by Alexander Hamilton.
- Write an essay comparing the visions of Hamilton and Jefferson.
- Present an essay to highlight key points from the comparison.
- Use print and digital sources to clarify multiple meanings.
- Understand the use of hyphens.
- **Language** Compare and contrast ideas using terms such as *but, however,* or *whereas.*

TEXT COMPLEXITY

Quantitative Measures	Thomas Jefferson: The Best of Enemies	Lexile: 1340L
Qualitative Measures	**Ideas Presented** Requires weighing multiple perspectives; some analysis of bias and author's motivations.	
	Structures Used More complex, multiple perspectives may be presented; more deviation from chronology.	
	Language Used Vocabulary not defined at point of use; mostly Tier II and III words; metaphor (rather than similes) used more; multiple technical words may be used in one sentence.	
	Knowledge Required More complex problems; experiences may be less familiar to many; cultural or historical references.	

RESOURCES

 Online **Ed**

- Unit 2 Response Log
- 🔊 Selection Audio
- 📖 Reading Studio:
  Notice & Note
- 🔲 Level Up Tutorial:
  Compare-Contrast Organization
- 📰 Writing Studio:
  Writing an Informative Text
- 💬 Speaking and Listening Studio:
  Giving a Presentation
- 🔬 Vocabulary Studio:
  Using Reference Sources
- ☑️ "Thomas Jefferson: The Best of Enemies" Selection Test

SUMMARIES

English

Thomas Jefferson and Alexander Hamilton were integral figures in the founding of the United States of America. Despite their shared goal of freedom from the British, the two had very different opinions on how the country should be governed after its liberation. Jefferson firmly believed that power belonged in the hands of the individual states, while Hamilton was a passionate proponent of a strong federal government. The two ultimately paved the way for major arguments that continue to resound throughout American politics today.

Spanish

Thomas Jefferson y Alexander Hamilton fueron figuras esenciales en la fundación de los Estados Unidos de América. A pesar de su meta compartida de libertad de los británicos, tenían opiniones muy diferentes sobre cómo se gobierna un país luego de su liberación. Jefferson creía firmemente que el poder pertenecía a los estados individuales, mientras que Hamilton proponía apasionadamente un gobierno federal firme. En última instancia, ambos prepararon el terreno para argumentos importantes que todavía resuenan en la política estadounidense.

SMALL-GROUP OPTIONS

Have students work in small groups and pairs to read and discuss the selection.

Think-Pair-Share

- After reading the selection, pose this question: *Who do you agree with more on how to run the government, Thomas Jefferson or Alexander Hamilton?*
- Have students think about the question individually and take notes.
- Then, have students work in pairs to listen, discuss, and formulate shared responses to the question.
- Finally, have each pair share their responses with the class.

Three-Minute Review

- After students read the selection, set a timer for three minutes.
- Have students work independently to write clarifying questions about what they read.
- After three minutes, ask volunteers to share their questions.
- Briefly discuss answers to each question.

Text X-Ray: English Learner Support
for Thomas Jefferson: The Best of Enemies

Use the Text X-Ray and the supports and scaffolds in the Teacher's Edition to help guide students at different proficiency levels through the selection.

INTRODUCE THE SELECTION
DISCUSS THE TERM *FOUNDING FATHERS*

Introduce the two terms *founders* and *founding fathers*. Note the root word *found*. Explain that *to found* means "to start" or "to begin." The past participle is *founded*. Give the following explanations:

- A *founder* is someone who starts something; for example, "the founder of a museum."
- *Founding fathers* is the term given to the men who developed the government of the United States.

Ask students if they can name any of the founders of the United States. Ask if there are people who are considered founders of their home country. Have students complete these frames: *The United States was ____ in 1776.* (founded) *The ____ wanted to created an independent country.* (founders/founding fathers)

CULTURAL REFERENCES

The following words or phrases may be unfamiliar to students:

- *taken aback* (paragraph 1): to be surprised
- *spearheaded* (paragraph 3): initiated or led
- *abolitionist* (paragraph 7): a person who initiated the end of slavery
- *backbiting* (paragraph 9): saying bad things about someone behind their back

LISTENING

Listen for Key Words

Explain that listening for key words and focusing on them in reading and discussion will help students be able to understand and express main ideas.

Use the following supports with students at varying proficiency levels:

- Write *liberty, central government,* and *states' rights*. Have students repeat them after you; review their meanings. Read paragraph 2 aloud slowly. Have students hold up one finger when they hear *liberty* and two fingers when they hear *central government*. Then, ask yes/no questions, such as *Did Hamilton want a strong central government?* (yes) *Did Jefferson agree?* (no) **SUBSTANTIAL**
- Read paragraph 2 aloud twice. Have students circle words related to politics and government. *(liberty, power, government, Constitution)* Have students report words and list them on the board. Then, help students orally summarize the paragraph. **MODERATE**
- Note that key phrases often use strong adjectives. Ask students to listen for and mark phrases with strong adjectives as you read paragraph 2 aloud. List phrases that students mark on the board and discuss how these phrases illustrate the two men's beliefs. **LIGHT**

SPEAKING

Explain When Events Occur

Tell students that looking for clues about when events happen can help them understand the text. Clues include dates and times and terms that indicate order, such as *first* or *earlier*.

Use the following supports with students at varying proficiency levels:

- Read the first sentence aloud to the class. Write the date "March 21, 1790." Ask: *What year did Jefferson become Secretary of State? What month and day?* Write the answer and have students echo read: *Jefferson became Secretary of State on March 21, 1790.* **SUBSTANTIAL**
- Read the first sentence aloud. Ask: *When did Jefferson arrive in New York? Where was he before?* Supply this frame: *Jefferson was in New York in _____. Before that, he was in _____.* **MODERATE**
- Ask volunteers to read aloud from the beginning of paragraph 1 to "holy writ for Americans." Have students identify events and order them using *first, next, then,* and *finally.* **LIGHT**

READING

Compare and Contrast

Explain that comparing and contrasting two viewpoints can help readers better understand each viewpoint. Note language that students can use to compare (*similar, and, same, both*) and to contrast (*but, whereas, however, different*).

Use the following supports with students at varying proficiency levels:

- Define "central government." Then have students echo read paragraph 2 and find and circle the words *strong* and *weak*. Have students contrast the two ideas: *Hamilton wanted a _____ central government, but Jefferson wanted a _____ central government.* **SUBSTANTIAL**
- Define *insufficient* and *concentrated*. Then have students read paragraph 2 and circle what each man wanted. Have students complete this frame: *Jefferson thought a _____ (weak) federal government was best, but Hamilton wanted a _____ (strong) federal government.* **MODERATE**
- Have student pairs read paragraph 2. Discuss the words *threat* and *jeopardized*. Ask students to identify differences between Hamilton and Jefferson; guide them to paraphrase information from the text. Have them compare and contrast the founders: *Hamilton and Jefferson both cared about _____. However, Hamilton thought _____, whereas Jefferson believed _____.* **LIGHT**

WRITING

Write an Essay

Help students complete the writing assignment on Student Edition page 123. Review how to form comparatives with words such as *strong/stronger, weak/weaker*. For more advanced students, discuss ways to structure a comparative essay.

Use the following supports with students at varying proficiency levels:

- Ask: *Did Jefferson and Hamilton have the same ideas?* Provide a frame: *Hamilton and Jefferson had _____ ideas. _____ wanted a stronger central government. Jefferson wanted a _____ central government.* Then, ask yes/no questions to help students compare the men. Help students write their ideas. **SUBSTANTIAL**
- Have students work in pairs to write some of Jefferson's ideas for the government and some of Hamilton's ideas. Then, have them turn those notes into a paragraph comparing the two sets of ideas. **MODERATE**
- Pair students. Have one student write a paragraph summarizing Hamilton's beliefs and the other student summarize Jefferson's beliefs. Then, have students combine their two paragraphs into one text that compares the two men's beliefs, editing and revising as needed. **LIGHT**

Connect to the
ESSENTIAL QUESTION

This article explores the serious disagreements that existed among the founders and will help students to understand our history as well as our current political system and how we share power and build alliances.

MENTOR TEXT

At the end of the unit, students will be asked to write a research report. "Thomas Jefferson: The Best of Enemies" provides a model for how a writer can use chronological order to present information and support a thesis with facts and examples.

THOMAS JEFFERSON: THE BEST OF ENEMIES

History Writing by **Ron Chernow**

? ESSENTIAL QUESTION:

How can we share power and build alliances?

112   Unit 2

LEARNING MINDSET

Effort   Explain to students that all learning takes effort, and that effort is the key to all types of growth. Encourage students to consider challenges and difficulties as opportunities for learning and growth. Suggest that focusing on the opportunity will help them be persistent in making the effort needed for learning and success.

QUICK START

Think about a time you had a disagreement with a friend. What happened as a result of the disagreement? Were there any long-term effects on your friendship? Discuss your experience with a partner.

ANALYZE INFORMATIONAL TEXTS

An **informational text** is a nonfiction text that presents fact-based information about a topic. History articles, like Chernow's piece, are a type of informative writing that focuses on important historical figures or events. Although the purpose of a history article is to inform readers, an author usually has a central idea to present about the event or people described. This central idea is contained in the **thesis** of the article, with the **body** of the article providing relevant supporting details and examples. The **conclusion** of the article summarizes important ideas and wraps up the piece in a satisfying way. As you read, identify the thesis, body, and conclusion of the essay.

Authors use organizational patterns to make their main point clear and to connect the supporting details. In this article, Chernow makes use of **chronological order,** which presents events in the order in which they happened. Use the following strategies when analyzing the sequence of events in an informational text.

- Look for words and phrases that identify time such as *in a year* or *three weeks earlier.*

- Look for words that signal order, such as *first* and *then* to see how events are related.

ANALYZE STRUCTURE

The overarching structure of Chernow's article is a point-by-point **comparison and contrast** of Jefferson and Hamilton that shows how and why they became "the best of enemies." In such a structure, a writer discusses a particular point of comparison about both subjects and then moves on to the next point. Chernow uses this structure to make his exposition of complex ideas clear, weaving in narrative elements to make the text more engaging.

Within these basic structural elements, Chernow employs literary devices, syntax, and diction to achieve his purpose.

- His straightforward **syntax,** or arrangement of words, and use of dashes to present information creates a clear, brisk style.

- His precise **diction,** or word choice, communicates a vivid picture of the two men and contributes to the author's tone of admiration for them.

- Chernow also uses **irony**—events that contrast with expectations—to add a lighthearted yet memorable note to his essay.

As you read, notice how Chernow uses structure and style to achieve his purpose:

GENRE ELEMENTS: HISTORY WRITING

- presents information about historical events or persons

- includes facts, dates, and information, presented in chronological order

- may employ literary devices to emphasize details and increase engagement

© Houghton Mifflin Harcourt Publishing Company

QUICK START

After students have read the Quick Start, have volunteers share the subject and result of their disagreement with a partner or with the class. Ask them to reflect on any positive effects of this disagreement, such as how they may have learned from their friend's perspective to refine their own views on the topic at hand. What did the disagreement teach them about this friendship? What might they have done differently?

ANALYZE INFORMATIONAL TEXTS

Review with students the features common to informational texts and prepare them to identify the thesis statement, supporting evidence and examples, and the conclusion. Remind students that a **thesis statement** in an informational text is an expression of the central idea and purpose of the piece of writing. Tell students that sections of the article describe a sequence of events. Help students understand the importance of Chernow's use of chronological order to set the stage for the great battles that would take place between Jefferson and Hamilton.

ANALYZE STRUCTURE

Explain to students that the structure of this article supports the author's purpose—to compare and contrast Jefferson's and Hamilton's beliefs. Clarify the definitions of stylistic features Chernow employs in this comparison.

- **Syntax:** Use comparisons with other genres (newspaper article, novel) to help students understand how Chernow's use of language contributes to the style of this article.

- **Diction:** Point out to students that a writer's choice of words can serve to highlight a comparison. Words with negative or positive connotations can help reveal the author's tone. As students read, have them pay attention to the author's word choice and think about how it reveals the author's tone, or attitude toward the men.

- **Situational Irony:** Explain to students that situational irony is a contrast between what is expected to happen and what does happen. Encourage students to look for examples of situational irony and think about its effect and why Chernow might have used the technique.

CRITICAL VOCABULARY

Have students use context clues to help them determine which vocabulary word completes each sentence. Encourage students to read all the sentences before completing them.

Answers:

1. *T*
2. *T*
3. *F*
4. *T*
5. *F*
6. *F*

■ English Learner Support

Use Cognates Tell Spanish speakers that the Critical Vocabulary words have Spanish cognates: *tepid/tibio; copious/copioso, cardinal/cardinal, rudiments/rudimentos, façade/fachada, anomalous/anómalo.* **ALL LEVELS**

LANGUAGE CONVENTIONS

Explain that hyphens are an important punctuation mark because they clarify meaning by joining words or word parts. Explain that there are rules for hyphenation. For example, use hyphenation when two or more words that come before a noun they modify act as a single idea. Some examples include: *state-of-the-art technology, well-known author,* and *off-site location.* Explain that the hyphens signal that all the words prior to the noun act as a single idea and are modifying the noun together. There are two exceptions to this rule: the word *very* and adverbs that end in *-ly* are not hyphenated.

ANNOTATION MODEL

Remind students of annotation strategies such as underlining important ideas and circling repeated words, dates, or related concepts. Students may follow this suggestion or use their own system for marking up the selection in their write-in text. They may want to color-code their annotation by using highlighters. Their notes in the margin may include questions about ideas that are unclear or topics they want to learn more about.

GET READY

CRITICAL VOCABULARY

| tepid | copious | cardinal | rudiments | façade | anomalous |

To see how many Critical Vocabulary words you already know, decide whether the following statements are true or false.

1. The outline of a story contains the **rudiments** of what it will eventually become.

2. The **cardinal** rule of learning to drive is: Safety first.

3. The **tepid** television ratings led the company to renew the series for a year.

4. The diligent student filled a notebook with **copious** notes.

5. The **façade** of the building shows a spacious and elegant interior.

6. The team of scientists was elated by the **anomalous** results of their experiment.

LANGUAGE CONVENTIONS

Hyphenation Hyphens are punctuation marks that join words to clarify meaning and improve style. Hyphens are often used to attach a prefix to a proper noun or to a date (as in *pre-Revolutionary* or *pre-1776*) or to join multiple adjectives *(He works two part-time jobs to make ends meet.).* Using hyphenated words can make writing concise and memorable. As you read the article, notice the way the writer uses hyphens.

ANNOTATION MODEL   NOTICE & NOTE

As you read, note how the author compares Hamilton and Jefferson and uses time order words to tell you the sequence of events. In the model, you can see one reader's notes about Chernow's article.

On March 21, 1790, Thomas Jefferson belatedly arrived in New York City to assume his duties as the first Secretary of State after a five-year ministerial stint in Paris. Tall and lanky, with a freckled complexion and auburn hair, Jefferson, 46, was taken aback by the adulation being heaped upon the new Treasury Secretary, Alexander Hamilton, who had streaked to prominence in his absence. Few people knew that Jefferson had authored the Declaration of Independence, ... Instead, the Virginian was eclipsed by the 35-year-old wunderkind from the Caribbean. . . .

author includes time references to events he will describe

compares age, accomplishments, background

BACKGROUND

Ron Chernow (b. 1949) is an award-winning author of several biographies, including Alexander Hamilton *(2004) and* Washington: A Life *(2010). In this magazine article from 2004, he explores the ideological differences that brought Thomas Jefferson (1743–1826) and Alexander Hamilton (1755/57–1804) into conflict when both served in President George Washington's first cabinet.*

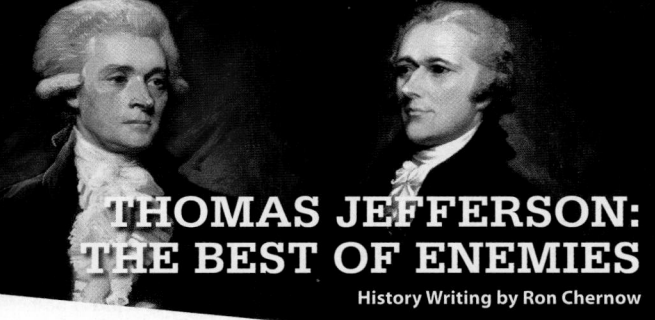

THOMAS JEFFERSON: THE BEST OF ENEMIES

History Writing by Ron Chernow

SETTING A PURPOSE

As you read, look for clues that reveal similarities and differences between Jefferson's and Hamilton's personalities and beliefs.

1   On March 21, 1790, Thomas Jefferson belatedly arrived in New York City to assume his duties as the first Secretary of State after a five-year ministerial stint in Paris. Tall and lanky, with a freckled complexion and auburn hair, Jefferson, 46, was taken aback by the adulation being heaped upon the new Treasury Secretary, Alexander Hamilton, who had streaked to prominence in his absence. Few people knew that Jefferson had authored the Declaration of Independence, which had yet to become holy writ for Americans. Instead, the Virginian was eclipsed by the 35-year-old wunderkind from the Caribbean, who was a lowly artillery captain in New York when Jefferson composed the famous document. Despite his murky background as an illegitimate orphan, the self-invented Hamilton was trim and elegant, carried himself with an erect military bearing and had a mind that worked with dazzling speed. At first, Hamilton and Jefferson socialized on easy terms, with little inkling that they were destined to become mortal foes. But their clash inside

Notice & Note

Use the side margins to notice and note signposts in the text.

ANALYZE INFORMATIONAL TEXTS

Annotate: Mark information in paragraph 1 about the long-term effects of the clash between Jefferson and Hamilton.

Infer: In your own words, state the author's thesis.

BACKGROUND

Thomas Jefferson and Alexander Hamilton both played integral roles in the founding of this country. Their shared objectives ended with the common goal of freedom from the British. However, they had very different opinions about how to create a sustainable government for the United States. Alexander Hamilton believed in a strong federal government, while Thomas Jefferson felt that more power belonged in the hands of the states. These arguments persist in American politics today.

SETTING A PURPOSE

Direct students to use the Setting a Purpose prompt to focus their reading.

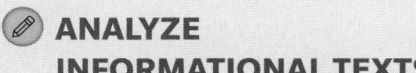 ANALYZE INFORMATIONAL TEXTS

Remind students that a **thesis** expresses the central idea and **author's purpose,** or reason for writing. Thesis statements can be one or two sentences long. Recognizing key details can help students determine the thesis. Call students' attention to words that indicate long-term effects, in contrast to those that emphasize immediate differences between the two men. (***Answer:*** *The author's thesis is that the disagreement between Jefferson and Hamilton was profound and had effects still being felt today.*)

For **speaking support** for students at varying proficiency levels, see the **Text X-Ray** on page 112D.

WHEN STUDENTS STRUGGLE ...

Understand Structure   Creating a Venn diagram can help students visualize similarities and differences. Have students reread the first part of the text and create and fill in a Venn diagram like the one shown to help them compare Jefferson and Hamilton.

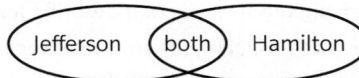

For additional support, go to the **Reading Studio** and assign the following **Level Up Tutorial: Comparison-Contrast Organization.**

ANALYZE STRUCTURE

Explain to students that the structure of this article supports one of the author's purposes: to compare and contrast Jefferson and Hamilton by comparing the two men point by point. Lead students to discuss how the contrasts support the author's thesis. (**Answer:** *Jefferson and Hamilton disagreed about how strong the federal government should be and about how to interpret the Constitution. The text says that Hamilton "advocated a vigorous central government marked by a strong President." Jefferson believed that "liberty was jeopardized by concentrated federal power."*)

For **listening** and **reading support** for students at varying proficiency levels, see the **Text X-Ray** on pages 112C–112D.

CRITICAL VOCABULARY

tepid: Thomas Jefferson did not enthusiastically support the new political structure; his support for it was tepid.

ASK STUDENTS to explain why Thomas Jefferson's enthusiasm was tepid about the new government. *(He supported the new United States in general but did not believe in a strong federal government with a lot of centralized power.)*

copious: Hamilton had many diverse talents. Jefferson recognized Hamilton's copious talents and saw that they made him powerful.

ASK STUDENTS to discuss why Hamilton's copious talents worried Jefferson. *(Hamilton's ability to write, speak, and charm others meant that he was easily able to persuade others to support his views, which Jefferson disagreed with.)*

 NOTICE & NOTE

ANALYZE STRUCTURE

Annotate: Underline words in paragraph 2 that reveal Hamilton's vision of government power. Circle words that tell you about Jefferson's vision.

Analyze: How would you describe the core difference between the men's views? Cite text evidence in your response.

tepid
(tĕp´ĭd) *adj.* lukewarm; indifferent.

copious
(kō´pē-əs) *adj.* extensive.

George Washington's first Cabinet proved so fierce that it would spawn the two-party system in America. It also produced two divergent visions of the country's future that divide Americans to the present day.

2   For Hamilton, the first Treasury Secretary, the supreme threat to liberty arose from insufficient government power. To avert that, he advocated a vigorous central government marked by a strong President, an independent judiciary and a liberal reading of the Constitution. As the first Secretary of State, Jefferson believed that liberty was jeopardized by concentrated federal power, which he tried to restrict through a narrow construction of the Constitution. He favored states' rights, a central role for Congress and a comparatively weak judiciary.

3   At first glance, Hamilton might seem the more formidable figure in that classic matchup. He took office with an ardent faith in the new national government. He had attended the Constitutional Convention, penned the bulk of the Federalist papers to secure passage of the new charter and spearheaded ratification efforts in New York State. He therefore set to work at Treasury with more unrestrained gusto than Jefferson—who had monitored the Constitutional Convention from his post in Paris—did at State. Jefferson's enthusiasm for the new political order was **tepid** at best, and when Washington crafted the first government in 1789, Jefferson didn't grasp the levers of power with quite the same glee as Hamilton, who had no ideological inhibitions about shoring up federal power.

4   Hamilton—brilliant, brash and charming—had the self-reliant reflexes of someone who had always had to live by his wits. His overwhelming intelligence petrified Jefferson and his followers. As an orator, Hamilton could speak extemporaneously for hours on end. As a writer, he could crank out 5,000- or 10,000-word memos overnight. Jefferson never underrated his foe's **copious** talents. At one point, a worried Jefferson confided to his comrade James Madison that Hamilton was a one-man army, "a host[1] within himself."

5   Whether in person or on paper, Hamilton served up his opinions promiscuously. He had a true zest for debate and never left anyone guessing where he stood. Jefferson, more than a decade older, had the quiet, courtly manner of a Virginia planter. He was emphatic in his views—Hamilton labeled him "an atheist in religion and a fanatic in politics"—but shrank from open conflict. Jefferson, a diffident speaker, mumbled his way through his rare speeches in a soft, almost inaudible voice and reserved his most scathing strictures for private correspondence.

6   The epic battle between these two Olympian[2] figures began not long after Jefferson came to New York City to assume his State

[1] **host:** an army or large group of troops.
[2] **Olympian:** like a god; one from Mount Olympus.

 ## ENGLISH LEARNER SUPPORT

Compare and Contrast Visualizing similarities and differences can help students better understand the text. Have students mark the text to compare and contrast the two men.

- Have students read the first two sentences and look for the names of the two men in this essay. Then have them highlight words that describe Jefferson. **SUBSTANTIAL**
- Have students read paragraphs 1–2. Have them circle words that show Jefferson's ideas or personality. Have them underline words that show Hamilton's ideas and personality. **MODERATE**

Department duties in March 1790. By then Hamilton was in the thick of a contentious campaign to retire massive debt inherited from the Revolution. America had suspended principal and interest payments[3] on its obligations, which had traded as low as 15¢ on the dollar. In an audacious scheme to restore public credit, Hamilton planned to pay off that debt at face value, causing the securities to soar from depressed levels. Jefferson and Madison thought the original holders of those securities—many of them war veterans—should profit from that appreciation even if they had already sold their paper to traders at depressed prices. Hamilton thought it would be impractical to track them down. With an eye on future U.S. capital markets, he wanted to enshrine the **cardinal** principle that current owners of securities incurred all profits and losses, even if that meant windfall gains for rapacious speculators who had only recently bought the securities.

7   That skirmish over Hamilton's public credit plan was part of a broader tussle over the U.S.'s economic future. Jefferson was fond of summoning up idyllic scenes of an agrarian America peopled by sturdy yeoman farmers.[4] That poetic vision neglected the underlying reality of large slave plantations in the South. Jefferson was a fine populist on paper but not in everyday life, and his defense of Virginia interests was inextricably bound up with slavery. Hamilton—derided as a pseudo aristocrat, an elitist, a crypto-monarchist[5]—was a passionate abolitionist with a far more expansive economic vision. He conceded that agriculture would persist for decades as an essential component of the economy. But at the same time he wanted to foster the **rudiments** of a modern economy—trade, commerce, banks, stock exchanges, factories and corporations—to enlarge economic opportunity.

8   Hamilton dreamed of a meritocracy, not an aristocracy, while Jefferson retained the landed gentry's disdain for the vulgar realities of trade, commerce and finance. And he was determined to undermine Hamilton's juggernaut.[6]

9   Because we celebrate Jefferson for his sonorous words in the Declaration of Independence—Hamilton never matched Jefferson's gift for writing ringing passages that were at once poetic and inspirational—we sometimes overlook Jefferson's consummate skills as a practicing politician. A master of subtle, artful indirection, he was able to marshal his forces without divulging his generalship. After Hamilton persuaded President Washington to create the Bank of the United States, the country's first central bank, Jefferson was aghast

---

3   **principal and interest payments:** the amount borrowed and the fees charged by the lender.
4   **yeoman farmers:** owners of small independent farms.
5   **crypto-monarchist:** one who secretly supports government rule by a king.
6   **juggernaut:** an extremely powerful force.

ANALYZE INFORMATIONAL TEXTS

Annotate: Mark words in paragraph 6 that show the sequence of events.

Infer: Why does the author include information about the order of events?

cardinal
(kär´dn-əl) *adj.* most important; prime.

rudiment
(rōō´də-mənt) *n.* basic form.

 ANALYZE INFORMATIONAL TEXTS

Remind students that writers use transitional words and phrases such as *first*, *next*, and *later* to indicate the order of events. Explain that writers also use verb tenses to show chronology. Point out the verb *had traded* in paragraph 6. Explain that this is the past perfect tense of *trade*. Writers use the past perfect tense (*had* plus the past particle of the verb) to express an action in the past that came before something else happened. In this case, America suspended principal and interest payments before Hamilton made his plan. (**Answer:** *Using specific time references locates the action in its historical context so readers can easily see how the events are related.*)

 ENGLISH LEARNER SUPPORT

Acquire Vocabulary   Read aloud from paragraph 7, sentences 4–5. Explain that a *populist* is a person who supports the common people. An *abolitionist* is a person who wants to end slavery. Have students write the definitions in their notebooks. Have them complete this frame: *Jefferson had ___ (populist) ideas, but he did not criticize ___ (slavery). In contrast, Hamilton was an ___ (abolitionist).*   **ALL LEVELS**

CRITICAL VOCABULARY

cardinal: Hamilton's beliefs about the future of the U.S. economy were guided by a cardinal, or most important, principle.

ASK STUDENTS what Hamilton's cardinal principle was. (*Current owners of securities incur all of the profits and losses. Former owners would have no claim to profit or obligation in loss.*)

rudiment: Hamilton's vision was to develop the rudiments of a modern economy to eventually change the basic economic system of the country.

ASK STUDENTS what, according to Hamilton, were the rudiments of a modern economy? (*trade, commerce, banks, stock exchanges, factories, and corporations*)

 ENGLISH LEARNER SUPPORT

Identify Verb Tenses   Students who speak Khmer and Korean may use the present perfect tense where the past perfect should be used: *Yesterday I have done that*. In the primary language, a past marker (e.g., *yesterday*) is inserted to indicate a completed action. Explain that the past tense expresses an action that began and ended in the past. The past perfect tense expresses an action that came before another action in the past. Draw a timeline on the board plotting each verb tense and have students copy it into their notebooks. Ask students to identify examples of each of these verb tenses on page 117. (past tense: *inherited, planned, thought, wanted*; past perfect: *had suspended, had traded, had bought*.)   **MODERATE**

ENGLISH LEARNER SUPPORT

Acquire Vocabulary Read paragraph 9 aloud and have students underline the words *subsidize, covertly, retaliate,* and *pseudonym.* Then, explain the meaning of the terms:

- *subsidize*: "to fund" or "to support financially"

- *covertly*: "in a hidden way"

- *retaliate*: "to fight back"

- *pseudonym*: "a false name"

Help students summarize the paragraph by providing these sentence frames. Students should complete each frame with the new vocabulary words. *Jefferson supported the National Gazette _____* (covertly). *In order to _____* (subsidize) *this paper, he gave Freneau a job. Hamilton was angry, so he _____* (retaliated). *He published articles, but he used _____* (pseudonyms), *not his real name.* **MODERATE/LIGHT**

at what he construed[7] as a breach of the Constitution and a perilous expansion of federal power. Along with Madison, he recruited the poet Philip Freneau to launch an opposition paper called the National Gazette. To subsidize the paper covertly, he hired Freneau as a State Department translator. Hamilton was shocked by such flagrant disloyalty from a member of Washington's Cabinet, especially when Freneau began to mount withering assaults on Hamilton and even Washington. Never one to suffer in silence, Hamilton retaliated in a blizzard of newspaper articles published under Roman pseudonyms. The backbiting between Hamilton and Jefferson grew so acrimonious that Washington had to exhort both men to desist.

10　Instead, the feud worsened. In early 1793, a Virginia Congressman named William Branch Giles began to harry Hamilton with resolutions ordering him to produce, on short deadlines, stupendous amounts of Treasury data. With prodigious bursts of energy, Hamilton complied with those inhuman demands, foiling his opponents. Jefferson then committed an unthinkable act. He secretly drafted a series of anti-Hamilton resolutions for Giles, including one that read, "Resolved, That the Secretary of the Treasury has been guilty of maladministration in the duties of his office and should, in the opinion of Congress, be removed from his office by the President of the United States." The resolution was voted down, and the effort to oust Hamilton stalled. Jefferson left the Cabinet in defeat later that year.

11　Throughout the 1790s, the Hamilton-Jefferson feud continued to fester in both domestic and foreign affairs. Jefferson thought Hamilton was "bewitched" by the British model of governance, while Hamilton considered Jefferson a credulous apologist for the gory excesses of the French Revolution. Descended from French

---

[7] **construed:** interpreted.

APPLYING ACADEMIC VOCABULARY

☐ contrary　☑ ideological　☐ publication　☐ revolution　☑ founder

Write and Discuss Have students discuss the questions with a partner using the words *ideological* and *founder* in their responses. Ask volunteers to share responses with the class.

- How does the writer's use of comparison create a picture of the **ideological** beliefs of Jefferson and Hamilton?

- Describe the roles of Jefferson and Hamilton as **founders** of the United States.

Huguenots[8] on his mother's side, Hamilton was fluent in French and had served as Washington's liaison with the Marquis de Lafayette and other French aristocrats who had rallied to the Continental Army. The French Revolution immediately struck him as a bloody affair, governed by rigid, Utopian thinking. On Oct. 6, 1789, he wrote a remarkable letter to Lafayette, explaining his "foreboding of ill" about the future course of events in Paris. He cited the "vehement character" of the French people and the "reveries" of their "philosophic politicians," who wished to transform human nature. Hamilton believed that Jefferson while in Paris "drank deeply of the French philosophy in religion, in science, in politics." Indeed, more than a decade passed before Jefferson fully realized that the French Revolution wasn't a worthy sequel to the American one so much as a grotesque travesty.[9]

12   If Jefferson and Hamilton define opposite ends of the political spectrum in U.S. history and seem to exist in perpetual conflict, the two men shared certain traits, feeding a mutual cynicism. Each scorned the other as excessively ambitious. In his secret diary, or Anas, Jefferson recorded a story of Hamilton praising Julius Caesar as the greatest man in history. (The tale sounds dubious, as Hamilton invariably used Caesar as shorthand for "an evil tyrant.") Hamilton repaid the favor. In one essay he likened Jefferson to "Caesar coyly refusing the proffered diadem"[10] and rejecting the trappings, but "tenaciously grasping the substance of imperial domination."

13   Similarly, both men hid a potent hedonism[11] behind an intellectual **façade**. For all their outward differences, the two

---

[8] **French Huguenots:** a group of Protestants who were persecuted in Catholic France; many fled to North America.
[9] **travesty:** an unreasonable distortion or parody.
[10] **"Caesar . . . diadem":** In Shakespeare's *Julius Caesar,* the Roman general refuses a crown three times, but republicans believe he really wanted to be named king.
[11] **hedonism:** the belief that personal pleasure is the primary goal in life.

ANALYZE INFORMATIONAL TEXTS

Annotate: Mark the references to time in paragraph 11.

Analyze: How did the men's view of the French Revolution change over time? Cite text evidence in your response.

façade
(fə-säd´) *n.* false or misleading appearance.

Thomas Jefferson: The Best of Enemies   119

● ANALYZE INFORMATIONAL TEXTS

Explain that the French Revolution had many parallels to the American Revolution, but ultimately took a different course. Whereas the American Revolution ended with a clean break from Britain and the formation of a new country, the French Revolution did not have a clear end. After overthrowing the French monarchy, revolutionaries instituted a "Reign of Terror," seeking to eliminate anyone suspected of being against the Revolution. Huge numbers of people were executed by the new regime. The fears Hamilton expressed in his 1789 letter, just a few months into the French Revolution, were ultimately justified. Jefferson, in Paris as minister to France when the French Revolution broke out, offered support to Lafayette. At this point, Jefferson saw the French Revolution as a parallel to the American Revolution.

Guide students to use paragraph 11 (starting on page 118) to identify Hamilton's and Jefferson's opinions and background. Ask students to consider how Hamilton's family background and ability to speak French likely shaped his views. (**Answer:** *Hamilton viewed the French Revolution with disdain—"gory excesses," "bloody affair, "rigid, utopian thinking," " foreboding of ill"—from the beginning. Jefferson initially believed in the nobility of the French Revolution but realized much later that it was not really an equivalent event to the American Revolution—"wasn't a worthy sequel," "grotesque travesty.")*

TO CHALLENGE STUDENTS

Organize Ideas Point out to students that writers of comparison-contrast essays sometimes organize their ideas according to subject-by-subject organization rather than point-by-point organization. Have students work in small groups to discuss how the impact of the article would be changed if the writer had chosen to use subject-by-subject organization—enumerating all of the points about Jefferson in one section, followed by all of the points about Hamilton. Have students summarize their thoughts in three bullet points to share with the class. Encourage students to support their opinions with textual evidence.

CRITICAL VOCABULARY

façade: Hamilton and Jefferson both presented a serious and dignified façade to the public but were revealed by their personal lives to be fallible humans.

ASK STUDENTS how scandal affected Hamilton's façade. *(He was mocked as "the amorous Treasury Secretary.")*

TEACH

LANGUAGE CONVENTIONS

Remind students that one use for hyphenation is when two words preceding a noun act as one modifier. Ask students to rewrite the sentence without using hyphenation and compare the results. (**Answer:** *Another way of saying "95-page pamphlet" is to say "pamphlet that was 95 pages long." Using a hyphen simplifies the sentence and makes it read more smoothly.*)

■ English Learner Support

Use Hyphens In Haitian, Creole, Hmong, Khmer, Spanish, and Vietnamese, adjectives commonly come after the noun. This might make hyphenating adjectives before a noun confusing to students. Remind them that in English, adjectives come before nouns, and if two adjectives modify the same noun and act as one idea, they should be hyphenated. Explain that a noun combined with an adjective is usually hyphenated. Give students example sentences such as: *She is a well respected teacher. I need an extra large shirt. That is a high risk activity. I want a full time job.* Have students copy the sentences and add hyphens. Point out the hyphen in *95-page pamphlet* in paragraph 13. **ALL LEVELS**

EL **ENGLISH LEARNER SUPPORT**

Acquire Vocabulary Explain that *confessed* means that Hamilton says it was true—he did have the affair. Ask students to decide which of the following are things people would confess to: a crime, cheating, finishing homework, stealing, eating lunch. Have intermediate and advanced students create their own sentences using the word *confessed*. **ALL LEVELS**

CRITICAL VOCABULARY

anomalous: At this time, the candidate with the most electoral votes became President and the runner-up became Vice President. In Jefferson's presidential election, something anomalous, or unusual, happened.

ASK STUDENTS to describe what was anomalous about this presidential election. (*Jefferson and Burr tied in the election, and it took 36 rounds of voting in the House to declare Jefferson the winner.*)

Thomas Jefferson

politicians stumbled into the two great sex scandals of the early Republic. In 1797 a journalist named James T. Callender exposed that Hamilton, while Treasury Secretary and a married man with four children, had entered into a yearlong affair with grifter Maria Reynolds, who was 23 when it began. In a 95-page pamphlet, Hamilton confessed to the affair at what many regarded as inordinate length. He wished to show that the money he had paid to Reynolds' husband James had been for the favor of her company and not for illicit speculation in Treasury securities, as the Jeffersonians had alleged. Forever after, the Jeffersonians tagged Hamilton as "the amorous Treasury Secretary" and mocked his pretensions to superior morality.

LANGUAGE CONVENTIONS
Annotate: Mark an example of hyphenation in paragraph 13.
Evaluate: How does hyphenation help make this sentence more concise?

14 By an extraordinary coincidence, during Jefferson's first term as President, Callender also exposed Jefferson's relationship with Sally Hemings. Callender claimed that "Dusky Sally," a.k.a. the "African Venus," was the President's slave concubine, who had borne him five children. "There is not an individual in the neighborhood of Charlottesville who does not believe the story," Callender wrote, "and not a few who know it." Jefferson never confirmed or denied Callender's story. But the likely truth of the Hemings affair was dramatically bolstered by DNA tests published in 1998, which indicated that a Jefferson male had sired at least one of Hemings' children.

15 The crowning irony of the stormy relations between Hamilton and Jefferson is that Hamilton helped install his longtime foe as President in 1801. Under constitutional rules then in force, the candidate with the majority of electoral votes became President; the runner-up became Vice President. That created an **anomalous** situation in which Jefferson, his party's presumed presidential nominee, tied with Aaron Burr, its presumed vice presidential nominee. It took 36 rounds of voting in the House to decide the election in Jefferson's favor. Faced with the prospect of Burr as President, a man he considered unscrupulous, Hamilton not only

anomalous
(ə-nŏm´ə-ləs) *adj.* unusual.

IMPROVE READING FLUENCY

Targeted Passage Have students work with partners to read paragraph 14. First, use the paragraph to model how to read informational text with appropriate phrasing and emphasis, calling students' attention to the author's use of parenthesis, quotations, commas, and other features that require the reader to adjust emphasis and pacing. Then, have partners take turns reading aloud paragraph 14, providing feedback and support for placing appropriate emphasis on hyphenated phrases and quotations.

opted for Jefferson as the lesser of two evils but also was forced into his most measured assessment of the man. Hamilton said he had long suspected that as President, Jefferson would develop a keen taste for the federal power he had deplored in opposition. He recalled that a decade earlier, in Washington's Cabinet, Jefferson had seemed like a man who knew he was destined to inherit an estate—in this case, the presidency—and didn't wish to deplete it. In fact, Jefferson, the strict constructionist, freely exercised the most sweeping powers as President. Nothing in the Constitution, for instance, permitted the Louisiana Purchase[12]. Hamilton noted that with rueful mirth.

---

[12]**Louisiana Purchase:** France's 1803 sale of its territory west of the Mississippi River to the United States.

CONTRASTS AND CONTRADICTIONS

Notice & Note: Mark a surprising fact that Chernow includes in the concluding paragraph of the article.

Analyze: What contradiction does this fact reveal? Explain.

CHECK YOUR UNDERSTANDING

Answer these questions before moving on to the **Analyze the Text** section on the following page.

1 What event sparked the beginning of the conflict between Hamilton and Jefferson?

   A Jefferson came back from France.

   B Hamilton arrived from the Caribbean.

   C Jefferson wrote the Declaration of Independence.

   D Hamilton attended the Constitutional Convention.

2 What is a main difference between the economic visions of America held by Jefferson and Hamilton?

   F Jefferson's vision was urban, while Hamilton's was rural.

   G Jefferson's vision was modern, while Hamilton's was agrarian.

   H Jefferson's vision included slavery, while Hamilton's was abolitionist.

   J Jefferson's vision included government controls, while Hamilton favored the aristocracy.

3 How did Hamilton respond to the accusations of illicit speculation?

   A He confessed to speculating in Treasury securities.

   B He confessed at length to having an extramarital affair.

   C He accused Jefferson of having an affair with Sally Hemings.

   D He accused the Jeffersonians of lying about his financial dealings.

© Houghton Mifflin Harcourt Publishing Company

TEACH

CONTRASTS AND CONTRADICTIONS

Remind students that **situational irony** is a contrast between what is expected to happen and what does happen. Ask students to frame their answers using this concept. (**Possible answer:** *Hamilton's support of Jefferson as the "lesser of two evils" is ironic because of their long-term dislike of each other. Jefferson's convenient decision to forego his previous stance on following a strict, narrow interpretation of the constitution shows a contradiction in his behavior as he comes over to Hamilton's way of thinking.*)

✏️ CHECK YOUR UNDERSTANDING

Have students answer the questions independently.

Answers:

   1. *A*

   2. *H*

   3. *B*

If they answer any questions incorrectly, have them reread the text to confirm their understanding. Then, they may proceed to ANALYZE THE TEXT on page 122.

(EL) ENGLISH LEARNER SUPPORT

Oral Assessment

1. Hamilton and Jefferson's conflict began when Jefferson came back from _____. (*France*)

2. _____ supported slavery, but _____ did not. (*Jefferson; Hamilton*)

3. Did Hamilton confess to an affair? (*Yes.*) **SUBSTANTIAL/MODERATE**

ANALYZE THE TEXT

Possible answers:

1. **DOK 4:** *Chernow effectively uses chronological order to show the development of the disagreement over time and effectively uses comparison-and-contrast to clearly delineate the differences between the two.*

2. **DOK 4:** *The words "brilliant," "brash and charming," "served up his opinions promiscuously" and "had a true zest for debate" reveal the most about Hamilton and establish the author's tone that he respected Hamilton.*

3. **DOK 3:** *Hamilton was a great speaker and a prolific writer. Everyone knew where he stood, and he never backed down from conflict. Jefferson was more reserved. While he was not a good speaker, he was a master politician and was able to manipulate his situation with Hamilton in the shadows. This affected the way they carried out their feud because Hamilton wrote and debated while Jefferson worked more behind the scenes.*

4. **DOK 4:** *Using a point-by-point comparison, Chernow creates a vivid picture of two men who not only hated each other but had very different views for the future of the United States. This made the shift in Hamilton's attitude and Jefferson's behavior seem all the more ironic. Hamilton ended up supporting Jefferson for President and Jefferson, as President, wielded his federal powers freely.*

5. **DOK 4:** *Each considered the other "excessively ambitious" and compared the other to Julius Caesar. Both were involved in sex scandals exposed by the same journalist. These similarities add interest to the article through situational irony. They also contribute an objective, even-handed tone that helps make Chernow's analysis more credible since he seems not to be favoring one over the other.*

RESEARCH

Review the research tip with students and make sure they understand how to access the *Federalist Papers* and information about them. Remind students to use credible sources for their research and to confirm information with multiple sources.

Extend   Prior to reading, have students review their annotations of Chernow's point-by-point comparison of Hamilton's views with Jefferson's. Suggest that they highlight key ideas in their summary of Hamilton's argument in the *Federalist Papers* and compare these ideas with their annotations from Chernow's article. Then, have them look for Jefferson's views on the same topics.

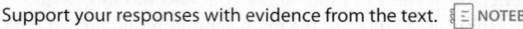

RESPOND

ANALYZE THE TEXT

Support your responses with evidence from the text.   📓 NOTEBOOK

1. **Evaluate** How effectively did Chernow use chronological order and the comparison-and-contrast structure to portray the idea that Hamilton and Jefferson were "destined to become mortal foes"?

2. **Analyze** An author's choice of words, or **diction,** can communicate a great deal about a subject. Reread Chernow's description of Hamilton in paragraphs 4 and 5, paying attention to the adjectives and adverbs. What words best communicate the author's tone toward Hamilton's personality and character?

3. **Cite Evidence** How did Hamilton's and Jefferson's different personal styles affect the ways they carried out their feud?

4. **Analyze** How does Chernow's point-by-point comparison of these two rivals add to the strength of his concluding paragraph?

5. **Notice & Note** Chernow points out that despite the two leaders' conflicts, they shared some common traits. In what ways were Jefferson and Hamilton similar, according to Chernow? How does describing their similarities strengthen the article?

RESEARCH

RESEARCH TIP
Quoted or paraphrased ideas from both primary and secondary sources must be attributed to their author using citations in the correct format. Complete these citations as you research and take notes on a topic, so you won't waste time at the end of a research project searching for source information.

The article mentions the *Federalist Papers* written by Alexander Hamilton. Research the *Federalist Papers* and answer these questions about them.

QUESTION	ANSWER
Why were the *Federalist Papers* written?	*to encourage support for ratification of the U.S. Constitution*
Who besides Hamilton contributed to the *Federalist Papers?*	*James Madison and John Jay*
What was Hamilton's position on the Bill of Rights? Why?	*He opposed the Bill of Rights. He thought it was unnecessary because nothing in the Constitution limited individual rights.*

Extend Read one of the *Federalist Papers* Hamilton wrote. Summarize Hamilton's argument and then add a paragraph outlining how you think Jefferson would have responded to Hamilton's views.

LEARNING MINDSET

Problem Solving Explain that flexible thinking is important to success in learning and in life. One way to practice flexible thinking is to see problems as opportunities for growth. Note that when students encounter problems as they read, analyze, or write, they can use many different strategies to solve these problems. Some approaches include being patient, changing strategies, asking for help, discussing the problem with a peer, or using resources to find answers. Explain that everyone has different approaches to problem solving. One of their jobs is to explore what strategies and solutions work best. As they analyze the essay and write their essays, they should look for opportunities to grapple with and solve problems.

CREATE AND PRESENT

Write an Essay Chernow states that the clash between Hamilton and Jefferson "produced two divergent visions of the country's future that divide Americans to the present day."

❏ Write an essay that provides a point-by-point comparison of these two visions.

❏ Use Chernow's article as a structural model and a source of content.

❏ Include a paragraph that explores whether these visions are relevant to Americans today. Use prior knowledge or conduct research to help you build your argument. Correctly cite any sources you use.

Present an Essay Present your essay to the class or a small group.

❏ Consider adding visuals to your presentation to enhance the audience's understanding.

❏ If available, use slide presentation software to create slides to accompany your essay. For example, you may use them to highlight important main ideas and add visual interest.

❏ Speak clearly and slowly, making eye contact with your audience as you present your essay.

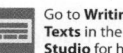

 Go to **Writing Informative Texts** in the **Writing Studio** for help.

Go to **Giving a Presentation** in the **Speaking and Listening Studio** for help.

RESPOND TO THE ESSENTIAL QUESTION

 How can we share power and build alliances?

Gather Information Review your annotations and notes on "Thomas Jefferson: The Best of Enemies." Then, add relevant information to your Response Log. As you determine which information to include, think about:

• important accomplishments of Jefferson and Hamilton
• differences between Jefferson and Hamilton
• how conflict between the two men influenced, enhanced, or impeded their ability to achieve their goals

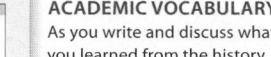

ACADEMIC VOCABULARY

As you write and discuss what you learned from the history article, be sure to use the Academic Vocabulary words. Check off each of the words that you use.

❏ **contrary**
❏ **founder**
❏ **ideological**
❏ **publication**
❏ **revolution**

CREATE AND PRESENT

Write an Essay Hamilton believed in a liberal reading of the Constitution, giving the federal government significant power, while Jefferson believed in a narrow reading of the Constitution, reserving most power for the states. Have students consider how the philosophies of today's two-party system relate to the philosophies of the two founders discussed in Chernow's article. Remind students that in a point-by-point comparison, the writer analyzes each topic, or point, and discusses the similarities and differences.

For **writing support** for students at varying proficiency levels, see the **Text X-Ray** on page 112D.

Present an Essay Demonstrate simple data visualization techniques that students can use to organize the information they present, such as a Venn diagram, mind map, or outline. Have students practice their presentations with a partner and give each other feedback on the structure of the presentation and the fluency of their delivery.

RESPOND TO THE ESSENTIAL QUESTION

Allow time for students to add details from "Thomas Jefferson: the Best of Enemies" to their Unit 2 Response Logs.

CRITICAL VOCABULARY

Answers:

1. *a*
2. *b*
3. *b*
4. *a*
5. *a*
6. *b*

VOCABULARY STRATEGY:
Use Print and Digital Resources

Show students this example of the entry for the Critical Vocabulary word *copious* from the *American Heritage Dictionary of the English Language.*

co·pi·ous (kō´pē-əs) *adj.* 1. Yielding or containing plenty; affording ample supply: *a copious harvest*. See Synonyms at *plentiful*. 2. Large in quantity; abundant: *copious rainfall*. 3. Abounding in matter, thoughts, or words; wordy: *"I found our speech copious without order, and energetic without rules"* (Samuel Johnson). [Middle English, from Latin *cōpiōsus*, from *cōpia*, abundance; see op- in the Appendix of Indo-European roots.]— co´pi·ous·ly *adv.* — co´pi·ous·ness *n.*

Explain that the entry has these elements:

- The word is broken into syllables with its pronunciation shown in parentheses using standard symbols to represent different sounds.
- Part of speech is shown next; in this case the word is an adjective.
- Three distinct but related definitions are listed, with an example of how each meaning of the word might be used. This is useful for choosing the correct definition for words with multiple meanings.
- Etymology, or word derivation, is shown in brackets. This English word is very similar to its Latin origin.
- Related words are shown, indicating how to turn this adjective into an adverb and a noun.

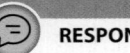

RESPOND

WORD BANK

tepid	rudiments
copious	façade
cardinal	anomalous

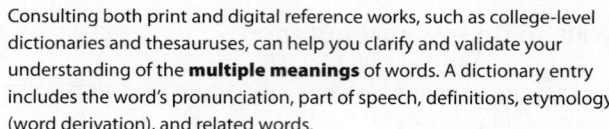

Go to **Using Reference Sources** in the **Vocabulary Studio** for help.

CRITICAL VOCABULARY

Practice and Apply Circle the letter of the best answer to each question. Then, explain your response.

1. Which of these responses is **tepid?**
   a. a shrug   **b.** a shout

2. An **anomalous** answer to a question is most likely to provoke
   a. satisfaction   **b.** confusion

3. Which type of print material has a **copious** number of pages?
   a. pamphlet   **b.** encyclopedia

4. A **façade** is most similar to which of the following?
   a. a mask   **b.** a hat

5. How does a musician learn the **rudiments** of playing an instrument?
   a. practicing   **b.** humming

6. Which of the following is a **cardinal** principle of American democracy?
   a. free markets   **b.** individual rights

VOCABULARY STRATEGY: Use Print and Digital Resources

Consulting both print and digital reference works, such as college-level dictionaries and thesauruses, can help you clarify and validate your understanding of the **multiple meanings** of words. A dictionary entry includes the word's pronunciation, part of speech, definitions, etymology (word derivation), and related words.

Practice and Apply Consult references to find additional information about each word below. Take notes in the chart. Then, discuss with a partner how this knowledge deepens your understanding of the article by Ron Chernow.

WORD	ADDITIONAL INFORMATION
tepid	*also refers to temperature; lack of enthusiasm*
copious	*synonym: plentiful*
cardinal	*synonyms: fundamental, primary, paramount*
rudiments	*related to the word "rudimentary," which means "existing at a basic level"*
façade	*public image, outward show*
anomalous	*also means "deviating from what people expect"*

ENGLISH LEARNER SUPPORT

Vocabulary Strategy

- Vietnamese and Hmong speakers might not articulate the *t* in *tepid* and *rudiment*. Say the words aloud, stressing the *t*, and have students repeat.
- Speakers of Spanish, Hmong, Cantonese, Haitian Creole, and Khmer might pronounce the *e* sound in *tepid* as a long *a* sound. Write words such as *set, say; jet, jay; met, may*. Say them aloud and have students repeat. Then, have them listen to repeat *tepid*.
   ALL LEVELS

LANGUAGE CONVENTIONS: Hyphenation

Following the conventions of punctuation is important for clear communication. "Thomas Jefferson: The Best of Enemies" contains several examples of hyphenated words. Using a hyphen joins words into compounds so that their meaning is clear. Using hyphenated words can also be a simple way of expressing an idea. Compare the phrase from the article to the alternative that does not use a hyphen.

Phrase from article:

> after a <u>five-year</u> ministerial stint in Paris

Nonhyphenated alternative:

> after a ministerial stint of <u>five years</u> in Paris

The hyphenated adjective creates a more succinct text and contributes to a straightforward style. Hyphens have several purposes that are demonstrated in the article.

USES OF HYPHENS	
PURPOSE	**EXAMPLES**
join parts of a compound with *all-, ex-, self-,* or *-elect*	the self-invented Hamilton the self-reliant reflexes
join numbers to a noun to make an adjective	35-year-old wunderkind the 95-page pamphlet
join a prefix to a proper noun	anti-Hamilton resolutions
join two or more compounds to a single base	5,000- or 10,000-word memos
join a prefix or suffix to a noun	crypto-monarchist runner-up

Some compounds do not use hyphens. They may be open, as in *stock exchange* or *pseudo aristocrat*. They may be closed, as in *courthouse* or *underrated*. Consult a dictionary or style guide if you are unsure whether a compound word should be hyphenated, open, or closed.

Practice and Apply Look back at the essay you wrote comparing Hamilton's and Jefferson's visions of the future. Review your writing to see if you have used hyphenation conventions correctly. See if you can add one or two hyphenated words to give your writing a more concise style or more clarity. Review your edits with a partner and compare your use of hyphens.

Go to **Hyphens** in the **Grammar Studio** for more help.

LANGUAGE CONVENTIONS: Hyphenation

Review the information about hyphens with students. Explain that hyphens can create more concise ways of expressing ideas. Remind students that there are rules for hyphen usage and that not all compound adjectives are hyphenated or are two words. Also point out that sometimes two adjectives that come before a noun are not hyphenated, such as *small, yellow house*. The house is small *and* yellow. The adjectives are not working as one modifier.

Illustrate the ideas of using hyphens and how it can make writing more concise by rewriting some of the examples as phrases without hyphens. For example:

- *a wunderkind who was 35 years old*
- *resolutions that were against Hamilton*
- *memos that were 5,000 or 10,000 words long*

Practice and Apply Students should review their essays for correct use of hyphenation. If they do not have any, they should add one instance of hyphenation. Have pairs work together and share the changes they made and explain the purpose of the hyphenation.

ENGLISH LEARNER SUPPORT

Language Conventions Use the following supports with students at varying proficiency levels:

- Have students look in paragraph 1 to find other phrases that use hyphenation and copy them in their notebooks. Ask yes/no questions about the purpose of hyphenation for each example. **SUBSTANTIAL**

- Have students choose three hyphenated phrases from the chart and use them to write original sentences. **MODERATE**

- Have students come up with three new hyphenated phrases that are not in the selection and write sentences using them. **LIGHT**

AMERICAN EXPERIENCE: ALEXANDER HAMILTON

Video by PBS

GENRE ELEMENTS
MEDIA

Explain to students that **media** is meant to be widely consumed. It is created expressly for the purpose of pushing a specific agenda, and usually for a specific audience. Elements of writing are used to create some media, but other factors can contribute to the whole, such as aural and visual effects.

LEARNING OBJECTIVES

- Consider the purpose and intended audience for an informational video and analyze the effectiveness of multimodal/digital text.
- Research the Constitutional Convention.
- Compare and contrast the article and the video.
- Create a multimedia presentation to present research.
- Use Vocabulary Words when writing and discussing video.
- **Language** Discuss the main idea and key details.

TEXT COMPLEXITY

Quantitative Measures	American Experience: Alexander Hamilton	Lexile: N/A
Qualitative Measures	**Ideas Presented** Simple, single meaning. Literal, explicit, and direct. Clear purpose.	
	Structures Used Primarily explicit. Perhaps several points of view.	
	Language Used Explicit, literal, familiar language.	
	Knowledge Required Requires no special knowledge.	

Online **Ed**

RESOURCES

- Unit 2 Response Log

- Reading Studio: Notice & Note

- Writing Studio: Organizing Ideas

- Speaking and Listening Studio: Using Media in a Presentation

- "American Experience: Alexander Hamilton" Selection Test

SUMMARIES

English

"American Experience: Alexander Hamilton" traces Hamilton's life from his tragic childhood to his rise to prominence in the American Revolution and in the founding of the United States. It examines Hamilton's unique perspective, intellectual genius, and strong personality, connecting these traits to his remarkable achievements and his demise. The documentary segment explains the influence of Hamilton on the establishment of the central government in the challenging aftermath of the Revolution.

Spanish

Alexander Hamilton detalla la vida de Hamilton, desde su trágica infancia, hasta su ascenso en la revolución americana y la fundación de los Estados Unidos. Examina la perspectiva única de Hamilton, su genio intelectual y fuerte personalidad al conectar estas características con sus logros extraordinarios y su fallecimiento. El documental explica la influencia de Hamilton en el establecimiento del gobierno central durante el desafiante período subsecuente a la Revolución.

SMALL-GROUP OPTIONS

Have students work in small groups and pairs to read and discuss the selection.

Send a Problem

- After watching the video, pose this question: *What do you think was the creator's purpose for making this video?*

- Call on a student to respond. Wait up to 11 seconds.

- If the student has no response, s/he must call on another student by name to answer the same question.

- Have students continue asking each other for assistance as needed, citing specific visual and audio examples from the video.

- Monitor responses and ask more questions as appropriate.

Double-Entry Journal

- Have students use notebooks for recording their double-entry notes.

- Show students how to create a two-column format by drawing a line from top to bottom on each page. The left side will be *Scenes from the Video* while the right side will be *My Notes*.

- Encourage students to take notes of particularly important or confusing scenes or quotes in the left column.

- Students will then write their own questions, restatements, or interpretations in the right column next to the quoted material.

Text X-Ray: English Learner Support
for "American Experience: Alexander Hamilton"

Use the Text X-Ray and the supports and scaffolds in the Teacher's Edition to help guide students at different proficiency levels through the selection.

INTRODUCE THE SELECTION
DISCUSS STATE AND FEDERAL GOVERNMENT

The beginning of the video explains that at the end of the Revolutionary War, the United States was *disunified*. Discuss with students the meaning of *unity*, and how its root can be seen as the word *unit* (meaning a single thing) and the word *United* in the name *United States*. Discuss the prefix *dis-* and how its addition to a root word can change the root word's meaning to its opposite. Ask students to think of other examples of words that use the prefix *dis-*.

Explain that *federal* means applying to the entire United States, a *federation* of individual states. After the Revolutionary War, the individual states were the most powerful political units. However, it was not clear how those states were going to work together. Alexander Hamilton's idea was to make the federal government into a strong political unit that would control how the states worked together.

The video states that Hamilton was an immigrant, and because he was not born in any of the individual states, he was better able to see the United States as a strong unit—one to strengthen and be loyal to. Ask students to think of reasons an immigrant might be more patriotic to an entire country than just to the small part of the country where he or she now lives.

CULTURAL REFERENCES

The following words or phrases may be unfamiliar to students:

- *Galloping consumption*: A disease that develops quickly (*galloping* refers to the running movement of a horse). *Consumption* was the term for tuberculosis at this time. Hamilton is saying that the country is sick and weak.
- *Republic*: This term describes a government run by people who are elected to do government jobs. This is different from governments in which people get positions of power when the person who has the job dies, such as in a country ruled by a king or queen.
- *Ratify:* This means to agree officially or to approve a treaty, amendment, etc.
- *Delegate*: This refers to a person authorized or elected to represent a district, state, etc., in discussions or government meetings held to reach an agreement.
- *Congress*: A meeting of a group; in this context, the Congress is the organization that governs the country.

LISTENING

Identify Central Ideas

Explain that the beginning of the video clip gives some important background information. Students should listen for key ideas about the situation and about Hamilton. This will help them follow the points made in the video segment.

Play the clip several times. Use the following supports with students at varying proficiency levels:

- Focus on the first two minutes of the clip. Ask yes/no questions about the country and the founders in the time just following the Revolution. For example, ask: *Did the country have problems?* (Yes.) *Is Hamilton different than most of the other Founders?* (Yes.) **SUBSTANTIAL**
- Ask questions about issues the United States faced just after the Revolution (*money problems, unity, states argued, who would control*). What did some of the Founders do after the end of the war? (*returned home; left the country to work as officials*) **MODERATE**
- Have students work with a partner to discuss the clip. After students discuss, ask questions to assess their understanding. For example: *How was Hamilton similar to and different from the other Founders? What problems was the country facing after the war?* **LIGHT**

SPEAKING

Discuss Main Idea and Key Details

Remind students that it is important to listen to and watch for the main idea and key details when viewing a video. Recognizing key details will help them understand the video.

Play the video twice. Use the following supports with students at varying proficiency levels:

- Ask students to identify the main idea and key details. Provide sentence frames: *Hamilton wants the states to become* _____. (united) *He helps write the* _____. (Constitution) *He writes* _____ *to get support for the Constitution.* (essays) **SUBSTANTIAL**
- Ask students to identify the main idea and key details. *What does Hamilton want?* (for the states to be united) *What does he do to achieve this?* (helps write the Constitution) *How does he try to get support for his ideas?* (He writes the Federalist Papers.) **MODERATE**
- Have partners ask and answer questions about the main idea and key details. Then have partners work with another pair and discuss the main idea and details they identified. **LIGHT**

READING

Acquire Vocabulary

Tell students that learning and using basic and academic vocabulary will help them understand the video and be able to express their knowledge and ideas.

Have students read the Background paragraph on page 127. Use the following supports with students at varying proficiency levels:

- Read the paragraph aloud several times. Then, have students choral read the paragraph. Ask students to find details about Hamilton's life and personality. If students have trouble, show them a sentence and ask them to find a key word or phrase. **SUBSTANTIAL**
- Tell students to write *life*, *personality*, and *influence* on sheets of paper. Have them read the paragraph. Then, have partners work together to identify details for each category. **MODERATE**
- Have students read the paragraph independently. Then, have them work with partners to summarize what points the video will focus on. **LIGHT**

WRITING

Write an Essay

Work with students to read the writing assignment on Student Edition p. 129.

Use the following supports with students at varying proficiency levels:

- Ask students to watch for things in the video that help tell the story, such as pictures of things mentioned, historic scenes, and actors playing historic people. Ask students to list those things and to each write a short sentence such as _____ *helped me understand the story.* **SUBSTANTIAL**
- Discuss the similarities and differences between the video and the article. Ask students what words, phrases, or ideas in the article helped them understand the video. Then, have students work with partners to write paragraphs that compare the video and the article. **MODERATE**
- Have each student write a paragraph comparing reading the article with watching the video, answering these questions: *How did the video help me answer questions I had from the article? Did I learn more from the article or the video?* Have pairs exchange papers and compare their answers. **LIGHT**

Connect to the
ESSENTIAL QUESTION

This video explores the context of the disagreements and power struggles between the Federalists and their opponents regarding the Constitution. This context will help students understand the stakes for the Founders as they debate the best way to govern their new country.

QUICK START

Encourage students to recall facts about Alexander Hamilton from Ron Chernow's article "Thomas Jefferson, The Best of Enemies," such as: *Hamilton was the first Treasury Secretary; he feuded with Jefferson; he favored a strong central government and president; he was an abolitionist; he had family ties to France; his extramarital affair was exposed.* Have students explore the relationship between Hamilton's background and personal circumstances and his views on the proper role of the central government. How did his connection to the country differ from that of his primary opponents? After students discuss, have volunteers share facts and questions.

DETERMINE AUTHOR'S PURPOSE

Note that the "author" of a video achieves his or her **purpose** by using sounds and images, as well as words. Instruct students to consider the author's purpose as they watch this video. What messages or ideas does the video seek to communicate? How do the sounds and images help achieve this purpose?

■ English Learner Support

Acquire Vocabulary Explain that a **documentary** is a video or film about a real person or event. It is not fiction; it provides information in the same way as an informative text. Give students sentence frames to discuss documentaries, such as "This video, _____[title]_____, is a documentary about _____." **SUBSTANTIAL**

ANALYZE EFFECTIVENESS
OF DIGITAL TEXT

Have students create charts like the ones on this page, listing **graphic features** and sound elements. As they watch the video, have them note examples of each type of feature.

MEDIA

AMERICAN EXPERIENCE: ALEXANDER HAMILTON

Video by **PBS**

? ESSENTIAL QUESTION:

How can we share power and build alliances?

QUICK START

List two facts you know about Alexander Hamilton. Then, list two questions that you have about him. Discuss your questions about him with a partner.

DETERMINE AUTHOR'S PURPOSE

The **purpose,** or intent, of an informational video is often to communicate a message about the subject. To achieve the purpose, the video's creator uses words as well as graphic features and sound elements. In a documentary about a historical person, the purpose is often to explain that person's accomplishments and significance to an audience.

ANALYZE EFFECTIVENESS OF DIGITAL TEXT

GENRE ELEMENTS: VIDEO

- is created for a specific purpose, usually to convey a message
- targets a particular audience
- includes graphic features and sound elements to convey ideas

Digital texts like videos convey ideas through graphic features and sound elements. You must determine if they are conveyed effectively. **Graphic features** can help viewers clarify their understanding of complex events.

STILLS	Images that are visually motionless, such as illustrations, maps, or photographs.
ANIMATION	Images that appear to move and seem alive are created through drawings, computer graphics, or photographs.
ACTOR PORTRAYALS	Actors playing the roles of historical or fictional people bring the subject matter to life and provide context.

Sound elements are what viewers hear in a video or embedded sound file.

MUSIC	Sounds created by singing, playing instruments, or using computer-generated tones can create a mood.
NARRATION	Narrator voice-overs guide the viewer; the words as well as the vocal quality of the narrator add to the experience.
SOUND EFFECTS	If reenactments or animations are used, sound effects—such as noises that suggest fighting in a war documentary—add realism.

© Houghton Mifflin Harcourt Publishing Company

126   Unit 2

 ENGLISH LEARNER SUPPORT

Practice Content-Area Vocabulary Tell students that there are different words that name the kinds of things we see and hear in videos. On the board, make two columns, one labeled *See* and the other labeled *Hear*. In the *See* column, list *images, pictures, stills,* and *animation*. Say each word aloud and have students repeat. Explain that *image* and *picture* are synonyms, or words that mean the same thing. A *still* is an image that is seen when a video is paused, or what is seen in a single moment. An *animation* is a cartoon. Next, under *Hear*, write *music, narration,* and *sound effects*. Say each word aloud and have students repeat. Explain that these are things that might be heard in a video, and give examples of each. **SUBSTANTIAL**

BACKGROUND

The PBS American Experience *documentary "Alexander Hamilton" traces Hamilton's life from his tragic childhood to his rise to prominence in the American Revolution and in the founding of the United States. It focuses on Hamilton's unique perspective, intellectual genius, and strong personality. It connects these characteristics to both his remarkable achievements and his demise. The segment of the documentary that you are about to watch explains the influence of Hamilton on the establishment of the central government in the challenging aftermath of the Revolution.*

SETTING A PURPOSE

As you view the video, evaluate how effectively the video uses graphic features and sound elements to achieve its purpose.

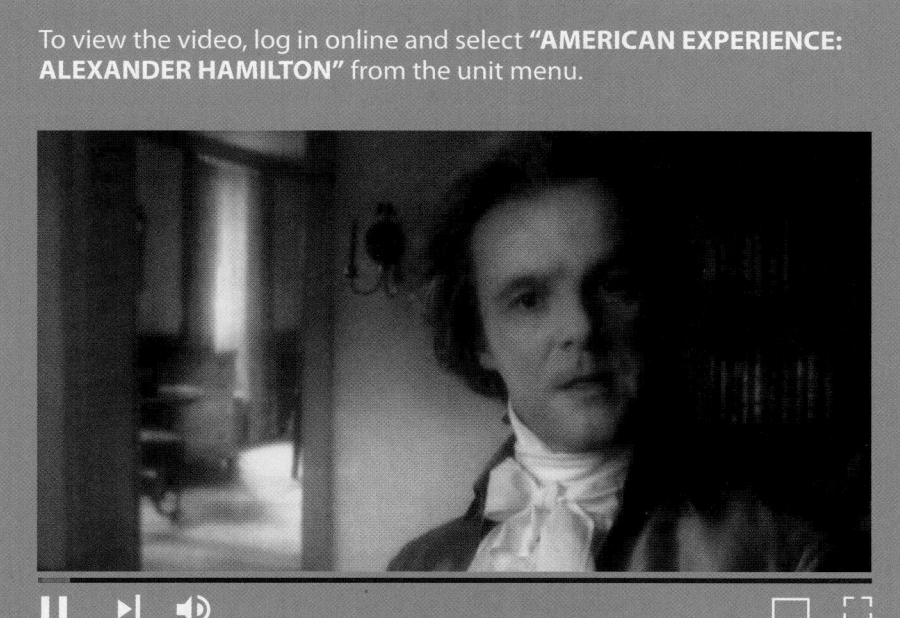

To view the video, log in online and select **"AMERICAN EXPERIENCE: ALEXANDER HAMILTON"** from the unit menu.

As needed, pause the video to make notes about what impresses you or about ideas you might want to talk about later. Replay the video so that you can clarify anything you do not understand.

American Experience: Alexander Hamilton   127

BACKGROUND

This segment of the documentary traces Hamilton's role in the transition from the Confederation Congress, formed immediately after the Revolutionary War, to the government under the Constitution. Hamilton's unique background, lacking allegiance to any particular state, is connected to his preference for a stronger central government, as well as his ability to diagnose the root of the many challenges facing the loose confederation of states after the War of Independence.

SETTING A PURPOSE

Direct students to use the Setting a Purpose prompt to focus their viewing.

 For **listening, speaking** and **reading support** for students at varying proficiency levels, see the **Text X-Ray** on pages 126C–126D.

WHEN STUDENTS STRUGGLE . . .

Organize Information Have students watch the video three times. Guide students to take notes about words, ideas, or events in the video they did not understand. Have them create three-column charts labeled *Words, Ideas,* and *Events* and list in the appropriate columns items from their notes. After a second viewing, have students list any additional questions. After the final viewing, ask students to share some questions and say whether those questions were answered. Lead a discussion to help students answer one another's questions.

ANALYZE MEDIA

Possible answers:

1. **DOK 4:** *Hamilton's views on states' rights and the central government were different from those of many others. This is reflected in the actor portrayals in the video, where Hamilton is seen writing alone or speaking directly to the audience, rather than engaged in conversation with the other Founders.*

2. **DOK 2:** *He was an outsider with no loyalty to any of the original states, which his contemporaries referred to as their countries. Therefore, he felt loyal to the whole nation, not just to a part of it. This gave him a strong sense of national identity at a time when most people's primary loyalty was to a state.*

3. **DOK 4:** *The creator's purpose is to show how Hamilton's unique perspective and force of personality gave him the tools needed to save the fledgling nation from chaos. The video uses narrator voice-over, actor reenacts, music, zoom-in-on and pan-through photographs and paintings, interviews with experts, and actors reading from primary documents. Often, more than one element is used at a time. This creates a varied and high-interest video that moves at a good pace and holds viewer attention.*

4. **DOK 4:** *The video uses the word "weak" to describe the Confederation Congress. The actor reads a primary document that explains Hamilton's opinion of the nation as suffering from an illness to which he has a "remedy" to make it "strong." The contrast is between "weak" and "strong" and "consumption" and "remedy."*

5. **DOK 4:** *According to the historians, Hamilton orchestrates a series of small meetings to float his ideas and, at the same time, creates a public image of great support for his ideas. The historians seem impressed by Hamilton's nerve. Hamilton's words reveal that he believes projecting confidence and strength is part of success as a leader. The combination of these two perspectives shows Hamilton's inner motivations, as well as an objective view of how his strategy played out.*

RESEARCH

Review the research tip with students and discuss what constitutes a credible source for research.

Extend Direct students to use their notes from watching the video to recall key conflicts about the Constitution. Does either painting appear to portray these conflicts? Ask students to identify elements in the paintings that distinguish the different personal qualities of the Founders.

 **RESPOND**

ANALYZE MEDIA

Support your answers with evidence from the video. NOTEBOOK

1. **Analyze** The video states that Hamilton was "almost alone in his determination to change the direction of the country." Explain whether graphic features and sound elements effectively reflect this statement.

2. **Summarize** According to the video, how did Hamilton's childhood in the Caribbean affect his approach to solving the nation's problems?

3. **Evaluate** Overall, what is the purpose of this video segment, and what graphic features and sound elements does the video's creator use to achieve this purpose?

4. **Analyze** How does the video characterize the Confederation Congress in the narrator's voice-over? How does the actor speaking Hamilton's own words show a contrast between the government's present state and Hamilton's dreams for a better government?

5. **Evaluate** According to the historians in the video, what is Hamilton's strategy for putting his ideas forward? How does Hamilton himself portray his actions? How effectively does the video use both Hamilton's own ideas and the ideas of others to create a full picture of a complex person?

RESEARCH TIP
To find credible sources, look for information on a site that tells who created and maintains it. If the site contains no information about those who created it—an "About Us" or similar explanation—you may need to use the name of the group in a search engine in order to discover more about the content creators.

RESEARCH

Hamilton was a delegate to the Constitutional Convention. Research this important meeting to find out more and answer the questions in the chart.

QUESTION	ANSWER
Which state did Alexander Hamilton represent at the Convention, and who else were delegates from that state?	*New York; John Lansing, Jr. and Robert Yates*
Which state did not send delegates to the Convention? What was the reason?	*Rhode Island did not attend because its leaders were distrustful of a strong federal government.*
Of the 55 men who went to the Convention, how many did not sign the Constitution? What were their reasons?	*George Mason, Elbridge Gerry, and Edmund Randolf did not sign the Constitution because it lacked a Bill of Rights.*

Extend A number of paintings depict the Constitutional Convention. Research and choose two to compare and contrast. What do they have in common, and how do they differ? If you were planning to use one of the paintings as a still in a documentary about the Convention, which one would you choose, and why? Briefly write your ideas and share them with a partner.

EL ENGLISH LEARNER SUPPORT

Oral Assessment To gauge comprehension and speaking skills, conduct an informal oral assessment. Walk around the class, talking with students and asking these questions:

- What problems did the United States face after the Revolution? *(financial problems; questions about being unified)* **MODERATE**

- Where was Hamilton from? *(the Caribbean)* **SUBSTANTIAL**

- How did this make Hamilton different from other Founders? *(The others felt very connected to and loyal to their states. Hamilton felt more connected to the whole country.)* **LIGHT**

- What kind of government did Hamilton want? *(a strong government)* **MODERATE**

CREATE AND PRESENT

Write an Essay Both this video segment and "Thomas Jefferson: The Best of Enemies" explore the contributions of Alexander Hamilton to the founding of the United States. Write an essay comparing and contrasting the two pieces.

❏ First, organize your thoughts. Make lists or charts to record the similarities and differences between the two selections.

❏ Make sure to compare the content, delivery, purpose, and audience of each.

❏ Evaluate the major differences between the video and article formats as well as differences in focus and message.

❏ Outline your main points of comparison. Include examples from each source that illustrate those main points.

❏ Be sure to begin your essay with a clear thesis statement and to end with a summarizing or concluding statement.

Present Your Ideas Communicate your ideas as a multimedia presentation.

❏ Use slide presentation software to communicate your main ideas.

❏ Include text examples from the article and embedded video or still images from the documentary to illustrate your points.

❏ Speak clearly and stay focused on your main points as you present your ideas.

 Go to **Writing Informative Texts: Organizing Ideas** in the **Writing Studio** for help.

 Go to **Using Media in a Presentation** in the **Speaking and Listening Studio** for help.

RESPOND TO THE ESSENTIAL QUESTION

? How can we share power and build alliances?

Gather Information Review your notes on "American Experience: Alexander Hamilton." Then, add relevant information to your Response Log. As you determine which information to include, think about:

• what made Hamilton unique among early leaders of the country
• how Alexander Hamilton built alliances with others
• his influence on the founding of the United States

UNIT 2 RESPONSE LOG

ACADEMIC VOCABULARY
As you write and discuss what you learned from the video, be sure to use the Academic Vocabulary words. Check off each of the words that you use.

❏ **contrary**
❏ **founder**
❏ **ideological**
❏ **publication**
❏ **revolution**

CREATE AND PRESENT

Write an Essay As students compare and contrast the article and video, remind them to focus on aspects of genre and presentation, as well as the information contained in each piece. Direct students to examine their list of similarities and differences in order to come up with a thesis statement. Explain that the thesis statement should briefly summarize the similarities and differences in the way Alexander Hamilton is portrayed in the two pieces.

 For **writing support** for students at varying proficiency levels, see the **Text X-Ray** on page 126D.

Present Your Ideas Provide assistance to students in how to embed video and still images using slide presentation software. Direct them to review the points in their essays to find one example that best supports each main point. Have them practice their presentations in pairs, and ask each listening student to summarize the presenter's thesis and main points to make sure that those are clear.

RESPOND TO THE ESSENTIAL QUESTION

Allow time for students to add details from "American Experience: Alexander Hamilton" to their Unit 2 Response Logs.

© Houghton Mifflin Harcourt Publishing Company

A SOLDIER FOR THE CROWN

Short Story by Charles Johnson

GENRE ELEMENTS
SHORT STORY

Tell students that a **short story** is a work of fiction that is built around a singular central idea and is written to be read in one sitting. Short stories generally feature a particular conflict that ends up being resolved by the end of the narrative. They also typically incorporate one main theme or message that the author wishes to convey to his or her audience.

LEARNING OBJECTIVES

- Analyze the structure and narrative methods of short stories.
- Evaluate the use of literary devices.
- Conduct research on what happened to loyalists during and after the American Revolution.
- Write an opinion essay about taking risks.
- Debate about Freeman's gamble.
- Understand and use prefixes and suffixes.
- Learn the rules for subject-verb agreement.
- **Language** Discuss character traits using key words.

TEXT COMPLEXITY

Quantitative Measures	A Soldier for the Crown	Lexile: 1250L
Qualitative Measures	**Ideas Presented** Probably requires weighing of multiple perspectives; some analysis of bias and author's motivations; some ambiguity.	
	Structures Used More complex, multiple perspectives may be presented; more deviation from chronology; tables and figures support understanding.	
	Language Used Vocabulary not defined at point of use; mostly Tier II and III words; metaphor (rather than similes) used more; multiple technical words may be used in one sentence.	
	Knowledge Required More complex problems; experiences may be less familiar to many; cultural or historical references.	

RESOURCES

- Unit 2 Response Log
- 🔊 Selection Audio
- 📖 Reading Studio: Notice & Note
- **LEVEL UP** Level Up Tutorial: Setting
- Writing Studio: Writing Arguments
- Vocabulary Studio: Word Structure
- ❗ Grammar Studio: Module 5: Lesson 1: Subject-Verb Agreement
- ✓ "A Soldier for the Crown" Selection Test

SUMMARIES

English

In "A Soldier for the Crown," author Charles Johnson explores the concept of freedom through a powerful narrative set during the American Revolution. In the story, the protagonist, Dorothy, seeks freedom from the racial enslavement of her day-to-day life as an African American. Dorothy also finds liberation in disguising her gender to live as a man, a decision that helps her assume more control over her life and actions.

Spanish

En "Un soldado de la corona", el autor Charles Johnson explora el concepto de la libertad a través de una poderosa narración en el contexto de la Revolución estadounidense. En la historia, la protagonista, Dorothy, busca la libertad de la esclavitud de su vida como afroamericana. Dorothy consigue liberarse al ocultar su género para vivir como hombre, una decisión que le ayuda a asumir más control sobre su vida y acciones.

 ## SMALL-GROUP OPTIONS

Have students work in small groups and pairs to read and discuss the selection.

Three-Minute Review

- After students read the selection, set a timer for three minutes.
- Have students work independently to write clarifying questions about what they read.
- After three minutes, ask volunteers to share their questions.
- Briefly discuss answers to each question.

Double-Entry Journal

- Have students use a notebook for recording their double-entry notes.
- Show students how to create a two-column format by drawing a line from top to bottom on each page. The left side will be "Quotes from the Text" while the right will be "My Notes."
- Encourage students to copy particularly important or confusing text passages in the left column.
- Students then write their own questions, restatements, or interpretations in the right column next to the quoted material.

Text X-Ray: English Learner Support
for "A Soldier for the Crown"

Use the Text X-Ray and the supports and scaffolds in the Teacher's Edition to help guide students at different proficiency levels through the selection.

INTRODUCE THE SELECTION
DISCUSS POINT OF VIEW

In this text, students will need to differentiate between points of view. Explain:

- First person means the narrator uses *I* and is a character in the story.
- Third person means the narrator talks about others, using *he, she, they*. A third-person narrator is not a character in the story.
- Second person means the narrator says *you*.

Ask students to provide examples from their own lives using sentences in each of the first, second, and third person. Discuss the types of situations in which each point of view might be used. Explain that in the text, the narrator speaks to the main character, who is a slave. During the American Revolution, some slaves had the chance to gain freedom by fighting in the war.

CULTURAL REFERENCES

The following words or phrases may be unfamiliar to students:

- *luck of the draw* (paragraph 2): outcome of chance, not in one's control
- *Continental Army* (paragraph 4): the name of the American army (the colonists) who fought against the British
- *regiment* (paragraph 14): unit of an army
- *bearing arms* (paragraph 14): carrying guns
- *seesawing war* (paragraph 15): change from one condition to another

LISTENING

Understand Characters

Explain that identifying character traits can give readers more insight into who the character is.

Have students listen as you read paragraph 2. Use the following supports with students at varying proficiency levels:

- As you read the text, pause and emphasize phrases that describe the character. Then, have students repeat phrases. Ask yes/no questions to check comprehension. For example: *Is the main character a slave?* (yes) *Does the main character like to take chances?* (yes) *Does the main character think taking a risk is a good thing?* (yes) **SUBSTANTIAL**
- After students listen to the text, have them identify key words about the character. Help them define words using brief sentence stems, such as: *The character likes to _____. The character thinks taking a risk is _____.* **MODERATE**
- After reading the text, ask: *What do we know about the main character? Why is this information important?* Encourage students to ask for clarification as needed. **LIGHT**

SPEAKING

Infer Emotion

Explain that making inferences about what and why characters feel can help readers understand characters, plot, and theme.

Use the following supports with students at varying proficiency levels:

- Read aloud the sentence in paragraph 4: "You know you are fortunate to be on board." Explain that "on board" means "on a ship." Then, read aloud the paragraph, pausing frequently to ask yes/no questions, such as *Is the character escaping slavery?* (yes) *Are other people trying to get on the boat?* (yes) *Does the character feel lucky?* (yes) **SUBSTANTIAL**
- Read aloud the first part of paragraph 4, through "*That might have been me.*" Ask: *Why does the character feel fortunate? What is the character doing?* Have students respond using complete sentences. **MODERATE**
- Have volunteers take turns reading paragraphs 4 and 5 aloud. Then, ask students to identify emotions the character feels in this passage. (*fortunate, grateful, determined*) Have students respond using complete sentences and tell why the character feels these ways. **LIGHT**

READING

Understand Plot

Explain that students can increase comprehension of the plot by asking and answering *what* and *why* questions.

Use the following supports with students at varying proficiency levels:

- Have students echo read paragraph 6 (the last two sentences) through paragraph 12. Help students complete these frames: *Titus and Caesar plan to _____ horses and _____ away. They do not plan to _____ the main character with them.* **SUBSTANTIAL**
- Have partners take turns reading aloud paragraphs 6–12. Ask: *What do Titus and Caesar plan? Why? How does the main character feel? What does the character want?* **MODERATE**
- Have students read paragraphs 6–12. Have them explain Titus and Caesar's plan, and why they don't want to take the main character. Ask: *What does the main character mean by "I'll tell"?* **LIGHT**

WRITING

Write an Opinion

Explain that writing about an opinion means stating what you believe. Writers use reasons to support what they believe. Work with students to complete the argumentative writing assignment on Student Edition page 139.

Use the following supports with students at varying proficiency levels:

- Modify the Write an Argumentative Essay task by having students write a short paragraph. Provide frames. *Taking risks is _____. I think taking risks is a _____ idea. I took a risk when _____.* **SUBSTANTIAL**
- After reviewing the checklist, provide students with sentence frames to help them start their essays: *I think taking risks is _____ because _____. The narrator takes a risk by _____. One risk I have taken is _____.* Have students exchange papers with a partner and work together to add more detail and support. **MODERATE**
- Remind students to use reasons or evidence to support their opinion. Point out that the words *because first, second,* and *last* can be used to signal a reason. Have pairs work together to find places to add reasons or evidence. **LIGHT**

Connect to the
? ESSENTIAL QUESTION

In "A Soldier for the Crown," Charles Johnson examines multiple levels of freedom. The protagonist, Dorothy, seeks freedom from the enslavement that is forced upon her because of her skin color. She also finds freedom in hiding her gender and living as a man, because this gives her more control over her life and the freedom to make decisions for herself.

A SOLDIER FOR THE CROWN

Short story by **Charles Johnson**

? ESSENTIAL QUESTION:

How do we gain our freedom?

130   Unit 2

 LEARNING MINDSET

Persistence Remind students that challenging moments are when growth and learning occur. Encourage students not to give up when they find something challenging. Explain that making an effort is a crucial part of increasing knowledge, intelligence, and ability. Being persistent in the face of challenges requires great effort, because these are moments that can have big pay-offs in terms of intellectual and academic growth. Model positive self-talk to students, such as "I know I can do this if I keep at it." Ask volunteers to offer other examples of positive self-talk that can help students be persistent.

QUICK START

Share with a partner a time you or someone you know risked something in hopes of a desirable outcome. Did subsequent events unfold as expected? Was the risk worthwhile?

ANALYZE LITERARY ELEMENTS

Point of view refers to the method an author uses to narrate a story. In a work written in the **first-person point of view,** the narrator is a character in the story and plot events are experienced from the narrator's limited perspective. When a writer uses the **third-person point of view,** the narrator is not a character in the story but an outside observer. A more unusual method of narration is the **second-person point of view,** in which the narrator addresses someone using the pronoun *you.* In "A Soldier for the Crown," the narrator addresses the main character, Alexander Freeman, but often speaks as if he or she has entered the mind of that character.

With the second-person point of view, the reader may not know if the author is addressing a character, the reader, or the self. The reader must piece together information the narrator reveals to understand plot events or characters' behaviors. Point of view can also shape the development of the theme—the underlying message of a story—by affecting how much readers know and when they learn key information.

GENRE ELEMENTS: SHORT STORY

- is told from a particular point of view that impacts the reader's understanding of events
- contains literary elements that influence the development of the plot
- expresses a theme or the author's message

ANALYZE AND EVALUATE PLOT

Plot is the sequence of events in a literary work. Charles Johnson uses literary elements to develop the events surrounding the main character, a gambler named Alexander Freeman, in "A Soldier for the Crown."

- **Suspense** is the excitement or tension that readers feel as they wait to find out how a story ends. The author builds suspense when he introduces the main character as a risk-taker and creates suspense about the story's outcome with statements such as, "But did you win *this* time?"

- **Setting** is the time and place in which events take place. Setting also includes the work's historical context. **Historical context** refers to the conditions and customs during the time period in which events occur. In "A Soldier for the Crown," the writer includes details that tell you the historical context. As you read, think about how the setting influences the events of the plot.

- **Ambiguity** is the uncertainty created when readers can interpret words, phrases, or events in more than one way. The author builds the story by forcing the reader to put together clues about Freeman. As you read, your understanding of these clues may change.

As you read, analyze the writer's use of literary elements and evaluate how they shape the author's portrayal of the plot.

QUICK START

After the students have read the Quick Start question, have them take turns sharing their stories about taking a risk in hopes of a positive result. Encourage students to examine the implications of the risk that was taken, including what could have gone wrong or what the other outcomes might have been. Have students use this reflection to decide whether or not the risk was worth taking.

ANALYZE LITERARY ELEMENTS

Remind students that some narrators are omniscient: that is, they know all the characters' thoughts, feelings, and actions. Other narrators are limited to knowing what a single character knows. Explain that the text students are about to read uses a second person point of view throughout the story. The narrator addresses the main character as "you." The narrator for this story is not completely omniscient; the narrator's perspective is closely aligned to the knowledge of the protagonist. Explain that this narrator can be considered limited omniscient. Tell students that as they read, they should think about how the focus of the narrator and the use of the second person affects the reader's experience of the story.

ANALYZE AND EVALUATE PLOT

Note that ambiguity is a tool authors can use to build suspense. Encourage students to be on the lookout for ambiguity in the text and to think about how ambiguity and word choice lead the reader to make assumptions about the main character. Tell students to look for areas in the story where the author's use of ambiguity seems particularly purposeful.

CRITICAL VOCABULARY

Discuss which of these vocabulary words can easily be broken down into simple, familiar words. Direct the students to the terms "unalienable" and "belatedly" and discuss the familiar words and prefixes within them. Demonstrate how those smaller parts can be used to help construct a definition for the word, even when the exact meaning in unknown.

Possible answers:

1. *She insisted that her rights could never be taken away and the court must guarantee them.*

2. *His carelessness and lack of concern for others' feelings were evident in his always apologizing too late.*

3. *The solution to the mystery proved difficult to find, despite the detective's hard work.*

4. *She served in the role of an interpreter for her parents.*

■ English Learner Support

Use Cognates Point out the Spanish cognates *capacity/capacidad* and *elusive/elusivo*. Then, point out the prefix and suffix in the term *unalienable*. Explain that *un-* works similarly to the Spanish prefix *in-* meaning *not*. The suffix *-able* makes a verb into an adjective. **ALL LEVELS**

LANGUAGE CONVENTIONS

Review the concept of noun and verb agreement with the students. Discuss how this can become more confusing as sentences get more complex and the noun and verb are further apart. Give some examples of sentences where the verb/noun agreement in number might be less clear, such as "many parts of the tradition are unusual to outsiders." Even though "tradition" is singular in this sentence, the actual subject is "many parts" of the tradition, so the verb must remain plural.

ANNOTATION MODEL

Remind students of annotation strategies such as underlining important details, circling key words, and making notes. Point out that they can use their own system for marking up the selection in their write-in text. They might want to color-code their annotations by using highlighters. Their notes in the margin should identify various types of evidence and examples, including: direct quotations; historical facts; timeline of events; and observational details.

 **GET READY**

CRITICAL VOCABULARY

| capacity | belatedly | unalienable | elusive |

To see how many Critical Vocabulary words you understand, restate each sentence using a different word or words for the boldfaced term.

1. She insisted that her rights were **unalienable** and the court must guarantee them.

2. His carelessness and lack of concern for others' feelings were evident in his always apologizing **belatedly.**

3. The solution to the mystery proved **elusive,** despite the detective's hard work.

4. She served in the **capacity** of an interpreter for her parents.

LANGUAGE CONVENTIONS

Subject-Verb Agreement The subject and verb in a clause must agree in number. That means that if the subject is singular, the verb must also be singular. A plural subject requires a plural verb.

The <u>document</u>, dated April 1783, <u>brings</u> a broad smile to your lips.

When a pronoun is the subject of a sentence, the verb also needs to agree in person—first, second, or third—and number. For example: *I am, he is, you are, they are.* As you read, notice how correct subject-verb agreement adds clarity to what is happening in the story.

ANNOTATION MODEL **NOTICE & NOTE**

As you read, notice the way the writer uses literary elements to develop the plot. Note examples of the use of point of view and how it links to plot, character, and theme. Mark any other details that stand out to you. In the model, you can see one reader's notes about "A Soldier for the Crown."

Before the war broke out, when you were still a servant in Master William Selby's house, you'd bet on anything—how early spring thaw might come, or if your older brother Titus would beat your cousin Caesar in a wrestling match—and most of the time you won.

What war broke out? Seems like it is in the past.

Second-person point of view reveals character traits.

 ENGLISH LEARNER SUPPORT

Practice Subject-Verb Agreement Remind students that verbs are action words, or what happens in a sentence, and the subject is who or what does the action. Have students identify the subjects and verbs in the Critical Vocabulary sentences 1, 3, and 4. Explain that the endings of verbs are different depending on the kind of subject and when the action is taking place. Making sure the verb has the right ending is called subject-verb agreement. Give examples of verb endings changing according to the subject in a present tense verb. (For example: *I insist, he insists*.) Then, give other examples of present tense verbs with different subjects, and ask students to give the correct verb ending. **ALL LEVELS**

BACKGROUND

Charles Johnson *(1948–), a writer, philosopher, artist, and educator, has often confronted the effects of race and racism. "Racism is based on our belief in a division between Self and Other, and our tendency to measure ourselves against others," he says. "Sad to say, it is also based on fear." Johnson's work has earned a MacArthur fellowship, the National Book Award for* Middle Passage *(1990), and the American Academy of Arts and Letters Award.*

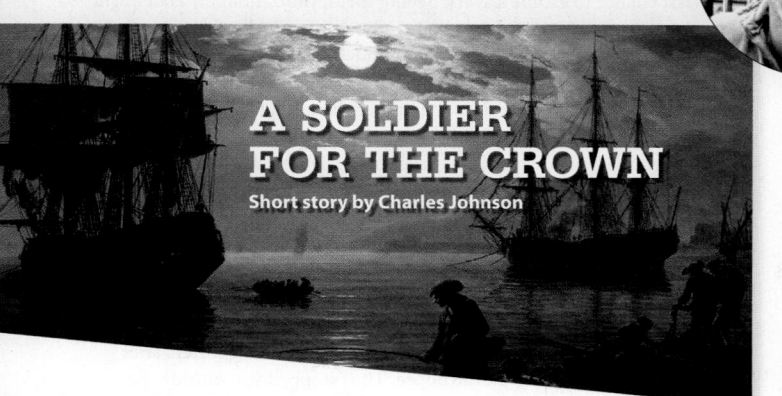

A SOLDIER FOR THE CROWN

Short story by Charles Johnson

SETTING A PURPOSE

As you read, pay attention to the way in which personal circumstance, social standing, and ideological differences affect the meaning of liberty.

1   YOU ALWAYS WERE a gambler.
2   Before the war broke out, when you were still a servant in Master William Selby's house, you'd bet on anything—how early spring thaw might come, or if your older brother Titus would beat your cousin Caesar in a wrestling match—and most of the time you won. There was something about gambling that you could not resist. There was suspense, the feeling that the future was not already written by white hands. Or finished. There was chance, the luck of the draw. In the roll of dice or a card game, there was always—what to call it?— an *openness*, a chance that the outcome would go this way or that. For or against you. Of course, in bondage to Master Selby there were no odds. Whichever way the dice fell or the cards came up, you began and ended your day a slave.
3   But did you win *this* time?
4   Standing by the wooden rail on a ship bound for Nova Scotia, crammed with strangers fleeing the collapse of their colonial world—women and children, whites and blacks, whose names

A Soldier for the Crown   133

Notice & Note

Use the side margins to notice and note signposts in the text.

ANALYZE AND EVALUATE PLOT

Annotate: Identify statements in paragraph 2 that introduce suspense.

Infer: What do these statements make you wonder about what will happen next?

BACKGROUND

Write the year "1783" on the board and discuss with the students why this time was significant for the United States and Canada. Remind students that this is the year that the American Revolution ended. Ask them if they know anything about the role of the black communities in the war, both in the United States and in Canada. Discuss the tactics used by both U.S. and British forces to enlist both enslaved people and free black people in the fighting. Point out that both sides offered freedom as an incentive to get more enslaved people to enlist.

SETTING A PURPOSE

Direct students to use the Setting a Purpose prompt to focus their reading.

 ## ANALYZE AND EVALUATE PLOT

Remind students an author may build suspense at the beginning of a story when a character is introduced. The author may not say everything readers need to know, but instead hint at what the character is like or how the characters behaves. Point out that the author does not directly describe the character or even give him or her a name. Have students think about what the author says about the character and what questions they have about him or her. Also point out that paragraph 3 is one sentence, and it is a question. Asking a question is a common way to build suspense. (***Possible answer:*** *The phrase "when you were still a servant" makes me wonder how the main character escaped slavery. "But did you win* this *time?" makes me wonder what "this time" refers to and what the main character might have won or lost.*)

For **listening**, **speaking**, and **reading support** for students at varying proficiency levels, see the **Text X-Ray** on pages 130C–130D.

 ## ENGLISH LEARNER SUPPORT

Understand Sentence Fragments Explain to students that fiction writers sometimes use sentence fragments—parts of a sentence that do not contain both a subject and a verb. Tell students that sentence fragments are often an addition to the previous sentence. Help students find two sentence fragments on this page and incorporate them into the preceding sentences. (*"Or finished," line 8: There was suspense, the feeling that the future was not already written or finished by white hands. "For or against you," lines 10–11: In the roll of dice or a card game, there was always . . . a chance that the outcome would go this way or that, for or against you.*) **LIGHT**

© Houghton Mifflin Harcourt Publishing Company • Image Credits: © John Storey/The LIFE Images Collection/Getty Images; © Photo: Josse/Leemage/Getty Images

ANALYZE LITERARY ELEMENTS

Remind students to look for words that might indicate feelings, such as adjectives that indicate emotion. Students might locate phrases, including *"That might have been me"* and *"you wonder what to call yourself now."* When students identify the phrase "You know you are fortunate to be on board," discuss what this might reveal (or not reveal) about the character's experience in this moment. (**Possible answer:** *Because the point of view is second person, the reader doesn't actually know how the character feels. The narrator is inferring the character's feelings, so the reader has to rely on what the narrator says and will later have to see if this information is correct.*)

ENGLISH LEARNER SUPPORT

Acquire Vocabulary Point out and explain the following words:

- *bondage:* synonym for *slavery.* Point out that it has the root word *bond,* meaning something that holds something tight to something else.
- *identities:* names or other information that a person is known by
- *loyalist:* someone who supported Britain during the Revolutionary War
- *traitor:* someone who turns against their country

Ask students to use each of the words in a sentence. Ask students to try to create sentences that use more than one of these words. **MODERATE**

LANGUAGE CONVENTIONS

Review different common pronoun/verb contractions with the students, such as *it's/it is* and *we're/we are.* Discuss the usage of the "to be" verb *are* as both a plural and a second person verb, and make sure students understand how it is used. (**Possible answer:** *Mark "You're" and "I'm." The subject "You're" is a contraction for "You are." "I'm" is a contraction for "I am." The first verb matches the subject "you," which is second person and agrees with the verb "are." "I" is singular, so it agrees with the singular verb "am.")*

ANALYZE LITERARY ELEMENTS

Annotate: Mark the phrase in paragraph 4 that reveals how the narrator thinks the main character feels.

Draw Conclusions: What effect does the second-person narration have?

LANGUAGE CONVENTIONS

Annotate: Read the dialogue in paragraphs 6–12. Mark the contraction with a first-person pronoun. Mark the contraction with the second-person pronoun.

Analyze: How do you know the subjects and verbs agree? How do the person and number of each subject affect the verb?

---

appear in Brigadier General Samuel Birch's *Book of Negroes*—you pull a long-shanked pipe from your red-tinted coat, pack the bowl with tobacco, and strike a friction match against a nail in your bootheel. You know you are fortunate to be on board. Now that the Continental Army is victorious, blacks who fought for the crown are struggling desperately to leave on His Majesty's ships departing from New York harbor. Even as your boat eased away from the harbor, some leaped from the docks into the water, swimming toward the ship for this last chance to escape slavery. Seeing them, you'd thought, *That might have been me.* But it wasn't; you've always been lucky that way, at taking risks. Running away from bondage. Taking on new identities. Yet you wonder what to call yourself now. A loyalist? A traitor? A man without a country? As the harbor shrinks, growing fainter in the distance, severing you forever from this strange, newly formed nation called the United States, you haven't the slightest idea after years of war which of these names fits, or what the future holds, though on one matter you *are* clear:

5   From the start, you were fighting for no one but yourself.

6   The day after Lieutenant General Sir Henry Clinton promised liberty to all blacks deserting the rebel standard and willing to fight on the side of the British, you learned that Titus and Caesar were planning to flee. In the evening, on your way to the quarters after finishing your duties in the house, Titus stopped you outside the barn, and asked, "Can you go back to the kitchen and sneak out some provisions for us?" Naturally, you'd asked him what for, and he put his fingers to his lips, shushing you. They planned to steal two horses, he said. Then ride to safety behind British lines. "You're leaving?" You were almost speechless with anger. "And you're not taking *me*?"

7   "How can I?" he asked. "You're only fifteen."

8   "What's that got to do with anything? I can fight!"

9   "You ever fired a gun?"

10   "No, but I can learn!"

11   "Once I'm free, and got the papers to prove it, I'll come back."

12   "Titus, if you don't take me, I'll *tell*."

13   For a heartbeat or two, Titus looked as if he might hit you. Grudgingly, he agreed to bring you along, despite your age and his declaration after your parents' deaths that he'd keep you from harm. You did as he requested, returning to the house and filling a sack with food, Master Selby's clothing, even some of the mistress's jewelry that the three of you might barter, then delivered all this to your brother and Caesar in the barn. The three of you left that night on two of the master's best horses, you riding behind Titus, your arms tightly circling his waist until you stopped to make camp in the woods. There, Caesar suggested that it would help if you all changed your names and appearances as much as possible since Master Selby was sure to post your descriptions. Titus said fine, he'd grow a beard and

---

APPLYING ACADEMIC VOCABULARY

☑ ideological ☐ contrary ☐ founder ☐ publication ☑ revolution

Write and Discuss Have students turn to a partner to discuss the following questions. Guide students to include the Academic Vocabulary words *ideological* and *revolution* in their responses. Ask volunteers to share their responses with the class.

- What **ideological** position does Freeman hold?
- What side of the American **Revolution** did Freeman fight for?

call himself John Free. Caesar liked that, said, "Then I'll be George Liberty." They waited for you to pick a name, poking sticks at the campfire, sending up sparks into the starless sky. "Give me time," you'd said, changing into buckskin breeches, blue stockings, and a checkered, woolen shirt. "I'll shave my hair off, and I'll think of *something* before we get there. I don't want to rush." What you didn't tell them that night was how thrilling, how sweet this business of renaming oneself felt, and that you wanted to toy with a thousand possibilities—each name promising a new nature—turning them over on your tongue, and creating whole histories for each before settling, as you finally did, on "Alexander Freeman" as your new identity.

14   Thus, it was Alexander Freeman, George Liberty, and John Free who rode a few days later, bone weary from travel, into the British camp. You will never forget this sight: scores of black men in British uniforms, with the inscription LIBERTY TO SLAVES on their breasts, bearing arms so naturally one would have thought they were born with a rifle in their hands. Some were cleaning their weapons. Others marched. Still others were relaxing or stabbing their bayonets at sacks suspended from trees or performing any of the thousand chores that kept a regiment well-oiled and ready. When you signed on, the black soldier who wrote down your names didn't question you, though he remarked he thought you didn't look very strong. The three of you were put immediately to work. Harder work, you recall, than anything you'd known working in Master Selby's house, but for the first time in fifteen years you fell to each task eagerly, gambling that the labor purchased a new lease on life.

15   Over the first months, then years of the seesawing war, you, Titus, and Caesar served His Majesty's army in more **capacities** than you had fingers on the hand: as orderlies[1] to the white officers, laborers, cooks, foragers, and as foot soldiers who descended upon farms abandoned by their white owners, burning the enemy's fortifications and plundering plantations for much-needed provisions; as spies slipping in and out of southern towns to gather information; and as caretakers to the dying when smallpox swept through your regiment, weakening and killing hundreds of men. Your brother among them. And it was then you nearly gave up the gamble. You wondered if it might not be best to take your chips off the table. And pray the promise of the Virginia Convention that black runaways to the British side would be pardoned was genuine. And slink back home, your hat in your hand, to Master Selby's farm—if it was still there. Or perhaps you and Caesar might switch sides, deserting to the ranks of General Washington who, pressured for manpower, **belatedly** reversed his opposition to Negroes fighting in the Continental Army. And then there was that magnificent Declaration penned by Jefferson, proclaiming that "We hold these truths to be self-evident, that all

---
[1] **orderlies:** soldiers who provide assistance to and perform tasks for an officer.

ANALYZE AND EVALUATE PLOT

Annotate: Mark the phrase in paragraph 13 that tells what Titus decided.

Infer: What questions from the beginning of this story are answered by his decision? What new question arises?

capacity
(kə-păs´ĭ-tē) *n.* ability to hold or have something; function or role.

belatedly
(bĭ-lā´tĭd-lē) *adv.* done too late or overdue.

WHEN STUDENTS STRUGGLE . . .

Analyze Story Elements   Point out that the characters are facing risks and rewards. Have students work in pairs to identify and list elements of the setting (*where: America; when: during the Revolution*), what this means for the characters (*slavery*), risks (*being captured, returned to slavery, dying in the war*), and rewards (*freedom*). Discuss how the setting shapes the risks and rewards the characters might face.

 For additional support, go to the **Reading Studio** and assign the following **Level Up tutorial: Setting**

ANALYZE AND EVALUATE PLOT

Review the dialogue that takes place before paragraph 13. Ask students to consider how this dialogue establishes the two characters as siblings, and what kind of relationship it indicates. Instruct students to keep this in mind as they read the first two sentences of paragraph 13 and answer the questions. (**Answer:** *This decision explains how the main character escapes slavery and why the siblings' parents are not in the story. It raises the question of what will happen to them, so it creates suspense. It's possible there will be tension between the characters, or the protagonist's age and lack of experience will be an issue.*)

EL ENGLISH LEARNER SUPPORT

Acquire Vocabulary   Point out and explain the following words:

• *score*: an old word meaning "twenty." This word works like the word *pair* ("two") or *dozen* ("twelve"). In the text, *scores* is used to describe a large number.

• *liberty*: the freedom to make one's own decisions

• *fortifications*: structures built to protect a place

• *provisions*: food and other necessary supplies

Have students use each of these words in a sentence. Then, have them think of synonyms for *liberty, fortifications,* and *provisions*. **MODERATE**

CRITICAL VOCABULARY

capacity: The narrator stresses the many roles that enlistees like the three brothers assumed for the Crown during the war. Serving in so many *capacities* meant that they were valuable to the British army.

ASK STUDENTS why the narrator enumerates the various capacities. (*to show they served the Crown in other ways besides fighting on the battlefield*)

belatedly: Washington originally opposed allowing Negroes in his army, but changed his mind, belatedly realizing he needed more soldiers.

ASK STUDENTS why the word *belatedly* fits Washington's change of mind. (*He might have admitted black soldiers in the first place but delayed.*)

ANALYZE LITERARY ELEMENTS

Remind students that when authors use second-person point of view, readers must make inferences about how the characters feel. In paragraph 19, the author relates what happens to Alexander, but the reader doesn't really know how Alexander feels. Tell students to look for clues that relate how Alexander must be feeling after Caesar dies. (**Answer:** *The reader gets an understanding of Alexander that the other characters do not. The pronoun "you" and details of the main character's thoughts and feelings help the reader to identify with the main character.*)

CRITICAL VOCABULARY

unalienable: The Declaration of Independence describes unalienable rights, which cannot be taken away from anyone, because people are born with these rights.

ASK STUDENTS whether enslaved people at the time of the story were deemed to have any unalienable rights. *(no)*

elusive: A British pass was extremely valuable and tremendously difficult to obtain. It was promised as a way to recruit enslaved people, but it proved elusive—many never received one.

ASK STUDENTS why a British pass would be elusive for enslaved people. (*The British were less interested in helping people become free than in using their status as enslaved people to motivate them to work and fight for the British army. The passes were not given immediately or readily.*)

---

unalienable
(ŭn-āl´yə-nə-bəl) *adj.*
impossible to be taken away.

ANALYZE LITERARY ELEMENTS
Annotate: Mark details in paragraph 19 that refer to Alexander's feelings.

Interpret: What is the effect of the second-person point of view on your understanding of Alexander?

elusive
(ĭ-lōō´sĭv) *adj.* difficult to define.

---

men are created equal, that they are endowed by their Creator with certain **unalienable** Rights, that among these are Life, Liberty and the pursuit of Happiness," words you'd memorized after hearing them. If the Continentals won, would this brave, new republic be so bad?

16   "Alex, those are just *words*," said Caesar. "White folks' words for other white folks."

17   "But without us, the rebels would lose—"

18   "So would the redcoats. Both sides need us, but I don't trust neither one to play fair when this thing is over. They can do that Declaration over. Naw, the words I want to see are on a British pass with my name on it. I'm stayin' put 'til I *see that*."

19   Caesar never did. A month later your regiment was routed by the Continental Army. The rebels fired cannons for six hours, shelling the village your side occupied two days before. You found pieces of your cousin strewn everywhere. And you ran. Ran. You lived by your wits in the countryside, stealing what you needed to survive until you reached territory still in British hands, and again found yourself a pawn in the middle of other men's battles—Camden, where your side scattered poorly trained regulars led by General Gates, then liberated slaves who donned their masters' fancy clothing and powdered wigs and followed along behind Gates as his men pressed on; and the disastrous encounter at Guilford Court House, where six hundred redcoats died and Cornwallis was forced to fall back to Wilmington for supplies, then later abandon North Carolina altogether, moving on to Virginia. During your time as a soldier, you saw thousands sacrifice their lives, and no, it wasn't as if you came through with only a scratch. At Camden you took a ball in your right shoulder. Fragments remain there still, making it a little hard for you to sleep on that side or withstand the dull ache in your shoulder on days when the weather is damp. But, miraculously, as the war began to wind down, you were given the **elusive**, long-coveted British pass.

20   On the ship, now traveling north past Augusta, you knock your cold pipe against the railing, shaking dottle from its bowl, then reach into your coat for the scrap of paper that was so difficult to earn. Behind you, other refugees are bedding down for the night, covering themselves and their children with blankets. You wait until one of the hands on deck passes a few feet beyond where you stand, then you unfold the paper with fingers stiffened by the cold. In the yellowish glow of the ship's lantern, tracing the words with your forefinger, shaping your lips silently to form each syllable, you read:

> This is to certify to whomfoever[2] it may concern, that the
> Bearer hereof . . . Alexander Freeman . . . a Negro, reforted
> to the Britifh Lines, in confequence of the Proclamations of
> Sir William Howe, and Sir Henry Clinton, late Commanders

---

[2] **whomfoever:** In the 1800s, handwritten and printed documents sometimes used the "long s," which looked like an *f* without the crossbar, in place of a lowercase *s*.

ENGLISH LEARNER SUPPORT

Analyze Details Tell students to pay close attention as you read aloud the beginning of paragraph 19, "Caesar never did . . . other men's battles." Discuss any questions students have about the section. Then, ask students to make a list of Alexander's actions in this section, or what he did. Have them share the actions they found with the class. For each action, ask students to list any details from the text that tell why Alexander did that action. Discuss the meaning of *pawn* (the lowest ranking piece in the game of chess) and ask students why Alexander might be called a pawn. **LIGHT**

in Chief in America; and that the said Negro has hereby his Excellency Sir Benjamin Hampton's Permiffion to go to Nova-Scotia, or wherever elfe he may think proper . . . By Order of Brigadier General Ruttledge

21 The document, dated April 1783, brings a broad smile to your lips. Once your ship lands, and you find a home, you will frame this precious deed of manumission.[3] At least in this sense, your gamble paid off. And for now you still prefer the adopted name Alexander Freeman to the one given you at birth—Dorothy.

22 Maybe you'll be Dorothy again, later in Nova Scotia. Of course, you'll keep the surname Freeman. And, Lord willing, when it's safe you will let your hair grow out again to its full length, wear dresses, and perhaps start a new family to replace the loved ones you lost during the war.

---

[3] **deed of manumission:** a document confirming a person's release from slavery.

ANALYZE AND EVALUATE PLOT

Annotate: Mark the sentence in paragraph 21 that reveals a surprising truth about the main character.

Infer: Why doesn't the narrator name the main character until the end? What ambiguity about the situation remains?

CHECK YOUR UNDERSTANDING

Answer these questions before moving on to the **Analyze the Text** section.

1 What is Dorothy doing when the story begins?

A Sailing away from New York to freedom

B Fleeing from Master Selby's farm

C Running away from the army after a battle

D Sailing with British troops for a new military campaign

2 Which most likely explains why Titus resists taking Dorothy with him?

F He does not take his promise to protect her seriously.

G He does not want her to slow down their escape.

H He does not think she will be safe because she is young and female.

J He thinks she would be happier staying on Master Selby's farm.

3 How does Dorothy gain the pass granting freedom?

A She takes Caesar's pass after he was killed in battle.

B She earns it through her service in the British army.

C She has to buy the pass from a British soldier.

D The British give passes to all African Americans.

ANALYZE AND EVALUATE PLOT

Ask the students what assumptions the use of the second person "you" allows. Encourage the students to reflect on why they might make assumptions about a character's gender when genderless pronouns like *you* or *I* are used. (**Answer:** *The main character is Dorothy. All along the reader assumes the main character is male, so this is a surprise and changes how we feel or understand the character. Dorothy's future remains quite uncertain.*)

CHECK YOUR UNDERSTANDING

Have students answer the questions independently.

Answers:

1. *A*

2. *H*

3. *B*

If they answer any questions incorrectly, have them reread the text to confirm their understanding. Then, they may proceed to ANALYZE THE TEXT on page 138.

 ENGLISH LEARNER SUPPORT

Oral Assessment Use the following questions to assess students' comprehension and speaking skills.

1. What is Dorothy doing when the story begins? (*She is on a boat. She is leaving America, going to be free.*)

2. Titus did not want to take Dorothy. Why? (*He was worried she would be in danger.*)

3. How did Dorothy get her freedom? (*She gets a pass that gives her freedom. She gets it for fighting in the British army.*) **ALL LEVELS**

ANALYZE THE TEXT

Possible answers:

1. **DOK 3:** *The setting creates suspense because it is during the American Revolution, and enslaved people and colonists are fighting for their independence. They are doing this on different sides of the battle. It is unclear if Freeman, who is an enslaved person will gain her freedom. She is taking a major gamble in running away and joining the British army. She can't be sure if the British will really free her.*

2. **DOK 4:** *The characters do not know whether the words of the Declaration will be interpreted to apply to them as enslaved people. There is even greater significance for Freeman because it is ambiguous whether the word "men" in the Declaration refers to all people or only to males, in which case it would not apply to her.*

3. **DOK 4:** *By detailing all of the options she faces—and the uncertainty of their outcome—the narrator underscores how profoundly risky her situation is, building more suspense about her eventual fate.*

4. **DOK 2:** *The use of the second person in paragraph 13 adds ambiguity to Freeman's choice of a new name and her cutting of her hair. The author is able to communicate that there is more to the scene than is directly stated.*

5. **DOK 3:** *The theme encompasses the ideas of chance and risk, but primarily focuses on the meaning of freedom, and how freedom will be different for a woman.*

RESEARCH

Remind students to use several reliable sources when doing research. Ask students to review how to determine the reliability of a source. Remind them that one element to look for is whether the source uses citations to back up what it says. Checking these citations is also a good way to assess credibility and to find more information.

Connect The *Smithsonian Source* website is a good resource for primary source documents and pamphlets. Remind students to compare the perspectives presented in the story and in research sources.

 **RESPOND**

ANALYZE THE TEXT

Support your responses with evidence from the text. NOTEBOOK

1. **Cite Evidence** How does the setting shape the writer's portrayal of the plot? Explain, citing details about the historical context.

2. **Analyze** Why does the conversation between Caesar and Freeman about the Declaration of Independence leave the reader with a sense of ambiguity, but hold greater significance once Freeman's identity is revealed?

3. **Analyze** Why does the writer include Freeman's reaction to Titus's death? How does it build suspense in the story?

4. **Interpret** What effect does the use of the second-person point of view have on the scene in paragraph 13? What idea is the author able to communicate by using this point of view?

5. **Draw Conclusions** The theme is the truth about life that the writer conveys. Theme can be suggested by what happens to the main character and the key events in the plot. What theme can you draw from these literary elements?

RESEARCH TIP
Narrow search terms by putting phrases like *American Revolution* in quotation marks.

RESEARCH

Tens of thousands of loyalists fled the United States after the American Revolution. Research what happened to loyalists during and after the American Revolution. Start by finding answers to these questions.

QUESTION	ANSWER
In what areas were most of the loyalists living?	*Most loyalists lived in the South, New York, and Pennsylvania.*
How were loyalists treated by the patriots? Why were they treated this way?	*The loyalist were treated badly by the patriots because they remained loyal to the King of England.*
How many loyalists left the United States? Where did they go?	*Approximately 100,000 loyalist fled, mostly to Canada.*

Connect What perspective on loyalists of the American Revolution does the writer present in the story? How do the answers to the research question support this perspective? What new information is introduced?

 LEARNING MINDSET

Problem Solving Remind students that there is not one set method of solving a problem. Encourage students to try different techniques, such as discussing the problem with different people or sticking with the problem and being patient with themselves. Suggest an exercise to the students where they identify and write down one problem per day that they have solved, whether large or small. That success can be a reminder to students when they work to solve another problem.

CREATE AND DEBATE

Write an Argumentative Essay Write a three- to four-paragraph opinion essay about whether taking risks is worthwhile. Consider whether some risks are worth taking even if they could have serious consequences.

❏ In the first paragraph, introduce your opinion about taking risks.

❏ Use details from the text as well as real-life examples to support your view on taking risks.

❏ Include your own commentary to support your opinion.

❏ Include a strong conclusion that restates your opinion and summarizes your reasons.

Have a Debate Have a debate about Freeman's "gamble" and if you think that gamble paid off.

❏ Divide into two groups: those who agree with Freeman's gamble and those who do not.

❏ Find details from the text and think about reasons that support your group's opinion. Consider the options Freeman had before and after her brother died. Also consider the setting and how it affected the characters' choices.

❏ Listen closely to the opposing group's ideas and present counterarguments.

Go to **Writing Arguments** in the **Writing Studio** for help.

RESPOND TO THE ESSENTIAL QUESTION

? How do we gain our freedom?

Gather Information Review your annotations and notes on "A Soldier for the Crown." Then, add relevant information to your Response Log. As you determine which information to include, think about:

• why individuals desire freedom
• the social and political factors that determine who is free
• the risks people take to gain freedom

UNIT 2 RESPONSE LOG

ACADEMIC VOCABULARY
As you write and discuss what you learned from "A Soldier for the Crown," be sure to use the Academic Vocabulary words. Check off each of the words that you use.

❏ **contrary**
❏ **founder**
❏ **ideological**
❏ **publication**
❏ **revolution**

CREATE AND DEBATE

Write an Argumentative Essay Remind students that they should be careful to support their opinion with evidence and quotations from the text. Explain that even though the essay is based on opinion, their writing will be more convincing if they include their own commentary that shows the basis of how their opinion was formed.

For **writing support** for students at varying proficiency levels, see the **Text X-Ray** on page 130D.

Have a Debate As a prewriting exercise before the debate, instruct students to make a pro-con list for making a decision about which group they will join. Students should list the reasons why they agree or disagree with the gamble that Freeman makes in the story.

RESPOND TO THE ESSENTIAL QUESTION

Allow time for students to add details from "A Soldier for the Crown" to their Unit 2 Response Logs.

CRITICAL VOCABULARY

Possible answers:

1. *My right to freedom of speech and freedom of religion are unalienable. They are protected by the Bill of Rights.*

2. *a birthday present from a relative who lives in a different state*

3. *some scientific theories*

4. *I could walk the dogs and help clean the cages.*

VOCABULARY STRATEGY:
Prefixes and Suffixes

Possible answers:

1. *base word—colony; other forms—colonize, colonist, colonial, colonization, colonialism, decolonization*

2. *base word—wood; other forms—wooden, woodenly, wooded, woodsy*

3. *base word—liberty; other forms—liberation, liberated, liberality, libertarian*

4. *base word—script; other forms—scripted, scriptorium, scripture, unscripted, inscriptive*

 RESPOND

WORD BANK
capacity
belatedly
unalienable
elusive

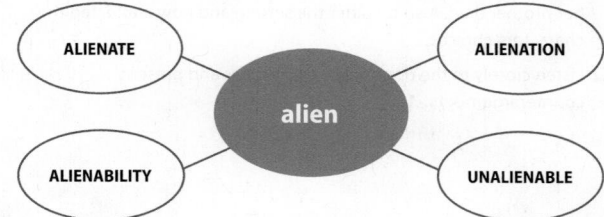 Go to **Analyzing Word Structure** in the **Vocabulary Studio** for help.

CRITICAL VOCABULARY

Practice and Apply Show your understanding of the vocabulary words by answering these questions.

1. What do you possess as an individual that is **unalienable?** Explain.

2. Describe a circumstance in which you receive something **belatedly.**

3. When have you tried to grasp something that proved **elusive?** Explain.

4. In what **capacity** might you help out at a local animal shelter?

VOCABULARY STRATEGY:
Prefixes and Suffixes

The Critical Vocabulary word *unalienable* is an example of a word built by adding the prefix *un-* and the suffix *-able* to the base word *alien*. Adding a prefix to the word changes the word's meaning. Adding a suffix changes the word's part of speech. As the word web shows, other prefixes and suffixes can be added to the base word *alien* with a variety of meanings and parts of speech.

```
ALIENATE        ALIENATION

        alien

ALIENABILITY    UNALIENABLE
```

Practice and Apply Each of the following words appears in the selection. For each one, identify the base word and at least three other words that can be formed by adding other prefixes or suffixes. Use print or online sources to help you identify forms of the word.

1. **colonial**

_____

2. **wooden**

_____

3. **liberty**

_____

4. **inscription**

_____

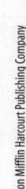 **ENGLISH LEARNER SUPPORT**

Work with Prefixes and Suffixes Discuss with students what prefixes and suffixes are. For speakers of Khmer, focus on suffixes, which are not used in Khmer. Ask students to give examples from their first language of words with prefixes or suffixes. Ask how a prefix or a suffix changes the meaning of the root word. For example, for Spanish speakers, have them think of the word *colón* and how its meaning changes in *colonial, colonizar, colonización.* Then, give examples from English. The word *alien* is a noun; *alienate* is a verb. *Liberty* is a noun; *liberate* is a verb. Ask students if they can continue the pattern with examples such as *narrator* and *narrate*; *annotation* and *annotate*; *evaluation* and *evaluate.* Discuss what each word means.
ALL LEVELS

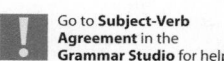
LANGUAGE CONVENTIONS:
Subject-Verb Agreement

The rules for **subject-verb agreement** are relatively simple—subjects and verbs should agree in number (singular or plural). When the subject is a pronoun, the verb must also agree in person—first person, second person, or third person.

First-Person Singular	I *ride* a bike to school every day.
Third-Person Singular	She *rides* a bike to school every day.
First-Person Plural	We *ride* our bikes to school together every day.

Compound subjects make subject-verb agreement more complicated. If two single subjects are joined by *and,* the subjects become a plural compound subject and need a plural verb, since both subjects are doing the action. If two subjects are joined by the words *or* or *nor,* they function in the sentence as a singular subject because *either one* is doing the action, but not both.

Plural Compound Subject	Terry **and** Raja *ride* their bikes to school every day.
Singular Compound Subject	Either Terry **or** Raja *rides* a bike to school every day.

If the subject is a **collective noun**—one that refers to several individuals— the verb may be singular or plural, depending on how the noun is used. The subject takes a singular verb if the subject is being viewed as a unit. It takes a plural verb if the focus is on the individual members of the collective group.

As a Unit	The **team** *takes* the bus to the game.
As Individuals	The **team** *take* turns at practice.

Practice and Apply Read the passage from the story that includes the escape from the Selby farm. Write a third-person narrative of what the three characters did to prepare and to flee. Use a mix of singular and compound subjects and choose the correct verb form to show subject-verb agreement.

> **!** Go to **Subject-Verb Agreement** in the **Grammar Studio** for help

LANGUAGE CONVENTIONS:
Subject-Verb Agreement

As students read through the explanations and examples of subject-verb agreement in different types of sentence structures, have them refer back to the story and look for examples of specific structures mentioned in the exercise. Have students pay attention to different variations in sentence structure, and how this affects the subject-verb agreement.

Practice and Apply Encourage students to include adjectives and descriptive language in their passages. After they write the passages and check that their subjects and verbs agree, ask students to incorporate four to five adjectives or descriptive phrases into their writing. Remind students that the more senses they use, the more engaging their writing will be. For example, they could incorporate a phrase that describes the smell of a room in the Selby's house, or the feel of Freeman's heart pounding as she rides away.

EL ENGLISH LEARNER SUPPORT

Practice Subject-Verb Agreement Remind students that when the subject of a sentence is a singular third-person noun or pronoun, such as *he, she, it,* a name (like Terry or Raja), or *the* ___ (such as *the team*), to make the verb agree, an *-s* must be added. Point out that some verbs, like *do* and *go* add an *-es* instead. Give students an example of a sentence with the first-person subject *I.* Then, change the subject to third person and have students restate the sentence, using the correct verb form. For example: *I take the bus.* → *She* → *She takes the bus.* Give more examples, using common verbs such as *write, think, like, do, go, say, feel,* and *need.* (Be aware that subject-verb agreement does not exist in Cantonese, Haitian, Creole, Hmong, Khmer, Tagalog, and Vietnamese. Extra help may be needed for some students.) **SUBSTANTIAL**

THE AUTOBIOGRAPHY
Autobiography by Benjamin Franklin

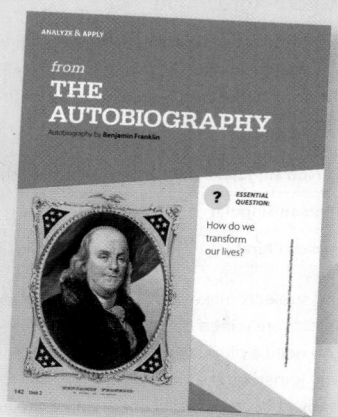

GENRE ELEMENTS
AUTOBIOGRAPHY

Explain to students that an **autobiography** is a piece of writing that comes from a first-person perspective. Autobiographies focus on significant moments and events from the author's life. In addition to facts and details, the author will also often include his or her thoughts or interpretations about what happened and why it was important.

LEARNING OBJECTIVES

- Evaluate a variety of graphic features.
- Research the life and accomplishments of Benjamin Franklin.
- Write an autobiographical essay.
- Discuss the process for writing an autobiography.
- Learn Latin roots and word families.
- Identify and understand Standard English conventions.
- **Language** Identify and describe a virtue that is relevant today.

TEXT COMPLEXITY

Quantitative Measures	The Autobiography	Lexile: 1390L
Qualitative Measures	**Ideas Presented** Probably requires weighing of multiple perspectives; some analysis of bias and author's motivations; some ambiguity.	
	Structures Used More complex, multiple perspectives may be presented; more deviation from chronology; tables and figures support understanding.	
	Language Used Vocabulary not defined at point of use; mostly Tier II and III words; metaphor (rather than similes) used more; multiple technical words may be used in one sentence.	
	Knowledge Required More complex problems; experiences may be less familiar to many; cultural or historical references.	

RESOURCES

- Unit 2 Response Log
- 🔊 Selection Audio
- 📖 Reading Studio: Notice & Note
- Level Up Tutorial: Main Ideas and Supporting Details.
- Writing Studio: Developing a Topic
- 💬 Speaking and Listening Studio: Participating in Collaborative Discussions
- Vocabulary Studio: Understanding Word Origins
- Grammar Studio: Module 4: Lesson 5: Sentence Structure
- ✅ from The *Autobiography* Selection Test

SUMMARIES

English

One of the greatest inventors in American history, Benjamin Franklin was also a prolific writer whose works ranged from essays and newspaper articles to almanacs, letters, and even ballads. His most famous piece of writing, however, was his autobiography, in which he details his quest to attain moral perfection. In this excerpt, Franklin creates a list of virtues he believes he must possess to be perfect. Although Franklin falls short of his objective and struggles to achieve Order, he comes away from the experiment feeling happier and better for having tried.

Spanish

Uno de los grandes inventores de la historia americana, Benjamin Franklin, era también un escritor prolífico, cuyo trabajo varió de los ensayos y artículos de prensa a los almanaques, las cartas e incluso las baladas. Sin embargo, su trabajo más famoso fue su autobiografía, en la cual detalla su búsqueda por la perfección moral. En este pasaje, Franklin enumera las 13 virtudes que él consideraba las características que debía poseer para ser perfecto. Luego, escribió un libro que enumeraba las virtudes y lo usaba para seguir la trayectoria de una virtud cada semana. A pesar de que Franklin se queda corto en su objetivo y lucha por alcanzar el orden, deja el experimento sintiéndose mejor y feliz por haberlo intentado.

 SMALL-GROUP OPTIONS

Have students work in small groups and pairs to read and discuss the selection.

Think-Pair-Share

- After reading Franklin's list of 13 virtues, pose this question: *Which of these virtues do you think is the hardest to possess?*
- Have students think about the question individually and take notes.
- Then, have students form pairs and listen, discuss, and formulate shared responses to the question.
- Finally, have pairs share their responses with the class.

Three-Minute Review

- As you read the text, pause after every two to three paragraphs.
- Direct students to reread the paragraphs and write clarifying questions. Set a timer for three minutes.
- After three minutes, ask: *What did you notice as you reread the text?*
- Invite volunteers to share clarifying questions.
- Guide small groups to discuss and answer the questions.

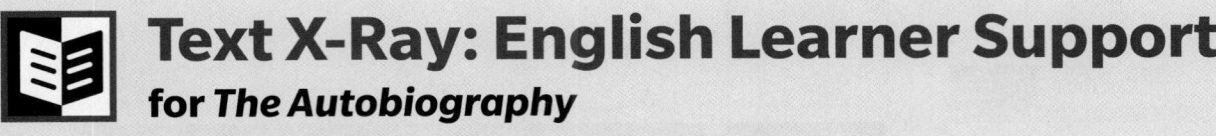

Text X-Ray: English Learner Support
for *The Autobiography*

Use the Text X-Ray and the supports and scaffolds in the Teacher's Edition to help guide students at different proficiency levels through the selection.

INTRODUCE THE SELECTION
DISCUSS VIRTUES AND HABITS

In this lesson, students will need to understand the idea of moral virtue and connect it to the concept of habit. Provide the following explanations to establish the ideas:

- A *virtue* is morally good behavior or character, like honesty or kindness.
- *Moral* means distinguishing between right and wrong.
- A *habit* is something a person does in a regular and repeated way.

On the board, write the terms *virtue* and *habit*, and draw a line connecting them. Explain to the students that Franklin believed that to be truly virtuous, you have to make virtue a habit. Ask for volunteers to offer examples of things they think are virtues and compile a list of ideas on the board. Then, ask students how they think they could become those particular virtues. Supply the following sentence frame:

If a person wants to be _____, he or she should get in the habit of _____.

CULTURAL REFERENCES

The following words or phrases may be unfamiliar to students:

- *punning* (paragraph 4): using a phrase in a humorous way so more than one meaning is suggested
- *should be/have* (paragraph 6): a now-more-commonly British phrase often used in place of "would." For example, the sentence "I should like to go" is the same as "I would like to go."
- *journeyman* (paragraph 9): a worker who has studied a skill under a master and is then qualified to go to work for someone else

LISTENING

Use Graphic Aids

Draw students' attention to the diagrams in the selection on pages 147 and 149. Explain that visual aids such as diagrams can be used to help identify and understand the main idea of a section of text.

Use the following supports with students at varying proficiency levels:

- Read aloud the list of virtues on page 146, and ask students to expand the abbreviations in the chart on page 147. Read slowly and clearly, asking students to repeat your pronunciations of the words and allowing time for them to check page 146 for the correct spelling of each virtue. **SUBSTANTIAL**
- Read aloud paragraph 6 while students examine the chart on page 147. Direct students to listen for information that helps them identify the purpose and meaning of each component of the chart. Define each virtue. Then assess comprehension by asking students what Franklin's plan will be for the next week, based on their understanding of the chart. **MODERATE**
- After students listen to the excerpt read aloud, have them work in pairs to discuss the excerpt. Ask them to explain why Franklin thinks it is important to create such a strict schedule and encourage students to think about the concept of *habit* when creating their answers. Have students summarize their partner's explanations in a few sentences. **LIGHT**

SPEAKING

Build Language Proficiency

Explain that some of the words in the list of virtues are common in modern English, while others are used less commonly. Guide students to think about how they would express virtues in contemporary English.

Use the following supports with students at varying proficiency levels:

- Read the virtues from page 146 aloud. Provide clarification. Then, write this sentence frame: _____ *(is still/is no longer) an important virtue.* Have students take turns saying this sentence aloud and filling in the blank with a virtue from the list. Provide pronunciation support as needed. **SUBSTANTIAL**
- Discuss the virtues as a class. Have students state their opinions. *The virtue _____ means that you must/ must not _____. I think _____ (is/is not) an important virtue because _____.* **MODERATE**
- Divide the class into small groups to discuss Franklin's list of virtues. Encourage an opinion-based discussion about which virtues students consider most important and why. Direct students to describe virtues in terms that make sense in their own lives, using a dictionary as needed. **LIGHT**

READING

Understand Structure

Explain to students that reading the first sentence of each paragraph is a useful pre-reading strategy that can help clarify the overall structure and some of the main points of an informative text.

Use the following support with students at varying proficiency levels:

- Echo read the first sentence of paragraph 1. Clarify words as necessary. Then ask: *What did Franklin want to achieve?* **SUBSTANTIAL**
- Create a three-column chart on the board with the labels *Goal, Action,* and *Result.* Have students read the first sentence of each paragraph in the selection to determine 1) what goal Franklin wants to achieve and 2) what actions he decides to take in pursuit of this goal. **MODERATE**
- Pair students and have them read together, focusing on the first sentence of each paragraph. Have them highlight the words in the topic sentence that reflect the main point and circle words in the rest of the paragraph that support the point. **LIGHT**

WRITING

Write an Autobiographical Essay

Direct students to the assignment on Student Edition page 153. Discuss Franklin's experiment and guide students to think about how they have learned skills in the past.

Use the following supports with students at varying proficiency levels:

- Work with students to remember a time they learned a new skill. Ask them to draw the steps they performed to learn this skill and title their drawing using the structure: *How I Learned to _____.* **SUBSTANTIAL**
- Ask students to write a short paragraph about a skill they learned and the steps they took to master it. Encourage students to use a topic sentence to structure their paragraph and to describe the steps in chronological order. **MODERATE**
- Have students write a short essay about a skill they learned, describing how and why they chose to learn it. Have them use topic sentences to structure their paragraphs by goal, action, and final result. **LIGHT**

Connect to the
ESSENTIAL QUESTION

Read aloud the Essential Question. Open the discussion of this idea by asking students if they know anyone who has transformed his or her life. Why? How did he or she do it? What is it like now?

from

THE
AUTOBIOGRAPHY

Autobiography by **Benjamin Franklin**

BENJAMIN FRANKLIN.
THE STATESMAN AND PHILOSOPHER.

142   Unit 2

? *ESSENTIAL QUESTION:*

How do we transform our lives?

QUICK START

It is said that virtues are the core of our character and that character determines destiny. Do you believe this? Why or why not? With a partner, list virtues you think shape your character and answer these questions.

MONITOR COMPREHENSION

When you **monitor comprehension,** you check your understanding as you read. Monitoring your comprehension can clarify ideas and help you when you are confused. Here are a few ways to monitor comprehension:

- **Reread** slowly and carefully when you face a long sentence or cannot follow the author's sequence of ideas.

- **Ask questions** about what is happening or why the writer shares certain information. This will deepen your understanding of the text.

- **Use background knowledge** to help you make sense of what you read.

- **Read an outside source** that can give you additional information.

In the excerpt from his autobiography, Benjamin Franklin describes his quest for moral perfection. As you read, be sure to monitor your comprehension so you can understand the key ideas and significant events that he conveys.

EVALUATE PRINT AND GRAPHIC FEATURES

Print and **graphic features** are text and visual tools that present and organize information. Captions, special print like boldface or italics, lists, and subheads are print features that help you understand what you read. Images, charts, and graphs are some of the graphic features that may also help. As you read, consider why Franklin chooses a different print or graphic feature for each part of the project and whether each feature is effective. Use a chart like this to keep track of the print and graphic features and the purpose of each. What information does Franklin organize and share by using them?

PRINT OR GRAPHIC FEATURE	PURPOSE
list, with bold headings	To identify and order (rank) the virtues he considers fundamental to moral perfection
chart	To collect data; to keep track of his performance
schedule	To plan his day; this is a support to help him reach his goals

GENRE ELEMENTS: AUTOBIOGRAPHY

- uses the first-person point of view
- focuses on significant events in author's life
- often includes thoughts about or interpretations of what is happening

QUICK START

Begin a discussion with this question: Is *perfection possible or at least worth striving for?* Provide this prompt for partners to discuss: "I hate to brag, but I'm really good at _____." After partner discussion, ask volunteers to share their lists of personal virtues, then describe their best virtue, explain why they consider it a virtue, and tell how they could improve. Ask volunteers to share their self-improvement plan or to explain why perfection is impossible.

MONITOR COMPREHENSION

Remind students that monitoring comprehension will help them ensure they understand what they read. Encourage them to stop at the end of a paragraph to ask themselves appropriate *who, what, when, where, why,* and *how* questions, such as *Who is the author's intended audience for this text?* and *Why is this detail important to include?* Ask volunteers to share other possible questions.

EVALUATE PRINT AND GRAPHIC FEATURES

Have students scan the selection and note the graphic elements (list, chart, schedule) before beginning to read. Discuss different reasons students use graphic features of each type. Remind them to consider as they read how these graphic elements help Franklin achieve his purpose.

TEACH

CRITICAL VOCABULARY

For unknown words, ask the students to decide if any of the words seem to be positive or negative. They can guess using associations; for example, *artifice* sounds like *artificial*, which means "fake" or "unnatural." They can also identify negative prefixes, such as *in-*, *un-*, and *e-* (from Latin: *ex-*, meaning *out*, as in *exit*).

Answers:

1. *artifice*
2. *unremitting*
3. *eradicate*
4. *felicity*
5. *affluence*
6. *contrive*
7. *trifling*
8. *incorrigible*

■ English Learner Support

Use Cognates Tell Spanish speakers that several of the Critical Vocabulary words have Spanish cognates: *artifice/ artificio, eradicate/erradicar, felicity/felicidad, incorrigible/ incorregible.* **ALL LEVELS**

LANGUAGE CONVENTIONS

Explain that a sentence fragment is a dependent clause that lacks one or more of the three elements of an independent clause: a subject, a main verb, and a complete thought.

ANNOTATION MODEL

Remind students of annotation strategies such as underlining important ideas and circling key words. Students may follow this suggestion or use their own system for marking up the selection in their write-in text. They may want to color-code their annotations by using highlighters. Their notes in the margin may include questions about ideas that are unclear or topics they want to learn more about.

 **GET READY**

CRITICAL VOCABULARY

| trifling | affluence | eradicate | artifice |
| unremitting | contrive | incorrigible | felicity |

To see how many Critical Vocabulary words you already know, use them to complete the sentences.

1. He thought sincerity was a better means to an end than _____.

2. Day and night, the pain was _____.

3. If we all work to clean the park, we can _____ litter.

4. The _____ at winning the award was shared by the whole family.

5. The rich furnishings of the house underscored the owners'_____.

6. How did he _____ to build that machine?

7. The little glass toys seemed silly and _____.

8. In trouble again, is he? He is _____.

LANGUAGE CONVENTIONS

Standard English When writing Standard English, writers follow conventions of sentence structure, usage, and punctuation that demonstrate an understanding of the language and audience. However, writers may not always use Standard English. They may include sentence fragments or dialogue that is written in a dialect, often to achieve a particular tone or style. Look for ways Franklin adheres to, and departs from, Standard English usage, and think about why he might be doing so.

ANNOTATION MODEL

NOTICE & NOTE

As you read, use the side margins to write any notes or questions. Mark any details in the text that stand out to you, including any graphic features. This model shows one student's notes about *The Autobiography*.

As I knew, or thought I knew, what was right and wrong, I did not see why I might not always do the one and avoid the other. But I soon found I had undertaken a task of more difficulty than I had imagined.

> He introduces uncertainty here.
>
> What difficulties will he face?

BACKGROUND

Benjamin Franklin *(1706–1790) was the oldest of the founders. He was 69 when he was sent as a delegate to the Second Continental Congress where he assisted Thomas Jefferson in drafting the Declaration of Independence. But by that time, he'd already had a remarkable life, finding success as a printer, publisher, scientist, inventor, businessman, philosopher, postmaster, and statesman. He was also a prolific writer, producing volumes of essays, travel journals, newspaper articles, almanacs, speeches, and more. His autobiography, however, was his masterpiece, and it is still popular today.*

from THE AUTOBIOGRAPHY
Autobiography by Benjamin Franklin

SETTING A PURPOSE

As you read, look for details that reveal Franklin's practical nature, even as he shows his faith in reason, order, and human perfectibility—common ideas in the 18th century.

1 It was about this time I conceived the bold and arduous project of arriving at moral perfection. I wished to live without committing any fault at any time; I would conquer all that either natural inclination, custom, or company might lead me into. As I knew, or thought I knew, what was right and wrong, I did not see why I might not always do the one and avoid the other. But I soon found I had undertaken a task of more difficulty than I had imagined. While my care was employed in guarding against one fault, I was often surprised by another; habit took the advantage of inattention; inclination was sometimes too strong for reason. I concluded, at length, that the mere speculative conviction that it was our interest to be completely virtuous, was not sufficient to prevent our slipping; and that the contrary habits must be broken, and good ones acquired and established, before we can have any dependence on a steady, uniform rectitude of conduct. For this purpose I therefore **contrived** the following method.

Notice & Note

Use the side margins to notice and note signposts in the text.

MONITOR COMPREHENSION

Annotate: Mark the words in the first paragraph that Franklin uses to describe the project.

Analyze: What questions do you have about Franklin's project so far?

contrive
(kən-trīv´) *v.* to plan skillfully; to design.

BACKGROUND

Franklin's writing— from humorous satires and wise sayings to serious political essays and scientific observations on electricity—as well as his diplomacy and charismatic personality made him an international celebrity. Although respected by the great minds of his age, he never lost his connection to the common people. In the words of John Adams: "His reputation is greater than that of Newton, Frederick the Great or Voltaire, his character more revered than all of them. There's scarcely a coachman or a footman or scullery maid who does not consider him a friend of all mankind."

SETTING A PURPOSE

Direct students to use the Setting a Purpose prompt to focus their reading.

MONITOR COMPREHENSION

Have students scan the paragraph. Remind them to reread sentences that they find confusing, and note details they think are important. Guide them to form a variety of questions about what Franklin is describing, why he makes particular choices, and how he will conduct his project. *(**Answer:** Possible questions include: What method will Franklin choose to follow? Why does Franklin expect moral perfection to be possible when he faces such difficulty?)*

CRITICAL VOCABULARY

contrive: Although today the word *contrive* often carries a negative connotation, in Franklin's day it was frequently used simply to mean *invent.* Franklin's use of the word serves to indicate that he put some thought and effort into his method. Explain that the noun *contrivance* means "a device, toll, plan, or design."

ASK STUDENTS why they think Franklin goes into so much detail concerning how he contrived his book. *(He wants to convey the idea that because this task is important, he has put a lot of thought into it.)*

 ENGLISH LEARNER SUPPORT

Retelling Read aloud the full sentence that begins "As I knew, or thought I knew. . . ." Ask students which is "the one" *(right)* and which is "the other" *(wrong).* Read the first sentence of the selection, providing definitions for words as needed. Ask students to explain what Franklin's "project" was, pointing out that it is related to "right" and "wrong" and his intention to "do the one and avoid the other." Then, ask students to write one to two sentences or phrases that explain what Franklin is talking about in this first portion of the text.
MODERATE

For **speaking** and **reading support** for students at varying proficiency levels, see the **Text X-Ray on page** 142D.

EVALUATE PRINT AND GRAPHIC FEATURES

Guide students to understand that Franklin's process for creating his list begins with reading other writers' categories and lists of virtues. He then chooses a method: to use more names (or categories), rather than fewer, and to put more ideas under each category. He decides to create a precept for each category. Explain that a precept is typically a short, pithy phrase that expresses a general rule about how to think or behave. (**Answer:** *The list allows Franklin to clearly define each virtue and makes the meaning clear to the reader.*)

Acquire New Vocabulary Pair students and provide each with a bilingual dictionary. Try to create pairs of students who share a native language. Students should look up each of the words on the virtues list in the bilingual dictionary to find the word in their native language. Have students create a new list with each English word followed by the word in their native language. Direct students to choose three English words and say them in a short English sentence or phrase to their partners. **SUBSTANTIAL**

CRITICAL VOCABULARY

trifling: Franklin stresses that silence is better than saying something that has little value. *Trifling* is the opposite of *important*. For example: Choosing a college is no trifling matter; it is a very important decision.

ASK STUDENTS what clue in the precept about Silence helps you understand the meaning of the word *trifling*? ("benefit") Ask: *What kind of speech benefits people?* (advice, praise, information) *What kind of speech doesn't have benefits?* (gossip, rumors, slander, etc.)

NOTICE & NOTE

2   In the various enumerations of the moral virtues I had met with in my reading, I found the catalogue more or less numerous, as different writers included more or fewer ideas under the same name. Temperance, for example, was by some confined to eating and drinking, while by others it was extended to mean the moderating every other pleasure, appetite, inclination, or passion, bodily or mental, even to our avarice and ambition. I proposed to myself, for the sake of clearness, to use rather more names, with fewer ideas annexed to each, than a few names with more ideas; and I included under thirteen names of virtues all that at that time occurred to me as necessary or desirable, and annexed to each a short precept, which fully expressed the extent I gave to its meaning.

3   These names of virtues, with their precepts were:

EVALUATE PRINT AND GRAPHIC FEATURES

Annotate: Mark where Franklin's list of virtues begins.

Analyze: Why does Franklin organize the virtues in this way?

1. **Temperance.** Eat not to dullness; drink not to elevation.

2. **Silence.** Speak not but what may benefit others or yourself; avoid **trifling** conversation.

3. **Order.** Let all your things have their places; let each part of your business have its time.

4. **Resolution.** Resolve to perform what you ought; perform without fail what you resolve.

5. **Frugality.** Make no expense but to do good to others or yourself; *i.e.,* waste nothing.

6. **Industry.** Lose no time; be always employed in something useful; cut off all unnecessary actions.

7. **Sincerity.** Use no hurtful deceit; think innocently and justly; and, if you speak, speak accordingly.

trifling
(trī´flĭng) *adj.* frivolous; inconsequential.

8. **Justice.** Wrong none by doing injuries, or omitting the benefits that are your duty.

9. **Moderation.** Avoid extremes; forbear resenting injuries so much as you think they deserve.

10. **Cleanliness.** Tolerate no uncleanliness in body, clothes, or habitation.

11. **Tranquillity.** Be not disturbed at trifles, or at accidents common or unavoidable.

12. **Chastity.** Rarely use venery but for health or offspring, never to dulness, weakness, or the injury of your own or another's peace or reputation.

13. **Humility.** Imitate Jesus and Socrates.[1]

---
[1] **Socrates** (sŏk´rə-tēz): Greek philosopher (470?–399 BC) who believed that true knowledge comes through dialogue and systematic questioning of ideas.

WHEN STUDENTS STRUGGLE. . .

Evaluate Graphic Features To identify Franklin's reasons for organizing the virtues in this way, tell students to focus on his explanations in paragraph 2. Have them think about the main idea of the paragraph (Franklin's thoughts about how to arrange or "catalogue" different virtues), and separate it from details he provides (such as the sentence "Temperance, for example . . . ."). Explain that identifying main ideas in the text can help readers understand how the text relates to or helps explain the purpose of the graphic features.

  For additional support, go to the **Reading Studio** and assign the following **LEVEL** **Level Up Tutorial: Main Ideas and Supporting Details.**

4   My intention being to acquire the *habitude* of all these virtues, I judged it would be well not to distract my attention by attempting the whole at once, but to fix it on one of them at a time; and, when I should be master of that, then to proceed to another, and so on, till I should have gone through the thirteen; and, as the previous acquisition of some might facilitate the acquisition of certain others, I arranged them with that view, as they stand above. Temperance first, as it tends to procure that coolness and clearness of head, which is so necessary where constant vigilance was to be kept up, and guard maintained against the **unremitting** attraction of ancient habits, and the force of perpetual temptations. This being acquired and established, Silence would be more easy; and my desire being to gain knowledge at the same time that I improved in virtue, and considering that in conversation it was obtained rather by the use of the ears than of the tongue, and therefore wishing to break a habit I was getting into of prattling, punning, and joking, which only made me acceptable to trifling company, I gave *Silence* the second place. This and the next, *Order,* I expected would allow me more time for attending to my project and my studies. *Resolution,* once become habitual, would keep me firm in my endeavors to obtain all the subsequent virtues; *Frugality* and Industry freeing me from my remaining debt, and producing **affluence** and independence, would make more easy the practice of Sincerity and Justice, etc., etc.

Form of the pages.

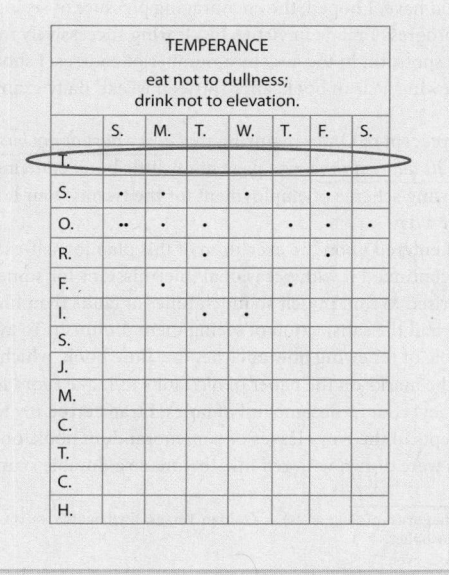

TEMPERANCE						
eat not to dullness; drink not to elevation.						
	S.	M.	T.	W.	T.	F.	S.
T.							
S.	•	•		•		•	
O.	••	•	•		•	•	•
R.			•			•	
F.		•			•		
I.			•	•			
S.							
J.							
M.							
C.							
T.							
C.							
H.							

MONITOR COMPREHENSION

Annotate: Mark the sentence in paragraph 4 describing the process Franklin chose.

Paraphrase: Reread the sentence slowly and carefully. Then, describe Franklin's process in your own words.

unremitting
(ŭn rĭ-mĭt´ĭng) *adj.* constant; never stopping.

affluence
(ăf´loo-əns) *n.* wealth.

EVALUATE PRINT AND GRAPHIC FEATURES

Annotate: Mark the area of the chart that shows Franklin succeeded in being temperate for most of the week.

Analyze: Does the information in the chart suggest Franklin will succeed on his project? Explain.

MONITOR COMPREHENSION

Guide students to identify individual steps in Franklin's process. Ask volunteers to paraphrase the cause-and-effect relationships Franklin describes. (**Possible answer:** *I wanted to acquire the habit of all of the virtues, so I decided to focus on one at a time. When I mastered one virtue, I would move on to the next one until I had gone through all 13. Because some virtues might help me to acquire others, I arranged them in a certain order.*)

EVALUATE PRINT AND GRAPHIC FEATURES

Make sure students understand that Franklin marks his failures (not adhering to the virtues). For this chart, fewer marks indicates a better performance. Franklin's explanation of how he marks the chart is on page 149. (**Possible answer:** *It makes it easier to see one's progress or failure at a glance and might keep one motivated.*)

CRITICAL VOCABULARY

unremitting: Franklin stresses the constant, *unremitting* pressure to fall back into old habits.

ASK STUDENTS why they think old habits have such unremitting attraction. (*People like what is familiar to them and find change difficult.*)

affluence: Franklin reasons that frugality and hard work will lead to wealth, or *affluence*.

ASK STUDENTS how they think frugality and industry can lead to affluence. (*Not wasting money and working hard can increase the chances of a person being affluent.*)

EXTREME OR ABSOLUTE LANGUAGE

Remind students to look for words that suggest something is always or never true, with no possibility of exceptions or doubt. Explain that absolute or extreme language is sometimes used to suggest intense feelings, and is not meant to be taken literally. Remind students that evidence in the text and the graphics may help them understand whether Franklin actually means to follow a strict schedule for every one of his tasks. (**Answer:** *Franklin has set lofty goals and has made plans to set about achieving them, so this is a case where extreme language is not an exaggeration. To achieve his genuine goal of moral perfection, he is taking an uncompromising stance.*)

 For **listening support** for students at varying proficiency levels, see the **Text X-Ray** on page 142C.

CRITICAL VOCABULARY

eradicate: Franklin says that he cannot completely eliminate all his bad habits at once, but must work to get rid of them, as a gardener works to *eradicate* weeds. Note that his phrase "bad herbs" is a phrase from the time period that simply means "weeds."

ASK STUDENTS how the comparison Franklin makes to a gardener eradicating weeds is relevant to his message. *(He is saying people must always be watching for their bad habits, and then immediately work to stop them before they once again "take root.")*

Conceiving then, that, agreeably to the advice of Pythagoras in his Golden Verses,[2] daily examination would be necessary, I contrived the following method for conducting that examination.

5   I made a little book, in which I allotted a page for each of the virtues. I ruled each page with red ink, so as to have seven columns, one for each day of the week, marking each column with a letter for the day. I crossed these columns with thirteen red lines, marking the beginning of each line with the first letter of one of the virtues, on which line, and in its proper column, I might mark, by a little black spot, every fault I found upon examination to have been committed respecting that virtue upon that day.

6   I determined to give a week's strict attention to each of the virtues successively. Thus, in the first week, my great guard was to avoid every[3] the least offense against *Temperance*, leaving the other virtues to their ordinary chance, only marking every evening the faults of the day. Thus, if in the first week I could keep my first line, marked T, clear of spots, I supposed the habit of that virtue so much strengthened, and its opposite weakened, that I might venture extending my attention to include the next, and for the following week keep both lines clear of spots. Proceeding thus to the last, I could go through a course complete in thirteen weeks, and four courses in a year. And like him who, having a garden to weed, does not attempt to **eradicate** all the bad herbs at once, which would exceed his reach and his strength, but works on one of the beds at a time, and, having accomplished the first, proceeds to a second, so I should have, I hoped, the encouraging pleasure of seeing on my pages the progress I made in virtue, by clearing successively my lines of their spots, till in the end, by a number of courses, I should be happy in viewing a clean book, after thirteen weeks' daily examination. . . .

7 The precept of *Order* requiring that *every part of my business should have its allotted time,* one page in my little book contained the following scheme of employment for the twenty-four hours of a natural day.

8   I entered upon the execution of this plan for self-examination, and continued it with occasional intermissions for some time. I was surprised to find myself so much fuller of faults than I had imagined; but I had the satisfaction of seeing them diminish. To avoid the trouble of renewing now and then my little book, which, by scraping out the marks on the paper of old faults to make room for new ones in a new course, became full of holes, I transferred my tables and precepts to the ivory leaves of a memorandum book, on which the lines were drawn with red ink, that made a durable stain, and on

---

2 **Pythagoras** (pĭ-thăg´ər-əs). . . **Golden Verses:** Pythagoras was a Greek philosopher.
3 **every:** even.

EXTREME OR ABSOLUTE LANGUAGE

Notice & Note: Mark the statement in paragraph 6 that contains extreme or absolute language.

Interpret: Explain whether Franklin is stating an uncompromising position or an exaggeration.

eradicate
(ĭ-răd´ĭ-kāt) *v.* tear up by the roots; eliminate.

APPLYING ACADEMIC VOCABULARY

☑ **contrary**   ☐ **founder**   ☐ **ideological**   ☑ **publication**   ☐ **revolution**

Write and Discuss   Have students turn to a partner to discuss the following questions. Guide students to include the Academic Vocabulary words *contrary* and *publication* in their responses. Ask volunteers to share their responses with the class.

- What did people appreciate about Franklin's **publication** of his autobiography?
- Why did some people have **contrary** opinions about Franklin's ideas?

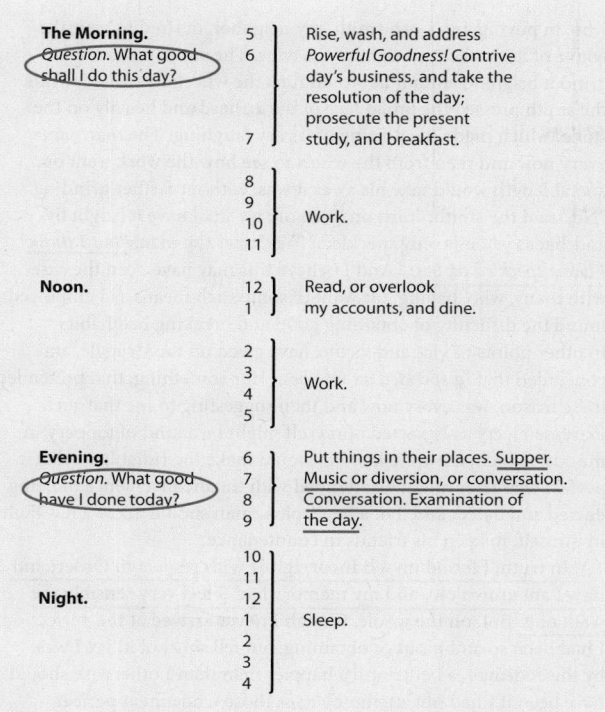

The Morning.	5	Rise, wash, and address
Question. What good shall I do this day?	6	*Powerful Goodness!* Contrive day's business, and take the resolution of the day; prosecute the present study, and breakfast.
	7	
	8	
	9	Work.
	10	
	11	
Noon.	12	Read, or overlook my accounts, and dine.
	1	
	2	
	3	Work.
	4	
	5	
Evening.	6	Put things in their places. Supper. Music or diversion, or conversation. Conversation. Examination of the day.
Question. What good have I done today?	7	
	8	
	9	
	10	
	11	
Night.	12	Sleep.
	1	
	2	
	3	
	4	

EVALUATE PRINT AND GRAPHIC FEATURES

Annotate: Circle the boldface text and underline the sentence fragments Franklin uses in his daily schedule.

Analyze: How do these features help the reader understand why Franklin wrote his book? Are they effective organizers?

those lines I marked my faults with a black-lead pencil, which marks I could easily wipe out with a wet sponge. After a while I went through one course only in a year, and afterward only one in several years, till at length I omitted them entirely, being employed in voyages and business abroad, with a multiplicity of affairs that interfered; but I always carried my little book with me.

9   My scheme of *Order* gave me the most trouble; and I found that, though it might be practicable where a man's business was such as to leave him the disposition of his time, that of a journeyman printer, for instance, it was not possible to be exactly observed by a master, who must mix with the world, and often receive people of business at their own hours. *Order,* too, with regard to places for things, papers, etc., I found extremely difficult to acquire. I had not been early accustomed to it, and, having an exceeding good memory, I was not so sensible of the inconvenience attending want of method. This article, therefore, cost me so much painful attention, and my faults in it vexed me so much, and I made so little progress in amendment, and had such frequent relapses, that I was almost ready to give up the attempt, and content myself with a faulty character in that respect, like the man

The Autobiography   149

EVALUATE PRINT AND GRAPHIC FEATURES

Explain that fragments should not be confused with imperative sentences. Guide students to notice that Franklin's notes are essentially instructions to guide and structure his day. The morning and afternoon are structured with commands to himself about what he must do. The evening has fewer commands. It is a time for relaxation, amusement, and reflection. (**Possible answer:** *They indicate he made the book primarily for himself.*)

ENGLISH LEARNER SUPPORT

Language Conventions Explain that *shall* is a synonym for *will* and that it is used in a similar way to *will*, but with an added sense of allowing or requiring that something happen. Have students say what Franklin *will* do. (e.g., *He will read.*) Then, have them say what Franklin *should* do. (*e.g., He should work.*) Then, ask students to create a sentence using *shall* instead of *should* or *will*. **MODERATE**

IMPROVE READING FLUENCY

Targeted Passage Have students work with a partner to read the beginning of paragraph 9 aloud. Instruct them to pay particular attention to when to pause, as indicated by commas, and to think about how to chunk words together to make meaning clear. Model this first by reading from paragraph 8, from "To avoid the trouble . . . memorandum book." Then, have students read paragraph 9, from "My scheme . . . their own hours."

 Go to the **Reading Studio** for additional support in developing fluency.

MONITOR COMPREHENSION

Note that Franklin is using the speckled ax as a metaphor. The speckled ax represents an idea. Franklin's conclusion that *"a speckled ax was best"* is reminiscent of pithy sayings he was known for using in works such as his *Poor Richard's Almanack*. A **pithy** saying is a concise, forceful statement that communicates a relatively complex idea. (**Possible answer:** *It is a way of telling the reader that Franklin has concluded the work was harder than he expected.*)

CRITICAL VOCABULARY

incorrigible: Have students break down the word *incorrigible*. Guide them to find the suffix *in-*, which indicates negation (like *un-*). Ask students to guess the meaning of *corrigible*. Explain that it means "reparable" or "correctable." Show that *corrigible* and *correctable* share the same root.

ASK STUDENTS what reasons Franklin gives for being incorrigible when it comes to order. (*He is old and his memory is bad.*)

artifice: Franklin's *artifice* was to improve himself by aiming for perfection. Though he did not achieve perfection, he made progress by trying to imitate it. Explain that today *artifice* usually has a negative connotation (implying fakeness). However, the word is related to "art" and "artful."

ASK STUDENTS why Franklin thought his artifice made him happy. (*It gave him something worthwhile to work toward, and whatever progress he made improved his life.*)

felicity: For Franklin, practicing good habits led to *felicity*, or happiness.

ASK STUDENTS if they believe striving to change themselves in positive ways increases their felicity. (*Having a goal to work toward generally makes people feel happier.*)

MONITOR COMPREHENSION

Annotate: Mark the phrase in paragraph 9 that tells the kind of ax the man decided was best.

Analyze: How does this story about the ax relate to Franklin's project?

incorrigible
(ĭn-kôr´ĭ-jə-bəl) *adj.* incapable of being reformed or corrected.

LANGUAGE CONVENTIONS
Annotate: Underline a short sentence in paragraph 10. Put brackets around a very long sentence.

Analyze: Explain how Franklin uses sentence variety in this paragraph.

artifice
(är´tə-fĭs) *n.* a clever means to an end.

felicity
(fĭ-lĭs´ĭ-tē) *n.* great happiness.

who, in buying an ax of a smith, my neighbor, desired to have the whole of its surface as bright as the edge. The smith consented to grind it bright for him if he would turn the wheel; he turned, while the smith pressed the broad face of the ax hard and heavily on the stone, which made the turning of it very fatiguing. The man came every now and then from the wheel to see how the work went on, and at length would take his ax as it was, without farther grinding. "No," said the smith, "turn on, turn on; we shall have it bright by-and-by; as yet, it is only speckled." "Yes," says the man, *"but I think I like a speckled ax best."* And I believe this may have been the case with many, who, having, for want of some such means as I employed, found the difficulty of obtaining good and breaking bad habits in other points of vice and virtue, have given up the struggle, and concluded that *"a speckled ax was best;"* for something, that pretended to be reason, was every now and then suggesting to me that such extreme nicety as I exacted of myself might be a kind of foppery in morals,[4] which, if it were known, would make me ridiculous; that a perfect character might be attended with the inconvenience of being envied and hated; and that a benevolent man should allow a few faults in himself, to keep his friends in countenance.

10   In truth, I found myself **incorrigible** with respect to Order; and now I am grown old, and my memory bad, I feel very sensibly the want of it. (But, on the whole, though I never arrived at the perfection I had been so ambitious of obtaining, but fell short of it, yet I was, by the endeavor, a better and a happier man than I otherwise should have been if I had not attempted it; as those who aim at perfect writing by imitating the engraved copies, though they never reach the wished-for excellence of those copies, their hand is mended by the endeavor, and is tolerable while it continues fair and legible.)

11   It may well be my posterity should be informed that to this little **artifice,** with the blessing of God, their ancestor owed the constant **felicity** of his life, down to his 79th year, in which this is written. What reverses may attend the reminder is in the hand of Providence; but, if they arrive, the reflection on past happiness enjoyed ought to help his bearing them with more resignation. To Temperance he ascribes his long-continued health, and what is still left to him of a good constitution; to Industry and Frugality, the early easiness of his circumstances and acquisition of his fortune, with all that knowledge that enabled him to be a useful citizen, and obtained for him some degree of reputation among the learned; to Sincerity and Justice, the confidence of his country, and the honorable employs it conferred upon him; and to the joint influence of the whole mass of the virtues, even in the imperfect state he was able to acquire them, all that

---

[4] **foppery in morals:** excessive regard for and concern about one's moral appearance.

TO CHALLENGE STUDENTS . . .

Write Creatively Have students work in groups to create a list of essential virtues. Instruct them to write a precept in Franklin's style to accompany each virtue. Before they write, have them examine Franklin's precepts and describe their style. (For example: *Precepts begin with an imperative; Franklin uses "but" to mean "except."*) When students complete their work, discuss the virtues with them, or have them present their lists and precepts to the class. Ask students to explain why and how they chose virtues.

evenness of temper, and that cheerfulness in conversation, which makes his company still sought for, and agreeable even to his younger acquaintance. I hope, therefore, that some of my descendants may follow the example and reap the benefit.

CHECK YOUR UNDERSTANDING

Answer these questions before moving on to the **Analyze the Text** section on the following page.

1 What reason did Franklin have for placing *Temperance* first?

A He hoped to achieve the most difficult goal first.

B Mastering it would make the others easier to achieve.

C Since it was mentioned by other writers, it must be most important.

D Temperance was the virtue he valued most.

2 Why did Franklin make a book with a chart for each of the virtues?

F To keep track of how well he was doing

G To share the information with the people he knew

H Because his friend Pythagoras told him to do it

J He preferred thinking in visual terms

3 What did Franklin think of the endeavor, once he realized he would not achieve his original goals?

A He believed the endeavor had been a waste of time and nothing had been gained.

B He decided that his ideas about reason and order were probably wrong.

C He was better and happier than he would have been if he hadn't tried.

D He believed he was a worse man than he had been when he started out.

The Autobiography 151

LANGUAGE CONVENTIONS

Guide students to recognize how using sentence variety can both create interest and allow authors to contrast different ideas. Have them identify the idea Franklin is communicating in each sentence of paragraph 10, then determine how using different sentence lengths allows him to express these ideas in an effective way. (***Possible answer:*** *Franklin uses sentence variety to contrast different ways of evaluating his progress. First, he uses a shorter sentence to admit to a fault or weakness in a frank, honest way. He then uses a longer sentence to analyze his progress in a more detailed way. This longer sentence shows that his attempt was not a complete failure, but helped him become a better and happier person.*)

CHECK YOUR UNDERSTANDING

Have students answer the questions independently.

Answers:

1. *B*

2. *F*

3. *C*

If students answer any questions incorrectly, have them reread the text to confirm their understanding. Then, they may proceed to ANALYZE THE TEXT on page 152.

ENGLISH LEARNER SUPPORT

Oral Assessment Use the following questions to assess students' comprehension and speaking skills.

1. Why did Franklin put Temperance first on his list? (*With Temperance, he could succeed with his other goals.*)

2. Why did Franklin make a chart for each virtue? (*to keep track of his faults*)

3. Did Franklin reach his goal? How did he feel? (*No. He was happy because he made progress.*) **MODERATE**

APPLY

ANALYZE THE TEXT

Possible answers:

1. **DOK 3:** *The print feature, the list of virtues, helped me understand Franklin's goals. The first graphic helped show how he tracked his progress toward achieving those goals. The second showed how he used a plan for organizing his day to achieve his goals.*

2. **DOK 3:** *As a result of his project, Franklin recognized humans could never be perfect, though they could make improvements in their moral behavior in the same way people aiming for "perfect writing" might "never reach the wished-for excellence" but find "their hand is mended by the endeavor."*

3. **DOK 2:** *They are unlikely to have benefited fully, as people generally need to learn their own lessons in life.*

4. **DOK 4:** *Although Franklin's exacting goals may make him seem self-righteous, he is also able to criticize himself in a direct and honest way, as when he admits he "never arrived at the perfection" he hoped to attain. While his plan may seem superficial, it has the result of making him feel like a "better and a happier man."*

5. **DOK 4:** *Answers will vary, but should cite examples of Franklin's uncompromising language and the results of his attempts to achieve this goal. Students may note the difficulty of trying to "conquer all that either natural inclination, custom, or company might lead" a person into, and Franklin's characterization of himself as "incorrigible."*

RESEARCH

Remind students to use multiple sources for research and to consider the reliability of the sources they use.

Extend Choices for additional reading include excerpts from *Poor Richard's Almanack*, letters, or other papers. Yale University provides access to many of Franklin's writings at franklinpapers.org.

RESPOND

ANALYZE THE TEXT

Support your responses with evidence from the text. ☰ NOTEBOOK

1. **Evaluate** How did the print and graphic features Franklin included help you understand his progress on his project?

2. **Draw Conclusions** How do you think Franklin's ideas about human perfectibility changed as a result of his endeavor? Cite specific details that suggest when his view changed.

3. **Infer** Do you think Franklin's descendants would have benefited from his example, as he hoped they would? Why or why not?

4. **Evaluate** Some critics consider Franklin to be self-righteous and materialistic; others have ridiculed his plan for moral perfection as regimented and superficial. Do you find any evidence for these charges in the excerpt? Explain.

5. **Notice & Note** Franklin's stated goal is "to live without committing any fault at any time." Does Franklin's extreme language convince you that this goal is important? Is this a reasonable expectation? Explain, citing evidence from the text.

RESEARCH TIP
For information about Franklin and the postal service, check the website of the United States Postal Service. The Franklin Institute is also a good source of information.

RESEARCH

Benjamin Franklin was a remarkable, brilliant, and accomplished person. Research his life and identify some of his accomplishments. Use what you learn to answer these questions.

QUESTION	ANSWER
What are two things Benjamin Franklin invented?	*Possible answers: lightning rod, bifocals, swim fins, the Franklin stove, glass harmonica*
What was Franklin's association with the postal service?	*He was postmaster of Philadelphia under the British and was appointed first Postmaster General by the Continental Congress.*
In what foreign country did Franklin work during the American Revolution, and what job did he have there?	*He went to France to represent Americans as their first ambassador.*

Extend Find another work written by Benjamin Franklin and compare the virtues and character flaws revealed in that work to those in *The Autobiography*. With a partner, discuss what it would have been like to spend time with the Ben Franklin portrayed in both selections.

WHEN STUDENTS STRUGGLE . . .

Reteaching: Evaluate Print and Graphic Features Explain that to evaluate print and graphic features, students should consider alternate ways of presenting information. Work with students to answer question 1. Review the list, the chart, and the schedule with students, and ask them to think about other ways Franklin could have presented the information in these features (for example, in a prose description). Guide students to recognize ways the print and graphic features emphasize information and make it easier to understand.

 For additional support, go to the **Reading Studio** and assign the following [LEVEL UP] **Level Up Tutorial: Analyzing Visuals.**

CREATE AND DISCUSS

Write an Essay Write an autobiographical essay about a time you tried to learn something new or improve existing skills. Review your notes on the Quick Start activity before you begin.

❏ Decide which project from your past would make an interesting topic for an autobiographical essay.

❏ Be sure to give details about your plans, your efforts, and the outcome of your project.

❏ Write a conclusion where you explain what you learned and whether you successfully achieved your goal.

Discuss Autobiographies In a small group, discuss what you learned about making goals and carrying out plans to meet them. Compare your experience to what you read about Franklin and to what others share.

❏ Talk about how reading Franklin's autobiography affected your thinking about planning and achieving goals.

❏ Share the types of projects, how you approached them, and what the outcomes were.

❏ Discuss any similarities between the projects in the group and even with Franklin's project.

❏ Summarize the lessons you learned from your experiences.

 Go to **Developing a Topic** in the **Writing Studio** for help.

 Go to **Participating in Collaborative Discussions** in the **Speaking and Listening Studio** for help.

RESPOND TO THE ESSENTIAL QUESTION

? How do we transform our lives?

Gather Information Review your annotations and notes on this excerpt from *The Autobiography*. Then, add relevant information to your Response Log. As you determine which information to include, think about:

• why we strive for self-improvement
• how to balance the desire for a big change with the need to set realistic goals
• the best way to pursue a goal

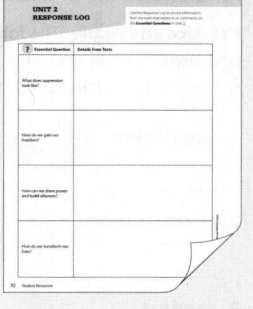

ACADEMIC VOCABULARY
As you write and discuss what you learned from *The Autobiography*, be sure to use the Academic Vocabulary words. Check off each of the words that you use.

❏ **contrary**
❏ **founder**
❏ **ideological**
❏ **publication**
❏ **revolution**

CREATE AND DISCUSS

Write an Essay As a prewriting activity, have a whole class discussion reviewing the features of the autobiography genre. Features include first-person narrative, significant life events, and often a dual perspective. In Franklin's case, his autobiography actually has two characters: his younger (or main character) self, and older (or narrator) self. However, only the narrator can reflect and comment on the actions and motives of the main character. Have students find examples in the text. Then, have students lists ideas and answers for each of the three bulleted items in the Student Edition.

For **writing support** for students at varying proficiency levels, see the **Text X-Ray** on page 142D.

Discuss Autobiographies Before students break into small groups, have the class review and summarize Franklin's main points about making plans and carrying them out. After groups discuss, call on volunteers to share their summaries with the class.

RESPOND TO THE ESSENTIAL QUESTION

Allow time for students to add details from *The Autobiography* to their Unit 2 Response Logs.

CRITICAL VOCABULARY

Possible Answers:

1. *A complicated science experiment might require unremitting attention.*

2. *Good news about a friend or family member would give me a feeling of felicity.*

3. *People would wear fancy or expensive clothes to show their affluence.*

4. *Pulling up weeds, using herbicides, or even applying household products are ways to eradicate weeds.*

5. *No, you should not spend much time on a trifling issue.*

6. *A villain is incorrigible.*

7. *Yes, a person would use artifice to perform a magic trick.*

8. *Someone might contrive a way to get the day off in order to visit family or attend an exciting event.*

VOCABULARY STRATEGY:
Latin Roots

Answers:

1. *The root is acquisitio, meaning "to acquire." Words in the family are acquire, acquisitive.*

2. *The root is circumstancia, meaning "to stand around." Words in the family are circumstantial, circumstantiate.*

3. *The root is conducere, meaning "to lead together." Words in the family are conductance, conduction, conductive, conductor.*

4. *The root is jus, meaning "law" or "right." Words in the family are judgment, just, judicial.*

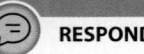

RESPOND

WORD BANK

trifling	eradicate
unremitting	incorrigible
affluence	artifice
contrive	felicity

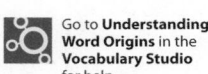

Go to **Understanding Word Origins** in the **Vocabulary Studio** for help.

CRITICAL VOCABULARY

Practice and Apply Show your understanding of the vocabulary words by answering these questions.

1. What is a project that requires **unremitting** attention?

2. What news might give you a feeling of **felicity?**

3. What would people wear to display their **affluence?**

4. How would you **eradicate** weeds from a field of grass?

5. Is a **trifling** issue something you should spend much time on?

6. Would you describe a hero or a villain as **incorrigible?**

7. Would someone use **artifice** to perform a magic trick?

8. Why might you **contrive** a way to get the day off?

VOCABULARY STRATEGY:
Latin Roots

A **root** is a word part that carries the core meaning of a word. In most cases, roots combine with other word parts to form whole words. Often, these word parts are prefixes or suffixes, but sometimes they are additional roots. Groups of words with the same root are called **word families**.

English has collected words and roots from around the world. Thousands of those roots came into English from Latin. Knowing some of the roots can help you figure out other words in the family. For example, the words *number, numerous,* and *enumeration* are all in one word family with the Latin root *numerus,* meaning "a number or quantity."

Practice and Apply The following words appear in the selection. For each one, use a general or etymological dictionary in print or online to identify the root or roots, and find at least one other word in the same word family.

1. acquisition

_____

2. circumstances

_____

3. conduct

_____

4. judge

_____

ENGLISH LEARNER SUPPORT

Spanish Word Families Spanish speakers may recognize the words used in the Vocabulary Strategy activity: *acquire/adquisición; circumstance/circunstancia; conduct/conducir; judge/juzgar.* Have these students identify word families using Spanish words.

- acquisition: *adquisición, adquirir, adquirido*
- circumstance: *circunstancia, circo, círculo*
- conduct: *conducir, conductor/a, conducta*
- judge: *juzgar, juez, juicio* **ALL LEVELS**

LANGUAGE CONVENTIONS:
Standard English

Standard English requires a writer to follow the **conventions** of sentence structure, usage, and punctuation that demonstrate a writer understands the expectations of the audience. Resources called **style guides** provide valuable assistance to writers in identifying departures from those conventions and suggesting ways to improve the text. Some word processing programs come with a grammar and style checker that a writer can use as a tool to check a text for possible errors. These checkers provide context-appropriate suggestions to correct such issues as sentence fragments, lack of subject-verb agreement, or punctuation problems. Print and online style guides explain the rules of Standard English and show examples of correct and incorrect usage to help illustrate those rules.

A style guide can also provide suggestions on how to undertake such tasks as varying sentence structure. It can provide examples of various sentence types, such as these examples from the selection:

Simple sentence: *It was about this time I conceived the bold and arduous project of arriving at moral perfection.*
Compound sentence: *I entered upon the execution of this plan for self-examination, and continued it with occasional intermissions for some time.*
Complex sentence: *As I knew, or thought I knew, what was right and wrong, I did not see why I might not always do the one and avoid the other.*

Practice and Apply Write four or five sentences stating your opinion of Franklin's character and judgment based on the excerpt from *The Autobiography*. Be sure to include a mix of sentence structures to give variety to your writing. Then, check your sentences against a style guide to ensure that you have structured sentences and used punctuation correctly.

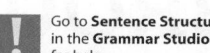

RESPOND

Go to **Sentence Structure** in the **Grammar Studio** for help.

LANGUAGE CONVENTIONS:
Standard English

On the board, demonstrate an error in subject-verb agreement and ask a volunteer to correct. It. Write a sentence fragment, then call on a volunteer to transform it into a complete sentence.

Provide explanations to students about each sentence type. A **simple sentence** has only one clause with one subject and one verb, or a compound subject and compound verb. A **compound sentence** consists of two or more independent clauses, correctly combined with a coordinator, conjunctive adverb, or semicolon. A **complex sentence** has at least one independent clause combined with at least one dependent, or subordinate, clause.

Practice and Apply

Answers will vary. *Examples:*

Simple: *Benjamin Franklin was smart and practical.*

Compound: *Franklin was interested in moral perfection, and he created a system to try to achieve it.*

Complex: *An intelligent and motivated man, Franklin created an ambitious project for himself, tracking his progress daily and reflecting on his experience.*

ENGLISH LEARNER SUPPORT

Connect Verbs Explain to Hmong speakers that in English two actions (verbs) must be connected with a conjunction (e.g., *and, if, but*). Note that Hmong speakers may use two or more main verbs in one clause without any connectors. For example, *I took a book studied at the library.*)

Have students practice creating simple sentences with two actions using the conjunction *and*. Provide this frame: *I _____ and _____* . **SUBSTANTIAL**

ON BEING BROUGHT FROM AFRICA TO AMERICA
Poem by Phillis Wheatley

SYMPATHY
Poem by Paul Laurence Dunbar

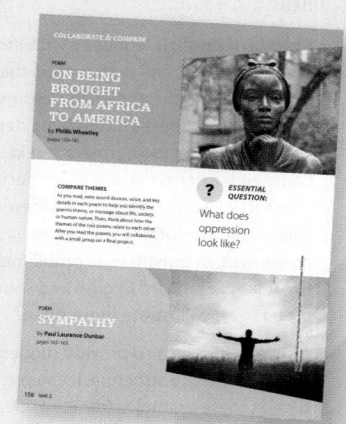

GENRE ELEMENTS
POEM

A poem is a piece of writing that relies heavily on imagery and figurative language to develop a theme (or multiple themes). It is usually shorter than prose, relying on more condensed and suggestive writing. Poetry can follow a prescriptive format (such as a sonnet, a limerick, or haiku) but it can also be free-form. Rhythm, rhyme, meter, and other devices can all be incorporated to assist the poem in adequately evoking themes and emotions.

LEARNING OBJECTIVES

- Identify words that express the speaker's emotion and attitude.
- Use the Internet and/or history books to research the slave trade.
- Write a prose adaptation of a poem.
- Analyze thematic development in poetry.
- Compare the themes of two poems.
- Assess how sound devices contribute to poetic voice.
- **Language** Discuss poetry using the words *stanza, rhyme,* and *rhythm*.

TEXT COMPLEXITY

Quantitative Measures	On Being Brought from Africa to America / Sympathy	Lexile: N/A
Qualitative Measures	**Ideas Presented** "On Being Brought": Multiple levels, abstract, difficult ideas. Use of symbolism, irony. "Sympathy": Multiple levels, use of symbolism, irony, satire. Some ambiguity.	
	Structures Used "On Being Brought": Clear, conventional. "Sympathy": Primarily explicit, conventional.	
	Language Used "On Being Brought": Implied meanings. Allusive, figurative language, perhaps archaic or formal. "Sympathy": Meanings are implied but support is offered. More figurative or ironic language.	
	Knowledge Required Requires no special knowledge. Situations and subjects familiar or easily envisioned.	

RESOURCES

- Unit 2 Response Log
- Selection Audio
- Reading Studio: Notice & Note
- Level Up Tutorials: Theme; Elements of Poetry
- Writing Studio: Writing Narratives
- Speaking and Listening Studio: Participating in a Collaborative Discussion; Giving a Presentation
- "On Being Brought from Africa to America"/"Sympathy" Selection Test

SUMMARIES

English

"On Being Brought from Africa to America" and "Sympathy" are poems written through the lens of the African American experience. In "On Being Brought from Africa to America," Phillis Wheatley delves into the feelings of a slave being brought to America, while Paul Laurence Dunbar's "Sympathy" deals more generally with feeling caged. Both poets are among the most lauded African American poets in the United States, and both poems reflect an important aspect of their history.

Spanish

"Ser traído desde África a América" y "Simpatía" son poemas escritos desde el punto de vista de la experiencia afroamericana. En "Ser traído desde África", Phillis Wheatley ahonda en los sentimientos de un esclavo llevado a América, mientras que "Simpatía" de Paul Laurence Dunbar trata generalmente de sentirse enjaulado. Ambos son de los más loados poetas afroamericanos de Estados Unidos y estos poemas reflejan un aspecto importante de su historia.

SMALL-GROUP OPTIONS

Have students work in small groups and pairs to read and discuss the selection.

Think-Pair-Share

- Pose a question to the class, such as *How are the two poems similar? How are the two poems different?*
- Have a students think about the question individually, making notes.
- Each student partners with another student to listen, discuss, and formulate a shared response.
- Call on students to respond to the entire class.

Send a Problem

- After reading "Sympathy," pose this question: *What was Paul Laurence Dunbar's motivation for writing this poem?*
- Call on a student to respond, citing evidence from the text. Wait up to 11 seconds.
- If the student has no response, s/he must call on another student by name to answer the same question.
- Have students continue asking each other for assistance as needed. Monitor responses and ask more questions as appropriate.

Text X-Ray: English Learner Support
for "On Being Brought from Africa to America" and "Sympathy"

Use the Text X-Ray and the supports and scaffolds in the Teacher's Edition to help guide students at different proficiency levels through the selection.

INTRODUCE THE SELECTION
DISCUSS OPPRESSION

Make sure students are aware of the history of slavery in the United States. Explain that slavery ended in the United States with the Civil War. Paul Laurence Dunbar was born less than ten years after slavery ended. Violence against African Americans and laws that severely limited their rights were extremely common long after slavery ended.

Introduce the word *oppression* to students. Discuss the relationship between its meaning and the root *press*. Point out that many words are built from this root, such as *compression* and *impression*. Discuss how these words are related in meaning to *oppression*. Prompt students to use the word *oppression* while discussing the selection and related topics.

CULTURAL REFERENCES

The following words or phrases may be unfamiliar to students:

- *Pagan* (p. 160, stanza 1): person who worships more than one god
- *soul* (p. 160, stanza 1): the part of a person that is not physical; In many religions, the soul is believed to live on after the body dies.
- *redemption* (p. 160, stanza 1): a key idea in Christianity; the belief is that people live in sin (error, badness), but by learning about God and Christianity, they are brought out of sin. Wheatley sees redemption from sin as so important that it outweighs being enslaved.
- *Cain* (p. 160, stanza 2): In the Bible, Cain and Abel were the sons of Adam and Eve. Cain killed his brother Abel.
- *alas* (p. 162, stanza 1): an old-fashioned word that expresses sadness and regret

LISTENING

Listen to Poetry

Tell students that listening to poetry is different from reading it. Direct them to listen for rhyme and rhythm, which are best heard aloud. Ask students to think about how hearing poetry aloud contributes to understanding.

Use the following supports with students at varying proficiency levels:

- Read the first 4 lines of "Sympathy" aloud. Explain that the poet is describing a place. Ask if it is inside or outside. Ask students to listen as you read again and to listen for words about nature. **SUBSTANTIAL**
- Read aloud the first stanza of "On Being Brought from Africa to America." Stress the last word of each line. Ask students which words rhyme. (*land, understand; too, knew*) Read aloud the second stanza, and ask students which words rhyme. (*eye, die; Cain, train*) **MODERATE**
- Read aloud the first stanza of "On Being Brought from Africa to America." Ask students to listen to identify two things mercy did in the poem. Guide students to note mercy brought the narrator from her Pagan land and taught her soul to understand. Note that the words rhyme. Reread the stanza and ask students which other words rhyme. **LIGHT**

SPEAKING

Focus on Sound and Rhythm

Explain that poetry is different from prose because it is built around the sound and rhythm of language. Tell students that recognizing sound devices helps them better understand the text.

Focus on the first stanza of "Sympathy." Use the following supports with students at varying proficiency levels:

- Read aloud the stanza. Help students recognize the rhyme by asking them *What rhymes with* grass? (glass and alas) *What rhymes with* steals? (feels) **SUBSTANTIAL**
- Read aloud the stanza. Ask students to identify the words that rhyme with *grass*, *slopes*, and *steals*. Then provide this sentence frame: *The rhyming words create a _____.* (rhythm) **MODERATE**
- Have volunteers read each line from the first stanza. Have students identify the rhyming words. Lead students in a discussion of the relationship between rhythm and meaning in the poem. **LIGHT**

READING

Understand Poetry

Explain that understanding poetry requires an investigation of its theme. Ask: *What universal ideas does "Sympathy" explore? Can you apply the ideas expressed in the poem to your own life?*

Focus on the second stanza of "Sympathy." Use the following supports with students at varying proficiency levels:

- Have students read the last line of the stanza. Ask: *Is the caged bird happy?* **SUBSTANTIAL**
- Have students read the stanza. Ask: *How does the caged bird feel? What does the bird do that shows his feelings?* Provide sentence frames: *The cage bird feels _____. The caged bird _____ against he bars.* **MODERATE**
- Have students read the first four lines. Review the definition of *fain* in the footnote. Ask: *What word would you use to describe the bird? What clues tell you how the bird feels?* **LIGHT**

WRITING

Write a Story

Work with students to read the assignment to Write a Prose Adaptation on Student Edition page 165. Explain that prose can have poetic elements, like strong images and carefully chosen words. Guide students to use their creativity to produce their prose adaptations.

Help student prepare to write their prose adaptation for Create and Present. Use the following supports with students at varying proficiency levels:

- Write *character(s)* and *setting* on the board. Explain each term. Ask students to share an idea for each of these elements. Record their ideas. If necessary, allow students to draw their ideas and help them express the ideas in words. **SUBSTANTIAL**
- Review *character(s), setting, plot,* and *detail.* Then, help students plan their stories by providing these sentence frames: *I will write about _____. The setting is _____. My character(s) will _____. One important detail I will use is _____.* **MODERATE**
- Have students work in pairs to create their prose adaptations. Circulate to help students. Then, have pairs exchange adaptations and peer edit. Have students revise based on the feedback. **LIGHT**

? Connect to the
ESSENTIAL QUESTION

These poems present the student with the divergent perspectives of two poets of color on their experiences of living in America. Comparing these perspectives will challenge the student to think about a familiar subject, America's history of racial injustice and oppression, in a more nuanced and difficult way.

COMPARE THEMES

Remind students that a **theme** is a message about life that a writer wants to communicate. Tell students that both of these poets use word choices and details in their poems to convey the theme, and because the theme is not stated directly, those elements will help them determine the message. Suggest students list the poetic elements in a graphic organizer with a separate column for each poem where they can make notes.

POEM

ON BEING BROUGHT FROM AFRICA TO AMERICA

by **Phillis Wheatley**
pages 159–161

COMPARE THEMES

As you read, note sound devices, voice, and key details in each poem to help you identify the poem's theme, or message about life, society, or human nature. Then, think about how the themes of the two poems relate to each other. After you read the poems, you will collaborate with a small group on a final project.

 ESSENTIAL QUESTION:

What does oppression look like?

POEM

SYMPATHY

by **Paul Laurence Dunbar**
pages 162–163

QUICK START

What are you grateful for in your life? What do you long for? Write your ideas in the chart.

GRATEFUL FOR	WISH FOR

ANALYZE SPEAKER

A poem's **speaker**, like the narrator of a story, is the voice that "talks" to the reader. Sometimes, the speaker can be identified with the poet; at other times—even if the poem relies on a first-person perspective—the speaker may be a **persona**, a fictional character adopted by the poet. As you read, note clues about the character of each poem's speaker. Note feelings and ideas being expressed, the speaker's use of language, hints about the speaker's experiences, and the speaker's tone.

ANALYZE THEME

The **theme** of a work is its message about life or human nature. This message may be stated directly, but readers often must **infer,** or make a logical guess, about it. To infer a poem's theme, note details about its speaker, its key ideas, the feelings it expresses, and the poet's use of imagery, language, and voice.

Use the chart to help you keep track of important details and clues that suggest each poem's theme or themes.

"ON BEING BROUGHT FROM AFRICA TO AMERICA"	"SYMPATHY"
Details and Suggested Theme(s)	Details and Suggested Theme(s)

The poems you are about to read give you the opportunity to compare how different texts treat similar themes. As you read the poems, think about the similarities and differences between them.

GENRE ELEMENTS: POETRY
- develops a theme (or multiple themes) in the work
- is more condensed and suggestive than prose
- uses a variety of sound devices to create voice, add emphasis, and convey meaning

QUICK START

After students have written their answers to the Quick Start, organize them into small groups for discussion. Challenge students to think about the extent to which they are permitted to pursue the things they long for in the society where they live. What social forces outside their control might act to keep them from fulfilling these longings? Challenge students to imagine scenarios in the past when the things they are grateful for would be drastically different, and to imagine how they might cope with this change.

ANALYZE SPEAKER

Review first-person pronouns such as *I, me, my,* and *we,* which can help students identify the speaker of a poem. Explain that while a speaker may give explicit details about his or her identity or experiences, in many cases students will need to make inferences based on the speaker's tone, word choices, and emotions. Encourage them to think about a possible subject of a poem, such as a forest scene in autumn. Ask how different speakers might describe the scene in different ways, based on their locations, attitudes, or experiences.

ANALYZE THEME

Review the poetic elements that will help students analyze the theme. For language, ask students to suggest pairs of words that have different connotations, such as *mercy* and *pity,* and discuss how each might help reveal the theme. Then, ask students for pairs of images that represent the same concept, such as solitude, but would have different emotional effects on the reader. Discuss how differences in point of view might help reveal the theme. Ask students to name other poetic elements and how they would contribute to theme.

On Being Brought from Africa to America / Sympathy   157

TEACH

ANALYZE SOUND DEVICES AND VOICE

Remind students that poetry is set apart from prose by a particular attention to and use of language. Rhyme and repetition help to direct readers' attention towards ideas, feelings, or messages. Sometimes, poets use rhyme in a way that "packs a punch," giving certain ideas a heavy emphasis. Poets can use repetition and variation to lead readers to see ideas, relationships, comparisons, contrasts, or other effects.

■ English Learner Support

Practice Vowel Sounds Display the final two lines of "On Being Brought from Africa to America." Note that when two vowels are combined, they often form a long vowel sound.

- Write the vowels on the board, say them, and have students repeat after you. Write *Cain* and *train*, say them, and have students repeat. Then, have students identify the vowel sound in the rhyme. **SUBSTANTIAL**

- Say *Cain* and *train* aloud and have students repeat them. Then, read the last stanza aloud. Have students identify words that use the long *a* sound (*sable, race, May*). **LIGHT**

✎ ANNOTATION MODEL

Remind students of annotation ideas such as underlining important details. Note that by circling repetition in poetry, they will gain a sense of how poetic effect is created. Point out that students may follow the suggestion in the model or use their own system for marking up the selection in their write-in text. They may want to color-code their annotation by using highlighters. Their notes in the margin may include questions about ideas that are unclear or reasons why certain words, phrases, or sound devices are important.

 **GET READY**

ANALYZE SOUND DEVICES AND VOICE

Poets use a number of different **sound devices**—such as rhyme, rhythm, alliteration, repetition, and meter—to emphasize ideas, add a musical quality, create mood, and reinforce meaning in their poems.

These devices also contribute to the **voice** of a poem, the unique style of the author or speaker. Wheatley and Dunbar use rhyme, rhythm, repetition, and alliteration, among other sound devices, as they develop their distinct voices.

Rhyme is the occurrence of similar or identical sounds at the end of two or more words. Rhyme that occurs within a single line of poetry, such as *suite, heat,* and *complete* is called **internal rhyme.** Rhyme that appears at the end of a set of lines is called **end rhyme.**

Rhythm refers to the "beat" of a poem and is created by the pattern of stressed and unstressed syllables. **Meter** is the repetition of a regular rhythmic unit in a line.

Repetition is a poetic device in which a sound, word, phrase, or line is repeated to emphasize the importance of an idea, as well as to create an appealing rhythm.

Alliteration is the repetition of consonant sounds at the beginnings of words, placing emphasis on those words, their sounds, and their meanings.

As you read, notice the way that the two poets use each of these sound devices to create their unique voices, draw attention to important ideas, convey meaning, and help suggest theme.

ANNOTATION MODEL

NOTICE & NOTE ✎

As you read, notice the use of sound devices and how these develop the voice and the theme of each poem. In the example below, you can see one reader's notes on "Sympathy."

I know what the caged bird feels, <u>alas!</u>

⟨When the⟩sun is bright on the upland slopes;

⟨When the⟩wind stirs soft through the springing grass,

And the river flows like a stream of glass;

⟨When the⟩first bird sings and the first bud opes,

The phrase "alas!" in the first line expresses the speaker's sorrow.

Repetition of "When the" draws attention to details about springtime, emphasizing the longings a caged bird might feel.

158 Unit 2

© Houghton Mifflin Harcourt Publishing Company

BACKGROUND

Phillis Wheatley *was the first African American to publish a book of poetry. Born in West Africa, probably in 1753, she was enslaved in 1761 and brought to Boston. There she was purchased by a local merchant, John Wheatley. He named the little girl Phillis, and she became the personal assistant of his wife, Susannah. Phillis learned to read and write English very quickly, and the Wheatley family tutored her in Latin, Greek, English literature, and the classics. Wheatley was quickly recognized as a prodigy, and respect for her talents grew. She published her first poem at age 13 in 1767. The poem was about two men who nearly drowned at sea, and it was printed in the* Newport Mercury.

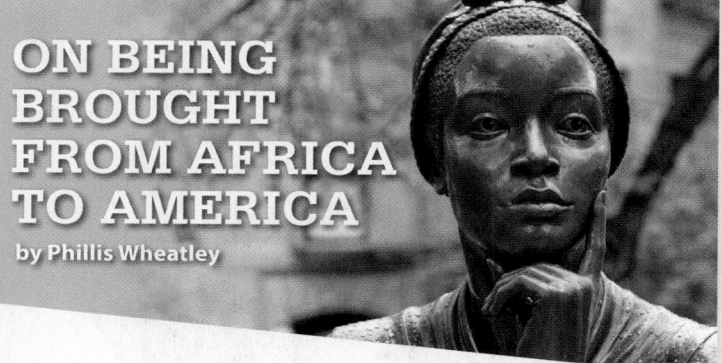

ON BEING BROUGHT FROM AFRICA TO AMERICA
by Phillis Wheatley

Wheatley went on to publish a number of other poems, increasing her fame, and by 1770 her work was known throughout the colonies.

In 1773, Wheatley published her first and only book of verse, Poems on Various Subjects, Religious and Moral. *To prove she was the actual author of the book, 17 men who lived in Boston, including John Hancock, had to verify that Wheatley wrote the poems. Their assertions appear in the preface of the book.*

Poems on Various Subjects *is considered a landmark achievement in U.S. history. With its publication, Wheatley became the first African American and first U.S. slave to publish a book of poems. She also became the third American woman to do so.*

Phillis was given her freedom after Susannah Wheatley's death in 1774. In 1778, she married John Peters. They had three children together—all died in infancy. The couple fell into extreme poverty, and Phillis was forced to work as a maid. Phillis Wheatley died in her early 30s in 1784.

BACKGROUND

In addition to writing poetry, Wheatley also translated works from Latin into English, surprising scholars in Boston by translating a tale from Ovid. Her literary accomplishments were held up as proof that the African people were intellectually capable, an idea pro-slavery forces wanted to suppress. Wheatley advocated for the emancipation of enslaved people. Her poem "To the Right Honourable William, Earl of Dartmouth" was written after Dartmouth was appointed by the British king as the Secretary of State for North America. It reflects Wheatley's hope that Dartmouth, who had abolitionist friends, would promote freedom for enslaved people. The notion that God's mercy brought the poem's narrator from Africa to America is complex. While many readers may have difficulty with the idea that the narrator feels grateful, Wheatley's focus on God's mercy conveys her deep and meaningful connection to her religion.

PREPARE TO COMPARE

Direct students to use the Prepare to Compare prompt to focus their reading.

ENGLISH LEARNER SUPPORT

Identify Thematic Elements Explain that religion is a theme of the poem. Have students identify words in the first stanza that reveal this theme (*mercy, Pagan, soul, God, Saviour, redemption*). Then, ask them to look at the last lines of each stanza and identify words Wheatley uses to show the effect of Christianity on people (*redemption, refin'd*).
LIGHT

TEACH

For **listening support** for students at varying proficiency levels, see the **Text X-Ray** on page 156C.

 ## ANALYZE THEME

As students analyze the theme of the poem, ask them to think about the transition the speaker experienced and what the speaker has gained from it. Discuss what challenge the speaker faces in America. Guide students to understand that the speaker is telling Christians who view African Americans as inherently sinful that they are wrong. People of color can "join th' angelic train" of Christianity, just as whites can. (**Answer:** *The words and phrases suggest the speaker is grateful for being brought from Africa to America and believes it was good for her. However, she recognizes the racism directed at her, even by other Christians, and speaks up against it, using an argument based on Christian principles.*)

 NOTICE & NOTE

Notice & Note

Use the side margins to notice and note signposts in the text.

ANALYZE THEME

Annotate: Mark the words or phrases in the poem that help develop the theme.

Interpret: What do these words and phrases suggest about the speaker's view of life in the Colonies?

PREPARE TO COMPARE

As you read, note how each of the following literary elements helps convey the theme of the poem and communicate information about the speaker's circumstances, thoughts, feelings, and character.

- *rhyme and rhythm*
- *alliteration*
- *word choice*
- *voice*

'Twas mercy brought me from my *Pagan* land,
Taught my benighted[1] soul to understand
That there's a God, that there's a *Saviour* too:
Once I redemption neither sought nor knew.

---

[1] **benighted:** ignorant.

160   Unit 2

ENGLISH LEARNER SUPPORT

Identify Contrasts Have students reread the title. Then, have them focus on the first stanza. Explain that the poet contrasts two places, Africa and America. Ask students what the contrast is based on *(religion, Christianity)*. Have students use a graphic organizer to note words associated with Africa and with America. Then, have them complete these sentence frames: *Wheatley says that Africa is a _____ land. She says that God's _____ took her away from Africa. When she came to America, she learned about _____.*   **MODERATE**

5 Some view our sable[2] race with scornful eye,
  "Their colour is a diabolic die."[3]
  Remember, *Christians, Negroes,* black as *Cain,*
  May be refin'd, and join th' angelic train.

  _____

  [2] **sable:** dark brown or black.
  [3] **diabolic die:** an evil or devilish coloring agent (dye).

ANALYZE SOUND DEVICES AND VOICE

Annotate: In lines 7 and 8, mark the end rhymes and the phrases in which they appear.

Evaluate: What contrast does the rhyme help emphasize? Why is this contrast significant?

CHECK YOUR UNDERSTANDING

Answer these questions about "On Being Brought from Africa to America" before moving on to the next selection.

1 A theme of "On Being Brought from Africa to America" is —

   A freedom rests on the ability to read

   B all people need understanding

   C bigotry toward African Americans is morally wrong

   D being brought to America from Africa was an act of oppression

2 Who is the speaker in the poem?

   F An enslaved woman in America

   G A free woman of color in America

   H A Christian slave owner

   J The friend of a Pagan slave

3 Which phrase reveals the speaker's attitude about going to America?

   A *'Twas mercy brought me*

   B *redemption neither sought nor knew*

   C *our sable race*

   D *May be refin'd*

4 How would you characterize the voice in "On Being Brought from Africa to America"?

   F Angry

   G Grateful

   H Disturbed

   J Indifferent

On Being Brought from Africa to America   161

ANALYZE SOUND DEVICES AND VOICE

Guide students to describe the rhyme pattern. It is fairly simple: each couplet, or two-line pair, rhymes. Use the students' annotations and responses to the question to guide them to think more about how the style of the poem contributes to its message. How does the use of rhyme affect the reader? Students might note that rhyme is pleasing and can attract the reader or listener to the message. Rhyme also can be used to convey emotion—points made by rhyme feel meaningful and important. (**Answer:** *The phrase "black as Cain" evokes the idea of sinfulness, but "th' angelic train" is the opposite, being holy. This contrast highlights the difference in how the addressees, white Christians, perceive African Americans and their spiritual potential to be good Christians.*)

■ English Learner Support

Interpret Poetry Assist students in annotating the poem. To support them with interpreting, guide students to complete these frames: *Wheatley's words _____ that she had a positive _____ of life in the Colonies.* **MODERATE**

CHECK YOUR UNDERSTANDING

Have students answer the questions independently.

Answers:

   1. *C*

   2. *F*

   3. *A*

   4. *G*

If students answer any questions incorrectly, have them reread the text to confirm their understanding. Then, they may proceed to the next selection.

EL ENGLISH LEARNER SUPPORT

Oral Assessment

1. What is a theme of the poem? (*It is wrong to treat African Americans badly.*)

2. Who is the speaker in the poem? (*a woman who is enslaved in America*)

3. Which phrase tells how the speaker feels about America? (*'Twas mercy brought me*)

4. Which describes the poetic voice in the poem? (*thankful, glad*) **SUBSTANTIAL**

BACKGROUND

Dunbar was a highly versatile writer. He published dialectic poems that contributed to his popularity, but they do not represent the majority of his writings. In addition to poems like "Sympathy," he wrote many short stories and novels in Standard English throughout his life. He originally dreamed of becoming a lawyer but did not have the financial resources to pursue that dream. The reception of his first book of poetry, *Oak and Ivy*, in which "Sympathy" appears, earned him the attention of a prominent attorney who offered him a job, but he declined in favor of continuing his literary career.

PREPARE TO COMPARE

Direct students to use the Prepare to Compare prompt to focus their reading.

 **ANALYZE SOUND DEVICES AND VOICE**

Guide students to note the repetition and analyze what it reveals about the speaker's thoughts and feelings. Point out the word *alas* after the first instance of the repeated phrase. Ask students to describe their response to that word. Mention that it may indicate something painful. Discuss the two different words that follow the repeated phrase in each stanza. Point out that *I know* shows a deeper understanding. Guide students to recognize that the effect of the repeated phrase in the last line of each stanza seems more powerful and plaintive than in the first lines. (**Possible answer:** *The poetic voice establishes itself as having particular (intimate) knowledge of, and affinity with, the caged bird.*)

 For **listening, speaking** and **reading support** for students at varying proficiency levels, see the **Text X-Ray** on pages 156C–156D.

 **NOTICE & NOTE**

BACKGROUND

Paul Laurence Dunbar *was born in Ohio in 1872, the son of former slaves. He was the only African American student in his high school class, and he published poems in the school newspaper, eventually becoming the editor. He self-published his first collection of poems titled* Oak and Ivy *in 1893. Dunbar was one of the premier African American poets in the United States. Dunbar continued publishing poetry and other writing until his death at age 33 in 1906.*

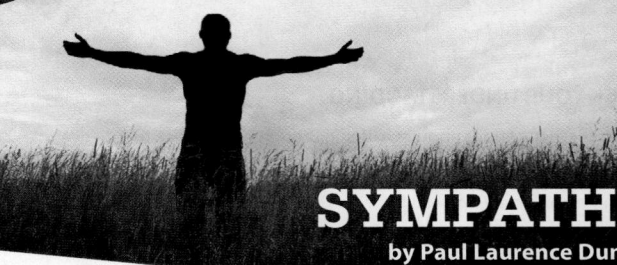

SYMPATHY
by Paul Laurence Dunbar

PREPARE TO COMPARE

As you read, look for how the author uses the following devices to convey the theme of the poem.

- *repetition and rhyme*
- *imagery and sensory detail*
- *alliteration*
- *voice*

Notice & Note

Use the side margins to notice and note signposts in the text.

ANALYZE SOUND DEVICES AND VOICE

Annotate: In stanzas 1 and 2, mark the phrase that is repeated.

Evaluate: How does the repetition of this phrase create a distinct poetic voice? Explain.

I know what the caged bird feels, alas!
    When the sun is bright on the upland slopes;
When the wind stirs soft through the springing grass,
And the river flows like a stream of glass;
5   When the first bird sings and the first bud opes[1],
And the faint perfume from its chalice steals—
I know what the caged bird feels!

---

[1] **ope:** *v.* open.

WHEN STUDENTS STRUGGLE . . .

Analyze Poetry To help students weigh the relative importance of so many unfamiliar phrases, instruct them to focus on the opening sentence of each stanza and make a list in their own words of the *what* and the *why*. For example, in the first stanza, students would write a list of "what the caged bird feels" in plain language; this list can then guide them in exploring the contrasts between what the bird longs for and what its reality is.

 For additional support, go to the **Reading Studio** and assign the following **Level Up Tutorial: Theme.**

I know why the caged bird beats his wing
　　Till its blood is red on the cruel bars;
10 For he must fly back to his perch and cling
　When he fain² would be on the bough a-swing;
　　And a pain still throbs in the old, old scars
　And they pulse again with a keener sting—
　I know why he beats his wing!

15 I know why the caged bird sings, ah me,
　　When his wing is bruised and his bosom sore,—
　When he beats his bars and he would be free;
　It is not a carol of joy or glee,
　　But a prayer that he sends from his heart's deep core,
20 But a plea, that upward to Heaven he flings—
　I know why the caged bird sings!

---

² **fain:** *adv.* happily, gladly.

ANALYZE THEME

Annotate: In lines 18–20, mark the words and phrases that refer to the bird's song.

Contrast: What two ways of interpreting the bird's song are noted by the speaker? How does the difference between these two help develop the theme?

CHECK YOUR UNDERSTANDING

Answer these questions about "Sympathy" before moving on to the **Analyze the Texts** section on the following page.

1 Which action stirs feelings in the caged bird?

A When it is caged

B When it hears the first bird sing

C When it feels pain from old scars

D When it prays

2 Which line in "Sympathy" describes what the bird wants to do?

F *When the sun is bright on the upland slopes;*

G *For he must fly back to his perch and cling*

H *When he fain would be on the bough a-swing;*

J *But a plea, that upward to Heaven he flings—*

3 Which line in the poem most directly refers to the conditions of slavery?

A *When the wind stirs soft through the springing grass,*

B *For he must fly back to his perch and cling*

C *It is not a carol of joy or glee,*

D *And a pain still throbs in the old, old scars*

 ANALYZE THEME

As students compare the words used to describe the bird's song, guide them to explore the human-like behavior of the imagined bird. What does this indicate about the unnatural situation of both the bird and the speaker? How else does the author use contrasting images in the poem? (**Answer:** *The speaker notes that though the song could be interpreted as a joyful carol, it is really a prayer. The bird is not singing out of celebration, but rather is suffering and asking for help.*)

CHECK YOUR UNDERSTANDING

Have students answer the questions independently.

Answers:

1. *B*

2. *H*

3. *D*

If students answer any questions incorrectly, have them reread the text to confirm their understanding. Then they may proceed to ANALYZE THE TEXT on page 164.

EL **ENGLISH LEARNER SUPPORT**

Identify Alliteration Read lines 15–17 aloud, and point out the words *beats* and *bars*. Explain that the /b/ sound at the beginning of these words is an example of alliteration. Repeat the lines, making sure to emphasize words that start with the same /b/ sound. Have students underline other *b* words that show alliteration and say the words aloud. **SUBSTANTIAL**

ANALYZE THE TEXTS

Possible answers:

1. **DOK 2:** *The lines show that the speaker is treated with suspicion and scorn by some people. They expand on the speaker's negative experience, which develops the theme that even tragic events can lead to personal growth.*

2. **DOK 2:** *The voice is sympathetic and understanding of the caged bird's plight. Natural events like "when the sun is bright" and "the first bird sings" are things the caged bird cannot experience, and the speaker feels the bird's frustration.*

3. **DOK 4:** *In Dunbar's poem, the first and third stanzas have an abaabcc rhyme scheme; the second stanza has a similar abaabaa rhyme scheme. The effect of this regular rhyme is to reflect the sense of constraint that the bird (and the speaker) feels. Dunbar also emphasizes a sense of constraint or confinement through using alliteration to highlight words such as "beats" and "bars."*

4. **DOK 3:** *The first stanza describes natural beauty ("upland slopes," "springing grass," and "faint perfume") that the caged bird cannot experience, which contrasts with the cruel and painful images of the second stanza that are the bird's reality. The bird's attempts at freedom despite injuries shows that oppression cannot stop the desire for freedom.*

5. **DOK 4:** *Answers will vary but should state the theme and use details from the poem to support the choice.*

RESEARCH

Instruct students to confirm information with multiple sources whenever possible. If necessary, review what constitutes a reliable source.

Extend Direct students to credible poetry sites on the Internet, such as poetryfoundation.org and poets.org.

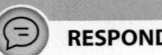 **RESPOND**

ANALYZE THE TEXTS

Support your responses with evidence from the texts. ▤ NOTEBOOK

1. **Interpret** Reread lines 5–6 of "On Being Brought from Africa to America." What do these lines tell you about the speaker's experience? How do these lines help develop the theme?

2. **Interpret** Reread lines 1–7 of "Sympathy." How would you describe the voice in this stanza? Cite text evidence to support your response.

3. **Analyze** How would you describe the rhyme scheme of the stanzas in the poem "Sympathy"? What words are emphasized through Dunbar's use of alliteration? What is the effect of each sound device?

4. **Contrast** What effect does the contrast between the imagery in the first stanza and the second stanza of "Sympathy" have? How does this contrast help develop the poem's theme?

5. **Connect** Think about the themes expressed by each poem. Which theme resonates with you the most? State the theme, and explain your response using details from the poem.

RESEARCH

RESEARCH TIP
If you use an Internet search to conduct your research, be sure to use reliable sources for the information you find. Look for sources authored or reviewed by experts on Dunbar's life and poetry.

Conduct research and answer the following questions to learn more about Paul Laurence Dunbar.

QUESTION	ANSWER
What other genres did Dunbar write in? Cite at least three examples.	*Possible answers: short stories, song lyrics, novels, essays, articles*
What well-known abolitionist did Dunbar write a poem about?	*Frederick Douglass*
What well-known book did a line from Dunbar's "Sympathy" give its title to?	*I Know Why the Caged Bird Sings by Maya Angelou*

Extend In what ways did Paul Laurence Dunbar influence African American writers who came after him? Write a paragraph that describes Dunbar's influence and legacy.

WHEN STUDENTS STRUGGLE . . .

Reinforce Meaning Encourage students to reread, pause, and reflect on each stanza before moving to the next one. Look at the title again together: "Sympathy." Decide what information one might expect to find in the poem. *(a difficult or painful situation or experience that would cause someone to care)*

 For additional support, go to the **Reading Studio** and assign the following ▣ **Level Up Tutorial: Elements of Poetry.**

CREATE AND PRESENT

Write a Prose Adaptation Choose the poem you like best, and write a prose adaptation that contains the same themes and supporting details as the poem.

- ❏ Give your story a title, and include elements of a short story, such as plot, character, narrator, and details about setting.
- ❏ Use the language and style appropriate for a short story.

Present a Theme Board With your group, present a theme board listing the major themes of "On Being Brought from Africa to America" and "Sympathy."

- ❏ Create three headings by writing the name of the first poem on the left side of the board, the phrase "Common Themes" at the center, and the name of the second poem on the right.
- ❏ Identify possible themes in the first poem, and list those themes below its title. Do the same thing for the second poem.
- ❏ Next, add text quotes and evidence from the poems for each theme.
- ❏ Then, determine the common themes of the two poems. Write those themes below "Common Themes" at the board's center.
- ❏ Finally, as a group, present your board to the class, explaining why you chose both the common and individual themes for each poem.

 Go to **Writing Narratives** in the **Writing Studio** for help.

 Go to **Participating in Collaborative Discussions** in the **Speaking and Listening Studio** for help.

RESPOND TO THE ESSENTIAL QUESTION

 ? What does oppression look like?

Gather Information Review your annotations and notes on "On Being Brought from Africa to America" and "Sympathy." Then, add relevant details to your Response Log. As you determine which information to include, think about:

- what the theme of each poem suggests about oppression
- what mechanisms of oppression are suggested by each poem
- the imagery the writers use in their descriptions of oppression

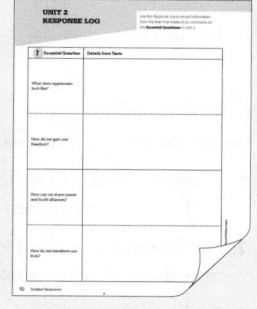

UNIT 2
RESPONSE LOG

ACADEMIC VOCABULARY
As you write and discuss what you learned from the poems, be sure to use the Academic Vocabulary words. Check off each of the words that you use.

- ❏ **contrary**
- ❏ **founder**
- ❏ **ideological**
- ❏ **publication**
- ❏ **revolution**

CREATE AND PRESENT

Write a Prose Adaptation Direct students to use their notes on the poem's theme to develop a scenario for a short story. Tell students to organize an outline to plan the elements of their story, including the characters, setting(s), and major events in the plot. Before they begin writing, ask them to reflect on the differences between a poem and a short story in order to anticipate challenges in writing their adaptation.

For **writing support** for students at varying proficiency levels, see the **Text X-Ray** on page 156D.

Present a Theme Board Divide students into mixed-ability groups and have them review their annotations of the poems for common themes. Review simple graphic organizers, such as Venn diagrams, to help students organize the themes and prepare supporting evidence. Instruct students to practice their presentation within the group, giving each other feedback on their delivery.

RESPOND TO THE ESSENTIAL QUESTION

Allow time for students to add details from "On Being Brought from Africa to America" and "Sympathy" to their Unit 2 Response Logs.

COMPARE THEMES

Remind students that themes are deeper, complex messages that texts convey about topics. Their task is not to summarize the poems, but rather to interpret and unpack them.

ANALYZE THE TEXTS

Possible answers:

1. **DOK 2:** *The voice in "On Being Brought from Africa to America" is that of an enslaved African American who has experienced prejudice, but is grateful to have found religious faith in her new homeland. The voice in "Sympathy" is that of a person who has experienced slavery or prejudice and feels trapped by racial oppression.*

2. **DOK 2:** *The speaker in "On Being Brought from Africa to America" seems to have an ambivalent attitude about slavery. She is glad she was brought to America, but shows disdain for people who believe enslaved African Americans cannot truly be Christians. In "Sympathy," the speaker appears to view slavery as a harsh and damaging form of oppression that deprives people of freedom and happiness.*

3. **DOK 3:** *Responses will vary. Possible response: I found the regular rhyme scheme in "Sympathy" to be the most engaging because it reflects the sense of constraint that the speaker feels.*

4. **DOK 2:** *In both poems, religion or religious faith is a source of comfort and refuge. In "On Being Brought from Africa to America," the speaker mentions experiencing "mercy" and "redemption" through religious faith. In "Sympathy," the speaker says that the caged bird sends a prayer to heaven, suggesting that religious faith allows oppressed people to hope for freedom.*

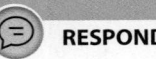

RESPOND

Collaborate & Compare

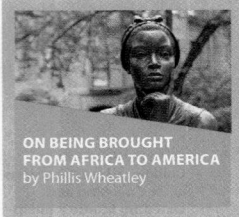

ON BEING BROUGHT FROM AFRICA TO AMERICA
by Phillis Wheatley

SYMPATHY
by Paul Laurence Dunbar

COMPARE THEMES

Both "On Being Brought from Africa to America" and "Sympathy" deal with the issues of slavery and oppression, although they address the topics in very different ways. Each has a specific **theme,** or message about life, society, and human nature that the poet develops over the course of the poem.

You can evaluate important details to determine the theme of a poem. You can also infer a theme based on the speaker's voice and point of view, and on sound devices. As you examine the poems to determine theme(s), consider:

- **Important details**—What information is provided by each poem's speaker?
- **Voice and point of view**—Who is speaking? What does the speaker feel, want, or believe?
- **Sound devices**—Does the poet use rhyme, repetition, or other sound devices to convey important information? What do the devices suggest?

With your group, complete the chart with details from both poems.

	"ON BEING BROUGHT FROM AFRICA TO AMERICA"	**"SYMPATHY"**
Important Details	*Africans viewed with "scornful eye"; Christianity as "angelic train"*	*Nature's beauty; bird's injuries, pain; its song as "prayer," "plea"*
Voice and Point of View	*An enslaved African American, who feels a sense of gratitude*	*A person who has experienced oppression and longs for freedom*
Sound Devices	*Regular rhythm; iambic pentameter; end rhyme; rhymed couplets*	*Regular rhythm; iambic and anapestic tetrameter, end rhyme, alliteration*

ANALYZE THE TEXTS

Discuss these questions in your group.

1. **Contrast** Review the notes you made on voice in the chart. In what ways does voice differ between the two poems? Explain.

2. **Make Inferences** What inference(s) can you make about the attitude toward slavery and oppression expressed by each poem?

3. **Evaluate** Both poems rhyme. Which poem's rhyme scheme did you find to be the most engaging? Explain why.

4. **Interpret** What role does religion or religious faith play in each poem? Cite evidence from the poems in your discussion.

COLLABORATE AND PRESENT

Now, your group can continue exploring the ideas expressed in the poems by analyzing and comparing their themes. You can use information from the earlier Create and Present activity, if you desire. Follow these steps:

1. **Determine the important details** With your group, review your chart and determine which details are most important. Decide how you want to present your analysis of the poems' themes using text evidence.

2. **Create theme statements** Decide as a group what the theme or themes are in each poem. You can use a chart to organize your ideas.

DETAIL FROM "ON BEING BROUGHT FROM AFRICA TO AMERICA"	DETAIL FROM "ON BEING BROUGHT FROM AFRICA TO AMERICA"	THEME
'Twas mercy brought me from my Pagan land . . .	[mercy] Taught my benighted soul to understand That there's a God, that there's a Saviour too	Even tragic events may lead to learning and growth.

DETAIL FROM "SYMPATHY"	DETAIL FROM "SYMPATHY"	THEME
A bird views nature's beauty from its cage.	The bird suffers injuries trying to escape the cage.	Oppression cannot stop the desire for freedom.

3. **Compare themes** Discuss with your group similarities and differences in the themes of the poems. Listen actively to members of your group, and ask each other to clarify any points that aren't clear. Doing this will strengthen what your group presents to the class.

4. **Present to the class** Now it's time to present your ideas to the class. Make sure your statement of each poem's theme(s) is clear and understandable. Discuss similarities and differences in the themes you have identified, ask for and answer questions from the class, and respond politely to any disagreements.

Go to **Giving a Presentation** in the **Speaking and Listening Studio** for help.

COLLABORATE AND PRESENT

1. **Determine the important details** Walk around the room as groups are discussing details. Encourage students to debate the significance of the details they identified. Prompt students to develop arguments about which details are most important.

2. **Create theme statements** Remind students that the topic of the poem is what it is about. The theme is a message or idea about the topic. Theme statements should address the deeper meaning(s) of the poems.

3. **Compare themes** Circulate as groups discuss. Encourage all students to participate. Tell students that asking questions is part of having a growth mindset. Students should work to get into the habit of asking about points they don't understand or are not sure about, and of challenging things they think are incorrect or unclear.

4. **Present to the class** Have groups plan how they will present their ideas to the class. Encourage most or all of the members of the group to take part in the presentation.

WHEN STUDENTS STRUGGLE . . .

Identify Themes Review the difference between the topic of a work and the theme (the work's insight into a human experience or the human condition). All the lines in a stanza usually support a main idea. Have students revisit the first stanza of "Sympathy." Ask them to identify key details and then make a theme statement. (**Possible answer:** *The theme is the longing for freedom. The details about nature show the contrast between a lack of liberty and a life of freedom.*)

 For additional support, go to the **Reading Studio** and assign the following **Level Up Tutorial: Theme.**

LETTER TO JOHN ADAMS

Letter by Abigail Adams

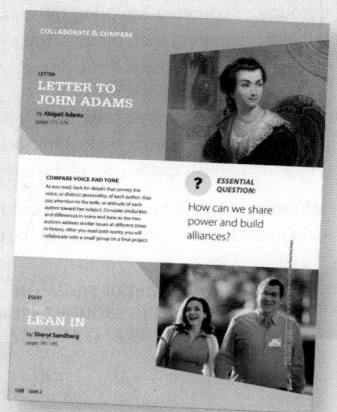

GENRE ELEMENTS
LETTERS

Remind students that **letters** are usually private correspondence between two people written from their perspectives. A letter will typically have a heading, which includes the date the writer wrote it. Due to their personal nature, letters tend to be less formal in tone than pieces of writing in other genres. They also more frequently feature multiple purposes and different motives for writing in comparison to other texts.

LEARNING OBJECTIVES

- Analyze author's purpose, voice, and tone.
- Research the Adams family's impact on American history.
- Write a letter to a notable figure from the American Revolution.
- Discuss the importance of letters in small groups.
- Analyze context and connotation to evaluate nuances in meaning.
- Learn and apply formal English.
- **Language** Verbalize inferences and opinions.

TEXT COMPLEXITY

Quantitative Measures	Letter to John Adams	Lexile: 1180
Qualitative Measures	**Ideas Presented** Requires weighing multiple perspectives. Some analysis of bias and the author's motivations. Some ambiguity.	
	Structures Used More complex, multiple perspectives may be presented; more deviation from chronology. Tables and figures support understanding.	
	Language Used Vocabulary not defined at point of use. Mostly Tier II and III words. Metaphor (rather than similes) used more. Multiple technical words may be used in one sentence.	
	Knowledge Required More complex problems. Experiences may be less familiar to many. Cultural or historical references.	

Online **Ed**

RESOURCES

- Unit 2 Response Log
- Selection Audio
- Reading Studio: Notice & Note
- Level Up Tutorial: Author's Purpose
- Writing Studio: Writing Informative Texts
- Speaking and Listening Studio: Participating in Collaborative Discussions
- Vocabulary Studio: Denotation and Connotation
- "Letter to John Adams"/from "Lean In" Selection Test

SUMMARIES

English

Abigail Adams, the wife of John Adams and a fierce supporter of the independence movement, wrote this letter while her husband was at the Second Continental Congress in Philadelphia, working to draft America's founding set of laws. She was sometimes criticized for being an active participant in the political world, especially given societal expectations of women at the time. John Adams replies to his wife's appeal in her letter to "remember the ladies" in an amused and dismissive manner.

Spanish

Abigail Adams, la esposa de John Adams y una defensora acérrima del movimiento independentista, escribió esta carta mientras su esposo estaba en el Segundo Congreso Continental de Filadelfia, trabajando para redactar el cuerpo de leyes fundadoras de Estados Unidos. Abigail era criticada por ser miembro activo en el mundo político, especialmente debido a las expectativas sociales impuestas sobre las mujeres en esa época. John Adams respondió de manera desdeñosa y entretenida a la revocación de su esposa de "recordar a las damas".

SMALL-GROUP OPTIONS

Have students work in small groups and pairs to read and discuss the selection.

Reciprocal Teaching

- Have students read the letter from Abigail Adams to her husband.
- After reading the letter, ask students to write three to five questions using these stems: *Why does Abigail say _____? Why did the _____? How did the _____?*
- Form teams of three students.
- Tell each student to offer two questions for group discussion.
- Groups should reach consensus on the answers and find supporting text evidence.

Activating Academic Vocabulary

- Provide a list of academic vocabulary words, such as *derive, tyrannical, impunity, abhor.*
- Read a section of the text (20 lines or so) and show students how the academic vocabulary words can inform their discussion of the section.
- Have students read a different section in pairs, and use the academic vocabulary words to discuss it.

Text X-Ray: English Learner Support
for "Letter to John Adams"

Use the Text X-Ray and the supports and scaffolds in the Teacher's Edition to help guide students at different proficiency levels through the selection.

INTRODUCE THE SELECTION
DISCUSS RIGHTS AND PROTECTIONS

In this lesson, students will need to discuss the concepts of liberty, rights, and protections. **Liberty** describes a state of personal freedoms. **Rights** are these individual freedoms. **Protections** are the legal and other measures taken by the state to secure these rights and keep them from being violated by the government.

Explain to students that while the delegates were working to secure the liberty of citizens and protect their rights from being violated by the government, not everyone was seen as having the same rights. Ask students to consider the similarities between Abigail Adams's views on liberty and the views of the founding fathers. Then, have volunteers give examples of rights protected by the government today. Supply the following sentence frames:

- All citizens today have the right to ____. (*free speech, freedom of religion*)
- ____ did not have the same liberty as the founding fathers. (*Women*)
- Their right to ____ was not protected by the constitution. (*vote*)

CULTURAL REFERENCES

The following words or phrases may be unfamiliar to students:

- *Gentery Lords* (paragraph 1): noble men who came from Britain
- *Riffel Men* (paragraph 1): British soldiers
- *shewen* (paragraph 1): shown
- *Colony* (paragraph 1): Virginia
- *ancestors* (paragraph 2): a family member or person from the past
- *tyrants* (paragraph 2): a cruel ruler or person with power who does not allow freedom and who does not care about the rights of people under his or her authority
- *bound by* (paragraph 2): required to follow
- *Code of Laws* (paragraph 2): Declaration of Independence
- *use us* (paragraph 3): treat us
- *Supreem Being* (paragraph 3): God

LISTENING

Identify Requests and Supporting Arguments

Remind students that Adams makes a request and provides arguments to persuade her husband. As students listen to the text, have them think about what arguments Adams makes and whether they are persuasive.

Read aloud paragraph 2. Use the following supports with students at varying proficiency levels:

- Ask yes/no questions to ensure comprehension. *Does Adams want women to have rights?* (Yes.) *Does she think women will be upset if they do not have rights?* (Yes.) **SUBSTANTIAL**
- Ask volunteers to identify and read aloud the requests Adams makes of her husband and the reasons she gives in support of her argument. Point out verbs to help students identify the requests. Ask guiding questions to determine comprehension of the main ideas. Provide the following sentence frames: *Adams wants _____. She says this is important because _____.* **MODERATE**
- Have students identify each request Adams makes. Ask a student to restate each request. Then, ask students to explain the reasons Adams gives in support of her requests. **LIGHT**

SPEAKING

Make and Support Inferences

Tell students they can use a text to make inferences about a writer. Remind them that inferences must be supported with evidence and reasoning. Note that Adams's personality comes across through the ideas and values she expresses.

Use the following supports with students at varying proficiency levels:

- Provide a list of adjectives to describe Adams, such as *curious, smart,* and *caring.* Provide other adjectives such as *shy, confused.* Have students repeat the adjectives. Provide definitions. Have students make statements about Adams, using these sentence frames: *I think she is _____. I don't think she is _____.* **SUBSTANTIAL**

- Help students brainstorm a list of adjectives to describe Adams. Then, guide them to provide antonyms or to supply adjectives that do not describe Adams. Have students make statements about Adams and support them. Provide this sentence frame: *I think Adams was _____ because she said/wanted _____.* **MODERATE**

- Have partners describe Adams. Guide them to connect their opinions and impressions of her to her arguments and tone. For example: *I think she cared about the Revolution and wanted to be involved.* **LIGHT**

READING

Analyze Author's Purpose

Remind students that an author's purpose is the reason he or she writes. Identifying key details can help determine the author's purpose. Have students identify words and phrases that show Adams's purpose(s).

Use the following supports with students at varying proficiency levels:

- Echo read from paragraph 2: "Remember the Ladies . . . if they could." Help students identify and circle words with positive and negative connotations. (*generous, favorable; unlimited, tyrants*) **SUBSTANTIAL**

- Have students read paragraph 3. Ask guiding questions to help students identify the main ideas. Then, ask them to explain Adams's purpose, offering suggestions such as: *to give an argument, to persuade, to provide reasons, to encourage.* Supply this sentence frame: *Adams's purpose is to _____.* **MODERATE**

- Have students reread paragraphs 2–3. Ask them to identify the phrase that best shows Adams's purpose. Then, have students discuss and share Adams's purpose in these paragraphs. **LIGHT**

WRITING

Write a Letter

Read the Create and Discuss prompt on Student Edition page 175. Explain that students will write a letter explaining an action they would like a leader to take.

Use the following supports with students at varying proficiency levels:

- Guide students to identify an issue. Supply key words such as *vote, support,* or *help* Provide frames: *Please free the _____. Please let _____ vote.* **SUBSTANTIAL**

- Have students work with a partner or small group to brainstorm a list of actions that Revolutionary leaders could take. Then, have them write two or three reasons in support of the action they will request. Supply key words such as *vote, support, oppose, demand,* or *assist.* **MODERATE**

- Have students work with a partner to draft a letter. Have pairs exchange drafts and provide feedback on their sentence structure. **LIGHT**

TEACH

? Connect to the ESSENTIAL QUESTION

Abigail Adams and Sheryl Sandberg, women from radically different historical periods, both write about questions of power and inequality.

COMPARE VOICE AND TONE

Point out that the tone writers use is always partly influenced by the culture and time period they live in. However, all writers also make choices about the voice and tone they use. This is particularly true in persuasive writing, where writers are usually very focused on the perspective and expectations of their intended audience. Ask students to consider what kinds of voice and tone might work well for persuasive writing, or for leading readers to think in a new or different way.

LETTER

LETTER TO JOHN ADAMS

by **Abigail Adams**
pages 171–173

COMPARE VOICE AND TONE

As you read, look for details that convey the voice, or distinct personality, of each author. Also pay attention to the tone, or attitude of each author toward her subject. Consider similarities and differences in voice and tone as the two authors address similar issues at different times in history. After you read both works, you will collaborate with a small group on a final project.

? ESSENTIAL QUESTION:

How can we share power and build alliances?

ESSAY

from

LEAN IN

by **Sheryl Sandberg**
pages 181–185

168   Unit 2

Letter to John Adams

QUICK START

How do you communicate with the people you know and love? Does how you communicate change in different circumstances? With a group, discuss how major events might affect how we communicate with others.

ANALYZE AUTHOR'S PURPOSE

An **author's purpose** is the reason he or she writes a text. Authors might write to persuade, inform, explain, express thoughts or feelings, motivate, or entertain. Most authors have more than one purpose for writing. For example, a writer may want to inform readers about an important topic, but he or she may also want to persuade readers to agree with certain ideas or values. You can determine an author's purpose by **making inferences,** or logical guesses, based on the use of key details, word choice, and tone in the text.

An author's purpose may depend on her particular audience. Abigail Adams has more than one purpose for writing to her husband, John. She was an important advisor, so she focused on issues of the day, but she was also his wife and shared news about their children.

As you read, look for clues to Abigail Adams's purposes for writing a letter to her husband. Use a chart like this to record details from the text and her purpose for including them.

ADAMS'S TEXT	INFERENCE ABOUT PURPOSE

ANALYZE LANGUAGE: Voice and Tone

An author's **voice** is his or her unique use of language, which allows the reader to "hear" a human personality in the writing. The elements of style that determine a writer's voice include syntax, diction, and tone.

Diction is a writer's choice of words. Diction includes both vocabulary (words) and **syntax** (arrangement of words). Diction can be formal or informal, common or technical, abstract or concrete. Diction can also reveal an author's **tone,** or attitude toward a subject.

As you read this letter, think about how the diction and syntax help communicate Adams's thoughts and her attitude toward the issues of freedom and liberty.

GENRE ELEMENTS: LETTER

- is addressed to a specific person or group
- may have a formal or informal tone, depending on writer's purpose
- may convey personal information, share opinions, or make requests

QUICK START

Encourage students to consider the different tones and styles they use to communicate with parents, siblings, close friends, casual acquaintances, teachers, and others. Have them give an example of how an important event might change the way they communicate with a person or group.

ANALYZE AUTHOR'S PURPOSE

Point out that **letters,** in particular, are primary texts that frequently have multiple **purposes.** Ask students what purposes a letter might have. Then, remind students to look for Adams's general purpose, but also to keep in mind secondary purposes.

ANALYZE LANGUAGE:
Voice And Tone

Point out that the **syntax** and **tone** Adams uses is, to some extent, typical of the time period during which she lived. Note that her complex sentence structure reflects her accomplishment as a reader and writer, but also suggests the complexity of her ideas. Tell students that, as they read, they should think about how Adams brings different ideas together into a single sentence.

WHEN STUDENTS STRUGGLE . . .

Evaluate Author's Purpose To help students evaluate Abigail Adams's letter, ask them to think about the author and the intended reader. Ask students if they have ever written a letter or message asking someone to do something or to consider a problem or idea. Ask them what strategies an author can use when writing for this purpose. Help them generate a list of strategies. While students read, have them be on the lookout to see if Adams uses any of the strategies they listed.

 For additional support, go to the **Reading Studio** and assign the following Level Up **Level Up Tutorial: Author's Purpose.**

CRITICAL VOCABULARY

Direct students to look over the choices in the word bank. Then, have them read all the sentences. Finally, have them select an answer for each sentence.

Answers:

1. *impunity*
2. *deprive*
3. *abhor*
4. *tyrannical*

■ English Learner Support

Use Cognates Tell Spanish speakers that the Critical Vocabulary words have Spanish cognates: *impunity/impunidad, abhor/aborrecer, tyrannical/tiránico.*
ALL LEVELS

LANGUAGE CONVENTIONS

Discuss with students the ways Adams's complex sentence structure reflects the complexity of the ideas she is expressing, as well as the complexity of the situation she is addressing. Her phrase, "I have sometimes been ready to think," suggests a certain inner conflict, or perhaps a sense that the point she wants to make is controversial and must be approached delicately. (The different colonies need to stick together, but she is not confident about the Virginians. She is also aware of the extremely problematic contradiction at the heart of the independence movement: it is built on ideas about freedom and rights, but many of the colonies have economic and social structures built upon the institution of slavery.) Adams's syntax helps to communicate all these issues, as well as to show her understanding of how these issues are connected. Her formal tone also reflects her status as an educated person. During Adams's lifetime, such formality and attention to phrasing was expected in a letter.

ANNOTATION MODEL

Remind students of annotation strategies such as underlining important ideas and circling repeated words. Students may follow this suggestion or use their own system for marking up the selection in their write-in text. They may want to color-code their annotation by using highlighters. Their notes in the margin may include questions about ideas that are unclear or topics they want to learn more about.

 **GET READY**

CRITICAL VOCABULARY

| deprive | tyrannical | impunity | abhor |

To see how many Critical Vocabulary words you already know, write the correct word after each definition.

1. exemption from punishment, penalty, or harm: _____

2. to keep from possessing or enjoying; deny: _____

3. to regard with horror or loathing; detest: _____

4. despotic and oppressive: _____

LANGUAGE CONVENTIONS

Formal English Today, formal English is used almost exclusively in formal situations, such as in legal documents and in speeches. However, you may notice that the language in a fairly informal piece of writing, such as a letter, composed in the past seems formal relative to writing today. Notice the formal language and complex syntax in the passage below.

> I have sometimes been ready to think that the passion for Liberty cannot be Eaquelly Strong in the Breasts of those who have been accustomed to deprive their fellow Creatures of theirs.

It was customary to capitalize nouns in certain categories, such as concrete objects, and nouns that the writer considered important. As you read, note Adams's use of formal English in the text and its effect on voice and tone.

ANNOTATION MODEL

NOTICE & NOTE

As you read, look for details that suggest Adams's purpose for writing a letter to her husband. Notice phrases that convey the writer's voice and suggest her tone. Here are one reader's notes about Abigail Adams's letter.

> I wish you would ever write me a Letter half as long as I write you; and tell me if you may where your Fleet are gone? What sort of Defence Virginia can make against our common Enemy? Whether it is so situated as to make an able Defence?

Her husband doesn't write as often as she'd like. Her tone seems urgent.

She repeats "Defence" and also capitalizes it. She must be greatly concerned about military matters.

BACKGROUND

Abigail Adams *was educated by her parents and grandparents since public education for women was limited. Access to her family's library grounded her in the classics, history, government, law, and philosophy. Married in 1764 to future U.S. President John Adams, Abigail had four children by the time John was sent to the Second Continental Congress in 1774. After that, John was absent more than he was at home. Abigail cared for the farm and the children, and she began the correspondence that would continue for the rest of her life. Her letters reflect life at the time but are also filled with her passion for politics and her intense patriotism.*

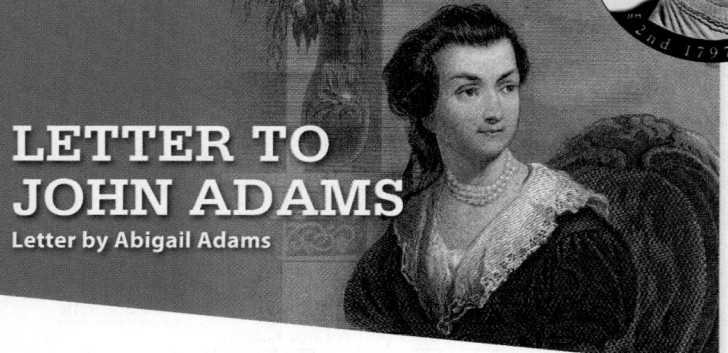

LETTER TO JOHN ADAMS

Letter by Abigail Adams

PREPARE TO COMPARE

As you read, make note of what Abigail Adams says about the treatment of women and how her tone supports what she says. This will help you compare her letter to the essay from Lean In *which follows.*

Abigail Adams to John Adams

Braintree March 31 1776

1   I wish you would ever write me a Letter half as long as I write you; and tell me if you may where your Fleet are gone? What sort of Defence Virginia can make against our common Enemy?[1] Whether it is so situated as to make an able Defence? Are not the Gentery Lords and the common people vassals,[2] are they not like the uncivilized Natives Brittain represents us to be? I hope their Riffel Men who have shewen themselves very savage and even Blood thirsty; are not a specimen of the Generality of the people. I am willing to allow the Colony great merrit for having

---

[1] **common Enemy:** Great Britain; Virginia and Massachusetts were the oldest colonies, and both were influential, but their cultures were very different. Adams is wondering here if Virginia will be helpful if the colonies break with Britain.

[2] **vassal** (văsʹsəl): a subordinate or dependent.

Notice & Note

Use the side margins to notice and note signposts in the text.

ANALYZE VOICE AND TONE

Annotate: Mark the four question marks in the opening sentences of the letter.

Infer: How does the series of questions help establish the voice and tone of the letter?

TO CHALLENGE STUDENTS . . .

Imitate Style Have students work in pairs to write a paragraph in the style of Adams's letter. Tell students to choose an issue and an intended reader whom they wish to persuade. Students should consider Adams's voice and syntax and imitate it. They may also wish to imitate the historical conventions for capitalization, by capitalizing certain important words that would normally not be capitalized using modern conventions.

BACKGROUND

Prior to the Revolution, Abigail Adams had been a strong supporter of the independence movement. She wrote her letter to John Adams while he was at the Second Continental Congress in Philadelphia, working to draft a set of laws for the new, independent country. When John Adams became the nation's second president, Abigail Adams remained actively engaged in the political debates of the day. This was a departure from the way Martha Washington had approached the role of First Lady. Abigail Adams was sometimes criticized for participating in political debates and discussions, rather than simply acting as a gracious hostess. After students read and analyze the text, ask whether they think John Adams and the other lawmakers did as she asked. *(They did not.)* You might wish to note that John Adams's reply to his wife's request to "remember the ladies" was genial, but ultimately dismissive. He teases her that men "know better than to repeal our Masculine systems," which would "subject Us to the Despotism of the Petticoat."

PREPARE TO COMPARE

Direct students to use the Prepare to Compare prompt to focus their reading.

✎ ANALYZE VOICE AND TONE

Guide students to analyze the types of questions Adams asks. Ask volunteers to describe what types of information Adams wants to know. Discuss the nature of each question, noting that Adams wants specific information about where the fleet is, but that most of her questions are broad and require a conversation or a complex response, rather than a simple answer. Ask students to think of words that describe a person who asks a lot of questions. Students may offer positive words such as *curious* or *inquisitive*. They may also think of negative words such as *nosy*. Note that Adams has been both admired and criticized for her engagement and involvement in politics. (***Possible answer:*** *It shows the voice is of someone who is knowledgeable and involved. It also underscores the passionate nature of the letter.)*

TEACH

QUOTED WORDS

Ask a volunteer to explain the "christian principal" Adams refers to. Guide students to understand that she invokes the notion of the Golden Rule or treating others as you would like to be treated. Ask students to explain who Adams is talking about, and what they are doing that violates the Golden Rule. Guide students to understand that she is referring to slavery. (**Answer:** *She would have recognized this as an instruction from God, so this shows it would have been very important to her.*)

■ English Learner Support

Learn New Expressions Read aloud the expression as it is commonly phrased: "Do unto others as you would have others do unto you." Explain that this expression means to treat people the way you would like to be treated. Note that "unto" is archaic language that means "to." **MODERATE**

 For **listening**, **speaking**, and **reading support** for students at varying proficiency levels, see the **Text X-Ray** on pages 168C–168D.

LANGUAGE CONVENTIONS

By using the "titles," she points out the masculine role (*Master*) she wants to see changed and proposes a new one (*Friend*). (**Possible answer:** *Her choice of dramatically different words makes the tone seem more passionate.*)

CRITICAL VOCABULARY

deprive: This word implies that something important or valuable is taken away, and that suffering or injustice is a result. It is unfair to *deprive* a person of rights, opportunities, or justice.

ASK STUDENTS how Adams's choice of *deprive* helps to convey her thoughts and feelings about the colonists of Virginia. (*She has already criticized the Virginia fighters as bloodthirsty. By describing the Virginians as depriving others of freedom, she alludes to the force and violence underlying slavery.*)

 NOTICE & NOTE

deprive
(dĭ-prīv´) *v.* to keep from possessing or enjoying; deny.

QUOTED WORDS

Notice & Note: Mark the "christian principal" that Adams, the daughter of a minister, refers to in paragraph 1.

Analyze: What does this reveal about her attitude toward slavery in the colony?

tyrannical
(tĭ-răn´ĭ-kəl): *adj.* characteristic of a tyrant or tyranny; despotic and oppressive.

impunity
(ĭm-pyōō´nĭ-tē): *n.* exemption from punishment, penalty, or harm.

abhor
(ăb-hôr´): *v.* to regard with horror or loathing; detest.

ANALYZE AUTHOR'S PURPOSE

Annotate: In paragraph 3, mark phrases describing the nature of men, according to Adams.

Draw Conclusions: What might her purpose for using these phrases be?

LANGUAGE CONVENTIONS

Annotate: Mark each "title" Adams refers to in paragraph 3.

Analyze: What effect does her choice of these words have on her tone?

---

produced a Washington but they have been shamefully duped by a Dunmore.[3] I have sometimes been ready to think that the passion for Liberty cannot be Eaquelly Strong in the Breasts of those who have been accustomed to **deprive** their fellow Creatures of theirs.[4] Of this I am certain that it is not founded upon that generous and christian principal of doing to others as we would that others should do unto us. . . .

2   I long to hear that you have declared an independancy—and by the way in the new Code of Laws which I suppose it will be necessary for you to make I desire you would Remember the Ladies, and be more generous and favourable to them than your ancestors. Do not put such unlimited power into the hands of the Husbands. Remember all Men would be tyrants if they could. If perticuliar care and attention is not paid to the Laidies we are determined to foment[5] a Rebelion, and will not hold ourselves bound by any Laws in which we have no voice, or Representation.

3   That your Sex are Naturally **Tyrannical** is a Truth so thoroughly established as to admit of no dispute, but such of you as wish to be happy willingly give up the harsh title of Master for the more tender and endearing one of Friend. Why then, not put it out of the power of the vicious and the Lawless to use us with cruelty and indignity with **impunity** Men of Sense in all Ages **abhor** those customs which treat us only as the vassals of your Sex. Regard us then as Beings placed by providence under your protection and in immitation of the Supreme Being make use of that power only for our happiness.

---

[3] **Dunmore:** Lord Dunmore was the last British governor of Virginia. In April 1775, in reaction to events in Boston, Dunmore had all the gunpowder in Williamsburg confiscated. Then, in November 1775, he offered freedom to any slaves or indentured servants who would leave and join the British to fight the colonists.

[4] **I have sometimes . . . of theirs:** Adams is referring to slavery, which was common in Virginia. She questioned whether those who denied slaves freedom would not really have a passion for freedom.

[5] **foment** (fō-měnt´): to arouse or incite.

 ENGLISH LEARNER SUPPORT

Analyze Ideas Remind students that Adams uses capital letters differently from how we use them today. She capitalizes words she considers important. Have students scan paragraph 2 to identify capitalized words that would not be capitalized in modern English. Ask students how Adams's use of capitalization affects their understanding of the text. For example, ask: *Is it easier to understand because some words are capitalized, or is it more confusing that words in the middle of sentences are capitalized?* Have students explain their responses. **MODERATE**

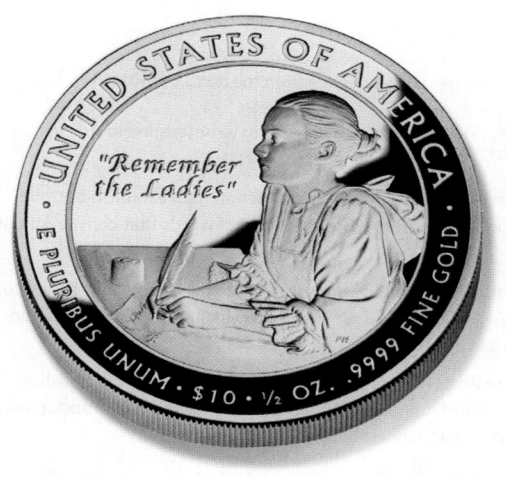

CHECK YOUR UNDERSTANDING

Answer these questions before moving on to the **Analyze the Text** section on the following page.

1 What is the complaint with which Abigail Adams begins the letter?

A Her husband's letters are too short.

B Her husband is in Philadelphia.

C Her husband is going to Virginia.

D Her husband is with the Fleet.

2 Why does Abigail Adams think Virginia might not be passionate about liberty?

F It is a new colony.

G It allows slavery.

H Washington lives there.

J There are no rifles.

3 What does Abigail Adams predict will happen if no laws protect women?

A Men will start becoming tyrannical.

B Men will imitate the supreme being.

C Men will give up the title of master.

D Women will incite a revolt of their own.

Letter to John Adams 173

ENGLISH LEARNER SUPPORT

Oral Assessment

1. What does Adams complain about in the beginning of the letter? (**Answer:** She wants longer letters.)

2. What does Adams dislike about the colony of Virginia? (**Answer:** Virginia has slavery.)

3. What does Adams think will happen if laws do not protect women? (**Answer:** Women will fight the government.) **SUBSTANTIAL**

ANALYZE AUTHOR'S PURPOSE

Following her blunt appraisal of men as naturally inclined to be tyrants, Adams ends on a conciliatory note. She draws a parallel between men like her husband and God. In so doing, she both encourages men to act for the good of others and perhaps also seeks to flatter her intended audience. (**Possible answer:** *She views God as being one whose power is used for good—"only for our happiness." She hopes men would consider behaving the same way.*)

CHECK YOUR UNDERSTANDING

Have students answer the questions independently.

Answers:

1. *A*

2. *G*

3. *D*

If students answer any questions incorrectly, have them reread the text to confirm their understanding. Then, they may proceed to ANALYZE THE TEXT on page 174.

CRITICAL VOCABULARY

tyrannical: Dictators who are not controlled by laws are *tyrannical.*

ASK STUDENTS to describe tyrannical behavior. (*throwing people in jail with no trial, executing political enemies, etc.*)

impunity: Adams says men have been cruel with *impunity.* She says this will continue unless laws prevent it.

ASK STUDENTS to give an example of acting with impunity. (*Breaking school rules, but not getting in trouble.*)

abhor: Adams's reference to Men of Sense must be understood in the context of the Enlightenment: sense/reason is a prime virtue or goal.

ASK STUDENTS to name something they abhor. (*Responses will vary.*)

ANALYZE THE TEXT

Possible answers:

1. **DOK 2:** *She is trying to determine whether Virginia is able to help the colonies defend themselves if they break with Great Britain.*

2. **DOK 4:** *Words are selected for precision and emotional impact, making it clear that Adams's voice is strong and the tone of the letter is passionate.*

3. **DOK 3:** *She refers to them as "savage" and "Blood thirsty", speaks disparagingly of their owning slaves, and mentions they were "shamefully duped" by the British governor. This helps support her argument that the Virginians may not be the best of allies.*

4. **DOK 3:** *You can tell their relationship allows for great honesty, and that Abigail is easily able to share her concerns about men's tyrannical nature, without fear of upsetting or offending her husband. She includes the information as part of her argument about why it is necessary to ensure rights for women in the new laws.*

5. **DOK 4:** *Answers will vary. She makes it clear that she doesn't approve of how women are treated, but the threat of rebellion might backfire (or make her point stronger). Text evidence might include the last statement in paragraph 2 in which Adams ties the potential response of women into the current rebellion by saying we (women) "will not hold ourselves bound by any Laws in which we have no voice, or Representation."*

RESEARCH

Review with students of the importance of using reliable sources. Remind them that online sources are not always reliable, and that to do good research they should consult a variety of sources. In addition to the Colonial Williamsburg Foundation, they might want to use the online *Encyclopedia Britannica*; mountvernon.org (which is home to a scholarly presidential library); monticello.org (run by the Thomas Jefferson Foundation); constitutioncenter.org; or sites affiliated with universities, such as millercenter.org (at the University of Virginia). Note, however, that some university sites (which typically end in .edu) sometimes provide access to student papers. These student papers may not always be completely accurate or reliable.

Extend John Quincy Adams was the son of John and Abigail Adams. Samuel Adams was John Adams's second cousin. Both Samuel and John Adams were active in the independence movement that led to the Revolution.

 RESPOND

ANALYZE THE TEXT

Support your responses with evidence from the text.   NOTEBOOK

1. **Summarize** What is Abigail Adams trying to determine in the first paragraph?

2. **Analyze** How does the writer's use of diction help establish both her voice and tone of the letter? Cite examples of words that convey Adams's tone.

3. **Cite Evidence** What details suggest that Abigail Adams may have a low opinion of Virginians as a whole? How does including this information support her purpose?

4. **Draw Conclusions** What can you determine about the relationship between John and Abigail Adams based on what she writes about men? Why do you think she includes this information?

5. **Evaluate** Do you think Abigail Adams does a good job of presenting her case for the need to pass laws that protect women? Support your response with evidence from the text.

RESEARCH TIP
Organizations that focus on the American Revolution, such as the Colonial Williamsburg Foundation, are excellent sources of information on the people and events from the founding of the United States.

RESEARCH

The influence and importance of the Adams family in America's early history was profound. Find at least one interesting fact about or quotation from each family member listed. Note how this fact or quote reveals the person's influence.

FAMILY MEMBER	INTERESTING INFORMATION	INFLUENCE
John Adams	*Principal author of oldest written constitution still in use*	*Was respected and trusted by other leaders*
Abigail Adams	*Advocate for women's rights and equal public education for women*	*As first lady, spoke out for what she believed*
Samuel Adams	*Helped plan Boston's resistance to the Tea Act*	*Worked with other colonial leaders*
John Quincy Adams	*Helped negotiate treaty that ended War of 1812*	*Trusted to deal with an important agreement*

Extend Explain why her relationships with John Adams and John Quincy Adams put Abigail Adams in a remarkable position to influence the country during this important period of time.

WHEN STUDENTS STRUGGLE . . .

Reteaching: Analyze Voice and Tone Have students look at paragraph 3 on page 172 and find two other "titles" Adams uses. (*Men of Sense, Beings*) Ask students what effect Adams creates by using these "titles." (**Possible answer:** *She makes both categories of people sound important and valuable. She inspires her intended reader to be a Man of Sense, and to think of women as Beings, rather than as "vassals of your Sex."*)

 For additional support, go to the **Reading Studio** and assign the following **Level Up Tutorial: Tone.**

CREATE AND DISCUSS

Write a Letter Write a letter to a historical figure you have studied who lived during the American Revolution.

- ❏ Decide on a person to whom you would like to write.
- ❏ Relate details about events with which you are familiar.
- ❏ Write in a formal style that is appropriate for the time period. Review "Letter to John Adams" for examples and inspiration.
- ❏ Encourage the person you are writing to to take some sort of action.
- ❏ Discuss anything else appropriate about life at that time.

Discuss with a Small Group Discuss why you think letters were so important at the time of the American Revolution. Compare your experience communicating with others with communication during Abigail Adams's day.

- ❏ Talk about how personal letters like Abigail Adams's can make history come to life.
- ❏ Discuss what information we get from letters that we may not get from secondary sources such as history articles.
- ❏ Read part of the letter you wrote and share what it was like writing your Revolutionary War letter.
- ❏ Discuss why you think letters have been so valued through the years.

RESPOND TO THE ESSENTIAL QUESTION

 ? How can we share power and build alliances?

Gather Information Review your annotations and notes on "Letter to John Adams." Then, add relevant information to your Response Log. As you determine which information to include, think about:

- the issues Adams raises in the letter
- Adams's attitude toward the circumstances of women at the time
- how Adams addresses building alliances and sharing power

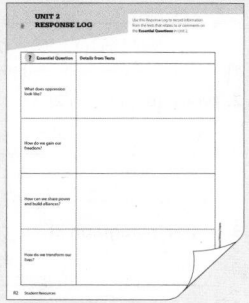

 Go to **Writing Informative Texts** in the **Writing Studio** for help with formal style.

Go to **Participating in Collaborative Discussions** in the **Speaking and Listening Studio** for help.

ACADEMIC VOCABULARY
As you write and discuss what you learned from the letter, be sure to use the Academic Vocabulary words. Check off each of the words that you use.

- ❏ **contrary**
- ❏ **founder**
- ❏ **ideological**
- ❏ **publication**
- ❏ **revolution**

CREATE AND DISCUSS

Write a Letter Encourage students to use both their knowledge about the historical figure and time period, and their creativity. Have students think through the tone and voice they will use in their letter. Remind students to think about what might be persuasive to their intended audience (the historical figure).

For **writing support** for students at varying proficiency levels, see the **Text X-Ray** on page 168D.

Discuss with a Small Group Circulate as groups discuss. Encourage students to share their thoughts and opinions about reading Adams's letter. Have students discuss why they chose the historical figure they did. Consider asking some volunteers to read parts of their letters aloud to the class.

RESPOND TO THE ESSENTIAL QUESTION

Allow time for students to add details from *Letter to John Adams* to their Unit 2 Response Logs.

CRITICAL VOCABULARY

Answers:

1. *tyrannical*

2. *abhor*

3. *impunity*

4. *deprive*

VOCABULARY STRATEGY:
Evaluate Nuances in Meaning

Answers:

1. *Negative; fooled, tricked. The word "shamefully" helps show the negative connotation.*

2. *Negative; an oppressive, cruel ruler. The words "unlimited power," Adams's hope that the Americans will "be more generous and favorable to them than your ancestors" help show the meaning and connotation.*

3. *Negative; a subordinate, a person who has a lower status. The words "common people" and "uncivilized" show the negative connotation.*

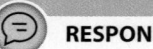 **RESPOND**

WORD BANK
deprive
tyrannical
impunity
abhor

 Go to **Denotation and Connotation** in the **Vocabulary Studio** for help.

CRITICAL VOCABULARY

Practice and Apply In the spaces provided, write the Critical Vocabulary word that best fits the sentence.

1. The Declaration of Independence accused King George of _____ behavior.

2. Law-abiding citizens generally _____ violence and lawlessness.

3. Some criminals seem to believe they can break laws with _____.

4. The laws being passed would _____ people of their rights.

VOCABULARY STRATEGY: Evaluate
Nuances in Meaning

In choosing to use the Critical Vocabulary word *impunity* in this letter, Abigail Adams was conscious not only of the word's **denotation,** or dictionary definition, but also of its **connotations** and **nuances**—its emotional connections and subtle shades of meaning and tone. The dictionary definition of *impunity* is "exemption from punishment, penalty, or harm," but the word's nuances, its shades of meaning, suggest an avoidance of a deserved penalty. The overall tone of the letter, the context in which *impunity* is used, and its nuances make the word's negative connotation clear.

Practice and Apply Write the denotation, or definition for each of the following words from Abigail Adams's letter. Then, note each word's nuances and state whether the connotation is negative or positive; finally, explain how you can tell.

1. duped (paragraph 1)

_____

_____

2. tyrant (paragraph 2)

_____

_____

3. vassal (paragraph 3)

_____

_____

 ENGLISH LEARNER SUPPORT

Vocabulary Strategy Guide students to locate the vocabulary words in the text. Then guide students to look for words and phrases near each vocabulary word that can help them understand the meaning of the word. For example, ask: *What word helps you understand the meaning of* vassals? *Based on that clue, what does* vassals *mean? Is the word positive or negative?* Provide these sentence frames: *The word _____ means _____. One word that helps me understand the meaning is _____. The word is _____.* **MODERATE**

LANGUAGE CONVENTIONS:
Formal English

Formal English combines **diction,** or word choice, with **syntax,** or the arrangement of words within sentences, closing adhering to the rules of grammar. In some cases, the topic or field dictates the style, requiring specific language and syntax—for example, in a legal document.

Abigail Adams used formal English because that is how educated people wrote in the 1700s. Although the letter is to her husband, her diction and syntax are formal. For example, in this sentence, while acknowledging that her husband is among those who happily treat women well, she pleads for laws that will protect women from those who are "Lawless."

> **That your Sex are Naturally Tyrannical is a Truth so thoroughly established as to admit of no dispute, but such of you as wish to be happy willingly give up the harsh title of Master for the more tender and endearing one of Friend.**

Today, although more casual forms of style are widely accepted, it is important to know how to write formally. For example, a letter to a potential employer, a report to a manager, or an essay produced for a college professor require use of formal English.

Practice and Apply Write a brief summary of "Letter to John Adams." Use formal, contemporary language, choosing words wisely, forming sentences carefully, and observing all rules of grammar.

LANGUAGE CONVENTIONS:
Formal English

Ask students to consider the ways in which Adams's **formal style** lends weight to her argument. Guide students to understand and discuss the ways in which her complex **syntax** serves to help her make her points. For instance, she offers a balanced, but forceful opinion about the Virginia colonists by beginning her sentence with an acknowledgement of merit, but then contrasting that merit with the ways that the Virginians allowed themselves to be "shamefully duped." Note the very different syntax of the simple, but extremely powerful sentence, "Remember all Men would be tyrants if they could." Adams sets off this key idea with a sentence structure that highlights and sets apart this phrase.

Practice and Apply Have students first create a list of the major issues in the letter. Then, have them write in a style that would be appropriate for a serious newspaper or a speech by an accomplished orator.

EL ENGLISH LEARNER SUPPORT

Language Conventions Note that Adams's style is different from the English we use today. Her diction and syntax were more complex. Help students understand the difference between formal and informal English by pointing out that when we talk to our friends we might use idioms or contractions. Use the following supports with students at varying proficiency levels:

• Review the sample sentence with students. Then, break it into parts and simplify it to help students understand the meaning.

Then, help students rewrite a passage from the text in informal language. **SUBSTANTIAL/MODERATE**

• Have pairs work together to rewrite a passage from the text in informal language. Tell students it may be necessary to break longer sentences into two sentences. Have pairs exchange papers and discuss their revisions. **LIGHT**

from LEAN IN
Essay by Sheryl Sandberg

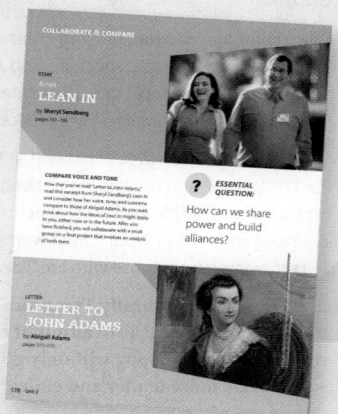

GENRE ELEMENTS
ESSAY

Remind students that an **essay** is a short work of nonfiction writing. An essay typically focuses on or recounts a particular subject or event, often directly tied to or experienced by its author. Due to their personal nature, essays can often be more informal than texts from other genres.

LEARNING OBJECTIVES

- Analyze author's purpose, voice, and tone.
- Conduct research on Sheryl Sandberg.
- Write an autobiographical essay.
- Hold a debate.
- Learn the meanings of idioms.
- Analyze and understand contested usage.
- **Language** Speak using formal and informal language.

TEXT COMPLEXITY

Quantitative Measures	Lean In	Lexile: 1000L
Qualitative Measures	**Ideas Presented** Requires weighing of multiple perspectives. Some analysis of bias and author's motivations. Some ambiguity.	
	Structures Used More complex, multiple perspectives may be presented; more deviation from chronology. Tables and figures support understanding.	
	Language Used Vocabulary not defined at point of use. Mostly Tier II and III words. Metaphor (rather than similes) used more. Multiple technical words may be used in one sentence.	
	Knowledge Required More complex problems. Experiences may be less familiar to many. Cultural or historical references.	

RESOURCES

- Unit 2 Response Log
- Selection Audio
- Reading Studio: Notice & Note
- LEVEL UP Level Up Tutorial: Author's Purpose
- Writing Studio: Writing Narratives
- Speaking and Listening Studio: Analyzing and Evaluating Presentations
- Vocabulary Studio: Idioms, Slang, and Figurative Language
- "Letter to John Adams"/*from* "Lean In" Selection Test

SUMMARIES

English

In this essay, American technology executive, activist, and author Sheryl Sandberg outlines her approach to leadership and her philosophy on life. She highlights themes like self-confidence, active participation in meetings, fostering a productive work-life balance, and nurturing a successful romantic partnership. The essay comes from Sandberg's book *Lean In: Women, Work, and the Will to Lead*, and shares its title with an initiative she founded.

Spanish

En este ensayo, la autora, activista y ejecutiva tecnológica americana, Sheryl Sandberg da una idea general de su enfoque en el liderazgo y su filosofía de vida. Destaca temas como la autoconfianza, la participación durante reuniones, fomentar un balance productivo entre la vida y el trabajo, y nutrir una relación romántica exitosa. El ensayo sale del libro de Sandberg, *Apóyate: mujeres, trabajo y el deseo de liderar* y comparte el título con una iniciativa que ella misma fundó.

SMALL-GROUP OPTIONS

Have students work in small groups and pairs to read and discuss the selection.

Send a Problem

- After reading the essay, pose this question: *What was Sheryl Sandberg's motivation for writing this essay?*
- Call on a student to respond, citing evidence from the text. Wait up to 11 seconds.
- If the student has no response, s/he must call on another student by name to answer the same question.
- Have students continue asking each other for assistance as needed. Monitor responses and ask more questions as appropriate.

Think-Pair-Share

- After reading the essay, pose this question: *How is my approach to life similar or different to Sheryl Sandberg's?*
- Have students think about the question individually and take notes.
- Then, have students form pairs and listen, discuss, and formulate shared responses to the question.
- Finally, have pairs share their responses with the class.

Text X-Ray: English Learner Support
for "Lean In"

Use the Text X-Ray and the supports and scaffolds in the Teacher's Edition to help guide students at different proficiency levels through the selection.

INTRODUCE THE SELECTION
DISCUSS VOICE AND TONE

Students will need to be able to discuss voice and tone in this lesson. Share the following explanations with them:

- *Voice* is the personality or style of a writer in a piece of writing.
- *Tone* refers to the author's attitude toward the subject.

Explain to students that voice and tone affect the level of formality in writing. For example, using contractions or slang makes a text informal. Read the sentence "I also felt a little nervous. . ." from paragraph 1 of the reading. Ask the students how the use of punctuation, repetition, and vocabulary affect the formality of the sentence, and to imagine how it could be phrased differently to be more formal.

Supply these sentence frames: *Sandberg's use of _____ makes this informal because _____. A more formal way of saying this would be _____.*

CULTURAL REFERENCES

The following words or phrases may be unfamiliar to students:

- *in sync* (paragraph 1): having the same ideas
- *at the root* (paragraph 3): at the basic level
- *sit at the table* (heading): be part of a group
- *milling around* (paragraph 7): moving around without purpose
- *barrier* (paragraph 9): something that stops someone from doing something
- *underplayed* (paragraph 11): not made to seem important
- *keep my hand up* (paragraph 12): talk; participate
- *lean in* (paragraph 15): work hard; make a priority
- *fosters* (paragraph 16): promotes; furthers
- *trends hold* (paragraph 18): if things stay the same
- *commitmentphobic* (paragraph 20): afraid of being in a relationship

LISTENING

Understand Tone

Explain to students that the tone of this selection is generally informal, and there are certain clues they can listen for to help understand the tone.

Use the following supports with students at varying proficiency levels:

- Explain to students that the word *okay* is an informal word. Read paragraph 1 of the selection and ask students to raise their hands when they hear the word *okay*. **SUBSTANTIAL**
- Discuss contractions before reading paragraphs one and two. As students listen, have them note the contractions they hear. Then, ask them what other clues tell them this text is informal. **MODERATE**
- Pair students and have them read paragraphs one and two to one another. Ask students to write down any informal language. After they finish reading, have the students compare notes. **LIGHT**

SPEAKING

Recognize Style

Explain to students that sometimes writers break grammar rules to achieve a certain style. Breaking grammar rules often mimics informal spoken English.

Work with students to read paragraphs 3 and 4. Use the following supports with students at varying proficiency levels:

- Explain that sentence fragments often occur when a sentence is missing a verb, or action word. Say the phrase "Fear of not being liked" aloud and ask students how this could be made into a complete sentence. Supply the sentence frame: *Women _____ a fear of not being liked.* **SUBSTANTIAL**
- Ask a student volunteer to read the paragraph aloud while other students listen for sentence fragments. Discuss what effect the sentence fragments have. **MODERATE**
- Pair students and have them read paragraphs 3 and 4 aloud. Have students choose a sentence, describe its structure, and say whether it is formal or informal. **LIGHT**

READING

Identify Purpose

Remind students that an author's purpose is the reason he or she writes a text. Have students work to identify words and phrases (such as "I think," or "my advice") that indicate the author's purpose.

Use the following supports with students at varying proficiency levels:

- Have students choral read paragraph 20. Ask students to identify a word or phrase that indicates the author's purpose ("my advice"). Supply the following sentence frame: *Sandberg's advice to _____ is _____.* **SUBSTANTIAL**
- Have students read paragraph 20. Ask students to summarize the author's purpose. Provide the sentence frames: *The author's purpose in this paragraph is to _____. The word _____ tells me that she is describing her purpose.* **MODERATE**
- Ask students to read paragraph 20 and take note of phrases that indicate the author's purpose. Then pair students to reread the essay and take turns describing the author's purposes. **LIGHT**

WRITING

Write About Personal Experiences

Review the Write an Essay assignment on Student Edition page 187. Explain that they will write an essay based on something they have done or learned.

Use the following supports with students at varying proficiency levels:

- Work with students to identify an accomplishment they are proud of. Supply the sentence frame: *I am proud of the time I _____.* Allow students to draw what they accomplished and use that drawing to complete the sentence frame. **SUBSTANTIAL**
- Have students write a paragraph describing a time when they accomplished a goal. Remind students to use complete sentences, and to try to include a descriptive adjective to make their paragraph more interesting. **MODERATE**
- Instruct students to develop two to three paragraphs about a time when they achieved or learned something. Student should use descriptive language to explain what they did or learned and how it made them feel. Have students share their paragraphs with a partner. **LIGHT**

Connect to the
ESSENTIAL QUESTION

Read the Essential Question aloud, and prompt students to respond to it from different angles. Ask them to examine this question in different contexts, such as "in the classroom," "on a national level," etc. Brainstorm what it means to "share power" or "build alliances." Ask students to reflect on what these two phrases could mean, and what forms they might take.

COMPARE VOICE AND TONE

Encourage students to look for similarities in voice or tone as they read. Even though both women were writing in very different times with disparate language, urge students to try to imagine how each writer might write in the other's time period.

ESSAY

from

LEAN IN

by **Sheryl Sandberg**
pages 181–185

COMPARE VOICE AND TONE

Now that you've read "Letter to John Adams," read this excerpt from Sheryl Sandberg's *Lean In* and consider how her voice, tone, and concerns compare to those of Abigail Adams. As you read, think about how the ideas of *Lean In* might apply to you, either now or in the future. After you have finished, you will collaborate with a small group on a final project that involves an analysis of both texts.

ESSENTIAL QUESTION:

How can we share power and build alliances?

LETTER

LETTER TO JOHN ADAMS

by **Abigail Adams**
pages 171–173

from **Lean In**

QUICK START

Sometimes it is hard to know what you really want—and harder to know what it might take to get it. Think of one or two goals you have for when you graduate high school. Then, list things that you would be willing to do or to give up to gain those goals. Share and discuss your list with a partner.

ANALYZE AUTHOR'S PURPOSE

An **author's purpose** is the reason he or she writes a text. The overall purpose might be to entertain, to inform, to describe, to express an idea or feeling, or to persuade. The purpose can also be a combination of these—to inform and persuade, for example. Purpose is related to both the text's **message,** the main idea the author wants to convey, and its intended **audience,** the readers the author wants to influence or affect. Authors support their purposes by adjusting tone and style to suit their audiences. As you read, think about Sandberg's purpose, the audience she addresses, and her style and tone.

ANALYZE LANGUAGE: Voice and Tone

Sandberg's **voice,** or writing personality, differs greatly from that of Abigail Adams. Because her subject matter targets a different audience, Sandberg's **tone,** or attitude, differs, as well. Voice and tone are communicated by **diction,** or word choice, and **syntax,** or how sentences are formed. Sandberg's diction and syntax are more modern and less formal than Adams's. As you read the essay from *Lean In,* use the chart to track some of the words or phrases Sandberg uses that Adams would not. Think about what these words reveal about Sandberg, her message, her tone, and her purpose.

WORD OR PHRASE	WHAT IT REVEALS
in sync	informal, modern, tech oriented

As you read this essay, think about how the diction and syntax help communicate the personality and attitudes of Sheryl Sandberg.

GENRE ELEMENTS: ESSAY
- is a short work of nonfiction on a single subject
- may use informal language
- can be autobiographical

QUICK START

Ask students to think about what fears they have related to their chosen goals. Have them ask themselves how those fears might present obstacles to those goals, and how they could work around or help diminish their fears.

ANALYZE AUTHOR'S PURPOSE

Remind students of the different **purposes** authors have for writing. Note that the style an author uses often reveals his or her purpose. Explain that in her essay, Sandberg's style is more formal than a letter or journal entry; however, Sandberg also writes in a very personal and relatively informal manner. Have students think about how these things connect to the author's purpose in writing her essay.

ANALYZE LANGUAGE: Voice and Tone

Instruct students to note places in Sandberg's essay where the **diction** and **syntax** are notably informal. Have them keep track of these notes as they go, and reflect on what this use of **informal language** and tone brings to the essay. Discuss other essays students have read—both formal and informal. Invite volunteers to explain which type of essay they respond to more and why.

CRITICAL VOCABULARY

Instruct students to examine the vocabulary words in the word bank and take guesses at their meanings. Then, have students read the sentences and guess which words complete each statement.

Answers:

1. *internalize*
2. *watershed*
3. *parity*
4. *demurred*

■ English Learner Support

Use Cognates Tell Spanish speakers that some of the Critical Vocabulary words have Spanish cognates: *internalize/interiorizar, parity/paridad.* **ALL LEVELS**

LANGUAGE CONVENTIONS

Ask students to consider why Sandberg might choose to break the conjunction rule in her essay. Read an example of this happening, beginning with the sentence before the one that begins with a conjunction. Ask the students if this type of pause sounds natural in spoken language. Then, have them consider that kind of effect the breaking of this rule might have on the tone and flow of the writing.

ANNOTATION MODEL

Remind students to underline important details and circle words that indicate themes or tone in the text. Point out that they may follow this suggestion or use their own system for marking up the selection in their write-in text. They may want to color-code their annotations by using highlighters. Their notes in the margin may include questions about ideas that are unclear or topics they want to learn more about.

 **GET READY**

CRITICAL VOCABULARY

| demurred | watershed | internalize | parity |

To see how many Critical Vocabulary words you already know, use them to complete the sentences.

1. All teams should _____ the ideals of good sportsmanship.

2. Finally getting a good pitcher was a _____ in the team's season.

3. In some countries, women cannot dream of achieving _____ with men.

4. She really didn't want to do it, so she _____.

LANGUAGE CONVENTIONS

Contested Usage The English language continually grows and changes, and over time grammatical rules relax or alter. The new usage often breaks with long-standing practices and tends to make writing less formal. The style of *Lean In* is informal, as is common in many essays. Most rules are carefully observed, but some of Sandberg's usage is contested. One rule of grammar she breaks with some regularity is "Don't begin a sentence with a conjunction."

> **But it does help to tell ourselves to fight our fears at every stage of our lives.**

As you read, keep an eye out for places where Sandberg uses conjunctions at the beginning of sentences, and note any other informal usage you see.

ANNOTATION MODEL

NOTICE & NOTE

As you read, note how Sandberg uses diction and syntax to express energy and emotion in the essay. Mark interesting passages and note how they contribute to the tone of the essay or convey the author's voice. In the model, you can see one reader's notes about *Lean In*.

> I headed to my first day of work as chief operating officer of a small company called Facebook. As I pulled out of my driveway, I remember feeling <u>excited</u>. I also felt a little <u>nervous</u> (. .)a little <u>anxious</u> (. .)okay, maybe even a little <u>scared</u> about this new challenge. It wasn't anything specific that concerned me.

The choice of words "excited," "nervous," "anxious," and "scared" makes the tone edgy—energy mixed with fear.

Use of "..." adds pauses, a sense of thoughtfulness.

BACKGROUND

Sheryl Sandberg *(1969–) Brilliant and motivated, with degrees in economics and business from Harvard, Sandberg became chief of staff in the U.S. Treasury Department, then vice president at Google, and in 2008, chief operating officer at Facebook.* Lean In *became her philosophy, book title, and also the name of an organization founded by Sandberg. Critics pointed out that her methods worked but came at a cost. That didn't slow Sandberg down. By 2014 she was a billionaire. In 2015 Sandberg's husband died suddenly, and Sandberg began to rethink some of her goals. Today, she is still with Facebook, but also helps women dealing with grief.*

from
LEAN IN
Essay by Sheryl Sandberg

PREPARE TO COMPARE

As you read, pay attention to both the style and content of the essay. Note details describing Sandberg's ideals for work and relationships.

1   On March 24, 2008, I headed to my first day of work as chief operating officer of a small company called Facebook. As I pulled out of my driveway, I remember feeling excited. I also felt a little nervous . . . a little anxious . . . okay, maybe even a little scared about this new challenge. It wasn't anything specific that concerned me. I knew the tech business well after spending more than six years at Google. I had shared many dinners with CEO[1] Mark Zuckerberg before he offered me the job, and I knew we were in sync about the importance of Facebook's mission. My fear was more the general anxiety you feel over the risks associated with a new job and the worry that you won't succeed.

2   I parked my car and went up to an industrial, open-plan office space. My desk faced Mark's and was near the very popular Rainbow Room, which was crammed with couches and video games. At the time, the office walls were bare. Today, those walls are filled with posters that reflect the company's philosophy

---

[1] **CEO:** chief executive officer, the highest-ranking executive at a company.

Notice & Note

Use the side margins to notice and note signposts in the text.

 ANALYZE VOICE

Annotate: Mark elements in paragraph 1 that help establish Sandberg's voice.

Analyze: What can you tell about the author from this paragraph? Explain.

BACKGROUND

Facebook, which Sheryl Sandberg played an integral role in the development of, was created by Mark Zuckerberg in 2004. Between 2004 and 2008, when Sandberg joined, the company grew immensely in size and popularity. Students may want to do more research on the development of Facebook to better understand Sandberg's role in the company.

PREPARE TO COMPARE

Direct students to use the Prepare to Compare prompt to focus their reading.

ANALYZE VOICE

Have students read paragraph 1 aloud to one another, as though they were trying to naturally read a script from a scene in a movie. Ask them to reflect on how natural this paragraph sounds in spoken English. Point out that when something is written in spoken English, it is almost always informal. (**Answer:** *She's smart, honest, and young. She wouldn't have had the jobs she had without having brains; she admits being scared; and shortened terms like "tech" and "in sync" suggest that she's young.*)

For **listening support** for students at varying proficiency levels, see the **Text X-Ray** on page 178C.

TO CHALLENGE STUDENTS . . .

Understand Tone After students read Sandberg's essay, instruct them to look at a few examples of other essays from places like the *New York Times*. Have them choose essays that interest them and identify the authors' tones. Students should keep notes on the type of language used by authors, as well as how formal or informal the writing seems. Afterwards, have them choose one essay and write a response paragraph to it. Ask students to write two versions of their paragraph—one using informal spoken language, as though it were addressed to their peers, and another in formal language, as though writing for an academic publication.

ANALYZE AUTHOR'S PURPOSE

Explain to students that a common device for organizing an essay and setting up purpose is to ask a question and then answer your own question in the following sentence or paragraph. (**Answer:** *She says it has special significance to women because they often have many fears. The question that ends paragraph 2, and the first sentence of paragraph 3, suggest the author's purpose might be to help women overcome fear.*)

LANGUAGE CONVENTIONS

Remind students that any type of word abbreviation in general makes a piece of writing more informal. Contractions and not writing out numbers are common examples, but also the shortened spellings of words like *you* as *u* and *through* as *thru* will make a piece seem extremely informal. (**Answer:** *It contributes to the chatty, informal tone of the writing.*)

> For **speaking support** for students at varying proficiency levels, see the **Text X-Ray** on page 178D.

CRITICAL VOCABULARY

demurred: When someone doesn't wish to do or accept something, they might *demur* and not accept.

ASK STUDENTS when someone demurs an invitation to join a group, what might be an appropriate response? (*to politely accept the refusal*)

 NOTICE & NOTE

ANALYZE AUTHOR'S PURPOSE

Annotate: In paragraph 2, mark the question that Sandberg refers to in paragraph 3.

Predict: Why do you think she says it has "special significance for women"? What does this suggest about her purpose?

LANGUAGE CONVENTIONS

Annotate: Sentence fragments lack a subject, predicate or both. Mark the sentence fragments in paragraph 3.

Skill: What is the function of this contested usage in Sandberg's writing? How does it impact your understanding?

demurred
(dĭ-mûrd´) *v.* disagreed or refused to accept a request or suggestion.

---

and encourage employees to take risks. "Proceed and be bold," declares one. "Move fast and break things," advises another. But the one that would have helped me on that first morning doesn't make a statement; it asks a question: "What would you do if you weren't afraid?"

3   This question speaks to everyone, but I think it has special significance for women. Fear is at the root of so many of the barriers that women face. Fear of not being liked. Fear of making the wrong decision. Fear of drawing negative attention. Fear of overreaching. Fear of being judged. Fear of failure. And for those who want to have children, the fear that we can't be both good employees and good mothers.

4   I know it's pointless to tell someone to be fearless. I regularly fail to convince even myself. But it does help to tell ourselves to fight our fears at every stage of our lives. In school, don't be afraid to raise your hand. When you are attending a meeting, don't be afraid to sit at the table. Don't be afraid to offer your opinion. Don't be afraid of waiting to find a life partner who will support you in achieving your dreams. And don't be afraid to be fully engaged in your career, even as you plan to have a family. By fighting these fears, women can pursue professional success and personal fulfillment—and freely choose one or the other . . . or both.

5   Five years ago, I dove into my new Facebook job as fearlessly as I could. And although at the time a lot of people questioned why I would want to go to work for a 23-year-old, no one asks me that question anymore.

6   It's your turn now. Please ask yourself: *What would I do if I weren't afraid?* And then go do it.

SUCCESS SECRET 1: SIT AT THE TABLE

7   A few years ago, I hosted a meeting for Treasury Secretary Tim Geithner at Facebook. We invited 15 executives from across Silicon Valley[2] for breakfast and a discussion about the economy. Secretary Geithner arrived with four members of his staff, two senior and two more junior, and we all gathered in our one nice conference room. After the usual milling around, I encouraged everyone to take a seat. Our invited guests, mostly men, sat down at the large conference table. Secretary Geithner's team, all women, took their food last and sat in chairs off to the side of the room. I motioned for the women to come sit at the table, waving them over publicly so they would feel welcomed. They **demurred** and remained in their seats.

8   The four women had every right to be at this meeting, but because of their seating choice, they seemed like spectators rather than participants. I knew I had to say something. So after the meeting, I pulled them aside to talk. I pointed out that they should

---

[2] **Silicon Valley:** The location in California of many of the large tech companies. So named because silicon is the element from which computer chips are made.

have sat at the table even without an invitation, but when publicly welcomed, they most certainly should have joined. At first, they seemed surprised, then they agreed.

9   It was a **watershed** moment for me. A moment when I witnessed an internal barrier altering women's behavior. A moment when I realized that in addition to facing institutional obstacles, women face a battle from within. We consistently underestimate ourselves. Multiple studies in multiple industries show that women often judge their own performance as worse than it actually is, while men judge their own performance as better than it actually is.

10   We hold ourselves back in ways both big and small, by lacking self-confidence, by not raising our hands, and by pulling back when we should be leaning in. We **internalize** the negative messages we get throughout our lives—the messages that say it's wrong to be outspoken, aggressive, or more powerful than men. We lower our own expectations of what we can achieve. We continue to do the majority of the housework and childcare. We compromise our career goals to make room for partners and children who may not even exist yet. Compared to our male colleagues, fewer of us aspire to senior positions.

11   Internal obstacles are rarely discussed and often underplayed. Throughout my life, I was told over and over about inequalities in the workplace and how hard it would be to have a career and a family. I rarely, however, heard anything about the ways I might hold myself back. These internal obstacles deserve a lot more attention because they are under our control. We cannot change what we are unaware of, and once we are aware, we cannot help but change.

12   I know that in order to continue to grow and challenge myself, I have to believe in my own abilities. I still face situations that I fear are beyond my qualifications. And I still sometimes find myself spoken over and discounted while men sitting next to me are not. But now I know how to take a deep breath and keep my hand up. I have learned to sit at the table.

watershed
(wôʹtər-shĕd) *n.* a turning point, a crucial dividing line.

internalize
(ĭn-tûrʹnə-līz) *v.* to make something, such as an idea or value, an important part of the kind of person you are.

ANALYZE TONE

Annotate: Mark in paragraph 11 the two examples of "internal obstacles."

Infer: The essay starts out bright and breezy, but the tone changes here. What is the relationship between the topic and the tone?

Lean In   183

ENGLISH LEARNER SUPPORT

Make Verbs and Nouns from Adjectives Help students make a word web to understand how the word *internal* becomes *internalize* and *internalization*. Write the word *internal* on the board and explain that it is an adjective. Demonstrate how the addition of suffixes changes the word from an adjective to a verb and then a noun. Have students repeat the words after you and note the pronunciation of the second *i* in *internalize* and *internalization*. Then, write the word *equal* on the board and ask students to add suffixes to change the adjective into a verb and a noun (*equalize, equality*). **MODERATE**

ANALYZE TONE

Encourage students to look for key words to find the answers to questions about the text. In this case, the author actually uses the phrase "internal obstacles," as well as similar terms like "internalize." These can be used as markers to help students orient themselves in the text when looking for answers to specific questions. (**Answer:** *The tone becomes more passionate, so the writer must consider "internal obstacles" to be serious.*)

CRITICAL VOCABULARY

watershed: In a *watershed* moment, someone might have a revelation that completely changes his or her life.

ASK STUDENTS if they've ever had a watershed moment that has caused their life to take a new direction. (*Answers will vary.*)

internalize: People often *internalize* strong emotions, such as grief or anger, instead of letting them out.

ASK STUDENTS if they can point to a moment when they internalized something that someone did or said to them. (*Answers will vary.*)

Lean In   **183**

ANALYZE AUTHOR'S PURPOSE

Explain to students that when dealing with a question that contains a general pronoun like *this*, the key is to read back a few sentences to see if they can find the specific noun that *this* is referring to. Often the answer is in the previous sentence. In this case, the students are looking for "what" exactly has to change in Sandberg's statement. (**Answer:** *The author moves from discussing the challenges to proposing changes that must occur for a solution to be reached. The author's purpose is to encourage a change in the expectations of women and a move towards true equality.*)

 ANALYZE VOICE

Remind students that when they are looking for personal information or anecdotes from the author, scan for first person pronouns like *I* or *my*. Reading for markers like this will help them find the relevant sections more quickly and efficiently. (**Answer:** *It shows she values marriage. Her marriage and her success are the sources for her ideas of how life should work for others.*)

CRITICAL VOCABULARY

parity: Partners working on a project might seek *parity* in the division of labor, so they are both doing the same amount of work.

ASK STUDENTS how parity might be achieved within a marriage. (*splitting the chores, listening to one another, sharing childcare*)

 NOTICE & NOTE

SUCCESS SECRET 2: MAKE YOUR PARTNER A REAL PARTNER

13   I truly believe that the single most important career decision that a woman makes is whether she will have a life partner and who that partner is. A woman who can find someone who is willing to share the burdens—and joys—of home life will go further in her work life. I don't know of a single woman in a leadership position whose life partner is not fully—and I mean fully—supportive of her career. No exceptions. And contrary to the popular notion that only unmarried women can make it to the top, the majority of the most successful female business leaders have partners.

14   In the last thirty years, women have made more progress in the workforce than in the home. When a husband and wife both work full-time, the mother does 40 percent more childcare and about 30 percent more housework than the father. So while men are taking on more household responsibilities, this increase is happening very slowly, and we are still far from **parity**. . . .

15   This has to change. Just as we need to encourage women to lean in to their careers, we need to encourage men to lean in to their families. If we expect and allow them to do more, they will do more. And everyone will benefit.

16   When husbands do more housework, wives are less depressed, marital conflicts decrease, and satisfaction rises. When women work outside the home and share breadwinning duties, couples are more likely to stay together. In fact, the risk of divorce reduces by about half when a wife earns half the income and a husband does half the housework. For men, participating in child rearing fosters the development of patience, empathy, and adaptability, characteristics that benefit them in all their relationships. For women, earning money increases their decision-making ability in the home, protects them in case of divorce, and can be important security in later years, as women often outlive their husbands. . . .

17   I could not do what I do without my husband, Dave. Still, like all marriages, ours is a work in progress. Dave and I have had our share of bumps on our path to achieving a roughly 50/50 split. After a lot of effort and seemingly endless discussion, we are truly partners.

18   The good news is that men in younger generations appear more eager to be real partners than previous generations did. A survey that asked participants to rate the importance of various job characteristics found that men in their 40s most frequently selected "work that challenges me" as very important, while men in their 20s and 30s most frequently selected having a job with a schedule that "allows me to spend time with my family." If these trends hold as this group ages, this could signal a promising shift toward greater equality.

19   Wonderful, sensitive men of all ages are out there. And the more that women value kindness and support in their boyfriends, the more men will demonstrate it.

parity
(păr´ ĭ-tē) *n.* equality, being equivalent.

ANALYZE AUTHOR'S PURPOSE

Annotate: Mark the sentence in paragraph 15 that signals a change in purpose from the first part of the essay.

Analyze: Explain the change. Why does Sandberg shift her purpose?

ANALYZE VOICE

Annotate: Mark words in paragraph 17 that show that Sandberg's voice has become more personal and autobiographical.

Draw Conclusions: How do these words reveal her personality? How does her life affect her ideas?

© Houghton Mifflin Harcourt Publishing Company

IMPROVE READING FLUENCY

Targeted Passage   Put students in pairs to read paragraphs 15–19. Instruct them to take turns reading paragraphs, and to read as though they are two actors reading a part. Have them make eye contact with one another every sentence or two that they read, and encourage them to try to speak naturally, as though in a conversation. This will help students gain better understanding of the author's own voice and tone and will give them a chance to practice oral reading skills with eye contact.

   Go to the **Reading Studio** for additional support in developing fluency.

20   So, when looking for a life partner, my advice to women is date all of them: the bad boys, the cool boys, the commitmentphobic boys, the crazy boys. But do not marry them. . . . When it comes time to settle down, find someone who wants an equal partner. Someone who thinks women should be smart, opinionated, and ambitious. Someone who values fairness and expects or, even better, wants to do his share in the home. And at the start of a romance, even though it may be tempting for you to show a more classic girlfriend-y side by cooking meals and taking care of errands, hold yourself back from doing this too much. If a relationship begins in an unequal place, it is likely to get more unbalanced if and when children are added to the equation. Instead, use the beginning of a relationship to establish the bar for the division of labor.

ANALYZE AUTHOR'S PURPOSE

Annotate: Mark Sheryl Sandberg's advice.

Infer: Why do you think she gives this advice? How does it support her overall purpose?

CHECK YOUR UNDERSTANDING

Answer these questions before moving on to the **Analyze the Text** section on the following page.

1 Why is Sandberg nervous when she starts at Facebook?

  A It was such a small company at the time.

  B She worried that she might not succeed.

  C She didn't know anything about technology.

  D She had never met Mark Zuckerberg before.

2 Sandberg thinks women could do better in business —

  F if they had more education

  G if they cared about business

  H if they didn't give in to fear

  J if they knew Mark Zuckerberg

3 For Sandberg, relationships are an important part of success —

  A because the right partner will be fully supportive

  B because the wrong partner will lead to divorce

  C because you can't get ahead if you're not married

  D because you can't get ahead if you are married

TEACH

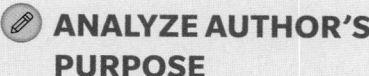 For **reading support** for students at varying proficiency levels, see the **Text X-Ray** on page 178D.

ANALYZE AUTHOR'S PURPOSE

When reading a text for advice, instruct students to look for verbs in the imperative form, such as *find*, *hold*, or *use*. Explain to students that these verbs often occur in an essay when the author is telling the reader to do something. In this case, it will help the students mark the sections of the text where the author is giving advice. (**Answer:** *Her advice to choose a partner who is willing to create an equal partnership and share duties reinforces her purpose, which is to point out the need for women's equality in the workplace and at home.*)

CHECK YOUR UNDERSTANDING

Have students answer the questions independently.

Answers:

  1. *B*

  2. *H*

  3. *A*

If students answer any questions incorrectly, have them reread the text to confirm their understanding. Then, they may proceed to ANALYZE THE TEXT on page 186.

 ENGLISH LEARNER SUPPORT

Oral Assessment Use the following questions to assess student comprehension and speaking skills.

  1. Why is Sandberg nervous when she starts at Facebook? *(She was worried she might fail.)*

  2. How does Sandberg think women can succeed in business? *(by overcoming their fear)*

  3. Why does Sandberg think relationships are important to being successful? *(because a good partner is supportive)* **SUBSTANTIAL/MODERATE**

ANALYZE THE TEXT

Possible answers:

1. **DOK 2:** *Be more assertive. Look for a partner who will support your career goals.*

2. **DOK 2:** *We can't stop being afraid because some things are scary. Because she goes on to talk about fighting our fears, it is clear that she knows fear will still exist.*

3. **DOK 3:** *This was the turning point when she realized that women were also held back by internal barriers, in addition to than external barriers.*

4. **DOK 3:** *She certainly makes a good case for it being a big factor, but not the biggest factor. The primary evidence she offers is her own happy marriage in addition to showing how this is better than other considerations.*

5. **DOK 4:** *Answers will vary. Possible answer: I like that she encourages us to be bolder. Fear often holds me back.*

RESEARCH

Remind students they should confirm any information they find by checking multiple websites and assessing the credibility of each one.

Connect As students research, they should try to find material that covers a broad range of time, both in terms of when articles were written and the span of Sandberg's life. Encourage students to look for articles written towards the beginning of Sandberg's career, and compare them with articles written more recently. Examining a wide range of articles over a larger span of time will help create a more comprehensive picture not only of Sandberg's career, but also of how she has been viewed in the public eye.

⟳ RESPOND

ANALYZE THE TEXT

Support your responses with evidence from the text. ▤ NOTEBOOK

1. **Summarize** In two or three sentences, summarize what the essay suggests could help women succeed in business. How does the summary help you identify Sandberg's message, audience, and purpose?

2. **Interpret** In paragraph 4, Sandberg writes that it is pointless to tell someone to be fearless. Explain what you think she means by this. How does this belief reveal her tone?

3. **Draw Conclusions** In paragraph 9, why does Sandberg describe the events from paragraph 8 as a "watershed moment"? How does this reveal her purpose?

4. **Evaluate** Do you think Sandberg makes a good case for a life partner being the biggest decision for a woman's career? Is it really bigger than education, interests, talent, or career choice? Explain.

5. **Connect** What aspects of Sandberg's essay do you think might relate to you and your choices or career interests? Use details from the text to support your response.

RESEARCH TIP
Start by searching for Sheryl Sandberg by name. Then, in addition to searching by name, add other terms, such as *Facebook, Google, billionaire, Harvard, husband,* or *family* to bring up articles more specific to what you're trying to find.

RESEARCH

Find newspaper and magazine articles about Sandberg. As you read, pick one or two topics, such as her career, her education, her relationships, or her family background, and look deeper into that topic. Consider how these aspects of her life might have affected her ideas. Keep track of your sources and the information you find in a chart like the one shown.

SOURCE/URL	FACT OR INSIGHT	POSSIBLE IMPACT
Response will vary.		

Connect Think about what you learned about Sandberg from the articles you selected. Did anything you learned conflict with what you learned about Sandberg in *Lean In*? Discuss your ideas with a partner.

WHEN STUDENTS STRUGGLE . . .

Reteaching: Understand Purpose Have students make a chart like the one shown here to organize some of the author's main points in this essay. Sandberg begins by detailing some experiences that lead to a realization. This realization helps her form some basic beliefs. These beliefs lead her to give her reader advice at the end of the essay. Have students reread the essay and use their charts to take notes on these three points to better understand Sandberg's purpose in her essay.

Experience	Beliefs	Advice

 For additional support, go to the **Reading Studio** and assign the following ᴸᴱⱽᴱᴸ **Level Up Tutorial: Author's Purpose.**

CREATE AND DEBATE

Write an Essay Write an autobiographical essay about something you have accomplished, something you have learned, or a relationship you value.

- ❏ Identify the accomplishment, lesson, or relationship.
- ❏ Share an anecdote that relates to the point you want to make.
- ❏ Include insights about anything that helped you reach your goal or build a relationship.
- ❏ Offer a suggestion for someone who might be interested in doing the same things.

Hold a Debate Not everyone agrees with Sandberg's approach to life. In a small group, talk about the pros and cons of some of Sandberg's ideas. Volunteer for a position you'd like to argue for or against, and then create a team with other students.

- ❏ Narrow the topic to some of Sandberg's ideas that can be debated in a reasonable amount of time.
- ❏ Use information from the essay, articles you've read, or your own experience.
- ❏ Outline the points you want to make for or against the selected issue or idea and state your position clearly.
- ❏ Hold a debate, listening carefully to the ideas of others and responding appropriately.

RESPOND TO THE ESSENTIAL QUESTION

 How can we share power and build alliances?

Gather Information Review your annotations and notes on *Lean In*. Then, add relevant information to your Response Log. As you determine which information to include, think about:

- advice that Sandberg offers
- Sandberg's purpose for writing
- Sandberg's ideas about success

Go to **Writing Narratives** in the **Writing Studio** for help with writing an essay.

Go to **Analyzing and Evaluating Presentations** in the **Speaking and Listening Studio** for help with holding a debate.

UNIT 2 RESPONSE LOG

Essential Question	Details from Texts
What does oppression look like?	
How do we gain our freedom?	
How can we share power and build alliances?	
How do we transform our lives?	

ACADEMIC VOCABULARY

As you write and discuss what you learned from the essay, be sure to use the Academic Vocabulary words. Check off each of the words that you use.

- ❏ **contrary**
- ❏ **founder**
- ❏ **ideological**
- ❏ **publication**
- ❏ **revolution**

CREATE AND DEBATE

Write an Essay Encourage students to create an outline before writing the bulk of their essay. Students may want to start by simply brainstorming responses to the items in the bullet point list, and then move on to organize that information into a basic outline of introduction, body, and conclusion.

For **writing support** for students at varying proficiency levels, see the **Text X-Ray** on page 178D.

Hold a Debate As a prewriting exercise, have students gather all their material and create a chart to organize their thoughts. Once they have decided their side, have them organize their points in support of their argument into a list on one side of their chart. On the other side, have students list arguments they think the other side might come up with, and try to brainstorm ways they can reasonably contradict those arguments.

RESPOND TO THE ESSENTIAL QUESTION

Allow time for students to add details from "Lean In" to their Unit 2 Response Logs.

CRITICAL VOCABULARY

Answers:

1. *b*

2. *b*

3. *b*

4. *a*

VOCABULARY STRATEGY:
Analyze Meaning of Idioms

Answers:

1. *a life-changing moment; a geographical term that refers to all water that empties into a single river, thus indicating a major change of path in life*

2. *being in agreement; to "sync" means to synchronize something*

3. *to be aimlessly moving around; unknown origin possibly linked to the random movement of grain in a mill*

 RESPOND

WORD BANK
demurred
watershed
internalize
parity

CRITICAL VOCABULARY

Practice and Apply Mark the letter of the best answer to each question. Then, explain your response.

1. A **watershed** event is more likely to be
   a. boring
   b. life-changing

2. People who achieve **parity** could be said to be
   a. subordinate
   b. equal

3. Someone who **demurred** when given a suggestion will have said
   a. yes
   b. no

4. If a person **internalizes** certain ideals, those ideals
   a. become part of the person
   b. are rejected by the person

 Go to the **Idioms, Slang, and Figurative Language** section of **Context Clues** in the **Vocabulary Studio** for more about idioms.

VOCABULARY STRATEGY: Analyze Meanings of Idioms

An **idiom** is a common figure of speech whose meaning is different from the literal meaning of its words. For example, *throw in the towel* comes from boxing, but it can be used in any situation where someone wants to quit. Idioms are more likely to appear in informal writing, and they often have nuanced meanings. For example, the idiom *throw in the towel* means "quit," but the connotation is quitting during a fight, probably that one cannot win.

Practice and Apply In her informal essay, Sandberg uses the following idioms. After each word or phrase, write the non-idiomatic definition of each word in the idiom. Then, write what the idiom means. Finally, explain any nuanced meanings or connotations of the idiom.

1. watershed moment

   _____

   _____

2. in sync

   _____

   _____

3. milling around

   _____

   _____

 ENGLISH LEARNER SUPPORT

Understand Idioms Explain that idioms are commonly used in informal settings, such as when people talk to friends or family members. Explain that idioms have meanings different from the literal meanings of the words. Write common idioms on the board and work with students to determine their meanings. For example: "raining cats and dogs" (raining heavily), "piece of cake" (easy), "back to the drawing board" (starting over), "ball is in your court" (it's your turn or up to you to decide). Ask students to share common idioms in their native languages and explain the idioms' meanings. **ALL LEVELS**

LANGUAGE CONVENTIONS:
Contested Usage

Some of the rules of grammar and usage have actually been contested, or deliberately broken, for decades. Contested usage is common in informal writing but is rarely accepted in formal writing. When breaking the rules, it is important to make certain that the writing is still clear and understandable, and it is best to break the rules only to create an effect or make a point.

One rule that Sandberg breaks frequently is the rule against beginning a sentence with a conjunction. In her essay, the conjunctions *And* and *But* begin several sentences. Her approach lends a chatty, personable tone to her writing, and it invites the reader in, making her advice more compelling.

> **And don't be afraid to be fully engaged in your career, even as you plan to have a family.**

Another rule that Sandberg breaks is the rule against using fragments. Complete sentences have a subject and a verb. However, Sandberg uses fragments for emphasis. Her use of fragments and repetition creates a rhythm and draws attention to her point—the number of things people fear.

> **Fear of making the wrong decision. Fear of drawing negative attention. Fear of overreaching. Fear of being judged. Fear of failure.**

Another common rule, though Sandberg does not break it in this essay, is the rule against ending sentences with prepositions. In informal writing, abiding by the rule can create awkward sentences. For example, "That is something I will not put up with" sounds much less awkward than "That is something up with which I will not put."

Practice and Apply   Write two or three sentences that employ contested usage. Then rewrite them employing the rules of formal English. With a partner, discuss which sentences sound better and where each type of sentence might be appropriate.

LANGUAGE CONVENTIONS:
Contested Usage

When working to understand contested usage and the difference between formal and informal texts, reading aloud is one of the best tools students can use. Have the students read the example sentences and other examples from the text aloud, pausing at the period breaks. Ask students to think about the rhythm of the writing, and what this type of sentence structure adds to the writing. Ask them to think about the question: *Is this type of writing more or less like spoken English?*

Practice and Apply   With their partner, have students work to flesh out their sentences into short paragraphs to give their contested usage sentences more context. Students should read one another's paragraphs and give feedback.

 ENGLISH LEARNER SUPPORT

Language Conventions   Use the following supports with students at varying proficiency levels:

- Help students annotate their texts to make it easier to spot contested usage. Students should underline the conjunction, circle the preposition, and highlight the sentence with the missing verb. **SUBSTANTIAL**

- Ask students to explain why each sentence is informal. Students should use the words *conjunction, preposition, subject,* and *verb* in their responses. Have students rewrite the sentences in formal English and discuss how the sentences are different.   **MODERATE**

- Review the usage issues with students. Ask students why they think these rules are contested and when it might be acceptable to break usage rules *(in informal settings)*. Have students write sentences that begin with a conjunction and sentences that are fragments. Then, have students exchange papers and correct the sentences so they are written in formal English.   **LIGHT**

COMPARE VOICE AND TONE

Before students work together to fill out their charts, remind them to think about some surface similarities between the two authors of the texts they are comparing. Ask students to think about what circumstantial things (e.g., being a woman) might contribute to the authors' tone in their writing.

ANALYZE THE TEXTS

Possible answers:

1. **DOK 2:** *It seems very likely the two women would agree. Adams talks about being friends and husbands making wives happy, and Sandberg talks about being partners and how both husbands and wives are happier when their contributions are more nearly equal.*

2. **DOK 4:** *Adams is clearly "leaning in" to the issues of her day, informed and definitely not shy about speaking up. She seems to epitomize Sandberg's advice to "sit at the table."*

3. **DOK 3:** *Both women use rapid-fire comments to express the importance of ideas: Adams with several questions at the beginning, Sandberg with the burst about different things women fear. Both also use word choice to underscore the things they care about.*

4. **DOK 3:** *Both works show that their authors are clearly focused on events around them, aware of what is going on, and interested in making a difference.*

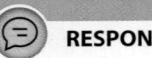

Collaborate & Compare

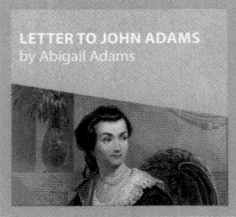

LETTER TO JOHN ADAMS
by Abigail Adams

from
LEAN IN
by Sheryl Sandberg

COMPARE VOICE AND TONE

"Letter to John Adams" and *Lean In* were written two centuries apart and under very different circumstances. You may have noticed differences in the voice and tone of each selection. However, there are some similarities between the texts as well. Review your annotations and notes to find similarities and differences in voice and tone in the two works.

In a small group, discuss how the voice and tone in these two works compare. Then, work together to complete the chart with examples from each text that illustrate tone or voice. In the third column, note if you think the examples are similar or different.

	"LETTER TO JOHN ADAMS"	*LEAN IN*	COMMENTS
Tone	. . . we are determined to foment a Rebelion . . .	. . . once we are aware, we cannot help but change.	Both are passionate about change.
Voice	. . . be more generous and favourable.to them . . .	I could not do without my husband, Dave.	Adams's voice is strong. Sandberg is personal and shares her life.

ANALYZE THE TEXTS

Discuss these questions in your group.

1. **Infer** Do you think the two women would agree on what makes an ideal marriage? Explain using examples from each text.

2. **Synthesize** How do Adams's comments about the approaching revolution suggest that she would have appreciated Sandberg's advice on pursuing success?

3. **Compare** Though the two writers have different styles, they have energy and passion in common. Use evidence from the texts—such as details related to style or tone—that demonstrate their energy and passion.

4. **Evaluate** What do these two works suggest about how involved the writers want to be in the world around them?

 ENGLISH LEARNER SUPPORT

Ask Questions Use the following questions to help students compare the selections.

1. How do you think Adams sees the ideal marriage? How do you think Sandberg sees the ideal marriage? Do you think their views are similar or different?

2. How does Adams show her strong feelings in her writing? How does Sandberg show her strong feelings? Give specific examples.

3. Do you think these writers want to change their world? Give specific examples.
   MODERATE

COLLABORATE AND PRESENT

Now, your group can continue exploring the ideas in these texts by collaborating to create an imagined dialogue between the two authors.

Go to **Giving a Presentation** in the **Speaking and Listening Studio** for help.

1. **Decide on topics** Discuss what each writer might want to know about the other one's life and concerns. For example, Adams might be glad to hear that slavery has ended, while Sandberg might be delighted to talk about the founding freedoms of the country.

2. **Conduct research** Find out more about each woman and the people in her life that would be of interest to the other writer. Combine this information with text taken from their writing to create an imagined discussion about freedom and relationships. You can alter the original text to make it feel more like part of a dialogue.

3. **Develop and combine ideas** You can use a chart like this to identify ideas, events, quotations, and concerns of the two individuals. Then, in the bottom box, combine the ideas and quotations to create a dialogue. Write enough dialogue that everyone in your group will have a few lines to read.

Abigail Adams	Sheryl Sandberg

Dialogue

4. **Present to the class** Decide who will read which lines of dialogue. Prepare a statement explaining what your dialogue hopes to accomplish and share it with the class. Make sure your listeners know who each speaker represents during the dialogue. Once everyone has had a chance to read his or her part, ask for input from the class. Ask for suggestions about other topics the two women might discuss, were they given the opportunity.

COLLABORATE AND PRESENT

Explain that though these authors may have very different backgrounds, they have many meeting points in terms of interest and basic experience.

1. **Decide on topics** Encourage students to discuss basic areas where the two writers might overlap in interests. Look for points of similarity, such as how both authors are women and have struggled because of that fact.

2. **Conduct research** As students research, urge them to look for specific commonalities and differences in the authors' backgrounds. Encourage them to look beyond the basic difference in era, and examine details which might affect anyone in any time.

3. **Develop and combine ideas** Instruct students to work together to add ideas to the chart, making sure each student gets to offer something for one of the boxes. As students write their dialogue, have them plan out who will read what and make sure the speaker changes at a natural break in lines and thought.

4. **Present to the class** Have students designate a speaker who will read the prepared statement. Encourage the students to read their lines in a way that sounds conversational, and not as though they are simply delivering a speech.

WHEN STUDENTS STRUGGLE . . .

Outline Ideas Some students may find it difficult to compare more than basic facts about authors who write in different times. Have students create a Venn diagram and list all the similarities and differences they can think of. Then, ask students to look deeper than facts such as, "both authors are women" or "the authors lived in different times." Tell students to ask questions about each author's purpose. Then, have them write the answers in their diagrams.

 For additional support, go to the **Reading Studio** and assign the following LEVEL UP **Level Up Tutorial: Taking Notes and Outlining.**

INDEPENDENT READING

READER'S CHOICE

Setting a Purpose Have students review their Unit 2 Response Log and think about what they've already learned about building a democracy. As they choose their Independent Reading selections, encourage them to consider what more they want to know.

NOTICE & NOTE

Explain that some selections may contain multiple signposts; others may contain only one. And the same type of signpost can occur many times in the same text.

LEARNING MINDSET

Curiosity Explain that curiosity leads to learning and a better understanding of literature and informational text. Being curious means asking questions and trying new things. Encourage students to explore different sides of a topic when they read, and to read sources with different opinions. Explain that they will gain a better understanding of the text and of the historical context by researching different viewpoints of the time.

 ESSENTIAL QUESTIONS

Review the four Essential Questions for this unit on page 95.

Reader's Choice

Setting a Purpose Select one or more of these options from your eBook to continue your exploration of the Essential Questions.

- Read the descriptions to see which text grabs your interest.
- Think about which genres you enjoy reading.

Notice & Note

In this unit, you practiced noticing and noting the signposts and asking big questions about nonfiction. As you read independently, these signposts and others will aid your understanding. Below are the anchor questions to ask when you read literature and nonfiction.

Reading Literature: Stories, Poems, and Plays	
Signpost	**Anchor Question**
Contrasts and Contradictions	Why did the character act that way?
Aha Moment	How might this change things?
Tough Questions	What does this make me wonder about?
Words of the Wiser	What's the lesson for the character?
Again and Again	Why might the author keep bringing this up?
Memory Moment	Why is this memory important?

Reading Nonfiction: Essays, Articles, and Arguments	
Signpost	**Anchor Question(s)**
Big Questions	What surprised me? What did the author think I already knew? What challenged, changed, or confirmed what I already knew?
Contrasts and Contradictions	What is the difference, and why does it matter?
Extreme or Absolute Language	Why did the author use this language?
Numbers and Stats	Why did the author use these numbers or amounts?
Quoted Words	Why was this person quoted or cited, and what did this add?
Word Gaps	Do I know this word from someplace else? Does it seem like technical talk for this topic? Do clues in the sentence help me understand the word?

© Houghton Mifflin Harcourt Publishing Company

ENGLISH LEARNER SUPPORT

Develop Fluency Select a passage from the text that matches students' reading abilities. Read the passage aloud while students follow along silently.

- Read aloud one sentence and have students repeat it after you. Then, have students reread the passage silently. Finally, ask short yes/no or either/or questions to check comprehension. **SUBSTANTIAL**
- Have students work with a partner to read the passage aloud. Then, have them reread silently. Ask 2 or 3 short questions to assess comprehension of key points or vocabulary. **MODERATE**

- Guide students to choose a passage that is challenging but not inaccessible. Have them read silently and make a list of key ideas. Then, ask students to orally summarize the main points. **LIGHT**

You can preview these texts in Unit 2 of your eBook.

Then, check off the text or texts that you select to read on your own.

SPEECH

Speech to the Virginia Convention
Patrick Henry

Discover the context for Henry's famous quotation, "Give me liberty or give me death!"

PUBLIC DOCUMENT

from **The United States Constitution: The Bill of Rights**

What rights did the founders believe were essential for the protection of citizens?

APHORISMS

from **Poor Richard's Almanack**
Benjamin Franklin

Discover some of Benjamin Franklin's wittier sayings about human nature.

HISTORY WRITING

Abigail Adams' Last Act of Defiance
Woody Holton

Learn how the wife of John Adams defied the patriarchal property laws of her time.

POEM

Democracy
Langston Hughes

How does a poet express his passionate plea for freedom?

Collaborate and Share   With a partner, discuss what you learned from at least one of your independent readings.

- Give a brief synopsis or summary of the text.
- Describe any signposts that you noticed in the text and explain what they revealed to you.
- Describe what you most enjoyed or found most challenging about the text. Give specific examples.
- Decide if you would recommend the text to others. Why or why not?

 Go to the **Reading Studio** for more resources on **Notice & Note**.

MATCHING STUDENTS TO TEXTS

Use the following information to guide students in choosing their texts.

Speech to the Virginia Convention   Lexile: 990L
  Genre: speech
  Overall Rating: Accessible

from **The United States Constitution: The Bill of Rights**   Lexile: 1580L
  Genre: public document
  Overall Rating: Challenging

from **Poor Richard's Almanack**   Lexile: 520L
  Genre: aphorisms
  Overall Rating: Accessible

Abigail Adams' Last Act of Defiance   Lexile: 1250L
  Genre: history writing
  Overall Rating: Challenging

Democracy
  Genre: poem
  Overall Rating: Accessible

Collaborate and Share   To assess how well students read the selections, walk around the room and listen to their conversations. Encourage students to be focused and specific in their comments.

 Online for Assessment

- Independent Reading Selection Tests

Encourage students to visit the **Reading Studio** to download a handy bookmark of **NOTICE & NOTE** signposts.

WHEN STUDENTS STRUGGLE . . .

Keep a Reading Log   As students read their selected texts, have them keep a reading log for each selection to note signposts and their thoughts about them. Use their logs to assess how well they are noticing and reflecting on elements of the texts.

Reading Log for (title)		
Location	**Signpost I Noticed**	**My Notes about It**

UNIT ② Tasks

- **WRITE A RESEARCH REPORT**
- **PRESENT A RESEARCH REPORT**

MENTOR TEXT

THOMAS JEFFERSON: THE BEST OF ENEMIES

Essay by RON CHERNOW

LEARNING OBJECTIVES

Writing Task

- Plan a research report explaining how people can share power and build alliances.
- Effectively organize ideas.
- Cite textual evidence in support of ideas.
- Develop a structured draft with a thesis statement.
- Use the mentor text to craft an interesting introduction and develop structure.
- Revise draft, incorporating feedback from peers.
- Edit draft to incorporate em dashes and to correct grammar and spelling.
- Publish the report as a podcast or blog.
- **Language** Write sentences correctly that paraphrase or include quotations.

Speaking and Listening Task

- Adapt research report for presentation.
- Practice effective verbal and nonverbal techniques.
- Practice with a partner or group.
- Listen actively and provide feedback to presenters.
- **Language** Share ideas about founding documents.

Assign the Writing Task in **Ed**.

Online

RESOURCES

- Unit 2 Response Log
- Writing Studio: Writing Informative Texts
- Listening and Speaking Studio: Giving a Presentation
- Grammar Studio: Module 14, Lesson 3: Dashes, Parentheses and Brackets

Language X-Ray: English Learner Support

Use the instruction below and the supports and scaffolds in the Teacher's Edition to help you guide students of different proficiency levels.

INTRODUCE THE WRITING TASK

Explain that a **research report** is a type of writing that presents information about a topic based on information gathered through research. Tell students that they can get information from articles, books, encyclopedias, and websites. Make sure students understand how to include information they gather. Provide sample sentence frames: *I can include research by _____ .* Show them how terms like *quoting* or *paraphrasing* can complete this sentence.

Brainstorm words and phrases related to the topic, such as *Constitution, Declaration of Independence,* and *two-party system.* Then, have students work with a partner to write a sentence about the topic of founding documents and their relationship to shared power and alliances. Tell students to use this sentence to begin their essays.

WRITING

Incorporate Research

Explain to students that whether they paraphrase a source or quote that source directly, they must give credit to that source in their writing. This is called citing sources.

Use the following supports with students at varying proficiency levels:

- Provide sentence frames to help students express their ideas: *The founders founded ____. They wrote important _____.* **SUBSTANTIAL**
- Explain the difference between quoting and paraphrasing by modeling phrases such as, *according to _____* and *_____ states that.* Then have students choose a different sentence and paraphrase it. Then have them write it as a direct quote. **MODERATE**
- Discuss the correct use of sources. Have students work in pairs to research and write their reports. Their reports should use at least one direct quote and one instance of paraphrasing. **LIGHT**

SPEAKING

Present a Report

Explain that students will adapt their written essays into a presentation. Tell students that they will not read their reports, but rather share some main points they learned. Provide the sentence frames: *My topic is _____. I believe that founding documents _____ .*

Use the following supports with students at varying proficiency levels:

- Have them identify the thesis statement in their reports. Then, work with students to complete the sentence frames. Have them practice saying the sentences to a partner. **SUBSTANTIAL**
- Have students complete the sentence frames and then add key details and a quotation. Pair students and have them practice reading their sentences with a partner. **MODERATE**
- Have students read their reports and identify the thesis, an important quotation, and key ideas. Have them complete the sentence frames and add additional sentences. Pair students and have them practice their presentations with a partner. **LIGHT**

WRITING

WRITE A RESEARCH REPORT

Inform students that they are going to be writing a research paper that draws from some of the texts they read in the unit. Review the elements of a research report. A **thesis statement** conveys the researcher's main conclusion, and it usually appears near the beginning or end of the introductory paragraph. The **body paragraphs** use examples and evidence to support the thesis statement. The **conclusion** summarizes the main points and leaves the reader with a compelling thought. Remind students to refer back to their Response Log for assistance as they begin planning and drafting their reports. Reflect with students on how a research report needs to include citations that come from reliable sources.

For **writing support** for students at varying proficiency levels, see the **Language X-Ray** on page 194B.

USE THE MENTOR TEXT

Point out that their research reports will be similar to the informational text "Thomas Jefferson: The Best of Enemies" in that it includes a thesis statement and evidence. Remind students that Chernow's essay uses a point-by-point comparison structure to present evidence for his thesis. The mentor text also illustrates the use of chronological order to organize and present information.

WRITING PROMPT

Review the prompt with students. Encourage them to ask questions about any part of the assignment that is unclear. Make sure they understand that the purpose of their report is to answer the question "How can we share power and build alliances?" using facts and examples from the texts they have read in Unit 2.

Write a Research Report

▤ Go to the **Writing Studio** for help writing a research report.

This unit focuses on what it takes to build and maintain a democracy, and how this relates to sharing power and building alliances among people and groups. For this writing task, you will write a research report—a type of informational writing grounded securely in careful research of a topic. Reports synthesize information from multiple relevant and credible primary and secondary sources. For an example of a well-written informational text you can use as a mentor text, review the article "Thomas Jefferson: The Best of Enemies."

As you write your research report, you can use the notes from your Response Log, which you filled out after reading the texts in this unit.

BUILDING A DEMOCRACY
THE REVOLUTIONARY PERIOD

Writing Prompt

Read the information in the box below.

This is the topic or context for your research report.

> The founding of the United States involved forming and documenting systems and shared fundamental principles.

Think carefully about the following question.

How might this Essential Question relate to a research report?

> How can we share power and build alliances?

Mark words that will help you begin your research.

Write a research report exploring how the founding documents, systems, or fundamental principles facilitate shared power and constructive alliances in our democracy.

Be sure to—

Review these points as you write and again when you finish. Make any needed changes.

- ❏ provide an introduction that catches the reader's attention, clearly states the topic, and includes a clear controlling idea or thesis statement
- ❏ support main ideas with evidence from sources
- ❏ examine sources you use for credibility, bias, and accuracy
- ❏ cite sources of any quoted text and ideas that are not your own
- ❏ organize information in a logical way
- ❏ connect related ideas effectively
- ❏ use appropriate word choice
- ❏ end by summarizing ideas or drawing an overall conclusion

---

⚙ LEARNING MINDSET

Asking for Help   Explain that asking for help is the most important learning tool that students have available. Every moment of confusion can also be treated as an opportunity to deepen understanding, if only the student will ask for help. There are several advantages to asking for help over struggling independently to solve problems. The first is that finding a way to ask the question is often the first step to better understanding the content. The second is that most people run into similar problems in their work; asking for help is almost always a way of assisting others in the class to better learn a topic. It might also help to highlight the fact that one's teacher is better able to succeed in his or her effort to teach a topic if the students are vocal in asking for help.

1 Plan

Before you start writing, you need to plan your report. First, consider your topic. Choose a topic that is not too narrow and not too broad. For example, you might compare other founding fathers or foundational documents, or you might explore the historical context that led to the creation of a foundational document. Remember to focus on how the founding documents, systems, or fundamental principles relate to our ability to share power and form alliances. Once you have a topic, formulate a research question. A good research question cannot be answered in a single word and should be open-ended. Next, find sources that will help you answer your research question. These should include primary and secondary sources, in either print or digital formats. Look for sources that are relevant and credible. Use the table below to assist you in planning your draft.

Research Report Planning Table	
Topic	
Research Question(s)	
Possible Sources	

Background Reading Review the notes you have taken in your Response Log that relate to the question, "How can we share power and build alliances?" Texts in this unit provide background reading that will help you formulate questions for your research. They also provide models of text structures and text features that will help you organize your report.

Go to **Writing Informative Texts: Developing a Topic** for help planning your research report.

Notice & Note
From Reading to Writing

As you plan your research report, apply what you've learned about signposts to your own writing. Remember that writers use common features, called signposts, to help convey their message to readers.

Think how you can incorporate **Signposts** into your essay.

 Go to the **Reading Studio** for more resources on **Notice & Note**.

Use the notes from your Response Log as you plan your research report.

UNIT 2 RESPONSE LOG

WRITING

1 PLAN

Explain to students that they are going to be doing more than just putting together other people's ideas. They need both a topic and an original approach to it. Have them think about looking at the topic through different "lenses" by creating fresh comparisons, by asking original questions, or by freewriting. As a class, work together to generate a list of research questions about a possible topic.

Then, review finding and using sources. Remind students that the first step in finding online sources is to choose search terms—terms that are neither so broad that they bring in a host of irrelevant sources nor so narrow that they leave out relevant sources. Point out the importance of evaluating sources and the importance of choosing only relevant and reliable sources. Finally, remind students to create source cards so they can create a Works Cited page.

■ English Learner Support

Acquire Academic Language Review the terms *topic, research,* and *sources.* Define each term and give examples. Help students complete the planning table. Allow students to use phrases or some words from their home language if necessary. Remind students to focus on the idea of shared power and alliances in the United States. **MODERATE**

NOTICE & NOTE

From Reading to Writing Remind students they can use **Quoted Words** to include the conclusions of experts or people who witnessed or participated in an event. Quoted Words can also be used to provide support for a point they are trying to make. Remind students to format direct quotations correctly and to give credit to the source.

Background Reading As students plan their reports, remind them to refer to the notes they took in the Response Log. They may also review the selections to find additional facts and examples to support ideas they want to include in their writing.

TO CHALLENGE STUDENTS

Use Sources Help students identify a range of primary and secondary sources to incorporate into their report. Direct students to online resources at the National Archives, the Smithsonian, and the Library of Congress. Guide students to use scholarly journals such as *The Journal of American History, The American Historical Review,* or *Perspectives on History.* Teach students to effectively use resources such as Google Scholar or Project Gutenberg to find primary, academic, and scholarly sources. Point out that researchers also must compare and contrast sources within a type. For example, a researcher might need to decide which of three biographies of an author will be the best source of information about the author's political views. Urge students to look for two or more sources per category for their topic.

WRITING

Organize Your Ideas Have students focus on identifying main ideas or points of comparison first and on understanding which details can be used to support them. If students used note cards, encourage them to group their cards by subject or idea and then put them in a logical order. Suggest that students create an outline after they have completed the graphic organizer. Have students draft a thesis statement after organizing their ideas and details.

■ English Learner Support

Write a Group Report Pair students of different proficiencies and have them work together to complete the graphic organizer and draft a report. If necessary, provide students with sentence frames to help them draft thesis statements. For example: *The founding documents created shared power and alliances because _____.* If students struggle, simplify the task by having them write an informative report about one founding document and its importance. **ALL LEVELS**

② DEVELOP A DRAFT

Point out that many research papers begin by providing interesting background information that leads up to the **thesis statement,** which is often the final sentence of the introductory paragraph. Explain that when writing the body paragraphs, students should incorporate information from their notes and graphic organizers and blend material from multiple sources. Remind students that they should only include information that supports the thesis. Explain that the **conclusion** to a research paper often includes a statement or restatement of the writer's individual interpretation. A thoughtful conclusion does more than just summarize main points—it leaves the reader with something compelling to think about. For example, a writer may include a thought-provoking question or a compelling quotation.

Point out that students can make changes to their writing plan during this stage. As they write, they may discover that they need a different example to support an idea, or that a particular detail belongs in a different paragraph. Encourage students to focus on getting down their ideas. Remind them to include specific, relevant details and examples from the texts to support each point of comparison.

 WRITING TASK

Go to **Writing Informative Texts: Organizing Ideas** for help organizing your ideas.

Organize Your Ideas After you have gathered ideas from your planning activities, you need to organize them in a way that will help you draft your research report. Identify the controlling idea, or thesis statement, which you will state in your introduction. A thesis is a succinct expression about your topic and research question that introduces the claim or main idea you intend to support with additional details, facts, and text evidence. You can use the chart below to map out the organizational structure of your report.

Thesis:

Main Idea/Point of Comparison 1:	Main Idea/Point of Comparison 2:	Main Idea/Point of Comparison 3:
Supporting Details	Supporting Details	Supporting Details

② Develop a Draft

You might prefer to draft your research report online.

Once you have completed your planning activities, you will be ready to begin drafting your research report. Refer to your graphic organizers as well as any notes you took as you studied the texts in this unit. These will provide a kind of map for you to follow as you write. Using a word processor or online writing application makes it easier to make changes or move sentences around later when you are ready to revise your first draft.

WHEN STUDENTS STRUGGLE . . .

Cite Sources Remind students that they need to include citations in their writing. Explain that introductory phrases in quotations in a research paper (such as *According to expert John Smith*) do the same job as dialogue tags (such as "he said" or "she replied") in fiction. These phrases help the reader keep track of the source of the quotation and help create a smooth, readable flow of language. Encourage students to look through their notes and add source phrases next to the corresponding information in the graphic organizer. Incorporating the source information will help them remember to cite sources as they write.

Use the Mentor Text

Author's Craft

A strong introduction is essential for capturing the reader's attention. In addition to your controlling idea or thesis statement, your introduction should include something that gets your reader interested in reading your report. Note how the writer begins in the middle of an action and immediately introduces the two "enemies" mentioned in the title of the article, "Thomas Jefferson: The Best of Enemies."

> On March 21, 1790, Thomas Jefferson belatedly arrived in New York City to assume his duties as the first Secretary of State after a five-year ministerial stint in Paris. Tall and lanky, with a freckled complexion and auburn hair, Jefferson, 46, was taken aback by the adulation being heaped upon the new Treasury Secretary, Alexander Hamilton, who had streaked to prominence in his absence.

The writer begins with Jefferson in motion—the reader can almost see him arriving in busy New York and being confused as to why this young upstart was getting so much attention.

Apply What You've Learned To capture your reader's attention and to make sure your topic is clear, consider plunging straight into a description of an event that is a significant moment in the development of a document or in the life of a historical person, or that is a turning point in some other way.

Genre Characteristics

Often a text about a historical person or event will use a combination of chronological order and another structure, such as cause and effect or compare and contrast. Chronological order invites the reader to see history as a narrative. Whatever structure is used, main ideas need supporting details and examples. Notice how the author of "Thomas Jefferson: The Best of Enemies" uses chronological order within an overall compare and contrast structure.

> Instead, the feud worsened. In early 1793, a Virginia Congressman named William Branch Giles began to harry Hamilton . . . With prodigious bursts of energy, Hamilton complied with those inhuman demands, foiling his opponents. Jefferson then committed an unthinkable act.

The author uses chronological structure in this passage, even though the overall article is compare and contrast. Words like "In early 1793" and "then" signal chronological order.

Apply What You've Learned In your plan, choose where you can use a secondary text structure to enhance your support for a main idea.

WHY THIS MENTOR TEXT?

"Thomas Jefferson: The Best of Enemies" is a good example of a well-researched article about the history and principles of the United States. Chernow includes facts, dates, and events to support his thesis. Use the instruction below to help students use the mentor text as a model for using sources in an engaging and informative way.

USE THE MENTOR TEXT

Author's Craft Point out that Chernow sets a scene to start his text. He gives information about when and why Jefferson comes to New York City, essentially having Jefferson enter the scene like a character. He then describes Jefferson's appearance and emotions. In doing so, he makes Jefferson seem real, accessible, and interesting to the reader. Ask students to consider how they can make the people or events they are writing about "come alive" and how they can begin their research papers in a way that interests the reader.

Genre Characteristics Explain to students that chronological order is often used when writing about history because it helps the reader keep track of events. Examining the order in which events occurred can also reveal important causes and effects. The advantage of chronological order is that it makes articles easy to understand by laying out how events unfolded, step by step. There are also disadvantages, however, because chronology alone can become dull for readers. Encourage students to use other types of structures to reveal or highlight important information.

ENGLISH LEARNER SUPPORT

Acquire Academic Language Review or define the terms *chronological order, cause and effect,* and *compare and contrast*. Help students list signal words that are used for each type of organizational structure. Have students copy the chart and use the words in their papers.

Chronological order	Cause and effect	Compare and contrast
first, next, then, later, finally in (year), on (date), before, after	*because, since, as a result, this led to, therefore, that's why, this is why*	*similar, different, alike, however, in contrast*

MODERATE/LIGHT

WRITING

③ REVISE

Remind students that revising means evaluating the development, organization, and language of their reports. Review the chart with students and explain how it can guide their revisions. As students revise, have them ask themselves if they included enough explanation and evidence to support each point. If needed, tell them to add explanations, including correctly cited facts and their own insights or interpretations.

Have students answer each question in the chart to determine how they can improve their drafts. Invite volunteers to model their revision techniques.

With a Partner Have students ask peer reviewers to evaluate the flow of ideas and their supporting evidence by answering the following questions:

- Which pieces of evidence are unclear? Why?
- What questions about the topic are unanswered?
- What transitions could be added to improve flow or clarity?

Students should use the reviewer's feedback to add relevant facts, details, examples, or quotations that further develop their main points.

 WRITING TASK

 Go to **Writing Informative Texts: Precise Language and Vocabulary** for help revising your report.

③ Revise

On Your Own Once you have written your draft, you'll want to go back and look for ways to improve your research report. As you reread and revise, think about whether you have achieved your purpose. The Revision Guide will help you focus on specific elements to make your writing stronger.

Revision Guide

Ask Yourself	Tips	Revision Techniques
1. Does my introduction engage the reader and contain a thesis statement that clearly identifies the topic?	**Highlight** sentences that get the audience interested. **Underline** your thesis statement.	**Add** vivid language and details to interest the reader. **Reword** your thesis statement to **clarify** the topic.
2. Do I present relevant text evidence to support my thesis statement and central ideas?	**Highlight** each central idea. **Underline** evidence that supports each idea and **note** evidence that seems weak.	**Add** evidence for any idea that is not supported. **Change** evidence that does not offer strong support.
3. Is my report logically organized with smooth transitions linking ideas and evidence?	**Note** major sections that reflect your organization. **Underline** each transitional word or phrase.	**Reorder** paragraphs if needed. **Add** transitions to **clarify** relationships between ideas.
4. Do I use formal, precise language and maintain an objective tone throughout?	**Highlight** slang and informal language. **Underline** instances of biased perspective.	**Reword** text to avoid informal language. **Replace** sentences that express an attitude or opinion.
5. Does my conclusion follow logically from the ideas I present?	**Note** where the conclusion summarizes your ideas.	**Add** a closing statement if needed to sum up the information your report presents.

ACADEMIC VOCABULARY
As you conduct your **peer review,** be sure to use these words.

- ❏ **contrary**
- ❏ **founder**
- ❏ **ideological**
- ❏ **publication**
- ❏ **revolution**

With a Partner Once you and your partner have worked through the Revision Guide on your own, exchange papers and evaluate each other's draft in a **peer review.** Focus on providing revision suggestions for at least three of the items mentioned in the chart. Explain why you think your partner's draft should be revised and what your specific suggestions are.

When receiving feedback from your partner, listen attentively and ask questions to make sure you fully understand the revision suggestions.

 ENGLISH LEARNER SUPPORT

Acquire Academic Language Review and define key terms in the "Ask Yourself" column:

- *thesis statement:* an expression of the main idea and purpose for writing
- *support:* facts, quotations, dates, or explanations that support the thesis
- *transitions:* words or phrases that connect ideas, such as *first, next, then,* and *finally*
- *objective:* unbiased; free of opinion
- *conclusion:* last section of a research paper that restates the thesis

Allow students to ask for clarification of these terms and their meanings.   **MODERATE**

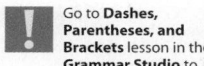

④ Edit

Once you have addressed the organization, development, and flow of ideas in your research report, you can look to improve the finer points of your draft. Edit for the proper use of standard English conventions and make sure to correct any misspellings or grammatical errors.

> ⚠ Go to **Dashes, Parentheses, and Brackets** lesson in the **Grammar Studio** to learn more.

Language Conventions

Dashes An em dash—the long dash you often see used in the middle of sentences—allows writers to make ideas in a long sentence clear, especially when there are already other punctuation marks in the sentence.

- Em dashes can be used in pairs, the same way we use parentheses.
- An em dash can also be used alone, to emphasize a word or short phrase at the end of a sentence.

The chart contains examples of em dash pairs from "Thomas Jefferson: The Best of Enemies."

from "Thomas Jefferson: The Best of Enemies"	Use of Em Dashes
He therefore set to work at Treasury with more unrestrained gusto than Jefferson—who had monitored the Constitutional Convention from his post in Paris—did at State.	This set of dashes gives additional information about something that happened previously but is relevant to the point.
Hamilton—brilliant, brash and charming—had the self-reliant reflexes of someone who had always had to live by his wits.	This set of dashes sets off a description of Hamilton.
He was emphatic in his views—Hamilton labeled him "an atheist in religion and a fanatic in politics"— but shrank from open conflict.	This set of dashes sets off a quotation from a primary document that helps support the author's point.

⑤ Publish

Finalize your research report and choose a way to share it with your audience. Consider these options:

- Present your report as a podcast.
- Post your report as a blog on a classroom or school website.

WHEN STUDENTS STRUGGLE . . .

Proofread for Parenthetical Documentation Remind students that every word and punctuation mark in every paper should be proofread; in research papers, however, it is especially important to proofread the documentation of sources. Have students work with a partner and take turns proofreading, with the writer reading aloud (including capitalization and punctuation marks) as the partner checks another copy of the draft.

④ EDIT

Suggest that students read their drafts aloud to assess how clearly and smoothly they have presented their ideas. If the text sounds choppy in places or if the connection between certain ideas is unclear, they should consider combining simple sentences into compound or complex sentences. Students should be checking for grammatical errors and misspellings.

LANGUAGE CONVENTIONS

Use Dashes Review the information about em dashes with students. Then discuss the example sentences in the chart, asking students to rewrite the sentences without the dashes and compare the effect. For example: *Hamilton was brilliant, brash and charming, and he had the self-reliant reflexes of someone who had always had to live by his wits.* Without the dashes, Hamilton's important characteristics are not emphasized.

■ English Learner Support

Use Punctuation Em dashes are not common in some languages or are used in different ways. For example, in Polish, em dashes are used to replace the open quotation mark and no end quotation mark is used. Point out how em dashes and hyphens are different. Then read aloud one of the example sentences and help students understand how em dashes are used by writing the sentence without the em dashes and phrase. Explain that the sentence is still grammatically correct and understandable, but some important information is lost. Have students add one or a pair of em dashes in their writing. **MODERATE/LIGHT**

⑤ PUBLISH

Students can present their essays as blog posts on a school website. Encourage others to read the essays and to write comments about them. The authors can then respond to the comments. **MODERATE/LIGHT**

WRITING

USE THE SCORING GUIDE

Have students read over the scoring guide and mark key words and ideas. Allow time for discussion and questions. If possible, provide examples of student writing (anonymously, preferably from several years in the past or another school) that model excellent, middle-of-the road, and weaker organization, development, and use of language and conventions. Then, have partners exchange final drafts of their research report. Ask them to score their partner's report using the scoring guide. Each student should write a paragraph explaining the reasons for the score he or she awarded in each category.

 **WRITING TASK**

Use the scoring guide to evaluate your research report.

	Organization/ Progression	Development of Ideas	Use of Language and Conventions
Writing Task Scoring Guide: Research Report			
4	• The organization is effective and logical throughout the report. • Transition words and phrases effectively link related ideas and evidence.	• The introduction engages the reader's attention and includes a thesis statement that clearly identifies the topic. • The topic is strongly developed with relevant facts, concrete details, interesting quotations, and examples from the texts. • The concluding section capably follows from and supports the ideas presented.	• The writing reflects a formal style and an objective, knowledgeable tone. • Language is vivid and precise. • Sentence structures vary and have a rhythmic flow. • Spelling, capitalization, and punctuation are correct. Grammar and usage are correct. • Quotations and citations are properly formatted.
3	• The organization is confusing in a few places. • Transitions are needed in a few places to link related ideas and evidence.	• The introduction could do more to attract the reader's curiosity; the thesis statement identifies a topic. • One or two key points could use additional support in the form of relevant facts, concrete details, quotations, and examples from the texts. • The concluding section mostly follows from and supports the ideas presented.	• The style is inconsistent in a few places, and the tone is subjective at times. • Vague language is used in a few places. • Sentence structures vary somewhat. • Some spelling, capitalization, and punctuation mistakes occur. Some grammatical and usage errors are repeated in the report. • Some errors are found in quotation and citation format.
2	• The organization is confusing in some places and often doesn't follow a pattern. • More transition words and phrases are needed throughout to link ideas and evidence.	• The introduction provides some information about a topic but does not include a thesis statement. • Most key points need additional support in the form of relevant facts, concrete details, quotations, and examples from the texts. • The concluding section is confusing and does not follow from the ideas presented.	• The style is too informal; the tone conveys subjectivity and a lack of understanding of the topic. • Vague, general language is used in many places. • Sentence structures barely vary, and some fragments or run-on sentences are present. • Spelling, capitalization, and punctuation are often incorrect but do not make reading the report difficult. Grammar and usage are incorrect in many places, but the writer's ideas are still clear. • Many errors are found in quotation and citation format.
1	• A logical organization is not used; information is presented randomly. • Transitions are not used, making the essay difficult to understand.	• The appropriate elements of an introduction are missing. • Facts, details, quotations, and examples from the texts are missing. • The report lacks an identifiable concluding section.	• The style and tone are inappropriate for the report. • Language is too vague or general to convey the information. • Repetitive sentence structure, fragments, and run-on sentences make the writing difficult to follow. • Spelling, capitalization, and punctuation are incorrect throughout. Grammatical and usage errors change the meaning of the writer's ideas. • Many errors are found in quotation and citation format.

Present a Research Report

 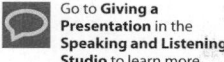

You will now adapt your research report for presentation to your classmates. You also will listen to their presentations, ask questions to better understand their ideas, and help them improve their work.

Go to **Giving a Presentation** in the **Speaking and Listening Studio** to learn more.

1 Adapt Your Report for Presentation

Review your research report and use the chart below to guide you as you adapt your report and create a script and presentation materials.

Presentation Planning Chart		
Title and Introduction	How will you revise your title and introduction to capture the listener's attention? Is there a more concise way to state your controlling idea or thesis?	
Audience	What information will your audience already know? What information can you exclude? What should you add?	
Effective Language and Organization	Which parts of your research report should be simplified? Where can you add transitions to help your listeners follow your train of thought?	
Visuals	What images or graphics would help clarify ideas or add interest? What text should appear on screen?	

PRESENT A RESEARCH REPORT

Introduce students to the Listening and Speaking task by discussing what makes reading an informational text different from hearing someone speak about the same topic. Point out that presenters often include visuals, videos, or sound clips to add information or support points. It is important for listeners to pay attention to these elements in order to better understand the topic. Listeners should also note when a speaker changes the volume of his or her voice because that might indicate important information. Point out that one benefit of listening to a presentation is the opportunity to ask questions after the presentation. When reading a text, readers cannot ask the author to clarify points or provide additional information.

1 ADAPT YOUR REPORT FOR PRESENTATION

Have students read the questions in the chart. Then work with the class to list some general principles for presenting information orally. (Examples: Use shorter sentences. Repeat important ideas. Use interesting examples to keep the audience engaged.) Point out that a strong presentation

- brings the subject matter to life
- is planned with the audience in mind
- uses technology effectively
- presents accurate, properly credited details from a variety of sources
- takes the form of explanation and discussion, not of reading aloud

Suggest that students make note cards or use a storyboard if they want to create a script in that form.

 For **speaking support** for students at varying proficiency levels, see the **Language X-Ray** on page 194B.

© Houghton Mifflin Harcourt Publishing Company

SPEAKING AND LISTENING

2 PRACTICE WITH A PARTNER OR GROUP

Review the information and tips with the class, ensuring that all the terms and ideas are clear. Explain that practicing will improve their delivery and soothe their nerves. In addition to practicing with a partner or group, students can practice in front of a mirror or before their friends or family members. Students can also practice by recording their presentations and watching it.

Remind group members that they should provide constructive feedback. For example, they might note that an important idea wasn't clear or that the speaker didn't speak loudly enough. They may also note that a visual aid might be helpful at a specific point in the presentation.

3 DELIVER YOUR PRESENTATION

Set aside time for all students to give their presentations. When everyone has finished, ask students to share their thoughts on how their classmates' feedback helped them improve their performance.

SPEAKING AND LISTENING TASK

As you work to improve your presentations, be sure to follow discussion rules:

- ❑ listen closely to each other
- ❑ don't interrupt
- ❑ stay on topic
- ❑ ask only helpful, relevant questions
- ❑ provide only clear, thoughtful, and direct answers

2 Practice with a Partner or Group

Once you've completed your draft, practice with a partner or group to improve both the presentation and your delivery.

Practice Effective Verbal Techniques

- ❑ **Enunciation** Replace words that you stumble over, and rearrange sentences so that your delivery is smooth.
- ❑ **Voice Modulation and Pitch** Use your voice to display enthusiasm and emphasis.
- ❑ **Speaking Rate** Speak slowly enough that listeners understand you. Pause now and then to let them consider important points.
- ❑ **Volume** Remember that listeners at the back of the room need to hear you.

Practice Effective Nonverbal Techniques

- ❑ **Eye Contact** Try to let your eyes rest on each member of the audience at least once.
- ❑ **Facial Expression** Smile, frown, or raise an eyebrow to show your feelings or to emphasize points.
- ❑ **Gestures** Stand tall and relaxed, and use natural gestures—shrugs, nods, or shakes of your head—to add meaning and interest to your presentation.

Provide and Consider Advice for Improvement

As a listener, pay close attention. Take notes about ways that presenters can improve their presentations and more effectively use verbal and nonverbal techniques. Paraphrase and summarize each presenter's key ideas and main points to confirm your understanding, and ask questions to clarify any confusing ideas.

As a presenter, listen closely to questions and consider ways to revise your presentation to make sure your points are clear and logically sequenced. Remember to ask for suggestions about how you might change onscreen text or images to make your presentation clearer and more interesting.

3 Deliver Your Presentation

Use the advice you received during practice to make final changes to your presentation. Then, using effective verbal and nonverbal techniques, present it to your classmates.

© Houghton Mifflin Harcourt Publishing Company

WHEN STUDENTS STRUGGLE . . .

Prepare and Practice When preparing to speak to a group or give a presentation, it is best to prepare at least five note cards (or index cards) ahead of time with the main ideas of the introduction, three supporting ideas or evidence, and a conclusion. These cards will provide reminders of the ideas that were worked out on paper ahead of time. It is best not to write down an entire speech and read it aloud. Instead, five note cards with simple bullet points or a short sentence on each allow the presenter to connect to the audience while also staying narrowly focused on the planned remarks. However, presenting in this way, without a written speech, does require practice. Direct students to prepare five note cards and then practice their presentations in pairs. Another important benefit of practice is working on accurate timing of the planned comments.

Reflect on the Unit

By completing your research report, you have created a writing product that pulls together and expresses your thoughts about the reading you have done in this unit. Now is a good time to reflect on what you have learned.

Reflect on the Essential Questions

• Review the four Essential Questions on page 95. How have your answers to these questions changed in response to the texts you read in this unit?

• What are some examples from the texts you read that show how people share power and build alliances?

Reflect on Your Reading

• Which selections were the most interesting or surprising to you?

• From which selection did you learn the most about how people share power and build alliances?

Reflect on the Writing Task

• What difficulties did you encounter while working on your research report? How might you avoid them next time?

• What part of the research report was the easiest and hardest to write? Why?

• What improvements did you make to your research report as you were revising?

UNIT 2 SELECTIONS
• The Declaration of Independence
• "Thomas Jefferson: The Best of Enemies"
• *American Experience*: "Alexander Hamilton"
• "A Soldier for the Crown"
• from *The Autobiography*
• "On Being Brought from Africa to America"
• "Sympathy"
• Letter to John Adams
• from *Lean In*

REFLECT ON THE UNIT

Have students reflect on the questions independently and write some notes in response to each one. Then have students meet with partners or in small groups to discuss their reflections. Circulate during these discussions to identify the questions that are generating the liveliest conversations. Wrap up with a whole-class discussion focused on these questions.

LEARNING MINDSET

Problem Solving Remind students that the process of understanding anything new is always a process of problem solving. Everyone experiences difficulties in learning of one kind or another, and everyone has different ways of solving the problem of learning. For some, it is best to write notes and create graphic organizers to restructure information as a way of understanding it. For others, it helps to take a break from study, then return to the material later, when refreshed. Although it might seem strange that stopping study is a way of learning, the brain needs a break in order to absorb new information. Taking short breaks is a good way of solving the problem of feeling overwhelmed when learning new information or skills.

Instructional Overview and Resources

	Instructional Focus	Online Ed Resources
 **Unit Introduction** **The Individual and Society**	**Unit 3 Essential Question** **Unit 3 Academic Vocabulary**	**Stream to Start:** The Individual and Society **Unit 3 Response Log**

ANALYZE & APPLY

from **"Song of Myself"** Poem by Walt Whitman Lexile N/A	**Reading** • Analyze Poetry • Analyze Theme and Structure **Writing:** Write an Argument **Speaking and Listening:** Debate a Position	◉ **Audio** **Close Read Screencast:** Modeled Discussion **Reading Studio:** Notice & Note **Writing Studio:** Writing Arguments **Speaking and Listening Studio:** Analyzing and Evaluating Presentations
"My Friend Walt Whitman" Essay by Mary Oliver Lexile 1030L	**Reading** • Analyze Essays • Analyze Development of Key Ideas **Writing:** Write an Essay **Speaking and Listening:** Discuss with a Small Group **Vocabulary:** Use Print and Digital Resources **Language Conventions:** Informal Style	◉ **Audio** **Reading Studio:** Notice & Note **Writing Studio:** Writing Informative Texts **Speaking and Listening Studio:** Participating in Collaborative Discussions **Vocabulary Studio:** Using Reference Resources
 **Poems by Emily Dickinson** Lexile N/A	**Reading** • Analyze Theme and Structure • Analyze Figurative Language • Analyze Sound Devices . **Writing:** Write a Poem **Speaking and Listening:** Discuss Poems	◉ **Audio** **Reading Studio:** Notice & Note **Writing Studio:** Writing as a Process **Speaking and Listening Studio:** Participating in Collaborative Discussions
 **"In the Season of Change"** Poem by Teresa Palomo Acosta Lexile N/A	**Reading** • Analyze Sound Devices • Analyze Lines and Stanzas • Analyze Imagery **Writing:** Write a Poem **Speaking and Listening:** Present a Poem	◉ **Audio** **Reading Studio:** Notice & Note **Writing Studio:** Writing as a Process **Speaking and Listening Studio:** Giving a Presentation

SUGGESTED PACING: 30 DAYS	**Unit Introduction**	*from* **Song of Myself**	**My Friend Walt Whitman**	**Poems by Emily Dickinson**				**In the Season of Change**
	1	2 3	4 5 6	7 8 9 10 11 12				13 14

English Learner Support	Differentiated Instruction	Assessment
• Understand Figurative Language • Build Background Knowledge		
• Text X-Ray • Acquire Academic Vocabulary • Use Available Support • Understand Inverted Word Order • Oral Assessment	**When Students Struggle** • Summarize • Reteaching: Analyze Theme **To Challenge Students** • Research the Poet's Attitudes	**Selection Test**
• Text X-Ray • Use Cognates • Understand Supporting Ideas and Details • Oral Assessment • Vocabulary Strategy • Language Conventions	**When Students Struggle** • Identify Thesis Statements • Reteaching: Analyzing Essays	**Selection Test**
• Text X-Ray • Punctuation and Print Cues • Analyze Language • Oral Assessment	**When Students Struggle** • Interpret Images	**Selection Test**
• Text X-Ray • Understand Sound Devices • Oral Assessment	**When Students Struggle** • Analyze Sound Devices • Reteaching: Analyze Author's Craft	**Selection Test**

from **Walden** /
from **Last Child in the Woods**
15 16 17 18 19 20

The Minister's Black Veil /
The Pit and the Pendulum
21 22 23 24 25

**Independent
Reading**
26 27

End of Unit
28 29 30

The Individual and Society **204B**

UNIT 3 Continued

	Instructional Focus	**Online Ed Resources**

COLLABORATE & COMPARE

from **Walden** Essay by Henry David Thoreau Lexile 1250L **Mentor Text** *from* **Last Child in the Woods** Informational Text by Richard Louv Lexile 1190L	**Reading** • Summarize • Analyze Author's Craft **Writing:** Write an Essay **Speaking and Listening:** Present an Essay **Vocabulary:** Draw Conclusions about Word Meanings **Language Conventions:** Rhetorical Questions	🔊 **Audio** **Reading Studio:** Notice & Note **Writing Studio:** Conducting Research **Speaking and Listening Studio:** Giving a Presentation **Vocabulary Studio:** Using Context Clues
Collaborate and Compare	**Reading:** Compare Main Ideas	**Speaking and Listening Studio:** Giving a Presentation
"The Minister's Black Veil" Short Story by Nathaniel Hawthorne Lexile 1260L	**Reading** • Analyze Literary Elements • Analyze Structure **Writing:** Write an Essay **Speaking and Listening:** Discuss with a Small Group **Vocabulary:** Nuances in Word Meanings **Language Conventions:** Appositives and Appositive Phrases	🔊 **Audio** **Reading Studio:** Notice & Note **Writing Studio:** Writing Arguments **Speaking and Listening Studio:** Participating in Collaborative Discussions **Vocabulary Studio:** Denotation and Connotation **Grammar Studio:** Appositives and Appositive Phrases
"The Pit and the Pendulum" Short Story by Edgar Allan Poe Lexile 1020L	**Reading** • Analyze Mood • Analyze Plot Structure **Writing:** Write an Adaptation **Speaking and Listening:** Present an Adaptation **Vocabulary:** Context Clues **Language Conventions:** Using Semicolons	🔊 **Audio** **Reading Studio:** Notice & Note **Writing Studio:** Writing Narratives **Speaking and Listening Studio:** Using Media in a Presentation **Vocabulary Studio:** Using Context Clues **Grammar Studio:** Semicolons and Colons
Collaborate and Compare	**Reading:** Compare Themes	**Speaking and Listening Studio:** Giving a Presentation

Online Ed

INDEPENDENT READING

The Independent Reading selections are only available in the eBook. 📖 **Go to the Reading Studio for more information on NOTICE & NOTE.**	 *from* Nature Essay by Ralph Waldo Emerson Lexile 990L	 *from* Self-Reliance Essay by Ralph Waldo Emerson Lexile 980L

END OF UNIT

Writing Task: Write an Explanatory Essay **Reflect on the Unit**	**Writing:** Write an Explanatory Essay **Language Conventions:** Use Semicolons	**Unit 3 Response Log** **Mentor Text:** *from* Last Child in the Woods **Writing Studio:** Writing Informative Texts **Grammar Studio:** Semicolons and Colons

English Learner Support	Differentiated Instruction	Online Ed Assessment
• Text X-Ray • Use Cognates • Use Prior Knowledge and Experiences • Homographs • Understand Contrasts • Oral Assessment • Explain with Increasing Specificity and Detail	**When Students Struggle** • Figurative Language • Audience **To Challenge Students** • Compare and Contrast	Selection Test
• Pronunciation Strategy		
• Text X-Ray • Use Visuals • Use Cognates • Develop Vocabulary • Oral Assessment • Vocabulary Strategy • Language Convention	**When Students Struggle** • Visualize Details • Reteaching: Effect of the Setting on the Plot **To Challenge Students** • Visual Art Connection • Puritans and Sin	Selection Test
• Text X-Ray • Vocabulary Strategy • Use Cognates • Language Conventions • Use High-Frequency Words • Demonstrate Comprehension • Understand Interjections • Use Context • Use Visuals • Oral Assessment	**When Students Struggle** • Use a Graphic Organizer • Unpack Syntax • Multiple-Meaning Words • Reteaching: Use Context **To Challenge Students** • Evaluate Writer's Craft • Mimic the Writer's Style	Selection Test
• Ask Questions	**When Students Struggle** • Determine the Theme	

"The Pointlessness of Unplugging" Article by Casey N. Cep **Lexile 1190L**	"The Raven" Poem by Edgar Allan Poe "Pastoral" Poem by Jennifer Chang	Selection Tests

END OF UNIT

| • Language X-Ray
• Identify Cognates
• Understand Text Structure
• Write and Revise
• Use Semicolons | **When Students Struggle**
• Add Relevant Evidence
• Use Semicolons

To Challenge Students
• Gather Additional Evidence | Unit Test |

DISCUSS THE QUOTATION

Tell students that this quotation is from "Self-Reliance," published in 1841 in Emerson's first volume of *Essays*. He had set forth his ideas of transcendental philosophy five years before in *Nature,* in which he emphasized self-reliance and individuality. In his essay "Self-Reliance," Emerson argues that people should trust their own judgment about what is right and wrong, rather than conform to other people's opinions. However, he also insists that we should feel free to change our beliefs, and he concludes by offering historical examples to support his view that "[t]o be great is to be misunderstood."

Ask students how this quotation illustrates Emerson's belief in individual judgment. How would he respond to the idea of herd mentality, in which people's behavior is influenced by their peers?

■ English Learner Support

Understand Figurative Language Tell students that the "iron string" in this quotation is an example of **figurative language,** in which a phrase goes beyond the literal meaning of the words. In this case, Emerson uses an iron string, such as a piano or guitar string, to represent the individual's conscience. Suggest that students try to put the quotation into their own words. **LIGHT**

THE INDIVIDUAL AND SOCIETY

LITERATURE OF THE AMERICAN RENAISSANCE

> " Trust thyself: every heart vibrates to that iron string. "
>
> —Ralph Waldo Emerson

204   Unit 3

LEARNING MINDSET

Setting Goals Remind students that setting goals is an important part of having a learning mindset, and that everyone learns at a different speed. Encourage students to set their own personal goals and track their progress to help them reach their goals.

Discuss the **Essential Questions** with your whole class or in small groups. As you read The Individual and Society, consider how the selections explore these questions.

? *ESSENTIAL QUESTION:*

In what ways do we seek to remain true to ourselves?

The transcendentalists broke with the Puritan tradition, which emphasized rigid obedience to the laws of society. Transcendentalism exalted the dignity of the individual and stressed the ideals of optimism, freedom, and self-reliance. The notion of the authentic self has become part of the national consciousness. This desire to be ourselves guides us in everything we do. How can we live our lives authentically in a world where so much seems to be false?

? *ESSENTIAL QUESTION:*

How do we relate to the world around us?

In the early 19th century, the Romantics reacted to the negative effects of industrialization—the commercialism, hectic pace, and lack of conscience—by turning to nature and to the self for simplicity, truth, and beauty. In today's world, technological advances are constantly changing the way we do everything, especially the ways we interact with others. How do we make sense of a world in which change seems to be the only constant?

? *ESSENTIAL QUESTION:*

What do we secretly fear?

Fear is a natural response to danger, either real or imagined. Without fear, we would not be able to protect ourselves from real threats. Many people fear the unknown or have seemingly irrational fears. Edgar Allan Poe and other Gothic writers were able to make fear exciting, and modern masters of horror, such as Stephen King and director John Carpenter, continue to use fear to entertain. Are your secret fears real or imagined?

? *ESSENTIAL QUESTION:*

When should we stop and reflect on our lives?

Reflecting on your life can help you learn from your mistakes, give you great ideas, and help you put things in perspective. Some people only pause to reflect during major milestones in their lives. People who frequently take time to reflect tend to be happier than those who don't. How might regularly thinking about your life, either in a journal or simply as you go about your day, help you?

The Individual and Society 205

Connect to the

ESSENTIAL QUESTIONS

Read aloud the Essential Questions and the paragraphs that follow them. Open the discussion of each idea by having students respond to the questions that conclude each paragraph.

? *ESSENTIAL QUESTION:*

In what ways do we seek to remain true to ourselves?

Tell students that although we strive to be individuals, it is often easier to give in to peer pressure or "herd mentality" than to stick up for our own beliefs. Invite students to share ways of resisting pressure to conform when it goes against their conscience. Then ask students to share ways in which they embrace their individuality.

? *ESSENTIAL QUESTION:*

How do we relate to the world around us?

Encourage students to discuss the ways they interact with others and with their physical environment. Ask them how have those interactions changed over time and why.

? *ESSENTIAL QUESTION:*

What do we secretly fear?

Challenge students to consider the things they secretly fear and whether those fears are caused by things that are beyond their control. Invite volunteers to share some of their fears with the class.

? *ESSENTIAL QUESTION:*

When should we stop and reflect on our lives?

Point out that setting goals and reflecting on our actions are important not just for learning but also for living our lives. Guide students in a discussion of the ways in which reflecting can help them achieve their goals.

LITERATURE OF THE AMERICAN RENAISSANCE

This essay provides students with a historical context for the Unit 3 selections. It presents a brief overview of the nationalism and industrialization that fueled America's growth and eventually led to conflict between the North and South. It also addresses how living in a newly developing culture influenced how American writers of this period wrote about the relationship between people and the world around them.

Westward Expansion America's western expansion began with the Louisiana Purchase in 1803, which doubled the country's size. In the years that followed, explorers and settlers pushed farther and farther west to make money and to gain land. The United States' annexation in 1845 of Texas from Mexico set off the Mexican-American War. Many Americans found the Mexican-American War to be immoral—a war fought mainly to expand slavery.

Nationalism vs. Sectionalism As the textile industry grew, so did the demand for cotton. The plantation owners who were the most powerful people in the South felt that slavery was necessary for increasing profits. Many in the North—where most of the textile mills were located—saw slavery as immoral and worked to have it abolished. Abolitionists—including women—began to join together to work for the emancipation of slaves.

COLLABORATIVE DISCUSSION

Ask students to share their timeline entries with the class and explain why they found them interesting.

LITERATURE OF THE AMERICAN RENAISSANCE

In 1812 tensions between the United States and Great Britain erupted in a two-year war. The War of 1812 is sometimes referred to as the second war for American independence. Victory in the war cemented the reality of independence and brought great changes to life in the United States, including a new spirit of nationalism. Written after the Battle of Baltimore in 1814, the American national anthem is just one manifestation of that spirit.

Because the war interrupted trade, Americans had to produce many of the goods they had imported in the past. This period marked the beginning of the Industrial Revolution in the United States, as the country shifted from its largely agrarian economy to become an industrial powerhouse. The growth of the factory system brought many people from farms into cities, where they worked long hours for low wages, often under harsh conditions.

Westward Expansion American settlers in search of new farmland and opportunities had been moving west since the late 1700s. This often led to direct conflict with Native American groups living on these lands. In 1830 the United States Congress passed the Indian Removal Act, forcing Native Americans to relocate west of the Mississippi River. Those who resisted were often brutally pushed off their lands.

By mid-century, Americans began to fully embrace the idea of "manifest destiny"—the belief that the United States was destined to expand to the Pacific Ocean and into Mexican Territory. The United States' annexation of Texas in 1845 sparked the Mexican-American War. Through the Treaty of Guadalupe Hidalgo, which ended the war, and later land purchases, the United States established the current borders of the "lower" 48 states.

Nationalism vs. Sectionalism As new territories achieved statehood, the northern and southern states wrangled over the balance between free and slave states. Economic interests also threatened American unity. Tariffs on manufactured goods from Britain forced southerners to buy more expensive northern-manufactured goods. From the South's point of view, the North was getting rich at the South's expense. Sectionalism, or the placing of the interests of one's own region ahead of the nation as a whole, began to take hold.

COLLABORATIVE DISCUSSION
Which events covered above illustrate the new spirit of nationalism in the United States? How did they contribute to nationalism?

Timeline:

- **1810**
- **1812–14** War of 1812 reaffirms U.S. independence from Great Britain.
- **1822** Factories built in Lowell, Massachusetts, made it one of the country's largest industrial cities.
- **1825** Erie Canal links the Great Lakes with the Hudson River.
- **1830** Congress passes the Indian Removal Act.

© Houghton Mifflin Harcourt Publishing Company

ENGLISH LEARNER SUPPORT

Build Background Knowledge To aid comprehension of the essay, provide students with the following definitions.

- *manifestation:* an indication of the existence, reality, or presence of something
- *agrarian:* relating to farming
- *embrace:* adopt or support willingly
- *manifest:* clearly apparent to the understanding; obvious

- *annexation:* the incorporation of territory into an existing political unit, such as a country
- *wrangled:* quarreled noisily or angrily
- *transcendent:* lying beyond the ordinary range of perception
- *conventions:* widely used and accepted devices or techniques

ALL LEVELS

Romantics and Transcendentalists American writers of this period were influenced by European romanticism but soon adapted it to their own culture. Ralph Waldo Emerson, a New England writer, led a group focused on transcendentalism. The term *transcendentalism* came from Immanuel Kant, a German philosopher who wrote about "transcendent forms" of knowledge that exist beyond reason and experience. Emerson gave this European philosophy a uniquely American spin, saying that every individual is capable of discovering higher truth through his or her own intuition.

A major target for the transcendentalists' criticism was their Puritan heritage, with its emphasis on material prosperity and rigid obedience to the laws of society. The transcendentalists disliked the commercial side of American life and the hectic pace of the Industrial Revolution. Instead, they stressed spiritual well-being, achieved through intellectual activity and a close relationship to nature. Emerson's friend Henry David Thoreau put his beliefs into practice by building a small cabin on Walden Pond and living there for two years, writing and studying nature.

In 1842 Emerson called for the emergence of a poet worthy of the new America—a fresh voice with limitless passion and originality. Two such poets were Walt Whitman and Emily Dickinson. Both wrote poetry that broke with the traditional conventions of poetic form and content. In this way they followed the transcendentalist ideals of individuals discovering the truth through intuition and following their own beliefs.

Romantics and Transcendentalists One common feature of the American version of Romanticism is the presence of an individual hero who turns away from society to chart his or her own course in life. The early Romantics looked to the beauty of nature for inspiration, emphasized emotions and the imagination over reason, and celebrated the individual spirit. Early Romantics included William Cullen Bryant, Washington Irving, James Fennimore Cooper, Henry Wadsworth Longfellow, James Russell Lowell, Oliver Wendell Holmes, and John Greenleaf Whittier.

Transcendentalism, an offshoot of Romanticism, emphasized living a simple life and a close relationship to nature, stressed individualism and self-reliance, believed in the inherent goodness of people, and encouraged spiritual well-being over financial well-being. In *Walden*, transcendentalist Henry David Thoreau presents an edited version of the journals he kept while living on his own by Walden Pond. He stressed individualism and the simple life. Walt Whitman's poem "Song of Myself" celebrates the beliefs, desires, and emotional responses of its first-person narrator, at times speaking of subjects that were considered taboo or offensive so openly that many readers over time have been offended by his frankness.

RESEARCH

To learn more about their chosen topic, encourage students to search for primary sources from the historical period. Have students choose excerpts from a source to present to the class.

RESEARCH

What about this historical period interests you? Choose a topic, event, or person to learn more about. Then, add your own entry to the timeline.

1837	1846–48
John Deere develops a steel plow for the western prairies.	Mexican-American War expands the western territory of the United States.

1850

1844	1848
Samuel B. Morse transmits the first successful telegraph message.	Discovery of gold in California leads to the first gold rush.

The Individual and Society 207

WHEN STUDENTS STRUGGLE . . .

Vocabulary Support Some students may experience difficulty understanding the meaning of the different movements discussed in this essay. Explain that *-ism* is a suffix that indicates that a word is a label for a particular doctrine or school of thought. Work with students to identify and list the different systems of belief mentioned in this essay, such as *nationalism*, *sectionalism*, *Romanticism*, and *transcendentalism*. Create a chart with each movement as a head and record students' ideas. Then, have students work with a partner and use information from the chart and this essay to summarize each movement and its central characteristics.

Dark Romantics The gothic tradition began in Europe, where writers such as Mary Shelley, author of *Frankenstein*, delighted readers with their deliciously creepy accounts of monsters, vampires, and humans with a large capacity for evil. Edgar Allan Poe was the master of the gothic form in the United States. He explored human psychology from the inside, using first-person narrators who were sometimes criminal or even insane. His plots involved extreme situations—not just murder, but live burials, physical and mental torture, and retribution from beyond the grave. In works such as *The Scarlet Letter* and "The Minister's Black Veil," Nathaniel Hawthorne examined the darker facets of the human soul, such as the psychological effects sin and guilt may have on human life.

CHECK YOUR UNDERSTANDING

Have students answer the questions independently.

Answers:

1. *D*

2. *H*

3. *C*

If students answer any question incorrectly, have them reread the text to confirm their understanding.

Dark Romantics Not all American Romantics were optimistic or had faith in the innate goodness of humankind. Edgar Allan Poe and Nathaniel Hawthorne have been called "dark" or "brooding" Romantics or "anti-transcendentalists." Their stories are characterized by a probing of the inner lives of their characters—an examination of the complex and often mysterious forces that motivate human behavior. Their stories are romantic, however, in their emphasis on emotion, nature, the individual, and the unusual. Both Poe and Hawthorne used elements that are common in Gothic fiction, such as grotesque characters, bizarre situations, and violent events, in order to explore the unknown.

CHECK YOUR UNDERSTANDING

Choose the best answer to each question.

1 Which of the following was a threat to nationalism in the United States?

   A The War of 1812

   B The Indian Removal Act

   C The Mexican-American War

   D Sectionalism

2 What is "manifest destiny"?

   F The shift from an agrarian to an industrial economy

   G The official act of removing Native Americans from their homelands

   H The belief that the United States was meant to expand to the Pacific Ocean

   J The balance of power between free and slave states

3 Which of the following is a characteristic of transcendentalism?

   A An emphasis on material prosperity

   B Rigid obedience to the laws of society

   C The belief that individuals can discover higher truths through intuition

   D An examination of the complex forces that motivate human behavior

ENGLISH LEARNER SUPPORT

Vocabulary: Figurative and Literal Language Even if students can define the meaning of a word, they may be confused when a writer uses a word in a figurative sense instead of a literal one. For example, the main meaning of the word *erupt* is "to throw or force something out violently, as lava, ash, and gases." When we hear the word, the image that comes to mind is that of a volcano. In the first line of this essay, the author uses the word *erupted* to indicate that the War of 1812 developed suddenly as a result of tensions. Ask students to work in small mixed-language–ability groups to identify other words that are being used in a figurative sense, such as *cemented* in the third sentence of this essay, and to explain how and why the author is using these words in a particular context. **ALL LEVELS**

ACADEMIC VOCABULARY

Academic Vocabulary words are words you use when you discuss and write about texts. In this unit, you will learn the following five words:

☑ **analogy**   ☐ **denote**   ☐ **quote**   ☐ **topic**   ☐ **unique**

Study the Word Network to learn more about the word **analogy.**

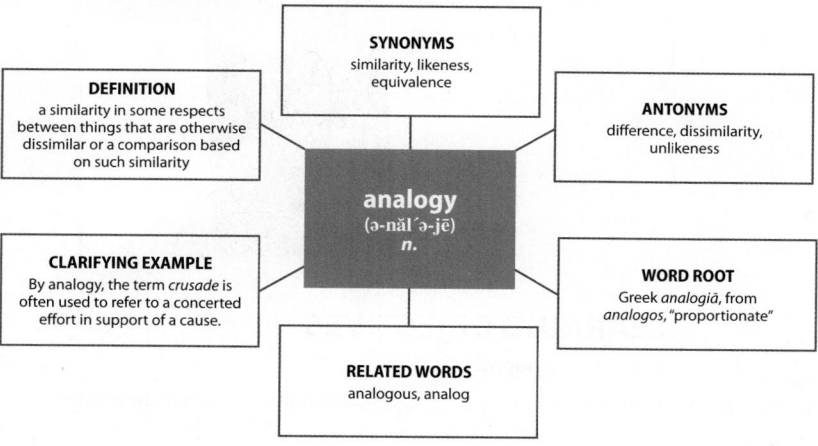

SYNONYMS
similarity, likeness, equivalence

ANTONYMS
difference, dissimilarity, unlikeness

DEFINITION
a similarity in some respects between things that are otherwise dissimilar or a comparison based on such similarity

analogy
(ə-năl´ə-jē)
n.

CLARIFYING EXAMPLE
By analogy, the term *crusade* is often used to refer to a concerted effort in support of a cause.

WORD ROOT
Greek *analogià*, from *analogos*, "proportionate"

RELATED WORDS
analogous, analog

Write and Discuss   Discuss your completed Word Network with a partner, making sure to talk through all of the boxes until you both understand the word, its synonyms, antonyms, and related forms. Then, fill out a Word Network for the remaining four words. Use a dictionary or online resource to help you complete the activity.

Go online to access the Word Networks.

RESPOND TO THE ESSENTIAL QUESTIONS

In this unit, you will explore four different **Essential Questions** about the individual and society. As you read each selection, you will gather your ideas about one of these questions and write about it in the **Response Log** that appears on page R3. At the end of the unit, you will have the opportunity to write an **explanatory essay** related to one of the Essential Questions. Filling out the Response Log after you read each text will help you prepare for this writing task.

You can also go online to access the Response Log.

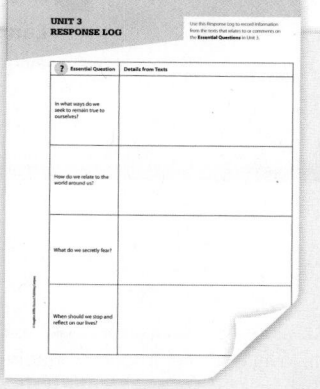

© Houghton Mifflin Harcourt Publishing Company

ACADEMIC VOCABULARY

As students complete Word Networks for the remaining four vocabulary words. Encourage them to include all the categories shown in the completed network if possible, but point out that some words do not have clear synonyms or antonyms.

analogy (ə-năl´ə-jē) *n.* a similarity in some respects between things that are otherwise dissimilar or a comparison based on such similarity (Spanish cognate: *analogía*)

denote (dĭ-nōt´) *tr.v.* to mark; indicate; to serve as a symbol or name for the meaning of; signify (Spanish cognate: *denotar*)

quote (kwōt) *v.* to repeat or copy words from a source such as a book, usually with an acknowledgment of the source; to give a quotation; *n.* a quotation

topic (tŏp´ĭk) *n.* the subject of a speech, essay, discussion, or conversation

unique (yo͞o-nēk´) *adj.* being the only one of its kind; remarkable or extraordinary (Spanish cognate: *único*)

RESPOND TO THE ESSENTIAL QUESTIONS

Direct students to the Unit 3 Response Logs. Explain that students will use it to record ideas and details from the selections that help answer one of the Essential Questions. When they work on the Writing Task at the end of the unit, their Response Logs will help them think about what they have read and make connections between the texts.

from SONG OF MYSELF

Poem by Walt Whitman

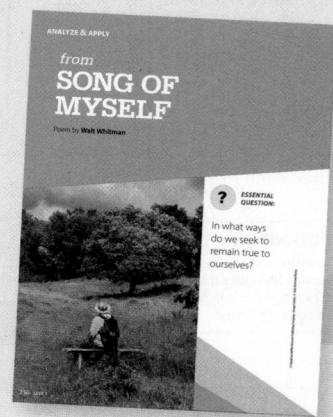

GENRE ELEMENTS
FREE VERSE

Free verse is a type of poetry that does not have elements of rhyme and meter. Instead, it uses uneven, unrhymed lines and stanzas that follow the natural rhythm of everyday speech. Free verse uses elements of traditional poetry like imagery and sound devices.

LEARNING OBJECTIVES

- Analyze a poem.
- Identify poetic elements used to help the reader determine themes.
- Evaluate whether Whitman emulates his own description of democratic attitudes.
- Write an argument that supports a position about Whitman's egoism.
- Defend a position in a class debate.
- Demonstrate comprehension using academic vocabulary.
- Analyze a poem by examining and annotating the text.
- **Language** Support a position using the words *claim*, *reason*, and *evidence*.

TEXT COMPLEXITY

Quantitative Measures	Song of Myself	Lexile: N/A
Qualitative Measures	**Ideas Presented** Multiple levels, subtle, implied meaning and purpose. Abstract, difficult ideas. Use of symbolism, irony, satire.	
	Structures Used Complex, narrow perspective. Deviation from chronological or sequential order.	
	Language Used Meanings are implied, but support is offered. Figurative language. Inference is demanded.	
	Knowledge Required Complexity in theme. Experiences may be less familiar to many. Cultural or historical references may make heavier demands.	

Online

RESOURCES

- Unit 3 Response Log
- Selection Audio
- Close Read Screencast: Modeled Discussion
- Reading Studio: Notice & Note
- Level Up Tutorials: Summarize; Reteaching: Analyze Theme
- Writing Studio: Writing Arguments
- Speaking and Listening Studio: Analyzing and Evaluating Presentations
- ☑ "Song of Myself"

SUMMARIES

English

Walt Whitman declares in the opening line that he is going to "celebrate" himself in his poem. He stops and stares at a blade of grass and ponders his life in relation to the world. Whitman imagines how to explain the grass to a child, which sparks his thinking about his relationship to those who have lived before him, the natural world, and everything in the universe. He imagines himself as various characters, or personas, and empathizes with their experiences. Finally, a hawk flies by and interrupts Whitman's daydream, and the poet "departs as air."

Spanish

Walt Whitman declara en la primera línea de su poema que va a "celebrarse a sí mismo". Se detiene y mira una brizna de hierba y reflexiona sobre su vida en relación con el mundo. Whitman imagina cómo explicarle la hierba a un niño, cosa que desata su atención acerca de aquellos que vivieron antes de él, el mundo natural y todo en el universo. Se imagina a sí mismo como muchos personajes o personas y siente empatía con sus experiencias. Finalmente, el vuelo de un halcón interrumpe su ensueño y el poeta "se aleja como el aire".

SMALL-GROUP OPTIONS

Have students work in small groups and pairs to read and discuss the selection.

Identify Elements of Poetry

- Organize the class into five groups. Assign each group one of the following elements of poetry: free verse, imagery, figures of speech, symbols, and direct statements.
- Ask students in each group to examine the text and identify at least five examples of their assigned element. Have students list the examples.
- Invite each group to share with the class. Have students explain what their assigned element is, share one or two of the best examples they identified, and explain why those examples demonstrate the element.

Think-Pair-Share

- Have each student reread the section "I understand the large hearts of heroes" and identify the various personas in the section (e.g., the skipper, the loose gown'd women, the hounded slave, the mash'd fireman).
- Ask students to choose one persona and think about why Whitman chose that persona to develop his theme. Have them jot down their ideas.
- Organize students into pairs. Ask them to share and discuss their ideas with each other.
- Display the following guiding questions to help steer students' discussion: *Do you agree with your partners assessment? Why or why not? Support your answers with citations from the poem.*

Text X-Ray: English Learner Support
for "Song of Myself"

Use the Text X-Ray and the supports and scaffolds in the Teacher's Edition to help guide students at different proficiency levels through the selection.

INTRODUCE THE SELECTION
DISCUSS "I CELEBRATE MYSELF" AND "SING MYSELF"

In this lesson, students need to understand Whitman's use of the words *celebrate* and *sing*. *Celebrate* can mean to mark a special occasion (e.g., celebrate a birthday) or to perform a religious ceremony (e.g., celebrate mass). *Sing* usually means to make music with your voice. Whitman uses both words to mean "praise, honor, or rejoice" in the selection.

Whitman's use of the phrases "celebrate myself" and "sing myself" reflect the American value of individualism. America was founded on the principle of independence, and the founders valued personal freedom over government control. Whitman was honoring and rejoicing in his own life, which reflects American individualism.

Ask students what freedoms they value and why. Provide sentence frames: *I value _____ because _____. I also value _____. This is important to me because _____.*

CULTURAL REFERENCES

The following words or phrases may be unfamiliar to students:

- *offspring* (section 6, line 24): a person's child or children; descendants
- *skipper* (section 33, line 3): the captain of a ship
- *mother of old, condemn'd for a witch* (section 33, line 13): This is an allusion to the witch hunts and witch trials that occurred during colonial times. Many women were accused of practicing witchcraft. As punishment, women were hanged, drowned, or burned.
- *hounded slave* (section 33, line 14): When a slave ran away, their owners chased them with hounds, or dogs.
- *marksmen* (section 33, line 18): someone shooting at a target
- *resuscitate* (section 33, line 35): to bring someone back to life; revive

LISTENING

Identify Metaphors

A metaphor is a figure of speech. It compares two things by saying one thing is another thing. For example, "her eyes are shining stars" compares someone's eyes to the stars. It helps the reader understand that her eyes were bright.

Read aloud section 6, lines 1–11. Explain that in the passage, Whitman uses metaphors that compare grass to other objects. Use the following supports with students at varying proficiency levels:

- Provide examples of metaphors for grass from the poem. For example, "the flag . . ."; "the handkerchief . . ."; ". . . a child." Ask yes/no questions to confirm understanding. For example: *Is Whitman saying the grass is a child?* (Yes) **SUBSTANTIAL**
- Have students listen as you read aloud and write the words they hear that are metaphors for grass. Then provide sentence frames to help students restate the metaphor: *The grass is a _____. The grass is a _____. The grass is a _____.* **MODERATE**
- As you read the poem, have students write words that are metaphors for grass. Organize students into pairs and ask them to share the words they identified and tell their partners what is being compared to grass and what they think the comparison means. **LIGHT**

SPEAKING

Talk about the Text

Display or draw the students' attention to the following lines:

"I celebrate myself, and sing myself" (section 1, line 1)

"I am the mash'd fireman with breast-bone broken, (section 33, line 26)

Use the following supports with students at varying proficiency levels:

- Chorally read each line several times with students. Explain, using words, gestures, or pictures, that in the first line, Whitman is honoring himself. Explain that in the second line, he compares himself to a fireman. Have the students work in pairs to restate the meaning of each line, using words, gestures, or drawing pictures. **SUBSTANTIAL**

- Have the students repeat the lines several times with a partner. Have students share with their partners what they think Whitman meant when he wrote these lines. **MODERATE**

- Have the students read the lines aloud to a partner and invite them to discuss what they think the lines mean. Ask: *How is the meaning of each line the same or different?* **LIGHT**

READING

Read and Analyze Free Verse

Review with the students the elements of free verse found on page 211.

Have students create a chart like the one found on page 211 (divide the first row into specific elements of free verse).

Use the following supports with students at varying proficiency levels:

- Read the first two stanzas chorally. Help students identify one example of each element and write the corresponding line number(s) in the chart. If students struggle, ask yes/no questions. **SUBSTANTIAL**

- Have students work in pairs to reread section 33, lines 1–23, and write "UL" next to *unrhymed lines*, "ES" next to examples of *everyday speech*, and "I" next to examples of *imagery*. Have students use their notes to complete the chart. **MODERATE**

- Have students work in pairs to read section 33. Have them identify examples of free verse and fill in the chart. Remind students that the free verse writing style is like everyday speech. **LIGHT**

WRITING

Make a Claim

To develop an *argument*, writers must make a *claim* and support it. A *claim* is the point the writer is trying to make. A *reason* tells why your claim is valid, and *evidence* provides specific examples that illustrate the reason.

Explain that an egoist is a philosopher who believes that self-interest drives people's actions. Use the following supports with students at varying proficiency levels:

- Display the sentences: *Whitman is an egoist* and *Whitman is not an egoist*. Return to the selection and point out one passage that supports each claim. Have students copy the claim they agree with. **SUBSTANTIAL**

- Have the students work in pairs to create a chart with two columns with the following heads: *Whitman is an egoist* and *Whitman is not an egoist*. Have students work in pairs to fill in the chart giving a reason for each claim and use evidence from the text to support their reason. **MODERATE**

- Have students work with a partner to develop a draft of the first two paragraphs of their argument. In the second paragraph, ask students to state three reasons for their claims, each supported by evidence from the text. **LIGHT**

? Connect to the
ESSENTIAL QUESTION

To be true to ourselves, we must know ourselves. In "Song of Myself," Whitman explores his own identity in relation to the world around him. He values self-knowledge and sees himself reflected in and connected to both nature and other people.

from

SONG OF MYSELF

Poem by **Walt Whitman**

? ESSENTIAL QUESTION:

In what ways do we seek to remain true to ourselves?

210   Unit 3

QUICK START

You have been asked to mentor students to help them consider a career path. Discuss with a partner the ways in which you could help other students answer questions such as, "What should you ask yourself when thinking about a job or career?" and "How do you know whether a career path is right for you?".

ANALYZE POETRY

"Song of Myself" is written in **free verse.** Poems written in free verse do not have regular patterns of rhyme and rhythm and may not have conventional stanzas. Because it uses varied line lengths and does not rhyme, free verse poetry often has a **rhythm,** or pattern of stressed and unstressed sounds, that is closer to that of everyday speech.

The **speaker** is the voice that is talking in a poem. In free verse, the speaker may be the poet, or a fictional character or narrator. The speaker may even change throughout the poem. As you read "Song of Myself," use a chart like this to help you analyze the relationships between the different elements of free verse poetry.

**GENRE ELEMENTS:
FREE VERSE**

• does not have regular patterns of rhyme and rhythm

• uses uneven, unrhymed lines and stanzas that sound like everyday speech

• includes elements of traditional poetry like imagery and sound devices

MY QUESTIONS	EVIDENCE FROM THE POEM
What characteristics of free verse are in the poems?	The poem uses no regular rhyme scheme or rhythm patterns and has uneven line lengths. The stanzas do not contain the same number of lines.
Who is the speaker? How do I know?	The speaker is the poet, Walt Whitman. He writes in the first person and refers to specific details about himself, such as his age.
How is the identity of the speaker related to the free verse writing style?	The poet is writing about himself and his ideas of individualism. Free verse allows him to express ideas in a more conversational way, rather than following strict forms.

QUICK START

After students read the Quick Start activity, discuss how there are many factors involved in choosing a job or career. Discuss as a class what some of the considerations are when thinking about a job. For example: What skills or education are needed? Is interest or pay rate a higher priority for an individual? How can one learn more about what jobs exist? This should help prepare students to think about what questions to ask a younger student.

ANALYZE POETRY

To help students understand the characteristics of free verse, share examples of a variety of poems (just a few lines each) that exhibit the elements that free verse is described as *not* having. Alternatively, you could ask students to share lines from poems they know that have regular rhyme schemes or meter/rhythm or conventional stanzas. Then explain that free verse does not adhere to strict poetic elements; instead it sounds more like the poet talking to you. Free verse lacks the structure of traditional verse, but it has a sense of immediacy.

For **reading support** for students at varying proficiency levels, see the **Text X-Ray** on page 210D.

ANALYZE THEME AND STRUCTURE

Review the elements in the chart with students. Then explain that the **themes** of identity and individuality that run through Whitman's poem are emphasized by the structure of the poem. The structure of the poem is inconsistent, with lines of different length and no regular rhythm. The refusal to follow standard poetic structures was one way Whitman showed his individuality. By using the language and structure of ordinary speech, he emphasizes the value he places on ordinary people.

Another theme is the interconnectedness of all people, which is clearer in the full poem. (You may want to note that the full poem has 52 sections and more than 1,300 lines.) It is significant that there is a section about "what is the grass," since the title of the collection in which the poem appeared is *Leaves of Grass*. Nature is another important element of Whitman's overall message.

■ English Learner Support

Acquire Academic Vocabulary Help students understand the word *structure* by suggesting things they know that have a structure or form, such as a building. Discuss how structure is related to function in buildings, such as a house versus a school. Relate how structure is also related to function in poetry. **LIGHT**

✎ ANNOTATION MODEL

Remind students that annotating the text, identifying important points, and making notes in the margins as they read can help them connect with what they are reading. Point out in this model that words are circled and underlined to emphasize who the speaker is in this poem and the connection the speaker feels with the reader. Explain that these annotations are just a suggestion; students can create their own system for annotating the text. They may want to color-code their annotations using highlighters. Their notes in the margin may include questions about ideas that are unclear or topics they want to learn more about.

 **GET READY**

ANALYZE THEME AND STRUCTURE

The **theme** or themes of a poem are the underlying message or messages that a poet wants to convey. The poet will not state the theme directly. It is up to you to infer it based on details in the text.

In the selections of "Song of Myself" that you are about to read, Whitman uses language, structure, and literary devices to communicate his themes. As you read, consider how the following elements impact your understanding of the poems and the themes they express.

ELEMENTS	HOW THEY REVEAL THEMES
Free verse	Look for words that stand out because of the poet's manipulation of lines, repeated words and phrases that create rhythm and heighten emotion in key places, and lists of people, things, or attributes that create rhythm and evoke imagery.
Imagery	Think about the types of images created by sensory language and why the poet wants readers to "see" these pictures.
Figures of speech	Comparisons in the form of similes and metaphors tell readers how the poet wants them to view certain ideas.
Symbols	A person, place, or thing that has meaning beyond itself is often central to the poem's meaning.
Direct statements	Sometimes the poet expresses ideas directly.

ANNOTATION MODEL

NOTICE & NOTE

As you read, note the themes the poet develops and the elements he uses to convey those themes. Pay attention to what the speaker reveals and how the structure of the poem helps convey meaning. This model shows one reader's notes about the beginning of "Song of Myself."

I celebrate myself, and sing myself,
And what I assume you shall assume,
For every atom belonging to me as good belongs to you.

The speaker stresses the idea of individuality by repeating the pronouns "I" and "myself." He also uses the pronoun "you," connecting himself to the audience of humankind.

BACKGROUND

Walt Whitman *(1819–1892) was not born into a prosperous family. The son of a house builder and one of nine children, he grew up in rural Long Island and Brooklyn, New York. Although he was a voracious reader, he did not have much formal education, and at age twelve began work as a printer. In his younger years, he showed little indication of literary promise, moving from job to job and working at various times as an office boy, a typesetter, a school teacher, and a carpenter.*

from

SONG OF MYSELF

Poem by Walt Whitman

In the 1840s, Whitman published poems, short stories, and even a novel, but they were fairly conventional efforts that did not stand out from the other literature of the day. Whitman had yet to find the inspiration that would unlock his voice as a writer. He soon found it in the writings of poet and philosopher Ralph Waldo Emerson. After reading Emerson's work, Whitman realized that he could celebrate all aspects of nature and humanity by using spiritual language.

In the early 1850s, Whitman quit his job as a journalist and devoted himself to writing his collection of poems entitled Leaves of Grass. He printed the volume in 1855. It soon ignited a flurry of reaction from readers because of its content and form, both of which were considered revolutionary. Many early readers scorned his efforts, and the book was so controversial that many of the original 800 copies were thrown away. Undeterred, Whitman continued working on the book for the rest of his life—revising or rearranging existing poems and adding new poems. The ninth and final edition, published in 1892, contained nearly 400 poems.

Whitman celebrated all aspects of American life—the unique and the commonplace, the beautiful and the ugly. Rejecting the rigidity of earlier poetic conventions, Whitman's poetry captures the vitality, optimism, and voice of America in a style that reflects the freedom and vastness of his beloved country. Today, Leaves of Grass is widely regarded as one of the most influential books of poetry in American literature.

Song of Myself   213

BACKGROUND

Whitman lived during a time of tremendous growth and change in the United States. The population was on the move with new states coming into existence across the Midwest. Philosophers of the day, such as Ralph Waldo Emerson, saw the opening of the nation as being a return to an ideal state, where people could live an idyllic existence of farming and nature. It was, however, also a time of turmoil, as the nation fought over whether the new states would be slave states or free states.

Whitman—sometimes called the "Bard of Democracy" because of his love for the American ideal—feared that the continued existence of slavery might harm democracy as a whole. For a short time, his work as a journalist turned toward keeping slavery out of new states.

The horrors of the Civil War had a tremendous emotional and physical impact on Whitman. He found part-time work in Washington, D.C., but spent most of the war visiting wounded soldiers. Hundreds of hospital visits led to more poems for his growing collection, including three written in memory of Abraham Lincoln.

Whitman continued to work on *Leaves of Grass* for the rest of his life. The only thing that stopped his work was his death, which came in 1892.

CLOSE READ SCREENCAST

Modeled Discussion   In their eBooks, have students view the Close Read Screencast, in which readers discuss and annotate the following key passages:

- from "I celebrate myself, and sing myself" (lines 10–13)
- from "A child said *What is the grass*?" (lines 13–20)

As a class, view and discuss one of these videos. Then have students pair up to do an independent close read of an additional passage from "I understand the large hearts of heroes" (lines 12–16). Students can record their answers on the Close Read Practice PDF.

 **Close Read Practice PDF**

SETTING A PURPOSE

Direct students to use the Setting a Purpose prompt to focus their reading.

 ## ANALYZE POETRY

Remind students poets use sensory details to create images in the reader's mind. Poets also use **repetition** of sounds and words to emphasize ideas and establish meaning. (**Possible answer:** *In line 6, "my tongue" and "my blood" underscores that this is about the speaker. Then, the repetition in line 7 of "born here" and "parents the same," and the inclusion of "their" emphasizes the connection with others.*)

 For **listening** and **reading support** for students at varying proficiency levels, see the **Text X-Ray** on pages 210C and 210D.

ANALYZE THEME AND STRUCTURE

Remind students that a **metaphor** is one of the structural elements Whitman uses to establish meaning. Metaphors are direct comparisons between two things that have something in common. Unlike similes, metaphors do not use the words *like* or *as*. (**Possible answer:** *Each new metaphor is introduced in a new stanza. The effect is to suggest that grass is everywhere, representing the personal, the spiritual, and the universal. This helps develop Whitman's theme of the interconnectedness of life.*)

 NOTICE & NOTE

Notice & Note

Use the side margins to notice and note signposts in the text.

ANALYZE POETRY

Annotate: Mark words and phrases that stand out to you in lines 6 and 7.

Analyze: How does the speaker express a relationship to the wider world in these lines?

ANALYZE THEME AND STRUCTURE

Annotate: Mark examples of metaphor in lines 3–11.

Analyze: How do these metaphors give structure to the poem? What theme do they suggest?

SETTING A PURPOSE

As you read, pay attention to Whitman's unique poetic style and how he uses the elements of a poem to develop a theme.

1   I celebrate myself, and sing myself

I celebrate myself, and sing myself,
And what I assume you shall assume,[1]
For every atom belonging to me as good belongs to you.

I loaf and invite my soul,
5 I lean and loaf at my ease observing a spear of summer grass.

My tongue, every atom of my blood, form'd from this soil, this air,
Born here of parents born here from parents the same, and their
      parents the same,
I, now thirty-seven years old in perfect health begin,
Hoping to cease not till death.

10 Creeds and schools in abeyance,[2]
Retiring back a while sufficed at what they are, but never forgotten,
I harbor for good or bad, I permit to speak at every hazard,
Nature without check with original energy.

6   A child said *What is the grass?*

A child said *What is the grass?* fetching it to me with full hands;
How could I answer the child? I do not know what it is any more
      than he.

I guess it must be the flag of my disposition, out of hopeful green
      stuff woven.

Or I guess it is the handkerchief of the Lord,
5 A scented gift and remembrancer designedly dropt,
Bearing the owner's name someway in the corners, that we may see
      and remark, and say *Whose?*

Or I guess the grass is itself a child, the produced babe of the
      vegetation.

---
[1] **assume:** Here, the word *assume* means "take on."
[2] **abeyance:** temporary suspension; inactivity.

EL ## ENGLISH LEARNER SUPPORT

Use Available Support Remind students to use all available resources when reading something unfamiliar, such as the unusual style and use of language seen in Whitman's work. Students should consider the background information, footnotes, and images in the lesson. They should also seek support from their peers and the teacher, as the rich imagery and unusual sentence structure make Whitman difficult to understand even for some native speakers. Discuss specific imagery and ideas. Encourage students to ask questions. Have students discuss elements and ideas found in the poem. Rephrase some of the more difficult lines in easier language to aid student understanding of the language. **ALL LEVELS**

Or I guess it is a uniform hieroglyphic,[1]
And it means, Sprouting alike in broad zones and narrow zones,
10 Growing among black folks as among white,
Kanuck, Tuckahoe, Congressman, Cuff,[2] I give them the same,
    I receive them the same.

And now it seems to me the beautiful uncut hair of graves.

Tenderly will I use you curling grass,
It may be you transpire from the breasts of young men,
15 It may be if I had known them I would have loved them,
It may be you are from old people, or from offspring taken soon out
    of their mothers' laps,
And here you are the mothers' laps.

The grass is very dark to be from the white heads of old mothers,
Darker than the colorless beards of old men,
20 Dark to come from under the faint red roofs of mouths.

O I perceive after all so many uttering tongues,
And I perceive they do not come from the roofs of mouths for
    nothing.

I wish I could translate the hints about the dead young men and
    women,
And the hints about old men and mothers, and the offspring taken
    soon out of their laps.

25 What do you think has become of the young and old men?
And what do you think has become of the women and children?

They are alive and well somewhere,
The smallest sprout shows there is really no death,
And if ever there was it led forward life, and does not wait at the
    end to arrest it,
30 And ceas'd the moment life appear'd.

All goes onward and outward, nothing collapses,
And to die is different from what any one supposed, and luckier.

---

[1] **hieroglyphic:** picture symbol used in a writing system to represent sounds or
words.
[2] **Kanuck, Tuckahoe, . . .Cuff:** *Kanuck, Tuckahoe,* and *Cuff* are slang terms, now
considered offensive, for a French Canadian, an inhabitant of the Virginia lowlands,
and an African American, respectively.

**ANALYZE THEME AND
STRUCTURE**
Annotate: In lines 27–32,
mark places where the poet
expresses his thoughts directly.

Cite Evidence: How do these
ideas relate to each other and
to Whitman's theme(s)?

Song of Myself **215**

ANALYZE THEME AND STRUCTURE

Remind students that the theme is the main message a poet wants to share. Poets do not directly state their themes. Readers must use details from the text to determine the theme. (**Possible answer:** *Whitman uses the example of young shoots of grass in line 28 to demonstrate the concept that life is always renewing itself. In line 31 he directly states the same idea in different words. The theme of the cyclical, interconnected nature of life that was introduced in the first section, "I celebrate myself, and sing myself," is thus further developed.*)

WHEN STUDENTS STRUGGLE . . .

Summarize Lead students to understand Whitman's answer to the question "What is the grass?" by encouraging them to summarize key passages. Ask students to read the following passages and summarize each passage: lines 8–11 (*Grass grows everywhere, among all people*); lines 12–17 (*Grass grows from the graves of all the dead*); and lines 27–32 (*Grass continues to grow, proving that life is more powerful than death*). Suggest students create a two-column chart labeled *Section* and *Summary*. Students can create summaries of each section as they read.

 For additional support, go to the **Reading Studio** and assign the following **Level Up Tutorial: Summarizing.**

ANALYZE THEME AND STRUCTURE

Remind students that sensory words are words that appeal to or refer to the senses—taste, touch, hearing, sight, smell. Whitman uses sensory details to help readers "see" what he is describing. (**Possible answer:** *By creating realistic sensory images, Whitman is establishing his empathy with the slave and confirming his statement from line 1: "I understand the large hearts of heroes."*)

 For **speaking** and **reading support** for students at varying proficiency levels, see the **Text X-Ray** on page 210D.

EL ENGLISH LEARNER SUPPORT

Understand Inverted Word Order Remind students that the normal order of an English sentence is subject-verb-object. On the board, write this part of line 10: "All this I swallow." Point out that in this line, the object (*this*) comes before the subject (*I*) and the verb (*swallow*). Rewrite the sentences as "I swallow all this." Ask students to rewrite these lines using standard English word order: "Heat and smoke I inspired" (line 28) and "Again gurgles the mouth of my dying general" (line 48). (*I inspired heat and smoke. The mouth of my dying general gurgles again.*) **MODERATE**

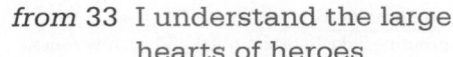
from 33 I understand the large hearts of heroes

I understand the large hearts of heroes,
The courage of present times and all times,
How the skipper saw the crowded and rudderless wreck of the
    steam-ship, and Death chasing it up and down the storm,
How he knuckled tight and gave not back an inch, and was faithful
    of days and faithful of nights,

5 And chalk'd in large letters on a board, *Be of good cheer,*
    we will not desert you;
How he follow'd with them and tack'd with them three days and
    would not give it up,
How he saved the drifting company at last,
How the lank loose-gown'd women look'd when boated from the
    side of their prepared graves,
How the silent old-faced infants and the lifted sick, and the
    sharp-lipp'd unshaved men;
10 All this I swallow, it tastes good, I like it well, it becomes mine,
I am the man, I suffer'd, I was there.

The disdain and calmness of martyrs,
The mother of old, condemn'd for a witch, burnt with dry wood,
    her children gazing on,
The hounded slave that flags in the race, leans by the fence,
    blowing, cover'd with sweat,
15 The twinges that sting like needles his legs and neck, the
    murderous buckshot and the bullets,
All these I feel or am.

I am the hounded slave, I wince at the bite of the dogs,
Hell and despair are upon me, crack and again crack the
    marksmen,
I clutch the rails of the fence, my gore dribs, thinn'd with the ooze
    of my skin,
20 I fall on the weeds and stones,
The riders spur their unwilling horses, haul close,
Taunt my dizzy ears and beat me violently over the head with
    whip-stocks.

Agonies are one of my changes of garments,
I do not ask the wounded person how he feels, I myself become the
    wounded person,
25 My hurts turn livid upon me as I lean on a cane and observe.

ANALYZE THEME AND STRUCTURE

Annotate: Mark sensory words and phrases in lines 17–22.

Analyze: How does Whitman's use of vivid imagery develop his theme in this section of the poem?

APPLYING ACADEMIC VOCABULARY

☑ **analogy**   ☑ **denote**   ☐ **quote**   ☐ **topic**   ☐ **unique**

Write and Discuss Have students turn to a partner to discuss the following questions. Guide students to include the academic vocabulary words *analogy* and *denote* in their responses. Ask volunteers to share their responses with the class.

- How does Whitman use **analogies** throughout the poems?
- How can you make a distinction between the **denotation** and connotation of Whitman's words?

✗   I am the mash'd fireman with breast-bone broken,
    Tumbling walls buried me in their debris,
    Heat and smoke I inspired,[1] I heard the yelling shouts of my
        comrades,
    I heard the distant click of their picks and shovels,
30 They have clear'd the beams away, they tenderly lift me forth.

    I lie in the night air in my red shirt, the pervading hush is for
        my sake,
    Painless after all I lie exhausted but not so unhappy,
    White and beautiful are the faces around me, the heads are bared
        of their fire-caps,
    The kneeling crowd fades with the light of the torches.

✗ 35 Distant and dead resuscitate,
    They show as the dial or move as the hands of me, I am the clock
        myself.

✗   I am an old artillerist, I tell of my fort's bombardment,
    I am there again.

    Again the long roll of the drummers,
40 Again the attacking cannon, mortars,
    Again to my listening ears the cannon responsive.

    I take part, I see and hear the whole,
    The cries, curses, roar, the plaudits for well-aim'd shots,
    The ambulanza slowly passing trailing its red drip,
45 Workmen searching after damages, making indispensable repairs,
    The fall of grenades through the rent roof, the fan-shaped
        explosion,
    The whizz of limbs, heads, stone, wood, iron, high in the air.

    Again gurgles the mouth of my dying general, he furiously waves
        with his hand,
    He gasps through the clot *Mind not me—mind—the entrenchments.*

---
[1] **inspired:** breathed in.

© Houghton Mifflin Harcourt Publishing Company • Image Credits: © Digital Storm/Shutterstock

ANALYZE POETRY
Annotate: Mark each place in "I understand the large hearts of heroes" where the speaker's persona changes or seems to change.

Connect: How does Whitman use stanzas to convey a change in the speaker's persona?

Song of Myself   **217**

 ANALYZE POETRY

Remind students that a stanza is a group of lines that form a section of a poem. Stanzas often express one idea. Point out that some of the lines to be marked are on the previous page. (**Possible answer:** *A different persona begins on lines 17, 23, 26, 35, and 37. A persona only changes at the beginning of a stanza. While not every stanza introduces a new persona, the change never occurs in the middle of a stanza. So Whitman uses stanzas to help signal a change.*)

For **speaking support** for students at varying proficiency levels, see the **Text X-Ray** on page 210D.

TO CHALLENGE STUDENTS...

Research the Poet's Attitudes Tell students that although Whitman identifies with the hounded slave in this poem, his attitude toward slavery was complex. Have small groups discuss why Whitman might have identified with the hounded slave. Encourage them to relate their thoughts to the theme that people and nature are interconnected.

TEACH

 ANALYZE THEME AND STRUCTURE

Explain to students that Whitman uses descriptive words and phrases to help readers visualize what he is describing or how he feels. Tell students to think about what they know of Whitman's ideas and the theme of the poems as they answer this question. (**Possible answer:** *The hawk swooping in flight symbolizes the freedom of nature. By comparing himself to the hawk, the speaker is associating himself with the free spirit of the natural world and telling the reader that the poem they are reading is his call to the world. If they listen the way he listens to the hawk, they might be able to understand him, even though his is "untranslatable."*)

For **listening support** for students at varying proficiency levels, see the **Text X-Ray** on page 210C.

NOTICE & NOTE

ANALYZE THEME AND STRUCTURE
Annotate: In lines 1–3, circle descriptive or action words associated with the spotted hawk. Underline descriptive or action words associated with the speaker.

Draw Conclusions: Why does the speaker compare himself to the hawk?

52 The spotted hawk swoops by

The spotted hawk swoops by and accuses me, he complains
   of my gab and my loitering.

I too am not a bit tamed, I too am untranslatable,
I sound my barbaric yawp[1] over the roofs of the world.

The last scud[2] of day holds back for me,
5 It flings my likeness after the rest and true as any on the
         shadow'd wilds,
It coaxes me to the vapor and the dusk.

I depart as air, I shake my white locks at the runaway sun,
I effuse[3] my flesh in eddies,[4] and drift it in lacy jags.

---
[1] **yawp:** a loud, harsh cry.
[2] **scud:** windblown mist and low clouds.
[3] **effuse:** spread out.
[4] **eddies:** small whirlwinds.

I bequeath myself to the dirt to grow from the grass I love,
10 If you want me again look for me under your boot-soles.

You will hardly know who I am or what I mean,
But I shall be good health to you nevertheless,
And filter and fiber your blood.

Failing to fetch me at first keep encouraged,
15 Missing me one place search another,
I stop somewhere waiting for you.

CHECK YOUR UNDERSTANDING

Answer these questions before moving on to the **Analyze the Text** section on the following page.

1 Which line best supports the idea that the speaker feels connected and relates to all of humankind?

A *My tongue, every atom of my blood, form'd from this soil, this air* (from "I celebrate myself . . ." line 6)

B *I do not ask the wounded person how he feels, I myself become the wounded person* (from "I understand . . ." line 24)

C *I sound my barbaric yawp over the roofs of the world* (from "The spotted hawk . . ." line 3)

D *I stop somewhere waiting for you* (from "The spotted hawk . . ." line 16)

2 According to the speaker in "I understand the large hearts of heroes," what is the common characteristic shared by all heroes?

F Heroes show deep love for all of humanity.

G Heroes are willing to die for their cause.

H Heroes are able to act despite pain.

J Heroes demonstrate courage.

3 Which symbol does the speaker most closely associate with his own spirit?

A The grass (from "A child said . . . ")

B The child (from "A child said . . . ")

C The slave (from "I understand . . . ")

D The hawk (from "The spotted hawk . . . ")

Song of Myself   219

CHECK YOUR UNDERSTANDING

Have students answer the questions independently.

Answers:

1. *B*

2. *J*

3. *D*

If they answer any questions incorrectly, have them reread the text to confirm their understanding. Then they may proceed to ANALYZE THE TEXT on page 220.

ENGLISH LEARNER SUPPORT

Oral Assessment   Use the following questions to assess students' comprehension and speaking skills.

1. What idea from "I understand" expresses that the speaker feels connected to people? *(The speaker becomes the wounded person.)*

2. What does the poet say that all heroes have in common? *(They all have courage.)*

3. What animal or person does the speaker feel he is most like? *(the hawk)*
LIGHT

ANALYZE THE TEXT

Possible answers:

1. **DOK 4:** *The speaker of "I celebrate myself . . ." identifies himself with all of humanity and the natural world. The subsequent poems develop this theme further with the speaker celebrating the universality of life and the human experience.*

2. **DOK 2:** *In "I celebrate myself . . ." the speaker announces that "every atom" within him belongs to everyone else. He expands on this theme in "I understand the large hearts of heroes" by assuming the identities of multiple people from diverse backgrounds facing a variety of circumstances.*

3. **DOK 2:** *To Whitman, grass is the unifying symbol of life. He points out that grass is everywhere (lines 9–11), growing out of the graves of young and old, men and women (lines 14–19). He sees the "smallest sprout" of grass as an indication that "there is really no death" (line 28).*

4. **DOK 2:** *Both poems assert that life continues unimpeded by death. In "A child said . . .," the speaker concludes that "there is really no death." In "The spotted hawk swoops by," the speaker claims that even in death "I stop somewhere waiting for you."*

5. **DOK 4:** *Whitman seeks to be a part of nature and to encompass all of human experience. Free verse allows him to expand on and explore this vast topic. He is free to vary the structure of his poem to reflect the variety and complexity of life.*

RESEARCH

Encourage students to read the preface more than once and to mark or jot down important ideas. Ask students to share any other information they learn in the preface to *Leaves of Grass* that might help a reader understand Whitman's work.

Extend Depending on what poem is selected, students may also want to contrast the poem with what they have read in this lesson. The poems written after the Civil War often differ in tone from those written before the war.

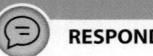 **RESPOND**

ANALYZE THE TEXT

Support your responses with evidence from the text. 📓 NOTEBOOK

1. **Analyze** "I celebrate myself . . ." is the first section of Whitman's poem "Song of Myself." In what ways does this section serve as an introduction to the themes and poetic vision described in these excerpts?

2. **Compare** How do the sections "I celebrate myself . . ." and "I understand the large hearts . . ." communicate Whitman's vision of a bond that unites all humanity?

3. **Infer** What does the grass symbolize in the section "A child said . . ."? How does this symbol relate to the deeper meaning of the poem?

4. **Interpret** Compare the themes of "A child said . . ." and "The spotted hawk swoops by." What insight do they share?

5. **Analyze** Think of Whitman's topics and the ideas he expresses in his poetry. Why is free verse the best form of poetry for him to use? Explain.

RESEARCH

RESEARCH TIP
When you use a search engine, add more terms to a broad topic to get more relevant results. For example, when searching for the preface to *Leaves of Grass*, including the word *preface* will bring better results than searching the book title only.

Walt Whitman has been described as a democratic and inclusive poet. He once described Americans as having "the fullest poetical nature." In the 1855 preface to *Leaves of Grass*, Walt Whitman outlines his vision of the American poet and describes what he or she should write about. With a partner, read the preface and use what you learn to answer these questions.

QUESTION	ANSWER
In the paragraph starting with "The American poets are to enclose . . . ," how would you paraphrase some of the characteristics Whitman lists?	*Whitman believed poets should reflect every voice. The poems should be new in form and theme. Poets should look to all things for inspiration.*
Find the passage beginning with "This is what you shall do: . . . " Whitman lists many things a poet should do. Which of them reflect inclusive or democratic attitudes?	*Loving the earth and the animals, standing up for the people, going about with uneducated people, mothers, and the young, giving aid to anyone who asks.*
How are Whitman's views about America and the role of the poet reflected in the portions of "Song of Myself" that you have read?	*Whitman embraces the diversity of humanity by connecting his life and experiences "I understand the large hearts of heroes." In "The spotted hawk swoops by," he compares the wild nature of animals to the human spirit.*

Extend Find another poem by Whitman that reflects his ideas about America. Discuss with your partner how the poem enhances or clarifies your understanding of Whitman's ideas.

WHEN STUDENTS STRUGGLE . . .

Reteaching: Analyze Theme Explain that poets share messages they want the reader to know or understand. To figure out the theme, students should determine who is speaking and look for details that help get across the message. Point out that Whitman is the speaker. Some of his important ideas are that people are connected to nature and others. Have students reread the poem looking for words that convey Whitman's message.

 For additional support, go to the **Reading Studio** and assign the following 📘 **Level Up Tutorial: Analyze Theme**.

CREATE AND DEBATE

Write an Argument Whitman has been accused of being an "egoist," or overly focused on himself, by some readers of his poetry. Use your reading of the selections from "Song of Myself" to write a three- or four-paragraph argument either supporting or refuting this claim.

❏ Write an introduction that introduces the claim of egoism and your position about the claim.

❏ Develop your argument in the body paragraph(s), using textual examples from "Song of Myself" to support your position.

❏ Anticipate and address any counterarguments to strengthen your argument.

❏ Conclude by summarizing your views on Walt Whitman and egoism.

Debate a Position With a small group of classmates who took your same position in the argument, prepare to defend that position in a class debate.

❏ Share your ideas and supporting examples with your group members.

❏ As a group, select key, well-supported claims that you will present in the debate.

❏ Anticipate the claims that the opposing side will make, and prepare rebuttal statements.

❏ Engage your audience by speaking clearly and using appropriate eye contact and volume.

❏ Always show respect in your interactions with the opposing side.

RESPOND TO THE ESSENTIAL QUESTION

 ? In what ways do we seek to remain true to ourselves?

Gather Information Review your annotations and notes on "Song of Myself." Then, add relevant information to your Response Log. As you determine which information to include, think about:

• what it means to be true to oneself
• how the individual is related to society as a whole
• the importance of personal identity

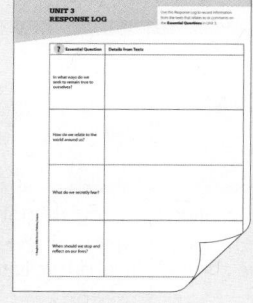

UNIT 3
RESPONSE LOG

| Essential Question | Details from Texts |

Go to **Writing Arguments** in the **Writing Studio** for help.

Go to **Analyzing and Evaluating Presentations** in the **Speaking and Listening Studio** for more on holding a debate.

ACADEMIC VOCABULARY
As you write and discuss what you learned from the poem, be sure to use the Academic Vocabulary words. Check off each of the words that you use.

❏ **analogy**
❏ **denote**
❏ **quote**
❏ **topic**
❏ **unique**

Song of Myself   221

CREATE AND DEBATE

Write an Argument You may wish to hold a discussion with students before they begin writing to see if there are different opinions on Whitman. If too many students have the same opinion, you may want to assign the underrepresented opinion to some of the more advanced students. Allow students time to reread the poems to look for evidence. Remind them that an argument includes a counterclaim, or an acknowledgement and refutation of what the opposition might say. After students have drafted their arguments, encourage them to try to identify any parts that need to be strengthened.

For **writing support** for students at varying proficiency levels, see the **Text X-Ray** on page 210D.

Debate a Position Have students gather with those who are on the same side of the debate to discuss the key points of the arguments. Have students present the opposing arguments and then discuss who has the most convincing rebuttal statements.

RESPOND TO THE ESSENTIAL QUESTION

Allow time for students to add details from "Song of Myself" to their Unit 3 Response Logs.

MY FRIEND WALT WHITMAN

Essay by Mary Oliver

GENRE ELEMENTS
ESSAY

An **essay** is a short work of nonfiction about one central topic. Near the beginning of an essay, the author includes a **thesis statement,** which tells the reader the author's argument or purpose. The body of the essay includes evidence to support the author's thesis, which are often examples or citations from another text. At the end of the essay, the author restates the thesis and summarizes the supporting evidence.

LEARNING OBJECTIVES

- Analyze an essay for the development of key ideas using annotation.
- Make connections between the author's works.
- Write an essay about a favorite author.
- Discuss the impact of literature on our lives.
- Define critical vocabulary words.
- Identify examples from the selection of an informal writing style.
- **Language** Express personal connections to the text.

TEXT COMPLEXITY

Quantitative Measures	My Friend Walt Whitman	Lexile: 1030
Qualitative Measures	**Ideas Presented** Much is explicit but moves to some implied meaning. Requires some inferential reasoning.	
	Structures Used Primarily explicit. Varies from simple chronological order. Largely conventional.	
	Language Used Mostly explicit, some figurative or allusive language. Some unconventional language.	
	Knowledge Required Some references to other texts. Begins to rely on outside knowledge.	

RESOURCES

- Unit 3 Response Log
- Selection Audio
- Reading Studio:
  Notice & Note
- Level Up Tutorials: Main Idea and
  Supporting Details; Prose Forms
- Writing Studio:
  Writing Informative Texts
- Speaking and Listening Studio:
  Participating in Collaborative
  Discussions
- Vocabulary Studio:
  Using Reference Resources
- "My Friend Walt Whitman"
  Selection Test

SUMMARIES

English

Mary Oliver describes her life growing up in a small town in Ohio in the 1950s. She tells how she was somewhat disconnected from the "mainstream of that time." While real people sometimes left, her "shadow-companions" from books remained constant. Walt Whitman was one of these companions. She thought of him as a brother. Oliver recounts how she skipped school and, instead, went to the woods and fields and immersed herself in Whitman's poetry. She described how his faith and certainty strengthened her own "when everything was needed" and taught her how powerful words can be.

Spanish

Mary Oliver describe su vida al crecer en un pueblo pequeño en Ohio en los años cincuenta. Comenta que estaba desconectada del "convencionalismo de la época". Mientras que las personas reales a veces se iban, los "compañeros de sombra" de sus libros permanecían constantes. Walt Whitman era uno de esos compañeros. Lo veía como su hermano. Oliver recuenta que, en lugar de ir a clases, iba a los bosques y a los campos a sumergirse en la poesía de Whitman. Describe cómo la fe y certeza de Whitman fortalecieron la suya cuando "todo hacía falta" y le enseñó lo poderosas que son las palabras.

SMALL-GROUP OPTIONS

Have students work in small groups and pairs to read and discuss the selection.

Gallery Walk

- Post four large blank posters around the room. At the top of each poster, write one *Analyze* question from the side margins on pages 225–227.
- Organize the class into four small groups and provide each group with a different colored marker with which to write on the posters.
- Have the students circulate around the room with their group to discuss the question and write a response on the poster.
- When all groups have responded, use the responses on the posters to guide the students in a group discussion about the questions.

Vocabulary Charades

- Organize the students into small groups and have the students write the Critical Vocabulary words and their definitions on slips of paper. Have them fold the paper and put the slips in a container.
- Demonstrate how to play charades by choosing a word not in the container and acting it out. Tell the students to try to guess the word.
- Allow the students time to act out all the words, giving each student a turn.
- Play charades for as long as time allows. You and/or the students can add more words from the selection into the container if desired.

Text X-Ray: English Learner Support
for "My Friend Walt Whitman"

Use the Text X-Ray and the supports and scaffolds in the Teacher's Edition to help guide students at different proficiency levels through the selection.

INTRODUCE THE SELECTION
DISCUSS WALT WHITMAN

In this section, students will need to understand who Walt Whitman is and the themes in his poetry to which Mary Oliver felt connected.

Review some main ideas found in Whitman's poetry. Display a word web like the one below and write *Walt Whitman* in the center. In the outer circles, identify ideas found in Whitman's poetry. Have students work together to find words or phrases from the selection associated with each idea and connect them to the outer circles of the web.

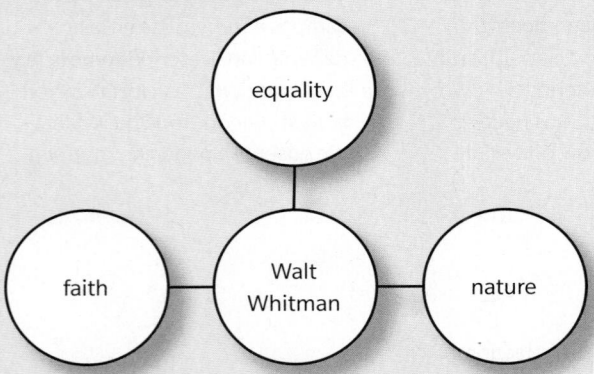

CULTURAL REFERENCES

The following words or phrases may be unfamiliar to students:

- *congenial* (paragraph 1): agreeable
- *shadow-companions* (paragraph 2): someone who is not really there
- *gypsy boy* (paragraph 3): a boy who wanders or travels
- *knapsack* (paragraph 4): backpack
- *truancy* (paragraph 4): unexcused absence from school
- *stood before me like a model of a delivery* (paragraph 5): were powerful examples
- *lit circle* (paragraph 5): short for *literature circle*; a place where students get together to discuss a piece of literature; a book club

LISTENING

Listen to Understand

To help students understand the meaning of the selection, read aloud and have the students answer comprehension questions. Read aloud the first two paragraphs.

Use the following supports with students at varying proficiency levels:

- Reread the paragraphs. Ask yes/no questions about the paragraphs to check for comprehension. For example: *Did Oliver have real friends?* (No.) *Did she read a lot of poetry?* (Yes.) **SUBSTANTIAL**
- Provide a copy of the paragraphs with key words removed, such as *few friends, loyal, poetry, usual,* and *writings*. As you reread the paragraphs, have students fill in the missing words. Ask simple questions to check for understanding. **MODERATE**
- As you read the paragraphs, have students jot down key words. Have students share the key words they listed and explain why they feel these words are important to understanding the paragraph. **LIGHT**

SPEAKING

Make Connections

Oliver made personal connections to Whitman's words. Students can make personal connections to Oliver's words, which will help them understand and remember their meaning.

Use the following supports with students at varying proficiency levels:

- Provide model sentences in positive and negative forms that help students express a personal connection to the text, such as *I like books* or *I do not like books*. Have students repeat the sentence that is true for them. Then have them make a connection to the text using this sentence frame: *I am like/not like the author because I like/do not like books*. **SUBSTANTIAL**
- Have students work in pairs to talk about personal connections with the text. Provide sentence frames: *I like _____. I am like the author because _____.* Have students complete the frames. **MODERATE**
- Have students work in pairs to share personal connections with the text. Have them use the word *because* to explain why. For example: *I feel a connection with the author because _____.* **LIGHT**

READING

Identify Key Ideas

Explain that Oliver uses quotations and personal experiences to support the main idea. A quotation is someone else's exact words. Personal experiences are things the author has done.

Use the following supports with students at varying proficiency levels:

- Lead students in an echo-reading of the last sentence of paragraph 4. Ask students if the author did this or if this is Whitman's words. **SUBSTANTIAL**
- Have students copy the chart on page 223. Supply students with key points, such as Whitman's quotations and phrases like *she skipped school, her friends were authors,* and *she learned from books*. As students read the selection, have them fill in the second column of the chart. **MODERATE**
- Have students copy the chart on page 223. Then pair students and have them read the text and identify two key points that are personal experiences and two that are quotations. **LIGHT**

WRITING

Write an Essay

Work with students to read the writing assignment on Student Edition page 229.

Use the following supports with students at varying proficiency levels:

- Display a model sentence like the following: *I admire J. K. Rowling because of her imagination*. Help students write a thesis statement by filling in the sentence frame. **SUBSTANTIAL**
- Provide a model thesis statement (see above). Point out that the word *because* tells why. Have partners write a thesis statement using the model. Have pairs find quotations from the author's work that support their thesis. **MODERATE**
- Have students work independently to write a thesis statement and find examples from the author's work that support the main idea. Have them exchange papers with a partner to check whether the examples are clear and related to the thesis. **LIGHT**

Connect to the
ESSENTIAL QUESTION

"My Friend Walt Whitman" demonstrates one of the ways we can relate to the world around us—through reading and connecting with different forms of literature. This personal essay explores how we can forge strong bonds with authors we have never met.

MY FRIEND WALT WHITMAN

Essay by **Mary Oliver**

? ESSENTIAL QUESTION:

How do we relate to the world around us?

222 Unit 3

QUICK START

In this essay, the author examines her life in relationship to the inspiration she got from the poetry of Walt Whitman. What inspires you? It may be a piece of writing, someone you know, or something else entirely. Discuss your ideas with the class.

ANALYZE ESSAYS

An **essay** is a short work of nonfiction on a single subject. Essays can be written for many purposes: to inform, persuade, express an idea or feelings, or entertain. An essay can be formal or informal. This essay is informal—it uses the first person and has a conversational tone.

Essays include a **thesis statement** that expresses the writer's main idea. The author may then use quotations, examples, and personal experiences to support the thesis. The organizational design of an essay often supports the writer's purpose, which in this case is to express her feelings about Whitman and poetry. As you read, look for the thesis statement and think about the essay's organizational design.

ANALYZE DEVELOPMENT OF KEY IDEAS

When reading an essay, it is important to analyze the development of key ideas. Writers **develop key ideas** by including a variety of evidence—such as facts, quotations, examples, statistics, or personal experiences. To analyze key ideas, think about how the details support the author's thesis and purpose.

One way that Oliver supports her ideas is to cite quotations from Walt Whitman's work. She also relates her own personal experiences. Take notes to keep track of the significant details and how they support your understanding of the writer's important ideas. As you list the details, you can begin to infer which ideas are key to the essay.

GENRE ELEMENTS: ESSAY

- includes a thesis statement to identify writer's argument or purpose
- offers details or evidence to support the thesis
- has a conclusion that restates the thesis and summarizes the evidence

TYPE OF EVIDENCE	DETAILS FROM TEXT	HOW IT SUPPORTS KEY IDEA
Quotations by Whitman	*Example: "This hour I tell things in confidence, I might not tell everybody but I will tell you."*	*Example: The quote makes a close connection between Whitman and his reader.*
Personal Experiences	*Example: She often skipped school, taking her books with her.*	*Example, Makes the point that her favorite writers were her best companions*

My Friend Walt Whitman 223

QUICK START

Have students read the Quick Start question and invite them to share what inspires them. Point out that the things that inspire us help us make sense of and relate to the rest of the world. For example, a great poem might help us understand another person's experience and lead us to be more caring. A fictional superhero's story might help give us direction and teach us values. Being inspired by nature might help us feel connected to the planet and make us live more responsibly.

ANALYZE ESSAYS

Have students recall essays they have written for other classes. Ask them how creating an initial thesis statement helped to organize their essay. Writing a thesis statement might feel like a difficult task, but, in the end, it makes writing an essay much easier. Discuss the benefits of having a clear thesis statement. *(It sets the purpose for the essay. It narrows the focus. It establishes expectations for the reader.)* Have students imagine they are going to write a short personal essay about their morning. What might their thesis statement be? Give them a couple minutes to think about it and to write their thesis statements. Encourage students to make their thesis statements detailed and concise. Thesis statements might revolve around such things as traffic, the weather, breakfast, or whether or not they got a good night's sleep.

ANALYZE DEVELOPMENT OF KEY IDEAS

Tell students that they will read this essay to look at how the author uses evidence to support key ideas. Point out that sometimes these features are called "main ideas and details." Being able to identify supporting evidence—and separating it from the other features of an essay—helps readers understand what the essay is about. Ask students to imagine an essay about the construction of the Statue of Liberty. Ask them what kind of key ideas and details they might see in that essay. *(Details might include the dimensions of the statue, how it was manufactured, and why it was given to the United States.)*

For **reading support** for students at varying proficiency levels, see the **Text X-Ray** on page 222D.

TEACH

CRITICAL VOCABULARY

Tell students to read all the words before looking at the definitions. Suggest that they identify any familiar roots, prefixes, and suffixes. Explain that considering the meanings of these word parts will help them define the words.

Answers:

1. *a*

2. *b*

3. *a*

4. *a*

5. *a*

■ English Learner Support

Use Cognates Tell students that four of the Critical Vocabulary words have a Spanish cognate: *bravado/bravata, delinquent/delincuente, inclination/inclinación, metaphysical/metafísico.* **ALL LEVELS**

LANGUAGE CONVENTIONS

Informal Style After students have read the information about informal style, tell students that Mary Oliver, the writer of this essay, is a highly respected poet. Ask students why they think she would use an informal style for this particular essay. *(The essay is very personal, so it makes sense that the style is more conversational.)*

Have students read the example sentence. Ask them to point out the elements that are personal. *(The use of "I"; "my friends"; "of course"; the use of a dash; "they were strangers")*

ANNOTATION MODEL

Remind students that a thesis statement is supported by evidence and details. As students read, they might want to underline or highlight evidence that supports the writer's thesis statement.

CRITICAL VOCABULARY

inclination   estrangement   delinquent   bravado   metaphysical

To see how many Critical Vocabulary words you already know, write the correct word after each definition.

1. Something that is immaterial or supernatural is _____.
   a. metaphysical   b. delinquent

2. If you have a tendency to act a certain way, you have _____.
   a. bravado   b. an inclination

3. When you feel a sense of alienation, you feel _____.
   a. estrangement   b. metaphysical

4. If you show bravery or defiance, you show _____.
   a. bravado   b. estrangement

5. When you ignore laws or duties, you _____.
   a. are delinquent   b. feel an inclination

LANGUAGE CONVENTIONS

Informal Style Informal writing is more like spoken language than formal writing is. It observes many of the same rules as formal style, but it is more casual. Contractions, idioms, and common phrases are often used in informal essays. Notice how Oliver uses the common phrase *of course* in her essay.

> I never met any of my friends, of course, in a usual way— they were strangers, and lived only in their writings.

As you read "My Friend Walt Whitman," look for ways in which the writing seems conversational rather than formal.

ANNOTATION MODEL

NOTICE & NOTE

As you read, think about how Mary Oliver develops key ideas in her essay. In the model, you can see one reader's notes about "My Friend Walt Whitman."

My town was no more or less congenial to the fact of poetry than any other small town in America—I make no special case of a solitary childhood. Estrangement from the mainstream of that time and place was an unavoidable precondition, no doubt, to the life I was choosing from among all the lives possible to me.

Poetry was not part of her life.

She feels out of place.

She had other options; what influenced her to make this choice?

BACKGROUND

Mary Oliver *(b. 1935) was born in Maple Heights, Ohio. Her first book of poetry,* No Voyage and Other Poems, *was published in the United Kingdom in 1963, when Oliver was 28. Oliver's life choice may have been influenced by Walt Whitman, but another major early influence was poet Edna St. Vincent Millay. Oliver is a prolific poet and has won numerous honors, including the Pulitzer Prize and National Book Award. Her poetry is known for its focus on the natural world and her effort to explore both the beauty and difficulty of nature. Oliver rarely grants interviews, saying she wants people to discover her through her writing.*

MY FRIEND WALT WHITMAN

Essay by Mary Oliver

SETTING A PURPOSE

As you read, pay attention to how Oliver develops key ideas in this essay. Who are her friends, why are they important, and what impact have they had on her life?

1   In Ohio, in the 1950s, I had a few friends who kept me sane, alert, and loyal to my own best and wildest **inclinations.** My town was no more or less congenial to the fact of poetry than any other small town in America—I make no special case of a solitary childhood. **Estrangement** from the mainstream of that time and place was an unavoidable precondition, no doubt, to the life I was choosing from among all the lives possible to me.

2   I never met any of my friends, of course, in a usual way—they were strangers, and lived only in their writings. But if they were only shadow-companions, still they were constant, and powerful, and amazing. That is, they said amazing things, and for me it changed the world.

> *This hour I tell things in confidence,*
> *I might not tell everybody but I will tell you.*[1]

---
[1] All text in italics, including italic text that is not set apart from the main text, is from Walt Whitman's poem "Song of Myself."

Notice & Note

Use the side margins to notice and note signposts in the text.

inclination
(ĭn-klə-nāʹshən) *n.* a characteristic disposition or tendency to act in a certain way; a propensity.

estrangement
(ĭ-strānjʹmənt) *n.* the condition of being detached or withdrawn; alienation.

ANALYZE ESSAYS

Annotate: In paragraph 2, mark Oliver's thesis statement.

Analyze: What unusual claim does Oliver make about her "friends"?

BACKGROUND

After students read the Background note, explain that Mary Oliver is particularly well suited to describe the relationship that we can have to literature. Not only did she grow up as a reader who found solace and inspiration in books, but she became a famous poet, sharing her ideas about nature and beauty with her readers. Her poems give readers new ways to think about how people relate to the world. This essay does the same.

SETTING A PURPOSE

Direct students to use the Setting a Purpose prompt to focus their reading.

ANALYZE ESSAYS

Explain that thesis statements are often bolder, clearer, and more independent than their surrounding sentences. (**Answer:** *She says that as a child, she never met any of her friends in the usual way and that they were strangers she met through their writing.*)

For **listening** and **speaking support** for students at varying proficiency levels, see the **Text X-Ray** on pages 222C – 222D.

CRITICAL VOCABULARY

inclination: The writer is talking about her preferences and tendencies as a child.

ASK STUDENTS to predict what the writer's "wildest" inclinations might have been as a child. (*A wild inclination might be to misbehave, skip school, or act mischievously.*)

estrangement: The essay makes the point that we don't always feel comfortable in the time and place in which we live.

ASK STUDENTS how the word *strange* might be related to estrangement. (*It might be the root word, or* estrangement *might mean "made to feel strange."*)

WHEN STUDENTS STRUGGLE . . .

Identify Thesis Statements   Remind students that the opening paragraphs of an essay will likely hold the thesis statement. Identifying a thesis statement will help them make sense of an essay as they read. Ask for volunteers to read the thesis statement on this page (in the marginal instruction, students have been told to annotate the sentence in paragraph 2). (*I never met any of my friends, of course, in a usual way—they were strangers, and lived only in their writings.*) Tell students to keep this sentence in mind as they encounter information and ideas throughout the essay.

 For additional support, go to the **Reading Studio** and assign the following **Level Up Tutorial: Main Idea and Supporting Details.**

TEACH

QUOTED WORDS

Remind students that quotations are a common feature of nonfiction writing, such as news articles and essays. Quotations usually come in two varieties: block quotes and in-line quotes. When used correctly, quotations serve important purposes. Discuss with students how Mary Oliver's use of quotations is creative and engaging. (**Answer:** *It is unique that she uses so many quotes throughout the essay, usually without introduction. She uses them both internally and in block quotes. The quotations support her purpose of telling the reader why she thinks of Whitman as her friend.*)

 For **reading support** for students at varying proficiency levels, see the **Text X-Ray** on page 222D.

LANGUAGE CONVENTIONS

Most essays students write for classes call for formal language. This means their writing should feature complete sentences, proper grammar, and full words (as opposed to contractions). Formal writing is not conversational; it is impersonal and usually objective. Mary Oliver used an informal style in her essay because she was writing for a general audience and wished to communicate very clearly. (**Answer:** *The phrase "I mean" helps give the essay a personal feel. The phrase is conversational, which puts the reader at ease. It also introduces a rephrasing of the previous thought; this signals that the writer is working to be as clear as possible for the benefit of the reader. This, too, makes the essay more accessible.*)

CRITICAL VOCABULARY

delinquent: The writer first describes other students' behavior as "delinquent" before suggesting that she, too, became guilty of it.

ASK STUDENTS what might constitute delinquent behavior. (*skipping school, misbehaving, property destruction*)

bravado: The words *bravado* and *bravery* are similar in meaning, but *bravado* connotes a certain attitude.

ASK STUDENTS why a young person might be attracted to a writer's bravado. (*They might find the writer's confidence and attitude appealing.*)

metaphysical: Whitman had varied interests, including intellectual and speculative ones.

ASK STUDENTS what might count for metaphysical curiosity. (*questions about the origins of life, the meaning of life, and so on*)

226 Unit 3

QUOTED WORDS

Notice & Note: Mark the Walt Whitman quotes on this page.

Analyze: What is unique about the way Oliver organizes her essay? How does this organization support her purpose?

delinquent
(dĭ-lĭng´kwənt) *adj.* failing to do what law or duty requires.

LANGUAGE CONVENTIONS
Annotate: Mark the informal phrase in the first sentence of paragraph 5.

Analyze: How does this phrase affect the essay and how the reader might react to it?

bravado
(brə-vä´dō) *n.* a show of bravery or defiance, often in order to make a false impression or mislead someone.

metaphysical
(mĕt-ə-fĭz´ĭ-kəl) *adj.* based on speculative or abstract reasoning.

---

3   Whitman was the brother I did not have. I did have an uncle, whom I loved, but he killed himself one rainy fall day; Whitman remained, perhaps more avuncular[2] for the loss of the other. He was the gypsy boy my sister and I went off with into the far fields beyond the town, with our pony, to gather strawberries. The boy from Romania[3] moved away; Whitman shone on in the twilight of my room, which was growing busy with books, and notebooks, and muddy boots, and my grandfather's old Underwood typewriter.

> *My voice goes after what my eyes cannot reach,*
> *With the twirl of my tongue I encompass worlds and volumes of worlds.*

4   When the high school I went to experienced a crisis of **delinquent** student behavior, my response was to start out for school every morning but to turn most mornings into the woods instead, with a knapsack of books. Always Whitman's was among them. My truancy was extreme, and my parents were warned that I might not graduate. For whatever reason, they let me continue to go my own way. It was an odd blessing, but a blessing all the same. Down by the creek, or in the wide pastures I could still find on the other side of the deep woods, I spent my time with my friend: my brother, my uncle, my best teacher.

> *The moth and the fisheggs are in their place,*
> *The suns I see and the suns I cannot see are in their place,*
> *The palpable is in its place and the impalpable is in its place.*

5   Thus Whitman's poems stood before me like a model of delivery when I began to write poems myself: I mean the oceanic power and rumble that travels through a Whitman poem—the incantatory[4] syntax, the boundless affirmation. In those years, truth was elusive—as was my own faith that I could recognize and contain it. Whitman kept me from the swamps of a worse uncertainty, and I lived many hours within the lit circle of his certainty, and his **bravado.** *Unscrew the locks from the doors! Unscrew the doors themselves from their jambs!* And there was the passion which he invested in the poems. The **metaphysical** curiosity! The oracular[5] tenderness with which he viewed the world—its roughness, its differences, the stars, the spider—nothing was outside the range of his interest. I reveled in the specificity of his words. And his faith—that kept my spirit buoyant surely, though his faith was without a name that I ever heard of.

---

[2] **avuncular:** of or having to do with an uncle.
[3] **boy from Romania:** This phrase refers to the gypsy in the previous sentence. The gypsies, also called Romani, are one of the largest minority groups in Romania.
[4] **incantatory:** in the manner of a verbal charm or spell.
[5] **oracular:** resembling or characteristic of an oracle; solemnly prophetic.

226 Unit 3

APPLYING ACADEMIC VOCABULARY

☐ **analogy**   ☐ **denote**   ☑ **quote**   ☐ **topic**   ☐ **unique**

Write and Discuss Have students turn to a partner to discuss the following question. Guide students to include the academic vocabulary word *quote* in their responses. Ask volunteers to share their responses with the class.

• What is your favorite **quote** of Whitman that Oliver uses? Explain why it is your favorite quote.

Do you guess I have some intricate purpose? Well I have . . . for the April rain has, and the mica on the side of a rock has.

6   But first and foremost, I learned from Whitman that the poem is a temple—or a green field—a place to enter, and in which to feel. Only in a secondary way is it an intellectual thing—an artifact, a moment of seemly and robust wordiness—wonderful as that part of it is. I learned that the poem was made not just to exist, but to speak— to be company. It was everything that was needed, when everything was needed. I remember the delicate, rumpled way into the woods, and the weight of the books in my pack. I remember the rambling, and the loafing—the wonderful days when, with Whitman, *I tucked my trowser-ends in my boots and went and had a good time.*

NOTICE & NOTE

ANALYZE DEVELOPMENT OF KEY IDEAS

Annotate: In paragraph 6, mark what Oliver learned from Whitman.

Analyze: How does this sentence develop a key idea expressed in the thesis statement?

CHECK YOUR UNDERSTANDING

Answer these questions before moving on to the **Analyze the Text** section on the following page.

1 How did Oliver think of Whitman?

  A As her uncle or Romanian cousin

  B As the brother she didn't have

  C As a somewhat interesting poet

  D As a poet she was forced to read

2 What triggered Oliver's truancy?

  F Students in her class displayed delinquent behavior.

  G Her parents did not believe in the school.

  H The school stopped teaching writing.

  J She was meeting her friend and goofing off.

3 What does Oliver mean when she writes that "the poem is a temple"?

  A Writing is a religious experience for her.

  B Whitman wrote religious poetry.

  C It allows her to explore her emotions.

  D She prefers traditional forms of poetry.

 ANALYZE DEVELOPMENT OF KEY IDEAS

Explain that key ideas support the thesis statement and make the argument more convincing. (**Answer:** *This supports the idea that Whitman was a friend who taught her many things, particularly to appreciate poetry.*)

■ ENGLISH LEARNER SUPPORT

Understand Supporting Ideas and Details Explain that, just as an entire essay has a thesis statement backed up by evidence, an individual paragraph or section of text has a key idea and supporting details as well. Draw students' attention to paragraph 3. Point out that the first sentence is the closest to a main idea—that the writer considered Whitman to be a member of her family. Have students volunteer details from the paragraph that support that main idea. Write these on the board. Then slowly read through the paragraph again until you discover all of the supporting ideas. **SUBSTANTIAL**

CHECK YOUR UNDERSTANDING

Have students answer the questions independently.

Answers:

  1. *B*

  2. *F*

  3. *C*

If they answer any questions incorrectly, have them reread the text to confirm their understanding. Then they may proceed to ANALYZE THE TEXT on page 228.

 ENGLISH LEARNER SUPPORT

Oral Assessment Use the following questions to assess students' comprehension and speaking skills.

  1. How did Oliver feel about Walt Whitman? (*Oliver felt that Whitman was like a brother.*)

  2. Why did Oliver begin to skip school? (*Many students in her class displayed delinquent behavior.*)

  3. Oliver says that Whitman's poems are like a temple. What does she mean? (*The poem allowed her to think about how she felt.*) **LIGHT**

ANALYZE THE TEXT

Possible answers:

1. **DOK 2:** *She means that her life was not all that unusual, at least not so unusual that it would account for her being "different." She wants the reader to know that her town and upbringing were like others and that is not the reason she felt so strongly about Whitman and books.*

2. **DOK 4:** *He was a constant companion who "said amazing things" that "changed the world" for her. He was like a brother to her ("Whitman was the brother I did not have.") and replaced other figures in her life, such as an uncle ("an uncle, whom I loved"). He inspired her with "his bravado" and faith ("that kept my spirit buoyant").*

3. **DOK 2:** *Her purpose is to entertain the reader by describing how her friends in childhood were her literary heroes, including Walt Whitman. She succeeds in doing so by claiming the following: Whitman was a constant companion who "said amazing things"; "Whitman was the brother I did not have"; he also took the place of a beloved uncle; while in the wilderness, she would spend "time with my friend"; "Whitman kept me from the swamps of a worse uncertainty"; "his faith . . . kept my spirit buoyant"; and so on.*

4. **DOK 3:** *The quotations provide support for Oliver's thesis statement that Whitman was like a childhood friend. The quotations are spread evenly throughout the text, even popping up sometimes without introduction. Using the quotations in this way helps Oliver make her point that Whitman was a constant companion and a major influence in her life.*

5. **DOK 4:** *The title of the poem, "Song of Myself," supports the ideas that the poem is about how one identifies oneself. In the essay, Oliver writes that she grew up with guidance from her favorite authors, people she thought of as friends. In a way, Whitman's "Song of Myself" was a guidebook for Oliver's childhood; it was her song, as well. In this way, the quotations support the main idea of the essay, because they show what a strong influence Whitman had on her early life.*

RESEARCH

The graphic organizer should include parallels and connections for each of the three poems.

Extend Students should cite examples from the essay of her views on nature, as well as views from at least one of her poems.

ANALYZE THE TEXT

Support your responses with evidence from the text. 📓 NOTEBOOK

1. **Interpret** In the first paragraph, Oliver writes that she makes "no special case of a solitary childhood." What do you think she means by this? Why do you think she includes this information?

2. **Analyze** How does Oliver support the idea that Whitman was her friend? Cite evidence from the text in your response.

3. **Infer** Oliver does not directly state her purpose for writing. It is up to you to infer it based on details in the text. What is Oliver's main purpose for writing? Cite text evidence in your response.

4. **Evaluate** How do the quotations from Whitman create an organizational design for the essay? How does this organizational design support Oliver's ideas?

5. **Notice & Note** The poem quoted throughout the essay is Walt Whitman's "Song of Myself." How does the title of this poem and the use of quotations support the main idea of Oliver's essay?

RESEARCH TIP
Use both Oliver's name and the title of the poem to easily find the works specified.

RESEARCH

Find and read the poems "Sleeping in the Forest," "Why I Wake Early," and "Song of the Builders" by Mary Oliver. Think about the essay you just read, and note in the chart below the parallels or connections you find between Oliver's poems and what you read in the essay. The parallels can be themes, phrases, words, or ideas.

POEM	PARALLELS AND CONNECTIONS
"Sleeping in the Forest"	*Notes should include specific references to the two texts.*
"Why I Wake Early"	*Notes should include specific references to the two texts.*
"Song of the Builders"	*Notes should include specific references to the two texts.*

Extend Mary Oliver is famous for poetry that focuses on nature. What general view of nature does Oliver express in her writing? In a small group, discuss Oliver's view on the natural world. Cite evidence from the essay and at least one of the poems in your discussion.

WHEN STUDENTS STRUGGLE . . .

Reteaching: Analyzing Essays Review the definition of a thesis statement: a sentence that expresses the writer's main idea or purpose for writing. Every essay should have a thesis statement, and the major details in an essay should support that statement. As a class, create a thesis statement for a possible essay about the discovery of a new dinosaur species. The thesis statement should be able to be supported by evidence. (*Example: "The discovery of this new dinosaur revolutionizes paleontology and the current understanding of how dinosaurs evolved."*)

 For additional support, go to the **Reading Studio** and assign the following 📘 **Level Up Tutorial: Prose Forms.**

CREATE AND DISCUSS

Write an Essay   Write an essay about an author whom you admire or whose work you enjoy. Focus on why you think the author's work is important and/or influential.

- ❏ Work on crafting a good thesis statement—what you are going to claim about the author.
- ❏ Include information about the author and quotes from his or her work. The quotes should support your thesis.
- ❏ Include a conclusion that summarizes your thesis statement.

Discuss with a Small Group   Discuss the impact of literature on our lives. Use your essay as the basis of your contribution to the discussion. To prepare for the discussion, you may want to think about the following questions:

- ❏ What are the different kinds of literature we read and why are they important?
- ❏ How do movies sometimes revise or change literature?
- ❏ What can we experience by reading various types of literature?

 Go to **Writing Informative Texts** in the **Writing Studio** for help with writing essays.

Go to **Participating in Collaborative Discussions** in the **Speaking and Listening Studio** for help.

RESPOND TO THE ESSENTIAL QUESTION

?   How do we relate to the world around us?

Gather Information   Review your annotations and notes on "My Friend Walt Whitman." Then, add relevant information to your Response Log. As you determine which information to include, think about:

- the impact reading Walt Whitman had on the writer
- how the quotes from Walt Whitman's work help develop the main idea
- the effect of the author's use of personal anecdotes

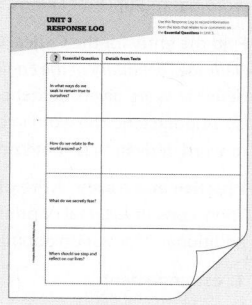

ACADEMIC VOCABULARY
As you write and discuss what you learned from the essay, be sure to use the Academic Vocabulary words. Check off each of the words that you use.

- ❏ **analogy**
- ❏ **denote**
- ❏ **quote**
- ❏ **topic**
- ❏ **unique**

CREATE AND DISCUSS

Write an Essay   Student essays should feature a specific author and explain why the students think the author's work is meaningful. Essays must include a well-crafted thesis statement that makes an argument about the author. Information about the author should support the thesis. The best essays will have quotations from the author. Remind students to revise their personal essays for clarity of content, accuracy, and depth of information. A conclusion should summarize the essay and reference the thesis statement.

For **writing support** for students at varying proficiency levels, see the **Text X-Ray** on page 222C.

Discuss with a Small Group   Discussions should demonstrate effective oral collaboration, including coming prepared to the discussion, listening to others, and offering insightful input.

RESPOND TO THE ESSENTIAL QUESTION

Allow time for students to add details from "My Friend Walt Whitman" to their Unit 3 Response Logs.

CRITICAL VOCABULARY

Answers:

1. *b; Possible answer: "When you are delinquent, you're not doing the things you should."*

2. *a; Possible answer: "When you have bravado, you act bravely. One way to act bravely is to stand up for yourself."*

3. *a; Possible answer: "Metaphysics is based on abstract reasoning, and philosophy is more abstract than something like engineering."*

4. *b; Possible answer: "When you fight with someone, you might alienate that person."*

5. *a; Possible answer: "Being on time is important to me."*

VOCABULARY STRATEGY:
Use Print and Digital Resources

Practice and Apply

Possible answers:

1. Estrangement *means "being made to feel strange or like a stranger." Students should provide additional information based on their research.*

2. Bravado *means "braveness." Students should provide additional information based on their research.*

3. Metaphysical *means "something that goes beyond the physical." Students should provide additional information based on their research.*

 RESPOND

WORD BANK
inclination
estrangement
delinquent
bravado
metaphysical

CRITICAL VOCABULARY

Practice and Apply Circle the letter of the best answer to each question. Then, explain your response.

1. An example of **delinquent** behavior is —
   a. doing homework   **b.** not doing chores

2. **Bravado** is more likely to result in —
   a. standing your ground   **b.** running away

3. An interest in the **metaphysical** might draw one to —
   a. philosophy   **b.** engineering

4. Which of the following might lead to **estrangement**?
   a. working with someone   **b.** arguing with someone

5. Which is an example of an **inclination** of an organized person?
   a. being on time   **b.** being spontaneous

Go to **Using Reference Resources** in the **Vocabulary Studio** for help with using digital and print resources.

VOCABULARY STRATEGY: Use Print and Digital Resources

Digital and print resources, such as online and print dictionaries, can provide additional information about unfamiliar words and help you verify the meaning of a word. Using print and digital resources is especially important when the context isn't enough to determine the word's meaning, when a word has multiple meanings, or when the word is archaic, or no longer used.

Find the entry for the Critical Vocabulary word *inclination* in the *American Heritage Dictionary of the English Language*. Notice that a number of definitions are given. Sentences using the word are also included to help the user understand the word in context. In many entries, the word's etymology or word derivation is shown in brackets. Related words are also shown.

Practice and Apply Write what you think each word listed below means. Then, consult a digital or print dictionary to confirm the meaning and find additional information about each word.

1. estrangement:

   _____

2. bravado:

   _____

3. metaphysical:

   _____

EL ## ENGLISH LEARNER SUPPORT

Vocabulary Strategy Oliver's essay includes many words that are cognates in Spanish. Work with students to discover cognates beyond the ones listed in the Get Ready section. Words with cognates include *solitary, possible,* and *extreme*. Read all of the sentences containing those words, using the cognates to help students understand the sentences. Work with students to write new sentences using three of the cognates you find.
ALL LEVELS

LANGUAGE CONVENTIONS:
Informal Style

Authors choose what style they will use based on their purpose for writing. Formal language is used for academic or business settings. Informal language is often used in personal essays, so it sounds more conversational, as if the author is talking to the reader. Informal language often includes slang, idioms, or colloquial phrases. Contractions appear regularly in informal writing. The writer may occasionally address the reader directly, using the second-person *you*. Oliver uses many aspects of informal style.

- Her sentences are long and sound as if they are part of a conversation.

  The boy from Romania moved away; Whitman shone on in the twilight of my room, which was growing busy with books, and notebooks, and muddy boots, and my grandfather's old Underwood typewriter.

- Here, Oliver interjects information in the middle of the sentence.

  Only in a secondary way is it an intellectual thing—an artifact, a moment of seemly and robust wordiness— wonderful as that part of it is.

- She begins a sentence with a conjunction.

  And there was the passion which he invested in the poems.

- She shows empathy for the reader and adds clarification in a relatable way.

  That is, they said amazing things, and for me it changed the world.

Practice and Apply Write a paragraph about Mary Oliver, Walt Whitman, or any other writer you admire, using an informal style. As you write, think about how you would talk to someone about the subject you've chosen. Remember that the writing still has to be clear, but it can be friendly and conversational.

LANGUAGE CONVENTIONS:
Informal Style

Explore the concept of formal versus informal writing by asking students what genres of writing most often feature the two respective styles. Formal writing is most appropriate for official reports, business letters, news articles, and most school essays. Informal writing, on the other hand, most often appears in friendly letters, blogs, texts, social media messages, and personal essays.

Remind students most instruction and practice in their language arts classes have emphasized formal writing. Stress that formal writing is still the most appropriate style to use when completing essays and reports for school.

However, creative writing, including some personal essays, offers the chance for writers to use an informal style. This style requires practice, just like the formal style. Informal style is not a rejection of grammar rules and the need for clarity; in fact, a writer using the informal style must work very hard to produce a clear, concise, and engaging text.

Practice and Apply Students' paragraphs should demonstrate an informal style by including such elements as contractions, direct address with the reader, dashes, beginning sentences with conjunctions, or a conversational tone. Paragraphs must be clear and communicate something about a writer students admire.

 ENGLISH LEARNER SUPPORT

Language Conventions Use the following supports with students at varying proficiency levels.

- Have students read the sentences on this page and point to the elements that show the informal style. (*dashes, sentence length, opening conjunction*) **SUBSTANTIAL**

- Have students rewrite the sentences on this page in a formal style. Sentences can be very simple, but they should reflect formality and proper grammar. **MODERATE**

- Have students write formal and informal versions of sentences they make up. Tell them to choose any subject they wish. **LIGHT**

POEMS BY EMILY DICKINSON

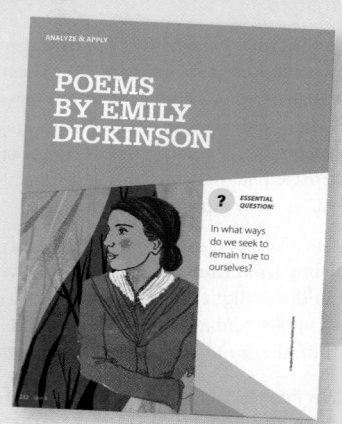

GENRE ELEMENTS
POETRY

Poetry is language arranged in lines and stanzas. The form and content of the poem combine to convey meaning. Poetry usually uses figurative language to express ideas, evoke emotions, and recreate experiences. It often contains patterns of meter and rhyme, and it uses the sound of words to connote ideas and create beauty.

LEARNING OBJECTIVES

- Analyze theme, structure, figurative language, and sound devices.
- Conduct research about Dickinson's letter writing.
- Write a poem using concrete images to express an abstract idea.
- Discuss the poem's images and ideas.
- **Language** Identify and write words that rhyme.

TEXT COMPLEXITY

Quantitative Measures	Poems by Emily Dickinson	Lexile: N/A
Qualitative Measures	**Ideas Presented** Multiple levels of complex meaning.	
	Structures Used Speaker is ironic.	
	Language Used Implied meanings, some figurative language.	
	Knowledge Required Moderately complex themes.	

RESOURCES

Online Ed

- Unit 3 Response Log
- Selection Audio
- Reading Studio:
  Notice & Note
- Level Up Tutorial:
  Figurative Language
- Writing Studio:
  Writing as a Process
- Speaking and Listening Studio:
  Participating in Collaborative
  Discussions
- Poems by Emily Dickinson
  Selection Test

SUMMARIES

English

In "The Soul selects her own Society," the speaker describes the experience of choosing a friend.

In "Because I could not stop for Death," the speaker describes a ride in death's carriage.

In "Much Madness is divinest Sense," the speaker notes that standards of "madness" and "sense" are determined by the majority.

In "Tell all the Truth but tell it slant," the speaker says that truth is best presented indirectly.

Spanish

En "El alma elige su propia sociedad", la voz narrativa describe la experiencia de escoger un amigo.

En "Porque no pude detenerme por la muerte", la voz narrativa describe un paseo en el carruaje de la muerte.

En "Mucha locura es el sentido más divino", la voz narrativa comenta que los estándares de la "locura" y el "sentido" son determinados por la mayoría.

En "Di toda la verdad, pero dila sesgada", la voz narrativa dice que es mejor presentar la verdad indirectamente.

SMALL-GROUP OPTIONS

Have students work in small groups and pairs to read and discuss the selection.

Line Up

- Organize students in groups of six or eight.
- Have each group form two parallel lines so each student is facing a partner.
- Ask Analyze questions from the side margins on pages 236–239, and have student partners discuss the answers.
- Signal one line to shift before asking a new question so each student has a new partner.

Hypothetical Questions

- Organize students in pairs.
- Display the following question starters:
  "When might you . . .?"
  "How might you . . .?"
  "Why might you . . .?"
- Have students take turns asking each other questions, using the sentence starters and the Academic Vocabulary words on page 241.
- Example questions may be:
  "When might you use an analogy in a poem?"
  "How might you denote friendship in a poem?"

Text X-Ray: English Learner Support
for Poems by Emily Dickinson

Use the Text X-Ray and the supports and scaffolds in the Teacher's Edition to help guide students at different proficiency levels through the selection.

INTRODUCE THE SELECTION
DISCUSS SOUND DEVICES

In this section, students will need to understand sound devices used in poetry, such as those listed under Analyze Sound Devices on page 234. To help students acquire the new vocabulary, provide the following learning strategies, model them, and allow time for students to practice.

If they run across unfamiliar punctuation, such as a dash, they should request assistance. For example, they might say, "Excuse me. What does this punctuation mean? Why does she use a dash?"

Students should listen not just to the words, but to the way someone's voice changes. Listening for voice changes can help them understand the meter and rhythm. Students should also listen for rhyming words.

Use simpler language to help students understand the sound devises. For example: *Rhyme scheme refers to the pattern of end rhyme, or words that sound the same at the end of each line, like* door *and* more.

Have students use the terms in sentence frames: ____ *and* ____ *help me understand the poem.* ____ *is the pattern of end rhyme. The words* ____ *and* ____ *are examples of end rhyme.*

CULTURAL REFERENCES

The following words or phrases may be unfamiliar to students:

- *chariots* (page 236, line 5): vehicles with two wheels pulled by horses
- *valve* (page 236, line 11): a mechanical device that opens and closes to control the flow of something (e.g., air, water)
- *carriage* (page 237, line 3): a vehicle with four wheels pulled by horses
- *madness* (page 238, line 1): foolish or dangerous thoughts or actions

LISTENING

Distinguish Sound Patterns

An important part of comprehending spoken English is recognizing and distinguishing sound and intonation patterns that occur in speech. Listening to and reading poetry is one way to practice this skill.

Choose one of the poems and read it aloud slowly and clearly as students follow along. Tell students to listen carefully for pauses and changes in pitch, volume, rhythm, and tempo as you read. Use the following supports with students at varying proficiency levels:

- Read the poem aloud, emphasizing the sound and intonation patterns that occur as you do. Then, have students repeat each line after you read it, imitating the sounds they hear. **SUBSTANTIAL**
- Have students work in pairs and read the poem chorally, trying to match the way they heard you read. Then, have students listen as their partners read the poem to evaluate how closely they match you. **MODERATE**
- Have students work in pairs and choose a different poem to practice. Have them read the poem chorally and then take turns listening as their partners read the poem. **LIGHT**

SPEAKING

Use Academic Vocabulary in Context

Students will be more likely to internalize new vocabulary if they have opportunities to use it in a variety of ways. Display the Academic Vocabulary words on page 241. Provide a citation from the text for each.

Explain how the citation represents the vocabulary word. For example: *In the lines "We paused before a House that seemed / A Swelling of the Ground—" (page 237, lines 17–18), the house is an analogy for a grave.*

Use the following supports with students at varying proficiency levels:

- Say the vocabulary word and have the students repeat. Then, chorally read the citation from the selection you have chosen. Explain the literal meaning through gestures or pictures. Use the vocabulary word in context (e.g., *The house is an analogy for a grave.*) Have the students repeat. **SUBSTANTIAL**
- Have students work with a partner to practice reading aloud the examples you have provided. Have them use your model sentences to make other sentences of their own. **MODERATE**
- Have students work in pairs to use the Academic Vocabulary words and the models you have provided. Have them extend your sentences, using the word *because*. For example, "The house is an analogy for a grave because 'A swelling of the Ground' implies the image of a grave." **LIGHT**

READING

Analyze How Form Is Used to Convey Meaning

Form refers to the physical arrangement of words or the length and placement of the lines and the grouping of lines into stanzas. For example, stanzas act like paragraphs and express a key idea.

Point out that poems do not follow the same form as prose. Display one of Dickinson's poems. Draw students' attention to the capitalization, punctuation, line length, and the grouping of lines into stanzas. Use the following supports with students at varying proficiency levels:

- Provide students with the summary for "The Soul selects her own Society" on Teacher Edition page 232B. Choral read the paragraph. Then show the poem. Point out how Dickinson uses form to convey that meaning. **SUBSTANTIAL**
- Have students work in pairs and read the summary of "The Soul selects her own Society." Ask them to work together to consider how the stanzas and punctuation help her express this main idea. **MODERATE**
- Have students work in pairs to read the summary of one of the poems. Then have students read the poem and discuss how Dickinson uses form to convey meaning. **LIGHT**

WRITING

Practice Spelling Words That Rhyme

Poets often use the sound of language, or sound devices, to create a certain quality in their poems. Dickinson often used rhyme. Rhyme is when two or more words have the same sound.

Point out that rhyme is about how words sound, not how they are spelled. Read aloud "Tell all the Truth but tell it slant," emphasizing the rhyming sounds in *lies—surprise* and *kind—blind*. Use the following supports with students at varying proficiency levels:

- Have students identify the words that rhyme and write them down. Have them write other words they know that rhyme with *kind* and *blind*. **SUBSTANTIAL**
- Have students create a two-columned chart labeled *lies—surprise* and *kind—blind*. Have them list words that fit each rhyme scheme. Explain that different letter combinations can rhyme. **MODERATE**
- Have students choose another poem and read the poem aloud in pairs. Have them identify rhyming words in the poem and list other words that rhyme with the words from the poem. **LIGHT**

Connect to the
ESSENTIAL QUESTION

Emily Dickinson's poems idealize individualism and often focus on being separate from others. She was contemptuous of fame and valued following her own instincts. Her style, with its unconventional punctuation and capitalization, reflects her individualism as much as the subjects she chooses.

POEMS BY EMILY DICKINSON

? ESSENTIAL QUESTION:

In what ways do we seek to remain true to ourselves?

232   Unit 3

© Houghton Mifflin Harcourt Publishing Company

LEARNING MINDSET

Curiosity   Explain to students that curiosity leads to learning. For example, being curious about events during Dickinson's lifetime leads to discovering how rapidly the world was changing at that time. Knowing about those changes can give students a deeper understanding of the literature and other arts of the time. Remind students that reading enables them to explore and discover new interests. It also will help them become better writers—and can even help them feel more at home in a wonderfully diverse world.

QUICK START

Emily Dickinson cherished her independence. Do you always feel free to just be you or can you be influenced by others? Think about whether it is easy or difficult to stand up for what you believe in. Share your ideas with the class.

ANALYZE THEME AND STRUCTURE

The **theme** of a poem is its underlying message—the point the poet wants to make about life. Most often, a reader has to infer the theme from details in the poem. In addition to her language, Dickinson uses elements of **structure** to convey important ideas and suggest themes. You can use the following structural elements to help you determine the theme.

- **Stanzas** Groups of lines make up the "paragraphs" of a poem. Each stanza may express a key idea that develops the theme.

- **Dashes** Dickinson uses the dash (—) in a variety of ways, including denoting an interruption or abrupt shift in thought, for emphasis, or to denote uncertainty or indecision. Think about how dashes can affect your interpretation of the theme.

- **Rhyme scheme** Rhyme is the occurrence of identical or similar sounds at the ends of words. In addition to being a sound device, rhyming words can serve to emphasize important ideas and concepts.

As you read, notice how Dickinson uses structure as well as language to develop the themes of her poems.

ANALYZE FIGURATIVE LANGUAGE

Figurative language is language that communicates ideas beyond the literal meaning of words. Dickinson uses figurative language to add engagement to her poems and convey important ideas. Study the types of figurative language in the chart. Then, add an example of each type of figurative language from Dickinson's poems.

GENRE ELEMENTS: POETRY
- is arranged in verse, or lines, and stanzas
- uses figurative language to convey ideas
- often has patterns of meter and rhyme

FIGURATIVE LANGUAGE	DEFINITION	EXAMPLE
Metaphor	a comparison of two unlike things that have something in common	
Simile	a comparison using the words *like* or *as* of two unlike things that have something in common	
Personification	the giving of human qualities to an object, animal, idea, or abstract concept	

QUICK START

Have students read the Quick Start question, and invite them to share their responses. Then mention that no one is completely independent. Discuss to what degree being independent and interdependent are both desirable and how students might protect one without losing the other.

ANALYZE THEME AND STRUCTURE

Tell students that writers usually have different themes in different poems, although they do have favorite themes. Some of Dickinson's most common themes are death, truth, fame, grief, emotions, freedom, and the importance of self. She believed that poetry could help her find both freedom and truth, and this is what drove her to continue to write. The freedom Dickinson sought was not political freedom but rather freedom from tradition and the opinions of others. Encourage students to look for evidence of these ideas in the poems on pages 236–239.

ANALYZE FIGURATIVE LANGUAGE

Explain to students that people frequently use figurative language in everyday speech. "It's like an oven in here" is a common simile for a room that is too warm. As soon as we make a comparison of one thing to another, we're using either similes or metaphors. Explain that personification applies human traits to something not human, such as, "The sun is smiling down on us." Dickinson's writing often focuses on abstract ideas, and figurative language helps her communicate by connecting the ideas to things that are more concrete or familiar.

ANALYZE SOUND DEVICES

Remind students that sound devices are among the most commonly used elements of poetry. However, not all poets use sound devices in the same way. Dickinson did not adhere strictly to traditional forms of meter and rhyme, but her particular "trademark" is her use of dashes. Point out that she also uses repetition of words and phrases as well as alliteration, such as "Soul selects Society," "Gazing Grain," and "Much Madness."

Encourage students to think about how the repetition, dashes, rhyme, and meter help draw attention to the ideas Dickinson is trying to communicate.

ANNOTATION MODEL

Remind students that annotating the text as they read, identifying important poetic elements, and making notes in the margins can help them connect with what they are reading. Point out that the model is a suggestion and students may follow it or create their own system. They may want to color-code their annotations using highlighters. Their notes in the margin may include questions about ideas that are unclear or topics they want to learn more about.

 **GET READY**

ANALYZE SOUND DEVICES

In addition to the rich imagery they contain, Dickinson's poems are distinctive for the way they sound. Dickinson uses these sound devices in her poetry.

- **Meter and rhythm** The basic unit of meter is a **foot,** which contains one stressed and at least one unstressed syllable. This pattern of stressed and unstressed syllables creates a rhythm that may emphasize ideas, reinforce subject matter, and bring out the musical quality of language in the poem.

- **Rhyme scheme** Rhyme scheme refers to the pattern of end rhyme in a poem. Poets use patterns of sounds that are alike or similar to create a certain aesthetic quality. When the sounds are similar rather than the same, this is called **slant rhyme.**

- **Repetition** Repetition is a technique in which a sound, word, phrase, or line is repeated for emphasis or unity. Repetition often helps to reinforce meaning and create an appealing rhythm.

- **Punctuation and line breaks** When reading a poem aloud, punctuation can tell you when a pause occurs. These pauses can signify an interruption in thought or a shift in thinking. Dickinson uses line breaks in unusual ways. For example:

> The Soul selects her own Society—
> Then—shuts the Door—
> To her divine Majority—
> Present no more—

Both the line break and the dash at the end of the second line insert a break where there would not be one naturally. The pause this creates emphasizes the finality of the phrase "shuts the Door." Her verse is also unusual for the time in the way that it slows down, speeds up, pauses dramatically, and sometimes trails off.

As you read, note Dickinson's use of sound devices and how they affect your understanding of the poems.

ANNOTATION MODEL   **NOTICE & NOTE**

As you read, notice Dickinson's use of sound devices and figurative language. Note details that suggest the theme of each poem. Here are one reader's notes on the beginning of one poem by Dickinson.

The Soul selects her own Society—   Personification: the soul
                                                      performs an action
Then⊖shuts the Door⊖
                                                      These dashes are
To her divine Majority—   jarring.

Present no more—

BACKGROUND

Emily Dickinson *(1830–1886) was not known as a poet during her lifetime. After her death, her sister discovered some 1,800 poems in her home, written mostly between 1858 and 1865. Dickinson spent her entire life in and around Amherst, Massachusetts. Although formal schooling was unusual for girls at the time, Dickinson attended school, including Amherst Academy and Mount Holyoke Female Seminary. She occupied her time reading and writing letters as well as singing, gardening, and taking walks in nature. In her youth, she was very social, attending numerous church activities and cultivating a number of close friendships.*

POEMS BY EMILY DICKINSON

According to letters she wrote to her brother Austin, Dickinson increasingly sensed a difference between herself and others, writing in one letter, "What makes a few of us so different from others? It's a question I often ask myself." As she grew older, Dickinson retreated from public life, growing more and more reclusive. In her later years, she mostly interacted with the outside world through reading and writing, corresponding through letters with a few close friends. During her most productive years, she occupied a bedroom in the family home in Amherst. Letters from this time suggest a troubled romantic attachment that was the source of her creative drive.

Dickinson first took an interest in writing poetry in her teens, and by the time she was 35 she had composed more than 1,100 poems in her concise lyrical style, capturing her astute observations on love, nature, art, grief, pain, and joy. She did share a small portion of these poems with select friends and family. A few of her poems were published in newspapers, but only anonymously and apparently without her consent.

Emily Dickinson died at age 55. When the first volume of her poems was published in 1890, it won great critical and public acclaim, and she is now considered one of the greatest American poets.

BACKGROUND

Emily Dickinson lived during a time of tremendous growth and change in the United States. Though she never traveled far from Amherst, active correspondence kept her informed of and engaged in the issues of her time. Her friend, adviser, and eventual editor, Thomas Wentworth Higginson, was an abolitionist and women's rights advocate. Another friend, Helen Hunt Jackson, fought for Native American rights.

The Civil War erupted during Dickinson's most productive poetic years. She closely followed the news of the conflict and discussed its progress in her correspondence. Her letters reveal that she was deeply moved when she received word that the son of another Amherst family was killed in the war. She also wrote of her delight when the president of the Confederacy, Jefferson Davis, was captured. Although specific works are not explicitly identified as "war poems," Dickinson scholars see evidence in several poems that her perspective was influenced by the events and tragedies of the time.

Dickinson's poetry was private, concerned with events on a small scale. However, while she remained in one house almost all her life, her thoughts and imagination ranged widely.

 ENGLISH LEARNER SUPPORT

Punctuation and Print Cues Nonstandard capitalization and punctuation may confuse students learning English. Tell students that these titles are also the first lines in the poems. Have students read the first title and determine whether it is a sentence. Ask them what they notice about punctuation and capitalization in the "sentence." *(It has no end punctuation; it begins with a capital letter; two internal words are capitalized.)* Discuss with them how they know the line is a sentence. *(It expresses a complete thought and includes a subject and verb.)* Have student pairs analyze the other three titles. Which are sentences? *(Tell all the Truth but tell it slant)* **MODERATE**

TEACH

SETTING A PURPOSE

Direct students to use the Setting a Purpose prompt to focus their reading.

 ## ANALYZE SOUND DEVICES

Remind students that repetition can provide emphasis and reinforce meaning. Explain that the word *moved* does not always refer to physical motion but can mean being moved emotionally. (**Possible answer:** *The repetition emphasizes the firmness of the decision regarding the choice the soul has made. She is not going to be moved to change her mind.*)

For **listening** and **reading support** for students at varying proficiency levels, see the **Text X-Ray** on pages 232C–232D.

 ## ANALYZE FIGURATIVE LANGUAGE

You may wish to discuss this stanza before students respond, as there is both a simile and a metaphor, with the attention being described as having valves, before the simile of the valves closing "Like Stone." You may also point out that the words *Door* in stanza 1 and *Gate* in stanza 2 have preceded stanza 3, so there is a continued concept of the Soul as something that could be closed off. (**Possible answer:** *The simile is that the* Valves of her attention *are* Like Stone, *with the Stone being solid and unmoved, underscoring the firmness of her determination to shut herself off.*)

 NOTICE & NOTE

Notice & Note

Use the side margins to notice and note signposts in the text.

ANALYZE SOUND DEVICES
Annotate: Mark the repeated word in the second stanza.
Interpret: What is the effect of repeating this word?

ANALYZE FIGURATIVE LANGUAGE
Annotate: Mark the simile in lines 11–12.
Analyze: What two things are being compared? What theme about the soul does this image suggest?

SETTING A PURPOSE

As you read Dickinson's poems, pay attention to the various ways she uses punctuation and line breaks, especially dashes, to create meaning and the concrete images she uses to represent abstract ideas.

The Soul selects her own Society

The Soul selects her own Society—
Then—shuts the Door—
To her divine Majority—
Present no more—

5 Unmoved—she notes the Chariots—pausing—
At her low Gate—
Unmoved—an Emperor be kneeling
Upon her Mat—

I've known her—from an ample nation—
10 Choose One—
Then—close the Valves of her attention—
Like Stone—

Illustration of Emily Dickinson's home.

236 Unit 3

APPLYING ACADEMIC VOCABULARY

❏ analogy ☑ denote ❏ quote ☑ topic ❏ unique

Write and Discuss Have students read the first line of each poem. Then have students write answers to the following questions. Guide students to use the Academic Vocabulary words *denote* and *topic* in their responses. Ask volunteers to share their responses with the class.

- What might the capital letters **denote**? (*They denote that the words are significant.*)
- How might the capitalized words help predict the **topic** of the poem? (*They give clues about what is important, and that helps readers predict the topic.*)

236 Unit 3

Because I could not stop for Death

Because I could not stop for Death—
He kindly stopped for me—
The Carriage held but just Ourselves—
And Immortality.

5 We slowly drove—He knew no haste
And I had put away
My labor and my leisure too,
For His Civility—

We passed the School, where Children strove
10 At Recess—in the Ring—
We passed the Fields of Gazing Grain—
We passed the Setting Sun—

Or rather—He passed Us—
The Dews drew quivering and chill—
15 For only Gossamer,[1] my Gown—
My Tippet—only Tulle[2]—

We paused before a House that seemed
A Swelling of the Ground—
The Roof was scarcely visible—
20 The Cornice[3]—in the Ground—

Since then—'tis Centuries—and yet
Feels shorter than the Day
I first surmised the Horses' Heads
Were toward Eternity—

---

[1] **Gossamer:** thin, soft material.
[2] **Tippet . . . Tulle:** shawl made of fine netting.
[3] **Cornice:** molding at the top of a building.

ANALYZE FIGURATIVE LANGUAGE

Annotate: In the first three stanzas, mark examples of personification.

Analyze: How does the personification of death affect the meaning of the poem?

ANALYZE THEME AND STRUCTURE

Annotate: Mark the word in the fourth stanza that signifies a shift in thinking.

Analyze: How does the speaker's perception of what is happening change in this stanza? Explain.

 ANALYZE FIGURATIVE LANGUAGE

Remind students that personification is attributing human qualities to things that are not human. (**Possible answer:** *It makes death seem less frightening. Death is simply doing a job.*)

ANALYZE THEME AND STRUCTURE

Consider what the speaker begins to feel in this stanza. (**Possible answer:** *The speaker is suddenly chilled and feels inadequately dressed for what is happening. It seems like the speaker has suddenly realized that this is actually death and not just a pleasant ride.*)

 For **speaking support** for students at varying proficiency levels, see the **Text X-Ray** on page 232D.

WHEN STUDENTS STRUGGLE...

Interpret Images Have students reread the first three stanzas and work in pairs to complete a two-column graphic organizer labeled *What the Poem Describes* and *What It Might Mean*. Share with them some interpretations before having them read the rest of the poem; for example, Stanzas 1 and 2: Death in his carriage stops for the speaker—the speaker has died; Stanza 3: They journey past a school and fields of grain—They are reviewing life stages.

For additional support, go to the **Reading Studio** and assign the following **Level Up Tutorial: Figurative Language.**

ANALYZE THEME AND STRUCTURE

Remind students that dashes are often used to set off important ideas. (**Possible answer:** *The dashes are setting off the speaker's definition of "Sense."*)

■ English Learner Support

Analyze Language Display lines 1–4 of "Much Madness."

1. Ask students: *What visual clues indicate significant words or relationships?* ("Madness" and "Sense" do not need to be capitalized, but they are, so they are probably significant.) Highlight these words.

2. Ask students: *What relationship is suggested by the way the words are arranged or used?* (*The placement of the words in lines 1 and 3, with the words reversed in line 3, suggests that these words are antonyms, or words with opposite meanings.*)

3. Work with students to paraphrase the lines.

Have student pairs practice this process with lines 5–8. Monitor progress.

NOTICE & NOTE

ANALYZE THEME AND STRUCTURE

Annotate: In line 3, mark the words that come between dashes.

Interpret: What is the function of the dashes in line 3?

Much Madness is divinest Sense

Much Madness is divinest Sense—
To a discerning Eye—
Much Sense—the starkest Madness—
'Tis the Majority
5 In this, as All, prevail—
Assent—and you are sane—
Demur—you're straightway dangerous—
And handled with a Chain—

Tell all the Truth but tell it slant

Tell all the Truth but tell it slant—
Success in Circuit⁴ lies
Too bright for our infirm Delight
The Truth's superb surprise
5 As Lightning to the Children eased
With explanation kind
The Truth must dazzle gradually
Or every man be blind—

_____

⁴ **Circuit:** indirect path.

ANALYZE FIGURATIVE LANGUAGE

Annotate: In lines 4–8, mark the simile.

Interpret: Using this simile, what does the speaker tell us about truth?

 **ANALYZE FIGURATIVE LANGUAGE**

Remind students that a simile compares two unlike things. Discuss the characteristics of the two things being compared. (**Answer:** _Truth can be shocking and dangerous._)

CHECK YOUR UNDERSTANDING

Have students answer the questions independently.

Answers:

1. _D_

2. _G_

3. _C_

If they answer any questions incorrectly, have them reread the text to confirm their understanding. Then they may proceed to ANALYZE THE TEXT on page 240.

CHECK YOUR UNDERSTANDING

Answer these questions before moving on to the **Analyze the Text** section on the following page.

1 What is the theme of "The Soul selects her own Society"?

A It's wrong not to be open to making new friends.

B You shouldn't give up if someone refuses to talk to you.

C The speaker blames herself for her loneliness.

D People only reveal their innermost thoughts and feelings to a very few friends.

2 In the fifth stanza of "Because I could not stop for Death," what is the speaker describing?

F An underground chapel

G Her own grave

H Her own fallen-down house

J The house of the person they are visiting

3 Which of the following is an example of personification?

A _I've known her—from an ample nation—_

B _In this, as All, prevail—_

C _The Truth must dazzle gradually_

D _The Roof was scarcely visible—_

 ENGLISH LEARNER SUPPORT

Oral Assessment Use the following questions to assess students' comprehension and speaking skills:

1. What message does Dickinson share in "The Soul selects her own Society"? (_People tell their thoughts and feelings only to close friends._)

2. What does the speaker describe in the fifth stanza of "Because I could not stop for Death"? (_her own grave_)

3. What does Dickinson personify, or give human qualities to, in "Tell all the Truth but tell it slant"? (_truth_) **LIGHT**

APPLY

ANALYZE THE TEXT

Possible answers:

1. **DOK 2:** *The repetition of sounds (Soul selects, Society, shuts) and words (Unmoved) emphasizes the finality of the poet's actions. Rhyme or near rhyme emphasizes exclusion: door, gate, stone. These support main ideas of finality and exclusion: the poet selects a friend or lover and then closes the door on all else.*

2. **DOK 2:** *Death is portrayed as a courteous carriage driver and dying as riding in the carriage Death drives. This metaphor contributes to the overall theme that death is ordinary and not very frightening.*

3. **DOK 4:** *The paradox is that madness, as the world defines it, is sense, while sense, as the world defines it, is madness. So madness is a trait of individuality, and sense is a trait of conformity (the Majority). The theme is that individuality will put you at odds with society.*

4. **DOK 4:** *The poet suggests telling the truth slant (that is, not straight), in Circuit (indirect), and with an explanation that makes it easier to take. Dickinson wants the truth told, but with gentleness, so as not to hurt. She sees Truth as being so dazzling that, like Lightning, it is fearful if not carefully introduced.*

5. **DOK 2:** *The dashes in Dickinson's work break up the flow of ideas, allowing other thoughts or definitions. One gets the feeling of someone talking with great emotion, but not formally. One can read the poems as if the poet were speaking energetically, interjecting thoughts and changing directions to emphasize ideas.*

RESEARCH

Depending on time available for the exercise, provide a list of sites where students can find suitable letters. Challenge students to look at multiple letters and compare what Dickenson shares with more than one correspondent.

Extend If time allows, show a scene from the play in class.

RESPOND

ANALYZE THE TEXT

Support your responses with evidence from the text. 📝 NOTEBOOK

1. **Interpret** Consider the sound devices Dickinson uses in "The Soul selects her own Society," such as repetition and rhyme. How do these sound devices support the important ideas in the poem?

2. **Interpret** An **extended metaphor** is a metaphor that is developed through several lines or sometimes an entire poem. What is the extended metaphor in "Because I could not stop for Death"? How does this impact the meaning of the poem?

3. **Analyze** A **paradox** is a statement that seems to contradict itself while suggesting an important truth. What paradox do you find in "Much Madness is divinest Sense"? What does this paradox suggest about the theme of the poem?

4. **Evaluate** In "Tell all the Truth but tell it slant," what are the different ways the speaker says the truth may be told? What theme about truth does she express through these ideas?

5. **Interpret** Dickinson uses dashes freely in her poems. How do the dashes affect the way you read the poem? How do they help clarify the meaning that she conveys?

RESEARCH

Although Emily Dickinson was reclusive for much of her life, she did maintain a lively correspondence with family members and friends. Do some research to find an example of Dickinson's letter writing. Then, answer the questions in the chart below.

RESEARCH TIP
If you enter *Emily Dickinson* or *Emily Dickinson writer,* you will likely get responses related to poetry. Be sure to enter search terms that are specific to ensure you receive information about her letters.

QUESTION	ANSWER
To whom did Dickinson address her letter?	*Answers will vary depending on the letter selected.*
What is the subject of the letter?	
What insight about Dickinson's life did you gain from reading the letter?	

Extend Excerpts from Dickinson's letters were included in the Tony Award–winning one-woman play *The Belle of Amherst,* starring Julie Harris. Recordings of the show are available on the Internet. Look up a scene from the show. Then, summarize the scene to the class. Be sure to include any new insights on Dickinson that you gained from watching the scene.

⚙ LEARNING MINDSET

Try Again Ask students to think about infants learning to walk. If babies gave up the first time they fell, they would never get anywhere. The same applies to our minds. We can learn from our mistakes and try again—sometimes just putting forth a bit more effort or possibly looking for a new approach. Making mistakes and trying again is how we learn.

In class, encourage students to take intellectual risks. Make sure students feel safe to try and fail so trying again seems natural. Don't reward failure or act like it isn't failure, but discuss what was learned and how it will go better next time.

CREATE AND DISCUSS

Write a Poem Create a poem that uses concrete images to describe one of these abstract ideas: friendship, adolescence, anger, or summer. As you write your poem:

- ❏ Include at least one example of figurative language. When creating your metaphors and similes, try to use imagery and descriptive language to create comparisons that a reader would not expect.
- ❏ Use sound devices such as rhyme or repetition to convey meaning.
- ❏ Express a theme about the idea you choose.

Discuss Poems Form groups or pairs with other students who wrote about the same idea that you did. Compare your poems with others in your group.

- ❏ Identify similarities and differences between the images in the poems.
- ❏ Evaluate the themes that each poem expresses.
- ❏ Discuss any ideas that the group found surprising.

 Go to **Writing as a Process** in the **Writing Studio** for help.

Go to **Participating in Collaborative Discussions** in the **Speaking and Listening Studio** for help.

RESPOND TO THE ESSENTIAL QUESTION

? In what ways do we seek to remain true to ourselves?

Gather Information Review your annotations and notes on the poems by Emily Dickinson. Then, add relevant information to your Response Log. As you determine which information to include, think about:

- why people sometimes want to be alone
- how valuable other people's opinions are to us
- the benefits of thinking differently from the crowd

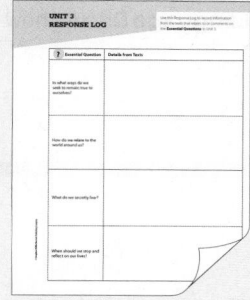

ACADEMIC VOCABULARY
As you write and discuss what you learned from the poem, be sure to use the Academic Vocabulary words. Check off each of the words that you use.

- ❏ analogy
- ❏ denote
- ❏ quote
- ❏ topic
- ❏ unique

CREATE AND DISCUSS

Write a Poem Encourage students to turn back to pages 233 and 234 to review the definitions of the elements they are being asked to include in their poems. Remind students that the point of a metaphor or simile is to illustrate a point. Explain that as they search for comparisons a reader would not expect, they should make sure readers can understand them.

 For **writing support** for students at varying proficiency levels, see the **Text X-Ray** on page 232D.

Discuss Poems Remind students to pay close attention to what others have written. Discussion should focus on how the figurative language and sound devices contribute to the theme of each person's poem.

RESPOND TO THE ESSENTIAL QUESTION

Allow time for students to add details from "Poems by Emily Dickinson" to their Unit 3 Response Logs.

IN THE SEASON OF CHANGE

Poem by **Teresa Palomo Acosta**

GENRE ELEMENTS
FREE VERSE

Remind students that traditional poetic forms have structured stanzas with a regular rhythm and rhyme scheme. Free verse has no set patterns of rhyme and meter and flows more naturally. It also gives greater emphasis to some poetic devices that can be used to impose rhythm, heighten emotion, and convey meaning. The poet's choice of line breaks highlights words and images that convey meaning and emotion.

LEARNING OBJECTIVES

- Analyze sound devices and the use of imagery.
- Conduct research about culture groups in Texas.
- Write a free-verse poem.
- Present an original free-verse poem.
- **Language** Discuss how free verse sounds like natural speech.

TEXT COMPLEXITY

Quantitative Measures	In the Season of Change	Lexile: N/A
Qualitative Measures	**Ideas Presented** Much is explicit, but moves to some implied meaning. Requires some inferential reasoning.	
	Structures Used Primarily explicit. Largely conventional.	
	Language Used Mostly explicit. Some figurative or allusive language. Some dialect or other unconventional language.	
	Knowledge Required Some references to events or other texts. Begins to rely on outside knowledge.	

Online **Ed**

RESOURCES

- Unit 3 Response Log
- Selection Audio
- Reading Studio: Notice & Note
- Level Up Tutorial: Elements of Poetry
- Writing Studio: Writing as a Process
- Speaking and Listening Studio: Giving a Presentation
- "In the Season of Change" Selection Test

SUMMARIES

English

In this free-verse poem, the speaker imagines what it would be like if she and poet Emily Dickinson were friends. She imagines they would love all the same heirlooms left to them by their great-grandmothers. The speaker describes how Dickinson's words inspired her and created a feeling of kinship between them that might have led to their having a conversation over rhubarb pie and coffee.

Spanish

En este poema de verso libre, la narradora imagina cómo sería si la poeta Emily Dickinson y ella fueran amigas. Se imagina que a ambas les encantarían las mismas reliquias familiares dejadas por sus bisabuelas. La narradora describe cómo las palabras de Dickinson la inspiraron y crearon un sentimiento de semejanza entre ellas, que las guiaría a tener una conversación mientras comían una tarta de ruibarbo y café.

SMALL-GROUP OPTIONS

Have students work in small groups and pairs to read and discuss the selection.

Numbered Heads Together

- Organize students into groups of four, then number off, 1-2-3-4, within the group.
- Ask: *How does the poet use imagery to describe her relationship to Emily Dickinson?*
- Allow time for students to discuss their responses in the group.
- Call a number from 1 to 4. The student who has been assigned that number responds for the group.

Reciprocal Teaching

- Provide students with a list of comprehension question stems before they begin reading the poem. For example:

  State _____ in your own words.
  What might happen if _____?

- As students read, have them write questions about the poem using the stems.
- Organize students into groups of three and have each student offer two questions to the group for discussion without duplicating each other.
- Have students discuss the questions and find evidence from the selection to support their responses.

Text X-Ray: English Learner Support
for "In the Season of Change"

Use the Text X-Ray and the supports and scaffolds in the Teacher's Edition to help guide students at different proficiency levels through the selection.

INTRODUCE THE SELECTION
DISCUSS FREE VERSE

Explain that free verse often uses informal language and does not adhere to the same grammatical rules as prose. Remind the students that free verse flows like natural speech. Authors use sound devices like alliteration (repetition of initial consonant sound), assonance (repetition of vowel sounds within a word), and consonance (repetition of consonant sounds within and at the end of words) to mimic natural speech. Free verse also uses imagery to help the reader make connections to personal experiences.

Provide sentence frames to help students discuss free verse: *Free verse sounds like _____. Poets do not follow _____ rules. Poets use _____ to make connections.*

CULTURAL REFERENCES

The following words or phrases may be unfamiliar to students:

- *doilies* (line 3): a cloth or paper that has a decorative pattern made of many small holes; lace
- *kinship* (line 20): a feeling of connectedness to someone
- *rhubarb pie* (line 25): a dessert made with the flesh of the thick pink or red stems of the rhubarb plant

LISTENING

Listen and Comprehend New Language

Students can learn new language structures, expressions, and basic as well as academic vocabulary as they listen to you read.

Have students listen as you read the poem aloud. Use the following supports with students at varying proficiency levels:

- Provide a bank of words and expressions you want students to recognize and learn their meanings. As you read, have students indicate with a "thumbs-up" when they hear you say a word or expression from the bank. **SUBSTANTIAL**

- Provide a bank of simple definitions for words and expressions you want students to recognize. As you read, have students indicate with a "thumbs-up" when they hear you say a word or expression that corresponds with a definition. **MODERATE**

- As students listen to you read the poem, have them jot down words and expressions they recognize but do not understand. Invite them to use their notes to ask clarifying questions, and use their questions to guide an individual or group discussion. **LIGHT**

SPEAKING

Identify Poetic Sound Devices

Remind students that poets create the natural rhythm of everyday speech in free verse using sound devices. Review assonance, consonance, and alliteration.

Use the following supports with students at varying proficiency levels:

- Read aloud the fourth stanza, one line at a time. Have students repeat after you. After students repeat each line, ask them if they recognized any sound devices. Provide sentence frames to help students express their ideas: *The poet used _____ in the last line.* (alliteration) *The words _____ start with the letter _____.* (despite, decrees, demanding; d) **SUBSTANTIAL**

- Have small groups take turns reading aloud the fourth stanza. Have them pause after each line to identify sound devices. Have students discuss the sound devices and how they reflect the rhythm of natural speech. If students need help, provide the sentence frames above. **MODERATE**

- Have students read aloud the poem in pairs. Have them pause after each stanza to identify sound devices and discuss the effect of the sound devices and how they reflect natural speech. **LIGHT**

READING

Build a Word Wall

As students read, their vocabulary and comprehension of English will increase. Creating environmental print by building a word wall will help them recognize and internalize new words they encounter.

Designate a space in the room where students can build a word wall. Supply slips of paper and markers. Prior to reading, have students scan the selection and circle words they already know. Have them read the selection. Use the following supports with students at varying proficiency levels:

- As you read the poem (or a stanza) together, have the students identify one new word. Work together to understand the word's meaning using context clues and images from the text. Have each student add one word to the wall by writing the word and drawing a related picture. **SUBSTANTIAL**

- Have students read the selection with a partner and identify three new words. Remind them to use context clues and images from the text to confirm meaning. Invite each student to add one word to the wall by writing the word and drawing a related picture. **MODERATE**

- Have pairs read the selection and identify five new words, expressions, or academic vocabulary; use resources to determine meaning; and choose one to add to the word wall. **LIGHT**

WRITING

Compose a Poem

By using all the resources students have acquired in the unit, they will be able to compose a free-verse poem like the one described on page 249 in the Create and Present section.

Model your thought processes by thinking aloud as you compose a simple poem in free verse. Have pairs generate ideas for their own poems. Use the following supports with students at varying proficiency levels:

- Invite students to draw or locate an image that represents a meeting with someone they admire. Help them label the picture, and, if they are able, use the words to describe the picture. **SUBSTANTIAL**

- Have students use the poem you composed as a model. Erase words from your poem and invite students to replace them with their own words. **MODERATE**

- Have pairs describe the meeting, person, emotions they want to evoke, and images they could use. Encourage them to use sound devices. **LIGHT**

ANALYZE & APPLY

IN THE SEASON OF CHANGE

Poem by **Teresa Palomo Acosta**

Connect to the
ESSENTIAL QUESTION

"In the Season of Change" is an exploration of how we relate to the world around us. The poet, Teresa Palomo Acosta, has found a deep connection to the 19th-century American poet Emily Dickinson, but she is also firmly grounded in her own present reality. While imagining a meeting with Dickinson, Acosta is able to consider their similarities and differences.

ESSENTIAL QUESTION:

How do we relate to the world around us?

242   Unit 3

QUICK START

Have you ever felt a connection to a well-known person? If you could share a meal with this person, what would you ask him or her? Write three questions you would ask. Then, role-play this encounter with a classmate.

ANALYZE SOUND DEVICES

"In the Season of Change" is an example of **free verse.** Free verse is poetry that does not have the regular meter or rhyming patterns of traditional poetry. Instead, free verse uses the natural rhythm of everyday speech. This poem also includes **sound devices** to contribute to the structure, rhythm, and meaning of the work. You will find the following sound devices in the poem:

- **Alliteration:** repetition of consonant sounds at the beginning of words

- **Assonance:** repetition of vowel sounds in nearby words

- **Consonance:** repetition of consonants within or at the end of a word

As you read, note examples of alliteration, assonance, and consonance in the chart. Think about the effect these sound devices have on the poem.

SOUND DEVICE	EXAMPLES
Alliteration	
Assonance	
Consonance	

GENRE ELEMENTS: FREE VERSE

- does not have regular meter or rhyme patterns
- flows like natural speech
- lines can break within or flow across stanzas
- uses imagery and sound devices to evoke emotions or draw connections

ANALYZE LINES AND STANZAS

In all poetry, **lines** are the core unit of a poem. **Line breaks** occur where a line of poetry ends. A line break can come at the end of a thought or sentence, but sometimes poets choose to break in the middle of a thought for effect. **Stanzas** are the groups of lines that form a unit of thought in a poem. When determining the meaning of a poem, consider the key ideas contained in each stanza. As you read, think about the effect line breaks have on the meaning of poem and consider the impact each stanza has on the message the writer expresses.

QUICK START

Have students read the Quick Start questions and invite them to share their written questions with the class. After the role-play sessions, have students report back on their exchanges. Ask what they think they might learn through actual conversation versus simply reading about their person.

ANALYZE SOUND DEVICES

Help students understand the terms **alliteration**, **assonance**, and **consonance**. Discuss why tools like these are useful in a free-verse poem. (*The poems don't rely on rhyme, meter, or formal structure; these sound devices add impact and meaning to a poem.*) Have students brainstorm examples of these terms that they have heard before. The most obvious examples will come from song lyrics, but movies, television shows, and video games might hold examples as well.

ANALYZE LINES AND STANZAS

Explain that poets often organize their ideas and images in compact units known as **stanzas**. Each stanza generally develops a separate idea, image, or example of figurative language. Recognizing stanzas helps readers trace the development of the poet's ideas. Tell students that identifying the central idea or image in each stanza and summarizing the stanza will help them trace the arc, and the sense, of the entire poem.

TEACH

ANALYZE IMAGERY

To help students understand how writers use **imagery,** guide the class in a collective writing exercise in which students write short descriptions of their morning using vivid sensory and/or figurative language. Descriptions should be short—a sentence or even just a few words—and written on small slips of paper. Instruct students to write three descriptions and put all of the slips into a bowl or jar. Pull slips out and read them to the class. Discuss which words contribute to the imagery and point out which notes express a deeper meaning.

ANNOTATION MODEL

Remind students of the annotation ideas on page 244, which suggest circling or underlining sound devices or use of imagery. Point out that they may follow this suggestion or use their own system for marking up the poem in their write-in text. They may want to color-code their notes by using highlighters—for example, sound devices in one color and imagery in another. The notes in the margin may include questions about language that is unclear.

 **GET READY**

ANALYZE IMAGERY

All poets use language to help them convey **themes,** or messages about life. Many of them convey themes through **imagery,** or vivid language that appeals to the senses. Imagery infuses a poem with meaning and allows readers to connect with similar emotions or experiences they've had. In "In the Season of Change," Teresa Palomo Acosta uses imagery to create a link with Emily Dickinson across time and cultures. In addition, she pairs Spanish terms with English terms—great-grandmothers/*bisabuelas*, rhubarb pie/*cafecito*, chatting/*chismeando*—to represent her heritage and emphasize both the similarities and the differences between her world and Dickinson's.

As you read "In the Season of Change," write down examples of imagery you find and note the senses they appeal to.

SENSE	IMAGERY
Sight	
Sound	
Smell	
Touch	
Taste	

ANNOTATION MODEL   NOTICE & NOTE

As you read, note the author's use of sound devices and the impact they have on meaning. Note the writer's use of imagery and the way she uses lines and stanzas to convey meaning. The model below shows one reader's notes for the first stanza of "In the Season of Change."

> If E. Dickinson and I had been friends,
> we would have each owned a treasure chest
> filled with doilies for laying under our silverware,
> for showing off atop our china cabinets.
> For softening the scars in the 300-year-old dining room tables
> we would have inherited
> from our great-grandmothers.

Consonance—words with the "n" sound

The poet's descriptions help me picture the furniture.

BACKGROUND

Teresa Palomo Acosta *(b. 1949) was born in McGregor, Texas, to Mexican parents who had migrated to Texas during the Great Depression. Acosta earned a degree in ethnic studies at the University of Texas and then a master's degree at the Columbia University School of Journalism. She went on to become a leading voice of multiculturalism in the United States. She says her writing helps her retell stories about herself and about the Chicana experience. Acosta is also the coauthor of Las Tejanas: 300 Years of History, a history of women of Spanish-Mexican origin in Texas.*

IN THE SEASON OF CHANGE

Poem by Teresa Palomo Acosta

SETTING A PURPOSE

As you read, note the details that suggest a sense of longing, and think about what the poet longs for.

If E. Dickinson and I had been friends,
we would have each owned a <u>treasure chest</u>
filled with <u>doilies</u> for laying under our <u>silverware</u>,
for showing off atop our <u>china cabinets</u>.
5 For softening the <u>scars in the 300-year-old dining room tables</u>
we would have inherited
from our <u>great-grandmothers</u>.

But our bisabuelas[1] never met,
exchanged glances or
10 sat next to each other in <u>church</u>.
And I only discovered E. Dickinson
in the few pages she was allowed
to enter in my <u>high school literature texts</u>.

---

[1] **bisabuelas** (bēs-ä-bwä′läs): great-grandmothers.

Notice & Note

Use the side margins to notice and note signposts in the text.

ANALYZE IMAGERY

Annotate: In the first and second stanzas, mark images that appeal to the senses.

Analyze: How does the poet use the images to describe her relationship to Emily Dickinson?

BACKGROUND

After students read the Background note, explain that Teresa Paloma Acosta's poem represents a bridge between different cultures. This is appropriate, considering how Acosta is a "leading voice of multiculturalism." Point out that multiculturalism involves understanding different cultures and how they interact. This poem touches on that theme, as well as others.

SETTING A PURPOSE

Direct students to use the Setting a Purpose prompt to focus their reading.

ANALYZE IMAGERY

Remind students that **imagery** can be created with a number of devices. It is often built with adjectives that appeal to the senses, but a poet can conjure images by writing about objects that connote a specific time or place, such as Paloma Acosta's mention of "doilies" and "china cabinets." (***Answer:*** *In the first stanza, the poet describes a cozy scene as the setting to an imaginary friendship with Dickinson. She creates the scene by connecting to the items both might have inherited from their great-grandmothers. The second stanza, in contrast, is spare and dry. It's colored by the words* never *and* only *and* few, *which describe the brief "meeting" Palomo Acosta had when she read a couple of Dickinson's poems in a high school textbook.*)

For **listening** and **reading support** for students at varying proficiency levels, see the **Text X-Ray** on pages 242C–242D.

WHEN STUDENTS STRUGGLE. . .

Analyze Sound Devices Tell students that free-verse poems require more attention to sound devices than poems with rigid structure and rhyme. Sometimes a reader can simply discover those devices by reading the poem aloud. Ask for a student to read aloud the first line of stanza 2: "But our bisabuelas never met." (Help them with the pronunciation of "bisabuelas" beforehand, if necessary.) Have students point out sound devices in this line. (*The line begins with alliteration and consonance and ends in assonance.*)

For additional support, go to the **Reading Studio** and assign the following **Level Up Tutorial: Elements of Poetry.**

TEACH

✏️ ANALYZE LINES AND STANZAS

Remind students that poets use line length to emphasize ideas and give meaning to a poem. (**Answer:** *The short lines in the first sentence emphasizes the closeness the poet feels to E. Dickinson. The longer lines in the second sentence emphasize the connection women feel to other women.*)

✏️ ANALYZE SOUND DEVICES

Ask for a volunteer to redefine **alliteration** before moving forward (the repetition of consonant sounds at the beginning of words). Point out how alliteration in line 22 connects the phrase "on our own" and gives it emphasis. Read the line aloud, replacing the phrase with "by ourselves" and ask students to comment on the difference. (**Answer:** *The sounds make the images flow together in rhythm. Even though the last line is separate, indicating a distance between two women, the alliteration helps connect the line back to the flow of the rest of the stanza.*)

📖 For **speaking support** for students at varying proficiency levels, see the **Text X-Ray** on page 242D.

 NOTICE & NOTE

ANALYZE LINES AND STANZAS

Annotate: Use brackets to mark each sentence in lines 14–21.

Infer: How does the line length reflect the ideas expressed in the stanza?

```
       ⎡Only years later did
    15  I finally pore over her words,
          believing that
          her songs held
          my name inscribed within.⎤
          ⎡And that they might fill the air
    20  with the ancient signs of kinship
          that women can choose to pass along.⎤

          And thus left on our own,
          E. Dickinson and I
          sat down at the same table,
    25  savoring her rhubarb pie and my cafecito²
          chatting and chismeando³
          and trading secrets
          despite decrees demanding silence between us:

          women from separate corners of the room.
```

ANALYZE SOUND DEVICES

Annotate: Mark the alliteration in lines 22–28.

Analyze: How does the alliteration serve to unify the lines in the stanza? What is the connection between the stanza and line 29?

² **cafecito** (kä-fā-sē´tô): little cup of coffee.
³ **chismeando** (chēs-mä-än´dô): gossiping.

246   Unit 3

ENGLISH LEARNER SUPPORT

Understand Sound Devices Help build comprehension of poetry's sound devices by leading shared readings of stanza 4. After each reading, point out a new sound device, such as the alliteration in line 26. Have student pairs choose a different stanza and decide which sound device they wish to look for. Instruct partners to take turns reading the stanza aloud line by line to locate the chosen sound device. Finally, have partners do a shared reading of the entire stanza. **MODERATE**

246   Unit 3

CHECK YOUR UNDERSTANDING

Answer these questions before moving on to the **Analyze the Text** section on the following page.

1 Which of the following phrases from the poem is an example of assonance?

   A *a treasure chest*

   B *high school literature texts*

   C *they might fill the air*

   D *despite decrees demanding*

2 How does the poet discover Dickinson?

   F The poet's grandmother introduces her.

   G She finds a few Dickinson poems in her literature book.

   H Her high school teacher spent a lot of time teaching Dickinson.

   J She found a book of Dickinson's poems in a china cabinet.

3 What do the lines her songs held / my name inscribed within mean?

   A Dickinson had known someone with the poet's name.

   B Someone had written in the poet's literature book.

   C The poet felt a strong kinship with Dickinson.

   D The poet put her name in the book to show it was hers.

CHECK YOUR UNDERSTANDING

Have students answer the questions independently.

Answers:

1. *D*

2. *G*

3. *C*

If they answer any questions incorrectly, have them reread the text to confirm their understanding. Then they may proceed to ANALYZE THE TEXT on page 248.

ENGLISH LEARNER SUPPORT

Oral Assessment   Use the following questions to assess students' comprehension and speaking skills.

1. In what way are Dickinson and the poet the same? *(They both love poetry.)*

2. How does the poet first find Dickinson's poems? *(The speaker found them in her literature book in high school.)*

3. Who is "her" in line 17? *(E. Dickinson)* Why does the poet say that she felt like her name was written in the poems? *(She felt connected to Dickinson.)* **MODERATE**

ANALYZE THE TEXT

Possible answers:

1. **DOK 2:** *She feels a "kinship" with Dickinson as a woman, despite the differences between them in time, culture, and place.*

2. **DOK 4:** *The first stanza sets up the imaginary relationship she would have liked to have had if they lived in the same time and place. The second stanza portrays the reality of the distance and time that makes the relationship impossible. The third stanza depicts how Dickinson's poem bridges the distance. The last stanza shows how the relationship has come full circle despite the barriers, because the speaker can still find relevance in Dickinson's words.*

3. **DOK 3:** *It reminds us of the poet's background and creates an interesting contrast. While it is clear that the poet is from a different background than Dickinson, the poem shows that the two cultures can coexist in one person (the poet).*

4. **DOK 2:** *The alliteration emphasizes that Acosta will always find meaning in Dickinson's poetry in spite of the obstacles described earlier in the poem.*

5. **DOK 4:** *The poet and Dickinson are separate because of their backgrounds and time periods, but Dickinson's poems reveal their similar thoughts and emotions. This shows that even though time and space may separate us, words are important because they can bring us together.*

RESEARCH

The graphic organizer should include the accurate meaning of each term.

Extend Responses should include the name of the poem and examples of Acosta's Hispanic heritage that are mentioned in it. Students should explain how the poem provides more insight into Acosta's life and culture.

 **RESPOND**

ANALYZE THE TEXT

Support your responses with evidence from the text. 📓 NOTEBOOK

1. **Infer** Why does the poet think that she and Dickinson could become friends?

2. **Analyze** How do the poem's stanzas give a structure to the poem? How does the structure support the poem's message?

3. **Evaluate** Think about the Spanish terms Acosta includes. What is the effect of using this imagery in the poem?

4. **Interpret** Poets may use sound devices to emphasize important ideas. What idea does Acosta emphasize by saying that she and Dickinson are sharing secrets "despite decrees demanding silence between [them]"?

5. **Connect** How do the lines "And thus left on our own, / E. Dickinson and I / sat down at the same table" help communicate the poem's theme?

RESEARCH TIP
If you find a reliable online source, check the webpage of the source for links to other sources and or related materials.

RESEARCH

Acosta coauthored a book on *Las Tejanas*—women in Texas who are descended from the original Spanish-speaking settlers of Texas and northern Mexico. However, there is some debate in Texas as to who qualifies as a *Tejana/Tejano* and who is *Criollo* or Mexican American. Research the meanings of these terms to find out more about these groups. Complete the chart below.

GROUP	CHARACTERISTICS
Tejano/Tejana	*Facts should reflect research from reliable sources.*
Criollo	*Facts should reflect research from reliable sources.*
Mexican American	*Facts should reflect research from reliable sources.*

Extend Find another poem by Acosta in which she shares something of her Hispanic heritage. How does the second poem help expand the reader's view of Acosta and her life?

WHEN STUDENTS STRUGGLE . . .

Reteaching: Analyze Author's Craft Review the definition of **imagery.** Then return to some of the examples of imagery in the poem and walk students through methodically. Begin with the first stanza. Point out the images of keepsakes and other family items that people preserve. Discuss with students how the vivid images in the poem create a bond between the poet and Dickinson.

 For additional support, go to the **Reading Studio** and assign the following 📘 **Level Up Tutorial: Elements of Poetry**.

© Houghton Mifflin Harcourt Publishing Company

CREATE AND PRESENT

Write a Poem Write a free verse poem in which you imagine a meeting with someone you admire. Review your response to the Quick Start activity before you begin.

❏ Decide on where your meeting will take place. Incorporate details about the place into your poem.

❏ Think carefully about how word choice and structure can help you convey your thoughts and feelings in the poem.

❏ Use sound devices, such as alliteration, assonance, and consonance, to make your poem more interesting and memorable.

Present a Poem Poetry lends itself to reading aloud. In small groups, share the poems you have written.

❏ Practice reading your poem aloud several times so that it flows naturally.

❏ Think of your presentation as somewhere between music and acting so you can get the most out of the sound and emotion of the poem.

❏ Use your voice to emphasize the imagery, sound, and the structure of the stanzas to draw listeners' attention to important ideas in your poem.

RESPOND TO THE ESSENTIAL QUESTION

? How do we relate to the world around us?

Gather Information Review your annotations and notes on "In the Season of Change." Then, add relevant information to your Response Log. As you determine which information to include, think about:

• how writing can be a way of connecting with the world around us
• how word choice, structure, and elements of poetry communicate emotions in a poem
• how writing, including poetry, can help us relate to people and see the world through different eyes

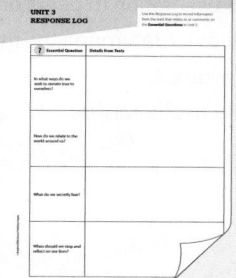

 Go to **Writing as a Process** in the **Writing Studio** for help.

Go to **Giving a Presentation: Delivering Your Presentation** in the **Speaking and Listening Studio** for help.

ACADEMIC VOCABULARY

As you write and discuss what you learned from the poem, be sure to use the Academic Vocabulary words. Check off each of the words that you use.

❏ **analogy**
❏ **denote**
❏ **quote**
❏ **topic**
❏ **unique**

CREATE AND PRESENT

Write a Poem Suggest that students think about the different elements of poetry before they begin writing. These include setting, stanza and line structure, sound devices, and the subject. Poems should be free verse and reflect a thoughtful approach to the above elements.

Tell students to review their poems once they finish and to make any edits necessary. Because poems are lyrical in nature, students should read them aloud to themselves. Their final poems should exhibit an attention to word choice, flow, and structure.

 For **writing support** for students at varying proficiency levels, see the **Text X-Ray** on page 242D.

Present a Poem As students practice, remind them that an important aspect of poetry is the expression of emotion. Suggest that they think about how the sound of their voices, their posture, and their body language might convey the feelings behind their writing.

Presentations should show evidence of practice and attention to detail. Students should vary their volume, pitch, and tone of voice to emphasize certain elements, such as word choice, structure, or key ideas.

RESPOND TO THE ESSENTIAL QUESTION

Allow time for students to add details from "In the Season of Change" to their Unit 3 Response Logs.

© Houghton Mifflin Harcourt Publishing Company

from **WALDEN**

Essay by Henry David Thoreau

MENTOR TEXT

from **LAST CHILD IN THE WOODS**

Informational text by Richard Louv

> This informational text serves as a **mentor text,** a model for students to follow when they come to the Unit 3 Writing Task: Writing an Explanatory Essay.

GENRE ELEMENTS
INFORMATIONAL TEXTS AND ESSAYS

Remind students that **informational texts and essays** have a purpose, usually expressed in the form of a thesis. In this lesson, students will identify the main (or central) ideas relevant to this thesis as well as pertinent details that support the main ideas, transitions that connect ideas, and the conclusions that draw everything together.

LEARNING OBJECTIVES

- Summarize author's thesis and main ideas.
- Evaluate author's use of literary devices and figures of speech.
- Identify and analyze rhetorical questions.
- Conduct research about the American frontier and Frederick Jackson Turner.
- Write an essay explaining key aspects of transcendentalism.
- Make an oral presentation to peers on transcendentalism.
- Use context clues to determine the meaning of words.
- Write rhetorical questions.
- **Language:** Discuss literary devices using the key word *compares*.

TEXT COMPLEXITY

Quantitative Measures	*from* **Walden** / *from* **Last Child in the Woods**	Lexile: 1250L/Lexile: 1190L
Qualitative Measures	**Ideas Presented** Much is explicit but moves to some implied meaning; requires some inferential reasoning.	
	Structures Used More complex perspective; more deviation from chronological or sequential order.	
	Language Used Explicit language as well as figurative language; complex sentence structure.	
	Knowledge Required More complexity in theme; experiences may be less familiar to many; historical and cultural references may make heavier demands.	

RESOURCES

- Unit 3 Response Log
- Selection Audio
- Reading Studio: Notice & Note
- Level Up Tutorial: Figurative Language; Audience
- Writing Studio: Conducting Research
- Speaking and Listening Studio: Giving a Presentation
- Vocabulary Studio: Using Context Clues
- *from* "Walden" / *from* "Last Child in the Woods" Selection Test

SUMMARIES

English

Walden, by transcendentalist Henry David Thoreau, is also called *Life in the Woods*. It is about Thoreau's search for a simpler, more ethical life immersed in nature, which he accomplished by moving to a rustic cabin in the woods surrounding Walden Pond. The book also focuses on the importance of independence and spiritual discovery.

Last Child in the Woods is a book about the loss of the modern child's exposure to nature. In it, author Richard Louv describes his exploration of the natural world during his own childhood and how he believes the loss of this exploration harms today's children.

Spanish

"De *Walden*", es un pasaje del libro del trascendentalista, Henry David Thoreau, también llamado *La vida en el bosque*. Trata de la búsqueda de una vida más simple y ética, sumergida en la naturaleza por parte de Thoreau, quien la consiguió al mudarse a una cabaña rústica en un bosque alrededor del lago Walden. El libro también se enfoca en la importancia de la independencia y el descubrimiento espiritual.

"De *El último niño en el bosque*" es un pasaje de un libro acerca de la pérdida moderna de la exposición infantil a la naturaleza. En él, Richard Louv describe su exploración del mundo natural durante su infancia y por qué cree que la pérdida de esa exploración afecta a los niños actualmente.

 ## SMALL-GROUP OPTIONS

Have students work in small groups and pairs to read and discuss the selection.

Reciprocal Teaching

- Have students read the two essays.
- After reading, ask students to write four or five questions comparing the essays, using these stems: *What do the two essays _____? In what ways do the authors _____? Why do the authors _____? How did the _____?*
- Form teams of three students, in which each student offers two questions for group discussion.
- Have the groups discuss the questions and reach consensus on the answers, using supporting text evidence.

Jigsaw with Experts

- Divide each essay into five or six parts.
- Assign each student a part to read silently, taking notes on the part assigned to them.
- Have students with the same part get into groups and, as "experts" of their part, discuss their part and what they believe is significant about it. Instruct them to write a two or three sentence summary of their part.
- Reread essays as a whole class, and have each group explain the meaning and significance of their section.

Text X-Ray: English Learner Support
for Walden and Last Child in the Woods

Use the Text X-Ray and the supports and scaffolds in the Teacher's Edition to help guide students at different proficiency levels through the selection.

INTRODUCE THE SELECTIONS
DISCUSS TRANSCENDENTALISM AND THE NATURAL WORLD

In this lesson, students will need to be able to understand transcendentalism and its relationship to nature.

Explain to students that transcendentalism was a literary movement associated with the belief that people and nature are good, and that society and its institutions can make people impure. Many transcendentalist writers expressed the belief that people are at their best when they are self-reliant and independent. Transcendentalism was the first American intellectual movement, and it helped give rise to public education as a means of helping an individual achieve self-reliance. It espouses the belief individuals can learn from nature.

Discuss with students what can be learned from nature and what they have learned from nature during their lives.

CULTURAL REFERENCES

The following words or phrases may be unfamiliar to students:

- *live deliberately* (paragraph 3, from *Walden*): focus one's life and efforts on what is basic and most important
- *crawdads* (paragraph 3, from *Last Child in the Woods*): another name for crayfish, freshwater crustaceans that resemble small lobsters and inhabit streams and rivers
- *patent-or-perish* (paragraph 8, from *Last Child in the Woods*): a phrase that has developed from the phrase *publish or perish*, which is referring to the pressure researchers are under to publish material (or patent material) in order to keep their positions at universities and be considered successful

LISTENING

Understand Figurative Language

Remind students that personification is a type of figurative language in which objects, animals, or ideas are given human qualities. Guide students' understanding of personification and its purpose in this essay.

Have students listen as you read paragraph 2 of the excerpt from *Walden*, which contains an example of personification. Use the following supports with the students at varying proficiency levels:

- Point out how Thoreau describes the pond. Display pictures of ponds covered with mist. Explain that this description is an example of personification. Ask students questions to ensure understanding. For example: *Does Thoreau personify the pond?* (Yes.) **SUBSTANTIAL**
- Point out the phrase "throwing off its nightly clothing of mist." Have partners work together to determine what Thoreau is describing and why the phrase is an example of personification. Then, have each partner say why they think Thoreau uses this phrase. **MODERATE**
- Ask students to work in pairs to ask and answer the following questions: *What object does Thoreau personify? What human qualities does he give to the object? How does it make you feel about the object?* Listeners should summarize what their partners say. **LIGHT**

SPEAKING

Understand Literary Devices

Guide students' understanding of intention and meaning behind literary devices, such as simile, metaphor, and analogy.

Use the following supports with students at varying proficiency levels:

- Read aloud the first sentence of paragraph 4 from the *Walden* excerpt. Point out that Thoreau says people "live meanly, like ants." Explain that *meanly* can mean "in a small or humble way." Have students describe ants. Then, have them refer to the list to explain why Thoreau compares people to ants. Provide a sentence frame: *Thoreau compares people to _____.* **SUBSTANTIAL**

- Tell students to look for comparisons Thoreau uses to describe people or life. Have partners discuss the meaning of two comparisons. Use questions to guide students: *What does Thoreau compare [people/life] to? What does the comparison show about [people/life]?* **MODERATE**

- Have students identify one simile and one metaphor in the text and discuss what they think these comparisons mean or why Thoreau used them. **LIGHT**

READING

Determine the Central Idea and Supporting Details

Help students to identify the central idea and to understand that it is the most important point the author wants to make. Then, help them identify supporting details.

Use the following supports with students of varying proficiency levels:

- In paragraph 3 of the *Walden* excerpt, ask students which words are repeated. Point out *life* and *live*. Explain that this shows that "life" is the topic of the paragraph. Help students find other details and key words to determine what Thoreau is saying about life. Provide sentence frames: *Thoreau thinks life should be _____. Thoreau thinks people should live _____.* **SUBSTANTIAL**

- Have student pairs read paragraph 3 and list words they think are important. Tell them to write a sentence describing the main idea, using some of the key words from their list. **MODERATE**

- Have students read paragraph 3 and write a sentence describing the central idea. Then, have students exchange sentences with a partner and discuss any differences. **LIGHT**

WRITING

Write an Essay

Modify the writing activity that appears on Student Edition page 263.

Have students create a two-column chart with the heads *Walden/Thoreau* and *Last Child in the Woods/Louv* and record words and phrases the authors use to describe the benefits of nature. Use the following supports with students of varying proficiency levels:

- Help students find words and phrases and add them to the chart. As you add words and phrases, explain them in different words. Work with students to write a paragraph on the topic. Have students copy the paragraph in their notebooks. **SUBSTANTIAL**

- Provide sentence frames for students to help them write their essays: *Thoreau says _____ about nature. Louv says _____. Both authors think _____.* Students should use details from their chart in their essay. **MODERATE**

- Have students work in pairs to write a draft of the essay. Encourage students to use quotations from the texts. Have pairs exchange papers and do a peer edit. **LIGHT**

? Connect to the
ESSENTIAL QUESTION

Nature, in its beauty and stillness, offers the chance to see ourselves as part of something vast and mysterious. In the excerpt from *Walden*, Thoreau reflects on that relationship. In the excerpt from *Last Child in the Woods*, Louv comments on technology's effect on the way young people view and interact with nature.

COMPARE MAIN IDEAS

Point out that both *Walden* and *Last Child in the Woods* are about the human relationship with nature. Ask students to reflect on that relationship. What is the value of being in nature? How have people's interactions with nature changed over time?

MENTOR TEXT

At the end of the unit, students will be asked to write an explanatory essay. The excerpt from *Last Child in the Woods* provides a model for how a writer can analyze and explain a topic with examples, details, and quotations.

COLLABORATE & COMPARE

ESSAY

from

WALDEN

by **Henry David Thoreau**
pages 253–257

COMPARE MAIN IDEAS

In the 19th century, Henry David Thoreau espoused the view that divinity was found in nature. The contemporary writer Richard Louv believes that humanity's essential connection to nature has been lost. As you read, consider what each author believes people gain from interacting with nature.

 ESSENTIAL QUESTION:

When should we stop and reflect on our lives?

INFORMATIONAL TEXT

from

LAST CHILD IN THE WOODS

by **Richard Louv**
pages 258–261

250   Unit 3

QUICK START

Humans have a complicated relationship with nature. Think of a positive experience and a negative experience you have had in a natural setting. Why were these experiences memorable? Discuss your thoughts with a partner.

SUMMARIZE

One way to identify a text's key ideas is to write an objective summary of it. When you **summarize**, you restate the central ideas in your own words. A summary is much shorter than the original text and includes only the most important supporting details. Use these strategies to summarize the texts.

- Skim titles, headings, and other text features to predict the key ideas.

- See if a topic sentence, usually at the beginning or end of a paragraph, explicitly states the paragraph's key idea.

- Infer a central idea from the details contained in a paragraph.

- If you are struggling, summarize individual paragraphs or sections first.

ANALYZE AUTHOR'S CRAFT

Author's craft refers to how an author expresses his or her ideas. Author's craft can make ideas more compelling and make a text more engaging. Two aspects of author's craft are literary devices and figures of speech.

GENRE ELEMENTS: INFORMATIONAL TEXTS AND ESSAYS

- clearly convey key ideas
- contain details that support key ideas
- use elements of author's craft including literary devices and figures of speech

ELEMENTS OF AUTHOR'S CRAFT	
Literary Devices: Language structures that produce a special effect or convey additional meaning to a text	**Rhetorical question** A question that requires no reply **Repetition** To repeat a sound, word, or phrase for emphasis or unity **Irony** A contrast between appearances and reality **Verbal irony** A contrast between what is said and what is meant
Figures of Speech: Language that communicates ideas beyond the literal meaning of the words used	**Simile** A comparison between two things, using *like* or *as* **Metaphor** A direct comparison that does not use *like* or *as* **Hyperbole** An exaggeration of the truth for emphasis or humorous effect **Personification** To give human traits to objects, animals, or ideas

As you read the texts, notice how each writer employs elements of author's craft to help readers understand the ideas he wants to communicate. Think about how these elements shape your perception of ideas.

from Walden / *from* Last Child in the Woods   251

QUICK START

Have students read the Quick Start question. Invite them to discuss their experiences with another student whom they feel comfortable, and explain that they should focus on why the experience was memorable to them. Invite volunteers to share their experiences with the class.

SUMMARIZE

Explain to students that summarizing a text will help them be sure they have a clear understanding of the text. Review the bulleted strategies for writing an objective summary. Students should use these strategies as they read the selections to clarify key ideas. Remind students that writers often restate an essay's central idea in the last paragraph.

ANALYZE AUTHOR'S CRAFT

Review the elements in the graphic organizer, and explain to students that they should be able to find an example of each of the elements as they read through the selections. Provide examples as needed if students are unfamiliar with any of the literary devices or figures of speech.

TEACH

CRITICAL VOCABULARY

Encourage students to read each Critical Vocabulary word before deciding on the correct answer.

Answers:

1. *b*
2. *a*
3. *a*
4. *b*
5. *b*
6. *a*
7. *b*
8. *b*

LANGUAGE CONVENTIONS

Rhetorical Questions Review the information about rhetorical questions. Explain that the example comes from *Walden,* and while Thoreau does not expect the reader to answer the question, it is asked to make the reader think. Invite students to talk about the question and give examples of what can make life so rushed and why that might be considered a "waste of life." Explain that although the question is rhetorical, it is a literary device designed to make the reader realize we should *not* live a life with such haste.

■ English Learner Support

Use Cognates Tell students that several of the Critical Vocabulary words have Spanish cognates: *abstraction/ abstracción, codify/codificar, superfluous/superfluo.*
ALL LEVELS

ANNOTATION MODEL

Remind students of the annotation marks they may use, such as underlining and circling words, ideas, or details. Point out that they may follow this suggestion or use their own system for marking up the selection in their write-in text. They may want to color-code their annotations by using highlighters. Their notes in the margin may include questions, concepts they are unclear about, or ideas they want to learn more about.

 **GET READY**

CRITICAL VOCABULARY

WORD BANK
superfluous	abstraction
unfathomed	codify
perturbation	remunerative
polarity	configuration

Circle the synonym for each Critical Vocabulary word.

1. abstraction
   a. fact   **b.** idea

2. codify
   a. order   **b.** allow

3. configuration
   a. formation   **b.** option

4. perturbation
   a. destruction **b.** disturbance

5. polarity
   a. convergence **b.** difference

6. remunerative
   a. paying   **b.** unpaid

7. superfluous
   a. essential   **b.** extra

8. unfathomed
   a. constrained **b.** vast

LANGUAGE CONVENTIONS

Rhetorical Questions Questions that are asked to make a point and without the expectation of an actual reply are called rhetorical questions. Note the example of a rhetorical question from *Walden* below.

> **Why should we live with such hurry and waste of life?**

In this case, Thoreau does not want readers to answer the question; he wants them to ponder what he has written and see things from his point of view. Note the use of rhetorical questions and why an author includes them.

ANNOTATION MODEL

NOTICE & NOTE

As you read, notice each author's key ideas and elements of author's craft that enhance their writing. Note any details that support the writer's key ideas. In the model, you can see one reader's notes about the essay from *Walden.*

I wanted to live deep and suck out all the <u>marrow of life</u>, to live so sturdily and <u>Spartan-like as to put to rout all that was not life</u>, to cut a broad swath and shave close, to drive life into a corner, and reduce it to its lowest terms, and, if it proved to be mean, why then to get the whole and genuine meanness of it, and publish its meanness to the world; or if it were sublime, to know it by experience, and be able to give a true account of it in my next excursion.

This is a strong statement and conveys an important idea: enthusiasm for life!

"Spartan-like" compares the way Thoreau wants to live—like a soldier. He uses more war imagery—describing an act of aggression.

BACKGROUND

Henry David Thoreau *(1817–1862) of Concord, Massachusetts, was a transcendentalist like his friend and mentor Ralph Waldo Emerson. After graduating from Harvard College and teaching school for a few years, Thoreau decided to become a nature poet. In 1845 he began his two-year experiment living in a cabin that he built in the woods near Walden Pond on property owned by Emerson. Walden (1854) is a collection of 18 essays based on his experiences. Thoreau's most famous essay, "Civil Disobedience" (1849), defends the right of an individual to follow his conscience rather than obey unjust laws.*

from
WALDEN
Essay by Henry David Thoreau

PREPARE TO COMPARE

As you read, note observations about "modern" life and the connection between humans and nature. You will compare these ideas with those of Richard Louv in the selection from Last Child in the Woods.

from Where I Lived, and What I Lived For

1   When first I took up my abode in the woods, that is, began to spend my nights as well as days there, which, by accident, was on Independence day, or the fourth of July, 1845, my house was not finished for winter, but was merely a defense against the rain, without plastering or chimney, the walls being of rough weather-stained boards, with wide chinks, which made it cool at night. The upright white hewn studs and freshly planed door and window casings gave it a clean and airy look, especially in the morning, when its timbers were saturated with dew, so that I fancied that by noon some sweet gum would exude from them. . . .

2   I was seated by the shore of a small pond, about a mile and a half south of the village of Concord and somewhat higher

Notice & Note

Use the side margins to notice and note signposts in the text.

SUMMARIZE
Annotate: Mark the title of this section of the essay.

Interpret: What is the most important idea the writer expresses in paragraph 1? How does the title help you predict this idea?

from Walden / *from* Last Child in the Woods   253

BACKGROUND

After students read the Background note, tell them that Thoreau and Emerson are regarded as the major transcendentalist writers of the 19th century. Transcendentalism was a philosophy that held that people could only learn the strongest truths by using their five senses—that is, through their intuition—rather than through logic. Transcendentalists also believed that humans are essentially good and all things are created equal. Thoreau's transcendentalist beliefs were expressed in his writings. In *Walden*, Thoreau is advocating for a return to nature, in which he believes humans may find life's deepest truths.

PREPARE TO COMPARE

Direct students to use the Prepare to Compare prompt to focus their reading.

 SUMMARIZE

Remind students to look at titles and headings as clues to the author's key ideas. (**Answer:** *In paragraph 1, Thoreau describes in detail his house in the woods as he took up residence. The header suggests that he is not only interested in the house, but in living there for a purpose, which he'll state in later parts of the essay.*)

For **listening support** for students at varying proficiency levels, see the **Text X-Ray** on page 250C.

TEACH

ANALYZE AUTHOR'S CRAFT

Tell students that Thoreau's style includes figurative language—language that communicates ideas beyond its literal meaning. **Personification** gives human characteristics to an animal, an object, or an idea. A **simile** is a comparison between two things, using the word *like* or *as*. (**Answer:** *Thoreau personifies the pond when he describes it "throwing off its nightly clothing of mist." He uses a simile to compare the mists to ghosts. From this figurative language, it is possible to infer that Thoreau's purpose was to help the reader see the landscape as he does: as a living being with its own spirit.*)

> For **speaking** and **reading support** for students at varying proficiency levels, see the **Text X-Ray** on page 250D.

CRITICAL VOCABULARY

superfluous: Thoreau says that feeling wretched, or miserable, is unnecessary.

ASK STUDENTS what is a solution for the *superfluous* wretchedness? (*simplicity; eliminating the excessive number of things or activities in one's life*)

ANALYZE AUTHOR'S CRAFT
Annotate: Mark an example of personification and an example of a simile in paragraph 2.

Analyze: How does this figurative language support a key idea in the paragraph?

superfluous
(soo-pûr´floo-əs) *adj.*
unnecessary.

than it, in the midst of an extensive wood between that town and Lincoln, and about two miles south of that our only field known to fame, Concord Battle Ground; but I was so low in the woods that the opposite shore, half a mile off, like the rest, covered with wood, was my most distant horizon. For the first week, whenever I looked out on the pond it impressed me like a tarn[1] high up on the side of a mountain, its bottom far above the surface of other lakes, and, as the sun arose, I saw it throwing off its nightly clothing of mist, and here and there, by degrees, its soft ripples or its smooth reflecting surface was revealed, while the mists, like ghosts, were stealthily withdrawing in every direction into the woods, as at the breaking up of some nocturnal conventicle.[2] The very dew seemed to hang upon the trees later into the day than usual, as on the sides of mountains. . . .

3   I went to the woods because I wished to live deliberately, to front only the essential facts of life, and see if I could not learn what it had to teach, and not, when I came to die, discover that I had not lived. I did not wish to live what was not life, living is so dear; nor did I wish to practice resignation, unless it was quite necessary. I wanted to live deep and suck out all the marrow of life, to live so sturdily and Spartan-like[3] as to put to rout all that was not life, to cut a broad swath and shave close, to drive life into a corner, and reduce it to its lowest terms, and, if it proved to be mean, why then to get the whole and genuine meanness of it, and publish its meanness to the world; or if it were sublime, to know it by experience, and be able to give a true account of it in my next excursion. For most men, it appears to me, are in a strange uncertainty about it, whether it is of the devil or of God, and have *somewhat hastily* concluded that it is the chief end of man here to "glorify God and enjoy him forever."

4   Still we live meanly, like ants; though the fable tells us that we were long ago changed into men; like pygmies we fight with cranes; it is error upon error, and clout upon clout, and our best virtue has for its occasion a **superfluous** and evitable[4] wretchedness. Our life is frittered away by detail. An honest man has hardly need to count more than his ten fingers, or in extreme cases he may add his ten toes, and lump the rest. Simplicity, simplicity, simplicity! I say, let your affairs be as two or three, and not a hundred or a thousand; instead of a million count half a dozen, and keep your accounts on your thumbnail. In the midst of this chopping sea of civilized life, such are the clouds and storms and quicksands and thousand-and-one items to be allowed for, that a man has to live, if he would not founder and go to the bottom and not make his port at all, by dead reckoning, and he must be a great calculator indeed who succeeds. Simplify, simplify. Instead of three meals a day, if it be necessary eat but one; instead of a hundred dishes, five; and reduce other things in proportion. . . .

---

[1] **tarn:** a small mountain lake or pool.
[2] **conventicle:** a secret or unlawful religious meeting.
[3] **Spartan-like:** in a simple and disciplined way, like the inhabitants of the ancient city-state of Sparta.
[4] **evitable:** avoidable.

ENGLISH LEARNER SUPPORT

Use Prior Knowledge and Experiences To help students practice speaking in small groups about a topic, ask student pairs to discuss their experiences walking or doing activities in nature. Provide the sentence frame: *One place I like to go when I am outdoors is ___. I like it because ___.* Then, invite them to briefly tell their experiences to a larger group. Finally, ask at least one volunteer to describe his or her experiences to the class. **ALL LEVELS**

© Houghton Mifflin Harcourt Publishing Company • Image Credits: © Jaromir Chalabala/Shutterstock

LANGUAGE CONVENTIONS

As students mark the question in the first line of the text, ask them if the subsequent text answers that question. Explain that because the question is not answered—and not expected to be answered—it is a rhetorical question. (**Answer:** *The rhetorical question forces the reader to pause and take note, which reinforces the argument that Thoreau is making.*)

EL ENGLISH LEARNER SUPPORT

Homographs Point out the word *excuse* (ik-ʹskyüs) in paragraph 5 and say it out loud. Explain that in this sentence, the word is used as a noun. Then, mark the verb *excuse* (ik-ʹskyüz) and use it in a sentence. Point out that these words are spelled the same but pronounced slightly differently. Explain that students must read the word in the context of the sentence to determine which meaning and pronunciation the author intends. **ALL LEVELS**

5   Why should we live with such hurry and waste of life? We are determined to be starved before we are hungry. Men say that a stitch in time saves nine, and so they take a thousand stitches today to save nine to-morrow. As for *work*, we haven't any of any consequence. We have the Saint Vitus' dance,[5] and cannot possibly keep our heads still. If I should only give a few pulls at the parish bell-rope, as for a fire, that is, without setting the bell, there is hardly a man on his farm in the outskirts of Concord, notwithstanding that press of engagements which was his excuse so many times this morning, nor a boy, nor a woman, I might almost say, but would forsake all and follow that

LANGUAGE CONVENTIONS
Annotate: Mark the rhetorical question in paragraph 5.

Analyze: What point is Thoreau making by asking this question?

---
[5] **Saint Vitus' dance:** a disorder of the nervous system, characterized by rapid, jerky, involuntary movements.

from Walden / *from* Last Child in the Woods   255

IMPROVE READING FLUENCY

Use Footnotes Some students may need to rely on the footnotes provided throughout the selections to help them understand the meanings of words. Point out the footnote for *Saint Vitus' dance.* After students read the phrase and confirm its meaning, have them go back and read the sentence again—this time with fluency and a consistent reading rate.

📖 Go to the **Reading Studio** for additional support in developing fluency.

ANALYZE AUTHOR'S CRAFT

Explain that **hyperbole** is an exaggeration for effect. Have students locate the hyperbole in paragraph 5. Ask students to think about what Thoreau is exaggerating and how they respond to his example. (**Answer:** *Thoreau is exaggerating people's interest in news and other people's affairs by saying that some don't want to sleep more than a half hour at a time because they want to know what's going on at all hours of the day and night. The effect of the hyperbole is to make the people who regard the news as indispensable as breakfast seem foolish and flighty. Thoreau's purpose is to make readers think about whether they are also fixated on other people's business.*)

SUMMARIZE

Ask students to read the last sentence in the selection, interpret the phrase, and then summarize to clarify Thoreau's key point. (**Answer:** *Thoreau means that the rewards his intellect craves can be found where he is living in nature. Thoreau is expressing that his mind is a useful and important tool he uses to find out the meaning of things through his exploration of nature.*)

CRITICAL VOCABULARY

unfathomed: Thoreau compares the world to a large cave, the deepest places in which have not been measured or explored.

ASK STUDENTS in what way the world might be *unfathomed* by someone who is overly concerned with news. (*Someone who is overly concerned with news might not notice the nuances of nature or be in touch with his or her own inner thoughts.*)

perturbation: Thoreau is asking the reader to stay calm at the beginning of the day and not get caught up in the day's business.

ASK STUDENTS what modern-day events might be likely to cause *perturbation* in the morning? (*phone calls, texts, car trouble, traffic*)

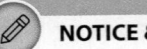

ANALYZE AUTHOR'S CRAFT
Annotate: Mark an example of hyperbole in paragraph 5.

Analyze: What is Thoreau exaggerating in this sentence? What effect does this exaggeration have on the reader? What does this use of hyperbole reveal about Thoreau's purpose?

unfathomed
(ŭn-făth´əmd) *adj.* located at the deepest place.

perturbation
(pûr-tər-bā´shən) *n.* disturbance or agitation.

SUMMARIZE
Annotate: Mark the last sentence of the selection.

Interpret: What does Thoreau mean when he says "the richest vein is somewhere hereabouts"? What key idea does this statement convey?

sound, not mainly to save property from the flames, but, if we will confess the truth, much more to see it burn, since burn it must, and we, be it known, did not set it on fire,—or to see it put out, and have a hand in it, if that is done as handsomely; yes, even if it were the parish church itself. Hardly a man takes a half hour's nap after dinner, but when he wakes he holds up his head and asks, "What's the news?" as if the rest of mankind had stood his sentinels. Some give directions to be waked every half hour, doubtless for no other purpose; and then, to pay for it, they tell what they have dreamed. After a night's sleep the news is as indispensable as the breakfast. "Pray tell me any thing new that has happened to a man any where on this globe,"—and he reads it over his coffee and rolls, that a man has had his eyes gouged out this morning on the Wachito River; never dreaming the while that he lives in the dark **unfathomed** mammoth cave of this world, and has but the rudiment of an eye himself.

6   For my part, I could easily do without the post-office. I think that there are very few important communications made through it. To speak critically, I never received more than one or two letters in my life—I wrote this some years ago—that were worth the postage. The penny-post is, commonly, an institution through which you seriously offer a man that penny for his thoughts which is so often safely offered in jest. And I am sure that I never read any memorable news in a newspaper. If we read of one man robbed, or murdered, or killed by accident, or one house burned, or one vessel wrecked, or one steamboat blown up, or one cow run over on the Western Railroad, or one mad dog killed, or one lot of grasshoppers in the winter,—we never need read of another. One is enough. . . .

7   Let us spend one day as deliberately as Nature, and not be thrown off the track by every nutshell and mosquito's wing that falls on the rails. Let us rise early and fast, or break fast, gently and without **perturbation;** let company come and let company go, let the bells ring and the children cry,— determined to make a day of it. . . .

8   Time is but the stream I go a-fishing in. I drink at it; but while I drink I see the sandy bottom and detect how shallow it is. Its thin current slides away, but eternity remains. I would drink deeper; fish in the sky, whose bottom is pebbly with stars. I cannot count one. I know not the first letter of the alphabet. I have always been regretting that I was not as wise as the day I was born. The intellect is a cleaver; it discerns and rifts its way into the secret of things. I do not wish to be any more busy with my hands than is necessary. My head is hands and feet. I feel all my best faculties concentrated in it. My instinct tells me that my head is an organ for burrowing, as some creatures use their snout and fore-paws, and with it I would mine and burrow my way through these hills. I think that the richest vein is somewhere hereabouts; so by the divining rod and thin rising vapors I judge; and here I will begin to mine.

WHEN STUDENTS STRUGGLE . . .

Figurative Language Students may experience difficulty identifying the hyperbole in paragraph 5. Encourage them to use the side columns to indicate possible places in the text that might indicate an extreme exaggeration or claim that is not meant to be taken literally. Then, have them look for clues that indicate exaggeration, such as "every half hour," "tell me any thing new," or "indispensable."

For additional support, go to the **Reading Studio** and assign the following [LEVEL UP] **Level Up Tutorial: Figurative Language**.

CHECK YOUR UNDERSTANDING

Have students answer the questions independently.

Answers:

1. *D*

2. *G*

3. *D*

If they answer any questions incorrectly, have them reread the text to confirm their understanding. Then they may proceed to the next selection.

CHECK YOUR UNDERSTANDING

Answer these questions about *Walden* before moving on to the next selection.

1 Where does Thoreau live during the time described in this essay?

  A In the village of Concord

  B In the small town of Lincoln

  C In a field not far from Lincoln

  D In the woods not far from Concord

2 What is Thoreau's main purpose for living there?

  F To escape modern life

  G To learn what is essential about life

  H To be more devoted to God and glorify Him

  J To become more like an animal than like a human

3 What are Thoreau's main complaints about human society?

  A It is dull and full of empty relationships.

  B It is shallow and full of terrifying cruelty.

  C It is violent and full of appalling suffering.

  D It is rushed and full of meaningless distractions.

© Houghton Mifflin Harcourt Publishing Company

from Walden / *from* Last Child in the Woods   257

 ENGLISH LEARNER SUPPORT

Oral Assessment Use the following question to assess students' comprehension and speaking skills.

  • Where is Thoreau living? *(in the woods near Concord)*

  • Does Thoreau want to learn what is important in life? *(yes)*

  • Does Thoreau think society is too busy? *(yes)*

  SUBSTANTIAL/MODERATE

from Walden / *from* Last Child in the Woods   **257**

BACKGROUND

Have students read the Background about Richard Louv. Explain that the book *Last Child in the Woods: Saving Our Children from Nature-Deficit Disorder* is an informational text. It presents information and the author's point of view with a reflective and serious tone. As they read, ask students to note similarities and differences between the this excerpt and the excerpt from *Walden*.

PREPARE TO COMPARE

Direct students to use the Prepare to Compare prompt to focus their reading.

 SUMMARIZE

As students identify the contrast the author is pointing out, ask them to imagine life without the things he mentions, such as cell phones, texting, social media, and video games. Discuss what they imagine the author's childhood might have been like without these things. Then, have students summarize the main idea. (***Answer:*** *Over a short time—one generation—children's experience of nature has changed drastically.*)

CRITICAL VOCABULARY

polarity: Louv describes a reversal of children's experience of nature from an intimate experience to an intellectual understanding of the environment in general.

ASK STUDENTS to discuss other ways there is a *polarity* between the way things were done in the past and today. (*Students may mention the way people communicated long ago and communication in the digital age.*)

258 Unit 3

 NOTICE & NOTE

BACKGROUND

Journalist **Richard Louv** *(b. 1949) is an active writer and speaker about the importance of reconnecting children to nature. He cofounded the Children & Nature Network, an organization whose vision is a "world in which all children play, learn and grow with nature in their everyday lives." He published the book* Last Child in the Woods: Saving Our Children from Nature-Deficit Disorder *in 2005, and received the Audubon Medal in 2008 for his work.*

from
LAST CHILD IN THE WOODS
Informational Text by Richard Louv

Notice & Note

Use the side margins to notice and note signposts in the text.

SUMMARIZE

Annotate: Mark sentences and phrases in paragraph 4 that contrast the author's childhood and the lives of children today.

Compare: What main idea does this comparison communicate?

polarity
(pō-lăr´ĭ-tē) *n.* separation to opposite sides.

PREPARE TO COMPARE

As you read the excerpt from Last Child in the Woods, *consider how Richard Louv's ideas on nature relate to Thoreau's.*

1   One evening when my boys were younger, Matthew, then ten, looked at me from across a restaurant table and said quite seriously, "Dad, how come it was more fun when you were a kid?"

2   I asked what he meant.

3   "Well, you're always talking about your woods and tree houses, and how you used to ride that horse down near the swamp." At first, I thought he was irritated with me. I had, in fact, been telling him what it was like to use string and pieces of liver to catch crawdads in a creek, something I'd be hard-pressed to find a child doing these days. Like many parents, I do tend to romanticize my own childhood— and, I fear, too readily discount my children's experiences of play and adventure. But my son was serious; he felt he had missed out on something important.

4   He was right. Americans around my age, baby boomers or older, enjoyed a kind of free, natural play that seems, in the era of kid pagers, instant messaging, and video games, like a quaint artifact. Within the space of a few decades, the way children understand and experience nature has changed radically. The **polarity** of the relationship has reversed. Today, kids are aware of the global threats

---

WHEN STUDENTS STRUGGLE...

Audience Students should realize that the author of the essay is older than they are. Point out that he refers to a conversation with his son, and he says "Americans around my age, baby boomers or older...." Students should realize he is giving background information. Invite students to think about whether the things he says about the current generation of children applies to their own lives.

 For additional support, go to the **Reading Studio** and assign the following **Level Up Tutorial: Audience**.

to the environment—but <u>their physical contact, their intimacy with nature, is fading</u>. That's exactly the opposite of how it was when I was a child.

5   As a boy, I was unaware that my woods were ecologically connected with any other forests. Nobody in the 1950s talked about acid rain or holes in the ozone layer or global warming. But I knew my woods and my fields; I knew every bend in the creek and dip in the beaten dirt paths. I wandered those woods even in my dreams. A kid today can likely tell you about the Amazon rain forest—but not about the last time he or she explored the woods in solitude, or lay in a field listening to the wind and watching the clouds move.

6   The shift in our relationship to the natural world is startling, even in settings that one would assume are devoted to nature. Not that long ago, summer camp was a place where you camped, hiked in the woods, learned about plants and animals, or told firelight stories about ghosts or mountain lions. <u>As likely as not today, "summer camp" is a weight-loss camp, or a computer camp.</u> For a new generation, nature is more **abstraction** than reality. Increasingly, nature is something to watch, to consume, to wear—to ignore. A recent television ad depicts a four-wheel-drive SUV racing along a breathtakingly beautiful mountain stream—while in the backseat two children watch a movie on a flip-down video screen, oblivious to the landscape and water beyond the windows.

7   A century ago, the historian Frederick Jackson Turner announced that the American frontier had ended. His thesis has been discussed and debated ever since. Today, a similar and more important line is being crossed.

8   Our society is teaching young people to avoid direct experience in nature. That lesson is delivered in schools, families, even organizations devoted to the outdoors, and **codified** into the legal and regulatory structures of many of our communities. Our institutions, urban/suburban design, and cultural attitudes unconsciously associate nature with doom—while disassociating[1] the outdoors from joy and solitude. Well-meaning public-school systems, media, and parents are effectively scaring children straight out of the woods and fields. In the patent-or-perish environment of higher education, we see the death of natural history as the more hands-on disciplines, such as zoology, give way to more theoretical and **remunerative** microbiology and genetic engineering. Rapidly advancing technologies are blurring the lines between humans, other animals, and machines. The postmodern notion that reality is only a construct—that we are what we program—suggests limitless human possibilities; but as the young spend less and less of their lives in natural surroundings, their senses narrow, physiologically and psychologically, and this reduces the richness of human experience.

9   Yet, at the very moment that the bond is breaking between the young and the natural world, a growing body of research links our

[1] **disassociating** (dĭs-ə-sō´sē-āt-ĭng): remove from association.

NOTICE & NOTE

ANALYZE AUTHOR'S CRAFT
Annotate: Mark an example of irony in paragraph 6.

Interpret: What point does Louv make through the use of irony?

abstraction
(ăb-străk´shən) *n.* something that is not part of the concrete, material world.

codify
(kŏd´ĭ-fī) *v.* to arrange or systematize.

remunerative
(rĭ-myōō´nər-ə-tĭv) *adj.* yielding suitable recompense, profitable.

 ANALYZE AUTHOR'S CRAFT

Tell students that **irony** can be used to emphasize a point. Remind them that irony expresses the difference between appearances and reality. (**Answer:** *Louv is making the point that even when children are in nature, they are not experiencing nature.*)

CRITICAL VOCABULARY

abstraction: An abstraction is an idea that is far from reality. The text uses the example of nature as something to wear.

ASK STUDENTS to name some ways nature can be an *abstraction* as something to wear. (*animal prints*)

codified: The author uses the word *codified* to signify an organizational structure.

ASK STUDENTS what connotation the word *codify* has in paragraph 8, referring to laws about the environment. (*negative*)

remunerative: The word *remunerative* refers to profits that can be made from nature.

ASK STUDENTS ways nature can be *remunerative*. (*plants used for pharmaceuticals*)

SUMMARIZE

As students choose significant details from the paragraph, write them on the board. Remind them that one of the strategies for summarizing is to infer a central idea from the details contained in a paragraph. (**Answer:** *The research suggests that exposure to nature has a positive effect on one's health and well-being. The possibility of improved health supports the idea that humanity and nature need to reconnect.*)

ENGLISH LEARNER SUPPORT

Understand Contrasts Help students locate the words *mental, physical, and spiritual health* and make sure they understand the meanings. Then, have students work in pairs to give examples of each.
ALL LEVELS

CRITICAL VOCABULARY

configuration: The author refers to the arrangement, or layout, and structure of cities, comparing them to the way nature is arranged.

ASK STUDENTS to describe how a city is *configured*.
(*A city has buildings arranged by streets, with people using those buildings.*)

NOTICE & NOTE

SUMMARIZE

Annotate: Mark two significant details about the research that the author cites in paragraph 9.

Analyze: How do these details support the author's key idea that children ought to reconnect with nature?

configuration
(kən-fĭg-yə-rā′shən) *n.* arrangement of parts or elements.

mental, physical, and spiritual health directly to our association with nature—in positive ways. Several of these studies suggest that thoughtful exposure of youngsters to nature can even be a powerful form of therapy for attention-deficit disorders and other maladies. As one scientist puts it, we can now assume that just as children need good nutrition and adequate sleep, they may very well need contact with nature.

10   Reducing that deficit[2]—healing the broken bond between our young and nature—is in our self-interest, not only because aesthetics or justice demands it, but also because our mental, physical, and spiritual health depends upon it. The health of the earth is at stake as well. How the young respond to nature, and how they raise their own children, will shape the **configurations** and conditions of our cities, homes—our daily lives. . . .

11   . . . I am encouraged to find that many people now of college age—those who belong to the first generation to grow up in a largely de-natured environment—have tasted just enough nature to intuitively understand what they have missed. This yearning is a source of power. These young people resist the rapid slide from the

---

[2] **deficit** (dĕf′ĭ-sĭt): inadequacy or insufficiency.

LEARNING MINDSET

Try Again Tell students that sometimes they may think they know the answer to a question, only to later find out they got it incorrect. Encourage students to go back to the text and reread until they figure it out.

real to the virtual, from the mountains to the Matrix. They do not intend to be the last children in the woods.

12   My sons may yet experience what author Bill McKibben has called "the end of nature," the final sadness of a world where there is no escaping man. But there is another possibility: not the end of nature, but the rebirth of wonder and even joy. Jackson's obituary for the American frontier was only partly accurate: one frontier did disappear, but a second one followed, in which Americans romanticized, exploited, protected, and destroyed nature. Now that frontier—which existed in the family farm, the woods at the end of the road, the national parks, and in our hearts—is itself disappearing or changing beyond recognition. But, as before, one relationship with nature can evolve into another. . . .

SUMMARIZE

Annotate: In paragraph 12, mark a sentence that summarizes Louv's final thought to his readers.

Analyze: How does this final thought help to conclude the essay?

CHECK YOUR UNDERSTANDING

Answer these questions before moving on to the **Analyze the Texts** section on the following page.

1 What event caused Louv to begin thinking about how children relate to nature?

   A The birth of his child

   B A conversation with his child

   C Taking his child on a camping trip

   D Looking at his child's science textbook

2 What was Louv's childhood like?

   F Playing outside and going fishing

   G Going to camp and studying nature

   H Wandering the streets of his small town

   J Playing video games and being with friends

3 What is the main thing Louv thinks people ought to do?

   A Clean up the environment.

   B Give children books about nature.

   C Help children reconnect with nature.

   D Work to make the world a better place.

from *Walden* / from Last Child in the Woods   261

TEACH

SUMMARIZE

Ask students if they think the essay ends on a positive note or on a negative note. (**Answer:** *This final thought concludes the essay on a note of hope for the future, allowing the readers to extend their imaginations into a positive future rather than dwell on the negative. The reader may now ask, "How do I help make this hopeful future happen?"*)

CHECK YOUR UNDERSTANDING

Have students answer the questions independently.

Answers:

1. *B*

2. *F*

3. *C*

If they answer any questions incorrectly, have them reread the text to confirm their understanding. Then they may proceed to ANALYZE THE TEXT on page 262.

ENGLISH LEARNER SUPPORT

Oral Assessment Use the following questions to assess students' comprehension and speaking skills.

• Why did the author start thinking about nature and children? (*a talk with his son*)

• What kinds of things did the author do when he was a boy? (*played outside and went fishing*)

• What does the author think people should do? (*help children do things outside*)

SUBSTANTIAL/MODERATE

ANALYZE THE TEXTS

Possible answers:

1. **DOK 2:** *Thoreau moved to the woods because he wanted to live a simpler life and learn from nature. He also says he wanted to share his experiences with the world. This fact, coupled with his writing style of long, informal sentences and abundant figurative language, reveals he wrote to share his transformative experience of living in the woods.*

2. **DOK 4:** *Thoreau's metaphor in this section compares civilized life to a choppy sea. He is expressing the idea that civilized like is too complex and chaotic.*

3. **DOK 2:** *Thoreau likens being distracted from living deliberately to being thrown off a track. This metaphor means something similar to being "derailed."*

4. **DOK 4:** *Louv uses opposites first to make the reader aware that children today experience nature differently than they did when he was young, and then he uses opposites to emphasize that the situation for children today can change, or turn around.*

5. **DOK 3:** *Answers will vary, but students may cite scientific evidence that "nature can even be a powerful form of therapy," "children . . . need contact with nature," and "our mental, physical, and spiritual health depends upon it." The science supports the author's personal experiences of enjoying "a kind of free, natural play" where he knew his "woods and . . . fields."*

RESEARCH

Possible student responses for each section of the graphic organizer:

Biographical details about Turner: American historian born in 1861 in Wisconsin; taught at the University of Wisconsin and Harvard University; president of American Historical Association; died 1934

Major writings: "The Significance of the Frontier in American History," Rise of the New West, 1819–1829 (1906); The United States, 1830–1850: The Nation and Its Sections (1935); The Frontier in American History (1920); and The Significance of Sections in American History (1932)

Opinion on the American frontier: Thought the frontier, and expansion, were essential to the American identity; "the existence of an area of free land, its continuous recession, and the advance of American settlement westward explain American development."

💬 **RESPOND**

ANALYZE THE TEXTS

Support your responses with evidence from the texts. 📓 NOTEBOOK

1. **Summarize** How does Thoreau describe his reasons for moving to the woods in the excerpt from *Walden*? How do these reasons relate to his purpose in writing *Walden*?

2. **Analyze** What is the metaphor that Thoreau uses to describe civilized life in paragraph 4? What meaning does he convey through this figure of speech?

3. **Interpret** What does Thoreau mean by saying we should not be "thrown off the track" in paragraph 7 of the excerpt from *Walden*?

4. **Analyze** How does Louv use contrasts—such as *death* and *rebirth*, *broken* and *healing*—to develop his essay's main ideas in the excerpt from *Last Child in the Woods*?

5. **Evaluate** Louv includes both scientific evidence and his own personal experiences in *Last Child in the Woods*. Which of the details best support his ideas about the relationship between humanity and nature? Cite text evidence in your response.

RESEARCH TIP
Narrowing the topic for Internet searches will help you find relevant sources. Using "Frederick Jackson Turner frontier" or "Frederick Jackson Turner biography" will give better results than "Frederick Jackson Turner."

RESEARCH

The essay excerpt from *Last Child in the Woods* makes a reference to historian Frederick Jackson Turner and his thesis that the American frontier had ended. Do some research to complete the chart below with details about Turner and his theory.

BIOGRAPHICAL DETAILS ABOUT TURNER	MAJOR WRITINGS	OPINION ON THE AMERICAN FRONTIER

TO CHALLENGE STUDENTS . . .

Compare and Contrast After students have done their research on Frederick Jackson Turner and filled out the graphic organizer, challenge them to analyze the information and use it to compare and contrast Turner's ideas with Richard Louv's. Have them write a paragraph to explain how their ideas about nature are similar and different.

CREATE AND PRESENT

Write an Essay Transcendentalism emphasized living a simple life and celebrating the truth found in nature, emotion, and imagination. How does the excerpt from *Walden* reflect these key aspects of transcendentalism? In your opinion, does the excerpt from *Last Child in the Woods* contain any transcendentalist ideas? Write an essay to describe your findings.

- ❏ Do any research you need to better understand transcendentalism.
- ❏ Describe the transcendentalist ideas in the two excerpts.
- ❏ Include text evidence to support your response.
- ❏ Close by stating your opinion on the value of these ideas today.

Present an Essay Present your essay to the class or a small group.

- ❏ Consider adding visuals to your presentation.
- ❏ Practice several times before presenting to an audience.
- ❏ Speak clearly and slowly, making eye contact with your audience as you present your essay.

 Go to **Conducting Research** in the **Writing Studio** for help.

Go to **Giving a Presentation** in the **Speaking and Listening Studio** for help.

RESPOND TO THE ESSENTIAL QUESTION

? When should we stop and reflect on our lives?

Gather Information Review your annotations and notes on the excerpts from *Walden* and *Last Child in the Woods*. Think about how each author reflects on his life experiences and views them as beneficial. Consider how experiencing nature relates to this reflection. Then, add relevant details to your Response Log.

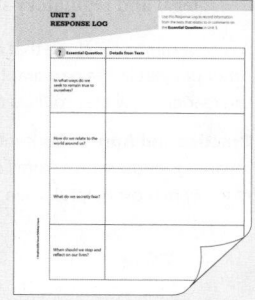

ACADEMIC VOCABULARY
As you write and discuss what you learned from the two excerpts, be sure to use the Academic Vocabulary words. Check off each of the words that you use.

- ❏ analogy
- ❏ denote
- ❏ quote
- ❏ topic
- ❏ unique

APPLY

CREATE AND PRESENT

Write an Essay If students are doing the research assignment in class, provide them with the research materials they will need to explore transcendentalism in the time you have allotted. If students are doing the essay portion for homework, encourage them to do their own online or library research.

For **writing support** for students at varying proficiency levels, see the **Text X-Ray** on page 250D.

Present an Essay Allow student groups time to practice their presentations to each other, or allow time to practice after class or after school.

RESPOND TO THE ESSENTIAL QUESTION

Allow time for students to add details from the *Walden* excerpt and the *Last Child in the Woods* excerpt to their Unit 3 Response Logs.

CRITICAL VOCABULARY

Answers:

1. *The pond would be deep;* unfathomed *means "located at the deepest place."*

2. *It makes them upset;* perturbation *is a state of agitation.*

3. *He found it unnecessary;* superfluous *means "not essential."*

4. *He thinks it is only learned about as a concept;* abstraction *is the opposite of* concrete.

5. *It benefits them;* remunerative *means "something is profitable."*

VOCABULARY STRATEGY:
Draw Conclusions about Word Meanings

Have students completely fill out the graphic organizer with details about the vocabulary words before they use a dictionary to check their work. Once they have either confirmed or corrected the meaning of each word based on the dictionary definition, encourage them to use each word in a sentence of their own to confirm understanding.

Answers:

maladies: *context clues—disorders; meaning—diseases, disorders, ailments*

ecologically: *context clues—woods, forests, acid rain, ozone layer, global warming; meaning—having to do with the relationships between organisms and their environment*

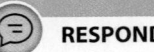 **RESPOND**

WORD BANK

superfluous	abstraction
unfathomed	codify
perturbation	remunerative
polarity	configuration

 Go to **Using Context Clues** in the **Vocabulary Studio** for help.

CRITICAL VOCABULARY

Practice and Apply Use your understanding of the Critical Vocabulary words to answer each question.

1. If Walden Pond was **unfathomed,** was it deep or shallow?

2. Many people experience **perturbation** when listening to the news. Does it make them upset or happy?

3. Thoreau found the post office **superfluous.** Did he think it was necessary or unnecessary?

4. Louv notes that nature has become an **abstraction** for children. Does this mean it is learned by experience or as a concept?

5. Both essayists suggest nature is **remunerative.** Does this mean it harms or benefits them?

VOCABULARY STRATEGY: Draw Conclusions about Word Meanings

Using **context clues**—nearby words, phrases, and sentences—can help you draw conclusions about the meanings of unfamiliar words. Consider the context in *Walden* for the Critical Vocabulary word *perturbation*:

> **Let us rise early and fast, or break fast, gently and without perturbation . . .**

The word *without* signals a contrast between *gently* and *perturbation*. You can guess that *perturbation* means "agitation or uneasiness." Sometimes you have to look at a wider context to find clues to a word's meaning.

The word *codified* appears in this sentence from *Last Child in the Woods*:

> **That lesson is delivered in schools, families, even organizations devoted to the outdoors, and codified into the legal and regulatory structures of many of our communities.**

A reader might conclude that *codified* means "written" or "added." However, other phrases in the paragraph, such as "legal and regulatory structures" let the reader know that *codified* means to be organized and systematized.

Practice and Apply Work with a partner to use context to determine the meanings of the words from *Last Child in the Woods*. Record which context clues were most helpful. Then, check your definitions by using a dictionary.

WORD	CONTEXT CLUES	MEANING
maladies		
ecologically		

ENGLISH LEARNER SUPPORT

Explain with Increasing Specificity and Detail Have students work in mixed-proficiency groups to fill out the chart of word meanings and context clues for the words *maladies* and *ecologically*. Provide the sentence frame: *The word* maladies *from the selection ___ means ___. I know this because ___.* Invite a student at lower English proficiency skills to summarize what they learned by filling out the sentence frame. Then, have a student at higher English proficiency skills speak in greater detail about the word. This should be done in a supportive way, helpfully correcting the partner if the sentence frame is completed incorrectly, or if it means using the word in another sentence. **SUBSTANTIAL/MODERATE**

LANGUAGE CONVENTIONS:
Rhetorical Questions

Questions that are asked to make a point without the expectation of a reply are called **rhetorical questions.** Rhetorical questions require that readers pause and reflect on some aspect of a writer's argument or claim. However, the writer either does not expect an answer to the question, or may choose to answer it in the course of making a point. Often, rhetorical questions suggest that the writer's view is obvious or common sense. In some instances, a rhetorical question serves as a transition from one topic to another.

Because *Walden* reflects on Thoreau's experiment with living simply and the lessons he learned from the experiment, these questions also suggest the kinds of questions that Thoreau may have asked himself while living alone in the woods.

Practice and Apply Review the essay you wrote in the Create and Present activity. Revise the essay so that it includes at least two rhetorical questions. For example, consider introducing one of your main ideas in the form of a question. Write your revision to the paragraph in the space below.

LANGUAGE CONVENTIONS:
Rhetorical Questions

Make sure students understand rhetorical questions by asking volunteers to give examples. Then, have students look for other examples of rhetorical questions in the selections and explain their purposes.

For example, Thoreau uses the rhetorical question, "Shall he turn his spring into summer?" This suggests that a person should not rush his growth or be in a "desperate haste to succeed."

Practice and Apply Invite pairs to share with the class their revised essays and explain their rhetorical questions and the purposes they serve.

COMPARE MAIN IDEAS

As students work on their graphic organizers, remind them to include the page number where they gathered any piece of text evidence. If they are summarizing ideas, remind them to use their own words and use complete sentences.

ANALYZE THE TEXTS

Answers:

1. **DOK 3:** *The images in* Walden *include serene images from nature, such as the sunrise, fishing in a stream, and creatures burrowing in the ground. The images in* Last Child *in the Woods include images such as playing in woods and fields, advertisements, and modern technology. The images in* Walden *are often used as metaphors or analogies for a thought process or the human condition, while the images in* Last Child in the Woods *emphasize the contrast between the author's childhood and that of his children.*

2. **DOK 2:** *In both essays, human progress, such as the development of newspapers, the post office, computers, and text messages, is seen as having negative effects on human beings. In* Walden, *the newspaper consumes so much of a person's thoughts, he barely lives his own life. In* Last Child in the Woods, *screens and technology consume children so they hardly experience the out-of-doors at all, except in textbooks.*

3. **DOK 4:** *The diction in* Walden *is made up of long sentences of simple words. This makes it seem conversational. Louv's essay is made up of shorter sentences, such as "He was right." It is also informal and conversational, though less rambling than Thoreau's. In both essays, the informal diction conveys the author's desire to communicate ideas in a straightforward way. Students' opinions of which author uses diction most effectively will vary.*

4. **DOK 4:** *Thoreau used cause and effect to describe why he decided to go live in the woods, what he hoped to gain from the experience, and its actual effects. Louv used compare and contrast to show how differently he and his children experienced nature. Students' opinions of which author had the more effective organizational structure will vary.*

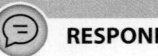 **RESPOND**

Collaborate & Compare

COMPARE MAIN IDEAS

from
WALDEN
by Henry David Thoreau

from
LAST CHILD IN THE WOODS
by Richard Louv

Both *Walden* and *Last Child in the Woods* are about the human relationship with nature. Even though the texts are from very different historical and social contexts, they discuss some of the same issues. Using examples from the works, complete the chart below with:

- main ideas about the effects of technology on people
- main ideas about the benefits of nature for people
- important images and details that relate to main ideas
- important comparisons that relate to main ideas

	from **WALDEN**	*from* **LAST CHILD IN THE WOODS**
Effects of Technology		
Benefits of Nature		
Important Images and Details		
Important Comparisons		

ANALYZE THE TEXTS

Discuss these questions in your group.

1. **Compare** With your group, review the images and details that you cited in your chart. In what ways are the images similar? In what ways are they different? Explain.

2. **Infer** Both essays describe the effects progress and technology have on human beings. According to each, what should be the attitude of people toward technology and toward nature? Cite text evidence in your discussion.

3. **Evaluate** Would you characterize the diction of each excerpt as formal or informal? In what other ways does the diction affect the tone of each piece? How does each author's diction reflect the purpose of each essay? Which author most effectively uses diction to achieve his purpose?

4. **Analyze** Authors can structure their essays in a variety of ways. Compare how Thoreau and Louv construct their arguments to best serve their purpose. For example, did they look at cause and effect or did they compare and contrast elements? Which author had the more effective organizational structure?

 ENGLISH LEARNER SUPPORT

Pronunciation Strategy Have students work in pairs and look up the Critical Vocabulary words in the dictionary. Guide them to use the pronunciation guide and point out each prefix and suffix. Allow students time to practice using the pronunciation guide to help them say the word. Stress syllable breaks, such as *con-fig-ur-a-tions* or *cod-i-fied*.
SUBSTANTIAL/MODERATE

COLLABORATE AND PRESENT

Now, your group can continue exploring the ideas in these texts by identifying and comparing their main ideas. Follow these steps:

1. **Decide on the most important ideas** With your group, review your chart to identify the most important ideas from each essay. Identify points you agree on, and resolve any disagreements through a discussion based on evidence from the texts.

2. **Compare main ideas** Compare the main ideas of the two essays. Listen actively to the members of your group and ask them to clarify any points you do not understand. Include similarities and differences in the chart.

SIMILARITIES	DIFFERENCES

3. **Synthesize information** Think about what insights you may have gained by reading these two texts in tandem. What connections did you make between the two pieces? What new understanding about nature and humanity's connection to it emerged from your reading? Record your ideas and any supporting details.

4. **Present to the class** Now it is time to present your ideas. Be sure to include a summary of the main ideas of each essay as well as a comparison of those ideas. Consider what new insights you may have learned by synthesizing the information from the two texts. You may adapt the charts you created or prepare other visuals to help convey information to the class.

RESPOND

Go to **Giving a Presentation** in the **Speaking and Listening Studio** for help.

© Houghton Mifflin Harcourt Publishing Company

COLLABORATE AND PRESENT

As groups explore main ideas in the texts, remind them to brainstorm as much as possible and use the graphic organizer to guide them. When they have settled on the most important ideas, circulate around the room and help focus their work so they can conclude with a presentation that involves all group members.

1. **Decide on the most important ideas** Encourage discussion about all of the ideas on the chart, and suggest that students cross off ideas they cannot support with text evidence from the selections.

2. **Compare main ideas** As students review and compare ideas, you may wish to choose a student who will be the class presenter so he or she will have time to practice and incorporate all of the ideas from the group.

3. **Synthesize information** Remind students that synthesizing requires the combining of ideas and facts with other information and prior knowledge in order to understand a subject better or to develop new ideas. In this activity, synthesizing will help students make comparisons between the two selections and develop their understanding of the connection between nature and humanity.

4. **Present to the class** As students give their presentations, remind other groups to listen attentively and politely, and save comments or questions for the end. Then, encourage a class discussion about each presentation.

THE MINISTER'S BLACK VEIL

Short Story by **Nathaniel Hawthorne**

GENRE ELEMENTS
SHORT STORY

Remind students that a short story is a brief work of fiction that centers on a single idea and uses suspense to maintain the reader's interest, as the plot—the sequence of events that make the narrative—is revealed. Short stories often feature a symbol that is central to the story's meaning. In this lesson, students will analyze the structure of "The Minister's Black Veil," as well as the use of suspense and ambiguity. Hawthorne's short stories explored the darker side of humanity, often through referring to human guilt and sin.

LEARNING OBJECTIVES

- Analyze the story's structure and how the author uses suspense, ambiguity, and symbolism.
- Research Nathaniel Hawthorne's biography to determine how his life shaped his work.
- Write an explanatory essay.
- Participate in a group discussion.
- Compare denotation with connotation of words.
- Identify and apply appositive words and phrases.
- **Language** Discuss the story using the key word *symbol*.

TEXT COMPLEXITY

Quantitative Measures	**The Minister's Black Veil**	Lexile: 1260L
Qualitative Measures	**Ideas Presented** Multiple levels of meaning, use of symbolism.	
	Structures Used Chronological order, mostly one point of view. Some inference demanded.	
	Language Used Some archaic language structure, some figurative language.	
	Knowledge Required Some reference to events, historical and cultural practices. Begins to rely on some outside knowledge.	

RESOURCES

- Unit 3 Response Log

- 🔊 Selection Audio

- 📖 Reading Studio:
  Notice & Note

- Level Up Tutorials: Symbol and
  Allegory; Setting: Effect on Plot

- Writing Studio: Writing Arguments

- 💬 Speaking and Listening Studio:
  Participating in Collaborative
  Discussions

- Vocabulary Studio: Denotation and
  Connotation

- ❗ Grammar Studio: Appositives and
  Appositive Phrases

- ☑ "The Minister's Black Veil"/"The Pit
  and the Pendulum" Selection Test

SUMMARIES

English

"The Minister's Black Veil" is a short story set in the 1800s in New England. Author Nathaniel Hawthorne, grandson of a judge involved in the Salem witch trials, wrote this short story about a minister who suddenly begins wearing a black veil over his face. The veil brings discomfort to the people in his community, who are not sure what it means or why he is wearing it.

Spanish

"El velo negro del ministro" es un cuento en el contexto del siglo XIX en Nueva Inglaterra. El autor, Nathaniel Hawthorne, nieto de un juez involucrado en los juicios de brujería de Salem, escribió este cuento acerca de un ministro quien de pronto empieza a ponerse un velo negro sobre la cara. El velo molesta a los miembros de la comunidad, quienes no están seguros de qué significa ni por qué lo usa.

 ## SMALL-GROUP OPTIONS

Have students work in small groups and pairs to read and discuss the selection.

Think-Pair-Share

- Have students read the short story.
- Ask students these questions:
  What is the main symbol in this story?
  What is ambiguous in this story, and how does ambiguity build suspense in this story?
- Have students work alone silently to answer these questions.
- Have students work in pairs to formulate a shared response.
- Discuss responses as a whole class.

Three Before Me

- After reading the story, have students individually write a "diary entry" by Mr. Hooper about the secret reason he was wearing the veil.
- Have each student ask three other students to edit his or her writing. Have students make the necessary edits in a final draft.
- Ask volunteers to read their final work aloud.
- Discuss these student-endings with the whole class, and ask what they think Hawthorne's intentions were for writing "The Minister's Black Veil." Then, discuss a possible modern-day equivalent of the minister's veil.

Text X-Ray: English Learner Support
for "The Minister's Black Veil"

Use the Text X-Ray and the supports and scaffolds in the Teacher's Edition to help guide students at different proficiency levels through the selection.

INTRODUCE THE SELECTION
DISCUSS HAWTHORNE'S AMBIGUITY

Nathaniel Hawthorne was a master in the use of ambiguity. To recognize the ambiguity in the story, students need to understand Hawthorne's life and the time in which he lived.

Explain that when something is ambiguous, it is unclear, uncertain, or doubtful. Then, provide the following details about Hawthorne:

- Hawthorne wrote at a time when advances in knowledge, science, and technology challenged many long-held religious beliefs. Hawthorne's own grandfather was a judge whose interpretation of religion resulted in many innocent people being sentenced to death for witchcraft.

- Hawthorne often wrote about religious communities, but in an ambiguous way. Many of his stories focus on dark or negative topics such as sin and guilt. His stories also contain ambiguity in descriptions of characters' thoughts, acts, and motivations.

Guide students to discuss Hawthorne's writing. Provide these sentence frames: *Hawthorne wrote about _____ and guilt. He wrote about _____. He often used ambiguity because _____.*

CULTURAL REFERENCES

The following words or phrases may be unfamiliar to students:

- *sexton* (paragraph 1): a church official responsible for duties such as ringing the bell
- *meetinghouse* (paragraph 1): a church or place where people attended religious services
- *parson* (paragraph 4): a minister or church official
- *parishioners* (paragraph 6): members of a church community

---

LISTENING

Understand Characters

Help students understand some of the characters and how they feel about Mr. Hooper. Explain that understanding how characters think or act will help them understand the story. Have students listen as you read paragraphs 7–9 on Student Edition page 272.

Then, use the following supports with students at varying proficiency levels:

- Read the dialogue aloud. Ask students yes/no questions to ensure comprehension of the characters. *Do the people like the veil?* (No.) *Do they think the parson has gone mad?* (Yes.) **SUBSTANTIAL**

- After reading aloud the lines, ask students to discuss how the characters feel about him. Listeners should add additional details. Provide sentence frames: *The people feel _____ about Mr. Hooper's veil. They think that ___.* **MODERATE**

- After reading aloud the lines. Have students discuss how the characters feel. Then pair students and have them take turns reading aloud paragraph 10. Have listeners summarize what was read. Then have students continue discussing the townspeople. **LIGHT**

SPEAKING

Discuss a Symbol

Explain that a symbol is a person, place, or thing that stands for something else. In this story, the veil is a symbol. Emphasize that students should focus on what the veil means in the context of this story and in the time and place it was written for a better understanding of the story.

Use the following supports with students at varying proficiency levels.

- Display a photo of a black veil. List feelings a person might express by wearing the veil, such as sadness or guilt. Guide students to decide which feeling from the list applies to Mr. Hooper. **SUBSTANTIAL**
- Have groups of students discuss what the veil may symbolize. Each group member should share an opinion and support it with evidence from the text. Provide sentence frames: *I think the veil symbolizes ____. I think this because ____.* **MODERATE**
- Pair students and have them discuss what the veil might symbolize. Have students support their opinions with details from the text. Provide sentence frames. *Based on _____, the veil symbolizes _____. Wearing the veil suggests that _____.* **LIGHT**

READING

Identify Conflict

Remind students that the conflict is the problem a character or characters must solve. Identifying the conflict can help students understand the story and begin to infer the theme.

Use the following supports with students at varying proficiency levels.

- Have students choral read paragraph 22. Clarify any unfamiliar words or phrases. Ask yes/no questions to ensure comprehension. *Does everyone in the village talk about the veil?* (Yes.) *Do you think they want to know why Mr. Hooper wears a veil?* (Yes.) **SUBSTANTIAL**
- Have students work in pairs to read paragraph 22 and identify details that help them infer the conflict. Provide sentence frames: *The townspeople talk of _____. They think it is _____. They want to know why he _____. I think one conflict is between _____ and _____.* **MODERATE**
- Have students work in pairs to read paragraphs 21 and 22. Have students discuss how Mr. Hooper and the townspeople react to the veil. Have students discuss the following questions: *What are the internal and external conflicts? How do the characters' actions reveal the conflict?* **LIGHT**

WRITING

Use New Vocabulary

Help students understand and use new vocabulary words using cognates, context clues, and resource materials.

- Help students identify words from the selection with cognates from their home language and use them to create a cognate chart. Suggest the students create a cognate wall at home or in their locker, adding to it with each selection they read. **SUBSTANTIAL**
- Have pairs of students identify three unfamiliar words from the story. Ask them to research and record the definition for each word, then write sentences using each of the words. **MODERATE**
- Tell pairs to list three or four unfamiliar words from the story. Ask them to predict the meanings using context clues or cognates from their home language. Then, have students confirm the meaning of each word in a dictionary and write an original sentence using each word. **LIGHT**

? Connect to the
ESSENTIAL QUESTION

In "The Minister's Black Veil," a minister's refusal to remove a veil from his face sparks uncertainty as members of the community wonder what terrible thing he might be hiding. Secrets and fear are intertwined as the minister's secrecy—and fear of revealing what is hidden—cause a reciprocal fear in others. Have students suggest reasons a person might hide something about him- or herself from others. What kind of fear might this reveal?

COMPARE THEMES

Have students read the Compare Themes note and reflect on why sin and guilt might have such a powerful psychological impact. Ask students to discuss why authors often explore dark themes in their works.

SHORT STORY

THE MINISTER'S BLACK VEIL

by **Nathaniel Hawthorne**
pages 271–285

COMPARE THEMES

As you read these two short stories, consider how Hawthorne and Poe explored the darker side of Romanticism. Hawthorne examined the psychological effects that sin and guilt have on human life. Poe explored human psychology through first-person narrators who were involved in physical and mental torture.

ESSENTIAL QUESTION:

What do we secretly fear?

SHORT STORY

THE PIT AND THE PENDULUM

by **Edgar Allan Poe**
pages 293–307

The Minister's Black Veil

QUICK START

How do you react in situations where you feel unsure? Discuss your ideas with a partner.

ANALYZE LITERARY ELEMENTS

In the early 1800s, Romanticism was a major literary movement reflecting a belief that the divine is embodied in nature and people are essentially good. Some American Romantics disagreed, feeling that these views did not account for the presence of suffering in the world and the conflict between good and evil. These **Dark Romantics** did share with other Romantics an interest in the spiritual world; however, they also sought to explore the darker mysteries of human existence.

To do so, Hawthorne and other authors used **literary elements**—character, setting, plot, and theme—to explore their ideas. The plot of a short story can arise not only from a character's **motivations,** or reasons for a character's behavior, but also from the setting of the story. In some stories, like Hawthorne's, the social context of the setting actively influences plot events and a character's actions. For example, in Puritan society, the meetinghouse was the central community gathering place for all religious and civil events. Congregation members sat according to social status and gender with the oldest and most distinguished sitting toward the front. Men and women, even from the same family, sat on opposite sides. This sin-obsessed community provides social context for "The Minister's Black Veil," and can help you understand plot events, character motivations, and the themes that emerge. As you read, notice the way these literary elements relate and impact your understanding.

ANALYZE STRUCTURE

The **structure** of a story is how the writer organizes and develops the plot. In "The Minister's Black Veil," Hawthorne uses suspense and ambiguity to advance the plot.

- **Suspense** is the tension created by the plot that leaves readers wondering what will happen next and how the central conflict will be resolved.
- **Ambiguity** is the uncertainty created when an author leaves elements of the text open to the reader's interpretation. Ambiguity often surrounds a **symbol**—an object that has a concrete meaning but also stands for something else—as symbols can have complex associations.

The black veil worn by one of the main characters is a central symbol in the story. As you read, note descriptions of the black veil, as well as the way other characters react to and comment on it. What meaning does Hawthorne attempt to convey through the symbol?

GENRE ELEMENTS: SHORT STORY

- contains literary elements such as plot, character, and setting, that relate and interact
- uses suspense to maintain readers' interest as the plot is revealed
- may center on a symbol that is central to the story's meaning

The Minister's Black Veil   269

QUICK START

Have students read the Quick Start activity and reflect on situations in which they felt unsure and how they acted or reacted in these situations. Then, have them share these ideas with a partner. If students have trouble recalling situations, have volunteers offer examples to spark ideas.

ANALYZE LITERARY ELEMENTS

Point out to students that so far in this unit, they have read works by writers who celebrate the individual and the imagination (Whitman and Dickinson) and by a writer who celebrates the natural world and the individual (Thoreau). Explain that the Dark Romantics delved into the individual as well, exploring the inner lives of their characters and the complex forces that motivate and sometimes warp human behavior. This deeply psychological subject matter is reflected in the literary elements of the stories of Poe and Hawthorne. Settings may evoke a dark or mysterious mood. Characters' fears, instabilities, and obsessions are revealed through their reactions to settings and plot events. The plot unfolds in ways designed to increase suspense and anxiety by withholding information.

ANALYZE STRUCTURE

Note that both suspense and ambiguity hinge on keeping information away from readers. When readers don't know a crucial piece of information or lack the information needed to clearly understand an event, they are left with a sense of heightened anxiety. Suspense and ambiguity can be effectively used to create rising action, increasing tension as the plot builds to a climax. The climax of a suspenseful story often includes a revelation of at least some of the hidden information. Some writers even choose to end a story with some questions left unanswered. This can have an unsettling effect on the reader, who anticipates a full resolution.

To help prepare students uncover the symbolism of the black veil, ask them to share their preliminary impressions of the symbolism of veils and, in particular, a black veil. Emphasize that students should focus on what the veil means in the context of this story and in the time and place it was written, America in the 1800s.

TO CHALLENGE STUDENTS . . .

Visual Art Connection   Explain that, like Romantic writers, Romantic painters focused on nature, inner struggles and passions, emotions, and imagination. Have students do some independent research on the work of an American Romantic painter. For instance, students might explore the paintings of Thomas Cole, John Singleton Copley, Edward Hicks, or John James Audubon.

Once they have completed their research, invite students to give a short multimedia class presentation on the painter and his or her work. Challenge students to draw parallels between the paintings and the selections in this unit.

TEACH

CRITICAL VOCABULARY

Encourage students to look for context clues that suggest the meaning of the bold word in each sentence. Students may also substitute each of the choices for the bold word in the sentence and see if it has the same meaning and makes sense.

Answers:

1. *a. believability*

2. *b. stubbornness*

3. *b. sadness*

4. *c. identifying mark*

5. *b. lessen*

6. *c. pretentious*

LANGUAGE CONVENTIONS

Appositives and Appositive Phrases Review the information about appositives and appositive phrases. Then, to help students recognize appositives as they read, display the following example from the selection:

Mr. Hooper, <u>a gentlemanly person about thirty</u>, though still a bachelor, was dressed with due clerical neatness . . .

Point out that the appositive renames Mr. Hooper in a way that gives more details about him.

ANNOTATION MODEL

Remind students of the ideas in Analyze Literary Elements and Analyze Structure on page 269. These areas suggest focusing on how literary elements interact with descriptions of the black veil and characters' reactions to the black veil. Point out that pupils may follow the method of marking the text shown in the Annotation Model or use their own system for marking up the selection in their write-in text. Students may want to color-code their annotations by using highlighters. Any notes that they have added to the margin may include questions about ideas that are unclear or topics they want to learn more about.

CRITICAL VOCABULARY

Choose the best definition of each Critical Vocabulary word.

emblem   pathos   ostentatious   obstinacy   plausibility   mitigate

1. Her explanation for being late lacked all **plausibility.**
   a. believability   b. responsibility   c. contrition

2. Nevertheless, she stuck to that explanation with great **obstinacy.**
   a. conviction   b. stubbornness   c. smugness

3. The **pathos** of the tale left the audience deeply moved.
   a. humor   b. sadness   c. outrage

4. Each product bore the **emblem** of the manufacturer.
   a. label   b. address   c. identifying mark

5. A sincere apology might serve to **mitigate** your punishment.
   a. intensify   b. lessen   c. eliminate

6. The **ostentatious** furnishings were a failed attempt to impress visitors.
   a. rich   b. valuable   c. pretentious

LANGUAGE CONVENTIONS

Appositives and Appositive Phrases Nouns that identify or rename another noun or a pronoun are called appositives. Appositives are single words; appositive phrases include modifiers of the appositive. An appositive comes immediately after the noun or pronoun to make the connection between the two clear, as in the example "My brother Mychal." As you read, note the author's use of appositives to provide information on the characters.

ANNOTATION MODEL

NOTICE & NOTE

As you read, note how the author uses details to signal the importance of the minister to the townspeople. Here are one reader's notes on "The Minister's Black Veil."

> "But what has the good Parson Hooper got upon his face?" cried the sexton in astonishment.
>
> All within hearing immediately turned about, and beheld the semblance of Mr. Hooper, pacing slowly his meditative way toward the meetinghouse. With one accord they started, expressing more wonder than if some strange minister were coming to dust the cushions of Mr. Hooper's pulpit.

seems like something is terribly wrong

Suspense! Character reactions make me wonder what the matter is. Will the writer tell us?

BACKGROUND

Nathaniel Hawthorne *(1804–1864) was born in Salem, Massachusetts. By the time he left for Bowdoin College in 1821, Hawthorne knew he wanted to write. After graduation, he lived alone for 12 years, dedicated to building his career. By 1842, he had achieved some success. When times were tough, Hawthorne had friends set him up with government jobs, whose dull routines choked his imagination and limited his time to write. Hawthorne, however, never stopped writing, often exploring the influence of Puritan beliefs on New England society. Today he is most celebrated for his short stories and for* The Scarlet Letter *(1850).*

THE MINISTER'S BLACK VEIL

Short Story by Nathaniel Hawthorne

PREPARE TO COMPARE

*The **theme** is the central message of a work of literature. Think about how a writer develops theme through the introduction and development of characters and the building of plot.*

1   The sexton stood in the porch of Milford meetinghouse, pulling lustily at the bell rope. The old people of the village came stooping along the street. Children, with bright faces, tripped merrily beside their parents, or mimicked a graver gait, in the conscious dignity of their Sunday clothes. Spruce¹ bachelors looked sidelong at the pretty maidens, and fancied that the Sabbath sunshine made them prettier than on weekdays. When the throng had mostly streamed into the porch, the sexton began to toll the bell, keeping his eye on the Reverend Mr. Hooper's door. The first glimpse of the clergyman's figure was the signal for the bell to cease its summons.

2   "But what has good Parson Hooper got upon his face?" cried the sexton in <u>astonishment.</u>

---

¹ **Spruce:** neat and clean.

Notice & Note

Use the side margins to notice and note signposts in the text.

ANALYZE STRUCTURE

Annotate: Mark the word in paragraph 2 that shows something unusual has occurred.

Analyze: How does this word choice build suspense in the story?

BACKGROUND

Explain that the setting of "The Minister's Black Veil" is a town in Puritan New England in the 1700s. Puritans were a moral and religious people who followed a strict interpretation of Bible lessons. They believed that, if they made individual compacts with God to avoid sin, God would bless them. Ministers based their preaching on images from scripture and everyday experiences. Since a Puritan community was thought to be a "pure" working model of the Puritan way of life, when someone in the community sinned, severe punishments—possibly even banishment—were issued because townspeople thought that person had corrupted the community.

PREPARE TO COMPARE

Direct students to use the Prepare to Compare prompt to focus their reading.

ANALYZE STRUCTURE

Remind students that writers often build **suspense** by withholding pertinent information from them. This technique causes readers to wonder and question. For instance, in this story, it is not just the reader who doesn't have all of the information. Many of the characters don't either. (***Answer:*** *The sexton shows "astonishment," indicating that whatever he sees is truly remarkable, which intrigues the reader.*)

ANALYZE STRUCTURE

Discuss how Hawthorne's general description of Mr. Hooper contrasts with his description of the veil and how this affects the reader's perception of the veil. Remind students of their discussion about where and when people might wear veils. They may have suggested veils are worn at weddings and funerals. (**Answer:** *The purpose of a veil is to hide, to gain privacy, or to promote modesty. Possible symbolic meanings of the color black are mystery, sorrow, mourning, or something hidden or secret.*)

■ English Learner Support

Use Visuals Before students answer the Analyze Structure question, show them photos of wedding veils and veils on women's funeral hats. Point out that, while not as commonly used today as they were in the past, some people still use these traditional veils. Ask students to show or describe traditional wedding and funeral garments from their known traditions. **ALL LEVELS**

For **listening support** for students at varying proficiency levels, see the **Text X-Ray** on page 268C.

ANALYZE LITERARY ELEMENTS

Draw attention to the word *perturbation* in paragraph 10 and tell students it means "unrest" or "uneasiness." Have pupils look for words and phrases that show this "perturbation" among the people in the congregation. (**Answer:** *Since the reactions are so widespread and extreme— "greatly at variance" with what was normal—it is clear that the minister is very important and that his abnormal appearance is deeply disturbing.*)

ANALYZE STRUCTURE

Annotate: Mark the words in paragraph 6 that describe what is on Mr. Hooper's face.

Interpret: What is the purpose of a veil? What are possible symbolic meanings of the black color?

ANALYZE LITERARY ELEMENTS

Annotate: Mark the phrases in paragraph 10 that tell you the reaction of the members of the congregation.

Infer: What can you infer about the minister's role in Puritan society from these reactions?

---

3   All within hearing immediately turned about, and beheld the semblance[2] of Mr. Hooper, pacing slowly his meditative way towards the meetinghouse. With one accord they started, expressing more wonder than if some strange minister were coming to dust the cushions of Mr. Hooper's pulpit.

4   "Are you sure it is our parson?" inquired Goodman[3] Gray of the sexton.

5   "Of a certainty it is good Mr. Hooper," replied the sexton. "He was to have exchanged pulpits with Parson Shute of Westbury; but Parson Shute sent to excuse himself yesterday, being to preach a funeral sermon."

6   The cause of so much amazement may appear sufficiently slight. Mr. Hooper, a gentlemanly person about thirty, though still a bachelor, was dressed with due clerical neatness, as if a careful wife had starched his band, and brushed the weekly dust from his Sunday's garb. There was but one thing remarkable in his appearance. Swathed about his forehead, and hanging down over his face, so low as to be shaken by his breath, Mr. Hooper had on a black veil. On a nearer view, it seemed to consist of two folds of crape,[4] which entirely concealed his features, except the mouth and chin, but probably did not intercept his sight, farther than to give a darkened aspect to all living and inanimate things. With this gloomy shade before him, good Mr. Hooper walked onward, at a slow and quiet pace, stooping somewhat and looking on the ground, as is customary with abstracted[5] men, yet nodding kindly to those of his parishioners who still waited on the meetinghouse steps. But so wonder-struck were they that his greeting hardly met with a return.

7   "I can't really feel as if good Mr. Hooper's face was behind that piece of crape," said the sexton.

8   "I don't like it," muttered an old woman, as she hobbled into the meetinghouse. "He has changed himself into something awful, only by hiding his face."

9   "Our parson has gone mad!" cried Goodman Gray, following him across the threshold.

10 A rumor of some unaccountable phenomenon had preceded Mr. Hooper into the meetinghouse, and set all the congregation astir. Few could refrain from twisting their heads towards the door; many stood upright, and turned directly about; while several little boys clambered upon the seats, and came down again with a terrible racket. There was a general bustle, a rustling of the women's gowns and shuffling of the men's feet, greatly at variance[6] with that hushed repose which should attend the entrance of the minister. But Mr. Hooper appeared not to notice the perturbation of his people. He entered with an almost noiseless step, bent his head mildly to the pews on each side,

---

[2] **semblance:** appearance.
[3] **Goodman:** a title used by Puritans that was equivalent to *mister*.
[4] **crape:** a black, silky fabric worn as a sign of mourning.
[5] **abstracted:** absent-minded; preoccupied.
[6] **at variance:** contrasting.

and bowed as he passed his oldest parishioner, a white-haired great-grandsire, who occupied an armchair in the centre of the aisle. It was strange to observe how slowly this venerable man became conscious of something singular in the appearance of his pastor. He seemed not fully to partake of the prevailing wonder till Mr. Hooper had ascended the stairs, and showed himself in the pulpit, face-to-face with his congregation, except for the black veil. That mysterious **emblem** was never once withdrawn. It shook with his measured breath as he gave out the psalm; it threw its obscurity between him and the holy page, as he read the Scriptures; and while he prayed, the veil lay heavily on his uplifted countenance. Did he seek to hide from the dread Being whom he was addressing?

11   Such was the effect of this simple piece of crape, that more than one woman of delicate nerves was forced to leave the meetinghouse. Yet perhaps the pale-faced congregation was almost as fearful a sight to the minister as his black veil to them.

12   Mr. Hooper had the reputation of a good preacher, but not an energetic one: he strove to win his people heavenward by mild persuasive influences, rather than to drive them thither by the thunders of the Word. The sermon which he now delivered was marked by the same characteristics of style and manner as the general series of his pulpit oratory. But there was something, either in the sentiment of the discourse itself, or in the imagination of the auditors, which made it greatly the most powerful effort that they had ever heard from their pastor's lips. It was tinged, rather more darkly than

emblem
(ĕm′bləm) *n.* an identifying mark or symbol.

The Minister's Black Veil   273

CRITICAL VOCABULARY

emblem: Hawthorne refers to the black veil as an emblem, or symbol, that was mysterious.

ASK STUDENTS to infer what makes this *emblem* mysterious and why the congregation dislikes it. *(The veil is an emblem of mystery because it covers up the minister's expression and separates him from the congregation. In addition, Mr. Hooper refuses to explain to his attendees why he wears it or what it means.)*

CONTRASTS AND CONTRADICTIONS

Remind students that contrasts and contradictions are instances where readers' expectations are challenged. Here, a **character** does something the reader may not expect. (**Answer:** *Given how unsettled everyone in the congregation is by Mr. Hooper wearing the veil, his inexplicable smile intensifies the reader's puzzlement over why he wears it.*)

ENGLISH LEARNER SUPPORT

Use Cognates Remind students that they can sometimes determine the meanings of English words by using cognates from their first language. Cognates share many of the same letters and sounds as well as meanings. For instance, students might be able to guess the meaning of *oratory* from a word in their first language that is derived from the same Latin word, *orare*, meaning "to speak." Have students work in pairs. Instruct them to take turns reading aloud while partners listen for other words in paragraphs 12–13 that are possible cognates. **MODERATE/LIGHT**

CRITICAL VOCABULARY

pathos: Hawthorne describes how the veil creates a feeling of pathos, or sorrow, as well as awe in the minister's congregation. Invite students to consider why the congregation might consider the minister's black veil to be a sad or pitiful sight.

ASK STUDENTS to give examples of situations that might ordinarily create a feeling of *pathos*. (*the sight of an abandoned dog; a sick child; a lonely, isolated person*)

ostentatious: Hawthorne describes the laughter of some of the congregation as ostentatious, or vulgar and showy.

ASK STUDENTS how the narrator's description of the laughter as "ostentatious" affects the tone, or the author's attitude, toward the subject. (*Describing the laughter as ostentatious creates a judgmental tone, as if the narrator disapproves of the laughter.*)

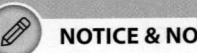

pathos
(pā´thŏs) *n.* something that evokes pity or sympathy.

ostentatious
(ŏs-tĕn-tā´shəs) *adj.* conspicuous and vulgar.

CONTRASTS AND CONTRADICTIONS

Notice & Note: Mark the words in paragraph 13 that show a surprising reaction by the minister.

Analyze: How does this reaction add suspense to the situation?

---

usual, with the gentle gloom of Mr. Hooper's temperament. The subject had reference to secret sin, and those sad mysteries which we hide from our nearest and dearest, and would fain conceal from our own consciousness, even forgetting that the Omniscient[7] can detect them. A subtle power was breathed into his words. Each member of the congregation, the most innocent girl, and the man of hardened breast, felt as if the preacher had crept upon them, behind his awful veil, and discovered their hoarded iniquity[8] of deed or thought. Many spread their clasped hands on their bosoms. There was nothing terrible in what Mr. Hooper said; at least, no violence; and yet, with every tremor of his melancholy voice, the hearers quaked. An unsought **pathos** came hand in hand with awe. So sensible were the audience of some unwonted attribute in their minister, that they longed for a breath of wind to blow aside the veil, almost believing that a stranger's visage would be discovered, though the form, gesture and voice were those of Mr. Hooper.

13   At the close of the services, the people hurried out with indecorous[9] confusion, eager to communicate their pent-up amazement, and conscious of lighter spirits the moment they lost sight of the black veil. Some gathered in little circles, huddled closely together, with their mouths all whispering in the centre; some went homeward alone, wrapped in silent meditation; some talked loudly, and profaned[10] the Sabbath day with **ostentatious** laughter. A few shook their sagacious heads, intimating[11] that they could penetrate the mystery; while one or two affirmed that there was no mystery at all, but only that Mr. Hooper's eyes were so weakened by the midnight lamp as to require a shade. After a brief interval, forth came good Mr. Hooper also, in the rear of his flock. Turning his veiled face from one group to another, he paid due reverence to the hoary[12] heads, saluted the middle-aged with kind dignity, as their friend and spiritual guide, greeted the young with mingled authority and love, and laid his hands on the little children's heads to bless them. Such was always his custom on the Sabbath day. Strange and bewildered looks repaid him for his courtesy. None, as on former occasions, aspired to the honor of walking by their pastor's side. Old Squire Saunders, doubtless by an accidental lapse of memory, neglected to invite Mr. Hooper to his table, where the good clergyman had been wont[13] to bless the food almost every Sunday since his settlement. He returned, therefore, to the parsonage, and at the moment of closing the door, was observed to look back upon the people, all of whom had their eyes fixed upon the minister. A sad smile gleamed

---

[7] **the Omniscient:** God; literally, the all-knowing.
[8] **iniquity:** sinfulness.
[9] **indecorous:** undignified; inappropriate.
[10] **profaned:** desecrated; treated irreverently.
[11] **intimating:** revealing.
[12] **hoary:** gray or white due to age.
[13] **wont:** habit.

faintly from beneath the black veil, and flickered about his mouth, glimmering as he disappeared.

14   "How strange," said a lady, "that a simple black veil, such as any woman might wear on her bonnet, should become such a terrible thing on Mr. Hooper's face!"

15   "Something must surely be amiss with Mr. Hooper's intellects," observed her husband, the physician of the village. "But the strangest part of the affair is the effect of this vagary,[14] even on a sober-minded man like myself. The black veil, though it covers only our pastor's face, throws its influence over his whole person, and makes him ghost-like from head to foot. Do you not feel it so?"

16   "Truly do I," replied the lady; "and I would not be alone with him for the world. I wonder he is not afraid to be alone with himself!"

17   "Men sometimes are so," said her husband.

18   The afternoon service was attended with similar circumstances. At its conclusion, the bell tolled for the funeral of a young lady. The relatives and friends were assembled in the house, and the more distant acquaintances stood about the door, speaking of the good qualities of the deceased, when their talk was interrupted by the appearance of Mr. Hooper, still covered with his black veil. It was now an appropriate emblem. The clergyman stepped into the room where the corpse was laid, and bent over the coffin, to take a last farewell of his deceased parishioner. As he stooped, the veil hung straight down from his forehead so that, if her eyelids had not been closed forever,

---

[14]**vagary:** oddity.

ANALYZE LITERARY ELEMENTS

Annotate: Mark the words and phrases in paragraph 18 that are spooky or disturbing.

Synthesize: How does this description reflect what you know about Dark Romanticism?

The Minister's Black Veil   275

ANALYZE LITERARY ELEMENTS

Remind students that the main literary elements are **plot, setting, theme,** and **character**. How these elements are described can evoke a **mood** or feeling. Here, the description of the setting and the actions of the minister evoke a spooky or disturbing mood. Point out that paragraph 18 continues on to page 276. (**Answer:** *Dark Romantic literature is characterized by exploration of the darker mysteries of human existence.*)

WHEN STUDENTS STRUGGLE . . .

Visualize Details   Tell students that visualizing details about the black veil can help them interpret its symbolism. Then, have the pupils mark details in the funeral scene that help them visualize the black veil, such as "he so hastily caught back the black veil" and "at the instant when the clergyman's features were disclosed, the corpse had slightly shuddered." Ask questions to help students interpret the veil as something that hides Parson Hooper's true self and sins, at least until death: *Why is he afraid to let even a corpse see behind his veil? Why does it seem as if the corpse shuddered, as if appalled, at the sight of his face? What kinds of things do people hide?*

 For additional support, go to the **Reading Studio** and assign the following LEVEL UP **Level Up Tutorial: Symbol and Allegory**.

the dead maiden might have seen his face. Could Mr. Hooper be fearful of her glance, that he so hastily caught back the black veil? A person, who watched the interview between the dead and the living, scrupled[15] not to affirm that, at the instant when the clergyman's features were disclosed, the corpse had slightly shuddered, rustling the shroud[16] and muslin cap, though the countenance retained the composure of death. A superstitious old woman was the only witness of this prodigy. From the coffin, Mr. Hooper passed into the chamber of the mourners, and thence to the head of the staircase, to make the funeral prayer. It was a tender and heart-dissolving prayer, full of sorrow, yet so imbued with celestial[17] hopes, that the music of the heavenly harp, swept by the fingers of the dead, seemed faintly to be heard among the saddest accents of the minister. The people trembled, though they but darkly understood him, when he prayed that they, and himself, and all of mortal race might be ready, as he trusted this young maiden had been, for the dreadful hour that should snatch the veil from their faces. The bearers went heavily forth, and the mourners followed, saddening all the street, with the dead before them, and Mr. Hooper in his black veil behind.

19   "Why do you look back?" said one in the procession to his partner.

20   "I had a fancy," replied she, "that the minister and the maiden's spirit were walking hand in hand."

---

[15] **scrupled:** was reluctant.
[16] **shroud:** a cloth in which people were wrapped before burial.
[17] **celestial:** relating to heaven.

21 "And so had I, at the same moment," said the other. That night, the handsomest couple in Milford village were to be joined in wedlock. Though reckoned a melancholy man, Mr. Hooper had a placid cheerfulness for such occasions, which often excited a sympathetic smile, where livelier merriment would have been thrown away. There was no quality of his disposition which made him more beloved than this. The company at the wedding awaited his arrival with impatience, trusting that the strange awe, which had gathered over him throughout the day, would now be dispelled. But such was not the result. When Mr. Hooper came, the first thing that their eyes rested on was the same horrible black veil, which had added deeper gloom to the funeral, and could portend nothing but evil to the wedding. Such was its immediate effect on the guests, that a cloud seemed to have rolled duskily from beneath the black crape, and dimmed the light of the candles. The bridal pair stood up before the minister. But the bride's cold fingers quivered in the tremulous[18] hand of the bridegroom, and her death-like paleness caused a whisper that the maiden who had been buried a few hours before was come from her grave to be married. If ever another wedding were so dismal, it was that famous one where they tolled the wedding knell.[19] After performing the ceremony, Mr. Hooper raised a glass of wine to his lips, wishing happiness to the new-married couple, in a strain of mild pleasantry that ought to have brightened the features of the guests, like a cheerful gleam from the hearth. At that instant, catching a glimpse of his figure in the looking glass, the black veil involved his own spirit in the horror with which it overwhelmed all others. His frame shuddered—his lips grew white—he spilt the untasted wine upon the carpet—and rushed forth into the darkness. For the Earth, too, had on her Black Veil.

22 The next day, the whole village of Milford talked of little else than Parson Hooper's black veil. That, and the mystery concealed behind it, supplied a topic for discussion between acquaintances meeting in the street, and good women gossiping at their open windows. It was the first item of news that the tavern keeper told to his guests. The children babbled of it on their way to school. One imitative little imp covered his face with an old black handkerchief, thereby so affrighting his playmates that the panic seized himself, and he well-nigh lost his wits by his own waggery.[20]

23 It was remarkable that, of all the busybodies and impertinent people in the parish, not one ventured to put the plain question to Mr. Hooper, wherefore he did this thing. Hitherto, whenever there appeared the slightest call for such interference, he had never lacked advisers, nor shown himself averse to be guided by their judgment. If he erred at all, it was by so painful a degree of self-distrust that

---

[18]**tremulous:** trembling.

[19]**If ever . . . wedding knell:** In Hawthorne's "The Wedding Knell," funeral bells ring during a wedding ceremony.

[20]**waggery:** silly humor.

ANALYZE STRUCTURE

Annotate: Mark the words in paragraph 21 that describe the minister's reaction to his own image.

Synthesize: How does this reaction intensify the suspense in the story?

ANALYZE STRUCTURE

Remind students that **ambiguity** is created when the reader is unsure how to interpret something in a story, such as an event, dialogue, or symbol. Until this moment, the black veil has been a symbol for others. Now it has a powerful symbolic value to the minister as well. But the story still does not reveal why this is, and the black veil becomes more mysterious because even the man wearing it is affected by its potent symbolism. (**Answer:** *The minister's apparent abhorrence at seeing himself makes his wearing the veil even more mysterious and shocking.*)

For **speaking support** for students at varying proficiency levels, see the **Text X-Ray** on page 268D.

ANALYZE STRUCTURE

Discuss with students that the essence of **suspense** is anticipation. Often, the anticipation involves the revelation of some eagerly awaited information. In this paragraph, the reader waits for and anticipates something. (***Answer:*** *The woman's relationship to the minister, as his fiancée, and the direct question that "made the task easier both for him and her" suggests that the minister will respond and the mystery will be cleared up. This builds the suspense to a peak point as readers await the actual question and the minister's answer.*)

ANALYZE STRUCTURE

Annotate: Mark the sentence in paragraph 24 that describes the fiancée's upcoming question to the minister.

Predict: How does the information in this paragraph build suspense in the story?

even the mildest censure[21] would lead him to consider an indifferent action as a crime. Yet, though so well acquainted with this amiable weakness, no individual among his parishioners chose to make the black veil a subject of friendly remonstrance.[22] There was a feeling of dread, neither plainly confessed nor carefully concealed, which caused each to shift the responsibility upon another, till at length it was found expedient to send a deputation to the church, in order to deal with Mr. Hooper about the mystery, before it should grow into a scandal. Never did an embassy so ill discharge its duties. The minister received them with friendly courtesy, but became silent, after they were seated, leaving to his visitors the whole burden of introducing their important business. The topic, it might be supposed, was obvious enough. There was the black veil, swathed round Mr. Hooper's forehead, and concealing every feature above his placid mouth, on which, at times, they could perceive the glimmering of a melancholy smile. But that piece of crape, to their imagination, seemed to hang down before his heart, the symbol of a fearful secret between him and them. Were the veil but cast aside, they might speak freely of it, but not till then. Thus they sat a considerable time, speechless, confused, and shrinking uneasily from Mr. Hooper's eye, which they felt to be fixed upon them with an invisible glance. Finally, the deputies returned abashed to their constituents, pronouncing the matter too weighty to be handled, except by a council of the churches, if, indeed, it might not require a general synod.[23]

24   But there was one person in the village unappalled by the awe with which the black veil had impressed all beside herself. When the deputies returned without an explanation, or even venturing to demand one, she, with the calm energy of her character, determined to chase away the strange cloud that appeared to be settling round Mr. Hooper, every moment more darkly than before. As his plighted wife,[24] it should be her privilege to know what the black veil concealed. At the minister's first visit, therefore, she entered upon the subject, with a direct simplicity, which made the task easier both for him and her. After he had seated himself, she fixed her eyes steadfastly upon the veil, but could discern nothing of the dreadful gloom that had so overawed the multitude: it was but a double fold of crape, hanging down from his forehead to his mouth, and slightly stirring with his breath.

25   "No," said she aloud, and smiling, "there is nothing terrible in this piece of crape except that it hides a face which I am always glad to look upon. Come, good sir, let the sun shine from behind the cloud. First lay aside your black veil: then tell me why you put it on."

26   Mr. Hooper's smile glimmered faintly.

---

[21] **censure:** disapproval or criticism.
[22] **remonstrance:** protest.
[23] **synod:** an assembly or court of church officials.
[24] **plighted wife:** fiancée.

27   "There is an hour to come," said he, "when all of us shall cast aside our veils. Take it not amiss, beloved friend, if I wear this piece of crape till then."

28   "Your words are a mystery too," returned the young lady. "Take away the veil from them, at least."

29   "Elizabeth, I will," said he, "so far as my vow may suffer me. Know, then, this veil is a type and a symbol, and I am bound to wear it ever, both in light and darkness, in solitude and before the gaze of multitudes, and as with strangers, so with my familiar friends. No mortal eye will see it withdrawn. This dismal shade must separate me from the world: even you, Elizabeth, can never come behind it!"

30   "What grievous affliction hath befallen you," she earnestly inquired, "that you should thus darken your eyes forever?"

31   "If it be a sign of mourning," replied Mr. Hooper, "I, perhaps, like most other mortals, have sorrows dark enough to be typified by a black veil."

32   "But what if the world will not believe that it is the type of an innocent sorrow?" urged Elizabeth. "Beloved and respected as you are, there may be whispers that you hide your face under the consciousness of secret sin. For the sake of your holy office, do away this scandal!"

33   The color rose into her cheeks, as she intimated the nature of the rumors that were already abroad in the village. But Mr. Hooper's mildness did not forsake him. He even smiled again—that same sad smile, which always appeared like a faint glimmering of light proceeding from the obscurity beneath the veil.

34   "If I hide my face for sorrow, there is cause enough," he merely replied; "and if I cover it for secret sin, what mortal might not do the same?"

35   And with this gentle but unconquerable **obstinacy** did he resist all her entreaties. At length Elizabeth sat silent. For a few moments she appeared lost in thought, considering, probably, what new methods might be tried to withdraw her lover from so dark a fantasy, which, if it had no other meaning, was perhaps a symptom of mental disease. Though of a firmer character than his own, the tears rolled down her cheeks. But, in an instant, as it were, a new feeling took the place of sorrow: her eyes were fixed insensibly on the black veil, when, like a sudden twilight in the air, its terrors fell around her. She arose, and stood trembling before him.

36   "And do you feel it then at last?" said he mournfully.

37   She made no reply, but covered her eyes with her hand, and turned to leave the room. He rushed forward and caught her arm.

38   "Have patience with me, Elizabeth!" cried he passionately. "Do not desert me, though this veil must be between us here on earth. Be mine, and hereafter there shall be no veil over my face, no darkness

ANALYZE LITERARY ELEMENTS

Annotate: Mark the phrases in paragraphs 31 and 34 that the minister uses to comment on his condition.

Analyze: What do these passages suggest about Hawthorne's theme?

obstinacy
(ŏb′stə-nə-sē) *n.* stubbornness.

ANALYZE LITERARY ELEMENTS

Remind students that the **theme** of a story often involves a message about life or the human condition. (**Answer:** *The phrases "I, perhaps, like most other mortals" and "what mortal might not do the same?" connect the minister's reasons for wearing his veil to all humanity, suggesting that everyone shares the minister's shame.*)

CRITICAL VOCABULARY

obstinacy: Hawthorne describes the minister as being extremely obstinate, or stubborn, about wearing the veil.

ASK STUDENTS to cite evidence from the story that demonstrates Mr. Hooper's *obstinacy*. (*Mr. Hooper responds to Elizabeth's first request that he remove the veil by saying he will wear it until the hour comes "when all of us shall cast aside our veils." Elizabeth asks him to at least reveal the meaning of his words and he does not give a clear answer. Elizabeth asks him what affliction has happened to him and he avoids a direct answer. Elizabeth says he is causing a scandal and he again avoids answering.*)

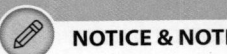

ANALYZE STRUCTURE

Point out that some of the questions readers had at the beginning of the story have been answered, and the story increasingly presents the inner thoughts of Mr. Hooper as if readers are allowed to go behind the veil to see inside his mind. (**Answer:** *The uncertainty over whether Mr. Hooper wears the veil because of a horrible sin he committed, because of sorrow, or for some other reason makes the story more complex and puts the reader in the same position as the people in Mr. Hooper's community. It suggests the theme that we can never know the secrets of another person's heart.*)

CRITICAL VOCABULARY

plausibility: Hawthorne says that the minister's horror at the sight of his veil in a mirror made the townspeople's belief that he had done some terrible thing plausible, or believable.

ASK STUDENTS to discuss other actions the minister took that lend *plausibility* to the idea that he feels he has done something terrible. Have them explain their ideas. (*He wore the veil at a wedding; he refused to take the veil off so that Elizabeth could see his face.*)

NOTICE & NOTE

between our souls! It is but a mortal veil—it is not for eternity! Oh! you know not how lonely I am, and how frightened to be alone behind my black veil. Do not leave me in this miserable obscurity forever!"

39   "Lift the veil but once, and look me in the face," said she.

40   "Never! It cannot be!" replied Mr. Hooper.

41   "Then, farewell!" said Elizabeth.

42   She withdrew her arm from his grasp and slowly departed, pausing at the door to give one long, shuddering gaze that seemed almost to penetrate the mystery of the black veil. But even amid his grief, Mr. Hooper smiled to think that only a material emblem had separated him from happiness, though the horrors which it shadowed forth must be drawn darkly between the fondest of lovers.

43   From that time no attempts were made to remove Mr. Hooper's black veil or, by a direct appeal, to discover the secret which it was supposed to hide. By persons who claimed a superiority to popular prejudice, it was reckoned merely an eccentric whim, such as often mingles with the sober actions of men otherwise rational, and tinges them all with its own semblance of insanity. But with the multitude, good Mr. Hooper was irreparably a bugbear.[25] He could not walk the streets with any peace of mind, so conscious was he that the gentle and timid would turn aside to avoid him, and that others would make it a point of hardihood to throw themselves in his way. The impertinence of the latter class compelled him to give up his customary walk, at sunset, to the burial ground, for when he leaned pensively over the gate, there would always be faces behind the gravestones, peeping at his black veil. A fable went the rounds that the stare of the dead people drove him thence. It grieved him to the very depth of his kind heart to observe how the children fled from his approach, breaking up their merriest sports, while his melancholy figure was yet afar off. Their instinctive dread caused him to feel, more strongly than aught else, that a preternatural[26] horror was interwoven with the threads of the black crape. In truth, his own antipathy to the veil was known to be so great that he never willingly passed before a mirror, nor stooped to drink at a still fountain, lest, in its peaceful bosom, he should be affrighted by himself. This was what gave **plausibility** to the whispers that Mr. Hooper's conscience tortured him for some great crime too horrible to be entirely concealed, or otherwise than so obscurely intimated. Thus, from beneath the black veil there rolled a cloud into the sunshine, an ambiguity of sin or sorrow, which enveloped the poor minister, so that love or sympathy could never reach him. It was said that ghost and fiend consorted with him there. With self-shudderings and outward terrors, he walked continually in its shadow, groping darkly

---

ANALYZE STRUCTURE

Annotate: Mark the sentences in paragraph 43 that describe Mr. Hooper's inner life beneath the veil.

Analyze: How does the ambiguity over why Mr. Hooper wears the veil affect the meaning of the story?

plausibility
(plô-zə-bəl´ ĭ-tē) *n.* likelihood; believability.

---

[25] **bugbear:** source of irrational fear.
[26] **preternatural:** inexplicable, supernatural.

TO CHALLENGE STUDENTS . . .

Puritans and Sin Students may be interested in learning more about the Puritans' beliefs so they can better understand the minister. Have interested students search the Internet to gather details about the Puritans' beliefs. Suggest that students investigate details about New England Puritans, original sin, predestination, and daily life. (*Puritans believed that all people were born with original sin and that God had predestined who would be saved from eternal damnation and who would be damned. The Puritans believed that they would receive God's grace and be saved if they adhered to strict moral values and a strong work ethic.*)

When students have finished their research, have them gather in small groups to discuss how the Puritans' belief about sin applies to the minister's situation.

within his own soul, or gazing through a medium that saddened the whole world. Even the lawless wind, it was believed, respected his dreadful secret, and never blew aside the veil. But still good Mr. Hooper sadly smiled at the pale visages of the worldly throng as he passed by.

44   Among all its bad influences, the black veil had the one desirable effect, of making its wearer a very efficient clergyman. By the aid of his mysterious emblem—for there was no other apparent cause—he became a man of awful power, over souls that were in agony for sin. His converts always regarded him with a dread peculiar to themselves, affirming, though but figuratively, that before he brought them to celestial light, they had been with him behind the black veil. Its gloom, indeed, enabled him to sympathize with all dark affections. Dying sinners cried aloud for Mr. Hooper, and would not yield their breath till he appeared; though ever, as he stooped to whisper consolation, they shuddered at the veiled face so near their own. Such were the terrors of the black veil, even when Death had bared his visage! Strangers came long distances to attend service at his church, with the mere idle purpose of gazing at his figure, because it was forbidden them to behold his face. But many were made to quake ere they departed! Once, during Governor Belcher's[27] administration, Mr. Hooper was appointed to preach the election sermon. Covered

---

[27] **Governor Belcher:** Jonathan Belcher (1682–1757), governor of Massachusetts Bay Colony from 1730 until 1741.

ANALYZE LITERARY ELEMENTS

Annotate: Mark the phrases in paragraph 44 that explain the role Mr. Hooper played in political life.

Infer: What can you infer about the role of the clergy in Puritan Massachusetts?

ANALYZE LITERARY ELEMENTS

Have students look for details that show Mr. Hooper participated in a political event. How long does the text say people were affected by his participation in the event? (**Answer:** *Mr. Hooper was called on to perform "the election sermon," which suggests that members of the clergy were seen as having moral authority over elected officials, giving them a very powerful role in society.*)

For **speaking support** for students at varying proficiency levels, see the **Text X-Ray** on page 268D.

with his black veil, he stood before the chief magistrate, the council, and the representatives, and wrought so deep an impression that the legislative measures of that year were characterized by all the gloom and piety of our earliest ancestral sway.

45   In this manner Mr. Hooper spent a long life, irreproachable[28] in outward act, yet shrouded in dismal suspicions; kind and loving, though unloved, and dimly feared; a man apart from men, shunned in their health and joy, but ever summoned to their aid in mortal anguish. As years wore on, shedding their snows above his sable veil, he acquired a name throughout the New England churches, and they called him Father Hooper. Nearly all his parishioners, who were of a mature age when he was settled, had been borne away by many a funeral: he had one congregation in the church, and a more crowded one in the churchyard; and having wrought so late into the evening, and done his work so well, it was now good Father Hooper's turn to rest.

46   Several persons were visible by the shaded candlelight in the death chamber of the old clergyman. Natural connections[29] he had none. But there was the decorously grave, though unmoved physician, seeking only to **mitigate** the last pangs of the patient whom he could not save. There were the deacons, and other eminently pious members of his church. There, also, was the Reverend Mr. Clark of Westbury, a young and zealous divine, who had ridden in haste to pray by the bedside of the expiring minister. There was the nurse, no hired handmaiden of death, but one whose calm affection had endured thus long, in secrecy, in solitude, amid the chill of age, and would not perish, even at the dying hour. Who, but Elizabeth! And there lay the hoary head of good Father Hooper upon the death pillow, with the black veil still swathed about his brow and reaching down over his face, so that each more difficult gasp of his faint breath caused it to stir. All through life that piece of crape had hung between him and the world: it had separated him from cheerful brotherhood and woman's love, and kept him in that saddest of all prisons, his own heart; and still it lay upon his face, as if to deepen the gloom of his darksome chamber, and shade him from the sunshine of eternity.

47   For some time previous, his mind had been confused, wavering doubtfully between the past and the present, and hovering forward, as it were, at intervals, into the indistinctness of the world to come. There had been feverish turns, which tossed him from side to side and wore away what little strength he had. But in the most convulsive struggles, and in the wildest vagaries of his intellect, when no other thought retained its sober influence, he still showed an awful solicitude lest the black veil should slip aside. Even if his bewildered soul could have forgotten, there was a faithful woman at his pillow, who, with averted eyes, would have covered that aged face, which

---

[28] **irreproachable:** without fault; blameless.
[29] **Natural connections:** relatives, kin.

mitigate
(mĭt´ĭ-gāt) *v.* to lessen.

LANGUAGE CONVENTIONS
Annotate: In paragraph 46, circle the nouns and underline the appositives that follow them.

Analyze: What information do the appositives reveal about the nouns they modify?

ENGLISH LEARNER SUPPORT

Develop Vocabulary Write and read aloud the first sentence of paragraph 45, emphasizing the contrasts that Hawthorne uses to describe Mr. Hooper's life. Circle the words *yet, though,* and *but* and have students repeat them after you. Tell students these three words all signal contrasts or differences. Have students practice using the words in sentences: *I like _____, but I don't like _____. We all thought the movie was boring, yet no one _____. He enjoyed the show, though _____.*
SUBSTANTIAL/MODERATE

LANGUAGE CONVENTIONS

Remind students that an **appositive** renames a noun and is often enclosed within commas directly after the noun it refers to. (**Answer:** *The appositives that describe Reverend Clark show where he lives and what he's like. The appositive that describes the nurse reveals her to be a long-time friend, not a hired hand who comes in to attend a dying person. The appositive modifying the "saddest of all prisons" explains the metaphor that Father Hooper had been living in an emotional prison because of his decision to wear the veil.*)

IMPROVE READING FLUENCY

Targeted Passage Have students work with partners to read paragraphs 45–47. First, use paragraph 45 to model how to read fictional text. Have students follow along in their books as you read the text with appropriate phrasing and emphasis. Then, have partners take turns reading the next two paragraphs aloud. Encourage students to provide feedback and support for pronouncing unusual or unknown words. Remind students that, when they are reading a story aloud for an audience, they should pace their reading so the audience has time to absorb and comprehend what is happening.

  Go to the **Reading Studio** for additional support in developing fluency.

CRITICAL VOCABULARY

mitigate: The minister's physician did what he could to mitigate, or ease, Mr. Hooper's pain.

ASK STUDENTS what the doctor might have done to mitigate Mr. Hooper's suffering. (*He might have provided medications to reduce pain or calm the patient.*)

ANALYZE LITERARY ELEMENTS

Direct attention to paragraph 53 and have students read carefully to understand what is happening. What does Reverend Clark try to do? Then, have pupils read back in paragraph 52 to find out why the reverend tried to take this action. (**Answer:** *Mr. Clark says that he wants to remove the veil in order to remove a shadow from the face of someone who lived a good life. He may also be curious about what the minister is hiding.*)

 ANALYZE LITERARY ELEMENTS

Note that both Mr. Hooper's actions and his words are reactions to Reverend Clark's action. (**Answer:** *He is fulfilling the "vow" he took, revealed in the scene with Elizabeth, that "No mortal eye will see [the veil] withdrawn.")*

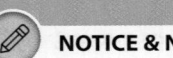 **NOTICE & NOTE**

she had last beheld in the comeliness of manhood. At length the death-stricken old man lay quietly in the torpor[30] of mental and bodily exhaustion, with an imperceptible pulse, and breath that grew fainter and fainter, except when a long, deep, and irregular inspiration[31] seemed to prelude the flight of his spirit.

48   The minister of Westbury approached the bedside.

49   "Venerable Father Hooper," said he, "the moment of your release is at hand. Are you ready for the lifting of the veil, that shuts in time from eternity?"

50   Father Hooper at first replied merely by a feeble motion of his head; then, apprehensive, perhaps, that his meaning might be doubtful, he exerted himself to speak.

51   "Yea," said he, in faint accents, "my soul hath a patient weariness until that veil be lifted."

52   "And is it fitting," resumed the Reverend Mr. Clark, "that a man so given to prayer, of such a blameless example, holy in deed and thought, so far as mortal judgment may pronounce; is it fitting that a father in the church should leave a shadow on his memory that may seem to blacken a life so pure? I pray you, my venerable brother, let not this thing be! Suffer us to be gladdened by your triumphant aspect, as you go to your reward. Before the veil of eternity be lifted, let me cast aside this black veil from your face!"

ANALYZE LITERARY ELEMENTS
Annotate: Mark the sentence in paragraph 53 that describes Reverend Mr. Clark's action.

Infer: What is the motivation for Mr. Clark's action?

53   And thus speaking, the Reverend Mr. Clark bent forward to reveal the mystery of so many years. But, exerting a sudden energy that made all the beholders stand aghast, Father Hooper snatched both his hands from beneath the bedclothes and pressed them strongly on the black veil, resolute to struggle, if the minister of Westbury would contend with a dying man.

54   "Never!" cried the veiled clergyman. "On earth, never!"

55   "Dark old man!" exclaimed the affrighted minister, "with what horrible crime upon your soul are you now passing to the judgment?"

ANALYZE LITERARY ELEMENTS
Annotate: Mark the sentence that describes Mr. Hooper's response to Mr. Clark.

Connect: Why does Mr. Hooper insist on keeping the veil in place?

56   Father Hooper's breath heaved; it rattled in his throat; but with a mighty effort, grasping forward with his hands, he caught hold of life, and held it back till he should speak. He even raised himself in bed; and there he sat shivering, with the arms of death around him, while the black veil hung down, awful, at that last moment, in the gathered terrors of a lifetime. And yet the faint, sad smile, so often there, now seemed to glimmer from its obscurity, and linger on Father Hooper's lips.

57   "Why do you tremble at me alone?" cried he, turning his veiled face round the circle of pale spectators. "Tremble also at each other! Have men avoided me, and women shown no pity, and children screamed and fled only for my black veil? What, but the mystery which it obscurely typifies, has made this piece of crape so awful? When the friend shows his inmost heart to his friend; the lover to his best beloved; when man does not vainly shrink from the eye of his

---

[30] **torpor:** lifelessness, inactivity.
[31] **inspiration:** inhalation of air into the lungs.

APPLYING ACADEMIC VOCABULARY

❑ analogy   ☑ denote   ❑ quote   ☑ topic   ☑ unique

Write and Discuss Have students turn to a partner to discuss the following questions. Guide students to include the Academic Vocabulary words *unique, topic,* and *denote* in their responses. Ask volunteers to share their responses with the class.

- What is **unique** about the minister's appearance when he appears in church?
- How does the **topic** of the minister's sermon relate to a theme of the story?
- What does the black veil **denote**?

Creator, loathsomely treasuring up the secret of his sin; then deem me a monster, for the symbol beneath which I have lived, and die! I look around me, and, lo! On every visage a Black Veil!"

58   While his auditors shrank from one another, in mutual affright, Father Hooper fell back upon his pillow, a veiled corpse, with a faint smile lingering on his lips. Still veiled, they laid him in his coffin, and a veiled corpse they bore him to the grave. The grass of many years has sprung up and withered on that grave, the burial stone is moss-grown, and good Mr. Hooper's face is dust; but awful is still the thought, that it mouldered beneath the Black Veil!

CHECK YOUR UNDERSTANDING

Answer these questions before moving on to the **Analyze the Text** section on the following page.

1 What is the topic of the first sermon Mr. Hooper gives when wearing the veil?

A Death

B Sorrow

C Secret sin

D Salvation

2 Why does the congregation send a deputation to talk to Mr. Hooper?

F To tell him he is fired

G To ask why he is wearing the veil

H To protest his behavior at the wedding

J To plead with him to marry Elizabeth

3 Which of the following does the story reveal about Puritan beliefs?

A Strict separation of church and state

B Strong belief in witches and witchcraft

C Exclusion of children from Sunday services

D Deep concern with sinfulness

 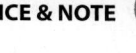

ANALYZE LITERARY ELEMENTS

Annotate: Circle the phrases that show the town's actions over time. Underline the actions Father Hooper suggests they should have done.

Draw Conclusions: What themes do Father Hooper's last words suggest?

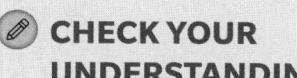

ANALYZE LITERARY ELEMENTS

Remind students that the elements of plot, setting, and characters are intertwined. Characters affect plot, setting affects characters, characters affect other characters, and so on. Point out that students should focus on paragraph 57. (**Answer:** *These words show that everyone is sinful and that no person has the right to judge another. Instead, people should be kinder to others and be honest about their own sins.*)

CHECK YOUR UNDERSTANDING

Have students answer the questions independently.

Answers:

1. *C*

2. *G*

3. *D*

If they answer any questions incorrectly, have them reread the text to confirm their understanding. Then they may proceed to ANALYZE THE TEXT on page 286.

 ENGLISH LEARNER SUPPORT

Oral Assessment Use the following questions to assess students' comprehension and speaking skills.

1. Mr. Hooper's sermon was about secret ____. *(sin)*

2. The church people ask Mr. Hooper why he wears ____. *(a veil)*

3. Puritans believed people were ____. *(sinful)*

SUBSTANTIAL/MODERATE

ANALYZE THE TEXT

Possible answers:

1. **DOK 4:** *He appears devoted to fulfilling what he apparently sees as a solemn oath to wear the veil but is also tormented by wearing it, confessing that he is "lonely" and "frightened to be alone" with the veil.*

2. **DOK 4:** *In his conversation with Elizabeth in paragraphs 25–41, Mr. Hooper speaks of having taken some kind of vow to wear the veil and his determination to wear it until death, but he never explains why he took that vow. Ambiguity gives the symbol more power by suggesting the complexity of human emotion.*

3. **DOK 2:** *The veil seems to symbolize the secret sin or darkness found in all humans. Secret sin is the subject of Mr. Hooper's first sermon after wearing the veil, establishing that link. His final speech before dying says that all people are wearing a black veil because they hide sins from friends, loved ones, and even God.*

4. **DOK 4:** *The veil suggests secret sin or guilt over secret sin, and Mr. Hooper's comments to Elizabeth and at the end connect his veil to all people, giving this sense of sinfulness a universal application. Another theme is loneliness and isolation, since Mr. Hooper has no spouse, close confidant, or even a friend.*

5. **DOK 4:** *The congregation was full of "busybodies" and "impertinent people" who had never hesitated to offer him advice in the past, and he had often taken that advice. The fact that they do not ask now may suggest that the people have become uncomfortable questioning something that seems to have such personal and symbolic meaning.*

RESEARCH

Possible answers are shown in the chart.

Extend You may wish to divide students into groups and have each group research a different author. In addition to the two mentioned, Hawthorne also knew Henry David Thoreau.

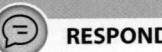

RESPOND

ANALYZE THE TEXT

Support your responses with evidence from the text. **NOTEBOOK**

1. **Analyze** Mr. Hooper's conversation with Elizabeth is the first time that readers learn about the minister from his own words. What insight does this conversation provide about Mr. Hooper's character?

2. **Evaluate** What evidence in the text hints at or suggests Mr. Hooper's reasons for wearing the black veil? What effect does the ambiguity surrounding the veil add to the overall meaning of the story?

3. **Interpret** What does the veil symbolize? How does the meaning of the symbol change over the course of the story? Cite specific details from the story to support your interpretation.

4. **Synthesize** What themes does the story suggest to you? Cite text evidence in your response.

5. **Notice & Note** Why is it surprising that no one in the congregation talks to Mr. Hooper about the veil when he first starts wearing it? What might this reaction reveal about Puritan society and beliefs?

RESEARCH TIP
Combine search terms, such as "Nathaniel Hawthorne" and "John Hathorne" by putting them in quotation marks to get more relevant search results.

RESEARCH

Nathaniel Hawthorne's life shaped his thought and work. Research some of the key points of his biography to learn the answers to these questions.

QUESTION	ANSWER
What famous event was his ancestor John Hathorne involved in?	*John Hathorne was one of the judges in the Salem witch trials of 1692.*
What political jobs did Hawthorne hold?	*He was assigned to the Custom House in Boston and in Salem and was named consul in Liverpool.*
Which of those jobs was used in part in The Scarlet Letter?	*The Scarlet Letter begins with an essay called "The Custom House," referring to his work in Salem.*

Extend Research Hawthorne's relationship with other famous authors of the period, such as Ralph Waldo Emerson and Herman Melville. How did he get along with them? What did he think of them? Share your ideas with the class.

WHEN STUDENTS STRUGGLE . . .

Reteaching: Effect of the Setting on the Plot Discuss with students the ways in which the setting of this story helps in the development of the plot. Ask for specific examples of how the setting interacts with the action and the characters.

 For additional support, go to the **Reading Studio** and assign the following **Level Up Tutorial: Setting: Effect on Plot**.

CREATE AND DISCUSS

Write an Essay Write an argumentative essay in which you interpret the real causes of the villagers' discomfort in the minister's presence.

❏ Choose one of the following pairs of scenes to analyze: (1) first sighting of Mr. Hooper and the parishioners' comments after services; (2) Mr. Hooper's participation in the funeral and the wedding; (3) the delegation's visit and the early days afterward.

❏ Determine your thesis statement on the cause of the villagers' discomfort.

❏ Craft the essay with clear organization and adequate evidence to support your position.

❏ Use the characteristics of the genre, such as making a clear statement of your position and addressing counterarguments.

Discuss with a Small Group Explore your views in a moderated discussion. Join with other students who chose the same two scenes as you did.

❏ Take turns presenting your interpretations of the congregation's behavior.

❏ When you ask questions about the clarity or coherence of others' positions, do so respectfully to engage in a meaningful discussion.

RESPOND TO THE ESSENTIAL QUESTION

 What do we secretly fear?

Gather Information Review your annotations and notes on "The Minister's Black Veil." Then, add relevant details to your Response Log. As you determine which information to include, think about:

• how difficult it can be to face fear alone
• how uncertainty complicates facing fear
• how peer pressure affects our ability to face fear

 Go to **Writing Arguments** in the **Writing Studio** for help.

Go to **Participating in Collaborative Discussions** in the **Speaking and Listening Studio** for help.

UNIT 3 RESPONSE LOG

ACADEMIC VOCABULARY
As you write and discuss what you learned from the story, be sure to use the Academic Vocabulary words. Check off each of the words that you use.

❏ **analogy**
❏ **denote**
❏ **quote**
❏ **topic**
❏ **unique**

CREATE AND DISCUSS

Write an Essay Review the basic structure of an argument with students: an introduction that includes a clear claim or thesis; evidence and reasoning that show the claim to be true; a counterargument that identifies and refutes an opposing claim; and a conclusion that wraps up the argument.

If students need help developing a counterargument, have them work with a partner whose interpretation is slightly different from their own. Have students summarize or read their claim and main reasons aloud. Partners should offer any reasons why they disagree. The point of disagreement can become the basis for the counterargument. Offer the following transitions for introducing a counterargument: *It might seem as if, Of course, Admittedly, One might object.*

For **writing support** for students at varying proficiency levels, see the **Text X-Ray** on page 268D.

Discuss with a Small Group Tell groups to have one or more members take notes on the discussion, summarizing the main points of each presentation. After groups discuss, have one person from each group report back to the class in a class discussion.

RESPOND TO THE ESSENTIAL QUESTION

Allow time for students to add details from "The Minister's Black Veil" to their Unit 3 Response Logs.

CRITICAL VOCABULARY

Possible answers:

1. *it showed the stricken faces of the victims of the horrible flooding*

2. *her upturned chin and crossed arms*

3. *his successful completion of the marathon*

4. *it made them feel inadequate in comparison*

5. *promoting its benefits to all groups*

6. *the statistics and other supporting evidence she gave*

VOCABULARY STRATEGY:

Nuances in Word Meanings

Possible answers:

1. **melancholy:** *a sad or gloomy state of mind; sad, sorrowful, gloomy*

2. **dread:** *terror or fear of something about to happen; fear, awe, apprehension*

3. **obstinacy:** *the quality of being stubborn, unwilling to change an opinion or a purpose; stubbornness, willfulness, bullheadedness*

4. **miserable:** *extremely unhappy; wretched, forlorn*

5. **horrible:** *extremely unpleasant or bad; terrible, gruesome, repellent*

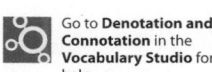 **RESPOND**

WORD BANK

emblem	obstinacy
pathos	plausibility
ostentatious	mitigate

 Go to **Denotation and Connotation** in the **Vocabulary Studio** for help.

CRITICAL VOCABULARY

Practice and Apply Complete each of the following sentence stems in a way that reflects the meaning of the Critical Vocabulary word.

1. The painting evoked **pathos** in the viewer because _____.

2. The **obstinacy** of her response was made clear by _____.

3. The runner treasured his race number as an **emblem** of _____.

4. The **ostentatious** display of wealth made visitors uncomfortable because _____.

5. Proponents of the new law sought to **mitigate** opposition by _____.

6. The **plausibility** of her statement was supported by _____.

VOCABULARY STRATEGY: Nuances in Word Meanings

When you analyze nuances in the meaning of words with similar **denotations,** or dictionary meanings, you look for subtle differences in shades of meaning. The **connotation** of a word refers to the feelings or ideas associated with it. For example, consider the connotation of the Critical Vocabulary word *ostentatious* in this sentence from "The Minister's Black Veil":

> Some gathered in little circles, huddled closely together, with their mouths all whispering in the centre; some went homeward alone, wrapped in silent meditation; some talked loudly, and profaned the Sabbath day with ostentatious laughter.

The word *ostentatious* carries a negative connotation of disapproval, in contrast to the synonym *loud*, which has a more neutral connotation. This emphasizes the narrator's reproach of the congregants' behavior on what should have been a solemn day of worship.

Practice and Apply Work with a partner to explore nuances in word meanings. Follow these steps:

- List five words from the story that have a strong positive or negative connotation.
- Use a dictionary and a thesaurus to find definitions and synonyms of the words.
- Discuss how synonyms with different connotations would affect meaning.

EL ENGLISH LEARNER SUPPORT

Vocabulary Strategy Give students additional practice in finding and comparing synonyms using the following sentence from the selection: "Though reckoned a melancholy man, Mr. Hooper had a placid cheerfulness for such occasions, which often excited a sympathetic smile, where livelier merriment would have been thrown away." Have students find synonyms for *melancholy* and *placid* and share them with the group. Ask students to substitute these synonyms in the sentence and read it aloud. Discuss how the use of the synonym or synonyms changes the sentences. **MODERATE/LIGHT**

LANGUAGE CONVENTIONS: Appositives and Appositive Phrases

An **appositive** is a noun or pronoun that identifies or renames another noun or pronoun, providing more information about the word it refers to. An **appositive phrase** is simply an appositive and its modifiers.

An appositive or an appositive phrase can be either **essential** or **nonessential**. An **essential appositive** provides information that is necessary to identify what is referred to by the preceding noun or pronoun.

In the following example, the appositive specifies which brother the writer is referring to:

> **Essential appositive:** "My brother **Mychal** was always active."

A **nonessential appositive** provides additional but supplementary information about the preceding noun or pronoun. Nonessential appositives are always set off from the word they refer to by commas or dashes.

> **Nonessential appositive:** "Elaine, **a diligent student,** reviewed her extensive notes the night before the test."

Appositive phrases can be used in place of dependent clauses to make sentences more concise:

> **Dependent clause:** "The Reverend Mr. Hooper, **who was a persuasive but not forceful preacher,** delivered sermons that guided rather than scolded."

> **Appositive phrase:** "The Reverend Mr. Hooper, **a persuasive but not forceful preacher,** delivered sermons that guided rather than scolded."

Practice and Apply Find two examples of appositive phrases in "The Minister's Black Veil" and identify whether they are essential or nonessential. Then, write two sentences that include either an appositive or an appositive phrase.

RESPOND

! Go to **Appositives and Appositive Phrases** in the Grammar Studio for help.

LANGUAGE CONVENTIONS: Appositives and Appositive Phrases

Review the examples and make sure students understand how appositives and appositive phrases can make sentences more concise and provide either essential or nonessential information.

Provide additional, simple examples to further clarify, if needed:

Essential appositive:
The architect <u>Frank Lloyd Wright</u> frequently incorporated nature into his designs.

Nonessential appositive:
The car, <u>an old and rusty bucket</u>, finally broke down.

Practice and Apply Have students work with a partner to locate and write examples of sentences with appositives.

Possible answers (all these examples are nonessential):

1. *as he passed his oldest parishioner, a white-haired great-grandsire, . . .*

2. *Mr. Hooper, a gentlemanly person about thirty, . . .*

3. *Each member of the congregation, the most innocent girl, and the man of hardened breast, . .*

4. *There, also, was the Reverend Mr. Clark, of Westbury, a young and zealous divine, . . .*

Students' sentences with appositives will vary; accept any responses that show correct understanding of this grammatical structure.

ENGLISH LEARNER SUPPORT

Language Convention Use the following supports with students at varying proficiency levels:

- Show an example and a non-example of a sentence with an appositive, such as *The cat is my favorite pet* (non-example) and *The cat, my favorite pet, likes to play* (example). Help students identify the sentence that uses the appositive. **SUBSTANTIAL**

- Give students examples of nouns and possible appositives, such as *The cat* and *my favorite pet*. Have them use these to make sentences with appositives. **MODERATE**

- Have students work with partners to find examples of appositives in a less-challenging text. Have them use these sentences as models for their own sentences and then have pupils share their examples. **LIGHT**

THE PIT AND THE PENDULUM

Short Story by Edgar Allan Poe

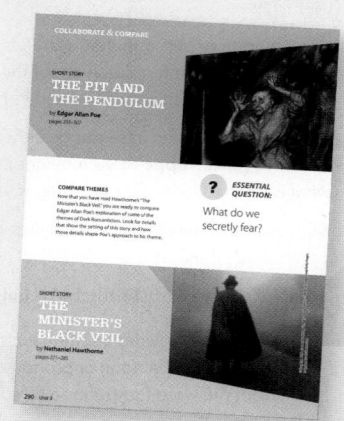

GENRE ELEMENTS
SHORT STORY

Remind students that a **short story** is a brief work of fiction that centers on a single idea and uses suspense to maintain the reader's interest. Short stories convey a particular mood, or atmosphere. Remind them that Poe is an American Gothic writer and in this story, Poe creates an atmosphere of terror.

LEARNING OBJECTIVES

- Analyze and identify mood and atmosphere as conveyed through diction and syntax.
- Research Edgar Allan Poe's literary impact on other writers.
- Write an adaptation of Poe's story.
- Present adaptation through visual or auditory medium.
- Use context clues to determine word meaning.
- Evaluate, understand, and apply the use of semicolons.
- **Language** Summarize a story using time-order words.

TEXT COMPLEXITY

Quantitative Measures	The Pit and the Pendulum	Lexile: 1020L
Qualitative Measures	**Ideas Presented** Multiple levels, use of symbolism, some ambiguity, greater demand for inference.	
	Structures Used More complex structure, narrow perspective, deviates from chronological order.	
	Language Used Some archaic language, figurative language, implied meanings, complex sentence structure.	
	Knowledge Required More complexity in theme. Experiences may be less familiar to many. Cultural and historical references may make heavier demands.	

Online **Ed**

RESOURCES

- Unit 3 Response Log
- Selection Audio
- Reading Studio: Notice & Note
- Level Up Tutorial: Plot: Sequence of Events
- Writing Studio: Writing Narratives
- Speaking and Listening Studio: Using Media in a Presentation
- Vocabulary Studio: Using Context Clues
- Grammar Studio: Semicolons and Colons
- "The Minister's Black Veil"/"The Pit and the Pendulum" Selection Test

SUMMARIES

English

"The Pit and the Pendulum" is identified as an American Gothic short story, a sub-genre of Romanticism that explores the dark side of human nature. It is a disturbing tale set during the Spanish Inquisition, when people who differed in religious beliefs from the dominant Christian tradition of the time were often tortured and put to death. In this story, the narrator is tried for this crime and slowly comes to realize the fate the inquisitors have planned for him.

Spanish

"El pozo y el péndulo" es se conoce como un cuento gótico americano, un subgénero del romanticismo que explora el lado oscuro de la naturaleza humana. Es una historia perturbadora en el contexto de la Inquisición española, donde la gente era torturada y ejecutada por tener opiniones religiosas diferentes a la mayoría cristiana. En el cuento se enjuicia por ese crimen al narrador, quien lentamente se da cuenta del destino que los inquisidores planean para él.

👥 SMALL-GROUP OPTIONS

Have students work in small groups and pairs to read and discuss the selection.

Three-Minute Review

- Read "The Pit and the Pendulum" aloud as a whole class.
- Pause the reading after each page and tell students that they have three minutes to reread silently, review notes, and develop clarifying questions about the text.
- After three minutes, students will submit questions.
- Read clarifying questions aloud and answer them with a brief discussion.

Double-Entry Journal

- Have students use a notebook or journal for recording notes.
- Instruct students to divide page down the middle with a line, then a write heading over each: "Quotes from Story" over the left column and "My Notes" over the right column.
- Instruct students to record significant or perplexing quotes in the left column.
- Instruct students to write their own interpretations, summaries, or questions in the right column.
- Discuss these notes with the whole class.

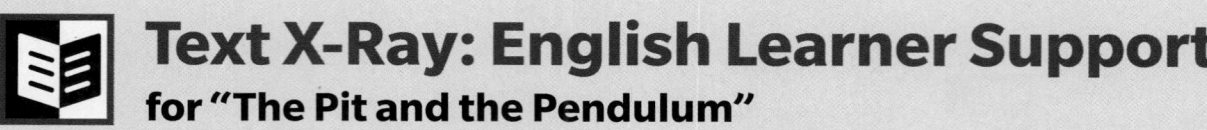

Text X-Ray: English Learner Support
for "The Pit and the Pendulum"

Use the Text X-Ray and the supports and scaffolds in the Teacher's Edition to help guide students at different proficiency levels through the selection.

INTRODUCE THE SELECTION
DISCUSS THE SPANISH INQUISITION

Edgar Allan Poe's setting for "The Pit and the Pendulum" is 15-century Toledo, Spain, during the Spanish Inquisition. This setting is less important for its religious and political background than for its legendary status as a period of terror and brutality. The Spanish Inquisition was an attempt by church and government leaders to root out heretics, or people who held religious beliefs that differed from those prescribed by the religious and government leaders of that time. While the tales of torture and death at the hands of the judges—called inquisitors—has sometimes been exaggerated, 150,000 people were tried for the crime of heresy and several thousand were sentenced to death. This made the Spanish Inquisition the perfect setting for Poe's macabre style of storytelling, despite being hundreds of years in Poe's past. Another element of history loosely connected to the end of Poe's tale is France's invasion and occupation of Toledo, Spain, which brought about the end of the Spanish Inquisition. Supply the following sentence frames:

- Poe used the _____ as the setting.
- This setting was good because Poe liked to write about _____.

CULTURAL REFERENCES

The following words or phrases may be unfamiliar to students:

- *Fate* (paragraph 1): The supernatural belief that some power controls and decides everything that happens, in a way that cannot be changed. This concept has origins in Greek myth.
- *painted figure of Time* (paragraph 18): Also referred to as "Father Time," this is a personification of time as an old man with a white beard, usually carrying a scythe and an hourglass.
- *grotesquerie* (paragraph 21): the quality of being eerie or grotesque

LISTENING

Listen for Understanding

Read paragraphs 10–13 aloud with students, directing them to take notes of sensory words, like *bathed in a clammy vapor* and *smell of decayed fungus*. Upon completion, have students work with a partner or small group to summarize the paragraphs.

Use the following supports with students at varying proficiency levels:

- Explain that the narrator of the story is being punished and is trying to explore the cell where he is being held. Reread the paragraphs to students, pausing after each to summarize what the narrator does or finds. For example, in paragraph 10, the narrator tries to measure his cell, but he falls. Have students copy the summaries into their notebooks. **SUBSTANTIAL**
- Have students get into pairs and compare the words and sensory descriptions they wrote down. Tell partners to discuss which details would belong in a summary of the paragraphs. Remind them that only the most important details should be included. **MODERATE**
- Have students work with a partner to write a summary of paragraphs 10–13 in their own words. Encourage them to refer to their notes as they compose the summaries. **LIGHT**

SPEAKING

Use Time-Order Words

Review a list of time-order words, such as *First...*, *Then...*, *After that...*, and *Next....* Have students use time-order words to summarize the order of events in the story.

Use the following supports with students at varying proficiency levels:

- Use time-order words to summarize the events of the story in chronological order. Have students repeat each sentence you say and then practice saying it aloud to a partner. Direct students to emphasize each time-order word when they say it. **SUBSTANTIAL**
- Have students work with a partner to orally summarize the events of the story in chronological order. Provide sentence frames that include time-order words, such as *First, the narrator _____* and *After that, the narrator _____.* **MODERATE**
- Have students take turns summarizing the events in the text using time-order words. Encourage them to refer to the list of time-order words as they summarize. **LIGHT**

READING

Read for Comprehension

Explain to students that paragraphs 15–16 help describe the narrator's cell. Have students read these paragraphs and use visual aids to help them comprehend the text.

Use the following supports with students at varying proficiency levels:

- Read the first two sentences of paragraph 15 aloud and start a drawing of the narrator's cell on the board. Continue reading the paragraphs aloud, stopping to summarize each new detail. Have students add to the drawing based on the details. **SUBSTANTIAL**
- Guide students to identify details about the narrator's cell in paragraphs 15 and 16. Work with students to make a list of descriptions of the size of the cell, using relevant phrases from the text. Then, help them list descriptions of the shape of the cell. Have students draw the cell, based on the lists. **MODERATE**
- Have students work with a partner to identify the central idea of the paragraphs and draw a picture of what is being described to help them understand the rest of the story. **LIGHT**

WRITING

Write a Summary

Work with students to write a summary of the story.

Use the following supports with students at varying proficiency levels:

- Provide this sentence frame to help students start writing: *A man reveals that he has been _____.* Help students complete the sentence frame. **SUBSTANTIAL**
- Have students work with a partner to list the main events of the story. Then have students use the list to summarize the story. **MODERATE**
- Work with students to develop a transition word bank to refer to as they write their summaries. For example, *then*, *after*, or *in the end*. Direct students to look for places in their writing where a transition word would make their ideas flow more smoothly. **LIGHT**

TEACH

Connect to the
ESSENTIAL QUESTION

In "The Pit and the Pendulum," Poe creates an atmosphere of terror as the narrator experiences the setting through his limited senses. Discuss with students how limiting sensory information creates a sense of fear or tension. For example, ask: *Why are people afraid of the dark? How can individuals' secret fears affect how they respond to the darkness?* Note that when we have limited information, our minds use imagination to fill in the gaps.

COMPARE THEMES

Have students read the Compare Themes note, and review the characteristics of Dark Romanticism before reading the story.

SHORT STORY
THE PIT AND THE PENDULUM

by **Edgar Allan Poe**
pages 293–307

COMPARE THEMES

Now that you have read Hawthorne's "The Minister's Black Veil," you are ready to compare Edgar Allan Poe's exploration of some of the themes of Dark Romanticism. Look for details that show the setting of this story and how those details shape Poe's approach to his theme.

ESSENTIAL QUESTION:

What do we secretly fear?

SHORT STORY
THE MINISTER'S BLACK VEIL

by **Nathaniel Hawthorne**
pages 271–285

290   Unit 3

The Pit and the Pendulum

QUICK START

Why do you think people like watching horror or suspense movies? What makes the experience of being frightened enjoyable?

ANALYZE MOOD

As a complement to the American Dark Romantics, the European Romantic period gave rise to the Gothic novel. These tales used the stone vaults and dark dungeons of medieval settings to evoke mystery and fear. The term **Gothic** was later applied to any fiction that depicted strange events in a haunting environment.

Poe, a master of Gothic style, sets "The Pit and the Pendulum" during the Spanish Inquisition, which was established in 1480 to punish people accused of heresy—having beliefs that differed from Catholic Church doctrine. The setting allows Poe to evoke an eerie mood. **Mood** refers to the atmosphere the writer creates in a work of literature. Poe uses unique diction and syntax to describe the narrator's situation and state of mind, creating a haunting mood. In the chart below, you can find examples from "The Pit and the Pendulum" that show how diction and syntax can impact the story's mood.

LITERARY ELEMENT	EXAMPLE FROM STORY	IMPACT ON MOOD
Diction word choice	"I was sick—sick unto death with that long agony"	"sick," "death," and "agony" are words that immediately create a frightening mood
Syntax sentence structure	"This only for a brief period; for presently I heard no more. Yet, for a while, I saw; but with how terrible an exaggeration!"	The narrator speaks in brief bursts, creating a tense mood.

As you read, note the way Poe uses diction and syntax to create a mood.

ANALYZE PLOT STRUCTURE

A writer's decisions on how to structure a plot contribute to a story's overall meaning. Typically, a short story begins by introducing the characters, setting the scene, and providing background information. Then, a conflict arises and builds to a resolution. In this story, however, Poe makes some choices to create an immediate atmosphere of terror.

As you read, think about how Poe structures the plot and uses literary elements like character, setting, and imagery to shape your understanding of events. Consider the beginning and ending story and how his choices build suspense and reveal the narrator's situation.

GENRE ELEMENTS: SHORT STORY
- is a short work of fiction that centers on a single idea
- can experiment with plot structure to build suspense
- conveys a particular mood or atmosphere

QUICK START

Have students read the Quick Start activity and share their experiences with horror movies with the group. Have students who do like the movies share their reasons, or how the movies make them feel.

ANALYZE MOOD

Explain that **mood,** or the feeling or atmosphere evoked by the story, is closely tied to the basic elements of a story: plot, setting, and character. In particular, mood is often set by descriptions of the setting. A gloomy or dark setting may lend itself to a spooky, frightening mood, for example. But the way the plot unfolds and how characters react to the setting and events also contribute to the mood.

Read through the examples with students, and point out that the story is narrated in first-person point of view. The mood will be governed by how the narrator tells the story, how he describes events and settings, and what he thinks and fears.

ANALYZE PLOT STRUCTURE

Explain that short-story writers, more than novelists, tend to begin a story by diving straight into the action. Discuss examples of movies or television shows that begin in the midst of a crisis or conflict. Note that this kind of beginning hooks readers' interest and begins the story with a great deal of energy.

TEACH

CRITICAL VOCABULARY

Encourage students to look for context clues that help them complete each sentence.

Answers:

1. *supposition*
2. *avert*
3. *lucid*
4. *indeterminate*
5. *prostrate*
6. *tumultuous*
7. *insuperable*
8. *pertinacity*

■ English Learner Support

Use Cognates Tell students that these Critical Vocabulary words have Spanish cognates: *lucid/lúcido; supposition/ suposición.* **ALL LEVELS**

LANGUAGE CONVENTIONS

Semicolons Review the definition of semicolons. Display the following example from the selection to help students recognize this distinctive sentence structure:

He who has never swooned, is not he who finds strange palaces and wildly familiar faces in coals that glow; is not he who beholds floating in midair the sad visions that the many may not view; is not he who ponders over the perfume of some novel flower—is not he whose brain grows bewildered with the meaning of some musical cadence which has never before arrested his attention.

Have students locate the semicolons. Point out that repetition helps the reader track who the sentence is talking about: "He who has never swooned." Encourage students to discuss how using semicolons supports Poe's purpose.

✎ ANNOTATION MODEL

Remind students of the ideas in Analyze Mood, which suggest noticing how diction and syntax help to create mood. Point out that they may follow the method of marking the text shown in the Annotation Model or use their own system for marking up the selection. They may want to color-code their annotations by using highlighters. Their notes in the margin may include questions about ideas that are unclear or topics they want to learn more about.

292 Unit 3

◎ **GET READY**

CRITICAL VOCABULARY

indeterminate	**tumultuous**	**insuperable**	**pertinacity**
lucid	**supposition**	**prostrate**	**avert**

Complete each sentence with the correct Critical Vocabulary word.

1. The _____ that she was honest proved to be a naïve one.

2. It's normal to _____ one's gaze from such a horrific sight.

3. She could describe the incident in a _____ way, even though it occurred years ago.

4. The ship left on a perilous voyage toward a distant and _____ shore.

5. The peasant lay _____ at the baron's feet, fearful of his decision.

6. His _____ feelings overwhelmed him and left him incapable of action.

7. The goal seemed _____, but the team labored to achieve it.

8. The woman devoted herself to her work with a _____ remarkable for her years.

LANGUAGE CONVENTIONS

Semicolons A writer's **style** is the particular way he or she uses language to communicate ideas. One characteristic of Edgar Allan Poe's distinctive style is his use of **semicolons** to create long, uninterrupted sentences.

As you read, note Poe's use of semicolons and how it impacts your understanding of the narrator's state of mind.

ANNOTATION MODEL

NOTICE & NOTE ✎

As you read, look for how Poe creates a particular mood through his use of diction and syntax. Note how he uses literary elements to develop the plot. Here are one student's notes about "The Pit and the Pendulum."

> I had swooned; but still will not say that all of consciousness was lost. What of it there remained I will not attempt to define, or even to describe; yet all was not lost. In the deepest slumber—(no!) In delirium—(no!) In a swoon—(no!) In death—(no!) even in the grave all *is not* lost. Else there is no immortality for man. Arousing from the most profound of slumbers, we break the gossamer web of *some* dream.

Punctuation shows agitation, excitement.

Preoccupation with death is spooky.

292 Unit 3

<section>© Houghton Mifflin Harcourt Publishing Company</section>

BACKGROUND

Edgar Allan Poe *(1809–1849) is considered one of literature's "most brilliant, but erratic stars." Poe explored such distinctive themes as madness, untimely death, and obsession. He was orphaned at an early age, and for most of his life he struggled to earn a living. The 1845 publication of his poem "The Raven" made Poe famous. This success, however, was soon marred by the death of his wife and his own illness. Although Poe's life was brief, his literary influence was great, especially on the development of the horror story and detective fiction.*

THE PIT AND THE PENDULUM

Short Story by Edgar Allan Poe

PREPARE TO COMPARE

You have analyzed how Hawthorne developed theme through the use of characterization and symbols. Look for clues in Poe's text for his theme and the literary elements he uses to develop it.

> *Impia tortorum longos hic turba furores*
> *Sanguinis innocui, non satiata, aluit.*
> *Sospite nunc patria, fracto nunc funeris antro,*
> *Mors ubi dira fuit vita salusque patent.*[1]
>
> *[Quatrain composed for the gates of a market to be erected upon the site of the Jacobin[2] Club House at Paris.]*

1   I was sick—sick unto death with that long agony; and when they at length unbound me, and I was permitted to sit, I felt that my senses were leaving me. The sentence—the dread sentence of death—was the last of distinct accentuation which reached my ears. After that, the sound of the inquisitorial voices seemed

---

[1] **Impia . . . patent:** *Latin:* Here the wicked crowd of tormentors, unsated, fed their long-time lusts for innocent blood. Now that our homeland is safe, now that the tomb is broken, life and health appear where once was dread death.

[2] **Jacobin** (jăk´ə-bĭn): a radical political group active in the French Revolution and later known for implementing the Reign of Terror.

The Pit and the Pendulum   293

Notice & Note

Use the side margins to notice and note signposts in the text.

ANALYZE PLOT STRUCTURE

Annotate: Mark the first two sentences of paragraph 1.

Analyze: What is happening to the narrator in these two sentences? How does the beginning of the story create dramatic tension?

BACKGROUND

Explain to students that "The Pit and the Pendulum" is set during the period of the Spanish Inquisition, which was established in 1480. The Spanish Inquisition jailed, tortured, tried, and executed thousands of people for heresy, or having opinions that differed from Catholic church doctrine. Poe uses this setting to convey the physical and psychological horror a man, who is convicted and sentenced to death under the courts of the Inquisition, experiences. Poe takes liberty with the history of the period to create his story.

PREPARE TO COMPARE

Direct students to use the Prepare to Compare prompt to focus their reading.

ANALYZE PLOT STRUCTURE

Remind students that the initial situation usually contains the seeds of the story's **conflict**. Point out that the story is in first person, so readers must "see" through his eyes and "listen" to his thoughts in order to understand what is happening. (**Answer:** *The narrator is in someone's custody—he has just been unbound—and has been sentenced to death. The effect is to heighten tension immediately, as the reader recognizes that the main character is in a life-or-death situation.*)

🗨 ENGLISH LEARNER SUPPORT

Use High-Frequency Words Explain to students that to appreciate the rising action, they should pay attention to the sequence of events. Point out these words and phrases from paragraph 1.

- *when*: at the same time
- *For a while*: for a short time
- *After that*: at a later time
- *And then*: next
- Explain their meanings, and have students read them chorally after you.
  SUBSTANTIAL/MODERATE
- Have students use the words and phrases in their own sentences.
  LIGHT

ANALYZE MOOD

Remind students that the mood is the overall feeling the story evokes. Direct students' attention to the sentence "I saw the lips of the black-robed judges," and encourage them to visualize the scene and the lips of the judges, using the description that follows. (**Possible answer:** *Descriptions such as: "thin even to grotesqueness" and "writhe with deadly locution" create a mood of horror.*)

CRITICAL VOCABULARY

indeterminate: The narrator could no longer understand the judges' voices as the voices became an indeterminate, or vague and unclear, hum.

ASK STUDENTS why the judges' voices turned into an "indeterminate hum" at that point in the story. (*The narrator had just heard his death sentence and was so overwhelmed with emotion, he could no longer understand the judges' words.*)

NOTICE & NOTE

indeterminate
(ĭn-dĭ-tûr′mə-nĭt) *adj.*
not precisely known.

ANALYZE MOOD

Annotate: Beginning with when he first sees them, mark the words the narrator uses to describe the lips of the judges.

Infer: What mood, or atmosphere, does this description help create?

---

merged in one dreamy **indeterminate** hum. It conveyed to my soul the idea of *revolution*—perhaps from its association in fancy with the burr of a millwheel. This only for a brief period; for presently I heard no more. Yet, for a while, I saw; but with how terrible an exaggeration! I saw the lips of the black-robed judges. They appeared to me white—whiter than the sheet upon which I trace these words—and thin even to grotesqueness; thin with the intensity of their expression of firmness—of immoveable resolution—of stern contempt of human torture. I saw that the decrees of what to me was Fate, were still issuing from those lips. I saw them writhe with a deadly locution.[3] I saw them fashion the syllables of my name; and I shuddered because no sound succeeded. I saw, too, for a few moments of delirious horror, the soft and nearly imperceptible waving of the sable draperies which enwrapped the walls of the apartment. And then my vision fell upon the seven tall candles upon the table. At first they wore the aspect of charity, and seemed white slender angels who would save me; but then, all at once, there came a most deadly nausea over my spirit, and I felt every fiber in my frame thrill as if I had touched the wire of a galvanic battery,[4] while the angel forms became meaningless specters, with heads of flame, and I saw that from them there would be no help. And then there stole into my fancy, like a rich musical note, the thought of what sweet rest there must be in the grave. The thought came gently and stealthily, and it seemed long before it attained full appreciation;[5] but just as my spirit came at length properly to feel and entertain it, the figures of the judges vanished, as if magically, from before me; the tall candles sank into nothingness; their flames went out utterly; the blackness of darkness supervened; all sensations appeared swallowed up in a mad rushing descent as of the soul into Hades.[6] Then silence, and stillness, and night were the universe.

2   I had swooned;[7] but still will not say that all of consciousness was lost. What of it there remained I will not attempt to define, or even to describe; yet all was not lost. In the deepest slumber—no! In delirium—no! In a swoon—no! In death—no! even in the grave all *is not* lost. Else there is no immortality for man. Arousing from the most profound of slumbers, we break the gossamer web of *some* dream. Yet in a second afterward, (so frail may that web have been) we remember not that we have dreamed. In the return to life from the swoon there are two stages; first, that of the sense of mental or spiritual; secondly, that of the sense of physical, existence. It seems probable that if, upon reaching the second stage, we could recall the impressions of the first, we should find these impressions eloquent in memories of the gulf beyond. And that gulf is—what? How at

---

[3] **locution:** style of speech.
[4] **galvanic battery:** a device for producing electricity with series of voltaic cells.
[5] **appreciation:** understanding.
[6] **Hades:** in Greek mythology, the underworld where the dead reside.
[7] **swooned:** fainted.

least shall we distinguish its shadows from those of the tomb? But if the impressions of what I have termed the first stage, are not, at will, recalled, yet, after long interval, do they not come unbidden, while we marvel whence they come? He who has never swooned, is not he who finds strange palaces and wildly familiar faces in coals that glow; is not he who beholds floating in midair the sad visions that the many may not view; is not he who ponders over the perfume of some novel flower—is not he whose brain grows bewildered with the meaning of some musical cadence which has never before arrested his attention.

3   Amid frequent and thoughtful endeavors to remember; amid earnest struggles to regather some token of the state of seeming nothingness into which my soul had lapsed, there have been moments when I have dreamed of success; there have been brief, very brief periods when I have conjured up remembrances which the **lucid** reason of a later epoch assures me could have had reference only to that condition of seeming unconsciousness. These shadows of memory tell, indistinctly, of tall figures that lifted and bore me in silence down—down—still down—till a hideous dizziness oppressed me at the mere idea of the interminableness of the descent. They tell also of a vague horror at my heart, on account of that heart's unnatural stillness. Then comes a sense of sudden motionlessness throughout all things; as if those who bore me (a ghastly train!) had outrun, in their descent, the limits of the limitless, and paused from the wearisomeness of their toil. After this I call to mind flatness and dampness; and that all is *madness*—the madness of a memory which busies itself among forbidden things.

4   Very suddenly there came back to my soul motion and sound— the **tumultuous** motion of the heart, and, in my ears, the sound of its beating. Then a pause in which all is blank. Then again sound, and motion, and touch—a tingling sensation pervading my frame. Then the mere consciousness of existence, without *thought*—a condition which lasted long. Then, very suddenly, thought, and shuddering terror, and earnest endeavor to comprehend my true state. Then a strong desire to lapse into insensibility. Then a rushing revival of soul and a successful effort to move. And now a full memory of the trial, of the judges, of the sable draperies, of the sentence, of the sickness, of the swoon. Then entire forgetfulness of all that followed; of all that a later day and much earnestness of endeavor have enabled me vaguely to recall.

5   So far, I had not opened my eyes. I felt that I lay upon my back, unbound. I reached out my hand, and it fell heavily upon something damp and hard. There I suffered it to remain for many minutes, while I strove to imagine where and *what* I could be. I longed, yet dared not to employ my vision. I dreaded the first glance at objects around me. It was not that I feared to look upon things horrible, but that I grew aghast lest there should be *nothing* to see. At length, with a wild desperation at heart, I quickly unclosed my eyes. My worst thoughts, then, were confirmed. The blackness of eternal night

© Houghton Mifflin Harcourt Publishing Company

lucid
(lo͞o´sĭd) *adj.* easily understood.

tumultuous
(to͝o-mŭl´cho͝o-əs)
adj. stormy, intense.

ANALYZE MOOD

Annotate: Mark the different changes in the narrator's thoughts and feelings in paragraph 4.

Interpret: How does Poe convey the rapid succession of ideas in the narrator's mind? How does this contribute to the mood?

The Pit and the Pendulum   295

WHEN STUDENTS STRUGGLE . . .

Use a Graphic Organizer Have students complete the graphic organizer to understand the different stages of the narrator's return to consciousness.

suddenly	then	then	then	then	then	then	now

 For additional support, go to the **Reading Studio** and assign the following ⬛ **Level Up Tutorial: Plot: Sequence of Events**.

ANALYZE MOOD

Remind students that both **diction**—word choice—and **syntax**—word order and arrangement—affect mood. Sentence length, an aspect of syntax, can slow the pace down or speed it up. Slower speeds and longer sentences may lend themselves to calm or tedious moods, while shorter sentences may heighten anxiety and excitement. (**Answer:** *Poe uses a string of short sentence, with successive changes often signaled by the word "Then." The effect on the reader is to convey fear and horror at the narrator's fate.*)

CRITICAL VOCABULARY

lucid: When the narrator remembers details of the time immediately after his trial, his memory is lucid, or clear and unclouded.

ASK STUDENTS whether the narrator's mind is lucid while he is being taken from the scene of his trial to his prison. *(The narrator is semiconscious, so his mind is not lucid.)*

tumultuous: When the narrator regained consciousness, his heart was beating tumultuously and hard.

ASK STUDENTS what the description of a tumultuously beating heart suggests to readers. *(a heart that is beating wildly and irregularly)*

ANALYZE PLOT STRUCTURE

Remind students that plot, characters, and setting are all connected. In this section, the plot involves the narrator's search for information about the setting—his own mysterious surroundings. (**Answer:** *The narrator's inability to see and locate the boundaries of wherever he is creates a sense of sensory deprivation. Not even being able to gather the slightest bit of information about his surroundings creates utter uncertainty and acute suspense.*)

🇪🇱 ENGLISH LEARNER SUPPORT

Demonstrate Comprehension Call students' attention to Poe's use of dashes in paragraphs 7 and 8. Explain to students that the dash (—) is a punctuation mark used to indicate a break or pause in a sentence, or to set off phrases or clauses that interrupt a sentence. Read aloud the sentences in which dashes appear, and have students listen. Then, ask students to identify which purpose the dashes in each of the examples serve. (*paragraph 7: interrupting clause; paragraph 8: pause or break*)

Explain that dashes often heighten suspense by creating a pause for effect, or to signal a significant moment of reflection or addition of information. Encourage students to watch for dashes as they read. **MODERATE/LIGHT**

CRITICAL VOCABULARY

supposition: Although he was in complete darkness and solitude, the narrator did not make a supposition, or assume, that he was dead.

ASK STUDENTS why the narrator rejected the supposition that he might be dead. (*He rejected it because he had thoughts and feelings about what he was experiencing.*)

 NOTICE & NOTE

supposition
(sŭp-ə-zĭsh´ən) *n.* a belief or assumption.

ANALYZE PLOT STRUCTURE

Annotate: Mark details in paragraph 6 that help you picture the narrator's situation.

Analyze: How do these details help build suspense?

encompassed me. I struggled for breath. The intensity of the darkness seemed to oppress and stifle me. The atmosphere was intolerably close. I still lay quietly, and made effort to exercise my reason. I brought to mind the inquisitorial proceedings, and attempted from that point to deduce my real condition. The sentence had passed; and it appeared to me that a very long interval of time had since elapsed. Yet not for a moment did I suppose myself actually dead. Such a **supposition**, notwithstanding what we read in fiction, is altogether inconsistent with real existence;—but where and in what state was I? The condemned to death, I knew, perished usually at the *autos-da-fé*,[8] and one of these had been held on the very night of the day of my trial. Had I been remanded to my dungeon, to await the next sacrifice, which would not take place for many months? This I at once saw could not be. Victims had been in immediate demand. Moreover, my dungeon, as well as all the condemned cells at Toledo, had stone floors, and light was not altogether excluded.

6   A fearful idea now suddenly drove the blood in torrents upon my heart, and for a brief period, I once more relapsed into insensibility. Upon recovering, I at once started to my feet, trembling convulsively in every fiber. I thrust my arms wildly above and around me in all directions. I felt nothing; yet dreaded to move a step, lest I should be impeded by the walls of the *tomb*. Perspiration burst from every pore and stood in cold big beads on my forehead. The agony of suspense grew at length intolerable, and I cautiously moved forward, with my arms extended, and my eyes straining from their sockets, in the hope of catching some faint ray of light. I proceeded for many paces; but still all was blackness and vacancy. I breathed more freely. It seemed evident that mine was not, at least, the most hideous of fates.

7   And now, as I still continued to step cautiously onward, there came thronging upon my recollection a thousand vague rumors of the horrors of Toledo. Of the dungeons there had been strange things narrated—fables I had always deemed them—but yet strange, and too ghastly to repeat, save in a whisper. Was I left to perish of starvation in the subterranean world of darkness; or what fate, perhaps even more fearful, awaited me? That the result would be death, and a death of more than customary bitterness, I knew too well the character of my judges to doubt. The mode and the hour were all that occupied or distracted me.

8   My outstretched hands at length encountered some solid obstruction. It was a wall, seemingly of stone masonry—very smooth, slimy, and cold. I followed it up! stepping with all the careful distrust with which certain antique narratives had inspired me. This process, however, afforded me no means of ascertaining the dimensions of my dungeon; as I might make its circuit, and return to the point whence I set out, without being aware of the fact; so perfectly uniform seemed the wall. I therefore sought the knife which had been in my pocket,

---

[8] **autos-da-fé** (ou-tōz-də-fā´): Portuguese for *acts of faith*; public executions of people condemned by the Inquisition and carried out by the civil authorities.

when led into the inquisitorial chamber; but it was gone; my clothes had been exchanged for a wrapper of coarse serge.[9] I had thought of forcing the blade in some minute crevice of the masonry, so as to identify my point of departure. The difficulty, nevertheless, was but trivial; although, in the disorder of my fancy, it seemed at first **insuperable**. I tore a part of the hem from the robe and placed the fragment at full length, and at right angles to the wall. In groping my way around the prison I could not fail to encounter this rag upon completing the circuit. So, at least I thought: but I had not counted upon the extent of the dungeon, or upon my own weakness. The ground was moist and slippery. I staggered onward for some time, when I stumbled and fell. My excessive fatigue induced me to remain **prostrate**; and sleep soon overtook me as I lay.

9 Upon awakening, and stretching forth an arm, I found beside me a loaf and a pitcher with water. I was too much exhausted to reflect upon this circumstance, but ate and drank with avidity. Shortly afterward, I resumed my tour around the prison, and with much toil, came at last upon the fragment of the serge. Up to the period when I fell I had counted fifty-two paces, and upon resuming my walk, I counted forty-eight more;—when I arrived at the rag. There were in all, then, a hundred paces; and, admitting two paces to the yard, I presumed the dungeon to be fifty yards in circuit. I had met, however, with many angles in the wall, and thus I could form no guess at the shape of the vault; for vault I could not help supposing it to be.

10 I had little object—certainly no hope—in these researches; but a vague curiosity prompted me to continue them. Quitting the wall, I resolved to cross the area of the enclosure. At first I proceeded with extreme caution, for the floor, although seemingly of solid material, was treacherous with slime. At length, however, I took courage, and did not hesitate to step firmly; endeavoring to cross in as direct a line as possible. I had advanced some ten or twelve paces in this manner, when the remnant of the torn hem of my robe became entangled between my legs. I stepped on it, and fell violently on my face.

11 In the confusion attending my fall, I did not immediately apprehend a somewhat startling circumstance, which yet, in a few seconds afterward, and while I still lay prostrate, arrested my attention. It was this—my chin rested upon the floor of the prison, but my lips and the upper portion of my head, although seemingly at a less elevation than the chin, touched nothing. At the same time my forehead seemed bathed in a clammy vapor, and the peculiar smell of decayed fungus arose to my nostrils. I put forward my arm, and shuddered to find that I had fallen at the very brink of a circular pit, whose extent, of course, I had no means of ascertaining at the moment. Groping about the masonry just below the margin, I succeeded in dislodging a small fragment, and let it fall into the abyss. For many seconds I hearkened to its reverberations as it dashed against the sides of the chasm in its descent; at length there was a

---

[9] **serge** (sûrj): a type of woolen fabric.

insuperable
(ĭn-sōō′pər-ə-bəl) *adj.*
impossible to overcome.

prostrate
(prŏs′trāt) *adj.* lying down with
the head facing downward.

ANALYZE MOOD
Annotate: Mark the details in paragraph 11 that appeal to the senses.

Interpret: How does the diction in this paragraph contribute to the story's mood?

WHEN STUDENTS STRUGGLE . . .

Unpack Syntax Explain to students that Poe often uses multiple modifying phrases in his sentences. Read aloud the first sentence of paragraph 11. Point out the modifying phrases in the sentence. Discuss how these modifiers build dramatic tension. Ask students to examine the third sentence of paragraph 10 and identify its modifying phrase. Then, ask how the modifier builds suspense.

 For additional support, go to the **Reading Studio** and assign the following **Level Up Tutorials: Prepositions and Prepositional Phrases** *and* **Modifiers and Placement of Modifiers**.

 ANALYZE MOOD

Discuss with students the images in this paragraph and which of the five senses they appeal to. Point out that sight, the dominant sense in most stories, is not available to the narrator. Yet three of the other senses are engaged. Poe's ability to describe this lengthy scene, relying mostly on touch, smell, and sound, shows his mastery of storytelling. (**Answer:** *His head is suspended over air rather than resting on the floor; he feels a "clammy vapor," which is unpleasant, and detects a smell of "decayed fungus," suggesting death; the pit is an "abyss," suggesting Hell. These vivid images make the terror the narrator feels seem real and contribute to an atmosphere of death and horror.*)

For **listening support** for students at varying proficiency levels, see the **Text X-Ray** on page 290C.

CRITICAL VOCABULARY

insuperable: The narrator feels that the challenge of measuring his cell is insuperable, or cannot be overcome.

ASK STUDENTS what other tasks might have been insuperable for the narrator. (*figuring out how much time had passed, escaping the cell*)

prostrate: The narrator fell prostrate, or facedown, on the floor.

ASK STUDENTS what the narrator's decision to remain prostrate for a time tells them about his state. (*He was so exhausted that he could not even move to a more comfortable position.*)

TEACH

ANALYZE STRUCTURE

Note to students that at the beginning of paragraph 12, the narrator says he "saw clearly" the fate that was meant for him but does not say what it is until later in the paragraph. He bases his understanding on what he already knows of the Inquisition. (**Answer:** *Dramatic tension is heightened due to uncertainty over what form the "most hideous moral horrors" will take and when the death sentence will be delivered.*)

ANALYZE MOOD

Point out to students that in paragraph 14, the narrator says he woke from sleep to find that he could see a little. So in paragraph 15 he begins comparing his previous understanding of the prison to his visual perception of the prison. (**Answer:** *He seems much calmer now than before and is using his reason to figure out a puzzle. Now that he can see a little and understands his environment better, he feels a little less afraid than he did when he could not comprehend his fate.*)

 For **listening support** for students at varying proficiency levels, see the **Text X-Ray** on page 290D.

ANALYZE PLOT STRUCTURE
Annotate: Mark the sentence in paragraph 12 that states the narrator's understanding of the fate that may await him.

Analyze: How does knowing the narrator's thoughts build suspense in the story?

ANALYZE MOOD
Annotate: Mark the phrases in paragraphs 15–16 that describe the dungeon.

Infer: What does the narrator's description suggest about his state of mind? Why does he feel that way?

---

sullen plunge into water, succeeded by loud echoes. At the same moment there came a sound resembling the quick opening, and as rapid closing of a door overhead, while a faint gleam of light flashed suddenly through the gloom, and as suddenly faded away.

12   I saw clearly the doom which had been prepared for me, and congratulated myself upon the timely accident by which I had escaped. Another step before my fall, and the world had seen me no more. And the death just avoided, was of that very character which I had regarded as fabulous and frivolous in the tales respecting the Inquisition. To the victims of its tyranny, there was the choice of death with its direst physical agonies, or death with its most hideous moral horrors. I had been reserved for the latter. By long suffering my nerves had been unstrung, until I trembled at the sound of my own voice, and had become in every respect a fitting subject for the species of torture which awaited me.

13   Shaking in every limb, I groped my way back to the wall; resolving there to perish rather than risk the terrors of the wells, of which my imagination now pictured many in various positions about the dungeon. In other conditions of mind I might have had courage to end my misery at once by a plunge into one of these abysses; but now I was the veriest of cowards. Neither could I forget what I had read of these pits—that the *sudden* extinction of life formed no part of their most horrible plan.

14   Agitation of spirit kept me awake for many long hours; but at length I again slumbered. Upon arousing, I found by my side as before, a loaf and a pitcher of water. A burning thirst consumed me, and I emptied the vessel at a draft. It must have been drugged; for scarcely had I drunk, before I became irresistibly drowsy. A deep sleep fell upon me—a sleep like that of death. How long it lasted of course, I know not; but when, once again, I unclosed my eyes, the objects around me were visible. By a wild sulphurous luster,[10] the origin of which I could not at first determine, I was enabled to see the extent and aspect of the prison.

15   In its size I had been greatly mistaken. The whole circuit of its walls did not exceed twenty-five yards. For some minutes this fact occasioned me a world of vain trouble; vain indeed! for what could be of less importance, under the terrible circumstances which environed me, than the mere dimensions of my dungeon? But my soul took a wild interest in trifles, and I busied myself in endeavors to account for the error I had committed in my measurement. The truth at length flashed upon me. In my first attempt at exploration I had counted fifty-two paces, up to the period when I fell; I must then have been within a pace or two of the fragments of serge; in fact, I had nearly performed the circuit of the vault. I then slept, and upon awaking, I must have returned upon my steps—thus supposing the circuit nearly double what it actually was. My confusion of mind prevented

---

[10] **sulphurous luster:** a pale, yellow glow.

TO CHALLENGE STUDENTS . . .

Evaluate Writer's Craft   When should a writer keep readers "in the dark"? Discuss with students the narrator's fear of the unknown. Then, ask them how the reader's situation mirrors that of the narrator. (*Like the narrator, the reader is "in the dark" about where the narrator is and what will happen to him.*)

Have students discuss in small groups whether they think it is more frightening to readers to show or describe something horrible or to hint at it. Tell students to support their opinions with references to other literature, dramas, or movies.

me from observing that I began my tour with the wall to the left, and ended it with the wall to the right.

16   I had been deceived, too, in respect to the shape of the enclosure. In feeling my way around I had found <u>many angles</u>, and thus deduced an idea of great irregularity; so potent is the effect of total darkness upon one arousing from lethargy or sleep! <u>The angles were simply those of a few slight depressions, or niches, at odd intervals. The general shape of the prison was square. What I had taken for masonry seemed now to be iron, or some other metal, in huge plates, whose sutures or joints occasioned the depression.</u> The entire surface of this metallic enclosure was rudely daubed in all the hideous and repulsive devices to which the charnel superstitions[11] of the monks has given rise. The figures of fiends in aspects of menace, with skeleton forms, and other more really fearful images, overspread and disfigured the walls. I observed that the <u>outlines of these monstrosities were</u>

---

[11] **charnel superstitions:** irrational beliefs about death and dying.

The Pit and the Pendulum   299

IMPROVE READING FLUENCY

Targeted Passage Have students work with partners to read the narrator's description of the prison. Have students echo you as you read paragraph 16 aloud. Model each sentence, and then have students read it aloud together. Finally, have students take turns reading aloud the paragraph to a partner. Encourage students to provide feedback and support for pronunciation and observing punctuation cues. Remind students that when they are reading aloud for an audience they should pace their reading so the audience has time to understand what is happening.

Go to the **Reading Studio** for additional support in developing fluency.

TEACH

ANALYZE PLOT STRUCTURE

Point out to students that the narrator woke from a drugged sleep in paragraph 14, yet it is only here in paragraph 17 that he reveals a very important piece of information about the way his situation has changed. Ask students for ideas about why Poe waited so long to reveal this important change—what it reveals about the role of the narrator's captors in the story. (**Answer:** *The narrator is now tied down on a platform and the water he needs has been taken away. These new and disturbing details considerably increase the dramatic tension since the reader sees that the narrator's situation appears worse than before.*)

ANALYZE MOOD

Once students have annotated the details that describe the pendulum, have them focus on the motion of the pendulum and how it is changing in order to begin evaluating the mood. (**Answer:** *The pendulum is descending and moving faster; the description of "a crescent of glittering steel" and the comparison to a razor makes the mood even more terrifying.*)

 NOTICE & NOTE

ANALYZE PLOT STRUCTURE

Annotate: Mark the words in paragraph 17 that tell you the narrator's situation has changed.

Synthesize: How do these descriptions shape your understanding of the plot?

ANALYZE MOOD

Annotate: Underline details in paragraph 20 that describe the pendulum.

Interpret: How does the description of the pendulum contribute to the mood?

sufficiently distinct, but that the colors seemed faded and blurred, as if from the effects of a damp atmosphere. I now noticed the floor, too, which was of stone. In the center yawned the circular pit from whose jaws I had escaped; but it was the only one in the dungeon.

17   All this I saw distinctly and by much effort: for my personal condition had been greatly changed during slumber. I now lay upon my back, and at full length, on a species of low framework of wood. To this I was securely bound by a long strap resembling a surcingle.[12] It passed in many convolutions about my limbs and body, leaving at liberty only my head, and my left arm to such extent that I could, by dint[13] of much exertion, supply myself with food from an earthen dish which lay by my side on the floor. I saw, to my horror, that the pitcher had been removed. I say to my horror; for I was consumed with intolerable thirst. This thirst it appeared to be the design of my persecutors to stimulate: for the food in the dish was meat pungently seasoned.

18   Looking upward I surveyed the ceiling of my prison. It was some thirty or forty feet overhead, and constructed much as the side walls. In one of its panels a very singular figure riveted my whole attention. It was the painted figure of Time as he is commonly represented, save that, in lieu of a scythe, he held what, at a casual glance, I supposed to be the pictured image of a huge pendulum such as we see on antique clocks. There was something, however, in the appearance of this machine which caused me to regard it more attentively. While I gazed directly upward at it (for its position was immediately over my own) I fancied that I saw it in motion. In an instant afterward the fancy was confirmed. Its sweep was brief, and of course slow. I watched it for some minutes, somewhat in fear, but more in wonder. Wearied at length with observing its dull movement, I turned my eyes upon the other objects in the cell.

19   A slight noise attracted my notice, and, looking to the floor, I saw several enormous rats traversing it. They had issued from the well, which lay just within view to my right. Even then, while I gazed, they came up in troops, hurriedly, with ravenous eyes, allured by the scent of the meat. From this it required much effort and attention to scare them away.

20   It might have been half an hour, perhaps even an hour, (for I could take but imperfect note of time) before I again cast my eyes upward. What I then saw confounded and amazed me. The sweep of the pendulum had increased in extent by nearly a yard. As a natural consequence, its velocity was also much greater. But what mainly disturbed me was the idea that it had perceptibly *descended*. I now observed—with what horror it is needless to say—that its nether extremity was formed of a crescent of glittering steel, about a foot in length from horn to horn; the horns upward, and the under edge evidently as keen as that of a razor. Like a razor also, it seemed massy

---

[12]**surcingle:** a belt used to hold a saddle or pack onto a horse's back.
[13]**dint:** force.

and heavy, tapering from the edge into a solid and broad structure above. It was appended to a weighty rod of brass, and the whole *hissed* as it swung through the air.

21   I could no longer doubt the doom prepared for me by monkish ingenuity in torture. My cognizance of the pit had become known to the inquisitorial agents—*the pit* whose horrors had been destined for so bold a recusant[14] as myself—*the pit*, typical of hell, and regarded by rumor as the Ultima Thule[15] of all their punishments. The plunge into this pit I had avoided by the merest of accidents, and I knew that surprise, or entrapment into torment, formed an important portion of all the grotesquerie of these dungeon deaths. Having failed to fall, it was no part of the demon plan to hurl me into the abyss; and thus (there being no alternative) a different and a milder destruction awaited me. Milder! I half smiled in my agony as I thought of such application of such a term.

22   What boots it[16] to tell of the long, long hours of horror more than mortal, during which I counted the rushing vibrations of the steel! Inch by inch—line by line—with a descent only appreciable at intervals that seemed ages—down and still down it came! Days passed—it might have been that many days passed—ere it swept so closely over me as to fan me with its acrid breath. The odor of the sharp steel forced itself into my nostrils. I prayed—I wearied heaven with my prayer for its more speedy descent. I grew frantically mad, and struggled to force myself upward against the sweep of the fearful scimitar.[17] And then I fell suddenly calm, and lay smiling at the glittering death, as a child at some rare bauble.

23   There was another interval of utter insensibility; it was brief; for, upon again lapsing into life there had been no perceptible descent in the pendulum. But it might have been long; for I knew there were demons who took note of my swoon, and who could have arrested the vibration at pleasure. Upon my recovery, too, I felt very—oh, inexpressibly sick and weak, as if through long inanition.[18] Even amid the agonies of that period, the human nature craved food. With painful effort I outstretched my left arm as far as my bonds permitted, and took possession of the small remnant which had been spared me by the rats. As I put a portion of it within my lips, there rushed to my mind a half formed thought of joy—of hope. Yet what business had I with hope? It was, as I say, a half formed thought— man has many such which are never completed. I felt that it was of joy—of hope; but I felt also that it had perished in its formation. In vain I struggled to perfect—to regain it. Long suffering had nearly

---

[14]**recusant:** a heretic or dissident.

[15]**Ultima Thule** (ŭl´tə-mə thōō´lē): according to ancient geographers, the most remote region of the world—here used figuratively to mean "most extreme achievement; summit."

[16]**What boots it?:** What good is it?

[17]**scimitar:** a curved sword of Middle Eastern origin.

[18]**inanition:** weakness from starvation.

ANALYZE PLOT STRUCTURE

Annotate: Mark the phrases in paragraph 21 that describe the narrator and his antagonists.

Synthesize: What do you learn about the narrator's crime? What details are left out? Explain.

The Pit and the Pendulum   301

ANALYZE PLOT STRUCTURE

Have students read the paragraph for details about the characters, including the prisoner and his captors. Point out that even though the captors are not seen much in the story, they have a large effect on the plot—almost as if acting from outside the story. (**Answer:** *The narrator identifies himself as a "bold recusant," or heretic, and his judges as "agents" of the Inquisition. The narrator's description does not include the reason why he is punished. The author may have chosen to omit this information to make the narrator more mysterious.*)

 ENGLISH LEARNER SUPPORT

Understand Interjections   Call students' attention to the word *oh* in paragraph 23. Read it aloud, noting the silent *h*, and have students echo you. Explain that *oh* is an interjection—a word or short phrase that expresses emotion and can stand alone. Explain that interjections are often used in casual conversation, so in Poe's writing they help to create the narrator's voice. In writing, interjections are usually followed by an exclamation point and that they may begin with the word *how*; for example, *How beautiful!*

Ask students to give examples of interjections from their first languages. Have students practice speaking with interjections with partners, using sentence frames such as: *Oh dear! I _____. Oh no! I _____. Amazing! I've never seen anything so _____.*
ALL LEVELS

 For **speaking support** for students at varying proficiency levels, see the **Text X-Ray** on page 290D.

ENGLISH LEARNER SUPPORT

Use Context   Call students' attention to the phrase "What boots it" in paragraph 22. Tell them that the word *boots* in this phrase means "gives an advantage or benefit." Although it is spelled the same, it is a different word from the one that refers to footwear. Explain that in addition to its verb form, *boot* can also be used as an adjective or an adverb.

- bootless: useless
- bootlessly: uselessly

Encourage students to watch for other archaic words as they read and to look them up in a dictionary. **LIGHT**

TEACH

 LANGUAGE CONVENTIONS

Point out to students that the pronoun *they* after the semicolon refers back to the subject "My eyes." (**Answer:** *In the first part of the sentence, the narrator's eyes are fixated on the pendulum. He then closes them as the tension increases.*)

pertinacity
(pûr-tn-ăs ´ĭ-tē) *n.* firm, unyielding intent.

LANGUAGE CONVENTIONS

Annotate: Mark the semicolon in paragraph 27.

Analyze: How does the semicolon help you comprehend the narrator's shift in thought?

annihilated all my ordinary powers of mind. I was an imbecile—an idiot.

24   The vibration of the pendulum was at right angles to my length. I saw that the crescent was designed to cross the region of the heart. It would fray the serge of my robe—it would return and repeat its operations—again—and again. Notwithstanding its terrifically wide sweep (some thirty feet or more) and the hissing vigor of its descent, sufficient to sunder these very walls of iron, still the fraying of my robe would be all that, for several minutes, it would accomplish. And at this thought I paused. I dared not go farther than this reflection. I dwelt upon it with a **pertinacity** of attention—as if, in so dwelling, I could arrest *here* the descent of the steel. I forced myself to ponder upon the sound of the crescent as it should pass across the garment— upon the peculiar thrilling sensation which the friction of cloth produces on the nerves. I pondered upon all this frivolity until my teeth were on edge.

25   Down—steadily down it crept. I took a frenzied pleasure in contrasting its downward with its lateral velocity. To the right—to the left—far and wide—with the shriek of a . . . spirit; to my heart with the stealthy pace of the tiger! I alternately laughed and howled as the one or the other idea grew predominant.

26   Down—certainly, relentlessly down! It vibrated within three inches of my bosom! I struggled violently, furiously, to free my left arm. This was free only from the elbow to the hand. I could reach the latter, from the platter beside me, to my mouth, with great effort, but no farther. Could I have broken the fastenings above the elbow, I would have seized and attempted to arrest the pendulum. I might as well have attempted to arrest an avalanche!

27   Down—still unceasingly—still inevitably down! I gasped and struggled at each vibration. I shrunk convulsively at its every sweep. My eyes followed its outward or upward whirls with the eagerness of the most unmeaning despair; they closed themselves spasmodically at the descent, although death would have been a relief, oh! how unspeakable! Still I quivered in every nerve to think how slight a sinking of the machinery would precipitate that keen, glistening axe upon my bosom. It was *hope* that prompted the nerve to quiver—the frame to shrink. It was *hope*—the hope that triumphs on the rack[19]— that whispers to the death-condemned even in the dungeons of the Inquisition.

28   I saw that some ten or twelve vibrations would bring the steel in actual contact with my robe, and with this observation there suddenly came over my spirit all the keen, collected calmness of despair. For the first time during many hours—or perhaps days—I *thought*. It now occurred to me that the bandage, or surcingle, which enveloped me, was *unique*. I was tied by no separate cord. The first stroke of

---

[19]**rack:** a device for torture that stretches the victim's limbs.

302   Unit 3

© Houghton Mifflin Harcourt Publishing Company

CRITICAL VOCABULARY

pertinacity: The narrator keeps his mind on his belief that the pendulum will cut only his robe with pertinacity, or unwavering firmness.

ASK STUDENTS why the narrator chooses to focus on the pendulum cutting his robe with such a "pertinacity of attention." (*because he is afraid to think about what will happen after the pendulum cuts the robe*)

WHEN STUDENTS STRUGGLE . . .

Multiple Meaning Words Point out to students the word *unique* in paragraph 28. Explain that while this word usually means "the only one of its kind," here Poe uses a secondary, or less common, meaning. Then, help students use context clues to guess this meaning. Point out that the narrator explains that if the cord were cut in one place, the entire thing could be removed. Guide students to conclude that Poe uses *unique* to mean "single."

 For additional support, go to the **Reading Studio** and assign the following **Level Up Tutorial: Multiple-Meaning Words**.

the razor-like crescent athwart[20] any portion of the band, would so detach it that it might be unwound from my person by means of my left hand. But how fearful, in that case, the proximity of the steel! The result of the slightest struggle how deadly! Was it likely, moreover, that the minions[21] of the torturer had not foreseen and provided for this possibility! Was it probable that the bandage crossed my bosom in the track of the pendulum? Dreading to find my faint, and, as it seemed, my last hope frustrated, I so far elevated my head as to obtain a distinct view of my breast. The surcingle enveloped my limbs and body close in all directions—*save in the path of the destroying crescent.*

29   Scarcely had I dropped my head back into its original position, when there flashed upon my mind what I cannot better describe than as the unformed half of that idea of deliverance to which I have previously alluded, and of which a moiety[22] only floated indeterminately through my brain when I raised food to my burning lips. The whole thought was now present—feeble, scarcely sane, scarcely definite,—but still entire. I proceeded at once, with the nervous energy of despair, to attempt its execution.

30   For many hours the immediate vicinity of the low framework upon which I lay, had been literally swarming with rats. They were wild, bold, ravenous; their red eyes glaring upon me as if they waited but for motionlessness on my part to make me their prey. "To what food," I thought, "have they been accustomed in the well?"

31   They had devoured, in spite of all my efforts to prevent them, all but a small remnant of the contents of the dish. I had fallen into an habitual seesaw, or wave of the hand about the platter, and, at length, the unconscious uniformity of the movement deprived it of effect. In their voracity the vermin frequently fastened their sharp fangs into my fingers. With the particles of the oily and spicy viand[23] which now remained, I thoroughly rubbed the bandage wherever I could reach it; then, raising my hand from the floor, I lay breathlessly still.

32   At first the ravenous animals were startled and terrified at the change—at the cessation of movement. They shrank alarmedly back; many sought the well. But this was only for a moment. I had not counted in vain upon their voracity. Observing that I remained without motion, one or two of the boldest leaped upon the framework, and smelt at the surcingle. This seemed the signal for a general rush. Forth from the well they hurried in fresh troops. They clung to the wood—they overran it, and leaped in hundreds upon my person. The measured movement of the pendulum disturbed them not at all. Avoiding its strokes they busied themselves with the anointed bandage. They pressed—they swarmed upon me in ever accumulating heaps. They writhed upon my throat; their cold

---

[20] **athwart:** across, from one side to the other.
[21] **minions:** followers, servants.
[22] **moiety:** one of two equal parts.
[23] **viand:** food.

© Houghton Mifflin Harcourt Publishing Company

ANALYZE PLOT STRUCTURE

Annotate: Mark the sentence in paragraph 29 that shows the narrator's shift from having an idea for freeing himself to beginning to implement it.

Analyze: What does Poe achieve by not having the narrator tell us his plan?

ANALYZE PLOT STRUCTURE

Have students point out words in paragraph 29 that describe the formation of the narrator's plan. Note that readers may not find out the substance of the plan, but they know it is "feeble, scarcely sane, scarcely definite." How does this description make the reader feel? (**Answer:** *He wants the reader to be curious about or surprised by the details of the plan.*)

304   Unit 3

© Houghton Mifflin Harcourt Publishing Company • Image Credits: © Culture Club/Getty Images

TO CHALLENGE STUDENTS . . .

Mimic the Writer's Style Discuss with students the elements of Poe's writing style, emphasizing the following:

- the use of dashes
- the use of italics
- the use of words with strong connotations

Have students choose a familiar scene, such as feeding a pet, doing laundry, or eating a meal, and describe it in a short paragraph mimicking Poe's style. Then, have students read their paragraphs aloud in small groups.

lips sought my own; I was half stifled by their thronging pressure; disgust, for which the world has no name, swelled my bosom, and chilled, with a heavy clamminess, my heart. Yet one minute, and I felt that the struggle would be over. Plainly I perceived the loosening of the bandage. I knew that in more than one place it must be already severed. With a more than human resolution I lay *still*.

33   Nor had I erred in my calculations—nor had I endured in vain. I at length felt that I was *free*. The surcingle hung in ribands from my body. But the stroke of the pendulum already pressed upon my bosom. It had divided the serge of the robe. It had cut through the linen beneath. Twice again it swung, and a sharp sense of pain shot through every nerve. But the moment of escape had arrived. At a wave of my hand my deliverers hurried tumultuously away. With a steady movement—cautious, sidelong, shrinking, and slow—I <u>slid from the embrace of the bandage and beyond the reach of the scimitar. For the moment, at least, *I was free.*</u>

34   Free!—and in the grasp of the Inquisition! I had scarcely stepped from my wooden bed of horror upon the stone floor of the prison, when the motion of the hellish machine ceased and I beheld it drawn up, by some invisible force, through the ceiling. This was a lesson which I took desperately to heart. My every motion was undoubtedly watched. Free!—I had but escaped death in one form of agony, to be delivered unto worse than death in some other. With that thought I rolled my eyes nervously around the barriers of iron that hemmed me in. Something unusual—some change which at first I could not appreciate distinctly—it was obvious, had taken place in the apartment. For many minutes in a dreamy and trembling abstraction, I busied myself in vain, unconnected conjecture. During this period, I became aware, for the first time, of the origin of the sulphurous light which illuminated the cell. It proceeded from a fissure, about half an inch in width, extending entirely around the prison at the base of the walls, which thus appeared, and were, completely separated from the floor. I endeavored, but of course in vain, to look through the aperture.

35   As I arose from the attempt, the mystery of the alteration in the chamber broke at once upon my understanding. I have observed that, although the outlines of the figures upon the walls were sufficiently distinct, yet the colors seemed blurred and indefinite. These colors had now assumed, and were momentarily assuming, a startling and most intense brilliancy, that gave to the spectral and fiendish portraitures an aspect that might have thrilled even firmer nerves than my own. Demon eyes, of a wild and ghastly vivacity, glared upon me in a thousand directions, where none had been visible before, and gleamed with the lurid luster of a fire that I could not force my imagination to regard as unreal.

ANALYZE PLOT STRUCTURE

Annotate: In the plot of a story, a resolution reveals the outcome of events. Mark the sentences in paragraph 33 that indicate a resolution.

Predict: The resolution usually comes at the end and ties up the loose story threads. Do you think the character's problems are over? What do you predict will happen?

 **ANALYZE PLOT STRUCTURE**

Remind students that during the falling action and resolution, the character has resolved the conflict. Poe, however, introduces a new conflict, which heightens the tension and adds suspense. (**Possible answer:** *I do not believe the character's problems are over because he still needs to escape from the pit. I predict he will not escape from the pit.*)

ANALYZE MOOD

Remind students that holding back information from the reader increases the tension on the story. This tension is called **suspense**. Students should consider how the suspense of not knowing for certain affects the mood. (**Answer:** *The metal walls are being heated from the outside by fire. Poe suggests rather than explicitly stating this change to increase the horrifying uncertainty of the scene and the generally disturbing mood.*)

EL ENGLISH LEARNER SUPPORT

Use Visuals Tell students that in paragraph 37 Poe uses several terms from geometry in his description of the changes in the room's size and shape. Help students to identify and define the following words, providing visuals to support understanding.

- *square*: having four equal sides and four right angles
- *acute*: forming an angle of less than 90 degrees
- *obtuse*: forming an angle of more than 90 degrees
- *lozenge:* a four-sided shape with two acute and two obtuse angles **ALL LEVELS**

CRITICAL VOCABULARY

avert: When he is about to fall into the pit, the narrator looks away, or averts his eyes.

ASK STUDENTS why the narrator averts his eyes before he falls. (*He doesn't want to see whatever is waiting for him in the pit.*)

 NOTICE & NOTE

ANALYZE MOOD

Annotate: Mark the words and phrases in paragraph 36 that provide clues to what is happening.

Analyze: What is happening? What effect on the mood does Poe achieve by not stating what is happening explicitly?

36   *Unreal!*—Even while I breathed there came to my nostrils the breath of the vapor of heated iron! A suffocating odor pervaded the prison! A deeper glow settled each moment in the eyes that glared at my agonies! A richer tint of crimson diffused itself over the pictured horrors of blood. I panted! I gasped for breath! There could be no doubt of the design of my tormentors—oh! most unrelenting! oh! most demoniac of men! I shrank from the glowing metal to the center of the cell. Amid the thought of the fiery destruction that impended, the idea of the coolness of the well came over my soul like balm. I rushed to its deadly brink. I threw my straining vision below. The glare from the enkindled roof illumined its inmost recesses. Yet, for a wild moment, did my spirit refuse to comprehend the meaning of what I saw. At length it forced—it wrestled its way into my soul—it burned itself in upon my shuddering reason.—Oh! for a voice to speak!—oh! horror!—oh! any horror but this! With a shriek, I rushed from the margin, and buried my face in my hands—weeping bitterly.

37   The heat rapidly increased, and once again I looked up, shuddering as with a fit of the ague.[24] There had been a second change in the cell—and now the change was obviously in the form. As before, it was in vain that I, at first, endeavored to appreciate or understand what was taking place. But not long was I left in doubt. The Inquisitorial vengeance had been hurried by my twofold escape, and there was to be no more dallying with the King of Terrors. The room had been square. I saw that two of its iron angles were now acute—two, consequently, obtuse. The fearful difference quickly increased with a low rumbling or moaning sound. In an instant the apartment had shifted its form into that of a lozenge. But the alteration stopped not here—I neither hoped nor desired it to stop. I could have clasped the red walls to my bosom as a garment of eternal peace. "Death," I said, "any death but that of the pit!" Fool! might I have not known that *into the pit* it was the object of the burning iron to urge me? Could I resist its glow? or, if even that, could I withstand its pressure? And now, flatter and flatter grew the lozenge, with a rapidity that left me no time for contemplation. Its center, and of course, its greatest width, came just over the yawning gulf. I shrank back—but the closing walls pressed me resistlessly onward. At length for my seared and writhing body there was no longer an inch of foothold on the firm floor of the prison. I struggled no more, but the agony of my soul found vent in one loud, long, and final scream of despair. I felt that I tottered upon the brink—I **averted** my eyes—

avert
(ə-vûrt′) *v.* to turn away.

38   There was a discordant hum of human voices! There was a loud blast of many trumpets! There was a harsh grating as of a thousand thunders! The fiery walls rushed back! An outstretched arm caught my own as I fell, fainting, into the abyss. It was that of General Lasalle. The French army had entered Toledo. The Inquisition was in the hands of its enemies.

---

[24]**ague:** an illness, like malaria, that causes fever and shivering.

APPLYING ACADEMIC VOCABULARY

❑ **analogy**   ❑ **denote**   ☑ **quote**   ☑ **topic**   ☑ **unique**

Write and Discuss Have students turn to a partner to discuss the following questions. Guide students to include the Academic Vocabulary words *unique, quote,* and *topic* in their responses. Ask volunteers to share their responses with the class.

- What is the **topic** of the story?
- How does Poe's **unique** use of descriptive language convey the narrator's terror?
- What lines would you **quote** as examples of Poe's style?

CHECK YOUR UNDERSTANDING

Answer these questions before moving on to the **Analyze the Text** section on the following page.

1 What are the rats doing when the narrator first encounters them?

A Fleeing the fire

B Trying to take his food

C Chewing on his bonds

D Crawling on his body

2 Which method of execution does the narrator fear the most?

F The pit

G The pendulum

H The fire

J The contracting walls

3 What detail contributes to the horrific mood?

A *I breathed more freely*

B *I found beside me a loaf and a pitcher with water*

C *at length I again slumbered*

D *I struggled violently, furiously, to free my left arm*

The Pit and the Pendulum   307

CHECK YOUR UNDERSTANDING

Have students answer the questions independently.

Answers:

1. *B*

2. *F*

3. *D*

If they answer any questions incorrectly, have them reread the text to confirm their understanding. Then they may proceed to ANALYZE THE TEXT on page 308.

 ENGLISH LEARNER SUPPORT

Oral Assessment   Use the following questions to assess students' comprehension and speaking skills:

1. There are rats in the story. What are they doing the first time the narrator runs into them? *(trying to take his food)*

2. What does the narrator fear most? *(the pit)*

3. Of these two details, which creates a mood of horror? "I found beside me a loaf and a pitcher with water" OR "I struggled violently, furiously, to free my left arm." *(I struggled violently, furiously, to free my left arm.)* **SUBSTANTIAL/MODERATE**

ANALYZE THE TEXT

Possible answers:

1. **DOK 4:** *Gothic elements include the narrator's fear and near madness; his mention of torture, suffering, and death; and his characterization of the judges of the Inquisition as fiendish and monstrous.*

2. **DOK 2:** *It suggests that his mind is not entirely sharp either because he is overwhelmed by his situation, weakened by hunger and thirst, or unhinged by his fear.*

3. **DOK 4:** *We learn he is highly emotional but also rational as he tries to reason about his situation, explore his prison, and find a way of escape. His hopefulness and resourcefulness help him to survive when he gets the rats to gnaw through his bonds.*

4. **DOK 2:** *The mood is tense, haunting, and frightening. Poe gradually reveals details of the narrator's prison and punishments, which adds to the tension. Vivid images such as the rats and the hot iron walls make the mood even more terrifying.*

5. **DOK 4:** *The opening focuses on the narrator's mental state after he is sentenced. The ending of the story is abrupt; the narrator may have been rescued or may have plunged into an abyss. The structure suggests that the overall meaning is concerned with the mind and its struggle between hope and despair, rationality and insanity.*

RESEARCH

Discuss search terms students can use to quickly find sources to answer each question in the chart.

1. *"The Old Dude's Ticker"*

2. *Arthur Conan Doyle, creator of Sherlock Holmes*

3. *Charles Baudelaire*

Extend Students will find ample sources by searching on "Edgar Allan Poe influence."

RESPOND

ANALYZE THE TEXT

Support your responses with evidence from the text. ⧉ NOTEBOOK

1. **Synthesize** Review the elements of Gothic fiction on the Get Ready page. Which of these elements does Poe include in "The Pit and the Pendulum"?

2. **Infer** The narrator is often uncertain about how much time has elapsed and about the physical details of the prison. What does this uncertainty suggest about the narrator's state of mind?

3. **Analyze** Poe's narrator's personal qualities are revealed through his responses to the horrors of imprisonment. How does discovering his character in this way affect your understanding of the plot? Cite text evidence in your response.

4. **Infer** How would you describe the mood of the story? How does Poe create this mood? Cite examples of diction and syntax in your response.

5. **Synthesize** How does Poe begin and end the story? What does this structure suggest about the story's overall meaning?

RESEARCH TIP
When searching for information on the literary influence of an author, be sure to use reliable sources, such as books by expert authors or websites that are reliable and accurate.

RESEARCH

Edgar Allan Poe's life, though brief, had a lasting literary impact, as he is credited with having influenced later writers. Find out more about Poe's literary heritage by answering these questions.

QUESTION	ANSWER
Which Stephen King story is modeled on Poe's "Tell-Tale Heart"?	
Which famous author of detective fiction wrote, "Where was the detective story until Poe breathed the breath of life into it?"	
Which French poet acclaimed Poe's poetry and helped establish his reputation as a poet?	

Extend Read more about Poe's influence on the horror story, the detective story, or science fiction. Write a brief paragraph summarizing your findings on the views of his influence.

WHEN STUDENTS STRUGGLE . . .

Reteaching: Use Context Make certain students understand the meaning of the word *context*. Write this sentence on the board: *And now, flatter and flatter grew the lozenge, with a rapidity that left me no time for contemplation.* Ask students how they might use context to determine the meaning of the word *contemplation*. (*Since the change occurred quickly, it seems likely the narrator would not be able to think about what was happening.*)

 For additional support, go to the **Reading Studio** and assign the following **Level Up Tutorial: Using Context Clues**.

CREATE AND PRESENT

Write an Adaptation Poe's "The Pit and the Pendulum" is an intense study of a man suffering petrifying terror, fighting despair, and trying desperately to find a method of escape. Such a dramatic work could be adapted to another form, such as a radio or television script or a graphic novel.

- ❏ Choose the medium you prefer for your adaptation.
- ❏ Break the overall narrative into individual scenes that accurately convey a sense of character, setting, plot, and the theme of the original work.
- ❏ Write a narrative that includes text, stage directions (if appropriate), and visuals.
- ❏ Review your adaptation to ensure that it builds dramatic tension and conveys the main character's state of mind and the work's mood.

Present an Adaptation Turn your adaptation into a presentation either by recording the script or making a visual presentation out of your graphic novel.

- ❏ Practice using volume, tone of voice, and expression to convey effectively the thoughts, feelings, and state of mind of the narrator.
- ❏ Scan or copy visuals into a digital format to facilitate displaying them to classmates.
- ❏ Give a dramatic reading of your script or graphic novel to classmates, using voice and nonverbal communication to add impact to the presentation.

RESPOND

 Go to **Writing Narratives** in the **Writing Studio** for help.

 Go to **Using Media in a Presentation** in the **Speaking and Listening Studio** for help.

RESPOND TO THE ESSENTIAL QUESTION

 What do we secretly fear?

Gather Information Review your annotations and notes on "The Pit and the Pendulum." Then, add relevant details to your Response Log. As you determine which information to include, think about the:

- fear of being in the power of another
- impact of the unknown on people's fears
- appeal of stories with elements of horror

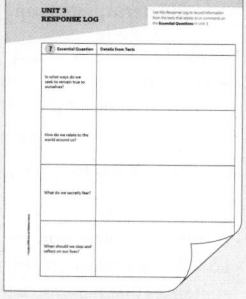

ACADEMIC VOCABULARY

As you write and discuss what you learned from the story, be sure to use the Academic Vocabulary words. Check off each of the words that you use.

- ❏ **analogy**
- ❏ **denote**
- ❏ **quote**
- ❏ **topic**
- ❏ **unique**

CREATE AND PRESENT

Write an Adaptation Review the options with students and provide examples of graphic novels, scripts, and videos that use still visuals plus a voiceover. Brainstorm other possibilities with students, encouraging them to think creatively about how to use visuals, music, and narration together to bring the story to life. Students may wish to search online for illustrations for the story to get ideas for their own presentations.

Have students work with partners or small groups to create their adaptations. They may wish to use a story sequence graphic organizer or storyboard app to plan.

For **writing support** for students at varying proficiency levels, see the **Text X-Ray** on page 290D.

Present an Adaptation Have students practice several times with their partners or small group. They may wish to record their presentation and replay it to see what works well and what needs improvement.

RESPOND TO THE ESSENTIAL QUESTION

Allow time for students to add details from "The Pit and the Pendulum" to their Unit 3 Response Logs.

APPLY

CRITICAL VOCABULARY

Answers:

1. *prostrate*

2. *lucid*

3. *pertinacity*

4. *averted*

5. *tumultuousness*

6. *indeterminate*

7. *insuperable*

8. *supposition*

VOCABULARY STRATEGY:
Context Clues

Suggest that pairs of students find and determine the meanings of three unknown words. When the pairs are finished, have volunteers share with the class the process of reasoning they used to determine the meaning of a word, using context clues.

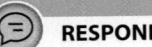 **RESPOND**

WORD BANK

indeterminate	insuperable
lucid	prostrate
tumultuous	pertinacity
supposition	averted

 Go to **Using Context Clues** in the **Vocabulary Studio** for help.

CRITICAL VOCABULARY

Practice and Apply Choose the correct term to complete each sentence.

1. The _____ figure of the dog sprawled on the hearth.

2. Her response was remarkably _____ for one so young.

3. "Determination is an admirable trait," he cautioned, "but _____ will not make up for lack of preparation."

4. By following well-thought-out plans, the team _____ the disaster.

5. The rebellion launched a period of _____ and wrenching change.

6. The staff was told to prepare for a(n) _____ number of visitors, making it difficult to secure sufficient supplies.

7. The odds were _____ for anyone with less determination than he.

8. The confident _____ that we would meet the deadline faded.

VOCABULARY STRATEGY:
Context Clues

When you come across an unfamiliar word in a text, you can use context clues, or information in surrounding phrases and sentences, to determine the word's meaning. For example, you can use context clues to determine the meaning of the word *indeterminate* in this passage from "The Pit and the Pendulum":

> I was sick—sick unto death with that long agony; and when they at length unbound me, and I was permitted to sit, I felt that my senses were leaving me. The sentence—the dread sentence of death—was the last of distinct accentuation which reached my ears. After that, the sound of the inquisitorial voices seemed merged in one dreamy indeterminate hum.

The word *dreamy* provides a clue that *indeterminate* means "not precisely known." The clause "I felt that my senses were leaving me" also hints at this meaning. In addition, the word *distinct* contrasts what the narrator hears when the sentence is announced from the sound of the voices that follow.

Practice and Apply Work with a partner to use context clues to help determine or clarify the meaning of unknown words. Follow these steps:

- Identify unfamiliar words in the story.
- Look for synonyms, antonyms, and other clues in surrounding words and sentences that help you infer the word's meaning. Consult a thesaurus if needed to identify synonyms and antonyms.
- Verify your preliminary determination of each word's meaning by checking the definition in a print or digital college-level dictionary.

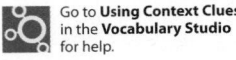 **ENGLISH LEARNER SUPPORT**

Vocabulary Strategy Give students additional practice in determining the meanings of words from the selection. Write *acrid* and *cessation* from the selection on the board. Have pairs of students find each word, then guide them to identify context clues in each sentence that help them understand its meaning. Have them share their ideas with the group.
ALL LEVELS

LANGUAGE CONVENTIONS:
Semicolons

Semicolons are used syntactically in various ways to help writers construct compound and compound-complex sentences.

One use is to separate two independent clauses that are linked by a conjunction (*and, or, but*), especially when one of the clauses contains a number of commas:

> How long it lasted of course, I know not; but when, once again, I unclosed my eyes, the objects around me were visible.

Semicolons are also used to separate parts of a compound sentence that are not joined by a coordinating conjunction or adverb:

> They shrank alarmedly back; many sought the well.

Semicolons are used to link an independent clause with another independent clause preceded by a **conjunctive adverb** (*then, however, thus,* or *therefore*) to closely connect the two ideas:

> With the particles of the oily and spicy viand which now remained, I thoroughly rubbed the bandage wherever I could reach it; then, raising my hand from the floor, I lay breathlessly still.

Semicolons are also used to separate items in a list when one or more of the items within the list has a comma:

Poe was a master of many genres, as evidenced by such impressive works as "The Raven" and "The Bells," lyric poems; "The Tell-Tale Heart" and "The Fall of the House of Usher," short stories; and many pieces of literary criticism.

Practice and Apply Write four original sentences, each following one of the four examples of uses of semicolons.

RESPOND

> ! Go to **Semicolons** and Colons in the **Grammar Studio** for help.

LANGUAGE CONVENTIONS:
Use Semicolons

Explain to students that Poe's varying use of sentence lengths is meant to reflect the inner emotional and mental state of the narrator. Semicolons helped him create sentences with several short parts occurring in a jarring rhythm—as shown in the first example. In this sentence, the pause of the semicolon after "I know not" covers quite a long time, in which the narrator sleeps. The semicolon in the third example joins two longer sentences to create the effect of actions done in tiring succession before the narrator can rest.

Review the four uses of semicolons with students, and provide additional examples as needed before students write their own sentences.

Practice and Apply Have partners share their four sentences. Partners can make sure the semicolons are used correctly. (*Sentences will vary.*)

The Pit and the Pendulum   311

ENGLISH LEARNER SUPPORT

Language Conventions Use the following supports with students at varying proficiency levels to practice using semicolons:

- Have students join two simple sentences into one compound sentence using a semicolon: *The pit was deep. The pendulum was sharp.* **SUBSTANTIAL**
- Have students join two simple sentences into one compound sentence using a semicolon, as above, then join these sentences using a conjunctive adverb such as *however* or *thus*: *The pit was deep and the pendulum was sharp. The man was terrified.* **MODERATE**
- Have students write several related simple sentences, then exchange sentences with a partner. Partners create new sentences using semicolons. **LIGHT**

COMPARE THEMES

Remind students that synthesizing information means taking individual pieces of information and combining them with other pieces of information and with prior knowledge or experience to gain a better understanding of a subject. Before students begin, have them revisit their notes about plot structure, literary elements, and mood. This will allow them to come prepared to their small group discussion.

ANALYZE THE TEXTS

Possible answers:

1. **DOK 3:** "The Minister's Black Veil" is set in a small New England town during the time of the Puritans; "The Pit and the Pendulum" is set in the depths of a prison in Spain during the Inquisition. A small town in which people consider their piety of utmost importance is an appropriate setting for probing the human nature of religious people. A prison is an appropriate setting in which to explore human responses to grotesque punishment.

2. **DOK 4:** In "The Minister's Black Veil," the reaction of the townspeople to the minister's veil is central to the theme. Hawthorne explores the changing response from initial shock and dismay to eventual awe at and approval of the minister for what is seen as heightened virtue. Since Hawthorne reveals little of the minister's actual thoughts, this response reinforces the theme of the secrets buried in the human heart and the possible misperceptions by others. In "The Pit and the Pendulum," the main character is essentially in the scene alone, though he is acted upon by unseen jailors. This arrangement intensifies the focus on his perception of the experience and his sense of persecution, reinforcing Poe's theme of the resilience or fragility of the individual psyche in an extreme situation.

3. **DOK 4:** Answers will vary, but should include clear examples of word choice, imagery, and plot details that contribute to the dark and ominous mood of each story and relate to the two authors' themes.

4. **DOK 4:** Hawthorne does not tell why the minister wears the veil. Poe does not reveal who the narrator is and only suggests why he is being punished. In both cases, this ambiguity makes the reader focus on the reaction to the circumstances rather than the circumstances themselves. Poe focuses on the narrator's response to torture, and Hawthorne focuses on the townspeople's response to the veil.

 RESPOND

Collaborate & Compare

COMPARE THEMES

Collaborate to Synthesize Comparing works of literature from the same historical period can deepen your understanding of each work's themes and provide an insight into issues and ideas important in that period. "The Minister's Black Veil" and "The Pit and the Pendulum" represent two different strains of American Romanticism. Poe is considered a master of Gothic literature. Hawthorne's work is subtler and more psychologically probing, but reflects a shared interest in the darker side of the human mind.

In a small group, complete the chart with similarities and differences in the two texts you read. One example is completed for you. Add rows as your group generates more ideas.

THE MINISTER'S BLACK VEIL
by Nathaniel Hawthorne

THE PIT AND THE PENDULUM
by Edgar Allan Poe

SIMILARITIES	DIFFERENCES
Both use suspense and ambiguity to create a sense of dread	"Minister": main character interacts with others "Pit": other characters unseen
Both use objects that evoke fear and death: pit, pendulum, veil	"Minster" takes place in small Puritan town; "Pit" takes place in dark prison
Both concern some kind of sin or crime the reader does not fully understand	"Minster" is in third person and spans many years; "Pit" is in first person and takes place in a short time

ANALYZE THE TEXTS

Discuss these questions in your group, paraphrasing and summarizing the text when needed and using academic vocabulary.

1. **Cite Evidence** What is the setting of each story? How does each setting relate to ideas and themes the writer presents?

2. **Synthesize** Compare and contrast the social context of the characters in both stories. How do their interactions with others contribute to the themes of the two works?

3. **Analyze** Select two short passages from each story and identify details that contribute to a dark and ominous mood. How do these details support the themes of each work? Consider word choice, imagery, and plot details in your response.

4. **Analyze** How does each author use ambiguity or uncertainty to add interest and to advance his themes? Cite an example of ambiguity in each story and describe its effect.

EL **ENGLISH LEARNER SUPPORT**

Ask Questions Use the following questions to help students synthesize and compare the selections.

1. What do you know and not know about the narrator in "The Pit and the Pendulum?" What do you know and not know about the minister in "The Minister's Black Veil"?

2. How are both Poe's narrator and Mr. Hooper alone? How is each one's situation different?

3. Where does each story take place? Why is each setting important to its story?
   MODERATE/LIGHT

COLLABORATE AND PRESENT

Now your group can continue exploring the ideas in these texts by identifying and comparing their themes. Follow these steps:

1. **Decide on the most important details** With your group, review your chart to identify the key similarities and differences in the two stories. Identify points you agree on and collaboratively offer ideas, resolving disagreements through discussions based on evidence from the texts.

2. **Create theme statements** Determine a theme statement for each story. Remember, it is up to you and your group to use details to infer the themes and determine the implicit meaning of the texts. You can use a chart to determine the themes each writer suggests.

Characters	Plot	Setting
Mr. Hooper, Elizabeth, physician, dead girl, Reverend Clark, Mr. Moody, people of the congregation	A minister begins wearing a mysterious veil, which frightens people. Over time, the veil becomes a sign of a shared human condition.	A small town full of pious yet gossipy Puritans whose religious beliefs focus on sin

Theme Statements

Sin and death are part of being human, so people should comfort and share their true selves with one another.

3. **Compare themes** With your group, discuss whether the themes of the stories are similar or different. Listen actively to the members of your group and ask them to clarify any points you do not understand. Be sure to use text evidence supplemented by original ideas.

4. **Present to the class** Finalize your ideas as a group. Create a formal presentation that has a logical structure, smooth transitions, accurate evidence, and well-chosen details. Present your ideas to the class. Be sure to include clear statements on the themes of each story. Compare and contrast the stories' themes to highlight the different purposes of the two authors. Think about using visuals to help convey information to the class. Make sure every member of the group takes part in the presentation.

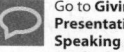 Go to **Giving a Presentation** in the **Speaking and Listening Studio** for help.

© Houghton Mifflin Harcourt Publishing Company

COLLABORATE AND PRESENT

Explain to students that the culmination of the small group's work together will be a presentation comparing the themes of the two stories. Review the requirements of Step 4 (Present to the class) before students begin their discussion.

1. **Decide on the most important details** Students should focus on points of comparison that seem most significant in determining the themes. Since students will need a clear sense of each story's theme to choose the best details, this initial step may take longer than the others. Plan adequate time and support to get students off to a good start. Groups may wish to begin using the graphic organizer to collect these details. They will need to create an additional graphic organizer for each story. A sample is shown for "The Minister's Black Veil."

2. **Create theme statements** Students now need to articulate a clear and concise statement of the theme for each story. Remind students that a theme is the message about human nature or society the author wants to share.

3. **Compare themes** Students should use their theme statements as well as the text evidence that support those statements for the comparison.

4. **Present to the class** Before groups present, have them divide up responsibilities and run through the presentation several times before giving it to the entire class. Encourage them to create charts or slides to help listeners understand their main ideas.

WHEN STUDENTS STRUGGLE . . .

Determine the Theme A theme can be difficult for students to determine because it must be inferred based on details in the text. Remind students that one way to infer the theme is to think about how the main characters act and interact, what motivates their behavior, how they solve the conflict, and how the characters change or do not change. Have students create a character chart with the following heads: *Actions, Motivations, Conflict, Change.* Have students reread each story and record details for each category. Then, have pairs determine the theme.

 For additional support, go to the **Reading Studio** and assign the following LEVEL **Level Up Tutorial: Theme.**

READER'S CHOICE

Setting a Purpose Have students review their Unit 3 Response Logs and think about what they've already learned about the role of the individual in society. As they choose their Independent Reading selections, encourage them to consider what more they want to know.

NOTICE NOTE

Explain that some selections may contain multiple signposts; others may contain only one. And the same type of signpost can occur many times in the same text.

 LEARNING MINDSET

Plan/Predict Encourage students to make a plan for completing their assignments, including mapping out the steps. Tell them that the table on this page will help them with this task.

 INDEPENDENT READING

 ESSENTIAL QUESTION:

Review the four Essential Questions for this unit on page 205.

Reader's Choice

Setting a Purpose Select one or more of these options from your eBook to continue your exploration of the Essential Questions.

- Read the descriptions to see which text grabs your interest.
- Think about which genres you enjoy reading.

NOTICE NOTE

In this unit, you practiced noticing and noting the signposts and asking big questions about nonfiction. As you read independently, these signposts and others will aid your understanding. Below are the anchor questions to ask when you read literature and nonfiction.

Reading Literature: Stories, Poems, and Plays	
Signpost	**Anchor Question**
Contrasts and Contradictions	Why did the character act that way?
Aha Moment	How might this change things?
Tough Questions	What does this make me wonder about?
Words of the Wiser	What's the lesson for the character?
Again and Again	Why might the author keep bringing this up?
Memory Moment	Why is this memory important?

Reading Nonfiction: Essays, Articles, and Arguments	
Signpost	**Anchor Question(s)**
Big Questions	What surprised me? What did the author think I already knew? What challenged, changed, or confirmed what I already knew?
Contrasts and Contradictions	What is the difference, and why does it matter?
Extreme or Absolute Language	Why did the author use this language?
Numbers and Stats	Why did the author use these numbers or amounts?
Quoted Words	Why was this person quoted or cited, and what did this add?
Word Gaps	Do I know this word from someplace else? Does it seem like technical talk for this topic? Do clues in the sentence help me understand the word?

© Houghton Mifflin Harcourt Publishing Company

ENGLISH LEARNER SUPPORT

Develop Fluency Select a passage from the text that matches students' reading abilities. Read the passage aloud while students follow along silently.

- Read aloud a brief passage from one of the selections to model for students. Then, have them read it back to you. Have students reread the passage three times. Check their comprehension by asking yes/no questions about the passage. **SUBSTANTIAL**

- Have pairs of students take turns reading and rereading the passage aloud to each other. Then, have the partners time each other to track

their improvement. **MODERATE**

- Allow more fluent readers to select their own texts. Set a specific time for them to read silently, such as 30 minutes. To check their comprehension, have them write a summary of what they have read. **LIGHT**

Go to the **Reading Studio** for additional support in developing fluency.

You can preview these texts in Unit 3 of your eBook.

Then, check off the text or texts that you select to read on your own.

ESSAY

from **Nature**

from **Self-Reliance**

Ralph Waldo Emerson

How can you live as an individual, relate to nature, and be your own master?

ARTICLE

The Pointlessness of Unplugging

Casey N. Cep

What happens when people unplug from their digital devices?

POEM

The Raven

Edgar Allan Poe

Does the raven relieve a grieving man of his painful burden of memories?

POEM

Pastoral

Jennifer Chang

Find out how a poet's vivid images and wordplay can place you in a field of flowers.

Collaborate and Share With a partner, discuss what you learned from at least one of your independent readings.

- Give a brief synopsis or summary of the text.
- Describe any signposts that you noticed in the text and explain what they revealed to you.
- Describe what you most enjoyed or found most challenging about the text. Give specific examples.
- Decide if you would recommend the text to others. Why or why not?

 Go to the **Reading Studio** for more resources on **Notice & Note**.

MATCHING STUDENTS TO TEXTS

Use the following information to guide students in choosing their texts.

from **Nature**   Lexile: 990L
from **Self-Reliance**   Lexile: 980L
   Genre: essay
   Overall Rating: Challenging

The Pointlessness of Unplugging   Lexile: 1190L
   Genre: article
   Overall Rating: Accessible

The Raven
   Genre: poem
   Overall Rating: Accessible

Pastoral
   Genre: poem
   Overall Rating: Challenging

Collaborate and Share To assess how well students read the selections, walk around the room and listen to their conversations. Encourage students to be focused and specific in their comments.

 Online **for Assessment**

- Independent Reading Selection Tests

 Encourage students to visit the **Reading Studio** to download a handy bookmark of **NOTICE & NOTE** signposts.

WHEN STUDENTS STRUGGLE . . .

Keep a Reading Log As students read their selected texts, have them keep a reading log for each selection to note signposts and their thoughts about them. Use their logs to assess how well they are noticing and reflecting on elements of their texts.

Reading Log for (title)		
Location	**Signpost I Noticed**	**My Notes about It**

UNIT ③ Task

- ## WRITE AN EXPLANATORY ESSAY

MENTOR TEXT

LAST CHILD IN THE WOODS
Essay by RICHARD LOUV

LEARNING OBJECTIVES

Writing Task

- Plan an explanatory essay, including a research question and sources.
- Perform background reading.
- Incorporate signposts.
- Effectively organize ideas.
- Develop a thesis related to the topic.
- Develop a draft.
- Use the Mentor Text to identify effective techniques.
- Use a revision chart to edit and improve the essay.
- Edit the essay to correct grammar and spelling.
- **Language** Ask for clarification using the key terms *detail* and *example*.

Assign the Writing Task in *Ed.*

Online
Ed

RESOURCES

- Unit 3 Response Log
- Writing Studio: Writing Informative Texts; Using Textual Evidence
- Grammar Studio: Module 3 Lesson 6: Semicolons and Colons

Language X-Ray: English Learner Support

Use the instruction below and the supports and scaffolds in the Teacher's Edition to help you guide students at different proficiency levels.

INTRODUCE THE WRITING TASK

Explain that an **explanatory essay** is a type of informational writing that examines and analyzes a topic or explains a topic. Make sure students understand they will be closely examining and writing their opinion about the essential question, *When should we stop and reflect on our lives?* Then, they will support their opinions with quotations and details from the texts.

Provide sentence frames to help students articulate their ideas, such as: *We should stop and reflect on our lives when _____. Stopping to reflect on our lives can help us _____.*

Brainstorm with students how the authors saw the individual and society interacting, and how they thought nature and self-reflection affected the relationship between individuals and society.

WRITING

Connect Ideas to Theme

Assist students as they connect their ideas and those of the authors to the concept of **reflection**. Have students create a word web or concept map to consider "When should we stop and reflect on our lives?"

Use the following supports with students at varying proficiency levels:

- Have students think about this question by suggesting words or phrases or drawing pictures in response. Add words to the web based on students' responses. **SUBSTANTIAL**
- Have students work with a partner to complete the organizer. Encourage them to review their notes about the unit selections as they add to the organizer. **MODERATE**
- Have students reread paragraph 3 of *Walden* and review the phrase *live deliberately*. Ask: *How does this phrase relate to the question?* Have students complete the graphic organizer. **LIGHT**

SPEAKING

Ask for Clarification

Have students present their essays to a partner. Provide a sentence frame for students to use as they ask for clarification. For example: *Why do you include this _____?*

- Provide a word bank to use with the sentence frame, such as: *statement, quotation, detail*. For example, *Why did you use this quotation?* Have students repeat the questions. **SUBSTANTIAL**
- Have partners write a list of words they can use when asking questions, such as: *thesis, claim, anecdote, quotation, detail, example,* and *restatement*. Have students use the word bank and sentence frame to orally state questions they can use to gain clarification. **MODERATE**
- Have students ask for clarification of the presentations after the discussion. Direct students to ask at least one *Why do you _____?* question about each presentation. **LIGHT**

WRITING

WRITE AN EXPLANATORY ESSAY

Introduce students to the Writing Task by reading the introductory paragraph with them. Remind students to refer to the notes they recorded in their Unit 3 Response Logs as they plan and draft their essays. Their Response Logs should contain ideas about relationships of the individual and society. Drawing on these different perspectives will make their own writing more interesting and well informed.

 For **writing support** for students at varying proficiency levels, see the **Language X-Ray** on page 316B.

USE THE MENTOR TEXT

Point out to students that their essays will be similar to the informational excerpt from *Last Child in the Woods* in that they will present facts and examples related to a topic. However, their essays will be shorter than the excerpt and will focus on the relationships of the individual and society.

WRITING PROMPT

Review the prompt with students. Encourage them to ask questions about any part of the assignment that is unclear. Make sure they understand that the purpose of their essays are to answer the question, using facts and examples from the texts they have read.

Write an Explanatory Essay

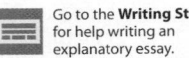 Go to the **Writing Studio** for help writing an explanatory essay.

This collection focuses on understanding ourselves and the relationship among self, society, and nature. For this writing task, you will write an explanatory essay—a type of informational writing that examines and analyzes a topic or explains a topic. For an example of a well-written explanatory essay you can use as a mentor text, review the excerpt from *Last Child in the Woods*.

As you write your explanatory essay, you can use the notes from your Response Log which you filled out after reading the texts in this unit.

Writing Prompt

Read the information in the box below.

This is the context for your explanatory essay.

> Society is made up of individuals who share space, share natural resources, and rely on each other.

Think carefully about the following question.

How might stopping and reflecting help people who rely on each other?

> When should we stop and reflect on our lives?

What information will you use to develop a topic and support a thesis in your explanatory essay?

Write an explanatory essay exploring this question, using your own ideas as well as ideas from two or more of the selections in this unit.

Review these points as you write and again when you finish. Make any needed changes.

Be sure to include—

- ❏ an introduction with a clear thesis statement about the relationships of the individual and society
- ❏ ideas from at least two selections from the unit
- ❏ a logically structured body that thoroughly develops the topic with relevant examples, details, and quotations from the texts
- ❏ transitions to clarify the relationships between sections of your essay and to link ideas with the textual evidence that supports them
- ❏ a conclusion that follows from the ideas in the body of the essay
- ❏ precise use of language with appropriate tone and style

 LEARNING MINDSET

Seeking Challenges Remind students that having the willingness to take on challenges is essential to having a learning mindset. In fact, overcoming challenges is key to developing skills and intelligence. Assure students they are not expected to be perfect, and making mistakes is part of the learning process. By taking risks and trying different strategies, students can learn to overcome challenges.

1 Plan

Before you start writing, you need to research and plan your essay. First, review your notes from the unit's selections on the individual and society. Work with a group to share ideas and discuss the following questions. Be prepared to discuss specific textual evidence.

- Which authors described ways to maintain a balance between the self and society? Did they engage with the outer world? Did they retreat from the issues of the day?
- Overall, did the authors present society and individuals in opposition or in harmony?

Now that you have discussed the topic with others, consider your own approach to the question "How can we maintain balance between the individual and society?" Decide which texts contain ideas about the connection between the self and society, and choose two or three that you feel best demonstrate these connections. Reread these selections, taking notes about what each one says about the relationship between the individual and society. Add quotations or ideas from the work. Be sure to note which selection you are using for quotations or ideas.

Explanatory Essay Planning Table	
Genre	
Topic	
Audience	
Ideas from Selection 1	
Ideas from Selection 2	
Ideas from Selection 3	

Background Reading Review the notes you have taken in your Response Log that relate to the question, "When should we stop and reflect on our lives?" Texts in this unit provide background reading that will help you formulate the key ideas you will include in your essay.

Go to **Using Textual Evidence: Summarizing, Paraphrasing, and Quoting** for help planning your explanatory essay.

Notice & Note

From Reading to Writing

As you plan your explanatory essay, apply what you've learned about signposts to your own writing. Remember that writers use common features, called signposts, to help convey their message to readers.

Think how you can incorporate **Contrasts and Contradictions** into your essay.

Go to the **Reading Studio** for more resources on **Notice & Note**.

Use the notes from your Response Log as you plan your explanatory essay.

Write an Explanatory Essay **317**

1 PLAN

Suggest that students write a working thesis based on the evidence they have identified. They can use this idea to help them choose which selections to review for supporting evidence. After reviewing their notes, they can refine their theses to fit the evidence from the selections they have chosen.

■ English Learner Support

Identify Cognates Suggest that English learners keep a list of cognates they find as they read the selections on which they will base their essays. Encourage them to try to use some of these cognates as they develop their essays. **MODERATE**

▶ NOTICE & NOTE

From Reading to Writing Remind students they can use Contrasts and Contradictions as they develop their essays. Tell them to explore differences between the points of views expressed in their chosen selections and why those differences are important.

Background Reading As students plan their essays, remind them to refer to the notes they took in their Response Logs. They may also review the selections to find additional facts and examples to support ideas they want to include in their writing.

TO CHALLENGE STUDENTS . . .

Gather Additional Evidence After students have gathered evidence from two or three selections in this unit, challenge them to look in outside sources for additional support for their theses. Ask students to consider how adding details, quotations, or examples from a greater variety of sources will help them develop their topics more thoroughly. Did they revise or refine their theses based on the additional evidence?

WRITING

Organize Your Ideas Suggest that students use a writing application to create an outline of their essays based on the organizational chart. Tell students their outlines should have one main section for each main idea in their essays. Provide the following sample based on the chart:

I. Introduction
(Thesis statement and detail)

II. Main Idea 1
(List Text Evidence)

III. Main Idea 2
(List Text Evidence)

IV. Main Idea 3
(List Text Evidence)

V. Conclusion

In this organizational pattern, each paragraph would introduce a specific idea about the relationships of the individual and society, such as how people share space, how they relate to natural resources, and how they rely on each other. By thinking about the details and examples they have gathered, students can select the best way to organize their essays.

② DEVELOP A DRAFT

Tell students they should establish a clear link between the thesis in their draft introductions and the main idea of each supporting paragraph. Although students should use the graphic organizer as a guide for writing, they should also be open to rearranging sections and taking their essays in a different direction if, while drafting, they discover a more effective way to make their key points or a more logical way to order them.

 Go to **Writing Informative Texts: Organizing Ideas** for help organizing your ideas.

Organize Your Ideas After you have gathered ideas from your planning activities, you need to organize them in a way that will help you draft your explanatory essay. Develop a strong thesis statement. Choose which textual evidence is the most relevant to your thesis statement and your main ideas. Select an interesting quotation or detail to accompany your thesis statement in the introduction. List some ideas for your concluding section. You can use the chart below to map out the organizational structure of your essay.

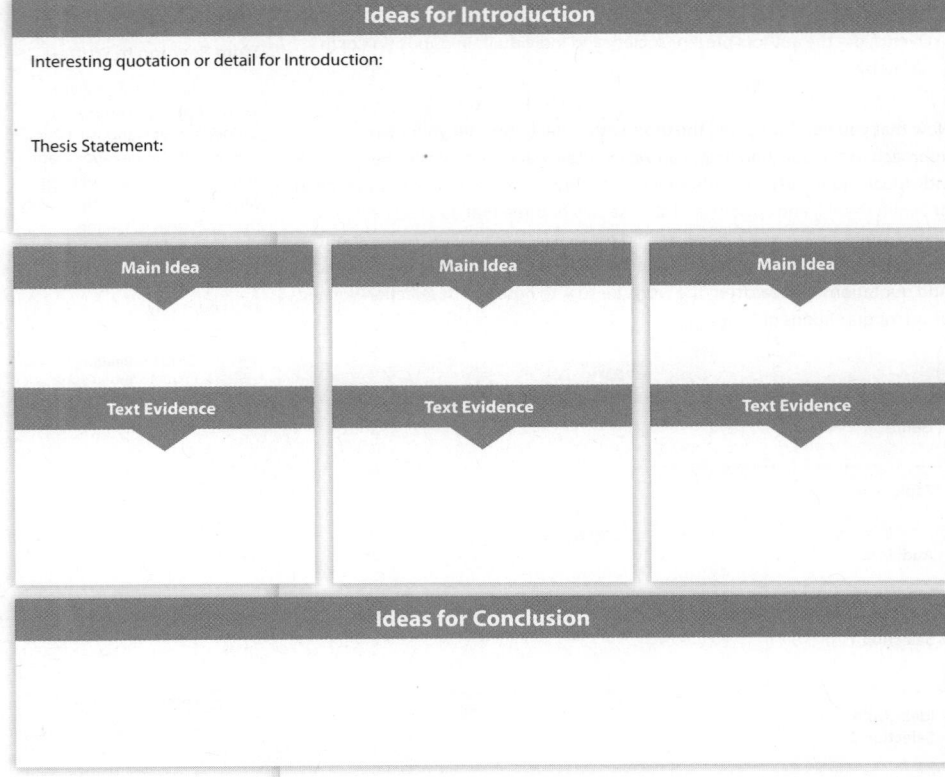

② Develop a Draft

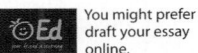 You might prefer to draft your essay online.

Once you have completed your planning activities, you will be ready to begin drafting your explanatory essay. Refer to your Graphic Organizers as well as any notes you took as you studied the texts in this unit. These will provide a kind of map for you to follow as you write. Using a word processor or online writing application makes it easier to make changes or move sentences around later when you are ready to revise your first draft.

© Houghton Mifflin Harcourt Publishing Company

WHEN STUDENTS STRUGGLE . . .

Add Relevant Evidence Have students work in pairs, using the following questions to help them evaluate the evidence in each other's draft:

- Which pieces of evidence are unclear? Why?
- What questions do you have about my central ideas?
- What types of evidence do you think would offer stronger support for my ideas?

Students should use the reviewer's feedback to add relevant facts, details, examples, or quotations to further develop their central ideas.

WRITING TASK

Use the Mentor Text

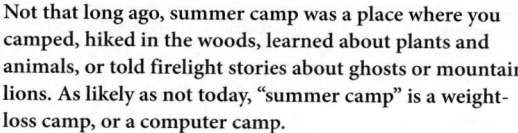

Structure and Purpose

Contrasts and comparisons are important in all types of writing. Fiction writers create characters with stark contrasts to highlight their differences or similarities. Informational writers include comparisons to help readers understand a new fact or process. Richard Louv compares his own childhood and modern childhood to show how the world has changed.

> Not that long ago, summer camp was a place where you camped, hiked in the woods, learned about plants and animals, or told firelight stories about ghosts or mountain lions. As likely as not today, "summer camp" is a weight-loss camp, or a computer camp.

Louv shows the way our attitudes toward nature have changed by using a "then and now" example regarding summer camp.

Apply What You've Learned Consider how you could use contrasts and comparisons to strengthen your main ideas. Can you compare being alone with being part of society, or being in nature with being in a city? What contrasts can help address the important distinctions between the individual and society?

Supporting Main Ideas

Writers of explanatory essays use a variety of evidence and details to support their thesis and main ideas. Personal experiences, quotations from famous authors, references to pop culture, and facts and statistics are all fair game—the art of the essay is tying it all together. Notice how Richard Louv uses examples from history and pop culture to introduce ideas and elaborate on them.

> A recent television ad depicts a four-wheel-drive SUV racing along a breathtakingly beautiful mountain stream—while in the backseat two children watch a movie on a flip-down video screen, oblivious to the landscape and water beyond the windows.

Louv gives an example of how children today do not appreciate nature. They would rather watch screens than look at nature.

Apply What You've Learned Choose one or two places in your plan where you can include evidence or details from history—for example, a charismatic individual or important event—or an element of pop culture, such as an advertisement or movie. Note these ideas in your Graphic Organizer.

WHY THIS MENTOR TEXT?

The excerpt from *Last Child in the Woods* provides a good example of explanatory writing. Use the instruction below to help students use the mentor text as a model for writing engaging introductions and for integrating facts and details into their essays.

USE THE MENTOR TEXT

Structure and Purpose Point out to students that this selection was not written as a stand-alone essay but as part of a longer book titled *Last Child in the Woods*. The selection begins with a dramatic scene that illustrates the main idea. Ask a volunteer to read aloud paragraph 4, where the author states the main idea of this excerpt. Then, ask students to identify the sentence in which Louv states his thesis. (*"Within the space of a few decades, the way children understand and experience nature has changed radically."*) Discuss possible reasons the author might have had for structuring the selection in this way and how it fit his purpose.

Supporting Main Ideas Have students reread the excerpt, identifying the main ideas as they do so. Then, have them examine the evidence and details Louv provides in support of those ideas. Ask volunteers to share the main ideas and their supporting details with the class. As they do so, have them identify each supporting detail as personal experience, history or pop culture, or fact or statistic. Ask them how the author makes use of direct or indirect quotations to support his thesis.

Write an Explanatory Essay 319

ENGLISH LEARNER SUPPORT

Understand Text Structure Have students work in pairs to decide how to organize their essays. Point out that they may focus each paragraph on a separate selection, or they may devote each paragraph to an idea and use information from all their chosen selections to support that idea. Provide students with the following questions to help them determine the most logical organization:

- How does the information I gathered from each text support my thesis?

- Does the evidence from each selection support different points about my thesis, or does each selection support similar ideas?

Encourage students to work with their partners to write two or three *How?* or *Why?* questions that their evidence helps answer about their theses.
LIGHT

WRITING

3 REVISE

Have students answer each question in the chart to determine how they can improve their drafts. Invite volunteers to model their revision techniques.

With a Partner Have students ask peer reviewers to evaluate their supporting evidence by answering the following questions:

- Which pieces of evidence are unclear? Why?
- What questions do you have about my main points?

Students should use the reviewer's feedback to add relevant facts, details, examples, or quotations that further develop their main points.

 WRITING TASK

3 Revise

 Go to **Writing Informative Texts: Precise Language and Vocabulary** for help revising your explanatory essay.

On Your Own Once you have written your draft, you'll want to go back and look for ways to improve your explanatory essay. As you reread and revise, think about whether you have achieved your purpose. The Revision Guide will help you focus on specific elements to make your writing stronger.

Revision Guide		
Ask Yourself	**Tips**	**Revision Techniques**
1. Does my introduction engage the reader and contain a thesis statement that clearly identifies the topic?	**Highlight** sentences that get the audience interested. **Underline** your thesis statement.	**Add** vivid language and details to interest the reader. **Reword** your thesis statement to **clarify** the topic.
2. Do I present relevant text evidence to support my thesis statement and central ideas?	**Highlight** each central idea. **Underline** evidence that supports each idea and **note** evidence that seems weak.	**Add** evidence for any idea that is not supported. **Change** evidence that does not offer strong support.
3. Is my essay logically organized with smooth transitions linking ideas and evidence?	**Note** major sections that reflect your organization. **Underline** each transitional word or phrase.	**Reorder** paragraphs if needed. **Add** transitions to **clarify** relationships between ideas.
4. Do I use formal, precise language?	**Highlight** slang and informal language.	**Reword** text to avoid informal language.
5. Does my conclusion follow logically from the ideas I present?	**Note** where the conclusion summarizes your ideas.	**Add** a closing statement if needed to sum up the information your essay presents.

ACADEMIC VOCABULARY

As you conduct your **peer review,** be sure to use these words.

- ❏ analogy
- ❏ denote
- ❏ quote
- ❏ topic
- ❏ unique

With a Partner Once you and your partner have worked through the Revision Guide on your own, exchange explanatory essays and evaluate each other's draft in a **peer review.** Focus on providing revision suggestions for at least three of the items mentioned in the chart. Explain why you think your partner's draft should be revised and what your specific suggestions are.

When receiving feedback from your partner, listen attentively and ask questions to make sure you fully understand the revision suggestions.

EL ENGLISH LEARNER SUPPORT

Write and Revise Encourage students to use a writing application to write their essays. Allow them to use simple sentences for their first drafts, and if necessary, to write in their native language when they have difficulty expressing their ideas in English. They can then use a translation application to help them interpret their words into English. Then, have them work in pairs with native speakers to revise their essays into idiomatic English. **SUBSTANTIAL/MODERATE**

4 Edit

Once you have addressed the organization, development, and flow of ideas in your explanatory essay, you can look to improve the finer points of your draft. Edit for the proper use of standard English conventions and make sure to correct any spelling or grammatical errors.

Language Conventions

Use Semicolons Authors have unique styles to communicate information. One characteristic of Richard Louv's style is his use of semicolons to form compound and compound-complex sentences. He often uses semicolons rather than a comma and conjunction to mimic the way people think or speak and to create a rhythm in his writing. Semicolons also add clarity to writing and can draw attention to specific ideas or closely connect two ideas.

Notice how Louv uses semicolons to connect ideas in *Last Child in the Woods*.

Purpose	Example
To separate two independent clauses that are linked by a conjunction when the sentence already contains a number of commas	The postmodern notion that reality is only a construct—that we are what we program—suggests limitless human possibilities; but as the young spend less and less of their lives in natural surroundings, their senses narrow, physiologically and psychologically, and this reduces the richness of human experience.
To separate parts of a compound sentence that are not joined by a coordinating conjunction or adverb	But my son was serious; he felt he had missed out on something important. But I knew my woods and my fields; I knew every bend in the creek and dip in the beaten dirt paths.

5 Publish

Finalize your explanatory essay and choose a way to share it with your audience. Consider these options:

- Present your essay as a speech or video recording.
- Post your essay as a blog on a classroom or school website.

WRITING TASK

! Go to **Semicolons and Colons** in the **Grammar Studio** to learn more.

---

4 EDIT

Have students look for places in their drafts where short sentences can be combined into compound sentences using semicolons. Encourage them to use transitional words and phrases. Point out that words and phrases such as *unlike, in contrast to, on the other hand, however,* and *nevertheless* signal that two things are different, whereas the words *also, similarly, like,* and *the same as* signal that two things are alike.

LANGUAGE CONVENTIONS

Use Semicolons Remind students that a compound sentence consists of two or more independent clauses. The clauses in compound sentences are joined with commas and coordinating conjunctions (*and, but, or, nor, yet, for, so*) or with semicolons, whereas a compound-complex sentence contains two or more independent clauses and one or more subordinate clauses.

■ English Learner Support

Use Semicolons Encourage English learners to work in pairs with native speakers to revise their essays, looking for simple sentences that can be combined into compound or compound-complex sentences. **MODERATE**

5 PUBLISH

Set aside a bulletin board "For Writers Only" in a place where students will have an opportunity to stop and read what is posted. Encourage students to post their essays for others to read, and encourage them to read and post comments on each other's writing.

WHEN STUDENTS STRUGGLE . . .

Use Semicolons Some students may have trouble using semicolons. Reassure them that semicolons are optional, and it is better to avoid them than to misuse them. Have students reread the three examples above and replace the semicolons with periods. Point out that this does not change the meaning of what is being said, only the rhythm of the writing.

WRITING

USE THE SCORING GUIDE

Allow students time to read the scoring guide and to ask questions about any words, phrases, or ideas that are unclear. Then, have partners exchange final drafts of their explanatory essays. Ask them to score their partner's essay using the scoring guide. Each student should write a paragraph explaining the reasons for the score he or she awarded in each category.

Use the scoring guide to evaluate your essay.

Writing Task Scoring Guide: Explanatory Essay

	Organization/Progression	Development of Ideas	Use of Language and Conventions
4	• The organization is effective and logical and appropriate to the task and purpose. • Transition words and phrases effectively link related ideas and evidence.	• The introduction engages the reader's attention and includes a thesis statement that clearly addresses the prompt. • The topic is strongly developed with relevant facts, concrete details, interesting quotations, and examples from the texts. • The concluding section follows from and supports the ideas presented.	• The writing reflects a formal style. • Language is vivid and precise. • Sentence structures vary and have a rhythmic flow. • Spelling, capitalization, and punctuation are correct. • Grammar and usage are correct.
3	• The organization is for the most part appropriate to the task and purpose. • Progression of ideas mostly flows smoothly. Transitions are needed in a few places to link related ideas and evidence.	• The introduction could do more to attract the reader's curiosity; the thesis statement identifies the topic. • One or two key points could use additional support in the form of relevant facts, concrete details, quotations, and examples from the texts. • The concluding section mostly follows from and supports the ideas presented.	• The style is inconsistent in a few places. • Vague language is used in a few places. • Sentence structures vary somewhat. • Some spelling, capitalization, and punctuation mistakes occur. • Some grammatical and usage errors are repeated in the report.
2	• The organization is confusing in some places and often doesn't follow a logical order. • More transition words and phrases are needed throughout to link ideas and evidence.	• The introduction provides some information about a topic, but the thesis statement is weak or unclear. • Most key points need additional support in the form of relevant facts, concrete details, quotations, and examples from the texts. • The concluding section is confusing and does not follow from the ideas presented.	• The style and tone are too informal. • Vague, general language is used in many places. • Sentence structures barely vary, and some fragments or run-on sentences are present. • Spelling, capitalization, and punctuation are often incorrect but do not make reading the report difficult. • Grammar and usage are incorrect in many places, but the writer's ideas are still clear.
1	• A logical organization is not used; information is presented randomly. • Transitions are not used, making the essay difficult to understand.	• The response to the prompt is vague or confused. • The thesis statement is missing or unclear. • Facts, details, quotations, and examples from the texts are missing or unrelated to the topic or thesis. • The essay lacks an identifiable concluding section.	• The style and tone are inappropriate for the essay. • Language is too vague or general to convey the information. • Repetitive sentence structure, fragments, and run-on sentences make the writing monotonous and difficult to follow. • Spelling, capitalization, and punctuation are incorrect throughout. • Many grammatical and usage errors change the meaning of the writer's ideas.

Reflect on the Unit

By completing your explanatory essay, you have created a writing product that pulls together and expresses your thoughts about the reading you have done in this unit. Now is a good time to reflect on what you have learned.

Reflect on the Essential Questions

- Review the four Essential Questions on page 205. How have your answers to these questions changed in response to the texts you've read in this unit?

- What are some examples from the texts you've read that show how people interact with others and society while remaining true to themselves?

Reflect on Your Reading

- Which selections were the most interesting or surprising to you?

- From which selection did you learn the most about the relationship between the individual and society?

Reflect on the Writing Task

- What difficulties did you encounter while working on your explanatory essay? How might you avoid them next time?

- What part of the explanatory essay was the easiest to write? the hardest to write? Why?

- What improvements did you make to your explanatory essay as you were revising?

UNIT 3 SELECTIONS

- from "Song of Myself"
- "My Friend Walt Whitman"
- Poems of Emily Dickinson: "The Soul selects her own Society," "Because I could not stop for Death," "Much Madness is divinest Sense," "Tell all the Truth, but tell it slant"
- "In the Season of Change"
- from *Walden*
- from *Last Child In the Woods*
- "The Minister's Black Veil"
- "The Pit and The Pendulum"

REFLECT ON THE UNIT

Have students reflect on the questions independently and write some notes in response to each one. Then, have students meet with partners or in small groups to discuss their reflections. Circulate during these discussions to identify the questions that are generating the liveliest conversations. Wrap up with a whole-class discussion focused on these questions.

LEARNING MINDSET

Self-Reflection Point out that self-reflection can be a valuable tool for improving students' skills. Reflection can help them realize where they made mistakes and how to avoid making them again. It can also help them figure out what worked well for them and how to use those successful strategies in the future.

Instructional Overview and Resources

	Instructional Focus	**Online Ed Resources**

**Unit Introduction
The Quest for Freedom**

Instructional Focus

Unit 4 Essential Question
Unit 4 Academic Vocabulary

Resources

Stream to Start: The Quest for Freedom

Unit 4 Response Log

ANALYZE & APPLY

Second Inaugural Address
Speech by Abraham Lincoln
Lexile 1160L

Reading
• Analyze Argumentative Texts
• Analyze Author's Purpose

Writing: Write a Letter

Speaking and Listening: Discuss and Evaluate a Speech

Vocabulary: Pronunciation

Language Conventions: Balanced Sentences

🔊 **Audio**

Close Read Screencast: Modeled Discussion

Reading Studio: Notice & Note

Writing Studio: Writing as a Process

Speaking and Listening Studio: Participating in Collaborative Discussions

---

"To My Old Master"
Letter by Jourdon Anderson
Lexile 1190L

Reading
• Analyze Letters
• Analyze Tone

Writing: Write a Biographical Essay

Speaking and Listening: Give a Presentation

Vocabulary: Use Sentence Structure to Determine Meaning of Words

Language Conventions: Noun Clauses

🔊 **Audio**

Reading Studio: Notice & Note

Writing Studio: Developing a Topic

Speaking and Listening Studio: Giving a Presentation

Vocabulary Studio: Words with Multiple Meanings

Grammar Studio: The Noun Clause

Civil War Photographs
Image Collection by Mathew Brady, Alexander Gardner, and Andrew J. Russell
Lexile N/A

Reading
• Make Connections
• Analyze Media Effectiveness

Writing: Write a Didactic Placard

Speaking and Listening: Hold a Debate

🔊 **Audio**

Reading Studio: Notice & Note

Speaking and Listening Studio: Analyzing and Evaluating Presentations

---

"An Occurrence at Owl Creek Bridge"
Short Story by Ambrose Bierce
Lexile 1000L

Reading
• Analyze Literary Elements
• Analyze Structure

Writing: Write a Short Story

Speaking and Listening: Share Your Story

Vocabulary: Etymology

Language Conventions: Sensory Language

🔊 **Audio**

Reading Studio: Notice & Note

Writing Studio: Writing Narratives

Vocabulary Studio: Word Origins

**SUGGESTED PACING:
30 DAYS**

Unit Introduction	Second Inaugural Address	To My Old Master	Civil War Photographs	An Occurrence at Owl Creek Bridge
1	2 3 4	5 6 7 8	9 10 11	12 13 14

English Language Support		Differentiated Instruction	Online Ed Assessment
• Learn New Expressions • Build Background Knowledge • Understand Prefixes		**When Students Struggle** • Concept Support	
• Text X-Ray • Analyze Details • Confirm Understanding • Oral Assessment • Use Cognates • Language Conventions		**When Students Struggle** • Develop Reading Fluency	**Selection Test**
• Text X-Ray • Use Cognates • Understand Tone • Oral Assessment • Sound Transfer • Language Conventions		**When Students Struggle** • Inferences • Make Inferences	**Selection Test**
• Text X-Ray • Connect with Images • Compare and Contrast Photographs • Oral Assessment		**When Students Struggle** • Analyze Images	**Selection Test**
• Text X-Ray • Understand Expressions • Use Cognates • Understand Point of View • Understand Plot	• Understand Sensory Language • Understand Imagery • Acquire Related Vocabulary • Oral Assessment • Build Vocabulary with Cognates • Use Language Details	**When Students Struggle** • Analyze Structure • Understand Complex Sentences • Analyze Plot **To Challenge Students** • Analyze Personification and Tone • Analyze Realism	**Selection Test**

Building the Transcontinental Railroad
15 16 17 18

Declaration of Sentiments / Speech to the American Equal Rights Association
19 20 21 22

Runagate Runagate / from Incidents in the Life of a Slave Girl
23 24 25

Independent Reading
26 27

End of Unit
28 29 30

UNIT 4 Continued

	Instructional Focus	Online Ed Resources

"Building the Transcontinental Railroad"
History Writing by Iris Chang
Lexile 1310L

Reading
• Analyze Informational Texts
• Analyze Author's Purpose

Writing: Write a Historical Report

Speaking and Listening: Discuss with a Small Group

Vocabulary: Context Clues

Language Conventions: Avoid Misplaced Modifiers

🔊 **Audio**

Reading Studio: Notice & Note

Writing Studio: Conducting Research

Speaking and Listening Studio: Participating in Collaborative Discussions

Vocabulary Studio: Using Context Clues

Grammar Studio: Placement of Modifiers

COLLABORATE & COMPARE

Mentor Text
Declaration of Sentiments
Argument by Elizabeth Cady Stanton
Lexile 1430L

Speech to the American Equal Rights Association
Speech by Sojourner Truth
Lexile 620L

Reading
• Analyze and Evaluate Arguments
• Analyze Author's Purpose

Writing: Write a Comparison-and-Contrast Essay

Speaking and Listening: Give a Dramatic Reading

Vocabulary: Suffixes

Language Conventions: Rhetorical Devices

🔊 **Audio**

Reading Studio: Notice & Note

Writing Studio: Writing Informative Texts

Speaking and Listening Studio: Giving a Presentation

Vocabulary Studio: Common Roots, Prefixes, and Suffixes

Collaborate and Compare

Reading: Compare Arguments

Speaking and Listening Studio: Participating in Collaborative Discussions

"Runagate Runagate"
Poem by Robert Hayden
Lexile N/A

Reading
• Analyze Speaker and Voice
• Analyze Sound Devices: Rhythm
• Analyze Language: Allusion

Writing: Write a Literary Analysis

Speaking and Listening: Present a Dramatic Reading

🔊 **Audio**

Reading Studio: Notice & Note

Speaking and Listening Studio: Giving a Presentation

from Incidents in the Life of a Slave Girl
Autobiography by Harriet Jacobs
Lexile 810L

Reading
• Analyze Literary Elements
• Analyze Language

Writing: Write an Autobiographical Sketch

Speaking and Listening: Share and Discuss Characters

Vocabulary: Synonyms

Language Conventions: Dialect and Idioms

🔊 **Audio**

Reading Studio: Notice & Note

Writing Studio: Writing Narratives

Speaking and Listening Studio: Participating in Collaborative Discussions

Vocabulary Studio: Synonyms and Antonyms

Collaborate and Compare

Reading: Compare Writer's Voice

English Language Support	Differentiated Instruction	Online Ed Assessment
• Text X-Ray • Use Cognates • Identify Chronological Words • Understand Modifiers • Understand Archaic Language • Understand Idioms • Understand Cause and Effect • Oral Assessment • Language Conventions	**When Students Struggle** • Understand Arguments • Reteach: Analyze Chronological Order **To Challenge Students** • Research Historical Detail • Use Research Techniques • Analyze Tone	**Selection Test**
• Text X-Ray • Use Cognates • Develop Vocabulary and Language Structures • Read with Accommodations and Support • Oral Assessment • Understand Idioms • Understand Similes • Use Patterns of Word Change • Use Rhetorical Devices • Ask Questions	**When Students Struggle** • Read for Meaning • Make Predictions • Reteach: Analyze Author's Purpose **To Challenge Students** • Imagery • Create a Podcast Interview	**Selection Test**
• Text X-Ray • Understand Sentence Structure • Use Reading Strategies • Oral Assessment	**When Students Struggle** • Understand Voice and Rhythm • Reteach: Analyze Allusions	**Selection Test**
• Text X-Ray • Use Cognates • Use Antonyms • Oral Assessment • Practice Pronunciation • Ask Questions	**When Students Struggle** • Understand Characterization • Reteach: Diction and Syntax **To Challenge Students** • Synthesize	**Selection Test**

UNIT 4 Continued

INDEPENDENT READING

The Independent Reading selections are only available in the eBook.

Go to the Reading Studio for more information on NOTICE & NOTE.

"Letter to Sarah Ballou"
Letter by Sullivan Ballou
Lexile 1230L

from *A Diary from Dixie*
Diary by Mary Chestnut
Lexile 680L

END OF UNIT

Writing Task: Write an Argument

Speaking Task: Debate an Issue

Reflect on the Unit

Writing: Write an Argument

Speaking and Listening: Debate an Issue

Unit 4 Response Log

Mentor Text: Declaration of Sentiments

Writing Studio: Writing Arguments

Grammar Studio: Verb Tense

Speaking and Listening Studio: Analyzing and Evaluating Presentations

English Learner Support	Differentiated Instruction	 Assessment

|  from "What to the Slave Is the Fourth of July?" Speech by Frederick Douglass **Lexile 1200L** |  "Go Down, Moses," "Follow the Drinking Gourd," "Swing Low, Sweet Chariot" Spirituals    "Imagine the Angels of Bread" Poem by Martín Espada | **Selection Tests** |

English Learner Support	Differentiated Instruction	Assessment
• Language X-Ray • Understand Implicit Language • Cooperative Learning • Build Background Knowledge • Use Transitional Phrases • Use Verb Tenses • Monitor Speaking Techniques	**When Students Struggle** • Develop Claims • Consistency in Verb Tense • Plan to Present an Argument **To Challenge Students** • Add Multimedia Elements	**Unit Test**

DISCUSS THE QUOTATION

Born in 1898, Paul Robeson was a gifted athlete, singer, actor, scholar, author, and political activist. He visited Moscow in the 1930s, and for the first time found a place where, as an African American, he did not feel racial prejudice. For the rest of his life he was an enthusiastic supporter of the Soviet regime. In the 1940s, he used his celebrity to campaign against racial segregation, but in the 1950s, the FBI tried to silence him by sabotaging his career—he was banned from performance venues, radio stations refused to play his songs, and his records were no longer available in stores. In 1956, he was called before the House Un-American Activities Committee, which was investigating suspected Communist sympathizers. This quotation is part of his response when he was asked why he came back to the United States.

Ask students to think about what it would be like to be the child of a slave living in a country where they were routinely denied equal rights. How would that experience shape their view of the world?

■ English Learner Support

Learn New Expressions Point out to students that the phrase "have a part of it" means that Robeson wanted to be involved in some way in making life better in the United States. **SUBSTANTIAL**

THE QUEST FOR FREEDOM

THE CIVIL WAR AND ITS AFTERMATH

> My father was a slave and my people died to build this country, and I'm going to stay here and have a part of it.
>
> —Paul Robeson

324   Unit 4

🧠 LEARNING MINDSET

Effort Remind students that effort is necessary for growth. By making an effort, students can develop their talents and abilities to effectively overcome many of their perceived limitations. Through hard work, they can develop a powerful love of learning and a positive mental attitude that views failures as opportunities to improve their abilities.

Discuss the **Essential Questions** with your whole class or in small groups. As you read The Quest for Freedom, consider how the selections explore these questions.

? ESSENTIAL QUESTION:

When is self-determination possible?

Self-determination is the ability to decide one's own fate or course of action freely and without compulsion. The United States fought a war of independence for that right, but even in the "land of the free," there were many who were denied the right of self-determination. Enslaved Africans were considered property and could be forced to do whatever their owners wanted. Women often lacked self-determination in many areas of their lives, as well. What obstacles to self-determination still exist?

? ESSENTIAL QUESTION:

What divides us as human beings?

Throughout history, human beings have found many things to divide us: race, nationality, ethnicity, language, religion, gender, politics, social class, and occupation. In the first half of the 19th century, slavery was one of many issues that divided America. What issues divide Americans today? How can we focus on our similarities so we can live together in an inclusive society?

? ESSENTIAL QUESTION:

How do we face defeat?

Early in the Civil War, the North faced defeat after defeat at the hands of the South's military leaders. Despite these early setbacks, the North endured and its victory at the Battle of Gettysburg marked the turning point in the Civil War. After the war, parts of the South were in ruins, and the reunited country faced a long, difficult period of healing and rebuilding. What makes some shrink from defeat? What makes others rise to the challenge?

? ESSENTIAL QUESTION:

What is the price of progress?

During the 19th century, the United States progressed at a rapid pace—new frontiers were being explored and new inventions pushed the boundaries of farming and industry. However, there were unintended consequences to this swift march of progress. The environment suffered as rivers were diverted, forests cleared, mines dug, and oil wells drilled. To many people, especially those in cities, life felt frantic and soulless. Today, some prioritize progress above all else while others warn to proceed with caution. Is progress always worth the cost?

© Houghton Mifflin Harcourt Publishing Company

The Quest for Freedom 325

Connect to the

ESSENTIAL QUESTIONS

Read aloud the Essential Questions and the paragraphs that follow them. Open the discussion of each idea by having students respond to the questions that conclude each paragraph.

? ESSENTIAL QUESTION

When is self-determination possible?

Ask students if they can think of any groups or classes of people in the United States that still lack self-determination. What kinds of barriers still exist that can limit an individual's self-determination?

? ESSENTIAL QUESTION

What divides us as human beings?

Point out that our nation is still divided on many issues. Guide students in a discussion of some of the issues that divide Americans today. Then, have them brainstorm ways in which those divisions can be healed.

? ESSENTIAL QUESTION

How do we face defeat?

Ask volunteers to share instances in which a defeat has led them to keep trying and finally succeed. How do they think their earlier defeat changed how they felt when they succeeded?

? ESSENTIAL QUESTION

What is the price of progress?

Ask students how progress continues to affect the environment. Are the effects of progress always bad? What can be done to limit the adverse effects of progress?

THE CIVIL WAR AND ITS AFTERMATH

The following essay provides students with a historical context for the Unit 4 selections. It presents a brief overview of the events leading up to the Civil War, the positive and negative effects of the war, and the rise of realism in American literature.

Abolition Tell students that not all abolitionists used peaceful methods. In Kansas, violence between proslavery and antislavery settlers led people to begin calling the territory Bleeding Kansas. Abolitionist John Brown played a role in Bleeding Kansas in 1856, killing five proslavery men as revenge for an attack on the antislavery town of Lawrence. Three years later, Brown again shocked the nation when he led a bloody raid on the federal arsenal at Harpers Ferry, hoping to spark a slave uprising.

A Country Divided Point out that during the first half of the 19th century, some states were free states that forbade slavery, while others were slave states that allowed slavery. As newly settled territories achieved statehood, Congress wanted to maintain a balance between the northern free states and the southern slave states so that neither would have an advantage. A series of acts and compromises set up different rules for how such areas as the Northwest Territory, the Missouri Territory, and the land acquired during the Mexican-American War (1846–1848) would be divided and admitted to the union as free states or slave states.

COLLABORATIVE DISCUSSION

Ask volunteers to share their expectations with the class and guide the class in a discussion of them.

THE CIVIL WAR AND ITS AFTERMATH

Since colonial times, there had been sharp regional differences between the industrial North and the agrarian South. By the mid-1800s, the economy of the South had come to depend on its workforce of more than 3 million enslaved people. While some Americans settled for compromise, others pushed for an end to slavery and other social injustices.

Abolition Abolitionists—white and black, male and female—led the fight by forming organizations, holding conventions, publishing newspapers, and swamping Congress with petitions for the sole purpose of ending what many considered an evil institution—slavery. Narratives by abolitionists, such as Harriet Beecher Stowe, and former slaves, such as Frederick Douglass, helped bring the evils of slavery to life for many readers. In fact, Stowe's 1852 novel, *Uncle Tom's Cabin*, is cited as a contributing cause of the Civil War.

At the same time some were working to change the system, others were working to circumvent it. The Underground Railroad, an informal network of abolitionists, helped thousands of slaves escape to freedom. Many of the people working to free slaves were themselves not entirely free. Working for abolition made women more aware of the rights they had been denied. Elizabeth Cady Stanton, Lucretia Mott, and other reformers fought for women's rights, including the right to vote.

A Country Divided By 1850 the country was equally divided into free and slave states. In Congress, the debate raged on, with some claiming a state's right to choose for itself on the issue of slavery. Addressing the Illinois Republican Convention in 1858, Abraham Lincoln warned, "A house divided against itself cannot stand." Although Lincoln promised not to abolish slavery, he vowed to stop its spread. For him, the issue was more than a question of what each state wanted; it was a question of right and wrong.

When Lincoln was elected president in 1860, the southern states seceded and formed the Confederate States of America. In 1861, Confederates fired on Fort Sumter in South Carolina, and the Civil War began. Both sides expected a quick victory, but romantic ideals of heroism soon gave way to a harsher reality. By the end of the war in April 1865, approximately 620,000 men had died, nearly as many as have died in all other wars that the United States has ever fought.

COLLABORATIVE DISCUSSION
Based on what you have learned, what would you expect to be the major themes of literature from this period?

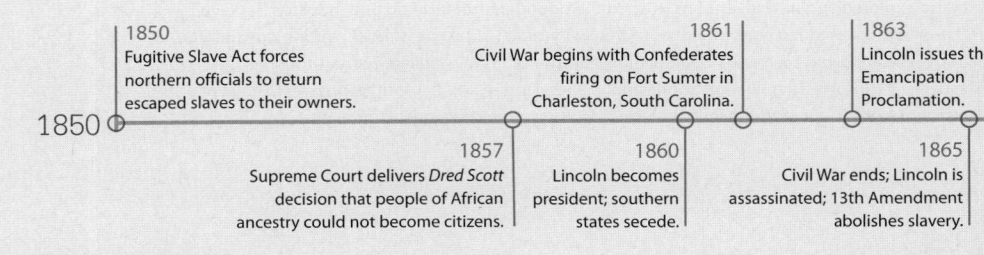

1850
1850 Fugitive Slave Act forces northern officials to return escaped slaves to their owners.

1857 Supreme Court delivers *Dred Scott* decision that people of African ancestry could not become citizens.

1860 Lincoln becomes president; southern states secede.

1861 Civil War begins with Confederates firing on Fort Sumter in Charleston, South Carolina.

1863 Lincoln issues the Emancipation Proclamation.

1865 Civil War ends; Lincoln is assassinated; 13th Amendment abolishes slavery.

326   Unit 4

 ENGLISH LEARNER SUPPORT

Build Background Knowledge To aid comprehension of the essay, provide students with the following definitions:

- *agrarian:* agricultural or farming
- *abolitionist:* someone who wants to do away with slavery
- *circumvent:* to go around or avoid

- *secede:* to withdraw formally from membership in a state or union
- *pronouncement:* a formal expression of opinion
- *unsentimental:* not showing emotion or tenderness   **ALL LEVELS**

Rebuilding a Nation With the end of the Civil War came the reunification of the United States. This period of healing and rebuilding came to be known as Reconstruction. During the war, Lincoln had issued the Emancipation Proclamation (1863), freeing all enslaved people in the South. After the war in 1865, the Thirteenth Amendment to the Constitution outlawed slavery everywhere in the United States. Despite the bitterness of the Civil War, Lincoln felt the South should not be punished for seceding. He wanted to bring the country back together peacefully and as quickly as possible. Unfortunately, Lincoln's plans for Reconstruction were cut short by his assassination within days of the war's end.

Some Republicans in Congress did not share Lincoln's views on Reconstruction. After his death, they imposed military rule on the South and passed laws to protect the rights of newly freed slaves, including the right to vote. During Reconstruction, projects that had been interrupted by the war resumed, and the United States continued its westward expansion. Construction of a transcontinental railroad had begun in 1862. In 1869 a golden spike was driven into the track at Promontory, Utah, marking the completion of the country's first nationwide railroad.

As Reconstruction dragged on, though, southerners gradually retook control of state governments in the South, passing laws to undermine the rights of African Americans. In 1877 a compromise allowed Republican Rutherford B. Hayes to become president in exchange for the end of federal control over the South. This event marked the end of Reconstruction.

Rebuilding a Nation After experiencing the horrors of a war in which family members had fought on opposite sides, the nation cautiously approached the process of healing its wounds and readmitting the Confederate states to the Union. Some southerners resisted the idea of granting equal rights to African Americans. Black codes passed in 1865 and 1866 by the governments of former Confederate states attempted to maintain white supremacy by severely restricting the rights of African Americans to do such things as own property and run certain businesses. Reconstruction technically abolished these laws. However, after Reconstruction ended in 1877, these laws were reenacted in the form of Jim Crow laws, which took their name from a derogatory term for African Americans. It was not until the Civil Rights Act passed in 1964 that full equal rights for all African Americans were guaranteed.

RESEARCH

To learn more about their chosen topic, encourage students to search for primary sources from the historical period. Have students choose excerpts from a source to present to the class.

RESEARCH

What about this historical period interests you? Choose a topic, event, or person to learn more about. Then add your own entry to the timeline.

1877
Compromise allows Hayes to become president; Reconstruction ends.

1880

1869
Transcontinental railroad is completed at Promontory, Utah.

WHEN STUDENTS STRUGGLE . . .

Concept Support After students read the section titled "A Country Divided," discuss the conflict between the high ideals held by the people who started the war and the terrible destruction that occurred once the war was underway. Have students work in pairs to make a two-column chart labeled *Positive* and *Negative*. In the first column, have them list the positive aspects of the Civil War, such as the end of slavery. In the second column, have them record the negative aspects of the war, such as the huge loss of life.

© Houghton Mifflin Harcourt Publishing Company • Image Credits: © Corbis via Getty Images

Rise of Realism The Civil War marked a time of great technological change and innovation in the tools of warfare. With new weapons came new and terrible kinds of destruction not previously experienced by troops. In his writing, Ambrose Bierce described the grim realities of the war that he encountered during his time as an officer in the Union Army. Although he was too young to have participated in the Civil War itself, Stephen Crane instead used his experiences working as a foreign war correspondent during conflicts like the Spanish-American War to write his classic 1895 Civil War novel *The Red Badge of Courage*. This book describes the carnage of battle and the inner feelings of a soldier struggling to find the courage to continue fighting in the war.

CHECK YOUR UNDERSTANDING

Have students answer the questions independently.

Answers:

1. *D*

2. *G*

3. *A*

If students answer any questions incorrectly, have them reread the text to confirm their understanding.

Rise of Realism The Civil War changed not only American society, but its literature as well. Northern and southern writers—black and white, male and female, high-ranking officers and lowly foot soldiers and the women they left behind—all expressed different perspectives on their wartime experiences through diaries and letters. In contrast to these personal accounts were the public pronouncements of President Lincoln, whose inspiring Gettysburg Address proved to be one of the most enduring works of the Civil War. After the war, writers rejected Romanticism and began writing honest, unsentimental, and ironic fiction. Called realists, writers such as Ambrose Bierce and Stephen Crane focused on the human tragedy of the war. These writers would have a notable impact on the writing that followed at the turn of the century.

CHECK YOUR UNDERSTANDING

Choose the best answer to each question.

1 What was the Underground Railroad?

  A The nation's first subway system

  B The nation's first transcontinental railroad

  C A railroad that ran from the southern United States to Canada

  D An informal network of abolitionists who helped slaves escape

2 Which of the following freed slaves in the South?

  F Lincoln's Gettysburg Address

  G Lincoln's Emancipation Proclamation

  H The Transcontinental Railroad

  J The end of Reconstruction

3 What was Reconstruction?

  A The period of rebuilding after the Civil War

  B The harsh new restrictions on African Americans

  C The compromise to allow Rutherford B. Hayes to become president

  D The process for constructing the first transcontinental railroad

ENGLISH LEARNER SUPPORT

Understand Prefixes Students may be unfamiliar with the meaning of prefixes that could help them decipher the meaning of complicated terms in this section. Review with students the meanings of prefixes such as *re-* ("again") and *trans-* ("across"). Have them work in pairs and use their understanding of the meaning of prefixes to figure out the meaning of words in "Rebuilding a Nation," such as *rebuilding, reunification, Reconstruction, retook,* and *transcontinental*. **MODERATE**

ACADEMIC VOCABULARY

Academic Vocabulary words are words you use when you discuss and write about texts. In this unit, you will learn the following five words:

☑ confirm ☐ definitely ☐ deny ☐ format ☐ unify

Study the Word Network to learn more about the word **confirm**.

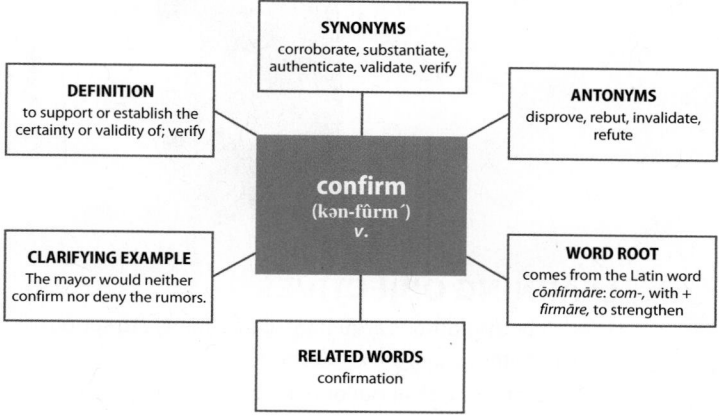

SYNONYMS
corroborate, substantiate, authenticate, validate, verify

DEFINITION
to support or establish the certainty or validity of; verify

ANTONYMS
disprove, rebut, invalidate, refute

confirm
(kən-fûrm´)
v.

CLARIFYING EXAMPLE
The mayor would neither confirm nor deny the rumors.

WORD ROOT
comes from the Latin word *cōnfirmāre*: *com-*, with + *firmāre*, to strengthen

RELATED WORDS
confirmation

Write and Discuss Discuss your completed Word Network with a partner, making sure to talk through all of the boxes until you both understand the word, its synonyms, antonyms, and related forms. Then, fill out a Word Network for the remaining four words. Use a dictionary or online resource to help you complete the activity.

Go online to access the Word Networks.

RESPOND TO THE ESSENTIAL QUESTIONS

In this unit, you will explore four different **Essential Questions** about the quest for freedom. As you read each selection, you will gather your ideas about these questions in the **Response Log** that appears on page R4. At the end of the unit, you will have the opportunity to write an **argument** related to one of the Essential Questions. Filling out the Response Log after you read each text will help you prepare for this writing task.

You can also go online to access the Response Log.

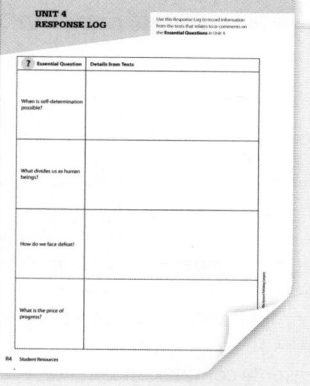

The Quest for Freedom   329

© Houghton Mifflin Harcourt Publishing Company

ACADEMIC VOCABULARY

Have students complete Word Networks for the remaining four vocabulary words. Encourage them to include all the categories shown in the completed network if possible, but point out that some words do not have clear synonyms or antonyms.

confirm (kən-fûrm´) *v.* to support or establish the certainty or validity of; verify (Spanish cognate: *confirmar*)

definitely (děf´ə-nĭt-lē) *adv.* in a clearly defined manner; explicitly precisely; decidedly

deny (dĭ-nī´) *tr.v.* to declare untrue; assert to be false; to refuse to believe

format (fôr´măt) *n.* a plan for the organization and arrangement of a specified production (Spanish cognate: *formato*)

unify (yo͞o´nə-fī) *v.* to make into or become a unit; consolidate (Spanish cognate: *unificar*)

RESPOND TO THE ESSENTIAL QUESTIONS

Direct students to the Unit 4 Response Log. Explain that students will use it to record ideas and details from the selections that help answer one of the Essential Questions. When they work on the Writing Task at the end of the unit, their Response Logs will help them think about what they have read and make connections between the texts.

SECOND INAUGURAL ADDRESS

Speech by Abraham Lincoln

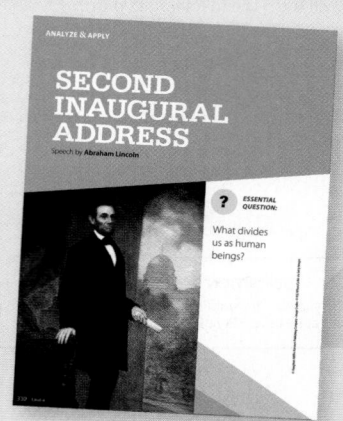

GENRE ELEMENTS
PERSUASIVE SPEECH

Remind students that a speech can be a type of **argumentative text.** The speaker presents a claim, or position about an issue, and attempts to persuade the audience to agree with this claim. The speaker provides specific pieces of information as support for the claim and uses word choices to appeal to the audience. In addition to the claim, supporting evidence, and persuasive strategy, a speech often includes a **call to action,** or request that the audience do something.

LEARNING OBJECTIVES

- Analyze the author's argument, cite evidence to support it, and identify the author's call to action.
- Conduct research about opposing consequences of the Civil War.
- Write a letter responding to Lincoln's address.
- Discuss and evaluate Lincoln's address.
- Use a dictionary to confirm correct pronunciation of words with silent letters.
- Identify examples of balanced statements.
- **Language** Discuss with a partner details from the selection.

TEXT COMPLEXITY

Quantitative Measures	**Second Inaugural Address**	Lexile: 1160
Qualitative Measures	**Ideas Presented** Most are implied but easy to infer.	
	Structures Used Both implicit compare-contrast and sequential order.	
	Language Used Mostly complex with varied sentence structure.	
	Knowledge Required Presents complex and abstract social studies concepts.	

RESOURCES

- Unit 4 Response Log
- Selection Audio
- Close Read Screencasts: Modeled Discussion
- Reading Studio: Notice & Note
- Level Up Tutorial: Academic Vocabulary and Word Knowledge
- Writing Studio: Writing as a Process
- Speaking and Listening Studio: Participating in Collaborative Discussions
- Second Inaugural Address Selection Test

SUMMARIES

English

Abraham Lincoln gave this speech after he had been elected to serve a second term as president. In it, he describes how the nation had changed since his first inauguration. The nation was divided and at war, fighting over slavery and the unity of the nation. He describes how each side asks the same God for assistance, and he questions if it is God's will for the war to continue until all the nation's wealth is destroyed and all lives lost. He then calls for all to end the war, heal the nation's wounds, and create a lasting peace.

Spanish

Abraham Lincoln dio este discurso luego de ser elegido para cumplir un segundo período como presidente. En el discurso, describe cómo la nación cambió desde su inauguración. La nación estaba dividida y en guerra, luchando debido a la esclavitud y la unidad. Describe cómo cada lado le pide ayuda al mismo Dios y se pregunta si es la voluntad de Dios que la guerra continúe hasta que se acaben todas las riquezas y se pierdan todas las vidas del país. Luego pide por el fin de la guerra, la sanación de las heridas de la nación y la creación de una paz duradera.

SMALL-GROUP OPTIONS

Have students work in small groups and pairs to read and discuss the selection.

Three-Way Talking Points

- Have students form groups of three. Assign a student in each group to represent the North, the South, and Abraham Lincoln.
- Explain that a talking point is a brief statement that supports a particular position on an issue.
- Have students work individually to write 3–5 talking points based on Lincoln's inaugural speech to support the view they represent.
- Discuss talking points by having the "North" or "South" student read a talking point followed by the counterpart reading a corresponding talking point. For each set of talking points, have "Lincoln" share a related talking point that shows Lincoln's view on the issue. Discuss all perspectives.

Tell Me What and Why

- Have students form equal-sized groups, and have each group select a "judge."
- Each group will write six questions, one for each paragraph of the speech, on a piece of paper. Three questions need to start with *Why* and three need to start with *What*. Each question must have only one correct answer.
- Pair each group with another group. Have each group place its questions in a bag and give them to the other group. Taking turns, a member of each group will select a question and have a set amount of time to answer it. The opposing group's judge will determine if the answer is correct. Have students play the game until all questions have been used.

 **Text X-Ray: English Learner Support**
for Second Inaugural Address

Use the Text X-Ray and the supports and scaffolds in the Teacher's Edition to help guide students at different proficiency levels through the selection.

INTRODUCE THE SELECTION
DISCUSS THE CIVIL WAR

In this lesson, students will need to be able to discuss the Civil War. Check for students' prior knowledge of the Civil War by asking questions such as: When did it happen? What were the causes of the Civil War? What did people in the North want? What did people in the South want? Why did they go to war? Display discussion prompts such as: *It happened in ___. The causes were ___ and ___. The people in the North wanted ___, but the people in the South wanted ___.*

CULTURAL REFERENCES

The following words or phrases may be unfamiliar to students:

- *civil war* (paragraph 2): a war between different groups in a country
- *the Union* (paragraph 2): the union of states—the United States
- *slaves* (paragraph 3): people legally owned by other people, and forced to work for them
- *the conflict* (paragraph 4): the war
- *the Almighty* (paragraph 5): God

LISTENING

Rephrase Author's Call to Action

Explain that the author's purpose is to persuade people to do something. He expresses what he wants them to do in his call to action, in the last paragraph.

Tell students they are going to listen to the author's call to action. Have students listen as you read the last paragraph of the selection aloud. Use the following supports with students at varying proficiency levels:

- Reread individual phrases in the final paragraph and ask students yes or no questions about Lincoln's call to action. For example, read "let us strive on to finish the work we are in" and ask: *Does Lincoln want people to hope for peace? (yes)* **SUBSTANTIAL**
- Reread individual phrases in the final paragraph and ask students to paraphrase the meaning of each phrase. Example: "to bind up the nation's wounds" means to heal that which divided people. **MODERATE**
- Ask students to identify five things Lincoln called on people to do in his final paragraph. **LIGHT**

SPEAKING

Discuss the Concepts of War and Unity

Tell students they are going to discuss the concepts of unity and war. Explain that during the Civil War the South broke from the Union and was willing to fight to stay separate. The North fought to keep the states united.

Read the last two sentences in paragraph 2. Use the following supports with students at varying proficiency levels:

- Display and read this paraphrase of the two sentences: *Both sides disapproved of war. But one side thought war was more important than keeping the nation together. The other side thought that keeping the nation together was more important.* Have students repeat it chorally. **SUBSTANTIAL**

- Read this paraphrase: *Both sides disapproved of war. But one side thought war was more important than the survival of the nation. The other side went to war rather than let the nation die.* Ask yes/no questions: *Did both sides approve of war? (yes) Did both sides want the nation to survive? (no)* **MODERATE**

- Ask questions and provide prompts such as these to help students discuss the two sentences: *Who disapproved of war? (Both sides disapproved.) What did one side think? (War was more important than the nation.) What did the other side think? (The nation was more important than war.)* **LIGHT**

READING

Understand the Speech

Work with students to comprehend the speech.

Use the following supports with students at varying proficiency levels:

- Read aloud the last two sentences of paragraph 4, pausing after phrases to let students echo read. Then, ask yes/no questions: *Does Lincoln think God is just? (yes) Does he think people should judge other people? (no) Does Lincoln think all prayer can be answered? (no)* **SUBSTANTIAL**

- Have volunteers in small groups read aloud a sentence from paragraphs 2 and 3 while group members read along silently. After one or two sentences, a group member should then ask a *Who, What, Where, When, Why,* or *How* question. The other group members can answer the question. **MODERATE**

- Have students silently read paragraphs 2 and 3. Tell them to note details about each paragraph in a *Who, What, Where, When, Why,* and *How* graphic organizer as they read. **LIGHT**

WRITING

Write Balanced Sentences

Review balanced sentences. Read the second sentence of selection paragraph 2. Explain each clause. Tell students they will write balanced sentences, using examples from the selection as models.

Use the following supports with students at varying proficiency levels:

- Display the balanced sentence from the text: "All dreaded it—all sought to avert it." Explain how it can be rewritten: *Everyone feared the war—everyone wanted to avoid it.* Have students copy it. **SUBSTANTIAL**

- Have students review the balanced sentence. Then, discuss their ideas for their own opening sentence for their speech. If necessary, provide a sentence frame: *Everyone feared war—_____.* Also, provide sentence frames as needed for adding more balanced sentences. **MODERATE**

- Have students work in small groups to discuss how to use the balanced sentence as a model. Then, have students work independently on their drafts. If their drafts lack balanced sentences, ask them questions, such as: *How could you change that sentence to a balanced sentence?* **LIGHT**

ANALYZE & APPLY

SECOND INAUGURAL ADDRESS

Speech by **Abraham Lincoln**

President Lincoln gave this address on March 4, 1865, as the Civil War was nearing an end. The issue of slavery had divided the nation. Although "Both parties deprecated war . . ." according to Lincoln, the division led to a terrible conflict with widespread effect.

? ESSENTIAL QUESTION:

What divides us as human beings?

330 Unit 4

© Houghton Mifflin Harcourt Publishing Company • Image Credits: © VCG Wilson/Corbis via Getty Images

 LEARNING MINDSET

Seeking Challenges Remind students that seeking challenges is how we grow, and that meeting challenges brings growth rather than certain success. Neither the United States as a nation nor Lincoln as a person succeeded every time. However, they serve as examples of seeking new challenges and benefiting from them.

QUICK START

Division within a school, community, or team is sometimes unavoidable. What are some actions you could take to bring people together? Take a few minutes to freewrite your ideas. Then, share your best idea with the class.

ANALYZE ARGUMENTATIVE TEXTS

Abraham Lincoln delivered his Second Inaugural Address in Washington, DC, as the American Civil War continued to rage. The address was not a victory speech, but recent events made it appear that the Union was close to winning the war. In his address, Lincoln made an argument to his fellow countrymen for the best way forward for the country.

In an argumentative text, a writer expresses a position to an audience on a particular issue. When you analyze an argument, it is important to identify and analyze its structural elements. As you read, add examples of the structural elements of Lincoln's argument in the chart.

GENRE ELEMENTS: SPEECH
- includes a clear claim or thesis
- supports ideas with evidence
- makes a call to action to the audience

ELEMENT	DEFINITION	EXAMPLE
Claim or Thesis	an expression of the writer's position on an issue	
Evidence	specific information, such as facts, quotations, and examples, that supports the thesis	
Appeal	a persuasive method intended to influence the beliefs of the audience	
Call to Action	an attempt to convince the audience to do something based on the argument	

ANALYZE AUTHOR'S PURPOSE

The reason why an author composed a text is called the **author's purpose.** The purpose of an argumentative text is to persuade the audience to believe in or do something. As you read, note that the structure of Lincoln's argument supports his desire to convince his audience to take action.

An author may use rhetorical devices to help achieve his or her purpose. **Rhetorical devices** are techniques that influence the way a text is understood by the audience. Lincoln uses the following rhetorical devices in his speech:

- **Diction:** the words the writer chooses to include

- **Parallelism:** the use of similar grammatical constructions to express ideas that are related

- **Allusion:** quotations or references to a familiar person, place, event, or literary work

As you read, note the ways Lincoln uses rhetorical devices to impact the audience's understanding of his argument and achieve his purpose.

Second Inaugural Address   331

QUICK START

After students read the Quick Start question, have them share ideas of how to bring people together. Encourage students to emphasize ideas that do more than just avoid division but rather heal the division or help people address it productively.

ANALYZE ARGUMENTATIVE TEXTS

Review the reasons why each of the elements of an argumentative text is necessary. Explain that without a clear thesis, readers would not know what argument the author was trying to defend. Arguments that are not well supported with evidence will not be persuasive. If students are not sure why emotional appeals are necessary, remind them that without them, the audience will not be involved or may not care enough to act. A clear conclusion centers the audience on what is important to the author, and a call to action makes sure that their interest and focus is not wasted.

ANALYZE AUTHOR'S PURPOSE

Discuss with students what they will see in the text if Lincoln's diction supports his purpose. How will the text show that? They may expect Lincoln to use words that supply strong evidence and evoke emotions. Explain why an author might use parallelism and allusions to support his purpose. For example, parallelism helps focus the audience on important evidence or ideas the author wants to communicate. Allusions can support emotional appeals or pieces of evidence.

TEACH

CRITICAL VOCABULARY

Encourage students to read all the sentences before deciding which word best completes each sentence. Remind them to look for context clues that match the precise meaning of each word.

Answers:

1. *venture*

2. *wring*

3. *engross*

4. *deprecate*

LANGUAGE CONVENTIONS

Tell students that a sentence is balanced when it has parts that are approximately equal in importance, grammatical structure, and length. Have students identify the parts in the quoted sentence and discuss how they are equal in each way.

ANNOTATION MODEL

- Remind students of the annotation ideas such as underlining important details and circling words that signal how the text is organized. Point out that they may follow this suggestion or use their own system for marking up the selection in their write-in text. They may want to color-code their annotations by using highlighters. Their notes in the margin may include the thesis, evidence and reasons, or emotional appeals Lincoln makes as well as questions about ideas that are unclear or topics they want to learn more about.

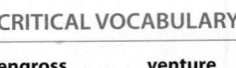

CRITICAL VOCABULARY

engross	venture	deprecate	wring

To see how many Critical Vocabulary words you already know, use them to complete the sentences.

1. If I were to _____ a guess, I would say that we will have a quiz today.

2. In that movie, the lawyer had to _____ a confession out of the criminal.

3. The filmmaker used special effects to help _____ the audience in the film.

4. I don't usually like to _____ anyone's work, but my brother did a poor job of mowing the lawn.

LANGUAGE CONVENTIONS

Balanced Sentences A **balanced sentence** is made up of two or more clauses that are parallel in structure, roughly equal in length, and combine contrasting ideas that are equally important. Lincoln's style in his Second Inaugural Address is marked by complex, balanced sentences and paragraphs. **Syntax** is the way an author arranges words in phrases, clauses, and sentences. Lincoln uses his distinctive syntax to create balanced sentences that support and emphasize particular ideas, as in the following example.

> **Both parties deprecated war; but one of them would make war rather than let the nation survive; and the other would accept war rather than let it perish.**

As you read the Second Inaugural Address, note other examples of balanced sentences. How do they emphasize Lincoln's ideas?

ANNOTATION MODEL   NOTICE & NOTE

As you read, notice how Lincoln builds his argument for restoring the Union. Note words and phrases that suggest his purpose. In the model, you can see one reader's notes about the Second Inaugural Address.

Then a statement, somewhat in detail, of course to be pursued, seemed fitting and proper. Now, at the expiration of four years, during which public declarations have been constantly called forth on every point and phase of the great contest which still absorbs the attention and engrosses the energies of the nation, little that is new could be presented.

"Then" and "Now" suggest changes over four years.

"The great contest" must be the war.

He's not going to focus too much on the war.

BACKGROUND

Abraham Lincoln *(1809–1865), elected president in 1860, had told the South in his First Inaugural Address, "In your hands, my dissatisfied fellow countrymen, and not in mine, is the momentous issue of civil war." Lincoln had promised to prevent the expansion of slavery. The southern states feared he would abolish slavery, and they eventually seceded. This led to the start of the Civil War. Four bloody years later, the Union forces had gained the upper hand in the conflict, Lincoln had issued the Emancipation Proclamation and had been reelected, and the Union was about to be restored. But Lincoln would not see it, as he would be assassinated less than six weeks after giving this speech.*

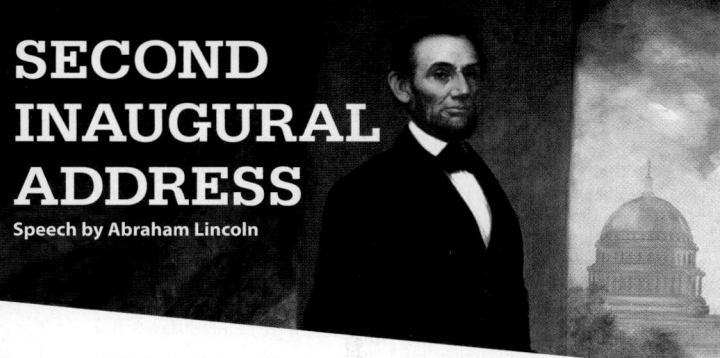

SECOND INAUGURAL ADDRESS

Speech by Abraham Lincoln

SETTING A PURPOSE

As you read, pay attention to the issues and ideas that are important to Lincoln. Note details that will help you understand what he valued and why he wanted the Union restored.

FELLOW COUNTRYMEN:

1   At this second appearing to take the oath of the presidential office, there is less occasion for an extended address than there was at the first. Then a statement, somewhat in detail, of course to be pursued, seemed fitting and proper. Now, at the expiration of four years, during which public declarations have been constantly called forth on every point and phase of the great contest which still absorbs the attention and **engrosses** the energies of the nation, little that is new could be presented. The progress of our arms, upon which all else chiefly depends, is as well known to the public as to myself; and it is, I trust, reasonably satisfactory and encouraging to all. With high hope for the future, no prediction in regard to it is **ventured**.

 2   On the occasion corresponding to this four years ago, all thoughts were anxiously directed to an impending civil war.

Notice & Note

Use the side margins to notice and note signposts in the text.

engross
(ĕn-grōs´) *v.* to completely engage the attention or interest.

venture
(vĕn´chər) *v.* to risk or dare.

CLOSE READ SCREENCAST

Modeled Discussion   In their eBooks, have students view the Close Read Screencast, in which readers discuss and annotate paragraph 2—Lincoln reminds listeners that four years ago a war was about to begin. As a class, view and discuss this video. Then, have student pairs do an independent close read of an additional passage—Lincoln's statement that the length of the war will be for God to decide (paragraph 5, beginning with "Fondly"). Students can record their answers on the Close Read Practice PDF.   **Close Read Practice PDF**

BACKGROUND

Thousands gathered on the wet, muddy grounds of the Capitol to hear Lincoln's speech. With a Union victory on the horizon, listeners may have been expecting a victory speech and a description of administration policy for Reconstruction. What they heard instead was an inspiring call to begin the hard work of reaching a peaceful reconciliation.

SETTING A PURPOSE

Direct students to use the Setting a Purpose prompt to focus their reading.

EL ENGLISH LEARNER SUPPORT

Analyze Details   Read aloud "the great contest which still absorbs the attention and engrosses the energies of the nation." Have students mark the subject of the clause. Ask which great contest Lincoln is referring to *(war)* and how it engages the nation. Ask: How is war like most contests? How is it not like most contests? *(Possible answer: No one wins.)*   **LIGHT**

CRITICAL VOCABULARY

engross: Lincoln points out that the war is still the most central concern of the nation.

ASK STUDENTS why war engrosses peoples' attention and energy. *(It deeply affects their lives and their countries.)*

venture: Lincoln does not want to directly predict the outcome of the war.

ASK STUDENTS why political figures might be reluctant to venture guesses about future events. *(If they are wrong, they could lose credibility.)*

ANALYZE AUTHOR'S PURPOSE

Discuss with students what Lincoln's purpose might be in bringing up his first inaugural address here. Point out that besides making clear his focus on unity, Lincoln is making clear how much better things are now in some ways than they were then. At that time, war was coming, and now the war is almost won. (**Answer:** *To Lincoln, the Union—the undivided United States—was of utmost importance. Lincoln's words explain both the war and Lincoln's desire for reunification.*)

LANGUAGE CONVENTIONS

Have students consider what effect a balanced style might have on Lincoln's audience and why he would want to create that effect. Since Lincoln expected that soon he would be helping his country rebuild and get over a big division, he wants to imply a common cause for both sides of the war as often as possible. (**Answer:** *By repeating "Neither," he emphasizes that both sides were surprised by the extent of the war and its impact.*)

For **speaking** and **reading support** for students at varying proficiency levels, see the **Text X-Ray** on page 330D.

CRITICAL VOCABULARY

deprecate: Both sides had openly disapproved of a civil war, but ultimately they both engaged in one.

ASK STUDENTS what, besides war, are leaders likely to deprecate. (*injustice, poverty, crime*)

wring: Lincoln uses the word *wringing* figuratively, to describe slave labor.

ASK STUDENTS to give examples of literal wringing. (*squeezing water from a washcloth*)

NOTICE & NOTE

ANALYZE AUTHOR'S PURPOSE

Annotate: Mark the words in paragraph 2 that tell what Lincoln spoke about during his First Inaugural Address.

Infer: What do these words tell the reader about Lincoln's view of the Union?

deprecate
(dĕp´rĭ-kāt) *v.* to express disapproval.

LANGUAGE CONVENTIONS

Annotate: Mark the words that are repeated at the beginning of sentences in paragraph 4.

Evaluate: How does the use of these repeated words create a balance in the paragraph?

wring
(rĭng) *v.* to obtain through force or pressure.

All dreaded it—all sought to avert it. While the inaugural address was being delivered from this place, devoted altogether to saving the Union without war, insurgent agents were in the city seeking to destroy it without war—seeking to dissolve the Union, and divide effects, by negotiation. Both parties **deprecated** war; but one of them would make war rather than let the nation survive; and the other would accept war rather than let it perish. And the war came.

3   One-eighth of the whole population were colored slaves, not distributed generally over the Union, but localized in the Southern part of it. These slaves constituted a peculiar and powerful interest. All knew that this interest was, somehow, the cause of the war. To strengthen, perpetuate, and extend this interest was the object for which the insurgents would rend the Union, even by war; while the government claimed no right to do more than to restrict the territorial enlargement of it.

4   Neither party expected for the war the magnitude or the duration which it has already attained. Neither anticipated that the cause of the conflict might cease with, or even before, the conflict itself should cease. Each looked for an easier triumph, and a result less fundamental and astounding. Both read the same Bible, and pray to the same God; and each invokes his aid against the other. It may seem strange that any men should dare to ask a just God's assistance in **wringing** their bread from the sweat of other men's faces; but let us judge not, that we be not judged. The prayers of both could not be answered—that of neither has been answered fully.

5   The Almighty has his own purposes. "Woe unto the world because of offences! for it must needs be that offences come; but woe to that man by whom the offence cometh." If we shall suppose that American slavery is one of those offences which, in the providence of God, must needs come, but which, having continued through his appointed time, he now wills to remove, and that he gives to both North and South this terrible war, as the woe due to those by

---

WHEN STUDENTS STRUGGLE . . .

Develop Reading Fluency Invite students to pick one or two paragraphs from the speech and note any words they are not sure how to pronounce. Have them look up the words to learn their correct pronunciations. Encourage students to note any silent letters or difficult letter combinations. Then, have students pair up and practice reading the paragraphs aloud to one another. Circulate among the teams to make sure words are being pronounced correctly.

 For additional support, go to the **Reading Studio** and assign the following **Level Up Tutorial: Academic Vocabulary and Word Knowledge.**

whom the offence came, shall we discern therein any departure from those divine attributes[1] which the believers in a living God always ascribe to him? Fondly do we hope—fervently do we pray—that this mighty scourge of war may speedily pass away. Yet, if God wills that it continue until all the wealth piled by the bondman's two hundred and fifty years of unrequited toil shall be sunk, and until every drop of blood drawn with the lash shall be paid by another drawn with the sword, as was said three thousand years ago, so still it must be said, "The judgments of the Lord are true and righteous altogether."

6   With malice toward none; with charity for all: with firmness in the right, as God gives us to see the right, let us strive on to finish the work we are in; to bind up the nation's wounds; to care for him who shall have borne the battle, and for his widow, and his orphan—to do all which may achieve and cherish a just and lasting peace among ourselves, and with all nations.

[1] **attributes:** qualities or characteristics.

CHECK YOUR UNDERSTANDING

Answer these questions before moving on to the **Analyze the Text** section on the following page.

1 What did Lincoln view as the primary reason for the war?

  A To punish the South

  B To preserve the Union

  C To divide the nation

  D To protect slavery

2 What does Lincoln say the North and South have in common?

  F Both expected the war to go on for a long time.

  G Both were determined to unite the country.

  H Both were looking to restrict slavery.

  J Both shared some of the same values.

3 What did Lincoln hope would happen when the war ended?

  A He hoped for healing and long-lasting peace.

  B He hoped the South would form its own nation.

  C He hoped that more territories would join the Union.

  D He hoped that more states would secede.

© Houghton Mifflin Harcourt Publishing Company

NOTICE & NOTE

QUOTED WORDS

Notice & Note: Lincoln includes quotations from the Bible in his speech. Mark the quotations in paragraph 5.

Analyze: How do these quotations relate to Lincoln's argument? Explain.

ANALYZE ARGUMENTATIVE TEXTS

Annotate: Mark the words in paragraph 6 that describe what Lincoln wants the country to be like in the future.

Analyze: What is Lincoln's call to action to his audience in this paragraph?

ENGLISH LEARNER SUPPORT

Oral Assessment   Use the following questions to assess students' comprehension and speaking skills.

1. Why did Lincoln say the war had to happen? *(to keep the country together)*

2. What did Lincoln say the two sides of the war have in common? *(both have the same values)*

3. What did Lincoln want to happen when the war ended? *(healing and peace)* **SUBSTANTIAL/MODERATE**

QUOTED WORDS

Note that Lincoln is making it clear that he thinks God is punishing the whole country, not just one part of the country or the other. (***Possible answer:*** *He is identifying the losses of the war with God's judgment on slavery. These religious references add authority to Lincoln's words and would appeal to the values of people in both the North and the South.*)

ANALYZE ARGUMENTATIVE TEXTS

Discuss with students that Lincoln's call to action in paragraph 6 echoes his thesis throughout the speech that the country seek to rebuild in a way that unifies the country and helps everyone. (***Answer:*** *Lincoln calls on his audience to care for every citizen, no matter which side.*)

For **listening support** for students at varying proficiency levels, see the **Text X-Ray** on page 330C.

ENGLISH LEARNER SUPPORT

Confirm Understanding   Use the following supports with students at varying proficiency levels:

- Display the word *departure* from paragraph 5 and draw lines to separate the syllables. Pronounce the word several times and have students repeat it after you. Point out the prefix *de-* which means "do or make the opposite of or reverse." Then, tell students *departure* means "the act of leaving." **SUBSTANTIAL**

- Have students pronounce the word *departure,* and explain that *departure* is a noun meaning "the act of leaving." **MODERATE**

CHECK YOUR UNDERSTANDING

Have students answer the questions independently.

Answers:

1. *B*

2. *J*

3. *A*

If they answer any questions incorrectly, have them reread the text to confirm their understanding. Then, they may proceed to ANALYZE THE TEXT on page 336.

APPLY

ANALYZE THE TEXT

Possible answers:

1. **DOK 4:** *Lincoln's claim is that the Union should be restored. He cites the desire of both sides for the war to end and the fact that each side shares the same morals and values to support his claim.*

2. **DOK 3:** *Similarities: deprecated war, didn't expect severity of war, expected easy victory, read same Bible, believed in same God; Differences: viewpoints on slavery, willingness to make war and dissolve Union; Highlighting these emphasizes the need for healing and peace.*

3. **DOK 4:** *Lincoln appeals to the moral sense that the North and South share; this appeal to the audience's beliefs builds to a call to action to convince people to help one another no matter what side of the war they were on.*

4. **DOK 4:** *Lincoln uses parallel structures ("With malice," "with charity," "with firmness," and "to finish," "to bind up," "to care for") to emphasize the shared feelings, intentions, and actions that must exist between the two sides for the nation to recover from war.*

5. **DOK 4:** *Lincoln clearly believed in God and would know that forgiveness is an important element of Christian belief, as is the command to love your enemy. The final paragraph is a logical outgrowth of these beliefs.*

RESEARCH

Remind students that when primary sources exist, they are the best sources to use. Encourage them to find some, and tell them that government websites or those run by universities will be particularly good places to find such sources, because they have the resources to maintain such collections.

Extend Encourage students to follow the event they are studying all the way to the present. Even when the division has healed, often these events have some visible effects on society today.

RESPOND

ANALYZE THE TEXT

Support your responses with evidence from the text. 📓 NOTEBOOK

1. **Analyze** What is the central claim of Lincoln's speech? What evidence does he provide to support his claim?

2. **Compare** What are the similarities between northerners and southerners that Lincoln outlines in the speech? What are their differences? How does highlighting these similarities and differences support Lincoln's purpose?

3. **Evaluate** An **ethical appeal** is a kind of appeal in which a writer links a claim to a widely accepted value. How does Lincoln use ethical appeals to build his argument? Cite text evidence in your response.

4. **Analyze** What rhetorical device does Lincoln use in the last paragraph of his speech? How does the use of this rhetorical device relate to Lincoln's purpose?

5. **Notice & Note** How does Lincoln's use of quotations from the Bible support his call to action in the final paragraph?

RESEARCH

Lincoln had a vision of a reunited and healing nation, but he was assassinated before he could put any policies in place. Research the aftermath of the Civil War. List two events that suggest the nation had begun to heal. Then, list two events that suggest the nation was still fractured.

RESEARCH TIP
Some issues pertaining to the Civil War are still divisive today. When researching, try to focus on scholarly sites. These sites generally have urls that end in .org or .edu. Be sure to evaluate any source for bias.

EVENTS THAT SUGGEST HEALING	EVENTS THAT SUGGEST FRACTURE
Answers will vary.	

Extend Choose one of the events you listed and research it more in depth. What were some long-term effects of this event? Share with the class what you learn.

336   Unit 4

🧠 LEARNING MINDSET

Seeking Challenges Remind students that seeking challenges in research doesn't have to mean getting the best source, though useful sources are also good goals, but sometimes going deeper into the topic or deeper into the research can be a great way to push themselves.

CREATE AND DISCUSS

Write a Letter Imagine you were in the audience when Lincoln gave his Second Inaugural Address. Write a letter in which you respond to Lincoln's speech. Be sure to touch on some of the topics he discussed, such as the consequences of actions, forgiveness, and the value of unity.

❏ State the reason why you are writing your letter. Strike a friendly tone if you agree with the ideas in Lincoln's speech. Respectfully note any disagreements.

❏ Discuss the elements of Lincoln's argument that struck you as compelling or significant.

❏ Include any relevant historical details in your correspondence.

Discuss and Evaluate a Speech Hold a group discussion in which you evaluate Lincoln's Second Inaugural Address.

❏ State whether you found Lincoln's claim to be clear and coherent.

❏ Evaluate the evidence. Did Lincoln adequately support his claim? Did he include a variety of evidence to support his claim?

❏ Note points of agreement and disagreement and respond respectfully.

RESPOND TO THE ESSENTIAL QUESTION

? What divides us as human beings?

Gather Information Review your annotations and notes on the Second Inaugural Address. Then, add relevant information to your Response Log. As you determine which information to include, think about:

- the causes of the Civil War
- the differences in outlook of the two sides
- how Lincoln presents his ideas

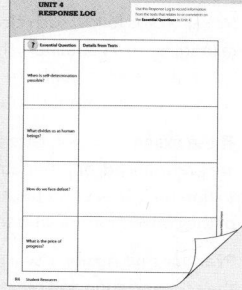

Go to **Writing as a Process** in the **Writing Studio** for help.

Go to **Participating in Collaborative Discussions: Listening and Responding** in the **Speaking and Listening Studio** for help.

ACADEMIC VOCABULARY
As you write and discuss what you learned from Lincoln's Second Inaugural Address, be sure to use the Academic Vocabulary words. Check off each of the words that you use.

❏ **confirm**
❏ **definitely**
❏ **deny**
❏ **format**
❏ **unify**

CREATE AND DISCUSS

Write a Letter Encourage students to respond to a part of the speech that interests them and then use what they know about the historical context to include relevant details and strong emotional elements in their letter, while keeping a friendly, respectful tone.

Discuss and Evaluate a Speech Have students look again at Lincoln's speech to identify the supporting reasons and evidence for his central claim. Have them create a chart with three columns: *Reasons, Evidence,* and *Effectiveness.* Then, have students jot notes in their charts and use them in the group discussion. Students can use the information in the third column to talk about how effectively Lincoln supported his central claim.

RESPOND TO THE ESSENTIAL QUESTION

Allow time for students to add details from the Second Inaugural Address to their Unit 4 Response Logs.

CRITICAL VOCABULARY

Answers:

1. *b. fascinating;* engrossed *means you are completely engaged and interested*

2. *a. dislike the app;* deprecate *means to expresses disapproval*

3. *a. risked failure;* ventured *means to risk or dare*

4. *b. forcing the hero to answer questions;* wring *means to obtain by force*

VOCABULARY STRATEGY:
Pronunciation

Answers:

1. *cliché* (klē-shā´): *a trite or overused expression or idea*

2. *subtle* (sut´l): *so slight as to be difficult to analyze or describe*

3. *indict* (ĭn-dīt´): *to accuse of wrongdoing or criticize severely*

4. *aisle* (īl): *a passage between rows of seats in a building such as a church or theater, an airplane, or a train*

5. *silhouette* (sĭl-oo-ĕt´): *an outline that appears dark against a light background*

6. *segue* (sĕg´wā): *a transition from one thing or one piece of music or film scene to another*

7. *colonel* (kûr´nəl): *an army officer of high rank, in particular, an officer above a lieutenant colonel and below a brigadier general*

8. *epitome* (ĭ-pĭt´ə-mē): *a person or thing that is a perfect example of a particular quality or type*

9. *circuit* (sûr´kĭt): *a roughly circular line, route, or movement that starts and finishes at the same place*

10. *respite* (rĕs´pĭt): *a short period of rest or relief from something difficult or unpleasant*

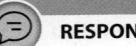 **RESPOND**

WORD BANK
engross
venture
deprecate
wring

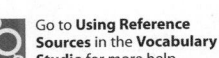 Go to **Using Reference Sources** in the **Vocabulary Studio** for more help.

CRITICAL VOCABULARY

Practice and Apply Choose the letter of the best answer to each question. Then, explain your response.

1. If you are **engrossed** in a book, you find the book _____.
   a. tedious
   b. fascinating

2. If you hear someone **deprecate** a new computer app, you know they _____.
   a. dislike the app
   b. like the app

3. If a classmate **ventured** to take on a difficult task, he or she _____.
   a. risked failure
   b. was certain of success

4. If you were watching a movie in which the villain was trying to **wring** information out of the hero, you'd know the villain was _____.
   a. patiently waiting for an answer
   b. forcing the hero to answer questions

VOCABULARY STRATEGY: Pronunciation

The Critical Vocabulary word *wring* has a silent first letter, so it is pronounced *ring*. Someone listening to Lincoln's speech would need to determine the correct word from its context, rather than its sound. This example shows why it is helpful to verify the pronunciation of an unfamiliar word by checking a dictionary. In *wring*, *write*, and all English words that begin with *wr*, the *w* is silent.

Not all words follow such clear patterns. For example, in the word *trough* (a long, narrow container), the *gh* sounds like *f* and the word rhymes with *off*, but in the word *through*, the *gh* is silent and the vowel combination *ou* is also pronounced differently—the word is pronounced like *threw*.

These examples emphasize that words are not always spelled the way they are pronounced, or pronounced the way they are spelled. Using a dictionary to find the correct pronunciation of a word will help you achieve a command of the conventions of written and spoken English.

Practice and Apply Use a print or digital college-level dictionary to confirm the pronunciation and meaning of the words below. Take turns with a partner practicing the pronunciations and using the words in sentences.

1. cliché
2. subtle
3. indict
4. aisle
5. silhouette

6. segue
7. colonel
8. epitome
9. circuit
10. respite

 ENGLISH LEARNER SUPPORT

Use Cognates Tell students that *subtle* is related to the Spanish word *sutil* and *circuit* is related to *circuito*. Similarly, *silhouette* corresponds to the Spanish word *silueta* and *colonel* is *coronel* in Spanish. **ALL LEVELS**

LANGUAGE CONVENTIONS:
Balanced Sentences

Lincoln wrote balanced sentences, both short and long, that help emphasize key ideas in his speeches. Consider this complex sentence in paragraph 5:

> **Yet, if God wills that it continue until all the wealth piled by the bondsman's two hundred and fifty years of unrequited toil shall be sunk, and until every drop of blood drawn with the lash shall be paid by another drawn with the sword, as was said three thousand years ago, so still it must be said, "The judgments of the Lord are true and righteous altogether."**

In this sentence, Lincoln balances the evils of war against the evils of slavery. The two ideas are connected through the syntax that Lincoln employs, creating balance between "blood drawn with the lash" and "drawn with the sword." He then concludes with another balanced statement about the enduring truth of God's judgments: "as was said three thousand years ago, so still it must be said." This extended, complex sentence is constructed by Lincoln to help make his meaning clear and strongly support his message.

Lincoln also creates balance in his shorter sentences. For example, in paragraph 2, Lincoln writes:

> **All dreaded it—all sought to avert it.**

These stylistic choices support Lincoln's message that the war was just and necessary, but in order to preserve the Union, it was time for the North and the South to come together once again and heal the nation's wounds.

Practice and Apply Review the letter you wrote for the Create and Discuss activity on page 337. Use the space below to revise your writing. Practice rewriting some of your sentences as balanced sentences to make your ideas more memorable and compelling as Lincoln did in his writing.

LANGUAGE CONVENTIONS:
Balanced Sentences

Note that many of Lincoln's balanced sentences also have multiple clauses, even his short sentences. Guide students to notice that complex sentences are more difficult to write smoothly than simpler sentences. Yet Lincoln makes it look easy. Also notice that this raises his speech to a level of formality that is less common today, even in presidential speeches.

To give them an idea of what it takes to make a balanced sentence, have students write a sentence about what they think about Lincoln's speech. Then, have them make it into a balanced sentence if it wasn't already one. Discuss why the task was challenging.

Practice and Apply Students should revise the letter they wrote and incorporate balanced sentences.

 For **writing support** for students at varying proficiency levels, see the **Text X-Ray** on page 330D.

ENGLISH LEARNER SUPPORT

Language Conventions Use the following supports with students at varying levels:

- Have students find balanced sentences in paragraph 2 of the Second Inaugural Address and underline the similar parts in the sentences. **MODERATE**
- Have students find balanced sentences in paragraph 2 of the address and then explain how the parts of each sentence are balanced. **LIGHT**

TO MY OLD MASTER

Letter by Jourdon Anderson

GENRE ELEMENTS
LETTER

Explain why some letters have literary or historical significance. Letters written as private communication between a sender and recipient may become public because they reveal information about a person or time period. For example, a letter may express the writer's feelings and ideas about issues, events, or other people. A letter may include information about a historical period or culture, such as details about social, cultural, and economic conditions as well as people's opinions and views about these conditions, events, and people.

LEARNING OBJECTIVES

- Identify text that expresses the writer's attitude and cite examples of the writer's tone.
- Conduct research to show cause-effect relationship of amendments on African American lives.
- Write a biographical essay about Frederick Douglass.
- Give a presentation about Frederick Douglass to a small group.
- Use context to determine the meaning of words.
- Identify noun clauses and their function.
- **Language** Identify supporting details in a text.

TEXT COMPLEXITY

Quantitative Measures	To My Old Master	Lexile: 1190L
Qualitative Measures	**Ideas Presented** Multiple levels and use of irony, with a demand for inference.	
	Structures Used Multiple, including problem-solution, cause-effect, and compare-contrast.	
	Language Used Extensive use of implied meanings and ironic language, but support is offered.	
	Knowledge Required Requires some knowledge about historical events and time periods.	

RESOURCES

- Unit 4 Response Log

- 🔊 Selection Audio

- 📖 Reading Studio: Notice & Note

- Level Up Tutorial: Making Inferences

- Writing Studio: Developing a Topic

- 💬 Speaking and Listening Studio: Giving a Presentation

- Vocabulary Studio: Words with Multiple Meanings

- ❗ Grammar Studio: The Noun Clause

- ✅ "To My Old Master" Selection Test

SUMMARIES

English

In 1865, Jourdon Anderson is living in Ohio. He writes a letter to Colonel P.H. Anderson, his former master on a plantation in Tennessee. The colonel wants Jourdon to return to work for him. Jourdon writes that he often felt uneasy about his old master. He mentions his current wages and situation and asks the colonel what he plans to offer. Jourdon also requests wages for his and his wife's past labor and a promise of safety and education for his children.

Spanish

El 7 de agosto de 1865, Jourdon Anderson escribió una carta desde Ohio, al coronel P.H. Anderson, quien había sido su amo cuando trabajaba como esclavo en una plantación en Tennessee. La carta es una respuesta a la petición del coronel de volver a vivir con él. Jourdon dice que su antiguo amo le inquieta. Le informa de su situación y salario actual y le pregunta al coronel qué planea ofrecerle. Le pide reivindicación salarial por su trabajo y el de su esposa y educación para sus hijos.

 ## SMALL-GROUP OPTIONS

Have students work in small groups and pairs after reading the text to discuss the selection.

Role Play and Discuss

- Have students form pairs, with one student taking the role of Jourdon and the other, the role of the colonel.

- Have students discuss each paragraph using comments or questions, such as "I want you to know . . ." and "Why . . ."

- Continue until both students have spoken at least twice. Repeat for each paragraph.

- Have students conclude by discussing how the colonel might respond after he gets this letter.

Draw a Conclusion and Vote

- Have students form small groups to discuss whether Jourdon will return to his old master.

- Each group should determine reasons to support their conclusion and write its top two reasons on the whiteboard.

- Have students vote for the top reason.

- Briefly discuss the results. Ask those who voted for a different reason to comment on their vote.

Text X-Ray: English Learner Support
for "To My Old Master"

Use the Text X-Ray and the supports and scaffolds in the Teacher's Edition to help guide students at different proficiency levels through the selection.

INTRODUCE THE SELECTION
DISCUSS ENSLAVED AND FREED PERSONS

In this lesson, students will need to discuss what life was like for an enslaved person working on a plantation in the South during the Civil War and what life was like for a free person. Read the background information and discuss the words *enslaved* and *freed*. Provide the following explanations:

- An enslaved person worked for a master and received no money for work. The master controlled where the person lived and what the person could do, such as go to school.
- A freed person could choose who to work for and receive money for work. The freed person was able to choose activities and where to work and live.

Have volunteers share information they know about an enslaved person (or slavery) and a freed person (or freedom). Provide the following sentence frames.

- A freed person can ____. An enslaved person cannot ____.
- When a person can/cannot ____ that person is a ____ person.

CULTURAL REFERENCES

The following words or phrases may be unfamiliar to students:

- *Yankees* (paragraph 1): northerners
- *Union soldier* (paragraph 1): soldier who fought for the North in the Civil War
- *better world* (paragraph 1): afterlife, or life after death
- *colored people* (paragraph 2): African Americans, or individuals born in Africa or whose parents or ancestors were born in Africa
- *wages* (paragraph 2): money paid for work
- *free papers* (paragraph 3): documents officially stating that a formerly enslaved person was free

LISTENING

Understand Tone and Irony

Explain tone is the author's attitude about a subject. Explain in this letter the writer uses a friendly tone, but some of his words suggest he does not have a kind attitude toward his old master. Describe this as irony, or words that mean something different than what they appear to mean.

Have students listen as you read the selection aloud. Use the following supports with students at varying proficiency levels:

- Tell students you will ask questions about what they just heard. Model that they should give a thumbs up if the answer is yes and a thumbs down if the answer is no. For example: *Does he sound like he is mad at his old master? Do you think he liked his old master?* **SUBSTANTIAL**
- Reread sentences from the selection aloud. Tell students to shake their heads up and down if the words express a positive attitude and to shake their heads sideways if they express a negative attitude. For example, "I have often felt uneasy about you" (paragraph 1). **MODERATE**
- After they listen to the selection, have students work in pairs and take turns reading sentences. Tell them to use facial expressions and gestures to express the author's attitude in each sentence and to identify any sentences that express irony. **LIGHT**

SPEAKING

Discuss Self-Determination

Demonstrate self-determination by having two students stand. Allow one student to move freely. Direct the other student to move only when you give commands. Ask: *Which student will get to a specific destination first?*

Use the following supports with students at varying proficiency levels:

- Provide sentence frames to help students discuss self-determination. *If a master buys clothes for an enslaved person, the enslaved person _____ (has/does not have) self-determination. If a person asks his former master for back pay, the person _____ (has/does not have) self-determination.* **SUBSTANTIAL**
- Have student pairs brainstorm things an enslaved person could do and things a freed person could do based on the selection. Then, discuss who has more self-determination and why. **MODERATE**
- Have small groups create a T-chart about the author's self-determination. Label the left column *Enslaved* and the right column *Freed*. Have students list examples from the selection of what the author could do as an enslaved person and as a freed person. Then, have students discuss how the author achieved self-determination. **LIGHT**
-

READING

Identify Supporting Details

Explain that a writer provides details to support key information. These details provide information that may emphasize or explain the meaning about a specific statement.

Use the following supports with students at varying proficiency levels:

- Read aloud sentences 5–8 of paragraph 1, pausing after phrases to let students echo read. Then, ask yes/no questions: *Would the author like to go back home? (yes) Does he think his master would treat him well? (no)* **SUBSTANTIAL**
- Have students create a word web with the words *old score* in the center. Then, have them silently read paragraph 3. Tell them to add words from the text that relate to "old score." **MODERATE**
- Have students silently read paragraph 3. Then, have them annotate their text to answer the question *What are the "old scores" the author is willing to forget and forgive?* **LIGHT**

WRITING

Write Sentences with Noun Clauses

Review noun clauses and explain they are used in place of the words *something* or *someone*. Give students a list of words that start noun clauses (Student Edition page 342).

Use the following supports with students at varying proficiency levels:

- Point at an object and say a sentence with the word *something* or *someone*. Then, repeat without that word and add a word to start the noun clause. Example: "I see something" followed by "I see that _____." Have students complete the sentence using a noun clause (e.g., "I see that the book is in the corner"). Write paired sentences on the board and have students copy them. **SUBSTANTIAL**
- Have each student write a sentence with the word *something* or *someone*. Then, have student pairs trade sentences and rewrite them using a noun clause. **MODERATE**
- Have each student write a paragraph using noun clauses. Then, have student pairs trade paragraphs and underline each noun clause. Tell them to test for noun clauses by substituting *something* or *someone* for the clause. Tell them to include sentences like these in their essays. **LIGHT**

? ESSENTIAL QUESTION

Jourdon Anderson, a freed slave, is finally free to determine what he and his family will do. He can now earn a living doing what he chooses. When his former master invites him and his family to return, he can choose whether or not to return.

TO MY OLD MASTER

Letter by **Jourdon Anderson**

? ESSENTIAL QUESTION:

When is self-determination possible?

340 Unit 4

QUICK START

What do you know about the system of slavery that existed in the United States before the Civil War? List five facts about slavery.

ANALYZE LETTERS

Letters are formal or informal communications that convey information to an individual or group. Letters have several structural characteristics, including a **date;** an **addressee;** a **salutation,** or greeting; a **body;** a **closing** word or phrase; and a **signature.** They are generally written as private correspondence, though letters can become public. For example, the letters of well-known figures may be published, typically after their deaths, due to interest in the life and ideas of the sender.

Some letters are published as historical artifacts that provide context on a period or culture. Jourdon Anderson certainly conveys a memorable point of view on the system of slavery in "To My Old Master." As you read, look for the pertinent examples and commentary that convey his feelings about the situation at the time.

ANALYZE TONE

Tone is a writer's attitude toward his or her subject. A writer can communicate tone through diction, details, and direct statements of his or her position.

Writers may also use literary devices to convey their attitude on a subject. One such device is **verbal irony**—a contrast between what is stated and what is meant. Sometimes irony can produce **understatement,** which creates emphasis by saying less than is actually true. These devices may be used to create a humorous or restrained tone.

As you read, note details that suggest the writer's tone in the chart.

LITERARY ELEMENT	EXAMPLE
Diction	
Details	
Direct statements	
Irony	

GENRE ELEMENTS: LETTER

- written by an individual to another person or to a group
- may be formal or informal
- a literary letter may be read by a wider audience because the author is well known or reveals information about a period or place
- an open letter is addressed to a specific person but published for a broad readership

QUICK START

Have students take turns sharing what they know about slavery. If misconceptions about slavery are mentioned—for instance, enslaved people were usually happy—discuss the misconceptions and use them to prompt a discussion about sources of information and about fiction versus reality.

ANALYZE LETTERS

Tell students that because letters are generally intended as private communication, they will often have a somewhat more personal tone than a speech or essay. Encourage them to look for ways that the personal nature of this letter makes it more powerful than if it were an essay or a more formal account.

ANALYZE TONE

Discuss the topic of the letter. Tell students that the letter does not just answer a question—whether or not the author will return to work on his old master's farm. It also tells us a lot about what the writer's life was like as a slave. Encourage students to determine what the author's stated attitude toward his old master is and compare it to the tone he uses.

TEACH

CRITICAL VOCABULARY

Discuss that many of these words are related to easier words. For instance, *recompense* is related to *compensate*, which means "to make satisfactory payment." Similarly, *virtuous* is the adjective form of *virtue*, which means "moral excellence and righteousness."

Answers:

1. *a. retribution*
2. *b. moral*
3. *b. inclined*
4. *a. payment*

ENGLISH LEARNER SUPPORT

Use Cognates Tell students that *virtuous* has a Spanish cognate in the word *virtuoso*. Also, *recompense* is a cognate for the Spanish *recompensa*.
ALL LEVELS

LANGUAGE CONVENTIONS

Noun Clauses Review the information about noun clauses. Tell students that noun clauses not only vary in the ways they are introduced, but also can function in various ways in sentences.

Give students this example of a noun clause introduced by *what*: "what I told you." Ask volunteers to use it as the subject of a sentence. *(What I told you was supposed to be a secret.)* Continue working with the class to devise other sentences using noun clauses with various introductory words and different functions in the sentences.

ANNOTATION MODEL

Remind students of the annotation ideas such as underlining the diction and details that contribute to the author's tone and circling the letter's structural elements. Point out that they may follow this suggestion or use their own system for marking up the selection in their write-in text. They may want to color-code their annotations by using highlighters. Their notes in the margin may include questions about ideas or statements that are unclear or topics they want to learn more about.

◎ GET READY

CRITICAL VOCABULARY

disposed	reckoning	recompense	virtuous

Circle the letter of the best definition of each Critical Vocabulary term.

1. The prisoner insisted that there would be a day of **reckoning** for the false charge.
   a. retribution   b. calculation   c. forgiveness

2. Fully devoted to his faith and its values, he lived a **virtuous** life.
   a. quiet   b. moral   c. rich

3. The audience was **disposed** to accept the speaker's appeal.
   a. opposed   b. inclined   c. touched

4. "Your gratitude is sufficient **recompense** for my labors," she said.
   a. payment   b. thanks   c. regard

LANGUAGE CONVENTIONS

Noun Clauses Subordinate clauses used as nouns are called noun clauses. A noun clause may be used as a subject, a direct object, an indirect object, a predicate nominative, or the object of a preposition. Because they are clauses, they include both subjects and verbs, but not in a form that allows them to stand alone as a sentence. Noun clauses are introduced either by pronouns, such as *that, what, who, whoever, which,* and *whose,* or by subordinating conjunctions, such as *how, when, where, why,* and *whether.* The example below contains a noun clause as an indirect object. As you read, note other examples of noun clauses in "To My Old Master."

> I would have gone back to see you all when I was working in the Nashville Hospital, but one of the neighbors told me <u>that Henry intended to shoot me if he ever got a chance.</u>

ANNOTATION MODEL **NOTICE & NOTE**

As you read, note how the author uses diction and details to communicate tone. In the model, you can see one reader's notes about "To My Old Master."

> <u>It would do me good to go back to the dear old home again, and see Miss Mary and Miss Martha and Allen, Esther, Green, and Lee.</u> Give my love to them all, and tell them I hope we will meet in the better world, if not in this. I would have gone back to see you all when I was working in the Nashville Hospital, <u>but one of the neighbors told me that Henry intended to shoot me if he ever got a chance.</u>

The tone seems warm and affectionate.

Wow! I wonder if this friendly tone is genuine?

BACKGROUND

Jourdon Anderson *(1826–1907) was enslaved for the first 38 years of his life working on a plantation in Tennessee. He and his wife were freed during the Civil War when Union troops came to the plantation where they worked. They took their children to Ohio, where Anderson found work and they lived in freedom. A year later, after the war ended, the man who had held them in slavery wrote Jourdon and asked him to come back to work, as the plantation was in dire straits. Jourdon dictated this letter, which was sent in response. Later, it was published in a newspaper.*

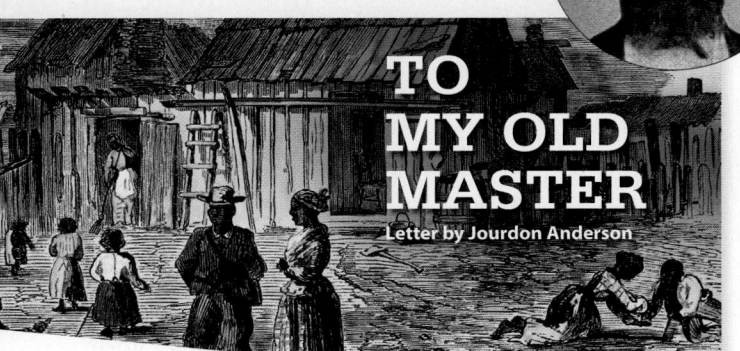

TO MY OLD MASTER

Letter by Jourdon Anderson

SETTING A PURPOSE

As you read, pay attention to the details Anderson includes about his situation. Think about whether he is seriously considering Colonel Anderson's offer to return to work.

Dayton, Ohio

August 7, 1865

To My Old Master, Colonel P.H. Anderson, Big Spring, Tennessee

1   Sir: I got your letter, and was glad to find that you had not forgotten Jourdon, and that you wanted me to come back and live with you again, promising to do better for me than anybody else can. I have often felt uneasy about you. I thought the Yankees would have hung you long before this, for harboring Rebs they found at your house. I suppose they never heard about your going to Colonel Martin's to kill the Union soldier that was left by his company in their stable. Although you shot at me twice before I left you, I did not want to hear of your being hurt, and am glad you are still living. It would do me good to go back to the dear old home again, and see Miss Mary and Miss Martha and Allen,

---

Notice & Note

Use the side margins to notice and note signposts in the text.

ANALYZE TONE

Annotate: Mark the sentence in paragraph 1 that describes Jourdan's surprising response to Colonel Anderson's action.

Draw Conclusions: What does the writer convey by describing his response to this incident?

BACKGROUND

Remind students that Reconstruction left many plantations struggling greatly. The end of slavery meant that plantations no longer had free labor. In addition, the South was required to pay very high costs for its part in the war. Together these factors left many landowners unable to support themselves in the same manner as before the Civil War. Many plantation owners sold their land at reduced prices.

SETTING A PURPOSE

Direct students to use the Setting a Purpose prompt to focus their reading.

ANALYZE TONE

Remind students that a paradox is a statement that seems to contradict itself but may nevertheless suggest an important truth. Analysis of their use can inform readers about the writer's intended purpose. (**Answer:** *Anderson says he is pleased no harm befell the man who shot at him twice, but he mentions this to remind the colonel that he has not forgotten their past.*)

> For **listening, speaking** and **reading support** for students at varying proficiency levels, see the **Text X-Ray** on pages 340C and 340D.

APPLYING ACADEMIC VOCABULARY

☐ **confirm**   ☐ **definitely**   ☑ **deny**   ☑ **format**   ☐ **unify**

Write and Discuss   Have students turn to a partner to discuss the following questions. Guide students to include the academic vocabulary words *deny* and *format* in their responses. Ask volunteers to share their responses with the class.

- Based on this text, would Anderson support or **deny** an argument that formerly enslaved people owe their masters something because of a long history together?
- What is the **format** of Anderson's communication with his former master?

TEACH

 ## LANGUAGE CONVENTIONS

Remind students that a noun clause is a subordinate clause used as a noun. Explain that if they can replace the clause with the word *something* or *someone* and the sentence still makes sense, it is a noun clause. (**Answer:** *It serves as a direct object that refers to the verb* know.)

ANALYZE TONE

Remind students to watch for ways the author's word choice establishes the tone. For instance, "which you say I can have" emphasizes the difference between the colonel's situation and that of Anderson. (**Answer:** *The Colonel cannot offer Anderson his freedom because Anderson is already free. Anderson and his family are treated better than they ever were while they were enslaved. The Colonel has nothing to offer Anderson that can improve on his current situation.*)

■ English Learner Support

Understand Tone Help students locate the clause "which you say I can have" and make sure they understand that *which* refers back to "freedom." Then, have pairs discuss why Anderson and the Colonel see Anderson's situation differently. **MODERATE**

CRITICAL VOCABULARY

disposed: Anderson says Mandy wants evidence that their former master was inclined to treat them kindly.

ASK STUDENTS for evidence about whether Anderson seems disposed to return to his former master's farm. (*He is not so disposed and that is why he is asking for an impossibly large sum of money.*)

recompense: Anderson and his relatives had to work for no pay.

ASK STUDENTS whether they think Anderson's former master would be able to pay the recompense if he wanted to. (*He probably could not because his farm is already in trouble.*)

reckoning: Anderson says that someday his former master will have to answer for having kept slaves.

ASK STUDENTS how losing his farm was a partial reckoning for Colonel Anderson's keeping slaves. (*His farm would not have lost so many workers if he had not depended on unpaid labor and abused them.*)

 NOTICE & NOTE

LANGUAGE CONVENTIONS
Annotate: Mark the noun clause in the first sentence of paragraph 2.

Analyze: What function does this noun clause serve in the sentence? What does it refer to?

ANALYZE TONE
Annotate: In paragraph 3, mark Anderson's response to the Colonel's offer of freedom.

Analyze: What contrast is there between Anderson and the Colonel's understanding of Anderson's situation?

disposed
(dĭ-spōzd´) *adj.* having a preference, disposition, or tendency.

recompense
(rĕk´əm-pĕns) *n.* payment in return for something, such as a service.

reckoning
(rĕk´ə-nĭng) *n.* a settlement of accounts.

Esther, Green, and Lee. Give my love to them all, and tell them I hope we will meet in the better world, if not in this. I would have gone back to see you all when I was working in the Nashville Hospital, but one of the neighbors told me that Henry intended to shoot me if he ever got a chance.

2   I want to know particularly what the good chance is you propose to give me. I am doing tolerably well here. I get twenty-five dollars a month, with victuals[1] and clothing; have a comfortable home for Mandy,—the folks call her Mrs. Anderson,—and the children—Milly, Jane, and Grundy—go to school and are learning well. The teacher says Grundy has a head for a preacher. They go to Sunday school, and Mandy and me attend church regularly. We are kindly treated. Sometimes we overhear others saying, "Them colored people were slaves" down in Tennessee. The children feel hurt when they hear such remarks; but I tell them it was no disgrace in Tennessee to belong to Colonel Anderson. Many darkeys would have been proud, as I used to be, to call you master. Now if you will write and say what wages you will give me, I will be better able to decide whether it would be to my advantage to move back again.

3   As to my freedom, which you say I can have, there is nothing to be gained on that score, as I got my free papers in 1864 from the Provost-Marshal-General of the Department of Nashville. Mandy says she would be afraid to go back without some proof that you were **disposed** to treat us justly and kindly; and we have concluded to test your sincerity by asking you to send us our wages for the time we served you. This will make us forget and forgive old scores, and rely on your justice and friendship in the future. I served you faithfully for thirty-two years, and Mandy twenty years. At twenty-five dollars a month for me, and two dollars a week for Mandy, our earnings would amount to eleven thousand six hundred and eighty dollars. Add to this the interest for the time our wages have been kept back, and deduct what you paid for our clothing, and three doctor's visits to me, and pulling a tooth for Mandy, and the balance will show what we are in justice entitled to. Please send the money by Adams's Express, in care of V. Winters, Esq., Dayton, Ohio. If you fail to pay us for faithful labors in the past, we can have little faith in your promises in the future. We trust the good Maker[2] has opened your eyes to the wrongs which you and your fathers have done to me and my fathers, in making us toil for you for generations without **recompense**. Here I draw my wages every Saturday night; but in Tennessee there was never any pay-day for the negroes any more than for the horses and cows. Surely there will be a day of **reckoning** for those who defraud the laborer of his hire.

---

[1] **victuals** (vĭt´lz): food fit for human consumption.
[2] **good Maker:** God.

WHEN STUDENTS STRUGGLE . . .

Inferences Often a writer will use language to imply something rather than say it directly. In his letter, Anderson says, "You will also please state if there has been any schools opened for the colored children in your neighborhood." Ask students why they think Anderson said that. Then explain that he does not say directly that there was not a school his children could go to before, but it is implied. The reader must infer what he is really saying. Have student pairs find more language in the letter that implies something different than what the words say literally.

 For additional support, go to the **Reading Studio** and assign the following Level Up Tutorial: Making Inferences.

4   In answering this letter, please state if there would be any safety for my Milly and Jane, who are now grown up, and both good-looking girls. You know how it was with poor Matilda and Catherine. I would rather stay here and starve—and die, if it come to that—than have my girls brought to shame by the violence and wickedness of their young masters. You will also please state if there has been any schools opened for the colored children in your neighborhood. The great desire of my life now is to give my children an education, and have them form **virtuous** habits.

5   Say howdy to George Carter, and thank him for taking the pistol from you when you were shooting at me.

From your old servant,

Jourdon Anderson.

virtuous
(vûr´chŏŏ-əs) *adj.* having or showing virtue, especially moral excellence.

ANALYZE LETTERS
Annotate: Mark the sentence that closes the letter.

Analyze: Why does the writer conclude with another example of the Colonel's poor behavior?

CHECK YOUR UNDERSTANDING

Answer these questions before moving on to the **Analyze the Text** section.

1 What message does Anderson send in paragraph 1 when explaining his worries for his former master's safety?

A The former master is fortunate not to have been punished.

B The former master is a hothead who always gets into trouble.

C Anderson wants to have nothing to do with the former master.

D Anderson will only return if the former master apologizes for shooting at him.

2 What does Anderson ask for to test the Colonel's sincerity?

F Freedom for himself and his family

G Wages earned while they were enslaved

H A role in the Nashville Hospital

J Greetings to his old friends

3 What does Anderson wish for his daughters?

A A return to their childhood homes

B Good marriages and jobs

C Safety and an education

D Good relations with the former master

 ENGLISH LEARNER SUPPORT

Oral Assessment Use the following questions to assess students' comprehension and speaking skills.

1. What is Anderson saying when he worries about his old master's safety in paragraph 1? *(His former master is lucky that he was not punished.)*

2. What does Anderson want from the Colonel to prove he's not lying? *(payment for their work when Anderson and his wife were enslaved)*

3. What does Anderson want his daughters to have? *(safety and an education)*
    MODERATE/LIGHT

 ANALYZE LETTERS

Encourage students to think about how they would close correspondence, either letters or digital communications and how this last sentence differs from what one might expect. (**Answer:** *Anderson adds a note to remind his former master of past injustices against him, indicating that he is not going to accept promises at face value.*)

CHECK YOUR UNDERSTANDING

Have students answer the questions independently.

Answers:

1. *A*

2. *G*

3. *C*

If they answer any questions incorrectly, have them reread the text to confirm their understanding. Then, they may proceed to ANALYZE THE TEXT on page 346.

CRITICAL VOCABULARY

virtuous: Anderson wants his children to behave in a moral way.

ASK STUDENTS whether Anderson thinks his former master has virtuous habits and why Anderson has that opinion. *(No, because he shot at Anderson and kept slaves.)*

ANALYZE THE TEXT

Possible answers:

1. **DOK 2:** *He states that he earns "twenty-five dollars a month," says the children are doing well and going to church, and says that they are "kindly treated." He includes these details to show that his life has improved since he got away from the Colonel.*

2. **DOK 4:** *It is ironic for the Colonel to try to grant freedom to someone who is already free. Anderson responds by pointing out that he has his freedom.*

3. **DOK 4:** *Anderson is trying to show how fair-minded he is—he's asking only for what they are due for what they have done in the past. He is also subtly reminding Colonel Anderson that he has acted unjustly in the past.*

4. **DOK 2:** *Anderson and his family frequently dealt with violence and oppressive conditions, making a return to his old life seem unappealing. Including these examples makes the Colonel's request seem absurd, as no one would willfully choose to return to such conditions.*

5. **DOK 4:** *The tone can be described as calm and reasonable. Anderson does not overstate his case; there are no angry denunciations of the recipient, just a straightforward presentation of the writer's position. By using a matter-of-fact way of contrasting the positive circumstances he is experiencing with the violence and exploitation he faced while he was enslaved, the writer powerfully conveys that he would not consider Colonel Anderson's offer.*

RESEARCH

Tell students that although the Civil War amendments are not particularly divisive now, they were much more so when they were enacted. Encourage them to look for evidence of how they would have been perceived at that time in some parts of the country.

Extend Have students find a few first-person sources about the freeing of the slaves as the word of the Emancipation Proclamation spread.

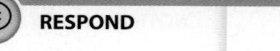 **RESPOND**

ANALYZE THE TEXT

Support your responses with evidence from the text. **NOTEBOOK**

1. **Infer** What details about his current situation does Anderson include in paragraph 2? Why does he include this information?

2. **Analyze** What is ironic about the Colonel's willingness to grant Anderson his freedom? How does Anderson respond?

3. **Analyze** One way writers convey tone is through **diction,** or word choice. In paragraph 3, what does Anderson mean when he asks for "what we are in justice entitled to"? Why did he choose these words to express this idea?

4. **Infer** Consider the details the writer includes about his life serving Colonel Anderson. How are these examples pertinent to the Colonel's request? What do they suggest about the writer's life at that time and his feeling toward Colonel Anderson's request?

5. **Synthesize** How would you describe the overall tone of the letter? Explain your answer, citing evidence from the text including examples of direct statements, verbal irony, and understatement.

RESEARCH

RESEARCH TIP
Be sure to evaluate the credibility of your sources. Government websites ending in .gov will have reliable information on these questions, as will general encyclopedias and many sites devoted to Civil War history.

The end of the Civil War saw a huge change in southern society due to the end of slavery. Find out how the three amendments to the U.S. Constitution known as the "Civil War amendments" dramatically changed the status of African Americans.

AMENDMENT	YEAR	EFFECT
Thirteenth	1865	Ended slavery in the United States and its possessions
Fourteenth	1868	Gave citizenship to anyone born in U.S. and equal protection under law to citizens
Fifteenth	1870	Gave right to vote to African American men

Extend President Abraham Lincoln declared many enslaved African Americans to be free when he issued the Emancipation Proclamation. Given that, why was the Thirteenth Amendment necessary? Find out and write a paragraph or two comparing the two government actions.

WHEN STUDENTS STRUGGLE . . .

Make Inferences Tell students that they can make a lot of inferences based on what Anderson says and doesn't say in his letter. For instance, since he still wishes well about the man who tried to shoot him, we can infer that he is a forgiving person. Ask what they could infer about Anderson from his asking for his wages for the time he worked as a slave. (*He doesn't want to go back, and he wants to remind the Colonel how he took advantage of Anderson and the others.*)

 For additional support, go to the **Reading Studio** and assign the following **Level Up Tutorial: Making Inferences.**

CREATE AND PRESENT

Write a Biographical Essay Numerous historical figures had a hand in helping African Americans gain their freedom. One of the most distinguished African Americans of the 19th century was Frederick Douglass, who escaped slavery and became an eloquent leader of the movement to abolish slavery. Research Douglass and write an essay about his life.

❏ Take notes on the details on key events in his life, including his escape from slavery, his role in reform movements, and his continued advocacy for African Americans' rights.

❏ Use reliable, authoritative sources; provide source information for all facts and quotations.

❏ Craft an essay with a logical structure, including an introduction, body, and conclusion that state a thesis about the impact of Douglass.

❏ Cite sources correctly in the final essay.

Give a Presentation Turn your essay into a presentation given to a small group of students.

❏ Practice reading your essay, speaking loudly enough to be heard, pronouncing all words clearly, and placing emphasis on the most important points.

❏ Present your essay to the group. When you are done, ask your listeners if they have any questions and respond to them.

❏ Listen to others in the group make their presentations and ask clarifying questions of them.

 Go to **Developing a Topic** in the **Writing Studio** for help.

Go to **Giving a Presentation: Delivering Your Presentation** in the **Speaking and Listening Studio** for help.

RESPOND TO THE ESSENTIAL QUESTION

 ? When is self-determination possible?

Gather Information Review your annotations and notes on "To My Old Master." Then, add relevant information to your Response Log. As you determine which information to include, think about:

• how people demonstrate strength of character and will

• how people choose to address wrongs and injustices

• what it means to make a moral choice

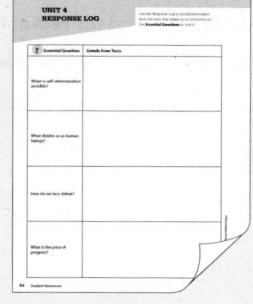

ACADEMIC VOCABULARY

As you write and discuss what you learned from the letter, be sure to use the Academic Vocabulary words. Check off each of the words that you use.

❏ **confirm**

❏ **definitely**

❏ **deny**

❏ **format**

❏ **unify**

CREATE AND PRESENT

Write a Biographical Essay Encourage students to find Frederick Douglass's autobiography to use as a primary source. Emphasize that a research paper needs a thesis, and encourage students to determine their thesis first in order to focus their writing.

📖 For **writing support** for students at varying proficiency levels, see the **Text X-Ray** on page 340D.

Give a Presentation Remind students that asking good clarifying questions is an extremely useful tool. Discuss what kinds of questions are designed to get more information on an interesting topic. Students should concentrate their focus on *how* or *why* questions to synthesize the information with other facts they know about the period, instead of asking *yes* or *no* questions.

RESPOND TO THE ESSENTIAL QUESTION

Allow time for students to add details from "To My Old Master" to their Unit 4 Response Logs.

CRITICAL VOCABULARY

Answers:

1. *recompense*

2. *disposed*

3. *reckoning*

4. *virtuous*

VOCABULARY STRATEGY:
Use Sentence Structure to Determine Meaning of Words

Answers:

1. *verb; to get rid of or throw out*

2. *adjective; having a preference, disposition, or tendency*

3. *noun; compensation or reward given for loss or harm suffered or effort made*

4. *verb; make amends to (someone) for loss or harm suffered; compensate*

5. *noun; an itemized bill or statement of a sum due*

6. *verb; to consider as being; regard as*

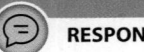 **RESPOND**

CRITICAL VOCABULARY

Practice and Apply Choose the correct word to complete each sentence.

WORD BANK
disposed
recompense
reckoning
virtuous

1. "We will _____ you fairly for your efforts on our behalf," the business owner told her lawyer.

2. Millions of fans were _____ to embrace the newest entry in the popular movie franchise.

3. The final _____ of the proceeds showed that the charity auction was a great success.

4. The children's education aimed to ensure that they would be _____ and not immoral.

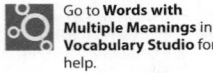 Go to **Words with Multiple Meanings** in the **Vocabulary Studio** for help.

VOCABULARY STRATEGY: Use Sentence Structure to Determine Meaning of Words

Many words in English can function as more than one part of speech. *Promising*, for instance, can be a gerund used to indicate the act of making a promise or an adjective meaning something likely to succeed. With words that have multiple meanings, you can use sentence structure to determine which meaning is appropriate in context.

Practice and Apply Read the following sentences. Write the part of speech and the correct meaning in context for each boldface word. Use a print or digital dictionary to validate your choices if necessary.

1. They **disposed** of the leftover supplies by dumping them in the trash.

2. The family was well **disposed** toward anyone who liked dogs.

3. Mr. and Mrs. Tomlinson offered a **recompense** for the return of their cat.

4. How will you **recompense** the employees who exceeded expectations?

5. If you give me the **reckoning,** I will settle the bill.

6. The producers were **reckoning** that more people would attend the show.

 ENGLISH LEARNER SUPPORT

Sound Transfer Note that the /k/ in *reckoning* and *recompense* may be a difficult sound for speakers of Spanish, Hmong, Cantonese, Haitian Creole, and Korean, as the sound either does not exist in the language, does exist but is pronounced somewhat differently, or is likely to be confused with another sound. Be sure to pronounce these words for students while they can see the letters: *clothing, care, recompense, reckoning*. Then, have them repeat chorally.
SUBSTANTIAL/MODERATE

LANGUAGE CONVENTIONS: Noun Clauses

Noun clauses are subordinate clauses used as nouns. They are introduced either by pronouns, such as *that, what, who, whoever, which,* and *whose,* or by subordinating conjunctions, such as *how, when, where, why,* and *whether.* However, these same words may introduce adjective clauses as well. For that reason, you need to consider how a clause functions within its sentence to determine which type of clause it is. One way of checking is to try substituting *something* or *someone* for the clause. If you do that and the sentence still makes sense, it is probably a noun clause.

This example is a noun clause serving as a direct object because you can say "I know *something.*"

I know <u>whose woods these are</u>.

This example is an adjective clause because you cannot say "The book *something* has clearly been read many times."

The book <u>that is tattered</u> has clearly been read many times.

Practice and Apply Look at the following sentences from "To My Old Master." Determine whether the boldface phrases are noun clauses and, if so, what function they serve in the sentence. Are they a subject, a direct object, an indirect object, a predicate nominative, or the object of a preposition?

1. I got your letter, and was glad to find **that you had not forgotten Jourdon** . . .

2. I would have gone back to see you all **when I was working in the Nashville Hospital,** . . .

3. I want to know particularly **what the good chance is you propose to give me.**

4. I will be better able to decide **whether it would be to my advantage to move back again.**

5. . . . please state if there would be any safety for my Milly and Jane, **who are now grown up,** . . .

RESPOND

Go to **The Noun Clause** in the **Grammar Studio** for help.

LANGUAGE CONVENTIONS: Noun Clauses

Discuss with students why the *something* test works, namely that *something* is a noun. If the clause is being used as a noun, it will make sense when a noun is substituted, but if the clause is being used as an adjective, it will only make sense when an adjective is substituted, and even then it will be out of order.

Practice and Apply After students have identified each noun clause and decided its function, have partners discuss the noun clauses to explain their reasoning.

ENGLISH LEARNER SUPPORT

Language Conventions Use the following supports with students at varying proficiency levels:

- Have students work in pairs to find and underline the clauses in the Practice and Apply sentences. **SUBSTANTIAL**

- Have students underline the words that introduce the clauses in the Practice and Apply sentences, and then work with a partner to decide whether each is a noun clause. **MODERATE**

- Have students write each of the Practice and Apply sentences with the clause replaced with *someone* or *something,* and then decide whether each is a noun clause. **LIGHT**

CIVIL WAR PHOTOGRAPHS

Image Collection by Mathew Brady, Alexander Gardner, and Andrew J. Russell

GENRE ELEMENTS
PHOTOJOURNALISM

Photography that shows people, places, and events from the past provides information, just like informational text does. **Photographs** reveal visual information that may be difficult to describe in words. For example, they may show facial expressions and body movements that communicate what a person is experiencing. Photographs often form a greater connection with an audience than text can, as they allow the viewer to visualize a setting or person and imagine what a person, place, or event was like.

LEARNING OBJECTIVES

- Make connections with photographs and analyze media effectiveness.
- Research photography creation and distribution during the Civil War.
- Write a didactic placard for a Civil War photograph.
- Debate whether the public should see violent war images.
- Use academic vocabulary words in writing.
- **Language** Express ideas and describe a photograph's message.

TEXT COMPLEXITY

Quantitative Measures	Civil War Photographs	Lexile: N/A
Qualitative Measures	**Ideas Presented** Most is explicit, but moves to some implied meaning.	
	Structures Used Explicit, visual imagery.	
	Language Used N/A	
	Knowledge Required Some references to events required for fuller understanding.	

Online Ed

RESOURCES

- Unit 4 Response Log
- Reading Studio: Notice & Note
- Level Up Tutorial: Historical and Cultural Context
- Speaking and Listening Studio: Analyzing and Evaluating Presentations
- Civil War Photographs Selection Test

SUMMARIES

English

Photographs taken between 1863 and 1865 show scenes from the American Civil War. The background photo shows a man next to a wagon in a forest. The next photograph shows photographer Mathew Brady in the field where the Battle of Gettysburg was fought. A September 1863 photograph shows a group of soldiers posing for a group portrait. Another shows Union soldiers at a wooden cottage where they lived in the winter. The last photograph shows the ruins of Richmond, Virginia, after the city surrendered on April 3, 1865.

Spanish

Cinco fotografías tomadas entre 1863 y 1865 muestran escenas de la Guerra Civil. La foto del fondo muestra a un hombre al lado de una carreta en un bosque. La siguiente fotografía muestra al fotógrafo Matthew Brady junto a un cerco roto alrededor del campo donde se libró la Batalla de Gettysburg. Una fotografía de septiembre de 1863 muestra a un grupo de oficiales posando para un retrato grupal. Otra muestra unos soldados de la Unión en la cabaña de madera donde se quedaron durante el invierno. La última fotografía muestra las ruinas de Richmond, Virginia, luego de la rendición de la ciudad el 3 de abril de 1865.

SMALL-GROUP OPTIONS

Have students work in small groups and pairs to view and discuss the selection.

Create a Message Poster

- Have students form four groups. Assign a photograph to each group. Distribute a copy of the photo and a poster board to each group.
- Tell students to discuss a message conveyed by their photograph. The message can be about topics such as the war, the challenges soldiers faced, or the friendships between soldiers.
- Have students decide on one of the messages they discussed and plan a poster that conveys the same message. The poster can include both images and text.
- Have each group create its poster and share it with the class.

It's in the Details

- Have students form four groups. Assign a photograph to each group. Have each group list the letters of the alphabet on paper, and record a word that describes an image in the photo for each letter. Students can list more than one word per letter, but the objective is to assign a word to as many letters as possible in a set time.
- Announce end of time, count the number of letters used, and celebrate the group that used the most letters.
- Then, give the groups a few minutes to write a sentence about their photographs using one or more words on their lists.

Text X-Ray: English Learner Support
for Civil War Photographs

Use the Text X-Ray and the supports and scaffolds in the Teacher's Edition to help guide students at different proficiency levels through the selection.

INTRODUCE THE SELECTION
DISCUSS PHOTOGRAPHY

Discuss how people today communicate via photos. Display these terms, say them aloud, and elicit or explain their meanings:

- *composition*: the manner in which parts or elements are combined to form the whole
- *foreground*: the part of the photo that is nearest to the viewer
- *background*: the part of the photo that appears to be in the distance, behind the subject
- *black and white*: the presentation of an image in black and white
- *digital photography*: photography using a digital camera, or one that stores images using data instead of film

Then, connect the discussion to Civil War photography. Ask:

- If people during the Civil War had today's technology, what types of photos would they send to their family and friends?
- Would they send photos of battle scenes? Why or why not?

CULTURAL REFERENCES

The following words or phrases may be unfamiliar to students:

- *battlefield* (photograph 1): place where a battle was fought
- *Confederate* (photograph 1): someone who supported the Confederate States of America (the southern states that seceded from the Union)
- *brigade* (photograph 1): an army unit
- *quarters* (photograph 3): shelter or place to live
- *surrendered* (photograph 4): gave up or yielded to the opposing side

LISTENING

Identify Details in a Photograph

Draw students' attention to the photo captions. Explain that a caption gives information about a photo and can help them identify specific details in the photo.

Have students listen as you read the caption aloud. Use the following supports with students at varying proficiency levels:

- Read the caption of the first photo to the students. Then, say individual words and phrases in the caption. Tell students to point to the matching detail in the photo. Repeat for each photo. **SUBSTANTIAL**
- Read each photo's caption aloud and have students paraphrase it. Provide sentence frames such as these: *This photo shows the (battlefield) at (Gettysburg) in (1863). In the background, we see _____. In the foreground, we see _____.* **MODERATE**
- Read each photograph's caption aloud. After each caption, tell students to retell what you read and point out details in the photo. **LIGHT**

SPEAKING

Interview the Photographer

Tell students to imagine they have the opportunity to interview the photographers who took these photos. Work with them to prepare interview questions and conduct interviews.

Brainstorm with the class a list of questions to ask the photographers about specific information and the photographer's message. Use the following supports with students at varying proficiency levels:

- Work with students in a small group. Have students say a *Wh-* question word (e.g., *Where*) and then ask them a question starting with that word *(Where was this photo taken?)* followed by a related *yes-no* question *(Was it taken in Washington, D.C.?)* Have students imagine they are the photographer and respond *yes* or *no*. Repeat this process with additional questions. **SUBSTANTIAL**
- Have students work with a partner and play the roles of the photographer and the interviewer. Interviewers should ask questions about a photo. **MODERATE**
- In groups of four, have one student play the photographer. The others are journalists. For each photo, have each journalist ask one question. After the photographer answers, have another student play the photographer for another photo and repeat the process. **LIGHT**

READING

Identify the Message in Photographs

Tell students that photographs and captions work together to tell a story or share a message. Discussing the photographs and captions will help students understand the photographs.

Use the following supports with students at varying proficiency levels:

- Chorally read the captions and have students study the photographs. Ask *yes/no* questions about each, such as: *Is the mood happy? Is it sad? Is the photograph effective?* **SUBSTANTIAL**
- Have students work in groups to read the captions and discuss the photographs. Provide sentence frames such as: *The caption tells me_____. The caption and photograph help me understand the war because ____. I think the photograph was trying to ____.* **MODERATE**
- Have students work in small groups to discuss each caption and photograph. Have students answer the following questions: *What does the photograph tell about the war? How does the caption help you understand the photograph? What is the photographer's message?* **LIGHT**

WRITING

Write a Didactic Placard

Work with students to read the writing assignment on page 359.

Use the following supports with students at varying proficiency levels:

- Work with students to write a short placard for the image. Help them include the date and name of the photographer. Write the information on the board and have students copy it in their notebooks. **SUBSTANTIAL**
- Provide sentence frames for the placard for the image. *This photograph was taken in ____ by ____. It shows ____.* **MODERATE**
- In addition to the date, name of photographer, and what the image shows, students should include in their placards why the image is important. **LIGHT**

Connect to the
ESSENTIAL QUESTION

Americans were divided on many issues, even before the United States won independence, but no other issue was more divisive than slavery. However, although blood was shed before the Civil War, slavery alone did not lead to combat. The southern states' belief that they could leave the United States and create their own, separate country is what triggered the start of the war. Of course, slavery provided the reason they wanted to leave. Essentially, the issue that divided people then, as now, was divergent and incompatible beliefs.

ANALYZE & APPLY

MEDIA

CIVIL WAR PHOTOGRAPHS

Image Collection by **Mathew Brady, Alexander Gardner,** and **Andrew J. Russell**

? ESSENTIAL QUESTION:

What divides us as human beings?

© Houghton Mifflin Harcourt Publishing Company • Image Credits: © Library of Congress Prints & Photographs Division

350   Unit 4

QUICK START

You've probably heard the saying, "A picture is worth a thousand words." Can you think of a photograph you've seen that exemplifies this saying? Share it with your group, and explain what you find compelling about it.

MAKE CONNECTIONS

In this lesson, you will examine photographs taken during the Civil War and make connections between them and other materials related to the topic. One way of making connections is to link what you are reading or seeing to your background knowledge or to other texts you have read. You might also relate a text to the world at large.

Think about what you know about the Civil War or the other texts you have read on the subject. As you view the photographs, make connections between them and what you already know, and think about what they add to your understanding of the topic. You may also have questions if what you see in the photographs relates to or conflicts with what you already know about the Civil War. Write down any questions that occur to you while viewing.

GENRE ELEMENTS: PHOTOJOURNALISM

- includes still images
- documents events of historical significance
- conveys a message through subject and composition

WHAT I'VE READ ON THE TOPIC	MY OWN KNOWLEDGE	WHAT PHOTOS TELL ME	QUESTIONS I HAVE ABOUT PHOTOS

QUICK START

Discuss in class the saying about a picture being worth a thousand words. What do students think that means and when might it not be true? As students look for photos to share in class, you can either encourage them to share photos they bring to class—because they would know the stories behind the photos—or, to save time, have them select images from those in this collection. Either way, they should share not only why the selected image is compelling, but also what words they think the picture suggests.

MAKE CONNECTIONS

Encourage students to think of everything they have heard about the Civil War from textbooks, TV, movies, or other sources. Using class time, you might want to discuss some key elements of the war, such as the number of casualties and how completely shattered the South was by the end of the conflict. Have students share any details that come to mind, especially from other sources.

ANALYZE MEDIA EFFECTIVENESS

Point out to your students that to be effective, a photograph needs to communicate clearly the information the photographer meant to transmit. Sometimes the photograph simply records something, such as crossing a finish line or showing what a specific bird looks like. However, photographers often have a message they want to get across. They work to find images that will get that message across. Many photographs will also elicit an emotional response. Encourage students to think about what emotions one would feel if the people in these photographs were friends, brothers, or fathers, or if, in the last image, Richmond was home.

 **GET READY**

ANALYZE MEDIA EFFECTIVENESS

The Civil War photographs produced by Mathew Brady and others were intended to reveal the terrible realities of the conflict to an audience that tended to romanticize war. The photos were important to soldiers, who did not want to burden family members with battlefield descriptions in their letters, and to families, who desperately wanted information about their loved ones. The photographs printed in newspapers and magazines motivated civilian efforts to send relief supplies to those who were fighting.

Photojournalists communicate the significant details and broad context of a story through the selection of **subjects,** or the central figures in a photograph, and **composition,** or the arrangement of visual elements. Civil War cameras could not capture motion, so photographers were limited to photographing their subjects before and after battle. Scenes from the camps, prisons, hospitals, and the aftermath of battles were typical settings.

As you view the photographs, think about the choices the photographer made and the ideas conveyed through the images. What message is the photographer sending? Who is the intended audience, and how might those people perceive the photographs? Are the photographs effective? If not, what would make them more powerful? Record your ideas in the chart.

PHOTOGRAPH	PHOTOGRAPHER'S MESSAGE	AUDIENCE PERCEPTION	EFFECTIVENESS
Photo 1			
Photo 2			
Photo 3			
Photo 4			

 ENGLISH LEARNER SUPPORT

Connect with Images Have students work with a partner or in a small group (if there are several students who share the same language). Assess how much they understand about the American Civil War and supply any information they lack that relates to the images. Let them discuss, in their native language if necessary, how the images help them gain information about the Civil War. Then, ask them to work together to formulate in English a statement about each photograph. Provide this sentence frame: *This photo helps me understand _____ during the American Civil War.* **SUBSTANTIAL**

BACKGROUND

Mathew Brady *(1823–1896),* **Alexander Gardner** *(1821–1882), and*
Andrew J. Russell *(1829–1902) took thousands of photographs of the Civil
War. When it began in 1861, advances in photography enabled these men
to take their photographic equipment to the camps and battlefields. Brady,
Gardner, and Russell braved not only harsh weather and rugged terrain but
also stray bullets in their quest to capture the realities of war.*

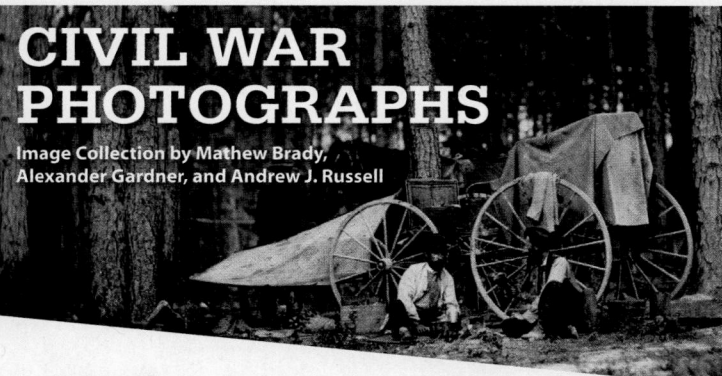

CIVIL WAR PHOTOGRAPHS

Image Collection by Mathew Brady,
Alexander Gardner, and Andrew J. Russell

*Before the late 1800s, important news was generally limited to text. News about
the progress of war, for example, appeared in newspapers and in soldiers' letters
to people back home. By the time of the Civil War, photographic technology
had advanced enough that photographers could be mobile. Those brave
enough to carry their equipment with them to the front lines were able to
show civilians the stark realities of war. The Civil War was the first war to be
documented in photographs, and it fundamentally changed war journalism.*

*There were still limitations to camera technology. Soldiers moving on
battlefields became blurry figures in a hazy landscape. However, preparations
for battle, the daily life of soldiers, and the gruesome aftermath of battle
could be captured. Photographers set up cameras in fields strewn with
corpses. They took photos of the wounded in hospitals and enemy soldiers in
prisons. The photos then had to be processed, which was an added difficulty.
Photographers set up portable darkrooms and rinsed the finished photos in
streams, but the photos could easily be ruined by dirt and debris. The courage
and determination of these photographers gave the nation a remarkable
historical record of an important time in its history.*

BACKGROUND

Mathew Brady (1823–1896) was among the earliest
photographers in U.S. history and one of the first Civil
War photographers. Though famous during his life for
his portraits of politicians, his enduring fame rests on the
remarkable images he took during the American Civil War.
Because he wanted a complete record of the conflict, he
hired a group of about 20 photographers who were willing
to brave the dangers of war to produce gritty, realistic
photos of the war's terrible realities. Though he spent
much time supervising his employees and getting them
supplies, he photographed some of the most important
and bloodiest battles of the war, including Bull Run,
Antietam, and Gettysburg. Many of his team's photos were
gathered and exhibited in 1862 under the title "The Dead
of Antietam." They showed the field of battle littered with
the dead—a sight that shocked and sobered viewers. While
the accomplishment was unparalleled, it ruined Brady, who
had spent $100,000 on the project. He never recovered
financially, dying alone and forgotten. Fortunately, his
images were not forgotten, and today he is better known
than he was when he was alive.

Alexander Gardner (1821–1882) first saw an exhibition
of Brady's photos on a visit to New York in 1851, and when
he emigrated from Scotland to the United States in 1856,
he began working for Brady. When the Civil War broke out,
Gardner was one of about 20 photographers sent out by
Brady to document it. However, Gardner wanted credit for
his images, rather than having them combined with Brady's.
He quit working for Brady and went out on his own.

Andrew J. Russell (1829–1902) was another
photographer who braved the harsh realities and very real
dangers of war to capture images of what combat was like.
He was an engineer with the United States Military Railroad
Construction Corps. During the Civil War, he was sent to
photograph military camps and battlefields.

The image at left, shot near Petersburg, Virginia, shows
how much equipment Brady and his employees had to carry
into the field—as well as how rough the living conditions
were for the photographers.

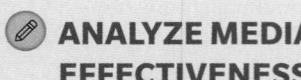

TEACH

SETTING A PURPOSE

Direct students to use the Setting a Purpose prompt to focus their reading.

ANALYZE MEDIA EFFECTIVENESS

Tell students they can list the elements under the image, rather than circling or marking them, if they would rather not draw on the photograph. Also relate that the purpose of the exercise is to notice how ordinary things are—they might recognize a pond, a fence, and so on. (**Possible answer:** *The pond is reflective, and the viewer might be reflective. The scene is quiet, but the fence is broken, which hints at the combat that occurred here. Though the scene seems peaceful, it also suggests a sense of loss and sadness.*)

For **listening support** for students at varying proficiency levels, see the **Text X-Ray** on page 350C.

SETTING A PURPOSE

As you examine each of these historic photographs, think about what story the photographer wanted to tell and how the image connects with your knowledge of the Civil War.

ANALYZE MEDIA EFFECTIVENESS

Annotate: What images in this photograph stand out to you?

Analyze: How does the composition of this photograph evoke a mood? What is surprising or unexpected about the photo?

Battlefield at Gettysburg, 1863. In the background is McPherson's (or Herbst's) Woods where Confederate Brigadier General James J. Archer's brigade was captured. Mathew Brady, photographer, in the foreground

© Houghton Mifflin Harcourt Publishing Company • Image Credits: © Library of Congress Prints & Photographs Division

September 1863, Culpeper, Virginia. Officers of the U.S. Horse Artillery Brigade commanded by Captain James M. Robertson (seated 2nd row, 4th from left). Alexander Gardner, photographer

MAKE CONNECTIONS
Annotate: What is happening in this photograph?

Connect: Does this photo remind you of any photos you have seen in the world at large? How does the photo connect to the overall war effort?

MAKE CONNECTIONS

Tell students to write their comments about what is happening in the photo in the space under the caption. Encourage them to notice the details and to think about what the details say about what life was like on the battlefield. (**Possible answer:** *This is similar to a class photo because it shows people united in a group with a common goal. It is something the people in the group would likely keep to remind them of the men with whom they served. It connects to the overall war effort by showing the people who would be fighting the war and illustrating how they lived during wartime—in the tents behind the men. They look confident and ready for battle.*)

WHEN STUDENTS STRUGGLE...

Analyze Images If students are having difficulty figuring out what they are supposed to be noticing in the images, walk them through the analysis of one or more photographs. Point out the elements in the image and talk through what they communicate. For example, point out the broken fence on page 354 and ask what might have happened there. Ask how the photo on this page might make parents back home feel good about what these men are doing. Ask if students would want to spend the winter in the hut on page 356, or how they would feel if their town looked like the one on page 357. Discuss what it is in each photo that catches their eye or makes them wonder what is happening.

 ## MAKE CONNECTIONS

Tell students they can identify the items and activities in the space below the caption, rather than on the photograph. Remind students that people had to stay still for a few minutes to keep from looking blurred in a photograph. Ask how knowing that helps students understand the poses. (**Possible answer:** *The photo could likely show people back home that, even though the accommodations are too small, the soldiers seem fine. These are all tasks that would probably be taking place at home, even if there was no war. Family members might find it reassuring.*)

MAKE CONNECTIONS

Annotate: What items and activities do you see in this photograph?

Interpret: Consider what you already know about the Civil War. What does this photo suggest to people back home who would want news of their loved ones?

1863(?), "Pine Cottage," winter quarters for Union soldiers.
Mathew Brady, photographer

The ruins of Richmond, Virginia, capital of the Confederacy, after the city surrendered on April 3, 1865. Andrew J. Russell, photographer

ANALYZE MEDIA EFFECTIVENESS

Annotate: What details in the photograph show that retreating Confederate troops burned bridges and munitions?

Evaluate: Richmond residents believed that General Robert E. Lee would never abandon the capital. What message would the photographer have wanted to convey? How do you think southerners reacted to this photo? How would northerners have reacted?

Civil War Photographs 357

 ANALYZE MEDIA EFFECTIVENESS

Students may not recognize the piles in the middle of the photo as cannonballs, so point them out and ask what the piles of cannonballs reveal to them about this site. (*Weapons and munitions were stored at this site.*) You may also need to explain that "munitions" refers to military weapons. (***Possible answer:*** *The message the photographer likely wanted to convey was that the South had lost, the war was as good as over—and possibly something about the huge human cost of the conflict. Southerners were probably devastated by the image. Richmond, their capital, was in ruins. Northerners, however, though probably saddened by the destruction, would be relieved at this evidence that the war was nearing an end.*)

For **speaking** and **reading support** for students at varying proficiency levels, see the **Text X-Ray** on page 350D.

 ENGLISH LEARNER SUPPORT

Compare and Contrast Photographs Have students compare and contrast the photographs with a partner or in a small group. Provide students sentence frames such as: *This photo shows _____, but that photo shows _____. Both photos show _____.* Remind students of transitional words they can use to compare and contrast, such as *both, similarly, however, but, unlike,* and *on the other hand.* Ask them what lessons they would hope images such as these would communicate to people. **ALL LEVELS**

ANALYZE MEDIA

Possible answers:

1. **DOK 3:** *Answers will vary depending on which two images students select. However, students should make comparisons using the images and captions and relate them to what they know of the Civil War.*

2. **DOK 4:** *Answers will vary depending on what students know about the Civil War, but should clearly communicate how the images and captions support or contradict what students already know.*

3. **DOK 4:** *Answers will vary, though they will likely vary more in response to the request for connections to other historical events.*

4. **DOK 4:** *Answers will vary, but it is likely students will agree that photographs at that time, since they couldn't be digitally manipulated, were probably more reliable than images today. That said, showing peaceful scenes in the midst of war might be said to manipulate information for the photographer's purpose.*

5. **DOK 4:** *Answers will vary, depending on the photo the student selects. However, students should include clear explanations of why they think the photo communicates effectively.*

RESEARCH

Tell students that, in addition to the sites mentioned in the research tip, sites related to photography or that offer biographies of the photographers featured in this selection might also offer insights and information.

Connect Answers will vary, but students should recognize that photojournalists covering modern wars still experience danger as they try to capture the stories of war for the public and for history. They don't have to transport huge pieces of equipment, but they do travel to unfamiliar places to do their work. While modern photojournalists capture the action of a battle, and even moving images, Civil War photographers had to tell the stories by documenting the aftermaths of battles or events surrounding the war.

 **RESPOND**

ANALYZE MEDIA

Support your responses with evidence from the text.   📓 NOTEBOOK

1. **Compare** Choose two of the images. How do these photos and captions present the experience of the Civil War? Do they present it similarly or differently? Explain.

2. **Connect** How do these images and captions confirm or contradict what you already knew about the time, place, and events of the Civil War?

3. **Connect** How do these images connect to what you know or have read about the Civil War? How do they connect to other historical events? Explain.

4. **Evaluate** Civil War photographer Alexander Gardner said that "verbal representations" of war "may or may not have the merit of accuracy; but photographic presentments of them will be accepted by posterity with an undoubting faith." Evaluate these photos against this statement. Which can be deemed faithful presentations of war and why?

5. **Critique** Which image and caption communicate the photographer's purpose and intended effect most powerfully? Explain.

RESEARCH

> **RESEARCH TIP**
> When doing historical research, look for websites published by museums and historical institutions that are reliable and accurate sources of information.

Today, many of us carry slim, lightweight digital cameras that allow us to capture and share images all over the world in an instant. During the Civil War, photography was much different. Do some research to answer the questions about how photographic images were created and distributed during the Civil War.

QUESTION	ANSWER
What equipment was needed?	*Heavy cameras and a portable dark room, carried by wagon*
How was a photograph developed?	*Photographs were developed using the wet-plate process.*
How did the public come to view the photograph?	*The public viewed the photographs at exhibits and later in newspapers.*

Connect Photojournalists in the Civil War went to great lengths and incurred great danger to capture their images. How are their jobs similar and different to that of a modern photojournalist covering wars?

 ENGLISH LEARNER SUPPORT

Oral Assessment To gauge comprehension and speaking skills, ask these questions:

- Did Mathew Brady want a permanent record of the war? *(Yes)* **SUBSTANTIAL**

- In what way did photography change how wars were reported? *(It forced people to confront the reality of what was happening.)* **MODERATE**

- How do you think Mathew Brady felt about the tendency of people to romanticize war? *(His images, which document the horrors of war, indicate that he did not like romanticizing war.)* **LIGHT**

CREATE AND DEBATE

Write a Didactic Placard When images and other objects are displayed in a museum, they are usually accompanied by a didactic placard—a sign that provides the viewer with context and information about the image or object. Find an image like those you have just studied, and write a didactic placard.

- ❏ Include an approximate date of the image.
- ❏ Say who the photographer is.
- ❏ Write a short paragraph explaining what the image shows and why it's important.
- ❏ Add other details about the image an audience would find interesting.

Hold a Debate Form two groups to debate the question, "Should the public be exposed to the violent images of war?"

- ❏ Think about how images might affect people's attitudes toward war.
- ❏ Use evidence to support your arguments. Consider the photographs in this lesson as well as other examples you have encountered.
- ❏ Listen to opposing viewpoints and respond respectfully when you disagree with a participant.

 Go to **Analyzing and Evaluating Presentations: Tracing a Speaker's Argument** in the **Speaking and Listening Studio** for helping with weighing reasons and evidence.

RESPOND TO THE ESSENTIAL QUESTION

? What divides us as human beings?

Gather Information Review your annotations and notes on the Civil War photographs. Then, add relevant information to your Response Log. As you determine which information to include, think about:

- the messages that war photography can convey
- how photographs and other media can shape people's opinions on an issue
- the emotional effects of violent imagery

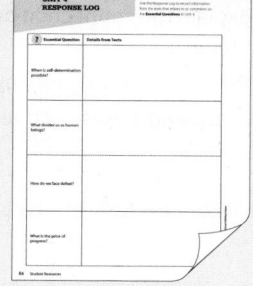

ACADEMIC VOCABULARY

As you write and discuss what you learned about photography during the Civil War, be sure to use the Academic Vocabulary words. Check off each of the words that you use.

- ❏ **confirm**
- ❏ **definitely**
- ❏ **deny**
- ❏ **format**
- ❏ **unify**

CREATE AND DEBATE

Write a Didactic Placard Share with students examples of didactic placards from museums to show them the format. Encourage students to include a few elements of history about the photographer and the event, rather than just explaining what the image shows.

 For **writing support** for students at varying proficiency levels, see the **Text X-Ray** on page 350D.

Hold a Debate Allow students time to research information that would support one side or the other. Before the debate, have students join with those who are on the same side of the debate to discuss the points of the arguments. Have students present the opposing arguments and then discuss who has the most convincing arguments.

RESPOND TO THE ESSENTIAL QUESTION

Allow time for students to add details from Civil War Photographs to their Unit 4 Response Logs.

AN OCCURRENCE AT OWL CREEK BRIDGE

Short Story by Ambrose Bierce

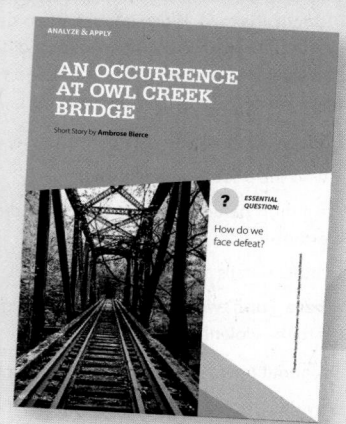

GENRE ELEMENTS
SHORT STORY

A **short story** is a brief fictional work. It has literary elements similar to those in a longer fictional work, such as plot, characters, setting, theme, and point of view. **Point of view** is the perspective from which a story is told. Parts of this story are told from an objective third-person point of view, in which the narrator tells only what happens without describing the thoughts or feelings of the characters. Other parts of the story are told from a third-person limited point of view, in which the narrator is able to describe the thoughts and feelings of one of the characters.

LEARNING OBJECTIVES

- Use literary elements to understand a story.
- Analyze the structure of a literary work.
- Conduct research to answer specific questions.
- Write a short story.
- Discuss your short story with a partner.
- Explain the connection between a word's meaning and its etymology.
- Revise your short story by adding sensory language.
- **Language** Answer questions about the author's message.

TEXT COMPLEXITY

Quantitative Measures	An Occurrence at Owl Creek Bridge	Lexile: 1000L
Qualitative Measures	**Ideas Presented** Multiple levels, subtle, implied meanings and purpose; abstract, difficult ideas.	
	Structures Used Complex plot line; deviates from chronological order; narrator may be unreliable.	
	Language Used Meanings are implied, but support is offered; more figurative language; more inference is demanded.	
	Knowledge Required Explores complex ideas; refers to texts or ideas that may be beyond students' experiences.	

Online

RESOURCES

- Unit 4 Response Log

- Selection Audio

- Reading Studio: Notice & Note

- Level Up Tutorial: Plot: Sequence of Events.

- Writing Studio: Writing Narratives

- Vocabulary Studio: Understanding Word Origins

- "An Occurrence at Owl Creek Bridge" Selection Test

SUMMARIES

English

Bierce's short story begins with Peyton Farquhar, a southern planter, standing on a bridge in Alabama, about to be hanged by Union soldiers for attempting to set fire to Owl Creek Bridge. He falls through the bridge and hangs for a moment before the rope breaks and he falls into the water. He unties his hands, dodges bullets, and swims ashore. He runs through the forest to his home, where he sees his wife. Then, he feels a pain on his neck and hangs, dead. His escape was a fantasy.

Spanish

El cuento de Bierce comienza con Peyton Farquhar, un hacendado sureño, parado en un puente en Alabama a punto de ser ahorcado por soldados de la Unión por tratar de incendiar el puente de Owl Creek. Peyton cae del puente y pende durante un momento antes de que la soga se rompa y caiga al agua. Se desata las manos, esquiva las balas y nada hasta la orilla. Corre a través del bosque, a su hogar, donde ve a su esposa. Luego siente un dolor en el cuello y cuelga, muerto. Su escape era una fantasía.

SMALL-GROUP OPTIONS

Have students work in small groups and pairs to read and discuss the selection.

Think-Pair-Share

- Have students silently read Section II.
- Ask the class the following question: What crime did Peyton Farquhar commit and how was he caught?
- Have students think about the question and make notes.
- Tell students to work with a partner to listen, discuss, and formulate a shared response.
- Call on students from each pair to share their responses with the entire class.

Reciprocal Teaching

- Have students silently read Section I.
- Present students with the following question stems: What must have happened before _____? What was the purpose of _____? Which statements reveal _____? Why did the executioners _____?
- Have students write three questions about the material, using the stems.
- Have students work in groups of three. Tell students to take turns sharing a question and discussing it. Students can form a consensus on the answer and use text evidence to support it.

Text X-Ray: English Learner Support
for "An Occurrence at Owl Creek Bridge"

Use the Text X-Ray and the supports and scaffolds in the Teacher's Edition to help guide students at different proficiency levels through the selection.

INTRODUCE THE SELECTION
DISCUSS THE CIVIL WAR

Explain that the story is set during the American Civil War (1861–1865), fought between the South and the North. Explain that Farquhar lives in the southern state of Alabama and is a slave owner. He is a "secessionist," which means that he supports the South's separating from the Union. Explain that "Yanks" are Yankees or Northerners.

Have volunteers share what they know about the Civil War. Supply the following sentence frames:

- The South did not want to be part of the ___. *(United States/Union)*
- The North and South fought over ____ . *(slavery)*

CULTURAL REFERENCES

The following words or phrases may be unfamiliar to students:

- *code of military etiquette* (paragraph 2): rules for how soldiers are expected to act
- *a civilian* (paragraph 3): a person who is not a soldier or military official
- *neck was in the hemp* (paragraph 3): neck had a rope tied around it
- *outside their lines* (paragraph 6): outside the territory held by soldiers or a group during a war
- *all is fair in love and war* (paragraph 8): a situation in which traditional rules do not apply
- *the voice of Niagara* (paragraph 25): the sound of rushing water in the Niagara Falls, a huge waterfall

LISTENING

Identify Imagery

Explain how Peyton Farquhar's senses are heightened, and he sees, hears, and feels things more intensely than usual. Authors use details to help the reader understand what characters are seeing and feeling.

Have students listen as you read aloud paragraph 20. After you have read the excerpt, use the following supports with students at varying proficiency levels:

- Display pictures of things mentioned in the excerpt (e.g., trees, leaves, locusts, spiders, dragon-flies, fish). Reread individual sentences and emphasize certain words. Have students point to the corresponding pictures. **SUBSTANTIAL**
- Ask students what Farquhar saw and heard. Provide sentence frames for their responses. For example: *He saw individual ___. (trees and leaves) He saw ___ and ___. (dragon-flies; fish) He heard what sounded like ____. (music)* **MODERATE**
- Ask students questions about what Farquhar saw and heard. *How did he see the trees and leaves? What kinds of animals did he see and hear? What did the animals sound like?* Invite students to list other examples of imagery. **LIGHT**

SPEAKING

Analyze the Author's Message

Review the author's message and ask students what they think the author wanted to communicate in this short story. Tell them they can get clues about the message by analyzing how the author portrays characters.

Use the following supports with students at varying proficiency levels:

- Ask students yes/no questions about the soldiers and Peyton Farquhar. *Do the soldiers want to execute (kill) Farquhar? (yes) Is Farquhar a soldier? (no) Does the author want readers to know that people in the North and the South did bad things during the war? (yes)* **SUBSTANTIAL**
- Have students work in groups of three, with each student completing a sentence frame. Then, have group members swap sentence frames and repeat the process (without repeating details). Frames: *The author described Peyton Farquhar as a ___ man who ___. The author described the soldiers as ___ men who ___. The author wanted readers to know ___.* **MODERATE**
- Have students work in small groups to discuss these questions: *Should the soldiers have executed Peyton Farquhar? What does the author want readers to know about the soldiers? What does the author want readers to know about Farquhar?* **LIGHT**

READING

Describe Setting

Tell students to visualize the setting as you read the text aloud. Explain they will be using the details in the paragraphs to describe the setting and position of people on the bridge.

Use the following supports with students at varying proficiency levels:

- Read the first three sentences of paragraph 1, pausing after each phrase to let students echo read. Then, have students create a diagram showing the details of what they read. Ask students questions about placement as they draw various items. **SUBSTANTIAL**
- Have student pairs read paragraph 1 and respond to it by drawing a diagram of the bridge and people on it. Tell them to refer to the passage to verify details. **MODERATE**
- Have students work with a partner to read paragraphs 1 and 2, underlining words and phrases that describe the scene. Then, have pairs create a drawing of the scene. **LIGHT**

WRITING

Write a Short Story

Read aloud the Create and Present prompt on Student Edition page 375. Review the elements of a short story: character, plot, setting, dialogue, and theme.

Use the following supports with students at varying proficiency levels:

- Make a plot diagram on the board and work with students to plot a simple story. Then, have them use the diagram to make a series of labeled drawings that tells the story. **SUBSTANTIAL**
- Provide students with a plot diagram and review how to use it. Then, have students work with a partner to plan and write a short story. Provide sentence frames: *One day ___ and ___ went to the ___. They ___, and then they ___. ___ said, "_____."* **MODERATE**
- Have students work with a partner to draft a short story. Encourage students to include dialogue and descriptive words and phrases to make the events and characters come to life. **LIGHT**

Connect to the
ESSENTIAL QUESTION

Discuss with students the meaning of the word *defeat*. Explain that the word is typically used to describe the losing side in a battle or contest. Although the question asks how we, as humans, face defeat, ask students to write down a couple of sentences describing how they personally react to defeat. Tell them to keep their reflections in mind as they read this story about a defeated man during the Civil War.

■ English Learner Support

Understand Expressions Make sure students understand that *face* is used here as a verb. In this context, it means to confront a situation and deal with it in a straightforward manner. Provide the following sentence frames to help students use the word *face* as a verb: *I will face _____. It's time to face _____.* If necessary, allow students to draw pictures or use their native languages to complete the sentence frames. **SUBSTANTIAL**

AN OCCURRENCE AT OWL CREEK BRIDGE

Short Story by **Ambrose Bierce**

360   Unit 4

? **ESSENTIAL QUESTION:**

How do we face defeat?

QUICK START

Think about a time when you were in a situation you felt like you could not change. How did you respond? Did your actions make a difference? Discuss your situation with a partner.

ANALYZE LITERARY ELEMENTS

The author's treatment of literary elements shapes your understanding of how the story unfolds and the overall meaning the writer conveys. One important literary element is **point of view,** the perspective from which the story is told. The **narrator** is the voice that tells the story; as a result, the reader only knows what the narrator is able to tell. Types of point of view include:

- **first-person:** told by a character in the work whose knowledge is limited by his or her own experiences

- **third-person omniscient:** told by a voice outside the story who knows the thoughts and feelings of all the characters

- **third-person limited:** told by a voice outside the story who focuses on one character's thoughts and feelings

The way literary elements relate influences your understanding of a story. For example, the author's choice of point of view may impact how you perceive the plot, setting, and characters. It can even impact the story's **theme,** or message about life. As you read, look for clues about point of view and note the way point of view relates to other literary elements throughout the story.

ANALYZE STRUCTURE

To analyze the **structure** of a literary work, you examine the relationship between its parts and its content. This story is divided into three numbered sections, each of which occurs at a different point in time. After you read each section, summarize the events that occur and note when they take place.

SECTION	WHAT HAPPENS	WHEN
I	Peyton Farquhar is on a bridge with soldiers who have captured him and want to hang him.	This happens at the beginning of the story, in part I.
II		
III		

GENRE ELEMENTS: SHORT STORY

- is a brief fictional work, usually written in prose
- is told from a point of view, which may shift depending on the structure of the story
- uses the relationship of literary elements to convey a theme

QUICK START

After students read the Quick Start questions, invite them to share how they knew a situation was out of their control. Ask them if, at their moment of realization, their reactions were based more on rational thoughts or emotions. Discuss with the class how instinct plays a role in a person's response to a situation that is out of their control.

ANALYZE LITERARY ELEMENTS

Help students understand how to distinguish between first-person and third-person point of view using pronouns. Tell them that first-person point of view will often use the pronoun *I,* whereas third-person point of view will make use of the pronouns *he, she,* or *they,* or refer to the characters by name. Write the following sentences on the board to model the differences, circling the identifying pronouns:

First-person point of view:

I sat up in bed, covered in sweat. My dreams foretold that my greatest fear was about to come true.

Third-person point of view:

She sat up in bed, covered in sweat. Her dreams foretold that her greatest fear was about to come true.

Amelia sat up in bed, covered in sweat. Her dreams foretold that her greatest fear was about to come true.

Ask students how they think point of view affects the plot and what readers perceive about the characters and their actions.

ANALYZE STRUCTURE

Explain to students that when a story's structure includes different time periods, readers must use textual evidence and context clues to put the parts together. Point out that the story begins with a character in crisis, so readers need to look for clues explaining how the crisis arose. Also emphasize that structuring the story out of sequence creates suspense.

Ask students to identify another literary work in which the author generated suspense by structuring the story out of sequence. After they mention some works, have them think of movies that use the same nonlinear approach to narrative structure.

TEACH

CRITICAL VOCABULARY

Encourage students to read all the sentences before deciding which word best completes each one. Remind them to look for context clues that match the precise meaning of each word. After they've chosen words to complete each sentence, suggest that they read the sentences aloud to make sure their selected words make sense.

Answers:

1. *ineffable; effaced*

2. *malign; summarily*

3. *poignant; undulations*

4. *presaging; interminable*

■ English Learner Support

Use Cognates Tell students that two of the Critical Vocabulary words have Spanish cognates: *interminable/interminable; ineffable/inefable.* **ALL LEVELS**

LANGUAGE CONVENTIONS

Sensory Language Reinforce with students how important the use of sensory language is in stimulating a reader's imagination and in helping him or her share experiences with a story's character. Encourage students to identify specific words or phrases that establish sensory details.

Have students use a chart like the one shown here to identify the words or phrases in the story that connect to the five senses. Tell students they can fill it in as they read.

Sight	Sound	Smell	Taste	Touch

✎ ANNOTATION MODEL

Remind students of the annotation ideas in Analyze Literary Elements on page 361, which suggest looking for clues that identify the narrator's point of view. Point out that they may circle or highlight specific pronouns or names used, which help determine the point of view. Their notes in the margin should reflect how the particular point of view impacts the story's theme.

 **GET READY**

CRITICAL VOCABULARY

summarily	effaced	presaging	malign
poignant	undulations	interminable	ineffable

To see how many Critical Vocabulary words you already know, use them to complete the sentences. Each sentence will use two vocabulary words.

1. Maya's previously _____ joy was quickly _____ when she received the bad news.

2. Isaac tried unsuccessfully not to harbor _____ thoughts about the school's principal after he had been _____ dismissed from his office.

3. His grandfather's _____ stories about the past filled Seamus with sadness, but as they stared at the rhythmic _____ of the waves, he felt a sense of peace.

4. Ari's dream, _____ a disaster in his village, went on for so long that it seemed _____.

LANGUAGE CONVENTIONS

Sensory Language Language that connects to the five senses (sight, sound, smell, taste, touch) is called sensory language. Writers use sensory language to create an image that readers are meant to visualize or a description that readers are meant to experience.

> **With their greater infrequency the sounds increased in strength and sharpness. They hurt his ear like the thrust of a knife; he feared he would shriek. What he heard was the ticking of his watch.**

In the example, Bierce appeals to the reader's sense of sound to make his character's experience vivid. As you read, note the way Bierce's sensory language brings scenes to life.

ANNOTATION MODEL   **NOTICE & NOTE**

As you read, notice clues that help identify the point of view of the story. Think about how the point of view relates to other literary elements, including plot, character, and theme. In the model, you can see one reader's notes on "An Occurrence at Owl Creek Bridge."

> ⟨A man⟩ stood upon a railroad bridge in northern Alabama, looking down into the swift water twenty feet below. ⟨The man's hands⟩ were behind his back, the wrists bound with a cord. A rope closely encircled his neck. It was attached to a stout cross-timber above his head and the slack fell to the level of his knees.

The details suggest third-person point of view.

This person is in danger.

BACKGROUND

Ambrose Bierce *(1842–1914) Born into a poor family, Bierce spent his early years on an Indiana farm until he left home at 15 to work at a newspaper. Three years later, he joined the Union army to fight in the Civil War. After the war, he moved to San Francisco and started publishing short stories in the 1870s. The contrast between soldiers' dreams of glory and the senselessness of warfare became a recurring theme in his work, as is seen in "An Occurrence at Owl Creek Bridge."*

AN OCCURRENCE AT OWL CREEK BRIDGE

Short Story by Ambrose Bierce

SETTING A PURPOSE

As you read, think about how the story is structured. How does its organization build suspense and keep you interested? How does it reveal the events leading up to the protagonist's dilemma to the reader?

I

©Chronicle/Alamy

1 A man stood upon a railroad bridge in northern Alabama, looking down into the swift water twenty feet below. The man's hands were behind his back, the wrists bound with a cord. A rope closely encircled his neck. It was attached to a stout cross-timber above his head and the slack fell to the level of his knees. Some loose boards laid upon the sleepers[1] supporting the metals of the railway supplied a footing for him and his executioners—two private soldiers of the Federal army, directed by a sergeant who in civil life may have been a deputy sheriff. At a short remove upon the same temporary platform was an officer in the uniform of his rank, armed. He was a captain. A sentinel at each end of the bridge stood with his rifle in the position known as "support," that is to say, vertical in front of the left shoulder, the hammer resting on the forearm thrown straight across the

---

[1] **sleepers:** railroad ties.

Notice & Note

Use the side margins to notice and note signposts in the text.

ANALYZE LITERARY ELEMENTS

Annotate: Mark details in paragraph 1 that tell where and when the story takes place.

Predict: What is going to happen to the man?

BACKGROUND

Help set the context for this story by describing important features of the American Civil War, the bloodiest battle on American soil, in which an estimated 620,000 soldiers died. Tell students that the Civil War was fought between two sides, the Union, or Federal, army and the Confederate army. The Union army represented the northern states that sought to keep all the states united; the Confederate army represented 11 southern states that sought to secede from, or leave, the Union. The author of this story, Ambrose Bierce, fought for the North, whereas the main character, Peyton Farquhar, aligned with the Confederate states.

Then, tell students Bierce began publishing short stories when realism was becoming the dominant literary style in American fiction. Although Bierce's true-to-life war stories inspired writers like Stephen Crane, his fiction often included surreal or ghostly events. Like Edgar Allan Poe, to whom he was often compared, Bierce was fascinated with strange and horrible deaths, and he described them with his characteristic dark humor and sense of irony. Bierce also went beyond realism in his experiments with narration, pioneering the use of multiple points of view in a single story.

SETTING A PURPOSE

Direct students to use the Setting a Purpose prompt to focus their reading.

✏ ANALYZE LITERARY ELEMENTS

Remind students that literary elements influence the reader's understanding of the story. Marking these details will help students identify the setting of the story. (**Answer:** *It appears the man has been captured and is standing on a railroad bridge, awaiting his execution by hanging.*)

📖 For **reading support** for students at varying proficiency levels, see the **Text X-Ray** on page 360D.

IMPROVE READING FLUENCY

Targeted Passage Tell students that when they read the beginning of a story aloud, they should read slowly enough for listeners to catch all of the important details that introduce them to the story's situation. Read aloud the story's first paragraph. After reading, discuss your pacing, pointing out places you chose to pause in the longer sentences. Then, have students practice reading this paragraph with a partner.

📖 Go to the **Reading Studio** for additional support in developing fluency.

TEACH

ANALYZE LITERARY ELEMENTS

Remind students of the different points of view and how to determine point of view by looking for pronouns. Students should also look for details that reveal who the narrator is; the narrator's **tone,** or attitude; and what type of information he or she is sharing. (**Answer:** *The narrator describes the man who is about to be hanged in a calm tone that suggests the narrator is detached and is able to report all aspects of the event factually. This objective narration prevents the reader from closely identifying with the man.*)

chest—a formal and unnatural position, enforcing an erect carriage of the body. It did not appear to be the duty of these two men to know what was occurring at the center of the bridge; they merely blockaded the two ends of the foot planking that traversed it.

2   Beyond one of the sentinels nobody was in sight; the railroad ran straight away into a forest for a hundred yards, then, curving, was lost to view. Doubtless there was an outpost farther along. The other bank of the stream was open ground—a gentle acclivity[2] topped with a stockade of vertical tree trunks, loopholed for rifles, with a single embrasure[3] through which protruded the muzzle of a brass cannon commanding the bridge. Midway of the slope between bridge and fort were the spectators—a single company of infantry in line, at "parade rest," the butts of the rifles on the ground, the barrels inclining slightly backward against the right shoulder, the hands crossed upon the stock.[4] A lieutenant stood at the right of the line, the point of his sword upon the ground, his left hand resting upon his right. Excepting the group of four at the center of the bridge, not a man moved. The company faced the bridge, staring stonily, motionless. The sentinels, facing the banks of the stream, might have been statues to adorn the bridge. The captain stood with folded arms, silent, observing the work of his subordinates, but making no sign. Death is a dignitary who when he comes announced is to be received with formal manifestations of respect, even by those most familiar with him. In the code of military etiquette silence and fixity are forms of deference.

3   The man who was engaged in being hanged was apparently about thirty-five years of age. He was a civilian, if one might judge from his habit, which was that of a planter. His features were good—a straight nose, firm mouth, broad forehead, from which his long, dark hair was combed straight back, falling behind his ears to the collar of his well-fitting frock-coat. He wore a mustache and pointed beard, but no whiskers; his eyes were large and dark gray, and had a kindly expression which one would hardly have expected in one whose neck was in the hemp. Evidently this was no vulgar assassin. The liberal military code makes provision for hanging many kinds of persons, and gentlemen are not excluded.

4   The preparations being complete, the two private soldiers stepped aside and each drew away the plank upon which he had been standing. The sergeant turned to the captain, saluted and placed himself immediately behind that officer, who in turn moved apart one pace. These movements left the condemned man and the sergeant standing on the two ends of the same plank, which spanned

ANALYZE LITERARY ELEMENTS

Annotate: Mark the phrases that indicate point of view in paragraph 3.

Evaluate: What point of view is used in paragraph 3? How does the point of view affect the perception of events?

---

[2] **acclivity:** an upward slope.

[3] **embrasure:** a flared opening in a wall for a gun, with sides angled so that the inside opening is larger than that on the outside.

[4] **stock:** the wooden part of the rifle that serves as a handle.

TO CHALLENGE STUDENTS . . .

Analyze Personification and Tone Have students identify the figure of speech in paragraph 2 (personification) and paraphrase it for the class. Then, have pairs write and exchange five sentences that personify death and fear. Have small groups discuss questions.

- How do the sentences in paragraph 2 explain the way soldiers are meant to react to death? How might that differ from civilian reactions?

- What do you think the "code of military etiquette" means? What evidence have you seen so far in the story that displays military etiquette?

- What is the narrator's tone in the lines about the military code?

three of the cross-ties of the bridge. The end upon which the civilian stood almost, but not quite, reached a fourth. This plank had been held in place by the weight of the captain; it was now held by that of the sergeant. At a signal from the former the latter would step aside, the plank would tilt and the condemned man go down between two ties. The arrangement commended itself to his judgment as simple and effective. His face had not been covered nor his eyes bandaged. He looked a moment at his "unsteadfast footing," then let his gaze wander to the swirling water of the stream racing madly beneath his feet. A piece of dancing driftwood caught his attention and his eyes followed it down the current. How slowly it appeared to move! What a sluggish stream!

5   He closed his eyes in order to fix his last thoughts upon his wife and children. The water, touched to gold by the early sun, the brooding mists under the banks at some distance down the stream, the fort, the soldiers, the piece of drift—all had distracted him. And now he became conscious of a new disturbance. Striking through the thought of his dear ones was a sound which he could neither ignore nor understand, a sharp, distinct, metallic percussion like the stroke of a blacksmith's hammer upon the anvil; it had the same ringing quality. He wondered what it was, and whether immeasurably distant or near by—it seemed both. Its recurrence was regular, but as slow as the tolling of a death knell.[5] He awaited each stroke with impatience and—he knew not why—apprehension. The intervals of silence grew progressively longer; the delays became maddening. With their greater infrequency the sounds increased in strength and sharpness. They hurt his ear like the thrust of a knife; he feared he would shriek. What he heard was the ticking of his watch.

6   He unclosed his eyes and saw again the water below him. "If I could free my hands," he thought, "I might throw off the noose and spring into the stream. By diving I could evade the bullets and, swimming vigorously, reach the bank, take to the woods and get away home. My home, thank God, is as yet outside their lines; my wife and little ones are still beyond the invader's farthest advance."

7   As these thoughts, which have here to be set down in words, were flashed into the doomed man's brain rather than evolved from it the captain nodded to the sergeant. The sergeant stepped aside.

II

8 Peyton Farquhar was a well-to-do planter, of an old and highly respected Alabama family. Being a slave owner and like other slave owners a politician he was naturally an original secessionist and ardently devoted to the Southern cause. Circumstances of

---

[5] **the tolling of a death knell:** the slow, steady ringing of a bell at a funeral or to indicate death.

ANALYZE LITERARY ELEMENTS

Annotate: Mark details in paragraph 4 that tell you the narrator's thoughts.

Evaluate: How do these details portray a shift in point of view?

ANALYZE STRUCTURE

Annotate: Mark details that suggest the main character is thinking about escaping.

Predict: Reread this section, starting with paragraph 3. What would you expect to happen next? Cite evidence to support your answer.

ANALYZE LITERARY ELEMENTS

Remind students that third-person point of view can be either omniscient or limited. Tell them Bierce was known for changing point of view throughout a story. They should look for clues that reveal the point of view and if it has shifted. (**Answer:** *The sensory details that signify the change in point of view include the main character seeing the "swirling water of the stream" and the "piece of dancing driftwood" that he thinks moves slowly. At this point, the narrator describes only the main character's sights and thoughts.*)

■ English Learner Support

Understand Point of View Write the pronouns used in third-person point of view (*he, she, they, them, his, her, theirs*) and first-person point of view (*I, me, mine, we, us, ours*). Have students copy the list in their notebooks. Explain the difference between first- and third-person pronouns and what they indicate. Tell students it is important to look at the pronouns in a story to determine the point of view. Read aloud the end of paragraph 4 twice. Have students raise their hands when they hear a pronoun. Have students keep track of the pronouns they hear. After you have finished reading, have students identify the point of view. **MODERATE**

ANALYZE STRUCTURE

Remind students that authors often **foreshadow** events, or give clues about what might happen. Point out to students that the author is prompting the reader to think the main character may yet escape. The main character's hope thrusts the plot forward. (**Answer:** *In paragraph 4, the narrator details that "this plank had been held in place by the weight of the captain; it was now held by that of the sergeant." This suggests there has been some movement. At the end of paragraph 7, the narrator states "The sergeant stepped aside," implying that the main character will be hanged.*)

 For **speaking support** for students at varying proficiency levels, see the **Text X-Ray** on page 360D.

WHEN STUDENTS STRUGGLE...

Analyze Structure After students complete Section I, help them add to the prereading event chart introduced on page 361. Have students use their charts to generate questions about Section I. Tell students to pause after each remaining section to add to the chart and list more questions. Urge them to read on to answer their questions.

Clarify that in the prereading chart, the heading *When* refers to an event's place in the story's sequence of events, not to its historical period.

 For additional support, go to the **Reading Studio** and assign the following **Level Up Tutorial: Plot: Sequence of Events.**

TEACH

 ## ANALYZE STRUCTURE

Remind students that the uniqueness of this story's structure arises from the relationship between its parts, or sections, and its content. (**Answer:** *The similar details link the two sections and help to structure the order of events in the reader's mind.*)

EL ENGLISH LEARNER SUPPORT

Understand Plot Explain that "Yanks" (paragraph 10) are Yankees or northerners—those fighting against the South. Clarify that the soldier who approaches Farquhar is dressed in the gray uniform of the southern army and appears as a comrade to him. Have students work in pairs to reread paragraph 17. Ask students to answer the following questions: *What do you learn about the soldier who approaches Farquhar? Why is this important?* (*Paragraph 17 reveals that the soldier is a Federal, or northern, scout in disguise. Farquhar takes information from a man he would consider an enemy.*)
ALL LEVELS

MEMORY MOMENT

Explain to students that the story's plot is interrupted by the narrator's recollection of how Farquhar's mission began. Remind students that a story's structure does not need to follow the chronological order of the events. (**Answer:** *This part of the story takes place before Section I. In Section II, the reader learns about events that precede Farquhar's capturing at the railroad bridge. The reader also learns about an important character, the Federal scout, who happens to be a spy, though Farquhar does not know this information.*)

CRITICAL VOCABULARY

summarily: The order conveys a dire warning to offenders that there will be no leniency and that execution will occur swiftly.

ASK STUDENTS why they think any civilian caught interfering with the railroad will be summarily hanged. (*The army hopes to deter people by relaying that they would have no trial or chance of escape.*)

 366 Unit 4

 ## NOTICE & NOTE

ANALYZE STRUCTURE
Annotate: Compare paragraph 10 with the description in paragraphs 1 and 2. Mark details that connect the two sections of the story.

Evaluate: What is the effect of including similar details in the two sections?

summarily
(sə-mĕr´ə-lē) *adv.* quickly and without ceremony.

MEMORY MOMENT

Notice & Note: Notice the placement of Section II in the story. When does this part of the story actually take place?

Analyze: What information about the characters do you learn in this section?

---

an imperious nature, which it is unnecessary to relate here, had prevented him from taking service with the gallant army that had fought the disastrous campaigns ending with the fall of Corinth,[6] and he chafed under the inglorious restraint, longing for the release of his energies, the larger life of the soldier, the opportunity for distinction. That opportunity, he felt, would come, as it comes to all in war time. Meanwhile he did what he could. No service was too humble for him to perform in aid of the South, no adventure too perilous for him to undertake if consistent with the character of a civilian who was at heart a soldier, and who in good faith and without too much qualification assented to at least a part of the frankly villainous dictum that all is fair in love and war.

9   One evening while Farquhar and his wife were sitting on a rustic bench near the entrance to his grounds, a gray-clad soldier rode up to the gate and asked for a drink of water. Mrs. Farquhar was only too happy to serve him with her own white hands. While she was fetching the water her husband approached the dusty horseman and inquired eagerly for news from the front.

10   "The Yanks are repairing the railroads," said the man, "and are getting ready for another advance. They have reached the Owl Creek bridge, put it in order and built a stockade on the north bank. The commandant has issued an order, which is posted everywhere, declaring that any civilian caught interfering with the railroad, its bridges, tunnels or trains will be **summarily** hanged. I saw the order."

11   "How far is it to the Owl Creek bridge?" Farquhar asked.

12   "About thirty miles."

13   "Is there no force on this side the creek?"

14   "Only a picket post[7] half a mile out, on the railroad, and a single sentinel at this end of the bridge."

15   "Suppose a man—a civilian and student of hanging—should elude the picket post and perhaps get the better of the sentinel," said Farquhar, smiling, "what could he accomplish?"

16   The soldier reflected. "I was there a month ago," he replied. "I observed that the flood of last winter had lodged a great quantity of driftwood against the wooden pier at this end of the bridge. It is now dry and would burn like tow."[8]

17   The lady had now brought the water, which the soldier drank. He thanked her ceremoniously, bowed to her husband and rode away. An hour later, after nightfall, he repassed the plantation, going northward in the direction from which he had come. He was a Federal scout.

---

[6] **Corinth:** a town in Mississippi that was the site of a Civil War battle in 1862.
[7] **picket post:** the camp of soldiers who are assigned to guard against a surprise attack.
[8] **tow** (tō): coarse, dry fiber.

© Houghton Mifflin Harcourt Publishing Company

WHEN STUDENTS STRUGGLE . . .

Understand Complex Sentences Point out that Bierce's long sentences can be difficult to understand. Help students use punctuation to break them into manageable chunks. Then, ask the following questions to determine comprehension:

- How do the Farquhars greet the visiting soldier? Do they view him as a friend?

- What does the soldier say about the Yanks? What order have they posted?

- What does Farquhar ask the soldier?

- What army is the soldier actually from?

III

18 As Peyton Farquhar fell straight downward through the bridge he lost consciousness and was as one already dead. From this state he was awakened—ages later, it seemed to him—by the pain of a sharp pressure upon his throat, followed by a sense of suffocation. Keen, **poignant** agonies seemed to shoot from his neck downward through every fiber of his body and limbs. These pains appeared to flash along well-defined lines of ramification[9] and to beat with an inconceivably rapid periodicity. They seemed like streams of pulsating fire heating him to an intolerable temperature. As to his head, he was conscious of nothing but a feeling of fullness—of congestion. These sensations were unaccompanied by thought. The intellectual part of his nature was already **effaced**; he had power only to feel, and feeling was torment. He was conscious of motion. Encompassed in a luminous cloud, of which he was now merely the fiery heart, without material substance, he swung through unthinkable arcs of oscillation[10], like a

poignant
(poin´yənt) *adj.* physically or mentally painful.

efface
(ĭ-fās´) *v.tr.* to rub or wipe out; erase.

---

[9] **flash . . . ramification:** spread out rapidly along branches from a central point.
[10] **oscillation:** the action of swinging back and forth.

CRITICAL VOCABULARY

poignant: The physical effects from the tightened noose create pain, but the knowledge of impending death creates an overwhelming sense of agony.

ASK STUDENTS to make a list of emotions they would consider poignant. *(melancholy, nostalgia)*

efface: Farquhar no longer has the ability to think rationally or logically. He is cut off from any intellectual reasoning.

ASK STUDENTS why they think Farquhar's power of intellect is effaced. *(As he drew closer to death, his body automatically reverts to pure instinct, fighting for a last chance to survive.)*

TEACH

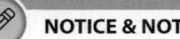
LANGUAGE CONVENTIONS

Bierce's use of sensory language helps readers connect to Farquhar's panic, by activating their sensory perceptions. Tell students that Bierce creates images, which allow the reader to experience, by proxy, being hanged. (**Answer:** *The sudden wrenching pains vividly show Farquhar's panic. This makes the character extremely vivid, as his fear grips the reader, and the reader panics with him.*)

vast pendulum. Then all at once, with terrible suddenness, the light about him shot upward with the noise of a loud plash; a frightful roaring was in his ears, and all was cold and dark. The power of thought was restored; he knew that the rope had broken and he had fallen into the stream. There was no additional strangulation; the noose about his neck was already suffocating him and kept the water from his lungs. To die of hanging at the bottom of a river!—the idea seemed to him ludicrous. He opened his eyes in the darkness and saw above him a gleam of light, but how distant, how inaccessible! He was still sinking, for the light became fainter and fainter until it was a mere glimmer. Then it began to grow and brighten, and he knew that he was rising toward the surface—knew it with reluctance, for he was now very comfortable. "To be hanged and drowned," he thought, "that is not so bad; but I do not wish to be shot. No; I will not be shot; that is not fair."

LANGUAGE CONVENTIONS

Annotate: Reread paragraph 19. Mark details and sensory language that illustrate Peyton Farquhar's panic.

Synthesize: How do these sensory details contribute to your understanding of his character?

19   He was not conscious of an effort, but a sharp pain in his wrist apprised him that he was trying to free his hands. He gave the struggle his attention, as an idler might observe the feat of a juggler, without interest in the outcome. What splendid effort!— what magnificent, what superhuman strength! Ah, that was a fine endeavor! Bravo! The cord fell away; his arms parted and floated upward, the hands dimly seen on each side in the growing light. He watched them with a new interest as first one and then the other pounced upon the noose at his neck. They tore it away and thrust it

© Houghton Mifflin Harcourt Publishing Company • Image Credits © little-known/Shutterstock

ENGLISH LEARNER SUPPORT

Understand Sensory Language Help students understand the narrator's use of vivid sensory language to describe Farquhar's pain as he is under the water and swims to the surface. Ask students to rephrase, in their own words, the following descriptions from paragraph 19: *"brain was on fire"* (head ached), *"his heart . . . gave a great leap"* (his heart was beating hard), *"body was racked and wrenched"* (body was twisted by the pain), *"insupportable anguish"* (unbearable pain), *"his chest expanded convulsively"* (he had difficulty catching his breath), *"his lungs engulfed a great draught of air, which instantly he expelled in a shriek"* (he took a great gulp of air, then yelled). **MODERATE/LIGHT**

fiercely aside, its **undulations** resembling those of a water-snake. "Put it back, put it back!" He thought he shouted these words to his hands, for the undoing of the noose had been succeeded by the direst pang that he had yet experienced. His neck ached horribly; his brain was on fire; his heart, which had been fluttering faintly, gave a great leap, trying to force itself out at his mouth. His whole body was racked and wrenched with an insupportable anguish![11] But his disobedient hands gave no heed to the command. They beat the water vigorously with quick, downward strokes, forcing him to the surface. He felt his head emerge; his eyes were blinded by the sunlight; his chest expanded convulsively, and with a supreme and crowning agony his lungs engulfed a great draught of air, which instantly he expelled in a shriek!

20   He was now in full possession of his physical senses. They were, indeed, preternaturally keen and alert. Something in the awful disturbance of his organic system had so exalted and refined them that they made record of things never before perceived. He felt the ripples upon his face and heard their separate sounds as they struck. He looked at the forest on the bank of the stream, saw the individual trees, the leaves and the veining of each leaf—saw the very insects upon them: the locusts, the brilliant-bodied flies, the gray spiders stretching their webs from twig to twig. He noted the prismatic colors in all the dewdrops upon a million blades of grass. The humming of the gnats that danced above the eddies of the stream, the beating of the dragon-flies' wings, the strokes of the water-spiders' legs, like oars which had lifted their boat—all these made audible music. A fish slid along beneath his eyes and he heard the rush of its body parting the water.

21   He had come to the surface facing down the stream; in a moment the visible world seemed to wheel slowly round, himself the pivotal point, and he saw the bridge, the fort, the soldiers upon the bridge, the captain, the sergeant, the two privates, his executioners. They were in silhouette against the blue sky. They shouted and gesticulated, pointing at him. The captain had drawn his pistol, but did not fire; the others were unarmed. Their movements were grotesque and horrible, their forms gigantic.

22   Suddenly he heard a sharp report and something struck the water smartly within a few inches of his head, spattering his face with spray. He heard a second report, and saw one of the sentinels with his rifle at his shoulder, a light cloud of blue smoke rising from the muzzle. The man in the water saw the eye of the man on the bridge gazing into his own through the sights of the rifle. He observed that it was a gray eye and remembered having read that gray eyes were keenest,

[11] **racked . . . anguish:** stretched and twisted with unendurable physical pain.

undulation
(ŭn´jə-lā´shən, ŭn´dyə-, -də-) *n.* a regular rising and falling or movement to alternating sides; movement in waves.

ANALYZE STRUCTURE
Annotate: Mark details in paragraphs 21 and 22 that describe the soldiers' reaction to Farquhar's escape.

Synthesize: Explain whether the details in this description are realistic. Cite text evidence in your response.

 ANALYZE STRUCTURE

Remind students to fill out the prereading chart for this section. Point out to them that the soldiers' reactions occur after Farquhar emerges from underwater. (**Answer:** *The soldiers' reactions seem to be at once realistic and fantastic. It makes sense they would try to follow up on a failed execution by shooting, but the men seem to behave as Farquhar would want them to, which suggests the descriptions are a fantasy. In addition, the words "grotesque and horrible, their forms gigantic" (paragraph 21) suggest fantastic images. Finally, Farquhar says he could see the "gray eye" (paragraph 22) of the shooter, which is unlikely, especially as the shooter misses Farquhar. All of these details suggest a scene Farquhar hopes for or dreams.*)

For **listening support** for students at varying proficiency levels, see the **Text X-Ray** on page 360C.

TO CHALLENGE STUDENTS . . .

Analyze Realism   Remind students that Section III includes surreal elements. As students read this section, challenge them to determine whether this section is realistic or surreal and why. Have them identify important details of both types, then use these details to discuss why Bierce uses both realistic and surreal details in his short story. Encourage them to add these details to their Response Logs and think about how these details support their answer to the Essential Question.

CRITICAL VOCABULARY

undulation: Farquhar frees himself of the noose underwater, releasing the rope to be borne away by the swirling river.

ASK STUDENTS why an inanimate object like a rope would undulate, imitating a live animal. (*The rope takes on the energy of the surrounding water, which moves in wavelike motions.*)

ANALYZE LITERARY ELEMENTS

Point out to students that the narrator's point of view in paragraphs 25–27 is limited to the thoughts and feelings of Farquhar. Although the narrator describes the actions of the other characters, we do not know what they are thinking or how they are feeling. (**Answer:** *These details make the action more immediate and tell readers about Farquhar's thoughts and feelings about his circumstances. As we share Farquhar's panic, the suspense helps us to understand the story's theme about dealing with defeat.*)

EL ENGLISH LEARNER SUPPORT

Understand Imagery Read paragraphs 23–29 aloud. Explain to students that descriptive words and phrases a writer uses to recreate sensory experiences are called **imagery.** Use the following supports with students at varying proficiency levels:

Help students note words or phrases that evoke the sense of sound and circle them in the text. (*"sound," "rang out," "beating . . . in his ears," "chant," "intonation," "roared," "heard," "loud, rushing sound"*) **SUBSTANTIAL**

Ask students to identify language that shows a musical description of the events. Then, ask them to write in their own words how a musical approach to sensory details can further enhance a reader's experience. (*"high voice in a monotonous singsong," "beating of the ripples," "aspirated chant," "measured intervals," "diminuendo."*) **LIGHT**

CRITICAL VOCABULARY

presaging: To achieve good performance from his soldiers, the lieutenant anticipates they will successfully shoot Farquhar.

ASK STUDENTS why they think the author chose to use *presaging* in this context. (*Presaging indicates knowledge of some degree of future events. Using it here indicates the lieutenant is trying to "enforce tranquility" on his men.*)

 NOTICE & NOTE

presaging
(prĕs´ĭj-ĭng) *adj.* predicting.

ANALYZE LITERARY ELEMENTS
Annotate: Mark details in paragraphs 25–27 that reveal Farquhar's perspective.

Analyze: How does learning about these events from Farquhar's perspective build suspense?

and that all famous marksmen had them. Nevertheless, this one had missed.

23   A counter-swirl had caught Farquhar and turned him half round; he was again looking into the forest on the bank opposite the fort. The sound of a clear, high voice in a monotonous singsong now rang out behind him and came across the water with a distinctness that pierced and subdued all other sounds, even the beating of the ripples in his ears. Although no soldier, he had frequented camps enough to know the dread significance of that deliberate, drawling, aspirated chant; the lieutenant on shore was taking a part in the morning's work. How coldly and pitilessly—with what an even, calm intonation, **presaging,** and enforcing tranquillity in the men—with what accurately measured intervals fell those cruel words:

24   "Attention, company! . . . Shoulder arms! . . . Ready! . . . Aim! . . . Fire!"

25   Farquhar dived—dived as deeply as he could. The water roared in his ears like the voice of Niagara, yet he heard the dulled thunder of the volley and, rising again toward the surface, met shining bits of metal, singularly flattened, oscillating slowly downward. Some of them touched him on the face and hands, then fell away, continuing their descent. One lodged between his collar and neck; it was uncomfortably warm and he snatched it out.

26   As he rose to the surface, gasping for breath, he saw that he had been a long time under water; he was perceptibly farther down stream—nearer to safety. The soldiers had almost finished reloading; the metal ramrods flashed all at once in the sunshine as they were drawn from the barrels, turned in the air, and thrust into their sockets. The two sentinels fired again, independently and ineffectually.

27   The hunted man saw all this over his shoulder; he was now swimming vigorously with the current. His brain was as energetic as his arms and legs; he thought with the rapidity of lightning.

28   "The officer," he reasoned, "will not make that martinet's[12] error a second time. It is as easy to dodge a volley as a single shot. He has probably already given the command to fire at will. God help me, I cannot dodge them all!"

29   An appalling plash within two yards of him was followed by a loud, rushing sound, *diminuendo,*[13] which seemed to travel back through the air to the fort and died in an explosion which stirred the very river to its deeps! A rising sheet of water curved over him, fell down upon him, blinded him, strangled him! The cannon had taken a hand in the game. As he shook his head free from the commotion of the smitten water he heard the deflected shot humming through

---

[12] **martinet's:** alluding to a strict disciplinarian or person who demands that regulations be followed exactly.

[13] *diminuendo* (dĭ-mĭn-yŏo-ĕn´dō) *Italian:* gradually decreasing in loudness.

the air ahead, and in an instant it was cracking and smashing the branches in the forest beyond.

30 "They will not do that again," he thought; "the next time they will use a charge of grape.[14] I must keep my eye upon the gun; the smoke will apprise me—the report arrives too late; it lags behind the missile. That is a good gun."

31 Suddenly he felt himself whirled round and round—spinning like a top. The water, the banks, the forests, the now distant bridge, fort and men—all were commingled and blurred. Objects were represented by their colors only; circular horizontal streaks of color—that was all he saw. He had been caught in a vortex and was being whirled on with a velocity of advance and gyration that made him giddy and sick. In a few moments he was flung upon the gravel at the foot of the left bank of the stream—the southern bank—and behind a projecting point which concealed him from his enemies. The sudden arrest of his motion, the abrasion of one of his hands on the gravel, restored him, and he wept with delight. He dug his fingers into the sand, threw it over himself in handfuls and audibly blessed it. It looked like diamonds, rubies, emeralds; he could think of nothing beautiful which it did not resemble. The trees upon the bank were giant garden plants; he noted a definite order in their arrangement, inhaled the fragrance of their blooms. A strange, roseate light shone through the spaces among their trunks and the wind made in their branches the music of æolian harps.[15] He had no wish to perfect his escape—was content to remain in that enchanting spot until retaken.

32 A whiz and rattle of grapeshot among the branches high above his head roused him from his dream. The baffled cannoneer had fired him a random farewell. He sprang to his feet, rushed up the sloping bank, and plunged into the forest.

33 All that day he traveled, laying his course by the rounding sun. The forest seemed **interminable**; nowhere did he discover a break in it, not even a woodman's road. He had not known that he lived in so wild a region. There was something uncanny in the revelation.

34 By night fall he was fatigued, footsore, famishing. The thought of his wife and children urged him on. At last he found a road which led him in what he knew to be the right direction. It was as wide and straight as a city street, yet it seemed untraveled. No fields bordered it, no dwelling anywhere. Not so much as the barking of a dog suggested human habitation. The black bodies of the trees formed a straight wall on both sides, terminating on the horizon in a point, like a diagram in a lesson in perspective. Overhead, as he looked up through this rift in the wood, shone great golden stars looking unfamiliar and grouped in strange constellations. He was sure

---

[14]**grape:** short for *grapeshot,* a cluster of several small iron balls fired in one shot from a cannon.

[15]**music of æolian** (ē-ō´lē-ən) **harps:** heavenly, or unearthly, music.

ANALYZE LITERARY ELEMENTS

Annotate: Mark details in paragraph 31 that describe Farquhar's movement.

Analyze: How does Farquhar feel while he is moving? How does he feel when he stops? From what point of view is the scene described?

interminable
(ĭn-tûr´mə-nə-bəl) *adj.* endless.

✎ ANALYZE LITERARY ELEMENTS

Remind students that the author's choice of point of view supports the theme of the story. The descriptive language helps the reader visualize what is happening. (**Answer:** *Farquhar is nervous and confused while he is moving, but once he stops he is relieved and then extremely happy. The author is using third-person limited point of view.*)

■ English Learner Support

Acquire Related Vocabulary Remind students that authors use descriptive words and phrases to help readers visualize what is happening. Read aloud paragraph 31. Then focus on the phrases below and show or act out what the phrases or words describe. Have students write the movement words or phrases in their notebooks so they can use them in their own writing.

- "whirled round and round—spinning like a top"
- "commingled and blurred"
- "vortex"
- "velocity"   **MODERATE**

CRITICAL VOCABULARY

interminable: Farquhar is seemingly lost in the woods, searching endlessly for a way out but unable to find one.

ASK STUDENTS to explain why the forest seemed interminable. (*The forest seemed interminable because it is difficult to see where it ends.*)

APPLYING ACADEMIC VOCABULARY

❑ confirm   ☑ definitely   ❑ deny   ❑ format   ☑ unify

Write and Discuss Have students turn to a partner to discuss the following questions. Guide students to include the academic vocabulary words *definitely* and *unify* in their responses. Ask volunteers to share their responses with the class.

- Do we know Peyton Farquhar has **definitely** escaped his execution?
- How did the Union lieutenant **unify** his soldiers, getting them to fire simultaneously?

malign
(mə-līn´) *adj.* evil in disposition, nature, or intent.

they were arranged in some order which had a secret and **malign** significance. The wood on either side was full of singular noises, among which—once, twice, and again, he distinctly heard whispers in an unknown tongue.

35   His neck was in pain and lifting his hand to it he found it horribly swollen. He knew that it had a circle of black where the rope had bruised it. His eyes felt congested; he could no longer close them. His tongue was swollen with thirst; he relieved its fever by thrusting it forward from between his teeth into the cold air. How softly the turf had carpeted the untraveled avenue—he could no longer feel the roadway beneath his feet!

36   Doubtless, despite his suffering, he had fallen asleep while walking, for now he sees another scene—perhaps he has merely recovered from a delirium. He stands at the gate of his own home. All is as he left it, and all bright and beautiful in the morning sunshine. He must have traveled the entire night. As he pushes open the gate and passes up the wide white walk, he sees a flutter of female garments; his wife, looking fresh and cool and sweet, steps down from the veranda to meet him. At the bottom of the steps she stands waiting, with a smile of **ineffable** joy, an attitude of matchless grace and dignity. Ah, how beautiful she is! He springs forward with extended arms. As he is about to clasp her he feels a stunning blow upon the back of the neck; a blinding white light blazes all about him

ineffable
(ĭn-ĕf´ə-bəl) *adj.* beyond description; inexpressible.

CRITICAL VOCABULARY

malign: Farquhar travels through a surreal landscape, which seems to maliciously plot against him.

ASK STUDENTS how is it possible that a natural environment can malign someone. (*A person's emotional state can be externalized, resulting in the belief that a natural environment carries human characteristics.*)

ineffable: The wife's joy summarizes Farquhar's own ecstasy at having escaped his death and returned home.

ASK STUDENTS to explain how an emotion like joy is ineffable. (*Joy is ineffable when it brings happiness beyond description.*)

WHEN STUDENTS STRUGGLE . . .

Analyze Plot Have students reread paragraphs 35–37 and ask them if they really think Farquhar has escaped, arriving back home to his wife. Have students volunteer to read sentences that indicate he is actually hanging from the bridge and has been dying all along. Tell them to fill in these details in the prereading chart. You may prompt them with the following questions: What physical condition is Farquhar in? What is really happening to Farquhar now? What is he visualizing or thinking about? How does Farquhar die?

For additional support, go to the **Reading Studio** and assign the following [LEVEL] **Level Up Tutorial: Plot Stages.**

with a sound like the shock of a cannon—then all is darkness and silence!

37　　Peyton Farquhar was dead; his body, with a broken neck, swung gently from side to side beneath the timbers of the Owl Creek bridge.

ANALYZE STRUCTURE

Annotate: Reread paragraphs 34–36. Mark details that suggest Peyton Farquhar is going to escape his situation.

Infer: What can you infer about how he is going to escape? Does this support or contradict what happens at the end of the story?

CHECK YOUR UNDERSTANDING

Answer these questions before moving on to the **Analyze the Text** section on the following page.

1 Why does the soldier who visited Farquhar give him such detailed information about the bridge?

　A He wants to help Farquhar become a war hero.

　B He made a plan to take action against the Union.

　C He was trying to trick Farquhar into committing a crime.

　D He only appears in Farquhar's imagination.

2 Which of the following details is an example of the use of third-person limited point of view?

　F *He wore a moustache and pointed beard.*

　G *The preparations being complete, the two private soldiers stepped aside.*

　H *Peyton Farquhar was a well-to-do planter.*

　J *By night fall he was fatigued, footsore, famishing.*

3 What is the significance of the ticking watch in the story?

　A It reminds the man of his family.

　B It represents hope and a desire to escape.

　C It tells the reader how much time has passed.

　D It conveys fear and anxiety in the situation.

ANALYZE STRUCTURE

Point out to students that the use of third-person point of view allows the narrator to surprise the reader by suggesting a false sequence of events. (**Answer:** *It can be inferred that to escape, he must actually die; this supports the unexpected ending of the story.*)

CHECK YOUR UNDERSTANDING

Have students answer the questions independently.

Answers:

　1. *C*

　2. *J*

　3. *D*

If they answer any questions incorrectly, have them reread the text to confirm their understanding. Then they may proceed to ANALYZE THE TEXT on page 374.

 ENGLISH LEARNER SUPPORT

Oral Assessment Use the following questions to assess students' comprehension and speaking skills.

1. Was the soldier a Union spy? (*Yes, the soldier was a Union spy. He was trying to trick Farquhar into committing a crime.*)

2. What point of view is the line "By night fall he was fatigued, footsore, famishing"? (*third-person limited point of view*)

3. Farquhar's watch keeps _____ . Why do you think the author includes this detail? (*ticking; the sound helps the reader experience the fear and anxiety of the main character*)
SUBSTANTIAL/INTERMEDIATE

ANALYZE THE TEXT

Possible answers:

1. **DOK 4:** *The writer structured the story to increase suspense and maintain interest. If it were told in chronological order, the story would be less suspenseful, and it might not be as interesting because readers would know Farquhar did not escape.*

2. **DOK 2:** *The narrator implies Farquhar attempted to burn down the bridge, preventing trains from carrying supplies to Union soldiers. ("a great quantity of driftwood . . . is now dry and would burn like tow.") The Union army specifically declares that "any civilian caught interfering . . . will be summarily hanged."*

3. **DOK 4:** *The shifts in point of view increase the suspense and make the story more exciting. When the point of view shifts from omniscient to limited in paragraph 4, readers know only how Farquhar feels. This draws them into Farquhar's experience. In Section III, the point of view again shifts from omniscient to limited. This enables readers to experience Farquhar's emotions and thoughts, creates suspense about his fate, and supports the fantasy. Without the departures into third-person omniscient point of view, readers would not recognize the fantasy.*

4. **DOK 4:** *Bierce uses many realistic details in Section I and the beginning of Section III. ("If I could free my hands . . . I might throw off the noose and spring into the stream. By diving I could evade the bullets and, swimming vigorously, reach the bank, take to the woods and get away home"; "he knew that the rope had broken and he had fallen into the stream.") However, the details get increasingly fantastic in Section III, which suggests the escape is unlikely to be real. ("what superhuman strength!"; "Their movements were grotesque . . . , their forms gigantic.")*

5. **DOK 4:** *A former soldier, Bierce knows that the best of intentions can meet the most tragic fates. The details in the story suggest that heroism is a foolish dream, and war is treacherous and dangerous, not glorious or ideal.*

RESEARCH

Advise students to search credible and official sources for information about the American Civil War. Suggest the National Archives or the CIA website.

Extend Many spies during the Civil War were women, who could gather information as they participated in social events. For example, the confederate spy Rose O'Neal Greenhow was a southern woman who socialized and dined with Washington's elite, the organizers of Union strategies.

 **RESPOND**

ANALYZE THE TEXT

Support your responses with evidence from the text. ☰ NOTEBOOK

1. **Analyze** Review the chart you filled out as you read. How would the story be different if it were told in chronological order? Why did the writer structure the story the way he did? Explain.

2. **Infer** What is the Union soldiers' reason for hanging Farquhar? Cite text evidence in your response.

3. **Evaluate** Citing at least two examples from the story, explain how the shifts in point of view impact the plot and build suspense. What would be different about the story if it were told entirely from the third-person omniscient point of view?

4. **Evaluate** Explain whether the author intended Farquhar's escape to be believable. Cite text evidence in your response.

5. **Notice & Note** Section II includes background details on Farquhar's desire for "the larger life of the soldier, the opportunity for distinction." Based on his dreams of glory and his ultimate fate, what theme does Bierce express about heroism and the realities of war?

RESEARCH

RESEARCH TIP
Coming up with short, targeted phrases related to your topic is a helpful way to find relevant search results, especially when conducting an online search.

Farquhar finds himself in danger as a result of an encounter with a spy who poses as his ally during the Civil War. Do some research on the use of spies at this time to answer the questions in the chart.

QUESTION	ANSWER
Who are some well-known spies?	*Harriet Tubman, Belle Boyd, Timothy Webster, Mary Bowser, Sam Davis, Rose O'Neal Greenhow*
Why were spies used?	*to gather intelligence and scout opposing troop movements and numbers*
Were spies typically effective?	*Yes, the strategies for intelligence gathering were helpful to both sides. Robert Smalls, for example, helped prevent a Confederate attack on the port at Fernandina, Florida.*

Extend Choose one of the well-known spies you learned about and create a brief presentation. Note details such as which side the spy was on in the conflict and why the spy became well known.

WHEN STUDENTS STRUGGLE . . .

Analyze Plot Prompt students to look over their completed prereading chart. Have them work in pairs to reorder the events into a sequential chronology. Suggest students cut up the chart into small pieces and arrange them in order, from beginning to end. Then, have them share their timelines with the class.

 For additional support, go to the **Reading Studio** and assign the following 🔼 **Level Up Tutorial: Plot: Sequence of Events.**

CREATE AND PRESENT

Write a Short Story Write your own short story, making sure to include specific details about the main character, plot, and setting. Also, consider what themes you want to develop throughout the story and how point of view might help that express your theme.

- ❏ Identify a clear topic. What is your purpose for telling this story?
- ❏ Decide on what point of view you will use to tell the story. How will this help to convey your message?
- ❏ Include literary elements, such as character and setting, to develop your theme.
- ❏ Determine your audience. Will they understand the themes you are developing? Provide them with any background information they need.

Share Your Story Find a partner and take turns sharing your story. Be sure to provide each other with feedback.

- ❏ Discuss the elements of a short story you included. Were you successful? Why or why not?
- ❏ Ask your partner what he or she thinks your theme is and confirm whether he or she is correct. Discuss what details you considered when developing your theme.
- ❏ Provide each other with feedback.

Go to **Writing Narratives** in the **Writing Studio** for help.

RESPOND TO THE ESSENTIAL QUESTION

? How do we face defeat?

Gather Information Review your annotations and notes on the story. Then, add relevant information to your Response Log. As you determine which information to include, think about:

- the way the conflict was developed and resolved
- how you learn about the main character and the danger he faces
- the way the theme is conveyed through literary elements

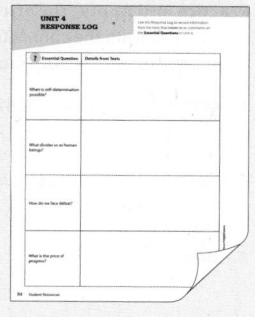

ACADEMIC VOCABULARY

As you write and discuss what you learned from the short story, be sure to use the Academic Vocabulary words. Check off each of the words that you use.

- ❏ **confirm**
- ❏ **definitely**
- ❏ **deny**
- ❏ **format**
- ❏ **unify**

CREATE AND PRESENT

Write a Short Story Encourage students to map out the plot of their story using a chart similar to the prereading one. The events in their stories can follow in a linear or non-linear way, but advise students that the story's structure should help support the theme. Similarly, tell students that whichever point of view they use, it should work to enhance the story's theme.

For **writing support** for students at varying proficiency levels, see the **Text X-Ray** on page 360D.

Share Your Story Tell students to listen carefully to their partner's story, paying close attention to the plot structure. Direct students to jot down a timeline of the sequence of events as they listen. Have them share any confusion about the plot structure with their partner, asking whether or not the lack of clarity was intentional.

RESPOND TO THE ESSENTIAL QUESTION

Allow time for students to add details from "An Occurrence at Owl Creek Bridge" to their Unit 4 Response Logs.

CRITICAL VOCABULARY

Answers:

1. summarily; because he did not put up the paintings quickly

2. poignant; because there was no physical or emotional pain in Troy's journey to his car

3. interminable; because a cabin cannot be endless

VOCABULARY STRATEGY:
Etymology

Answers:

1. confirm: make sure; strengthen belief

2. definitely: when something is defined

3. deny: refuse to give something

4. format: to give something shape or organization

5. unify: to bring separate entities together

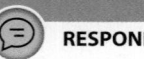 **RESPOND**

WORD BANK

summarily	presaging
poignant	interminable
effaced	malign
undulations	ineffable

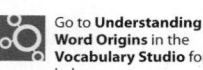 Go to **Understanding Word Origins** in the **Vocabulary Studio** for help.

CRITICAL VOCABULARY

Practice and Apply Underline the words that are used incorrectly in the sentences.

1. Carlito was asked to put up paintings on the newly **effaced**, white walls, which he did <u>summarily</u>—it took him the entire day.

2. As the waves' **undulations** became more rapid, heavy clouds formed, **presaging** rain; this caused Troy to make a <u>poignant</u> journey from the door to the car.

3. To punish her brother for his **malign** behaviors, Niko sent him to an <u>interminable</u> cabin. When he arrived, the confusion on his face was **ineffable.**

VOCABULARY STRATEGY: Etymology

Etymology is the study of the origin of words and how the meaning of words has evolved over time. The word *etymology*, for example, derives from the Greek word *etumos*, meaning "true." Etumologia was the study of words' true meanings. This evolved into etymology, from the Old French word *ethimologie*.

Knowing the etymology of a word provides an enhanced perspective about its most effective use. You can identify subtle differences with similar or related words, both now and from the past. You also begin to see patterns and relationships between languages, which enriches your ability to communicate with others and understand what you are reading. When reading anything from the past, understanding the etymology of words can help clarify meanings that might otherwise become lost or misconstrued.

Practice and Apply The etymologies of the words below have been provided. Explain the connection between the definition of the word and its etymology using the clues provided.

1. **confirm** – Latin: *con* – together; *firmare* – strengthen

2. **definitely** – Latin: *definitus* – bounded, limited

3. **deny** – Latin: *denagare* – refuse, reject

4. **format** – Latin: *formare* – shape

5. **unify** – Latin: *unificare* – make one

 ENGLISH LEARNER SUPPORT

Build Vocabulary with Cognates Remind students that two of the Critical Vocabulary words have Spanish cognates: *interminable/interminable* and *ineffable/inefable*. Have students pair up and use their knowledge of the cognates to create a word web to help them better understand the vocabulary words. Students should include a definition, any synonyms, and a sample phrase or sentence using the word. **ALL LEVELS**

LANGUAGE CONVENTIONS:
Sensory Language

Sensory language is language that appeals to one of the five senses—touch, sight, sound, taste, and hearing. In "An Occurrence at Owl Creek Bridge," the author uses sensory language to bring the story to life. When Farquhar is under water, for example, the narrator uses vivid sensory language to describe the protagonist's pain (paragraph 19).

> His neck ached horribly; his brain was on fire; his heart, which had been fluttering faintly, gave a great leap, trying to force itself out at his mouth.

In this sentence, Bierce appeals to the senses of sight and touch. He says that the character's "brain was on fire", which means he is experiencing pain and is disoriented. He also says that "his heart . . . gave a great leap", meaning his heart was beating hard and fast. Notice that the sensory language in this passage makes the text more vibrant.

Practice and Apply Review the story you wrote in the Create and Present section. Choose three instances where you can add sensory language to make your story more effective and memorable. Write your revised sentences in the space below.

© Houghton Mifflin Harcourt Publishing Company

An Occurrence at Owl Creek Bridge   377

LANGUAGE CONVENTIONS:
Sensory Language

Remind students that sensory language uses precise words and phrases to describe feelings and actions. In addition to the example in the text, write these two sentences on the board, illustrating how sensory language can be used to create vivid imagery.

Initial sentence: *John waited until he heard the door shut.*

Revision: *John's skin tingled with anticipation, waiting for the soft sound of the door's latch clicking into place.*

Point out to students that the revised sentence uses details to appeal to the reader's sense of touch and hearing.

Practice and Apply After students have finished reviewing their short stories, have their partners suggest passages that would benefit from stronger sensory language. Tell students to pay attention to what senses are engaged by the writing. Remind them to select language that expresses a consistent tone throughout their narrative.

EL ENGLISH LEARNER SUPPORT

Use Language Details Use the following supports with students at varying proficiency levels:

- Work with students to create a word map to which they add five modifying words that help describe each of the five senses: sight, smell, touch, taste, and hearing. If necessary, students can draw pictures to represent sensory words. **SUBSTANTIAL**

- Have students work with their partners to create a word map of sensory language. Have partners add at least three sensory words to their stories. **MODERATE**

- Have students choose three sentences from their stories where they used some descriptive language. Challenge them to rewrite the sentences to add sensory language that appeals to more than one sense. **LIGHT**

BUILDING THE TRANSCONTINENTAL RAILROAD

History Writing by Iris Chang

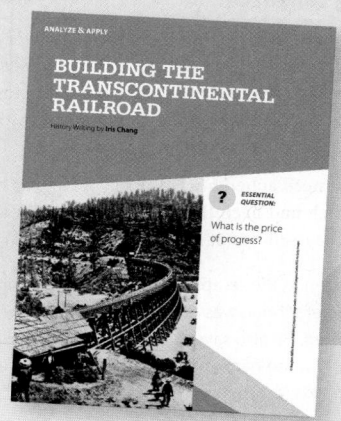

GENRE ELEMENTS
HISTORY WRITING

History writing is an account of events that happened in the past. It places events in their historical, social, or economic context and provides information that explains the motivations and causes of events as well as their effects. Usually presented in chronological order, history writing may present cause-effect and problem-solution relationships. It is based on factual information found in primary and secondary sources and written in third person.

LEARNING OBJECTIVES

- Analyze informational texts and author's purpose.
- Conduct research about Chinese immigration.
- Write a historical report.
- Participate in group discussion.
- Use context clues to determine word meanings.
- Edit sentences to correct misplaced modifiers.
- **Language** Make comparisons using connecting words.

TEXT COMPLEXITY

Quantitative Measures	Building the Transcontinental Railroad	Lexile: 1310L
Qualitative Measures	**Ideas Presented** Much is explicit but moves to some implied meaning; requires some inferential reasoning.	
	Structures Used More complex; narrow perspective; more deviation from chronological or sequential order.	
	Language Used Mostly explicit.	
	Knowledge Required More complexity in theme; experiences may be less familiar to many; cultural or historical references may make heavier demands.	

Online **⊙ Ed**

RESOURCES

- Unit 4 Response Log
- Selection Audio
- Reading Studio:
  Notice & Note
- Level Up Tutorials: Analyzing
  Arguments; Chronological Order
- Writing Studio:
  Conducting Research
- Speaking and Listening Studio:
  Participating in Collaborative
  Discussions
- Vocabulary Studio:
  Using Context Clues
- Grammar Studio:
  Placement of Modifiers
- "Building the Transcontinental
  Railroad" Selection Test

SUMMARIES

English

During the building of the transcontinental railroad, Chinese workers faced discrimination. However, they showed that they were capable workers and often worked harder and more quickly than other laborers. After the railroad was completed, many Chinese workers dispersed throughout the United States.

Spanish

Durante la construcción del ferrocarril transcontinental, los trabajadores chinos fueron discriminados. Sin embargo, mostraron que no solo era trabajadores diligentes, sino que trabajaban más duro y rápido que los demás. Luego de la construcción del ferrocarril, muchos trabajadores chinos se dispersaron a través de Estados Unidos.

SMALL-GROUP OPTIONS

Have students work in small groups and pairs to read and discuss the selection.

Numbered Heads Together

- Have students form groups of four and number off 1, 2, 3, and 4.
- Ask: What words or phrases does the writer use to show she thinks Chinese railroad workers worked harder than the white railroad workers?
- Have students discuss their responses in their groups.
- Call the number for each group and have the "numbered" students share their ideas with the class.

Sticky Note Peer Review

- After students have finished writing their historical report, ask them to review their peers' writing and provide constructive feedback.
- Have students work in small groups and take turns reading their papers aloud.
- As one student reads, have listeners write the following on sticky notes: 1) positive comments, such as words they liked; 2) suggestions; and 3) questions they have about the report.
- Have listeners initial their sticky notes and give them to the writer.

Text X-Ray: English Learner Support
for "Building the Transcontinental Railroad"

Use the Text X-Ray and the supports and scaffolds in the Teacher's Edition to help guide students at different proficiency levels through the selection.

INTRODUCE THE SELECTION
DISCUSS PREJUDICE

In this lesson, students will need to understand the concept of prejudice and how it applied to Chinese railroad workers in the 1800s. Define the word *prejudice*: a feeling of dislike for a person or people because of their sex, race, or country of origin. Explain to students that thousands of workers were needed to build the transcontinental railroad. However, the Central Pacific was able to hire only a few hundred to start building the line east from California. When those workers demanded higher pay, the company hired Chinese immigrants willing to work for low wages. This situation, along with cultural differences, led to feelings of animosity and prejudice.

Ask students to give examples of prejudice they have observed in their lives. Supply the following sentence frames:

- Prejudice is when someone _____.
- A person who _____ is showing prejudice.

CULTURAL REFERENCES

The following words or phrases may be unfamiliar to students:

- *transcontinental* (title): across the continent
- *from sea to shining sea* (paragraph 1): from the Atlantic Ocean in the east to the Pacific Ocean in the west
- *territories* (paragraph 1): areas that were not yet states
- *Sierra Nevada* (paragraph 5): a rugged mountain range in California and Nevada
- *Confederate prisoners* (paragraph 5): southerners who had been captured during the Civil War
- *bankruptcy* (paragraph 27): a declaration saying that a person or company is out of money
- *recently freed American blacks* (paragraph 28): formerly enslaved people who gained their freedom during the Civil War

LISTENING

Understand Differences

Have students listen as you read aloud paragraphs 6–8. Tell them to jot down words and phrases they hear that describe the white workers and the Chinese workers.

Use the following supports with students at varying proficiency levels:

- Tell the students you will repeat some words or phrases that they just heard. Ask them to raise their right hand if the word or phrase describes the Chinese workers and to raise their left hand if the word or phrase describes the white workers. **SUBSTANTIAL**
- Have students describe the Chinese workers and the white workers using the words they wrote down. Provide these sentence frames: *Many of the Chinese/white workers were _____. Railroad executives believed the Chinese workers _____.* **MODERATE**
- Have students work in pairs. Tell them to use the words and phrases they wrote down as the passage was read aloud to describe one group of workers, without identifying the group, and ask *Who am I?* **LIGHT**

SPEAKING

Identify Character Traits

Have students discuss the character traits of individuals and groups in the selection, such as the white workers, the Chinese workers, and the railroad owners. Circulate around the room to provide assistance as needed.

Use the following supports with students at varying proficiency levels:

- Display and read aloud this sentence: *"One character trait that the Chinese workers showed was endurance."* Explain that endurance is the willingness to keep working no matter how difficult it is. Have students repeat the sentence to you and practice saying it to a partner. **SUBSTANTIAL**

- Have students work with a partner to identify character traits. Provide a list of characters or groups for them to discuss, including railroad workers, railroad executives, and Chinese immigrants. Display the following sentence frame: *The (name a person or group) was/were (name a character trait) because the passage says they/he/she (read a quote from the passage).* **MODERATE**

- Have students work in pairs. One student can read aloud a sentence from the selection about a group of people (examples: Chinese laborers, white laborers, railroad executives). The other student can explain what the sentence shows about the group's character traits. Provide this example: *The Chinese workers had courage, since they worked even in dangerous conditions.* **LIGHT**

READING

Analyze Author's Purpose

Read the last sentences of paragraph 4. Explain that they provide the author's purpose: to inform readers of Chinese workers' contributions to the transcontinental railroad.

Use the following supports with students at varying proficiency levels:

- Read aloud various sentences from the selection. Tell students to nod yes or shake their heads no based on whether each shows how Chinese workers made the railroad a reality. **SUBSTANTIAL**

- Have students read silently and find two examples of Chinese workers helping to make the railroad a reality. Have students read each example aloud to a partner. **MODERATE**

- Have students work in pairs. Tell them to skim the selection and find text evidence that best describes how Chinese workers helped to make the transcontinental railroad a reality. Have students read the evidence aloud to their partners and defend their choices. **LIGHT**

WRITING

Compare Research Findings

Help students use connecting words as they compare and contrast Chang's account to their research findings for their historical investigations.

Use the following supports with students at varying proficiency levels:

- Display and read aloud a paragraph comparing Chang's account with a different account of the building of the transcontinental railroad. Include comparison words such as *while, similarly,* and *however.* Have students copy the paragraph into their notebooks. **SUBSTANTIAL**

- Supply sentence frames that students can use to compare Chang's account to another account of the building of the transcontinental railroad. For example: *While Chang describes _____ (topic or fact), [author] describes _____ (different topic or fact).* **MODERATE**

- Help students prepare a bank of comparison/contrast words, such as *in the same way, however,* and *in contrast.* Encourage students to use a variety of the words as they write. **LIGHT**

? **Connect to the**
ESSENTIAL QUESTION

The text recognizes that building the transcontinental railroad was a huge boon to American economic and public progress. Point out to students that the author discusses the price of this progress in both monetary and human terms.

BUILDING THE TRANSCONTINENTAL RAILROAD

History Writing by **Iris Chang**

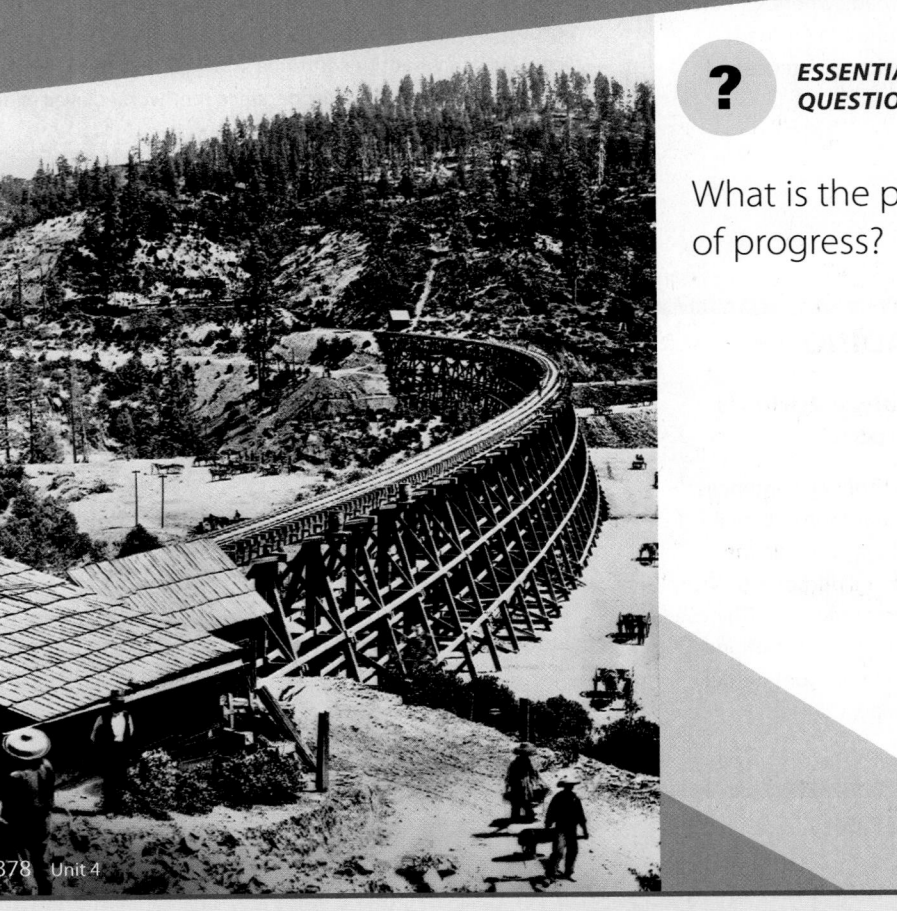

? ***ESSENTIAL QUESTION:***

What is the price of progress?

QUICK START

The text you are about to read explores the human cost of progress in the mid-1800s. With a partner, think of an innovation that made it possible to solve a problem or move forward. What negative effects resulted?

ANALYZE INFORMATIONAL TEXTS

"Building the Transcontinental Railroad" is a **historical narrative,** an account of real events that happened in the past. Writers of historical narratives try to accurately depict events as they happened. As you read, notice the inclusion of details such as economic or cultural factors that tell you about what life was like at the time.

Writers of historical narratives like Chang usually present events in **chronological order,** or the order in which they occurred. This organizational design allows Chang to develop the sequence of events over the course of the text. Dates and time-order signal words, such as *finally, later,* and *then,* help show the connections between events. As you read, use the chart to record important events and dates.

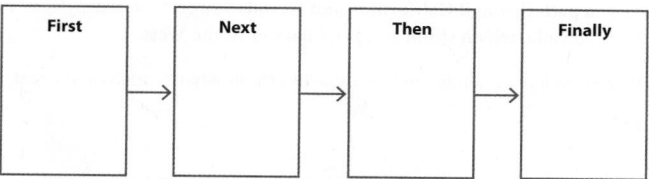

ANALYZE AUTHOR'S PURPOSE

An **author's purpose** is her reason for writing. An author's purpose may be suggested by her diction and the way she describes events. For example, phrases that reveal Iris Chang's **tone,** or attitude toward her topic, might suggest her purpose for telling the story of Chinese laborers. An author might also include particular information from primary or secondary sources that supports her purpose.

Ask yourself these questions to determine and analyze Iris Chang's purpose:

- What is Chang's attitude toward the treatment of Chinese laborers?

- What details and events does Chang emphasize in the account?

- How do certain descriptions and quotations add power to Chang's message?

GENRE ELEMENTS: HISTORY WRITING

- written in the third person
- usually presents events in chronological order
- places events in their historical, social, or economic context
- based on facts from primary and secondary sources

QUICK START

After students read the Quick Start question, prompt them to think about technological innovations that have changed the world during their lifetimes. Many students will point to the smartphone or other computer-related technology. Discuss with them the negative aspects of this technology, such as social isolation, cyberbullying, low-wage factory workers, and privacy issues.

ANALYZE INFORMATIONAL TEXTS

Ask students to think of other historical narratives they have read, such as *Incidents in the Life of a Slave Girl* by Harriet Jacobs or *Of Plymouth Plantation* by William Bradford. Based on their previous encounters with historical narratives, ask students what they expect to learn about in "Building the Transcontinental Railroad." Students might note facts about who built the railroad and how it was built, important dates, and names of important people.

Tell students that the most direct way for authors to indicate chronological sequence is through the use of words for time, such as dates, hours, minutes, or phrases (*that afternoon* or *the following day*). Ask students to name other words that signal chronological order. (*first, next, later*) Remind students to complete a chart like the one on page 379 as they read the selection.

ANALYZE AUTHOR'S PURPOSE

Make the point that a historical narrative, while informational, can also be subjective. In addition to facts, dates, and important figures, the author's **tone** will reveal her purpose for writing about Chinese immigrant laborers. Tell students it's important to look for clues to determine her tone and purpose. Have students write the three questions in their logs, leaving room to note details, figurative language, and diction, which will help provide insight into the author's purpose.

TEACH

CRITICAL VOCABULARY

Encourage students to read all the sentences before deciding which word best completes each one. Remind them to look for context clues that help them determine the meaning of each word. After they've chosen words to complete each sentence, suggest that they read the sentences aloud to make sure their selected words make sense.

Answers:

1. *formidable*

2. *expedience*

3. *diligence*

4. *systematize*

■ English Learner Support

Use Cognates Tell students that two of the Critical Vocabulary words have Spanish cognates: *diligence/ diligencia* and *formidable/formidable*. **ALL LEVELS**

LANGUAGE CONVENTIONS

Misplaced Modifiers Explain to students that a misplaced modifier is a modifier that is placed too far from the word it modifies. When modifiers are misplaced, the intended meaning of the sentence is unclear. Prepositional phrases and participial phrases are often misplaced. Review the example sentences:

- Misplaced modifier: *Industrious and reliable, the managers were impressed with the Chinese laborers.*

- Correctly placed modifier: *The managers were impressed with the industrious and reliable Chinese laborers.*

■ English Learner Support

Understand Syntax Explain that different languages place modifiers, such as adjectives and adverbs, in different locations in a sentence. Provide an example sentence: *The careful workers completed the task quickly.* Help students identify the modifiers and the words they modify. Guide them to substitute different modifiers in the sentence. **ALL LEVELS**

ANNOTATION MODEL

Remind students of the annotation ideas such as underlining and circling text and making notes in the margin. Students may follow these suggestions or use their own system for marking up the selection in their write-in text. They may want to color-code their annotations by using highlighters.

 **GET READY**

CRITICAL VOCABULARY

formidable	expedience	diligence	systematize

To see how many Critical Vocabulary words you already know, write the correct word that completes the sentence.

1. If something inspires awe or fear, it is _____.

2. A means of achieving an end is _____.

3. The man's _____ made his work consistent and thorough.

4. If you _____ a proposal, you turn it into a specific plan.

LANGUAGE CONVENTIONS

Misplaced Modifiers Modifiers change or limit the meaning of other words. For example, adjectives modify nouns by telling you something specific about them. Good writers like Iris Chang place modifiers near the words they modify, which adds to the clarity of her work. Note how the adjectives in the example below help you understand the challenge, and enhance the image, of the Sierra Nevada mountains.

> **The first and largest challenge was figuring out how to cut a path through California's and Nevada's rugged Sierra Nevada, which stood as a final barrier to the West.**

As your read, pay attention to how modifiers clarify what happens in the text.

ANNOTATION MODEL   NOTICE & NOTE

As you read, note the details that suggest Chang's purpose for writing. Notice words that suggest chronological order, the organizational design of the text. In the model, you can see one reader's notes about "Building the Transcontinental Railroad."

Making the vision real, however, was dangerous and frustrating. The territory between the coasts was unsettled and there was no reliable transport or route. Crossing the continent meant braving death by disease, brigands, Native Americans, starvation, thirst, heat, or freezing. This was true especially for those headed straight to the gold hills of California, but the gold rushers weren't the only ones frustrated by the lack of a safe passage between the settled East and the new state of California in the sparsely populated West. Californians themselves were impatient at waiting months to receive mail and provisions.

There were many dangers and challenges at this time.

important ideas about the need for the railroad

BACKGROUND

Iris Chang (1968–2004) was a historian who sought to shed light on acts of injustice. Her international bestseller, The Rape of Nanking, documents previously unpublished accounts of brutal violence by the Japanese military during their occupation of China prior to World War II. In The Chinese in America, Chang traces her ethnic group's immigration experiences and achievements from the mid-19th century to the present day. This chapter from her book details the role of Chinese laborers in building a vital transportation link that fueled westward expansion in the United States.

BUILDING THE TRANSCONTINENTAL RAILROAD
History Writing by Iris Chang

SETTING A PURPOSE

As you read, pay attention to the details that reveal Chang's attitude toward her subject and her purpose for writing.

1 *From sea to shining sea.* In the decade of the 1840s, Americans were consumed by this vision, articulated in the doctrine of Manifest Destiny, which proclaimed it the right and duty of the United States to expand its democratic way of life across the entire continent, from the Atlantic to the Pacific, from the Rio Grande in the south to the 54th parallel in the north. The country was feeling confident (during this decade, it acquired the territories of Texas, California, and Oregon), its population was increasing, and many wanted to push west, especially to California, made famous by gold and Richard Henry Dana's recounting of his adventures there, in *Two Years Before the Mast*.

2 Making the vision real, however, was dangerous and frustrating. The territory between the coasts was unsettled and there was no reliable transport or route. Crossing the continent meant braving death by disease, brigands,[1] Native Americans, starvation, thirst, heat, or freezing. This was true especially for

[1] **brigands:** bandits.

Notice & Note

Use the side margins to notice and note signposts in the text.

ANALYZE INFORMATIONAL TEXTS

Annotate: Mark two statements of time in paragraph 1 that indicate chronological order is the organizational design of the text.

Predict: What other details provide clues about when the events took place?

BACKGROUND

Inform students that large-scale Chinese immigration to the United States began in the 1840s and 1850s, with most immigrants arriving at San Francisco. However, most Chinese immigrants at that time were declared ineligible to become citizens, vote, hold office, own land, or testify against a white person in court.

SETTING A PURPOSE

Direct students to use the Setting a Purpose prompt to focus their reading.

ANALYZE INFORMATIONAL TEXTS

Point out to students that Chang immediately establishes the beginning of her narrative: the 1840s. Tell them that by stating the exact time period, she places informational details that follow in historical context. (**Answer:** *The gold rush and the acquisition of Texas, California, and Oregon suggest the events take place as the United States is spreading westward.*)

ENGLISH LEARNER SUPPORT

Identify Chronological Words Help students recognize the chronological text structure by pointing out the phrase "in the decade of the 1840s" in the second sentence of paragraph 1. Explain that a decade is a span of ten years. Provide students with a word bank of chronological terms they can use to understand the sequence of events in the selection, including *during, first, later,* and *finally,* as well as references to years or seasons. Have them use the word bank to find another chronological phrase in the first paragraph. (*during this decade*)
SUBSTANTIAL/ MODERATE

ANALYZE AUTHOR'S PURPOSE

Remind students to consider the author's tone to help determine her purpose. Point out that Chang uses a tone of reverence for describing the role of the Chinese laborers. For example, rather than simply stating that the Chinese laborers helped to an extent, she modifies the phrase by saying they helped to a "great extent." (**Answer:** *Chang wants readers to know that the Chinese played a pivotal role in the building of the railroad. Including these details suggests that her purpose is to inform readers of their achievements.*)

For **reading support** for students at varying proficiency levels, see the **Text X-Ray** on page 378D.

CRITICAL VOCABULARY

formidable: The railroad engineers had the extremely difficult task of laying track over and through formidable areas.

ASK STUDENTS to list the formidable challenges that the builders of the transcontinental railroad faced. (*the Sierra Nevada, Rocky Mountains, and the deserts of Nevada and Utah*)

those headed straight to the gold hills of California, but the gold rushers weren't the only ones frustrated by the lack of a safe passage between the settled East and the new state of California in the sparsely populated West. Californians themselves were impatient at waiting months to receive mail and provisions. Washington, too, recognized the economic as well as political benefits of linking the country's two coasts. In the West lay rich farmland waiting for settlement, gold and silver to be mined and taxed. What was needed was a transcontinental railroad to move more people west and natural resources safely and profitably to major markets back east.

3   There were only two overland routes west—over the Rockies or along the southern route through Apache and Comanche territory—both hazardous. It took longer, but was almost always safer, to get to California from anywhere east of the Missouri by sea. This meant heading east to the Atlantic Ocean or south to the Gulf of Mexico, boarding a ship that would sail almost to the southern tip of South America, passing through the Strait of Magellan, and heading back north to California. The sea voyage could be shortened considerably by disembarking on the eastern coast of Central America, traveling by wagon across the isthmus,[2] and then hitching a ride on the first steamer headed north.[3]

ANALYZE AUTHOR'S PURPOSE

Annotate: In paragraph 4, mark the role of the Chinese in building the transcontinental railroad.

Draw Conclusions: Why do you think Chang includes this information? What does its inclusion suggest about her purpose for writing?

formidable
(fôr´mĭ-də-bəl) *adj.* difficult and intimidating.

4   The need for a transcontinental railroad was so strongly argued that Congress, with the support of President Lincoln, passed legislation to finance the railroad with government bonds, even though the country was already at war. Two companies divided the task of actual construction. In 1862, the Central Pacific Railroad Corporation, headed by the "Big Four"—Leland Stanford, Collis P. Huntington, Charles Crocker, and Mark Hopkins—was awarded the contract to lay tracks eastward from Sacramento, while its rival, the Union Pacific, was awarded the path westward from Omaha, Nebraska, which was already connected to the East through existing rail lines. The goal was to meet in the middle, connecting the nation with a continuous stretch of railroad tracks from the Atlantic to the Pacific. The Union Pacific's job—laying track over plains—was much easier, while the Central Pacific had to go over steep mountains. The Central Pacific engineers promised that the **formidable** physical obstacles could be overcome, and to a great extent, it was Chinese labor, and even, here and there, Chinese ingenuity, that helped make the transcontinental railroad a reality.

5   The first and largest challenge was figuring out how to cut a path through California's and Nevada's rugged Sierra Nevada, which stood as a final barrier to the West. The workers of the Central Pacific had

---

[2] **isthmus** (ĭs´məs): a thin strip of land between two bodies of water.
[3] Eventually, U.S. engineers would build the Panama Canal in the early twentieth century. [Author's note]

APPLYING ACADEMIC VOCABULARY

☑ **confirm**   ☐ **definitely**   ☑ **deny**   ☐ **format**   ☐ **unify**

Write and Discuss   Have students turn to a partner to discuss the following questions. Guide students to include the Academic Vocabulary words *confirm* and *deny* in their responses. Ask volunteers to share their responses with the class.

- What details in the text **confirm** that Chinese laborers were industrious and inventive?
- How did the Central Pacific Railroad company **deny** the Chinese proper recognition for their efforts?

the dangerous task of ramming tunnels through these mountains, and then laying tracks across the parched Nevada and Utah deserts. Some engineers, watching the project from afar, said this was impossible. In a major recruitment drive for five thousand workers, the Central Pacific sent advertisements to every post office in the state of California, offering high wages to any white man willing to work. But the appeal secured only eight hundred. Why toil for wages when an instant fortune was possible in the mines? Many men who did sign on were, in the words of company superintendent James Strobridge, "unsteady men, unreliable. Some of them would stay a few days, and some would not go to work at all. Some would stay until payday, get a little money, get drunk, and clear out." The company thought of asking the War Department for five thousand Confederate prisoners to put to work, but Lee's surrender at the Appomattox Court House ended the war and this plan.

6 Fortunately for the Central Pacific, Chinese immigrants provided a vast pool of cheap, plentiful, and easily exploitable labor. By 1865, the number of Chinese in California reached close to fifty thousand, at least 90 percent of them young men. In the spring of that year, when white laborers demanded higher pay and threatened to strike, Charles Crocker, the Central Pacific's chief contractor, ordered Superintendent Strobridge to recruit Chinese workers. The tactic worked, and the white workers agreed to return, as long as no Chinese were hired, but by then the Central Pacific had the upper hand and hired fifty Chinese anyway—former miners, laundry men, domestic servants, and market gardeners—to do the hard labor of preparing the route and laying track. Many claimed the railroad did this as a reminder to the white workers that others were ready to replace them. Needless to say, this did not contribute to harmony between the whites and the Chinese.

7 Of course prejudice against the Chinese railroad workers did not start with the white laborers. Initially, Superintendent Strobridge was unhappy with their being hired. "I will not boss Chinese!" he roared, suggesting that the Chinese were too delicate for the job. (The Chinese averaged four feet ten inches in height and weighed 120 pounds.) Crocker, however, pointed out that a race of people who had built the Great Wall of China could build a railroad. Grudgingly, Strobridge put the Chinese to work, giving them light jobs, like filling dump carts.

8 To the surprise of many—but apparently not the Chinese themselves—the first fifty hired excelled at their work, becoming such disciplined, fast learners that the railroad soon gave them other responsibilities, such as rock cuts. In time, the Central Pacific hired another fifty Chinese, and then another fifty, until eventually the company employed thousands of Chinese laborers—the overwhelming majority of the railroad workforce. E. B. Crocker,

ANALYZE AUTHOR'S PURPOSE

Annotate: Mark the words in paragraph 6 that Chang uses to describe Chinese immigrants.

Interpret: What do these words suggest about Chang's attitude toward those doing the hiring?

ANALYZE INFORMATIONAL TEXTS

Annotate: Mark the phrases in paragraph 8 that signal chronological order.

Analyze: How do these phrases help you understand the sequence of events?

 ANALYZE AUTHOR'S PURPOSE

Remind students that word choice can reveal an author's purpose. Point out to students that some of the words and phrases Chang uses to describe the Chinese immigrants are factual, while others are more expressive and subjective. Tell students that the more subjective descriptions add to the author's purpose. (**Answer:** *It suggests that those who needed workers were happy to take advantage of the flood of Chinese immigrants.*)

 ANALYZE INFORMATIONAL TEXTS

Remind students to look for time-order signal words in order to establish a chronology of events. Point out that paragraph 8 contains two sections that convey a sequence of events: first, the rate at which Chinese laborers were hired; second, Leland Stanford's evolving stance on Chinese immigration. (**Answer:** *These words help the reader understand that people did not want to work with Chinese immigrants at first, but that immigrants continued to be hired because they proved to be such good workers.*)

For **listening support** for students at varying proficiency levels, see the **Text X-Ray** on page 378C.

WHEN STUDENTS STRUGGLE...

Understand Arguments If students have trouble keeping track of the arguments that were used to justify excluding Chinese workers, have them reread paragraphs 7–9. Then, have them complete a two-column point/counterpoint chart listing the reasons Superintendent Strobridge gave for not hiring Chinese workers and evidence Charles and E. B. Crocker found for hiring them.

For additional support, go to the **Reading Studio** and assign the following **Level Up Tutorial: Analyzing Arguments.**

ANALYZE AUTHOR'S PURPOSE

Remind students that **historical narratives** will include primary sources, such as quotations, in order to support the author's purpose. Tell students that the quotations here serve to underline Chang's description of the railroad executives as "delighted" and "fervent." (**Answer:** *It suggests that she wants to make it clear that the Chinese were valuable workers.*)

EL ENGLISH LEARNER SUPPORT

Understand Modifiers Read the first sentence of paragraph 9 aloud. Guide students to identify and circle adjectives in the sentence (such as *fervent* and *delighted*) and underline the nouns or noun phrases they modify (*advocates* and *railroad executives*). Remind students that adjectives usually appear close to the nouns they modify. **MODERATE**

For **speaking support** for students at varying proficiency levels, see the **Text X-Ray** on page 378D.

CRITICAL VOCABULARY

expedience: The attitudes of the railroad companies toward Chinese workers stemmed from their own economic interests.

ASK STUDENTS to relate how expedience guided Leland Stanford's attitude toward the Chinese. (*In order to advance his own goals, Stanford modified his stance on Chinese immigration to gain the support of important people.*)

 NOTICE & NOTE

expedience
(ĭk-spē´dē-əns) *n.* a self-interested means to an end.

ANALYZE AUTHOR'S PURPOSE

Annotate: Mark the phrase in paragraph 9 that tells how the railroad executives felt about the Chinese workers.

Analyze: What does this suggest about Chang's purpose for writing this work?

brother of Charles, wrote to Senator Cornelius Cole (R-Calif.) that the Chinese were nearly equal to white men in the amount of work they could do and far more reliable. Leland Stanford, the railroad's president, and later the founder of Stanford University, praised the Chinese as "quiet, peaceable, patient, industrious and economical." (Stanford's position on the Chinese was governed by **expedience**. In 1862, to please the racist sentiments of the state, he called the Chinese in California the "dregs" of Asia, a "degraded" people. A few years later, he was praising the Chinese to President Andrew Johnson and others in order to justify the Central Pacific's mass hiring of Chinese. Later still—notably in 1884, when he ran for the U.S. Senate—he would ally himself with those who favored a ban on Chinese immigration.)

9 Delighted by the productivity of the Chinese, railroad executives became fervent[4] advocates of Chinese immigration to California. "I like the idea of your getting over more Chinamen," Collis Huntington, one of the "Big Four" executives at the Central Pacific, wrote to Charlie Crocker in 1867. "It would be all the better for us and the State if there should a half million come over in 1868."

10 The Central Pacific printed handbills and dispatched recruiters to China, especially the Guangdong province, to find new workers. It negotiated with a steamship company to lower their rates for travel. And, fortuitously[5] for the Central Pacific, Sino-American diplomacy would create more favorable conditions for Chinese immigration to the United States. In 1868, China and the U.S. government signed the Burlingame Treaty. In exchange for "most favored nation" status in trade, China agreed to recognize the "inherent and inalienable right of man to change his home and allegiance and also the mutual advantage of free migration and emigration of their citizens and subjects respectively from one country to the other for purposes of curiosity or trade or as permanent residents."

11 The new Chinese recruits docked at San Francisco and were immediately transported by riverboat to Sacramento, and then by the Central Pacific's own train to the end of the laid tracks, which was a moving construction site. There they were organized into teams of about a dozen or so, with each team assigned its own cook and headman, who communicated with the Central Pacific foreman. The Chinese paid for their own food and cooked it themselves—they were even able to procure special ingredients like cuttlefish, bamboo shoots, and abalone. At night they slept in tents provided by the railroad, or in dugouts in the earth. At the peak of construction, Central Pacific would employ more than ten thousand Chinese men.

12 The large number of Chinese made white workers uncomfortable. As Lee Chew, a railroad laborer, later recalled in a spasm of national

---

[4] **fervent:** avid, enthusiastic.
[5] **fortuitously:** luckily; by favorable chance.

TO CHALLENGE STUDENTS . . .

Research Historical Detail To enhance appreciation of the detailed series of historical developments that resulted in Chinese immigration to the United States, have students look up the following terms:

• Burlingame Treaty

• most favored nation

Invite students to give brief talks to the class elaborating on how these terms relate to Chinese immigration.

pride, the Chinese were "persecuted not for their vices but for their virtues. No one would hire an Irishman, German, Englishman or Italian when he could get a Chinese, because our countrymen are so much more honest, industrious, steady, sober and painstaking." Crocker explicitly acknowledged this work ethic. After recruiting some Cornish miners from Virginia City, Nevada, to excavate one end of a tunnel and the Chinese the other, he commented, "The Chinese, without fail, always outmeasured the Cornish miners. That is to say, they would cut more rock in a week than the Cornish miners did. And here it was hard work, steady pounding on the rock, bone-labor." The Cornish eventually walked off the job, vowing that "they would not work with Chinamen anyhow," and soon, Crocker recalled, "the Chinamen had possession of the whole work."

13   White laborers began to feel that Chinese **diligence** forced everyone to work harder for less reward. Crocker recalled that one white laborer near Auburn was questioned by a gentleman about his wages. "I think we were paying $35 a month and board to white laborers, and $30 a month to Chinamen and they boarded themselves," Crocker said. "The gentleman remarked, 'That is pretty good wages.' 'Yes,' says he, 'but begad if it wasn't for them damned nagurs we would get $50 and not do half the work.' "

14   Some white laborers on the Central Pacific whispered among themselves about driving the Chinese off the job, but when Charles Crocker got wind of this, he threatened to replace all the whites with Chinese. Eventually the white workers gave up, placated[6] perhaps by being told that they alone could be promoted to the position of foreman. The more Chinese workers, the fewer whites in the labor

---

[6] **placated:** made peaceful or less angry.

diligence
(dĭl´ə-jəns) *n.* consistent, thorough effort and dedication.

ANALYZE INFORMATIONAL TEXTS
Annotate: Reread paragraph 14. Underline what white laborers wanted to do. Circle how the executives reacted.

Connect: Why do you think Chang includes this information?

ANALYZE INFORMATIONAL TEXTS

Point out to students that Chang uses this event to support her claim. Tell students that by describing a tense racial situation, Chang is placing events in their social context. (**Answer:** *Chang describes the feelings of whites and the reactions of executives to underscore how valuable the railroad executives felt the Chinese were.*)

ENGLISH LEARNER SUPPORT

Understand Archaic Language Tell students that the quotations on this page reflect the way some Americans spoke in the 1800s. Explain the following terms: *Chinamen* was a disrespectful word used to refer to Chinese people. *Nagurs* was a disrespectful word used to refer to groups of people the speaker considered inferior.

Tell students that when they read historical quotations, they should watch for archaic language and look up any words they don't understand in a dictionary. Then, ask students to determine how the use of these words affects the tone of the quotations. (*It gives them a hostile tone.*)
MODERATE

CRITICAL VOCABULARY

diligence: It became obvious that the Chinese worked harder than the Cornish miners, causing resentment among the latter group.

ASK STUDENTS why non-Chinese workers reacted negatively to Chinese diligence. (*Non-Chinese workers objected to Chinese diligence because it led to higher employer expectations.*)

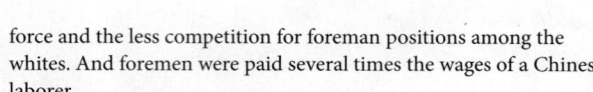
NOTICE & NOTE

ANALYZE AUTHOR'S PURPOSE

Tell students that Chang uses these historical events to support her statement from paragraph 4 that "it was Chinese labor, and even, here and there, Chinese ingenuity, that helped make the transcontinental railroad a reality." Point out that Chang includes details about the hardworking spirit of the Chinese workers and another paragraph (18) describing Chinese skill and ingenuity. (**Answer:** *Chang's diction suggests a tone of admiration for the courage of the Chinese laborers, since she lists the dangerous tasks that only they were willing to do. She also uses a deeply critical tone when referring to the railroad companies, whose actions led "countless workers" to "perish.")*

ANALYZE AUTHOR'S PURPOSE

Annotate: Mark in paragraphs 17 and 18 what Chinese workers did and what happened to some of them.

Analyze: What tone is suggested by the diction in these paragraphs?

force and the less competition for foreman positions among the whites. And foremen were paid several times the wages of a Chinese laborer.

15   In the process of laying the track across northern California, Nevada, and Utah, hundreds of men—Chinese, Irish, German, and others—cleared a path through some of the world's largest trees, some with stumps so deeply rooted that ten barrels of gunpowder were often needed to unearth them. It was dangerous work—work that loosened boulders, started landslides, and filled the air with flying debris. Even more dangerous was the work that began upon reaching the Sierra Nevada.

16   Ideally, the roadbed[7] through the mountains would be tunneled through by heavy machinery. This machinery was unavailable, however, because it was expensive and difficult to transport (entire bridges would have had to be rebuilt for such machinery to reach the current site). Thus the Chinese were forced to chisel tunnels through the granite using only handheld drills, explosives, and shovels. In some places they encountered a form of porphyritic[8] rock so hard it was impervious[9] to frontal attack, even with gunpowder. Work proceeded, on average, seven inches a day, at a cost of as much as a million dollars for one mile of tunnel.

17   In the summer of 1866, to move farther faster, the railroad kept several shifts of men going day and night. Shoulder to shoulder, hour after hour, the Chinese railroad workers chipped away at the rock, breathing granite dust, sweating and panting by the dim flickering glow of candlelight, until even the strongest of them fainted from exhaustion.

18   Finally, to speed up the process, the Central Pacific brought in nitroglycerin. Only the Chinese—a people experienced with fireworks—were willing to handle this unpredictable explosive, pouring it into the tunnel through holes drilled in the granite. Countless workers perished in accidental blasts, but the Central Pacific did not keep track of the numbers.

19   Still the workers struggled on. One terrifying challenge lay at Cape Horn, the nickname for a three-mile stretch of gorge above the American River three miles east of Colfax, California, and fifty-seven miles east of Sacramento. Through much of the way, a flat roadbed had to be carved along a steep cliff, and a Chinese headman suggested to Strobridge that they employ an ancient method used to create fortresses along the Yangtze River gorges: they could dangle supplies down to the work site in reed baskets, attached to ropes secured over the tops of mountains.

---

[7] **roadbed:** the path or foundation on which railroad tracks are laid.
[8] **porphyritic** (pôr´fə-rĭt´ĭk): rock containing relatively large, visible crystals.
[9] **impervious:** immune or resistant.

IMPROVE READING FLUENCY

Targeted Passage Tell students that proper names can cause hiccups in their pace of reading. Read aloud paragraph 19 and have students read along with you. Suggest to students that they may want to practice pronouncing proper names several times before reading a text out loud. After reading, discuss your pacing, pointing out proper names that may be difficult to pronounce (*Colfax, Sacramento, Strobridge, and Yangtze*). Ask students who are familiar with the names to give their pronunciations. Then, have students practice reading this paragraph with a partner.

 Go to the **Reading Studio** for additional support in developing fluency.

20   Reeds were shipped out immediately from San Francisco to Cape Horn. At night the Chinese workers wove them into wicker baskets and fastened them to sturdy ropes. When everything was ready, workers were lowered in the baskets to drill holes and tamp in dynamite, literally sculpting the rail bed out of the face of sheer rock. The lucky ones were hauled up in time to escape the explosions; others, peppered with shards of granite and shale, fell to their deaths in the valley below.

21   Disease swept through the ranks of the exhausted railroad workers, but the Chinese fared better than whites. Caucasian laborers, subsisting largely on salt beef, potatoes, bread, coffee, and rancid butter, lacked vegetables in their diet, while the Chinese employed their own cooks and ate better-balanced meals. White workers succumbed to dysentery after sharing communal dippers from greasy pails, but the Chinese drank fresh boiled tea, which they kept in whiskey barrels or powder kegs suspended from each end of a bamboo pole. They also avoided alcohol and, "not having acquired the taste of whiskey," as one contemporary observed, "they have fewer fights and no blue Mondays." Most important, they kept themselves clean, which helped prevent the spread of germs. The white men had "a sort of hydrophobia," one writer observed, whereas the Chinese bathed every night before dinner, in powder kegs filled with heated water.

22   In the Sierras, the railroad workers endured two of the worst winters in American history. In 1865, they faced thirty-foot drifts and spent weeks just shoveling snow. The following year brought the "Homeric winter" of 1866–67, one of the most brutal ever recorded, which dropped forty feet of snow on the crews and whipped up drifts more than eighty feet high. Power snowplows, driven forward by twelve locomotives linked together, could scarcely budge the densest of these drifts. Sheds built to protect the uncompleted tracks collapsed under the weight of the snow, which snapped even the best timber. On the harshest days, travel was almost impossible; as horses broke the icy crust, sharp edges slashed their legs to the bone. They received mail from a Norwegian postal worker on cross-country skis.

23   Making the best of the situation, the Chinese carved a working city under the snow. Operating beneath the crust by lantern light, they trudged through a labyrinth of snow tunnels, with snow chimneys and snow stairs leading up to the surface. Meanwhile, they continued to shape the rail bed out of rock, using materials lowered down to them through airshafts in the snow.

24   The cost in human life was enormous. Snow slides and avalanches swept away entire teams of Chinese workers. On Christmas Day 1866, the *Dutch Flat Enquirer* announced that "a gang of Chinamen employed by the railroad . . . were covered up by a snow slide and four or five died before they could be exhumed. Then snow

ANALYZE AUTHOR'S PURPOSE
Annotate: Mark the direct quotations from a primary source in paragraph 21.

Infer: What is the purpose of including this account in the narrative?

LANGUAGE CONVENTIONS
Annotate: Adjectives, adverbs, and prepositional phrases are examples of modifiers. Mark two modifiers in paragraph 22.

Evaluate: How does Chang's careful placement of modifiers help make the situation clear?

ANALYZE AUTHOR'S PURPOSE

Explain that in order to support their purposes, history writers often include eyewitness accounts to add descriptive detail and to help readers form a picture of the time, the place, the people, and the actions involved. (**Answer:** *The account helps support the idea that Chinese laborers were often more reliable than white workers. The observer provides details to show that the Chinese workers bathed more frequently, drank less alcohol, and got sick less often than white workers did.*)

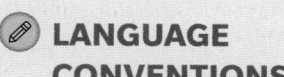 LANGUAGE CONVENTIONS

Remind students that modifiers are used to enhance the meaning of a sentence, add details, and provide clarity. Tell them that using too many modifiers, or misplacing them, can confuse the reader. (**Answer:** *The modifiers paint a vivid picture of cold weather and deep snow, hardship, and difficulty. The accurate use of modifiers helps readers comprehend a large amount of information.*)

 ENGLISH LEARNER SUPPORT

Understand Idioms   Explain that in paragraph 22, the word "Homeric" refers to the epic poetry of the ancient poet Homer, and describes something that is epic, large-scale, or impressive. The phrase "Homeric winter" describes a particularly severe winter, with significant amounts of snow and ice. Ask students what else might happen during a Homeric winter, and have them use this phrase in a sentence. (**Sample answer:** *A Homeric winter would be extremely cold.*)
MODERATE/LIGHT

ANALYZE AUTHOR'S PURPOSE

Remind students that a writer's tone is his or her attitude toward the topic. Discuss with students their impressions of the winter of 1866 through 1867 and how Chang's word choices helped shape their views. Point out that in this paragraph, Chang presents the historical details in a fairly straightforward manner. Tell students that Chang may have thought the facts were impressive enough and that excessive figurative language was not needed to convey the degree of hardship. (**Answer:** *The tone is one of respect and awe because laborers faced extreme hardship and still persevered.*)

CRITICAL VOCABULARY

systematize: The whites' abuse of the Chinese was not limited to isolated incidents.

ASK STUDENTS why prejudice is especially harmful when it is systematized. (*When it is systematized, a whole society practices discrimination and harms entire groups of people for long periods of time.*)

ANALYZE AUTHOR'S PURPOSE

Annotate: Mark in paragraph 25 obstacles the laborers faced.

Draw Conclusions: Why does the writer include such vivid details? What tone, or attitude, does the inclusion of these details suggest?

systematize
(sĭs´tə-mə-tīz) *v.* to form something into an organized plan or scheme.

fell to such a depth that one whole camp of Chinamen was covered up during the night and parties were digging them out when our informant left." When the snow melted in the spring, the company found corpses still standing erect, their frozen hands gripping picks and shovels.

25   Winter was only one obstacle. Other conditions also affected the workers. Landslides rolled tons of soil across the completed track, blocking its access and often smothering workers. Melting snow mired wagons, carts, and stagecoaches in a sea of mud. Once through the mountains, the crews faced terrible extremes of weather in the Nevada and Utah deserts. There the temperature could plummet to 50 degrees below zero—freezing the ground so hard it required blasting, as if it were bedrock—or soar above 120, causing heat stroke and dehydration.

26   The Chinese labored from sunrise to sunset six days a week, in twelve-hour shifts. Only on Sundays did they have time to rest, mend their clothes, talk, smoke, and, of course, gamble.[10] The tedium of their lives was aggravated by the **systematized** abuse and contempt heaped on them by the railroad executives. The Chinese worked longer and harder than whites, but received less pay: because the

---

[10]Gambling was as addictive for Chinese railroad workers as whiskey among their white counterparts. Chinese gamblers left their mark on Nevada, where casinos credit the nineteenth-century Chinese railroad workers with introducing the game of keno, based on the Chinese lottery game of *pak kop piu*. [Author's note]

TO CHALLENGE STUDENTS . . .

Use Research Techniques   How can writers bring history back to life? Ask students what techniques a writer might use to find reliable descriptions and statistics about a century-old event. (*A writer would search in libraries and online for documents from that time and place, such as newspapers, diaries, and letters. The writer would also consult biographies of people who played an important part in the events, as well as recent history books and articles on the subject.*)

Have students choose a historical event that interests them and perform a brief search for primary and secondary sources about it. Have students share their topics, search methods, and results with the class.

Chinese had to pay for their own board, their wages were two-thirds those of white workers and a fourth those of the white foremen. (Even the allocation for feed for horses—fifty dollars a month for each—was twenty dollars more than the average Chinese worker earned.) Worst of all, they endured whippings from their overseers, who treated them like slaves.

27   Finally the Chinese rebelled. In June 1867, as the Central Pacific tottered[11] on the brink of bankruptcy (Leland Stanford later described a two-week period when there was not a dollar of cash in the treasury), some two thousand Chinese in the Sierras walked off the job. As was their way in a strange land, they conducted the strike politely, appointing headmen to present James Strobridge a list of demands that included more pay and fewer hours in the tunnels. They also circulated among themselves a placard written in Chinese, explaining their rights. In retrospect, it is surprising that they managed to organize a strike at all, for there are also reports of frequent feuds erupting between groups of Chinese workers, fought with spades, crowbars, and spikes. But organize they did.

28   The Central Pacific reacted swiftly and ruthlessly. An enraged Charles Crocker contacted employment agencies in an attempt to recruit ten thousand recently freed American blacks to replace the Chinese. He stopped payments to the Chinese and cut off the food supply, effectively starving them back to work. Because most of them could not speak English, could not find work elsewhere, and lacked transportation back to California, the strike lasted only a week. However, it did achieve a small victory, securing the Chinese a raise of two dollars a month. More important, by staging the largest Chinese strike of the nineteenth century, they demonstrated to their current and future employers that while they were willing and easily managed workers, if pushed hard enough they were able to organize to protect themselves, even in the face of daunting odds.

29   Later, the railroad management expressed admiration at the orderliness of the strike. "If there had been that number of whites in a strike, there would have been murder and drunkenness and disorder," Crocker marveled. "But with the Chinese it was just like Sunday. These men stayed in their camps. They would come out and walk around, but not a word was said; nothing was done. No violence was perpetuated[12] along the whole line."

30   The Chinese were certainly capable, however, of violence. As the railroad neared completion, the Chinese encountered the Irish workers of the Union Pacific for the first time. When the two companies came within a hundred feet of each other, the Union Pacific Irish taunted the Chinese with catcalls and threw clods of dirt.

---
[11] **tottered:** wobbled unsteadily.
[12] **perpetuated:** sustained.

ANALYZE INFORMATIONAL TEXTS

Annotate: Mark words in paragraph 27 that suggest chronological order.

Summarize: Restate the sequence of events in the paragraph.

CONTRASTS AND CONTRADICTIONS

Notice & Note: Underline the word in the first sentence of paragraph 30 that suggests a contrast.

Analyze: How does the information in paragraph 30 contrast with what Chang has said previously? Why does Chang include these details?

ANALYZE INFORMATIONAL TEXTS

Point out that the Chinese workers' strike is one episode within the overall sequence of events of the building of the railroad. It has its own sequence, which can be viewed as a subsequence of the main sequence. (**Answer:** *As the company approached bankruptcy, two thousand Chinese walked off their jobs. They presented demands to the company and circulated a placard. The Central Pacific stopped payments and food deliveries to the strikers. After a week, the strikers were forced to go back to work.*)

CONTRASTS AND CONTRADICTIONS

Point out to students that contrasts and contradictions in historical narratives can create a nuanced view of the subject. Explain to students that Chang creates a more informative historical record by contrasting earlier descriptions. (**Answer:** *She has previously described the Chinese as remarkably peaceful. Here, she says they could be violent. I think she includes it to show they could express anger even though they were disciplined, hard workers.*)

 ENGLISH LEARNER SUPPORT

Understand Cause and Effect   Define the terms *cause* and *effect* and help student pairs identify cause-and-effect relationships in paragraphs 26-28.

- A *cause* is an event or action that directly results in another event or action.
- An *effect* is a direct or logical outcome of the cause.

Have pairs add causes and effects of the strike to a graphic organizer. Then, ask them to describe the causes and effects. Supply sentence frames: *Chinese railroad workers decided to strike because _____. One effect of the strike was _____. Another effect was _____.*   **MODERATE**

ANALYZE INFORMATIONAL TEXTS

Explain that a chronological narrative may be unified around an overall main action that includes a sequence of several events. In this passage, the event is a one-day contest to see how many miles of track the workers could lay. (**Answer:** *The date and time help me understand when this happened. Crocker originally did not want Chinese workers. By this time, he was proud of them and knew he could rely on them to beat the Union Pacific. The time tells me how quickly and hard the Chinese worked.*)

ANALYZE AUTHOR'S PURPOSE

Explain to students that sometimes an author will state his or her attitude clearly. Point out to students that Chang uses the word *nonetheless* to express disapproval that the Chinese workers did not receive fair treatment considering their enormous contributions to the building of the railroad. (**Answer:** *She mentions that the railroad couldn't have been completed without the Chinese, but people tried to write the Chinese out of history. They didn't even get the things they were promised, such as money to go home.*)

ANALYZE INFORMATIONAL TEXTS

Annotate: Mark the date and time in paragraph 31.

Evaluate: How does the use of dates and times help you understand the bet and how Crocker felt about the Chinese laborers?

ANALYZE AUTHOR'S PURPOSE

Annotate: Mark sentences in paragraph 32 that reveal Chang's attitude toward the Chinese and how they were treated.

Cite Evidence: What information in paragraph 32 relates to Chang's desire to bring attention to the Chinese laborers?

When the Chinese ignored them, the Irish swung their picks at them, and to the astonishment of the whites, the Chinese fought back. The level of antagonism continued to rise. Several Chinese were wounded by blasting powder the whites had secretly planted near their side. Several days later, a mysterious explosion killed several Irish workers. The presumption was that the Chinese had retaliated in kind. At that point, the behavior of white workers toward the Chinese immediately improved.

31   If relations were often tense between the Chinese and the Irish, there were also moments of camaraderie.[13] In April 1869, the Central Pacific and Union Pacific competed to see who could throw down track the fastest. The competition arose after Charlie Crocker bragged that the Chinese could construct ten miles of track a day. (In some regions, the Union Pacific had averaged only one mile a week.) So confident was Crocker in his employees that he was willing to wager $10,000 against Thomas Durant, the vice president of Union Pacific. On the day of the contest, the Central Pacific had eight Irish workers unload materials while the Chinese spiked, gauged, and bolted the track, laying it down as fast as a man could walk. They broke the Union Pacific record by completing more than ten miles of track within twelve hours and forty-five minutes.

32   On May 10, 1869, when the railways from the east and west were finally joined at Promontory Point, Utah, the Central Pacific had built 690 miles of track and the Union Pacific 1,086 miles. The two coasts were now welded together. Before the transcontinental railroad, trekking across the country took four to six months. On the railroad, it would take six days. This accomplishment created fortunes for the moguls of the Gilded Age, but it also exacted a monumental sacrifice in blood and human life. On average, three laborers perished for every two miles of track laid, and eventually more than one thousand Chinese railroad workers died, with twenty thousand pounds of their bones shipped to China.[14] Without Chinese labor and know-how, the railroad would not have been completed. Nonetheless, the Central Pacific Railroad cheated the Chinese railway workers of everything they could. They tried to write the Chinese out of history altogether. The Chinese workers were not only excluded from the ceremonies, but from the famous photograph of white American laborers celebrating as the last spike, the golden spike, was driven into the ground. Of more immediate concern, the Central Pacific immediately

---

[13] **camaraderie:** friendly companionship.

[14] Years later, some of the Chinese railroad workers would journey back to the Sierra Nevada to search for the remains of their colleagues. On these expeditions, known as *jup seen you* ("retrieving deceased friends"), they would hunt for old grave sites, usually a heap of stones near the tracks marked by a wooden stake. Digging underneath the stones, they would find a skeleton next to a wax-sealed bottle, holding a strip of cloth inscribed with the worker's name, birth date, and district of origin. [Author's note]

TO CHALLENGE STUDENTS . . .

Analyze Tone Have student pairs read paragraphs 32 and 33. Have them discuss how the tone of the paragraphs changes and why Chang shifted her tone. Students should use text evidence to support their analysis of the tone. (**Possible answers:** *The tone at the beginning is one of admiration, celebrating the triumph with phrases such as "finally joined," "two coasts were now welded together," and "accomplishment created fortunes." Later, the tone turns more bitter as Chang reveals how the Chinese workers were not properly recognized: "monumental sacrifice . . . human life"; "more than one thousand . . . shipped to China"; "cheated the Chinese . . . they could." Finally, the tone is one of sadness, as evidenced by the words "homeless as well as jobless, in a harsh and hostile environment," "straggled," "survive."*) Have pairs present their ideas to the class.

laid off most of the Chinese workers, refusing to give them even their promised return passage to California. The company retained only a few hundred of them for maintenance work, some of whom spent their remaining days in isolated small towns along the way, a few living in converted boxcars.

33　　The rest of the Chinese former railway workers were now homeless as well as jobless, in a harsh and hostile environment. Left to fend for themselves, some straggled by foot through the hinterlands[15] of America, looking for work that would allow them to survive, a journey that would disperse them throughout the nation.

_____

[15]**hinterlands:** remote areas.

CHECK YOUR UNDERSTANDING

Answer these questions before moving on to the **Analyze the Text** section on the following page.

1 Why did the Central Pacific hire so many Chinese workers?

A Americans generally preferred Chinese workers.

B The Chinese had experience building railroads.

C The Chinese were diligent and effective workers.

D The government required hiring Chinese workers.

2 Why did Crocker remind Strobridge that the Chinese had built the Great Wall of China?

F To show the Chinese could do demanding work

G To demonstrate knowledge about Chinese history

H To bring harmony between Chinese and white workers

J To suggest the Chinese build a wall as well as the railroad

3 When white workers plotted to drive off the Chinese workers, Charles Crocker —

A offered the white workers more money to stay on the job

B threatened to replace all the whites with Chinese workers

C encouraged them to follow through with their plans

D fired all the white workers for having a bad attitude

CHECK YOUR UNDERSTANDING

Have students answer the questions independently.

Answers:

1. C

2. F

3. B

If they answer any questions incorrectly, have them reread the text to confirm their understanding. Then they may proceed to ANALYZE THE TEXT on page 392.

ENGLISH LEARNER SUPPORT

Oral Assessment　Use the following questions to assess students' comprehension and speaking skills:

1. Were Chinese workers hard working? (*The Chinese were diligent and hardworking.*)

2. Crocker said the Chinese built _____. (*the Great Wall of China*)

3. Crocker threatened to replace white workers with _____ . (*Chinese workers*)
SUBSTANTIAL/MODERATE

ANALYZE THE TEXT

Possible answers:

1. **DOK 2:** *Her purpose is to inform readers about the contribution to America made by Chinese workers. Comments such as "They tried to write the Chinese out of history altogether" support the idea that she felt they needed to be remembered.*

2. **DOK 4:** *Chang's tone is that of a well-informed, fair-minded historian, sympathetic toward the struggles and achievements of Chinese workers. Examples of diction and details include "the Chinese fought back," "broke the Union Pacific record," and "tried to write the Chinese out of history altogether."*

3. **DOK 2:** *Americans believed the United States should expand democracy across the continent, the population was increasing and needed farmland to grow food, crossing the continent was dangerous and sailing around it took months, and growing cities back east needed the resources the West offered.*

4. **DOK 4:** *Chang's use of quotations gives authenticity to her presentation and supports her view of the Chinese by showing that it was shared by some of the people who participated in this project.*

5. **DOK 4:** *This detail adds depth to Chang's portrayal of the Chinese workers. The writer shows that they are human beings with feelings and beliefs.*

RESEARCH

Help students get started by showing Guangdong province on a map and pointing out that its easily accessible coastline contributed to its high rate of emigration. Then, see if they can find a few Chinese sources that show the Chinese point of view of events during that time. If there are students in the class who can read Chinese, encourage them to participate in this task.

Extend Help students understand that the problems the Chinese faced were a product of the times, but some problems still exist today. For example, Taiping Rebellion was one of several events that created instability in southern China during the mid-19th century. This particular event was unique to that place and time, but people from all over the world continue to immigrate to the United States in order to escape political instability and oppression.

⊜ **RESPOND**

ANALYZE THE TEXT

Support your responses with evidence from the text. ▤ NOTEBOOK

1. **Infer** What is Iris Chang's purpose for writing "Building the Transcontinental Railroad"? Cite evidence from the text that helps you infer her purpose.

2. **Analyze** What **tone,** or attitude, does Chang convey on the topic of Chinese workers? Provide examples of details and diction that reflect her attitude.

3. **Cause and Effect** According to Chang, what economic, social, and political forces caused the United States to decide that building the railroad was important?

4. **Evaluate** Chang includes quotations from primary sources in the text. How does Chang's use of these quotations contribute to the effectiveness of her message? Cite specific examples in your response.

5. **Notice & Note** Why does the author present the contradiction between how the Chinese usually acted and instances when they could be assertive or aggressive? What does this add to your understanding of the Chinese workers?

RESEARCH

RESEARCH TIP
If using the Internet, do not include the words *United States* or any other country in your search terms. Doing so will yield results on the Chinese experience in that country, rather than what they faced in China.

In the mid-1800s, people from China, especially Guangdong (Canton), were leaving their country by the thousands and settling all over the world. Research the events and circumstances in China at that time. What would induce so many thousands to leave during this period? Add what you find to the chart below.

DATES	EVENTS
1850s	*Taiping Rebellion resulted in many deaths and an unstable society.*

Extend Review the events in your chart. Were the problems they faced particular to people in China at the time or did they confront issues that are still relevant to people today? Discuss your ideas with a partner.

WHEN STUDENTS STRUGGLE . . .

Reteach: Analyze Chronological Order Review words that signal chronological order, and explain that many history writers use this organizational pattern to structure their writing. To help students determine the chronological sequence in "Building the Transcontinental Railroad," have pairs work together to complete the pre-reading chart (page 379). Encourage them to expand the chart to include more of the narrative's events.

 For additional support, go to the **Reading Studio** and assign the following 🔼 **Level Up Tutorial: Chronological Order.**

CREATE AND DISCUSS

Write a Historical Report Research the building of the Transcontinental Railroad—the purpose, the need, the people involved. Compare your findings with Iris Chang's account. Then, write a report that compares Chang's account and the accounts you discover in your research.

❏ Start with a paragraph that sets the historical context.

❏ Include a thesis statement that expresses what you found and how it compares to Chang's narrative.

❏ Explain each similarity and difference between Chang's account and your own.

❏ End with a conclusion that restates your thesis statement.

Discuss with a Small Group Engage in a group discussion to evaluate the effectiveness of Chang's account based on the details and events she includes, her links among ideas, and her points of emphasis.

❏ Consider the information Chang emphasizes and the information that was included in the other sources you explored.

❏ Support your evaluation with evidence from the text and from your research.

❏ Discuss why people at the time thought this railroad was so important. Consider its impact on the growth of the nation.

 Go to **Conducting Research** in the **Writing Studio** for help.

Go to **Participating in Collaborative Discussions** in the **Speaking and Listening Studio** for help.

RESPOND TO THE ESSENTIAL QUESTION

? What is the price of progress?

Gather Information Review your annotations and notes on "Building the Transcontinental Railroad." Then, add relevant information to your Response Log. As you determine which information to include, think about:

• the details that help reveal the author's purpose
• how the author conveys a particular tone toward her subject
• how the time period and setting impact actions and attitudes

ACADEMIC VOCABULARY

As you write and discuss what you learned from the "Building the Transcontinental Railroad," be sure to use the Academic Vocabulary words. Check off each of the words that you use.

❏ **confirm**
❏ **definitely**
❏ **deny**
❏ **format**
❏ **unify**

CREATE AND DISCUSS

Write a Historical Report Remind students of the key elements of a historical narrative: third-person point of view; chronological order of events; factual information, including primary and secondary resources; and the economic, social, or other context to the events. Then, tell students that they should include these elements to support their thesis.

 For **writing support** for students at varying proficiency levels, see the **Text X-Ray** on page 378D.

Discuss with a Small Group Explain to students that Chang chose to focus on the Chinese contribution to the railroad because she wanted to tell their story. Tell students to discuss the research they found that might contradict or supplement Chang's account. Remind students to support their discussion points with specific evidence from the text. Listeners should build on ideas and ask questions for clarification.

RESPOND TO THE ESSENTIAL QUESTION

Allow time for students to add details from "Building the Transcontinental Railroad" to their Unit 4 Response Logs.

CRITICAL VOCABULARY

Possible answers:

1. *I studied every night for my driver's exam, reading the whole manual carefully.*

2. *Zach became friends with Eli because he knew that Eli made good grades in science and could help him with his homework.*

3. *While building the transcontinental railroad, laborers had to carve paths through mountains to build the transcontinental railroad. This was a formidable or seemingly impossible task.*

4. *I systematized the process by using a spreadsheet to keep track of my college applications.*

VOCABULARY STRATEGY:
Context Clues

Answers:

1. *The doctrine of Manifest Destiny was a term used to describe the inevitable westward expansion of the United States.*
    Context clues: "proclaimed it the right and duty," "expand," "across the entire continent"
    Possible sentence: The discovery of gold in California created intense interest in the western territories, leading to the support of Manifest Destiny.

2. *Parched is used to describe something that is deprived of natural moisture.*
    Context clues: "dangerous," "deserts"
    Possible sentence: I found myself lost in the woods, parched, and unfortunately out of fresh water.

3. *Prejudice can be defined as an irrational attitude of hostility directed against an individual, a group, a race, or their supposed characteristics.*
    Context clues: "unhappy with their being hired," "the Chinese were too delicate for the job," "Grudgingly"
    Possible sentence: Even if cases of blatant racism are rarer today than in the past, prejudice against minorities remains ubiquitous.

4. *Placated means soothed or mollified.*
    Context clues: "gave up," "they alone could be promoted"
    Possible sentence: My dad was placated when my mom apologized with a dinner out at the steakhouse.

 **RESPOND**

WORD BANK
formidable
expedience
diligence
systematize

Go to **Using Context Clues** in the **Vocabulary Studio** for help.

CRITICAL VOCABULARY

Practice and Apply Use your knowledge of the Critical Vocabulary words in your written responses.

1. Describe something you did with **diligence.**

2. Identify an action that someone took that was driven by **expedience.**

3. Tell about a **formidable** task that you have studied in history.

4. Explain how to **systematize** the college application process.

VOCABULARY STRATEGY:
Context Clues

Context clues—the words and ideas in the surrounding phrases and sentences—can help you determine the meaning of an unknown word. For example, the writer might include an example, an explanation, a definition, or suggest a similarity or contrast. Notice how the highlighted context clues in the examples from "Building the Transcontinental Railroad" can help you determine the meaning of the boldfaced words.

CONTEXT CLUE	EXAMPLE
Suggest a **similarity:** diligence is hard work	. . . Chinese **diligence** forced everyone to work harder for less reward.
Suggest a **contrast:** something formidable is difficult to overcome	The Central Pacific engineers promised that the **formidable** physical obstacles could be overcome, . . .

Practice and Apply Use context clues in "Building the Transcontinental Railroad" to determine the meaning of the following words and terms. Confirm the meaning of each word in a dictionary and then use it in a new sentence.

1. doctrine of Manifest Destiny (paragraph 1)

2. parched (paragraph 5)

3. prejudice (paragraph 7)

4. placated (paragraph 14)

LANGUAGE CONVENTIONS:
Misplaced Modifiers

Modifiers are words or groups of words that change or limit the meaning of other words. For example, adjectives and adjectival phrases modify nouns by telling which one, what kind, how many, or how much. Adverbs and adverbial phrases modify verbs, adjectives, and other adverbs by telling where, when, how, or to what extent. Chang's careful placement of modifiers contributes to the clarity and readability of her text.

In less professional writing, a modifier is sometimes placed in the wrong place or so far away from the word it modifies that the intended meaning of the sentence is unclear. To correct a sentence with a misplaced modifier, you must first find the word being modified. Then, place the modifying word or phrase as close as possible to the word it modifies.

Read the following sentence with a misplaced modifier:

> **The railroad workers gathered the necessary supplies to finish the tunnel before starting.**

The placement of the prepositional phrase *before starting* creates confusion, because it seems to modify "to finish the tunnel." Finishing the tunnel before starting would be impossible.

Here the sentence has been revised for clarity so that the prepositional phrase properly functions as the adverb modifying the verb *gathered*.

> **Before starting, the railroad workers gathered the necessary supplies to finish the tunnel.**

Practice and Apply Revise the following sentences to correct the misplaced modifiers. Refer to the text if you are unsure about the intended meaning of a sentence.

1. Disembarking the ship and crossing the Isthmus of Panama on the sea voyage by wagon could shorten the trip to the West Coast considerably.

2. The Union Pacific Railroad was contracted to build westward from Omaha, Nebraska, across the plains already connected to other railways in the East.

3. Unpredictable and dangerous, many workers were killed by the explosives.

4. Everyone praised the railroad workers' accomplishments at the ceremony.

Go to **Placement of Modifiers** in the **Grammar Studio** for help.

LANGUAGE CONVENTIONS:
Misplaced Modifiers

Remind students that using modifiers is an important part of good writing. However, misplaced modifiers can confuse the reader. Tell students that partner reading is one way to detect unclear sentences caused by misplaced modifiers. Point out that although a sentence may make sense to them, a reader might be confused.

Review the first sample sentence and ask students why the modifier is misplaced. Before reviewing the revision, ask students to revise the sentence themselves.

Practice and Apply After each student has finished revising the sentences, have them read their sentences aloud in small groups. Tell the listeners to mark any confusion about what words are being modified.

Possible answers:

1. *On the sea voyage, disembarking the ship and crossing the Isthmus of Panama by wagon could shorten the trip to the West Coast considerably.*

2. *The Union Pacific Railroad was contracted to build westward across the plains from Omaha, Nebraska, which was already connected to other railways in the East.*

3. *Many workers were killed by the unpredictable and dangerous explosives.*

4. *At the ceremony, everyone praised the railroad workers' accomplishments.*

ENGLISH LEARNER SUPPORT

Language Conventions Use the following supports with students at varying proficiency levels:

• Read aloud these words from paragraph 19: "Through much of the way, a flat roadbed had to be carved along a steep cliff." Help students identify modifiers and the words they modify. Students can hold up one finger for a modifier and two fingers for the word it modifies. **SUBSTANTIAL**

• Have students work with a partner or in small groups to reread paragraphs 19 and 20. Have students make a chart to identify modifiers and the words they modify. Point out that a modifier may be only one word or a whole phrase. **MODERATE**

• After students complete the Practice and Apply activity, have them work in pairs to compare their revised sentences. Ask the pairs to discuss their reasoning for the changes they made. **LIGHT**

© Houghton Mifflin Harcourt Publishing Company

MENTOR TEXT

DECLARATION OF SENTIMENTS
Argument by Elizabeth Cady Stanton

SPEECH TO THE AMERICAN EQUAL RIGHTS ASSOCIATION
Speech by Sojourner Truth

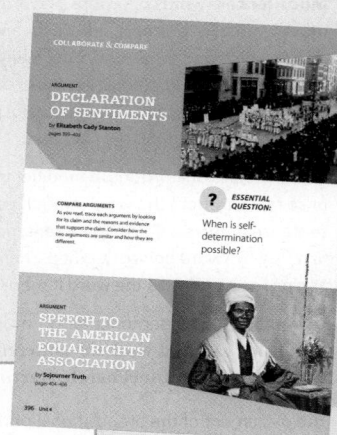

This argument serves as a **mentor text,** a model for students to follow when they come to the Unit 4 Writing Task: Writing an Argument.

GENRE ELEMENTS
ARGUMENT

Remind students that the purpose of an **argument** is to clearly state a claim or opinion using reasons and evidence to support that claim. An argument may feature **rhetorical devices** for additional support. In this lesson, students will examine features of two arguments and then compare and contrast the effectiveness of those strategies in an essay and a dramatic reading.

LEARNING OBJECTIVES

- Identify claims to evaluate an argument.
- Analyze author's purpose and determine meaning.
- Conduct research on Lucretia Mott and women's rights.
- Compare and contrast two arguments while citing evidence.
- Present a dramatic reading of an effective argument.
- Use suffixes to become familiar with patterns of word change.
- Examine how rhetorical devices develop an argument.
- **Language** Discuss the elements of an argument, using key terms *claim, reasons,* and *evidence.*

TEXT COMPLEXITY

Quantitative Measures	Declaration of Sentiments / Speech to the American Equal Rights Association	Lexile: 1430L / Lexile: 620L
Qualitative Measures	**Ideas Presented** Connections between ideas are mostly explicit and clear.	
	Structures Used Organization is genre-specific and slightly complex.	
	Language Used Complex sentence structure with some use of archaic, ambiguous, or figurative language.	
	Knowledge Required References to historical events and other texts may make moderately complex demands.	

Online Ed

RESOURCES

- Unit 4 Response Log

- 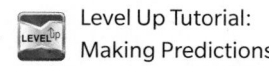 Selection Audio

- Reading Studio: Notice & Note

- Level Up Tutorial: Making Predictions

- Writing Studio: Writing Informative Texts

- Speaking and Listening Studio: Giving a Presentation

- Vocabulary Studio: Common Roots, Prefixes, and Suffixes

-  Declaration of Sentiments / Speech to the American Equal Rights Association Selection Test

SUMMARIES

English

Declaration of Sentiments was written by a group of women in 1848. Elizabeth Cady Stanton was asked to finish and polish a draft of the document, which became an inspiration for the women's suffrage movement.

In Speech to the American Equal Rights Association, from 1867, Sojourner Truth refers to the end of slavery and the granting of rights to African American men. Yet she argues that unless women and men have equal rights, people will not truly be free.

Spanish

Un grupo de mujeres escribió la Declaración de Seneca Falls en 1848. Se le pidió a Elizabeth Cady Stanton terminar y pulir el borrador del documento, que luego sería una fuente de inspiración para el movimiento a favor del sufragio femenino. En su Discurso a la Asociación Americana por la Igualdad de Derechos, en 1867, Sojourner Truth se refiere al fin de la esclavitud y a los derechos otorgados a los hombres afroamericanos. Sin embargo, sostiene que a menos que entre las mujeres y los hombres haya igualdad de derechos, nadie será realmente libre.

SMALL-GROUP OPTIONS

Have students work in small groups and pairs to read and discuss the selections.

Jigsaw with Experts

- Divide each selection into three to five parts.

- Have students count off or assign each student a numbered part from one of the selections.

- Instruct each group to discuss their section. Prompts for discussion include: *Who is the subject of this section? What part of an argument is this section? What does the author want?*

- Have students reform groups with a representative from each section. Direct students to discuss their sections and then discuss and compare both texts.

Three-Minute Review

- Read the selections aloud to students, pausing after every two or three paragraphs in Declaration of Sentiments and after each paragraph in Speech to the American Equal Rights Association.

- Instruct students to reread the paragraphs and write a clarifying question. Set a timer for three minutes. After three minutes, ask: *What did you notice as you reread the text?*

- Invite volunteers to share clarifying questions.

- Guide small groups to discuss and answer the questions.

Text X-Ray: English Learner Support

for Declaration of Sentiments and Speech to the American Equal Rights Association

Use the Text X-Ray and the supports and scaffolds in the Teacher's Edition to help guide students at different proficiency levels through the selection.

INTRODUCE THE SELECTION
DISCUSS *INALIENABLE RIGHTS*

In this lesson, students will need to understand the concept of inalienable rights, as described in foundational American documents. Explain the phrases *inalienable rights* and *life, liberty, and the pursuit of happiness.*

Ask students:

- What rights do you have as young people?
- What rights do adults have in America?
- Do you think these rights have to be earned?

Supply the following sentence frames for student responses:

- _____ is an example of an inalienable right.
- One example of an inalienable right is _____.

To aid responses, consider physical gestures or visual images of activities such as driving a car, holding hands, or playing a sport.

CULTURAL REFERENCES

The following words or phrases may be unfamiliar to students:

- *inalienable rights* (paragraph 2, from Declaration of Sentiments): freedoms that belong to all people and cannot be taken away
- *sphere of action* (paragraph 18, from Declaration of Sentiments): group of interests or daily activities
- *the pulpit and the press* (paragraph 21, from Declaration of Sentiments): the church and the media
- *root and branch* (paragraph 1, from Speech to the American Equal Rights Association): completely
- *colored* (paragraph 1, from Speech to the American Equal Rights Association): African American

---

LISTENING

Identify Rhetorical Devices

Explain to students that the use of repetition helps convey one's point. Explain that **diction** (words) and **syntax** (sentence structure) can be repeated to have an effect on the reader.

Have students listen as you read aloud paragraphs 4–10 of Declaration of Sentiments. Use the following supports with students at varying proficiency levels:

- Ask students questions about what they heard. Model that they should give a thumbs-up if they agree or the answer is yes, and a thumbs-down if the answer is no or they disagree. Ask students: *Are words repeated? (yes) What words are repeated? ("He has") Do the repeated words come at the end of the sentence? (no) Does the repetition make you feel negative? (yes)* **SUBSTANTIAL**

- Help students recognize the repetition of syntax in paragraphs 4–10. Have them underline the subject and circle the verb in the first sentence of each paragraph. Ask: *Why does the author repeat the same word order?* **MODERATE**

- Read the excerpt aloud again. Have students underline the repeated words in each sentence. Then ask: *Is another word repeated? (yes) What is it? ("right")* Direct students to list as many details as they can that come after the repeated beginning of the sentences. *How does this pattern help support the main idea? (The repetition signals all the rights that were refused to women.)* **LIGHT**

SPEAKING

Describe Features of an Argument

Have students discuss the key features of an argument using the terms *claim, reasons,* and *call to action*. Circulate around the room to ensure they are using these terms correctly.

Read aloud paragraph 1 of Speech to the American Equal Rights Association. Use the following supports with students at varying proficiency levels to help them identify the claim:

- Ask the following questions: *Does Truth think slavery has been completely destroyed? (no) Does she think people are truly free? (no) Does she want women to have the same rights as men? (yes)* **SUBSTANTIAL**
- Provide these sentence frames to help students determine the claim of paragraph 1: *Although slavery is over, people are not free because _____. Truth states that since men and women have similar _____, they should have the same _____.* Ask: *What is the central claim of this paragraph?* **MODERATE**
- Have student pairs find and state the central claim of the paragraph. **LIGHT**

READING

Identify Conjunctions that Indicate a Counterargument

Tell students that an argument must address a counterargument. Explain that contrasting conjunctions help indicate when a counterargument is introduced in the text.

Read paragraphs 13–17 of Declaration of Sentiments. Use the following supports with students at varying proficiency levels:

- Read paragraphs 13 and 16 and point out the use of the word *but* as a contrasting conjunction. Display sentences: "She receives but a scanty remuneration." *(She receives some pay, but it is very little.)* "He allows her in Church . . . but a subordinate position." *(She has a position, but it is low.)* **SUBSTANTIAL**
- Ask students to reread paragraphs 13 and 16 and identify words that indicate a contrast. *(but)* Have students summarize each of the counterarguments in these paragraphs. **MODERATE**
- Explain to students that a strong counterargument simultaneously provides support for the central claim. For additional context support, direct students to look at what comes on either side of the contrasting conjunction—the word *but*. **LIGHT**

WRITING

Write a Compare-and-Contrast Essay

Work with students to read the writing assignment on Student Edition page 409. Review the prompt to ensure students understand that they will write an essay identifying the similarities and differences in Declaration of Sentiments and the Declaration of Independence.

Use the following supports with students at varying proficiency levels:

- Provide students with a Venn diagram to compare and contrast the features of the two arguments. Help students identify diction and syntax that is similar and add it to the center of the diagram. Help them identify one to two differences (such as the use of the words *her* and *women*). Add these to the outer parts of the diagram. Then, model a compare and contrast paragraph on the board. Have students copy the paragraph. **SUBSTANTIAL**
- Provide students with a Venn diagram to organize their thoughts and sentence frames to craft their paragraphs, such as: *The Declaration of Sentiments and the Declaration of Independence use similar _____. The words that are similar are _____ and _____. These words are used at _____. This is known as _____. One difference is that the author of the Declaration of Independence believes all men _____. Stanton thinks _____.* **MODERATE**
- Ask students to use compare-and-contrast transitions such as *both, similarly, but, unlike,* and *on the other hand* in their essays. Then, have students exchange drafts with a partner and suggest any additional places for transitions. **LIGHT**

Connect to the
ESSENTIAL QUESTION

The fight for equality and equal rights was a fight for the power of self-determination—the ability to have a say in what you can do and what you can be. Both Sojourner Truth and Elizabeth Cady Stanton point out some barriers to a person's ability to access this power.

MENTOR TEXT

At the end of the unit, students will be asked to write an argument based on current barriers to self-determination. Declaration of Sentiments provides a model for how a writer can present an argument supported by facts and examples.

COMPARE ARGUMENTS

All arguments have the same basic elements—a main claim and supporting reasons—but how these are introduced and developed can vary greatly. Some variance comes about because of the writer's style, but some is due to the audience and format of the argument. Declaration of Sentiments was a written document meant for many women to sign and for people to read. Sojourner Truth's speech was presented before a live audience. It was meant to be listened to. As you compare, consider how the presentation and audience affect the way each argument unfolds.

COLLABORATE & COMPARE

ARGUMENT
DECLARATION OF SENTIMENTS

by **Elizabeth Cady Stanton**
pages 399–403

ESSENTIAL QUESTION:

When is self-determination possible?

COMPARE ARGUMENTS

As you read, trace each argument by identifying its claim and the reasons and evidence that support the claim. Consider how the two arguments are similar and how they are different.

ARGUMENT
SPEECH TO THE AMERICAN EQUAL RIGHTS ASSOCIATION

by **Sojourner Truth**
pages 404–406

396   Unit 4

QUICK START

In 1848 women in the United States did not have many of the rights that they do today. Generate a question about what life was like for women at that time.

ANALYZE AND EVALUATE ARGUMENTS

An **argument** expresses a position on an issue or problem and supports it with reasons and evidence. A sound argument contains the following:

ELEMENT	DEFINITION
claim	the writer's position on an issue or central idea
support	any material that serves to prove a claim; usually consists of reasons and evidence
reasons	declarations made to justify an action, a decision, or a belief
evidence	specific references, quotations, facts, examples, and opinions that support a claim

When analyzing an argument, consider the writer's claim and support. To evaluate arguments, distinguish between valid and invalid claims based on the evidence presented. Does the writer present enough evidence? Is the evidence relevant? Which types of evidence are effective? As you read, think about whether Stanton and Truth have similar or different claims. Consider the ways they support their claims and how that influences your perception of their arguments.

ANALYZE AUTHOR'S PURPOSE

The purpose of an argument is to convince the audience to agree, to recognize the validity of a position, or to take a certain action. Authors may use **rhetorical devices** to achieve their purposes and make their arguments more compelling. Note the following rhetorical devices as you read.

- **repetition**—repeated words and phrases. Writers may use repetition to emphasize ideas.

- **parallelism**—the use of components in a sentence that are grammatically similar. It may be used to tell readers that ideas are equally important.

- **allusion**—a reference to another familiar person, place, or event. Writers may use allusion to make a connection.

Stanton's text alludes to the Declaration of Independence written by Thomas Jefferson. Stanton went beyond simple adaptation by incorporating the style and content, as well as the format of Jefferson's text. As you read, think about why Stanton links her text with the Declaration of Independence and how this influences her audience and supports her purpose.

GENRE ELEMENTS: ARGUMENT

- contains a clearly stated claim or opinion
- includes reasons and evidence that support the claim
- may feature rhetorical devices to support the argument

QUICK START

Have students read the Quick Start activity and consider what they already know about the lives of women in 1848. Have students meet with their groups and discuss their knowledge before writing their questions. Have groups write their questions on slips of paper or index cards. Then, as a class, read each one aloud and see if the reading has given students additional insights.

ANALYZE AND EVALUATE ARGUMENTS

Have students read the information about the general structure of an argument. Note that, although all arguments have these basic elements, they may occur in a variety of orders. Additionally, the type of evidence used to support the reasons and evidence can vary greatly. For instance, students will notice that Stanton uses no personal language or examples, while Truth speaks largely from her own life experience and sense of right and wrong.

ANALYZE AUTHOR'S PURPOSE

Review what students have already learned about finding author's purpose from reading other texts, including how audience and genre affect purpose and how that purpose affects the author's tone and diction. Explain that the two selections they will read are arguments, so their purpose is to persuade. A persuasive text can be informative, but the information serves the greater purpose of persuasion. Likewise, the diction of these two selections has stark differences. However, in each case, the diction suits the purpose of convincing an audience of an important truth.

Read through the information on rhetorical devices, and have students offer examples from their study of the Declaration of Independence. It will also be helpful to have this founding document on hand as students read the first selection.

TEACH

CRITICAL VOCABULARY

Encourage students to read all the synonyms before deciding which word best matches the meaning of each one.

Answers:

1. *transient*
2. *evince*
3. *consolation*
4. *delinquency*
5. *abject*
6. *supposition*

■ English Learner Support

Use Cognates Tell students that several Critical Vocabulary words have Spanish cognates: *transient/transeúnte, consolation/consuelo, supposition/suposición.* **ALL LEVELS**

LANGUAGE CONVENTIONS

Rhetorical Devices Review the information about rhetorical devices on page 397. Remind students that rhetorical devices support the purpose of the text.

Read the sample sentence aloud, emphasizing the word *that* so students can hear the parallelism. Point out that the quoted sentence is also an allusion to the Declaration of Independence.

✎ ANNOTATION MODEL

Remind students of the ideas in Analyze and Evaluate Arguments and Analyze Author's Purpose on page 397, which suggest noticing claims and reasons, rhetorical devices, and links with the Declaration of Independence. Point out that they may follow the method of marking the text shown in the Annotation Model or use their own system for marking up the selection in their write-in text. Students may want to color-code their annotations by using highlighters. Their notes in the margin may include questions about ideas that are unclear or topics students want to learn more about.

 **GET READY**

CRITICAL VOCABULARY

To see how many Critical Vocabulary words you already know, write a word from the Word Bank that is a synonym for each word below.

WORD BANK

transient   delinquency
evince   abject
supposition   consolation

1. fleeting _____
2. reveal _____
3. comfort _____
4. misbehavior _____
5. hopeless _____
6. hypothesis _____

LANGUAGE CONVENTIONS

Rhetorical Devices Allusion, repetition, and parallelism are rhetorical devices writers use to make their arguments memorable. In the passage below by Elizabeth Cady Stanton, notice the use of parallelism to emphasize ideas.

> We hold these truths to be self-evident; <u>that</u> all men and women are created equal; <u>that</u> they are endowed by their Creator with certain inalienable rights; <u>that</u> among these are life, liberty, and the pursuit of happiness; <u>that</u> to secure these rights . . .

As you read, look for rhetorical devices and consider how they emphasize important ideas and make arguments more powerful.

ANNOTATION MODEL

NOTICE & NOTE

As you read, notice the elements of the argument. Note how the writer supports her purpose by including particular details. In the model, you can see one reader's notes about the Declaration of Sentiments.

> When, in the course of human events, it becomes necessary for <u>one portion of the family of man to assume among the people of the earth a position different from that which they have hitherto occupied</u>, but one to which the laws of nature, and of nature's God entitle them,

Stanton suggests that women need to change their traditional status.

> <u>We hold these truths to be self-evident; that all men and women are created equal;</u> that they are endowed by their Creator with certain inalienable rights; that among these are life, liberty, and the pursuit of happiness;

Stanton uses language from the Declaration of Independence. What does her piece have in common with it?

BACKGROUND

The 1848 Declaration of Sentiments was presented at the Seneca Falls Convention, the birthplace of the women's rights movement in the United States. **Elizabeth Cady Stanton** *(1815–1902) and Lucretia Mott (1793–1880) had first discussed the idea for the conference at the World Anti-Slavery Convention in London in 1840. Active abolitionists, the women had been denied the right to participate in the convention because of their gender.*

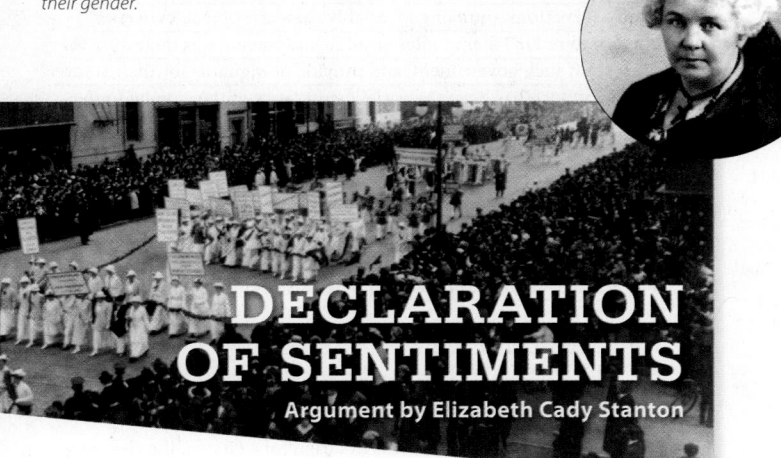

DECLARATION OF SENTIMENTS

Argument by Elizabeth Cady Stanton

PREPARE TO COMPARE

As you read, think about the problem Stanton identifies and how she crafts her argument to propose a solution for it. What change is Stanton arguing for?

Put forth at Seneca Falls, N. Y., July, 19th *and* 20th, 1848.

1 When, in the course of human events, it becomes necessary for one portion of the family of man to assume among the people of the earth a position different from that which they have hitherto occupied, but one to which the laws of nature, and of nature's God entitle them, a decent respect to the opinions of mankind requires that they should declare the causes that impel them to such a course.

2 We hold these truths to be self-evident; that all men and women are created equal; that they are endowed by their Creator with certain inalienable rights; that among these are life, liberty, and the pursuit of happiness; that to secure these rights governments are instituted, deriving their just powers from the consent of the governed. Whenever any form of Government becomes destructive of those ends, it is the right of those who suffer from it, to refuse allegiance to it, and to insist upon the

Notice & Note

Use the side margins to notice and note signposts in the text.

ANALYZE AUTHOR'S PURPOSE
Annotate: Mark details in paragraphs 1 and 2 that echo the language of the Declaration of Independence.

Interpret: What does adapting the language of the Declaration of Independence imply about the audience for, and purpose of, the argument?

BACKGROUND

Declaration of Sentiments was written by a group of women in 1848. Stanton was asked to finish and polish the draft and also add the ninth resolution, which called for women to be given the right to vote. The document was signed by 68 women and 32 men. While this resolution was the impetus for the women's suffrage movement, the Declaration of Sentiments didn't gain historical recognition until the passing of the Nineteenth Amendment in 1920.

PREPARE TO COMPARE

Direct students to use the Prepare to Compare prompt to focus their reading.

ANALYZE AUTHOR'S PURPOSE

Remind students that the **purpose** is the reason the writer wrote the text. Discuss with students the similarities between the Declaration of Sentiments and the Declaration of Independence, reading aloud the first two paragraphs of the Declaration of Independence as needed. (**Answer:** *The purpose of the Declaration of Independence was to declare that the United States is an independent country and to convince its audience, the public, that it must and should be independent. Similarly, Stanton appeals to the nation at large and wants to convince the entire nation that women should have the same rights as men.*)

ENGLISH LEARNER SUPPORT

Develop Vocabulary and Language Structures Discuss with students how gender-sensitive language has evolved since the Declaration of Sentiments was written. Point out that until the last 30 years, terms like *man* were thought to represent all people. Give examples of gender-specific terms and their gender-sensitive replacements (*fireman—firefighter, man-made—synthetic*). Draw students' attention to the phrase "one portion of the family of man" in the first paragraph. Explain that today we might say "one portion of humanity." Have students scan the selection to identify other examples of gender-specific language and instruct them to revise as necessary. **ALL LEVELS**

TEACH

 **ANALYZE AND EVALUATE ARGUMENTS**

Point out the word *prove* to students. Have them look for the statement the author says she is going to "prove." (**Answer:** *Stanton creates a convincing portrait of women as oppressed citizens: They cannot vote, they have no voice in forming laws, and they have fewer rights than all men do.*)

LANGUAGE CONVENTIONS

Encourage students to read paragraphs 4–10 aloud with a partner to better detect the repetition and parallelism. (**Answer:** *Stanton's sentence structure uses "he" as its subject, followed by the helping verb "has." This repeated structure, or parallelism, emphasizes the subject "he" as perpetrator of the abuse and lends equal importance to each of these injustices. The repetition of "right" alludes to the rights the founders of the country fought for and established, suggesting those rights should be available to women.*)

> For **listening support** for students at varying proficiency levels, see the **Text X-Ray** on page 396C.

CRITICAL VOCABULARY

transient: A government should not change in reaction to transient, or fleeting, issues.

ASK STUDENTS why the issue of women's rights in 1848 isn't a transient cause. (*The inequity that women endured had existed since the founding of the country.*)

evince: Stanton revealed, or evinced, a pattern in events related to the obstruction of women's rights.

ASK STUDENTS what Stanton claims evinces a plan to oppress women. (*She cites a "long train of abuses" as evidence.*)

supposition: Stanton notes that people make the supposition, or assumption, that men are superior to women.

ASK STUDENTS how Stanton's purpose for writing is related to that supposition. (*Part of her purpose is to challenge this supposition.*)

400 Unit 4

 NOTICE & NOTE

transient
(trăn´zē-ənt) *adj.* temporary; short-term.

evince
(ĭ-vĭns´) *v.* to reveal or give evidence of.

ANALYZE AND EVALUATE ARGUMENTS
Annotate: Mark the statement in paragraph 3 that is supported by the evidence in paragraphs 4–10.

Analyze: How does the evidence build Stanton's portrait of women as oppressed citizens?

LANGUAGE CONVENTIONS
Annotate: Underline examples of repetition and parallelism in paragraphs 4–10.

Evaluate: How does the use of these rhetorical devices emphasize important ideas in this section?

supposition
(sŭp-ə-zĭsh´ən) *n.* the act of supposing; an assumption.

400 Unit 4

institution of a new government, laying its foundation on such principles, and organizing its powers in such form as to them shall seem most likely to effect their safety and happiness. Prudence, indeed, will dictate, that governments long established should not be changed for light and **transient** causes; and accordingly, all experience hath shown that mankind are more disposed to suffer, while evils are sufferable, than to right themselves by abolishing the forms to which they are accustomed. But when a long train of abuses and usurpations, pursuing invariably the same object, **evinces** a design to reduce them under absolute despotism, it is their duty to throw off such government, and provide new guards for their future security. Such has been the patient sufferance of the women under this government, and such is now the necessity which constrains them to demand the equal station, to which they are entitled.

3   The history of mankind is a history of repeated injuries and usurpations on the part of man toward woman, having in direct object the establishment of an absolute tyranny over her. To prove this, let facts be submitted to a candid world.

4   He has never permitted her to exercise her inalienable right to the elective franchise.[1]

5   He has compelled her to submit to laws, in the formation of which she had no voice.

6   He has withheld from her rights which are given to the most ignorant and degraded men—both natives and foreigners.

7   Having deprived her of this first right of a citizen, the elective franchise, thereby leaving her without representation in the halls of legislation, he has oppressed her on all sides.

8   He has made her, if married, in the eye of the law, civilly dead.

9   He has taken from her all right in property, even to the wages she earns.

10   He has made her, morally, an irresponsible being, as she can commit many crimes with impunity, provided they be done in the presence of her husband. In the covenant[2] of marriage, she is compelled to promise obedience to her husband, he becoming, to all intents and purposes, her master—the law giving him power to deprive her of her liberty, and to administer chastisement.[3]

11   He has so framed the laws of divorce, as to what shall be the proper causes of divorce, in case of separation, to whom the guardianship of children shall be given; as to be wholly regardless of the happiness of women—the law, in all cases, going upon the false **supposition** of the supremacy of man, and giving all power into his hands.

12   After depriving her of all rights as a woman, if single and the owner of property, he has taxed her to support a government, which recognizes her only when her property can be made profitable to it.

---
[1] **inalienable right to the elective franchise:** unassailable right to vote.
[2] **covenant:** agreement or contract.
[3] **chastisement:** punishment.

WHEN STUDENTS STRUGGLE . . .

Read for Meaning Explain that sentences can be broken down into groups of words that express a thought, often separated by commas or semicolons. Display this text: *He has monopolized nearly all the profitable employments; | and from those she is permitted to follow, | she receives but a scanty remuneration.* Explain that the separators show phrases or clauses. Read the text, showing how to break up the sentence. Have students practice phrase-cued reading.

For **reading support** for students at varying proficiency levels, see the **Text X-Ray** on page 396D.

13   He has monopolized nearly all the profitable employments; and from those she is permitted to follow, she receives but a scanty remuneration.[4]

14   He closes against her all avenues to wealth and distinction, which he considers most honorable to himself. As a teacher of Theology, Medicine or Law, she is not known.

15   He has denied her the facilities for obtaining a thorough education—all colleges being closed against her.

16   He allows her in Church as well as State, but a subordinate position, claiming Apostolic[5] authority for her exclusion from the

---
[4] **scanty remuneration:** minimal payment.
[5] **Apostolic:** from the Apostles, the initial followers of Jesus.

APPLYING ACADEMIC VOCABULARY

❑ confirm   ❑ definitely   ☑ deny   ☑ format   ☑ unify

Write and Discuss: Have students discuss the following questions and include the Academic Vocabulary words *deny, format,* and *unify* in their responses.

- According to Stanton, which rights did men **deny** to women?
- How does Stanton want women to **unify** to accomplish the goals set forth in the essay?
- How does Stanton's writing reflect the **format** of the Declaration of Independence?

ANALYZE AND EVALUATE ARGUMENTS

Point out that paragraph 20 is all one long sentence. Note its stacked phrases as students consider how Stanton supports her idea. (**Answer:** *Stanton repeats and summarizes the evidence she listed and explained earlier in the writing and uses the summary to move her argument to its conclusion.*)

■ English Learner Support

Read with Accommodations and Support   Help students understand paragraph 20 before answering the Analyze and Evaluate Arguments question. Break the paragraph into simpler sentences, and work with students to paraphrase phrases such as "this entire disfranchisement of one half the people of this country" and to substitute simpler synonyms for words such as *degradation (decline, lowering), aggrieved (wronged),* and *fraudulently (dishonestly, deceitfully).* Once you have rewritten the paragraph with student input, read it aloud and have students read it with partners. **SUBSTANTIAL/MODERATE**

CRITICAL VOCABULARY

delinquency: Moral misbehaviors, or delinquencies, are tolerated in men, while women who commit the same acts suffer social exclusion.

ASK STUDENTS why Stanton emphasizes that delinquencies are tolerated for men but not for women. *(to show that bias regarding moral misconduct is yet another double standard)*

abject: According to Stanton, men strive to reduce women's self-confidence so they can more easily control them.

ASK STUDENTS why women of the time might have lived an abject life. *(Women were dependent on men and had no choice but to be submissive.)*

402   Unit 4

---

delinquency
(dĭ-lĭng´kwən-sē) *n.*
shortcoming or misbehavior.

abject
(ăb´jĕkt) *adj.* miserable and submissive.

ANALYZE AND EVALUATE ARGUMENTS

Annotate: In paragraph 20, mark what Stanton says she wants for women.

Analyze: How does the evidence in this paragraph support this idea?

---

ministry, and with some exceptions, from any public participation in the affairs of the Church.

17   He has created a false public sentiment, by giving to the world a different code of morals for man and woman, by which moral **delinquencies** which exclude women from society, are not only tolerated but deemed of little account when committed by man.

18   He has usurped the prerogative of Jehovah himself, claiming it as his right to assign for her a sphere of action, when that belongs to her conscience and her God.

19   He has endeavored in every way that he could, to destroy her confidence in her own powers, to lessen her self-respect, and to make her willing to lead a dependent and **abject** life.

20   Now, in view of this entire disfranchisement of one half the people of this country, their social and religious degradation—in view of the unjust laws above mentioned and because women do feel themselves aggrieved, oppressed and fraudulently deprived of their most sacred rights, we insist that they have immediate admission to all the rights and privileges, which belong to them as citizens of these United States.

21   In entering upon the great work before us, we anticipate no small amount of misconception, misrepresentation and ridicule; but we shall use every instrumentality within our power to effect our object. We shall employ agents, circulate tracts, petition the State and National Legislatures, and endeavor to enlist the pulpit and the press in our behalf. We hope this Convention will be followed by a series of Conventions, embracing every part of the country.

22   Firmly relying upon the final triumph of the Right and the True, we do this day affix our signatures to this declaration.

ANALYZE AUTHOR'S PURPOSE

Annotate: Mark the actions Stanton says she and the other women will take.

Infer: Why does Stanton include these details in her argument?

CHECK YOUR UNDERSTANDING

Answer these questions about Declaration of Sentiments before moving on to the next selection.

1 Which point does Stanton make about taxation?

A Women are not even allowed to pay taxes.

B Women pay more taxes divorced than they do married.

C Women pay more taxes than men do, though they earn less money.

D Women pay taxes but are not recognized or represented in government.

2 Which point does Stanton make about women's employment?

F Women are not allowed to be employed.

G Women are hired only for jobs that men don't want.

H Women are not allowed the education needed for higher paying jobs.

J Women have few ways to save money so they accumulate real wealth.

3 What lines from the text serve as Stanton's call to action?

A *We hold these truths to be self-evident*

B *The history of mankind is a history of repeated injuries*

C *He has endeavored in every way that he could*

D *We insist that they have immediate admission to all the rights and privileges*

ANALYZE AUTHOR'S PURPOSE

Note that the argument came to its main point in paragraph 20. Thus, these final paragraphs may seem anticlimactic. However, Stanton's purpose is not only to make a point about the rights of women. (**Answer:** *She lists them as evidence of her seriousness and determination and belief that she is in the right. She leverages the force of her conviction to help persuade her audience and goes beyond persuasion that change is needed to a statement of what the women signing the document are planning to do to take action.*)

CHECK YOUR UNDERSTANDING

Have students answer the questions independently.

Answers:

1. *D*

2. *H*

3. *D*

If they answer any questions incorrectly, have them reread the text to confirm their understanding. Then they may proceed to the next selection.

 ENGLISH LEARNER SUPPORT

Oral Assessment Use the following questions to assess students' comprehension and speaking skills.

1. Does Stanton say women pay taxes? *(Yes, women must pay taxes, but they are not represented in government.)*

2. Does Stanton say women can get the best jobs? *(No, women cannot get the best jobs, because they cannot get the education needed for better jobs.)*

3. Stanton wants people to give women _____. *(immediate admission to all rights and privileges)*

SUBSTANTIAL/MODERATE

BACKGROUND

Sojourner Truth is perhaps best known for her speech "Ain't I a Woman?" an impromptu speech given at the Ohio Women's Rights Convention in 1851, about 15 years before this speech. After escaping from slavery, with her baby daughter in her arms, she fought for abolition of slavery and was active during the Civil War, working to recruit African American soldiers to fight in the Union army. The Speech to the American Equal Rights Association was delivered after a long career working for the rights of women, prisoners, and African Americans.

PREPARE TO COMPARE

Direct students to use the Prepare to Compare prompt to focus their reading.

ANALYZE AUTHOR'S PURPOSE

Remind students that the **author's purpose** is the reason he or she writes and that an important part of understanding purpose is considering the writer's audience. In this case, the text is a speech delivered to the American Equal Rights Association. What can readers infer about the audience from the name of the association? What does Truth say about the audience? (**Answer:** *Truth uses this distinction to point out that she is concerned with equal rights for all, rather than just the war's outcome. Truth's purpose for writing is to convince her audience that slavery should be dead in all its forms, and she draws the distinction so that the audience will focus on what she views as the larger issue of equal rights for all.*)

 ENGLISH LEARNER SUPPORT

Understand Idioms Display for students some of the idiomatic language on this page, such as *answer for* and *a great stir*. Direct student pairs or small groups to use a dictionary to find the meaning of these idioms (*to be held responsible for* and *a great deal of attention and change is happening*). Invite volunteers to explain their meanings to the group. Clarify that idiomatic phrases are more often found in less formal text and speech. Part of the power of Sojourner Truth's words is that they are from the heart—from her own deep feelings and experiences—and not overly formal.
ALL LEVELS

 **NOTICE & NOTE**

BACKGROUND

Sojourner Truth *(c. 1797–1883) was born into slavery. After being sold several times and bearing five children, she escaped from slavery in 1827 and lived the rest of her life as a free woman. A religious woman, she changed her name from Isabella Baumfree to Sojourner Truth in 1843. As an advocate for the rights of African Americans and women, Truth delivered this candid address to a progressive audience not long after the signing of the Emancipation Proclamation, which freed 3 million enslaved people.*

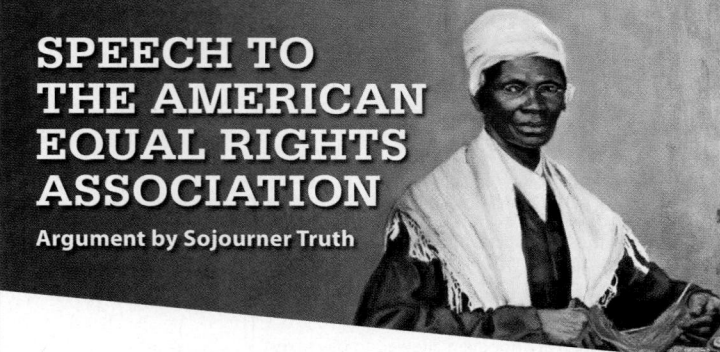

SPEECH TO THE AMERICAN EQUAL RIGHTS ASSOCIATION

Argument by Sojourner Truth

PREPARE TO COMPARE

In her Declaration of Sentiments, Elizabeth Cady Stanton called for the government and society to grant women equal rights. As you read the words of Sojourner Truth, consider how her claim and reasoning are similar to and different from Stanton's.

May 9, 1867

Notice & Note

Use the side margins to notice and note signposts in the text.

ANALYZE AUTHOR'S PURPOSE

Annotate: Mark text that illustrates a distinction between Truth and her audience.

Connect: Why does Truth point out this difference? How might it compel an audience to react?

1   My friends, I am rejoiced that you are glad, but I don't know how you will feel when I get through. <u>I come from another field— the country of the slave.</u> <u>They have got their liberty—so much good luck to have slavery partly destroyed; not entirely.</u> I want it root and branch destroyed. <u>Then we will all be free indeed.</u> I feel that if I have to answer for the deeds done in my body just as much as a man, I have a right to have just as much as a man. There is a great stir about colored men getting their rights, but not a word about the colored women; and if colored men get their rights, and not colored women theirs, you see the colored men will be masters over the women, and it will be just as bad as it was before. So I am for keeping the thing going while things are stirring; because if we wait till it is still, it will take a great while to get it going again. . . . I want women to have

---

WHEN STUDENTS STRUGGLE . . .

Make Predictions Because this is a challenging text, have students make predictions about what they will read based on the title of the speech and what they know about the author. Ask: What do you already know about the author and her audience? What do you think Truth is going to say to the audience? Have students write their predictions. After students read the selection, have them work with a partner to discuss and then evaluate their predictions.

 For additional support, go to the **Reading Studio** and assign the following **Level Up Tutorial: Making Predictions.**

their rights. <u>In the courts women have no right, no voice; nobody speaks for them.</u> I wish woman to have her voice there among the pettifoggers.[1] If it is not a fit place for women, it is unfit for men to be there.

2   I am above eighty years old; it is about time for me to be going. I have been forty years a slave and forty years free, and would be here forty years more to have equal rights for all. I suppose I am kept here because something remains for me to do; I suppose I am yet to help to break the chain. <u>I have done a great deal of work; as much as a man, but did not get so much pay.</u> I used to work in the field and

---
[1] **pettifoggers:** legal practitioners known for dealing with petty cases and using sometimes questionable methods.

ANALYZE AND EVALUATE ARGUMENTS

Annotate: Mark the reasons Truth says women ought to "have their rights."

Analyze: What is Sojourner Truth's main claim? How do these reasons support her argument?

 ANALYZE AND EVALUATE ARGUMENTS

Encourage students to read the entire speech, then reread it to consider the main ideas of each paragraph. Point out that the first five lines are a sort of introduction, with Truth's first main point beginning with "I feel that . . ." (**Answer:** *She is arguing for full civil rights for women and her reasons are (1) they have no voice in the courts and are therefore still in a kind of slavery, (2) they work as hard as men and have the same needs, so should have the same rights.*)

For **speaking support** for students at varying proficiency levels, see the **Text X-Ray** on page 396D.

TO CHALLENGE STUDENTS . . .

Imagery Have students analyze Sojourner Truth's image of "root and branch" in paragraph 1. Have them answer the following questions in a small group discussion:

- What metaphor does this image represent?
- How does the metaphor help express her purpose?

Have students create a visual based on this image that illustrates the meaning of Sojourner Truth's metaphor.

ANALYZE AUTHOR'S PURPOSE

Encourage students to look for additional information they can infer about the audience from the second paragraph, noting that Truth addresses the audience directly with *you*. (**Answer:** *She compares her audience to a slaveholder to emphasize the need for additional work on the equal rights front. She notes that the changes she advocates will hurt—cut like a knife—her audience, because they are used to having power. Both images boldly address the audience in unflattering terms, giving the audience a sense that she feels she has nothing to lose and is going to speak the truth.*)

■ English Learner Support

Understand Similes Help students locate the two similes ("like a slaveholder" and "like a knife"). Make sure they understand the meanings. Then, have students work in pairs to show how these similes relate to Truth's argument. (*She explains that her audience is used to being slaveholders and cannot think otherwise, and that it must hurt a lot to let one's slaves go, as much as it hurts when a knife cuts the skin.*)
LIGHT

CRITICAL VOCABULARY

consolation: Sojourner Truth says it is a consolation, or a comfort, for men to know they will not have to provide money for women.

ASK STUDENTS why this might be a consoling thought. (*It might be pleasant for the men to think they can keep more of their money in the future and not be bothered by women asking for things.*)

consolation
(kŏn-sə-lā´shən) *n.* act of giving comfort.

ANALYZE AUTHOR'S PURPOSE
Annotate: A **simile** is a comparison of unlike things that includes the words *like* or *as*. Mark two similes Sojourner Truth uses toward the end of paragraph 2.

Interpret: How do these similes relate to Truth's argument to her audience?

bind grain, keeping up with the cradler;[2] but men doing no more, got twice as much pay; so with the German women. They work in the field and do as much work, but do not get the pay. We do as much, we eat as much, we want as much. I suppose I am about the only colored woman that goes about to speak for the rights of the colored women. I want to keep the thing stirring, now that the ice is cracked. What we want is a little money. You men know that you get as much again as women when you write, or for what you do. When we get our rights we shall not have to come to you for money, for then we shall have money enough in our own pockets; and may be you will ask us for money. But help us now until we get it. It is a good **consolation** to know that when we have got this battle fought we shall not be coming to you any more. You have been having our rights so long, that you think, like a slaveholder, that you own us. I know that it is hard for one who has held the reins for so long to give up; it cuts like a knife. It will feel all the better when it closes up again. I have been in Washington about three years, seeing about these colored people. Now colored men have the right to vote. There ought to be equal rights now more than ever, since colored people have got their freedom.

_____
[2] **cradler:** worker who uses a scythe-like tool for reaping grain in a crop field.

APPLYING ACADEMIC VOCABULARY

☐ **confirm** ☑ **definitely** ☐ **deny** ☑ **format** ☐ **unify**

Write and Discuss Have students turn to a partner to discuss the following questions. Guide students to include the Academic Vocabulary words *format* and *definitely* in their responses. Ask volunteers to share their responses with the class.

- How does the **format** of the speech reflect its purpose and audience?
- What does Sojourner Truth **definitely** believe to be true?

CHECK YOUR UNDERSTANDING

Have students answer the questions independently.

Answers:

1. *A*

2. *J*

3. *C*

If they answer any questions incorrectly, have them reread the text to confirm their understanding. Then they may proceed to ANALYZE THE TEXT on page 408.

CHECK YOUR UNDERSTANDING

Answer these questions before moving on to the **Analyze the Texts** section on the following page.

1 What doubt does Sojourner Truth express at the beginning of her speech?

A She is unsure about how the audience will react.

B She doubts that women can achieve as much as men.

C She is unsure about the value of speaking out for equal rights.

D She doubts that someone of her age can be effective.

2 Why does Sojourner Truth think she is still alive at her advanced age?

F Because long life runs in her family

G Because she stopped working so hard

H Because she has had good health all her life

J Because there is still something for her to do

3 Which of the following supports the idea of full civil rights for women?

A *I come from another field—the country of the slave.*

B *There is a great stir about colored men getting their rights.*

C *They work in the field and do as much work, but do not get the pay.*

D *I know that it is hard for one who has held the reins for so long to give up. . . .*

ENGLISH LEARNER SUPPORT

Oral Assessment Use the following questions to assess students' comprehension and speaking skills.

1. Is Truth sure her audience will like what she says? *(No, she is unsure that her audience will like what she has to say.)*

2. Does Truth believe she still has work to do? *(Yes, she believes she still has work to do in life.)*

3. Truth says men and women should have _____ rights. *(equal; She thinks that if women work as hard as men, they should receive the same rights as men.)* **SUBSTANTIAL/MODERATE**

ANALYZE THE TEXTS

Possible answers:

1. **DOK 4:** *Stanton claims that it has become necessary to change the status of women from the one that they hold to one that God and nature entitles them to. She says she is obligated to state the reasons for this change due to her "decent respect to the opinions of mankind," implying that those reasons are forthcoming.*

2. **DOK 3:** *By using the wording of the groundbreaking and historical Declaration of Independence, to which the United States owes its formation, Stanton invokes the clout of that document for her own argument. At the same time, she emphasizes the inequity inherent in it by adding "and women." Use of the famous language—changed only to illustrate her point—makes the inequity apparent.*

3. **DOK 2:** *The phrase "to demand the equal station" sums up the point of the entire piece; the lack of equality can no longer be abided, and this document is a demand to end that situation.*

4. **DOK 2:** *She means that what she has to say may spoil their happy mood; they are full of rejoicing that slavery is over, but she is planning to show that it isn't completely over. This reflects her purpose in writing, since her point is to convince others of the need to solve a problem, and she has to first convince them there is a problem.*

5. **DOK 4:** *Sojourner Truth uses repetition of the simple words "men" and "women," "free" and "slave" throughout the speech, drawing a comparison between the oppression of women and slavery. She also uses parallelism to make her point about the equality of men and women clear: "We do as much, we eat as much, we want as much."*

RESEARCH

Have students work with a partner to research Lucretia Mott. Remind students to use reliable sources and to check more than one source to ensure the information they find is correct.

 RESPOND

ANALYZE THE TEXTS

Support your responses with evidence from the texts. ⧉ NOTEBOOK

1. **Analyze** In an argument, a **claim** is an author's position on an issue. What claim does Stanton make in paragraph 1, and how does she say she will support the claim elsewhere in the document?

2. **Draw Conclusions** In paragraph 2, Stanton exactly repeats the language used in the Declaration of Independence, except for the addition of the phrase "and women." How does using this sentence—and the addition of this phrase—contribute to the persuasiveness of her argument?

3. **Interpret** In paragraph 2, Stanton writes, "Such has been the patient sufferance of the women under this government, and such is now the necessity which constrains them to demand the equal station, to which they are entitled." What does this reveal about Stanton's purpose in writing the Declaration of Sentiments?

4. **Interpret** Sojourner Truth begins her speech "My friends, I am rejoiced that you are glad, but I don't know how you will feel when I get through." What does she mean by this, and how does it reflect the purpose of her argument?

5. **Analyze** Which rhetorical devices does Sojourner Truth use in her speech to the American Equal Rights Association? How does her use of these devices contribute to the power and persuasiveness of the speech?

RESEARCH

Stanton wrote the Declaration of Sentiments, but the idea for it also came from Lucretia Mott. Find out more about Mott and her views.

RESEARCH TIP
Wiki sites, such as Wikipedia, and personal blogs should not be relied on as a source of factual information. However, these sites may lead you to keywords for further searches or to links for other, more reliable sources.

VIEWS ON SLAVERY	WRITING	LEADERSHIP ACCOMPLISHMENTS
She was a Quaker, a leading abolitionist, and member of Philadelphia Female Anti-Slavery Society. She worked to abolish slavery.	*Discourse on Women (1850)*	*founder and president of the Philadelphia Female Anti-Slavery Society; helped establish Swarthmore College (1864); elected head of American Equal Rights Association (1866)*

WHEN STUDENTS STRUGGLE . . .

Reteaching: Analyze Author's Purpose Remind students that the purpose of an argument is to persuade the audience to agree with you. Knowing the audience is very important to writing a convincing argument.

Have students record the following items in a four-column chart: author, purpose, details about the audience, and main points of each argument.

For additional support, go to the **Reading Studio** and assign the following ▸LEVEL▸ **Level Up Tutorial: Reading for Details.**

CREATE AND DISCUSS

Write an Comparison-and-Contrast Essay Write an essay in which you compare the the Declaration of Sentiments with the Declaration of Independence (page 103).

❏ Formulate a thesis statement where you tell which argument you found most effective.

❏ Determine your method of organization. Choose between the block method where you discuss one argument and then the other or the point-by-point method where you organize by discussing each argument one characteristic at a time.

❏ Be sure to evaluate the writers' claims and the evidence they used to support the claim. Discuss whether the evidence was convincing.

❏ Conclude with a statement that confirms your thesis statement and that flows from the evidence you cited.

Give a Dramatic Reading Choose one of the arguments to present as a dramatic reading.

❏ Study the text you choose carefully. Mark up a copy indicating which words you will emphasize and when you might speed up or slow down.

❏ Consider when you will incorporate hand gestures and other nonverbal techniques.

❏ Present your dramatic reading to the class.

RESPOND TO THE ESSENTIAL QUESTION

 When is self-determination possible?

Gather Information Review your annotations and notes on Declaration of Sentiments and Speech to the American Equal Rights Association and highlight those that help answer the Essential Question. Then, add relevant information to your Response Log.

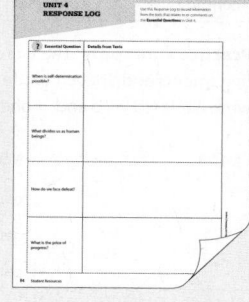

RESPOND

Go to **Writing Informative Texts: Developing a Topic** in the **Writing Studio** for help.

Go to **Giving a Presentation: Delivering Your Presentation** in the **Speaking and Listening Studio** for delivery techniques.

ACADEMIC VOCABULARY
As you write and discuss what you learned from the two speeches, be sure to use the Academic Vocabulary words. Check off each of the words that you use.

❏ **confirm**

❏ **definitely**

❏ **deny**

❏ **format**

❏ **unify**

CREATE AND DISCUSS

Write a Comparison-and-Contrast Essay Have students work in pairs to create a Venn diagram comparing the Declaration of Sentiments to the Declaration of Independence. Remind them to pay attention to each author's purpose and themes, as well as the repetition of words and the use of parallelism. Have students work independently to formulate a thesis statement and to draft their essays. Then, have them share their drafts with their partners for a peer review before revising for a final draft.

 For **writing support** for students at varying proficiency levels, see the **Text X-Ray** on page 396D.

Give a Dramatic Reading Have students choose the text they want to present and practice reading it several times, marking where they will emphasize words and phrases, where they should change tempo, and where they will use gestures.

RESPOND TO THE ESSENTIAL QUESTION

Allow time for students to add details from the "Declaration of Sentiments" and the "Speech to the American Equal Rights Association" to their Unit 4 Response Logs.

CRITICAL VOCABULARY

Possible answers:

1. *People who live abject lives probably have very difficult and deprived lives.*

2. *Stanton's long list of facts evinces the inequality that women have faced as the hands of men.*

3. *She hopes for the knowledge that women will not always have to come to men for money.*

4. *Stanton was referring to social misconduct, for which she believed women would be judged much more harshly than men.*

5. *Stanton states that the denial of women's rights had persisted for years and years, as described in her reference to "a long train of abuses and usurpations."*

6. *She makes the supposition that women deserve the same rights as men.*

VOCABULARY STRATEGY:
Suffixes

Review the chart and suffixes with students. Have them brainstorm other words that end in -*tion* and -*able*.

Answers:

• *Verbs: educate, declare, participate, associate, console*

• *Adjectives: educable, declarable, consolable*

RESPOND

CRITICAL VOCABULARY

WORD BANK

transient	delinquency
evince	abject
supposition	consolation

Go to **Common Roots, Prefixes, and Suffixes** in the **Vocabulary Studio** for help with suffixes.

CRITICAL VOCABULARY

Practice and Apply Use your knowledge of the Critical Vocabulary words to answer each question in a complete sentence.

1. If people live in **abject** poverty, what are their lives like?

2. What reaction does Stanton's long list of facts about man's treatment of woman **evince?**

3. What **consolation** does Sojourner Truth hope for?

4. When Stanton refers to moral **delinquencies,** is she more likely referring to major crimes or social misconduct?

5. Why does Stanton claim that the denial of women's rights has not been a **transient** situation?

6. What **supposition** does Stanton make about women's rights?

VOCABULARY STRATEGY: Suffixes

The word *supposition*, from Declaration of Sentiments, is formed by adding the noun suffix -*tion* to the verb *suppose*. The word *consolation*, from Speech to the American Equal Rights Association, is formed by adding the noun suffix -*tion* to the verb *console*. The chart below shows other words that change their spelling when suffixes are added. Once you become familiar with these patterns of word changes, you can use them to more easily recognize unfamiliar words by connecting them to more common root words.

VERB FORM	NOUN: -*TION*, -*SION* "STATE OF BEING"	ADJECTIVE: -*ABLE* "CAPABLE OF BEING"
invoke	invocation	
conceive	conception	conceivable
certify	certification	certifiable
concede	concession	

Practice and Apply The words in the chart are found in Declaration of Sentiments and Speech to the American Equal Rights Association. For each, write a related verb and, if one exists, a related adjective.

VERB	NOUN	ADJECTIVE
	education	
	declaration	
	participation	
	association	
	consolation	

🄴🄻 ENGLISH LEARNER SUPPORT

Use Patterns of Word Change Have students form nouns from the following verbs and then use both the nouns and the verbs correctly in written sentences: *vacate, process.* Invite volunteers to share their sentences orally. Use the following scaffolds:

• Display the noun-ending -*ing* to help students form nouns from the verbs. Remind students that the silent *e* is dropped before adding the noun suffix. **SUBSTANTIAL**

• Use sentence frames such as these to help students form sentences: *We will <u>vacate</u> the campground on time. We went on <u>vacation</u>. The bride <u>processed</u> down the aisle. We joined in the <u>procession</u>.* **MODERATE**

• Have students work with partners to create original sentences and share them aloud with the class. **LIGHT**

LANGUAGE CONVENTIONS:
Rhetorical Devices

Rhetorical devices are ways of using language that increase the power and clarity of a writer's or speaker's message. In their arguments, Stanton and Truth make effective use of rhetorical devices to keep their audiences engaged and to convey the precise meanings and emotions they intend. In the chart, review the examples of rhetorical devices from the two arguments.

RHETORICAL DEVICE	EXAMPLE
An **allusion** is an indirect reference to a famous person, place, event, or literary work.	The use of "We hold these truths to be self-evident . . ." is an allusion Stanton makes to the Declaration of Independence.
Parallelism is the use of repeated grammatical structures.	Truth uses parallel structure to make her points memorable and powerful, such as in the sentences, "We do as much, we eat as much, we want as much" and "I suppose I am kept here because something remains for me to do; I suppose I am yet to help to break the chain."
Repetition is a way of emphasizing an idea through the repeated use of a word or phrase.	Truth emphasizes the need for women to have the same access as men to money using repetition: "What we want is a little <u>money</u>. . . . When we get our rights we shall not have to come to you for <u>money</u>, for then we shall have <u>money</u> enough in our own pockets; and may be you will ask us for <u>money</u>."

Practice and Apply Look back at the essay you wrote as part of the Create and Discuss activity. Consider how adding two or more rhetorical devices can make your points memorable and effective. Revise to add these devices. Write your original and revised sentences below.

ORIGINAL SENTENCES	REVISED SENTENCES

LANGUAGE CONVENTIONS:
Rhetorical Devices

Review the information about rhetorical devices with students. Point out that parallelism and repetition have a similar function; they provide emphasis and make the words memorable. In addition, they are often used together for an even greater effect.

Have students find additional examples of parallelism and repetition in the selections. Have them share their examples with the class, explaining whether the example features parallelism, repetition, or a combination.

Practice and Apply Have partners compare their original and revised sentences. Encourage them to read the sentences aloud to their partner and provide feedback on the effectiveness of the change. *(Sentences will vary.)*

EL   ENGLISH LEARNER SUPPORT

Use Rhetorical Devices Note that students with Cantonese and Korean language backgrounds are used to a more repetitive sentence structure. Use the following supports with students at varying proficiency levels:

- Help students write two or three sentences that begin with the same word or phrase to practice repetition.
- Have students write two or three sentences that begin with the same word or phrase to practice repetition. Then, combine the sentences into one sentence with a parallel structure.

- Have students work with partners to identify examples of repetition and parallel structure in another famous speech. Invite them to share their examples and explain why they are effective.

COMPARE ARGUMENTS

Before students begin, have them revisit their notes about purpose and structure from the two selections. This will allow them to come prepared to their small-group discussion.

ANALYZE THE TEXTS

Possible answers:

1. **DOK 2:** *Declaration of Sentiments points out that, even though the Declaration of Independence asserted "all men are created equal," nothing was said about women. The remedy is "immediate admission to all the rights and privileges." Speech to the American Equal Rights Association asserts that, even though slavery is abolished, a kind of slavery still remains as long as women, and particularly women of color, are not valued as much as men and cannot vote as men do. She recognizes that abolishing slavery as an institution is good, but the next step has to be equal rights.*

2. **DOK 4:** *Both arguments spend the majority of their text outlining the grievance each writer has, then spends a few lines or phrases at the end demanding some kind of positive action. It is clear that each woman feels her main purpose is to convince her audience that there is a problem. However, each argument is strengthened by turning the complaint or grievance into an action because it adds to the objectivity of her tone and presents a hopeful solution to the dire problem each presents.*

3. **DOK 2:** *Stanton's argument appeals to logic by mimicking the very formal diction, tone, and structure of the Declaration of Independence and employs the parallelism of the Declaration of Independence. For example, "he" in her sentences refers to all men, showing them to be as despotic as the king. Her purpose is to draw a sweeping parallel in no uncertain terms. Sojourner Truth appeals to emotion by using simpler words, shorter sentences, and an informal style that emphasizes she is speaking out of her own personal experience, even as she applies her experience to a more general principle. This lends authenticity to her argument.*

4. **DOK 4:** *In the final few paragraphs, Stanton uses the pronouns "us" and "we," indicating she is speaking for a larger group than just herself, perhaps on behalf of all women. Truth also uses "us" and "we": "when we have got this battle fought," "our rights," "you think, like a slaveholder, that you own us." This, too, shows she is speaking on behalf of herself and many others. This works because it opens the argument up and pushes it toward a generalization that feels satisfyingly important.*

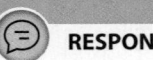

Collaborate & Compare

DECLARATION OF SENTIMENTS
by Elizabeth Cady Stanton

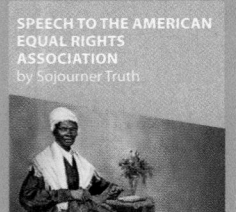

SPEECH TO THE AMERICAN EQUAL RIGHTS ASSOCIATION
by Sojourner Truth

COMPARE ARGUMENTS

Both Declaration of Sentiments and Speech to the American Equal Rights Association argue for an expansion of rights and freedom. Even though the arguments feature different styles and levels of formality, they contain some of the same characteristics. Fill in the chart with examples of the following:

- ❏ a **claim,** or the writer's position on an issue
- ❏ **evidence,** or the information that supports the claim. Types of evidence include facts, statistics, quotations, and personal experiences.
- ❏ **appeals,** or messages to the audience. Two common appeals are **logical appeals,** which rely on reasoning and intellect, and **emotional appeals,** which evoke strong feelings such as fear or pity in the reader.
- ❏ a **call to action,** or an attempt to get the audience to do something in response to the argument.

	DECLARATION OF SENTIMENTS	SPEECH TO THE AMERICAN EQUAL RIGHTS ASSOCIATION
Claim	*He has monopolized; He has denied; He has closed*	*I want to keep the thing stirring, . . . the ice is cracked*
Evidence	*We hold these truths . . . ; women are created equal*	*We do as much, we eat as much, we want as much.*
Appeals	*a long train of abuses and usurpations*	*In the courts women have no right, no voice*
Call to Action	*all the rights and privileges, which belong to them*	*root and branch destroyed; equal rights now*

ANALYZE THE TEXTS

Discuss these questions in your group.

1. **Compare** With your group, review the claims you cited in your chart. In what ways are the claims similar? In what ways are they different?

2. **Evaluate** Does each writer include enough evidence to support her claim? Are there other types of evidence they could have included to strengthen their arguments? Explain.

3. **Interpret** Explain whether each argument appeals to logic or to emotion. Cite evidence from the text in your response.

4. **Analyze** How does each writer strike a balance between arguing *against* something and arguing *for* something? How does including a positive call to action affect the argument?

 ENGLISH LEARNER SUPPORT

Ask Questions Use the following questions to help students synthesize and compare the selections: **1.** Which text is more formal? Which is more casual? Why do you think so? **2.** How does Declaration of Sentiments help you understand the difficulty Sojourner Truth faced because she was a woman? What additional challenges did she face? **3.** Which argument relies more on personal experience? Which relies more on logic? **4.** What goals did Sojourner Truth and Elizabeth Cady Stanton share? **MODERATE/LIGHT**

COLLABORATE AND DISCUSS

Now your group can continue exploring the ideas in these texts by having a group discussion in which you evaluate the strengths and weaknesses of each argument. Follow these steps:

1. **Evaluate the arguments** With your group, review your notes and determine the criteria you will use to assess the arguments. Some questions that you might ask about the arguments include:
   - Do the authors convince you that their claims are valid?
   - What is the strongest evidence the authors include? Is there any other evidence they could have included?
   - Do the authors use appeals convincingly?

2. **Choose and organize details** Choose passages from each text that demonstrate the strengths and weaknesses of each argument. Organize them using the chart.

		DECLARATION OF SENTIMENTS	SPEECH TO THE AMERICAN EQUAL RIGHTS ASSOCIATION
Strengths		to demand the equal station, to which they are entitled	I want women to have their rights. I wish woman to have her voice. . . There ought to be equal rights now more than ever.
		all men and women are created equal	We do as much, we eat as much, we want as much.
Weaknesses		a history of . . . repeated injuries and usurpations on the part of man toward woman, having in direct object the establishment of an absolute tyranny over her	You have been having our rights so long, that you think, like a slaveholder, that you own us.

3. **Have a group discussion** Choose a format in which you will present your group's ideas about the two arguments. Share your views of their strengths and weaknesses and determine whether each argument was convincing. Invite your audience to ask questions and address their concerns respectfully.

Go to **Participating in Collaborative Discussions** in the **Speaking and Listening Studio** for help with having a discussion.

Collaborate & Compare   413

COLLABORATE AND DISCUSS

Explain that small groups will continue exploring ideas through a group discussion. Review the following steps:

1. **Evaluate the arguments** Have students review their notes and consider the listed questions to decide how to assess the two arguments.

2. **Choose and organize details** Students can then choose passages from the selections that best illustrate the strengths and weaknesses of each argument. Have students use the chart to categorize strengths and weaknesses.

3. **Have a group discussion** Have each small group present their ideas about the two arguments, identifying strengths and weaknesses, assessing each argument's effectiveness, and inviting other students to ask questions. Remind students to participate with respect for everyone's opinion.

TO CHALLENGE STUDENTS . . .

Create a Podcast Interview After students plan and practice their presentations, pair students and have them create a podcast in which they interview Stanton and Truth. Students may choose to read the quotations they chose and then ask the author of the quotation a question. Partners should respond as if they were Stanton or Truth. Encourage students to speak in the same style that the authors used (formal or informal). Allow time for students to conduct research, write their scripts, and record their podcasts. Have students play their podcasts for the class.

RUNAGATE RUNAGATE

Poetry by Robert Hayden

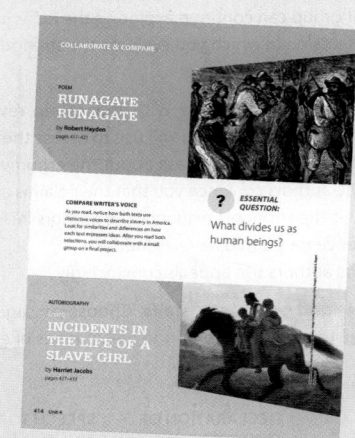

GENRE ELEMENTS
POETRY

In this lesson, students examine how a poem creates meaning. This lesson will focus on analyzing two of the ways poets enrich their poems: the use of allusion and syntax.

LEARNING OBJECTIVES

- Analyze a poem for voice.
- Research historical figures for deeper understanding of allusion.
- Paraphrase a text to maintain meaning.
- Present research aloud to a group.
- Examine connotations of synonyms.
- Analyze language for allusions.
- **Language** Identify subject pronouns.

TEXT COMPLEXITY

Quantitative Measures	Runagate Runagate	Lexile: N/A
Qualitative Measures	**Ideas Presented** Work on multiple levels and demand inference.	
	Structures Used free verse; lack of standard grammatical structures may be confusing.	
	Language Used Complex language with extensive figurative and implied meaning.	
	Knowledge Required Cultural and historical references are essential to understanding.	

Online

RESOURCES

- Unit 4 Response Log
- Selection Audio
- Reading Studio: Notice & Note
- Level Up Tutorial: Elements of Poetry
- Speaking and Listening Studio: Giving a Presentation
- "Runagate Runagate" Selection Test

SUMMARIES

English

Written in multiple voices, Robert Hayden's poem depicts the Underground Railroad, which helped lead escaped slaves to freedom in the 1800s. As the poet journeys towards freedom, the choral voices that arise remind him of all those who have gone before him. These voices work to form a community, offering power and determination to continue the challenging quest. Allusions to leaders such as Harriet Tubman and John Brown give the poet the final push toward freedom.

Spanish

Escrito con muchas voces narrativas, el poema de Robert Hayden describe el ferrocarril subterráneo que llevaba a esclavos escapados a la libertad durante el siglo XIX. Mientras el poeta viaja camino a la libertad, un coro de voces le recuerda al poeta aquellos quienes vinieron antes que él. Esas voces forman una comunidad, que ofrece poder y aplomo para continuar la difícil búsqueda. Las alusiones a grandes líderes como Harriet Tubman y John Brown le dan al poeta el empuje final hacia a la libertad.

SMALL-GROUP OPTIONS

Have students work in small groups and pairs to read and discuss the selection.

Chunking the Text/Think-Pair-Share

- Read the entire poem aloud with students.
- Chunk the text into the following lines: 1–7, 8–18, 19–31, 32–36, 37–52, 53–60, 60–72.
- Tell students to go back and reread each of the chunks, pausing after each to Think-Pair-Share.
- Instruct students to think about the following questions for each chunk and jot down some notes: *Who is speaking? Who are the "characters"? What is happening? Where is it happening?*
- Direct students to share their responses with one another after each chunk.
- As a whole class, reread the entire poem, pausing to let students share their responses to the questions after each chunk.

Double-Entry Journal/ Visualization

- Instruct students to create two columns in their notebooks, or if using a consumable workbook, to draw vertical lines to the right of the poem.
- Ask students to reread the poem aloud in their small groups, pausing at each stanza break.
- Ask students: *What images stand out in each stanza? How do these images help you understand the meaning of the poem? Do these images have positive or negative connotations?*
- Have students discuss each stanza and then draw images that help them to understand the content of the poem.

 # Text X-Ray: English Learner Support
for "Runagate Runagate"

Use the Text X-Ray and the supports and scaffolds in the Teacher's Edition to help guide students at different proficiency levels through the selection.

INTRODUCE THE SELECTION
DISCUSS ALLUSIONS

In this lesson, students will need to be able to identify allusions and understand how the historical, cultural, and theological references develop the poem.

Explain to students that this poem is about the experience of enslaved Africans escaping from slavery. Explain that the poem uses **allusions,** or references to well-known stories and historical events or people. These allusions help give meaning to the poem by evoking emotion. In this instance, it is the power and support to people moving towards freedom.

CULTURAL REFERENCES

The following words or phrases may be unfamiliar to students:

- *Runagate* (title): nickname given to an escaped slave who is "running" past the plantation "gates"
- *Harriet Tubman* (line 38): woman who escaped slavery and made trips to rescue other enslaved people
- *Moses* (line 54): person who, according to religious texts, helped free his people (the Israelites) from slavery in Egypt
- *Garrison, Alcott, Emerson* (line 55): American writers who opposed slavery (William Lloyd Garrison, Louisa May Alcott, Ralph Waldo Emerson)
- *John Brown* (line 56): American who tried to abolish slavery using weapons and violence

LISTENING

Relate Rhythm to Meaning

Remind students that how poetry sounds when read aloud gives meaning to the words. The **rhythm,** or pattern of stressed and unstressed syllables, may change throughout the poem to highlight certain emotions or feelings.

Use the following supports with students at varying proficiency levels:

- Read aloud lines 18–20, demonstrating that the rhythm conveys urgency and movement. Reread the text, having students clap, tap, or snap along. **SUBSTANTIAL**
- Read aloud lines 19–31. Encourage students to raise their hands when they hear a word that conveys movement. Read slowly and enunciate the rhythm. **MODERATE**
- Read aloud lines 61–72. Have students clap, tap, or snap their fingers as you read the poem aloud. Ask them to identify the movement words. Ask students to identify changes in the poem: *Does the rhythm change? How is it different? Does the format of the poem change? What does this tell you about the voices in the poem?* **LIGHT**

SPEAKING

Practice Fluency

Tell students that the poem uses rhythm so that its sound also gives meaning. Use gestures to communicate the meaning. Explain that you will reread the poem aloud together to practice fluency. Direct students to listen for rhythm.

Use the following supports with students at varying proficiency levels:

- Working with students as a group, read lines 1–10 of the poem aloud and have students echo-read. Encourage students to move their fingers along the text as they read. Read the section over aloud at least three times. **SUBSTANTIAL**

- Working with students as a group, read lines 19–31 together and have students choral-read. Then, have students practice saying the lines aloud with partners. **MODERATE**

- Direct students to memorize a line or two from lines 61–72 of the poem. Have students practice reciting the lines, without notes, with partners. Invite students to recite their lines to the class. **LIGHT**

READING

Infer Subjects of Sentences

Explain to students that the syntax of the poem is irregular. Review subject pronouns with students: *I, you, he, she, we, you* (plural) and *they.* Then, explain that you will identify the subject pronouns of key stanzas.

Use the following supports with students at varying proficiency levels:

- Help students skim and scan lines 1–10 and identify the subject of the sentence using context clues. ("I," line 6) Ask students: *Who is the subject? (an escaped slave) What does he do? (runs, falls, stumbles) Who is chasing him? (hunters and hounds)* **SUBSTANTIAL**

- Ask students to summarize lines 1–10, using the third person to describe the "I" in the poem. **MODERATE**

- Guide students to identify the verbs in lines 1–10. Ask students: *Why does the speaker start by describing actions?* Have them discuss with partners. **LIGHT**

WRITING

Write an Analysis

Work with students to read the writing assignment on page 423.

Use the following supports with students at varying proficiency levels:

- Work with students to develop the key ideas of the first stanza. Help them identify verbs and nouns that are central to the ideas of the stanza. Display the following sentences and have students copy them in their journals. Ask them to provide the line number where they can find the quoted words in the poem. *The poem begins with a fugitive slave who "runs, fall, stumbles" (line ___) towards freedom. He is chased by hunters and hounds (line ___).* **SUBSTANTIAL**

- Have students write sentences about the first stanza. Provide sentence frames to facilitate student comprehension of grammatical terms: *The poet uses nouns such as ____ and ____ to show the Runagate's fear (lines ___).* **MODERATE**

- Review the first stanza with students. Ask about the difference between *the* and *a*. Ask students to discuss: *Why would the night be definite or specific? Does the word* the *make the night more or less frightening?* **LIGHT**

? Connect to the
ESSENTIAL QUESTION

Ask students to think about the idea of *preconceptions*. Discuss the meaning of the word, breaking it down into its two parts: *pre* and *conceive*. Encourage students to reflect on how preconceptions can influence our responses and interactions with others. Then, discuss how this is related to the question, "What divides us as human beings?"

COMPARE WRITER'S VOICE

Encourage the students to examine the differences in time periods between the two pieces as they compare. Remind them that "Runagate Runagate" was written much later, from the perspective of someone who is mixing his own experiences and feelings during a time of segregation and violence with a reflection on slavery.

COLLABORATE & COMPARE

POEM
RUNAGATE RUNAGATE

by **Robert Hayden**
pages 417–421

COMPARE WRITER'S VOICE

As you read, notice how both texts use distinctive voices to describe slavery in America. Look for similarities and differences on how each text expresses ideas. After you read both selections, you will collaborate with a small group on a final project.

ESSENTIAL QUESTION:

What divides us as human beings?

AUTOBIOGRAPHY
from
INCIDENTS IN THE LIFE OF A SLAVE GIRL

by **Harriet Jacobs**
pages 427–433

414   Unit 4

LEARNING MINDSET

Questioning   Remind students that learning is hard work. However, in the end it is very rewarding. For centuries, scientists have struggled to answer questions. It is because of their constant searching that they get answers. Likewise, we obtain new knowledge by answering questions. Have students work individually to each come up with a question about the information on this page. For example, students may ask what *Runagate* means. Encourage volunteers to share their questions. Discuss that they may not know the answers yet, but can work to learn them as they read.

Runagate Runagate

QUICK START

If you were going to write a poem about slavery in America, which words would you include? Make a list of three to five words that you might incorporate into your piece.

ANALYZE SPEAKER AND VOICE

Two important related characteristics in poetry are speaker and voice. A **speaker** is a persona who talks to the reader in poetry, similar to a narrator in fiction. A poem may have more than one speaker. The **voice** is the human personality that comes through in a work. The voice in a poem is developed through the author's unique use of language, including word choice, repetition, and rhyme. As a result, you may learn about the author's personality, beliefs, and attitudes.

As you read "Runagate Runagate," use a chart like the one below to help you analyze the details in the poem and what they suggest about the voice.

DETAIL	VOICE
Runs falls rises stumbles on from darkness into darkness	The experience of a runaway is uncertain and dangerous.

ANALYZE SOUND DEVICES: Rhythm

Rhythm is the sound produced by the arrangement of stressed and unstressed syllables, along with the intervals of time that fall between them. A good poet creates a relationship between rhythm and content by carefully selecting words and controlling line lengths and format. Even the title Hayden chooses for his poem—"Runagate Runagate"—uses rhythm to heighten its meaning. Imagine that the poet had chosen "Escaped Slave" instead; the experience of reading the poem would be very different.

Poets, like musicians, manipulate rhythm to express ideas and emotions. As you read, pay attention to when, how, and why its rhythm rushes you along, slows you down, or suddenly makes you stop and change direction.

GENRE ELEMENTS: POETRY

- uses rhythm and may use rhyme
- may contain more than one speaker
- has a definite voice
- includes deliberate word choice that conveys important ideas

---

QUICK START

As the students think about their words, encourage them to draw from a range of different types of words. Having a mixture of nouns, adjectives, and verbs will help get them into a more creative and poetic mindset about language and the subject matter of the selection.

ANALYZE SPEAKER AND VOICE

Remind students that sometimes reading aloud can help give insight into a piece of writing. When looking for clues about tone and voice, especially in poetry, reading lines aloud and listening for rhythm, repetition, and other tools that might be used to build tension or communicate emotion will create a clearer picture of the voice and tone for a given section.

ANALYZE SOUND DEVICES: Rhythm

Tell students that repetition is a device used to affect the rhythm in a poem. Repetition may include words or phrases, such as the title of the poem, or may be a repetition of sounds within a word or letters at the beginning of words. Encourage students to look for different kinds of repetition as they read, and reflect on how different kinds of repetition affect the rhythm.

TEACH

ANALYZE LANGUAGE:
Allusion

Encourage students to use the Internet to research allusions in the poem. Researching the different names and other references in the work will lead to a deeper understand of the author's intended meaning.

✎ ANNOTATION MODEL

As students mark up the poem, encourage them to use different symbols to indicate different rhythmic devices and types of repetition. Explain that this will help them create a visual map of the poem's rhythm. Remind them to look past word or phrase repetition alone, and to look at sounds within the words that are repeated.

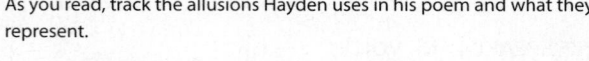

GET READY

ANALYZE LANGUAGE: Allusion

An **allusion** is a reference to a well-known historical or literary person, event, or composition. Allusions can evoke specific feelings or ideas associated with the thing to which the writer refers. Writers choose allusions that their readers will understand, such as references to the Bible. Hayden employs several, including Ezekiel (line 59). For an allusion to succeed, the reader must recognize it.

As you read, track the allusions Hayden uses in his poem and what they represent.

ALLUSION	MEANING
John Brown	well-known abolitionist
Ezekiel	

ANNOTATION MODEL

NOTICE & NOTE

As you read, mark up the text to identify aspects of rhythm and allusions that you recognize. Make notes in the margin that help you identify the speakers and voice in the poem. This model shows one reader's notes for the first lines of "Runagate Runagate."

Runs falls rises stumbles on from darkness into darkness and the darkness thicketed with shapes of terror and the hunters pursuing and the hounds pursuing and the night cold and the night long and the river	The verbs runs, falls, rises are all stressed, creating a frantic rhythm. "Darkness" and "night" help create a setting.

BACKGROUND

Robert Hayden *(1913–1980) endured a childhood marred by poverty, a broken family, and a dysfunctional foster home. Plagued by depression, vision problems, and bullying peers, the Detroit native withdrew into a world of books. He researched African American folklore for the Federal Writers' Project in 1936, published his first book of poems in 1940, and earned a master's degree in English. Hayden then began his own lengthy career as a teacher while continuing to produce volumes of poetry. Much of his award-winning work explores the history and legacy of racial injustice in America.*

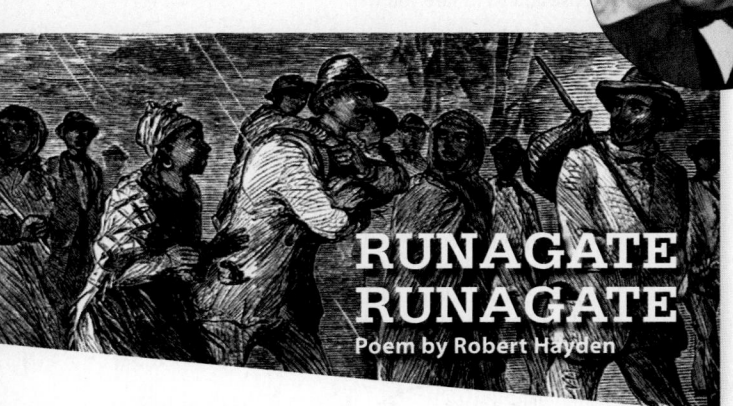

RUNAGATE RUNAGATE

Poem by Robert Hayden

PREPARE TO COMPARE

As you read, note the features associated with slavery that are described by the poem's speakers. This information will help you compare the poem with the autobiographical excerpt from Incidents in the Life of a Slave Girl, *which follows it.*

I.

Runs falls rises stumbles on from darkness into darkness
and the darkness thicketed with shapes of terror
and the hunters pursuing and the hounds pursuing
and the night cold and the night long and the river
5   to cross and the jack-muh-lanterns[1] beckoning beckoning
and blackness ahead and when shall I reach that somewhere
morning and keep on going and never turn back and keep on going
                    Runagate[2]
                        Runagate
10   Runagate

---

[1] **jack-muh-lanterns:** a mythical goblin, popular in African American folklore.
[2] **Runagate:** a fugitive slave.

Notice & Note

Use the side margins to notice and note signposts in the text.

ANALYZE SOUND DEVICES
Annotate: Mark the point where the rhythm changes in this stanza.

Interpret: What effect does this change have on the poem?

Runagate Runagate   417

BACKGROUND

Hayden was born Asa Bundy Sheffey. He studied with W.H. Auden and admired the work of Carl Sandburg, Langston Hughes, and Jean Toomer. He was the first African American to serve as Consultant in Poetry to the Library of Congress—a position we now call Poet Laureate.

PREPARE TO COMPARE

Direct students to use the Prepare to Compare prompt to focus their reading.

 ## ANALYZE SOUND DEVICES

Encourage students to use visual clues in this poem to help them find the major changes. Remind students that reading aloud can help them understand how the rhythm changes. (***Answer:*** *The repetition of the word "Runagate" evenly alternates stressed and unstressed syllables. The change heightens the sense of urgency and reflects a sound almost like breathing hard while running.*)

For **speaking** and **reading support** for students at varying proficiency levels, see the **Text X-Ray** on page 414D.

EL ENGLISH LEARNER SUPPORT

Understand Sentence Structure Hayden does not use regular sentence structure in this poem. Capital letters signal the beginnings of sentences, but he omits the subjects of these sentences so that they must be inferred. Ask questions to help students infer the subject and actions in the first 10 lines: (Line 1) Who runs, falls, rises, and stumbles? *(an escaped slave)* (Line 3) What are the hunters and hounds doing? *(pursuing the escaped slave)* (Line 4) What is cold and long? *(The night is cold and long.)* Encourage students to formulate questions about lines 5–7, such as what he will cross and when he will get where he is going.
SUBSTANTIAL/MODERATE

ANALYZE SPEAKER AND VOICE

Encourage students to think about the content of each line and what events are being described. Sometimes the shift in voice can be confusing, but remind students that a slave or escaped slave probably wouldn't say "notify subscriber" or refer to other slaves as "them." Looking for clues in pronouns can help students find the shifts in speaker. (**Answer:** *The changes in pronouns in line 19 is clearly from the perspective of someone who used to be a slave. Lines 21–29 refer to the slaves at auction with the possessive my, so this is clearly changing to the slaveholder's perspective. The voice shifts back in line 30.*)

ANALYZE ALLUSION

Remind students that **allusions** are references to things that the writer hopes will evoke specific feelings or associations. Tell students that the subjects of allusions in older works may no longer be well known. Encourage students to use the Internet to research Harriet Tubman if they are confused about her appearance in the poem. (**Answer:** *Harriet Tubman was an escaped slave who helped many other slaves reach freedom.*)

 For **listening support** for students at varying proficiency levels, see the **Text X-Ray** on page 414C.

 NOTICE & NOTE

Many thousands rise and go
many thousands crossing over

O mythic North
O star-shaped yonder Bible city

ANALYZE SPEAKER AND VOICE
Annotate: Circle the individual stanzas in lines 19–31.

Interpret: How can you tell that there are different speakers in these lines?

15 Some go weeping and some rejoicing
some in coffins and some in carriages
some in silks and some in shackles

Rise and go or fare you well

No more auction block for me
20 no more driver's lash for me

If you see my Pompey, 30 yrs of age,
new breeches, plain stockings, negro shoes;
if you see my Anna, likely young mulatto[3]
branded E on the right cheek, R on the left,
25 catch them if you can and notify subscriber.[4]
Catch them if you can, but it won't be easy.
They'll dart underground when you try to catch them,
plunge into quicksand, whirlpools, mazes,
turn into scorpions when you try to catch them.

30 And before I'll be a slave
I'll be buried in my grave

North star and bonanza gold
I'm bound for the freedom, freedom-bound
and oh Susyanna don't you cry for me[5]

ANALYZE ALLUSION
Annotate: Mark the reference to a well-known person in lines 37–41.

Interpret: How does this allusion connect to the topic of the poem?

35   Runagate

                    Runagate

II.

Rises from their anguish and their power,

Harriet Tubman,

woman of earth, whipscarred,
40 a summoning, a shining

Mean to be free

---

[3] **mulatto:** of mixed white and black ancestry.
[4] **subscriber:** a person placing a notice for a fugitive slave.
[5] **oh Susyanna don't you cry for me:** an allusion to the chorus of "Oh! Susanna" by Stephen Foster.

APPLYING ACADEMIC VOCABULARY

☐ format   ☑ definitely   ☐ unify   ☑ confirm   ☐ deny

Write and Discuss Have students turn to partners to discuss the following questions. Guide students to include the academic vocabulary words *confirm* and *definitely* in their responses. Ask volunteers to share their responses with the class.

- How can you **confirm** a reference to an allusion?
- Does an allusion have a **definite** meaning?

And this was the way of it, brethren brethren,
way we journeyed from Can't to Can.
Moon so bright and no place to hide,
45   the cry up and the patterollers[6] riding,
hound dogs belling[7] in bladed air.

---

[6] **patterollers:** people who watched and restricted the movement of black slaves at night.
[7] **belling:** barking.

ENGLISH LEARNER SUPPORT

Use Reading Strategies Direct student attention to the stanza on page 419. Read the stanza aloud to the class, and then write the stanza on the board. Use vertical lines to break each line into simple clauses: for example, "way we journeyed | from Can't to Can." Focus on helping students break down the text into phrases to help them understand what the author is saying. Afterwards, review the entire line and check for improved comprehension. **SUBSTANTIAL**

TEACH

✏️ ANALYZE SOUND DEVICES

Remind students that pauses can be indicated both by space and by punctuation. Review the difference between commas and semicolons, and encourage students to keep this difference in mind as they read. Encourage students to try reading the lines aloud, following the cues for pauses and thinking about what kinds of pauses each device creates. (**Answer:** *Lines 51–52 have the rhythm of speech. Harriet Tubman is speaking. Lines 53–58 have more pauses. These lines sounds like someone reading a poster or bulletin.*)

ANALYZE SOUND DEVICES

Annotate: Pauses between some syllables or words contribute to the rhythm of the lines. Reread lines 51–58 silently and mark any visual cues you see for pauses.

Compare: Contrast the rhythms and meanings in lines 51–52 and lines 53–58.

And fear starts a-murbling, Never make it,
we'll never make it. *Hush that now,*
and she's turned upon us, levelled pistol
50 glinting in the moonlight:
Dead folks can't jaybird-talk,[8] she says
you keep on going now or die, she says

Wanted__Harriet Tubman__alias The General
Alias Moses__Stealer of Slaves

55 In league with Garrison__Alcott__Emerson
Garrett__Douglass__Thoreau__John Brown

Armed and known to be Dangerous

Wanted__Reward__Dead or Alive

Tell me, Ezekiel, oh tell me do you see
60 mailed[9] Jehovah coming to deliver me?

Hoot-owl calling in the ghosted air,
five times calling to the hants[10] in the air.
Shadow of a face in the scary leaves,
shadow of a voice in the talking leaves:

65 Come ride-a my train

Oh that train, ghost-story train
through swamp and savanna movering movering,
over trestles of dew, through caves of the wish,
Midnight Special on a sabre track movering movering,
70 *first stop Mercy and the last Hallelujah.*

Come ride-a my train

Mean mean mean to be free.

---

[8] **jaybird-talk:** talk like fools.
[9] **mailed:** covered with a flexible armor made of rings or plates.
[10] **hants:** ghosts.

WHEN STUDENTS STRUGGLE . . .

Understand Voice and Rhythm Use modeling and choral reading to prepare students for independent fluent reading. Read aloud lines 42–60 as students follow the text. Reread lines 42–60 with students reading along chorally. Then, divide students into two groups, and have them read alternate lines aloud chorally. Ask students where rhythm changes suggest a new speaker. (*lines 51, 53, and 59*)

 For additional support, go to the **Reading Studio** and assign the following ⬛ᴸᵉᵛᵉˡ **Level Up Tutorial: Elements of Poetry.**

CHECK YOUR UNDERSTANDING

Answer these questions about "Runagate Runagate" before moving on to the next selection.

1 Which of the following words best describes the speaker in the poem?

A Frightened

B Sarcastic

C Determined

D Hesitant

2 Which of the following lines features a rushing rhythm?

F *No more auction block for me / no more driver's lash for me*

G *And fear starts a-murbling, Never make it, / we'll never make it.*

H *I'm bound for the freedom, freedom-bound / and oh Susyanna don't you cry for me*

J *Runagate / Runagate*

3 Which of the following items is an example of an allusion?

A *O star-shaped yonder Bible city*

B *my Pompey, 30 yrs of age*

C *Dead folks can't jaybird-talk, she says*

D *Hoot-owl calling in the ghosted air*

 © Houghton Mifflin Harcourt Publishing Company

CHECK YOUR UNDERSTANDING

Have students answer the questions independently.

Answers:

1. *C*

2. *J*

3. *A*

If they answer any questions incorrectly, have them reread the text to confirm their understanding. Then they may proceed to ANALYZE THE TEXT on page 422.

EL ENGLISH LEARNER SUPPORT

Oral Assessment Use the following questions to assess students' comprehension and speaking skills.

1. Was the speaker's voice determined? *(yes)*

2. Does "Runagate / Runagate" have a rushing rhythm? *(yes)*

3. The poem is about people escaping from _____ *(slavery)*

SUBSTANTIAL/MODERATE

APPLY

ANALYZE THE TEXT

Possible answers:

1. **DOK 4:** *The speaker uses all action verbs without punctuation to describe running without thought because he or she is so scared. The repetition of the words* darkness, pursuing, *and* night *shows an ominous setting that the speaker is trying to escape.*

2. **DOK 1:** *Allusions: star-shaped yonder Bible city, Ezekiel, Jehovah; the Bible talks about people being freed from slavery, so biblical allusions and imagery can suggest hope for fugitive slaves.*

3. **DOK 2:** *The first speaker seems to be calm and in charge, calling her party "brethren brethren" and showing a fugitive slave how to run by saying "journeyed from Can't to Can"; the second speaker is in her group and scared of the unknown, saying "no place to hide," "hound dogs belling," "fear starts a-murbling," but he or she listens to the authority of the first speaker ("you keep on going now or die, she says").*

4. **DOK 4:** *In these lines, the rhythm is more regular and predictable and includes rhyming words; the speaker appears to be calling out to God and then receiving an answer.*

5. **DOK 4:** *He is an abolitionist who is against slavery.*

RESEARCH

Remind students that different types of sources will contain different information, and they should double check facts in multiple sources before entering them into their charts.

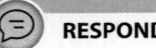 **RESPOND**

ANALYZE THE TEXT

Support your responses with evidence from the text. NOTEBOOK

1. **Analyze** The opening stanza portrays a frightened speaker fleeing through darkness. How does its rhythm reflect and enhance the speaker's experience?

2. **Identify** What allusions to religion or the Bible can you find in the poem? Why might religious imagery and biblical allusions be appropriate for this topic?

3. **Interpret** Consider the stanza that begins "And this was the way of it" (lines 42–52). Who are the two speakers in the stanza, and how do the rhythms of their speech reflect the differences in their attitudes?

4. **Synthesize** Read the two stanzas in lines 59–64, starting with the one that begins "Tell me, Ezekiel." How do the rhythms in these stanzas differ from most other parts of the poem? How do the rhythms and the meanings of the verses combine to convey a certain feeling or form an allusion?

5. **Analyze** How would you describe the writer's voice in "Runagate Runagate"? What beliefs does he reveal through the details of the poem?

RESEARCH

RESEARCH TIP
When conducting online research, check a few different sources to make sure the facts are accurate. Use only credible sources, such as encyclopedias and websites of institutions with specific expertise.

"Runagate Runagate" references the Underground Railroad and Harriet Tubman, who was probably the most famous conductor working on it. Do some research on Tubman and fill out the chart with what you learn.

HARRIET TUBMAN'S EARLY LIFE	ESCAPE FROM SLAVERY	WORK ON THE UNDERGROUND RAILROAD	LATER WORK
Born a slave; beaten mercilessly; hit with an iron, causing head injury	*Was going to be sold, so she escaped with her brothers*	*Called Moses; never lost a passenger; communicated in codes*	*Worked for the Union Army and for "women's" suffrage*

 LEARNING MINDSET

Asking for Help Emphasize to students that asking for help is a sign of strength. It shows that the student realizes faster progress can be made by getting outside help. In addition, getting information from someone else can give students new ideas and a broader understanding of a topic. Model for students how they might ask for help in getting started on researching the topics of Harriet Tubman and the Underground Railroad.

CREATE AND PRESENT

Write a Literary Analysis Write a literary analysis in which you analyze the poet's voice in "Runagate, Runagate."

- ❑ Write an opening paragraph in which you describe the writer's voice.
- ❑ Identify examples of word choice that may reflect the writer's beliefs and attitudes.
- ❑ Review the poem for examples of repetition, rhythm, and rhyme that suggest important ideas.
- ❑ Restate your idea in a conclusion.

Present a Dramatic Reading With your group, take turns reading the poem aloud, interpreting the different speakers' attitudes. Then, present your dramatic reading.

- ❑ With your group, decide how each part of the poem should be read.
- ❑ Vary tone of voice.
- ❑ Rehearse your reading.
- ❑ Explain to the class why you chose to present the poem the way you did.

 Go to **Giving a Presentation: Delivering Your Presentation** in the **Speaking and Listening Studio** for help with delivery techniques.

RESPOND TO THE ESSENTIAL QUESTION

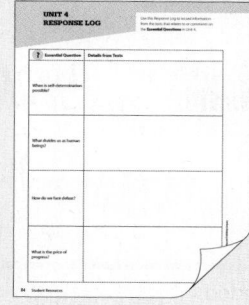

? What divides us as human beings?

Gather Information Review your annotations and notes on "Runagate, Runagate." Then, add relevant details to your Response Log. As you determine which information to include, think about:

- what the fugitive slaves fear
- where the fugitives are going
- what motivates the poem's speakers

ACADEMIC VOCABULARY

As you write and discuss what you learned from the poem, be sure to use the Academic Vocabulary words. Check off each of the words that you use.

- ❑ **confirm**
- ❑ **definitely**
- ❑ **deny**
- ❑ **format**
- ❑ **unify**

CREATE AND PRESENT

Write a Literary Analysis Review the structure of an analytical essay with the students. Remind them that they should focus each body paragraph of their essays on one particular point of analysis, and to state the main point in the topic sentence of each paragraph. Explain that this will help keep their essays focused and clear.

For **writing support** for students at varying proficiency levels, see the **Text X-Ray** on page 414D.

Present a Dramatic Reading As a prewriting exercise, have each student work on a different section of the poem and identify the voices in his or her section. Encourage students to take notes on the changes of voice and the effects of those changes before working together on their dramatic readings.

RESPOND TO THE ESSENTIAL QUESTION

Allow time for students to add details from "Runagate Runagate" to their Unit 4 Response Logs.

WHEN STUDENTS STRUGGLE . . .

Reteach: Analyze Allusions Review the term *allusion*. Then, have students reread the poem. Focus on the allusion to Frederick Douglass in line 56. Ask: *Why might Hayden have alluded to Douglass in this poem? How is the subject of the allusion related to the topic of the poem? Does the allusion create positive or negative associations and feelings? Does the allusion help convey the theme of the poem?* Have students work in small groups to analyze the allusion and write sentences that answer the questions.

 For additional support, go to the **Reading Studio** and assign the following **Level Up Tutorial: Elements of Poetry.**

from INCIDENTS IN THE LIFE OF A SLAVE GIRL

Autobiography by Harriet Jacobs

GENRE ELEMENTS
AUTOBIOGRAPHY

Explain to students that an **autobiography** is a first-person account of a person's life. Point out that this autobiographical account of a person who was enslaved may also be called a slave narrative. The events are selected and arranged to create a compelling story, containing narrative elements such as plot, conflict, suspense, direct and indirect characterization, and theme. Remind students that although a slave narrative resembles fiction, it is a true account of an enslaved person's journey from degradation to emancipation. The purpose of a slave narrative was to generate empathy from Americans and make them realize that slavery was immoral.

LEARNING OBJECTIVES

- Examine direct and indirect characterization.
- Research slave narratives.
- Write an autobiographical sketch.
- Discuss research findings in a group.
- Analyze connotative and denotative meanings.
- Examine dialect and idioms using context clues.
- **Language** Discuss a narrative using the terms *character* and *point of view*.

TEXT COMPLEXITY

Quantitative Measures	Incidents in the Life of a Slave Girl	Lexile: 740L
Qualitative Measures	**Ideas Presented** Mostly explicit; a few inferences needed.	
	Structures Used Clear structure and chronological order.	
	Language Used Mostly explicit with some dialect and idioms that may be difficult for ELL students.	
	Knowledge Required May require knowledge of historical or cultural institutions.	

Online **Ed**

RESOURCES

- Unit 4 Response Log
- 🔊 Selection Audio
- 📖 Reading Studio: Notice & Note
- Level Up Tutorials: Character Traits; Author's Style
- Writing Studio: Writing Narratives
- 💬 Speaking and Listening Studio: Participating in Collaborative Discussions
- Vocabulary Studio: Synonyms and Antonyms
- ☑ *Incidents in the Life of a Slave Girl* Selection Test

SUMMARIES

English

This excerpt begins with Linda's realization that her master, Mr. Flint, will take control of her children in order to further suppress her. To save her children, Linda decides to flee. She hopes that their father, a white man, will buy them. She hides at a friend's house while Mr. Flint searches for her, offering a reward for her capture. Linda's children, aunt, and brother are put in jail to pressure them to provide information about her escape.

Spanish

Este pasaje de la narrativa de esclavos *Incidentes en la vida de una esclava* comienza con la comprensión de Linda de que su amo, el Sr. Flint, tomará control de sus hijos para seguir reprimiéndola. Para salvar a sus hijos, Linda decide huir, esperando que su padre, un hombre blanco, los compre. Se esconde en la casa de una amiga mientras que el Sr. Flint la busca y ofrece una recompensa por su captura. Los hijos, la tía y el hermano de Linda son llevados a la cárcel para presionarlos para que den información sobre su escape.

 ## SMALL-GROUP OPTIONS

Have students work in small groups and pairs to read and discuss the selection.

Think-Pair-Share

- Write the following questions for students to think about as they read: *When in your life do you experience freedom? What conflicts do you have when you have to "fight" for this freedom?*
- After students read, have them jot down quick responses to the questions.
- Ask students to share and discuss their responses with a partner. Then, ask the partners to share what they discussed with the larger group.

Double-Entry Journal

- Instruct students to make two columns in their notebooks or to draw a vertical line to the right of the text in their consumable versions.
- Explain that the left side will be text evidence and the right side will be for their responses.
- Direct students to record any quotes from the text that evoke an emotional response, evoke a question, indicate conflict, or seem important.
- Explain that on the right side, students are to write their responses to those quotes.
- Have students share with the class what they recorded.

Text X-Ray: English Learner Support
for *Incidents in the Life of a Slave Girl*

Use the Text X-Ray and the supports and scaffolds in the Teacher's Edition to help guide students at different proficiency levels through the selection.

INTRODUCE THE SELECTION
DISCUSS ELEMENTS OF A NARRATIVE TEXT

In this lesson, students will need to be able to analyze and discuss the various elements of a narrative text, including characters and point of view, while understanding the historical context of slavery. Provide the following explanations: A **narrative** relates, or tells about, an event or series of events. A narrative can be imaginary, as in a short story, or it can be factual, as in a news story or autobiography. **Characters** are the people who take part in the action of the story. The main character is the most important person in the story. A minor character is less important but helps to move the action along. In the **first-person point of view,** the narrator is a character who tells everything in his or her own words and uses the pronouns *I, me,* and *my*. In the **third-person point of view,** events are related by a voice outside the action, not by one of the characters. A third-person narrator uses pronouns such as *he, she,* and *they*.

Supply the following sentence frames: *A narrative ___ an ___ or ___. A character can be a ___ character or a ___ character. Point of view is ___ when the narrator uses the pronouns ___ , ___, and ___. Point of view is ___ when a person outside the action tells the events. This voice uses the pronouns ___ , ___, and ___.*

CULTURAL REFERENCES

The following words or phrases may be unfamiliar to students:

- *house servant* (paragraph 1): an enslaved person who works in the house, not the field
- *you are killing me* (paragraph 3): you are adding stress to my life
- *lashes* (paragraph 10): harsh blows with a whip, given as a punishment
- *fugitives* (paragraph 11): escaped slaves
- *chick'n hearted* (paragraph 15): fearful

LISTENING

Understand Dialect

Tell students that they will listen to an audio version of the text in order to hear the use of **dialect,** a way of speaking specific to a certain region or group of people. Explain to students that Sally's dialect reflects typical speech of slaves.

Use the following supports with students at varying proficiency levels:

- Have students read along, underlining the text with their index fingers as they listen to the audio. Instruct students to raise their hands when they hear **dialect.** Pause the audio frequently to allow students to ask you questions about what they hear. Replay audio as needed. **SUBSTANTIAL**
- Play the audio and have students listen and follow along. Ask students to take notes about words they don't understand. Pause the audio frequently to allow students to discuss how to ask questions about what they don't understand. For example: *What does "chile" mean? (child)* **MODERATE**
- Play the audio of the text and have students listen and follow along. Encourage them to ask questions about words and ideas that they don't understand. If possible, have them ask each other questions about the dialect. **LIGHT**

SPEAKING

Discuss Point of View and Characterization

Have students discuss the features of narrative text. Explain that autobiographies are written in first-person point of view. Other characters are revealed through direct statements or indirect clues.

After reading the text, use the following supports with students at varying proficiency levels:

- Display these sentences and read them aloud: *The first-person point of view shows me the events from Linda's perspective. I learn about other characters through Linda's statements.* Have students repeat the sentences back to you and then practice saying them with a partner. **SUBSTANTIAL**
- To help students express ideas about point of view and characterization, display sentences frames: _____ *point of view shows me the events from Linda's perspective. Linda's statements tell me more about the other* _____. Ask students to complete the sentences and say them to a partner. **MODERATE**
- Have student pairs discuss examples of characterization. Have pairs decide whether the following are examples of direct or indirect characterization: "I knew she was a faithful friend." (paragraph 3, indirect); "Anxious as I was . . . " (paragraph 13, direct). **LIGHT**

READING

Examine Characterization

Explain to students that **characterization** is created in a narrative through a character's actions, words, and feelings. Students can learn about a character through either the narrator or through other characters.

Display a word web for notes about characters. Put a name in the center with three surrounding circles for actions, words, and feelings. Use the following supports with students at varying proficiency levels:

- Complete the word web as a group, and have students copy it. Have students choose Mr. Flint, Linda, or Sally. Use facial expressions and gestures to help students understand character traits. **SUBSTANTIAL**
- Have student pairs complete word webs. Guide pairs to identify character traits using context clues: actions (verbs), words (quotation marks), and feelings (adjectives). Students can choose from these characters: Mr. Flint, Linda, Sally. **MODERATE**
- Read using a Three-Minute Review. Pause every two to three paragraphs and have students complete word webs. Instruct students to share their findings with a small group. **LIGHT**

WRITING

Write an Autobiographical Sketch

Reread "Write an Autobiographical Sketch" from Student Edition page 435. Review first-person pronouns and conjugations of key verbs such as *to have* and *to be*.

Use the following supports with students at varying proficiency levels:

- Select a character. Then, write a paragraph on the board, addressing *who*, *what*, *where*, *when*, and *why*. Have students copy the paragraph into their notebooks. **SUBSTANTIAL**
- Provide sentence frames for students to craft their own responses: I am a _____ (*who*). I have _____ (*character trait*). The problem I am having is _____ (*what*) because _____ (*why*). First, I _____ (*what*) in _____ (*when/where*). Next, I _____ (*what*) After that, I _____ (*what*) I want ___ (*character trait*). **MODERATE**
- Offer students an outline format to write their responses: 1) Who is the character? Where does he or she live? 2) What does the character want? Why? 3) How will the character get it? **LIGHT**

TEACH

AUTOBIOGRAPHY

from

INCIDENTS IN THE LIFE OF A SLAVE GIRL

by **Harriet Jacobs**
pages 427–433

? Connect to the
ESSENTIAL QUESTION

This excerpt explores the roles played by enslaved people, slave owners, as well as those who necessitated and those who aided the author's escape from slavery. Students will read examples of how divisions across gender, race, and class operated, and how those divisions were overcome.

COMPARE WRITER'S VOICE

Point out that this excerpt is taken from an autobiography, while "Runagate, Runagate" is a poem exploring similar themes. Ask students to share examples of other texts dealing with slavery. Prompt them to reflect on the following questions: *What are the advantages of dealing with these themes in one genre as opposed to the other? How does the author's purpose for each piece relate to the choice of genre?*

COMPARE WRITER'S VOICE

Now that you've read "Runagate Runagate," read the autobiographical excerpt from *Incidents in the Life of a Slave Girl* and explore how this connects with some of the ideas from the poem. As you read, think about how the narrator's point of view compares to other stories you've heard about slavery. After you are finished, you will collaborate with a small group on a final project that involves an analysis of both texts.

? ESSENTIAL QUESTION:

What divides us as human beings?

POEM

RUNAGATE RUNAGATE

by **Robert Hayden**
pages 417–421

from **Incidents in the Life of a Slave Girl**

QUICK START

Think about how you would tell the story of your life. How would you seek to portray yourself? Freewrite some adjectives that might describe yourself as presented in your autobiography.

ANALYZE LITERARY ELEMENTS

Critics have noted, not always admiringly, that Jacobs's autobiography resembles a novel. Even though the events Jacobs describes are true, she employs literary elements to tell a compelling story.

- Linda, the main character, experiences both internal and external conflicts resulting from slavery. (Jacobs wrote *Incidents in the Life of a Slave Girl* under the pseudonym Linda Brent.) An **internal conflict** is a struggle within a character. An **external conflict** is a struggle between a character and an outside force. These conflicts result in **suspense,** or excitement and tension, as readers wonder about the outcome of events.

- The point of view in which a story is told affects how readers learn about characters and events. In an autobiography, the story is told in the **first-person point of view,** and the narrator is part of the action, using pronouns such as *I, me,* and *we.* As a result, the reader's impressions come through Linda's eyes.

- This point of view influences how the narrator reveals the characters' personalities through **characterization,** which can be direct or indirect. With **direct characterization,** the writer states what a character is like, such as, "He is a friendly neighbor." In **indirect characterization,** the narrator uses subtle clues to describe a character's personality. These details may include information about the character's appearance, behavior, or manner; a character's own thoughts, words, or actions; and how other characters react to the character.

As you read, notice the writer's use of literary elements and how they relate.

ANALYZE LANGUAGE

In this autobiography, the writer's use of language shapes the way readers perceive the events of her life and the characters in her story. **Diction** is a writer's choice of words and can be formal or informal, showy, or full of slang. Another element of language to consider is **syntax,** or the way words are arranged in sentences. A writer's voice will emerge from the work's diction and syntax. For example, at the start of the excerpt the narrator says she did not do her work "with a willing mind." This word choice reveals her attitude toward her situation.

As you read the excerpt from *Incidents in the Life of a Slave Girl,* pay attention to how language shapes the reader's perception of events in the autobiography.

© Houghton Mifflin Harcourt Publishing Company

GENRE ELEMENTS: AUTOBIOGRAPHY

- is told in first-person point of view
- has setting, conflict, and characters, like a story
- may include dialogue

from Incidents in the Life of a Slave Girl   425

QUICK START

After students have read the Quick Start prompt, review the definition of *adjective* before they begin freewriting. When they have finished, invite them to share their work. Ask students to reflect on how the focus would change if someone wrote their biography, such as a parent, friend, teacher, or person with whom they have had a disagreement. Challenge students to add complexity to their autobiographies by including negative and positive adjectives.

ANALYZE LITERARY ELEMENTS

Review the definitions of literary terms with students and prepare them to identify examples of these features in the excerpt. Draw students' attention to the possible relationships between point of view and characterization. Ask them to consider why critics might not approve of the use of literary elements in this autobiography. To help students analyze the characterization of Linda in the excerpt, direct them to look at her behaviors and motivations and to analyze how her motivations and actions affect the development of the plot.

ANALYZE LANGUAGE

After reviewing the terms *diction* and *syntax* with students, direct their attention to the use of dialect in the excerpt. How does the narrator's voice compare to the voices of other characters from this excerpt? Review with students the characteristics of autobiography as a genre and ask what role they might expect diction and syntax to play in texts from different genres. How does the author's use of dialect contribute to characterization in this text? Invite students to consider how the author's language contributes to the sense that this autobiography is like a novel, as well as how these linguistic features interact with the literary elements of the text.

TEACH

CRITICAL VOCABULARY

Present students with strategies for determining the meaning of unfamiliar words, such as analyzing prefixes or identifying parts of speech. Challenge students to give examples of antonyms for the vocabulary words.

Answers:

1. *d. proposal*
2. *b. persuaded*
3. *c. encouragement*
4. *a. obligated*
5. *b. irresponsible*
6. *c. news*

■ English Learner Support

Use Cognates Tell Spanish speakers that some of the Critical Vocabulary words have Spanish cognates: *proposition/proposición, induced/inducer, provocation/provocación.* Give examples of how the words are used in English sentences. **SUBSTANTIAL**

LANGUAGE CONVENTIONS:
Dialect and Idioms

Dialect Have students work in mixed-ability groups to list as many idioms as they can within a short time limit, such as two to three minutes. Ask students to share any unfamiliar idioms offered by other members of their groups. Allow students to guess the meaning of the idiom before the answer is announced. Ask students: *Are any of these idioms associated with a particular region or dialect?*

ANNOTATION MODEL

Remind students of annotation strategies, such as underlining important ideas and circling key words, dates, or related concepts. Students may follow this suggestion or use their own system for marking up the selection in their write-in text. They may want to color-code their annotation by using highlighters. Notes in the margin may include ideas that are unclear or topics they want to learn more about.

 **GET READY**

WORD BANK
proposition　　tidings
induced　　compelled
provocation　　reckless

CRITICAL VOCABULARY

Select the answer that is a synonym for the Critical Vocabulary word.

1. **proposition**
   a. knowledge　　**b.** entertainment　　**c.** event　　**d.** proposal

2. **induced**
   a. destroyed　　**b.** persuaded　　**c.** mulled　　**d.** pleaded

3. **provocation**
   a. resolution　　**b.** conclusion　　**c.** encouragement　　**d.** explanation

4. **compelled**
   a. obligated　　**b.** allowed　　**c.** secured　　**d.** satisfied

5. **reckless**
   a. nervous　　**b.** irresponsible　　**c.** bleak　　**d.** energetic

6. **tidings**
   a. folktales　　**b.** money　　**c.** news　　**d.** trinkets

LANGUAGE CONVENTIONS: Dialect and Idioms

Dialect Dialect is a type of language spoken by people in a particular place. Writers use dialect to evoke a specific setting or to develop characters. Dialect can include specialized vocabulary words and colloquial expressions.

Writers might also use **idioms,** or expressions in which the literal meanings of the word do not add up to the actual meaning. For example, the phrase *under the weather* means "to feel sick."

ANNOTATION MODEL

NOTICE & NOTE

As you read, note the author's use of language and literary elements. In the model, you can see one reader's notes on the first paragraph of the text.

> Mr. Flint was hard pushed for house servants, and rather than lose me he had <u>restrained his malice</u>. I did my work faithfully, though not, of course, with a willing mind. They were evidently <u>afraid I should leave them</u>. Mr. Flint wished that I should sleep in the great house instead of the servants' quarters. <u>His wife agreed to the proposition</u>, but said I mustn't bring my bed into the house, because it would scatter feathers on her carpet.

There may be a conflict between Linda and Mr. Flint.

Direct: Linda says they are afraid.

Indirect: Linda hints that Mrs. Flint is obedient to her husband.

BACKGROUND

Harriet Jacobs *(1813–1897) was born into slavery in North Carolina. At age12, she was given to the daughter of Dr. James Norcom. Norcom made inappropriate advances toward Jacobs, and to avoid him she started a relationship with Samuel Sawyer ("Mr. Sands"), with whom she had two children. Norcom then sent Jacobs and her children to work elsewhere, and she made the painful decision to flee and leave her children. Sawyer bought the children to save them from plantation life, while Jacobs hid in an attic for seven years before escaping to New York. In 1861, she published her account under the name Linda Brent.*

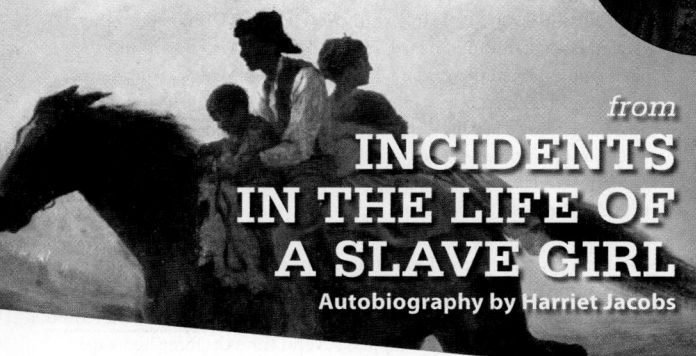

from
INCIDENTS IN THE LIFE OF A SLAVE GIRL
Autobiography by Harriet Jacobs

PREPARE TO COMPARE

As you read, pay attention to the first-person point of view and how it affects the characterization of the people in the narrator's life. Note details that show how Linda's motivations and actions affect plot development.

The Flight

1 MR. FLINT was hard pushed for house servants, and rather than lose me he had restrained his malice. I did my work faithfully, though not, of course, with a willing mind. They were evidently afraid I should leave them. Mr. Flint wished that I should sleep in the great house instead of the servants' quarters. His wife agreed to the **proposition**, but said I mustn't bring my bed into the house, because it would scatter feathers on her carpet. I knew when I went there that they would never think of such a thing as furnishing a bed of any kind for me and my little one. I therefore carried my own bed, and now I was forbidden to use it. I did as I was ordered. But now that I was certain my children were to be put in their power, in order to give them a stronger hold on me, I resolved to leave them that night. I remembered the grief this step would bring upon my dear old

> **Notice & Note**
>
> Use the side margins to notice and note signposts in the text.
>
> ---
>
> **proposition**
> (prŏp-ə-zĭsh´ən) *n.* a plan suggested for acceptance; a proposal.

BACKGROUND

The female slave narrative was intended to influence white northern middle-class women. Many of the trials that Jacobs endures, such as separation from her children, resonated with white women who cared for their own children and saw themselves as the protectors of morality. This slave narrative's purpose was to cause white women to empathize with slave women and to recognize that slavery was immoral.

PREPARE TO COMPARE

Direct students to use the Prepare to Compare prompt to focus their reading.

CRITICAL VOCABULARY

proposition: Mrs. Flint likes her husband's idea, but makes one modification to his proposition: Linda must not bring her bed into the great house.

ASK STUDENTS to describe Mr. Flint's proposition and its effects on Linda. *(Mr. Flint proposes that Linda sleep in the house, and Linda realizes that she won't be able to bring her bed in or stay near her children.)*

 **ANALYZE LITERARY ELEMENTS**

Remind students of the distinction between direct and indirect characterization and guide them to look for the sentence in paragraph 3 that most directly describes what the narrator thinks of Sally. (**Answer:** *She uses direct characterization to show that Sally is trustworthy and that Linda can count on her.*)

 **LANGUAGE CONVENTIONS**

Suggest that students use graphic organizers to keep track of the relationships between the characters. Encourage students to reflect on the questions: *What is the relationship between Sally and Linda's grandmother? How does this affect our reading of Sally's idiomatic language here?* (**Answer:** *She is worried that Linda will make things worse if she runs away, so she is trying to tell Linda not to add to her troubles.*)

CRITICAL VOCABULARY

induced: It was not easy to persuade Linda to go against her grandmother's advice; it took the threat of her children being used against her to induce her to flee.

ASK STUDENTS how this change in Linda's circumstance induced her to risk everything to escape from Mr. Flint. (*Linda realizes that Mr. Flint might use her children to get her to do what he wants, and resolves to leave.*)

NOTICE & NOTE

induced
(ĭn-dōōst´) *v.* led or moved, as to a course of action, by influence or persuasion.

ANALYZE LITERARY ELEMENTS

Annotate: Mark the sentence in paragraph 3 that gives Linda's characterization of Sally.

Interpret: How does Linda characterize her?

LANGUAGE CONVENTIONS

Annotate: Mark a colloquial idiom that Sally uses in the last sentence of paragraph 3.

Analyze: What does this phrase add to your knowledge of Sally?

---

grandmother; and nothing less than the freedom of my children would have **induced** me to disregard her advice. I went about my evening work with trembling steps. Mr. Flint twice called from his chamber door to inquire why the house was not locked up. I replied that I had not done my work. "You have had time enough to do it," said he. "Take care how you answer me!"

2   I shut all the windows, locked all the doors, and went up to the third story, to wait till midnight. How long those hours seemed, and how fervently I prayed that God would not forsake me in this hour of utmost need! I was about to risk everything on the throw of a die; and if I failed, O what would become of me and my poor children? They would be made to suffer for my fault.

3   At half past twelve I stole softly down stairs. I stopped on the second floor, thinking I heard a noise. I felt my way down into the parlor, and looked out of the window. The night was so intensely dark that I could see nothing. I raised the window very softly and jumped out. Large drops of rain were falling, and the darkness bewildered me. I dropped on my knees, and breathed a short prayer to God for guidance and protection. I groped my way to the road, and rushed towards the town with almost lightning speed. I arrived at my grandmother's house, but dared not see her. She would say, "Linda, you are killing me;" and I knew that would unnerve me. I tapped softly at the window of a room, occupied by a woman, who had lived in the house several years. I knew she was a faithful friend, and could be trusted with my secret. I tapped several times before she heard me. At last she raised the window, and I whispered, "Sally, I have run away. Let me in, quick." She opened the door softly, and said in low tones, "For God's sake, don't. Your grandmother is trying to buy you and de chillern. Mr. Sands was here last week. He tole her he was going away on business, but he wanted her to go ahead about buying you and de chillern, and he would help her all he could. Don't run away, Linda. Your grandmother is all bowed down wid trouble now."

4   I replied, "Sally, they are going to carry my children to the plantation tomorrow; and they will never sell them to any body so long as they have me in their power. Now, would you advise me to go back?"

5   "No, chile, no," answered she. "When dey finds you is gone, dey won't want de plague[1] ob de chillern; but where is you going to hide? Dey knows ebery inch ob dis house."

6   I told her I had a hiding-place, and that was all it was best for her to know. I asked her to go into my room as soon as it was light, and take all my clothes out of my trunk, and pack them in hers; for I knew Mr. Flint and the constable would be there early to search my room. I feared the sight of my children would be too much for my full heart; but I could not go out into the uncertain future without one last look. I bent over the bed where lay my little Benny and baby Ellen.

---

[1] **plague:** nuisance.

Poor little ones! fatherless and motherless! Memories of their father came over me. He wanted to be kind to them; but they were not all to him, as they were to my womanly heart. I knelt and prayed for the innocent little sleepers. I kissed them lightly, and turned away.

7   As I was about to open the street door, Sally laid her hand on my shoulder, and said, "Linda, is you gwine all alone? Let me call your uncle."

8   "No, Sally," I replied, "I want no one to be brought into trouble on my account."

9   I went forth into the darkness and rain. I ran on till I came to the house of the friend who was to conceal me.

10   Early the next morning Mr. Flint was at my grandmother's inquiring for me. She told him she had not seen me, and supposed I was at the plantation. He watched her face narrowly, and said, "Don't you know any thing about her running off?" She assured him that she did not. He went on to say, "Last night she ran off without the least **provocation**. We had treated her very kindly. My wife liked her. She will soon be found and brought back. Are her children with you?" When told that they were, he said, "I am very glad to hear that. If they are here, she cannot be far off. If I find out that any of my niggers have had any thing to do with this damned business, I'll give

ANALYZE LITERARY ELEMENTS

Annotate: Mark the phrases Linda uses in paragraph 10 to characterize Mr. Flint when he talks to her grandmother.

Evaluate: What type of characterization is this, and what do the phrases show about Mr. Flint?

provocation
(prŏv-ə-kāˊshən) *n.* the act of provoking or inciting.

IMPROVE READING FLUENCY

Targeted Passage   In paragraph 10, *narrowly* means "closely" or carefully" Mr. Flint is looking for any hints to Linda's whereabouts. Explain to students that when they encounter a multiple-meaning word, they should examine the surrounding words to determine which meaning the writer used. To give students an example, point out the multiple-meaning word *die* in paragraph 2. Write possible meanings of *die* on the board. Tell students that the words *throw of a* are clues to the correct meaning of *die*. Ask students which meaning is used in this sentence.

 Go to the **Reading Studio** for additional support in developing fluency.

ANALYZE LITERARY ELEMENTS

Remind students of the difference between direct and indirect characterization. Guide them to consider the contrast between Linda's characterization of Mr. Flint and the motivations he claims to hold. (**Answer:** *Indirect characterization is the use of subtle clues to reveal a character's personality. These clues show that he does not trust the grandmother to be truthful and that he tries to manipulate her by pretending to be kind.*)

For **reading support** for students at varying proficiency levels, see the **Text X-Ray** on page 424D.

CRITICAL VOCABULARY

provocation: Mr. Flint claims not to understand Linda's motivation for leaving, saying that he and his wife have done nothing to provoke such a drastic action.

ASK STUDENTS what provocation ultimately caused Linda to flee Mr. Flint. (*He was threatening the freedom of her children by moving them into the great house.*)

'em five hundred lashes." As he started to go to his father's, he turned round and added, persuasively, "Let her be brought back, and she shall have her children to live with her."

11   The **tidings** made the old doctor rave and storm at a furious rate. It was a busy day for them. My grandmother's house was searched from top to bottom. As my trunk was empty, they concluded I had taken my clothes with me. Before ten o'clock every vessel northward bound was thoroughly examined, and the law against harboring[2] fugitives was read to all on board. At night a watch was set over the town. Knowing how distressed my grandmother would be, I wanted to send her a message; but it could not be done. Every one who went in or out of her house was closely watched. The doctor said he would take my children, unless she became responsible for them; which of course she willingly did. The next day was spent in searching. Before

tidings
(tī′dĭngs) *pl.n.* information or news.

---

[2] **harboring:** sheltering or protecting.

TO CHALLENGE STUDENTS...

Synthesize Remind students that the law against harboring fugitives was read to every northbound ship (paragraph 11). Have students research to learn about fugitive slave laws. Ask students to write a short paragraph that might have been read aboard these ships. Encourage pairs to share their paragraphs with the class. Ask them to explain what would probably have happened to Linda had she been found.

CRITICAL VOCABULARY

tidings: The tidings from Mr. Flint infuriate the old doctor.

ASK STUDENTS what these tidings were that caused the doctor's reaction. (*news of Linda's departure*)

night, the following advertisement was posted at every corner, and in every public place for miles round:—

12   *$300 REWARD! Ran away from the subscriber,[3] an intelligent, bright, mulatto[4] girl, named Linda, 21 years of age. Five feet four inches high. Dark eyes, and black hair inclined to curl; but it can be made straight. Has a decayed spot on a front tooth. She can read and write, and in all probability will try to get to the Free States. All persons are forbidden, under penalty of the law, to harbor or employ said slave. $150 will be given to whoever takes her in the state, and $300 if taken out of the state and delivered to me, or lodged in jail. DR. FLINT.*

For a week, Linda hides in the house of an unnamed friend. Her pursuers come so close to finding her that she rushes from the house into the bushes, where she is bitten by a poisonous snake or lizard. She suffers greatly until an old woman treats her with a folk remedy. Vowing "give me liberty or death," she refuses to return to the Flints. Then a sympathetic white woman, an old friend of her grandmother's, offers to conceal Linda in a small storage room in her house. The woman makes them promise never to tell, as she is the wife of a prominent slaveholder. The woman sends her cook, Linda's friend Betty, to meet Linda and take her to the house.

Months of Peril

13 I went to sleep that night with the feeling that I was for the present the most fortunate slave in town. Morning came and filled my little cell with light. I thanked the heavenly Father for this safe retreat. Opposite my window was a pile of feather beds. On the top of these I could lie perfectly concealed, and command a view of the street through which Dr. Flint passed to his office. Anxious as I was, I felt a gleam of satisfaction when I saw him. Thus far I had outwitted him, and I triumphed over it. Who can blame slaves for being cunning? They are constantly **compelled** to resort to it. It is the only weapon of the weak and oppressed against the strength of their tyrants.

14   I was daily hoping to hear that my master had sold my children; for I knew who was on the watch to buy them. But Dr. Flint cared even more for revenge than he did for money. My brother William, and the good aunt who had served in his family twenty years, and my little Benny, and Ellen, who was a little over two years old, were thrust into jail, as a means of compelling my relatives to give some information about me. He swore my grandmother should never see one of them again till I was brought back. They kept these facts from me for several days. When I heard that my little ones

---

[3] **the subscriber:** the person placing the notice, Dr. Flint.
[4] **mulatto:** of mixed black and white ancestry.

ANALYZE LANGUAGE

Annotate: Mark Linda's diction in paragraph 13 that describes her actions.

Evaluate: How does Linda's language shape your perception of her?

compelled
(kəm-pĕld´) *v.* forced (a person) to do something; drove or constrained.

▶ TOUGH QUESTIONS

Annotate: Mark details in paragraph 14 that tell you what happened to Linda's family.

Analyze: What inner struggle does Linda face at this point in the story?

from Incidents in the Life of a Slave Girl   431

WHEN STUDENTS STRUGGLE . . .

Understand Characterization Urge students to read paragraph 13 and visualize the scene Linda describes and identify how they feel about her. Then, remind them that characterization is built from descriptions of a character's words, actions, and attitude. Help them complete a chart to identify information about Linda that created their response.

  For additional support, go to the **Reading Studio** and assign the following **Level Up Tutorial: Character Traits.**

© Houghton Mifflin Harcourt Publishing Company

ANALYZE LANGUAGE

Review the definition of *diction* with students and direct them to look for language in paragraph 13 that indicates a common theme. Ask students to consider the role Linda's diction plays in persuading the reader against judgment of her "cunning" actions in this passage. (**Answer:** *She is grateful for having a refuge and safety. She is clever, courageous, and determined to be free.*)

▶ TOUGH QUESTIONS

Remind students of the distinction between internal and external conflict. Guide them to analyze the information in paragraph 14 according to whether the conflicts Linda experiences are internal or external. Ask students to compare the type of conflict introduced here with those presented in the first paragraph of the excerpt. (**Answer:** *Linda is faced with an internal conflict. She must face the consequences her escape will have for her family, and the difficulty of leaving her children behind.*)

CRITICAL VOCABULARY

compelled: In order to protect her children, Linda is compelled by her circumstances to risk everything in a chance for escape.

ASK STUDENTS why Linda feels the need to defend her actions in this passage, saying that she and other slaves are compelled to resort to cunning regardless of what they might prefer. (*The purpose of the narrative is to gain the sympathy of readers and encourage them to oppose slavery.*)

reckless
(rĕk´lĭs) *adj.* heedless or careless, rash.

were in a loathsome jail, my first impulse was to go to them. I was encountering dangers for the sake of freeing them, and must I be the cause of their death? The thought was agonizing. My benefactress[5] tried to soothe me by telling me that my aunt would take good care of the children while they remained in jail. But it added to my pain to think that the good old aunt, who had always been so kind to her sister's orphan children, should be shut up in prison for no other crime than loving them. I suppose my friends feared a **reckless** movement on my part, knowing, as they did, that my life was bound up in my children. I received a note from my brother William. It was scarcely legible, and ran thus: "Wherever you are, dear sister, I beg of you not to come here. We are all much better off than you are. If you come, you will ruin us all. They would force you to tell where you had been, or they would kill you. Take the advice of your friends; if not for the sake of me and your children, at least for the sake of those you would ruin."

15   Poor William! He also must suffer for being my brother. I took his advice and kept quiet. My aunt was taken out of jail at the end of a month, because Mrs. Flint could not spare her any longer. She was tired of being her own housekeeper. It was quite too fatiguing to order her dinner and eat it too. My children remained in jail, where brother William did all he could for their comfort. Betty went to see them sometimes, and brought me tidings. She was not permitted to

---

[5] **benefactress:** a woman who gives aid.

CRITICAL VOCABULARY

reckless: Linda realizes that many people thought her behavior was reckless.

ASK STUDENTS why William thinks it would be reckless for Linda to come to him. (*It would put him and Linda's children in danger.*)

enter the jail; but William would hold them up to the grated window while she chatted with them. When she repeated their prattle, and told me how they wanted to see their ma, my tears would flow. Old Betty would exclaim, "Lors, chile! what's you crying 'bout? Dem young uns vil kill you dead. Don't be so chick'n hearted! If you does, you vil nebber git thro' dis world."

NOTICE & NOTE

LANGUAGE CONVENTIONS
Annotate: Mark the words in paragraph 15 that appear to be dialect.

Draw Conclusions: Why do you think Linda includes the dialect spoken by Betty?

CHECK YOUR UNDERSTANDING

Answer these questions before moving on to the **Analyze the Text** section on the following page.

1 What prompts Linda to make the decision to escape?

A She learns that her grandmother is going to be moving away.

B She is told by Mrs. Flint she cannot move her bed into the family's house.

C She learns the Flints are going to take her children in order to control her.

D She overhears the Flints deciding that they are going to sell her.

2 What of the following actions do the Flints *not* take after they find out Linda has left?

F They search her grandmother's house and northbound ships.

G They send people north to find out where she is.

H They offer a reward for her capture.

J They jail her relatives.

3 Why does Linda want the Flints to sell her children?

A She want Mr. Sands to buy them so they can be with their father.

B She thinks another owner will treat them with more kindness.

C She wants them to learn other skills at another household.

D She believes other owners will allow them to have freedom.

from Incidents in the Life of a Slave Girl   433

TEACH

LANGUAGE CONVENTIONS

Direct students to consider the specific circumstances in which the author includes dialect. How does the use of dialect contribute to characterization? Students may wish to make a chart that describes the language and style of each character in order to understand the role of dialect in characterization. (**Answer:** *Using the actual language Betty spoke adds realism to her character and to the 19th-century slavery era setting.*)

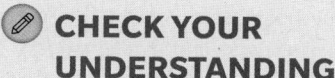 For **listening support** for students at varying proficiency levels, see the **Text X-Ray** on page 424C.

CHECK YOUR UNDERSTANDING

Have students answer the questions independently.

Answers:

1. C

2. G

3. A

If they answer any questions incorrectly, have them reread the text to confirm their understanding. Then they may proceed to ANALYZE THE TEXT on page 434.

ENGLISH LEARNER SUPPORT

Oral Assessment Use the following questions to assess students' comprehension and speaking skills.

1. Why does Linda decide to escape? *(because the Flints will use her children to control her)*

2. When Linda leaves, what do the Flints *not* do? *(send people north to find her)*

3. Why does Linda want the Flints to sell her children? *(She hopes their father will buy them.)*
SUBSTANTIAL/MODERATE

ANALYZE THE TEXT

Possible answers:

1. **DOK 4:** *Paragraph 1: She is hardworking. Paragraph 6: She loves her children deeply. Paragraph 8: She is considerate of others and takes responsibility for her own actions.*

2. **DOK 2:** *She describes the Flints as blind to their own cruelty, unfeeling, and selfish, and herself as a loving mother and oppressed victim.*

3. **DOK 2:** *He can't imagine that the threat of putting her children to work would upset and provoke Linda. He doesn't view Linda as having a mother's normal feelings, but rather sees her as a disobedient possession.*

4. **DOK 4:** *Students may say that Jacobs's emotional style contributes to the power of her work and enables readers to feel anger. Others may say the use of slave dialect robs these characters of dignity.*

5. **DOK 4:** *Linda faces a variety of conflicts, including the effect her behavior has on herself, her children, and others. These conflicts show the cruelty of slavery.*

RESEARCH

Encourage students to look at a variety of types of websites to determine the popularity of a text. Students could use articles, reviews, and book sales sites to gather their information.

Connect As students research different slave narratives, remind them to also research and take into consideration the author's background. Some slave narratives may be autobiographical accounts, others may be second-hand stories or biographies. Ask students to take note of the different types of authorship as they research.

RESPOND

ANALYZE THE TEXT

Support your responses with evidence from the text. NOTEBOOK

1. **Analyze** How does the writer present herself? Discuss what you learn about her character and values from her attitude toward work (paragraph 1), her thoughts as she visits her children (paragraph 6), and her insistence upon escaping alone (paragraph 8).

2. **Summarize** Contrast the writer's portrayal of herself with her portrayal of the Flints. What does she reveal about the Flints' character and values?

3. **Interpret** A writer's use of language can shape the way readers perceive events and characters. What does Mr. Flint's remark that Linda ran off "without the least provocation" tell you about him (paragraph 10)? How does he view Linda?

4. **Evaluate** When writers create a work for a particular audience, it can influence which details they include. How might the knowledge that she was writing for a primarily northern, white audience have influenced Jacobs's characterizations?

5. **Notice & Note** Describe the different conflicts that Linda faces in this excerpt. What do these conflicts reveal about the institution of slavery and the sacrifices forced by it?

RESEARCH TIP
You can find a lot of information about a book title on book review sites. They sometimes recommend works similar to that title.

RESEARCH

Slave narratives comprised a popular genre in 19th-century American literature. Do some research to find out what some of the most popular titles were and what the stories were about.

TITLE	SUMMARY

Connect Compare one of the titles you researched to the excerpt you just read. What similarities do they share? You may focus on events, character, or the writer's attitude.

© Houghton Mifflin Harcourt Publishing Company

WHEN STUDENTS STRUGGLE . . .

Reteach: Diction and Syntax Review the meanings of the terms *diction* and *syntax*. Point to examples in the text, illustrating how diction and syntax are related to dialect. Ask the students to think about the ways they talk, such as using the words "like" and "you know" regularly when they speak. Have students try to re-write a few of the author's sentences using their own diction, incorporating colloquial words and contemporary slang from their own vocabulary.

For additional support, go to the **Reading Studio** and assign the following LEVEL UP **Level Up Tutorial: Author's Style.**

CREATE AND DISCUSS

Write an Autobiographical Sketch Write a three- or four-paragraph autobiographical sketch about an incident from your own life using the literary elements that you learned about on page 425. Remember that—though Jacobs was writing a nonfiction account about true events and people—she chose to write her autobiography using elements of fiction to create a more compelling story. Review your notes about characterization before you begin.

- ❏ Write in first-person point of view, using pronouns like *I* and *me*.
- ❏ Use direct or indirect characterization to reveal the personality of characters in your sketch.

Share and Discuss In a small group, discuss the autobiographical sketch you chose to write. Which personality traits did you reveal in your characters? How did the story change as a result?

- ❏ Discuss the characters in your sketch and answer any questions others might have about them.
- ❏ Finally, see if other group members have suggestions to help you improve your sketch.

 Go to **Writing Narratives: Point of View and Characters** in the **Writing Studio** for help with writing a narrative.

 Go to **Participating in Collaborative Discussions** in the **Speaking and Listening Studio** for help.

RESPOND TO THE ESSENTIAL QUESTION

? What divides us as human beings?

Gather Information Review your annotations and notes on the excerpt from *Incidents in the Life of a Slave Girl*. Then, add relevant details to your Response Log. As you determine which information to include, think about:

- the writer's description of other characters
- the internal and external conflicts that the writer faces
- what separates the writer from other characters in the text

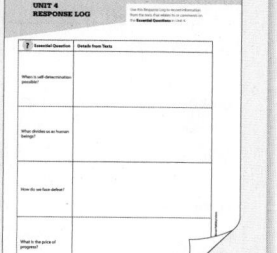

ACADEMIC VOCABULARY
As you write and discuss what you learned from the excerpt from *Incidents in the Life of a Slave Girl*, be sure to use the Academic Vocabulary words. Check off each of the words that you use.

- ❏ confirm
- ❏ definitely
- ❏ deny
- ❏ format
- ❏ unify

APPLY

CREATE AND DISCUSS

Write an Autobiographical Sketch As they write, remind students to include sensory detail in their texts. Encourage them to think about other intense experiences they have had, and what they remember feeling, tasting, smelling, or hearing during those experiences. Tell students that description is stronger when more than one sense is used. Strong description draws readers into the text and helps them experience the story more vividly.

Share and Discuss Characters Encourage students to be open to feedback from their peers. Each student should work to say one complimentary thing about their peers' work, and give one suggestion for making it stronger. Model positive language for giving constructive feedback.

For **writing and speaking support** for students at varying proficiency levels, see the **Text X-Ray** on page 424D.

RESPOND TO THE ESSENTIAL QUESTION

Allow time for students to add details from the excerpt from *Incidents in the Life of a Slave Girl* to their Unit 4 Response Logs.

CRITICAL VOCABULARY

Answers:

1. *induced*

2. *reckless*

3. *proposition*

4. *compelled*

5. *tidings*

6. *provocation*

VOCABULARY STRATEGY:
Synonyms

Ask students to give examples from their lives of words or phrases that can have different connotations and denotations. Encourage them to discuss how these differences can lead to misunderstandings between people.

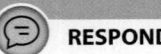 **RESPOND**

WORD BANK

proposition	tidings
induced	compelled
provocation	reckless

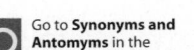 Go to **Synonyms and Antonyms** in the **Vocabulary Studio** for help.

CRITICAL VOCABULARY

Practice and Apply For each of the following words, list the vocabulary word that is the most opposite in meaning. Discuss your answers with a partner.

1. discouraged _____

2. cautious _____

3. refusal _____

4. blocked _____

5. silence _____

6. compliment _____

VOCABULARY STRATEGY: Synonyms

Synonyms are words that have the same or almost the same meaning. There can be shades of meanings between synonyms. Many words have two kinds of meaning. There's the **denotative meaning,** or dictionary definition, and the **connotative meaning,** which is a feeling or tone associated with it. For example, *giggle* and *snicker* both mean "to laugh," but *snicker* has the connotation of a mean type of laughter.

Practice and Apply To learn more about the Critical Vocabulary words, fill out the following chart with a synonym for each word and its connotation. If you need to, check your work with a dictionary or thesaurus.

WORD	SYNONYM	CONNOTATION
proposition	*scheme*	*plan of action*
induced	*coaxed*	*persuaded one to comply*
provocation	*incitement*	*cause or reason for behaving a certain way*
tidings	*communication*	*messages, greetings, possibly good wishes*
compelled	*coerce*	*required or forced by circumstance*
reckless	*devil-may-care*	*behaving without thought or concern for others*

 ENGLISH LEARNER SUPPORT

Practice Pronunciation Point to each of the vocabulary words and say each aloud, modeling correct pronunciation. Have the students repeat the words after you. Help students with tricky sounds and pronunciations such as the following:

- *proposition, provocation:* the last syllable is pronounced /shun/
- *induced:* the final sound is pronounced /t/
- *compelled:* the final sound is pronounced /d/
- *reckless:* the *ck* is pronounced /k/
  SUBSTANTIAL

LANGUAGE CONVENTIONS: Dialect and Idioms

Dialect is a way of speaking that is particular to a specific area or group of people. Jacobs's use of dialect allows her to portray her characters with authenticity. Her autobiography provides a glimpse into her community in North Carolina during the early years of the 19th century. Writers often spell dialect the way it would be pronounced and use nonstandard English to capture characters and make them appear authentic.

> Lors, chile! what's you crying 'bout. Dem young uns vil kill you dead. Don't be so chick'n hearted!

Standard English: "Lord, child! What are you crying about? Those kids will get you killed. Don't be so scared!

Idioms are common expressions where the literal meanings of the words are not the same as the actual meaning. For example, the idiom "it's raining cats and dogs" means that it is raining heavily; cats and dogs aren't actually falling from the sky. Take a look at the following example of an idiom from *Incidents in the Life of a Slave Girl*, and think about what the words actually mean compared to their literal definition.

> I was about to risk everything on the throw of a die.

Actual Meaning: I was about to do something really risky, gambling with my life in a game of chance.

Practice and Apply Answer the following questions about idioms and dialect.

1. Linda imagines her grandmother saying, "Linda, you are killing me." What does she mean by this idiom?

2. In the following chart, write the dialogue as it would be said in standard English.

DIALECT	STANDARD ENGLISH
Your grandmother is all bowed down wid trouble now.	*Your grandmother is burdened with troubles now.*
When dey finds you is gone, dey won't want de plague ob de chillern.	*When they find out you are gone, they won't want the trouble of the children.*
Dey knows ebery inch ob dis house.	*They know every inch of this house.*
Linda, is you gwine all alone?	*Linda, are you going all alone?*
If you does, you vil nebber git thro' dis world.	*If you do, you will never get through this world.*

LANGUAGE CONVENTIONS:
Dialect and Idioms

As students read for different dialects and use of idioms, encourage them to look for signposts such as use of apostrophes, words that seem misspelled, and sayings that don't seem to fit the rest of the content. These markers will help students pick out the instances of dialect and various idioms used throughout the text. Have students underline or highlight examples as they go back through the selection.

Practice and Apply As they read the sentences, tell students that when they are having trouble figuring out a piece of dialect, reading the word or phrase aloud can help them understand the standard English counterpart.

from Incidents in the Life of a Slave Girl   437

COMPARE WRITER'S VOICE

Before students begin, have them revisit their notes about author's background, genre, voice, and tone from the two selections. This will help them to come prepared to their small group discussion and will give them material for completing the diagram.

ANALYZE THE TEXTS

Possible answers:

1. **DOK 4:** *In Hayden's poetry, he gives each speaker a distinct persona, which is shown in rhythm or with word choices. For example, he uses different words for running, with no punctuation, to show a scared fugitive slave. For a brave, confident speaker like Harriet Tubman, he uses strong, positive words. In Jacobs's autobiography, she shows her voice as Linda by using first-person point of view and characterization. Much of Linda's voice is also shown in her diction and syntax.*

2. **DOK 2:** *In Hayden's poetry, the speakers aren't named. They are just personas. In Jacobs's autobiography, each character represents a real person in her life.*

3. **DOK 4:** *Hayden lived later and might have wanted to give just a snapshot of slavery and what feelings might be associated with it, so poetry was a good fit for him. Jacobs lived through slavery and probably wanted to share her true story, so an autobiography made sense.*

4. **DOK 3:** *Hayden—"And before I'll be a slave / I'll be buried in my grave." Jacobs—"Who can blame slaves for being cunning? They are constantly compelled to resort to it. It is the only weapon of the weak and oppressed against the strength of their tyrants."*

RESPOND

Collaborate & Compare

POEM
RUNAGATE RUNAGATE
by Robert Hayden

AUTOBIOGRAPHY
from **INCIDENTS IN THE LIFE OF A SLAVE GIRL**
by Harriet Jacobs

COMPARE WRITER'S VOICE

When you compare how a literary element is treated in multiple texts on the same topic, you synthesize the information, making connections and extending key ideas. It's easier to do this when the texts you're comparing are the same genre, such as two poems. But you can get a more thorough understanding of the topic by comparing texts from different genres, such as a poem and an autobiography.

In a small group, complete the Venn diagram with similarities and differences between the writer's voices in the two texts you read. One example is completed for you.

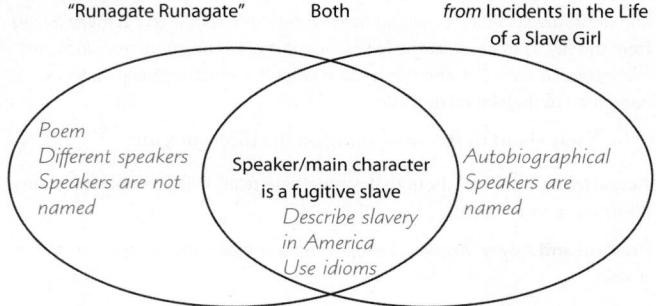

"Runagate Runagate"   Both   *from* Incidents in the Life of a Slave Girl

Poem
Different speakers
Speakers are not named

Speaker/main character is a fugitive slave
Describe slavery in America
Use idioms

Autobiographical
Speakers are named

ANALYZE THE TEXTS

Discuss these questions in your group.

1. **Analyze** How does each author use word choice to portray the speakers or characters in their works?

2. **Contrast** What differences are there between the two works?

3. **Evaluate** Why do you think each author chose their particular genre to convey their impressions of slavery?

4. **Cite Evidence** Both writers strongly condemn slavery. Find an example from each work that shows their feelings.

ENGLISH LEARNER SUPPORT

Ask Questions Use the following questions to help students compare and contrast the two texts utilizing what they learned from earlier activities.

1. What are some of the main differences between these two styles of writing?

2. How do the two authors use voice differently? Do both authors change voice within the selections?

3. What are some examples from the writing that show the authors' feelings about slavery?
MODERATE/LIGHT

RESEARCH AND SHARE

Now, your group can continue exploring the ideas in these texts by collaborating on research to share in a group presentation. Follow these steps:

1. **Find Sources** Though the texts you read are from different genres, each contains a strong message against slavery. Build on what you know about slavery by seeking out at least two more sources on the topic from other genres. You may consider a work of fiction such as *Uncle Tom's Cabin* by Harriet Beecher Stowe, an informational text, or a primary source.

2. **Gather Information** Gather information from each source on the topic of slavery, including the view of why it is unjust.
   - ❑ Think about what important ideas on slavery are presented in each text. Note the significant details that support these ideas.
   - ❑ As you read each additional source, consider if this introduces new information to what you already know. Reflect on what you have learned and adjust your understanding as needed.

TEXT	IDEAS ABOUT SLAVERY	EXAMPLES
"Runagate Runagate"		
from Incidents in the Life of a Slave Girl		

3. **Synthesize** Now that you have gathered information, synthesize what you have learned. Has a strong message about slavery emerged from what you read? Think about whether you have a new understanding of the topic.

4. **Share What You Learn** How will you share your ideas with the class? Listen to what others have to say, ask questions to request and clarify information, and build on the ideas of others as you discuss your findings.

RESEARCH TIP

Simply searching for the term *slavery* will give you unfocused results. Consider adding the genre or a historical period to your search term to get more targeted results.

Collaborate & Compare **439**

RESEARCH AND SHARE

Remind students to double-check their resources carefully, and make sure to think carefully on the "sensitivity" portion of Step 2.

1. **Find Sources** Primary sources on slavery, including images and documents, are readily available online. Remind students to search for information from reliable sources such as universities and libraries.

2. **Gather Information** Encourage students to look beyond the surface of their sources and try to imagine what the perspective and experience of the slave might have been. Students can refer directly to relevant information in both selections to aid their imagination.

3. **Synthesize** Have students combine the views and examples they have gathered with their prior knowledge in order to develop their understanding of slavery.

4. **Share What You Learn** Have students divide up responsibilities and each take on a part of the presentation and preparation. Each student should participate in either the sharing or the question answering.

WHEN STUDENTS STRUGGLE . . .

Find Sources Encourage students to discuss how they might search for websites containing information about slavery. Ask students what search terms they might use and write them on the board. *(Examples: slave, runaway, primary sources, images)* Discuss the importance of using websites that are credible, or believable. For example, a text that is on a government website such as the Library of Congress is more likely to be credible than a website created by an individual person.

READER'S CHOICE

Setting a Purpose Have students review their Unit 4 Response Logs and think about what they've already learned about the continuing work of bringing freedom and justice to all members of American society. As they choose their Independent Reading selections, encourage them to consider what more they want to know.

NOTICE NOTE

Explain that some selections may contain multiple signposts; others may contain only one. And the same type of signpost can occur many times in the same text.

 LEARNING MINDSET

Persistence Encourage students not to give up when something is challenging. Remind them that challenges are a part of learning, and we can often learn as much from our failures or mistakes as from our successes.

 INDEPENDENT READING

? **ESSENTIAL QUESTIONS:**

Review the four Essential Questions for this unit on page 325.

Reader's Choice

Setting a Purpose Select one or more of these options from your eBook to continue your exploration of the Essential Questions.

- Read the descriptions to see which text grabs your interest.
- Think about which genres you enjoy reading.

Notice Note

In this unit, you practiced noticing and noting the signposts and asking big questions about nonfiction. As you read independently, these signposts and others will aid your understanding. Below are the anchor questions to ask when you read literature and nonfiction.

Reading Literature: Stories, Poems, and Plays	
Signpost	**Anchor Question**
Contrasts and Contradictions	Why did the character act that way?
Aha Moment	How might this change things?
Tough Questions	What does this make me wonder about?
Words of the Wiser	What's the lesson for the character?
Again and Again	Why might the author keep bringing this up?
Memory Moment	Why is this memory important?

Reading Nonfiction: Essays, Articles, and Arguments	
Signpost	**Anchor Question(s)**
Big Questions	What surprised me? What did the author think I already knew? What challenged, changed, or confirmed what I already knew?
Contrasts and Contradictions	What is the difference, and why does it matter?
Extreme or Absolute Language	Why did the author use this language?
Numbers and Stats	Why did the author use these numbers or amounts?
Quoted Words	Why was this person quoted or cited, and what did this add?
Word Gaps	Do I know this word from someplace else? Does it seem like technical talk for this topic? Do clues in the sentence help me understand the word?

 ENGLISH LEARNER SUPPORT

Develop Fluency Select a passage from the text that matches students' reading abilities. Read the passage aloud while students follow along silently.

- Give students time to read the passage silently before you read it to them. Then, have students read the passage several times on their own. Check their comprehension by asking yes/no questions about the passage. **SUBSTANTIAL**

- Have students read the passage silently, noting any words they do not know. Then, have them look up those words before they reread the

selection. Check their comprehension by asking questions about the passage that can be answered with a few words. **MODERATE**

- Allow more fluent readers to select their own texts. Set a specific time for students to read silently (for example, 30 minutes). Check their comprehension by having them outline what they have read. **LIGHT**

 Go to the **Reading Studio** for additional support in developing fluency.

You can preview these texts in Unit 4 of your eBook.

Then, check off the text or texts that you select to read on your own.

LETTER

Letter to Sarah Ballou
Sullivan Ballou

What does a Civil War officer write to his wife when he is not sure of surviving an upcoming battle?

DIARY

from **A Diary from Dixie**
Mary Chesnut

How does a wealthy southern woman respond to the South's imminent defeat in the Civil War?

SPEECH

from **What to the Slave Is the Fourth of July?**
Frederick Douglass

How should a former slave respond to the celebration of freedom while many are still enslaved?

SPIRITUALS

Go Down, Moses

Follow the Drinking Gourd

Swing Low, Sweet Chariot

Experience the longing and hopefulness of enslaved people through the words of three traditional spirituals.

POEM

Imagine the Angels of Bread
Martín Espada

Can the experience of injustice and suffering lead to hope and inspire action?

Collaborate and Share   With a partner, discuss what you learned from at least one of your independent readings.

• Give a brief synopsis or summary of the text.

• Describe any signposts that you noticed in the text and explain what they revealed to you.

• Describe what you most enjoyed or found most challenging about the text. Give specific examples.

• Decide if you would recommend the text to others. Why or why not?

 Go to the **Reading Studio** for more resources on **Notice & Note.**

INDEPENDENT READING

MATCHING STUDENTS TO TEXTS

Use the following information to guide students in choosing their texts.

Letter to Sarah Ballou   **Lexile: 1230L**
   Genre: letter
   Overall Rating: Accessible

from **A Diary from Dixie**   **Lexile: 680L**
   Genre: diary
   Overall Rating: Accessible

from **What to the Slave Is the Fourth of July?**   **Lexile: 1200L**
   Genre: speech
   Overall Rating: Challenging

Go Down, Moses
Follow the Drinking Gourd
Swing Low, Sweet Chariot
   Genre: spirituals
   Overall Rating: Accessible

Imagine the Angels of Bread
   Genre: poem
   Overall Rating: Challenging

Collaborate and Share   To assess how well students read the selections, walk around the room and listen to their conversations. Encourage students to be focused and specific in their comments.

 Online **for Assessment**

• Independent Reading Selection Tests

 Encourage students to visit the **Reading Studio** to download a handy bookmark of **NOTICE & NOTE** signposts.

WHEN STUDENTS STRUGGLE...

Keep a Reading Log   As students read their selected texts, have them keep a reading log for each selection to note signposts and their thoughts about them. Use their logs to assess how well they are noticing and reflecting on elements of their texts.

Reading Log for (title)		
Location	**Signpost I Noticed**	**My Notes about It**

Shutterstock; © Science History Images/Alamy © Buyenlarge/Getty Images

UNIT (4) Tasks

- **WRITE AN ARGUMENT**
- **DEBATE AN ISSUE**

MENTOR TEXT

DECLARATION OF SENTIMENTS

Argument by Elizabeth Cady Stanton

LEARNING OBJECTIVES

Writing Task

- Write an argument identifying current barriers to self-determination.
- Develop a central claim.
- Analyze a text for supporting evidence.
- Support a claim with reasons and examples.
- Anticipate opposing arguments in a counterargument.
- Develop a rebuttal with supporting evidence.
- Revise drafts, incorporating feedback from peers.
- Use a rubric to evaluate writing.
- Publish writing to share with an audience.
- **Language** Respond to a prompt in writing.

Speaking Task

- Adapt writing for a debate.
- Use effective verbal and nonverbal techniques.
- Participate in an informal debate.
- **Language** Participate in a discussion using the key terms *claim* and *evidence*.

Assign the Writing Task in *Ed*.

Online

RESOURCES

- Unit 4 Response Log
- Writing Studio: Writing Arguments
- Grammar Studio: Verb Tense
- Speaking and Listening Studio: Analyzing and Evaluating Presentations

Language X-Ray: English Learner Support

Use the instruction below and the supports and scaffolds in the Teacher's Edition to help you guide students at different proficiency levels.

INTRODUCE THE WRITING TASK

Explain that an argumentative essay is a type of writing in which an author takes a position on an issue. An effective argument makes a clear claim, develops that claim with strong evidence, and offers a solution to the issue. The argument should also anticipate possible opposing claims and explain why the opposing claims are not valid.

Reread the directions with students to make sure they understand that they will be using the texts from the unit as their supporting evidence. Define *self-determination* and *barriers* and, if necessary, use gestures to clarify the meanings. Ask students to repeat the directions back to you to clarify their understanding of the assignment.

WRITING

Develop a Central Claim

Work with students to examine ideas about the nature of self-determination based on their prior knowledge. Then, guide students to write a central claim that responds to the prompt and find supporting evidence in the unit texts.

Use the following supports with students at varying proficiency levels:

- Work with students to write about self-determination. Provide a sentence frame: *When I do what I want, I have self-_____.* **SUBSTANTIAL**

- Guide students to write sentences about self-determination. Use the following sentence frames: *In Declaration of Sentiments, a barrier to self-determination was _____. (group of people) experienced this barrier. _____ (solution) is one way to break this barrier.* **MODERATE**

- Work with students to examine the barriers to self-determination in the mentor text and *Incidents in the Life of a Slave Girl.* Have students locate examples of barriers, add citations to the planning table, and extend their central claims to include text evidence. **LIGHT**

SPEAKING

Discuss Argumentative Writing

Explain to students that they will adapt their own work and then participate in a debate. Offer students the following sentence frame for discussion: *What is the _____? (claim, counterclaim, supporting evidence, solution, etc.)*

Use the following supports with students at varying proficiency levels:

- Provide students with these sentences to ask their peers: *What is your claim? What is your evidence?* **SUBSTANTIAL**

- Direct students to develop an argumentative writing word bank with a peer. Tell students to list words and phrases related to an argument. Then, instruct students to describe the use of these components in their own papers. **MODERATE**

- Direct students to develop an argumentative writing word bank with a peer, listing words and phrases that relate to an argument. Then, have students discuss the use of these words and phrases in a peer's paper. **LIGHT**

WRITING

WRITE AN ARGUMENT

Introduce students to the Writing Task by reading the introductory paragraph with them. Remind students to refer to the notes they recorded in the Unit 4 Response Log as they plan and draft their arguments. The Response Log should contain ideas about self-determination. Drawing on these different perspectives will make their own writing more interesting and well informed.

 For **writing support** for students at varying proficiency levels, see the **Language X-Ray** on page 442B.

USE THE MENTOR TEXT

Point out that students' essays will be similar to the Declaration of Sentiments in that they will present arguments supported by facts and examples related to the topic of self-determination. However, their essays will be shorter than this document and will focus on current barriers to self-determination and what should be done to remedy them.

WRITING PROMPT

Review the prompt with students. Encourage them to ask questions about any part of the assignment that is unclear. Make sure they understand that the purpose of their essays is to answer the question using facts and examples from the texts they have read.

Write an Argument

 Go to the **Writing Studio** for help writing arguments.

This unit focuses on the continuing work of bringing freedom and justice to all members of American society. For this writing task, you will write an argument. For an example of a well-written argument you can use as a mentor text, review Declaration of Sentiments.

As you write your argument, you can use the notes from your Response Log, which you filled out after reading the texts in this unit.

Writing Prompt

Read the information in the box below.

This is the context for your argument.

> America's founding documents emphasize liberties and rights for all, but fully realizing this goal takes work.

Think carefully about the following question.

What obstacles or barriers to self-determination exist today?

> When is self-determination possible?

How can you use the unit texts to develop and support a claim in your argument?

Write an argument in which you identify a current barrier to self-determination and specify what should be done to remedy it, so that self-determination is possible for more members of our society.

Be sure to—

- ❏ make a clear and persuasive claim
- ❏ ask questions that help develop your claim and research the answers by locating relevant sources and synthesizing the information they provide
- ❏ develop the claim with valid reasons and relevant evidence
- ❏ anticipate counterarguments, or opposing claims, and address them with a well-supported rebuttal or defense

Review these points as you write and again when you finish. Make any needed changes.

- ❏ establish clear, logical relationships among claims, rebuttals, reasons, and evidence
- ❏ write a satisfying conclusion that effectively summarizes the claim
- ❏ demonstrate appropriate and precise use of language, maintaining a formal tone through the use of standard English
- ❏ correctly cite sources you use, even when you summarize or paraphrase

---

 LEARNING MINDSET

Belonging Emphasize that everyone is a valuable member of the class and has something to offer. Encourage students to feel comfortable asking fellow students and the teacher for help, and encourage students to offer to help their fellow students.

① Plan

Before you start writing, you need to plan your argument. Review Elizabeth Cady Stanton's Declaration of Sentiments and at least two other unit texts and identify each writer's message about self-determination.

Then, answer the following questions, either on your own or with a partner or small group.

- What are the essential "ingredients" for self-determination?
- What barriers exist to obtaining these ingredients?

Record ideas from the texts and the discussion questions below.

Argument Planning Table	
Ideas about self-determination from the texts	
"Ingredients" of self-determination	
Existing barriers to self-determination	

Background Reading Review the notes you have taken in your Response Log that relate to the question "When is self-determination possible?" Texts in this unit provide background reading that will help you formulate key points in your argument.

 Go to **Writing Arguments: Introduction** to learn more.

Notice & Note

From Reading to Writing

As you plan your argument, apply what you've learned about signposts to your own writing. Remember that writers use common features, called signposts, to help convey their message to readers.

Think how you can incorporate **Quoted Words** into your argument.

 Go to the **Reading Studio** for more resources on **Notice & Note.**

Use the notes from your Response Log as you plan your argument.

WRITING

① PLAN

Allow time for students to review the unit texts and complete the planning table, either on their own, with partners, or in groups. Suggest that the class brainstorm a list of the "ingredients" necessary for self-determination.

■ English Learner Support

Understand Implicit Language Ask students what they think the word *ingredients* means. *(It is usually used to name the items that are combined in a recipe to make a particular kind of dish.)* Then, have students discuss this question with a partner: *What do you think it means here? (It refers to all the things that are necessary to ensure self-determination.)* Work with students to fill in the chart, providing text that they can copy into their charts as needed. **SUBSTANTIAL**

▶ NOTICE & NOTE

From Reading to Writing

Remind students they can use **Quoted Words** to include the opinions or conclusions of someone who is an expert on the topic. Students can also use Quoted Words to provide support for points they are trying to make. Remind students to format direct quotations correctly and to cite sources.

Background Reading As students plan their arguments, remind them to refer to the notes they took in the Response Log. They may also review the selections to find additional facts and examples to support ideas they want to include in their writing.

TO CHALLENGE STUDENTS . . .

Add Multimedia Elements Challenge students to incorporate graphic features such as photographs, drawings, or charts to help support their arguments. These features will be especially useful when they present their arguments later. After they have shared their presentations, discuss how the visual aids helped make their arguments more persuasive.

WRITING

Organize Your Ideas Remind students that the purpose of an argument is to persuade readers that the writer's opinion or belief is correct. Students' claims should reflect their analysis and synthesis of ideas about the texts they have chosen for this task. Encourage students to begin by writing their claims. Remind students that a **claim** is their position on the issue or argument. Point out that their claims will be the focus of their arguments, so they should make sure they are clear and precise. Remind students that they must support their claims with logical reasons, and each reason should be supported by relevant evidence from the texts. The evidence should be credible, reliable, and relevant to the text. Tell students that they may also use anecdotes to appeal to their audience's ethical beliefs. If students find that they cannot support their claims, tell them to rework their claims or to choose different questions to address in their arguments. After students have chosen their supporting evidence, have them consider counterarguments or opposing claims. A **counterargument** is the claim made to oppose another argument. To determine the counterarguments, students should consider what others might believe. Remind students they will need evidence to support their counterarguments.

② DEVELOP A DRAFT

Encourage students to focus their first drafts on getting down their ideas. Remind them to include and address counterclaims so that they can demonstrate that they have thoroughly considered their claims. Once they are sure that their arguments are both logical and convincing, they can focus on refining the language.

■ English Learner Support

Cooperative Learning Simplify the writing task by working as a class to complete the graphic organizer and create an outline. Begin by asking yes/no questions. For example: *Was being a slave a barrier to self-determination? Was not being allowed to vote a barrier to self-determination?* Then ask, *What is a barrier to self-determiniation today? Why?* Elicit words or phrases that students can use in their claims and reasons. Turn their reasons into sentences and write them in the graphic organizer. Repeat the process until students have at least one reason and one piece of evidence. Then, write the argument as a group. **SUBSTANTIAL**

 WRITING TASK

 Go to **Writing Arguments: What Is a Claim?** for help developing a claim for your argument.

Organize Your Ideas Based on the ideas in the texts and your answers to the discussion questions, write a clearly worded claim about a current barrier to self-determination and what should be done to remedy it. Then, develop several reasons that support your claim, and add details, examples, and quotations to support each reason. Make sure you use textual evidence from the unit selections.

Finally, develop a rebuttal to a potential counterargument. How would you argue against opposing claims and convince your audience to agree with you? You may want to conduct further research in print or digital sources, noting relevant facts, details, or examples that support your rebuttal. You can use the chart below to map out the organizational structure of your argument.

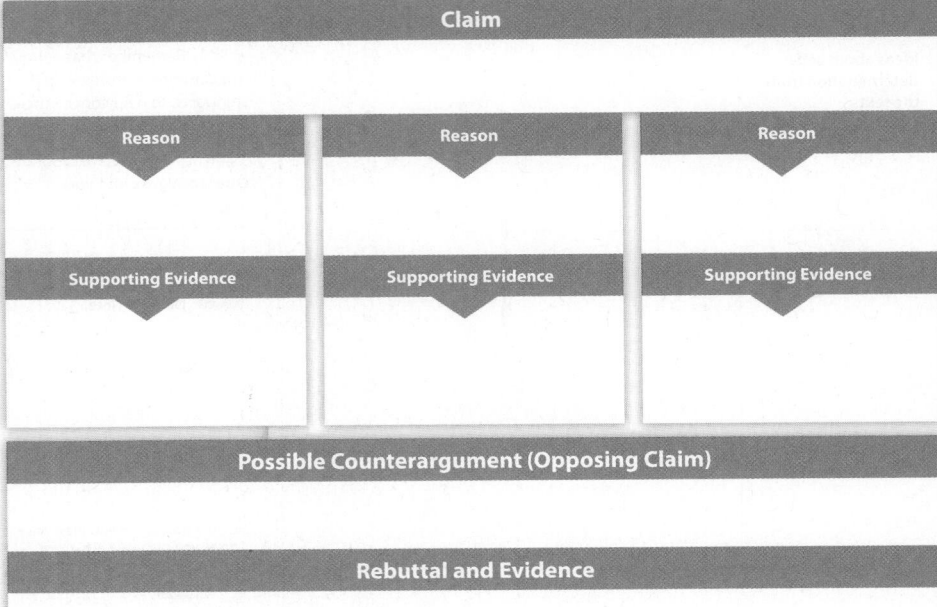

② Develop a Draft

 You might prefer to draft your argument online.

Once you have completed your planning activities, you will be ready to begin drafting your argument. Refer to your graphic organizers, as well as any notes you took as you studied the texts in this unit. These will provide a kind of map for you to follow as you write. Using a word processor or an online writing application makes it easier to make changes or move sentences around later when you are ready to revise your first draft.

WHEN STUDENTS STRUGGLE . . .

Develop Claims Have small groups review the selections and discuss similarities and differences between the way each author addresses the theme of self-determination. Suggest that they record notes from the discussion in a chart. Remind students to follow turn-taking rules and to offer comments and elaborate on each other's ideas. Students may use these discussions to help them develop their claims and to choose which two texts they will analyze in addition to Declaration of Sentiments.

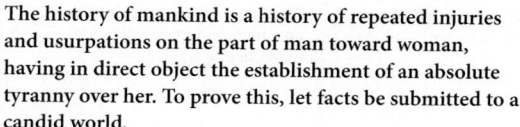

Use the Mentor Text

▶ **Author's Craft**
Clarity is of the utmost importance when writing an argument. You are trying to convince your audience that your claim is true. Precise word choice makes your argument easy to follow. Bold, direct statements communicate your personal sense of the truth of your words.

> The history of mankind is a history of repeated injuries and usurpations on the part of man toward woman, having in direct object the establishment of an absolute tyranny over her. To prove this, let facts be submitted to a candid world.

Stanton does not mince words. She uses strong, direct language: "injuries and usurpations," "absolute tyranny," and "facts." Her tone is unafraid and her word choice is precise.

Apply What You've Learned Stanton could have said, "In my view, here are some problems we should consider solving," instead of "To prove this, let facts be submitted to a candid world." Read your argument and find places where there is weak language, such as "in my opinion" or "it seems," and eliminate these phrases. Make your statements bold and clear, but not combative.

▶ **Genre Characteristics**
An argument often ends with a call to action—a statement of what the writer wants the audience to believe or do as a result of the argument presented.

> Now, in view of this entire disfranchisement of one half the people of this country, their social and religious degradation—in view of the unjust laws above mentioned and because women do feel themselves aggrieved, oppressed and fraudulently deprived of their most sacred rights, we insist that they have immediate admission to all the rights and privileges, which belong to them as citizens of these United States.

Stanton's call to action begins with "Now" to signal what should be done. She repeats "in view" to remind the audience of the pertinent parts of her argument. She uses the bold word "insist" to strengthen her call to action.

Apply What You've Learned Consider what action you want your audience to take, or what you want them to believe to be true, when they have finished reading your argument. Make sure to include this in your draft, using bold, clear language and a transitional word or phrase.

WHY THIS MENTOR TEXT?

Declaration of Sentiments provides a good example of an argument. Use the instruction below to help students use the mentor text as a model for building an argument.

USE THE MENTOR TEXT

Author's Craft Ask a volunteer to read aloud the first paragraph of Declaration of Sentiments. Point out that Stanton begins by using the language of the Declaration of Independence, which invites comparison with that document in which the American colonists claimed their rights. By doing so, Stanton lends credibility to her claim that women have been systematically denied the rights of citizenship enjoyed by men. Invite students to offer examples of famous quotations, interesting facts, or personal anecdotes that could be used in an introduction. Then, read the example and notes. Ask students what direct language they could use in their arguments.

Genre Characteristics Remind students that the purpose of an argument is to convince the audience to agree, to recognize the validity of a position, or to take a certain action. Writers may use rhetorical devices to achieve their purpose and make their arguments more compelling. Stanton makes use of rhetorical devices such as repetition, parallelism, and allusion in Declaration of Sentiments. After an opening that alludes to the Declaration of Independence, Stanton makes the claim in paragraph 3 that is quoted under Author's Craft. Note that she backs up this claim in paragraphs 4–19 with a list of examples. Finally note how she ends her argument with a call to action. Ask students what other calls to action Stanton could have made.

 ENGLISH LEARNER SUPPORT

Build Background Knowledge To aid comprehension of the sample text above, provide students with the following definitions:

- *usurpation:* the taking of someone's power or property by force
- *establishment:* the act of starting something that will last a long time
- *disfranchisement:* the act of keeping a group of people from having the right to vote

- *degradation:* the act of treating someone poorly or placing them on a lower level
- *aggrieved:* feeling anger because of unfair treatment
- *fraudulently:* by means of dishonest methods   **ALL LEVELS**

WRITING

3 REVISE

Explain that during the revising stage, students should assess the organization and strength of their arguments. They may need to reorganize information to make their arguments clearer and more logical. Tell students that they should use transitional words or phrases in their arguments. Some sample transitions are listed below.

To introduce a counterargument:

- *Others may argue*
- *According to*

To return to their original claim:

- *However*
- *On the other hand*

To conclude their argument:

- *Therefore*
- *In conclusion*

With a Partner Pair students and have them do peer reviews. Have students ask peer reviewers to evaluate their arguments by answering the following questions:

- Does my introduction capture your attention?
- Is my claim stated clearly?
- Can you think of any opposing claims I have missed?
- Which reasons or pieces of evidence are unclear?
- What questions do you have about my main points?
- Is my conclusion logical?

Students should use the reviewer's feedback to add relevant facts, details, examples, or quotations that further develop their main points.

 **WRITING TASK**

3 Revise

 Go to **Writing Arguments: Creating a Coherent Argument** for help revising your argument.

On Your Own Once you have written your draft, you'll want to go back and look for ways to improve your argument. As you reread and revise, think about whether you have achieved your purpose. The Revision Guide will help you focus on specific elements to make your writing stronger.

Revision Guide		
Ask Yourself	**Tips**	**Revision Techniques**
1. Does the introduction clearly state my claim and capture the reader's attention?	**Underline** your claim. **Highlight** your engaging opener.	**Clarify** or **replace** your claim. **Add** an attention-getting quotation, detail, or analogy.
2. Are counterarguments anticipated and refuted?	**Note** counterarguments (opposing claims) and **highlight** text that refutes them.	**Add** text to show the weakness of opposing claims.
3. Are reasons and evidence organized consistently and logically throughout?	**Highlight** reasons that support the claim. **Underline** evidence that supports each reason.	**Reorder** your reasons and evidence for emphasis, such as the strongest reason first or last.
4. Does my conclusion follow logically from the body of the argument and summarize my claim?	**Underline** the conclusion. **Highlight** sentences that summarize the claim.	**Clarify** your conclusion by adding a summary statement if needed.

ACADEMIC VOCABULARY
As you conduct your **peer review,** be sure to use these words.

- ❏ confirm
- ❏ definitely
- ❏ deny
- ❏ format
- ❏ unify

With a Partner Once you and your partner have worked through the Revision Guide on your own, exchange arguments and evaluate each other's draft in a **peer review.** Focus on providing revision suggestions for at least three of the items mentioned in the chart. Explain why you think your partner's draft should be revised and what your specific suggestions are.

When receiving feedback from your partner, listen attentively and ask questions to make sure you fully understand the revision suggestions.

 ENGLISH LEARNER SUPPORT

Use Transitional Phrases Point out that writers use transitional phrases to introduce and refute counterclaims. Work with students to look for and mark words and phrases in the text that they might use to express counterclaims in their own arguments. *(Opponents of this view may say that . . .; While . . .; Those who disagree often suggest . . ., Yet . . .)* Make a list from students' annotations and from class discussion and display it. **MODERATE**

Edit

Once you have addressed the organization, development, and flow of ideas in your argument, you can look to improve the finer points of your draft. Edit for the proper use of standard English conventions and make sure to correct any misspellings or grammatical errors. Correctly cite any outside sources you used.

Language Conventions

Verb Tenses The tense of a verb indicates the time of the action or state of being. An action or state can occur in the present, past, or future, or it can be an ongoing or continuing action or state. Elizabeth Cady Stanton uses a number of verb tenses in the Declaration of Sentiments.

Example	Verb Tense
He <u>has compelled</u> her to submit to laws, in the formation of which she had no voice.	The **present perfect tense** describes an action or state that began in the past and still continues, communicating that Stanton wants to change ongoing actions, and not simply right past wrongs.
We <u>hold</u> these truths to be self-evident; that all men and women are created equal; . . .	The use of **present tense** describes actions occurring now, giving urgency to Stanton's argument.
We <u>shall employ</u> agents, circulate tracts, petition the State and National Legislatures, and endeavor to enlist the pulpit and the press in our behalf.	The use of **future tense** describes actions that Stanton intends to do in the future, giving her closing a sense of hope and possibility.

 Publish

Finalize your argument and choose a way to share it with your audience. Consider these options:

- Present your argument as a persuasive speech or video recording.
- Post your argument as a blog on a classroom or school website.

> **!** Go to **Verb Tense** in the **Grammar Studio** to learn more.

4 EDIT

Remind students that, in the editing stage, they should proofread their essays to make sure they are free of grammar, spelling, and punctuation errors. Suggest that they read their drafts aloud to assess how clearly and smoothly they have presented their ideas.

LANGUAGE CONVENTIONS

Verb Tenses Review the chart and the different verb tenses. Remind students that consistency in verbs promotes not only accurate grammar but also parallel structure. Encourage them to edit their own work to make verb tenses consistent.

■ English Learner Support

Use Verb Tenses Remind students that there are three main verb tenses in English: present, past, and future. Only the present and past tenses can be formed by a single verb alone. Point out that the future tense is formed by using a helping verb such as *will* or *shall* before the main verb. Note that students who speak Cantonese and Korean tend to use the present for the future: *I come tomorrow.* In Vietnamese, verbs do not change to express tense. **SUBSTANTIAL**

5 PUBLISH

After they finalize their essays, suggest that students consider sending their argument essays to local newspapers or posting them on websites devoted to dealing with the issues they addressed.

WHEN STUDENTS STRUGGLE . . .

Consistency in Verb Tense Have students read through their essays to identify all of the verbs they have used. Help them label each verb as past, present, or future. After they have determined which tense they have used most, have them go over their essays to check for consistency, correcting tenses as necessary. Refer students to the chart on Student Edition page 447 to help them correct verb tenses.

WRITING

USE THE SCORING GUIDE

Allow students time to read the scoring guide and to ask questions about any words, phrases, or ideas that are unclear. Then have partners exchange final drafts of their arguments. Ask them to score their partner's argument using the scoring guide. Each student should write a paragraph explaining the reasons for the score he or she awarded in each category.

Use the scoring guide to evaluate your argument.

Writing Task Scoring Guide: Argument

	Organization/Progression	Development of Ideas	Use of Language and Conventions
4	• The reasons and textual evidence are organized consistently and logically throughout the argument. • Varied transitions logically connect reasons and textual evidence to the writer's claim.	• The introduction is memorable and persuasive; the claim clearly states a position. • Valid reasons and relevant evidence from the texts convincingly support the writer's claim. • Counterarguments, or opposing claims, are anticipated and effectively refuted. • The concluding section effectively summarizes the claim.	• The writing reflects a formal style; precise language; and an objective, or controlled, tone. • Sentence beginnings, lengths, and structures vary and have a rhythmic flow. • Spelling, capitalization, and punctuation are correct. • Grammar and usage are correct.
3	• The organization is confusing in a few places. • Transitions are needed in a few places to link related ideas and evidence.	• The introduction could do more to capture the reader's attention; the claim states a position on an issue. • Most reasons and evidence from the texts support the writer's claim, but they could be more convincing. • Counterarguments, or opposing claims, are anticipated, but the rebuttal needs to be developed more. • The concluding section restates the claim.	• The style is informal in a few places, the language is sometimes unclear, and the tone is defensive at times. • Sentence beginnings, lengths, and structures vary somewhat. • Several spelling and capitalization mistakes occur, and punctuation is inconsistent. • Some grammatical and usage errors are repeated in the argument.
2	• The organization of reasons and textual evidence is logical in some places, but it often doesn't follow a pattern. • Many more transitions are needed to connect reasons and textual evidence to the writer's claim.	• The introduction is ordinary; the claim identifies an issue, but the writer's position is not clearly stated. • The reasons and evidence from the texts are not always logical or relevant. • Counterarguments, or opposing claims, are anticipated but not addressed logically. • The concluding section includes an incomplete summary of the claim.	• The style becomes informal in many places, the language is often imprecise, and the tone is often dismissive of other viewpoints. • Sentence structures seldom vary, and some fragments or run-on sentences are present. • Spelling, capitalization, and punctuation are often incorrect but do not make reading the argument difficult. • Grammar and usage are often incorrect, but the ideas are still clear.
1	• An organizational strategy is not used; reasons and textual evidence are presented randomly. • Transitions are not used, making the argument difficult to understand.	• The introduction is missing. • Significant supporting reasons and evidence from the texts are missing. • Counterarguments, or opposing claims, are neither anticipated nor addressed. • The concluding section is missing.	• The style and language are inappropriate, and the tone is disrespectful. • Repetitive sentence structure, fragments, and run-on sentences make the writing hard to follow. • Spelling and capitalization are often incorrect, and punctuation is missing. • Many grammatical and usage errors change the meaning of the writing.

Debate an Issue

You will now adapt your argument for a classroom debate. You also will listen to other debates, ask questions to better understand the ideas your classmates are debating, and respond appropriately to help them improve their arguments.

Go to **Analyzing and Evaluating Presentations: Tracing a Speaker's Argument** in the **Speaking and Listening Studio** to learn more.

① Adapt Your Argument for a Debate

Review your argument, and use the chart below to guide you as you adapt your argument for a debate.

Debate Planning Chart		
Introduction and Claim	How will you revise your introduction and claim to make a strong statement about the best way to extend liberties and rights to all Americans?	
Reasons, Evidence, and Rebuttals	How will you organize your reasons and evidence to clearly support your claim? What are the potential opposing claims? How will you refute these with a rebuttal supported by evidence?	
Effective Language and Organization	Which parts of your argument should be simplified? Where can you add transitions to help your listeners better follow your train of thought?	
Gestures and Vocal Expression	How can you use gestures and tone of voice to convey your point convincingly?	

DEBATE AN ISSUE

Remind students that the purpose of a debate is similar to the purpose of writing an argument: to persuade others to believe or support a claim about an issue by providing valid reasons and sufficient evidence. Students should begin by considering both sides of the argument and reviewing their claims and opposing claims. They should acknowledge credible aspects of opposing claims while emphasizing their limitations. It is also important that the moderator be familiar with both sides so that he or she can keep the debate on track.

① ADAPT YOUR ARGUMENT FOR A DEBATE

As students adapt their arguments, suggest that they consider adding rhetorical techniques such as those that Stanton uses in Declaration of Sentiments. For instance, students might choose to use repetition or parallelism to emphasize certain points. They might add vivid or direct language to make their claims more compelling. Remind students to make sure they clearly link their debate points to their claims and reasons. Encourage them to use transitions as well as varied syntax to create cohesion and to clarify relationships between their introductions, arguments and counterarguments, and conclusions. Review gestures and vocal expression categories. Tell students they should practice making their points before the live debate.

 For **speaking support** for students at varying proficiency levels, see the **Language X-Ray** on page 442B.

 ENGLISH LEARNER SUPPORT

Monitor Speaking Techniques Remind students to use verbal and nonverbal elements to persuade fellow debaters to agree with their claims. After partners practice for the debate, have them use the following questions to help them determine how they might better incorporate speaking techniques to make their arguments more persuasive.

- Which words do I need to pronounce more clearly?
- What parts of my argument should I emphasize more strongly?
- Where should I make better eye contact, use gestures, or adjust my tone of voice to add emphasis?
- Do I need to adjust the volume or speed of my speech?
- In what places could I add connecting words or phrases to show relationships between my ideas and evidence? **ALL LEVELS**

② PRACTICE FOR THE DEBATE

Review the information and tips with the class, ensuring that all the terms and ideas are clear. Remind students that the purpose of practicing their arguments is to gain useful feedback from their peers. Emphasize that speaking before a group makes most people feel nervous, so everyone should be as supportive and helpful as possible.

③ HOLD A DEBATE

Set aside time for an informal debate. After the conclusion of the debate, ask students to share their thoughts on how their classmates' feedback helped them improve their performances.

SPEAKING AND LISTENING TASK

As you work to improve your debating skills, remember to

❏ state your claim clearly

❏ make sure your claim reflects your actual opinion

❏ present reasons and evidence that clearly support your claim

❏ maintain a reasonable tone

❏ when others oppose your opinion, respond calmly

② Practice for the Debate

With a partner, practice presenting and defending your argument. Take turns reading the introductions to your arguments. Then, begin an informal debate.

Practice Effective Verbal and Nonverbal Techniques

❏ **Enunciation** Choose words and phrases that flow easily.

❏ **Voice and Pitch** Use your voice to show enthusiasm and emphasis.

❏ **Speaking Rate** Speak slowly enough that listeners understand you. Pause now and then to let them consider important points.

❏ **Volume** Listeners at the back of the room need to hear you.

❏ **Eye Contact** Try to let your eyes rest on each member of the audience.

❏ **Facial Expression** Smile, frown, or raise an eyebrow to show your feelings or to emphasize points.

❏ **Gestures** Stand tall and relaxed, and use natural gestures—shrugs, nods, or shakes of your head—to add meaning and interest.

Provide and Consider Advice for Improvement

As a listener, pay close attention. Take notes about ways the debaters can improve their arguments and more effectively use verbal and nonverbal techniques. Summarize each debater's claim, reasons, and evidence to confirm your understanding, and ask questions to clarify any confusing ideas.

As a presenter, listen closely to questions and consider ways to revise your argument or improve your delivery to make sure your points are clear and persuasive. Remember to ask for suggestions about how you might make your argument clearer and more interesting.

③ Hold a Debate

Debates can have a formal structure, but this debate will be informal. Ask a student or the teacher to act as moderator.

- First, have each group member take a turn presenting his or her claim.
- Next, the moderator should invite others in the group to comment on or question each claim. The moderator should allow the debate to flow naturally but may step in as needed to restore order.
- Listen closely to what is said so you can respond appropriately and build on others' ideas. Maintain a respectful tone toward your fellow debaters, even when you disagree with their ideas.
- Conclude the debate by summarizing the main points of agreement and disagreement among group members for each claim.

WHEN STUDENTS STRUGGLE . . .

Plan to Present an Argument Point out that understanding both sides of the argument can help students support a position in a debate. Have students review Declaration of Sentiments independently and then join small groups to discuss the claim and the evidence Stanton provides. Next, have groups list other arguments for or against Stanton's claim. Suggest that students organize their notes in a chart. They can use the information they gather to help them develop their claims and counterclaims.

Reflect on the Unit

By completing your argument, you have created a writing product that pulls together and expresses your thoughts about the reading you have done in this unit. Now is a good time to reflect on what you have learned.

Reflect on the Essential Questions

• Review the four Essential Questions on page 325. How have your answers to these questions changed in response to the texts you've read in this unit?

• What are some examples from the texts you've read that show how people gain self-determination or overcome differences and defeat?

• How did the texts help you consider the costs and benefits of progress and change?

Reflect on Your Reading

• Which selections were the most interesting or surprising to you?

• From which selection did you learn the most about the quest for freedom and justice?

Reflect on the Writing Task

• What difficulties did you encounter while working on your argument? How might you avoid them next time?

• Which part of the argument was the easiest and hardest to write? Why?

• What improvements did you make to your argument as you were revising?

UNIT 4 SELECTIONS

• Second Inaugural Address

• "To My Old Master"

• Image Collection: Civil War Photographs

• "An Occurrence at Owl Creek Bridge"

• "Building the Transcontinental Railroad"

• Declaration of Sentiments

• Speech to the American Equal Rights Association

• "Runagate Runagate"

• from *Incidents in the Life of a Slave Girl*

REFLECT ON THE UNIT

Have students reflect on the questions independently and write some notes in response to each one. Then have students meet with partners or in small groups to discuss their reflections. Circulate during these discussions to identify the questions that are generating the liveliest conversations. Wrap up with a whole-class discussion focused on these questions.

LEARNING MINDSET

Try Again Encourage students to learn from their mistakes and to try again in a different way. Remind them that it is all right, and even expected, to make mistakes; that's how we learn. Encourage volunteers to share mistakes they have made and what they learned from them.

Instructional Overview and Resources

	Instructional Focus	Online ⦿Ed Resources
Unit Introduction **America Transformed**	**Unit 5 Essential Questions** **Unit 5 Academic Vocabulary**	**Stream to Start:** America Transformed **Unit 5 Response Log**

ANALYZE & APPLY

	Instructional Focus	Online ⦿Ed Resources
"To Build a Fire" Short Story by Jack London Lexile 970L	**Reading** • Analyze Character • Analyze Setting **Writing:** Write a How-to Guide **Speaking and Listening:** Present a How-to Demonstration **Vocabulary:** Allusions and Word Origins **Language Conventions:** Consistent Tone	🔊 **Audio** **Close Read Screencast:** Modeled Discussion **Reading Studio:** Notice & Note **Writing Studio:** Writing Informative Texts **Speaking and Listening Studio:** Giving a Presentation **Vocabulary Studio:** Understanding Word Origins
"The Lowest Animal" Essay by Mark Twain Lexile 1040L	**Reading** • Analyze Author's Purpose: Satire • Analyze Tone **Writing:** Write a Satire **Speaking and Listening:** Present a Satire **Vocabulary:** Nuances in Word Meaning **Language Conventions:** Anaphora and Parallelism	🔊 **Audio** **Reading Studio:** Notice & Note **Writing Studio:** Writing as a Process **Speaking and Listening Studio:** Giving a Presentation
"Why Everyone Must Get Ready for the Fourth Industrial Revolution" Article by Bernard Marr Lexile 1320L	**Reading** • Evaluate Graphic Features • Evaluate Counterarguments **Writing:** Write an Argument **Speaking and Listening:** Present an Argument **Vocabulary:** Context Clues **Language Conventions:** Capitalization	🔊 **Audio** **Reading Studio:** Notice & Note **Writing Studio:** Writing Arguments **Speaking and Listening Studio:** Giving a Presentation **Vocabulary Studio:** Using Context Clues **Grammar Studio:** Capital Letters
MENTOR TEXT **"The Story of an Hour"** Short Story by Kate Chopin Lexile 970L	**Reading** • Analyze Point of View • Make and Confirm Predictions **Writing:** Write a Short Story **Speaking and Listening:** Discuss with a Small Group **Vocabulary:** Multiple-Meaning Words **Language Conventions:** Craft Effective Sentences	**Reading Studio:** Notice & Note **Writing Studio:** Writing Narratives **Speaking and Listening Studio:** Participating in Collaborative Discussions **Vocabulary Studio:** Words with Multiple Meanings

SUGGESTED PACING: 30 DAYS

Unit Introduction	To Build a Fire	The Lowest Animal	Why Everyone Must Get Ready for the Fourth Industrial Revolution	The Story of an Hour
1	2 3 4 5	6 7 8	9 10 11 12	13 14 15

English Learner Support		**Differentiated Instruction**	**Online Ed Assessment**
• Learn New Language Structures • Build Background Knowledge • Build Vocabulary		**When Students Struggle** • Concept Support	
• Text X-Ray • Use Cognates • Analyze Setting • Use Prior Knowledge • Ask Yes/No Questions • Illustrate the Text • Retell the Story	• Repeat the Story • Confirm Understanding • Analyze Character • Understand Allusion • Oral Assessment • Understand Sound Transfer • Language Conventions	**When Students Struggle** • Analyze Character **To Challenge Students** • Analyze Setting • Analyze Character	**Selection Test**
• Text X-Ray • Use Cognates • Understand Multiple-Meaning Words	• Idioms • Oral Assessment • Sound Transfer • Language Conventions	**When Students Struggle** • Make Generalizations **To Challenge Students** • Analyze the Writer's Views	**Selection Test**
• Text X-Ray • Use Cognates • Identify Contrasts • Summarize Counterarguments	• Oral Assessment • Use Academic Vocabulary • Review Grammar Points	**When Students Struggle** • Identify Arguments and Counterarguments **To Challenge Students** • Write an Argument	**Selection Test**
• Text X-Ray • Use Cognates • Prepositions and Prepositional Phrases • Preteach Vocabulary	• Oral Assessment • Vocabulary Strategy • Understand Sentence Structure	**When Students Struggle** • Recognize Irony • Reteach: Point of View	**Selection Test**

Chicago
16 > 17 > 18 >

from **The Jungle / Food Product Design from Fast Food Nation**
19 > 20 > 21 > 22 > 23 > 24 > 25 >

Independent Reading
26 > 27 >

End of Unit
28 > 29 > 30 >

	Instructional Focus	**Online** Ed Resources

"Chicago"
Poem by Carl Sandburg
Lexile N/A

Reading
• Characteristics of Poetry
• Create Mental Images
• Analyze Diction and Syntax

Writing: Write a Poem

Speaking and Listening: Present a Dramatic Reading

Reading Studio: Notice & Note

Speaking and Listening Studio: Giving a Presentation

COLLABORATE & COMPARE

from *The Jungle*
Novel by Upton Sinclair
Lexile 1310L

Reading
• Analyze Author's Purpose
• Synthesize Information

Writing: Write a Literary Analysis

Speaking and Listening: Give a Presentation

Vocabulary: Word Families

Language Conventions: Prepositions and Prepositional Phrases

🔊 **Audio**

Reading Studio: Notice & Note

Writing Studio: Using Textual Evidence

Speaking and Listening Studio: Giving a Presentation

Vocabulary Studio: Word Families

Grammar Studio: Prepositions and Prepositional Phrases

"Food Product Design"
from *Fast Food Nation*
Investigative Journalism by Eric Schlosser
Lexile 1290L

Reading
• Analyze Author's Purpose
• Synthesize Information

Writing: Write a Rhetorical Analysis

Speaking and Listening: Present an Interview

Vocabulary: Understand Technical Terms

Language Conventions: Dashes

🔊 **Audio**

Reading Studio: Notice & Note

Writing Studio: Using Textual Evidence

Speaking and Listening Studio: Giving a Presentation

Vocabulary Studio: Specialized Vocabulary

Grammar Studio: Dashes

Collaborate & Compare

Reading: Compare Author's Purpose

Speaking and Listening Studio: Using Media in a Presentation

Online Ed INDEPENDENT READING

The Independent Reading selections are only available in the eBook.

Go to the Reading Studio for more information on **NOTICE & NOTE.**

"The Men in the Storm"
Short Story by Stephen Crane
Lexile 1200L

"A Journey"
Short Story by Edith Wharton
Lexile 870L

END OF UNIT

Writing Task: Write a Short Story

Reflect on the Unit

Writing: Write a Short Story

Language Conventions: Active and Passive Voice

Unit 5 Response Log

Mentor Text: "The Story of an Hour"

Writing Studio: Writing Narratives

Grammar Studio: Module 8: Lesson 7: Active and Passive Voice

English Learner Support		Differentiated Instruction	Online Ed Assessment
• Text X-Ray • Recognize Directionality • Use Visual Support • Oral Assessment		**When Students Struggle** • Understand Personification • Reteaching: Analyze Diction and Syntax **To Challenge Students** • Contrast Line Breaks	**Selection Test**
• Text X-Ray • Use Cognates • Identify Prepositional Phrases • Understand Quotation Marks • Identify Antecedents • Understand Complex Sentences	• Understand Prepositions • Understand Similes • Oral Assessment • Use Prefixes and Suffixes • Language Conventions	**When Students Struggle** • Use Graphic Organizers	**Selection Test**
• Text X-Ray • Understand Author's Purpose • Use Linguistic Support • Build Oral Fluency	• Oral Assessment • Vocabulary Strategy • Language Conventions	**When Students Struggle** • Understand Details • Determine Author's Purpose • Reteach: Author's Purpose **To Challenge Students** • Imitate Style • Debate an Issue • Collaborative Discussion	**Selection Test**
• Ask Questions		**When Students Struggle** • Use Graphic Organizers	
"A Wagner Matinee" Short Story by Willa Cather **Lexile 1470L**	"Evidence that Robots Are Winning the Race for American Jobs" Article by Claire Cain Miller **Lexile 1240L**	"Healthy Eaters, Strong Minds: What School Gardens Teach Kids" Article by Paige Pfleger **Lexile 1180L**	**Selection Tests**
• Language X-Ray • Understand Theme • Develop Plot • Use Figurative Language	• Understand Academic Language • Use Helping Verbs	**When Students Struggle** • Plan Plot • Use Helping Verbs **To Challenge Students** • Practice Creative Writing	**Unit Test**

DISCUSS THE QUOTATION

Much of Philip K. Dick's science fiction asks the question "What is reality?" He always hoped to find the answer. In 1972, he was asked by a Canadian college student to define *reality* in one sentence. His response was the quotation that opens this unit. Dick wrote more than 30 novels and more than 100 short stories between 1952 and his death in 1982. His novels include *The Man in the High Castle* and *Do Androids Dream of Electric Sheep?* (which was adapted for film as *Blade Runner*).

Ask students to think about what reality means to them. Have them try to define *reality* in their own words.

■ English Learner Support

Learn New Language Structures Students may have difficulty with the quotation because of the way it is worded. They may not be used to seeing the words *that* and *which* used together as they are here. Explain that the phrase *that which* usually means *what* or *whatever*. Then, tell them that this quotation could be rephrased more simply as "Reality is whatever doesn't go away when you stop believing it."
SUBSTANTIAL/MODERATE

AMERICA TRANSFORMED

AN AGE OF REALISM

> " **Reality is that which, when you stop believing in it, doesn't go away.** "
>
> —Philip K. Dick

452   Unit 5

LEARNING MINDSET

Plan/Predict Remind students that planning is essential to complete work efficiently and exceptionally. Encourage students to make a plan for completing each assignment, including mapping out the steps. Explain that planning will help them learn discipline, which will help them in future endeavors.

Discuss the **Essential Questions** with your whole class or in small groups. As you read America Transformed, consider how the selections explore these questions.

? *ESSENTIAL QUESTION:*

To what degree do we control our lives?

Life was difficult for many Americans in the years following the Civil War. Native Americans, African Americans, immigrants, factory workers, laborers, and farmers struggled daily against poverty and oppression. To many, it seemed that life was unfair—that despite their efforts, they could not escape their fate. Naturalist writers such as Stephen Crane and Upton Sinclair saw human beings as helpless creatures moved by forces beyond their understanding or control. Do people control their own destiny, or are they simply victims of circumstances?

? *ESSENTIAL QUESTION:*

Why do humans cause harm?

After the Civil War, rich and powerful people took advantage of those who lacked the power to defend themselves. The U.S. government forced Native Americans off their land. White southerners enacted Jim Crow laws to restrict newly freed African Americans. "Robber baron" industrialists exploited their workers. Slumlords rented unsanitary tenements to immigrants. Banks foreclosed on farmers' land, and women were discouraged from pursuing interests outside the home. How do we identify harmful acts and keep from harming others?

? *ESSENTIAL QUESTION:*

What are the consequences of change?

In the post–Civil War era, the United States was undergoing rapid change. Millions of immigrants came to America seeking a better life. Oligarchs and industrialists amassed huge fortunes by concentrating resources and exploiting immigrants and others who flooded the cities in search of work. Laborers worked long hours in dangerous conditions for low wages. How can the changes brought about by progress have both positive and negative consequences?

? *ESSENTIAL QUESTION:*

What makes a place unique?

In the late 19th century, the United States was growing at such a rapid pace that many Americans mourned the loss of their regional identities. People were proud of the things that made them unique. Writers captured this sentiment by depicting the character of the country's distinct regions. What is it exactly that makes a place unique?

America Transformed 453

Connect to the

ESSENTIAL QUESTIONS

Read aloud the Essential Questions and the paragraphs that follow them. Open the discussion of each idea by having students respond to the questions that conclude each paragraph.

? *ESSENTIAL QUESTION:*

To what degree do we control our lives?

Guide students in a discussion of the types of outside forces that limit personal control over our lives, such as laws and economic circumstances, and what we can do to try to control our destiny. Students might say that people can pursue higher education to learn a profession or trade.

? *ESSENTIAL QUESTION:*

Why do humans cause harm?

Point out that, throughout history, groups of people in power have committed acts that were harmful to other, less powerful, groups. Challenge students to identify ways in which this still happens in the United States and what can be done to change this.

? *ESSENTIAL QUESTION:*

What are the consequences of change?

Invite students to brainstorm the positive and negative consequences of progress. Create a T-chart of pros and cons to record students' ideas. Then, ask students whether they think such change is mainly positive or negative and why.

? *ESSENTIAL QUESTION:*

What makes a place unique?

Ask students what sets their region apart from other regions of the United States. Tell them to consider the landscape and natural resources, history and culture, and the ethnic backgrounds of the people who live there.

AN AGE OF REALISM

This essay provides students with a historical context for the Unit 5 selections. It presents a brief overview of life and literary movements in the United States at the end of the 19th century.

The Gilded Age In 1873, the novelist Mark Twain and his neighbor, newspaper editor and essayist Charles Dudley Warner, published a novel called *The Gilded Age*. The term *gild* means "to cover with a thin layer of gold," and the title was meant to contrast the greed and political corruption of the era with a true "golden age"— a period of great peace, prosperity, and happiness. Historians have adopted its title to describe the period from about 1870 to 1900, during which wealthy industrialists enjoyed showing off the vast fortunes they had made. They built palatial mansions, draped their wives and daughters in diamonds, and threw extravagant parties. They did everything except gild themselves.

The Have-Nots In 1890, journalist Jacob Riis published his groundbreaking work of social criticism, *How the Other Half Lives*, in which he combined photographs with harsh accounts of life in New York's worst slums. Riis had immigrated to the United States from Denmark 20 years earlier at the age of 21 and had worked as a farmhand, ironworker, bricklayer, carpenter, and salesman before becoming a police reporter for the *New York Tribune*. Riis's experiences of the worst aspects of life in the city's tenements and lodging houses informed his book, and it was a success. It shocked many New Yorkers and led to the enforcement of the city's housing policies.

COLLABORATIVE DISCUSSION

Ask groups to share key ideas from their discussions with the class.

AN AGE OF REALISM

After the Civil War, the transcontinental rail system carried thousands of settlers to the West. The huge herds of bison that had roamed the plains were decimated, and Native Americans were driven off their land to make way for settlers. By the 1880s most Native Americans were confined to reservations, usually on land deemed worthless by white settlers.

The Gilded Age A very small group of men controlled the vast share of the country's growing industry, including the enormously profitable steel, railroad, oil, and meatpacking sectors. This era became known as the "Gilded Age." It was a time of sparkle and glitter, luxury and excess, and it was dominated by "robber barons" like railroad mogul Cornelius Vanderbilt, oil tycoon John D. Rockefeller, and steel magnate Andrew Carnegie.

Many ordinary people had more money, too, and all sorts of new things to spend it on. The rising middle class could take the train to the amusement parks and shop in new department stores. Even some blue-collar workers could afford inventions such as automobiles, telephones, and electricity.

Women chafed under the social and economic restrictions imposed on them. An increasing number of those from the middle class achieved the goal of a university education as a step toward a broader role in society. Women's rights activist Susan B. Anthony credited the bicycle with doing "more to emancipate women than anything else in the world." The movement to secure their right to vote was reinvigorated as women sought a larger voice in every aspect of public life.

The Have-Nots The railroad industry fueled industrial growth, and new manufacturing centers grew up around railroad hubs in Pittsburgh, Cleveland, Detroit, and Chicago. The urban centers grew rapidly. People from the country streamed into these areas in search of work, and immigrants came to America looking for a better life. Unfortunately, many of these new city dwellers found themselves working 16-hour days in airless, dangerous sweatshops for low wages.

Farmers and African Americans also faced hard times. Farmers borrowed money from banks, but high interest rates meant many of them lost their land. Failures of the Reconstruction Act left many African Americans

COLLABORATIVE DISCUSSION

In a small group, discuss the timeline. What literary or other kinds of events had the most impact on the era?

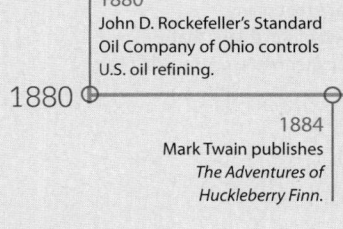

1880
John D. Rockefeller's Standard Oil Company of Ohio controls U.S. oil refining.

1892
New York's Ellis Island becomes the busiest entry point for European immigrants.

1880

1884
Mark Twain publishes *The Adventures of Huckleberry Finn*.

ENGLISH LEARNER SUPPORT

Build Background Knowledge To aid comprehension of the essay, provide students with the following definitions:

- *decimated:* destroyed large numbers or part of (a group of people or organisms)
- *tycoon:* a wealthy and powerful businessperson
- *magnate:* a person with great wealth and power in business or industry
- *emancipate:* to free from someone else's power or control

- *reinvigorated:* gave new life or energy to
- *colloquial:* using an informal or conversational style
- *decry:* to say publicly that something is bad or wrong
  ALL LEVELS

powerless and poor. People knew they were missing out on the prosperity that others were enjoying, and it made them angry. Workers began to form labor unions; and many farmers, white and black, joined the Populist Party, hoping to make the government more responsive to their needs.

Realism, Naturalism, and Muckrakers The changing world was reflected in the work of many authors. Realist writers portrayed ordinary lives as they were, without romance or sentimentality, through a variety of genres and forms. Some writers began to capture the customs, characters, and landscapes of the nation's distinct regions—a type of writing that came to be called regionalism. Mark Twain, Kate Chopin, and Willa Cather, among others, celebrated America's diversity in settings ranging from Mississippi River towns and the city of New Orleans to the plains of Nebraska. The publication in 1884 of Twain's *The Adventures of Huckleberry Finn* marked the high point of regionalism. It was the first novel written entirely in "American"—the colorful, colloquial, and frequently ungrammatical voice of its young narrator, Huck Finn. Twain often used humor to make serious points, and his novel tackled the issue of racism in America.

The social conditions in America's growing industrial cities, with their great disparities of wealth, led to the rise of the literary movement called naturalism, a starker form of realism. Looking to the theories of

Regionalism, Naturalism, and Muckrakers Mark Twain and other regionalist writers used local color to record for the future the unique characteristics of their areas. Their versions of life in the West captured the imaginations of readers in the more settled communities of the East, Midwest, and South. For those who could not hop aboard the new transcontinental train and see the country for themselves, reading all about it was the next best thing. Americans were endlessly fascinated by tales of life in mining camps, on the cattle ranches, and in frontier towns. Writers carefully recorded how ordinary people spoke, dressed, acted, thought, and looked.

RESEARCH

To learn more about their chosen topic, encourage students to search for primary sources from the historical period. Have students choose excerpts from a source to present to the class.

RESEARCH
What about this historical period interests you? Choose a topic, event, or person to learn more about. Then, add your own entry to the timeline.

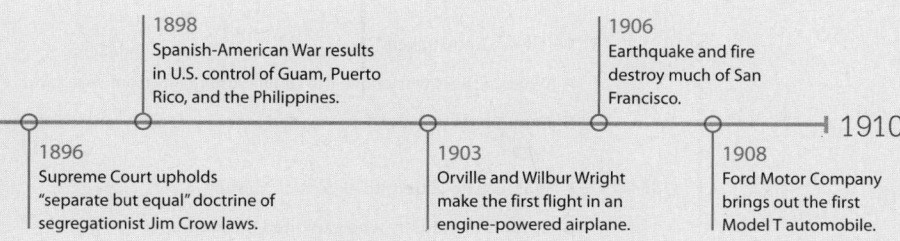

1898
Spanish-American War results in U.S. control of Guam, Puerto Rico, and the Philippines.

1906
Earthquake and fire destroy much of San Francisco.

1910

1896
Supreme Court upholds "separate but equal" doctrine of segregationist Jim Crow laws.

1903
Orville and Wilbur Wright make the first flight in an engine-powered airplane.

1908
Ford Motor Company brings out the first Model T automobile.

America Transformed 455

ENGLISH LEARNER SUPPORT

Build Vocabulary Use the following supports for students at varying proficiency levels:

- To help students internalize the words defined at the bottom of page 454, have them create their own vocabulary cards. For each word, students should make a card listing the word, its definition, an illustration (if appropriate), and an example sentence. Have students work with a partner to review and help revise each other's cards. **SUBSTANTIAL/MODERATE**

- Have students use a dictionary or other classroom resource to include synonyms and antonyms for each of the words defined at the bottom of page 454. After they have completed their cards, have them work with a partner to compare synonyms and antonyms and discuss the different meanings of each. Then, have pairs present their synonyms, antonyms, and explanations to the class. **ADVANCED/ADVANCED HIGH**

In the United States, naturalism was influenced by Charles Darwin's theory of natural selection. The English philosopher Herbert Spencer tried to apply that theory to human society as "social Darwinism." Social Darwinists used the idea of "survival of the fittest" to justify the huge gap between rich and poor.

The work of naturalist writers, such as Theodore Dreiser, reflected the harsh new reality many people faced. Despite their grim attitudes, many naturalist writers were quite popular. Some writers, like Frank Norris, gave a voice to ordinary people and portrayed the rich and influential in an unflattering light.

CHECK YOUR UNDERSTANDING

Have students answer the questions independently.

Answers:

1. *A*
2. *G*
3. *C*

If students answer any questions incorrectly, have them reread the text to confirm their understanding.

Charles Darwin and other scientists, naturalist writers like Stephen Crane saw human beings as helpless creatures moved by forces beyond their understanding or control. While Crane and others gave voice to ordinary people living in cities, Jack London captured readers with his tales of an arctic world completely outside readers' everyday experiences. In novels such as *The Age of Innocence* and *The House of Mirth,* Edith Wharton combined naturalism with her own experiences to decry the stifling small-mindedness of upper-class society.

Reform-minded journalists were part of a progressive movement that aimed to restore economic opportunities and correct injustices in American life. Their work expressed naturalist influences in other ways. One group, known as "muckrakers," sought to expose the political and economic corruption that resulted from the excessive power of large corporations. Among this group was Upton Sinclair, whose novel *The Jungle* tells the story of a Lithuanian immigrant who works in the Chicago meatpacking industry. The novel's descriptions of the appalling conditions in packing plants and the contaminated meat they produced helped lead to the passage of new laws regulating the food industry.

CHECK YOUR UNDERSTANDING

Choose the best answer to each question.

1 Why was this period referred to as the "Gilded Age"?

   A It was a time of luxury and excess for some.

   B Many people discovered gold in the West.

   C Industry was run by philanthropists.

   D The majority of Americans belonged to the middle class.

2 *Huckleberry Finn* was the first novel to —

   F tackle the issue of racism

   G be written entirely in "American"

   H expose corruption in large corporations

   J be written by an African American

3 Who were "muckrakers"?

   A White settlers who drove the Native Americans from their land

   B Immigrants who lived in crowded tenements and worked for low wages

   C Writers who sought to expose corruption

   D Leaders of industry who exploited their workers

WHEN STUDENTS STRUGGLE . . .

Concept Support   Charles Darwin's theory of natural selection described a process of evolution in which those individuals or groups whose traits were best adapted to their environment tend to survive and pass those traits on to their offspring. Herbert Spencer's term *survival of the fittest* referred to a social order based on Darwin's theory. This social theory is referred to as "social Darwinism."

ACADEMIC VOCABULARY

Academic Vocabulary words are words you use when you discuss and write about texts. In this unit, you will learn the following five words:

☑ **ambiguous**   ☐ **clarify**   ☐ **implicit**   ☐ **revise**   ☐ **somewhat**

Study the Word Network to learn more about the word **ambiguous**.

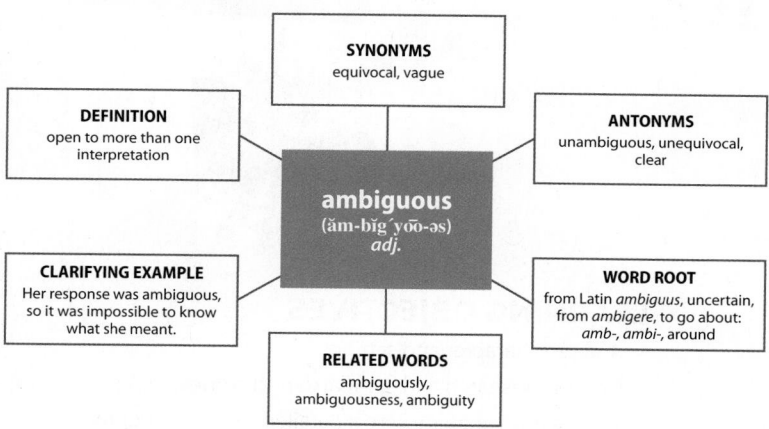

Write and Discuss Discuss the completed Word Network with a partner, making sure to talk through all of the boxes until you both understand the word, its synonyms, antonyms, and related forms. Then, fill out a Word Network for the remaining four words. Use a dictionary or online resource to help you complete the activity.

 Go online to access the Word Networks.

RESPOND TO THE ESSENTIAL QUESTIONS

In this unit, you will explore four different **Essential Questions** about self-determination, power struggles, change, and a sense of place. As you read each selection, you will gather your ideas about one of these questions and write about it in the **Response Log** that appears on page R5. At the end of the unit, you will have the opportunity to write a **short story** related to one of the Essential Questions. Filling out the Response Log after you read each text will help you prepare for this writing task.

 You can also go online to access the Response Log.

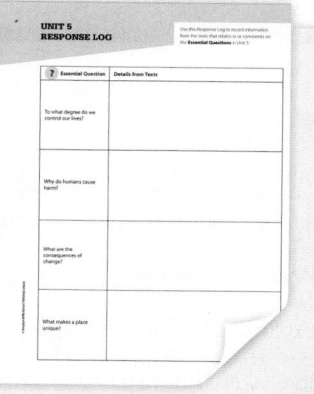

America Transformed 457

ACADEMIC VOCABULARY

As students complete Word Networks for the remaining four vocabulary words, encourage them to include all the categories shown in the completed network if possible, but point out that some words do not have clear synonyms or antonyms.

ambiguous (ăm-bĭgʹyo͞o -əs) *adj.* open to more than one interpretation (Spanish cognate: *ambiguo*)

clarify (klărʹə-fī) *v.tr.* to make clear or easier to understand (Spanish cognate: *clarificar*)

implicit (ĭm-plĭsʹĭt) *adj.* implied or understood though not directly expressed (Spanish cognate: *implícito*)

revise (rĭ-vīzʹ) *v.intr.* to alter or edit; to reconsider and change or modify (Spanish cognate: *revisar*)

somewhat (sŭmʹwŏt) *adv.* to some extent or degree

RESPOND TO THE ESSENTIAL QUESTIONS

Direct students to the Unit 5 Response Logs. Explain that students will use it to record ideas and details from the selections that help answer one of the Essential Questions. When they work on the Writing Task at the end of the unit, their Response Logs will help them think about what they have read and make connections between the texts.

TO BUILD A FIRE
Short Story by Jack London

GENRE ELEMENTS
SHORT STORY

A **short story** is a brief fictional work that includes elements such as characters, a conflict, a setting, and a theme. The theme is the author's message. It is usually revealed by how the conflict is resolved or the consequences of the main character's actions. Readers can learn about a character's motivations and traits through his or her words, thoughts, and actions. In some short stories, the setting also shapes the character's motivations and behavior.

LEARNING OBJECTIVES

- Analyze character and setting.
- Conduct research and compare short stories.
- Write a how-to guide with a detailed set of instructions.
- Present a how-to demonstration orally.
- Use strategies to identify allusions and word origins.
- Write a short narrative using the author's calm, unemotional tone.
- **Language** Write an informative text that describes a task.

TEXT COMPLEXITY

Quantitative Measures	To Build a Fire	Lexile: 970L
Qualitative Measures	**Ideas Presented** Multiple levels; use of irony; some ambiguity; greater demand for inference.	
	Structures Used Primarily explicit; some variation from simple chronological order; largely conventional.	
	Language Used Mostly explicit; some allusive language.	
	Knowledge Required More complexity in theme; experiences may be less familiar to many; historical references may make heavier demands.	

Online

RESOURCES

- Unit 5 Response Log
- Selection Audio
- Close Read Screencast: Modeled Discussion
- Reading Studio: Notice & Note
- Level Up Tutorials: listed at point of use
- Writing Studio: Writing Informative Texts
- Speaking and Listening Studio: Giving a Presentation
- Vocabulary Studio: Understanding Word Origins
- "To Build a Fire" Selection Test

SUMMARIES

English

A man walks through the freezing, icy wilderness to a Yukon mining camp. The temperature is 75 degrees below zero. The man's dog, a husky, reluctantly follows along. The man gets wet when he falls through the ice of a creek. He desparately tries to build a fire, hoping to dry his clothes and stay warm. However, snow falls on his small fire, and the man finds his hands are too numb from the cold to light it again. The cold overcomes him, and he dies. The dog continues on to the camp without the man.

Spanish

Un hombre atraviesa a pie la gélida y helada geografía de Yukón para llegar a un campamento minero. La temperatura es de 75 grados bajo cero. El perro del hombre, un husky siberiano, lo sigue a regañadientes. El hombre se moja al caer en el hielo de un riachuelo. Desesperado, intenta encender una fogata para secar su ropa y calentarse. Sin embargo, cae nieve sobre el fuego y el hombre se da cuenta de que no podrá volver a encenderlo porque sus manos están demasiado entumecidas por el frío. El hombre muere, vencido por el frío. El perro retoma la marcha rumbo al campamento sin el hombre.

SMALL-GROUP OPTIONS

Have students work in small groups and pairs to read and discuss the selection.

Double-Entry Journal

- Tell students to use a notebook or journal to record double-entry journal notes as they read.
- Have students draw a line from top to bottom in the middle of a page to create two columns. Add headings: *Quotes from the Text* (left column); *My Notes* (right column).
- Tell students to use the left column to record passages from the text that provide important information about the character, setting, conflict, or theme.
- Have students write notes, interpretations, or questions in the right column.

Reciprocal Teaching

- After students have read the selection, provide the following sentence frames: *Three words that describe the man are _____, _____, and _____. The man was doomed to experience difficulty because _____. If the man had had the wolf's instincts, he _____. The man should not have ignored _____. Things would have been different for the man if _____. The dog was _____ but _____ to his master.*
- Tell students to use the frames to write three to five questions about the selection.
- Have students form small groups of three. In each group, have students take turns asking a question for discussion without duplicating another student's question.
- Direct the groups to reach a consensus on the answer to each question and identify text evidence to support it.

Text X-Ray: English Learner Support
for "To Build a Fire"

Use the Text X-Ray and the supports and scaffolds in the Teacher's Edition to help guide students at different proficiency levels through the selection.

INTRODUCE THE SELECTION
DISCUSS THE SETTING

Students may benefit from knowing more about the time and place of the story. Explain that gold was discovered along the Klondike River in Canada's Yukon Territory in 1896. Many miners went to the Yukon Territory in search of gold. The trip was very dangerous and took a long time. The Yukon Territory is a wild, mountainous, and forested area in northwest Canada, near the Arctic Circle. During the winter, the days are very short, and it is very cold and snowy.

Discuss with students the difficulties of traveling in such a hostile environment.

CULTURAL REFERENCES

The following words or phrases may be unfamiliar to students:

- *hairline* (paragraph 2): something that looks like a very thin line
- *warm-whiskered* (paragraph 5): having thick facial hair
- *brute* (paragraph 6): an animal
- *snaps* (paragraph 7): periods of extremely cold weather
- *old-timer* (paragraph 20): someone who has been doing something for a long time
- *wires* (paragraph 21): commands from the brain that tell muscles what to do

LISTENING

Identify the Setting

Tell students that the first paragraph of a short story usually provides information about the setting, such as where it is, what it looks like, and who is present in it.

Read aloud paragraph 1. Use the following supports with students at varying proficiency levels:

- Work with students to pick out words that describe the setting, such as "cold," "gray," and "no sun." Then, work with students to write a sentence describing the setting. **SUBSTANTIAL**
- Provide students with a Five Ws graphic organizer. Tell them to jot notes in it as you read. After you read, have students work in small groups to review the paragraph and add additional notes to their graphic organizers to describe the setting. **MODERATE**
- Tell students they will be playing a game to see who can come up with the most words and phrases used in paragraph 1 to describe the setting. Provide students with a Five Ws graphic organizer. Tell them to jot notes in it as you read. After you have read the paragraph aloud, give students three minutes to add additional notes in each column. Then, have students meet in small groups to compare their notes and tally their results. **LIGHT**

SPEAKING

Discuss Character Traits

Have students discuss the character traits of the man by elaborating on a specific trait: his imagination. Tell students to use what the man says, thinks, and does to discuss this trait and similar traits.

Read the third and fourth sentences from paragraph 3 aloud. ("The trouble . . . not in the significances.") Then, use the following supports with students at varying proficiency levels:

- Ask students yes/no questions to identify examples of the man showing his lack of imagination. For example: *He knows it is cold but doesn't think about the danger of cold. Does this show imagination? (no) He takes off a mitten and is surprised by the cold. Does this show a lack of imagination? (yes)* **SUBSTANTIAL**
- Have students work in small groups to complete the following sentence frames orally. *The man was without imagination because ____. If the man had imagination he could have ____. Something that shows the man had no imagination was ____.* **MODERATE**
- Have students work in small groups to discuss the following question: *What did the man say, think, and do that showed he had no imagination?* **LIGHT**

READING

Identify Sensory Details

Review sensory language, or details based on sight, sound, touch, smell, and taste. Tell students they can create sensory images in their minds by using an author's words to imagine they are experiencing something through their senses.

Display names and images for the five senses. Use the following supports with students at varying levels:

- Read aloud examples of sensory images from the selection, and ask students to identify the sense used in the passage by touching their eyes, ears, hands, noses, or lips. **SUBSTANTIAL**
- Have students in small groups skim paragraphs 10–12 to find information to complete the sentence frames orally: *The man tried to stay warm by touching ____. The man tried to avoid danger by looking ____. The man became aware of danger when he heard ____.* Then, have students discuss sensory details based on smell and taste the author could have added to these paragraphs. **MODERATE**
- Tell students to read independently and identify two examples of sensory language. Then, have each student share the examples, as the other students identify the sense used in the passage. **LIGHT**

WRITING

Write a How-to Guide

Work with students to read and begin the writing assignment on Student Edition page 479.

Use the following supports with students at varying proficiency levels:

- As a class, make a list of simple things students know how to do well. Work with students to write or illustrate the steps. Write the guide as a class, and have students copy the steps in their notebooks. **SUBSTANTIAL**
- Pair or group students and have them decide on a process they could teach. Have students list or draw the steps. Provide sentence frames to help them write the guide: *First, you need to ____. Next, you ____. Finally, you need to ____.* **MODERATE**
- Pair students and have them write and illustrate a how-to guide. Remind them to list the steps in a logical order and to use transitions between steps. Have partners exchange papers with another pair and do a peer review. Reviewers should ensure that steps are clear and illustrations are helpful. **LIGHT**

Connect to the
ESSENTIAL QUESTION

"To Build a Fire" takes the reader deep into the freezing wilderness of the far north. In this story, the protagonist, known only as "the man," endures a harrowing experience as he struggles against subzero temperatures and rugged landscape. Despite being an experienced outdoorsman, the man must fight for his survival.

TO BUILD A FIRE

Short Story by **Jack London**

458   Unit 5

? ESSENTIAL QUESTION:

To what degree do we control our lives?

LEARNING MINDSET

Grit Tell students that mental toughness is a key ingredient to success. This quality is often called grit. This is one of the keys to having a learning mindset. It means more than just not giving up—it means being willing to keep working on a problem, despite all challenges. The brain is a muscle, and it gets stronger the more it is used. Accordingly, be sure to recognize students for effort and critical thinking, not just for concrete results.

QUICK START

What concerns might someone have while traveling through wilderness? Would weather be an issue? If so, why? Discuss your answers with a group.

ANALYZE CHARACTER

To make characters come to life, writers can describe their appearances or use the actions, feelings, or words of other characters to reveal personality traits. Another technique is to describe in detail the characters' **behavior**—how they act and the choices they make. A character's behavior is driven by his or her **motivations**—the stated or implied reasons behind a character's actions. In other words, motivation is the *why* that drives a character to do something.

A character's behavior can lead to conflicts or moral dilemmas and determine how they are resolved. It can also suggest a work's theme. As you read, note how the writer creates believable characters. Use a chart like the one below to record behaviors and infer the underlying motivations.

CHARACTER	BEHAVIOR	MOTIVATION
Man		
Dog		

ANALYZE SETTING

Setting is the time and place in which the events of a story take place. When writers depict the setting, they describe details about the environment. They also may reflect the historical and cultural context of the time. "To Build a Fire" reflects two movements of the time period: realism and naturalism.

- **Realism** is a 19th-century literary movement known for careful observation of contemporary life. It often focused on how the middle or lower classes were affected by progress. Realist writers attempted to present life objectively and without sentimentality. In so doing, they depicted the social, cultural, political, and economic forces shaping post-Civil War society.

- **Naturalism** is an offshoot of realism. Naturalists were influenced by the work of Charles Darwin and sought to describe the effect of natural and social forces on the individual. Naturalism typically renders common people and life as they are, shows that environment and instinct determine behavior, and paints human destiny as beyond the control of the individual.

As you read, look for details that realistically depict the setting and how the environment determines what happens to the main character. Also, note the characteristics of realism and naturalism that are reflected in the story.

GENRE ELEMENTS: SHORT STORY
- features a conflict centered around a main character
- features a theme, or message about life that the author wants to share
- may have a setting that reflects the historical, economic, and cultural reality of the time

QUICK START

Have students read the Quick Start questions and play a game of Would You Rather? (Wilderness Edition). Have students pose the questions to the rest of the class. For example: "Would you rather cross a raging river or walk 50 miles across a desert with no water?" "Would you rather walk across a glacier barefoot or eat what's left of a carcass after the vultures have lost interest?" Have students justify their answers and discuss the ways that nature can challenge us.

ANALYZE CHARACTER

Ask students to do a brief character analysis of one of their favorite characters. The character can come from any medium they wish. Instruct students to list at least one behavior and one motivation that shape who their characters are. Have volunteers share their analyses. As a class, discuss how these factors reveal character traits. Behaviors shed light on how characters think and what they consider important. Motivations, likewise, reveal what a character wants or needs.

ANALYZE SETTING

After students read the descriptions of realism and naturalism, have them speculate on which of the following storylines would likely be produced by authors of those movements:

- A sailor marooned on a desert island fights for survival during a typhoon.
- A factory worker protests unsafe working conditions and faces threats from management.

Have students propose their own realistic and naturalistic storylines, as well as counterexamples.

TEACH

CRITICAL VOCABULARY

Tell students to read all the words before reading the questions and answer options. Suggest they identify any familiar roots, prefixes, and suffixes. Explain that considering the meanings of these word parts will help them define the words.

Answers:

1. *b*
2. *b*
3. *a*
4. *a*
5. *b*

■ English Learner Support

Use Cognates Tell students that four of the Critical Vocabulary words have a Spanish cognate: *intangible/ intangible; panic/pánico; imperative/imperativo; extremity/ extremidad.* **ALL LEVELS**

LANGUAGE CONVENTIONS

Tone Discuss with students the difference between diction and syntax. Instruct students to write a sentence with unique and interesting diction. Next, have them write a sentence with interesting syntax. Ask for volunteers to read their sentences aloud, and have them explain how their sentences demonstrate diction and syntax.

Have students read the boldfaced passage. Ask them to point out how the passage is unemotional. (*The passage lacks descriptive detail or any hint of the character's feelings.*)

ANNOTATION MODEL

Point out to students that a story set in the outdoors will have many examples of naturalism. Therefore, it might be excessive to mark every single instance in the story. Instead, students might mark the most representative ones or their favorites.

 **GET READY**

CRITICAL VOCABULARY

intangible	apprehension	panic	imperative	extremity

To show your knowledge of the Critical Vocabulary, circle the best answer.

1. Which of the following is an example of an **extremity**?
  a. lungs   **b.** feet

2. If you experience **panic,** what are you feeling?
  a. calm   **b.** fear

3. Which of the following is **intangible**?
  a. the source of ideas   **b.** the source of a river

4. If you feel **apprehension,** what are you feeling?
  a. anxiety   **b.** happiness

5. If something is **imperative,** which is it?
  a. boring   **b.** urgent

LANGUAGE CONVENTIONS

Tone An author's attitude toward his or her subject or toward the reader is reflected in the **tone** of the work. For example, the tone might be serious, ironic, playful, or detached. Note that London's diction includes descriptive vocabulary and many of his sentences are syntactically complex. These give the story an almost clinical tone—unemotional and detached.

> **It was a steep bank, and he paused for breath at the top, excusing the act to himself by looking at his watch. It was nine o'clock.**

As you read, note how the author's language contributes to a consistent tone.

ANNOTATION MODEL   **NOTICE & NOTE**

As you read, note the features of naturalism and how London creates a realistic, natural setting. In the model, you can see one reader's notes about "To Build a Fire."

Day had broken cold and gray, <u>exceedingly cold and gray</u>, when the man turned aside from the main Yukon trail <u>and climbed</u> the high earth bank, where a dim and (little-traveled trail) led eastward through the fat spruce timberland. It was a steep bank, and he <u>paused for breath</u> at the top, excusing the act to himself by looking at his watch.

Weather will probably be a factor in the story.

"little-traveled" sounds lonely; maybe he'll get lost

If he's pausing for breath, is he in good enough shape for taking this trail in the cold?

BACKGROUND

Jack London *(1876–1916) not only wrote adventure stories, he lived them. London traveled as a hobo across the United States, tried his luck in the Klondike Gold Rush, escaped a typhoon on a seal-hunting ship, and sailed the South Seas in his own boat, the Snark. London's formal education was limited, but he read widely using public libraries. Many of his works, including the story "To Build a Fire," have themes involving survival and humans versus nature. His novel* The Call of the Wild *(1903) brought London fame and is still one of his best-known works. London died in California at age 40.*

TO BUILD A FIRE

Short Story by Jack London

SETTING A PURPOSE

As you read, pay attention to the details that depict the protagonist's dealings with the natural setting as well as details that contrast the actions of the man with those of the dog.

1   Day had broken cold and gray, exceedingly cold and gray, when the man turned aside from the main Yukon trail and climbed the high earth bank, where a dim and little-traveled trail led eastward through the fat spruce timberland. It was a steep bank, and he paused for breath at the top, excusing the act to himself by looking at his watch. It was nine o'clock. There was no sun or hint of sun, though there was not a cloud in the sky. It was a clear day, and yet there seemed an **intangible** pall[1] over the face of things, a subtle gloom that made the day dark, and that was due to the absence of sun. This fact did not worry the man. He was used to the lack of sun. It had been days since he had seen the sun, and he knew that a few more days must pass before that cheerful orb, due south, would just peep above the skyline and dip immediately from view.

---

[1] **pall:** overspreading atmosphere of gloom and depression.

Notice & Note

Use the side margins to notice and note signposts in the text.

intangible
(ĭn-tăn´jə-bəl) *adj.* unable to be defined or understood.

 ENGLISH LEARNER SUPPORT

Analyze Setting   Using a whiteboard, project this page. Invite students to mark up the text on this page (paragraph 1), highlighting words or phrases that describe the setting. Point out that most authors try to describe their settings early in a story so the reader knows where the story is happening. Authors might not tell you exactly where the story is set, but they will often provide details to give you a hint. **MODERATE**

TEACH

BACKGROUND

After students read the Background note, explain that Jack London lived at a time when the American frontier was coming to an end. Most of the western territories in the country were being turned into states, and the wars with Native Americans were winding down. Pastures were being fenced off, ending the days of the open range. The country's attention was beginning to turn to cities and the benefits of industrialization. However, there were still large swaths of the country that remained wild, especially in the Arctic regions of the northwest. London sought out these places and used them as settings for many of his stories.

SETTING A PURPOSE

Direct students to use the Setting a Purpose prompt to focus their reading.

For **listening support** for students at varying proficiency levels, see the **Text X-Ray** on page 458C.

CRITICAL VOCABULARY

intangible: London describes the pall over the scene as intangible, meaning that it is something the man senses but not something that can be directly seen or touched.

ASK STUDENTS what other intangible qualities a gray, gloomy day might have. *(The day might also be depressing, foreboding, melancholic, unhappy, demoralizing, or even hopeless.)*

ANALYZE CHARACTER

Paragraph 3 provides details that explicitly describe the protagonist's character. Tell students that passages like this can be a huge benefit while reading. A sentence beginning with a phrase like, "The trouble with him was that . . ." deserves close attention. (**Answer:** *It suggests he will have difficulty because he does not tend to see the significance of his surroundings. In this case, the extremely cold temperature is significant because it is very dangerous.*)

 ## ANALYZE SETTING

Remind students that authors don't always tell you *why* something is important. However, if the author includes many details about something, such as the weather, then it is likely important. (**Answer:** *Students' answers will vary but should assume that the extremely cold weather will cause problems for the protagonist.*)

 For **speaking support** for students at varying proficiency levels, see the **Text X-Ray** on page 458D.

2   The man flung a look back along the way he had come. The Yukon lay a mile wide and hidden under three feet of ice. On top of this ice were as many feet of snow. It was all pure white, rolling in gentle undulations where the ice jams of the freeze-up had formed. North and south, as far as his eye could see, it was unbroken white, save for a dark hairline that curved and twisted from around the spruce-covered island to the south, and that curved and twisted away into the north, where it disappeared behind another spruce-covered island. This dark hairline was the trail—the main trail—that led south five hundred miles to the Chilkoot Pass, Dyea, and salt water; and that led north seventy miles to Dawson, and still on to the north a thousand miles to Nulato, and finally to St. Michael on the Bering Sea, a thousand miles and half a thousand more.

3   But all this—the mysterious, far-reaching hairline trail, the absence of sun from the sky, the tremendous cold, and the strangeness and weirdness of it all—made no impression on the man. It was not because he was long used to it. He was a newcomer in the land, a cheechako,[2] and this was his first winter. The trouble with him was that he was without imagination. He was quick and alert in the things of life, but only in the things, and not in the significances. Fifty degrees below zero meant eighty-odd degrees of frost. Such fact impressed him as being cold and uncomfortable, and that was all. It did not lead him to meditate upon his frailty as a creature of temperature, and upon man's frailty in general, able only to live within certain narrow limits of heat and cold, and from there on it did not lead him to the conjectural[3] field of immortality and man's place in the universe. Fifty degrees below zero stood for a bite of frost that hurt and that must be guarded against by the use of mittens, earflaps, warm moccasins, and thick socks. Fifty degrees below zero was to him just precisely fifty degrees below zero. That there should be anything more to it than that was a thought that never entered his head.

4   As he turned to go on, he spat speculatively. There was a sharp, explosive crackle that startled him. He spat again. And again, in the air, before it could fall to the snow, the spittle crackled. He knew that at fifty below, spittle crackled on the snow, but this spittle had crackled in the air. Undoubtedly it was colder than fifty below—how much colder he did not know. But the temperature did not matter. He was bound for the old claim[4] on the left fork of Henderson Creek, where the boys were already. They had come over across the divide from the Indian Creek country, while he had come the roundabout way to take a look at the possibilities of getting out logs in the spring

---

[2] **cheechako:** Chinook jargon for "newcomer" or "tenderfoot."
[3] **conjectural:** based on guesswork or uncertain evidence.
[4] **claim:** piece of land staked out by a miner.

ANALYZE CHARACTER

Annotate: Mark words or phrases in paragraph 3 that describe the man.

Infer: What does this description of the man suggest about how he will fare during his journey?

ANALYZE SETTING

Annotate: In paragraphs 4–5, mark words that describe the weather conditions.

Predict: How will the weather affect the events of the story?

CLOSE READ SCREENCAST

Modeled Discussion   In their eBooks, have students view the Close Read Screencast, in which readers discuss and annotate key details of the environment in paragraph 4.

As a class, view and discuss the video. Then, have students pair up to do an independent close read of paragraph 38. Students can record their answers on the Close Read Practice PDF.

 Close Read Practice PDF

from the islands in the Yukon. He would be into camp by six o'clock; a bit after dark, it was true, but the boys would be there, a fire would be going, and a hot supper would be ready. As for lunch, he pressed his hand against the protruding bundle under his jacket. It was also under his shirt, wrapped up in a handkerchief and lying against the naked skin. It was the only way to keep the biscuits from freezing. He smiled agreeably to himself as he thought of those biscuits, each cut open and sopped in bacon grease, and each enclosing a generous slice of fried bacon.

5   He plunged in among the big spruce trees. The trail was faint. A foot of snow had fallen since the last sled had passed over, and he was glad he was without a sled, traveling light. In fact, he carried nothing but the lunch wrapped in the handkerchief. He was surprised, however, at the cold. It certainly was cold, he concluded, as he rubbed his numb nose and cheekbones with his mittened hand. He was a warm-whiskered man, but the hair on his face did not protect the high cheekbones and the eager nose that thrust itself aggressively into the frosty air.

6   At the man's heels trotted a dog, a big native husky, the proper wolf dog, gray coated and without any visible or temperamental difference from its brother, the wild wolf. The animal was depressed by the tremendous cold. It knew that it was no time for traveling. Its instinct told it a truer tale than was told to the man by the man's judgment. In reality, it was not merely colder than fifty below zero; it was colder than sixty below, than seventy below. It was seventy-five below zero. Since the freezing point is thirty-two above zero, it meant that one hundred and seven degrees of frost obtained. The dog did not know anything about thermometers. Possibly in its brain there was no sharp consciousness of a condition of very cold such as was in the man's brain. But the brute had its instinct. It experienced a vague but menacing **apprehension** that subdued it and made it slink along at the man's heels, and that made it question eagerly every unwonted[5] movement of the man, as if expecting him to go into camp or to seek shelter somewhere and build a fire. The dog had learned fire, and it wanted fire, or else to burrow under the snow and cuddle its warmth away from the air.

7   The frozen moisture of its breathing had settled on its fur in a fine powder of frost, and especially were its jowls, muzzle, and eyelashes whitened by its crystaled breath. The man's red beard and moustache were likewise frosted, but more solidly, the deposit taking the form of ice and increasing with every warm, moist breath he exhaled. Also, the man was chewing tobacco, and the muzzle of ice held his lips so rigidly that he was unable to clear his chin when he expelled the juice. The result was that a crystal beard of the color and

---
[5] **unwonted:** unusual.

ANALYZE CHARACTER
Annotate: Mark details in paragraph 6 that describe the dog's behavior.

Analyze: How does the dog's behavior differ from the man's?

apprehension
(ăp-rĭ-hĕn´shən) *n.* fear or anxiety; dread.

ANALYZE CHARACTER
Tell students that the term *foil* refers to a character who presents a contrast to the main character in order to emphasize the main character's traits. In this story, the dog acts as a foil to the man. For example, the dog has an intuitive knowledge of the environment, highlighting the man's ignorance. (**Answer:** *The dog moves tentatively and slinks along, while the man tends to crash through the woods.*)

ENGLISH LEARNER SUPPORT
Use Prior Knowledge Tap into students' prior knowledge by asking them what they think it is like to be outside in extremely cold weather. To help generate ideas, show examples of people dressed for extreme cold, such as mountain climbers or scientists in Antarctica, from news stories or Internet sites. Read paragraph 5 aloud, and have students raise their hands when they hear a way the man reacts to the extreme cold. Make sure students understand the man's nose is numb—has lost feeling—because of the cold and he rubs it to warm it up and restore the feeling.
SUBSTANTIAL

WHEN STUDENTS STRUGGLE...
Analyze Character As students read the story, have them record the inner thoughts of the protagonist in the side margin of their books. The man does not have a rich inner monologue, so the amount of information is not excessive, but the thoughts he has as his experience unfolds are, in fact, significant. Tracking his thoughts will give students an idea of what direction the story is headed.

 For additional support, go to the **Reading Studio** and assign the following **Level Up Tutorial: Character Motivation.**

CRITICAL VOCABULARY
apprehension: Many creatures feel fear, so it is not a surprise that the dog might feel apprehension in this extreme environment.

ASK STUDENTS when they have felt apprehension. (*Answers might include before a test, during a storm, or at a contest.*)

TEACH

 ANALYZE CHARACTER

Remind students that motivations are a key to discovering character. Spend a moment discussing the definition of the word *motivation* ("the reason we do something"). In a story, a motivation shows what is important to a character. (**Answer:** *His motivation seems primarily to be centered on his next two meals. This motivation might not be strong enough to drive him through the extreme challenges ahead.*)

 ANALYZE SETTING

Setting is often reduced to the location of a story, such as London, England, or New York City. Point out that setting can include many more details than that, including weather, climates, landscapes, cities or towns, and time periods. (**Answer:** *Answers will vary, but students might predict the man will eventually crash through the ice and get wet because the springs are nearly impossible to spot.*)

For **reading support** for students at varying proficiency levels, see the **Text X-Ray** on page 458D.

 **NOTICE & NOTE**

solidity of amber was increasing its length on his chin. If he fell down it would shatter itself, like glass, into brittle fragments. But he did not mind the appendage.[6] It was the penalty all tobacco chewers paid in that country, and he had been out before in two cold snaps. They had not been so cold as this, he knew, but by the spirit thermometer[7] at Sixty Mile he knew they had been registered at fifty below and at fifty-five.

8   He held on through the level stretch of woods for several miles, crossed a wide flat, and dropped down a bank to the frozen bed of a small stream. This was Henderson Creek, and he knew he was ten miles from the forks. He looked at his watch. It was ten o'clock. He was making four miles an hour, and he calculated that he would arrive at the forks at half past twelve. He decided to celebrate that event by eating his lunch there.

9   The dog dropped in again at his heels, with a tail drooping discouragement, as the man swung along the creek bed. The furrow of the old sled trail was plainly visible, but a dozen inches of snow covered the marks of the last runners. In a month no man had come up or down that silent creek. The man held steadily on. He was not much given to thinking, and just then particularly, he had nothing to think about save that he would eat lunch at the forks and that at six o'clock he would be in camp with the boys. There was nobody to talk to; and, had there been, speech would have been impossible because of the ice muzzle on his mouth. So he continued monotonously to chew tobacco and to increase the length of his amber beard.

10   Once in a while the thought reiterated[8] itself that it was very cold and that he had never experienced such cold. As he walked along he rubbed his cheekbones and nose with the back of his mittened hand. He did this automatically, now and again changing hands. But rub as he would, the instant he stopped his cheekbones went numb, and the following instant the end of his nose went numb. He was sure to frost his cheeks; he knew that, and experienced a pang of regret that he had not devised a nose strap of the sort Bud wore in the cold snaps. Such a strap passed across the cheeks, as well, and saved them. But it didn't matter much, after all. What were frosted cheeks? A bit painful, that was all; they were never serious.

11   Empty as the man's mind was of thought, he was keenly observant, and he noticed the changes in the creek, the curves and bends and timber jams, and always he sharply noted where he placed his feet. Once, coming around a bend, he shied abruptly, like a startled horse, curved away from the place where he had been walking, and retreated several paces back along the trail. The creek,

---

[6] **appendage:** something attached to another object.
[7] **spirit thermometer:** alcohol thermometer. In places where the temperature often drops below the freezing point of mercury, alcohol is used in thermometers.
[8] **reiterated:** repeated.

ANALYZE CHARACTER
Annotate: In paragraph 9, mark the description of the man's thought process.

Infer: What motivations do the man's thoughts reveal? How could these lead to a dilemma that advances the plot?

ANALYZE SETTING
Annotate: In paragraph 11, mark the clues that convey how dangerous the trail is.

Predict: What do you think will happen, based on the details about the springs? How do these details help develop the theme?

464   Unit 5

APPLYING ACADEMIC VOCABULARY

☑ **ambiguous**   ❑ **clarify**   ☑ **implicit**   ❑ **revise**   ❑ **somewhat**

Write and Discuss   Have students turn to a partner to discuss the following questions. Guide students to include the Academic Vocabulary words *ambiguous* and *implicit* in their responses. Ask volunteers to share their responses with the class.

- Why do you think the identity of the protagonist was left **ambiguous**?
- What realities about human survival are **implicit** when it comes to extremely cold weather?

he knew, was frozen clear to the bottom—no creek could contain water in that arctic winter—but he knew also that there were springs that bubbled out from the hillsides and ran along under the snow and on top of the ice of the creek. He knew that the coldest snaps never froze these springs, and he knew likewise their danger. They were traps. They hid pools of water under the snow that might be three inches deep, or three feet. Sometimes a skin of ice half an inch thick covered them, and in turn was covered by the snow. Sometimes there were alternate layers of water and ice skin, so that when one broke through he kept on breaking through for a while, sometimes wetting himself to the waist.

12   That was why he had shied in such **panic**. He had felt the give under his feet and heard the crackle of a snow-hidden ice skin. And to get his feet wet in such a temperature meant trouble and danger. At the very least it meant delay, for he would be forced to stop and build a fire, and under its protection to bare his feet while he dried his socks and moccasins. He stood and studied the creek bed and its banks, and decided that the flow of water came from the right. He reflected awhile, rubbing his nose and cheeks, then skirted to the left, stepping gingerly and testing the footing for each step. Once clear of the danger, he took a fresh chew of tobacco and swung along at his four-mile gait.

panic
(păn´ĭk) *n.* sudden, overpowering feeling of fear.

To Build a Fire   465

ENGLISH LEARNER SUPPORT

Ask Yes/No Questions Read aloud paragraphs 11–12 as students follow along. As you read, pause to clarify the idiom *clear to* as "all the way to," the meaning of the multiple-meaning word *spring* as a source of water that flows from underground, and other terms and expressions students may find confusing or unfamiliar (*coldest snaps, skin of ice, shied, skirted, gingerly*).

To confirm understanding and help students predict what will happen next, ask them yes/no questions or questions that can be answered in one word. Possible questions: *Do springs freeze over in cold weather? (no) Are springs always easy to see? (no) The man jumped in panic. Did he fall into the water? (no) Would the man have to stop walking if he fell into the water? (yes) If the man got wet, would he have to stop and build a fire? (yes) Was the man more careful after he heard the crack? (yes)* **SUBSTANTIAL**

TO CHALLENGE STUDENTS . . .

Analyze Setting By now, students should see that the setting plays a major role in "To Build a Fire." It is not simply a backdrop in which the plot occurs. Have students make a list of stories they have read, seen, or played (in a video game) in which the setting is significant. Stories can come from any medium they wish. Give students a few minutes to list the stories and their settings. Next, hold a discussion in which students share their top three settings and explain why those settings were so significant to their stories.

CRITICAL VOCABULARY

panic: When the man feels panic, he jumps "like a startled horse." This is an indication of what panic feels like.

ASK STUDENTS how they think they might respond to panic. (*Answers will vary but might include screaming, running, hiding, sweating, or shaking.*)

ENGLISH LEARNER SUPPORT

Illustrate the Text Read the text on page 466 aloud. Speak slowly and emphasize the verbs and the action in the story. This passage provides the opportunity for students to connect a scene of action with active verbs and explicit details. Next, ask students to draw and label what they just heard in a three- or six-panel comic strip. Labels might include the man, the dog, the creek, and the dog's ice-covered foot. **MODERATE**

13   In the course of the next two hours he came upon several similar traps. Usually the snow above the hidden pools had a sunken, candied appearance that advertised the danger. Once again, however, he had a close call; and once, suspecting danger, he compelled the dog to go on in front. The dog did not want to go. It hung back until the man shoved it forward, and then it went quickly across the white, unbroken surface. Suddenly it broke through, floundered to one side, and got away to firmer footing. It had wet its forefeet and legs, and almost immediately the water that clung to it turned to ice. It made quick efforts to lick the ice off its legs, then dropped down in the snow and began to bite out the ice that had formed between the toes. This was a matter of instinct. To permit the ice to remain would mean sore feet. It did not know this. It merely obeyed the mysterious prompting that arose from the deep crypts[9] of its being. But the man knew, having achieved a judgment on the subject, and he removed the mitten from his right hand and helped tear out the ice particles. He did not expose his fingers more than a minute, and was astonished at the swift numbness that smote[10] them. It certainly

---

[9] **crypts:** hidden recesses.
[10] **smote:** powerfully struck.

© Houghton Mifflin Harcourt Publishing Company • Image Credits: © zlikovec/Shutterstock

IMPROVE READING FLUENCY

Targeted Passage The passage on page 466 contains a lot of action. It is a good opportunity for students to practice "readers' theater," in which they act out the action of the story. As one student reads aloud—or as you read and they follow along—have two students play the role of the man and the dog crossing the sunken pool.

 Go to the **Reading Studio** for additional support in developing fluency.

was cold. He pulled on the mitten hastily, and beat the hand savagely across his chest.

14   At twelve o'clock the day was at its brightest. Yet the sun was too far south on its winter journey to clear the horizon. The bulge of the earth intervened between it and Henderson Creek, where the man walked under a clear sky at noon and cast no shadow. At half past twelve, to the minute, he arrived at the forks of the creek. He was pleased at the speed he had made. If he kept it up, he would certainly be with the boys by six. He unbuttoned his jacket and shirt and drew forth his lunch. The action consumed no more than a quarter of a minute, yet in that brief moment the numbness laid hold of the exposed fingers. He did not put the mitten on, but instead struck the fingers a dozen sharp smashes against his leg. Then he sat down on a snow-covered log to eat. The sting that followed upon the striking of his fingers against his leg ceased so quickly that he was startled. He had had no chance to take a bite of biscuit. He struck the fingers repeatedly and returned them to the mitten, baring the other hand for the purpose of eating. He tried to take a mouthful, but the ice muzzle prevented. He had forgotten to build a fire and thaw out. He chuckled at his foolishness, and as he chuckled he noted the numbness creeping into the exposed fingers. Also, he noted that the stinging which had first come to his toes when he sat down was already passing away. He wondered whether the toes were warm or numb. He moved them inside the moccasins and decided that they were numb.

15   He pulled the mitten on hurriedly and stood up. He was a bit frightened. He stamped up and down until the stinging returned into the feet. It certainly *was* cold, was his thought. That man from Sulphur Creek had spoken the truth when telling how cold it sometimes got in the country. And he had laughed at him at the time! That showed one must not be too sure of things. There was no mistake about it, it was cold. He strode up and down, stamping his feet and threshing his arms, until reassured by the returning warmth. Then he got out matches and proceeded to make a fire. From the undergrowth, where high water of the previous spring had lodged a supply of seasoned twigs, he got his firewood. Working carefully from a small beginning, he soon had a roaring fire, over which he thawed the ice from his face and in the protection of which he ate his biscuits. For the moment the cold of space was outwitted. The dog took satisfaction in the fire, stretching out close enough for warmth and far enough away to escape being singed.

16   When the man had finished, he filled his pipe and took his comfortable time over a smoke. Then he pulled on his mittens, settled the earflaps of his cap firmly about his ears, and took the creek trail up the left fork. The dog was disappointed and yearned back toward the fire. This man did not know cold. Possibly all the generations

---

NOTICE & NOTE

ANALYZE CHARACTER

Annotate: In paragraph 14, mark what the man forgets to do and how he feels.

Infer: What does this action tell you about the man and how nature might be affecting him? What affect will these actions have on him?

ANALYZE CHARACTER

One of the features of realism is the presence of quotidian details—often small details of everyday life. The text in paragraph 14 is a good example of this. It describes a scene in which the man tries to sit down and eat, only to be frustrated by his freezing fingers. Toward the end of the paragraph, the man realizes he has forgotten a key task—building a fire in order to warm up. (**Answer:** *It says that he is forgetful or is getting more so. It is possible that nature is taking its toll by slowly wearing him out, causing him to become forgetful. In the long run, these effects could become extremely dangerous for him.*)

 ENGLISH LEARNER SUPPORT

Retell the Story Read paragraph 14 aloud slowly. Then, as a class, have students retell this part of the story using short, simple sentences. The passage is long, so have students choose other students to pick up the retelling. **LIGHT**

✏ ANALYZE SETTING

Remind students that naturalism was partially inspired by the work of Charles Darwin. Darwin, a 19th-century scientist, explained how nature shapes the behavior and evolution of species. Naturalists, in turn, sought to describe the effects of natural forces on the individual. Tell students to watch for instances where the rules of the natural world make it difficult for the man because the man is not very fit for the environment. (**Answer:** *The paragraph supports Darwin's theories because the dog is much better suited for the environment than the man. This is the case because the dog and its species have adapted to the freezing environment over countless generations. Meanwhile, the man has not; he is from a different region and does not have the adaptations that would make him suited for the extreme cold.*)

✏ LANGUAGE CONVENTIONS

Remind students that the tone of a story reflects the author's attitude toward the subject or the audience. Diction and syntax are used to create tone. London has used very specific words and phrases to maintain a consistent tone in order to comment on man's place in nature. (**Answer:** *The tone of the story—unemotional and detached—is created by using fairly simple language and sentence structure. Much of the language is also quite cold, discussing the deadly dangers of the environment in a dispassionate way. London feels that the gold seekers are not well suited to survive in this environment.*)

CRITICAL VOCABULARY

imperative: Having gotten wet, the man's next act—starting a fire—is crucial, or imperative.

ASK STUDENTS why starting a fire is imperative in this situation. (*It is the only way to dry out his footgear. Otherwise, it will freeze solid.*)

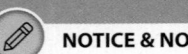

NOTICE & NOTE

ANALYZE SETTING

Annotate: In paragraph 16, mark the words that contrast what the dog and the man understand about the cold.

Summarize: How does this paragraph support the influence of Charles Darwin's theories in naturalist writings?

imperative
(ĭm-pĕr´ə-tĭv) *adj.* of great importance; essential.

LANGUAGE CONVENTIONS

Annotate: Mark details in paragraph 19 that reveal the story's tone.

Analyze: How does this tone reflect the author's attitude about man's ability to control nature?

---

of his ancestry had been ignorant of cold, of real cold, of cold one hundred and seven degrees below freezing point. But the dog knew; all its ancestry knew, and it had inherited the knowledge. And it knew that it was not good to walk abroad in such fearful cold. It was the time to lie snug in a hole in the snow and wait for a curtain of cloud to be drawn across the face of outer space whence this cold came. On the other hand, there was no keen intimacy between the dog and the man. The one was the toil slave of the other, and the only caresses it had ever received were the caresses of the whiplash and of harsh and menacing throat sounds that threatened the whiplash. So the dog made no effort to communicate its apprehension to the man. It was not concerned in the welfare of the man; it was for its own sake that it yearned back toward the fire. But the man whistled, and spoke to it with the sound of whiplashes, and the dog swung in at the man's heels and followed after.

17   The man took a chew of tobacco and proceeded to start a new amber beard. Also, his moist breath quickly powdered with white his mustache, eyebrows, and lashes. There did not seem to be so many springs on the left fork of the Henderson, and for half an hour the man saw no signs of any. And then it happened. At a place where there were no signs, where the soft, unbroken snow seemed to advertise solidity beneath, the man broke through. It was not deep. He wet himself halfway to the knees before he floundered out to the firm crust.

18   He was angry, and cursed his luck aloud. He had hoped to get into camp with the boys at six o'clock, and this would delay him an hour, for he would have to build a fire and dry out his footgear. This was **imperative** at that low temperature—he knew that much; and he turned aside to the bank, which he climbed. On top, tangled in the underbrush about the trunks of several small spruce trees, was a high-water deposit of dry firewood—sticks and twigs, principally, but also larger portions of seasoned branches and fine, dry, last year's grasses. He threw down several large pieces on top of the snow. This served for a foundation and prevented the young flame from drowning itself in the snow it otherwise would melt. The flame he got by touching a match to a small shred of birch bark that he took from his pocket. This burned even more readily than paper. Placing it on the foundation, he fed the young flame with wisps of dry grass and with the tiniest dry twigs.

19   He worked slowly and carefully, keenly aware of his danger. Gradually, as the flame grew stronger, he increased the size of the twigs with which he fed it. He squatted in the snow, pulling the twigs out from their entanglement in the brush and feeding directly to the flame. He knew there must be no failure. When it is seventy-five below zero, a man must not fail in his first attempt to build a fire— that is, if his feet are wet. If his feet are dry, and he fails, he can run

---

WHEN STUDENTS STRUGGLE . . .

Analyze Character Some students may have difficulty visualizing what is happening to the main character because of unfamiliar words. Encourage them to focus on familiar, concrete nouns, verbs, and modifiers in the text, such as *cold, deep, fire,* or *dry,* rather than on less familiar ones, such as *advertised* or *seasoned.* Ask students to choose a paragraph on page 468 and retell it in their own words.

For additional support, go to the **Reading Studio** and assign the following 🔲 **Level Up Tutorial: Characters and Conflict.**

along the trail for a half a mile and restore his circulation. But the circulation of wet and freezing feet cannot be restored by running when it is seventy-five below. No matter how fast he runs, the wet feet will freeze the harder.

20   All this the man knew. The old-timer on Sulphur Creek had told him about it the previous fall, and now he was appreciating the advice. Already all sensation had gone out of his feet. To build the fire, he had been forced to remove his mittens, and the fingers had quickly gone numb. His pace of four miles an hour had kept his heart pumping blood to the surface of his body and to all the **extremities**. But the instant he stopped, the action of the pump eased down. The cold of space smote the unprotected tip of the planet, and he, being on that unprotected tip, received the full force of the blow. The blood of his body recoiled before it. The blood was alive, like the dog, and like the dog it wanted to hide away and cover itself up from the fearful cold. So long as he walked four miles an hour, he pumped that blood, willy-nilly,[11] to the surface; but now it ebbed away and sank down into the recesses of his body. The extremities were the first to feel its absence. His wet feet froze the faster, and his exposed fingers numbed the faster, though they had not yet begun to freeze. Nose and cheeks were already freezing, while the skin of all his body chilled as it lost its blood.

21   But he was safe. Toes and nose and cheeks would be only touched by the frost, for the fire was beginning to burn with strength. He was feeding it twigs the size of his finger. In another minute he would be able to feed it with branches the size of his wrist, and then he could remove his wet footgear, and, while it dried, he could keep his naked feet warm by the fire, rubbing them at first, of course, with snow. The fire was a success. He was safe. He remembered the advice of the old-timer on Sulphur Creek, and smiled. The old-timer had been very serious in laying down the law that no man must travel alone in the Klondike after fifty below. Well, here he was; he had had the accident; he was alone; and he had saved himself. Those old-timers were rather womanish, some of them, he thought. All a man had to do was to keep his head and he was all right. Any man who was a man could travel alone. But it was surprising, the rapidity with which his cheeks and nose were freezing. And he had not thought his fingers could go lifeless in so short a time. Lifeless they were, for he could scarcely make them move together to grip a twig, and they seemed remote from his body and from him. When he touched a twig, he had to look and see whether or not he had hold of it. The wires were pretty well down between him and his finger ends.

---
11 **willy-nilly:** without choice.

extremity
(ĭk-strĕm´ĭ-tē) *n.* the outermost or farthest point or portion; the hand or foot.

ANALYZE CHARACTER
Annotate: In paragraph 21, mark what the old-timer said and how the man reacts to it.

Evaluate: How does the man's attitude toward the old-timer's advice continue to evolve?

To Build a Fire   469

ANALYZE CHARACTER

Many good stories have characters who change over time. The path a character goes down is often called a "character arc." In this story, the protagonist's attitude about the old-timer changes over time. The man's attitude is closely related to the dangerousness of his situation—as the situation gets more precarious, he becomes more and more receptive to the old-timer's ideas. (**Answer:** *The man grows to appreciate the old-timer's advice in paragraph 24. Early on, he laughed at the advice. Gradually, he comes to realize that the advice was wise.*)

TO CHALLENGE STUDENTS . . .

Analyze Character   Challenge students to write the action on page 469 in a different genre. Tell them that they can change the tone and even the theme of the story, if they wish. Possible genres include a poem, a melodrama, a folk song, or a screenplay. Regardless of their choice of genre, their piece should keep a spotlight on the character, including his behaviors and motivations, as London's story does. Afterward, discuss with students how character is a literary element that transcends different genres.

CRITICAL VOCABULARY

extremity: The words *extremity* and *extreme* are indeed related. One definition of *extremity* is something at the extreme end of something, such as a hand or foot.

ASK STUDENTS why one's extremities might get colder faster than other parts of one's body. (*Because extremities are farther from the body's core, they are more exposed to the elements.*)

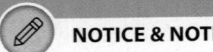

LANGUAGE CONVENTIONS

While characters often change throughout a story (as part of a character arc), the tone usually does not. An author usually uses a consistent tone in order to set the mood and to say something about the subject or theme of the story. (**Answer:** *The tone has not changed and is still consistent, up to this point.*)

22 All of which counted for little. There was the fire, snapping and crackling and promising life with every dancing flame. He started to untie his moccasins. They were coated with ice; the thick German socks were like sheaths of iron halfway to the knees; and the moccasin strings were like rods of steel all twisted and knotted as by some conflagration.[12] For a moment he tugged with his numb fingers, then, realizing the folly of it, he drew his sheath knife.

23 But before he could cut the strings it happened. It was his own fault, or, rather, his mistake. He should not have built the fire under the spruce tree. He should have built it in the open. But it had been easier to pull the twigs from the bush and drop them directly on the fire. Now the tree under which he had done this carried a weight of snow on its boughs. No wind had blown for weeks, and each bough was fully freighted. Each time he had pulled a twig he had communicated a slight agitation to the tree—an imperceptible agitation, so far as he was concerned, but an agitation sufficient to bring about the disaster. High up in the tree one bough capsized its load of snow. This fell on the boughs beneath, capsizing them. This process continued, spreading out and involving the whole tree. It grew like an avalanche, and it descended without warning upon the man and the fire, and the fire was blotted out! Where it had burned was a mantle of fresh and disordered snow.

LANGUAGE CONVENTIONS

Annotate: Mark the sentences in paragraph 24 that indicate the story's tone.

Analyze: Is the tone still consistent or has it changed? If it has changed, how so?

24 The man was shocked. It was as though he had just heard his own sentence of death. For a moment he sat and stared at the spot where the fire had been. Then he grew very calm. Perhaps the old-timer on Sulphur Creek was right. If he had only had a trail mate, he would have been in no danger now. The trail mate could have built the fire. Well, it was up to him to build the fire over again, and this second time there must be no failure. Even if he succeeded, he would most likely lose some toes. His feet must be badly frozen by now, and there would be some time before the second fire was ready.

25 Such were his thoughts, but he did not sit and think them. He was busy all the time they were passing through his mind. He made a new foundation for a fire, this time in the open, where no treacherous tree could blot it out. Next he gathered dry grasses and tiny twigs from the high-water flotsam.[13] He could not bring his fingers together to pull them out, but he was able to gather them by the handful. In this way he got many rotten twigs and bits of green moss that were undesirable, but it was the best he could do. He worked methodically, even collecting an armful of the larger branches to be used later when the fire gathered strength. And all the while the dog sat and watched

---

[12]**conflagration:** large fire.
[13]**high-water flotsam:** branches and debris washed ashore by a stream or river during the warm months, when the water is high.

IMPROVE READING FLUENCY

Targeted Passage The paragraphs on page 470 are very dramatic. Have students take part in a choral reading of the first two (or more) paragraphs on the page. When students read together, it reduces the pressure on them and invests the entire group in the story. Encourage students to comprehend what they are reading, not just to say the words. In the second paragraph (paragraph 23), the man's fire has been extinguished, and he is in great danger. Ask students what they think might happen next.

 Go to the **Reading Studio** for additional support in developing fluency.

him, a certain yearning wistfulness in its eyes, for it looked upon him as the fire provider, and the fire was slow in coming.

26 When all was ready, the man reached in his pocket for a second piece of birch bark. He knew the bark was there, and, though he could not feel it with his fingers, he could hear its crisp rustling as he fumbled for it. Try as he would, he could not clutch hold of it. And all the time, in his consciousness, was the knowledge that each instant his feet were freezing. This thought tended to put him in a panic, but he fought against it and kept calm. He pulled on his mittens with his teeth, and threshed his arms back and forth, beating his hands with all his might against his sides. He did this sitting down, and he stood up to do it; and all the while the dog sat in the snow, its wolf brush of a tail curled around warmly over its forefeet, its sharp wolf ears pricked forward intently as it watched the man. And the man, as he beat and threshed with his arms and hands, felt a great surge of envy as he regarded the creature that was warm and secure in its natural covering.

27 After a time he was aware of the first faraway signals of sensation in his beaten fingers. The faint tingling grew stronger till it evolved into a stinging ache that was excruciating, but which the man hailed with satisfaction. He stripped the mitten from his right hand and fetched forth the birch bark. The exposed fingers were quickly going numb again. Next he brought out his bunch of sulphur matches. But the tremendous cold had already driven the life out of his fingers. In his effort to separate one match from the others, the whole bunch fell in the snow. He tried to pick it out of the snow, but failed. The dead fingers could neither touch nor clutch. He was very careful. He drove the thought of his freezing feet, and nose, and cheeks, out of his mind, devoting his whole soul to the matches. He watched, using the sense of vision in place of that of touch, and when he saw his fingers on each side of the bunch, he closed them—that is, he willed to close them, for the wires were down, and the fingers did not obey. He pulled the mitten on the right hand, and beat it fiercely against his knee. Then, with both mittened hands, he scooped the bunch of matches, along with much snow, into his lap. Yet he was no better off.

28 After some manipulation he managed to get the bunch between the heels of his mittened hands. In this fashion he carried it to his mouth. The ice crackled and snapped when by a violent effort he opened his mouth. He drew the lower jaw in, curled the upper lip out of the way, and scraped the bunch with his upper teeth in order to separate a match. He succeeded in getting one, which he dropped on his lap. He was no better off. He could not pick it up. Then he devised a way. He picked it up in his teeth and scratched it on his leg. Twenty times he scratched before he succeeded in lighting it. As it flamed he held it with his teeth to the birch bark. But the burning brimstone

ANALYZE SETTING

Annotate: Mark the sentences in paragraph 27 that depict the man's struggle with nature.

Draw Conclusions: How do these details represent naturalist ideas?

© Houghton Mifflin Harcourt Publishing Company

ANALYZE SETTING

The close relationship between naturalism and realism can be seen in paragraph 27. Realism focused on the real, factual details of life, rather than on symbolic or emotional details (which were common in earlier literary movements). That focus is obvious in this paragraph, as the author describes trying to light a match in minute detail. Naturalism, meanwhile, focused on the details of nature, in particular, and how the rules of nature—and the universe, in general—are usually beyond our control. (**Answer:** *The details make it clear that the elements of nature are a dangerous reality for the man. In fact, he is slowly succumbing to them.*)

WORDS OF THE WISER

One of the signposts of fiction is **Words of the Wiser**. In this device, a wiser character offers advice or insight about life to the protagonist. While this wiser character (the old-timer) isn't present in the flesh, he makes an appearance via a recollection by the man. (**Answer:** *He initially laughed at the warning, thinking it was overly cautious. Now he realizes that the old-timer was right.*)

 ENGLISH LEARNER SUPPORT

Confirm Understanding Make sure students understand what is happening during this important event in the story. Read aloud paragraphs 29–30, using pantomime, gestures, and simpler language to communicate what is happening. (*Since the man dropped the match, he must try again to light one. He beats his hands against his chest. He still can't feel his hands, so he takes off his mittens and used the heels of his hands to hold the whole bunch of matches.*) Clarify the meaning of *mittens, matches, twigs,* and *moss* by projecting images of them. Show students the "heels" of your hands and demonstrate picking things up using them. Demonstrate shivering, poking the fire, and "cherishing" the flame. Finally, have students act out the event or create an illustration of the scene to show their understanding. **SUBSTANTIAL**

 **NOTICE & NOTE**

WORDS OF THE WISER

Notice & Note: Mark the advice the "old-timer on Sulphur Creek" had offered to the man.

Contrast: What did the main character think of the warning initially, and what does he think now?

went up his nostrils and into his lungs, causing him to cough spasmodically.[14] The match fell into the snow and went out.

29   The old-timer on Sulphur Creek was right, he thought in the moment of controlled despair that ensued: After fifty below, a man should travel with a partner. He beat his hands, but failed in exciting any sensation. Suddenly he bared both hands, removing the mittens with his teeth. He caught the whole bunch between the heels of his hands. His arm muscles, not being frozen, enabled him to press the hand heels tightly against the matches. Then he scratched the bunch along his leg. It flared into flame, seventy sulphur matches at once! There was no wind to blow them out. He kept his head to one side to escape the strangling fumes, and held the blazing bunch to the birch bark. As he so held it, he became aware of sensation in his hand. His flesh was burning. He could smell it. Deep down below the surface he could feel it. The sensation developed into pain that grew acute. And still he endured it, holding the flame of matches clumsily to the bark that would not light readily because his own burning hands were in the way, absorbing most of the flame.

30   At last, when he could endure no more, he jerked his hands apart. The blazing matches fell sizzling into the snow, but the birch bark was alight. He began laying dry grass and the tiniest twigs on the flame. He could not pick and choose, for he had to lift the fuel between the heels of his hands. Small pieces of rotten wood and green moss clung to the twigs, and he bit them off as well as he could with his teeth. He cherished the flame carefully and awkwardly. It meant life, and it must not perish. The withdrawal of blood from the surface of his body now made him begin to shiver, and he grew more awkward. A large piece of green moss fell squarely on the little fire. He tried to poke it out with his fingers, but his shivering frame made him poke too far, and he disrupted the nucleus of the little fire, the burning grasses and tiny twigs separating and scattering. He tried to poke them together again, but in spite of the tenseness of the effort, his shivering got away with him, and the twigs were hopelessly scattered. Each twig gushed a puff of smoke and went out. The fire provider had failed. As he looked apathetically[15] about him, his eyes chanced on the dog, sitting across the ruins of the fire from him, in the snow, making restless, hunching movements, slightly lifting one forefoot and then the other, shifting its weight back and forth on them with wistful eagerness.

31   The sight of the dog put a wild idea into his head. He remembered the tale of the man, caught in a blizzard, who killed a steer and crawled inside the carcass, and so was saved. He would kill

[14]**spasmodically:** in a sudden, violent manner; fitfully.
[15]**apathetically:** with little interest or concern; indifferently.

WHEN STUDENTS STRUGGLE . . .

Analyze Character If students have trouble comprehending the action amid all the details, ask the following questions: *What danger is the man in? How serious is the danger? What is the man's attitude toward the danger? Is his attitude likely to help him or not? What do you think will happen next?* Encourage students to make predictions and to search for evidence in the text to confirm or revise their predictions.

 For additional support, go to the **Reading Studio** and assign the following **Level Up Tutorial: Making Inferences About Characters.**

the dog and bury his hands in the warm body until the numbness went out of them. Then he could build another fire. He spoke to the dog, calling it to him; but in his voice was a strange note of fear that frightened the animal, who had never known the man to speak in such a way before. Something was the matter, and its suspicious nature sensed danger—it knew not what danger, but somewhere, somehow, in its brain arose an apprehension of the man. It flattened its ears down at the sound of the man's voice, and its restless, hunching movements and the liftings and shiftings of its forefeet became more pronounced; but it would not come to the man. He got on his hands and knees and crawled toward the dog. This unusual posture again excited suspicion, and the animal sidled mincingly[16] away.

32   The man sat up in the snow for a moment and struggled for calmness. Then he pulled on his mittens, by means of his teeth, and got up on his feet. He glanced down at first in order to assure himself that he was really standing up, for the absence of sensation in his feet left him unrelated to the earth. His erect position in itself started to drive the webs of suspicion from the dog's mind; and when he spoke peremptorily,[17] with the sound of whiplashes in his voice, the dog rendered its customary allegiance and came to him. As it came within reaching distance, the man lost his control. His arms flashed out to the dog, and he experienced genuine surprise when he discovered that his hands could not clutch, that there was neither bend nor feeling in the fingers. He had forgotten for the moment that they were frozen and that they were freezing more and more. All this happened quickly, and before the animal could get away, he encircled its body with his arms. He sat down in the snow, and in this fashion held the dog, while it snarled and whined and struggled.

33   But it was all he could do, hold its body encircled in his arms and sit there. He realized that he could not kill the dog. There was no way to do it. With his helpless hands he could neither draw nor hold his sheath knife nor throttle the animal. He released it, and it plunged wildly away, its tail between its legs and still snarling. It halted forty feet away and surveyed him curiously, with ears sharply pricked forward. The man looked down at his hands in order to locate them, and found them hanging on the ends of his arms. It struck him as curious that one should have to use his eyes in order to find out where his hands were. He began threshing his arms back and forth, beating the mittened hands against his sides. He did this for five minutes, violently, and his heart pumped enough blood up to the surface to put a stop to his shivering. But no sensation was aroused in his hands. He had an impression that they hung like weights on the

---

[16] **sidled mincingly:** moved sideways with small steps.
[17] **peremptorily:** in a commanding way.

ANALYZE SETTING

Annotate: Mark the point in paragraph 31 where the narrative shifts from the man's perspective to the dog's perspective.

Compare: One naturalist idea is that humans are simply animals. How do the thoughts of the man and the instincts of the dog suggest that London views them both as animals trying to survive?

To Build a Fire   473

ANALYZE SETTING

Remind students that naturalism was a popular literary movement in the late 1800s, a time when scientists were beginning to put humans in context with the rest of the animal kingdom. Much of this thinking was influenced by the work of Charles Darwin. (**Answer:** *The thoughts of the man and instincts of the dog are similar. Both creatures are fearful and interested in survival.*)

TO CHALLENGE STUDENTS . . .

Analyze Character   In "To Build a Fire," nature is portrayed as an uncontrollable force, almost cruel in its impersonal, punishing treatment of the man. In paragraphs 31–33, the man, out of desperation, shows signs of cruelty as well when he attempts to kill the dog. Have students discuss what drives the man to do this and how this reflects his poor choices of how to react to nature.

TEACH

 ANALYZE CHARACTER

Tell students that they should always be looking for motivations behind a character's behavior. Most good stories will make it clear what a character's motivations are. At times, the man's motivation in this story has been simply getting to his next meal. However, in paragraph 34, the man realizes he needs to take drastic action to save himself. This motivation propels him to begin running. (***Answer:*** *The man's actions reflect his new desperation. He is desperately running because he fears that he is close to death. At this moment, his primary motivation is to stay alive.*)

■ English Learner Support

Analyze Character Help students find the moment that the man begins running (sentence 3 of paragraph 34). This sentence includes the word *panic* (which was also an earlier Critical Vocabulary word). After feeling panic, he begins to run. Explain that locating turning points like these in stories helps the reader follow the action. **SUBSTANTIAL**

ANALYZE CHARACTER
Annotate: Mark the words in paragraph 34 that show a shift in the man's attitude.

Evaluate: How do the man's actions reflect a change in his attitude? What underlying motivations drive his choices and actions now?

ends of his arms, but when he tried to run the impression down, he could not find it.

34   A certain fear of death, dull and oppressive, came to him. This fear quickly became poignant[18] as he realized that it was no longer a mere matter of freezing his fingers and toes, or of losing his hands and feet, but that it was a matter of life and death, with the chances against him. This threw him into a panic, and he turned and ran up the creek bed along the old, dim trail. The dog joined in behind and kept up with him. He ran blindly, without intention, in fear such as he had never known in his life. Slowly, as he plowed and floundered through the snow, he began to see things again—the banks of the creek, the old timber jams, the leafless aspens, and the sky. The running made him feel better. He did not shiver. Maybe, if he ran on, his feet would thaw out; and, anyway, if he ran far enough, he would reach the camp and the boys. Without doubt he would lose some fingers and toes and some of his face; but the boys would take care of him, and save the rest of him when he got there. And, at the same time, there was another thought in his mind that said he would never get to the camp and the boys; that it was too many miles away, that the freezing had too great a start on him, and that he would soon be stiff and dead. This thought he kept in the background and refused

---

[18]**poignant:** painfully affecting feelings; touching.

to consider. Sometimes it pushed itself forward and demanded to be heard, but he thrust it back and strove to think of other things.

35   It struck him as curious that he could run at all on feet so frozen that he could not feel them when they struck the earth and took the weight of his body. He seemed to himself to skim along above the surface, and to have no connection with the earth. Somewhere he had once seen a winged Mercury,[19] and he wondered if Mercury felt as he felt when skimming over the earth.

36   His theory of running until he reached camp and the boys had one flaw in it: He lacked the endurance. Several times he stumbled, and finally he tottered, crumpled up, and fell. When he tried to rise, he failed. He must sit and rest, he decided, and next time he would merely walk and keep on going. As he sat and regained his breath, he noted that he was feeling quite warm and comfortable. He was not shivering, and it even seemed that a warm glow had come to his chest and trunk. And yet, when he touched his nose or cheeks, there was no sensation. Running would not thaw them out. Nor would it thaw out his hands and feet. Then the thought came to him that the frozen portions of his body must be extending. He tried to keep this thought

---

[19] **Mercury:** in Roman mythology, messenger of the gods, who is depicted wearing winged sandals and a winged hat.

ENGLISH LEARNER SUPPORT

Understand Allusion Paragraph 35 includes an allusion to Roman mythology. Explain that an allusion is a reference to something outside of the core text or subject matter. Students most likely make allusions frequently. For example, students make an allusion when they refer to a famous person while talking about someone they know (e.g., "He's like Einstein in our science class!").

You can easily explain this particular allusion by projecting an image of "a winged Mercury" on the board. Point out how Mercury has wings on his ankles and is usually depicted as being weightless and swift. **LIGHT**

IMPROVE READING FLUENCY

Targeted Passage Divide students into pairs, and have them read paragraphs 35–36. If necessary, begin by reading the two paragraphs aloud, using the appropriate emphasis. Tell students to take turns reading the paragraphs. The nonreading students should follow along. Once finished, have them give each other feedback and any necessary support for pronouncing difficult words.

  Go to the **Reading Studio** for additional support in developing fluency.

ANALYZE SETTING

Setting has a major impact in most stories, but setting is especially important in the stories of the naturalism movement. Many naturalists wrote about the closely observed facts and rules of nature and made the point that humans were subservient to those rules. In this way, the natural world was a driving force in many of those stories, as it is in "To Build a Fire." (**Answer:** *Throughout the story, the extreme cold and rugged landscape have been the main causes of the man's troubles. These perils are so severe, in fact, that they are a deadly threat to the protagonist.*)

ANALYZE CHARACTER

As the man becomes less physically active, the reader learns more of his thoughts. This change is meaningful for the reader. Students should pay close attention to these thoughts because they are signaling a turning point in the story. (**Answer:** *The man is seeing visions of his own death. The reader can assume at this point that the man is near death or likely to die. His final realization is that the old-timer was right and that he should have heeded the old-timer's advice.*)

NOTICE & NOTE

ANALYZE SETTING
Annotate: Mark details in paragraph 37 that indicate the man's fate is sealed.

Analyze: In what ways has the setting driven the plot and led to this moment?

ANALYZE CHARACTER
Annotate: Mark details in paragraph 38 that show the man is dying.

Draw Conclusions: How do his thoughts signal the resolution of the story? What is the man's final realization?

---

down, to forget it, to think of something else; he was aware of the panicky feeling that it caused, and he was afraid of the panic. But the thought asserted itself, and persisted, until it produced a vision of his body totally frozen. This was too much, and he made another wild run along the trail. Once he slowed down to a walk, but the thought of the freezing extending itself made him run again.

37 And all the time the dog ran with him, at his heels. When he fell down a second time, it curled its tail over its forefeet and sat in front of him, facing him, curiously eager and intent. The warmth and security of the animal angered him, and he cursed it till it flattened down its ears appeasingly. This time the shivering came more quickly upon the man. He was losing in this battle with the frost. It was creeping into his body from all sides. The thought of it drove him on, but he ran no more than a hundred feet when he staggered and pitched headlong. It was his last panic. When he had recovered his breath and control, he sat up and entertained in his mind the conception of meeting death with dignity. However, the conception did not come to him in such terms. His idea of it was that he had been making a fool of himself, running around like a chicken with its head cut off—such was the simile that occurred to him. Well, he was bound to freeze anyway, and he might as well take it decently. With this newfound peace of mind came the first glimmerings of drowsiness. A good idea, he thought, to sleep off to death. It was like taking an anesthetic.[20] Freezing was not so bad as people thought. There were lots worse ways to die.

38 He pictured the boys finding his body next day. Suddenly he found himself with them, coming along the trail and looking for himself. And, still with them, he came around a turn in the trail and found himself lying in the snow. He did not belong with himself anymore, for even then he was out of himself, standing with the boys and looking at himself in the snow. It certainly was cold, was his thought. When he got back to the States, he could tell the folks what real cold was. He drifted on from this to a vision of the old-timer on Sulphur Creek. He could see him quite clearly, warm and comfortable, and smoking a pipe.

39 "You were right, old hoss; you were right," the man mumbled to the old-timer of Sulphur Creek.

40 Then the man drowsed off into what seemed to him the most comfortable and satisfying sleep he had ever known. The dog sat facing him and waiting. The brief day drew to a close in a long, slow twilight. There were no signs of a fire to be made, and, besides, never in the dog's experience had it known a man to sit like that in the snow and make no fire. As the twilight drew on, its eager yearning for the fire mastered it, and with a great lifting and shifting of forefeet, it

---

[20]**anesthetic:** medication that causes loss of the sensation of pain.

© Houghton Mifflin Harcourt Publishing Company

WHEN STUDENTS STRUGGLE . . .

Analyze Character If students find it difficult to interpret the man's mental state, tell them that sometimes an author uses signal words and phrases to show that a passage reflects a character's thoughts or feelings. For example, in paragraph 37, "His idea of it was . . ." signals that the rest of the sentence will state the man's thoughts. Ask students to identify other such signal words on page 476. (*"He pictured" and "He drifted on from this to a vision"*)

For additional support, go to the **Reading Studio** and assign the following Level Up **Level Up Tutorial: Methods of Characterization.**

whined softly, then flattened its ears down in anticipation of being chidden[21] by the man. But the man remained silent. Later, the dog whined loudly. And still later it crept close to the man and caught the scent of death. This made the animal bristle and back away. A little longer it delayed, howling under the stars that leaped and danced and shone brightly in the cold sky. Then it turned and trotted up the trail in the direction of the camp it knew, where there were the other food providers and fire providers.

---
[21] **chidden:** scolded.

CHECK YOUR UNDERSTANDING

Answer these questions before moving on to the **Analyze the Text** section on the following page.

1 How does the man's attitude change toward the old-timer on Sulphur Creek?

  A He begins to distrust him.

  B He begins to respect him.

  C He intends to ignore him.

  D He hopes not to meet him.

2 Why did the man watch the terrain so carefully as he walked?

  F He was looking for rabbit holes under the snow.

  G He thought he would lose the trail if he didn't watch.

  H He feared breaking through to water under the snow.

  J He was looking for the matches he had dropped.

3 Why did the man think he would make it to his camp?

  A He thought he knew and understood the cold.

  B The camp was close and the path was well traveled.

  C The boys he would be meeting had marked the route.

  D The old-timer on Sulphur Creek told him he would.

ANALYZE CHARACTER

Annotate: In paragraph 40, mark the actions the dog associates with humans.

Interpret: What are the dog's motives for staying with the man? How does this behavior relate to naturalism?

 ANALYZE CHARACTER

As students have hopefully realized by now, the dog is a major character in the story. As with any character, the students should study the dog's motivations and behaviors. (**Answer:** *The dog stays with the man in order to get food and warmth [from a fire]. This behavior relates to naturalism because the dog is following its primary, instinctual motivations: seeking food and safety.*)

 CHECK YOUR UNDERSTANDING

Have students answer the questions independently.

Answers:

1. *B*

2. *H*

3. *A*

If they answer any questions incorrectly, have them reread the text to confirm their understanding. Then they may proceed to ANALYZE THE TEXT on page 478.

 ENGLISH LEARNER SUPPORT

Oral Assessment Use the following questions to assess students' comprehension and speaking skills.

1. Does the man change his mind about the old-timer on Sulphur Creek? How? (*Yes. The man grows to have more respect for the old-timer.*)

2. Why did the man walk very carefully through the snow? (*He was afraid he would break through the ice and fall in the water.*)

3. The man thought he could make it to the camp. Why did he think this? (*He thought he knew enough about the cold.*) **MODERATE**

ANALYZE THE TEXT

Possible answers:

1. **DOK 3:** *The story includes many realistic details, such as "exceedingly cold and gray" and "dim and little-traveled trail." These details help the reader picture the difficult and potentially dangerous landscape. They also help demonstrate the man's ignorance of nature and belief in the superiority of man over nature.*

2. **DOK 4:** *Examples include the fact that the old-timer has survived a long time by understanding, rather than ignoring, the environment; the man's inability to keep a fire going and his subsequent death; and the survival of the dog. The story supports the idea that only the fittest, or best adapted, survive.*

3. **DOK 4:** *The moral dilemma occurs when the man considers killing the dog. However, the man realizes that he has no way of killing it. His failed attempt to build a second fire most likely doom him to death. The dangerous setting—the freezing cold, in particular—ensures that the man's mistakes are deadly.*

4. **DOK 3:** *At first, the man's motivations are primarily food and comfort related. He wants to get to the camp where he can eat and warm up. Along the way, he becomes somewhat cautious while walking, in order not to fall into freezing water. Toward the end, he realizes he is in great danger. This motivation propels him to struggle to survive.*

5. **DOK 4:** *Over time, the man realizes that the old-timer was in fact wise and that his advice was good. London might be conveying the idea that people are inherently ignorant and arrogant and that people should be open to new information.*

RESEARCH

Students' responses should reflect an understanding of the stories they read. They should include specific details about the stories' themes, what becomes of the protagonists, and what their fate says about survival.

Connect Students' discussions should reflect an understanding of the distinction between Romanticism and Naturalism. Students should also be aware that the difficult social conditions of the late 1800s led many writers to tell stories of people's struggle for survival.

RESPOND

ANALYZE THE TEXT

Support your responses with evidence from the text. ☰ NOTEBOOK

1. **Cite Evidence** What details from the story reflect what you know about realism? How do these details impact your understanding of the story?

2. **Analyze** Works of naturalism often address the theme of survival of the fittest. Give examples that show how London's story develops this theme. What message does the story convey about the survival of the fittest?

3. **Analyze** What moral dilemma does the man face when his second fire fails? How do this dilemma and his subsequent actions influence the plot? How does the setting enhance the seriousness of this scene?

4. **Evaluate** At the beginning of the story, what motivates the man to travel? How do his motivations change over the course of his journey?

5. **Notice & Note** As the man tries a second time to start a fire, he remembers the advice of the old-timer. How has the man's opinion of the old timer's advice changed? What message do you think London intends to convey by describing this change?

RESEARCH

RESEARCH TIP
Use literature anthologies, or collections of works, to find other stories by Jack London. Literature anthologies can be found online or in the library.

Naturalism suggests that larger forces such as nature or fate control human lives. Think about this story, and find and read two other stories by London. How does he address the ideas of nature or fate in these stories? Use the chart to record the stories, their themes, and whether the characters can survive or are doomed from the start.

STORY BY LONDON	THEME	DETAILS ABOUT CHARACTER'S FATE
Answers will vary.		

Connect Naturalism was considered to be a reaction to romanticism. With a partner, discuss how the work of Jack London and other naturalists serves as a contrast to romanticism and how social conditions helped change literary style.

LEARNING MINDSET

Questioning Tell students that people with a learning mindset are constantly asking questions about the world around them. The clearer and more complete their questions are, the more likely they are to get useful answers. Remind students to make their questions succinct (concise) and clear. If the answer they get is not helpful to them, students should ask, "Was my question clearly stated?" "Can I improve my question?"

CREATE AND PRESENT

Write a How-to Guide In the story, the old-timer gives the protagonist instructions for surviving in the wilderness. Think of something you do well, and write a detailed set of instructions that teaches others how to do it.

❏ Choose a task that has several steps. Brainstorm a list of supplies or tools that should be on hand before starting.

❏ List the steps in logical order. Mentally step through the process to make sure that you are including all the relevant information.

❏ Keep directions simple, but complete. Revise for brevity and clarity.

❏ Include drawings or photos that illustrate parts of the process.

Present a How-to Demonstration In a small group, take turns giving and following the instructions you wrote. Evaluate how well the task was laid out, and give feedback on how to clarify any confusing parts.

❏ Practice your demonstration a few times, and plan out how to coordinate speaking and demonstrating.

❏ Offer additional advice for simplifying the process.

❏ Ask if your audience has any questions, and respond to them. When it is your turn to listen and follow along, ask any questions you have.

 Go to **Writing Informative Texts** in the **Writing Studio** for help.

Go to **Giving a Presentation** in the **Speaking and Listening Studio** for help.

RESPOND TO THE ESSENTIAL QUESTION

? To what degree do we control our lives?

Gather Information Review your annotations and notes on "To Build a Fire." Then, add relevant information to your Response Log. As you determine which information to include, think about:

• the author's viewpoint or ideas about nature
• the choices or mistakes the main character makes that lead to the outcome
• how different choices would affect the outcome

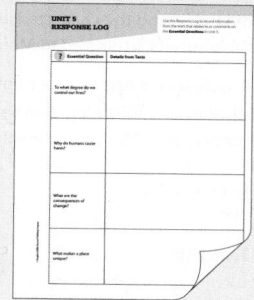

ACADEMIC VOCABULARY
As you write and discuss what you learned from the story, be sure to use the Academic Vocabulary words. Check off each of the words that you use.

❏ **ambiguous**
❏ **clarify**
❏ **implicit**
❏ **revise**
❏ **somewhat**

CREATE AND PRESENT

Write a How-to Guide Emphasize to students that they can write instructions for anything they know well. Help students brainstorm a list of ideas, such as making a favorite meal, installing new computer programs or apps, building a birdhouse, or changing a car battery. Suggest that students use a graphic organizer, such as a sequence chain, to help them plan their steps. Remind students to use transitions between steps, such as *first, next, then,* and *last.* Students can draw illustrations or look online for illustrations or diagrams.

 For **writing support** for students at varying proficiency levels, see the **Text X-Ray** on page 458D.

Present a How-to Demonstration Encourage students to create a presentation that includes a slide for the supplies or tools and a slide for each step. Students should include illustrations for the more complicated steps, or they can include videos of individual steps or part of the process. If students are teaching something that can be demonstrated in the classroom, suggest that students bring in some of the tools or supplies or demonstrate a few simple steps. Tell students to be prepared for questions or additional explanations.

RESPOND TO THE ESSENTIAL QUESTION

Allow time for students to add details from "To Build a Fire" to their Unit 5 Response Logs.

CRITICAL VOCABULARY

Answers:

1. a strong work ethic, enthusiasm, leadership skills

2. thinking that you don't know the material well enough, fear of failure

3. a house fire, an act of crime, or a natural disaster

4. to avoid serious injury or death if an accident occurs

5. because it could be difficult getting defensive forces out to those areas

VOCABULARY STRATEGY:
Allusions and Word Origins

Answers:

1. from Ceres, the Roman goddess of agriculture; the English meaning is related because cereal is food

2. from Mars, the Roman god of war; the English meaning is related because "martial" is usually related to war or an act of force

3. from Echo, a character from Greek mythology; the English meaning is related because of the story of Echo

4. from Nemesis, an avenging or punishing god in Greek mythology

5. from the Muses, characters from Greek mythology; the English meaning is related because the Muses were said to be the source of music, poetry, and so on

---

 RESPOND

CRITICAL VOCABULARY

WORD BANK
intangible
apprehension
panic
imperative
extremity

Practice and Apply Answer the questions to demonstrate your knowledge of the Critical Vocabulary.

1. What are some **intangible** characteristics that make athletes successful?

2. Why might you feel **apprehension** right before an important exam?

3. Under what circumstances might someone feel **panic**?

4. Why is it **imperative** that you wear a seat belt when riding in a car?

5. Why is it hard for a country to defend the **extremities** of its territory?

 Go to **Understanding Word Origins** in the **Vocabulary Studio** for more details.

VOCABULARY STRATEGY: Allusions and Word Origins

Many English words are derived from Greek and Roman mythology. For example, the word *panic* alludes to the Greek god Pan. His voice and looks were said to instill fear in people. *Panic* literally means "of or relating to Pan," but more commonly refers to fear-induced agitation. You may also know the word *mercurial*. It is an **allusion,** or indirect reference, to the Roman god Mercury, who served as messenger to the other gods. *Mercurial* often means having the characteristics of eloquence, shrewdness, swiftness, and thievishness attributed to Mercury. It can also mean "quick" or "changeable."

Practice and Apply Use print or digital resources to determine from which allusions the following words derived. Note the English meaning and how it is connected to the characteristics of the mythical being.

1. cereal

2. martial

3. echo

4. nemesis

5. music

EL ## ENGLISH LEARNER SUPPORT

Understand Sound Transfer The /j/ sound, as in *jacket*, may be unknown or confusing to speakers of Spanish, Vietnamese, Hmong, Cantonese, and Korean. Make sure students can produce and perceive this sound to help them with language acquisition.

Multiple words in the story contain this sound, including *just, jams, conjectural, jacket, judgment, jowls,* and *juice*. Have the class repeat these words, focusing on the /j/ sound.
ALL LEVELS

LANGUAGE CONVENTIONS:
Consistent Tone

Tone is the author's attitude toward the subject or his or her audience. Within the literary style known as naturalism, nature is considered a powerful, unfeeling force with control over human life. Naturalists value an objective narrative approach, which they view as scientific.

> **But before he could cut the strings it happened. It was his own fault, or, rather, his mistake. He should not have built the fire under the spruce tree. He should have built it in the open. But it had been easier to pull the twigs from the bush and drop them directly on the fire.**

The passage uses a detached, unemotional tone, even though this situation is extremely dangerous and is a key turning point in the story. London uses realism in this scene to provide detail, but does not add his own thoughts. The passage continues:

> **Now the tree under which he had done this carried a weight of snow on its boughs. No wind had blown for weeks, and each bough was fully freighted. Each time he had pulled a twig he had communicated a slight agitation to the tree—an imperceptible agitation, so far as he was concerned, but an agitation sufficient to bring about the disaster.**

These lines continue to focus on realistic detail, explaining the natural forces that are at work whether or not the man pays attention. The only indication that disaster is imminent comes from the character, not the author.

> **The man was shocked. It was as though he had just heard his own sentence of death.**

Practice and Apply Try to emulate London's style. Choose a terrible event or situation, and write about it in a realistic style, using a calm, unemotional tone. Remember that word choice and sentence structure can affect tone.

LANGUAGE CONVENTIONS:
Consistent Tone

Tone makes a huge difference to a story, and authors work hard to craft it. Using diction and syntax, authors shape their language to give a very specific impression to the reader. London used detached, unemotional language to convey certain ideas about the natural world and our role in it. If he had used another tone, the story would have come across much differently. Read the following passage to the class. It is a rewrite of the first boldfaced passage on page 481, and it has been given a different tone.

Boom, it happened in a flash! The disaster was all his fault, and he was really gonna kick himself for this one, if his foot wasn't already frozen. Building the fire under a tree was as dumb as building a house of cards in a room full of cats. So stupid! He should've been like that gabby old-timer—that guy was pretty boring but he sure knew a lot. But building the fire under the tree was just so easy. All you had to do was reach up to get new firewood—easy peasy.

Discuss with the class how the tone of this passage differs from London's tone and the implications of using a different tone. *(The tone of this passage is silly and unserious. It would be difficult to convey a serious point when using such a silly tone.)*

Practice and Apply Students' passages should have a realistic style. This includes the use of facts and observations, rather than opinions and conjectures. The style should be calm and unemotional.

 ENGLISH LEARNER SUPPORT

Language Conventions Use the following supports with students at varying proficiency levels.

- Read the first boldfaced passage to students. Ask students if the passage describes facts or emotions. *(facts)* **SUBSTANTIAL**

- Have students read aloud the first passage as a group. Then, have groups discuss whether the passage focuses on facts or emotions and what effect this has. **MODERATE**

- Point out that the original passage uses very plain language to describe a frightening event. Have students rewrite the passage in their own words. Tell them that while they do not need to use the same language London uses, their version should use a similar unemotional tone. **LIGHT**

THE LOWEST ANIMAL

Essay by Mark Twain

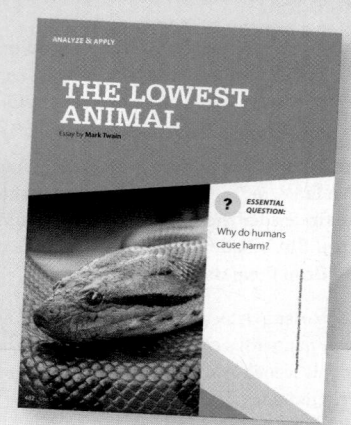

GENRE ELEMENTS
SATIRE

Satire is a literary device that is often used to criticize a person, thing, or idea. While satire uses techniques such as humor and exaggeration, its primary purpose is not to entertain but to inform readers about the negative aspects of humans and society. Satire is often used to bring about political or social change. In some cases, it is used to present ideas that are forbidden by a government or may be unacceptable to many people. Many cartoons use satire to make a political statement or point out the absurdity of a person's actions.

LEARNING OBJECTIVES

- Analyze author's purpose and tone.
- Research Mark Twain and his use of satire.
- Write a satire using Twain's techniques.
- Present a satire before an audience.
- Identify word nuances.
- Write sentences using parallelism and anaphora.
- **Language** Express ideas using vocabulary words.

TEXT COMPLEXITY

Quantitative Measures	The Lowest Animal	Lexile: 1040L
Qualitative Measures	**Ideas Presented** Some analysis of bias and author's motivations.	
	Structures Used Primarily explicit; one perspective; varies·from chronological order.	
	Language Used Vocabulary not defined at point of use; mostly Tier II and III words.	
	Knowledge Required Explores complex ideas; refers to ideas that may be beyond students' knowledge; may require specialized knowledge.	

RESOURCES

- Unit 5 Response Log
- Selection Audio
- Reading Studio:
  Notice & Note
- Level Up Tutorial:
  Making Generalizations
- Writing Studio:
  Writing as a Process
- Speaking and Listening Studio:
  Giving a Presentation
- "The Lowest Animal" Selection Test

SUMMARIES

English

Mark Twain describes conducting several experiments to test the theory that humans had ascended from the lower animals. He concluded humans had descended, not risen, from higher animals. He made this conclusion based on his observations that humans acted in ways that animals did not. Humans were the only species to exhibit greed, revenge, and miserliness. They also were indecent, vulgar, and obscene. And they were the only species to engage in war.

Spanish

Mark Twain describe la realización de varios experimentos para probar la teoría de que los humanos han ascendido de animales inferiores. Concluye que los humanos descendieron, no ascendieron, de animales superiores. Llegó a su conclusión al observar que los humanos actuaban de formas en que los animales no. Los humanos eran la única especie que exhibía codicia, venganza y mezquindad. También eran indecentes, vulgares y obscenos y eran la única especie que hacía la guerra.

SMALL-GROUP OPTIONS

Have students work in small groups and pairs to read and discuss the selection.

Activating Academic Vocabulary

- Draw students' attention to the Academic Vocabulary words found on page 457.
- During instruction and class discussion, model the appropriate use of each word.
- Challenge the students to use the Academic Vocabulary words in oral discussions, written responses, and assessments.

Think-Pair-Share

- After students have read the selection, pose the following question to the class: *How did the author use the scientific method to determine the difference between a snake and an earl?*
- Tell students to think about the question and jot down notes.
- Have students form pairs to discuss the question and formulate a shared response.
- Call on students to share their pair's response with the class.

Text X-Ray: English Learner Support
for "The Lowest Animal"

Use the Text X-Ray and the supports and scaffolds in the Teacher's Edition to help guide students at different proficiency levels through the selection.

INTRODUCE THE SELECTION
DISCUSS DARWIN AND THE "ASCENT OF MAN"

Tell students that Charles Darwin was a scientist who developed the theory of evolution, which describes a process by which living things change over time. In this essay, Mark Twain says that Darwin characterizes evolution as "the ascent of man from the lower animals"; however, Twain characterizes evolution as the "descent of man."

Explain that the word *ascent* means "a climb or path upward," and the word *descent* means "a climb or path downward." These words can be used in either a literal way (to describe a walk up or down the stairs) or a metaphorical way (to describe a path to a better or worse state of being). Ask students to name or describe examples of *ascent* and *descent*.

CULTURAL REFERENCES

The following words or phrases may be unfamiliar to students:

- *"lower animals"* (paragraph 1): animals considered to be simpler or less intelligent than humans
- *Great Plains, buffalo hunt* (paragraph 7): Before the United States expanded many buffalo lived in certain regions and were hunted for sport, or entertainment.
- *English earl* (paragraph 7): a nobleman from England
- *made accumulations* (paragraph 8): hoarded food for winter

LISTENING

Identify Satire

Remind students that **satire** is humor, irony, or exaggeration used to make a statement about people or society. Help them identify satirical statements read aloud from the selection. As needed, use tone and gestures to help them identify the author's attitude.

Use the following supports with students at varying proficiency levels:

- Read aloud short sentences or phrases from the selection that are clearly ironic or not meant to be taken seriously, such as "the earl was descended from the anaconda" (paragraph 7) or "in another cage I confined an Irish Catholic from Tipperary, and as soon as he seemed tame, I added a Scottish Presbyterian from Aberdeen" (paragraph 21). Have students give a thumbs up if they think the author is being serious and a thumbs down if they do not. Guide students to understand that Twain did not actually lock people together and did not really believe humans descended from anacondas. **SUBSTANTIAL**
- Read paragraph 15 to students. Pause after each sentence to ask students if they think it contains satire. Guide students to explain their reasons. **MODERATE**
- Have pairs of students read one or two paragraphs, taking turns reading the sentences aloud. Ask students to discuss whether they think the sentences contain satire and why. **LIGHT**

SPEAKING

Make Connections

Have students discuss Mark Twain's descriptions of humans and animals and connect them to their own experiences and observations. Circulate around the room to assess their use of new vocabulary and provide support as needed.

Read aloud paragraph 8. Then, display and reread the last sentence: "He is avaricious and miserly, they are not." Use the following supports with students at varying proficiency levels:

- Explain the meanings of *avaricious* (greedy) and *miserly* (stingy). Have the students practice repeating the sentence back to you and then practice saying it and acting it out with a partner. **SUBSTANTIAL**
- Explain the meanings of *avaricious* (greedy) and *miserly* (stingy). Provide these sentence frames: *Humans are avaricious when they _____. Humans are miserly when they _____.* **MODERATE**
- Have students discuss the sentence with a partner, using a dictionary to define unfamiliar terms. Ask partners to come up with examples of how humans are "avaricious and miserly" and animals "are not." **LIGHT**

READING

Paraphrase Text

Tell students paraphrasing is putting another person's words into your own words. Demonstrate by giving students an example. Say, "Take out a writing instrument," and then ask a volunteer to paraphrase what you said.

Use the following supports with students at varying proficiency levels:

- Read aloud one or two sentences from the essay. Then, model your thinking process as you paraphrase aloud the sentences. Ask students yes–no questions as you paraphrase, such as *Should I use [word from the essay]? Or [a synonym]?* **SUBSTANTIAL**
- Have pairs of students read paragraph 14. Ask one partner to paraphrase the paragraph. Then, have the other partner paraphrase it. Have them discuss their paraphrases, noting words they used from the paragraph and what they put in their own words. **MODERATE**
- Have students read paragraph 14 silently, then work with a partner to write a paraphrase of the paragraph. **LIGHT**

WRITING

Write Sentences Using Anaphora

Review **anaphora,** or the repetition of a word or phrase at the beginning of successive sentences or lines. Model an example, and work with students to create their own examples.

Use the following supports with students at varying proficiency levels:

- Tell students they will use repetition to write a paragraph describing themselves. Provide the following sentence frame: *I am _____.* Have them write it down three times, and help them complete each sentence with a different word. **SUBSTANTIAL**
- Give students simple sentence frames such as the following: *Today is _____. I am _____. People are _____.* Have each student write down a sentence frame and complete it with a short phrase. Then, have students pass their papers to the person on their right, who then writes a new sentence that begins in the same way and ends differently. **MODERATE**
- Have students work in small groups to create a group poem. Have one student write the first line of a poem and then pass the paper to another student, who writes the next line by repeating the first words in the original line. Repeat until every student has written a line of the poem. **LIGHT**

Connect to the
ESSENTIAL QUESTION

"The Lowest Animal" is a satire about some ways that humans cause harm to each other and to other animals.

ANALYZE & APPLY

THE LOWEST ANIMAL

Essay by **Mark Twain**

? ***ESSENTIAL QUESTION:***

Why do humans cause harm?

482   Unit 5

QUICK START

Mark Twain was a keen observer of human behavior and social institutions. In this work, he humorously compares humans and animals. With a small group, brainstorm a list of animals and discuss how their characteristics and behaviors are like those of humans.

ANALYZE AUTHOR'S PURPOSE: Satire

An **author's purpose** is what the writer hopes to accomplish by writing. An author may want to describe, inform, narrate, entertain, analyze, persuade, or do several of these at once. Different techniques are used to achieve different purposes. **Satire** is a literary form that ridicules the shortcomings of people or institutions in an attempt to bring about change. Techniques you may find in satire include:

- **Humor:** describing something in a way that causes laughter or amusement

- **Exaggeration:** overstating something to draw attention to it and make a point

- **Absurdity:** describing extreme situations that are impossible to take seriously

- **Irony:** stating the opposite of what is really meant

As you read, note Twain's use of these techniques and the emotional response they trigger. What is Twain's purpose for writing this satire?

ANALYZE TONE

The **tone** of a work is the writer's attitude toward its subject. Twain's subject is a comparison of humans to other animals. As you read, analyze how Twain's **diction** (the words chosen) and **syntax** (the construction of sentences) help establish his tone. Notice how his tone is different when speaking of humans as opposed to animals. You can use a chart like this to make notes about the words used to establish this difference in tone.

ATTITUDE TOWARD HUMANS	ATTITUDE TOWARD ANIMALS

GENRE ELEMENTS: SATIRE

- exposes the vices and folly of humans and society

- uses humor, irony, exaggeration, understatement, and other techniques

- is often intended to bring about social or political change

QUICK START

Have students read the Quick Start note, and invite them to share similarities they see between humans and other animals. Point out that sometimes our strongest drives (hunger, need for shelter, desire to protect) are similar to those instincts that inspire animals to act. Ask students which they think are more important: the differences or the similarities between themselves and animals.

ANALYZE AUTHOR'S PURPOSE: SATIRE

Remind students that satire does not always have to be extreme and greatly exaggerated. When the humor is more subtle, or the exaggeration less blatant, it is still satire. Tell them to watch for where Twain is more or less pointed in his satire and what inspires his harshest words.

ANALYZE TONE

Tell students that writers choose words with different shades of meaning, both to shape their tone and to make their writing more effective. As they read, students should consider how Twain's tone toward various human and animal subjects supports his purpose.

TEACH

CRITICAL VOCABULARY

Tell students to note the prefixes and suffixes on most of these vocabulary words. For example, remembering that *trans-* means "across" or "changing through" will be helpful.

Answers:

1. *transition*
2. *atrocious*
3. *caliber*
4. *disposition*

■ English Learner Support

Use Cognates Tell students that two of the Critical Vocabulary words have a Spanish cognate: *disposition/disposición, transition/transición*. **ALL LEVELS**

LANGUAGE CONVENTIONS

Note how the use of anaphora and parallelism in prose can make the prose feel formal and serious. As they read, encourage students to realize that this adds to the effect, since Twain is writing a satire and did not actually perform scientific experiments.

✎ ANNOTATION MODEL

Remind students that as they look for satirical elements, they may see some signs of the author's tone. Others will be revealed in the author's syntax. As students read, they might also want to underline or highlight syntax and diction that stands out to them.

CRITICAL VOCABULARY

disposition	caliber	transition	atrocious

To see how many Critical Vocabulary words you already know, write the correct word after its definition.

1. process of change _____

2. evil or brutal _____

3. level of ability _____

4. character or temperament _____

LANGUAGE CONVENTIONS

Anaphora and Parallelism Authors may use literary devices to make a point. **Anaphora**—the repetition of a word or phrase at the beginning of successive lines, clauses, sentences, or paragraphs—is more commonly used in poetry. However, Twain uses it here to underscore his ideas. **Parallelism,** or the use of similar grammatical structures, also helps emphasize ideas. Note the anaphora and parallelism in the beginnings of paragraphs 4, 5, and 6.

> That the human race <u>is</u> . . .
> That the quadrupeds <u>are</u> . . .
> That the other families . . . <u>are</u> . . .

As you read "The Lowest Animal," note where Twain uses these devices.

ANNOTATION MODEL

NOTICE & NOTE

As you read, note the elements of satire—exaggeration, irony, and other techniques—that underscore Twain's points. You may also make notes on words that reveal tone or suggest the author's purpose. In the model, you can see one reader's notes about "The Lowest Animal."

I have been studying the traits and dispositions of the "lower animals" (so-called) and contrasting them with the traits and dispositions of man. I find the result humiliating to me. For it obliges me to renounce my allegiance to the Darwinian theory of the Ascent of Man from the Lower Animals, since it now seems plain to me that that theory ought to be vacated in favor of a new and truer one, this new and truer one to be named the Descent of Man from the Higher Animals.

Saying "so-called" sounds pretty sarcastic.

"Humiliating" sounds like an exaggeration.

He says he believed in Darwin, but here he says humans descended from higher animals. This sounds ironic.

BACKGROUND

Mark Twain (1835–1910) was the pen name of Samuel Langhorne Clemens, the American author best known for his novel The Adventures of Huckleberry Finn, based on his own boyhood in Missouri. As a journalist, moralist, and lecturer, he frequently used humor to communicate his ideas. In his later years, Twain wrote many satirical essays commenting on the human race. This essay, first published in 1962, was probably written in 1896. In it, Twain refers to Charles Darwin's theory of evolution, first published in On the Origin of Species in 1859.

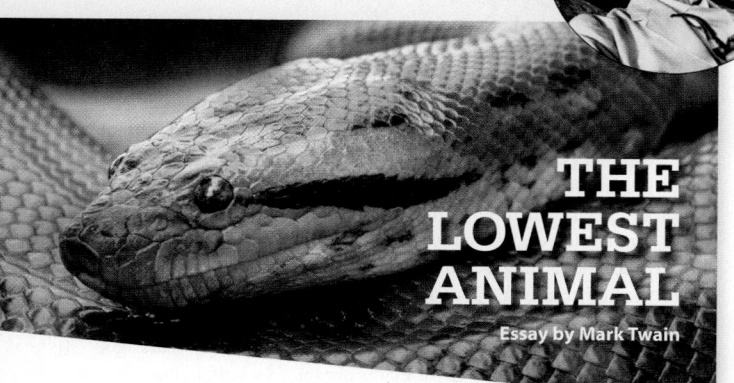

THE LOWEST ANIMAL

Essay by Mark Twain

SETTING A PURPOSE

As you read, notice how Twain uses elements of satire throughout the essay. Think about how he describes the various "painstaking" experiments he performed.

1 I have been studying the traits and **dispositions** of the "lower animals" (so-called) and contrasting them with the traits and dispositions of man. I find the result humiliating to me. For it obliges me to renounce[1] my allegiance to the Darwinian theory of the Ascent of Man from the Lower Animals, since it now seems plain to me that that theory ought to be vacated in favor of a new and truer one, this new and truer one to be named the Descent of Man from the Higher Animals.

2 In proceeding toward this unpleasant conclusion, I have not guessed or speculated or conjectured, but have used what is commonly called the scientific method.[2] That is to say, I have subjected every postulate[3] that presented itself to the crucial test of actual experiment and have adopted it or rejected it according

---

[1] **renounce:** give up; reject.
[2] **scientific method:** research method in which a hypothesis is tested by careful, documented experiments.
[3] **postulate:** assumption.

Notice & Note

Use the side margins to notice and note signposts in the text.

disposition
(dĭs-pə-zĭsh´ən) *n.* character or temperament.

ANALYZE AUTHOR'S PURPOSE: SATIRE

Annotate: Mark the words that suggest Twain's purpose in paragraph 1 is to entertain.

Analyze: How can you tell that Twain is trying to entertain rather than inform?

The Lowest Animal 485

BACKGROUND

Have students read the Background note. Then, tell students that as Twain grew older and experienced grief and financial reversals, his writing turned darker. Some of this writing was not published at the time, either because magazines rejected it or because Twain was reluctant to let readers see the changes in his worldview.

SETTING A PURPOSE

Direct students to use the Setting a Purpose prompt to focus their reading.

ANALYZE AUTHOR'S PURPOSE: SATIRE

Discuss with students that the author's purpose is his or her reason for writing a specific text. Writers may want to express many things, but often writers communicate these messages while trying to inform, persuade, entertain, analyze, or describe. Writers often do two of these things at once. As they read on, students may feel that Twain—whose tone becomes darker and more serious—is trying to persuade as well as entertain readers. (**Answer:** *Twain mentions the scientific method and science texts, which could suggest he is trying to inform. However, he is conveying ideas about humanity with humor, so his primary purpose seems to be to entertain.*)

CRITICAL VOCABULARY

disposition: Twain wants to compare the character of animals to the character of human beings.

ASK STUDENTS how Twain describes the dispositions of human beings. (*He describes them as being inferior to animals' dispositions.*)

LANGUAGE CONVENTIONS

Tell students that by using the anaphora, Twain isn't just imitating a style of formal speech, he is intentionally imitating formal scientific papers of his period. He is pretending that he is writing a serious paper following the scientific method. (**Answer:** *The repetition undercuts the scientific approach Twain says he is pursuing. His "generalizations" are almost meaningless, scientifically.*)

ENGLISH LEARNER SUPPORT

Understand Multiple-Meaning Words Tell students that the word *speculated* (first sentence in paragraph 2) is an example of a word with more than one meaning. It can mean "guessed" or "invested money." Discuss what the word means here. (*It means "guessed."*) What context clues helped you arrive at an answer? (*The sentence includes two synonyms for "speculated," which are apparent because of the word "or."*) Encourage students to use context clues to understand multiple-meaning words. **MODERATE**

For **listening support** for students at varying proficiency levels, see the **Text X-Ray** on page 482C.

CRITICAL VOCABULARY

caliber: Twain discusses how humans can vary, for example, by their mental calibers or abilities.

ASK STUDENTS to name two of the factors that Twain says can affect a person's mental caliber. (*climate and environment*)

transition: Twain compares the results of his anaconda experiments with the acts of the English earl and states that his findings suggest the earl descended from the anaconda.

ASK STUDENTS what Twain means by saying that "a good deal" was lost in the transition from snake to human being. (*During the process of change, humans became cruel, proving that the snake is a superior creature to the human being.*)

caliber
(kăl´ə-bər) *n.* level of ability.

LANGUAGE CONVENTIONS
Annotate: Mark the repeated phrase at the beginning of paragraphs 4, 5, and 6.

Analyze: How does anaphora contribute to the humor in this section?

transition
(trăn-zĭsh´ən) *n.* process of change.

to the result. Thus, I verified and established each step of my course in its turn before advancing to the next. These experiments were made in the London Zoological Gardens and covered many months of painstaking and fatiguing work.

3   Before particularizing any of the experiments, I wish to state one or two things which seem to more properly belong in this place than further along. This in the interest of clearness. The massed experiments established to my satisfaction certain generalizations, to wit:

4   1. That the human race is of one distinct species. It exhibits slight variations—in color, stature, mental **caliber**, and so on—due to climate, environment, and so forth; but it is a species by itself and not to be confounded with any other.

5   2. That the quadrupeds[4] are a distinct family, also. This family exhibits variations—in color, size, food preferences, and so on; but it is a family by itself.

6   3. That the other families—the birds, the fishes, the insects, the reptiles, etc.— are more or less distinct, also. They are in the procession. They are links in the chain which stretches down from the higher animals to man at the bottom.

7   Some of my experiments were quite curious. In the course of my reading, I had come across a case where, many years ago, some hunters on our Great Plains organized a buffalo hunt for the entertainment of an English earl—that, and to provide some fresh meat for his larder.[5] They had charming sport. They killed seventy-two of those great animals and ate part of one of them and left the seventy-one to rot. In order to determine the difference between an anaconda[6] and an earl—if any—I caused seven young calves to be turned into the anaconda's cage. The grateful reptile immediately crushed one of them and swallowed it, then lay back satisfied. It showed no further interest in the calves and no disposition to harm them. I tried this experiment with other anacondas, always with the same result. The fact stood proven that the difference between an earl and an anaconda is that the earl is cruel and the anaconda isn't; and that the earl wantonly destroys what he has no use for, but the anaconda doesn't. This seemed to suggest that the anaconda was not descended from the earl. It also seemed to suggest that the earl was descended from the anaconda, and had lost a good deal in the **transition**.

8   I was aware that many men who have accumulated more millions of money than they can ever use have shown a rabid hunger for more, and have not scrupled[7] to cheat the ignorant and the helpless

---

[4] **quadrupeds:** four-footed animals.
[5] **larder:** supply of food or place where food supplies are kept.
[6] **anaconda:** long, heavy snake that crushes its prey.
[7] **scrupled:** hesitated because of feelings of guilt.

out of their poor servings in order to partially appease[8] that appetite. I furnished a hundred different kinds of wild and tame animals the opportunity to accumulate vast stores of food, but none of them would do it. The squirrels and bees and certain birds made accumulations, but stopped when they had gathered a winter's supply and could not be persuaded to add to it either honestly or by chicane.[9] In order to bolster up a tottering reputation, the ant pretended to store up supplies, but I was not deceived. I know the ant. These experiments convinced me that there is this difference between man and the higher animals: He is avaricious and miserly, they are not.

9　　In the course of my experiments, I convinced myself that among the animals man is the only one that harbors[10] insults and injuries, broods over them, waits till a chance offers, then takes revenge. The passion of revenge is unknown to the higher animals.

10　　Roosters keep harems,[11] but it is by consent of their concubines;[12] therefore no wrong is done. Men keep harems, but it is by brute force, privileged by **atrocious** laws which the other sex was allowed no hand in making. In this matter man occupies a far lower place than the rooster.

---

[8] **appease:** satisfy; pacify.
[9] **chicane** (shĭ-kān´): clever deception; trickery.
[10] **harbors:** clings to.
[11] **harems:** groups of females who mate and live with one male.
[12] **concubines:** secondary wives.

ANALYZE AUTHOR'S PURPOSE: SATIRE

Annotate: Mark assertions in paragraph 8 that should not be taken literally.

Analyze: How are Twain's "experiments" an example of absurdity?

atrocious
(ə-trō´shəs) *adj.* evil or brutal.

ANALYZE AUTHOR'S PURPOSE: SATIRE

Tell students that something is absurd when it is far past what is possible. Even if it is said in a serious, practical manner, if it is drastically improbable, then it is absurd. (**Answer:** *It would be very difficult for one man to actually conduct experiments where vast stores of food were made available to a hundred different animals and to observe what the animals then did with the food over time. The idea that Twain tried "chicane," or trickery, to attempt to get the animals to store more food than they needed is amusing and ridiculous.*)

For **speaking support** for students at varying proficiency levels, see the **Text X-Ray** on page 482D.

WHEN STUDENTS STRUGGLE...

Make Generalizations Note that nowhere in his essay does Twain pretend that every person corresponds to the general statements he makes about people. And yet many people have agreed that he is right about enough people that he has a point. That means Twain made effective generalizations. Have students work with a partner to find generalizations in "The Lowest Animal."

For additional support, go to the **Reading Studio** and assign the following **LEVEL UP** **Level Up Tutorial: Making Generalizations.**

CRITICAL VOCABULARY

atrocious: Twain writes of despicable, or atrocious, laws that allow men to have multiple wives at the same time, although women had no say in making the laws.

ASK STUDENTS whether they believe that Twain would still believe that laws allowing men to have harems were atrocious if women were allowed to craft the laws. (*Answers will vary, but students may believe Twain would still find the laws bad but less unfair.*)

ANALYZE TONE

Discuss that part of identifying an author's attitude involves comparing the author's opinion to other ways the author could have said the same thing. Twain could have said the same thing about humans in a much less disgusted way, so his tone stands out. (**Answer:** *Twain thinks better of animals than of humans. "Man, with his soiled mind, covers himself." "He [man] is the only one that does it—or has occasion to.")*

 ENGLISH LEARNER SUPPORT

Idioms Draw out the meaning of the idiomatic phrase *saving grace* in paragraph 11 ("a redeeming quality"). Ask students to explain how this phrase contributes to the reader's understanding of the difference between cats and human beings.

 NOTICE & NOTE

ANALYZE TONE
Annotate: Circle words in paragraph 12 that reveal Twain's attitude toward humans. Underline words that describe his feelings about animals.

Cite Evidence: How does Twain's diction help you discern his attitude toward "higher animals" and toward humans?

11   Cats are loose in their morals, but not consciously so. Man, in his descent from the cat, has brought the cat's looseness with him but has left the unconsciousness behind—the saving grace which excuses the cat. The cat is innocent, man is not.

12   Indecency, vulgarity, obscenity—these are strictly confined to man; he invented them. Among the higher animals there is no trace of them. They hide nothing; they are not ashamed. Man, with his soiled mind, covers himself. He will not even enter a drawing room with his breast and back naked, so alive are he and his mates to indecent suggestion. Man is the Animal that Laughs. But so does the monkey, as Mr. Darwin pointed out, and so does the Australian bird that is called the laughing jackass. No—Man is the Animal that Blushes. He is the only one that does it—or has occasion to.

13   At the head of this article we see how "three monks were burnt to death" a few days ago and a prior was "put to death with atrocious cruelty." Do we inquire into the details? No; or we should find out that the prior was subjected to unprintable mutilations. Man—when he is a North American Indian—gouges out his prisoner's eyes; when he is King John,[13] with a nephew to render untroublesome, he uses a red-hot iron; when he is a religious zealot[14] dealing with heretics[15] in the Middle Ages, he skins his captive alive and scatters salt on his back; in the first Richard's[16] time, he shuts up a multitude of Jewish families in a tower and sets fire to it; in Columbus's time he captures a family of Spanish Jews and—but *that* is not printable; in our day in England, a man is fined ten shillings for beating his mother nearly to death with a chair, and another man is fined forty shillings for having four pheasant eggs in his possession without being able to satisfactorily explain how he got them. Of all the animals, man is the only one that is cruel. He is the only one that inflicts pain for the pleasure of doing it. It is a trait that is not known to the higher animals. The cat plays with the frightened mouse; but she has this excuse, that she does not know that the mouse is suffering. The cat is moderate—unhumanly moderate: She only scares the mouse, she does not hurt it; she doesn't dig out its eyes, or tear off its skin, or drive splinters under its nails—man fashion; when she is done playing with it, she makes a sudden meal of it and puts it out of its trouble. Man is the Cruel Animal. He is alone in that distinction.

---

[13] **King John:** king of England from 1199 to 1216, known for seizing the throne from his nephew Arthur.
[14] **zealot** (zĕl´ət): overly enthusiastic person; fanatic.
[15] **heretics:** people who hold beliefs opposed to those of the church.
[16] **first Richard's:** refers to Richard I (1157–1199), also called Richard the Lion-Hearted, king of England from 1189 to 1199.

APPLYING ACADEMIC VOCABULARY

❑ **ambiguous**   ☑ **clarify**   ❑ **implicit**   ❑ **revise**   ☑ **somewhat**

Write and Discuss Have students turn to a partner to discuss the following question. Guide students to include the Academic Vocabulary words *clarify* and *somewhat* in their responses. Ask volunteers to share their responses with the class.

• Is Twain right about humans, wrong about humans, or **somewhat** right and **somewhat** wrong? Use reasons to **clarify** your response.

14   The higher animals engage in individual fights, but never in organized masses. Man is the only animal that deals in that atrocity of atrocities, war. He is the only one that gathers his brethren about him and goes forth in cold blood and with calm pulse to exterminate his kind. He is the only animal that for sordid wages will march out, as the Hessians[17] did in our Revolution, and as the boyish Prince Napoleon did in the Zulu war,[18] and help to slaughter strangers of his own species who have done him no harm and with whom he has no quarrel.

15   Man is the only animal that robs his helpless fellow of his country—takes possession of it and drives him out of it or destroys him. Man has done this in all the ages. There is not an acre of ground on the globe that is in possession of its rightful owner, or that has not been taken away from owner after owner, cycle after cycle, by force and bloodshed.

---

[17] **Hessians** (hĕsh´ənz): German soldiers who served for pay in the British army during the American Revolution.

[18] **Prince Napoleon . . . Zulu war:** In search of adventure, Prince Napoleon, son of Napoleon III, joined the British campaign against Zululand (part of South Africa) in 1879.

ANALYZE AUTHOR'S PURPOSE: SATIRE

Annotate: Mark the contrast Twain describes at the beginning of paragraph 14.

Analyze: Is Twain using the techniques of satire? If so, which ones and to what effect?

 ANALYZE AUTHOR'S PURPOSE: SATIRE

Have students discuss the elements of satire and give examples of how Twain could have made this section more satirical. For instance, he could have led us to imagine animals like turtles massing in legions and each toting miniature weapons. But his tone is dark and unhappy with humans; he did not do that. (**Answer:** *Twain uses exaggeration to make his point about war.*)

For **reading support** for students at varying proficiency levels, see the **Text X-Ray** on page 482D.

TO CHALLENGE STUDENTS . . .

Analyze the Writer's Views Tell students that although Twain's attitude toward humanity is very negative in this piece, he wrote many stories and essays that celebrate the creativity and skill of humanity. Have them discuss why his views could vary so much without being contradictory.

ANALYZE TONE

Twain was an atheist and saw religion as a cause for irrational and even unethical behavior. This affects his tone in this section. (**Answer:** *The ways in which humanity stands out, such as failing to love one's neighbor, are not positive. Twain's tone is very accusatory and negative. He gives multiple examples to make his point.*)

 ANALYZE AUTHOR'S PURPOSE: SATIRE

Note that elements of absurdity often involve exaggeration. For instance, here the cat and the dog being quick friends is perhaps not common but not unbelievable. But as Twain mentions other animals, like rabbits and foxes, he has exaggerated past the point of reason and it becomes absurd. (**Answer:** *The experiment is an example of absurdity, since the situation is clearly extreme and ridiculous. There is also humor, since the experiment is described in a way designed to make readers laugh.*)

 **NOTICE & NOTE**

ANALYZE TONE

Annotate: In paragraph 18, mark the ways Twain says that humanity is unique.

Draw Conclusions: Does Twain regard humanity's uniqueness as a positive trait? What about his tone helps you determine this? Explain.

ANALYZE AUTHOR'S PURPOSE: SATIRE

Annotate: In paragraph 20, mark each animal Twain says he put in the cage.

Evaluate: What elements of satire are evident in paragraph 20? Explain.

16   Man is the only Slave. And he is the only animal who enslaves. He has always been a slave in one form or another, and has always held other slaves in bondage under him in one way or another. In our day he is always some man's slave for wages and does that man's work; and this slave has other slaves under him for minor wages, and they do *his* work. The higher animals are the only ones who exclusively do their own work and provide their own living.

17   Man is the only Patriot. He sets himself apart in his own country, under his own flag, and sneers at the other nations, and keeps multitudinous uniformed assassins on hand at heavy expense to grab slices of other people's countries and keep *them* from grabbing slices of *his*. And in the intervals between campaigns, he washes the blood off his hands and works for "the universal brotherhood of man"— with his mouth.

18   Man is the Religious Animal. He is the only Religious Animal. He is the only animal that has the True Religion—several of them. He is the only animal that loves his neighbor as himself, and cuts his throat if his theology isn't straight. He has made a graveyard of the globe in trying his honest best to smooth his brother's path to happiness and heaven. He was at it in the time of the Caesars, he was at it in Mahomet's[19] time, he was at it in the time of the Inquisition, he was at it in France a couple of centuries, he was at it in England in Mary's day,[20] he has been at it ever since he first saw the light, he is at it today in Crete—he will be at it somewhere else tomorrow. The higher animals have no religion. And we are told that they are going to be left out, in the hereafter. I wonder why. It seems questionable taste.

19   Man is the Reasoning Animal. Such is the claim. I think it is open to dispute. Indeed, my experiments have proven to me that he is the Unreasoning Animal. Note his history, as sketched above. It seems plain to me that whatever he is, he is *not* a reasoning animal. His record is the fantastic record of a maniac. I consider that the strongest count against his intelligence is the fact that with that record back of him, he blandly sets himself up as the head animal of the lot; whereas by his own standards, he is the bottom one.

20   In truth, man is incurably foolish. Simple things which the other animals easily learn he is incapable of learning. Among my experiments was this. In an hour I taught a cat and a dog to be friends. I put them in a cage. In another hour I taught them to be friends with a rabbit. In the course of two days I was able to add a fox, a goose, a squirrel, and some doves. Finally a monkey. They lived together in peace, even affectionately.

---

[19] **Mahomet's:** Muhammad (c. A.D. 570–632) was an Arab prophet and founder of Islam.

[20] **in Mary's day:** during the reign of Queen Mary (1553–1558), who was given the nickname "Bloody Mary" when she ordered the deaths of many Protestants.

21   Next, in another cage I confined an Irish Catholic from Tipperary, and as soon as he seemed tame, I added a Scottish Presbyterian from Aberdeen. Next a Turk from Constantinople, a Greek Christian from Crete, an Armenian, a Methodist from the wilds of Arkansas, a Buddhist from China, a Brahman from Benares. Finally, a Salvation Army colonel from Wapping. Then I stayed away two whole days. When I came back to note results, the cage of Higher Animals was all right, but in the other there was but a chaos of gory odds and ends of turbans and fezzes and plaids and bones and flesh— not a specimen left alive. These Reasoning Animals had disagreed on a theological detail and carried the matter to a higher court.

CHECK YOUR UNDERSTANDING

Answer these questions before moving on to the **Analyze the Text** section on the following page.

1 Twain's admiration of Darwin is undermined by what?

A Reading the work of other scientists

B Studying the behavior of animals

C Studying the behavior of humans

D Rereading Darwin's books and ideas

2 Why does Twain consider the behavior of cats superior to that of humans?

F Cats are always moral.

G Cats aren't conscious of morals.

H Humans don't think about morals.

J Humans don't understand cats.

3 Which of the following is an example of exaggeration?

A *He has made a graveyard of the globe....*

B *Man has done this in all the ages.*

C *He is the only Religious Animal.*

D *They lived together in peace, even affectionately.*

The Lowest Animal   491

© Houghton Mifflin Harcourt Publishing Company

TEACH

✏ CHECK YOUR UNDERSTANDING

Have students answer the questions independently.

Answers:

1. *C*

2. *G*

3. *A*

If they answer any questions incorrectly, have them reread the text to confirm their understanding. Then they may proceed to ANALYZE THE TEXT on page 492.

EL   ENGLISH LEARNER SUPPORT

Oral Assessment   Use the following questions to assess students' comprehension and speaking skills.

1. What weakens Twain's praise of Darwin? *(studying the behavior of humans)*

2. Why does Twain think cats behave better than people do? *(Cats don't think about morals.)*

3. Twain said, "He has made a graveyard of the globe." Why is this an example of an exaggeration? *(The whole world is not one giant graveyard.)* **SUBSTANTIAL**

ANALYZE THE TEXT

Possible answers:

1. **DOK 4:** *Twain's tone, or attitude, toward humans is critical. Toward animals, it is respectful.*

2. **DOK 4:** *It becomes clear in the rest of the essay that Twain is being absurd and has, in fact, not done any experiments. The fictional experiments he lists are ridiculous; for most of his claims, he mentions no associated experiments.*

3. **DOK 2:** *Twain writes that the hunting party left 71 dead buffalo to rot. Later in the paragraph, he writes that the earl is cruel while the anaconda is not. So clearly, this was the opposite of both charming and sport.*

4. **DOK 4:** *Twain's overall purpose is to make a point about the immorality of human beings (despite their many religions), as compared to other animals. His use of satire is quite effective because it grabs the reader's attention and enlivens an otherwise dull or preachy moral topic.*

5. **DOK 4:** *Twain's tone seems lighthearted early in the piece, as he uses humor to point out humanity's flaws. As the piece goes on, Twain's attitude becomes more serious, as when he describes intentional acts of cruelty done by humans, which should be a cause of shame.*

RESEARCH

Mark Twain wrote many other pieces, including many that are not satires. Encourage students to watch for the elements of satire in any piece that they choose.

Extend Students may also want to consider not only what role satire has to play in our world today but where satire appears. For instance, some satire may appear in social media. Is it effective there?

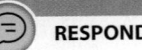 **RESPOND**

ANALYZE THE TEXT

Support your responses with evidence from the text. **NOTEBOOK**

1. **Analyze** In paragraph 1, what tone does Twain use in his discussion of humans? What tone does he use in his discussion of animals?

2. **Evaluate** In paragraph 2, Twain says that he reached his conclusions by following the scientific method. Explain whether this claim is intended to be taken seriously.

3. **Infer** When describing a buffalo hunt, Twain writes, "They had charming sport." (paragraph 7) How does the diction and syntax in the rest of the passage reveal the irony of this statement?

4. **Evaluate** What is Twain's overall purpose in writing this essay? How effective is his use of satire in achieving that purpose?

5. **Analyze** How does Twain's tone, or attitude, change over the course of the piece? Cite text evidence in your response.

RESEARCH

RESEARCH TIP
Sites that teach about Twain or about satire are good sources of information on the types of satire Twain uses. Search for *Twain* and *satire* both separately and together to get different results.

Use print and digital resources to research Mark Twain and his use of satire. Use what you learn to answer these questions.

QUESTION	ANSWER
What is an example of another satire written by Mark Twain?	*Answers will vary.*
What ideas does Twain satirize in this piece?	
What change might Twain have been hoping to achieve by writing about this issue?	

Extend There is a prestigious award given by the Kennedy Center called "The Mark Twain Prize." What questions do you have about this award? Think of two questions you have. Then, conduct research to find the answers to your questions.

WHEN STUDENTS STRUGGLE . . .

Make Generalizations Remind students that Twain makes generalizations because he is speaking about humans in general, not about particular humans. These generalizations are big statements about a topic—humans, for instance—that support an author's point, even though they do not fit every individual.

 For additional support, go to the **Reading Studio** and assign the following **LEVELUP Level Up Tutorial: Making Generalizations.**

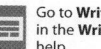
CREATE AND PRESENT

Write a Satire Twain holds up common characteristics and elements of everyday life to ridicule throughout "The Lowest Animal." What are some aspects of daily living that might be worthy of satire today? Write a paragraph in which you use Twain's techniques to satirize something humans do day in and day out.

❏ Choose an aspect of everyday life that is worthy of satire.

❏ Remember that satire can include humor and does not need to be as serious as Twain's work.

❏ Include elements of satire in your work, such as exaggeration, irony, or humor.

Present a Satire Twain was a famous lecturer and often presented his material before an audience. Choose a passage from "The Lowest Animal" to present to a small group.

❏ Practice reading your passage aloud, so the presentation flows easily.

❏ Use pacing, gestures, and vocal inflection to emphasize humorous, ironic, or sarcastic elements of your satire.

❏ Practice with a partner to ensure you convey Twain's points clearly to get the desired response to Twain's humor.

 Go to **Writing as a Process** in the **Writing Studio** for help.

 Go to **Giving a Presentation: Delivering Your Presentation** in the **Speaking and Listening Studio** for help.

RESPOND TO THE ESSENTIAL QUESTION

? Why do humans cause harm?

Gather Information Review your annotations and notes on "The Lowest Animal." Then, add relevant information to your Response Log. As you determine which information to include, think about:

- Twain's major point for writing
- the way Twain demonstrates that humans cause harm
- how satire helped Twain make his points

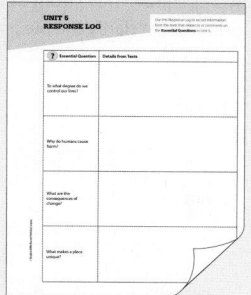

ACADEMIC VOCABULARY

As you write and discuss what you learned from the satire, be sure to use the Academic Vocabulary words. Check off each of the words that you use.

❏ **ambiguous**

❏ **clarify**

❏ **implicit**

❏ **revise**

❏ **somewhat**

CREATE AND PRESENT

Write a Satire Students' texts should include some of the elements of satire discussed, though there may not be room for all elements in one paragraph. Encourage students to find their own style instead of trying to exactly imitate Twain.

Present a Satire Encourage students to read their pieces first while their partner isn't looking at the text. That will help their partner notice pacing issues. Then, partners should have a copy of the text and check to see whether the various satirical points they read are brought out by the reading.

RESPOND TO THE ESSENTIAL QUESTION

Allow time for students to add details from "The Lowest Animal" to their Unit 5 Response Logs.

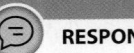

APPLY

CRITICAL VOCABULARY

Answers:

1. *caliber*

2. *atrocious*

3. *transition*

4. *disposition*

VOCABULARY STRATEGY: Nuances in Word Meaning

As a class, discuss the words that have similar meanings to *atrocious* but have slightly different nuances. Encourage students to discuss the differences between the words and give examples of when they might use each one.

RESPOND

WORD BANK
disposition
caliber
transition
atrocious

Go to **Using Reference Sources** in the **Vocabulary Studio** for more help.

CRITICAL VOCABULARY

Practice and Apply Write the word that best completes each statement.

1. The boss of a company wants to hire someone with skills that are of a high _____ for the job.

2. Many people agree that the effects of war can be _____.

3. Leaving home to go to college can be a challenging _____ for some students.

4. A salesperson needs to have a very outgoing _____ if he or she is going to be successful.

VOCABULARY STRATEGY: Nuances in Word Meaning

In "The Lowest Animal," Twain used the word *atrocious* to describe laws that allow men in some nations to keep harems. Twain chose a word with a very strong nuance, or shade of meaning. He wanted to emphasize how evil or brutal he thought the laws were. By choosing a word with a specific nuance, a writer can express his or her ideas with greater precision. Adjectives that have similar meanings but different nuances might be arranged on a continuum, as shown, with the word representing the least degree on the left and the greatest on the right.

BAD	HARMFUL	WICKED	CRUEL	ATROCIOUS

Practice and Apply For each word in the chart below, create a continuum of four other words that have similar meanings but show different nuances. Words should move from weakest to strongest. Consult print or digital resources to clarify the precise meaning of words.

1. cold	*cool*	*chilly*	*freezing*	*sub-zero*
2. hot	*warm*	*stifling*	*roasting*	*scorching*
3. happy	*pleased*	*glad*	*joyful*	*blissful*
4. smell	*fragrance*	*scent*	*odor*	*stench*
5. pretty	*cute*	*fine-looking*	*beautiful*	*stunning*

ENGLISH LEARNER SUPPORT

Sound Transfer Note that /r/ in *atrocious, caliber,* and *transition* may be a difficult sound for speakers of Spanish, Hmong, Cantonese, Haitian Creole, and Korean, as the sound either does not exist in the language, does exist but is pronounced somewhat differently, or is likely to be confused with another sound. Display these words and other words with the /r/ sound, and have students repeat each word chorally. **SUBSTANTIAL/MODERATE**

LANGUAGE CONVENTIONS: Anaphora and Parallelism

In "The Lowest Animal," Mark Twain uses a particular type of repetition known as **anaphora,** the repetition of a word or words at the beginning of successive lines, clauses, sentences, or paragraphs. This literary device is particularly effective in poetry, but it also has a place in argumentative prose. Consider this example from two sentences in paragraph 12.

> **Man is the Animal that Laughs. . . . No—Man is the Animal that Blushes.**

These sentences also share a **parallel construction,** meaning that they use similar grammatical structures to express ideas that are related or equal in value. By using these literary devices, Twain emphasizes his central ideas and creates a rhythm that strengthens the rhetorical effect. Here are other examples of anaphora from this essay. These appear at the beginning of successive paragraphs, beginning with paragraph 15.

> **Man is the only animal that robs his helpless fellow of his country. . . .**
> **Man is the only Slave.**
> **Man is the only Patriot.**
> **Man is the Religious Animal.**
> **Man is the Reasoning Animal.**

Twain uses these devices to build a cumulative list of the aspects of human conduct that he wants to satirize. Clearly, Twain's use of anaphora is deliberate. In his hands, it has an artistic effect and he successfully uses it to hammer home the point he wants to make, which is that humans are not the highest animals (though they may believe otherwise).

Practice and Apply Look back at the satire you wrote. Revise your writing to include the use of anaphora and parallelism.

LANGUAGE CONVENTIONS: Anaphora and Parallelism

Illustrate the importance that anaphora and parallelism have in Twain's style in this essay by rewriting several of the example sentences without anaphora or parallelism. Some examples are shown here.

From paragraph 12:

Man is the Animal that Laughs. Or perhaps it would be better to say Man is the Animal that Blushes.

From paragraph 15:

Humans are the only animals that rob helpless fellows of their country. . . .
People make other people slaves.
Only humans are patriots.
And religious animals are all people.
In fact, only humans reason.

Have students analyze why these revisions are worse. (*The first revisions de-emphasizes the change Twain is making and how it deprecates humans. In the second set of sentences, Twain's stress on "Man is the only animal that . . ." is lost.*)

Practice and Apply Students' paragraphs should use anaphora and parallelism to emphasize key points in their text.

 For **writing support** for students at varying proficiency levels, see the **Text X-Ray** on page 482D.

 ENGLISH LEARNER SUPPORT

Language Conventions Use the following supports with students at varying levels:

- Have students explain to a partner why the sentences are examples of parallelism and anaphora. **MODERATE**

- Have students work with a partner to revise their paragraphs to use anaphora and parallelism. **LIGHT**

WHY EVERYONE MUST GET READY FOR THE FOURTH INDUSTRIAL REVOLUTION

Article by Bernard Marr

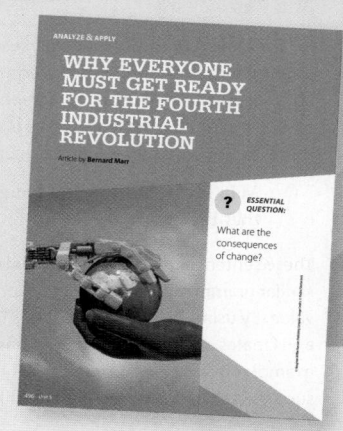

GENRE ELEMENTS
MULTIMODAL TEXT

Multimodal text uses two or more modes to convey information. For example, it may contain graphics, sound, video, or other media components. In some cases, these modes provide information to clarify or illustrate ideas or thoughts expressed in the written text. In other cases, these modes provide new information not mentioned in the written text. Graphics, for example, are often useful for presenting complex information in an easy-to-understand way and showing relationships between ideas.

LEARNING OBJECTIVES

- Identify the elements and message of a multimodal text.
- Conduct research to identify the causes and effects of three industrial revolutions.
- Write an argument for or against the likely occurrence of a fourth industrial revolution.
- Present an argument orally.
- Use context clues to understand word meanings.
- Use capitalization in writing.
- **Language** Create a graphic using details from the selection.

TEXT COMPLEXITY

Quantitative Measures	Why Everyone Must Get Ready for the Fourth Industrial Revolution	Lexile: 1320L
Qualitative Measures	**Ideas Presented** Much is explicit; some implied meaning; requires some inferential reasoning.	
	Structures Used More complex; more deviation from chronological or sequential order.	
	Language Used Mostly explicit.	
	Knowledge Required More complexity in theme; cultural and historical references may make heavier demands.	

Online 📶 **Ed**

RESOURCES

- Unit 5 Response Log
- 🔊 Selection Audio
- 📖 Reading Studio
  Notice & Note
- **LEVEL UP** Level Up Tutorial:
  Analyzing Arguments
- 📰 Writing Studio:
  Writing Arguments
- 💬 Speaking and Listening Studio:
  Giving a Presentation
- 🔵 Vocabulary Studio:
  Using Context Clues
- ❗ Grammar Studio: Module 12:
  Capital Letters
- ☑ "Why Everyone Must Get Ready for
  the Fourth Industrial Revolution"
  Selection Test

SUMMARIES

English

The author argues that soon a fourth industrial revolution will change the way people work and live. This new revolution will differ from earlier revolutions, which were primarily technology related, by impacting all industries, economies, and disciplines. It will have possible advantages for businesses and the natural environment, but will also have the potential to result in security risks and greater inequality between the rich and poor. Yet despite these drawbacks, history has shown that industrial revolutions have eventually been followed by periods of social and political change that benefited a wide scope of people.

Spanish

El autor argumenta que pronto una cuarta revolución industrial cambiará la manera en que se trabaja y se vive. Esta nueva revolución será diferente de las pasadas, que se relacionaban principalmente con el impacto de la tecnología en las industrias, economías y disciplinas. Tendrá posibles ventajas para los negocios y el medioambiente, pero también tendrá el potencial de causar riesgos de seguridad y una mayor desigualdad entre los ricos y pobres. A pesar de estos inconvenientes, la historia prueba que las revoluciones industriales han sido seguidas por períodos de cambio sociopolítico que beneficiaron a la mayoría.

 ## SMALL-GROUP OPTIONS

Have students work in small groups and pairs to read and discuss the selection.

Reciprocal Teaching

- Provide students with a list of sample questions before they begin reading the selection. For example:

  What is the fourth industrial revolution?

  What evidence does the author provide to support his claim?

- As students read, have them write additional questions about the selection.

- Organize students into groups of three and have each student offer two questions to the group for discussion without duplicating each other.

- Have students discuss the questions and find evidence from the selection to support their responses.

Three-Minute Review

- Have students work in small groups to discuss this question: *How would a fourth industrial revolution change people's lives?*

- Pause the discussion after a few minutes and direct the students to work independently.

- Set the timer for three minutes.

- Tell students to reread material, reflect on their discussion, and write clarifying questions.

- Solicit clarifying questions from volunteers. Engage in a brief discussion.

Text X-Ray: English Learner Support
for "Why Everyone Must Get Ready for the Fourth Industrial Revolution"

Use the Text X-Ray and the supports and scaffolds in the Teacher's Edition to help guide students at different proficiency levels through the selection.

INTRODUCE THE SELECTION
DISCUSS INDUSTRIAL REVOLUTION

In this lesson, students will need to be able to address the meaning of the term *industrial revolution*. Read aloud paragraphs 1 and 2 and point out this term. Explain that a revolution is a change to society that affects the way people live, work, and play. Industrial revolutions are a change created by the use of machines to make things that people used to make by hand.

Have volunteers share examples of things that are made by machines. Supply the following sentence frames:

- People use machines to _____.
- I like machines that _____ because _____.
- I use a computer to _____.

CULTURAL REFERENCES

The following words or phrases may be unfamiliar to students:

- *assembly lines* (paragraph 1): lines of workers in a factory who each complete a task to help make a product
- *spectrum* (paragraph 9): a range
- *at risk* (paragraph 9): in danger of something harmful happening
- *polarization* (paragraph 11): the division of two opposite groups or ideas
- *social safety nets* (paragraph 11): aid for people who are poor or need help
- *a safe bet to say* (paragraph 12): almost certain

LISTENING

Practice Paraphrasing

Work with students as you read sentences from the selection aloud. Explain that students can paraphrase them, or restate them in different words, to understand the author's ideas.

Use the following supports with students at varying proficiency levels:

- Read aloud paragraph 4. Explain that the phrase "well on its way" means it has already begun. Then, tell students to listen and repeat after you as you paraphrase this sentence: *It has already started and will change many jobs.* Repeat the process with other short sentences. **SUBSTANTIAL**
- Work with students in a group. Read aloud a sentence from the selection, and then repeat it. Explain any unfamiliar words. Have students work together to paraphrase the sentence. Repeat the process with other sentences. **MODERATE**
- As you read sentences aloud, have students write paraphrases. Then, have partners compare their paraphrases with each other and to the text. **LIGHT**

SPEAKING

Understand Counterarguments

Tell students that a **counterargument** is an idea or claim that opposes the author's main argument. Authors mention counterarguments to help readers understand the topic and to respond to opposing ideas.

Use the following supports with students at varying proficiency levels:

- Display and read aloud a claim and counterclaim. For example: *The fourth industrial revolution will be good for people. The fourth industrial revolution will cause harm to workers.* Have students repeat each. **SUBSTANTIAL**
- Have students work in pairs to say arguments and counterarguments. Give them the following sentence frames to work with: *I think ____ is the best [singer, sport, subject, food, movie] because ____. ____ is not the best because ____. I agree ____ is good, but it is not the best because ____.* **MODERATE**
- Have students work in pairs. Direct one student to make a claim on a topic of his or her choosing and the other student to make a counterargument. Have students switch roles and repeat the process several times. **LIGHT**

READING

Understand Arguments by Analyzing Text

Tell students that in an essay, the author strengthens an argument by anticipating counterarguments and explaining why they are invalid or incorrect.

Read paragraphs 6–10 with students. Use the following supports with students at varying levels:

- Read paragraph 8 aloud to students. Ask: *Does the author think new technology is always helpful?* (no) Help students identify words from the paragraph that support this conclusion. **SUBSTANTIAL**
- Read paragraphs 6–10 aloud. Ask students to raise their right hand when you read an argument and to raise their left hand when you read the counterargument. Then, ask them to find words that helped them to identify the argument and counterargument. **MODERATE**
- Have students read paragraphs 6–10 independently. Then, have student pairs make a T-chart showing the pros and cons of the fourth industrial revolution. Have them use their chart to write a statement expressing the author's argument and a statement expressing his counterargument. **LIGHT**

WRITING

Create a Graphic

Review types of graphics and their uses, including bar graphs, pie charts, timelines, drawings, and infographics.

Use the following supports with students at varying proficiency levels:

- Have students create a drawing showing what life may be like during the fourth industrial revolution. Have them label details on their drawing in English or in their home language. **SUBSTANTIAL**
- Have students work in small groups to identify information from the selection that can be shown in a pie chart, bar graph, or timeline. Then, have the students work together to create the graphic and add labels, captions, or other text to explain their graphic. **MODERATE**
- Have students work in small groups to create a graphic that describes the fourth industrial revolution. Students should decide what type of graphic to make, identify details from the selection to show, and write two or three sentences to describe their graphic and why they chose it. **LIGHT**

Connect to the
ESSENTIAL QUESTION

This text explains the concept that society is currently undergoing a new phase of industrial revolution. It considers the potential impacts of this revolution, including the negative consequences that could arise from it. The author argues that patterns of previous industrial revolutions suggest that negative effects may well occur, but they are likely to spark political and social transformations. The author concludes that the fourth industrial revolution will undoubtedly lead to major change and that everyone must prepare to understand and adapt to these changes.

ANALYZE & APPLY

WHY EVERYONE MUST GET READY FOR THE FOURTH INDUSTRIAL REVOLUTION

Article by **Bernard Marr**

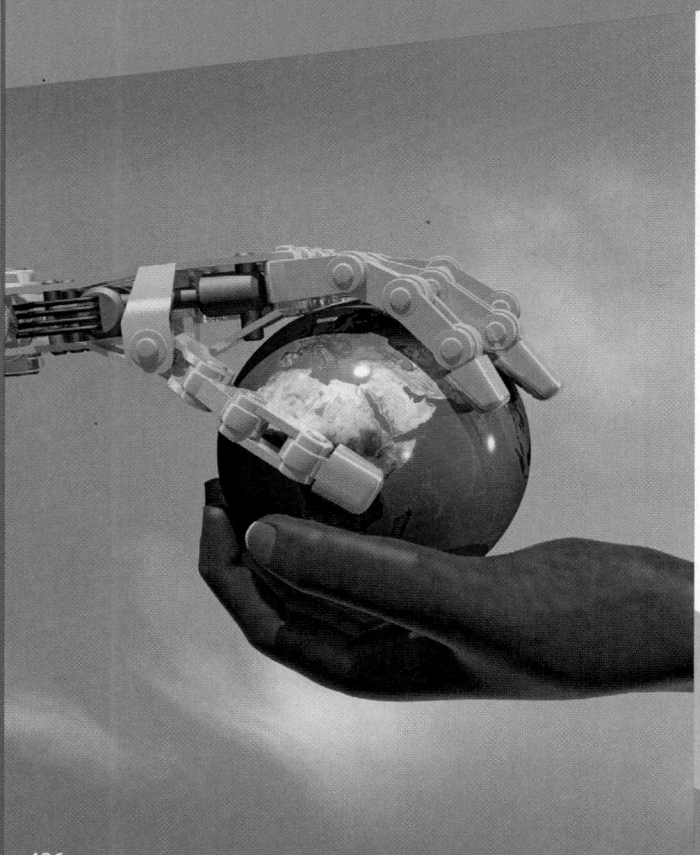

? ESSENTIAL QUESTION:

What are the consequences of change?

496   Unit 5

QUICK START

Think about a time when you went through a big change in your life. Did you have a sense that the change was going to happen? Take notes about what happened leading up to the change and how the change affected your life.

EVALUATE GRAPHIC FEATURES

Authors of argumentative texts make a claim and then support the claim with evidence and facts. In a multimodal text, writers use **graphic features** to support their claims. Graphic features help convey complex information in a way that makes the information easily accessible and understandable. Graphic features include lists, diagrams, maps, charts, timelines, and photos.

To evaluate how effectively a graphic feature supports the author's claim, ask yourself these questions:

- What information is being presented?

- How does the graphic feature support the author's claim?

- Does the information connect to the supporting evidence in the text?

EVALUATE COUNTERARGUMENTS

Authors of effective arguments not only build their arguments using supporting evidence—facts, examples, quotations, expert opinions, and statistics—but they also consider **counterarguments,** or opposing points. A writer of an argument acknowledges counterarguments but then explains why the primary claim still holds true. If the writer's argument does not hold up when presented with a counterargument, the writer's claim might be weak and the argument ineffective.

A writer might address a counterargument using a rebuttal or a concession. A **rebuttal** is a statement that proves a counterargument is false or invalid. A **concession** is an acknowledgment that an aspect of the counterargument has merit. In order to effectively make a concession, an author must explain why his or her claim still holds true despite the merits of the opposing viewpoint.

When evaluating counterarguments and concessions, ask yourself these questions:

- Is a counterargument addressed?

- Is the counterargument effectively rebutted, or disproved? If so, how?

- If not, does the writer make a concession?

- Has the writer effectively defended why his or her claim still holds true despite the concession?

GENRE ELEMENTS: MULTIMODAL TEXT

- uses two or more modes of conveying information

- may have graphic features to express or clarify ideas

- can include sound, video, and other media components

Why Everyone Must Get Ready For the Fourth Industrial Revolution   497

QUICK START

After students write their notes, have them discuss in small groups. Prompt students to consider positive, negative, and neutral consequences of the changes they experienced. Have groups discuss how individuals, communities, and societies can rise to the challenges that come with major changes. After groups discuss, bring the class together to report on group discussions. On the board, list the types of consequences that students identify and strategies for preparing for or adapting to change.

EVALUATE GRAPHIC FEATURES

Discuss the term *multimodal*, noting that *mode* means "way." Explain that written, visual, and aural texts are different modes of communication. Note that just as readers must develop literacy to understand and analyze written texts, they must also develop visual (graphic) literacy skills to be able to "read" and interpret visual elements of a text. Ask students to consider and discuss the types of graphic features that they find most helpful or interesting. Lead them to discuss what types of information can be best expressed visually (such as steps in a process or sharp contrasts). Effective graphic features often help readers visualize an important concept. Note that graphic features also serve to draw a reader's interest. Encourage students to examine and analyze graphic features before reading and then again after reading. In their post-reading consideration of a graphic feature, they should ask themselves what ideas are represented, as well as what other ideas are presented or more deeply explored by the written text.

EVALUATE COUNTERARGUMENTS

Point out that part of a reader's job is to consider what counterarguments a writer may not have addressed. Readers should also think about what constitutes an effective rebuttal. This is true even when you agree with or are attracted to a writer's argument. Encourage students to look for weaknesses in arguments. As they read the selection, ask them to think about other points the author might have included.

TEACH

CRITICAL VOCABULARY

Encourage students to read both sentences carefully before deciding which one uses the word correctly. Remind them to look for context clues to help determine the meaning of each word. Have them think about the prefixes *re-* (again) and *auto-* (self) and other words that use the same prefixes (such as *renaissance, retake, retrace* and *automatic, autobiography, automobile*).

Answers:

1. *a*

2. *b*

3. *b*

4. *a*

■ English Learner Support

Use Cognates Tell Spanish speakers that several of the Critical Vocabulary words have Spanish cognates: *augment/ aumentar, aumentada; regenerate/regenerar; postulate/ postular; automation/automatización.* **ALL LEVELS**

LANGUAGE CONVENTIONS

Capitalization Have a student read the text about capitalization aloud. Then, ask students to explain the reason for each instance of capitalization in the example sentence. Ask if anyone can explain why *of* in "House of Representatives" is not capitalized. *(Prepositions of four words or less are not capitalized in titles.)* Tell students to be on the lookout for words that are and are not capitalized in titles as they read the selection.

ANNOTATION MODEL

Remind students of annotation strategies such as underlining important ideas. They might want to circle or highlight phrases that signal arguments and counterarguments. Students may follow this suggestion or use their own system for marking up the selection in their write-in text. They may want to color-code their annotation by using highlighters. Their notes in the margin may include questions about ideas that are unclear or topics they want to learn more about.

CRITICAL VOCABULARY

| augment | regenerate | postulate | automation |

To see how many Critical Vocabulary words you already know, mark the letter of the sentence that uses the word correctly.

1. **a.** Video games can be **augmented** by using virtual reality goggles.
   b. She **augmented** her car in the traffic accident.

2. **a.** It's amazing how much our house **regenerates** with an air conditioner.
   b. If a plant is not cut too close to the ground, it **regenerates.**

3. **a.** I was upset by the **postulates** I saw on my son's leg.
   b. The scientist **postulates** a new theory.

4. **a.** The car industry grew when **automation** was added to the factories.
   b. The CEO wore a suit for the **automation.**

LANGUAGE CONVENTIONS

Capitalization In standard English, the first word of a sentence or direct quotation is capitalized. Proper nouns and adjectives formed from proper nouns are capitalized, as well as job titles, titles of books and newspapers, and, of course, titles before names. Geographical names and the names of organizations and government bodies are also capitalized.

> In <u>U.S. H</u>istory 101, we learned about the <u>S</u>enate and <u>H</u>ouse of <u>R</u>epresentatives.

ANNOTATION MODEL   **NOTICE & NOTE**

As you read, note the author's claim and details that support his argument, as well as any responses to counterarguments. Notice the way graphic features enhance the writer's argument. In the model, you can see one reader's notes about the article on the fourth industrial revolution.

> <u>Many experts suggest that the fourth industrial revolution will benefit the rich much more than the poor</u>, especially as low-skill, low-wage jobs disappear in favor of automation.
>
> <u>But this isn't new.</u> Historically, industrial revolutions have always begun <u>with greater inequality followed by periods of political and institutional change.</u>

Author identifies a counterargument.

Author effectively defends the claim against the counterargument.

BACKGROUND

Bernard Marr *lives near London, England, and is a best-selling author of many business books, such as* Big Data *and* The Intelligent Company. *Marr also contributes weekly columns to* Forbes *and* LinkedIn, *and his advice is sought out by publications like the* Wall Street Journal, *the* Guardian, *and* the Financial Times. *He has also worked as an advisor for many organizations around the world, including the United Nations, Microsoft, and T-Mobile.*

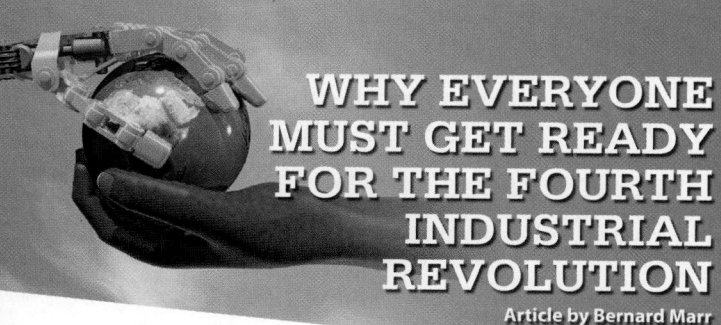

WHY EVERYONE MUST GET READY FOR THE FOURTH INDUSTRIAL REVOLUTION

Article by Bernard Marr

SETTING A PURPOSE

While reading the article, pay attention to the change the author says is coming and the possible consequences it may have for people. Write down any questions you have.

1 First came steam and water power; then electricity and assembly lines; then computerization . . . So what comes next?

2 Some call it the fourth industrial revolution, or industry 4.0, but whatever you call it, it represents the combination of cyber-physical systems,[1] the Internet of Things, and the Internet of Systems.[2]

3 In short, it is the idea of smart factories in which machines are **augmented** with web connectivity and connected to a system that can visualize the entire production chain and make decisions on its own.

4 And it's well on its way and will change most of our jobs.

5 Professor Klaus Schwab, Founder and Executive Chairman of the World Economic Forum, has published a book entitled *The*

---

[1] **cyber-physical systems:** systems composed of physical elements (such as robotics) and computer algorithms.

[2] **Internet of Things, and the Internet of Systems:** respectively, tangible things and systems connected to the Internet, such as smartphones or ATMs.

Notice & Note

Use the side margins to notice and note signposts in the text.

augment
(ôg-mĕnt´) *v.* to make (something already developed or well under way) greater, as in size, extent, or quantity.

LANGUAGE CONVENTIONS

Annotate: Mark the instances of capitalization in paragraph 5.

Interpret: Why are these particular words capitalized?

BACKGROUND

The first phase of industrial revolution began in Great Britain in the late 18th century. It spread rapidly through Europe and the United States and then worldwide. It was driven by new technology, especially the new steam engine developed by James Watt in 1768. This led to major transformations in how people worked and lived, including the rise of factories and an increase in urbanization. The second phase of industrial revolution was characterized by further innovations in technology and automation. Social and political changes prompted by growing income disparity also grew during this phase, with the development of labor unions playing a significant role. While contemporary writers don't fully agree on the limits of the third industrial revolution, it is defined by the development and widespread use of computers that began in the 1980s. In each phase of industrial revolution, technology has made work easier for humans but has also made certain professions obsolete, threatening the lifestyle and livelihoods of individuals impacted by the transformations. Since the first phase of the industrial revolution, a tension has existed between the progress and promise of modernity and potential negative impacts on individuals and society.

SETTING A PURPOSE

Direct students to use the Setting a Purpose prompt to focus their reading.

LANGUAGE CONVENTIONS

Have students annotate individually. Call on different students to explain the reasons for each instance of capitalization. (**Answer:** *beginning of a sentence, proper noun, job title, organization name, book title*)

For **listening support** for students at varying proficiency levels, see the **Text X-Ray** on page 496C.

CRITICAL VOCABULARY

augment: The text notes that the capabilities of machines can be augmented, or increased, by connecting them to the Internet or to other systems.

ASK STUDENTS how augmented machines can lead to the creation of "smart" factories. (*Augmented machines can do more tasks independently, requiring less human effort and input.*)

© Houghton Mifflin Harcourt Publishing Company • Image Credits: © PixOne/Shutterstock

EVALUATE COUNTERARGUMENTS

Have students discuss Marr's attitude toward the fourth industrial revolution. Guide students to note the positive potential consequences detailed in paragraph 7. In paragraph 8, have students note words that signal the acknowledgment of a counterargument (*but, outlines his concerns, postulates*). Ask students to consider how thoroughly Marr examines and rebuts the counterargument and how he could strengthen his points. Point out that in paragraph 5, he stresses a fundamental difference between previous industrial revolutions and the fourth one. His counterargument does not address this issue. (**Answer:** *The risks may cause the fourth industrial revolution to fail to take hold. For example, if companies fail to use technology, the revolution will not come into being as quickly as expected.*)

 EVALUATE GRAPHIC FEATURES

Ask students to interpret the icons for each stage of industrial revolution. Have them identify which part of the text the graphic best illustrates and discuss possible reasons for the size and location of the graphic on the page. (**Answer:** *The graphic feature identifies the four industrial revolutions visually. It provides background information.*)

> For **reading support** for students at varying proficiency levels, see the **Text X-Ray** on page 496D.

CRITICAL VOCABULARY

regenerate: The text notes the potential of technology to help regenerate the environment.

ASK STUDENTS why it is necessary to regenerate the natural environment. (*Industrialization has damaged the environment. People will likely still need natural resources; thus, it is important to regenerate the environment.*)

postulate: Writers postulate a thesis and then attempt to support it with facts and reasoned arguments.

ASK STUDENTS to paraphrase what Marr postulates in paragraph 6. (*New technologies will impact everything.*)

automation: Automation makes work easier but also eliminates the need for workers.

ASK STUDENTS to discuss why automation might benefit the rich more than the poor. (*Automation might make production cheaper, benefiting business and factory owners.*)

regenerate
(rĭ-jĕn´ə-rāt) *v.* to form, construct, or create anew.

postulate
(pŏs´chə-lāt) *v.* to assume or assert the truth, reality, or necessity of, especially as a basis of an argument.

EVALUATE COUNTERARGUMENTS
Annotate: In paragraph 8, mark the details that suggest risks.

Analyze: How do these risks form the basis of a counterargument against the writer's claim?

Fourth Industrial Revolution in which he describes how this fourth revolution is fundamentally different from the previous three, which were characterized mainly by advances in technology.

6   In this fourth revolution, we are facing a range of new technologies that combine the physical, digital and biological worlds. These new technologies will impact all disciplines, economies and industries, and even challenge our ideas about what it means to be human.

7   These technologies have great potential to continue to connect billions more people to the web, drastically improve the efficiency of business and organizations and help **regenerate** the natural environment through better asset management, potentially even undoing all the damage previous industrial revolutions have caused.

8   But there are also grave potential risks. Schwab outlines his concerns that organizations could be unable or unwilling to adapt to these new technologies and that governments could fail to employ or regulate these technologies properly. In the book he **postulates** that shifting power will create important new security concerns, and that inequalities could grow rather than shrink if things are not managed properly.

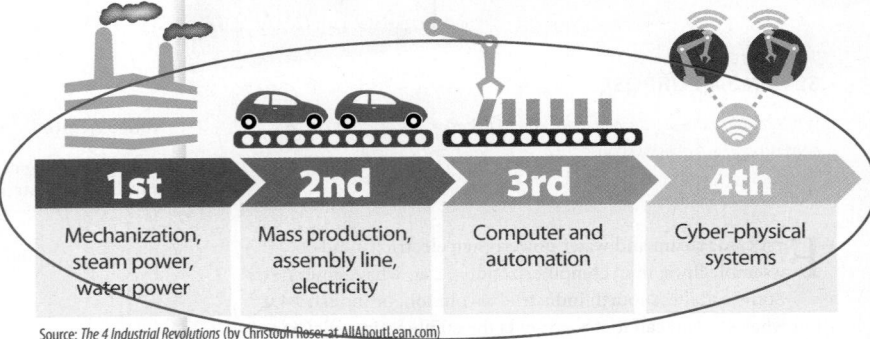

Source: *The 4 Industrial Revolutions (by Christoph Roser at AllAboutLean.com)*

EVALUATE GRAPHIC FEATURES
Annotate: Mark the graphic feature that is used on the page.

Evaluate: How does the graphic feature connect with the writer's argument?

automation
(ô-tə-mā´shən) *n.* the automatic operation or control of equipment, a process, or a system.

9   For example, as **automation** increases, computers and machines will replace workers across a vast spectrum of industries, from drivers to accountants and estate agents to insurance agents. By one estimate, as many as 47 percent of U.S. jobs are at risk from automation.

10   Many experts suggest that the fourth industrial revolution will benefit the rich much more than the poor, especially as low-skill, low-wage jobs disappear in favor of automation.

11   But this isn't new. Historically, industrial revolutions have always begun with greater inequality followed by periods of political and institutional change. The industrial revolution that began at the beginning of the 19th century originally led to a huge polarization of wealth and power, before being followed by nearly 100 years of

---

 ENGLISH LEARNER SUPPORT

Identify Contrasts   Read paragraphs 7 and 8 aloud. Discuss that the positive view reflects Marr's opinion and the negative view is Schwab's.

- Make a T-chart with headings *Positive* and *Negative*. Say words and phrases from the text—*connect billions more people, improve efficiency, regenerate,* and so on—and have students identify the words as positive or negative. Add them to the chart.

- Have students complete this frame orally: *Marr has a ____ viewpoint about ____ , but Schwab identifies some possible ____ consequences.*   **MODERATE**

change including the spread of democracy, trade unions, progressive taxation and the development of social safety nets.

12   It seems a safe bet to say, then, that our current political, business, and social structures may not be ready or capable of absorbing all the changes a fourth industrial revolution would bring, and that major changes to the very structure of our society may be inevitable.

13   Schwab said, "The changes are so profound that, from the perspective of human history, there has never been a time of greater promise or potential peril. My concern, however, is that decision makers are too often caught in traditional, linear (and non-disruptive) thinking or too absorbed by immediate concerns to think strategically about the forces of disruption and innovation shaping our future."

14   The future is happening around us. And we must rise to the challenge to meet it and thrive in the new industrial revolution.

EVALUATE COUNTERARGUMENTS

Annotate: Mark the words in paragraph 11 that signal the author is addressing a counterargument.

Evaluate: How does the author effectively address this counterargument?

CHECK YOUR UNDERSTANDING

Answer these questions before moving on to the **Analyze the Text** section on the following page.

1 According to the author, what is the fourth industrial revolution?

A Computers and automation

B Mass production, assembly line, electricity

C Cyber-physical systems

D Mechanization, water power, steam power

2 According to the author, how will the fourth revolution be different from the previous three?

F It will combine a range of technologies that impact all disciplines.

G It will result in people making a lot of money.

H It will involve great risks for some people and very little risk for others.

J It will improve efficiencies of businesses.

3 The graphic feature included in this text could best be described as a —

A map

B chart

C graph

D diagram

 ENGLISH LEARNER SUPPORT

Oral Assessment Use the following questions to assess students' comprehension and speaking skills.

1. According to the author, what is the fourth industrial revolution? (*cyber-physical systems*)

2. How does the author say the fourth revolution will be different from the previous three? (*It will combine a range of technologies that impact all disciplines.*)

3. How can the graphic feature on page 500 best be described? (*as a diagram*)
SUBSTANTIAL/MODERATE

TEACH

EVALUATE COUNTERARGUMENTS

Note that Marr's own viewpoint becomes more evident in paragraph 11. His central claim, that historical patterns suggest that industrial revolutions lead to political and institutional change, is evidence-based, in the sense that he cites facts that can be checked and verified. Students might note, however, that Marr relies heavily on the historical pattern he identifies, although he has also stated that the fourth industrial revolution is fundamentally different than previous ones. Ask students to discuss to what extent Marr grapples with potential downsides he has acknowledged. What is his stance on how to cope with such downsides? Marr stresses that it's important to rise to the challenge of the current revolution and seems to agree with Schwab that it's important to think strategically. Guide students to note that Marr could strengthen his text by including concrete explanations and examples of what he means by rising to the challenge and thinking strategically. (**Answer:** *The author concedes that inequality could be an issue, but he insists we need to rise to the challenge. He cites the previous industrial revolution as an example of how inequality is eventually overcome by institutional change.*)

■ English Learner Support

Summarize Counterarguments Ask students to define and discuss the terms *concession* and *rebuttal* orally. Have them identify the concession and rebuttal in paragraphs 10 and 11. Then, have students copy and complete this frame: *Marr acknowledges that the fourth industrial revolution might _____. He addresses this by pointing out that _____.* (*Marr acknowledges that the fourth industrial revolution might benefit the rich more than the poor. He addresses this by pointing out that industrial revolutions have always begun with inequality but are followed by periods of change.*) **LIGHT**

CHECK YOUR UNDERSTANDING

Have students answer the questions independently.

Answers:

1. *C*

2. *F*

3. *D*

If they answer any questions incorrectly, have them reread the text to confirm their understanding. Then, they may proceed to ANALYZE THE TEXT on page 502.

APPLY

ANALYZE THE TEXT

Possible answers:

1. **DOK 4:** *The author uses examples, statistics, and other information from a book by Professor Klaus Schwab. Schwab is a professor and is an expert in the field, so the information is reliable. He does not say where the statistic comes from, so that may not be reliable. There is sufficient evidence to support his claim.*

2. **DOK 4:** *The new technology will connect billions of people to the web; businesses and organizations will be able to perform more efficiently; and it will also help with the environment and could possibly undo damage caused by previous industrial revolutions. He includes this information because he wants to show the reader what the fourth industrial revolution could mean or do.*

3. **DOK 4:** *The writer includes a counterargument that industrial revolutions breed inequality. The writer concedes that inequality is an issue but points out that in prior industrial revolutions, the issue has eventually resolved itself.*

4. **DOK 4:** *Wi-Fi symbols are pictured by the machines and computers, showing how they're all connected.*

5. **DOK 4:** *While the graphic feature contains historical context and clarifies ideas, it does not offer specific evidence that supports the writer's claim.*

RESEARCH

Review the defining characteristics of the earlier industrial revolutions with the class. Suggest credible sources they can use for research such as *Britannica*, Google Scholar, or news sources such as *The Economist, The Atlantic,* or the BBC. Remind students to read critically and examine and compare multiple sources to confirm information. Encourage them to use the library to consult books as well as online sources, since digital access to scholarly, credible historical information may be limited. For online searches, suggest using *phases* or *stages of industrial revolution*.

Extend Remind students to go beyond the comparisons Marr makes. Encourage students to consider technological, historical, social, and political contexts when making their comparisons.

≡ RESPOND

ANALYZE THE TEXT

Support your responses with evidence from the text. ▤ NOTEBOOK

1. **Evaluate** What evidence does the author provide to support his claim? Is the evidence sufficient and reliable? Explain.

2. **Analyze** In paragraph 7, what does the author argue are benefits of the fourth industrial revolution? Why does the author include this information?

3. **Evaluate** Identify one of the counterarguments in the article and explain how the writer addresses the counterargument. Note any rebuttals and concessions.

4. **Synthesize** How does the text's graphic feature show that machines are augmented by the Internet in the fourth industrial revolution?

5. **Evaluate** Does the text's graphic feature contribute to the effectiveness of the writer's argument? Explain.

RESEARCH

RESEARCH TIP
For more in-depth information on a topic, check the bottom of the page in an article or encyclopedia entry for sources in footnotes. Often they're linked to other sources with more information.

The author refers to three other industrial revolutions that came before the fourth industrial revolution. Research what led to these revolutions and the effects they had on society. You can fill out a chart like this one to help you.

INDUSTRIAL REVOLUTION	CAUSES	EFFECTS
First	steam power, coal, iron	economic growth, urbanization, middle class
Second	electricity, railroads, assembly line, mass production	machines did human jobs, manufacturing costs declined, new markets
Third	electricity, railroads, assembly line, mass production	most jobs involve computers

Extend After reading about the fourth industrial revolution and doing research on the previous industrial revolutions, think about how they compare. Identify one way in which the fourth industrial revolution is similar to a previous one. Then, identify one way it is different from those that came before it.

502 Unit 5

WHEN STUDENTS STRUGGLE . . .

Identify Arguments and Counterarguments As students read paragraphs 7–10, have them list possible positive and negative impacts in a T-chart. Ask them what answer Marr gives to the possible negative impacts of the fourth industrial revolution. In paragraphs 13 and 14, what problem does Schwab identify? What is Marr's ultimate answer to the potential negative consequences of the current revolution?

 For additional support, go to the **Reading Studio** and assign the following [LEVEL UP] **Level Up Tutorial: Analyzing Arguments.**

CREATE AND PRESENT

Write an Argument Write a one-paragraph argument in favor of the idea that the fourth industrial revolution will occur or the idea that the fourth industrial revolution will not occur. Be sure to:

❏ Include a clear claim in which you state your position.

❏ Include evidence to support your claim.

❏ Address one counterargument to your stance and defend your claim against it.

Present an Argument With a small group, practice presenting your argument. Then present your argument to the class.

❏ Rehearse your argument a few times before presenting it to the class.

❏ Consider adding a graphic element to make your ideas clear.

❏ Remember to speak slowly and use eye contact to connect with your audience.

❏ Allow time for your audience to respond with questions or comments.

❏ Be prepared to defend your argument.

 RESPOND

 Go to **Writing Arguments** in the **Writing Studio** for help.

Go to **Giving a Presentation** in the **Speaking and Listening Studio** for help.

RESPOND TO THE ESSENTIAL QUESTION

? What are the consequences of change?

Gather Information Review your annotations and notes on "Why Everyone Must Get Ready for the Fourth Industrial Revolution." Then, add relevant information to your Response Log. As you determine which information to include, think about:

- benefits that could result from the fourth industrial revolution
- negative consequences that might occur
- whether or not the fourth revolution is inevitable

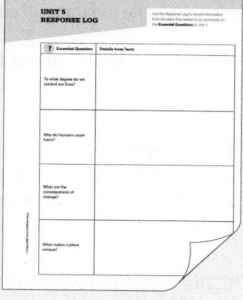

ACADEMIC VOCABULARY
As you write and discuss what you learned from the article, be sure to use the Academic Vocabulary words. Check off each of the words that you use.

❏ **ambiguous**

❏ **clarify**

❏ **implicit**

❏ **revise**

❏ **somewhat**

APPLY

CREATE AND PRESENT

Write an Argument Have students exchange paragraphs and peer edit. In addition to providing corrections and feedback for mechanics and writing quality, have peer editors identify the claim statement, evidence, and counterargument. Have them provide feedback about each of these elements, including suggestions for revising or strengthening them. Encourage students to think of counterarguments their partners have not addressed.

Present an Argument Have groups discuss possible graphic elements that each presenter could include. Encourage groups to think of different types of graphic elements that can effectively support the argument or draw the audience's attention. Remind students that speaking to the class is not the same as reading aloud from a text. Students should know their argument well and think about how to use rhythm and intonation to make their points clearly and to keep listeners' attention.

 For **speaking** and **writing support** for students at varying proficiency levels, see the **Text X-Ray** on page 496D.

RESPOND TO THE ESSENTIAL QUESTION

Allow time for students to add details from "Why Everyone Must Get Ready for the Fourth Industrial Revolution" to their Unit 5 Response Logs.

TO CHALLENGE STUDENTS . . .

Write an Argument Modify the Create and Present activity, asking students to consider Marr's argument that history suggests that social, political, and institutional changes will follow and counteract negative consequences of the fourth industrial revolution. Encourage students to consider why and how such changes occurred in the past and what, if any, parallel situations, groups, opinions, or cultural currents exist today. Challenge students to think deeply about whether or not fundamental differences exist between today's world and the past. If students have different viewpoints, consider holding an in-class debate.

CRITICAL VOCABULARY

Possible answers:

1. *He or she has researched the theory and thinks it's true.*

2. *She wants her building to be bigger or more complex.*

3. *He can revive or regrow the injured cells.*

4. *Lunches might be moved on a conveyor belt from the kitchen to students.*

VOCABULARY STRATEGY:
· Context Clues

Answers:

1. *The word* risks *is a context clue, meaning that there are possible difficulties. That tells me that* grave *means something like "serious."*

2. Broad *means "wide" or "vast" and then many types of jobs are listed.* Spectrum *must mean "a range of things."*

3. Polarization *is being used to talk about "wealth and power," but context clues like* democracy, unions, *and* social safety nets *are almost opposites of this. I think* polarization *in this sentence must mean "a division between the rich and the not rich."*

 **RESPOND**

WORD BANK
augment
regenerate
postulate
automation

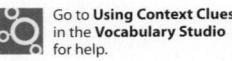 Go to **Using Context Clues** in the **Vocabulary Studio** for help.

CRITICAL VOCABULARY

Practice and Apply Answer each question with a sentence that shows your understanding of the Critical Vocabulary words.

1. What can you assume a scientist has done if he or she **postulates** a theory?

2. Why might an architect decide that her plans need to be **augmented**?

3. What does a medical researcher mean when he says that he can **regenerate** injured cells?

4. If a school instituted **automation** in the lunchroom, what might you expect?

VOCABULARY STRATEGY:
Context Clues

As you read, you can look at **context clues**—such as examples, definitions, restatements, synonyms, or antonyms—to help you determine the meaning of unfamiliar words. For example, the author uses *regenerate* in the sentence "These technologies have great potential to . . . help regenerate the natural environment through better asset management, potentially even undoing all the damage previous industrial revolutions have caused." Marr helps define *regenerate* with the imagery suggested by "natural environment" and "undoing all the damage previous industrial revolutions have caused." Using these context clues, the reader can determine that *regenerate* means "to form, construct, or create anew."

Practice and Apply State the meaning of each boldfaced word in these sentences from the article. Then, mark the context clues that helped you determine the meaning of each word.

1. But there are also **grave** potential risks.

2. For example, as automation increases, computers and machines will replace workers across a broad **spectrum** of industries, from drivers to accountants and estate agents to insurance agents.

3. The industrial revolution that began at the beginning of the 19th century originally led to a huge **polarization** of wealth and power, before being followed by nearly 100 years of change including the spread of democracy, trade unions, progressive taxation and the development of social safety nets.

 ENGLISH LEARNER SUPPORT

Use Vocabulary Review the pronunciation of each Critical Vocabulary word and have students repeat. Review definitions. Modify the Practice and Apply questions and have students answer orally: *What does a scientist do before he postulates a theory? How can an architect augment plans for a building? What does it mean to regenerate injured (hurt) cells? Can you imagine automation in the lunchroom? What could be automated?*
SUBSTANTIAL/MODERATE

LANGUAGE CONVENTIONS: Capitalization

When writing, it is important to use capitalization appropriately. The following list includes examples of words that should be capitalized.

- Names of people, titles before names, and ethnic and national groups
  Jack London, Professor Wilson, African Americans

- First word in a sentence or quotation
  She stopped suddenly. He said, "What's wrong?"

- Adjectives formed from proper nouns
  Chinese cooking, Pacific coast

- Geographical names such as cities, states, and countries
  Austin, Virginia, United States

- Names of organizations, government bodies, and historical periods and events
  Girl Scouts, House of Representatives, World War II

- Titles of works, such as books, newspapers, songs, and artwork, except for internal articles (*a, the, an*), coordinating conjunctions, the *to* in infinitives, and prepositions
  Life on the Mississippi, The New York Times, The Star-Spangled Banner

Practice and Apply   Rewrite the following sentences with proper capitalization.

1. My father is a member of the atlanta city council.

2. I'd like to go to the yucatán peninsula and see cancún someday.

3. She said, "the director starts each day by reading *usa today.*"

4. The playwright tennessee williams, known for writing groundbreaking plays, was inducted into the american theater hall of fame.

Go to **Capital Letters** in the **Grammar Studio** for help.

LANGUAGE CONVENTIONS:
Capitalization

Point out that a person's title usually involves the person's name. Therefore, *Professor Wilson* is capitalized, whereas *The professor arrived in the classroom* does not use capitalization for *professor* because it is simply a noun. Give examples of coordinating conjunctions such as *and, but, or*, and *for*.

Practice and Apply   Have student volunteers write corrected sentences on the board. Have the class decide together if the capitalization is done correctly, noting the reason for each instance of capitalization. (**Answers:** *My father is a member of the Atlanta City Council. I'd like to go to the Yucatán Peninsula and see Cancún someday. She said, "The director starts each day by reading USA Today." The playwright Tennessee Williams is known for writing groundbreaking plays, and he was inducted into the American Theater Hall of Fame.*)

ENGLISH LEARNER SUPPORT

Review Grammar Points   Review infinitive verbs and gerunds, conjunctions, and prepositions. Cantonese does not require an infinitive marker equivalent to the use of *to ___* in English. In Hmong, verbs can be connected without a conjunction such as *and* in Practice and Apply sentences 2 and 4. Note the gerund *writing* in sentence 4. Neither Khmer nor Korean include the *-ing* verb form, and learners with Haitian Creole background may use present-tense verbs instead of gerunds.   **MODERATE**

Have students suggest an example sentence that demonstrates one of these differences between their native language and English. Ask volunteers to share examples.   **LIGHT**

MENTOR TEXT

THE STORY OF AN HOUR

Short Story by Kate Chopin

This short story serves as a mentor text, a model for students to follow when they come to the Unit 5 Writing Task: Write a Short Story.

GENRE ELEMENTS
SHORT STORY

Remind students that making predictions when reading a short story is important because it helps you analyze the author's message. To do this, readers look for clues that the writer places in the text. Instruct students to pay close attention to the point of view the author uses to tell the story. This will affect how a reader perceives the sequence of events, which may vary greatly if told from another character's point of view.

LEARNING OBJECTIVES

- Analyze point of view.
- Make and confirm predictions.
- Research critical reviews of novels.
- Write a short story.
- Participate in group discussions.
- Find meanings for multiple-meaning words.
- Write effective sentences with varied sentence structures.
- **Language** Describe characters using lesson vocabulary.

TEXT COMPLEXITY

Quantitative Measures	The Story of an Hour	Lexile: 970L
Qualitative Measures	**Ideas Presented** Multiple levels of meaning; use of irony and greater demand for inference.	
	Structures Used Chronological order, mostly one point of view; some inference demanded.	
	Language Used Mostly explicit but some figurative language and implied meanings.	
	Knowledge Required Complex theme; some historical and cultural references.	

RESOURCES

- Unit 5 Response Log
- 🔊 Selection Audio
- 📖 Reading Studio:
  Notice & Note
- LEVEL UP Level Up Tutorial:
  Irony; Point of View
- 📰 Writing Studio:
  Writing Narratives
- 💬 Speaking and Listening Studio:
  Participating in Collaborative Discussions
- ⚛ Vocabulary Studio:
  Words with Multiple Meanings
- ✅ "The Story of an Hour" Selection Test

SUMMARIES

English

"The Story of an Hour" is a short story about a woman who receives tragic news and how she ultimately responds to this news. The author uses situational irony to send a message to readers about the pitfalls of relationships, particularly for women in the early 1900s. American women did not have the right to vote during Chopin's lifetime. For survival, a woman in her day had to rely on her father, her husband, or even the superior rights of a male child.

Spanish

"La historia de una hora" es el cuento de una mujer que recibe una noticia trágica y de cómo responde a ésta a la larga. El autor usa la ironía situacional para enviar un mensaje a los lectores acerca de las dificultades de las relaciones, específicamente para las mujeres al principio del siglo XX. Las mujeres americanas no tenían derecho al voto durante la vida de Chopin. Para sobrevivir, una mujer debía depender de su padre, esposo, o incluso de los derechos superiores de un hijo varón.

 ## SMALL-GROUP OPTIONS

Have students work in small groups and pairs to read and discuss the selection.

Think-Pair-Share

- Have the students read the short story.
- Ask students questions: *From whose point of view is the story being told? Why do you think the author chose this point of view?*
- Instruct students to find a passage that supports their answer to the following question: *How would the author's message change if the story had been told from the point of view of someone else?*
- Have students think about the questions, taking notes. Then, have student pairs discuss the questions and develop shared responses.
- Discuss responses as a whole class.

Three Before Me

- After reading the story, instruct students to individually choose a passage and rewrite it from another point of view. This can be the point of view of a character or even a newspaper reporter.
- Have each student ask three other students to edit his or her writing.
- Have students make the necessary edits in a final draft.
- Ask volunteers to read their final passages aloud.
- Discuss these student passages with the whole class, asking how they think the passages change the meaning of the story.

Text X-Ray: English Learner Support
for "The Story of an Hour"

Use the Text X-Ray and the supports and scaffolds in the Teacher's Edition to help guide students at different proficiency levels through the selection.

INTRODUCE THE SELECTION
DISCUSS MARRIAGE AND WOMEN'S RIGHTS

In this lesson, students will need to understand marriage and women's rights in the context of U.S. history. Explain that during the 19th and early 20th centuries, most women in the United States were not allowed to vote. Married middle-class women were not expected to work outside the home, and in some states, married women were not allowed to own property. While widows also had limited rights, they often had more freedom to travel and to make choices than married women did.

Ask students to name rights or freedoms they value. Encourage them to give reasons why these rights or freedoms are important to them.

CULTURAL REFERENCES

The following words or phrases may be unfamiliar to students:

- *broken sentences* (paragraph 2): sentences with many pauses or hesitations
- *telegram* (paragraph 2): a written message that was transmitted as Morse code by an electronic device called a telegraph, then translated and written out by the telegraph operator on the receiving end
- *peddler* (paragraph 5): a person who sells goods by going door to door
- *joy that kills* (final paragraph): overwhelming joy that causes sudden shock and results in death

LISTENING

Understand Irony

Assist students' understanding of irony. Explain that situational irony is when something happens that is the opposite of what one would expect. Dramatic irony occurs when the reader knows something a character does not.

Read paragraphs 21–23 aloud to students. Use the following supports with students at varying proficiency levels:

- Remind students that *irony* is the expression of something unexpected. Discuss the meaning of the word *unexpected*. Reread each sentence aloud to students and explain what happens in each. Ask them to raise their hands if they think the event is unexpected. **SUBSTANTIAL**
- After reading the paragraphs aloud, ask students what happens to Mrs. Mallard at the end of the story. *(She dies of heart disease.)* Then ask: *What causes Mrs. Mallard's death? What do other characters think causes her death?* If needed, read the paragraphs again. Guide students to recognize the difference between what actually causes the death *(shock at seeing her husband again)* and what the other characters think caused it *(joy)*. **MODERATE**
- Have students work together in pairs to summarize the events that occur in paragraphs 21–23. Then, have the partners discuss examples of irony in the paragraphs. Ask them to determine whether the examples are situational irony or dramatic irony. **LIGHT**

SPEAKING

Describe Characters Using Critical Vocabulary

List the following vocabulary words: *abandonment, vacant, illumination, composed.* Guide students to use these words in sentences describing the characters.

Use the following supports with students at varying proficiency levels:

- Say aloud the following sentences about the characters, and have students repeat them. Explain the meaning of each as needed. *Mrs. Mallard wept with <u>abandonment</u>. Then, she showed a <u>vacant</u> stare. Finally, she had a sense of <u>illumination</u>.* **SUBSTANTIAL**
- Have students say the vocabulary words. Provide sentence frames for students to use in a discussion: *Mrs. Mallard had a vacant stare when ___. Mr. Mallard seemed composed when ___. Mrs. Mallard ___ with abandonment when ___. Mrs. Mallard had a sense of illumination when ___.* **MODERATE**
- Review the meaning and pronunciation of each vocabulary word. Have student pairs compose and say sentences using each vocabulary word to describe a character from the story. **LIGHT**

READING

Make Predictions

Assist students as they make and review predictions.

Use the following supports with students at varying proficiency levels:

- Read paragraphs 1–2 aloud and summarize details about Mrs. Mallard. Provide a sentence frame: *I predict Mrs. Mallard will feel _____.* Help students choose a word to predict how Mrs. Mallard will feel when she hears about her husband. Later, discuss their predications. **SUBSTANTIAL**
- Have student pairs read paragraphs 1–2 and note details. Provide a sentence frame so students can predict how Mrs. Mallard will react when she hears about her husband's death: *I predict Mrs. Mallard will _____.* Later, have partners discuss if their prediction was correct. **MODERATE**
- Have students read paragraphs 1–2 independently and take notes. Have them write a prediction about how Mrs. Mallard will react to the news about the accident. After students read the story, have them compare and discuss their predictions with a partner. **LIGHT**

WRITING

Write Prepositional Phrases

Remind students that a preposition is a word used to show the relationship between a noun or pronoun and another word in the sentence.

List *near, in, before, of,* and *with.* Use the following supports with students at varying proficiency levels:

- Display text: "Her husband's friend Richards was there, too, near her. It was he who had been in the newspaper office. . ." Have students write the sentences and underline the prepositional phrases. Point out that both phrases help show where someone is. **SUBSTANTIAL**
- Display the first sentence of paragraph 5. Help partners identify a prepositional phrase in the sentence. Then, have them work together to write another sentence with the same preposition. **MODERATE**
- Display the first sentence of paragraph 5. Have partners identify the prepositions and prepositional phrases. Have them write sentences using the same prepositions. **LIGHT**

Connect to the
ESSENTIAL QUESTION

No one has complete control of anything, of course. Circumstances make that impossible; but some choices, such as the choice of love and independence, make control a little more possible. But within that reality, some have more control than others, and some want more control than they have.

MENTOR TEXT

At the end of the unit, students will be asked to write a realistic short story. "The Story of an Hour" provides a model of a well-planned and well-written short story.

ANALYZE & APPLY

THE STORY OF AN HOUR

Short Story by **Kate Chopin**

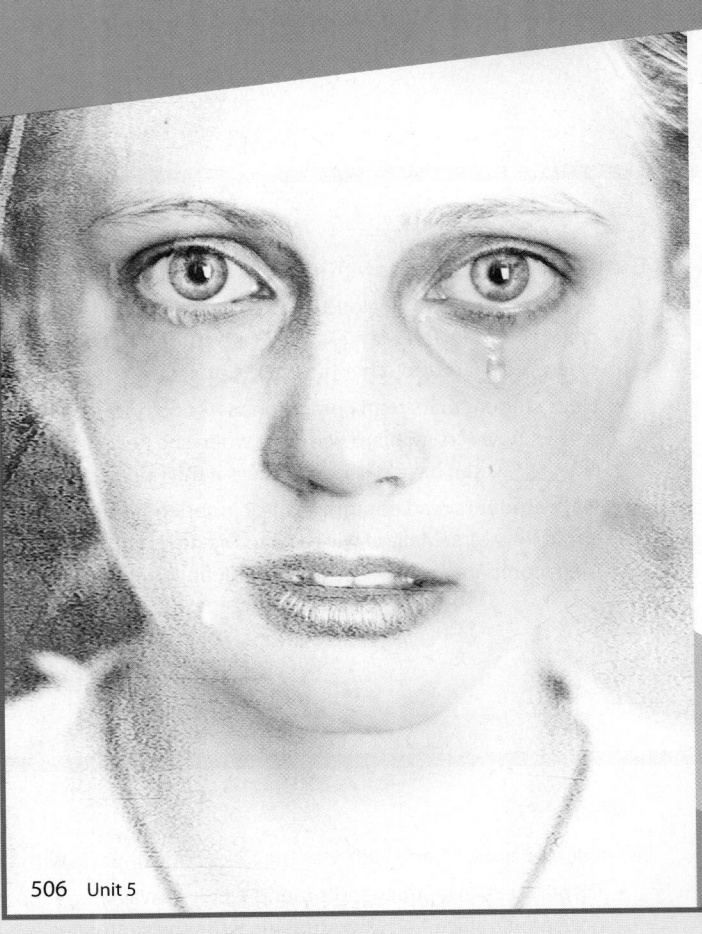

? *ESSENTIAL QUESTION:*

To what degree do we control our lives?

506   Unit 5

QUICK START

Have you ever gotten news that led you to expect one thing and then something entirely different happened? Make a few notes on your experience. Then, discuss your example with a partner.

ANALYZE POINT OF VIEW

Point of view refers to the perspective from which a story is told. "The Story of an Hour" is told from a **third-person point of view,** where the narrator is not a character in the story, but observes the action from the outside looking in. Point of view may also be characterized by what the narrator knows or shares. If the narrator tells readers what only one character thinks and feels, the point of view is **limited.** An **omniscient** narrator describes the thoughts and feelings of all the characters. Authors choose point of view carefully because it impacts how the readers perceive the plot and conflict. Point of view also helps convey the theme, or deeper message about life, that the author wants to communicate through a story.

MAKE AND CONFIRM PREDICTIONS

When reading a story, you can **make predictions,** or anticipate events in the story, regarding what will happen. Good predictions are based on details in the text, including what you learn about the conflict, the characters, and the narrator. As you read, you can confirm your predictions as events develop. Notice the author's use of literary elements and how they hint at what might happen. Use the chart to record and confirm your predictions.

Students' responses will vary.

CLUES FROM THE TEXT	PREDICTION	CONFIRM PREDICTION

GENRE ELEMENTS: SHORT STORY

• follows a sequence of events

• usually centers around a main conflict and resolution

• is written from a specific point of view

QUICK START

If students are struggling to think of an incident where inaccurate information affected them, suggest they think of a time when what happened was completely different from what they had hoped for or even prepared for. Explain that the point is not to analyze the news but rather to analyze their feelings surrounding a time when something happened that was unexpected. You may want to have a brief class discussion of why the unexpected can be unsettling.

ANALYZE POINT OF VIEW

Explain that one way to decide if the third-person point of view is omniscient or limited is to pay attention to whose thoughts, actions, and motives the author reveals. If readers have no idea what most characters are thinking, feeling, or doing, then the point of view is **limited.** If the text contains insights into what multiple characters are thinking or has statements about what multiple characters are doing, the point of view is **omniscient.**

MAKE AND CONFIRM PREDICTIONS

Explain that making and confirming predictions adds to the enjoyment of reading a story. We enjoy wondering what will happen next, and we enjoy the reaction when something unexpected happens. Making and confirming predictions is a way of processing what is being read that involves the reader in the action of the plot. Making predictions is like being a detective looking for clues. Using prior knowledge from reading books, from watching movies or TV, and from your own life all feed into making predictions.

CRITICAL VOCABULARY

Encourage students to think about how these words are used in other contexts or to think about how parts of the words might impact the meaning of the words. For example, a vacant lot is an empty lot. Also, suggest that students think about the part of speech for each word; two are adjectives and two are nouns.

Answers:

1. *abandonment*
2. *illumination*
3. *composed*
4. *vacant* .

■ English Learner Support

Use Cognates Tell the students that all four of the Critical Vocabulary words have Spanish cognates: *abandonment/abandono, illumination/illuminación, composed/compuesto, vacant/vacante.* **ALL LEVELS**

LANGUAGE CONVENTIONS

Effective Sentences Relate to students that, in addition to improving fluency, varied sentence structure makes writing more interesting and easier to read. Sentence length should also be included in this concept. Having a variety of sentence lengths makes writing more readable.

✎ ANNOTATION MODEL

Remind students that annotating the text as they read—identifying important details or possible clues—and making notes in the margins can help them connect better with what they are reading. Point out that in this sample the underlined words provide details that might be clues to what will happen. The words that are circled tell us about another character and underscore what is stated in the underlined sentence. This type of information might help students make predictions about the characters and about the plot. Explain that these are just suggestions, and students can use them as a guideline or create their own systems. They may want to color-code their annotations using highlighters. Their notes in the margin may include predictions, questions about ideas that are unclear, words to look up, or topics they want to learn more about.

◎ **GET READY**

CRITICAL VOCABULARY

abandonment	vacant	illumination	composed

To see how many Critical Vocabulary words you already know, use them to complete the sentences.

1. The excited child danced to the music with _____.

2. After working on the problem for years, a solution came to the mathematician in a moment of _____.

3. The defendant was _____ as the verdict was read.

4. She sat looking at the TV screen with a _____ stare.

LANGUAGE CONVENTIONS

Effective Sentences The patterns of words and phrases in sentences is called **syntax.** Writers will use several sentence patterns in order to add variety to their work. By varying syntax, authors can create rhythm, convey mood, and express ideas clearly. Notice how Chopin uses different sentence patterns and unusual syntax in the example to express the way that Mrs. Mallard feels.

> **There stood, facing the open window, a comfortable, roomy armchair. Into this she sank, pressed down by a physical exhaustion that haunted her body and seemed to reach into her soul.**

As you read, notice the way Chopin uses a variety of sentence structures to convey ideas effectively.

ANNOTATION MODEL

NOTICE & NOTE

As you read, note details that reveal the point of view. Notice clues in the text that you might use to make predictions about what will happen in the story. This model shows one reader's notes about the beginning of "The Story of an Hour."

> Knowing that Mrs. Mallard was afflicted with a heart trouble, great care was taken to break to her as gently as possible the news of her husband's death.
>
> It was her sister Josephine who told her, in broken sentences; veiled hints that revealed in half concealing.

Mrs. Mallard's heart condition makes her sensitive to bad news. This may be important.

third-person point of view

BACKGROUND

Kate Chopin *(1851–1904) wrote more than one hundred short stories and two novels. Her work features intelligent and sensitive female characters and is often set in Louisiana where she spent her married life. Her first novel,* At Fault *(1890), received little attention when it was published. Her second,* The Awakening *(1899), told the story of a woman who leaves her family and eventually commits suicide. It was widely condemned by critics as shocking and morbid. However, since its rediscovery in the 1950s, it has been hailed as an insightful work that foreshadowed the feminist movement in literature.*

THE STORY OF AN HOUR

Short Story by Kate Chopin

SETTING A PURPOSE

As you read, make notes about how much control Mrs. Mallard has over her life and how this changes during the course of the story.

1 Knowing that Mrs. Mallard was afflicted with a heart trouble, great care was taken to break to her as gently as possible the news of her husband's death.

2 It was her sister Josephine who told her, in broken sentences; veiled hints that revealed in half concealing. Her husband's friend Richards was there, too, near her. It was he who had been in the newspaper office when intelligence of the railroad disaster was received, with Brently Mallard's name leading the list of "killed." He had only taken the time to assure himself of its truth by a second telegram, and had hastened to forestall any less careful, less tender friend in bearing the sad message.

3 She did not hear the story as many women have heard the same, with a paralyzed inability to accept its significance. She wept at once, with sudden, wild **abandonment**, in her sister's arms. When the storm of grief had spent itself she went away to her room alone. She would have no one follow her.

Notice & Note

Use the side margins to notice and note signposts in the text.

ANALYZE POINT OF VIEW
Annotate: Mark the clues in paragraphs 1–3 that indicate the point of view.

Evaluate: Which type of third-person narrator is Chopin using? What is the effect of this point of view?

abandonment
(ə-băn´dən-mĕnt) *n.* a lack of restraint or inhibition.

BACKGROUND

Chopin was 32 years old and a widow with six children when she began to write fiction. Her short stories appeared in respected magazines, and many were also published in collections: *Bayou Folk* (1894) and *A Night in Acadie* (1897). Her work was praised for its depiction of Creoles, African Americans, and other inhabitants of Louisiana, which was the focus of her work. Her work was largely forgotten after her death, but the short stories and her second novel, *The Awakening*, are now widely read, having gained praise for their depictions of sensitive women in situations they did not like. While best known for her fiction, Chopin also wrote nonfiction essays and book reviews.

SETTING A PURPOSE

Direct students to use the Setting a Purpose prompt to focus their reading.

 ## ANALYZE POINT OF VIEW

Remind students that the two types of third-person narrator are omniscient and limited. (**Answer:** *omniscient; it allows the reader to know more than any single character in the story knows*)

 For **reading support** for students at varying proficiency levels, see the **Text X-Ray** on page 506D.

CRITICAL VOCABULARY

abandonment: Mrs. Mallard cried, abandoning all inhibition.

ASK STUDENTS why Mrs. Mallard's weeping with wild abandonment is significant at this point in the story. (*The response suggests she is terribly saddened by her husband's death.*)

ANALYZE POINT OF VIEW

Remind students that an omniscient narrator knows what all the characters are seeing and thinking, but generally reveals only details that help tell the story. (**Answer:** *The third-person point of view enables the author to show the things Mrs. Mallard is noticing—lovely, life-affirming things. This suggests that the message might be that life goes on after a death—and may even improve.*)

For **writing support** for students at varying proficiency levels, see the **Text X-Ray** on page 506D.

NOTICE & NOTE

ANALYZE POINT OF VIEW
Annotate: Mark text in paragraphs 4–6 that show what Mrs. Mallard is seeing.

Interpret: How do you think the author's use of third-person point of view hints at the story's theme, or larger message about life?

4   There stood, facing the open window, a comfortable, roomy armchair. Into this she sank, pressed down by a physical exhaustion that haunted her body and seemed to reach into her soul.

5   She could see in the open square before her house the tops of trees that were all aquiver with the new spring life. The delicious breath of rain was in the air. In the street below a peddler was crying his wares. The notes of a distant song which someone was singing reached her faintly, and countless sparrows were twittering in the eaves.

6   There were patches of blue sky showing here and there through the clouds that had met and piled one above the other in the west facing her window.

ENGLISH LEARNER SUPPORT

Prepositions and Prepositional Phrases Explain that Chopin often uses prepositional phrases to clarify details. A **preposition** is a word used to show the relationship between a noun or pronoun and another word in the sentence. Examples include *above, down, near, in, with,* and *among.* A **prepositional phrase** includes a preposition and its object and modifiers. Help students identify a few prepositional phrases and discuss what they clarify. You may want to supply a list of common prepositions. **MODERATE**

7   She sat with her head thrown back upon the cushion of the chair, quite motionless, except when a sob came up into her throat and shook her, as a child who has cried itself to sleep continues to sob in its dreams.

8   She was young, with a fair, calm face, whose lines bespoke repression and even a certain strength. But now there was a dull stare in her eyes, whose gaze was fixed away off yonder on one of those patches of blue sky. It was not a glance of reflection, but rather indicated a suspension of intelligent thought.

9   There was something coming to her and she was waiting for it, fearfully. What was it? She did not know; it was too subtle and elusive to name. But she felt it, creeping out of the sky, reaching toward her through the sounds, the scents, the color that filled the air.

10   Now her bosom rose and fell tumultuously. She was beginning to recognize this thing that was approaching to possess her, and she was striving to beat it back with her will—as powerless as her two white slender hands would have been.

11   When she abandoned herself a little whispered word escaped her slightly parted lips. She said it over and over under her breath: "free, free, free!" The **vacant** stare and the look of terror that had followed it went from her eyes. They stayed keen and bright. Her pulses beat fast, and the coursing blood warmed and relaxed every inch of her body.

12   She did not stop to ask if it were or were not a monstrous joy that held her. A clear and exalted perception enabled her to dismiss the suggestion as trivial.

13   She knew that she would weep again when she saw the kind, tender hands folded in death; the face that had never looked save with love upon her, fixed and gray and dead. But she saw beyond that bitter moment a long procession of years to come that would belong to her absolutely. And she opened and spread her arms out to them in welcome.

14   There would be no one to live for her during those coming years; she would live for herself. There would be no powerful will bending hers in that blind persistence with which men and women believe they have a right to impose a private will upon a fellow creature. A kind intention or a cruel intention made the act seem no less a crime as she looked upon it in that brief moment of **illumination**.

15   And yet she had loved him—sometimes. Often she had not. What did it matter! What could love, the unsolved mystery, count for in face of this possession of self-assertion which she suddenly recognized as the strongest impulse of her being!

16   "Free! Body and soul free!" she kept whispering.

MAKE AND CONFIRM PREDICTIONS

Annotate: Mark clues in paragraph 7 that describe the impact her husband's death has had on Mrs. Mallard.

Predict: How do you think Mrs. Mallard will cope after learning about the death of her husband?

vacant
(vā´kənt) *adj.* blank, expressionless.

MAKE AND CONFIRM PREDICTIONS

Annotate: Mark details in paragraph 13 that tell you what Mrs. Mallard is thinking about.

Cite Evidence: Do these details confirm or disprove predictions you made about the story? Explain.

illumination
(ĭ-lōō-mə-nā´shən) *n.* awareness or enlightenment.

© Houghton Mifflin Harcourt Publishing Company

MAKE AND CONFIRM PREDICTIONS

Remind students that connecting with previous experience or prior knowledge helps with making predictions. For example, what does sitting alone motionless except for an occasional sob usually mean? (**Answer:** *Mrs. Mallard may spend a lot of time in her room, crying. She will grieve for her lost husband.*)

MAKE AND CONFIRM PREDICTIONS

Explain that a good writer will often play with what the reader is likely to know, to make predicting more difficult. This is how writers create surprises in texts. The writer makes it seem like the plot is developing in one way, but the events will take a turn in a less predictable direction. (**Answer:** *The previous text seemed to suggest that Mrs. Mallard was deeply grieved by the loss of her husband. Now, suddenly, she seems to be okay with it. She welcomes the years ahead on her own. She wanted to be free, and now she has her freedom. A possible alternative prediction might wonder what effect her weak heart will have on the years ahead.*)

WHEN STUDENTS STRUGGLE . . .

Recognize Irony Students may struggle with the idea of making and confirming predictions when they read paragraphs 9–11. Mrs. Mallard was just weeping at news of her husband's death, but suddenly, she seems to be happy. Explain that irony is a tool writers use to surprise readers. To decide if something is irony, students can make a list of what they expect (the prediction) and then what actually happens.

    For additional support, go to the **Reading Studio** and assign the following **Level Up Tutorial: Irony.**

CRITICAL VOCABULARY

vacant: Mrs. Mallard's stare was without emotion or expression; like a vacant building, it was empty.

ASK STUDENTS how they would describe a vacant stare. *(looking off in the distance, not noticing anything around)*

illumination: Mrs. Mallard's mind was illuminated in a moment of clarity; one might say "the light went on."

ASK STUDENTS what Mrs. Mallard realizes in her "moment of illumination." *(the fact that one cannot be in a relationship and still live for oneself)*

LANGUAGE CONVENTIONS

Remind students that varied sentence structure adds interest, but also note that it can help add emphasis that can make meaning clearer. (**Answer:** *This sentence uses repetition to create a rhythm that conveys Mrs. Mallard's lighthearted feelings and joy. The repetition also emphasizes all of the days ahead that Mrs. Mallard would enjoy all by herself.*)

EL ENGLISH LEARNER SUPPORT

Preteach Vocabulary Many words in this story may be unfamiliar to English learners. On page 512, words such as *imploring, importunities, unwittingly, goddess,* and *descended* might need to be explained to help students understand the events in the story. Allow students time to scan the text to identify unfamiliar words before reading the story. Discuss and help students understand the words before reading the text.
ALL LEVELS

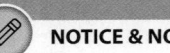

NOTICE & NOTE

LANGUAGE CONVENTIONS

Annotate: In paragraph 19, mark the sentence that effectively conveys an idea about how Mrs. Mallard feels.

Analyze: How does this sentence create mood and convey Mrs. Mallards feelings?

17   Josephine was kneeling before the closed door with her lips to the keyhole, imploring for admission. "Louise, open the door! I beg; open the door—you will make yourself ill. What are you doing, Louise? For heaven's sake open the door."

18   "Go away. I am not making myself ill." No; she was drinking in a very elixir of life[1] through that open window.

19   Her fancy was running riot along those days ahead of her. <u>Spring days, and summer days, and all sorts of days that would be her own.</u> She breathed a quick prayer that life might be long. It was only yesterday she had thought with a shudder that life might be long.

20   She arose at length and opened the door to her sister's importunities. There was a feverish triumph in her eyes, and she carried herself unwittingly like a goddess of Victory. She clasped her sister's waist, and together they descended the stairs. Richards stood waiting for them at the bottom.

---

[1] **elixir of life:** a medicine that restores vigor or the essence of life.

512   Unit 5

APPLYING ACADEMIC VOCABULARY

❏ **ambiguous**   ☑ **clarify**   ❏ **implicit**   ☑ **revise**   ❏ **somewhat**

Write and Discuss Have students turn to a partner to discuss the following questions. Guide students to include the academic vocabulary words *clarify* and *revise* in their responses. Ask volunteers to share their responses with the class.

- How does the narrator **clarify** the character's feelings as the story progresses?
- How did you need to **revise** your expectations about the story as you read?

21 Someone was opening the front door with a latchkey. It was Brently Mallard who entered, a little travel-stained, **composedly** carrying his grip-sack² and umbrella. He had been far from the scene of accident, and <u>did not even know there had been one</u>. He stood <u>amazed</u> at <u>Josephine's piercing cry</u>; at <u>Richards' quick motion</u> to screen him from the view of his wife.

22 But Richards was too late.

23 When the doctors came they said <u>she had died of heart disease—</u> of joy that kills.

_____

² **grip-sack:** a small traveling bag or satchel.

CHECK YOUR UNDERSTANDING

Answer these questions before moving on to the **Analyze the Text** section on the following page.

1 Why do you think the short story is titled "The Story of an Hour"?

  A The accident happened over an hour-long period.

  B The story takes place in an hour.

  C It is all the time Mrs. Mallard needed to grieve.

  D It is the amount of time it takes before she accepts the death.

2 Who informs Mrs. Mallard about her husband's death?

  F A servant

  G Richards

  H The doctors

  J Josephine

3 What causes Mrs. Mallard's death, according to the doctors?

  A The fright at seeing a ghost

  B Pneumonia

  C Heart disease

  D A broken heart

© Houghton Mifflin Harcourt Publishing Company

composed

(kəm-pōzd´) *adj.* self-possessed; calm.

ANALYZE POINT OF VIEW

Annotate: Mark words and phrases in paragraph 21 that show how each character feels or what they know.

Evaluate: How does the author's use of third-person point of view affect your understanding of the plot and conflict?

ENGLISH LEARNER SUPPORT

Oral Assessment Use the following questions to assess students' comprehension and speaking skills.

1. Think about the amount of time needed for the events in this story. How do you think the title of the story is related to that amount of time? *(The story takes place in about an hour.)*

2. How does Mrs. Mallard find out about her husband's death? *(Josephine tells her.)*

3. What do the doctors say caused Mrs. Mallard's death? *(She had heart disease.)*
SUBSTANTIAL

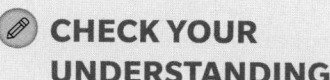 **ANALYZE POINT OF VIEW**

Remind students that this story uses the third-person omniscient point of view. (**Answer:** *The author uses the third-person omniscient point of view to show readers what multiple characters know or do. The text shows that Brently Mallard is actually alive, which causes Josephine to scream and Richards to try to keep Mrs. Mallard from seeing him. Throughout the story, knowing the thoughts and actions of multiple characters creates suspense.*)

For **listening** and **speaking support** for students at varying proficiency levels, see the **Text X-Ray** on pages 506C–506D.

CHECK YOUR UNDERSTANDING

Have students answer the questions independently.

Answers:

  1. *B*

  2. *J*

  3. *C*

If they answer any questions incorrectly, have them reread the text to confirm their understanding. Then they may proceed to ANALYZE THE TEXT on page 514.

CRITICAL VOCABULARY

composed: Mr. Mallard arrived home, calm and composed.

ASK STUDENTS what is ironic about Mr. Mallard being composed when he returns home. (*Everyone believed he died in the train wreck, so it is ironic that he comes home looking calm and composed.*)

ANALYZE THE TEXT

Possible answers:

1. **DOK 4:** *Josephine and Richards expect Mrs. Mallard to be so upset that her heart condition might be aggravated. Instead, although Mrs. Mallard weeps at first, she then imagines complete freedom without her husband. Mr. Mallard returns home expecting his wife to be happy to see him. Instead, his wife dies from the surprise of seeing him still alive. The theme of the story is that freedom was desirable (a "monstrous joy") but unlikely in that era.*

2. **DOK 3:** *She initially had been portrayed as frail, and would likely be unable to sustain a shock due to her heart trouble. In paragraph 11, her heart sounds fine, with her pulse beating fast, pumping blood, and warming and relaxing her.*

3. **DOK 2:** *Rather than being heartbroken at the loss of a husband whom she acknowledges was kind and loving, she is revitalized by the thought of being completely free. The idea that even a kind intention was unacceptable if it required her to live for someone else underscores the theme of freedom.*

4. **DOK 2:** *Chopin shows Mrs. Mallard as a "goddess of Victory," strong and independent. She has been revitalized. I predicted she would flourish now that she has the freedom she desired. My prediction was not correct because she dies when she finds out her husband is still alive.*

5. **DOK 4:** *Paragraph 14 says "There would be no one to live for her during those coming years," and "there would be no powerful will bending hers in that blind persistence with which men and women believe they have a right to impose a private will upon a fellow creature."*

RESEARCH

Point out the research tip to students. Add that recommended reading lists can be useful resources as well, because these list only books that are now well regarded. An encyclopedia article written during the author's lifetime may reveal whether the author was accepted initially.

Extend Reassure students that this is intended to generate thoughts and opinions. There is no "correct" answer. You might encourage students to think of reasons other than criticism that could cause an author to change a title.

ANALYZE THE TEXT

Support your responses with evidence from the text. 📝 NOTEBOOK

1. **Analyze** **Irony** is a contrast between appearance and reality. What examples of irony do you find in the story? What theme does the irony reveal?

2. **Evaluate** What is surprising about how the narrator describes Mrs. Mallard in paragraph 11 compared to the earlier description of her "heart trouble"?

3. **Infer** In paragraph 14, the narrator begins to reveal Mrs. Mallard's true feelings about being a widow. What does this point of view suggest about the story's theme?

4. **Confirm Predictions** Think about what happens to Mrs. Mallard at the end of the story. Was there evidence in the story that allowed you to predict what would happen? Explain, citing evidence in your response.

5. **Connect** In 1894, when "The Story of an Hour" was published in *Vogue* magazine, women were expected to stay at home and care for their husbands and children. What evidence can you find in Chopin's story that supports this perspective?

RESEARCH TIP
Articles and literary websites are useful sources for information about written works. A search for novels that were criticized when published may lead to lists of such books, but be sure to double-check the content for credibility and accuracy.

RESEARCH

When Chopin's second novel, *The Awakening*, was published, it was denounced by the critics, who called her work "morbid, poisonous, and vulgar." Research other classic American novels that received negative criticism. What did the critics claim? How are these novels perceived today?

NOVEL TITLE	CRITIC'S OPINION	OPINION TODAY
Possible answer: The Great Gatsby	*"no more than a glorified anecdote"*	*seen as one of the great 20th century novels; Jay Gatsby seen as a mythological creation*
Possible answer: O Pioneers!	*"is neither a skilled storyteller nor the least bit an artist"*	*ahead of its time; proto-feminist*

Extend Chopin's short story "The Story of an Hour" was originally titled "The Dream of an Hour." She changed the title when the story was published in another magazine. Discuss with a partner the kind of criticism that might have caused her to make this change.

WHEN STUDENTS STRUGGLE . . .

Reteach: Point of View Demonstrate first-person narrative (*I went to the store*) and third-person (*He went to the store*). Note the difference in pronouns. Then, explain that if the narrator can tell you what everyone is doing or thinking, the narrator is said to be omniscient, which means "all knowing." Point out that the author uses third-person pronouns and clearly knows what everyone is thinking, so the point of view used is third-person omniscient.

For additional support, go to the **Reading Studio** and assign the following 📖 **Level Up Tutorial: Point of View.**

CREATE AND DISCUSS

Write a Short Story Write a brief story that takes place in an hour. You can review your Quick Start notes for ideas.

❑ Decide what point of view you will use to tell your story. Think about what impact the point of view might have on how you reveal events.

❑ Include a main conflict and a resolution.

❑ Create realistic characters and an interesting setting.

❑ Think about the theme, or message, you want to share. Consider how the resolution of the conflict can suggest the theme.

Discuss with a Small Group Take turns reading your stories aloud. Then, give one another feedback.

❑ Offer one thing that the author did really well.

❑ Describe something the author might do differently or clarify for readers.

❑ Revise your story based on the feedback you receive.

RESPOND TO THE ESSENTIAL QUESTION

? To what degree do we control our lives?

Gather Information Review your annotations and notes on "The Story of an Hour." Then, add relevant information to your Response Log. As you determine which information to include, think about:

- what Mrs. Mallard thinks will happen to her
- how Mrs. Mallard feels about her life so far
- what happens to Mrs. Mallard

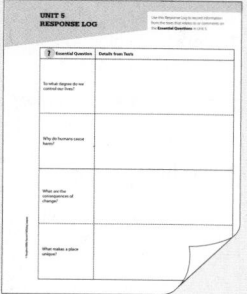

Go to **Writing Narratives** in the **Writing Studio** for help.

Go to **Participating in Collaborative Discussions** in the **Speaking and Listening Studio** for help with having a group discussion.

ACADEMIC VOCABULARY
As you write and discuss what you learned from the short story, be sure to use the Academic Vocabulary words. Check off each of the words that you use.

❑ **ambiguous**

❑ **clarify**

❑ **implicit**

❑ **revise**

❑ **somewhat**

CREATE AND DISCUSS

Write a Short Story Review the differences among the various points of view, giving examples of each. Make sure students understand the difference between third-person limited and third-person omniscient. Because the Quick Start activity focused on something that happened to the students, reassure them that an interesting setting is simply a setting that is well crafted, with details that make it vivid. The setting does not need to be exotic to be interesting.

Discuss with a Small Group Encourage students to listen attentively, so their comments are based on characteristics of the writing. Suggest they listen primarily for what the story is and whether it holds their attention. Once the story is understood, fine points of style can be discussed.

RESPOND TO THE ESSENTIAL QUESTION

Allow time for students to add details from "The Story of an Hour" to their Unit 5 Response Logs.

APPLY

CRITICAL VOCABULARY

Possible answers:

1. horseback riding; riding a horse might make you feel free, excited, and a bit reckless

2. a boring movie; a boring movie might cause you to be lost in your own thoughts

3. by recognizing a problem in an experiment and then figuring out the solution

4. before a big game or speech; it is important to be calm and collected to do well

VOCABULARY STRATEGY:
Multiple-Meaning Words

Possible answers:

1. time: to record the speed or duration of; a duration or period
   The coach will time the runners to see who is fastest.
   What time are we going to the movies?

2. patches: small pieces of cloth used to mend a hole or tear; small plots or pieces of land
   Mother sewed patches over the knees of my torn jeans.
   We looked for clear patches of grass in the wooded area.

3. spread: a cloth covering for a bed, table, etc.; a banquet of food; to open to a fuller extent or width; stretch
   The spread for my bed is a paisley pattern.
   If you spread out the blanket, we can sit on the grass.

4. fancy: highly decorated; to have a liking or enthusiasm for
   The fancy restaurant was a real treat.
   I fancy a bit of classical music.

RESPOND

CRITICAL VOCABULARY

WORD BANK
abandonment
vacant
illumination
composed

 Go to **Words with Multiple Meanings** in the **Vocabulary Studio** for help.

Practice and Apply Write a short answer for each of the following questions. Explain your responses.

1. What outdoor activity is likely to inspire wild **abandonment**?

2. What might cause a person to have a **vacant** stare?

3. How might a scientist experience a moment of **illumination**?

4. When is it helpful to maintain a **composed** demeanor?

VOCABULARY STRATEGY:
Multiple-Meaning Words

In the English language, many words have more than one meaning. The meaning of a word often changes according to its part of speech. For example, the vocabulary word *composed* means "self-possessed" and "calm" when used as an adjective to describe someone. *Compose* is also a verb. The past tense verb *composed* can mean "created a literary or musical piece" or "arranged aesthetically or artistically."

When you come across a multiple-meaning word, first, think about how it is used in the sentence. For example, is it an adjective or verb? Then, use context clues—examples, synonyms, or antonyms—to help you determine what it means in the sentence. It is useful to refer to an online or print dictionary to find all of the word's meanings and see which one best fits the sentence.

Practice and Apply Find two meanings for each of the words below. Use a dictionary to check your work. Then write sentences for both meanings.

1. time

2. patches

3. spread

4. fancy

EL ENGLISH LEARNER SUPPORT

Vocabulary Strategy Give students practice determining meanings of words using prefixes and suffixes. Point out that both *abandoned* and *abandonment* appear in the story. Knowing that the root word is *abandon*, that the suffix *-ed* shows the past tense, and that the suffix *-ment* means "the action or process of" can help students understand the meaning of *abandonment*. Display the words *inability, countless, reflection, suspension, suggestion, persistence*, and *unsolved*. Have student pairs use a print or digital dictionary to identify and define prefixes and suffixes. Then, have them create definitions for each word.
ALL LEVELS

LANGUAGE CONVENTIONS: Craft Effective Sentences

Chopin's distinct writing style comes from making effective choices to create her own unique **syntax**—the pattern of words and phrases in her sentences. By varying syntax, writers can adjust the rhythm of their sentences to convey mood and ideas effectively. They can also improve fluency and clarity. Tools such as punctuation, word choice, and well-chosen details all contribute to a writer's syntax and overall style. Authors also use a variety of sentence structures and sentence beginnings to craft effective sentences. The chart shows some of the techniques Chopin used.

WRITING TOOL	PURPOSE	EXAMPLE
Exclamations	to convey excitement or emphasis	What did it matter! (paragraph 15)
Dash	to set off ideas by calling attention to them	When the doctors came they said she had died of heart disease—of joy that kills. (paragraph 23)
Sensory details	to create a full, vivid picture for the reader; to enhance characterization	But now there was a dull stare in her eyes, whose gaze was fixed away off yonder on one of those patches of blue sky. (paragraph 8)
Precise words and phrases	to communicate ideas effectively	The notes of a distant song which someone was singing reached her faintly, and countless sparrows were twittering in the eaves. (paragraph 5)
Repetition	to create rhythm and mood; to emphasize a particular point or idea	When she abandoned herself a little whispered word escaped her slightly parted lips. She said it over and over under her breath: "free, free, free!" (paragraph 11)

Practice and Apply Write a paragraph about someone's response to shocking news. Craft effective sentences by using some of the techniques above. When you have finished, share your paragraph with a partner and discuss the techniques you used to vary your sentences. Then, revise your paragraph based on your discussion.

LANGUAGE CONVENTIONS: Craft Effective Sentences

Relate that syntax—how sentences are put together—differs not only by purpose, but also by writer and format. Every writer has his or her own style, but short stories have requirements different from a newspaper, for example.

Explain that the most important consideration is clarity in presentation. This means complex sentences have to be understandable to communicate the intended ideas in a way the reader can figure out. The point of varied syntax is adding interest and emphasis, not simply being "clever." The point of writing is communication. Varied syntax simply gives the writer more tools for communicating.

Practice and Apply Have partners discuss how effectively varied syntax expresses the information and emotion of someone receiving shocking news.

ENGLISH LEARNER SUPPORT

Understand Sentence Structure Use the following supports with students at varying proficiency levels:

• Read aloud the first sentence in paragraph 4: "There stood, facing the open window, a comfortable, roomy armchair." Explain that this sentence has unusual syntax because the subject (armchair) is at the end of the sentence. Help students restate the sentence in a more traditional order to aid comprehension: "An armchair stood facing the window." **SUBSTANTIAL**

• Have students work with a partner to restate two additional sentences from the story that have unusual syntax or word order. Example from paragraph 2: "It was her sister Josephine who told her." Restate as: "Her sister Josephine told her." **MODERATE**

• Have students work individually to write a sentence with nontraditional syntax and then rewrite the same sentence in a more traditional order. Ask for volunteers to share their sentences with the class. **LIGHT**

CHICAGO
Poem by Carl Sandburg

GENRE ELEMENTS
FREE VERSE POEM

A **free verse poem** does not contain regular meter or use a particular rhyme scheme. Free verse poets vary the lengths of lines or stanzas to convey meaning, separate different ideas, or create a mood or effect. In many free verse poems, the rhythm mirrors everyday speech, although the poet might also use sounds to convey a certain feeling or mood.

LEARNING OBJECTIVES

- Create mental images.
- Analyze diction and syntax.
- Research literary criticism of Carl Sandburg.
- Write a poem.
- Present a dramatic reading.
- Apply academic vocabulary.
- **Language** Identify and explain figures of speech.

TEXT COMPLEXITY

Quantitative Measures	Chicago	Lexile: N/A
Qualitative Measures	**Ideas Presented** Multiple levels of meaning, use of symbolism, simile, personification.	
	Structures Used Complex, deviates from chronological order. Some inference demanded.	
	Language Used Implied meanings, figurative language, complex sentence structure.	
	Knowledge Required Some reference to events, historical and cultural practices. Begins to rely on some outside knowledge.	

RESOURCES

- Unit 5 Response Log

- Selection Audio

- Reading Studio: Notice & Note

- Level Up Tutorial: Tone

- Speaking and Listening Studio: Giving a Presentation

- "Chicago" Selection Test

SUMMARIES

English

"Chicago" is a free verse poem about the city of Chicago, Illinois, by Carl Sandburg. In 1912, when Sandburg lived in Chicago, it was an industrial city, and the hub of the railroads linking the East and West Coasts. It was known for its hard-working people, yet vied for a more prominent status in America with the older cities of New York, Boston, and Philadelphia. This poem was part of Sandburg's collection of poems called *The Chicago Poems*, which made Sandburg a significant American writer.

Spanish

"Chicago" es un poema de verso libre de Carl Sandburg acerca de Chicago, Illinois. En 1912, cuando Sandburg vivía allí, Chicago era una ciudad industrial y el centro de los ferrocarriles que unían las costas este y oeste. Era conocida por su gente trabajadora, pero competía con otras ciudades más antiguas como Nueva York, Boston y Filadelfia por un estatus más prominente. El poema era parte de la colección de poemas de Sanburg llamada *Los poemas de Chicago*, e hizo de Sandburg un escritor americano importante.

SMALL-GROUP OPTIONS

Have students work in small groups and pairs to read and discuss the selection.

Think-Pair-Share

- Have students read the poem. Remind them that when poets use personification, they give a nonhuman thing (such as a city) human characteristics.

- Ask, *In what ways does Sandburg personify the city? What impression does this give you of the city?*

- Instruct students to reread the poem silently and list each example of personification that Sandburg makes.

- Have students work in pairs to formulate a shared response.

- Discuss responses as a whole class.

Three Before Me

- After they read the poem, direct students to write down their own thoughts about the poem, or the background research they have completed about Chicago. Responses can be about a personal connection to the city, the way it was a destination of immigrants and migrants, or even a connection to one of the figures of speech in the poem.

- Have each student ask three other students to edit his or her writing.

- Have students make the necessary edits in a final draft.

- Ask students to volunteer to read their final work aloud.

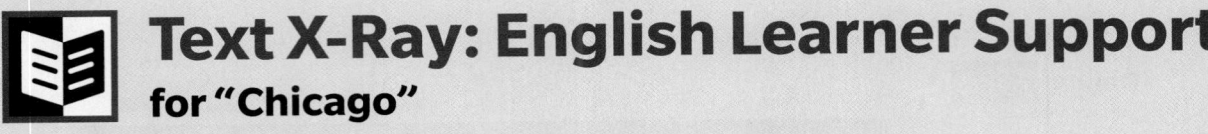

Text X-Ray: English Learner Support
for "Chicago"

Use the Text X-Ray and the supports and scaffolds in the Teacher's Edition to help guide students at different proficiency levels through the selection.

INTRODUCE THE SELECTION
DISCUSS THE CITY OF CHICAGO

To understand the poem, students will need some background information about Chicago and its history. Tell students that at the time Carl Sandburg wrote the poem, Chicago was known as a mostly working-class city. It was a transportation hub and the home of many factories. Sandburg described Chicago as "the city of the big shoulders" in order to compare it to a large, strong laborer—similar to the workers in the city's factories and stockyards.

Ask students what traits other cities or towns might have if they were people. Encourage them to think about a place where they live now or have lived in the past and describe it as "the city/town of the _____."

CULTURAL REFERENCES

The following words or phrases may be unfamiliar to students:

- *luring the farm boys* (line 6): Farmland surrounded the city, and young farm workers would often go in to the city for excitement.
- *crooked* (line 7): unjust or corrupt
- *the marks of wanton hunger* (line 8): the signs of significant hunger or poverty
- *give them back the sneer* (line 9): looking back at them with a scornful smile"
- *flinging magnetic curses* (line 11): talking in a tough, vulgar way
- *slugger* (line 11): a fighter, or a batter in a game of baseball

LISTENING

Understand Stanzas and Lines

Explain that stanzas are groups of lines that form a unit in a poem. Stanzas express one thought or idea. Line length is an essential element of the poem's meaning and rhythm. Line breaks may coincide with a grammatical unit. However, a line break may occur at the middle of a grammatical unit to create a pause or effect. Poets use a variety of line lengths to convey meaning.

Use the following supports with students at varying proficiency levels:

- Read the first stanza aloud, emphasizing each line. Ask students yes/no questions to ensure understanding. *Is the third line the longest? (Yes.) Does this stanza describe Chicago? (Yes) Does the poet say Chicago is the hog butcher of the world? (Yes.)* **SUBSTANTIAL**
- Read the first stanza aloud and have students follow along in the text. Ask how the short lines and long lines sound different. Then, read the stanza again. Ask what the rhythms and sounds of the stanza help students understand about Chicago. **MODERATE**
- Read lines 1–8 aloud twice. The first time, try to keep a steady rhythm for all of the lines and phrases. The second time, vary the rhythm, using a faster pace and more energetic tone for shorter lines or phrases and a slower pace and more thoughtful tone for longer lines. Ask students to discuss with a partner the differences between the two ways of reading the poem. Have partners decide which way better reflects the meaning of the poem. **LIGHT**

SPEAKING

Present Research

Help students plan and deliver a brief presentation on research about Sandburg or Chicago.

Use the following supports with students at varying proficiency levels:

- Work with students in a group. Provide a few simple questions to research. Have students repeat the questions. As a class, search online for the answers. Then, have students share answers aloud. Provide these sentence frames: *Sandburg moved to Chicago in _____. Sandburg was born in _____.* **SUBSTANTIAL**

- Have pairs conduct interest-based research into the history of Chicago and speak about what they found interesting in their research. Have students take notes about their research and discuss key ideas of their findings in a small group. **MODERATE**

- Have students conduct interest-based research into the history of Chicago. Have them use note cards to write an introduction for a presentation and list main ideas using past-tense verbs. Then, have them give a one-minute presentation to the class. **LIGHT**

READING

Visualize Details

Assist students in identifying descriptive language to help them create vivid mental pictures.

Use the following supports with students at varying proficiency levels:

- Read aloud the last five lines, and have students follow along in the text. Use gestures to help students understand the actions. Have them create drawings to illustrate the lines. **SUBSTANTIAL**

- Have pairs read lines 10–17. Ask students to circle descriptive words and action words that help them picture Chicago or the people. Provide these sentence frames for discussion: *The words _____ help me picture _____. This description shows that Chicago is _____.* **MODERATE**

- Have students read lines 10–26 and identify vivid descriptive words and action words that help them visualize Chicago. Then, have them write a response in which they identify and explain three or four additional words or phrases that could be used to describe the scene. **LIGHT**

WRITING

Write Figures of Speech

Explain that authors often use figures of speech, or words used to mean something other than their literal meanings, to create a mood or effect.

Use the following supports with students at varying proficiency levels:

- Read line 12 aloud to students and point out the phrase "fierce as a dog." Tell them that the word *as* shows that this line contains a simile, or comparison of two different things. Help students complete the sentence frame *Sandburg compares Chicago to a dog because _____.* Have students write the sentence in their notebooks. **SUBSTANTIAL**

- Read lines 12–20 aloud with students. Ask them to identify one thing that Sandburg compares to Chicago. Ask: *What does the comparison help you understand about Chicago?* Then, have students write a simile of their own about a place. Provide this sentence frame: *_____ is as _____ as (a) _____.* **MODERATE**

- Have students work in pairs to read lines 12, 19, and 20 and identify the similes. Then, have them write individual answers to question: *What is being compared in each of these pairs, and why?* **LIGHT**

Connect to the
? ESSENTIAL QUESTION

In "Chicago," poet Carl Sandburg captures the unique character of the city of Chicago as Sandburg knew it in the early 1900s. The speaker personifies the city and praises its vitality and hard-working energy, while also portraying its crime, corruption, and poverty in a series of vivid mental images.

CHICAGO

Poem by **Carl Sandburg**

? ESSENTIAL QUESTION:

What makes a place unique?

518   Unit 5

QUICK START

The poem you are about to read describes life in a large city. With a partner, generate three questions you have about living in a city. You might consider where people live and work, the sights and sounds that are part of life, or the difficulties residents might face. Share your questions with the class.

CHARACTERISTICS OF POETRY: Stanzas and Line Breaks

"Chicago" is a free verse poem. A **free verse** poem does not have regular patterns of rhythm and rhyme. Additionally, its stanzas and lines can be any length. However, that does not mean the stanzas and line breaks are random, or that the poem has no rhythm or sound devices. Rather, these elements support the ideas and feelings the poet is trying to express. Stanza and line length can also help create a unique voice for the speaker of the poem.

FREE VERSE POEM ELEMENTS	POSSIBLE EFFECTS
Line length	Shorter lines may create an energetic, fast-paced feeling, while longer lines may create a slower, more thoughtful effect.
Stanza length	Shorter stanzas can add urgency to a poem; stanzas may signal a change in time or space, a change in speaker, or a change in the speaker's tone.
Line breaks	Line breaks in the middle of sentences create tension, while ending lines with punctuation often creates a sense of resolution or stability. Line breaks can cause a sense of suspense or surprise when they set up a reader's expectation that is challenged after the break.
Natural rhythm	The rhythm of free verse poems echoes the cadences of natural speech or song.

CREATE MENTAL IMAGES

Free verse poems often contain vivid imagery that appeals to a reader's senses. Using the imagery as the basis of mental images will deepen your understanding of the poem. To create mental images, follow these steps:

- Pay attention to the descriptions in the stanzas, especially to any details that appeal to the senses.

- Carefully form mental images based on the descriptions. Consider the tone of the poem. What is the writer's attitude toward what he describes?

- Use your imagination to fill in anything left out of the description.

As you read the poem, create mental images from each stanza to help you visualize the city he describes.

GENRE ELEMENTS: FREE VERSE POEM

- does not contain formal meter or rhyme scheme

- uses line length and stanza breaks to convey meaning

- contains rhythm that mirrors everyday speech

Chicago   519

QUICK START

Have students read the Quick Start activity and share with a partner their experiences living and visiting large cities. Then, have partners brainstorm questions they have, writing them down as they discuss. Have pairs choose three of their questions to share with the class.

CHARACTERISTICS OF POETRY: Stanzas and Line Breaks

Provide an example of a poem that has a regular rhyme scheme and **line** length, such as one of Shakespeare's sonnets. Have a volunteer read aloud the poem, noticing its rhyme and metrical rhythm. Then, have another volunteer read aloud a **stanza** of "Chicago." Discuss how the sound and pacing of the poems compare. Then, have students discuss how the poems look different—one is blocky and rectangular and the other is sprawling.

Note that the structure of a poem can support the poem's meaning. In "Chicago," the speaker describes a city of contrasts. For example, images of strength and hard work contrast with images of violence and children going hungry. Ask students to discuss how the structure of the poem supports the character of Chicago.

CREATE MENTAL IMAGES

Explain that "Chicago" relies heavily on **imagery,** both to describe scenes from the city and to describe the **personified** Chicago. Before students read the poem, point out these two kinds of images. In lines 6–8, the speaker uses the phrase "I have seen" to alert the reader to particularly important images of the city. Students can try to create a mental image of what the speaker says he has seen. Line 10 introduces a character who is the city personified, a "city with lifted head singing." Images that follow this line all relate to this character, who becomes a **symbol** of the city.

ANALYZE DICTION AND SYNTAX

Students often confuse mood and tone, so spend some time reinforcing the similarities and differences between these two aspects of a text. Emphasize that **tone** is the speaker's or poet's feeling toward the subject and **mood** is the reader's feeling evoked by the poem. These are often similar feelings, because writers often want to help the reader share his or her perspective on a subject. In "Chicago," the speaker describes the city in ways designed to help the reader share his mixed feelings about it: though it is flawed, it is alive and admirable. Throughout, the speaker shares positive and negative descriptions of the city, which express his complicated feelings toward the city and evoke similar feelings in the reader.

Walk through the examples with students, identifying the mood and the tone of each. Make a list on the board or chart paper of words that describe tone and mood, and have students add to the list as they read the poem.

 ## ANNOTATION MODEL

Remind students of the ideas in Characteristics of Poetry, Create Mental Images, and Analyze Diction and Syntax on pages 519 and 520, which suggest noticing line and stanza breaks, vivid images that help create mental images, and words that create tone and mood. Point out to students that they may follow the method of marking the text shown in the Annotation Model or use their own system for marking up the selection in their write-in text. They may want to color-code their annotations by using highlighters. Their notes in the margin may include questions about ideas that are unclear or that they want to learn more about.

ANALYZE DICTION AND SYNTAX

Poets convey tone, mood, and voice through **diction** (word choice), **syntax** (arrangement of words), and choice of details. **Mood** is the feeling or atmosphere that a writer creates for a reader. **Tone** is the attitude or feeling the poet or poem's speaker has toward the subject of the poem. Sometimes the tone of a poem can be difficult to perceive and describe. Other times, tone is obvious in the first stanza. In these lines from "Chicago," Carl Sandburg's diction and syntax create a tone of admiration for a hard-working city.

> Fierce as a dog with tongue lapping for action, cunning
> as a savage pitted against the wilderness,
> Bareheaded,
> Shoveling,
> Wrecking,
> Planning,
> Building, breaking, rebuilding,

Often, a poet is trying to shape the reader's perceptions of the poem's subject to mirror his or her own. For example, consider how Sandburg uses a sorrowful tone and a lonely mood to convey a particular image to the reader.

> And they tell me you are brutal and my reply is: On the
> faces of women and children I have seen the marks
> of wanton hunger.

ANNOTATION MODEL   **NOTICE & NOTE**

As you read, notice how the writer uses stanzas and line breaks to convey meaning. Also note images and how diction and syntax convey the mood and tone of the poem. Here is one student's notes about the beginning of the poem.

> Hog Butcher for the World,
> Tool Maker, Stacker of Wheat,
> Player with Railroads and the Nation's Freight Handler;
> <u>Stormy, husky, brawling,</u>
> <u>City of the Big Shoulders:</u>
>
> They tell me you are (wicked) and I believe them, for I have seen your painted women under the gas lamps luring the farm boys.
> And they tell me you are (crooked) and I answer: Yes, it is true I have seen the gunman kill and go free to kill again.

Short lines give this opening stanza energy.

These words convey a tone of admiration of the city's strength.

The shift to a new stanza signals a change in tone. The images are not as admirable. The lines are longer; the poem feels more like a conversation.

BACKGROUND

Carl Sandburg (1878–1967) grew up in America's heartland in Galesburg, Illinois. Given to wanderlust from an early age, he traveled throughout the country, soaking up America's sights and sounds. When he ran out of money, he returned to the Midwest, writing for journals in Chicago and later settling there with Lillian Steichen, whom he married in 1908. Sandburg became a reporter, editorial writer, and columnist for the Chicago Daily News and began publishing his verse in Poetry, a prominent literary magazine. His first collection of poems, Chicago Poems, was published in 1916.

CHICAGO
Poem by Carl Sandburg

SETTING A PURPOSE

As you read, consider how Sandburg uses the elements of poetry to communicate the nature of Chicago. Note any questions you have as you read.

Hog Butcher for the World,
Tool Maker, Stacker of Wheat,
Player with Railroads and the Nation's Freight Handler;
Stormy, husky, brawling,
5   City of the Big Shoulders:

They tell me you are wicked and I believe them, for I
   have seen your painted women under the gas lamps
   luring the farm boys.
And they tell me you are crooked and I answer: Yes, it
   is true I have seen the gunman kill and go free to
   kill again.
And they tell me you are brutal and my reply is: On the
   faces of women and children I have seen the marks
   of wanton[1] hunger

---

[1] **wanton:** without limitation.

Notice & Note

Use the side margins to notice and note signposts in the text.

ANALYZE DICTION AND SYNTAX

Annotate: Circle the harsh words in lines 6–9. Underline the language in line 10 that contrasts with this harshness.

Analyze: What do these contrasts reveal about Sandburg's feelings toward the city as well as its critics?

BACKGROUND

After students read the Background note, tell them that when Carl Sandburg died in 1967, President Lyndon Johnson noted, "Carl Sandburg was more than the voice of America, more than the poet of its strength and genius. He was America." Explain that Sandburg had gained a reputation as the poet of the common people, partly because of the way he celebrated the spirit of the hard-working people of America and partly because of his interesting and accessible poetry readings, during which he would intersperse his poetry with engaging commentary and folk songs. Reading this poem, it is easy to imagine the poet reading "Chicago" aloud to a group of enthusiastic listeners.

SETTING A PURPOSE

Direct students to use the Setting a Purpose prompt to focus their reading.

ANALYZE DICTION AND SYNTAX

Remind students that **diction** is the poet's word choice, which can set the poem's **tone,** or attitude toward the subject of the poem. Here, the subject of the poem is the city of Chicago, so the tone is the attitude toward the city. Students should look for individual words, phrases, and images that communicate the tone. (**Possible answer:** *The words* wicked, crooked, kill, brutal, *and* hunger *all create a harsh, violent tone. Yet the phrase "my city" suggests the speaker's affection for Chicago in spite of these flaws. The image of Chicago "with lifted head singing so proud to be alive" reveals his pride in and admiration for it. He is dismissive and defiant toward critics who "sneer" at the city.*)

For **listening support** for students at varying proficiency levels, see the **Text X-Ray** on page 518C.

TO CHALLENGE STUDENTS . . .

Contrast Line Breaks Have students work in pairs to dig deeper into line breaks. Challenge them to compare the first and last stanzas, focusing on line breaks. (If needed, point out that, in this poem, new lines begin with a capital letter. The lines that begin with a lowercase letter are a continuation of the previous line.) Students should note that the first stanza includes punctuation at the end of every line, while the final stanza does not, and that although some of the same nicknames for Chicago are used in the final stanza as in the first, some occur over line breaks in the final stanza. Once students have noted these differences, have them discuss their effect.

TEACH

 CHARACTERISTICS OF POETRY: STANZAS AND LINE BREAKS

Point out that new lines begin with a capital letter in this poem, so a lowercase letter at the beginning of a line indicates that the line is continued from the previous one. Often in this poem, the "line" of the poem does not always correlate to the line on the page. For example, lines 10, 11, and 12 are more than one "line" on the page, but each are one "line" of the poem. This makes the shift in line length even more dramatic. Have students consider how the rhythm of the lines helps the reader picture the "tall bold slugger" and reflects other aspects of the busy industrial city of Chicago. (**Answer:** *The shift from very long lines to very short lines emphasizes the description of the "tall bold slugger" and creates energy surrounding his character and behavior. It seems to echo the rhythm of an industrial city with its factories, trains, and construction tools.*)

■ **English Learner Support**

Recognize Directionality Before students answer the Characteristics of Poetry question, remind them that even though English is read left to right, poems often have structural elements that make the vertical appearance of the poem important. Show students that the different line lengths, as they run left to right, create a vertical pattern: sections of short lines alternating with sections of very long lines. **SUBSTANTIAL/MODERATE**

For **reading** and **writing support** for students at varying proficiency levels, see the **Text X-Ray** on page 518D

NOTICE & NOTE

CHARACTERISTICS OF POETRY: STANZAS AND LINE BREAKS

Annotate: Mark the word that begins an important shift in line length in lines 12–17.

Analyze: How does this shift reflect the content and meaning of these lines?

And having answered so I turn once more to those who
 sneer at this <u>my city</u>, and I give them back the sneer
 and say to them:
10 Come and show me another city with <u>lifted head singing</u>
 <u>so proud to be alive and coarse and strong and cunning.</u>
Flinging magnetic curses amid the toil of piling job on
 job, here is a tall bold slugger set vivid against the
 little soft cities;
Fierce as a dog with tongue lapping for action, cunning
 as a savage pitted against the wilderness,
  <u>Bareheaded,</u>
  Shoveling,
15 Wrecking,
  Planning,
  Building, breaking, rebuilding,

522 Unit 5

WHEN STUDENTS STRUGGLE . . .

Understand Personification In lines 18–22, use questions to help students understand the personification of Chicago in the poem:

• What mental pictures does this description bring to your mind? Would you like to know this person? Why or why not? (*Students' responses should be consistent with the text description and should convey a personal response.*)

• In what ways is the description positive? In what ways is it negative? (***Possible answer:*** *It is positive in its depiction of strength and enjoyment, and negative in using the words* ignorant *and* bragging.)

• Is the person described here an appropriate symbol for a great American city? Why or why not? (***Possible answers:*** *Yes, because he displays a city's strength, energy, and hard work. No, because a city is composed of many kinds of people of both genders.*)

Under the smoke, dust all over his mouth, laughing with
    white teeth,
Under the terrible burden of destiny laughing as a young
    man laughs,
20 Laughing even as an ignorant fighter laughs who has
    never lost a battle,
Bragging and laughing that under his wrist is the pulse, and
    under his ribs the heart of the people,
                      Laughing!
Laughing the stormy, husky, brawling laughter of
    Youth, half-naked, sweating, proud to be Hog
25 Butcher, Tool Maker, Stacker of Wheat, Player with
    Railroads and Freight Handler to the Nation.

NOTICE & NOTE ✏

CREATE MENTAL IMAGES

Annotate: Mark words and phrases that appeal to the senses in lines 18–22.

Analyze: What characteristics of the city do these images convey?

CHECK YOUR UNDERSTANDING

Answer these questions before moving on to the **Analyze the Text** section on the following page.

1 How is stanza 1 different from stanza 2?

  A Stanza 1 has a rhyme scheme and stanza 2 does not.

  B Stanza 1 is about Chicago and stanza 2 is not.

  C Stanza 2 contains vivid images and stanza 1 does not.

  D Stanza 2 contains long lines and stanza 1 does not.

2 What proof of Chicago's reputation as brutal does the poem's speaker give?

  F The speaker thinks the people who live in Chicago are insensitive.

  G The speaker has seen dogs fighting in the streets.

  H The speaker thinks the people who live in Chicago grab all the wealth.

  J The speaker has seen hungry women and children.

3 According to the poem, how does Chicago feel about its reputation?

  A Sad

  B Angry

  C Proud

  D Sorrowful

Chicago   523

EL ENGLISH LEARNER SUPPORT

Oral Assessment Use the following questions to assess students' comprehension and speaking skills.

1. How are line lengths in stanzas 1 and 2 different? (*The lines in stanza 2 are longer.*)

2. What imagery shows that Chicago is brutal? (*hungry women and children*)

3. How does Chicago feel about what people think of it? (*It is proud.*)
   SUBSTANTIAL/MODERATE

✏ CREATE MENTAL IMAGES

Remind students that while imagery often appeals to the sense of sight, images are more effective when they combine several senses. Suggest that students look for images that appeal to sight, smell, touch, and sound. (**Answer:** *These images all convey the characteristics of life and vitality. The emphasis on the sound of laughter and the rhythm of a heart beating suggests the city is joyful and alive. The contrast of the smoke and the dirt with the white teeth in a laughing mouth suggests the characteristics of youth and defiance.*)

■ English Learner Support

Use Visual Support Since the imagery in the poem is essential to understanding the poem's meaning, make sure students have enough experience with big cities to create mental images from the words of the poem. Have students examine and describe the photos included with the selection using sentence frames like these: *This image shows _____. This image helps me understand line _____ because it shows _____. These images all show _____.*

Provide additional photos from this period of Chicago's history, including images of the industrial landscape and workers. **MODERATE**

✏ CHECK YOUR UNDERSTANDING

Have students answer the questions independently.

Answers:

1. *D*

2. *J*

3. *C*

If they answer any questions incorrectly, have them reread the text to confirm their understanding. Then they may proceed to ANALYZE THE TEXT on page 524.

ANALYZE THE TEXT

Possible answers:

1. **DOK 2:** *Although the structure of different parts of the poem is tied to its content, such as short, one-word lines that evoke setting one brick on another to describe building and rebuilding, the poem as a whole does not have a form. Its varying approach to the line length and stanza structure suggests Chicago is complex, always moving, and hard to categorize or pin down.*

2. **DOK 4:** *The tone is loud, dramatic, and boisterous, with long lines and lists of epithets. Examples include "Under the smoke, dust all over his mouth, laughing with white teeth / Under the terrible burden of destiny laughing as a young man laughs" and "Bareheaded, / Shoveling, / Wrecking, / Planning, / Building, breaking, rebuilding."*

3. **DOK 4:** *The long, flowing, rhythmic lines demonstrate Chicago's uncontainable energy. The short lines show the city's variety, brashness, and unpredictability.*

4. **DOK 4:** *The description is appropriate. This symbolic person displays strength, energy, and hard work. He is unrefined, authentic, and defiant—traits Americans often value. The description is not appropriate. A city is composed of many kinds of people, strong and weak, of both genders. It includes children and those who feel oppressed. This symbolic person is an idealistic view of certain aspects of an American city, but it does not represent the diversity in a real city.*

5. **DOK 4:** *The poem does have a sentimental tone toward the city. It portrays a defiant, stubborn, strong place. The poem is full of confidence and is an idealized or romanticized version of Chicago that is appropriate to someone who lives in and loves his or her own city. However, one could say that the negative images, while overshadowed by the positive in terms of energy, do occupy a lot of space in the poem and provide a realistic undercurrent that counteracts the sentimental tone.*

RESEARCH

Help students develop keywords for effective searches, such as "Carl Sandburg Robert Frost Chicago Poems."

Extend "Before men invented the alphabet, so that poems could be put down in writing, they spoke their poems," Sandburg wrote in defense of his technique. "When one man spoke to another in a certain time-beat and rhythm, if it happened that his words conveyed certain impressions and moods to his listeners, he was delivering poetry to them, whether he knew it or they knew it."

 RESPOND

ANALYZE THE TEXT

Support your responses with evidence from the text.   **NOTEBOOK**

1. **Interpret** How does the structure of the poem as a whole reflect its subject matter? Consider the stanzas and line breaks in your response.

2. **Analyze** What is the tone of the poem? Cite examples of diction or syntax from the poem that help create the tone.

3. **Analyze** What other stylistic devices underscore Sandburg's characterization of Chicago as a brash, vibrant city? Consider such elements as line and stanza length, rhythm, imagery, simile, and anaphora. Cite examples from the text.

4. **Evaluate** Explain whether the person described beginning in line 18 is an appropriate symbol for a great American city. Cite examples of particular images in your response.

5. **Connect** Although Carl Sandburg has been an extremely popular American poet for almost a century, some readers consider his work sentimental. Does Sandburg portray the city sentimentally or realistically—or both?

RESEARCH TIP
For literary criticism and analysis, you are likely to find more sources in a database of journals than in a simple Internet search.

RESEARCH

William Carlos Williams (1883–1963), a contemporary of Carl Sandburg, called Sandburg's poetry a "formless mass." What did others have to say about Sandburg or his poetry, especially *Chicago Poems*? Research to find a quotation from each of the following people or publications to complete the chart.

POET, CRITIC, OR PUBLICATION	QUOTATION
Robert Frost	*"artificial and studied ruffian"*
Amy Lowell	*"propagandist"*
The Dial	*"gross, simple-minded, sentimental, and sensual."*

Extend What did Sandburg have to say in defense of his technique to the critics of his poetry and its "formlessness"? Find a quotation that gives his perspective on poetic form and diction.

WHEN STUDENTS STRUGGLE . . .

Reteaching: Analyze Diction and Syntax Help students identify the complex tone by looking at the contrasting emotions expressed. Read aloud lines 6–10. Point out the phrase "my city," which suggests affection, and "with lifted head singing so proud to be alive," revealing pride. He dismisses critics who "sneer" at the city. The speaker admits the city's faults: the "painted women . . . luring the farm boys," "the gunman" who goes free, and the hungry faces.

 For additional support, go to the **Reading Studio** and assign the following **Level Up Tutorial: Tone.**

CREATE AND PRESENT

Write a Poem Using "Chicago" as inspiration, write a poem about a location in which you use vivid imagery, rhythm, line length, and stanza structure to express the mood and tone of the place.

- ❏ Use the line lengths and stanza structure of "Chicago" as a model.
- ❏ Use diction (word choice) that conveys a clear tone.
- ❏ Use line length to control the pace and flow of the poem.
- ❏ Include images that evoke a mood, or feeling about the place, in the reader.

Present a Dramatic Reading Present your poem to a small group as a dramatic reading.

- ❏ Mark up your poem with notes indicating where you intend to slow down, speak forcefully or quietly, and pause.
- ❏ Practice several times before presenting to an audience.
- ❏ Remember to speak clearly and with an appropriate volume, using eye contact to connect with your audience.

Go to **Giving a Presentation: Delivering Your Presentation** in the **Speaking and Listening Studio** for help.

RESPOND TO THE ESSENTIAL QUESTION

? What makes a place unique?

Gather Information Review your annotations and notes on Sandburg's "Chicago." Then, add relevant information to your Response Log. As you determine which information to include, think about:

- the features and people of Chicago that Sandburg describes
- the defense Sandburg offers for Chicago's faults
- the mental images of the city that Sandburg creates

ACADEMIC VOCABULARY

As you write and discuss what you learned from the poem, be sure to use the Academic Vocabulary words. Check off each of the words that you use.

- ❏ ambiguous
- ❏ clarify
- ❏ implicit
- ❏ revise
- ❏ somewhat

APPLY

CREATE AND PRESENT

Write a Poem Before students begin writing their poems, have them brainstorm phrases, words, and images they can use in it. Remind students that it is best to choose a location they have a personal connection to—one that has strong sensory associations in their own memory, rather than a place they have seen on television or in movies. Have them visualize this location. What does it look, smell, feel, and sound like? Have them write down descriptive words and phrases as well as vivid images that come to mind as they hold this mental picture in their minds. As they begin to write, they can use these words and phrases.

Another important aspect of the poem will be the speaker's voice. Encourage students to make bold decisions about the voice of the speaker. Is the speaker speaking to the location, as the location, or as an inhabitant of the location? Is the speaker praising, criticizing, or defending the location?

Present a Dramatic Reading Remind students to present the dramatic reading as the speaker of the poem, not as the poet. Have them "get into character" as the speaker as an actor plays a role. Are there props or items of clothing that would help evoke this speaking character?

RESPOND TO THE ESSENTIAL QUESTION

Allow time for students to add details from "Chicago" to their Unit 5 Response Logs.

APPLYING ACADEMIC VOCABULARY

❏ **ambiguous** ☑ **clarify** ☑ **implicit** ❏ **revise** ❏ **somewhat**

Write and Discuss Have students turn to a partner to discuss the following questions. Guide students to include the academic vocabulary words *clarify* and *implicit* in their responses. Ask volunteers to share their responses with the class.

- How does the speaker's use of imagery **clarify** what makes Chicago unique?
- What characteristics of Chicago are stated explicitly in the poem? What characteristics are **implicit** in the poem's imagery?

from **THE JUNGLE**
Novel by Upton Sinclair

GENRE ELEMENTS
NOVEL

A **novel** is an extended work of fiction that usually has a wide range of characters and a complex plot. Other elements of a novel include a theme, or message about life, and setting. Some novels feature realistic settings and characters in order to make readers think about a contemporary issue.

LEARNING OBJECTIVES

- Analyze author's purpose and synthesize information.
- Research journalists of the Progressive Era.
- Write a literary analysis.
- Give a presentation.
- Identify and define words in word families.
- Use prepositional phrases to combine sentences.
- **Language** Describe the author's tone and purpose.

TEXT COMPLEXITY

Quantitative Measures	*from* The Jungle	Lexile: 1310L
Qualitative Measures	**Ideas Presented** Simple single meaning, literal, explicit, and direct. Purpose is clear.	
	Structures Used Primarily explicit, largely conventional.	
	Language Used Mostly explicit, some dialect or unconventional language.	
	Knowledge Required More complexity in theme, experiences less familiar.	

Online Ed

RESOURCES

- Unit 5 Response Log
- Selection Audio
- Reading Studio:
  Notice & Note
- Level Up Tutorial: Cause-and-Effect
  Organization
- Writing Studio:
  Using Textual Evidence
- Speaking and Listening Studio:
  Giving a Presentation
- Vocabulary Studio:
  Word Families
- Grammar Studio:
  Prepositions and Prepositional
  Phrases
- from *The Jungle*/from "Fast Food
  Nation" Selection Test

SUMMARIES

English

The Jungle is a novel written by Upton Sinclair about the deplorable conditions in the slaughterhouses and meat-packing businesses of Chicago in the early 1900s. Sinclair went undercover to investigate the industry, earning him the title *muckraker*, a journalist who uncovered corruption or social hardship in order to motivate reform.

Spanish

La jungla es una novela escrita por Upton Sinclair acerca de las condiciones deplorables de los mataderos y empacadoras de carne de Chicago al principio del siglo XX. Sinclair trabajó encubierto e investigó la industria, lo que le dio el título de periodista sensacionalista, un periodista que dejaba al descubierto la corrupción o dificultades sociales para motivar las reformas.

SMALL-GROUP OPTIONS

Have students work in small groups and pairs to read and discuss the selection.

Jigsaw with Experts

- Divide the excerpt from *The Jungle* into six parts.
- Have students count off until each student is assigned a part, 1–6.
- Ask students to read their parts and take notes, then break into groups of students with the same number to discuss for understanding.
- Direct students to form new groups that include one representative for each part.
- Have the groups discuss their respective parts, then regroup for a class discussion about the text as a whole.

Double-Entry Journal

- Model the structure of the two-column format by dividing the board into two columns, then write the heading *Quotes from* The Jungle on the left side and *My Notes* on the right.
- Instruct students to record important or confusing quotes from the text on the left, then write their own interpretations, summaries, questions, or restatements on the right.
- Have students get into pairs or small groups to discuss their entries.

# Text X-Ray: English Learner Support
for The Jungle

Use the Text X-Ray and the supports and scaffolds in the Teacher's Edition to help guide students at different proficiency levels through the selection.

INTRODUCE THE SELECTION
DISCUSS FOOD REGULATION

In this lesson, students will need to understand the history of food regulation in the United States. Explain that when Sinclair's novel was published in 1906, few laws or regulations controlled how factories processed food or its ingredients. Soon after the book was published, the government passed the Pure Food and Drug Act—one of the first major laws regulating food production. Since then, additional laws introduced regulations about food ingredients, labels, and factory conditions. Ask the following questions:

- What are some possible dangers of eating food from unsafe factories?
- Why should the government regulate factories?

Provide these sentence frames:

- The government should regulate factories because _____.
- Unsafe factory conditions can _____.

CULTURAL REFERENCES

The following words or phrases may be unfamiliar to students:

- *alchemists* (paragraph 2): people who practiced alchemy, an early form of chemistry during the Middle Ages, aimed at turning cheap metals into gold
- *rubbers* (paragraph 2): rubber boots, usually worn in the rain to keep feet dry and protected
- *the horses were being canned* (paragraph 2): the horses were being packaged to sell as meat
- *Packingtown* (paragraph 3): the area of Chicago where meat was packed
- *inferno* (paragraph 3): a region of hell or a place resembling hell

LISTENING

Listen for Tone

Help students analyze the author's tone in paragraph 2. Explain that tone is a word for the author's attitude toward the characters or topic, and that students will often need to infer the tone based on details from the text.

Read the first half of paragraph 2 aloud. Use the following supports with students at varying proficiency levels:

- Explain the meaning of the term *positive*. Ask: *Does the author have a positive attitude about the characters?* Point out and paraphrase details in the paragraph to help them answer. Have students use a thumbs-up for "yes" and a thumbs-down for "no." **SUBSTANTIAL**
- After you read the passage, provide students with a list of words to describe an author's tone or attitude (such as *sympathetic, amused, positive, negative, bitter, thoughtful,* and *urgent*). Define any unfamiliar terms. Then, have students decide with a partner which words from the list best describe the author's tone. **MODERATE**
- As you read, ask students to note words or phrases that show the author's attitude toward the factory workers and the factory conditions. Then, have them discuss the author's tone with a partner. Have them use their notes to support their ideas. **LIGHT**

SPEAKING

Discuss Author's Purpose

Help students talk about the author's purpose—to inform, to entertain, or to persuade—in small groups or with a partner.

Use the following supports with students at varying proficiency levels:

- Review the major purposes for writing: to inform, to entertain, and to persuade. Have students say each purpose aloud. Model a sentence identifying the author's purpose for writing *The Jungle* and providing evidence for it. Have students repeat the sentence after you. **SUBSTANTIAL**
- Have partners discuss the author's purpose. Ask them to use sentences with connecting words to identify and support the purpose. Provide sentence frames: *I think the author's purpose is _____, because _____ . Another piece of evidence to support the purpose is _____.* **MODERATE**
- Explain that an author's tone often provides clues about his or her purpose. Have pairs discuss the author's purpose, citing evidence from their notes from the Listening exercise. **LIGHT**

READING

Identify Cause and Effect

Discuss with students the concept of cause and effect in *The Jungle* (example—cause: working with sharp knives; effect: cuts on hands).

Use the following supports with students at varying proficiency levels:

- Read the second sentence of paragraph 4 aloud to students. Tell them that the first part of the sentence (*Let a man so much as scrape his finger*) is a cause. Help students identify the words in the sentence that describe the effect (*he might have a sore*). **SUBSTANTIAL**
- Have students read the first five sentences of paragraph 4 (through ". . . like a fan"). Point out one cause and effect in the paragraph. Have students work with a partner to identify another cause and effect. Provide a sentence frame, such as: _____ *since* _____. **MODERATE**
- Have students read the first half of paragraph 4, then work with a partner to identify causes and effects in the paragraph. Provide a word bank of cause/effect words, such as *because, since, consequently*, and *as a result*, for them to use in their discussions. **LIGHT**

WRITING

Take Notes and Summarize

Help students take notes and write summaries while reading for meaning.

Use the following supports with students at varying proficiency levels:

- Read the first four sentences of the selection aloud. Pause to summarize or paraphrase sentences in simpler words. Guide students to write key words and phrases in their notes. **SUBSTANTIAL**
- Read aloud the second half of paragraph 1 (starting with "It seemed that . . .") while students take notes. Ask: *What is this part mainly about?* (the process of killing old or diseased cattle) *How does the author describe it?* Guide them to use their responses to write a short summary. **MODERATE**
- Have students work in pairs to read the second half of paragraph 1 (starting with "It seemed that . . .") and note important words and images. Then, ask them to summarize the image described in this passage (a worker slaughtering diseased cattle) in writing. **LIGHT**

Connect to the
ESSENTIAL QUESTION

Upton Sinclair's tough look at the ugly side of American industry ushered in a new era of public awareness and reform. This excerpt will give students the context to think critically about the positive and negative results of the industrial revolution in the United States.

COMPARE AUTHOR'S PURPOSE

Ask students how the excerpt's genre reflects the author's purpose in this selection. How else might the author have chosen to present his information? What effect does the author's use of the novel format have on the reader, and how does this genre choice support his purpose? Direct students to consider how they respond differently to novels and journalistic texts.

NOVEL

from
THE JUNGLE

by **Upton Sinclair**
pages 529–533

COMPARE AUTHOR'S PURPOSE

Journalists report on the world as it is—even if they sometimes present that world in a fictional environment, as Upton Sinclair does in *The Jungle*. However, an author's purpose for writing may include reasons beyond simply informing readers. Look for details in these two selections that convey a strong message and suggest the author's purpose.

ESSENTIAL QUESTION:

What are the consequences of change?

INVESTIGATIVE JOURNALISM

FOOD PRODUCT DESIGN

from
FAST FOOD NATION

by **Eric Schlosser**
pages 541–551

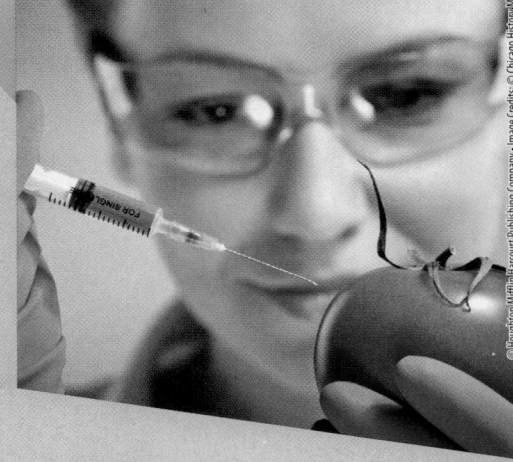

LEARNING MINDSET

Grit   Remind students that working hard at a difficult task will help them grow more than if they just completed tasks that were easy for them. Ask students to recall a challenge they have worked hard to overcome and to reflect on how the experience of putting in hard work, rather than just the experience of gaining the desired result, has helped shape who they are today. Tell students that the ability to persist in the face of discouraging results or uncertainty will help them in life no matter what they choose to pursue.

from THE JUNGLE

QUICK START

Have you ever heard of a food product being recalled by a government agency or by the manufacturer? Think about what might happen if there were no one overseeing the safety and quality of our food.

ANALYZE AUTHOR'S PURPOSE

An **author's purpose,** or reason for writing, can be to inform, to entertain, or to persuade. In the last case, an author may want to move people to take a particular action. That means he or she likely targets a particular **audience** with a focused **message.** Upton Sinclair offers vivid and realistic details about work in the slaughterhouse. Since the text is fiction he does not need to include factual verification. However, these details help to convey a strong message about the topic and serve as the basis of a call to action. By reading the brutally frank language that Sinclair employs in *The Jungle*—and the volume and variety of those details—a reader can determine Sinclair's purpose and message.

GENRE ELEMENTS: NOVEL

- is an extended work of fiction
- has a purpose that can be determined through examination of key details
- conveys a strong message about a topic

SYNTHESIZE INFORMATION

When you **synthesize information,** you combine information and prior knowledge to gain a better understanding of a subject or to create a new idea. Most often, you synthesize information when you read multiple texts on a topic. However, you may also synthesize information when you bring your experience and knowledge to a text. You combine what you already know with what you learn from a text, or even in several texts, to create a new understanding. You can use a graphic to help you synthesize information.

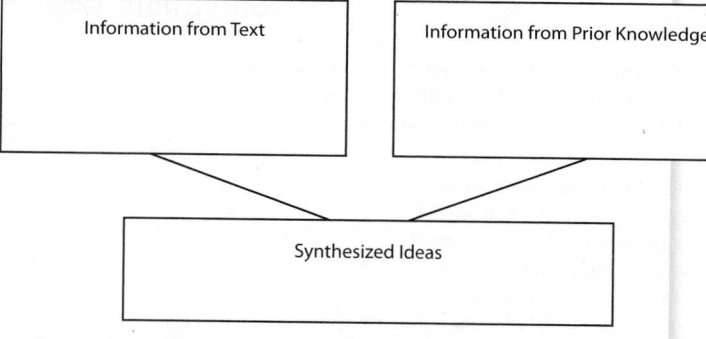

As you read the excerpt from *The Jungle,* note the key information and ideas the author presents and think about what you already know that will help you make connections to form new ideas.

QUICK START

Have students read the Quick Start question, and invite them to share their thoughts with the class. To promote further discussion, share the following information with students and discuss any questions:

- Soldiers in the Spanish American War died from eating badly preserved "embalmed beef."
- Until the early 1900s, there were few laws for the food industry. Food manufacturers added chemicals not meant for consumption.
- Thanks to *The Jungle* and food-safety pioneer Dr. Harvey W. Wiley, the Pure Food and Drug Act and Meat Inspection Act became law in 1906.

ANALYZE AUTHOR'S PURPOSE

Point out that Sinclair spent several months in Chicago visiting the stockyards. He originally went as a journalist, but he left as a novelist. His choice to write a novel was affected by his purpose and audience. Have students think about why writing a novel might have suited his purpose more than writing a news article. Guide students to realize that he could give more information in a novel and that he might have believed that a wider segment of the population would read a novel than read a newspaper article. Writing a novel also allowed him to make the story more personal. By creating characters, he humanized the story, which affected his readers more.

SYNTHESIZE INFORMATION

Tell students that synthesizing information will help them better understand a subject. Work with students to begin filling out the portion of the chart labeled "Information from Prior Knowledge" by posing the following questions: *Do you know anyone who has been injured at work? Do you read ingredients on food labels? Have you read articles or watched documentaries on this subject before? How do you think information you read will compare with a novel on a similar topic?*

TEACH

CRITICAL VOCABULARY

Encourage students to read all the sentences before deciding which word provides the best definition for each Critical Vocabulary term. Remind them to look for context clues that match the precise meaning of each word.

Answers:

1. *b*
2. *c*
3. *b*
4. *a*

■ English Learner Support

Use Cognates Tell students that two of the Critical Vocabulary words have Spanish cognates: *oblige/obligor* and *ingenious/ingenioso*. **ALL LEVELS**

LANGUAGE CONVENTIONS

Tell students that prepositional phrases can modify a noun or pronoun. This type of phrase is an adjective phrase. Prepositional phrases are called adverb phrases when they modify verbs, adjectives, or adverbs. Then, discuss the sample sentence and ask students to identify the type of phrase. Also discuss why the first prepositional phrase is followed by a comma.

■ English Learner Support

Identify Prepositional Phrases If students have difficulty identifying prepositions, provide the following sentence frame: *The rabbit hopped ___ the log.* If the word makes sense in this frame, that word is a preposition. **MODERATE**

ANNOTATION MODEL

Remind students of annotation strategies such as underlining important details and circling words that signal how the text is organized. Point out that they may follow this suggestion or use their own system for marking up the selection in their write-in text. They may want to color-code their annotations by using highlighters. Their notes in the margin may include questions about ideas that are unclear or topics they want to learn more about.

 **GET READY**

CRITICAL VOCABULARY

oblige   ingenious   ostensibly   sceptical

Circle the letter of the best definition of each Critical Vocabulary term.

1. Her **ingenious** solution was one the others had not thought of.
   a. expert   b. inventive   c. naive

2. He was **sceptical** about the story because the child fidgeted and looked away.
   a. negative   b. stern   c. doubtful

3. As a financial adviser, she felt **obliged** to explain the investment's risks.
   a. grateful   b. compelled   c. pleased

4. The vice-chair ran the meeting but the chair was **ostensibly** in charge.
   a. supposedly   b. rarely   c. tentatively

LANGUAGE CONVENTIONS

Prepositions Words that show the relationship between a noun or a pronoun and another word in a sentence are called prepositions. A preposition is always followed by a word or words that are its object. The preposition, its object, and words that modify the object form a **prepositional phrase.**

> Then one Sunday evening, Jurgis sat puffing his pipe <u>by the kitchen stove</u> . . .

As you read, note the writer's use of prepositional phrases and the relationships they describe.

ANNOTATION MODEL   **NOTICE & NOTE**

As you read, notice clues that suggest the author's purpose. Note the ways the author uses language to convey a message and shape the reader's response. This model shows one reader's notes about the excerpt from *The Jungle*.

> Jurgis heard of these things little by little, in the gossip of those who were <u>obliged to perpetrate them</u>. It seemed as if every time you met a person from a new department, you heard of new swindles and new crimes. There was, for instance, a Lithuanian who was a cattle butcher for the plant where Marija had worked, which killed meat for canning only; and to hear this man describe the animals which came to his place would have been <u>worthwhile for a Dante</u> or a Zola.

The language here is sinister—"obliged" suggests coercion; "perpetrate" has connotations of criminal behavior.

Mention of Dante (Inferno) turns the matter from the criminal to the hellish.

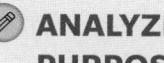

BACKGROUND

Upton Sinclair *(1878–1968) was sent by a newspaper to Chicago to investigate working conditions in the stockyards, where animals were processed into meat. His research led not only to an investigative report but to his most famous novel,* The Jungle *(1906), which he was forced to self-publish after several publishers turned down the manuscript. The novel exposed unsanitary conditions in the meatpacking industry and led to reforms. Jurgis Rudkus, the main character, is a Lithuanian immigrant who works in the stockyards.*

from

THE JUNGLE
Novel by Upton Sinclair

PREPARE TO COMPARE

As you read, make note of the writer's voice, or use of sentence structure, diction, and tone. This will help you infer the author's purpose and compare this text with the investigative journalism article "Food Product Design" that follows it.

1   Jurgis heard of these things little by little, in the gossip of those who were **obliged** to perpetrate them. It seemed as if every time you met a person from a new department, you heard of new swindles and new crimes. There was, for instance, a Lithuanian who was a cattle butcher for the plant where Marija had worked, which killed meat for canning only; and to hear this man describe the animals which came to his place would have been worthwhile for a Dante or a Zola.[1] It seemed that they must have agencies all over the country, to hunt out old and crippled and diseased cattle to be canned. There were cattle which had been fed on "whiskey

---

[1] **a Dante or a Zola:** Dante Alighieri (1265–1321), Florentine poet who wrote the *Inferno*, about a journey through Hell; Emile Zola (1840–1902), French novelist and playwright who focused on social and political ills.

Notice & Note

Use the side margins to notice and note signposts in the text.

oblige
(ə-blīj´) *v.* to compel or require (someone) to do something.

ANALYZE AUTHOR'S PURPOSE

Annotate: In paragraph 1, mark the vivid images in the two sentences about cattle and the workers who slaughter them.

Infer: What response is the author trying to provoke in the reader with these images?

BACKGROUND

Have students read the information about the author. Tell them that as a child in Baltimore, Sinclair was exposed to the enormous inequality in American society. His mother's family was wealthy. His father was an alcoholic whose family had lost its fortune during the Civil War. Moving back and forth from wealth to poverty in his childhood led Sinclair to embrace socialism and its promise of a just society. Introduce students to the term *muckraker*, used to describe Sinclair and other writers who exposed the ugly side of life—the corruption and injustices that polite society ignored. Point out that while Sinclair's muckraking was often unpopular, it was also effective. In 1906, the same year *The Jungle* was published, Congress passed the Pure Food and Drug Act and the Meat Inspection Act. Much of the credit belonged to Sinclair and his vivid description of the meat industry. Sinclair also wrote influential books about the automobile industry, the oil industry, and the rise of Adolf Hitler.

PREPARE TO COMPARE

Direct students to use the Prepare to Compare prompt to focus their reading.

ANALYZE AUTHOR'S PURPOSE

Point out that paragraph 1 continues on the next page. Remind students that an author's **diction,** or word choice, helps determine the effectiveness of his or her writing. Point out that Sinclair's diction creates strong imagery, helping the reader see, feel, and smell life in the slaughterhouse. (***Answer:*** *They are all meant to provoke the reader's outrage that food could be prepared in such foul conditions.*)

For **writing support** for students at varying proficiency levels, see the **Text X-Ray** on page 526D.

CRITICAL VOCABULARY

obliged: Workers were forced to do things they considered wrong.

ASK STUDENTS to identify a task that workers were obliged to do. (*They were obliged to slaughter diseased animals.*)

TEACH

SYNTHESIZE INFORMATION

Remind students that when you **synthesize** information, you think about your previous experiences or knowledge. Here they are being asked to think about modern laws they may be familiar with. Encourage students to think of the discussion that you had at the beginning of the lesson and refer to the notes they took in their charts. (**Answer:** *A company that sold meats that were not chicken as chicken and sold the same food as though it were different grades of quality would be punished, if caught.*)

EL **ENGLISH LEARNER SUPPORT**

Understand Quotation Marks Review with students the different uses of quotation marks in written English, such as indicating direct speech or signaling made-up terms or verbal irony. Explain that verbal irony occurs when someone states one thing but means another. Discuss the uses of quotation marks on this page, such as "steerly," "potted chicken," and "De-vyled." For example, "potted chicken" was not really chicken and "deviled ham" was actually waste ends of smoked beef that couldn't be sliced. Ask students why they think Sinclair used these terms. **LIGHT**

 For **listening support** for students at varying proficiency levels, see the **Text X-Ray** on page 526C.

CRITICAL VOCABULARY

ingenious: Sinclair suggests that devising the product sold as "deviled ham" required creative intelligence.

ASK STUDENTS what might have been ingenious about the mixture known as deviled or "de-vyled" ham. (*Creating a product that people would want from ingredients that they would otherwise reject required intelligence.*)

530 Unit 5

SYNTHESIZE INFORMATION

Annotate: Mark the details in paragraph 2 that suggest fraudulent sales practices.

Synthesize: What would happen today to a company that tried to do this? Consider your background knowledge of the topic in your response.

ingenious
(ĭn-jēn´yəs) *adj.* having great inventive skill and imagination.

malt," the refuse of the breweries, and had become what the men called "steerly"—which means covered with boils. It was a nasty job killing these, for when you plunged your knife into them they would burst and splash foul-smelling stuff into your face; and when a man's sleeves were smeared with blood, and his hands steeped in it, how was he ever to wipe his face, or to clear his eyes so that he could see? It was stuff such as this that made the "embalmed beef" that had killed several times as many United States soldiers as all the bullets of the Spaniards; only the army beef, besides, was not fresh canned, it was old stuff that had been lying for years in the cellars.

2   Then one Sunday evening, Jurgis sat puffing his pipe by the kitchen stove, and talking with an old fellow whom Jonas had introduced, and who worked in the canning-rooms at Durham's; and so Jurgis learned a few things about the great and only Durham canned goods, which had become a national institution. They were regular alchemists at Durham's; they advertised a mushroom-catsup, and the men who made it did not know what a mushroom looked like. They advertised "potted chicken"—and it was like the boarding-house soup of the comic papers, through which a chicken had walked with rubbers on. Perhaps they had a secret process for making chickens chemically—who knows? said Jurgis's friend; the things that went into the mixture were tripe,[2] and the fat of pork, and beef suet, and hearts of beef, and finally the waste ends of veal, when they had any. They put these up in several grades, and sold them at several prices; but the contents of the cans all came out of the same hopper. And then there was "potted game" and "potted grouse," "potted ham," and "deviled ham"—de-vyled, as the men called it. "De-vyled" ham was made out of the waste ends of smoked beef that were too small to be sliced by the machines; and also tripe, dyed with chemicals so that it would not show white, and trimmings of hams and corned beef, and potatoes, skins and all, and finally the hard cartilaginous gullets of beef, after the tongues had been cut out. All this **ingenious** mixture was ground up and flavored with spices to make it taste like something. Anybody who could invent a new imitation had been sure of a fortune from old Durham, said Jurgis's informant, but it was hard to think of anything new in a place where so many sharp wits had been at work for so long; where men welcomed tuberculosis[3] in the cattle they were feeding, because it made them fatten more quickly; and where they bought up all the old rancid butter left over in the grocery stores of a continent, and "oxidized" it by a forced-air process, to take away the odor, rechurned it with skim milk, and sold it in bricks in the cities! Up to a year or two ago it had been the custom

---

[2] **tripe:** the rubbery lining of the stomach of cattle or other ruminants, used as food.
[3] **tuberculosis:** an infectious disease that causes the growth of nodules on lung tissue.

 ENGLISH LEARNER SUPPORT

Identify Antecedents Remind students that a pronoun should have an antecedent, or the noun or pronoun it replaces or refers to. Read aloud the sentence at the top of page 530 that begins with "It was a nasty job." Point out that the word *it* in "steeped in it" is a pronoun. Ask students to find the noun it replaces (*blood*). Then, explain that authors sometimes break certain grammar rules for style purposes. Draw students' attention to the next sentence that begins with "It was stuff." Point out that here the pronoun *it* does not refer to a specific word. Have students read the entire sentence. Have them find an example where the word *it* replaces a noun. (*It stands for the army beef.*) **LIGHT**

to kill horses in the yards—**ostensibly** for fertilizer; but after long agitation the newspapers had been able to make the public realize that the horses were being canned. Now it was against the law to kill horses in Packingtown, and the law was really complied with—for the present, at any rate. Any day, however, one might see sharp-horned and shaggy-haired creatures running with the sheep—and yet what a job you would have to get the public to believe that a good part of what it buys for lamb and mutton is really goat's flesh!

3   There was another interesting set of statistics that a person might have gathered in Packingtown—those of the various afflictions of the workers. When Jurgis had first inspected the packing plants with Szedvilas, he had marveled while he listened to the tale of all the things that were made out of the carcasses of animals, and of all the lesser industries that were maintained there; now he found that each one of these lesser industries was a separate little inferno, in its way as

ostensibly
(ŏ-stĕn´sə-blē) *adv.* apparently.

The Jungle   531

ENGLISH LEARNER SUPPORT

Understand Complex Sentences Read aloud the last sentence in paragraph 2 on page 531, and have students work backward to understand the sentence. Because this is a long sentence, it may be helpful to simplify it and break it into parts. For example: *Any day, one might see sharp-horned and shaggy-haired creatures running with sheep. It would be hard to get the public to believe that what they buy as lamb and mutton was actually goat.* First, review the use of the hyphenated words and explain that the words are hyphenated because they both modify the noun. In this case, the noun is *creatures.* Sinclair is describing the creatures as having sharp horns and shaggy hair. Ask students to think about both sentences and identify what these creatures are (*goats*). Then, read the whole sentence as it is written. Explain to students that dashes, like parentheses, can be used to set off information that signals an abrupt break in thought or a thought the writer wants to emphasize. Here, Sinclair wants to emphasize that the people who think they are eating lamb or mutton are really eating goat. However, no one would actually believe this. Sinclair is shocked by this idea and wants to emphasize it.

MODERATE/LIGHT

WHEN STUDENTS STRUGGLE...

Use Graphic Organizers Ask students to reread the first 5 lines of paragraph 4 on page 532. Help them see how Sinclair is describing the effects of unsafe working conditions. Discuss with students the causes and effects. (*cause: working with sharp knives, effect: cuts on hands; cause: pulling hides, effect: loss of fingernails*) Then, have them read the rest of the paragraph and work in pairs to fill out a cause-and-effect table for the workers' afflictions.

 For additional support, go to the **Reading Studio** and assign the following **Level Up Tutorial: Cause-and-Effect Organization.**

CRITICAL VOCABULARY

ostensibly: The meat industry wanted the public to believe that horses were being killed only for use in fertilizers.

ASK STUDENTS why ostensibly killing horses only for fertilizer was important for the slaughterhouse owners. (*The slaughterhouse owners knew people would not want to eat horsemeat.*)

TEACH

 ANALYZE AUTHOR'S PURPOSE

Explain that authors often have more than one **purpose** when writing. Point out that Sinclair wanted to inform readers about what really happened in the meatpacking industry. He also had other purposes. His choice of details about the harm workers suffered helps the reader infer another purpose. (**Answer:** *Readers might have demanded government regulations to improve the working conditions in slaughterhouses.*)

🖉 **LANGUAGE CONVENTIONS**

Review terms associated with describing a writer's style. Have students read the passage aloud to determine the effect the prepositional phrases have on pacing. (**Answer:** *The prepositional phrases allow him to convey a great deal of information in one long, clear sentence that reads at a pace that feels like the workers running along. This helps the reader feel what the workers felt.*)

■ **English Learner Support**

Understand Prepositions Cantonese speakers may omit prepositions because there is no exact equivalent in Cantonese, although there are words to mark location and movement. Write a list of common prepositions on the board, including the ones from the paragraph: *upon, through, at, under, above.* Review what each word means. Then, work with students to identify the prepositional phrases on pages 532–533. **SUBSTANTIAL**

For **reading support** for students at varying proficiency levels, see the **Text X-Ray** on page 526D.

CRITICAL VOCABULARY

sceptical: Sinclair observes that an outsider might not believe all the talk about corruption in the meat industry.

ASK STUDENTS why people might be sceptical of the stories they heard about corruption. (*Without hard evidence, people might be sceptical and think these stories were unfounded rumors.*)

532   Unit 5

sceptical
(skĕp´tĭ-kəl) *adj.* marked by or given to doubt; questioning.

ANALYZE AUTHOR'S PURPOSE
Annotate: In the first half of paragraph 4, mark examples of injury or disease.

Analyze: What actions do you think Sinclair is hoping to inspire by including this information?

horrible as the killing-beds, the source and fountain of them all. The workers in each of them had their own peculiar diseases. And the wandering visitor might be **sceptical** about all the swindles, but he could not be sceptical about these, for the worker bore the evidence of them about on his own person—generally he had only to hold out his hand.

4   There were the men in the pickle rooms, for instance, where old Antanas had gotten his death; scarce a one of these that had not some spot of horror on his person. Let a man so much as scrape his finger pushing a truck in the pickle rooms, and he might have a sore that would put him out of the world; all the joints in his fingers might be eaten by the acid, one by one. Of the butchers and floorsmen, the beef boners and trimmers, and all those who used knives, you could scarcely find a person who had the use of his thumb; time and time again the base of it had been slashed, till it was a mere lump of flesh against which the man pressed the knife to hold it. The hands of these men would be criss-crossed with cuts, until you could no longer pretend to count them or to trace them. They would have no nails,— they had worn them off pulling hides; their knuckles were swollen so that their fingers spread out like a fan. There were men who worked in the cooking rooms, in the midst of steam and sickening odors, by artificial light; in these rooms the germs of tuberculosis might live for two years, but the supply was renewed every hour. There were the beef luggers, who carried two-hundred-pound quarters into the refrigerator cars, a fearful kind of work, that began at four o'clock in the morning, and that wore out the most powerful men in a few years. There were those who worked in the chilling rooms, and whose special disease was rheumatism;[4] the time limit that a man could work in the chilling rooms was said to be five years. There were the wool pluckers, whose hands went to pieces even sooner than the hands of the pickle men; for the pelts of the sheep had to be painted with acid to loosen the wool, and then the pluckers had to pull out this wool with their bare hands, till the acid had eaten their fingers off. There were those who made the tins for the canned meat, and their hands, too, were a maze of cuts, and each cut represented a chance for blood poisoning. Some worked at the stamping machines, and it was very seldom that one could work long there at the pace that was set, and not give out and forget himself, and have a part of his hand chopped off. There were the "hoisters," as they were called, whose task it was to press the lever which lifted the dead cattle off the floor. They ran along upon a rafter, peering down through the damp and the steam, and as old Durham's architects had not built the killing room for the convenience of the hoisters, at every few feet they

LANGUAGE CONVENTIONS
Annotate: In paragraph 4, mark the prepositional phrases in the sentence beginning, "They ran along. . . ."

Infer: Why does Sinclair use multiple prepositional phrases here?

---

[4] **rheumatism** (ro͞o´mə-tĭz´əm): a disease that causes inflammation and pain in muscles and joints.

532   Unit 5

APPLYING ACADEMIC VOCABULARY

❑ **ambiguous**   ☑ **clarify**   ❑ **implicit**   ❑ **somewhat**   ☑ **revise**

Write and Discuss Have students turn to a partner to discuss the following questions. Guide students to include the academic vocabulary words *clarify* and *revise* in their responses. Ask volunteers to share their responses with the class.

- How did Sinclair's exposure of the meat industry help **clarify** people's understanding of how power could be abused?
- How were readers forced to **revise** their opinions about the benefits of unregulated business practices?

would have to stoop under a beam, say four feet above the one they ran on, which got them into the habit of stooping, so that in a few years they would be walking like chimpanzees. Worst of any, however, were the fertilizer men, and those who served in the cooking rooms. These people could not be shown to the visitor—for the odor of a fertilizer man would scare any ordinary visitor at a hundred yards, and as for the other men, who worked in tank rooms full of steam, and in some of which there were open vats near the level of the floor, their peculiar trouble was that they fell into the vats; and when they were fished out, there was never enough of them left to be worth exhibiting—sometimes they would be overlooked for days, till all but the bones of them had gone out to the world as Durham's Pure Leaf Lard!

NOTICE & NOTE

ANALYZE AUTHOR'S PURPOSE

Annotate: Mark the closing dependent clause of the last sentence in paragraph 4.

Analyze: Why does Sinclair build the sentence so that it concludes with this disturbing detail?

CHECK YOUR UNDERSTANDING

Answer these questions before moving on to the **Analyze the Text** section on the following page.

1 How does Jurgis learn about what happened in the canning department at Durham?

  A By working in the department for several months

  B By reading accounts in the newspapers

  C By talking to workers in that department

  D By hearing stories from his wife Marija

2 According to the company, what was the advantage of cattle that had tuberculosis?

  F They were easier to kill.

  G They fattened more quickly.

  H They had better flavor.

  J They could be sold as veal.

3 Why was the time men were able to work in the chilling rooms limited to five years?

  A Their hands were disfigured by acid.

  B They lost fingers from butchering the cold beef.

  C They sickened from tuberculosis.

  D They tended to get rheumatism.

TEACH

ANALYZE AUTHOR'S PURPOSE

Explain that the way an author chooses to arrange information has an important effect on his or her writing. Draw students' attention to the choices Sinclair makes in concluding this selection. (**Answer:** *The idea that workers fell into vats, died, and ended up as part of the lard the company sold could shock a reader into realizing that he or she may have committed cannibalism. This would have produced revulsion, anger, and outrage.*)

EL ENGLISH LEARNER SUPPORT

Understand Similes Inform students that comparisons using the word *like* or as, such as "they would be walking like chimpanzees" in the text, are called similes. Explain how similes can be used to create images. Ask student pairs to write a simile that creates a vivid image. **LIGHT**

CHECK YOUR UNDERSTANDING

Have students answer the questions independently.

Answers:

1. *C*

2. *G*

3. *D*

If they answer any questions incorrectly, have them reread the text to confirm their understanding. Then they may proceed to ANALYZE THE TEXT on page 534.

EL ENGLISH LEARNER SUPPORT

Oral Assessment Use the following questions to assess students' comprehension and speaking skills:

1. How does Jurgis learn about what happened in the canning department? *(He talked to workers in the department.)*

2. According to the company, why was it good when the cattle had tuberculosis? *(They got fat faster.)*

3. Why were men only able to work in the chilling room for five years? *(They got rheumatism.)* **MODERATE/LIGHT**

ANALYZE THE TEXT

Possible answers:

1. **DOK 4:** *He uses images that evoke disease, poison, foulness, and criminality; the effect of piling these images on one another is to emphasize the corruption and evil of the practices being described.*

2. **DOK 4:** *Advantage: By writing fiction, Sinclair could express himself freely, without documenting each assertion. Disadvantage: People might not believe what Sinclair wrote was true, and the meat industry could accuse him of making up details to suit his purpose.*

3. **DOK 2:** *By referring ironically to the "alchemists" at Durham's, Sinclair suggests that the meat industry performed fantastic feats by creating food out of disgusting ingredients. Medieval alchemists attempted to turn base metals into gold.*

4. **DOK 3:** *Sinclair's topic in the third and fourth paragraphs is the poor conditions that meat industry workers endured. His message is that these conditions are harmful and inhumane.*

5. **DOK 4:** *While the injuries and illnesses the workers suffered are effectively described, they likely had less impact because readers were more concerned about the issues that directly affected them—the quality of their food and the fraud being perpetrated on them. Today, food and worker safety carry equal weight so readers care about both.*

RESEARCH

Review with students what constitutes a credible source. Remind students to confirm their information with multiple sources and to use correct formatting when citing sources.

Extend Direct students to keep in mind the instructions regarding synthesizing information and the graphic organizer on page 527. What connections can they draw between Sinclair's concerns in the novel and his policies and platforms from his political campaign?

 RESPOND

ANALYZE THE TEXT

Support your responses with evidence from the text. 📓 NOTEBOOK

1. **Synthesize** Describe the imagery Sinclair uses throughout the selection. What is the effect of this imagery on his message?

2. **Analyze** What are the advantages and disadvantages of Sinclair's decision to turn his research into a novel rather than journalistic articles?

3. **Infer** What does Sinclair mean when he says "They were regular alchemists at Durham's" (paragraph 2)?

4. **Draw Conclusions** What is Sinclair's topic in the third and fourth paragraphs of the selection? What message does he communicate about the topic?

5. **Synthesize** Which message likely resonated most strongly with Sinclair's contemporary audience—the company's unsafe and fraudulent practices or the suffering of its workers? Why do you think so? What effect do they have on readers today?

RESEARCH

RESEARCH TIP
When researching individuals or issues that may be considered controversial, be sure to evaluate the credibility and objectivity of your sources.

Upton Sinclair is counted among the "muckrakers," a group of journalists and writers from the Progressive Era who investigated and exposed corruption and injustice in government, corporations, and society as a whole. With a partner, research to find the answers to the questions below.

QUESTION	ANSWER
What is the origin of the word *muckrakers*?	*President Theodore Roosevelt used the term in a speech, taking it from a character in John Bunyan's* Pilgrim's Progress.
What laws were passed in part as a result of public outrage following publication of Sinclair's *The Jungle*?	*The Meat Inspection Act, the Pure Food and Drug Act*
Who was the muckraker who took on the powerful Standard Oil monopoly?	*Ida M. Tarbell, a teacher, author, and journalist*

Extend Sinclair later entered politics and ran for governor of California several times in the 1920s and 1930s. Find out about his most successful campaign, which was in 1934 during the Great Depression. Discuss his policies and the outcome of the campaign with your partner.

⚙️ **LEARNING MINDSET**

Questioning Remind students that asking specific, detailed questions will help them further their understanding of the subject at hand. Questioning is key to learning both in the classroom and out of the classroom. For students who are reluctant to ask questions, suggest they write a question down before asking it aloud, noting any references in the text to which their question refers. If students are afraid of appearing less intelligent for asking questions, remind them that the questions they ask will also help other students with their learning.

CREATE AND DISCUSS

Write a Literary Analysis Explore whether Sinclair's information and ideas have been presented effectively by writing a brief literary analysis.

❏ Think about Sinclair's purpose for writing. Was he seeking to entertain, to inform, to persuade, or a combination of these?

❏ Determine Sinclair's message. Did he convey this message effectively?

❏ Consider the genre characteristics of fiction and whether they supported Sinclair's purpose and the effectiveness of his message.

❏ Write a paragraph in which you discuss the effectiveness of the text. Did Sinclair's decision to write a fiction support his message? Provide specific examples in your response.

Give a Presentation With a small group, give a presentation to your class about whether Sinclair conveyed his message effectively.

❏ State whether Sinclair effectively conveyed his message to his audience.

❏ Cite well-chosen details from the text that support your view.

❏ Employ eye contact, gestures, and other techniques to emphasize ideas.

Go to **Using Textual Evidence** in the **Writing Studio** for help.

Go to **Giving a Presentation: Delivering Your Presentation** in the **Speaking and Listening Studio** for help.

RESPOND TO THE ESSENTIAL QUESTION

? What are the consequences of change?

Gather Information Review your annotations and notes on *The Jungle*. Then, add relevant details to your Response Log. As you determine which information to include, think about:

• how change affects social groups differently
• what can cause a change in society
• how views or beliefs shape the way people experience change

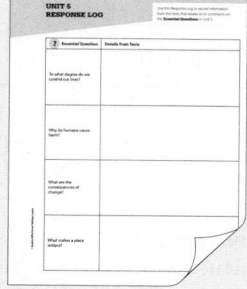

ACADEMIC VOCABULARY
As you write and discuss what you learned from the excerpt, be sure to use the Academic Vocabulary words. Check off each of the words that you use.

❏ **ambiguous**
❏ **clarify**
❏ **implicit**
❏ **revise**
❏ **somewhat**

CREATE AND PRESENT

Write a Literary Analysis Once students have written a first draft, direct them to review their literary analysis, focusing on how effectively they have described Sinclair's purpose, evaluated his message, and explained whether his use of fiction supported his message. Invite students to peer edit each other's drafts for content and style.

Give a Presentation Organize students in pairs to peer edit their presentations, focusing on delivery. Ask the listening students to take notes on how easy the presentation is to understand, how clearly the presenter communicates his or her points, and how effectively the presenter uses nonverbal techniques.

RESPOND TO THE ESSENTIAL QUESTION

Allow time for students to add details from *The Jungle* to their Unit 5 Response Logs.

CRITICAL VOCABULARY

Answers:

1. Answer should be close to the correct definition, which is "to compel or require (someone) to do something."

2. Answer should be close to the correct definition, which is "having great inventive skill and imagination."

3. Answer should be close to the correct definition, which is "apparently."

4. Answer should be close to the correct definition, which is "marked by or given to doubts; questioning."

VOCABULARY STRATEGY:
Word Families

Explain that Greek and Latin contributions to English vocabulary can sometimes have similar spellings but different meanings. For example, the Greek prefix *bio* means "life" and forms English words such as *biology*. The Latin prefix *bi* means "two," as in *biped*.

Some confusing Greek and Latin roots include

- *aud* (L: to hear); *aut* (G: self)
- *dent* (L: tooth), *dendre* (G: tree)
- *ped* (L: foot); *ped* (G: child)
- *spir* (L: to breathe); *spir* (G: coil)

Possible answers:

1. pathos (*noun*): a quality that arouses feelings of sadness; antipathy (*noun*): strong dislike; apathetic (*adjective*): showing little feeling; sympathize (*verb*): to share someone's feelings

2. spectacle (*noun*): an impressive sight; spectator (*noun*): a person who watches an event; specimen (*noun*): an object for people to look at; inspect (*verb*): to look at closely

3. mediocre (*adjective*): ordinary, middling; mediate (*verb*): to settle differences by intervening between two parties; medium (*noun*): a person who allegedly interprets the spirit world for the living world; median (*noun*): the middle number in a set of numbers

4. chronic (*adjective*): lasting a long time; chronology (*noun*): sequence of events; synchronize (*verb*): to make happen at the same time; chronometer (*noun*): a clock

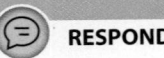 **RESPOND**

WORD BANK
oblige
ingenious
ostensibly
sceptical

Go to **Word Families** in the **Vocabulary Studio** for help.

CRITICAL VOCABULARY

Practice and Apply Go on a Critical Vocabulary scavenger hunt to find examples of the four words in advertisements, news articles, or other uses in print or online. Write your own definition of each word based on at least two examples. Note that the preferred spelling of *sceptical* in American dictionaries is now *skeptical*.

1. **oblige**

2. **ingenious**

3. **ostensibly**

4. **sceptical**

VOCABULARY STRATEGY:
Word Families

A **word family** is a group of words that have the same root and similar meanings. The Critical Vocabulary word *oblige* is part of the word family with the Latin root *ligare*, meaning "to bind." *Oblige* is formed by adding the prefix *ob-* meaning "to" so that it means "to be required or bound to do something." Words may include a variety of prefixes or suffixes and act as different parts of speech. Knowing the meaning of the common root will help you determine the meaning of words in a word family.

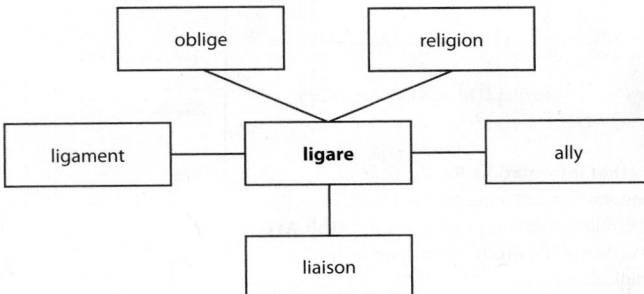

Practice and Apply Work with a partner to create a list of at least four words related to each root below. Write the part of speech and definition next to each word. Consult a dictionary to confirm the meaning and etymology of the words you list.

1. Greek root *path–* meaning "to feel or suffer"

2. Latin root *spec–* meaning "to see or look at"

3. Latin root *medi–* meaning "middle"

4. Greek root *chron–* meaning "time"

536   Unit 5

 ENGLISH LEARNER SUPPORT

Use Prefixes and Suffixes Explain to students that a prefix is a small word part added to the beginning of a root word or base word. A prefix changes the meaning of a word. Explain that a suffix is a word part that is added to the end of a root word or base word. A suffix usually changes the word's part of speech. Review some common prefixes and suffixes and how they can change the meaning of simple words, such as *happy, power, read, stop, correct,* and *care*. Point out that some English prefixes have similar Spanish prefixes, such as *re-* and *pre-*. Note that some of the possible answers in the Vocabulary Strategy activity, such as *sympathize, spectator, mediate,* and *chronic,* have prefixes and/or suffixes. **MODERATE**

LANGUAGE CONVENTIONS: Prepositions and Prepositional Phrases

A **preposition** shows the relationship between a noun or a pronoun and another word in a sentence. Common prepositions include *in, of, for, by, above, below, before,* and *after.* A preposition is always followed by a word or group of words that serves as its object. The preposition, its object, and modifiers of the object form a **prepositional phrase.** Prepositional phrases can be as short as two words: *at home.* They can be longer if the object is modified: *in his comfortable, welcoming home.*

Prepositional phrases can function in a sentence as either an adjective or an adverb:

As an adjective modifying *man*: The man *near the door* looks suspicious.
As an adverb modifying *rose*: The jet rose *into the sky.*

Prepositional phrases must be as near as possible to the word they modify.
Incorrect: The waves *against the rocks* crashed noisily.
Correct: The waves crashed *against the rocks* noisily.

You can use prepositional phrases to improve the fluency and clarity of sentences.

Practice and Apply Use prepositional phrases to revise each group of sentences into one sentence that has greater clarity and fluency.

1. There was a podium. The speaker stood there. She gave a spellbinding speech. She told her life story.

2. The chef cooked a meal. It took an hour to make it. It was hard work. He served the meal. His customers ate it.

3. The runner struggled. He felt disheartened. The finish line seemed far off. Then he felt an adrenaline rush. He ran faster.

4. The couple signed the mortgage. They used a pen. Now they owned the country house.

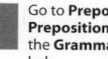
RESPOND

! Go to **Prepositions** and **Prepositional Phrases** in the **Grammar Studio** for help.

LANGUAGE CONVENTIONS: Prepositions and Prepositional Phrases

Review the sample sentences with students, and help them understand the difference between adjective phrases and adverb phrases. Ask students why putting a prepositional phrase as close to the word it modifies is important. Then, choose a paragraph from the text that contains prepositional phrases, such as paragraph 3, and have students find as many prepositions and prepositional phrases as they can and determine how the phrase is being used.

Practice and Apply After students have completed the exercise, direct them to review their speeches for any incorrect uses of prepositions, or places where they could combine sentences using prepositional phrases.

Possible answers:

1. *The speaker stood at the podium and gave a spellbinding speech about her life.*

2. *After an hour of hard work cooking, the chef served the meal to his customers.*

3. *The runner struggled, disheartened by the distance to the finish line, but then he ran faster, spurred by an adrenaline rush.*

4. *The couple signed the mortgage with a pen and became owners of a house in the country.*

 ENGLISH LEARNER SUPPORT

Language Conventions Use the following supports with students at varying proficiency levels:

- Take the answers for Practice and Apply activity and remove the prepositions, converting sentences into sentence frames. Write the prepositions on the board. Have students fill in the missing prepositions. **SUBSTANTIAL**

- Have students work with a partner and find at least three other prepositional phrases in the selection. Have students determine what word the phrase is modifying. **MODERATE**

- Ask students to write two sentences using prepositional phrases. One sentence should use the phrase as an adjective. The other sentence should use the phrase as an adverb. Have students exchange papers with a partner. Have the partners identify the phrases and the word each modifies. **LIGHT**

FOOD PRODUCT DESIGN
from FAST FOOD NATION

Investigative Journalism by Eric Schlosser

GENRE ELEMENTS
INVESTIGATIVE JOURNALISM

Investigative journalism is a type of informational text with the purpose to inform or persuade. Investigative journalists expose actions or events hidden from public view. They do so using facts and quotations from reputable sources. The investigative journalist may also encourage people to take action based on the information presented. Pieces of investigative journalists are usually published in newspapers and magazines, or on websites.

LEARNING OBJECTIVES

- Analyze author's purpose and intended audience.
- Synthesize information from two texts.
- Research key phrases from food labels.
- Write a rhetorical analysis.
- Present an interview.
- Understand technical terms.
- Analyze how writers use dashes.
- **Language** Identify and define multiple-meaning words.

TEXT COMPLEXITY

Quantitative Measures	**Food Product Design**	Lexile: 1290L
Qualitative Measures	**Ideas Presented** More than one purpose; implied meaning easily identified from context.	
	Structures Used Generally sequential order of main ideas; organization and large amount of details adds complexity.	
	Language Used Many unfamiliar academic and complex domain-specific words add difficulty.	
	Knowledge Required Some specialized knowledge required.	

RESOURCES

- Unit 5 Response Log
- 🔊 Selection Audio
- 📖 Reading Studio:
  Notice & Note
- LEVEL UP Level Up Tutorial:
  Reading for Details; Author's Purpose
- Writing Studio:
  Using Textual Evidence
- 💬 Speaking and Listening Studio:
  Participating in Collaborative Discussions
- Vocabulary Studio:
  Specialized Vocabulary
- ❗ Grammar Studio: Dashes
- ☑ from *The Jungle*/from "Food Product Design" from *Fast Food Nation* Selection Test

SUMMARIES

English

Journalist Eric Schlosser discusses the role that the flavor industry plays in well-known fast food chains in America. He meets with chemists and scientists in various laboratories. There he witnesses "natural" flavors being created by artificial means. Schlosser discusses both the history and biology of food cravings, stressing the importance of smell and taste. Schlosser points out that today, many foods are no longer natural.

Spanish

En este pasaje, el periodista Eric Schlosser discute el papel de la industria del sabor en las cadenas de comida rápida más conocidas de Estados Unidos. Schlosser va al corazón de la industria del sabor, en Nueva Jersey, para conocer a químicos y científicos en varios laboratorios. Dentro de estos espacios industriales, Schlosser presencia la creación de sabores "naturales" por medios artificiales. Schlosser discute la historia y biología de las ansias de comida, haciendo hincapié en la importancia del olor y el sabor al formar memorias y relaciones con la comida. Schlosser señala que a pesar de que sea natural para los humanos tener una relación con la comida, muchas comidas ya no son naturales.

 ## SMALL-GROUP OPTIONS

Have students work in small groups and pairs to read and discuss the selection.

Think-Pair-Share

- After students have read and analyzed the text, pose this prompt: *Describe a time when you have eaten fast food. What memories or details do you associate with the fast food? Why? Do you remember mostly the flavors or the experience?*
- Direct students to respond in writing.
- Have students share their responses with a peer.
- Finally, ask students to share commonalities between their experiences aloud with the class.

Numbered Heads Together

- Have students form groups of four and number off 1, 2, 3, 4 within the group.
- Ask the following questions: *After reading, how do you feel about fast food? Would you read the nutrition labels on your food now? Why or why not?*
- Tell students to discuss their answers in their groups.
- Call out a number from 1 to 4. Have that numbered student respond aloud for the group.

Text X-Ray: English Learner Support
for "Food Product Design" *from* Fast Food Nation

Use the Text X-Ray and the supports and scaffolds in the Teacher's Edition to help guide students at different proficiency levels through the selection.

INTRODUCE THE SELECTION
DISCUSS FAST FOOD

Explain to students that the concept of "fast food" was created in the United States. Emphasize the notion of speed over quality. If necessary, utilize visuals of TV dinners or fast food chain logos or slogans.

Ask students to discuss the brand slogans from personal experiences. Have students complete the following stems:

- *I ate fast food when I went to _____ . When I ate the food, I felt _____ .*
- *Eating at _____ is different from eating at my family's house because _____ .*

Then, direct students to share their sentences with one another.

CULTURAL REFERENCES

The following words or phrases may be unfamiliar to students:

- *natural flavor* and *artificial flavor* (paragraphs 2 and 3): common phrases on ingredient lists for foods; both describe substances made in a laboratory through chemical processes
- *nondisclosure form* (paragraph 6): a legal document that people sign as a promise they will keep information secret
- *Willy Wonka's chocolate factory* (paragraph 6): a reference to a book about an eccentric person's wild and magical candy factory
- *consumer likeability* (paragraph 21): the quality of being appreciated or liked by someone buying a product
- *mouthfeel* (paragraph 22): physical sensations within the mouth, produced by qualities of food

LISTENING

Identify Details

Draw students' attention to the words in the passage that describe flavors and tastes. As you read aloud, direct students to jot down descriptive words or phrases that they hear.

Instruct students to listen as you read aloud paragraphs 6–7. Use the following supports with students at varying proficiency levels:

- Tell students that you will repeat some words or phrases that they just heard. Ask them to raise their hand if the words relate to food or flavor. Use the following words and phrases from paragraphs 6–7: *huge pale blue building, thin cloud of steam, white lab coats, brightly colored liquids, white frosting, sport drinks*. **SUBSTANTIAL**
- Ask students to list what the author saw in the IFF plant using the words they wrote down as you read aloud. Have them circle the words and phrases that describe foods or flavors. **MODERATE**
- Have partners share and combine the lists of words and phrases they heard. Have them use a T-chart to classify the descriptions that relate to the IFF plant and those that relate to the foods or flavors developed there. **LIGHT**

SPEAKING

Discuss Details

Have students discuss how the details of the selection help inform the reader of the author's purpose. Circulate around the room to assess use of new vocabulary and provide support as needed.

Direct students to paragraph 7. Use the following supports with students at varying proficiency levels:

- Read aloud paragraph 7 and write this sentence on the board: *The author describes the IFF plant to show readers the real way foods get their flavors.* Read the sentence and have students repeat the sentence back to you and then practice saying it to a partner. **SUBSTANTIAL**
- Have students discuss the purpose of the paragraph using sentence frames: *The author describes _____. The author wants readers to understand _____.* **MODERATE**
- Have students discuss with a partner the following questions: What does paragraph 7 describe? Why did the author include this description? **LIGHT**

READING

Define Multiple-Meaning Words in Context

Explain to students that words in English may have multiple meanings. For example, the word *fries* is important at the beginning of this text because it refers to two meanings: 1) a familiar kind of fast food, a noun, and 2) the action of cooking the food, a verb.

Use the following supports with students at varying proficiency levels:

- Read paragraphs 1 and 2 aloud. When you read the words *fries* and *fry*, pause and ask students: *Which meaning is appropriate for each case?* Offer visuals and allow non-verbal students to point to their response. **SUBSTANTIAL**
- Read aloud paragraphs 7 and 8. Ask students to identify sentences that contain words with multiple meanings (*pilot* and *trade*). Write sentences on the board to illustrate the multiple meanings. For example: *The pilot flew the plane. The product was tested in a pilot study. We trade lunches. She works in the perfume trade.* **MODERATE**
- Instruct students to create Frayer model (definition, characteristics, examples, non-examples) flash cards for their new multiple-meaning words: *fry/fries, pilot, trade.* Have students share and compare their examples and non-examples with a partner. **LIGHT**

WRITING

Distinguish Main Idea from Details

Explain that each paragraph contains many details, but students should identify and summarize what is important. Have students practice identifying main ideas and details by writing summaries in their own words.

Use the following supports with students at varying proficiency levels:

- Read aloud paragraph 4. Then, read the following sentence: *The flavor industry is secretive.* Have student locate and write a detail that supports the main idea. For example: *Flavors are made in distant factories.* **SUBSTANTIAL**
- Have partners work together to read paragraph 4 and write its main idea in their own words. If necessary, provide the following sentence frame: *Food companies will not ____ because they want people to believe ____.* **MODERATE**
- Have students work with partners to write the main idea and three supporting details of paragraph 4 in their own words. **LIGHT**

Connect to the
ESSENTIAL QUESTION

Upton Sinclair and Eric Schlosser, writers from two different historical periods, both write about the industrialization of food manufacturing and the resultant human cost. Both selections explore the ways that the food industry's focus on concerns aside from human welfare, such as profit, efficiency, and marketability, can end up causing unintended harm to workers and consumers.

COMPARE AUTHOR'S PURPOSE

Point out that in addition to being written in different time periods, the two selections employ different types of writing. The selection from *The Jungle* is fiction, whereas the selection from *Fast Food Nation* is nonfiction. Discuss how both are being used to persuade, and how the authors may have some purposes in common despite the differences in genre. Ask students to consider how each genre might have its own advantages when it comes to persuasive writing, and which they find to be most effective.

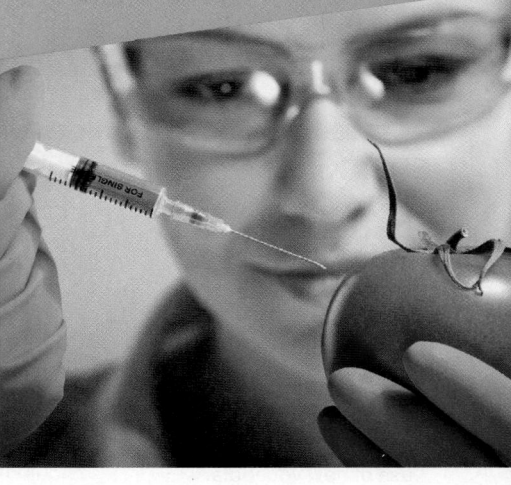

INVESTIGATIVE JOURNALISM
FOOD PRODUCT DESIGN

from
FAST FOOD NATION

by **Eric Schlosser**
pages 541–551

COMPARE AUTHOR'S PURPOSE

Now that you have read the selection from Sinclair's *The Jungle*, read Eric Schlosser's journalistic account of the modern food industry. Look for parallels in the way information is conveyed and in each author's purpose. After you have finished, you will work with a small group to analyze both texts.

? ESSENTIAL QUESTION:

Why do humans cause harm?

NOVEL

from
THE JUNGLE

by **Upton Sinclair**
pages 529–533

538   Unit 5

Food Product Design
from **Fast Food Nation**

QUICK START

Smell is a powerful sense and often evokes fond memories. Think of a food aroma you like and what it reminds you of. Describe how the aroma makes you feel and why you like it.

ANALYZE AUTHOR'S PURPOSE

As an investigative journalist, Eric Schlosser's general **purpose** for writing is to inform or to persuade—or to do some combination of the two. An investigative journalist may also want to encourage people to take a particular action based on the information he or she presents. Analyzing the details in the selection will allow you to infer Schlosser's specific purpose for writing this text. Ask yourself what overall **message** is suggested by the content, diction, style, and rhetoric that Schlosser employs. Use those ideas to infer his purpose for writing and determine what action he might want his audience to take.

GENRE ELEMENTS: INVESTIGATIVE JOURNALISM

- uses facts and quotations to support ideas
- exposes actions or events hidden from public view
- appears in newspapers, magazines, or on websites

SYNTHESIZE INFORMATION

When you **synthesize information** from different texts, you connect information that you read to create a new understanding of the subject. Seeing information presented in different genres of text—and in distinct eras—can broaden your understanding of the subject. You may notice details that are similar between texts or connect ideas that are expressed in different ways. Using a graphic like the one below can help you organize your thoughts as you synthesize information about food production.

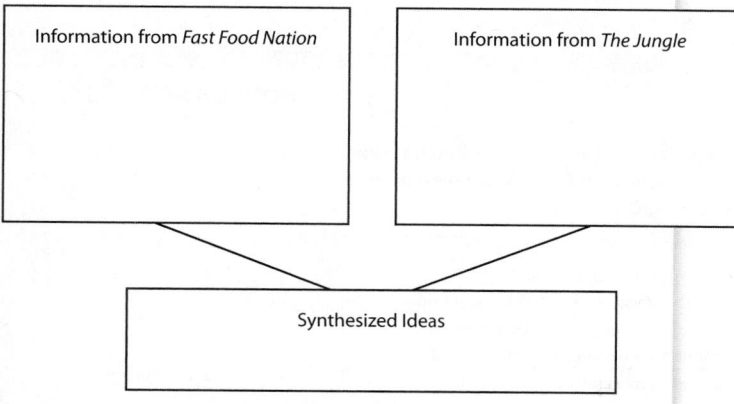

QUICK START

If students are struggling to come up with examples, suggest that they try to think of the aromas of certain foods cooking or scents associated with their favorite activities, such as reading or sports. Ask students to think of the emotions associated with the activity and to consider whether the aromas bring those emotions vividly to mind.

ANALYZE AUTHOR'S PURPOSE

Review the terms *diction, style,* and *rhetoric,* including *rhetorical devices.* Ask students to think about other selections they have read or heard in which the author used diction, style, or rhetoric to achieve a specific purpose. For example, Abraham Lincoln, Thomas Jefferson, and Martin Luther King, Jr., used several rhetorical devices, including repetition, to emphasize ideas and persuade their audiences. Have students predict how Schlosser might use these literary devices and how they will suggest his purpose.

SYNTHESIZE INFORMATION

Have students create graphic organizers like the one shown, and fill in information they recall from *The Jungle*. If time allows, you may want to complete the chart as a class. Then, as students read "Food Product Design" from *Fast Food Nation*, they can record important details about food production. Tell students to look for both information that parallels *The Jungle* and information that does not.

TEACH

CRITICAL VOCABULARY

Instruct students to examine the vocabulary words in the word bank to determine which words they are familiar with. Then, have students read the sentences and use context clues to complete the sentences.

Answers:

1. *catalyst*
2. *stem*
3. *infinitesimal*
4. *conjure*
5. *volatile*

LANGUAGE CONVENTIONS

Dashes Review the information about dashes, and ask students if they know of other instances in which an author might use a dash. *(to emphasize an idea or give examples)* Read aloud the sentence from "Food Product Design" without the information set off by dashes. Then, read the sentence as written. Ask students how their understanding of the information changes. Students should notice that the information set off by dashes helps them understand the process. Without the information, the sentence is not as clear.

ANNOTATION MODEL

Remind students of annotation strategies, such as underlining important ideas and circling repeated words. Students may follow this suggestion or use their own system for marking up the selection in their write-in text. They may want to color-code their annotations by using highlighters. Their notes in the margin may include questions about ideas that are unclear or topics they want to explore further.

CRITICAL VOCABULARY

stem	volatile	infinitesimal	catalyst	conjure

Use the Critical Vocabulary words to complete the sentences.

1. The chemical proved to be the _____ for an unexpected result.

2. "Who'd have thought that an entire industry would _____ from such a tiny device?" he mused.

3. The odds of the team winning were _____, but they played anyway.

4. The artist was able to _____ an image of the novel's mysterious main character.

5. The new serum proved to be _____ and evaporated in the open air.

LANGUAGE CONVENTIONS

Dashes Writers use dashes to insert supplementary or parenthetical information into a sentence. Dashes can indicate an abrupt interruption in thought, or they can insert a pause in a sentence before providing extra information. Dashes are also used to set off a definition of a term or to offer information not essential to the main topic of the sentence.

In "Food Product Design," dashes in this sentence enclose extra information.

> **Benzaldehyde derived through a different process—by mixing oil of clove and the banana flavor, amyl acetate—does not contain any cyanide.**

As you read, notice the writer's use of dashes and consider what functions they serve in his sentences.

ANNOTATION MODEL

NOTICE & NOTE

As you read, note how the author uses language to suggest his purpose and shape the reader's response. In this model, you can see one reader's notes about "Food Product Design."

> Open your refrigerator, your freezer, your kitchen cupboards, and look at the labels on your food. You'll find "natural flavor" or "artificial flavor" in just about every list of ingredients. The similarities between these two broad categories of flavor are far more significant than their differences.

The audience must be everyday people.

The author's message may be about food flavorings.

BACKGROUND

Eric Schlosser (b. 1959) became a journalist after studying history in college. In 1998, the magazine Rolling Stone published his two-part investigative series on the fast-food industry. Schlosser then expanded the articles into a best-selling book, Fast Food Nation: The Dark Side of the All-American Meal (2001), which examines the effects of the fast-food industry on workers, consumers, and the landscape. Later that same year, the book was made into a movie, with Schlosser cowriting the screenplay.

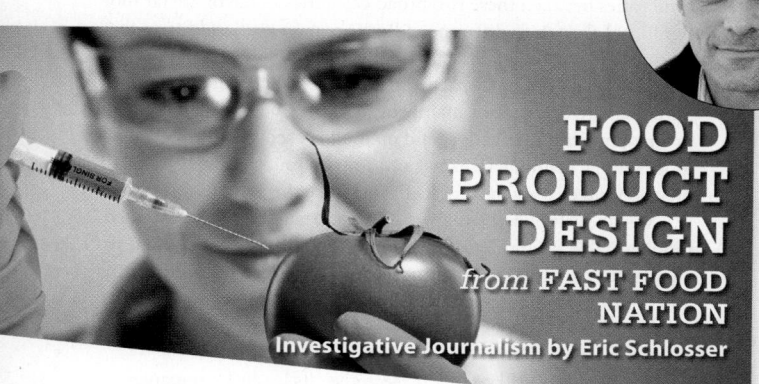

FOOD PRODUCT DESIGN
from FAST FOOD NATION
Investigative Journalism by Eric Schlosser

PREPARE TO COMPARE

Two authors writing on a similar subject may not necessarily have the same purpose. Differences seem even more likely in two texts written almost a century apart. What can you infer about Schlosser's purpose in this text? Does it differ from Sinclair's purpose?

Notice & Note

Use the side margins to notice and note signposts in the text.

1   The taste of McDonald's french fries has long been praised by customers, competitors, and even food critics. James Beard loved McDonald's fries. Their distinctive taste does not **stem** from the type of potatoes that McDonald's buys, the technology that processes them, or the restaurant equipment that fries them. Other chains buy their french fries from the same large processing companies, use Russet Burbanks, and have similar fryers in their restaurant kitchens. The taste of a fast food fry is largely determined by the cooking oil. For decades, McDonald's cooked its french fries in a mixture of about 7 percent cottonseed oil and 93 percent beef tallow. The mix gave the fries their unique flavor—and more saturated beef fat per ounce than a McDonald's hamburger.

2   Amid a barrage of criticism over the amount of cholesterol in their fries, McDonald's switched to pure vegetable oil in 1990. The switch presented the company with an enormous challenge:

stem
(stĕm) *v.* to have or take origin or descent.

BACKGROUND

After students have read the Background note, ask if any of them have seen or heard of the movie, and if so, what they learned about fast food. Then, tell students that Schlosser's book set off a "revolution" of the way people think about and eat food. The book has been translated into more than twenty languages.

Then, ask students to think about the things they eat and labels they might have read. They might be surprised to know that the Code of Federal Regulations defines *natural flavor* as containing "flavoring constituents derived from a spice, fruit or fruit juice, vegetable or vegetable juice, edible yeast, herb, bark, bud, root, leaf or similar plant material, meat, seafood, poultry, eggs, dairy products, products of fermentation thereof, whose significant function in food is flavoring rather than nutritional."

PREPARE TO COMPARE

Direct students to use the Prepare to Compare prompt to focus their reading.

For **reading support** for students at varying proficiency levels, see the **Text X-Ray** on page 538D.

CRITICAL VOCABULARY

stem: Schlosser is referring to the reason McDonald's fries taste so good. He explains that it is not because of their potatoes or the equipment used.

ASK STUDENTS to think of examples of things that stem from other things. *(kindness stems from empathy, detention stems from rule-breaking)*

ANALYZE AUTHOR'S PURPOSE

Remind students that authors choose their words carefully to emphasize ideas or help readers visualize what is being described. An author's word choice can reveal his or her purpose. (**Answer:** *By asserting—and supporting—the idea that the use of natural and artificial flavors is so widespread in American processed foods, Schlosser establishes that this topic is relevant to all readers.*)

ANALYZE AUTHOR'S PURPOSE

Tell students that authors include many facts and details that support their central ideas and purposes. (**Answer:** *The many details impress the reader with the thoroughness of the research and establish his credibility as a reporter.*)

For **writing support** for students at varying proficiency levels, see the **Text X-Ray** on page 538D.

NOTICE & NOTE

ANALYZE AUTHOR'S PURPOSE

Annotate: Mark the words and phrases in paragraph 3 that suggest a widespread use of natural flavors in the United States.

Analyze: How do these details suggest that the topic is important? Explain.

ANALYZE AUTHOR'S PURPOSE

Annotate: Mark the words in paragraph 5 that identify the location of the food flavor facilities.

Analyze: How does this collection of details support the author's purpose?

how to make fries that subtly taste like beef without cooking them in tallow. A look at the ingredients now used in the preparation of McDonald's french fries suggests how the problem was solved. At the end of the list is a seemingly innocuous, yet oddly mysterious phrase: "natural flavor." That ingredient helps to explain not only why the fries taste so good, but also why most fast food—indeed, most of the food Americans eat today—tastes the way it does.

3   Open your refrigerator, your freezer, your kitchen cupboards, and look at the labels on your food. You'll find "natural flavor" or "artificial flavor" in just about every list of ingredients. The similarities between these two broad categories of flavor are far more significant than their differences. Both are man-made additives that give most processed food its taste. The initial purchase of a food item may be driven by its packaging or appearance, but subsequent purchases are determined mainly by its taste. About 90 percent of the money that Americans spend on food is used to buy processed food. But the canning, freezing, and dehydrating techniques used to process food destroy most of its flavor. Since the end of World War II, a vast industry has arisen in the United States to make processed food palatable. Without this flavor industry, today's fast food industry could not exist. The names of the leading American fast food chains and their best-selling menu items have become famous worldwide, embedded in our popular culture. Few people, however, can name the companies that manufacture fast food's taste.

4   The flavor industry is highly secretive. Its leading companies will not divulge[1] the precise formulas of flavor compounds or the identities of clients. The secrecy is deemed essential for protecting the reputation of beloved brands. The fast food chains, understandably, would like the public to believe that the flavors of their food somehow originate in their restaurant kitchens, not in distant factories run by other firms.

5   The New Jersey Turnpike runs through the heart of the flavor industry, an industrial corridor dotted with refineries and chemical plants. International Flavors & Fragrances (IFF), the world's largest flavor company, has a manufacturing facility off Exit 8A in Dayton, New Jersey; Givaudan, the world's second-largest flavor company, has a plant in East Hanover. Haarmann & Reimer, the largest German flavor company, has a plant in Teterboro, as does Takasago, the largest Japanese flavor company. Flavor Dynamics has a plant in South Plainfield; Frutarom is in North Bergen; Elan Chemical is in Newark. Dozens of companies manufacture flavors in New Jersey industrial parks between Teaneck and South Brunswick. Indeed, the area produces about two-thirds of the flavor additives sold in the United States.

6   The IFF plant in Dayton is a huge pale blue building with a modern office complex attached to the front. It sits in an industrial

---

[1] **divulge:** to make known (something private or secret).

© Houghton Mifflin Harcourt Publishing Company

WHEN STUDENTS STRUGGLE . . .

Understand Details Tell students that in text that contains a great deal of detailed information, readers decide which information is necessary to understand in depth and which is less important. Tell students that in a paragraph containing a lot of details, reading the first and last sentences carefully and skimming the details can often provide the information they need. Ask students to try this technique with paragraph 5. Have them state the main point of the paragraph and leave out the secondary details.

For additional support, go to the **Reading Studio** and assign the following **LEVEL UP** **Level Up Tutorial: Reading for Details**.

park, not far from a BASF plastics factory, a Jolly French Toast factory, and a plant that manufactures Liz Claiborne cosmetics. Dozens of tractor-trailers were parked at the IFF loading dock the afternoon I visited, and a thin cloud of steam floated from the chimney. Before entering the plant, I signed a nondisclosure form, promising not to reveal the brand names of products that contain IFF flavors. The place reminded me of Willy Wonka's chocolate factory. Wonderful smells drifted through the hallways, <u>men and women in neat white lab coats cheerfully went about their work, and hundreds of little glass bottles sat on laboratory tables and shelves.</u> The bottles contained powerful but fragile flavor chemicals, <u>shielded from light by the brown glass and the round plastic caps shut tight.</u> The long chemical names on the little white labels were as mystifying to me as medieval Latin. They were the odd-sounding names of things that would be mixed and poured and turned into new substances, like magic potions.

7   I was not invited to see the manufacturing areas of the IFF plant, where it was thought I might discover trade secrets. Instead, I toured various laboratories and pilot kitchens, where the flavors of well-established brands are tested or adjusted, and where whole new flavors are created. IFF's snack and savory lab is responsible for the flavor of potato chips, corn chips, breads, crackers, breakfast cereals, and pet food. The confectionery lab devises the flavor for ice cream, cookies, candies, toothpastes, mouthwashes, and antacids. Everywhere I looked, I saw famous, widely advertised products sitting on laboratory desks and tables. The beverage lab is full of brightly colored liquids in clear bottles. It comes up with the flavor for popular soft drinks, sport drinks, bottled teas, and wine coolers, for all-natural juice drinks, organic soy drinks, beers, and malt liquors. In one pilot kitchen I saw a dapper chemist, a middle-aged man with an elegant tie beneath his lab coat, carefully preparing a batch of cookies with white frosting and pink-and-white sprinkles. In another pilot kitchen I saw a pizza oven, a grill, a milk-shake machine, and a french fryer identical to those I'd seen behind the counter at countless fast food restaurants.

8   In addition to being the world's largest flavor company, IFF manufactures the smell of six of the ten best-selling fine perfumes in the United States. It makes the smell of Estée Lauder's Beautiful, Clinique's Happy, Ralph Lauren's Polo, and Calvin Klein's Eternity. It also makes the smell of household products such as deodorant, dishwashing detergent, bath soap, shampoo, furniture polish, and floor wax. All of these aromas are made through the same basic process: the manipulation of **volatile** chemicals to create a particular smell. The basic science behind the scent of your shaving cream is the same as that governing the flavor of your TV dinner.

9   The aroma of a food can be responsible for as much as 90 percent of its flavor. Scientists now believe that human beings acquired the sense of taste as a way to avoid being poisoned. Edible plants generally taste sweet; deadly ones, bitter. Taste is supposed to help

---

SYNTHESIZE INFORMATION

Annotate: Mark the words in paragraph 6 that describe the lab and what it contains.

Compare: How do Schlosser's details compare and contrast with Sinclair's descriptive details in *The Jungle*? How are the presentations by the two authors similar?

volatile
(vŏl´ə-tl) *adj.* evaporating readily at normal temperatures and pressures.

 SYNTHESIZE INFORMATION

Remind students that **synthesizing information** means taking information from two or more texts to better understand a topic. Ask volunteers to summarize some of the details of Sinclair's description of the meat-packing factory. (**Answer:** *Schlosser portrays a clean place in contrast to the filthy, hot, dangerous factory that Sinclair described, but both authors establish that they are revealing deliberately hidden secrets.*)

For **listening** and **speaking support** for students at varying proficiency levels, see the **Text X-Ray** on pages 538C and 538D.

 ENGLISH LEARNER SUPPORT

Understand Author's Purpose Remind students of common purposes for writing a text: to inform, to persuade, and/or to entertain. Have student pairs use the following frames to gather details and make inferences about the author's purpose in paragraph 7.

- The "snack and savory lab" produces flavors for ___. (*many different crunchy snacks, such as crackers and potato chips, and for pet food*)

- The "confectionery lab" produces flavors for ___. (*things such as candies and mouthwash*)

- The "beverage lab" produces liquid flavors for ___. (*drinks such as bottled teas and soda*)

- The company also produces scents for perfumes and the following household products: ___. (*deodorant, bath soap, etc.*)

(**Sample inference:** *The contrasts between food flavors made for both people and pets and scents made for perfumes and cleaning supplies supports the author's purpose to inform readers about food additives in the United States.*) **LIGHT**

CRITICAL VOCABULARY

volatile: The word volatile describes certain chemicals that are dangerous.

ASK STUDENTS why the author chose a word with a negative connotation to describe the chemicals. (*to imply that additives can be dangerous*)

TEACH

WORD GAPS

Point out to students that there are times when Schlosser uses technical terms, and he also defines these terms. (**Answer:** *Schlosser does not assume that the reader will understand technical terms like "olfactory epithelium." He recognizes that his readers aren't experts and need explanations, and he uses everyday language to make sure his audience will understand the information.*)

NOTICE & NOTE

us differentiate food that's good for us from food that's not. The taste buds on our tongues can detect the presence of half a dozen or so basic tastes, including: sweet, sour, bitter, salty, astringent,[2] and umami (a taste discovered by Japanese researchers, a rich and full sense of deliciousness triggered by amino acids in foods such as shellfish, mushrooms, potatoes, and seaweed). Taste buds offer a relatively limited means of detection, however, compared to the human olfactory system, which can perceive thousands of different chemical aromas. Indeed "flavor" is primarily the smell of gases being released by the chemicals you've just put in your mouth.

10   The act of drinking, sucking, or chewing a substance releases its volatile gases. They flow out of the mouth and up the nostrils, or up the passageway in the back of the mouth, to a thin layer of nerve cells called the olfactory epithelium, located at the base of the nose, right between the eyes. The brain combines the complex smell signals from the epithelium with the simple taste signals from the tongue, assigns a flavor to what's in your mouth, and decides if it's something you want to eat.

11   Babies like sweet tastes and reject bitter ones; we know this because scientists have rubbed various flavors inside the mouths

WORD GAPS

Annotate: Mark an example of technical language in paragraph 10.

Infer: Does Schlosser assume the reader will grasp the meaning of this technical language? Explain.

---

[2] **astringent:** sharp and penetrating; pungent or severe.

APPLYING ACADEMIC VOCABULARY

☐ **infinitesimal**   ☑ **stem**   ☐ **catalyst**   ☐ **conjure**   ☑ **volatile**

Write and Discuss Have students turn to a partner to discuss the following questions. Guide students to include the academic vocabulary words *stem* and *volatile* in their responses. Ask volunteers to share their responses with the class.

- Does learning **stem** from hard work, or vice versa?
- What types of materials or chemicals are **volatile**?

of infants and then recorded their facial reactions. A person's food preferences, like his or her personality, are formed during the first few years of life, through a process of socialization. Toddlers can learn to enjoy hot and spicy food, bland health food, or fast food, depending upon what the people around them eat. The human sense of smell is still not fully understood and can be greatly affected by psychological factors and expectations. The color of a food can determine the perception of its taste. The mind filters out the overwhelming majority of chemical aromas that surround us, focusing intently on some, ignoring others. People can grow accustomed to bad smells or good smells; they stop noticing what once seemed overpowering. Aroma and memory are somehow inextricably linked. A smell can suddenly evoke a long-forgotten moment. The flavors of childhood foods seem to leave an indelible mark, and adults often return to them, without always knowing why. These "comfort foods" become a source of pleasure and reassurance, a fact that fast food chains work hard to promote. Childhood memories of Happy Meals can translate into frequent adult visits to McDonald's, like those of the chain's "heavy users," the customers who eat there four or five times a week.

12   The human craving for flavor has been a largely unacknowledged and unexamined force in history. Royal empires have been built, unexplored lands have been traversed, great religions and

Food Product Design *from* Fast Food Nation   545

ENGLISH LEARNER SUPPORT

Use Linguistic Support Ask students to volunteer to read aloud paragraph 11, with a different student reading each sentence, if possible. Help students with unfamiliar words and discuss the main idea of each sentence after it is read. **MODERATE**

TO CHALLENGE STUDENTS . . .

Imitate Style Have students work in pairs to write a paragraph in the style of Schlosser's text. Tell students to choose an issue in their own community and to decide which audience they wish to persuade. Students should try to imitate Schlosser's voice and syntax. Encourage students to use factual details as evidence.

TEACH

LANGUAGE CONVENTIONS

Remind students that authors use dashes to set off parenthetical or additional information. Authors use dashes for specific reasons. (**Answer:** *The author uses the dashes to set off a group of parenthetical elements that identify the types of "corporate empires" he has in mind as he compares them to the global empires built in the Age of Exploration.*)

ANALYZE AUTHOR'S PURPOSE

Point out that entertaining the reader is a valid secondary purpose even for serious nonfiction with an informational main purpose. (**Answer:** *The story supports his argument that flavorings are chemicals, rather than food; it supports the idea that the flavor and food companies are inventive in the way they employ discoveries, however they occur; it also provides the reader some entertainment.*)

CRITICAL VOCABULARY

infinitesimal: Schlosser writes that flavorings are added to food in tiny amounts.

ASK STUDENTS to compare the meanings of *infinitesimal* with the related but more familiar word *infinite*. (*Infinitesimal refers to extreme smallness, whereas infinite refers to never-ending quantities.*)

NOTICE & NOTE

LANGUAGE CONVENTIONS

Annotate: Mark the phrases set off by dashes in paragraph 12.

Explain: What is the purpose of the dashes in this passage?

ANALYZE AUTHOR'S PURPOSE

Annotate: Mark the sentences in paragraph 13 that describe the discovery of grape flavor.

Infer: What is the author's purpose in including this anecdote?

infinitesimal
(ĭn-fĭn-ĭ-tĕs´ə-məl)
adj. immeasurably or incalculably minute.

---

philosophies have been forever changed by the spice trade. In 1492 Christopher Columbus set sail to find seasoning. Today the influence of flavor in the world marketplace is no less decisive. The rise and fall of corporate empires—of soft drink companies, snack food companies, and fast food chains—is frequently determined by how their products taste.

13   The flavor industry emerged in the mid-nineteenth century, as processed foods began to be manufactured on a large scale. Recognizing the need for flavor additives, the early food processors turned to perfume companies that had years of experience working with essential oils and volatile aromas. The great perfume houses of England, France, and the Netherlands produced many of the first flavor compounds. In the early part of the twentieth century, Germany's powerful chemical industry assumed the technological lead in flavor production. Legend has it that a German scientist discovered methyl anthranilate, one of the first artificial flavors, by accident while mixing chemicals in his laboratory. Suddenly the lab was filled with the sweet smell of grapes. Methyl anthranilate later became the chief flavoring compound of grape Kool-Aid. After World War II, much of the perfume industry shifted from Europe to the United States, settling in New York City near the garment district and the fashion houses. The flavor industry came with it, subsequently moving to New Jersey to gain more plant capacity. Man-made flavor additives were used mainly in baked goods, candies, and sodas until the 1950s, when sales of processed food began to soar. The invention of gas chromatographs and mass spectrometers—machines capable of detecting volatile gases at low levels—vastly increased the number of flavors that could be synthesized. By the mid-1960s the American flavor industry was churning out compounds to supply the taste of Pop Tarts, Bac-Os, Tab, Tang, Filet-O-Fish sandwiches, and literally thousands of other new foods.

14   The American flavor industry now has annual revenues of about $1.4 billion. Approximately ten thousand new processed food products are introduced every year in the United States. Almost all of them require flavor additives. And about nine out of every ten of these new food products fail. The latest flavor innovations and corporate realignments are heralded in publications such as *Food Chemical News, Food Engineering, Chemical Market Reporter,* and *Food Product Design*. The growth of IFF has mirrored that of the flavor industry as a whole. IFF was formed in 1958, through the merger of two small companies. Its annual revenues have grown almost fifteenfold since the early 1970s, and it now has manufacturing facilities in twenty countries.

15   The quality that people seek most of all in a food, its flavor, is usually present in a quantity too **infinitesimal** to be measured by any traditional culinary terms such as ounces or teaspoons. Today's sophisticated spectrometers, gas chromatographs, and headspace vapor analyzers provide a detailed map of a food's flavor components, detecting chemical aromas in amounts as low as one part per billion.

WHEN STUDENTS STRUGGLE . . .

Determine Author's Purpose   Share these strategies for guided or independent analysis.

- Highlight key sentences or phrases that reflect the topic of the passage or paragraph.
- Write a note stating the purpose of each phrase or sentence.
- Review your notes to determine the author's larger purpose.

For additional support, go to the **Reading Studio** and assign the following Level Up **Level Up Tutorial: Author's Purpose**.

The human nose, however, is still more sensitive than any machine yet invented. A nose can detect aromas present in quantities of a few parts per trillion—an amount equivalent to 0.000000000003 percent. Complex aromas, like those of coffee or roasted meat, may be composed of volatile gases from nearly a thousand different chemicals. The smell of a strawberry arises from the interaction of at least 350 different chemicals that are present in minute amounts. The chemical that provides the dominant flavor of bell pepper can be tasted in amounts as low as .02 parts per billion; one drop is sufficient to add flavor to five average size swimming pools. The flavor additive usually comes last, or second to last, in a processed food's list of ingredients (chemicals that add color are frequently used in even smaller amounts). As a result, the flavor of a processed food often costs less than its packaging. Soft drinks contain a larger proportion of flavor additives than most products. The flavor in a twelve-ounce can of Coke costs about half a cent.

16   The Food and Drug Administration does not require flavor companies to disclose the ingredients of their additives, so long as all the chemicals are considered by the agency to be GRAS (Generally Regarded As Safe). This lack of public disclosure enables the companies to maintain the secrecy of their formulas. It also hides the fact that flavor compounds sometimes contain more ingredients than the foods being given their taste. The ubiquitous phrase "artificial strawberry flavor" gives little hint of the chemical wizardry and manufacturing skill that can make a highly processed food taste like a strawberry.

17   A typical artificial strawberry flavor, like the kind found in a Burger King strawberry milk shake, contains the following ingredients: amyl acetate, amyl butyrate, amyl valerate, anethol, anisyl formate, benzyl acetate, benzyl isobutyrate, butyric acid, cinnamyl isobutyrate, cinnamyl valerate, cognac essential oil, diacetyl, dipropyl ketone, ethyl acetate, ethyl amylketone, ethyl butyrate, ethyl cinnamate, ethyl heptanoate, ethyl heptylate, ethyl lactate, ethyl methylphenylglycidate, ethyl nitrate, ethyl propionate, ethyl valerate, heliotropin, hydroxyphrenyl-2-butanone (10 percent solution in alcohol), α-ionone, isobutyl anthranilate, isobutyl butyrate, lemon essential oil, maltol, 4-methylacetophenone, methyl anthranilate, methyl benzoate, methyl cinnamate, methyl heptine carbonate, methyl naphthyl ketone, methyl salicylate, mint essential oil, neroli essential oil, nerolin, neryl isobutyrate, orris butter, phenethyl alcohol, rose, rum ether, γ-undecalactone, vanillin, and solvent.

18   Although flavors usually arise from a mixture of many different volatile chemicals, a single compound often supplies the dominant aroma. Smelled alone, that chemical provides an unmistakable sense of the food. Ethyl-2-methyl butyrate, for example, smells just like an apple. Today's highly processed foods offer a blank palette: whatever chemicals you add to them will give them specific tastes. Adding methyl-2-peridylketone makes something taste like popcorn. Adding ethyl-3-hydroxybutanoate makes it taste like marshmallow.

© Houghton Mifflin Harcourt Publishing Company

NOTICE & NOTE

SYNTHESIZE INFORMATION

Annotate: Mark the equipment and the statistics cited in paragraphs 14–16.

Summarize: What point does Schlosser support by including technical and statistical details? How do these details compare to details Sinclair includes in *The Jungle*?

ANALYZE AUTHOR'S PURPOSE

Annotate: Mark the details in paragraph 18 about the chemicals and what they do.

Infer: What is the author's purpose for including this information on the chemicals?

TEACH

SYNTHESIZE INFORMATION

Remind students to think about the details Sinclair uses in *The Jungle*. Then, think about these details Schlosser includes and why he might include such specific information. (**Answer:** *Schlosser is trying to show how intricate the process of creating is and how technology has changed the way we flavor food. This attention to detail is different from Sinclair's more general descriptions, which fits Sinclair's purpose. Sinclair was not trying to inform or instruct readers on the actual process; he was trying to persuade readers that the process was dangerous to the workers and consumers. Since Sinclair was writing a novel, this much detail would have distracted from the characters and plot.*)

ANALYZE AUTHOR'S PURPOSE

Note that Schlosser does not include definitions of any of these technical terms. Ask students why he might not define technical terms here, but did define terms in other instances. (**Answer:** *He may have intended to overwhelm the reader with the complexity of artificial flavors, as well as to make the reader feel that there is something suspicious about foods containing such flavors.*)

TO CHALLENGE STUDENTS . . .

Debate an Issue Have students have a debate, with one side for and one side against updating and revising the labeling requirements for food products, including those for "natural flavors." Direct them to suggest a course of action, anticipate and address opposing arguments, and provide evidence to support their claims. Encourage students to do additional research to strengthen their evidence.

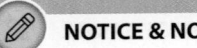

NOTICE & NOTE

SYNTHESIZE INFORMATION

Remind students of Sinclair's discussion of lamb meat. Have students think about why Sinclair included this information and how it is similar to Schlosser's inclusion of consumer preferences. (**Answer:** *Both authors describe consumer preferences that have nothing to do with the reality of what they're eating. In both cases, food companies are fooling them, but in Schlosser's example, consumers are actually fooling themselves by preferring a less healthful alternative.*)

SYNTHESIZE INFORMATION

Annotate: Mark the sentence in paragraph 19 about consumer preferences.

Compare: How is the discussion in the end of this paragraph reminiscent of Sinclair's discussion of lamb meat in *The Jungle*?

The possibilities are now almost limitless. Without affecting the appearance or nutritional value, processed foods could even be made with aroma chemicals such as hexanal (the smell of freshly cut grass) or 3-methyl butanoic acid (the smell of body odor).

19   The 1960s were the heyday of artificial flavors. The synthetic versions of flavor compounds were not subtle, but they did not need to be, given the nature of most processed food. For the past twenty years food processors have tried hard to use only "natural flavors" in their products. According to the FDA, these must be derived entirely from natural sources—from herbs, spices, fruits, vegetables, beef, chicken, yeast, bark, roots, etc. Consumers prefer to see natural flavors on a label, out of a belief that they are healthier. The distinction between artificial and natural flavors can be somewhat arbitrary and absurd, based more on how the flavor has been made than on what it actually contains. "A natural flavor," says Terry Acree, a professor of food science technology at Cornell University, "is a flavor that's been derived with an out-of-date technology." Natural flavors and artificial flavors sometimes contain exactly the same chemicals, produced through different methods. Amyl acetate, for example, provides the dominant note of banana flavor. When you distill it from bananas with a solvent, amyl acetate is a natural flavor. When you produce it by mixing vinegar with amyl alcohol, adding

sulfuric acid as a **catalyst**, amyl acetate is an artificial flavor. Either way it smells and tastes the same. The phrase "natural flavor" is now listed among the ingredients of everything from Stonyfield Farm Organic Strawberry Yogurt to Taco Bell Hot Taco Sauce.

20   A natural flavor is not necessarily healthier or purer than an artificial one. When almond flavor (benzaldehyde) is derived from natural sources, such as peach and apricot pits, it contains traces of hydrogen cyanide, a deadly poison. Benzaldehyde derived through a different process—by mixing oil of clove and the banana flavor, amyl acetate—does not contain any cyanide. Nevertheless, it is legally considered an artificial flavor and sells at a much lower price. Natural and artificial flavors are now manufactured at the same chemical plants, places that few people would associate with Mother Nature. Calling any of these flavors "natural" requires a flexible attitude toward the English language and a fair amount of irony.

21   The small and elite group of scientists who create most of the flavor in most of the food now consumed in the United States are called "flavorists." They draw upon a number of disciplines in their work: biology, psychology, physiology, and organic chemistry. A flavorist is a chemist with a trained nose and a poetic sensibility. Flavors are created by blending scores of different chemicals in tiny amounts, a process governed by scientific principles but demanding a fair amount of art. In an age when delicate aromas, subtle flavors, and microwave ovens do not easily coexist, the job of the flavorist is to **conjure** illusions about processed food and, in the words of one flavor company's literature, to ensure "consumer likeability." The flavorists with whom I spoke were charming, cosmopolitan, and ironic. They were also discreet, in keeping with the dictates of their trade. They were the sort of scientist who not only enjoyed fine wine, but could also tell you the chemicals that gave each vintage its unique aroma. One flavorist compared his work to composing music. A well-made flavor compound will have a "top note," followed by a "dry-down," and a "leveling-off," with different chemicals responsible for each stage. The taste of a food can be radically altered by minute changes in the flavoring mix. "A little odor goes a long way," one flavorist said.

22   In order to give a processed food the proper taste, a flavorist must always consider the food's "mouthfeel"— the unique combination of textures and chemical interactions that affects how the flavor is perceived. The mouthfeel can be adjusted through the use of various fats, gums, starches, emulsifiers, and stabilizers. The aroma chemicals of a food can be precisely analyzed, but mouthfeel is much harder to measure. How does one quantify a french fry's crispness? <u>Food technologists are now conducting basic research in rheology, a branch of physics that examines the flow and deformation of materials. A number of companies sell sophisticated devices that attempt to measure mouthfeel.</u> The Universal TA-XT2 Texture Analyzer, produced by the Texture Technologies Corporation, performs calculations based on data derived from twenty-five separate probes. It is essentially a mechanical mouth. It gauges the most important

---

catalyst
(kăt′l-ĭst) *n.* a substance, usually used in small amounts relative to the reactants, that modifies and increases the rate of a reaction without being consumed in the process.

conjure
(kŏn′jər) *v.* to influence or effect by or as if by magic.

WORD GAPS

Notice & Note: Mark details that help you understand what "rheology" means in paragraph 22.

Analyze: Why do companies employ specialists from scientific branches such as rheology?

WORD GAPS

Remind students that authors often define technical terms, and they set those definitions off with different types of punctuation. Authors may continue to explain a term in the following sentences. Remind students to look for context clues when determining the meaning of a word. (**Answer:** *Schlosser defines "rheology" and then continues to explain what companies are doing. Companies employ specialists to get the "mouthfeel" of food right to make sure that consumers like it.*)

 ENGLISH LEARNER SUPPORT

Build Oral Fluency The vocabulary word *conjure* presents an opportunity for students to practice pronunciation. Direct students to the pronunciation in the margin, and ask them to pronounce the word. Correct any errors. For example, some students might pronounce a long *u* in the second syllable. Invite students to point out other words in the text that they find hard to pronounce and have them repeat the words after you. **SUBSTANTIAL**

CRITICAL VOCABULARY

catalyst: In the chemical process that Schlosser describes, sulfuric acid is the substance that causes the reaction to happen.

ASK STUDENTS what would happen in a chemical process if no catalyst were added. (*The chemicals might not combine, or they would combine more slowly.*)

conjure: When the glass bottles were opened, it seemed as though specific foods had suddenly appeared in the room.

ASK STUDENTS what smells conjure good memories for them. (*Responses will vary. For example, students might say the smell of turkey reminds them of the holidays and their family.*)

APPLYING ACADEMIC VOCABULARY

☑ **conjure**   ☑ **infinitesimal**   ☐ **volatile**   ☐ **stem**   ☑ **catalyst**

Write and Discuss Have students turn to a partner to discuss the following questions. Guide students to include the academic vocabulary words *conjure, infinitesimal,* and *catalyst* in their responses. Ask volunteers to share their responses with the class.

- If you were a magician, what would you **conjure**?
- Which is more **infinitesimal,** a bacterium or a planet?
- Name an influential public speaker who is thought of as a **catalyst** for change.

SYNTHESIZE INFORMATION

Ask students to think back to what Sinclair wrote about the practices of the meatpacking company. If necessary, remind them of what Sinclair wrote. *(Both companies are not fully honest with consumers in saying what is in or who's behind their food products)*

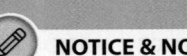

rheological properties of a food—the bounce, creep, breaking point, density, crunchiness, chewiness, gumminess, lumpiness, rubberiness, springiness, slipperiness, smoothness, softness, wetness, juiciness, spreadability, spring-back, and tackiness.

23 Some of the most important advances in flavor manufacturing are now occurring in the field of biotechnology. Complex flavors are being made through fermentation, enzyme reactions, fungal cultures, and tissue cultures. All of the flavors being created through these methods—including the ones being synthesized by funguses—are considered natural flavors by the FDA. The new enzyme-based processes are responsible for extremely lifelike dairy flavors. One company now offers not just butter flavor, but also fresh creamy butter, cheesy butter, milky butter, savory melted butter, and super-concentrated butter flavor, in liquid or powder form. The development of new fermentation techniques, as well as new techniques for heating mixtures of sugar and amino acids, have led to the creation of much more realistic meat flavors. The McDonald's Corporation will not reveal the exact origin of the natural flavor added to its french fries. In response to inquiries from *Vegetarian Journal*, however, McDonald's did acknowledge that its fries derive some of their characteristic flavor from "animal products."

24 Other popular fast foods derive their flavor from unexpected sources. Wendy's Grilled Chicken Sandwich, for example, contains beef extracts. Burger King's BK Broiler Chicken Breast Patty contains "natural smoke flavor." A firm called Red Arrow Products Company specializes in smoke flavor, which is added to barbecue sauces and processed meats. Red Arrow manufactures natural smoke flavor by charring sawdust and capturing the aroma chemicals released into the air. The smoke is captured in water and then bottled, so that other companies can sell food which seems to have been cooked over a fire.

SYNTHESIZE INFORMATION

Annotate: Mark the sentence in paragraph 25 that explains why Grainger disagrees with the author's suggestion.

Compare: How is the refusal to place IFF's logo on products similar to the marketing practices of the meatpacking company Sinclair wrote about?

25 In a meeting room at IFF, Brian Grainger let me sample some of the company's flavors. It was an unusual taste test; there wasn't any food to taste. Grainger is a senior flavorist at IFF, a soft-spoken chemist with graying hair, an English accent, and a fondness for understatement. He could easily be mistaken for a British diplomat or the owner of a West End brasserie with two Michelin stars. Like many in the flavor industry, he has an Old World, old-fashioned sensibility which seems out of step with our brand-conscious, egocentric age. When I suggested that IFF should put its own logo on the products that contain its flavors—instead of allowing other brands to enjoy the consumer loyalty and affection inspired by those flavors—Grainger politely disagreed, assuring me such a thing would never be done. In the absence of public credit or acclaim, the small and secretive fraternity of flavor chemists praises one another's work. Grainger can often tell, by analyzing the flavor formula of a product, which of his counterparts at a rival firm devised it. And he enjoys walking down supermarket aisles, looking at the many products that contain his flavors, even if no one else knows it.

TO CHALLENGE STUDENTS . . .

Collaborative Discussion Divide students into small groups, and have them discuss how reading this selection has affected their ideas about fast food. Have students create a chart in which they list specific facts or passages from the selection that surprised them, changed their ideas, or confirmed their existing ideas. Ask them to comment on the effect each example had on them.

26   Grainger had brought a dozen small glass bottles from the lab. After he opened each bottle, I dipped a fragrance testing filter into it. The filters were long white strips of paper designed to absorb aroma chemicals without producing off-notes. Before placing the strips of paper before my nose, I closed my eyes. Then I inhaled deeply, and one food after another was conjured from the glass bottles. I smelled fresh cherries, black olives, sautéed onions, and shrimp. Grainger's most remarkable creation took me by surprise. After closing my eyes, I suddenly smelled a grilled hamburger. The aroma was uncanny, almost miraculous. It smelled like someone in the room was flipping burgers on a hot grill. But when I opened my eyes, there was just a narrow strip of white paper and a smiling flavorist.

✎ CHECK YOUR UNDERSTANDING

Have students answer the questions independently.

Answers:

1. C

2. J

3. A

If they answer any questions incorrectly, have them reread the text to confirm their understanding. Then, they may proceed to ANALYZE THE TEXT on page 552.

CHECK YOUR UNDERSTANDING

Answer these questions before moving on to the **Analyze the Text** section on the following page.

1 What caused the growth of the flavor industry after World War II?

A The rise of fast-food chains

B The shift toward healthier eating

C The spread of processed foods

D The arrival of German chemists in the United States

2 How much of food's flavor is probably a function of smell?

F 30 percent

G 50 percent

H 75 percent

J 90 percent

3 Which industry spearheaded the development of food flavors?

A Chemical

B Agriculture

C Medical

D Dairy

ENGLISH LEARNER SUPPORT

Oral Assessment Use the following questions to assess students' comprehension and speaking skills.

1. Why were there more flavor companies after World War II? (*There was an increase in processed food.*)

2. Smell affects food's flavor. How much of a food's flavor is actually smell? (*90 percent*)

3. What industry was most important in the development of food flavors? (*chemical*)
   MODERATE/LIGHT

ANALYZE THE TEXT

Possible answers:

1. **DOK 4:** *The first two paragraphs connect the reader to a familiar product to engage his or her attention before using McDonald's dilemma to bring the focus of the text onto Schlosser's actual subject, the science and art of flavoring.*

2. **DOK 3:** *Schlosser includes so much detail about the IFF plant in order to impress the reader in specific ways with the power and capacity of the flavor industry, as well as the extent of its influence.*

3. **DOK 3:** *Similarities: The two types of flavors are identical in chemical composition and are manufactured at the same plants. Differences: The chemicals in natural flavorings are extracted from plants or animals, while those in artificial flavorings are produced through reactions of other chemicals. Schlosser explains these terms in detail in order to make his point that neither kind of flavoring truly occurs naturally.*

4. **DOK 3:** *Schlosser's audience will most likely be surprised, shocked, and angry. They might think more about what they eat and read the labels on the foods they buy. Readers might tell other people of what they learned so more people are aware of what is happening in the food industry.*

5. **DOK 4:** *Schlosser wants to educate the public so they know what they are eating. He may want to convince people not to eat processed foods, although his statement that 90 percent of Americans' food spending is on processed foods marks that as a monumental task. He might hope that the information would prompt citizens to push legislators to pass some new laws governing the use of flavoring.*

RESEARCH

Remind students to use reliable sources and to confirm their findings in more than one source. Help students brainstorm phrases they can use to locate the information. Remind them of the best way to use search engines, such as using quotation marks around phrases.

Extend Allow students to work in pairs to complete the activity. Before students begin, ask volunteers for examples of how to create a guide. Students can use the guide as a model.

⊜ RESPOND

ANALYZE THE TEXT

Support your responses with evidence from the text. ⊟ NOTEBOOK

1. **Synthesize** What do the first two paragraphs suggest about the author's purpose? Cite text evidence in your response.

2. **Draw Conclusions** Why does Schlosser include so much detail about his visit to the IFF plant in New Jersey?

3. **Compare** What are the similarities and differences between "artificial flavors" and "natural flavors"? Why does Schlosser explain the terms in such detail?

4. **Draw Conclusions** What might Schlosser want his audience to do after reading this selection?

5. **Notice & Note** What is Schlosser's purpose in listing all the chemical ingredients in "a typical artificial strawberry flavor, like the kind found in a Burger King strawberry milk shake" (paragraph 17)?

RESEARCH TIP
When researching information on the website of a nonprofit organization, it is best to check other sources to ensure the information is accurate.

RESEARCH

The author explores the definition of *natural flavors* in this extensive piece of investigative reporting. Many other phrases appear on food labels or packages. Investigate the following phrases, explain their meaning, and state any cautions that should be understood when interpreting that phrase.

PHRASE	DEFINITION	CAUTION
For plant foods: "certified organic"	*crops must be grown without synthetic fertilizers/pesticides; cannot be genetically engineered/irradiated*	*Organic plants may produce more toxins.*
For animal foods: "no antibiotics"	*animal was given no antibiotics while alive*	*could be used for animals raised in conditions considered by some as unhealthful*
For poultry: "free range"	*could be used for animals raised in conditions considered by some as unhealthful*	*amount of time not specified; other living conditions not limited; government standard does not apply to egg-producing chickens*

Extend Food packages have nutritional labels that must meet certain standards. Find out which nutrients are listed and what information is provided. Make an easy-to-follow guide to a nutrient label for consumers.

WHEN STUDENTS STRUGGLE . . .

Reteach: Author's Purpose Remind students that authors can have more than one purpose. While Schlosser's purpose is largely to inform his readers, he has another purpose, which is revealed by his word choice and the details he chooses to include. Ask students what types of words Schlosser uses and how those might indicate his purpose. Have students work with a partner to create a chart in which they list details that Schlosser provides that indicate his other purposes for writing.

 For additional support, go to the **Reading Studio** and assign the following LEVEL UP **Level Up Tutorial: Author's Purpose.**

CREATE AND PRESENT

Write a Rhetorical Analysis One of Schlosser's purposes for writing is to convince people to take action based on the information he shared about the "flavor industry." Write a rhetorical analysis in which you evaluate whether Schlosser achieved this purpose.

- ❏ Write a thesis statement in which you state whether Schlosser's essay convinced you that taking action is necessary.
- ❏ Cite details from Schlosser's text, including anecdotes, scientific evidence, and technical language.
- ❏ Explain whether these details adequately support his purpose and whether you are convinced to take action.

Present an Interview Work with a partner to turn the information in Eric Schlosser's text into an interview. One will take the role of the host of a talk show posing questions to the other, who will play Schlosser as an author on tour promoting his book.

- ❏ Decide what you will address in the interview. Research Schlosser's book or other sources to find additional information you need.
- ❏ Write the interview script, using book passages as the basis of your questions and answers. Include follow-up questions.
- ❏ Use volume, speaking rate, and tonal changes to indicate reactions to questions and answers and communicate information effectively.
- ❏ Choose diction carefully to reach a wide audience; include explanations of difficult or unfamiliar concepts.

RESPOND TO THE ESSENTIAL QUESTION

 Why do humans cause harm?

Gather Information Review your annotations and notes on "Food Product Design." Then, add relevant details to your Response Log. As you determine which information to include, think about:

- the way information can influence decision making
- how our experiences shape our preferences
- the power of the individual in complex modern society

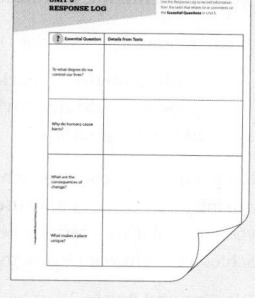

 Go to **Using Textual Evidence** in the **Writing Studio** for help.

Go to **Participating in Collaborative Discussions: Listening and Responding** in the **Speaking and Listening Studio** for to apply group tips to one-to-one discussions.

ACADEMIC VOCABULARY

As you write and discuss what you learned from the excerpt, be sure to use the Academic Vocabulary words. Check off each of the words that you use.

- ❏ **ambiguous**
- ❏ **clarify**
- ❏ **implicit**
- ❏ **revise**
- ❏ **somewhat**

CREATE AND PRESENT

Write a Rhetorical Analysis Explain to students that a rhetorical analysis is an evaluation of whether the author achieved his or her purpose for writing. Remind them that authors use various strategies, depending on their purpose. Point out that students may also want to examine the structure of Schlosser's text in their analysis.

Present an Interview Encourage students to think about questions the public might want to know about the fast food industry. If possible, give students an opportunity to rehearse the interview before presenting it to the class. If recording audio or video is possible, have them record themselves performing the interview. Then, have them watch or listen to the recording to look for ways to improve it before presenting it to the class. Encourage students to think about the roles they are taking (interviewer or author on book tour) and create an idea of the character they will be performing.

RESPOND TO THE ESSENTIAL QUESTION

Allow time for students to add details from "Food Product Design" to their Unit 5 Response Logs.

CRITICAL VOCABULARY

Answers:

1. *the catalyst triggers or helps the desired chemical reaction between the ingredients that create the flavor.*

2. *"natural flavor" that is manufactured in processing plants.*

3. *the chemicals are present in such tiny quantities.*

4. *the process is so mysterious and so different from that found in nature, that it seems almost magical.*

5. *they might explode or suddenly change state.*

VOCABULARY STRATEGY:
Understand Technical Terms

Answers:

Students will have a rich array of possible terms from which to choose, from additives *and* nondisclosure forms *in the early paragraphs through the many chemicals and scientific instruments listed in the middle to* Michelin stars *and* fragrance testing filters *at the end. Students should verify the meanings they infer and give plausible rationales for Schlosser's decision to suggest meaning or not, focusing on the relevance of the term to his purpose.*

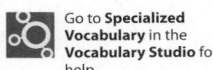 **RESPOND**

CRITICAL VOCABULARY

WORD BANK
stem
volatile
infinitesimal
catalyst
conjure

Practice and Apply Complete each sentence to show your knowledge of the correct meaning of each Critical Vocabulary word.

1. Producing artificial flavors requires a **catalyst** like sulfuric acid because —

2. The taste of fast-food french fries now **stems** from —

3. Everyday measuring spoons cannot be used to measure the **infinitesimal** amounts of chemicals in a particular flavor because —

4. Some chemists seem to **conjure** foods because —

5. **Volatile** chemicals have to be kept in closed containers because —

 Go to **Specialized Vocabulary** in the **Vocabulary Studio** for help.

VOCABULARY STRATEGY:
Understand Technical Terms

Schlosser's style involves the use of specialized vocabulary in the form of technical terms. By examining the context for each term, you can understand how they serve Schlosser's purpose. Sometimes Schlosser defines the terms.

> Legend has it that a German scientist discovered <u>methyl anthranilate</u>, one of the first artificial flavors, by accident while mixing chemicals in his laboratory.

At other times, Schlosser does not define the meaning of technical terms.

> Adding <u>methyl-2-peridylketone</u> makes something taste like popcorn. Adding <u>ethyl-3-hydroxybutanoate</u> makes it taste like marshmallow.

Neither of these sentences actually defines the technical terms, but you can infer from how they are used that they are names of chemicals. As you encounter such terms when analyzing the selection, ask yourself why Schlosser might want to use them instead of simpler words.

Practice and Apply Work with a partner to find five other technical terms that Schlosser uses. Try to figure out the meaning of each term from its context, verifying your prediction using print or digital resources. Reach a consensus on why Schlosser might have wanted to use each term and why he did or did not provide context clues to its meaning.

EL **ENGLISH LEARNER SUPPORT**

Vocabulary Strategy Help students understand that authors often provide context clues, such as definitions, restatements, or examples, to help readers understand new or difficult terms. Read aloud the first example sentence. Then, project the sentence. Point out the comma after the term *methyl anthranilate*. Explain that a comma after an unfamiliar word often signals that the author is providing additional information about the term. Read aloud the information after the comma and point out that this explains the term. Have students find another example of an unfamiliar or technical term, and help them look for context clues that explain the word. **ALL LEVELS**

LANGUAGE CONVENTIONS: Dashes

Sometimes a writer wants to interrupt the main thought of a sentence with a word, expression, phrase, or sentence called a **parenthetical element**. Usually such parenthetical elements are set off with parentheses or with commas. However, writers sometimes use dashes to set off elements in a sentence. If the break in thought is abrupt, the parenthetical element is set off with dashes.

> **That ingredient helps to explain not only why the fries taste so good, but also why most fast food—indeed, most of the food Americans eat today—tastes the way it does.**

Sometimes dashes are used to create pauses, often for ironic, satirical, or dramatic effect.

> **The mix gave the fries their unique flavor—and more saturated beef fat per ounce than a McDonald's hamburger.**

Practice and Apply Add the italicized parenthetical elements to the following sentences, setting them off with dashes.

1. Flavors made from natural ingredients are sometimes considered healthier. *herbs, fruits, vegetables, chicken, yeast, and bark*

2. The french fries are delicious. *and very fattening*

3. Flavorists create the flavor in most of the food we eat. *scientists with trained noses and poetic sensibilities*

4. One remarkable creation took Schlosser by surprise. *a strip of paper that smelled just like a grilled hamburger*

Go to **Dashes** in the **Grammar Studio** for help.

LANGUAGE CONVENTIONS: Dashes

Review the information about dashes and then review each example sentence. Help students understand why authors might choose to use dashes rather than commas or parentheses. Note that dashes are more obvious, and therefore signal to the reader a break in thought or important information. Have students find another example in the text and explain why the author used dashes.

Practice and Apply

Answers:

1. *Flavors made from natural ingredients—herbs, fruits, vegetables, chicken, yeast, and bark—are sometimes considered healthier.*

2. *The French fries are delicious—and very fattening.*

3. *Flavorists—scientists with trained noses and poetic sensibilities—create the flavors in most of the food we eat.*

4. *One remarkable creation took Schlosser by surprise—a strip of paper that smelled just like a grilled hamburger.*

ENGLISH LEARNER SUPPORT

Language Conventions Use the following supports with students at varying proficiency levels:

- Have students find other sentences in "Food Product Design" that use dashes. Have students choral read the sentences and then copy them into their notebooks. Help students understand why the author used the dashes. Provide sentence frames with possible answer options. For example: *The author used the dashes to (give an example, provide a definition, add information).* **SUBSTANTIAL**

- Have students work with a partner to write original sentences using dashes. Then, have students exchange sentences with another pair. Partners should write why they think the writers used dashes in their sentences. **MODERATE**

- Have students write one sentence modeled on each of the examples from "Food Product Design." Then, have them explain to a partner why the dashes in each sentence perform the same function as the corresponding example. **LIGHT**

COMPARE AUTHOR'S PURPOSE

Remind students that *The Jungle* is a novel. Ask students to discuss how a novel can also be a type of investigative journalism. *(It can address an issue of concern in the real world and can be based on thorough real-world research. Readers of* The Jungle *were aware that the author's main purpose was to expose real-world injustice.)*

Have students work with a partner to complete the graphic organizer. If necessary, review the terms *style* and *tone*.

ANALYZE THE TEXTS

Possible answers:

1. **DOK 4:** *The setting of* The Jungle *is an early 1900s meatpacking plant; that of "Food Product Design" is a modern chemical processing lab. Each workplace reflects the main topic of its selection: the mistreatment of animals and workers in Sinclair's case; the development of chemical flavorings in Schlosser's.*

2. **DOK 3:** *The Jungle is a literary text, and "Food Product Design" is informational nonfiction. Sinclair's tone is a mix of barely suppressed outrage and amazement at the inhumanity and corruption of the meatpacking plant with a healthy dose of anger at the treatment of the workers. He presents many facts in a reportorial style while also using vivid language that appeals to emotion. Both come through his characters' observations and reactions. Schlosser's tone is more purely informational journalism tempered by irony to convey both appreciation for the work of the flavorists and concern about their art.*

3. **DOK 3:** *Students' choices of passages will vary. Possible answer: Vivid imagery helps both writers achieve their purposes by capturing the readers' attention and creating an emotional response.*

4. **DOK 4:** *Both writers, using a mix of information and irony, deal with the various claims of food companies and the mysterious or complicated ingredients of processed foods. Schlosser relates scientific facts. Sinclair uses descriptions and a tone of outrage.*

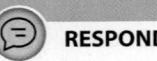 **RESPOND**

Collaborate & Compare

from
THE JUNGLE
Novel by Upton Sinclair

FOOD PRODUCT DESIGN
from **FAST FOOD NATION**
Investigative Journalism
Eric Schlosser

COMPARE AUTHOR'S PURPOSE

Sinclair and Schlosser are both investigative journalists; however, Sinclair wrote fiction about the food industry while Schlosser wrote nonfiction. The content and style of each work allows you to infer each author's specific purpose. As you analyze each selection, ask yourself these questions:

- What are the topics the author writes about?
- What messages does the author communicate about the topics?
- What tone or attitude does the author express?
- What is distinctive about each author's style and rhetoric?
- What action does the author want readers to take?

In a small group, complete the table with similarities and differences between the two authors, noting how these characteristics reflect their purposes. Then, work together to write a paragraph comparing their purposes.

	SINCLAIR: *THE JUNGLE*	SCHLOSSER: "FOOD PRODUCT DESIGN"
Topics		
Tone		
Style		
Readers' action		

ANALYZE THE TEXTS

Discuss these questions in your group.

1. **Analyze** What are the workplace settings described in each selection? How does the workplace relate to each author's purpose?

2. **Compare** How does the tone of each selection reflect the different genres and the different authors' purposes?

3. **Cite Evidence** Select two passages from each selection that contain vivid imagery. How do these passages help each author achieve his purpose?

4. **Synthesize** What similar topics do these selections address? What are similarities and differences in the approaches that the writers use to present these topics?

 ENGLISH LEARNER SUPPORT

Ask Questions Use the following questions to help students compare the selections.

1. Were you surprised with what you learned about the food industry? What surprised you the most? *(Possible response: I was surprised to learn that much of what we eat isn't what we think. I was most surprised by the fact that most of what we taste is actually what we smell.)*

2. What has changed about the way food is prepared since *The Jungle* was published? *(There are more rules about how food is prepared. There are more chemicals used to make food taste good.)* **MODERATE/LIGHT**

RESEARCH AND SHARE

Now, your group can continue exploring the ideas in these texts by collaborating on research to share as a multimedia presentation. Follow these steps:

1. **Conduct research** Find out more about food processing today compared with the practices mentioned in *The Jungle*. Include how foods are changed or enhanced as described in the example from "Food Product Design." Discuss your research within your group and list the similarities and differences to those of Sinclair's era.

2. **Decide on the most important topics** Decide as a group on the topics and key information to present as a comparison to earlier times. Discuss one or more multimedia elements that could be used to clarify and enhance the information. Use a chart to take notes on your discussion.

TOPIC	KEY POINTS	MEDIA

Go to **Using Media in a Presentation** in the **Speaking and Listening Studio** for help.

3. **Develop a plan** Choose one topic from the chart to use as the basis of the presentation. Discuss which medium would be the most effective presentation tool. Then, outline the content and organize the other elements of the presentation. Assign group members tasks such as writing narration and finding media to use. Be sure to reserve time to rehearse.

4. **Present to the class** Now it is time to present to the class. Make sure the narration is clear and concise, and coordinate the media with the content. Allow time after each key point for questions from the class.

© Houghton Mifflin Harcourt Publishing Company

Collaborate & Compare   557

RESEARCH AND SHARE

Divide students into small groups. Review with students any software they will be using to complete their presentations and invite them to discuss strategies for collaborating and dividing the work load.

1. **Conduct research** Review with students what constitutes acceptable source material and how they can identify reputable sources. Remind students to confirm information with more than one source. Review proper citation format.

2. **Decide on the most important topics** Review the graphic organizers from earlier in the unit that students have used to synthesize information. Have students work together to complete the graphic organizer.

3. **Develop a plan** Circulate and review with each group their strategies for sharing the work and managing their time. Suggest that students think about features of different media and how they relate to their purpose and desired audience for this presentation.

4. **Present to the class** Make sure students have taken time to rehearse their presentation within the group, providing feedback on each other's delivery. Suggest that students think of possible questions their audience might have and practice answering them.

WHEN STUDENTS STRUGGLE...

Use Graphic Organizers Students may benefit from the use of graphic organizers at each level of this project. During the research stage, they may want to use note cards to keep track of information and sources. Suggest they use an outline to develop the presentation and use note cards during their presentations. They should write one idea on each card. Remind them not to read from the cards, but to glance at them to remind them of their main ideas. Encourage students to practice their presentations before presenting to the class.

 For additional support, go to the **Reading Studio** and assign the following **Level Up Tutorial: Taking Notes and Outlining.**

READER'S CHOICE

Setting a Purpose Have students review their Unit 5 Response Logs and think about what they've already learned about the power humans wield and how they interact with and build unique places. As they choose their Independent Reading selections, encourage them to consider what more they want to know.

NOTICE & NOTE

Explain that some selections may contain multiple signposts; others may contain only one. And the same type of signpost can occur many times in the same text.

LEARNING MINDSET

Seeking Challenges Remind students that having the willingness to take on challenges is essential to having a learning mindset. In fact, overcoming challenges is key to developing skills and intelligence. Assure students that they are not expected to be perfect and that making mistakes is part of the learning process. By taking risks and trying different strategies, students can learn to overcome challenges.

 INDEPENDENT READING

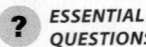 **ESSENTIAL QUESTIONS**

Review the four Essential Questions for this unit on page 453.

Reader's Choice

Setting a Purpose Select one or more of these options from your eBook to continue your exploration of the Essential Questions.

- Read the descriptions to see which text grabs your interest.
- Think about which genres you enjoy reading.

Notice & Note

In this unit you practiced noticing and noting the signposts and asking big questions about nonfiction. As you read independently, these signposts and others will aid your understanding. Below are the anchor questions to ask when you read literature and nonfiction.

Reading Literature: Stories, Poems, and Plays	
Signpost	**Anchor Question**
Contrasts and Contradictions	Why did the character act that way?
Aha Moment	How might this change things?
Tough Questions	What does this make me wonder about?
Words of the Wiser	What's the lesson for the character?
Again and Again	Why might the author keep bringing this up?
Memory Moment	Why is this memory important?

Reading Nonfiction: Essays, Articles, and Arguments	
Signpost	**Anchor Question(s)**
Big Questions	What surprised me? What did the author think I already knew? What challenged, changed, or confirmed what I already knew?
Contrasts and Contradictions	What is the difference, and why does it matter?
Extreme or Absolute Language	Why did the author use this language?
Numbers and Stats	Why did the author use these numbers or amounts?
Quoted Words	Why was this person quoted or cited, and what did this add?
Word Gaps	Do I know this word from someplace else? Does it seem like technical talk for this topic? Do clues in the sentence help me understand the word?

 ENGLISH LEARNER SUPPORT

Develop Fluency Select a passage from the text that matches students' reading abilities. Read the passage aloud while students follow along silently.

- Read aloud a brief passage from one of the selections to model it for students. Then, have them read it back to you. Have students reread the passage three times. Check their comprehension by asking yes/no questions about the passage. **SUBSTANTIAL**
- Have pairs of students take turns reading and rereading the passage aloud to each other. Have them time each other to track their improvement. **MODERATE**

- Allow more fluent readers to select their own texts. Set a specific time for them to read silently, such as 30 minutes. To check their comprehension, have them write a summary of what they have read. **LIGHT**

 Go to the **Reading Studio** for additional support in developing fluency.

You can preview these texts in Unit 5 of your eBook.

Then, check off the text or texts that you select to read on your own.

SHORT STORY

The Men in the Storm.
Stephen Crane

Wait outside in a blizzard with a group of homeless men as they anxiously line up to be let into a charity house.

SHORT STORY

A Journey
Edith Wharton

Find out how a woman, accompanied by her gravely ill husband, copes with a cross-country train journey.

SHORT STORY

A Wagner Matinee
Willa Cather

A concert triggers memories and revives life-changing questions for a young man and his aging aunt.

ARTICLE

Evidence that Robots Are Winning the Race for American Jobs
Claire Cain Miller

Real-life data give rise to new predictions as to whether humans or robots are winning the race for jobs.

ARTICLE

Healthy Eaters, Strong Minds: What School Gardens Teach Kids
Paige Pfleger

Why are teenagers across the country digging in the dirt, and what do they get from it?

Collaborate and Share   Join a partner to discuss what you learned from at least one of your independent readings.

- Give a brief synopsis or summary of the text.
- Describe any signposts that you noticed in the text, and explain what they revealed to you.
- Describe what you most enjoyed or found most challenging about the text. Give specific examples.
- Decide if you would recommend the text to others. Why or why not?

 Go to the **Reading Studio** for more resources on **Notice & Note.**

WHEN STUDENTS STRUGGLE . . .

Keep a Reading Log As students read their selected texts, have them keep a reading log for each selection to note signposts and their thoughts about them. Use their logs to assess how well they are noticing and reflecting on elements of their texts.

Reading Log for (title)		
Location	**Signpost I Noticed**	**My Notes about It**

MATCHING STUDENTS TO TEXTS

Use the following information to guide students in choosing their texts.

The Men in the Storm   **Lexile: 1200L**
  Genre: Short Story
  Overall Rating: Challenging

A Journey   **Lexile: 870L**
  Genre: Short Story
  Overall Rating: Accessible

A Wagner Matinee   **Lexile: 1470L**
  Genre: Short Story
  Overall Rating: Challenging

**Evidence that Robots
Are Winning the Race for
American Jobs**   **Lexile: 1240L**
  Genre: Article
  Overall Rating: Accessible

**Healthy Eaters, Strong Minds:
What School Gardens
Teach Kids**   **Lexile: 1180L**
  Genre: Article
  Overall Rating: Accessible

Collaborate and Share To assess how well students read the selections, walk around the room and listen to their conversations. Encourage students to be focused and specific in their comments.

Online **Ed** **for Assessment**

- Independent Reading Selection Tests

Encourage students to visit the **Reading Studio** to download a handy bookmark of **NOTICE & NOTE** signposts.

UNIT  5 Task

• WRITE A SHORT STORY

MENTOR TEXT

THE STORY OF AN HOUR

Short Story by Kate Chopin

LEARNING OBJECTIVES

Writing Task

- Write a short story that connects to one of the Essential Questions.
- Develop theme, setting, plot, conflict, and characterization.
- Use strategies to plan writing.
- Use the Mentor Text as a model for point of view, irony, figurative language, and foreshadowing.
- Use description to create imagery.
- Incorporate figurative language into writing.
- Revise draft for improvement.
- Conduct a peer review.
- **Language** Write a short story using sensory details to create imagery.

Assign the Writing Task in **Ed.**

Online

RESOURCES

- Unit 5 Response Log

- Writing Studio: Writing Narratives

- Grammar Studio: Module 8: Lesson 7: Active and Passive Voice

Language X-Ray: English Learner Support

Use the instruction below and the supports and scaffolds in the Teacher's Edition to help you guide students of different proficiency levels.

INTRODUCE THE WRITING TASK

Explain that a **short story** is a creative piece of writing that has a beginning, middle, and end. Often, authors' ideas for short stories come from personal experiences, but they do not have to be entirely based on the truth. Remind students that the theme of their stories will address one of the Essential Questions. Provide sentence frames to help students respond to the Essential Questions.

Sample sentence frames: *One consequence of change is _____. We control our lives when _____.* Then, use a Think-Pair-Share to get students to brainstorm about personal experiences that relate to their responses. Ask: *Who was with you? What did you do? Why?* As they share details about personal experiences with a partner, have students jot down words or phrases that may help to shape their short stories.

WRITING

Use Imagery

Ask students to consider their five senses. Use gestures, images, or manipulatives to communicate about sensory experiences with students.

Use the following supports with students at varying proficiency levels:

- Provide a list of words related to the five senses. Display a model paragraph that describes a setting using one word from each sense category. Have students copy the paragraph. **SUBSTANTIAL**

- Give students sentence frames to help them complete opening paragraphs describing either the setting or main character of their story. Sample frames: ___ (I/he/she) heard a ___ noise. It sounded like ___. ___ (I/he/she) wore ___ because the day was ___ outside. **MODERATE**

- Direct students to complete their drafts, making sure to include details that relate to each of the five senses. **LIGHT**

SPEAKING

Record a Podcast

Help students prepare a podcast of their story, as suggested in the Publish step of the Student Edition, page 565.

Direct students to use a free text-to-audio speech software program. Work with students to type or upload their stories into the software. Use the following supports with students at varying levels:

- Allow students to listen and read along with the synthetic voice while recording their podcasts. **SUBSTANTIAL**

- Direct students to record 1–2 minutes of their story for their podcast. Have students listen to their own voices and compare their pronunciation with the pronunciation of the audio software. **MODERATE**

- Allow students to share their podcasts in a small group. Ask students to paraphrase one another's stories as a way of retelling information and confirming understanding. **LIGHT**

WRITE A SHORT STORY

Introduce students to the Writing Task by reading the introductory paragraph with them. Remind students to refer to the notes they recorded in their Unit 5 Response Logs as they plan and draft their short stories. The Response Logs should contain ideas about the choices people make and the consequences of those choices. Drawing on these different perspectives will make their own writing more interesting and well informed.

For **writing support** for students at varying proficiency levels, see the **Language X-Ray** on page 560B.

USE THE MENTOR TEXT

Point out that students' short stories should be similar in format to "The Story of an Hour." Tell them they will use fiction to explore one of the two essential questions: "To what degree do we control our lives?" and "What are the consequences of change?"

WRITING PROMPT

Review the prompt with students. Encourage them to ask questions about any part of the assignment that is unclear. Make sure they understand that the purpose of their short story is to answer the question using ideas and themes from the texts they have read and insights from their own experiences.

Write a Short Story

Go to **Writing Narratives** in the **Writing Studio** for help.

This unit focuses on stories and essays that ask important questions about the power humans wield and how they interact with and build unique places. For this writing task, you will write a realistic short story that has a theme connected to one of the Unit Essential Questions. For an example of a well-written short story you can use as a mentor text, review Kate Chopin's short story "The Story of an Hour."

As you write your short story, you can use the notes from your Response Log, which you filled out after reading the texts in this unit.

Writing Prompt

Read the information in the box below.

This is the topic or context for your short story.

> The choices you make determine a lot about how you live your life, but they can also bring change and affect others.

How do your own experiences give you insight into these Essential Questions, and how might you transform those experiences into a fictional story?

Think carefully about these two Essential Questions.

> To what degree do we control our lives?
> What are the consequences of change?

How can you use a short story to explore one of these Essential Questions?

Write a short story that explores one of these questions and expresses something you have found to be true about life or the world.

Review these points as you write and again when you finish. Make any needed changes.

Be sure to—

- ☐ build a strong plot that centers around a conflict
- ☐ show how characters interact with the plot events and with each other
- ☐ use descriptive details to paint a vivid setting.
- ☐ develop a theme that relates to one of the Essential Questions above

---

LEARNING MINDSET

Try Again When writing, students often have trouble in their first drafts coming up with an opening that makes their reader want to continue, or a conclusion that provides a true sense of closure. Explain that sometimes it is necessary to set a piece of writing aside and go on to another task for a while. If students have trouble, tell them to concentrate on getting the main part of their stories written. Then, they can go back with a fresh perspective and rework or fine-tune their exposition or resolution.

1 Plan

First, choose one of the Essential Questions, and create a word map to generate ideas for your story. You can use the map below, adding bubbles as needed, or use sticky notes on a larger sheet of paper to create your map. Include ideas for characters, setting, plot, and conflict. Remember that your story should be fictional, but it can incorporate elements from your own experiences. In fact, using observations, events, and even people from your own life as ideas for fictional characters and conflicts will provide your story with authenticity.

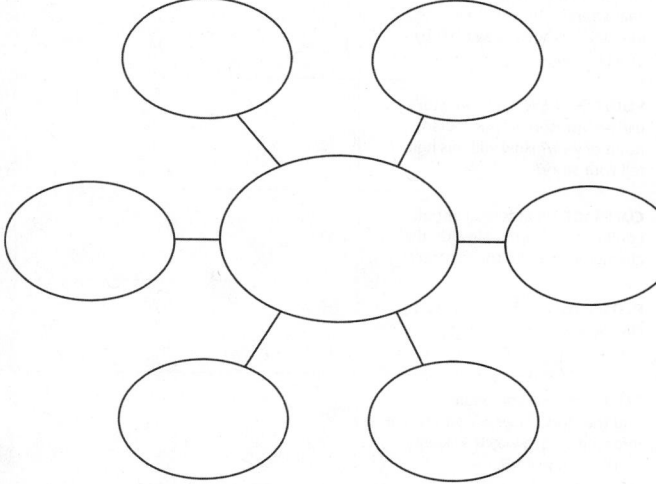

Background Reading Review the notes you have taken in your Response Log that relate to the questions "To what degree do we control our lives?" and "What are the consequences of change?" Texts in this unit provide background reading that will help you formulate the theme and plot of your story.

 Go to **Writing Narratives: Point of View and Characters** for help planning your short story.

Notice & Note

From Reading to Writing

As you plan your short story, apply what you've learned about signposts to your own writing. Remember that writers use common features, called signposts, to help convey their message to readers.

Think about how you can incorporate **Words of the Wiser** into your short story.

 Go to the **Reading Studio** for more resources on **Notice & Note**.

Use the notes from your Response Log as you plan your short story.

UNIT 5 RESPONSE LOG

Essential Question	Details from Texts
To what degree do we control our lives?	
Why do humans cause harm?	
What are the consequences of change?	
What makes a place unique?	

1 PLAN

Ask students to discuss the plots of stories they have read in class. Ask: *What happened in those stories? What did the characters want? What problems did they face? How did they solve them?* Have each student complete a concept map and then review it with another student. Explain that talking through something or thinking out loud can help them fine-tune their ideas or come up with new ideas. Remind students to think of plots that illustrate the theme of their story, either to what degree we control our lives or the consequences of change.

■ English Learner Support

Understand Theme Tell students that the theme of a story is the story's main message about life that the author wants to share. Emphasize that the theme is not the topic of a story, nor is it the plot—which is what happens. Help students understand that theme is revealed through the setting, plot, and characters. Most short stories have just one theme, but longer fiction, such as novels, may have several. Ask students to share themes from their favorite books, either in English or in their native language. If students struggle, discuss the themes of well-known fairy tales. **ALL LEVELS**

▶ NOTICE & NOTE

From Reading to Writing Remind students they can use **Words of the Wiser** to help them develop their plots. Tell them that the main character and another character are usually by themselves in a quiet, serious moment, and the wiser figure shares his or her wisdom or advice in an effort to help the main character solve the problem or make a decision.

Background Reading As students plan their stories, remind them to refer to the notes they took in their Response Logs. They may also review the selections to find additional facts and examples to support ideas they want to include in their writing.

TO CHALLENGE STUDENTS . . .

Practice Creative Writing Have students choose an alternate form for their writing assignment, such as a play or a narrative poem. Remind them that no matter what form they choose, they must consider characters, setting, and plot, and how each works together to develop the theme. After students have finished their work, have them exchange projects with another student. Have each student write a short review of the other student's work, examining its strengths and making positive suggestions for improvement.

WRITING

Organize Your Ideas Give students time to create a plot diagram independently. Have them organize their ideas from brainstorming, but encourage them to add or alter ideas if necessary to create an engaging plot. As students work, monitor their progress by making sure students' plots include a well-defined conflict, along with complications contributed by the characters' actions and motivations; a believable climax; and a clear resolution. Suggest students write a psychological profile of their main character before beginning their stories. Explain to students that the profile should relay aspects of the character's background that contribute to his or her personality and behavior. Encourage students to include specific details in their stories, such as the date, time of day, geographic location, weather, condition of buildings or furniture, and aspects of nature.

2 DEVELOP A DRAFT

Tell students that the exposition and the resolution of their stories are very important. The expositions should grab their readers' attention and introduce the setting and main characters. Remind students that as they reach the climax, they should reveal details of the final outcome. Tell students that by the end of the story, characters often change in some way because they have resolved the conflict. Emphasize that their readers should be left with something to think about.

■ English Learner Support

Develop Plot Draw a diagram of a hill on the board. Tell students the hill represents the "shape" of the story. Work with students to determine where on the hill the exposition, rising action, climax, and resolution should go. Consider using a simple story to illustrate the plot stages. Then, have students create a diagram for their own story. After students have completed their diagrams, ask them whether the "shape" of their story makes sense, or whether they change where they place events on the hill. **LIGHT**

WRITING TASK

 Go to **Writing Narratives: Narrative Structure** for more help.

Organize Your Ideas After you have gathered ideas from your planning activities, you need to organize them in a way that will help you draft your short story. You can use the chart below to decide on the elements of your story.

SETTING: Where does the story take place? Why is this important? How does setting influence plot and characters?	
CHARACTERS: Who are the characters? What are their personality traits? How do they grow or change?	
POINT OF VIEW: Will your story use first-person or third-person point of view? How will this help tell your story?	
CONFLICT: What is the central conflict or problem? How do the characters react to the conflict?	
PLOT: What are the rising action, climax, and falling action?	
PLOT: How will you begin and end the story? How will you reveal information in a way that keeps readers interested?	
LITERARY DEVICES: How could you use flashback or flash-forward? How could you use irony?	
THEME: How will you communicate a message about life that rings true?	

 You might prefer to draft your short story online.

2 Develop a Draft

Once you have completed your planning activities, you will be ready to begin drafting your short story. Refer to your Graphic Organizer and the chart of story elements, as well as any notes you took as you studied the texts in this unit. These will provide a kind of map for you to follow as you write. Using a word processor or online writing application makes it easier to make changes or move sentences around later when you are ready to revise your first draft.

© Houghton Mifflin Harcourt Publishing Company

WHEN STUDENTS STRUGGLE . . .

Plan Plot Work with students to fill in a plot plan using the events of "The Story of an Hour." Then, have students work in pairs to complete a plot diagram using the events of a movie they have both seen. Have each pair write their plot plan on the board and explain why they categorized each event as a part of the rising action, climax, or resolution.

Use the Mentor Text

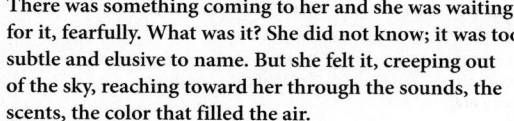

Author's Craft

Authors use many strategies to maintain reader interest and curiosity. For example, dramatic irony—in which the reader or another character knows more than the main character—gives readers a sense of suspense that increases their interest. Foreshadowing, such as in this example from "The Story of an Hour," also piques readers' curiosity and keeps them reading.

> There was something coming to her and she was waiting for it, fearfully. What was it? She did not know; it was too subtle and elusive to name. But she felt it, creeping out of the sky, reaching toward her through the sounds, the scents, the color that filled the air.

Chopin uses third-person limited point of view to foreshadow future events. The emotions of "waiting . . . fearfully" come through vividly as readers see the future through her eyes.

Apply What You've Learned Read your story and consider where you might increase the sense of suspense through foreshadowing or dramatic irony. Add these to your Graphic Organizer and work them into your story as you revise.

Figurative Language

Figurative language is a feature of nearly every type of writing. Both metaphors and similes compare something the reader is familiar with to something in the text, to help the reader visualize the characters, setting, or plot events. Notice how Kate Chopin uses figurative language to help readers create mental images of her character.

> When the storm of grief had spent itself she went away to her room alone. She would have no one follow her. . . .
>
> She sat with her head thrown back upon the cushion of the chair, quite motionless, except when a sob came up into her throat and shook her, as a child who has cried itself to sleep continues to sob in its dreams.

Chopin uses a metaphor to help describe the violence of Mrs. Mallard's grief. She uses a simile to help describe Mrs. Mallard's spasms of sobbing.

Apply What You've Learned Choose one or two places in your story where you can use either a metaphor or a simile to help evoke a mental image of what a character is doing or feeling. Add these to your Graphic Organizer and work them into your short story as you revise.

Write a Short Story   563

WHY THIS MENTOR TEXT?

"The Story of an Hour" provides a good example of a short story because it centers around a single conflict and setting and has a minimal number of characters. Chopin uses sensory details to set the scene and uses dialogue that reveals her characters' traits. Use the instruction below to help students use the mentor text as a model for writing their short stories.

USE THE MENTOR TEXT

Author's Craft Ask a volunteer to read the end of "The Story of an Hour," from paragraph 20 to the end. Point out this is an example of dramatic irony. In this case, it is ironic because the readers share knowledge of the main character's true feelings that the other characters lack. Tell students this is because Chopin has used a limited third-person point of view, focusing on Mrs. Mallard and allowing readers to know her inner feelings but no one else's. Ask the class to look for other instances of dramatic irony in the story.

Figurative Language Point out that similes and metaphors are just two examples of figurative language. Explain that another form of figurative language, **imagery,** helps to provide a mental picture by appealing to the senses. Another literary device is **personification,** in which human thoughts and feelings are attributed to nonhuman things. Have students scan the story and mark all the instances of figurative language they can find. Then, invite them to call out the examples and discuss the mental images the figurative language creates.

ENGLISH LEARNER SUPPORT

Use Figurative Language Tell students that both similes and metaphors are forms of figurative language that compare two things. The main difference between the two is that a simile uses the word *like* or *as* to make the comparison. "Dark as night" and "run like the wind" are examples of similes. A metaphor makes the comparison by applying a word or phrase to something to which it is not literally applicable. "America is a melting pot" and "the classroom was a zoo" are examples of metaphors. Work as a class or have students work in small groups to write other similes and metaphors. **MODERATE/LIGHT**

WRITING

3 REVISE

Have students answer each question in the chart to determine how they can improve their drafts. Have students pay particular attention to the conflict and the resolution. Inform students that a story's conflict does not need to be completely resolved, but some closure or character change must occur. Explain to students that a satisfying ending can raise questions about what happens next. Many good stories leave readers wanting more.

With a Partner Remind students that in peer review they should offer positive, constructive responses to each other's writing. Tell students peer reviewers should let their partners know when they come to story passages they find confusing. They do not have to solve the problem for the writers, but they should call their partners' attention to it and offer clear suggestions for revision. Encourage students to share positive feedback as well, pointing out where the writer excelled. When they have worked their way through one partner's story, they should switch roles and review the second student's draft.

 Go to **Writing Narratives: The Language of Narrative** for help revising your short story.

3 Revise

On Your Own Once you have written your draft, you'll want to go back and look for ways to improve your short story. As you reread and revise, think about whether you have achieved your purpose. The Revision Guide will help you focus on specific elements to make your writing stronger.

Revision Guide

Ask Yourself	Tips	Revision Techniques
1. Does my short story introduce characters, establish setting, and initiate the conflict?	**Highlight** details about the characters and setting. **Underline** the central conflict.	**Add** details about the characters and setting. **Add** a sentence that initiates the conflict.
2. Is a clear point of view developed consistently?	**Note** the point of view. **Underline** phrases that indicate point of view.	**Reword** sentences to make the point of view consistent.
3. Is the plot fully developed, and is pacing used effectively?	**Note** events that build toward the climax. **Highlight** details unrelated to the conflict.	**Add** details that create complications. **Delete** details that slow down the action.
4. Does my short story successfully convey the theme?	**Note** events and details that reveal the theme.	**Clarify** the theme by **adding** events and details.
5. Does the conclusion resolve the conflict or offer a satisfying concluding scene?	**Underline** sentences that resolve the conflict or conclude the story in a satisfying way.	**Add** or **change** sentences so that the conflict is resolved or the ending speaks clearly.

ACADEMIC VOCABULARY
As you conduct your **peer review,** be sure to use these words.

☐ ambiguous
☐ clarify
☐ implicit
☐ revise
☐ somewhat

With a Partner Once you and your partner have worked through the Revision Guide on your own, exchange short stories and evaluate each other's draft in a **peer review.** Focus on providing revision suggestions for at least three of the items mentioned in the chart. Explain why you think your partner's draft should be revised and what your specific suggestions are.

When receiving feedback from your partner, listen attentively and ask questions to make sure you fully understand the revision suggestions.

564　Unit 5

EL ENGLISH LEARNER SUPPORT

Understand Academic Language To help students understand how to develop a conclusion, introduce the following vocabulary:

- *setting:* where and when a story takes place
- *character motivation:* what leads a character to do or think a certain way
- *character traits:* what the character looks like or how he or she behaves
- *dialogue:* words characters say to each other

- *conflict:* a disagreement or problem
- *resolution:* a solution to a problem

Encourage students to use this academic vocabulary when they provide feedback. **ALL LEVELS**

4 Edit

Language Conventions

Active and Passive Voice The voice of a verb tells whether its subject performs or receives the verb's action. If the subject performs the action, the verb is in the **active voice,** and if the subject receives the action, the verb is in the **passive voice.** It is generally advisable to write using the active voice. This reduces wordiness and produces clear writing. However, the passive voice has its uses. It shifts the emphasis away from the person doing the action and onto the person receiving the action.

Consider these examples from Chopin's "The Story of an Hour":

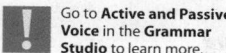 Go to **Active and Passive Voice** in the **Grammar Studio** to learn more.

Sentence from Text	Notes about Voice
Knowing that Mrs. Mallard was afflicted with a heart trouble, great care was taken to break to her as gently as possible the news of her husband's death.	The use of **passive voice**—"was afflicted," "was taken"—focuses attention on Mrs. Mallard rather than the persons or things doing the afflicting or taking care. It also creates the sense that people surrounding Mrs. Mallard are in accord in taking "great care" so their individuality is minimized, while hers is emphasized.
She wept at once, with sudden, wild abandonment, in her sister's arms.	This use of **active voice**—"She wept"—emphasizes the urgency and immediacy of her action.

5 Publish

Finalize your short story and choose a way to share it with your audience. Consider these options:

- Publish a printed book with illustrations or artwork.
- Prepare and record a podcast of your short story.

WHEN STUDENTS STRUGGLE . . .

Use Helping Verbs Tell students that one way they can identify passive voice is the use of a helping verb. In the passive voice, the helping verb is a form of *to be*—*am, is, are, was,* or *were.* However, not every sentence that includes a form of *to be* is in the passive voice. In the phrase "the car is red," the word *is* is the main verb in the sentence, not a helping verb, so the sentence is not in the passive voice. Have students review their stories and mark every place where they have used a form of *to be* and decide whether it is an example of the passive voice. If they are not sure, help them decide.

4 EDIT

Tell students that making sure their stories are free of errors in grammar, spelling, and punctuation will enhance their readers' understanding and pleasure. Have them rewrite sentences where the passive voice could be replaced by the active voice. Remind them that dialogue requires care in formatting and punctuation. Have students look for places where they can add transitions or combine sentences to add interest or clarify relationships.

LANGUAGE CONVENTIONS

Active and Passive Voice Review the information about active and passive voice with students. Point out that in the first example sentence, there are two instances of the passive voice. The first one—"Mrs. Mallard was afflicted with a heart trouble"—is unavoidable. Ask students how the second part of the sentence—"great care was taken to break to her"—can be rewritten to avoid using passive voice. (*"they took great care to break to her"*) Then, have students reread their stories to see if there are any instances where they used the passive voice but could rework the sentences to use the active voice instead.

■ English Learner Support

Use Helping Verbs Tell students the passive voice always uses a form of the verb *to be* followed by a past participle. In this case, the verb *to be* is considered a helping verb. Forms of *to be* include *am, is,* and *are* in the present tense and *was* and *were* in the past tense. Past participles are verb forms that usually end with either *-ed* or *-en,* such as *afflicted* or *taken* in the example from the story. However, there are many irregular past participles, such as *paid* and *caught.* Sometimes it can be difficult to tell whether a word is a past participle or not. For example, in the sentence "I am tired," *tired* is an adjective, not a past participle.
SUBSTANTIAL/MODERATE

5 PUBLISH

Brainstorm with students additional ways to publish their short stories. For example, they might submit them to a school literary magazine or they might present them for a live audience in a coffeehouse or other informal setting.

WRITING

USE THE SCORING GUIDE

Allow students time to read the scoring guide and to ask questions about any words, phrases, or ideas that are unclear. Then, have partners exchange final drafts of their short stories. Ask them to score their partner's story using the scoring guide. Each student should write a paragraph explaining the reasons for the score he or she awarded in each category.

WRITING TASK

Use the scoring guide to evaluate your short story.

	Writing Task Scoring Guide: Short Story		
	Organization/Progression	**Development of Ideas**	**Use of Language and Conventions**
4	• The sequence of events is effective, clear, and logical. • The organization keeps the reader interested. • Effective transitions clearly show the sequence of events.	• The story begins memorably, clearly introducing the setting, a main character, and conflict. • The plot is thoroughly developed. • The story reveals a significant theme related to an Essential Question. • The story ends by resolving the conflict or offering some satisfying concluding scene.	• The point of view is effective and consistent throughout the story. • Vivid descriptive details reveal the setting and characters. • Sentence structures vary and have a rhythmic flow. • Spelling, capitalization, and punctuation are correct. • Grammar and usage are correct.
3	• The sequence of events is mostly clear and logical. • The pace could move along more quickly to hold the reader's interest. • A few more transitions are needed to explain the sequence of events.	• The story introduces the setting, a main character, and a conflict, but the opening could be more engaging. • The plot or sequence of events is adequately developed. • The story suggests a theme related to an Essential Question. • More details are needed to create a satisfying conclusion.	• The point of view is mostly consistent. • A few more details are needed to vividly describe the setting and characters. • Sentence structures mostly vary. • Several spelling, capitalization, and punctuation mistakes occur. • Some grammatical and usage errors are repeated.
2	• The sequence of events is confusing in a few places. • The pace often lags. • More transitions are needed throughout to clarify the sequence of events.	• The story's opening is uneventful; it identifies a setting and a main character but only hints at a conflict. • Development of the plot is uneven in a few places. • A theme related to an Essential Question is only hinted at. • The conclusion is unintentionally unsatisfying.	• The point of view shifts or is confusing. • Descriptive details are ordinary or infrequent. • Sentence structures vary somewhat. • Spelling, capitalization, and punctuation are often incorrect, but the story is understandable. • Grammar and usage are often incorrect, but the writer's ideas are still clear.
1	• There is no clear sequence of events, making it easy for the reader to lose interest in the narrative. • The pace is ineffective. • Transitions are not used, making the story difficult to understand.	• The opening is missing critical information about the setting and main character, and doesn't set up a conflict. • The plot or sequence of events is barely developed. • There is no theme related to an Essential Question. • The story lacks a clear resolution.	• The story lacks a clear point of view. • Descriptive details are rarely or never used to develop setting and characters. • A repetitive sentence structure makes the writing monotonous. • Spelling, capitalization, and punctuation are incorrect throughout. • Many grammatical and usage errors change the meaning of the writer's ideas.

Reflect on the Unit

By completing your short story, you have created a writing product that uses strategies about how to tell a story drawn from the reading you have done in this unit. Now is a good time to reflect on what you have learned.

Reflect on the Essential Questions

- Review the four Essential Questions on page 453. How have your answers to these questions changed in response to the texts you've read in this unit?

- What are some examples from the texts you've read that show how people cause harm or adapt to change?

Reflect on Your Reading

- Which selections were the most interesting or surprising to you?

- From which selection did you learn the most about people and how they interact with others, their environments, or the places they live?

Reflect on the Writing Task

- What difficulties did you encounter while working on your short story? How might you avoid them next time?

- What parts of the short story were the easiest and hardest to write? Why?

- What improvements did you make to your short story as you were revising?

UNIT 5 SELECTIONS
- "To Build a Fire"
- "The Lowest Animal"
- "Why Everyone Must Get Ready for the Fourth Industrial Revolution"
- "The Story of an Hour"
- "Chicago"
- from *The Jungle*
- "Food Product Design" from *Fast Food Nation*

REFLECT ON THE UNIT

Have students reflect on the questions independently, and write some notes in response to each one. Then, have students meet with partners or in small groups to discuss their reflections. Circulate during these discussions to identify the questions that are generating the liveliest conversations. Wrap up with a whole-class discussion focused on these questions.

LEARNING MINDSET

Questioning Encourage students to always feel comfortable asking questions, either of themselves or others. Let them know that asking questions is about being open to new ideas and trying new things. It shows they are curious, and it leads to learning new things.

Instructional Overview and Resources

	Instructional Focus	**Online Ed Resources**
Unit Introduction **Contemporary Voices and Visions**	**Unit 6 Essential Question** **Unit 6 Academic Vocabulary**	**Stream to Start:** Contemporary Voices and Visions **Unit 6 Response Log**

ANALYZE & APPLY

	Instructional Focus	**Resources**
"A Rose for Emily" Short Story by William Faulkner Lexile 1120L	**Reading** • Make and Confirm Predictions • Analyze Literary Elements: Setting and Characterization **Writing:** Write a Literary Analysis **Speaking and Listening:** Discuss with a Small Group **Vocabulary:** Foreign Words and Phrases **Language Conventions:** Choose Effective Point of View	🔊 **Audio** **Reading Studio:** Notice & Note **Writing Studio:** Writing as a Process **Speaking and Listening Studio:** Preparing for Discussion **Vocabulary Studio:** Foreign Words
"Mending Wall" Poem by Robert Frost Lexile N/A	**Reading** • Analyze Poetry • Analyze Diction and Syntax • Analyze Author's Message **Writing:** Write a Poem **Speaking and Listening:** Present a Poem	🔊 **Audio** **Reading Studio:** Notice & Note **Writing Studio:** Writing as a Process **Speaking and Listening Studio:** Giving a Presentation
The Crucible Drama by Arthur Miller Lexile N/A	**Reading** • Analyze Dramatic Elements • Analyze Characters and Motivation • Analyze Literary Devices **Writing:** Write an Essay **Speaking and Listening:** Have a Discussion **Vocabulary:** Determine the Meaning of Idioms **Language Conventions:** Creating Effective Dialogue	🔊 **Audio** **Close Read Screencast:** Modeled Discussion **Reading Studio:** Notice & Note **Writing Studio:** Writing an Informative Text **Speaking and Listening Studio:** Using Media in a Presentation; Participating in Collaborative Discussions **Vocabulary Studio:** Idioms

SUGGESTED PACING:
30 DAYS

Unit Introduction	A Rose for Emily	Mending Wall	The Crucible	The Crucible	My Dungeon Shook: Letter to My Nephew
1	2 3 4	5 6	7 8 9 10 11	12	13 14

English Learner Support	Differentiated Instruction	Online Ed Assessment
• Learn New Expressions • Build Background Knowledge • Understand Multiple-Meaning Words	**When Students Struggle** • Summarize the Text	

• Text X-Ray • Use Cognates • Describe Setting • Ask Questions • Express Opinions • Improve Reading Fluency • Oral Assessment • Practice Vowel Sounds • Language Conventions	**When Students Struggle** • Understand Plot • Analyze Character • Analyze Literary Elements: Characterization • Reteach: Analyze Literary Elements: Setting **To Challenge Students** • Analyze Characterization • Analyze Theme	**Selection Test**
• Text X-Ray • Use Cognates • Understand Punctuation • Oral Assessment	**When Students Struggle** • Reteach: Analyze Diction and Syntax **To Challenge Students** • Interpret Symbolism	**Selection Test**
• Text X-Ray • Clarify and Reinforce Meaning • Understand Multiple-Meaning Words • Provide Contextual Support • Decode Words with Prefixes • Use Prior Knowledge • Use Synonyms • Analyze Idioms • Use Context to Understand Archaic Language • Interpret Stage Directions • Identify Cognates • Support Comprehension • Understand Suffixes • Analyze Language • Understand Similes • Acquire Vocabulary • Understand Homographs • Understand Figurative Language • Understand Homophones • Understand Phrasal Verbs • Use Possessive Nouns • Understand Language Structures • Understand Language Conventions • Understand Adverbs • Describe Dramatic Elements • Recognize Double Negatives • Use Adverbial Phrases • Understand Metaphors • Use Contractions • Oral Assessment	**When Students Struggle** • Understand Chronological Order • Understand Setting • Summarize • Understand Motivation • Analyze Conflict • Vocabulary Support • Understand Symbols • Summarize Plot • Interpret Confusing Pronouns • Support Comprehension • Understand Metaphors and Similes • Understand Characters • Find Meaning of Domain-Specific Terms • Analyze Dialogue • Understand Plot Structure • Understand Character Motivation • Use a Graphic Organizer **To Challenge Students** • Evaluate Author's Purpose • Extend Knowledge • Interpret Stage Directions • Investigate Text References • Analyze Dialogue • Make Inferences • Analyze Theme • Analyze Mood • Conduct Research • Direct a Scene • Analyze Motivation • Research and Contrast Productions • Research Andover • Evaluate Resolution • Analyze Genre	**Selection Test**

Speech on the Vietnam War, 1967	Ambush	The Universe as Primal Scream	How It Feels to Be Colored Me/ *from* The Warmth of Other Suns	Poetry/The Latin Deli: An Ars Poetica	Independent Reading	End of Unit
15 16 17	18 19	20 21	22 23	24 25	26 27	28 29 30

UNIT 6 Continued

	Instructional Focus	Online Ed Resources
The Crucible Production Images by Walter Kerr Theatre, New York Lexile N/A	**Reading** • Make Connections • Analyze Effectiveness of Multimodal Text **Writing:** Write a Treatment **Speaking and Listening:** Present Your Ideas	**Reading Studio:** Notice & Note **Speaking and Listening Studio:** Using Media in a Presentation
"My Dungeon Shook: Letter to My Nephew" Open Letter by James Baldwin Lexile 1040L	**Reading** • Analyze Rhetorical Devices • Analyze Audience and Message **Writing:** Write an Open Letter **Speaking and Listening:** Present Your Letter **Vocabulary:** Analyze Denotation and Connotation **Language Conventions:** Varied Sentence Structure	🔊 **Audio** **Reading Studio:** Notice & Note **Writing Studio:** Writing as a Process **Speaking and Listening Studio:** Giving a Presentation **Vocabulary Studio:** Denotation and Connotation **Grammar Studio:** Sentence Structure
"Speech on the Vietnam War, 1967" Speech by Martin Luther King Jr. Lexile 1290L	**Reading** • Analyze and Evaluate Arguments • Analyze and Evaluate Rhetorical Devices **Writing:** Write an Article **Speaking and Listening:** Have a Group Discussion **Vocabulary:** Suffixes **Language Conventions:** Imperative Mood	🔊 **Audio** **Reading Studio:** Notice & Note **Writing Studio:** Writing Arguments **Speaking and Listening Studio:** Analyzing and Evaluating Presentations **Vocabulary Studio:** Common Roots, Prefixes, and Suffixes **Grammar Studio:** Correct Use of Verbs
"Ambush" Short Story by Tim O'Brien Lexile 950L	**Reading** • Analyze Characterization • Analyze Text Structure **Writing:** Use a Story Frame **Speaking and Listening:** Discuss Your Story **Vocabulary:** Connotation and Denotation **Language Conventions:** Transitions	🔊 **Audio** **Reading Studio:** Notice & Note **Writing Studio:** Writing Narratives **Speaking and Listening Studio:** The Content of Your Presentation: Narrative **Vocabulary Studio:** Connotation and Denotation
"The Universe as Primal Scream" Poem by Tracy K. Smith Lexile N/A	**Reading** • Analyze Poetry • Analyze and Evaluate Literary Devices **Writing:** Write a Literary Analysis **Speaking and Listening:** Discuss the Poem	🔊 **Audio** **Reading Studio:** Notice & Note **Speaking and Listening Studio:** Participating in Collaborative Discussions

English Learner Support	Differentiated Instruction	Online Ed Assessment
• Text X-Ray • Understand Multiple-Meaning Words • Analyze Images	**When Students Struggle** • Use a Graphic Organizer • Reteach: Analyze Effectiveness of Multimodal Text **To Challenge Students** • Research Ivo van Hove	**Selection Test**
• Text X-Ray • Use Cognates • Word Definitions • Synonyms • Multiple-Meaning Words • Oral Assessment • Sound Transfer • Language Conventions	**When Students Struggle** • Author's Purpose • Reteach: Author's Purpose	**Selection Test**
• Text X-Ray • Use Cognates • Preteach Vocabulary • Master the Terms • Recognize Affixes • Confirm Understanding of Devices • Oral Assessment • Vocabulary Strategy • Language Conventions	**When Students Struggle** • Analyze Chronology • Analyze the Argument **To Challenge Students** • Analyze Allusions	**Selection Test**
• Text X-Ray • Use Cognates • Homonyms • Oral Assessment • Connotation and Denotation • Language Conventions	**When Students Struggle** • Setting • Reteach: Setting **To Challenge Students** • Compare to History	**Selection Test**
• Text X-Ray • Understand Idioms • Preteach Vocabulary • Oral Assessment	**When Students Struggle** • Develop Reading Fluency • Reteach: Imagery	**Selection Test**

UNIT 6 Continued

	Instructional Focus	Online Ⓔd Resources

COLLABORATE & COMPARE

Mentor Text

"How It Feels to Be Colored Me"
Essay by Zora Neale Hurston
Lexile 950L

Reading
• Analyze Development of Ideas
• Analyze Tone

Writing: Write an Argumentative Essay

Speaking and Listening: Discuss Other Perspectives

Vocabulary: Synonyms and Antonyms

Language Conventions: Sentence Variety

🔊 **Audio**

Reading Studio: Notice & Note

Writing Studio: Writing Arguments

Speaking and Listening Studio: Participating in Collaborative Discussions

Vocabulary Studio: Synonyms and Antonyms

Grammar Studio: Sentence Structure

---

from *The Warmth of Other Suns*
History Writing by Isabel Wilkerson
Lexile 1240L

Reading
• Analyze Informational Texts
• Determine Author's Message and Audience

Writing: Write a Historical Essay

Speaking and Listening: Discuss Your Essay

Vocabulary: Word Families

Language Conventions: Spelling

🔊 **Audio**

Reading Studio: Notice & Note

Writing Studio: Conducting Research

Speaking and Listening Studio: Participating in Collaborative Discussions

Vocabulary Studio: Analyzing Word Structure

Grammar Studio: Spelling

Collaborate & Compare

Reading: Compare Ideas Across Genres

Speaking and Listening Studio: Preparing for Discussion

Poetry
Poem by Marianne Moore
Lexile N/A

The Latin Deli: An Ars Poetica
Poem by Judith Ortiz Cofer
Lexile N/A

Reading
• Determine Theme
• Evaluate Figurative Language

Writing: Write a Compare and Contrast Essay

Speaking and Listening: Discuss Your Findings

🔊 **Audio**

Reading Studio: Notice & Note

Writing Studio: Writing Informative Texts

Speaking and Listening Studio: Participating in Collaborative Discussions

---

Collaborate & Compare

Reading: Compare Themes

Speaking and Listening Studio: Delivering Your Presentation

English Learner Support	Differentiated Instruction	Online **Ed** Assessment
• Text X-Ray • Use Cognates • Identify Important Details • Listen for Key Words • Understand Italics • Oral Assessment • Understand Prefixes • Sentence Structure	**When Students Struggle** • Understand Ideas • Reteach: Analyze Ideas and Details **To Challenge Students** • Create Tone	**Selection Test**
• Text X-Ray • Use Cognates • Recognize Dated Language • Pronounce Stressed Syllables • Use Context Clues • Assimilate Cultural Knowledge • Oral Assessment • Use Spelling Strategies	**When Students Struggle** • Identify Evidence • Reteach: Determine Author's Message and Audience	
• Compare Texts	**When Students Struggle** • Practice Close Reading	
• Text X-Ray • Explain Metaphors • Improve Reading Fluency • Understand Theme • Oral Assessment	**When Students Struggle** • Understand Theme • Understand Imagery • Reteach: Figurative Language **To Challenge Students** • Evaluate Form	**Selection Test**
• Analyze Poetry	**When Students Struggle** • Reteach: Analyze Theme	

UNIT 6 Continued

Instructional Focus

 INDEPENDENT READING

The Independent Reading selections are only available in the eBook.

 Go to the Reading Studio for more information on NOTICE & NOTE.

 Poems of the Harlem Renaissance
Poems by Langston Hughes, Jean Toomer, Countee Cullen, Arna Bontemps

 "Martin Luther King, Jr.: He Showed Us the Way"
Essay by César Chávez
Lexile 1120L

END OF UNIT

Writing Task: Write a Personal Essay

Reflect on the Unit

Writing: Write a Personal Essay

Language Conventions: Sensory Language

Unit 6 Response Log

Mentor Text: "How It Feels to Be Colored Me"

Writing Studio: Writing Informative Texts

Grammar Studio: Commas with Introductory Elements

English Learner Support	Differentiated Instruction	 Online Ed Assessment

"Mother Tongue"
Essay by Amy Tan
Lexile 1120L

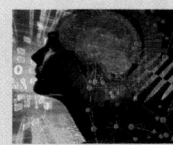
"Reality Check"
Short Story by David Brin
Lexile 920L

"YouTube Stars Stress Out, Just Like the Rest of Us"
Article by Neda Ulaby
Lexile 1160L

Selection Tests

• Language X-Ray

• Learn New Expressions

• Express Ideas

• Understand Academic Language

• Understand Personal Essays and Pronouns

• Use Sensory Language

When Students Struggle
• Develop a Draft
• Use Sensory Language

To Challenge Students
• Connect Art to Theme

Unit Test

DISCUSS THE QUOTATION

Don DeLillo has been called "the chief shaman of the paranoid school of American fiction." In his works, he portrays an America obsessed by materialism and stupefied by empty mass culture and politics. Throughout his work, DeLillo has explored the quest for connection and the replacement of reality by virtual reality. This quotation is from his 1997 novel *Underworld*, which earned him a National Book Award and was hailed by some critics as the "great American novel." At the end of the book, a nun from the Bronx dies, but instead of the Christian heaven she expects, she finds herself in cyberspace, where she muses that everything is linked to everything else.

Ask students to think about all the ways in which people and things are connected in the modern world. Have them support their ideas with examples.

■ English Learner Support

Learn New Expressions Make sure that students understand that the phrase *in the end* in the DeLillo quotation means "finally," "after a long time," "when all things are considered," or "ultimately." **SUBSTANTIAL/MODERATE**

CONTEMPORARY VOICES AND VISIONS

MODERN AND CONTEMPORARY LITERATURE

> " Everything is connected in the end. "
>
> —Don DeLillo

568   Unit 6

LEARNING MINDSET

Growth Mindset Remind students that a growth mindset means believing you can get smarter by taking on challenges and pushing yourself. Encourage students to look at this final unit as an opportunity to set higher goals and stretch past their comfort zone.

Discuss the Essential Questions with your whole class or in small groups. As you read Contemporary Voices and Visions, consider how the selections explore these questions.

? *ESSENTIAL QUESTION:*

How do we deal with rejection or isolation?

Everyone experiences rejection. While people may feel distressed at the time, most are able to cope with rejection. Repeated rejection, especially when it is based on unchangeable characteristics such as race or ethnicity, can be devastating. So can ostracism, or feeling excluded or isolated. What can we do to counteract rejection or social isolation?

? *ESSENTIAL QUESTION:*

For whom is the American Dream relevant?

Over the years, the American Dream has meant many things—political and religious freedom; economic opportunity; and the chance to achieve a better life through talent, education, and hard work. For most of our history, people of color were excluded from this dream. The Harlem Renaissance and the civil rights movement of the 1950s and 1960s were landmarks in the struggle of African Americans to realize that dream. Do you believe everyone can achieve the American Dream?

? *ESSENTIAL QUESTION:*

When should personal integrity come before civic duty?

In the years after World War II, Congress held hearings to identify Communist sympathizers. Many artists, writers, and entertainers were called to testify. Playwright Arthur Miller was one of those called. When he refused to "name names" of people with Communist leanings, he was cited for contempt of Congress. His play *The Crucible* uses the Salem witch trials as a metaphor for this anti-Communist "witch hunt." What ideals would you be willing to stand up for?

? *ESSENTIAL QUESTION:*

What would we do if there were no limits?

Limits may be imposed by others or they may be self-imposed. Many people place limits on themselves, telling themselves that there is no point in trying to do something because they won't succeed. Others have accomplished the seemingly impossible. For example, J. K. Rowling was a destitute single mother before publishing the best-selling Harry Potter books; NASA successfully reached the moon and is now exploring the surface of Mars. What limits do you place on yourself? What could you accomplish without these limits?

Connect to the
ESSENTIAL QUESTIONS

Read aloud the Essential Questions and the paragraphs that follow them. Open the discussion of each idea by having students respond to the questions that conclude each paragraph.

? *ESSENTIAL QUESTION:*

How do we deal with rejection or isolation?

Point out that bullying is one form of rejection, and may have devastating effects, including self-harm, suicide, or violence against others. Ask students how people can deal with rejection or isolation in a positive way, or a way that is not harmful to themselves or others.

? *ESSENTIAL QUESTION:*

For whom is the American Dream relevant?

Tell students that in 2017, the UN reported that "[t]he American Dream is rapidly becoming the American Illusion, as the United States now has the lowest rate of social mobility of any of the rich countries." Ask students what they think it takes to achieve the American Dream today.

? *ESSENTIAL QUESTION:*

When should personal integrity come before civic duty?

Remind students that Americans have engaged in sit-ins, boycotts, and other acts of civil disobedience to protest racial discrimination, war, and other forms of injustice. Guide the class in a discussion of the issues they would be willing to take a stand for.

? *ESSENTIAL QUESTION:*

What would we do if there were no limits?

Challenge students to embrace a learning mindset in all aspects of their lives so that they won't limit themselves. Ask them what they would like to accomplish and how they could set about doing it.

MODERN AND CONTEMPORARY LITERATURE

This essay provides students with a historical context for the Unit 6 selections. It presents a brief overview of the events that strongly influenced writers of the past century, including two world wars, the civil rights movement, and technological advances that both revolutionized how people communicate and affected the quality of life on Earth.

Effects of War New weapons made the carnage created by World War I much greater than any previous war. Witnessing this destruction drove modernist writers to doubt the worth of a civilization that could allow such a conflict to take place. Where realist writers had tried to capture the reality around them, modernists turned away from a world that they ultimately found themselves unable to replicate using traditional forms of literature. Many focused instead on the individual's inner life, sometimes using a technique called stream of consciousness in which they ignored narrative plot and complete sentences in favor of the scattered thoughts running through a character's mind.

COLLABORATIVE DISCUSSION

Ask volunteers to share the events they chose with the class, along with their reasons for choosing them.

MODERN AND CONTEMPORARY LITERATURE

In the first 30 years of the 20th century, Americans faced a world war, an economic boom followed by the Great Depression, and shifting attitudes toward women's place in society. Beginning in 1916 and continuing through the 1920s, a Great Migration took place as millions of black farmers and sharecroppers moved north in search of opportunity and freedom from oppression and racial hostility. Thousands of these migrants settled in Harlem, a Manhattan neighborhood that became the cultural center of African American life.

Effects of War World War I (1914–1918) was perhaps the most influential force on American writers of the early 20th century. Modernist writers, many of whom spent time living and writing in Europe, responded to the social and political upheaval of the war by experimenting with innovative styles and forms, and by focusing on the alienation of the individual in modern society. During the Roaring Twenties, young people rebelled against the values of the past. Women shortened their skirts and cut their hair as they entered the workplace in large numbers. Workers formed unions and demanded reforms in a wide variety of industries. As the Great Depression took hold in the 1930s, many artists and writers turned to Communism or Communist ideas.

World War II (1939–1945) was a catastrophe of epic dimensions: it was the first war in history in which more civilians died than soldiers. The United States and the Soviet Union, allies during the war, emerged as rival superpowers and engaged in a decades-long Cold War, competing in a deadly arms race that threatened the world with a nuclear apocalypse. In an effort to contain the spread of Communism, the U.S. military became heavily involved in civil wars in Korea and then in Vietnam. Americans were deeply divided over their country's involvement in these conflicts, particularly that of Vietnam. Students, pacifists, and even some returning veterans protested the American role in the Vietnam War and wanted the United States to withdraw, while "hawks" wanted to win the war through still greater military involvement.

Although the Cold War ended with the breakup of the Soviet Union in 1991, American warfare did not. In that same year, U.S. troops were sent to protect Kuwait from the Iraqi invasion. In 2001 the September 11 attacks on the

COLLABORATIVE DISCUSSION

In a small group, discuss events from the historical essay that you believe had a lasting effect on American life and literature. Why do you think this is so?

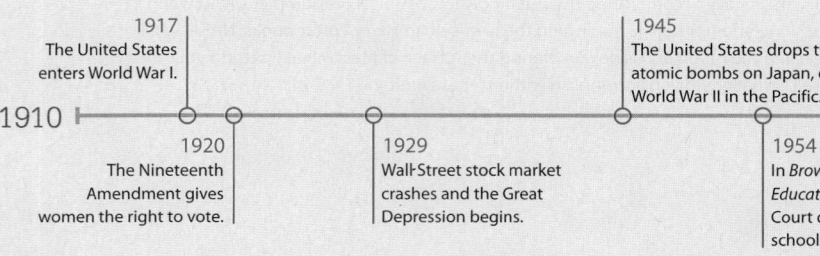

1917
The United States enters World War I.

1910

1920
The Nineteenth Amendment gives women the right to vote.

1929
Wall Street stock market crashes and the Great Depression begins.

1945
The United States drops two atomic bombs on Japan, ending World War II in the Pacific.

1954
In *Brown v. Board of Education*, the Supreme Court declares segregated schools unconstitutional.

🔵 ENGLISH LEARNER SUPPORT

Build Background Knowledge Provide support to help students with background knowledge and vocabulary. Divide the following words among pairs of students and have them write the words and definitions to display.

- *sharecroppers:* farmers, especially in the southern United States, who raise crops for the landowner and are paid part of the money from the sale of the crops
- *innovative:* introducing new ideas or methods
- *catastrophe:* a terrible disaster

- *alienation:* the act of causing someone to feel that he or she no longer belongs to a particular group
- *segregation:* the policy of keeping people of different races, religions, etc., separate from one another
- *momentum:* the strength or force that allows something to continue or to grow stronger or faster as time passes
- *nonrenewable:* not able to be replaced after use
- *implications:* possible future effects or results **ALL LEVELS**

World Trade Center and the Pentagon led to U.S. invasions of Afghanistan and Iraq. In recent years, international terrorism and the spread of nuclear weapons have brought on a heightened feeling of insecurity.

Struggle for Equality The civil rights movement of the 1950s and 1960s is perhaps the most important catalyst for social change in modern times. In 1954 the Supreme Court struck down school segregation as unconstitutional. In the late 1950s and early 1960s, Dr. Martin Luther King Jr. advocated nonviolent civil disobedience, eventually leading Congress to pass the 1964 Civil Rights Act, which outlawed segregation in public places and guaranteed legal equality to African Americans. In the years that followed, other groups drew on the ideals and tactics of the civil rights movement in the struggle to end discrimination based on gender, ethnicity, and sexual orientation.

As the civil rights movement gathered momentum, African American writers gained wider recognition. In a variety of genres, authors made powerful statements about the harmful effects of racism and the need for change. While earlier writers of color often focused on the experience of discrimination, contemporary authors also explore the individual, culture, and a sense of place from an African American perspective.

Struggle for Equality The Harlem Renaissance flourished during the first half of the 20th century, from 1918 to 1937. This important literary and artistic movement helped African Americans draw inspiration from their cultural heritage, as well as establish a sense of self that was separate from the way in which they had been viewed previously by white society. These young writers considered themselves the founders of a new era in literature. They looked inward and expressed what it meant to be black in a white-dominated world. They represented what came to be called "the New Negro," a sophisticated and well-educated African American with strong racial pride and self-awareness. They shared a deep pride in their heritage and asserted their cultural identity through their work. The power of this literary movement inspired and ensured the success of the later civil rights movement.

RESEARCH

To learn more about their chosen topic, encourage students to search for primary sources from the historical period. Have students choose excerpts from a source to present to the class.

RESEARCH
What about this historical period interests you? Choose a topic, event, or person to learn more about. Then, add your own entry to the timeline.

1977
First practical home computer, Apple II, hits the market.

2001
Hijackers fly commercial planes into World Trade Center and Pentagon, killing thousands.

2015

1965
First U.S. combat forces land in Vietnam.

2012
The number of smartphone users worldwide tops 1 billion.

Contemporary Voices and Visions   571

© Houghton Mifflin Harcourt Publishing Company • Image Credits: ©Scharfsinn/Shutterstock

WHEN STUDENTS STRUGGLE . . .

Summarize the Text Direct students to different paragraphs in the essay and have them summarize the information and then discuss how it relates to the overall topic. Ask students to reread the last paragraph on the next page. Have them summarize what it talks about (new technologies may have improved life, but they are using up fuel sources that cannot be replaced and polluting the environment). Ask students what point the author makes.

For additional support, go to the **Reading Studio** and assign the following [LEVEL UP] **Level Up Tutorial: Summarizing.**

Technology and the Environment Contemporary literature provides modern readers with a set of common references and terms that they can use when discussing fears raised by technology, the environment, and tense political issues. For example, Ray Bradbury's science-fiction novel *Fahrenheit 451* describes a futuristic society in which firemen burn all books to suppress ideas, and it is often alluded to when referring to real-world censorship. Writers such as Joseph Heller and Kurt Vonnegut question authority, conventional values, and the nature of reality. DeLillo's postmodern novel *Underworld* spans the second half of the 20th century, where the proliferation of garbage poses a greater threat than violence. Postmodernism asks, What is fiction? What is truth?

CHECK YOUR UNDERSTANDING

Have students answer the questions independently.

Answers:

1. *A*
2. *G*
3. *B*

If students answer any questions incorrectly, have them reread the text to confirm their understanding.

Technology and the Environment In 1910, automobiles, telephones, and electricity were not yet common conveniences for most people. Today, robotics has transformed manufacturing and medicine, and advances in communications technology—especially the Internet and smartphones—give people around the world instant access to information. A big question of our time is how to make the best use of this technology in a way that enhances the quality of life for all.

These advances in technology have not come without costs, especially to the environment. Cars, trucks, and planes, as well as electric power plants, have largely relied on nonrenewable fossil fuels such as oil, coal, and natural gas. The supply of these natural resources once seemed infinite, but we now know that they will eventually be exhausted. In addition, our use of these fuels has polluted the earth, air, and water on which all life depends, and has contributed to global climate change. Writers of fiction and nonfiction seek to understand the implications of these challenges for life today and for the future of the human race.

CHECK YOUR UNDERSTANDING

Choose the best answer to each question.

1 What was a result of the Great Migration?

  A Harlem became the cultural center of African American life.

  B Modernist writers spent time living and working in Europe.

  C Young people rebelled against the values of the past.

  D Fossil fuels polluted the air and water and led to global warming.

2 What was one effect the Cold War had on the United States?

  F Many American artists and writers turned to Communism.

  G The United States became involved in other countries' civil wars.

  H Congress struck down school segregation and passed civil rights legislation.

  J Millions of African Americans moved north in search of a better life.

3 How did the civil rights movement affect the country?

  A It led many people to protest against the war in Vietnam.

  B People used its tactics to end other types of discrimination.

  C The Civil Rights Act changed the way people communicated.

  D It influenced writers to reject conventional values.

572   Unit 6

ENGLISH LEARNER SUPPORT

Understand Multiple-Meaning Words Display multiple-meaning words from this essay: *boom, epic, engaged, arms, apocalypse, hawks* (all from page 570), *counter, drew* (page 571), *exhausted* (page 572). Assign students in mixed-language–ability groups 2 or 3 words to look up in a dictionary. Students should identify alternative meanings for each word and then try out each meaning in context to determine which meaning is being used. **ALL LEVELS**

ACADEMIC VOCABULARY

Academic Vocabulary words are words you will use when you discuss and write about texts. In this unit, you will learn the following five words:

☑ contemporary ☐ global ☐ infinite ☐ simulated ☐ virtual

Study the Word Network to learn more about the word **contemporary.**

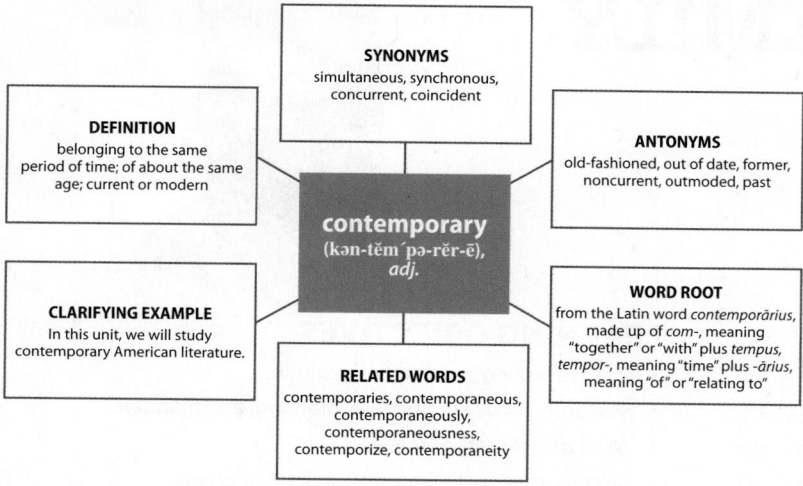

SYNONYMS
simultaneous, synchronous, concurrent, coincident

DEFINITION
belonging to the same period of time; of about the same age; current or modern

ANTONYMS
old-fashioned, out of date, former, noncurrent, outmoded, past

contemporary
(kən-tĕm´pə-rĕr-ē), adj.

CLARIFYING EXAMPLE
In this unit, we will study contemporary American literature.

WORD ROOT
from the Latin word *contemporārius,* made up of *com-,* meaning "together" or "with" plus *tempus, tempor-,* meaning "time" plus *-ārius,* meaning "of" or "relating to"

RELATED WORDS
contemporaries, contemporaneous, contemporaneously, contemporaneousness, contemporize, contemporaneity

Write and Discuss Discuss the completed Word Network with a partner, making sure to talk through all of the boxes until you both understand the word, its synonyms, antonyms, and related forms. Then, fill out a Word Network for the remaining four words. Use a dictionary or online resource to help you complete the activity.

Go online to access the Word Networks.

RESPOND TO THE ESSENTIAL QUESTIONS

In this unit, you will explore four different **Essential Questions** about life and literature in the contemporary world. As you read each selection, you will gather your ideas about one of these questions and write about it in a the **Response Log** that appears on page R6. At the end of the unit, you will have the opportunity to write a **personal essay** related to one of the Essential Questions. Filling out the Response Log after you read each text will help you prepare for this writing task.

You can also go online to access the Response Log.

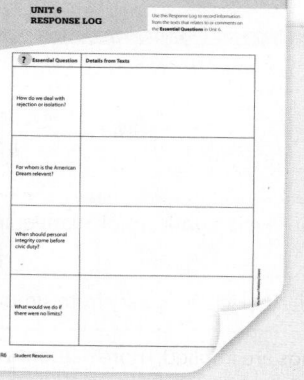

ACADEMIC VOCABULARY

Have students complete Word Networks for the remaining four vocabulary words. Encourage them to include all the categories shown in the completed network if possible, but point out that some words do not have clear synonyms or antonyms.

> **contemporary** (kən-tĕm´pə-rĕr-ē) *adj.* belonging to the same period of time; of about the same age; current or modern (Spanish cognate: *contemporáneo*)
>
> **global** (glō´bəl) *adj.* worldwide; total
>
> **infinite** (ĭn´fə-nĭt) *adj.* having no boundaries or limits; immeasurably great or large
>
> **simulated** (sĭm´yə-lā-tĭd) *adj.* made in resemblance of or as a substitute for another; performed or staged in imitation of a real event or activity (Spanish cognate: *simulado*)
>
> **virtual** (vûr´chōō-əl) *adj.* existing or resulting in essence or effect though not in actual form; existing in the mind (Spanish cognate: *virtual*)

RESPOND TO THE ESSENTIAL QUESTIONS

Direct students to the Unit 6 Response Logs. Explain that students will use it to record ideas and details from the selections that help answer one of the Essential Questions. When they work on the Writing Task at the end of the unit, their Response Logs will help them think about what they have read and make connections between the texts.

A ROSE FOR EMILY

Short Story by William Faulkner

GENRE ELEMENTS
SHORT STORY

A **short story** is a brief fictional work. It usually tells how one or more characters resolve a main conflict. Throughout the story, the author provides clues, or details, about the conflict and how it will be resolved. The author also provides details about the setting, which may play a role in the conflict. For example, this short story takes place over a 75-year period, from the 1860s to the 1920s or 1930s, when gender roles and social class expectations were different than they are today.

LEARNING OBJECTIVES

- Analyze setting and characterization.
- Research 1870s architecture, clothing, and manners.
- Write a brief literary analysis.
- Discuss an aspect of the story in a small group.
- Identify meaning and origins of foreign words.
- Write a paragraph using the first-person plural point of view.
- **Language** Describe the setting by listing details from the text.

TEXT COMPLEXITY

Quantitative Measures	A Rose for Emily	Lexile: 1120L
Qualitative Measures	**Ideas Presented** Multiple levels, subtle, implied meanings and purpose; abstract, difficult ideas; use of symbolism, irony.	
	Structures Used Primarily explicit; may vary from simple chronological order.	
	Language Used Meanings are implied; more inference is demanded.	
	Knowledge Required Cultural or historical references may make heavier demands.	

Online **Ed**

RESOURCES

- Unit 6 Response Log
- 🔊 Selection Audio
- 📖 Reading Studio:
  Notice & Note
- LEVEL UP Level Up Tutorial:
  Plot: Sequence of Events; Setting;
  Character Motivation
- 📊 Writing Studio:
  Writing as a Process
- 💬 Speaking and Listening Studio:
  Preparing for Discussion
- 🔬 Vocabulary Studio:
  Foreign Words
- ✓ "A Rose for Emily" Selection Test

SUMMARIES

English

In this story, a townsperson recalls, through a series of flashbacks, Emily Grierson, whose father prevents her from marrying. Emily later is courted by a man the townspeople consider unacceptable; he appears to desert her. Forty years later, at Emily's death, the townspeople discover that she poisoned her suitor and has kept his corpse in a bedroom.

Spanish

En esta historia un vecino recuerda, a través de una serie de *flashbacks*, a Emily Grierson, cuyo padre le impide casarse. Luego, Emily es cortejada por un hombre a quien los vecinos del lugar consideran inaceptable; él aparentemente la abandona. Cuarenta años después, al morir Emily, los vecinos del lugar descubren que ella envenenó a su pretendiente y mantuvo su cadáver en la habitación.

 ## SMALL-GROUP OPTIONS

Have students work in small groups and pairs to read and discuss the selection.

Three-Minute Review

- After students have read the selection, set a timer for three minutes.
- Have students work independently to write clarifying questions about what they read.
- After three minutes, ask volunteers to share their questions.
- Briefly discuss answers to each questions.

Ask a Question

- Read aloud paragraph 53, which describes where Emily died.
- Pose the following question: *Did Emily die in her own bed or the one with her boyfriend?*
- Tell students to provide evidence from the text to support their answers.
- Call on a student to respond. Wait 11 seconds for a response.
- If the student answers, ask another question and repeat process.
- If the student does not answer, have the student repeat the question and call on someone to answer it.
- Redirect or ask another question at any time.

Text X-Ray: English Learner Support
for "A Rose for Emily"

Use the Text X-Ray and the supports and scaffolds in the Teacher's Edition to help guide students at different proficiency levels through the selection.

INTRODUCE THE SELECTION
DISCUSS THE THEME OF DEATH

Tell students "A Rose for Emily" is about the life and death of a southern aristocrat, or grand lady. She lives in a grand house on a street that had once been one of the best streets in town. Her father had been a wealthy and important man. It is also the story about the passing of a way of life. By the time she dies, life in Emily's town is very different from the way it was when she was young. The author gives numerous clues about the theme of death, both of an individual and a way of life.

Direct students to skim the text and circle words such as *decay, faded,* and *dust* that show things are old and less vibrant. Discuss how these words are clues to the theme of death. Then, have students underline phrases such as *next generation* and *modern ideas* that represent the new way of life that is replacing the old way.

CULTURAL REFERENCES

The following words or phrases may be unfamiliar to students:

- *august names* (paragraph 2): names of important people
- *eyesore* (paragraph 2): ugly place
- *battle of Jefferson* (paragraph 2): an 1864 battle in the U.S. Civil War
- *hereditary obligation* (paragraph 3): a responsibility passed from generation to generation
- *on the books* (paragraph 11): in the official records
- *were not received* (paragraph 15): were not allowed to visit
- *lime* (paragraph 24): a chemical that reduces the odor of decaying bodies

LISTENING

Recall Details

Tell students that identifying details can help them analyze the setting and understand Emily's situation more. Read aloud paragraph 5, which describes part of Emily's house.

Have students listen as you read aloud paragraph 5. Use the following supports with students at varying proficiency levels:

- Have students draw a picture showing the hall or parlor of Emily's house. Help them to write a sentence describing their picture or to add labels for items in it. **SUBSTANTIAL**
- Have students work in pairs. Direct them to take notes as they listen to answer these questions: *What did her parlor [or hall] look like? What items were in the parlor?* **MODERATE**
- Tell students to listen without taking notes. Then, have them list as many details about the parlor and hall as they can remember without using their books. Have them share the items on the list in small groups. **LIGHT**

SPEAKING

Make Inferences

Tell students that they can use clues in the story to help them make inferences about why something happened. Read aloud paragraph 25 and have students discuss their inferences.

Use the following supports with students at varying proficiency levels:

- Reread sentences from the paragraph, such as "None of the young men were quite good enough for Miss Emily." Ask students yes/no questions, such as *Were the young men good enough for Emily?* (no) *Did Emily's father want her to have a boyfriend?* (no) **SUBSTANTIAL**

- Have students work in small groups. Direct them to make an inference about why Emily's father did not want her to have a boyfriend or to marry. To help them express their ideas, display this sentence frame: *Emily's father did not want her to have a boyfriend because _____.* **MODERATE**

- Have students work in pairs to discuss this question: *Why did Emily's father not want her to have a boyfriend or to marry?* Have them make an inference using text evidence. **LIGHT**

READING

Analyze Characters

Tell students that authors of fictional texts provide clues to help readers understand the characters in their stories.

Work with students to reread paragraph 26. Use the following supports with students at varying proficiency levels:

- Lead students in echo reading the first two sentences of paragraph 26. Ask yes/no questions as you read, such as: *Were the townspeople happy that Emily was poor?* (yes) *Could they pity Miss Emily?* (yes) **SUBSTANTIAL**

- Direct pairs of students to skim the paragraph for clues and complete the following frames: *The townspeople thought Emily _____. The townspeople liked that Emily _____.* **MODERATE**

- Encourage students to reread the paragraph silently. Then, direct small groups to answer the question: *Why were the townspeople glad Miss Emily became poor after her father died?* Have them use text evidence to support their responses during their discussion. **LIGHT**

WRITING

Write a Reflection

Work with students to read the writing assignment on Student Edition page 589.

Use the following supports with students at varying proficiency levels:

- Work with students to create a three-column chart with the headings *Characters, Setting,* and *Clues.* Help them identify words and phrases in the story that hint at the ending. Then, use the details to write a paragraph on the board. Have students copy the paragraph into their notebooks. **SUBSTANTIAL**

- Provide sentence frames that students can use to craft their essays: *I can/cannot believe that _____. I knew she was _____, but I can't believe she _____. I am surprised because _____.* **MODERATE**

- Remind students of transitions they can use, such as *on the one hand, on the other hand, however, first, next,* and *finally.* Have pairs find three places in their essays to add transitions. **LIGHT**

Connect to the
ESSENTIAL QUESTION

"A Rose for Emily" tells the story of a woman who was prevented from marrying by her oppressive father. Over time, the isolated woman develops very peculiar habits, some of which cause conflict with her fellow townspeople.

ANALYZE & APPLY

A ROSE FOR EMILY

Short Story by **William Faulkner**

? **ESSENTIAL QUESTION:**

How do we deal with rejection or isolation?

574 · Unit 6

© Houghton Mifflin Harcourt Publishing Company • Image Credits: © siam.pukkato/Shutterstock

QUICK START

Certain scenes from books and movies can create a creepy atmosphere so effectively that they can leave you shaky and repulsed. What books and movies have presented a scene or atmosphere that made you shudder? What works top your "creepiness scale"? Discuss your ideas in a small group.

MAKE AND CONFIRM PREDICTIONS

When you **make predictions,** you use clues in the text to make a reasonable guess about what will happen in a story. Watching for clues about the characters, setting, and plot can help you predict what will happen next and how the conflicts will be resolved. Sometimes, your predictions will be correct; other times, a story will surprise you with a plot twist. As you read, make inferences and predictions and note whether your predictions were correct. Use a chart like this one to help you make and confirm predictions.

CLUES FROM THE TEXT	PREDICTION	CONFIRM OR CORRECT PREDICTION
Clues should be specific details from the story.	*Predictions should be a logical guess as to what might happen.*	*If prediction was incorrect, present a revision.*

ANALYZE LITERARY ELEMENTS: Setting and Characterization

The **setting** of a work refers to the time and place in which the action occurs. A story can be set in the past, present, or future, or a combination thereof, and in real or imaginary places. In addition, settings can evoke a larger historical, social, or economic backdrop that adds context and deeper meaning to the events. This story takes place at the turn of the 20th century in a fictional small town in the deep South. In the description below, Faulkner includes details about social and economic conditions to bring the setting to life.

> It was a big, squarish frame house that had once been white, decorated with cupolas and spires and scrolled balconies in the heavily lightsome style of the seventies, set on what had once been our most select street. But garages and cotton gins had encroached and obliterated even the august names of that neighborhood; only Miss Emily's house was left. . . .

In "A Rose for Emily," setting impacts how the reader understands Miss Emily's behaviors and motivations and the townspeople's reactions to them. As you read, notice details that reveal the social and economic setting and how it affects your perception of characters and events.

GENRE ELEMENTS: SHORT STORY

- adds context to setting with historical, economic, and social details
- usually centers around one main conflict
- typically includes details that hint at how the main conflict will be resolved

---

TEACH

QUICK START

Have students read the Quick Start questions and point out to them that authors looking to create a "creepy" story will choose their setting carefully. Some settings are creepier than others. Have students suggest a setting for a story that is creepy and then one that is not. Have them repeat this until you begin to see patterns in what is generally thought of as creepy.

MAKE AND CONFIRM PREDICTIONS

Tell students that with some stories, particularly mysteries, readers can't help but try to predict the ending. Ask students if they think they are good at predicting the conclusions of stories. Ask them what they think makes a story predictable or not. Then, tell students that making predictions is an important reading strategy and keeps readers interested in the text. Have students provide examples of books or movies that have had predictable endings. Then, ask students to provide examples of stories that had surprise endings.

ANALYZE LITERARY ELEMENTS: Setting and Characterization

Take a moment to explain to students what the Deep South was like around the turn of the century. During this period, the region was still recovering from the Civil War (which ended in 1865). The physical landscape—including both rural and urban areas—had been heavily damaged in the war, and the population had suffered major losses. At the turn of the century, the economy was still largely agricultural and struggling. Southern writers of the early 20th century, such as William Faulkner and Flannery O'Connor, used the setting of the Deep South as a prominent feature in their stories. Tell students to look for evidence of this as they read the story.

Remind students that the setting can impact the plot, conflict, and characters. Tell students to keep the setting of the Deep South in mind as they read the story and think about how the setting affected Miss Emily and the townspeople.

CRITICAL VOCABULARY

Encourage students to read all of the phrases before deciding which word best fits each definition. Remind them to look for context clues that might point to the meaning of each word.

Answers:

1. *virulent*

2. *cabal*

3. *tableau*

4. *acrid*

5. *circumvent*

6. noblesse oblige

7. *vindicate*

8. *archaic*

■ English Learner Support

Use Cognates Tell students that one of the Critical Vocabulary words has a Spanish cognate: *archaic/arcaico*.
ALL LEVELS

LANGUAGE CONVENTIONS

Point of View To begin a discussion about the first-person plural point of view, have students list the most common points of view used in literature. These include first-person singular and third person. Ask students why first-person plural is an unusual point of view to choose. Have they ever read a story with this point of view?

Have students make up sentences using each point of view. Ask volunteers to share their examples. *(Examples: First-person singular: "I am looking forward to the holidays." Third person: "A tear fell down Anna's face." First-person plural: "We were surprised to find that Anna was crying.")*

ANNOTATION MODEL

Remind students of the annotation ideas on page 575, which suggest noting how details about the setting impact their understanding of.the characters and plot. Point out that they may follow this suggestion or use their own system for marking up the selection in their write-in text. They may want to color-code their annotations by using highlighters. Their notes in the margin may include questions about the characters, events, or setting or ideas that they are unclear about.

 **GET READY**

CRITICAL VOCABULARY

archaic	vindicate	cabal	virulent
tableau	*noblesse oblige*	circumvent	acrid

To see how many Critical Vocabulary words you already know, match each with the correct definition below.

1. Said of an attack that is extremely malicious or hateful: _____

2. A group united in a secret plot: _____

3. A dramatic scene or picture: _____

4. Having a sharp, pungent, or bitter taste or smell: _____

5. To avoid or get around by artful maneuvering: _____

6. The expectation that those of high standing will behave well: _____

7. To justify or prove the validity of something: _____

8. Something that suggests an earlier period of time: _____

LANGUAGE CONVENTIONS

Point of View A key decision in narrative writing is choosing an effective point of view, the narrative perspective from which events in a story are told. In "A Rose for Emily," Faulkner has selected the unusual first-person plural point of view, telling the tale from the townspeople's perspective, which is reflected by his use of the pronouns *we*, *us*, and *our*. It offers the intimacy of a first-person narrative, but adds a sense of uncertainty because the narrator isn't one person but a group of people.

ANNOTATION MODEL   **NOTICE & NOTE**

As you read, notice clues that will help you make predictions about the characters or events. Note details about setting that relate to character behavior and motivation. You can see one reader's notes about "A Rose for Emily" below.

> When Miss Emily Grierson died, <u>our whole town went to her funeral</u>: the men through a sort of respectful affection for a <u>fallen monument</u>, the women mostly out of curiosity to see the inside of the house, which <u>no one save an old manservant—a combined gardener and cook—had seen in at least ten years</u>.

Miss Emily was probably an important person in the town.

Why has no one been in the house?

BACKGROUND

William Faulkner *(1897–1962) struggled to find his ideal subject matter. When he finally decided to focus on his home state of Mississippi, he blossomed. He turned out masterpieces at a remarkable rate, including* The Sound and the Fury *(1929) and* As I Lay Dying *(1930). Many of his short stories and novels take place in his imaginary world of Yoknapatawpha County and populated with a variety of characters. His first readers found Faulkner's world too hard to understand. Today, Faulkner's works are revered for their strong themes and narrative technique.*

A ROSE FOR EMILY

Short Story by William Faulkner

SETTING A PURPOSE

As you read, think about how the setting, the townspeople's expectations, and the events of Emily's life reflect the larger historical, cultural, and economic context of the time. Be aware that contemporary readers may find some language derogatory or offensive.

I

1   When Miss Emily Grierson died, our whole town went to her funeral: the men through a sort of respectful affection for a fallen monument, the women mostly out of curiosity to see the inside of her house, which no one save an old manservant—a combined gardener and cook—had seen in at least ten years.

2   It was a big, squarish frame house that had once been white, decorated with cupolas and spires and scrolled balconies in the heavily lightsome style of the seventies,[1] set on what had once been our most select street. But garages and cotton gins had encroached and obliterated even the august names of that neighborhood; only Miss Emily's house was left, lifting its stubborn and coquettish decay above the cotton wagons and the gasoline pumps—an eyesore among eyesores. And now Miss

---

[1] **the seventies:** the 1870s.

Notice & Note

Use the side margins to notice and note signposts in the text.

ANALYZE LITERARY ELEMENTS: SETTING

Annotate: Mark details in paragraph 2 that describe the setting.

Analyze: What do these details tell you about the social and economic conditions of the time? How do they shape your perceptions about Emily?

BACKGROUND

After students read the Background note, explain that many of Faulkner's stories are labeled as a subgenre of fiction called Southern Gothic. Stories in this subgenre are often very atmospheric, with dark and gloomy settings. They often involve ruins or elements from the past that live on in everyday life. In much of southern literature from this period, the past—particularly the previous several decades—is very present, due to the traumatic nature of the Civil War, which ended in 1865. Authors in this subgenre work hard to create settings that are evocative and that can help propel a story.

SETTING A PURPOSE

Direct students to use the Setting a Purpose prompt to focus their reading.

ANALYZE LITERARY ELEMENTS: SETTING

Remind students that setting impacts characters and also reveals a lot about them. It is important to pay attention to the setting, particularly in the exposition to get a sense of the time, place, and characters. Then, note the style of home being described in the introduction would today be called "Victorian." An image search on the Internet for "Victorian house" will yield many examples of this style. Explain that these houses were highly decorated in an effort to display a family's wealth—or at least good taste—to the community. (**Answer:** *The details show that the town has been through many social and economic changes. The street being described once had many beautiful and elaborate homes, but now mostly has cotton gins and gasoline pumps. Emily has lived there a long time, but now she lives in the only house on the street. The details make me feel sorry for her, since she might be alone.*)

ENGLISH LEARNER SUPPORT

Describe Setting   Have students circle or highlight words in their text that describe Emily's house. Tell them that the description of the house is the author's first step in describing the setting of the story. Have students write a sentence describing the setting, using this sentence frame: *The setting of the story is _____ and _____.* **MODERATE**

ANALYZE LITERARY ELEMENTS: CHARACTERIZATION

Explain that authors have many ways of developing characters. In paragraph 3, Faulkner describes the character of Emily by discussing how the town treated her, rather than by describing her directly. The paragraph also reveals important information about the townspeople, who seem to act as one person. (**Answer:** *The town had a tradition of taking care of its citizens. Like a human character, it has an obligation.*)

ANALYZE LITERARY ELEMENTS: CHARACTERIZATION

Annotate: Mark the phrase in paragraph 3 that suggests what the town thinks about Miss Emily.

Interpret: What does paragraph 3 tell you about the town and its traditions?

Emily had gone to join the representatives of those august names where they lay in the cedar-bemused[2] cemetery among the ranked and anonymous graves of Union and Confederate soldiers who fell at the battle of Jefferson.

3   Alive, Miss Emily had been a tradition, a duty, and a care; a sort of hereditary obligation upon the town, dating from that day in 1894 when Colonel Sartoris, the mayor—he who fathered the edict that no Negro woman should appear on the streets without an apron—remitted her taxes, the dispensation dating from the death of her father on into perpetuity.[3] Not that Miss Emily would have accepted charity. Colonel Sartoris invented an involved tale to the effect that Miss Emily's father had loaned money to the town, which the town, as a matter of business, preferred this way of repaying. Only a man of Colonel Sartoris' generation and thought could have invented it, and only a woman could have believed it.

4   When the next generation, with its more modern ideas, became mayors and aldermen, this arrangement created some little dissatisfaction. On the first of the year they mailed her a tax notice. February came, and there was no reply. They wrote her a formal letter, asking her to call at the sheriff's office at her convenience. A week later the mayor wrote her himself, offering to call or to send

---

[2] **cedar-bemused:** almost lost in cedar trees.
[3] **remitted . . . perpetuity:** released her from paying taxes forever from the time of her father's death.

WHEN STUDENTS STRUGGLE . . .

Understand Plot   When a story jumps back and forth in time, it can be useful for students to use a timeline to keep track of the plot and character development. Provide a blank timeline which students can use to keep track of events as they read the story. For example, a significant year in paragraph 3 is 1894, when Emily's father dies and the mayor cancels all of her taxes.

   For additional support, go to the **Reading Studio** and assign the following [LEVEL UP] **Level Up Tutorial: Plot: Sequence of Events.**

his car for her, and received in reply a note on paper of an **archaic** shape, in a thin, flowing calligraphy in faded ink, to the effect that she no longer went out at all. The tax notice was also enclosed, without comment.

5   They called a special meeting of the Board of Aldermen. A deputation waited upon her, knocked at the door through which no visitor had passed since she ceased giving china-painting lessons eight or ten years earlier. They were admitted by the old Negro into a dim hall from which a stairway mounted into still more shadow. It smelled of dust and disuse—a close, dank smell. The Negro led them into the parlor. It was furnished in heavy, leather-covered furniture. When the Negro opened the blinds of one window, they could see that the leather was cracked; and when they sat down, a faint dust rose sluggishly about their thighs, spinning with slow motes in the single sun-ray. On a tarnished gilt easel before the fireplace stood a crayon portrait of Miss Emily's father.

6   They rose when she entered—a small, fat woman in black, with a thin gold chain descending to her waist and vanishing into her belt, leaning on an ebony cane with a tarnished gold head. Her skeleton was small and spare; perhaps that was why what would have been merely plumpness in another was obesity in her. She looked bloated, like a body long submerged in motionless water, and of that pallid hue. Her eyes, lost in the fatty ridges of her face, looked like two small pieces of coal pressed into a lump of dough as they moved from one face to another while the visitors stated their errand.

7   She did not ask them to sit. She just stood in the door and listened quietly until the spokesman came to a stumbling halt. Then they could hear the invisible watch ticking at the end of the gold chain.

8   Her voice was dry and cold. "I have no taxes in Jefferson. Colonel Sartoris explained it to me. Perhaps one of you can gain access to the city records and satisfy yourselves."

9   "But we have. We are the city authorities, Miss Emily. Didn't you get a notice from the sheriff, signed by him?"

10 "I received a paper, yes," Miss Emily said. "Perhaps he considers himself the sheriff . . . I have no taxes in Jefferson."

11 "But there is nothing on the books to show that, you see. We must go by the—"

12 "See Colonel Sartoris. I have no taxes in Jefferson."

13 "But, Miss Emily—"

14 "See Colonel Sartoris." (Colonel Sartoris had been dead almost ten years.) "I have no taxes in Jefferson. Tobe!" The Negro appeared. "Show these gentlemen out."

---

archaic
(är-kā´ĭk) *adj.* relating to, being, or characteristic of a much earlier period.

ANALYZE LITERARY ELEMENTS: SETTING
Annotate: In paragraph 5, mark the words and phrases that suggest the room has not been used in a while.

Draw Conclusions: What does the setting suggest about Miss Emily's social and economic circumstances?

ANALYZE LITERARY ELEMENTS: CHARACTERIZATION
Annotate: In paragraphs 8–14, mark the lines in the exchange between Miss Emily and the city authorities that reveal more about Miss Emily.

Draw Conclusions: What does the exchange reveal about Miss Emily and about the city authorities?

✏ ANALYZE LITERARY ELEMENTS: SETTING

Remind students that setting entails more than a story's location. It also includes details of the environment. These details can be loaded with meaning, and a reader should pay close attention to them to learn more about a character. (**Answer:** *The furniture is old and neglected, and no one has cleaned recently. She hasn't had visitors in a very long time. The furniture hints at her former wealthy status, but she seems to have fallen on hard times and withdrawn from society.*)

📖 For **listening support** for students at varying proficiency levels, see the **Text X-Ray** on page 574C.

✏ ANALYZE LITERARY ELEMENTS: CHARACTERIZATION

Dialogue is an effective way for authors to reveal character traits. Tell students that they should pay attention to the description of the delivery of speech, as well as to the actual lines of speech. For example, the fact that Emily's "voice was dry and cold" says something about her personality. (**Answer:** *She is accustomed to getting her way. She doesn't have a grip on reality. The authorities want Emily to get with the times and pay her taxes, but they also respect her age and standing in the town.*)

TO CHALLENGE STUDENTS . . .

Analyze Characterization   The dialogue in paragraphs 8 through 14 is both entertaining and enlightening. Emily's treatment of the city authorities is so dismissive, curt, and rude that it comes off as humorous. Have students read this well-crafted scene very closely to study how Faulkner achieves this tone. In particular, have students dissect Emily's response to being asked about getting a note from the sheriff: " . . . Perhaps he considers himself the sheriff . . ." (**Answer:** *The response shows just how stubborn and contrary Emily is. She refuses even to acknowledge the authority of the current sheriff, preferring to live in the past when her family went unquestioned.*)

CRITICAL VOCABULARY

archaic: It makes sense that Emily would have many archaic things in her house, given her disinterest in going out.

ASK STUDENTS to list several things that are *archaic*. (*Possible answers include old traditions, such as formal balls; superstitions; and old technology, such as typewriters.*)

ENGLISH LEARNER SUPPORT

Ask Questions Use the following questions to guide students' understanding of paragraphs 15–24. Allow pairs of students to discuss each question in their home languages before answering.

- After her father's death, did Emily leave the house much? *(no)*

- What do neighbors complain most about? *(a smell)*

- Is the judge mean or kind toward Emily? *(kind)*

- Is the judge willing to accuse Emily of creating the smell? *(no)*

- Is the Board of Aldermen willing to ignore the smell? *(no)*

- Does Emily catch the group of men sneaking around her property? *(yes)* **SUBSTANTIAL**

II

15 So she vanquished them, horse and foot, just as she had vanquished their fathers thirty years before about the smell. That was two years after her father's death and a short time after her sweetheart—the one we believed would marry her—had deserted her. After her father's death she went out very little; after her sweetheart went away, people hardly saw her at all. A few of the ladies had the temerity[4] to call, but were not received, and the only sign of life about the place was the Negro man—a young man then—going in and out with a market basket.

16 "Just as if a man—any man—could keep a kitchen properly," the ladies said; so they were not surprised when the smell developed. It was another link between the gross, teeming world and the high and mighty Griersons.

17 A neighbor, a woman, complained to the mayor, Judge Stevens, eighty years old.

18 "But what will you have me do about it, madam?" he said.

19 "Why, send her word to stop it," the woman said. "Isn't there a law?"

20 "I'm sure that won't be necessary," Judge Stevens said. "It's probably just a snake or a rat that nigger of hers killed in the yard. I'll speak to him about it."

21 The next day he received two more complaints, one from a man who came in diffident deprecation.[5] "We really must do something about it, Judge. I'd be the last one in the world to bother Miss Emily, but we've got to do something." That night the Board of Aldermen met—three graybeards and one younger man, a member of the rising generation.

22 "It's simple enough," he said. "Send her word to have her place cleaned up. Give her a certain time to do it in, and if she don't . . ."

23 "Dammit, sir," Judge Stevens said, "will you accuse a lady to her face of smelling bad?"

24 So the next night, after midnight, four men crossed Miss Emily's lawn and slunk about the house like burglars, sniffing along the base of the brickwork and at the cellar openings while one of them performed a regular sowing motion with his hand out of a sack slung from his shoulder. They broke open the cellar door and sprinkled lime there, and in all the outbuildings. As they recrossed the lawn, a window that had been dark was lighted and Miss Emily sat in it, the light behind her, and her upright torso motionless as that of an idol. They crept quietly across the lawn and into the shadow of the locusts that lined the street. After a week or two the smell went away.

---

[4] **temerity** (tə-měr´ ĭ-tē): foolish boldness.
[5] **diffident deprecation:** timid disapproval.

APPLYING ACADEMIC VOCABULARY

☑ **contemporary** ☐ **global** ☐ **infinite** ☐ **simulated** ☑ **virtual**

Write and Discuss Have students turn to a partner to discuss the following questions. Guide students to use the Academic Vocabulary words *contemporary* and *virtual* in their responses.

- Why would you want to warn **contemporary** readers about the language in this story?

- If you were to make a website for Faulkner's fictitious Yoknapatawpha County government, what kind of **virtual** features would you include?

25   That was when people had begun to feel really sorry for her. People in our town, remembering how old lady Wyatt, her great-aunt, had gone <u>completely crazy</u> at last, believed that the Griersons held themselves a little too high for what they really were. None of the young men were quite good enough for Miss Emily and such. We had long thought of them as a **tableau**, Miss Emily a slender figure in white in the background, her father a spraddled silhouette in the foreground, his back to her and clutching a horsewhip, the two of them framed by the backflung front door. So when she got to be thirty and was still single, we were not pleased exactly, but **vindicated**; even with <u>insanity</u> in the family she wouldn't have turned down all of her chances if they had really materialized.

26   When her father died, it got about that the house was all that was left to her; and in a way, people were glad. At last they could pity Miss Emily. Being left alone, and a pauper, she had become humanized. Now she too would know the old thrill and the old despair of a penny more or less.

27   The day after his death all the ladies prepared to call at the house and offer condolence and aid, as is our custom. Miss Emily met them at the door, dressed as usual and with no trace of grief on her face. She told them that her father was not dead. She did that for three days, with the ministers calling on her, and the doctors, trying to persuade her to let them dispose of the body. Just as they were about to resort to law and force, she broke down, and they buried her father quickly.

28   We did not say she was crazy then. We believed she had to do that. We remembered all the young men her father had driven away, and we knew that with nothing left, she would have to cling to that which had robbed her, as people will.

III

29 She was sick for a long time. When we saw her again, her hair was cut short, making her look like a girl, with a vague resemblance to those angels in colored church windows—sort of tragic and serene.

30   The town had just let the contracts for paving the sidewalks, and in the summer after her father's death they began the work. The construction company came with niggers and mules and machinery, and a foreman named Homer Barron, a Yankee—a big, dark, ready man, with a big voice and eyes lighter than his face. The little boys would follow in groups to hear him cuss the niggers, and the niggers singing in time to the rise and fall of picks. Pretty soon he knew everybody in town. Whenever you heard a lot of laughing anywhere about the square, Homer Barron would be in the center of the group. Presently we began to see him and Miss Emily on Sunday afternoons driving in the yellow-wheeled buggy and the matched team of bays from the livery stable.

© Houghton Mifflin Harcourt Publishing Company

MAKE AND CONFIRM PREDICTIONS

Annotate: Mark words in paragraph 25 that suggest mental instability in the Grierson family.

Predict: How does this paragraph confirm what paragraph 15 suggested about Emily? What do you predict was the cause of the smell?

tableau
(tăb´lō) *n.* a dramatic scene or picture.

vindicate
(vĭn´dĭ-kāt) *v.* to demonstrate or prove the validity of; justify.

ENGLISH LEARNER SUPPORT

Express Opinions Remind students that an opinion is a belief or view that a person has that is not a proven fact. Read aloud paragraph 25. Then, ask students to express their opinions about Emily and her past. For example, *Do you feel sorry for Emily? Do you think Emily's father was nice?* Provide sentence frames such as these: *I feel sorry for her because _____. I think her father was _____. I believe the townspeople were _____.* **MODERATE**

MAKE AND CONFIRM PREDICTIONS

"A Rose for Emily" invites predictions from the reader because the townspeople are engaged in making predictions, too. Faulkner has made Emily a mysterious figure by giving her inexplicable behaviors and an obstinate, uncommunicative manner. As the townspeople grow confused and intrigued, so does the reader. This helps hold the reader's attention. (**Answer:** *In paragraph 15, she seemed stubborn, like she wanted to cling to the past. Paragraph 25 confirms that she may not have a grip on reality. This suggests that the smell was caused by something far worse than the townspeople imagined, such as a dead body.*)

For **speaking** and **reading support** for students at varying proficiency levels, see the **Text X-Ray** on page 574D.

CRITICAL VOCABULARY

tableau: Faulkner describes the tableau as if discussing a painting, with characters in the foreground and background.

ASK STUDENTS what else might be considered a tableau. *(Answers might include a dramatic painting, an elaborate wedding, or a presidential inauguration.)*

vindicate: The townspeople felt vindicated when Emily ended up single.

ASK STUDENTS what they think it is like to feel vindicated. *(Answers might include happy, satisfied, reassured, or proud.)*

MAKE AND CONFIRM PREDICTIONS

When making predictions about a character, the reader should look for any odd behaviors. Discuss with students some of Emily's strange behaviors in this scene, beginning with paragraph 34. Her actions make her look rather suspicious, as does her refusal to answer the question. (**Answer:** *herself, the cousins, someone else—but probably not rats*)

CRITICAL VOCABULARY

noblesse oblige: The older women in town, knowing that Emily valued her dignity, expected her to behave with a certain *noblesse oblige.*

ASK STUDENTS to describe some characteristics of someone exhibiting *noblesse oblige.* (*Answers may include dressing well, having good manners and posture, and being dignified in public.*)

NOTICE & NOTE

noblesse oblige
(nō-blĕs´ ō-blēzh´) *n.* the responsibility of people in a high social position to behave in a noble fashion.

MAKE AND CONFIRM PREDICTIONS
Annotate: In paragraph 34, mark what Emily is buying.

Predict: For what or whom might she want to use this purchase?

31   At first we were glad that Miss Emily would have an interest, because the ladies all said, "Of course a Grierson would not think seriously of a Northerner, a day laborer." But there were still others, older people, who said that even grief could not cause a real lady to forget **noblesse oblige**—without calling it *noblesse oblige.* They just said, "Poor Emily. Her kinsfolk should come to her." She had some kin in Alabama; but years ago her father had fallen out with them over the estate of old lady Wyatt, the crazy woman, and there was no communication between the two families. They had not even been represented at the funeral.

32   And as soon as the old people said, "Poor Emily," the whispering began. "Do you suppose it's really so?" they said to one another. "Of course it is. What else could . . ." This behind their hands; rustling of craned silk and satin behind jalousies[6] closed upon the sun of Sunday afternoon as the thin, swift clop-clop-clop of the matched team passed: "Poor Emily."

33   She carried her head high enough—even when we believed that she was fallen. It was as if she demanded more than ever the recognition of her dignity as the last Grierson; as if it had wanted that touch of earthiness to reaffirm her imperviousness.[7] Like when she bought the rat poison, the arsenic. That was over a year after they had begun to say "Poor Emily," and while the two female cousins were visiting her.

34   "I want some poison," she said to the druggist. She was over thirty then, still a slight woman, though thinner than usual, with cold, haughty black eyes in a face the flesh of which was strained across the temples and about the eye-sockets as you imagine a lighthouse-keeper's face ought to look. "I want some poison," she said.

35   "Yes, Miss Emily. What kind? For rats and such? I'd recom—"

36   "I want the best you have. I don't care what kind."

37   The druggist named several. "They'll kill anything up to an elephant. But what you want is—"

38   "Arsenic," Miss Emily said. "Is that a good one?"

39   "Is . . . arsenic? Yes, ma'am. But what you want—"

40   "I want arsenic."

41   The druggist looked down at her. She looked back at him, erect, her face like a strained flag. "Why, of course," the druggist said. "If that's what you want. But the law requires you to tell what you are going to use it for."

42   Miss Emily just stared at him, her head tilted back in order to look him eye for eye, until he looked away and went and got the arsenic and wrapped it up. The Negro delivery boy brought her

---

[6] **jalousies** (jăl´ə-sēz): blinds or shutters containing overlapping slats that can be opened or closed.
[7] **imperviousness** (ĭm-pûr´vē-əs-nəs): an inability to be affected or disturbed.

582   Unit 6

IMPROVE READING FLUENCY

Targeted Passage Paragraphs 34–41 contain amusing dialogue. Have students take turns echo reading these paragraphs. This dialogue is a good opportunity for students to read with expression. In the humorous exchange, the druggist is put in an awkward situation by Emily, who refuses to explain herself and her odd request.

  Go to the **Reading Studio** for additional support in developing fluency.

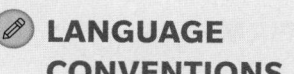

the package; the druggist didn't come back. When she opened the package at home there was written on the box, under the skull and bones: "For rats."

IV

43 So the next day we all said, "She will kill herself"; and we said it would be the best thing. When she had first begun to be seen with Homer Barron, we had said, "She will marry him." Then we said, "She will persuade him yet," because Homer himself had remarked—he liked men, and it was known that he drank with the younger men in the Elks' Club—that he was not a marrying man. Later we said, "Poor Emily" behind the jalousies as they passed on Sunday afternoon in the glittering buggy, Miss Emily with her head high and Homer Barron with his hat cocked and a cigar in his teeth, reins and whip in a yellow glove.

LANGUAGE CONVENTIONS

Annotate: Mark the pronoun that identifies the narrator in paragraph 43.

Evaluate: What effect does the point of view chosen by the author have on the telling of the story?

A Rose for Emily   583

LANGUAGE CONVENTIONS

Remind students that first-person plural is an unusual choice for a narrator. Most stories are written in first-person singular or third person. Discuss with students why the author might have made the point of view first-person plural rather than first-person singular. (**Answer:** *It has the effect of making the town a character. The reader sees Emily through the town's eyes. The reader only knows how the town sees her, and like the townspeople, the reader has no idea what Emily has been doing for ten years. She is a mystery to everyone.*)

WHEN STUDENTS STRUGGLE . . .

Analyze Character In paragraph 43, Emily makes an appearance in public. As students read the story, have them record instances of these public appearances and how other people react to them. They can record instances in the side margin of their write-in text. Point out that Faulkner isn't just writing about an eccentric character; he is writing about an entire town that is nosy and judgmental.

For additional support, go to the **Reading Studio** and assign the following **Level Up Tutorial: Character Motivation.**

TEACH

✏️ MAKE AND CONFIRM PREDICTIONS

Tell students that as they read, they should try to confirm their previous predictions. If they are unable to confirm a prediction, then they should revise it, adjusting it to account for new information. This engagement with the text is part of an active reading process. (**Answer:** *Maybe he left town. Maybe Emily locked him up. Maybe he died.*)

CRITICAL VOCABULARY

cabal: The townspeople came together in a cabal to help Emily avoid her cousins.

ASK STUDENTS what the difference is between a cabal and a club. (*Answers might include that a cabal's actions are secret, while a club is usually public.*)

circumvent: You circumvent something you want to avoid, rather than something pleasant. Miss Emily's allies helped her avoid the cousins.

ASK STUDENTS what they can imagine themselves circumventing. (*Answers might include a traffic jam, people arguing in the hallway, or a large puddle.*)

virulent: The townspeople thought Emily's father's actions were virulent, or malicious.

ASK STUDENTS how they think the word *virulent* might relate to *virus*. (*Answers will vary but might include that the words come from the same root, which is why* virulent *has a negative connotation. Something virulent can be hard to shake, much like a virus.*)

---

44 Then some of the ladies began to say that it was a disgrace to the town and a bad example to the young people. The men did not want to interfere, but at last the ladies forced the Baptist minister—Miss Emily's people were Episcopal—to call upon her. He would never divulge what happened during that interview, but he refused to go back again. The next Sunday they again drove about the streets, and the following day the minister's wife wrote to Miss Emily's relations in Alabama.

45 So she had blood-kin under her roof again and we sat back to watch developments. At first nothing happened. Then we were sure that they were to be married. We learned that Miss Emily had been to the jeweler's and ordered a man's toilet set in silver, with the letters H. B. on each piece. Two days later we learned that she had bought a complete outfit of men's clothing, including a nightshirt, and we said, "They are married." We were really glad. We were glad because the two female cousins were even more Grierson than Miss Emily had ever been.

46 So we were not surprised when Homer Barron—the streets had been finished some time since—was gone. We were a little disappointed that there was not a public blowing-off,[8] but we believed that he had gone on to prepare for Miss Emily's coming, or to give her a chance to get rid of the cousins. (By that time it was a **cabal**, and we were all Miss Emily's allies to help **circumvent** the cousins.) Sure enough, after another week they departed. And, as we had expected all along, within three days Homer Barron was back in town. A neighbor saw the Negro man admit him at the kitchen door at dusk one evening.

47 And that was the last we saw of Homer Barron. And of Miss Emily for some time. The Negro man went in and out with the market basket, but the front door remained closed. Now and then we would see her at a window for a moment, as the men did that night when they sprinkled the lime, but for almost six months she did not appear on the streets. Then we knew that this was to be expected too; as if that quality of her father which had thwarted her woman's life so many times had been too **virulent** and too furious to die.

48 When we next saw Miss Emily, she had grown fat and her hair was turning gray. During the next few years it grew grayer and grayer until it attained an even pepper-and-salt iron-gray, when it ceased turning. Up to the day of her death at seventy-four it was still that vigorous iron-gray, like the hair of an active man.

49 From that time on her front door remained closed, save for a period of six or seven years, when she was about forty, during which she gave lessons in china-painting. She fitted up a studio in one of the downstairs rooms, where the daughters and granddaughters of

---

[8] **blowing-off:** here, a celebration.

---

cabal
(kə-bäl´) *n.* a group united in a secret plot.

circumvent
(sûr-kəm-vĕnt´) *v.* to avoid or get around by artful maneuvering.

MAKE AND CONFIRM PREDICTIONS

Annotate: Mark the sentence in paragraph 47 that raises a question about Homer Barron.

Predict: Why do you think people never saw Homer Barron again?

virulent
(vîr´yə-lənt) *adj.* extremely hostile or malicious.

© Houghton Mifflin Harcourt Publishing Company

Colonel Sartoris' contemporaries were sent to her with the same regularity and in the same spirit that they were sent to church on Sundays with a twenty-five-cent piece for the collection plate. Meanwhile her taxes had been remitted.

50   Then the newer generation became the backbone and the spirit of the town, and the painting pupils grew up and fell away and did not send their children to her with boxes of color and tedious brushes and pictures cut from the ladies' magazines. The front door closed upon the last one and remained closed for good. When the town got free postal delivery, Miss Emily alone refused to let them fasten the metal numbers above her door and attach a mailbox to it. She would not listen to them.

51   Daily, monthly, yearly we watched the Negro grow grayer and more stooped, going in and out with the market basket. Each December we sent her a tax notice, which would be returned by the post office a week later, unclaimed. Now and then we would see her in one of the downstairs windows—she had evidently shut up the top floor of the house—like the carven torso of an idol in a niche, looking or not looking at us, we could never tell which. Thus she passed from generation to generation—dear, inescapable, impervious, tranquil, and perverse.

52   And so she died. Fell ill in the house filled with dust and shadows, with only a doddering Negro man to wait on her. We did not even know she was sick; we had long since given up trying to get any information from the Negro. He talked to no one, probably not even to her, for his voice had grown harsh and rusty, as if from disuse.

53   She died in one of the downstairs rooms, in a heavy walnut bed with a curtain, her gray head propped on a pillow yellow and moldy with age and lack of sunlight.

V

54   The Negro met the first of the ladies at the front door and let them in, with their hushed, sibilant voices and their quick, curious glances, and then he disappeared. He walked right through the house and out the back and was not seen again.

55   The two female cousins came at once. They held the funeral on the second day, with the town coming to look at Miss Emily beneath a mass of bought flowers, with the crayon face of her father musing profoundly above the bier[9] and the ladies sibilant and macabre; and the very old men—some in their brushed Confederate uniforms— on the porch and the lawn, talking of Miss Emily as if she had been a contemporary of theirs, believing that they had danced with her and courted her perhaps, confusing time with its mathematical progression, as the old do, to whom all the past is not a diminishing

---

[9] **bier:** coffin along with its stand.

© Houghton Mifflin Harcourt Publishing Company

ANALYZE LITERARY ELEMENTS: SETTING

Annotate: In paragraphs 48–52, mark words that indicate the passing of time.

Draw Conclusions: What contrast between Miss Emily and the townspeople is illustrated by the passing of time?

ANALYZE LITERARY ELEMENTS: CHARACTERIZATION

Annotate: In paragraph 52, mark words and phrases that describe the manservant.

Draw Conclusions: The old manservant enters the story just after we meet Emily. What does the repeated mentioning of his age suggest about his role as a character? What does his character help you understand about the town?

ANALYZE LITERARY ELEMENTS: SETTING

Remind students that the time period is an element of setting, along with location. A story set during colonial times, for example, will be different than one set in the present-day United States. As students read, have them take note of changes in the time period. (**Answer:** *The townspeople are moving on with their lives and adapting to the changing times, but Emily is frozen in time. She has no contact with anyone and resists all efforts to modernize.*)

ANALYZE LITERARY ELEMENTS: CHARACTERIZATION

Explain that authors include characters for specific reasons. Sometimes minor characters, like this manservant, help readers understand the other characters, the plot, and the setting. (**Answer:** *He serves mainly as a device to track the time, as the story moves from present to past to further past to present. His name is used only once and he's seen as a servant more than a person, which identifies his social standing in the town. His age and description suggest that the town thinks of him as a relic of a bygone era, just like they do of Miss Emily.*)

WHEN STUDENTS STRUGGLE . . .

Analyze Literary Elements: Characterization Remind students to keep adding entries to their timeline. Below are a few significant moments to include:

- Emily takes a "sweetheart" (Homer)
- Homer seems to desert her
- Emily dies

 For additional support, go to the **Reading Studio** and assign the following 🔺 **Level Up Tutorial: Plot: Sequence of Events.**

AHA MOMENT

Point out that paragraph 56 is building tension for the reader. The narrator seems certain that the mysterious room at the top of the stairs holds a secret of some sort. Perhaps that secret will answer questions that the townspeople had about Emily. Suggest that students read these final sentences very carefully. Paragraphs 57 and 58 will show them whether their predictions about this odd and mysterious protagonist were accurate. (**Possible answer:** *Since the townspeople knew there was a room that would have to be forced open, they suspected there might be something frightening in it, possibly related to Homer Barron.*)

CRITICAL VOCABULARY

acrid: The air of the room is described as acrid, which would be unusual for a normal room in a house.

ASK STUDENTS what would be the usual response to smelling something acrid. *(revulsion, disgust, nausea, and so on)*

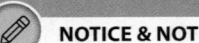

NOTICE & NOTE

road but, instead, a huge meadow which no winter ever quite touches, divided from them now by the narrow bottleneck of the most recent decade of years.

56   Already we knew that there was one room in that region above stairs which no one had seen in forty years, and which would have to be forced. They waited until Miss Emily was decently in the ground before they opened it.

57   The violence of breaking down the door seemed to fill this room with pervading dust. A thin, **acrid** pall[10] as of the tomb seemed to lie everywhere upon this room decked and furnished as for a bridal: upon the valance curtains of faded rose color, upon the rose-shaded lights, upon the dressing table, upon the delicate array of crystal and the man's toilet things backed with tarnished silver, silver so tarnished that the monogram was obscured. Among them lay a collar and tie, as if they had just been removed, which, lifted, left upon the surface a pale crescent in the dust. Upon a chair hung the suit, carefully folded; beneath it the two mute shoes and the discarded socks.

58   The man himself lay in the bed.

---

[10]**acrid pall:** bitter-smelling gloom.

acrid
(ăk´rĭd) *adj.* unpleasantly sharp, pungent, or bitter to the taste or smell.

AHA MOMENT

Annotate: Reread paragraphs 56–58. In paragraph 56, mark what the townspeople knew.

Infer: Explain whether the townspeople expected to find something frightening or suspicious when they went into the room. Cite text evidence in your response.

TO CHALLENGE STUDENTS . . .

Analyze Theme Have students determine the theme of "A Rose for Emily" and how the setting impacted the theme. Then, have students work in small groups to discuss the details from the text that helped them determine the theme. Remind students that themes should be expressed as a statement, not a single word. Also, note that there may be more than one theme in a story and that readers may interpret stories differently.

59   For a long while we just stood there, looking down at the profound and fleshless grin. The body had apparently once lain in the attitude of an embrace, but now the long sleep that outlasts love, that conquers even the grimace of love, had cuckolded him.[11] What was left of him, rotted beneath what was left of the nightshirt, had become inextricable from the bed in which he lay; and upon him and upon the pillow beside him lay that even coating of the patient and biding dust.

60   Then we noticed that in the second pillow was the indentation of a head. One of us lifted something from it, and leaning forward, that faint and invisible dust dry and acrid in the nostrils, we saw <u>a long strand of iron-gray hair.</u>

[11] **cuckolded him:** made his wife or lover unfaithful to him.

MAKE AND CONFIRM PREDICTIONS

Annotate: In paragraph 60, mark what else the townspeople found in Emily's bed.

Confirm: Think about your previous prediction about Emily's actions. Were you right, or is this ending a surprise? Explain.

CHECK YOUR UNDERSTANDING

Answer these questions before moving on to the **Analyze the Text** section on the following page.

1 How did Emily react to her father's death?

A She wept and could not be comforted.

B For days, she denied that he was dead.

C She sent for her relatives from Alabama.

D For days, she celebrated his being gone.

2 Why did Emily buy the rat poison?

F To kill herself

G To kill the rats

H To kill Homer

J To kill her father

3 How did people's attitudes toward Emily change when the cousins arrived?

A They became Emily's allies.

B They became suspicious of Emily.

C They became friends with the cousins.

D They became more distant than before.

A Rose for Emily   587

TEACH

 MAKE AND CONFIRM PREDICTIONS

The author has already included a major revelation—there has been a dead body in Emily's upper bedroom for years. But the author has one more surprise. Point out to students that literature doesn't have to be cryptic or symbolic in order to have an impact. (**Possible answer:** *I predicted that Emily did something "crazy." It is crazy that she killed someone. I am surprised and horrified because I never would have guessed she'd sleep beside him.*)

CHECK YOUR UNDERSTANDING

Have students answer the questions independently.

Answers:

1. *B*

2. *H*

3. *A*

If they answer any questions incorrectly, have them reread the text to confirm their understanding. Then they may proceed to ANALYZE THE TEXT on page 588.

 ENGLISH LEARNER SUPPORT

Oral Assessment Use the following questions to assess students' comprehension and speaking skills.

1. What did Emily do after her father's death? (*She said he wasn't dead.*)

2. Why did Emily buy the rat poison? (*so she could kill Homer*)

3. How did the townspeople behave differently toward Emily when her cousins visited? (*They began helping her.*) **MODERATE**

ANALYZE THE TEXT

Possible answers:

1. **DOK 3:** *Clues that triggered predictions might include Emily buying poison, comments about her being crazy, and Homer never being seen again after he went in the house. Clues that helped at the end might include the smell, comments about her being crazy, and buying the silver toilet set and suit.*

2. **DOK 3:** *Her conflict over the taxes reveals her presumption of special treatment. Her marriage gifts reveal her plan to make a gentleman out of Homer, which would fit with her entitled self-image. Her appearance changes from slender maiden to corpulent matron, but her pale skin and elevated nose are constant. The town thinks the family holds themselves "a little too high" and is glad when Emily sinks into poverty.*

3. **DOK 4:** *The town's attitude is mixed: on the one hand, Emily is a "fallen monument" they must look after; on the other hand, they resent her Grierson pride and enjoy pitying "poor Emily." Faulkner shows that people in small towns like to know their neighbors' business and have expectations about the social hierarchy and customary behavior.*

4. **DOK 4:** *The story documents Emily's lost wealth and social status, the disparaging treatment of African Americans, and the town's acceptance of progress and modernization. It reflects life both immediately after the Civil War and decades on, as the social order changed and the South began to modernize. Prominent families whose fortunes had been tied to slavery found themselves impoverished, their way of life forever changed, and their social influence diminished. African Americans were no longer slaves but were still treated as second-class citizens.*

5. **DOK 4:** *Homer wronged Emily by courting her without intending to marry her. She didn't want to be rejected, especially when the town suspected they had had premarital relations. Her father had driven away her young suitors, so she didn't want to let her last chance at marriage slip away. She killed him to make sure he couldn't leave her.*

RESEARCH

Students' findings should reflect original research as well as an effort to connect those details to the story.

Extend Help students brainstorm keyword search terms and websites for images.

 **RESPOND**

ANALYZE THE TEXT

Support your responses with evidence from the text.   NOTEBOOK

1. **Cite Evidence** Look back through your annotations and review the clues you used to support your predictions. Which ones helped you understand the ending? Did any clues cause you to adjust or correct your predictions as you read? Explain.

2. **Cite Evidence** How does Faulkner characterize Emily so effectively? Citing evidence, explain what each of the following reveals about her character:
   • her conflict with the aldermen over her taxes
   • her gifts for Homer
   • her physical appearance at various stages in her life
   • what the townspeople say about the Griersons

3. **Analyze** What contradictions are revealed in the town's attitude toward Emily? Explain what you think Faulkner is saying about small-town life in the South with this story.

4. **Synthesize** Drawing from Faulkner's description of the town and events, what was the larger historical, social, and economic context in the South when this story takes place?

5. **Notice & Note** What is Emily's motivation for murdering Homer? Consider Homer's intentions, Emily's father's reaction to her suitors, and the opinion of the townspeople in your response.

RESEARCH

RESEARCH TIP
In addition to searching for 1870s architecture, you could also search for Victorian architecture. The Victorian era was the period during which Queen Victoria ruled the British Empire. It lasted from 1837 to 1901 and had a tremendous effect on the United States.

Miss Emily's house and life are anchored in the 1870s. Details about customs, transportation, and social behavior are woven throughout the story. Research what architecture, clothing, and manners were like in this period. Try to find information that matches details in the story. Record what you learn in the chart.

LIFE IN THE 1870s	EXAMPLES
Architecture	*Details might include information about Victorian houses, their high level of detail, and home owners' efforts to display their wealth.*
Clothing	*Details might include information like women's dress styles (bustles) and the importance of looking presentable in public.*
Manners	*Details might include how people tried to act dignified in public, maintained customs like making visits, and treated African Americans as second-class citizens.*

Extend Print images of the architecture and clothing of the period, and share the images with the class.

WHEN STUDENTS STRUGGLE . . .

Reteach: Analyze Literary Elements: Setting Remind students that the time period is an important component of setting. Setting affects the characters, plot, and conflict. Have students review their timelines. Point out that the story begins not too long after the end of the Civil War (1865). Ask students why they think Faulkner wanted this story to take place so soon after the war and how this setting affected the characters and conflict.

 For additional support, go to the **Reading Studio** and assign the following **Level Up Tutorial: Setting.**

CREATE AND DISCUSS

Write a Literary Analysis Write a brief essay in which you analyze the surprise ending of "A Rose for Emily." Think about the details Faulkner uses to describe the characters and setting and the clues he includes that hint at the ending.

❏ Reread the text and review your annotations about Emily, the setting, and the townspeople.

❏ Write an introduction that states your opinion on whether the ending of Faulkner's story is believable.

❏ Use details from the text to support your view.

❏ Write a conclusion that restates your opinion.

Discuss with a Small Group In a small group, discuss whether the townspeople bear any responsibility for what becomes of Emily.

❏ Think about why they thought Emily bought the arsenic and their feeling on the consequences of this decision.

❏ Consider why they didn't discuss Homer Barron's disappearance.

❏ Review the story to gather more evidence and clarify your opinion.

❏ Cite evidence to support your opinion. Be sure to listen attentively to each person involved in the discussion.

Go to **Writing as a Process** in the **Writing Studio** for help.

Go to **Preparing for Discussion** in the **Speaking and Listening Studio** for help.

RESPOND TO THE ESSENTIAL QUESTION

 How do we deal with rejection or isolation?

Gather Information Review your annotations and notes on "A Rose for Emily." Then, add relevant information to your Response Log. As you determine which information to include, think about:

• how Faulkner evokes the time and place through details related to the historical, social, and economic context
• how the setting and characters contribute to or reflect a feeling of isolation
• the importance of point of view in the story

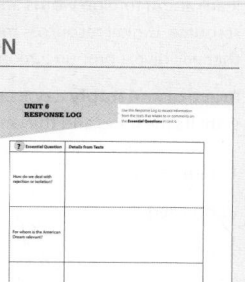

ACADEMIC VOCABULARY

As you write and discuss what you learned from "A Rose for Emily," be sure to use the Academic Vocabulary words. Check off each of the words that you use.

☑ **contemporary**
❏ **global**
❏ **infinite**
❏ **simulated**
☑ **virtual**

CREATE AND DISCUSS

Write a Literary Analysis Emphasize to students that their essays should include many supporting details from the story. Essays should be well organized and contain a clear introduction that states their opinion. Details from the story can be presented as quotations, paraphrases, or details. The conclusion should restate their opinion. Suggest that students use a graphic organizer to help them plan their analysis.

For **writing support** for students at varying proficiency levels, see the **Text X-Ray** on page 574D.

Discuss with a Small Group As students discuss the topic of the townspeople's responsibility, they should reference the story as much as possible. If they need a refresher on the townspeople's opinions, have them review the story to gather more details. During the discussion, students should listen actively and speak using appropriate discussion rules.

RESPOND TO THE ESSENTIAL QUESTION

Allow time for students to add details from "A Rose for Emily" to their Unit 6 Response Logs.

CRITICAL VOCABULARY

Answers:

1. *noblesse oblige*
2. *tableau*
3. *circumvent*
4. *cabal*
5. *acrid*
6. *vindicate*
7. *virulent*
8. *archaic*

VOCABULARY STRATEGY:
Foreign Words and Phrases

Answers:

1. *a social blunder; French*
2. *an inference that does not follow from the premises or evidence; Latin*
3. *in one group or body; all together; French*
4. *an accomplished, presumably irreversible deed or fact; French*
5. *unrestricted power to act at one's own discretion; unconditional authority; French*
6. *an established or usual way of doing things; Latin*
7. *made or carried out in good faith; sincere; authentic; genuine; Latin*
8. *for the specific purpose, case, or situation at hand and for no other; formed or concerned with one specific purpose; improvised and often impromptu; Latin*
9. *a temperamental, conceited person; Italian*
10. *the existing condition or state of affairs; Latin*

RESPOND

WORD BANK

archaic	cabal
tableau	circumvent
vindicate	virulent
noblesse oblige	acrid

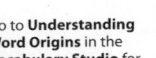

Go to **Understanding Word Origins** in the **Vocabulary Studio** for help.

CRITICAL VOCABULARY

Practice and Apply Fill in the word that best completes each sentence.

1. Out of _____ the princess treated her subjects quite well.
2. The museum's visitors were impressed with the splendid _____ in the main gallery.
3. Some people put a lot of effort into trying to _____ the rules.
4. The people who wanted to overthrow the government formed a(n) _____.
5. A(n) _____ smell told us we'd left the plastic bowl too near the fire.
6. She knows that further scientific inquiry will _____ her theory.
7. The _____ emotions of the crowd spilled over into violence.
8. Compared to modern cellphones, old dial phones seem _____.

VOCABULARY STRATEGY: Foreign Words and Phrases

English borrows many words from other languages. In "A Rose for Emily," *tableau* and *noblesse oblige* are two examples of words that were borrowed from the French. Some foreign words change pronunciation in the English language, but their spellings and general meanings remain the same. To learn about foreign words and phrases used in English, use a print or digital resource. Digital resources may also offer the advantage of an audio function that will give a pronunciation of the word or phrase in addition to a definition.

Practice and Apply Look up each of the following words or phrases and state its meaning and the language it comes from.

1. faux pas
2. non sequitur
3. en masse
4. fait accompli
5. carte blanche
6. modus operandi
7. bona fide
8. ad hoc
9. prima donna
10. status quo

EL ENGLISH LEARNER SUPPORT

Practice Vowel Sounds Speakers of Spanish, Hmong, Cantonese, Haitian Creole, and Korean may be unfamiliar with the short *u* sound, as in *cup*. Display the following words from the text with a short *u* sound: *just, but, pumps,* and *stubborn.* Then, have students repeat the words with you and then with a partner. **ALL LEVELS**

LANGUAGE CONVENTIONS: Point of View

Part of what makes "A Rose for Emily" so interesting is the first-person plural point of view—using *we* and related pronouns to tell the story. Usually, the first-person point of view is singular, an *I* who acts as both narrator and character. Faulkner's use of the plural creates a curious mixture of intimacy and anonymity. That is, the voice behind the *we* sounds personal, even though the readers don't know exactly whose voice it is:

> **We learned that Miss Emily had been to the jeweler's and ordered a man's toilet set in silver, with the letters H.B. on each piece. Two days later we learned that she had bought a complete outfit of men's clothing, including a nightshirt, and we said, "They are married."**

This kind of narration has the effect of making the town appear as a complete entity with a personality and opinions all its own.

The first-person plural also affects the tone and intent of the story. Think about how the following lines would be different if they were told in the first-person singular, *I*.

> **That was when people had begun to feel really sorry for her. People in our town, remembering how old lady Wyatt, her great-aunt, had gone completely crazy at last, believed that the Griersons held themselves a little too high for what they really were. None of the young men were quite good enough for Miss Emily and such. We had long thought of them as a tableau, Miss Emily a slender figure in white in the background, her father a spraddled silhouette in the foreground, his back to her and clutching a horsewhip, the two of them framed by the backflung front door.**

Practice and Apply Try using the first-person plural point of view to create a narrative of your own. Choose a group—a family, for example, or a sports team—and describe, in a paragraph, an event or experience from their point of view. Be sure to use the correct pronouns—*we, us, our, ours*—in your narrative.

LANGUAGE CONVENTIONS: Point of View

Point of view can greatly affect how a reader understands the characters and theme. Review the examples and discuss the effect of the first-person plural point of view.

Then, explain that although the first-person plural point of view is relatively unusual for literature, it has been used very effectively by speechmakers throughout history. Read the following excerpt from President Lincoln's Gettysburg Address and see if students can identify the speaker and occasion:

Four score and seven years ago our fathers brought forth on this continent, a new nation, conceived in liberty, and dedicated to the proposition that all men are created equal.

Now we are engaged in a great civil war, testing whether that nation, or any nation so conceived and so dedicated, can long endure. We are met on a great battlefield of that war. We have come to dedicate a portion of that field, as a final resting place for those who here gave their lives that that nation might live. It is altogether fitting and proper that we should do this.

But, in a larger sense, we can not dedicate—we can not consecrate—we can not hallow—this ground.

Discuss with students how the use of the first-person plural point of view serves to unite listeners in a single cause.

Practice and Apply Students' paragraphs should correctly use the first-person plural point of view. This includes using the correct pronouns.

ENGLISH LEARNER SUPPORT

Language Conventions Use the following supports with students at varying proficiency levels:

- Review first-person pronouns and have students write them in their notebooks. Then, read aloud the first boldface passage in the Language Conventions activity. Ask students to raise their right hand when they hear a singular pronoun and their left hand when they hear a plural pronoun. **SUBSTANTIAL**

- Have students discuss both passages in the Language Conventions activity as a group. Provide these sentence frames: *Using the first-person plural helps me understand Emily/the townspeople because _____. If the point of view were first-person singular, the story would change because _____.* **MODERATE**

- Have students rewrite the first passage in the first-person singular. Then, have partners discuss the effect of changing the point of view. **LIGHT**

MENDING WALL

Poem by Robert Frost

GENRE ELEMENTS
BLANK VERSE

While many poems have lines that rhyme, others are written in **blank verse,** or unrhymed lines of iambic pentameter. Each line of a poem written in iambic pentameter has a specific pattern. It consists of a total of ten syllables. The first syllable is unstressed and the next is stressed. This pattern repeats five times, or for five pairs of syllables. At the end of every line is a pause. Iambic pentameter reflects people's natural speech rhythm, or cadence.

LEARNING OBJECTIVES

- Analyze a poem's diction and syntax and the author's message.
- Conduct research to locate specific information.
- Write a poem in blank verse about isolation or separation.
- Present a poem.
- Use vocabulary words in discussions and writing.
- **Language** Discuss with a partner the author's message.

TEXT COMPLEXITY

Quantitative Measures	**Mending Wall**	Lexile: N/A
Qualitative Measures	**Ideas Presented** Much explicit, but moves to some implied meaning. Requires some inferential reasoning.	
	Structures Used Primarily explicit.	
	Language Used Meanings are implied. More inference is demanded.	
	Knowledge Required Requires no special knowledge.	

RESOURCES

- Unit 6 Response Log
- 🔊 Selection Audio
- 📖 Reading Studio: Notice & Note
- **LEVEL UP** Level Up Tutorial: Elements of Poetry
- 📑 Writing Studio: Writing as a Process
- 💬 Speaking and Listening Studio: Giving a Presentation
- ✅ "Mending Wall" Selection Test

SUMMARIES

English

Two neighbors work together to mend a stone wall. Each stays on his own side of the wall. The speaker says that they do not need a stone wall where apple trees and pines stand on each side. The other man replies, "Good fences make good neighbors," something the man learned from his father. The speaker wonders why they need a wall and what they are walling in and walling out. However, he knows that his neighbor will not go against what he has been taught.

Spanish

Dos vecinos trabajan juntos para arreglar una pared de piedra. Cada uno se queda en su lado de la cerca. Mientras trabajan, el narrador comenta que no necesitan una pared de piedra que separe los manzanos y pinos que hay de ambos lados. El otro hombre responde, "buenas cercas hacen buenos vecinos", algo que el hombre aprendió de su padre. El narrador reflexiona sobre esto y se pregunta por qué necesitan una pared y qué están emparedando. Se da cuenta de que su vecino no irá en contra de lo que se le enseñó.

 ## SMALL-GROUP OPTIONS

Have students work in small groups and pairs to read and discuss the selection.

Send a Problem

- Read line 41: "He moves in darkness as it seems to me."
- Pose the following question: *What does the speaker mean?*
- Call on a student to respond. Wait 11 seconds for a response.
- If the question is answered, pose another question and repeat the process.
- If it is not answered, have the student repeat the question and call on someone to answer it.
- Redirect or ask another question at any time.

Reciprocal Teaching

- Have students read the poem. Then, provide the following question stems:

  Why did the speaker _____?

  Why did the neighbor _____?

  What might have happened if _____?

- Tell students to use the stems to write three to five questions.
- Have students form groups of three.
- Have each student ask their group at least two of their questions. Have groups discuss each answer until they reach a consensus.

Text X-Ray: English Learner Support
for "Mending Wall"

Use the Text X-Ray and the supports and scaffolds in the Teacher's Edition to help guide students at different proficiency levels through the selection.

INTRODUCE THE SELECTION
DISCUSS WALLS AND SEPARATION

Explain that the poem is about a wall that marks a property line, or division between two neighbors' properties.

Ask students what kinds of walls, fences, or other barriers separate them from their neighbors. Then, ask students to name reasons for having walls or fences between neighbors and reasons why walls or fences may have negative effects. Display phrases such as *on the one hand* and *on the other hand,* and use them in examples to help students contrast the advantages and disadvantages of barriers.

CULTURAL REFERENCES

The following words or phrases may be unfamiliar to students:

- *walk the line* (line 13): walk along the wall that separates the neighbors' properties
- *Spring is the mischief in me* (line 28): spring makes me feel mischievous
- *put a notion in his head* (line 29): convince him to consider an idea
- *Isn't it where there are cows?* (lines 30–31): Aren't walls used to keep cows from wandering?
- *elves* (line 36): imaginary helpers

LISTENING

Identify Rhythm

Review iambic pentameter with students. Explain that it is composed of ten syllables that alternate unstressed and stressed syllables. Remind students that iambic pentameter is not always regular. Read aloud a few lines of the poem and emphasize the stressed syllables.

Use the following supports with students at varying proficiency levels:

- Read lines 20–24 aloud with correct stresses while students listen. Then, have students read and tap along while you reread these lines. **SUBSTANTIAL**
- Read lines 20–24 aloud, one or two lines at a time, and have students mark the stressed syllables. Repeat for another one or two lines. **MODERATE**
- Read lines 25–29 aloud. Have students work in pairs to mark the stressed syllables of the lines. Then, have each pair compare their marked stresses with another pair. **LIGHT**

SPEAKING

Analyze Author's Message

Explain that an author's message may be difficult to interpret, but the author gives details that are clues to the message. Ask questions to help students discuss their interpretations of the author's message.

Use the following supports with students at varying proficiency levels:

- Ask students yes/no questions, such as *Did the speaker want to keep the wall?* and *Did the neighbor want to keep the wall?* Point out and explain details in the text to help them interpret the author's message. **SUBSTANTIAL**

- Review lines 27–34 with students. Ask: *Did the gaps in the wall bring the two neighbors closer or keep them apart? How?* Then, have students discuss the questions in small groups and provide reasons for their answers to analyze the author's message. **MODERATE**

- Have students work in small groups to discuss whether gaps in the wall brought the two neighbors closer or kept them apart and to use text evidence to support their ideas. Tell them to come to a consensus on their interpretation of the author's message, and have groups share their answers with the class. **LIGHT**

READING

Paraphrase a Poem

Work with students to reread lines from the poem. Tell them they will paraphrase, or retell, the poem or part of the poem in their own words.

Use the following supports with students at varying proficiency levels:

- Work with students to read lines 25–26 and help them paraphrase the lines. Then, have students draw a picture of the paraphrase. **SUBSTANTIAL**

- Have students work in pairs to read lines 15–19 and discuss what the lines mean. Then, have pairs work together to paraphrase the lines. **MODERATE**

- Have students work in pairs to paraphrase lines 5–11. Have each pair exchange their paraphrase with another pair. **LIGHT**

WRITING

Synthesize Author's Message

Work with students to read the writing assignment on Student Edition page 599.

Use the following supports with students at varying proficiency levels:

- Work with students as they brainstorm a list of things that keep people apart. Ask simple yes/no questions about the items. After students choose one idea, help them create a mind map with words and phrases to describe that idea. **SUBSTANTIAL**

- Have students write a line of blank verse using the word *fence* or *wall* and add it to their mind maps. **MODERATE**

- Have students write one or two lines of blank verse and add them to their mind maps. **LIGHT**

? Connect to the
ESSENTIAL QUESTION

"Mending Wall" is a poem about things that separate us and things that bring us together. Robert Frost uses a wall as a symbol to discuss different aspects of life, both personal and social. While Frost and his neighbor work together to rebuild the wall between their properties, Frost meditates on the many ways we are isolated from each other.

MENDING WALL

Poem by **Robert Frost**

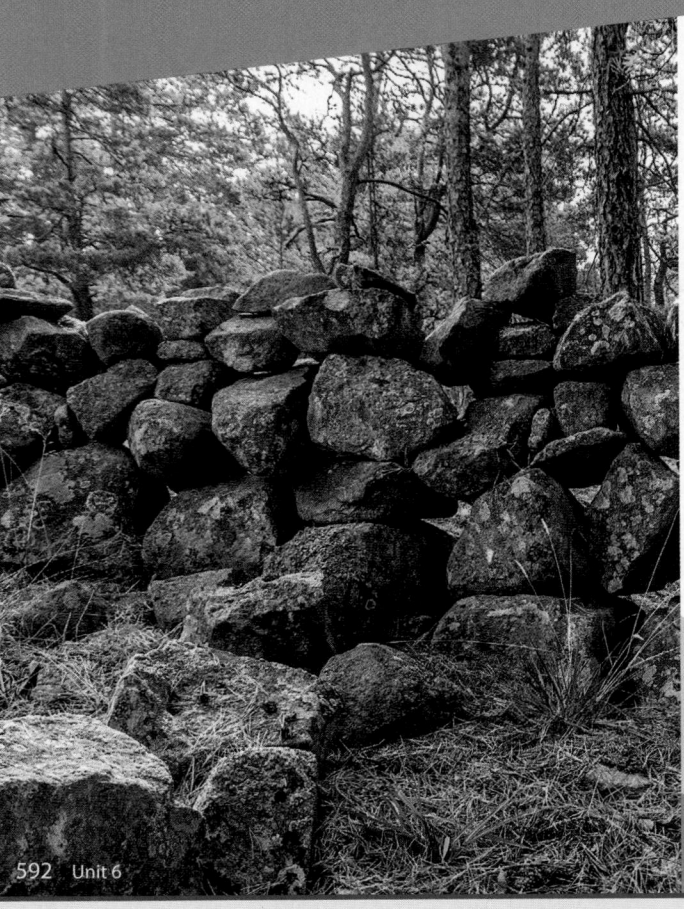

 ESSENTIAL QUESTION:

How do we deal with rejection or isolation?

© Houghton Mifflin Harcourt Publishing Company • Image Credits: © Ullrich Gnoth/Alamy

QUICK START

Think about activities you like to do alone and those you like to do with someone else. For instance, some people prefer to study alone while others would rather study with a friend or in a group. Write down your ideas in the chart below and share them with the group.

BETTER TO DO ALONE	BETTER TO DO WITH SOMEONE
Ideas might include studying or exercising.	*Ideas might include taking long walks or going to the movies.*

ANALYZE POETRY

"Mending Wall" is written in **blank verse,** a poetic structure of unrhymed lines of iambic pentameter. In other words, each line has five pairs of syllables. In most pairs, an unstressed syllable is followed by a stressed syllable. Note the stressed (in italics) and unstressed syllables in "Mending Wall."

> And *on* a *day* we *meet* to *walk* the *line*
> And *set* the *wall* be*tween* us *once* a*gain.*

The stressed and unstressed syllables imitate the rhythms of English speech. So do the line breaks, which emphasize natural pauses or stops in speech. This rhythm appealed to Frost because of his love of the speech patterns of the New Hampshire farmers who were his neighbors. As you read, note the way elements of poetry such as rhythm and repetition affect the poem's meaning.

ANALYZE DICTION AND SYNTAX

Diction refers to the author's word choice while **syntax** refers to how sentences are structured. Diction and syntax can contribute to the following literary elements in a poem.

- **Tone,** or the attitude toward the subject: Is Frost's language and sentence structure simple and direct, or complex? What attitude does this convey?

- **Mood,** or the atmosphere in a work of literature: Think about what types of words Frost uses in the poem and how they create a distinct mood.

- **Voice,** or the personality that emerges from a work: How does the language convey this personality?

As you read, notice the way diction and syntax contribute to the tone, mood, and voice in the poem.

GENRE ELEMENTS: BLANK VERSE

- imitates the cadence of English speech
- employs iambic pentameter
- has lines that do not rhyme

QUICK START

Have students read the Quick Start activity and share their thoughts with the class. Discuss how wanting to do something alone isn't a "bad" thing. Point out that sometimes we choose to do things alone, while other times we choose to be with others.

ANALYZE POETRY

Tell students that **blank verse** is one of the most common forms of poetry in the modern era of English literature. The form's lack of rhyme and its focus on rhythm make blank verse highly versatile. Have students read aloud the two lines of verse on this page and note the rhythm of the iambic pentameter. As a class, write two lines of verse in a similar meter to familiarize themselves with the structure.

ANALYZE DICTION AND SYNTAX

Make sure that students understand the difference between **diction** and **syntax** and how both affect **tone, mood,** and **voice.** Ask students to predict what kind of diction and syntax Frost might use in "Mending Wall." Remind them that the poem describes a conversation with a neighboring farmer and that Frost loved the rhythms and patterns of the New Hampshire farmers' ways of speaking. *(Answers will vary. The diction will likely include mostly simple words, due to the setting. The syntax is harder to predict, but most likely it will not be too complex or formal.)*

TEACH

ANALYZE AUTHOR'S MESSAGE

Point out to students that the **author's message** is often challenging to determine because it has to be inferred based on details. Ask students to share an author's message from one of their favorite works—such as a novel, short story, poem, or movie—and justify their opinion with supporting details. Then, discuss ambiguity and how it makes determining the message even more difficult. Note that two readers may interpret a poem differently due to ambiguity.

 ENGLISH LEARNER SUPPORT

Use Cognates Direct students to the following Spanish cognates: *repair/reparar* (line 6) and *exactly/ exactamente* (line 37). Have students read the lines and discuss the meanings of the words with cognates.

MODERATE

 ANNOTATION MODEL

Point out the annotations shown in the model. Explain that students may follow this suggestion or use their own system for marking up the selection in their write-in text. They may want to color-code their annotations by using highlighters. Their notes in the margin may include questions about the theme or sensory details that help them imagine the men and the wall.

 **GET READY**

ANALYZE AUTHOR'S MESSAGE

An **author's message** is the main idea or theme of a particular work. Readers must use details from a text to determine the author's message. In this poem, the speaker asks his neighbor about the wall, which signals to the reader that his message will be about separations people create. His use of repetition also helps emphasize his message. Frost wants his neighbor, and therefore the reader, to think about walls.

> He only says, "Good fences make good neighbors."
> Spring is the mischief in me, and I wonder
> If I could put a notion in his head:
> "*Why* do they make good neighbors? . . ."

It is up to you to determine the author's message. Authors do not state the message in their work directly. One literary element that can make it a challenge to determine a message is **ambiguity.** Something is ambiguous if it can be interpreted in more than one way. The statement "good fences make good neighbors" is an example of an ambiguous sentence. Your task as the reader is to determine the meaning Frost intends to convey and support your interpretation with details in the text.

Ambiguity can add richness and beauty to a work of literature. Since Frost is intentionally vague about his neighbor and about the value of walls, readers may be able to support more than one interpretation of the work. As you read "Mending Wall," notice when you encounter ambiguity and think about how different lines relate to the poem's message.

 **ANNOTATION MODEL**   **NOTICE & NOTE**

As you read, note details that reveal how Frost uses diction, syntax, and rhythm to create mood. Notice how Frost uses ambiguity as he conveys his message. The model shows one reader's notes about the beginning of "Mending Wall."

> Something there is that doesn't love a wall,
> That sends the frozen-ground-swell under it,
> And spills the upper boulders in the sun;
> And makes gaps even two can pass abreast.
> The work of hunters is another thing:
> I have come after them and made repair
> Where they have left not one stone on a stone,

The rhythm is slow and natural, like someone in a thoughtful mood. The images show how a wall that seems solid really isn't—it can be broken.

The wall must be important for the speaker to "make repair."

© Houghton Mifflin Harcourt Publishing Company

BACKGROUND

Robert Frost *(1874–1963) was born in San Francisco, but his family moved to New England when Frost's father died. Frost worked as a teacher but later became a farmer while trying to establish himself as a poet. At age 38 Frost uprooted the family and moved to England. There he was able to publish his first book of poetry, A Boy's Will. During World War I, in 1915 Frost and his family returned to the United States. He was greeted as a leading American poet and was celebrated for his skill at capturing American colloquial speech. However, a series of personal tragedies affected his later poems which conveyed a bleak outlook on life.*

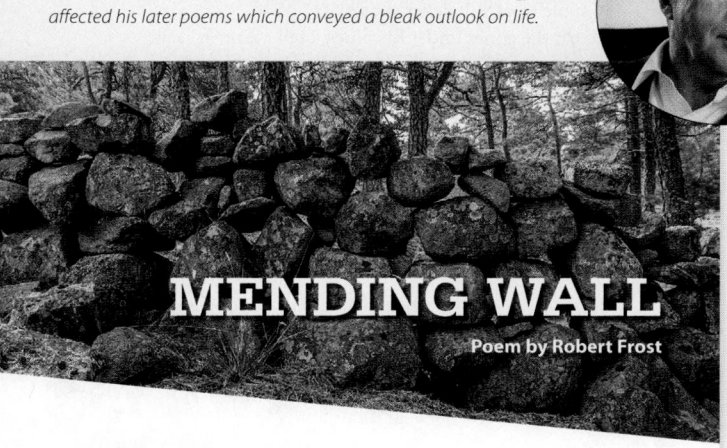

MENDING WALL

Poem by Robert Frost

SETTING A PURPOSE

As you read, pay attention to the details that convey what each person thinks of the wall.

Something there is that doesn't love a wall,
That sends the frozen-ground-swell under it,
And spills the upper boulders in the sun;
And makes gaps even two can pass abreast.
5 The work of hunters is another thing:
I have come after them and made repair
Where they have left not one stone on a stone,
But they would have the rabbit out of hiding,
To please the yelping dogs. The gaps I mean,
10 No one has seen them made or heard them made,
But at spring mending-time we find them there.
I let my neighbor know beyond the hill;
And on a day we meet to walk the line
And set the wall between us once again.
15 We keep the wall between us as we go.
To each the boulders that have fallen to each.
And some are loaves and some so nearly balls

Notice & Note

Use the side margins to notice and note signposts in the text.

ANALYZE DICTION AND SYNTAX

Annotate: Mark the phrases in lines 1–5 that appeal to your senses.

Compare: How does this imagery help create a particular mood?

ANALYZE POETRY

Annotate: Mark the stressed syllables in lines 14–15.

Interpret: What is the significance of the repeated phrase in these lines?

BACKGROUND

After students read the Background note, explain that Robert Frost bridged the literary traditions of the 19th and 20th centuries. He incorporated elements of poetry from both periods. He was also known as a regionalist writer, despite his broad national acclaim. One of his primary subjects was New England, and many of his poems describe its landscape and people in great detail.

SETTING A PURPOSE

Direct students to use the Setting a Purpose prompt to focus their reading.

ANALYZE DICTION AND SYNTAX

Point out to students that the diction (word choice) in these lines is quite simple, but the syntax is unusual. The line "Something there is that doesn't love a wall" sounds odd, but his placement of the word "something" at the beginning of the poem is meaningful. He is making it clear from the beginning that a wall is not a natural phenomenon and that there are natural forces always working against it. (***Answer:*** *The imagery suggests stones lying on the ground that have fallen from the wall they were part of. It creates a mood that is sad and weary.*)

ANALYZE POETRY

Repetition is often a part of rhythm in both poetry and music. Have students offer examples of repetition in music. Possible examples include the recurrence of themes in classical music, the basic structure of pop songs, and the automated beats of electronic music. (***Answer:*** *It emphasizes the separation that the neighbors want to maintain.*)

EL ENGLISH LEARNER SUPPORT

Understand Punctuation Read aloud lines 1–9 (the first two sentences of the poem) and have students follow along. Then, reread the lines and have them circle the punctuation. Explain that periods mark the end of a sentence and indicate a significant pause, while commas and semicolons are used to separate parts of a sentence and indicate smaller pauses. Colons are used to introduce something. Ask students to work with a partner to read aloud the first two sentences of the poem, first paying attention to the punctuation, and then not paying attention. What difference do they notice? **MODERATE/LIGHT**

ANALYZE AUTHOR'S MESSAGE

Because a poet does not explicitly state the message of a poem, it is up to the reader to interpret the message. This can be a challenge for a reader who wants to fully understand a poem. Sometimes, however, there are clues that are more obvious than others, as in lines 30–34. (**Answer:** *There are times when walls make sense, but not all the time, and one should make sure one knows the difference.*)

For **listening, reading,** and **speaking support** for students at varying proficiency levels, see the **Text X-Ray** on pages 592C–592D.

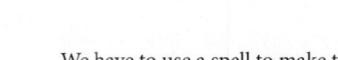

We have to use a spell to make them balance:
"Stay where you are until our backs are turned!"
20 We wear our fingers rough with handling them.
Oh, just another kind of out-door game,
One on a side. It comes to little more:
There where it is we do not need the wall:
He is all pine and I am apple orchard.
25 My apple trees will never get across
And eat the cones under his pines, I tell him.
He only says, "Good fences make good neighbors."
Spring is the mischief in me, and I wonder
If I could put a notion in his head:
30 "*Why* do they make good neighbors? Isn't it
Where there are cows? But here there are no cows.
Before I built a wall I'd ask to know

ANALYZE AUTHOR'S MESSAGE

Annotate: In lines 32–34, mark what the speaker would want to know before building a wall.

Analyze: What message about walls is expressed in these lines?

TO CHALLENGE STUDENTS . . .

Interpret Symbolism   Remind students that in poetry, concrete objects are often used to symbolize abstract ideas. "Mending Wall" at one level presents a realistic portrait of rural life, but it can also be read as symbolic. Encourage students to consider the wall in the poem at the purely symbolic level. What do they think the wall stands for beyond its basic meaning as a physical barrier or demarcation of property?

Ask students to write a short poem in their own style that uses a wall as a symbol. Have volunteers read their poems to the class, and offer classmates a chance to interpret the symbolism.

What I was walling in or walling out,
And to whom I was like to give offence.
35 Something there is that doesn't love a wall,
That wants it down." I could say "Elves" to him,
But it's not elves exactly, and I'd rather
He said it for himself. I see him there
Bringing a stone grasped firmly by the top
40 In each hand, like an old-stone savage armed.
He moves in darkness as it seems to me,
Not of woods only and the shade of trees.
He will not go behind his father's saying,
And he likes having thought of it so well
45 He says again, "Good fences make good neighbors."

AGAIN AND AGAIN

Notice & Note: Mark the phrase that the neighbor repeats.

Draw Conclusions: Why does the neighbor repeat this phrase?

CHECK YOUR UNDERSTANDING

Answer these questions before moving on to the **Analyze the Text** section on the following page.

1 Why do the hunters damage the wall?

A They want to force a rabbit out of hiding.

B They believe in the value of walls.

C They need a gap they can pass through.

D They don't understand why the wall is there.

2 What notion does the speaker want to put in his neighbor's head?

F To hire someone else to repair the wall

G To combine their resources to buy cattle

H To ask himself why walls make good neighbors

J To wait until autumn to repair the wall

3 Why does the speaker think the wall is unnecessary?

A There are cows in the neighborhood.

B There are not enough stones available.

C There is nothing to keep out or keep in.

D The hunters are annoyed by the wall.

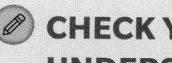

AGAIN AND AGAIN

Remind students that there are many reasons a poet might repeat a word or phrase. Repetition is a good way to create rhythm. It is also useful for drawing attention to a specific detail or concept that is meaningful in the poem. Repeating something is an obvious way to make a reader think twice about it. (**Answer:** *to reaffirm his belief in the value of boundaries*)

✎ CHECK YOUR UNDERSTANDING

Have students answer the questions independently.

Answers:

1. *A*

2. *H*

3. *C*

If they answer any questions incorrectly, have them reread the text to confirm their understanding. Then they may proceed to ANALYZE THE TEXT on page 598.

 ENGLISH LEARNER SUPPORT

Oral Assessment Use the following questions to assess students' comprehension and speaking skills.

1. Hunters make holes in the wall. Why do they do this? (*to make rabbits run away*)

2. What does the speaker want his neighbor to think about? (*whether or not walls are necessary*)

3. The speaker thinks the wall is not useful. Why? (*It does not have anything to keep out or in.*)
MODERATE

APPLY

ANALYZE THE TEXT

Possible answers:

1. **DOK 2:** *to emphasize that the speaker does not love the wall and that nature seems also not to love the wall*

2. **DOK 2:** *The speaker's feelings about the wall are somewhat ambiguous. Sometimes it seems like he wants the wall because he values good relations with his neighbor, while at other times it seems like he does not want it. He is silent when the neighbor says that walls make good neighbors, but then he internally questions why they need a wall at all.*

3. **DOK 4:** *His thoughts and speech are in the same relaxed rhythm, indicating thoughtfulness and a friendly humor as he challenges his neighbor in a way that is not offensive.*

4. **DOK 4:** *The neighbor is described as an armed savage living in the past, moving in darkness, which is not only actual darkness from shade but possibly spiritual darkness or ignorance. This reinforces the message that walls may not always be useful or necessary and should be questioned.*

5. **DOK 4:** *It emphasizes the difference between the speaker and his neighbor. For example, the speaker says "Something there is that doesn't love a wall" in lines 1 and 35. The neighbor says, "Good fences make good neighbors" in lines 27 and 45. The message is that walls are not natural—nature and animals break walls, but people keep building them. Walls can be useful at times, but they can make us feel isolated, especially when there are no reasons to have physical barriers.*

RESEARCH

Help students brainstorm search terms they can use for research. Remind students to use credible sources. Responses in the graphic organizer should include specific information from students' research. At Kennedy's inauguration, Frost recited his poem "The Gift Outright." He was originally going to read the poem "Dedication," which he had written for the occasion, but, in a last-minute change, he recited his older poem.

Extend Students' paragraphs should reflect research from credible sources.

 RESPOND

ANALYZE THE TEXT

Support your responses with evidence from the text. NOTEBOOK

1. **Infer** Why do you think Frost repeats the line "Something there is that doesn't love a wall"?

2. **Interpret** How does Frost use ambiguity to present the message about walls and neighbors? What evidence supports the idea that the speaker believes "Good fences make good neighbors"? What details suggest otherwise?

3. **Analyze** What tone does the speaker convey when he thinks of their activity as an "out-door game" and says his apple trees will never eat his neighbor's pine cones?

4. **Analyze** How do lines 39–42 characterize the neighbor? How does this relate to the message of the poem? Cite specific details in your response.

5. **Notice & Note** What ideas does the use of repetition in the poem emphasize? Cite at least two examples in your response.

RESEARCH TIP
Sites that focus on poetry, such as the Poetry Foundation and Academy of American Poets, are good places to find information about poets.

RESEARCH

Robert Frost is one of the most celebrated American poets. He was even asked to appear at President John F. Kennedy's inauguration. Conduct research to answer the questions below.

QUESTIONS	ANSWERS
What poem did Frost read at the inauguration?	*Frost recited his poem "The Gift Outright."*
Name a poem by Frost that Kennedy incorporated into his speeches.	*Kennedy often included lines from "Stopping by Woods on a Snowy Evening" in his campaign speeches*

Extend Kennedy and Frost were aware of each other even before Kennedy became president. Write a paragraph in which you describe their relationship before Kennedy became president. Include information on why Kennedy might have felt compelled to invite Frost to his inauguration.

WHEN STUDENTS STRUGGLE . . .

Reteach: Analyze Diction and Syntax Define *diction* and *syntax* again for students and find examples of each in the poem. Point out that the poem's diction features everyday American speech. Point out some of Frost's more unusual sentence structures, which create rhythm ("Spring is the mischief in me . . . ," line 28; "Something there is that . . . ," lines 1, 35).

For additional support, go to the **Reading Studio** and assign the following LEVEL UP **Level Up Tutorial: Elements of Poetry.**

CREATE AND PRESENT

Write a Poem In "Mending Wall," there is a stone wall between two neighbors, but walls are not the only things that keep neighbors or people apart. Write a short poem in blank verse exploring the idea of what keeps people apart and how people feel about this separation or isolation.

- ❏ Decide what you want your message to be.
- ❏ Review the elements of blank verse to make sure your style is correct.
- ❏ Think of descriptive words and images to communicate your message.
- ❏ Read your poem aloud to yourself to make sure you capture the rhythm of real speech.

Present a Poem Read your poem aloud to your group. Then, ask them if your message is clear.

- ❏ Revise your poem before you present it to make sure the message can be understood.
- ❏ Practice reading your poem aloud a few times before presenting so your reading is fluent.
- ❏ Speak clearly and read slowly enough so your audience can comprehend your ideas and appreciate your word choice and use of imagery.

 Go to **Giving a Presentation: Delivering Your Presentation** in the **Speaking and Listening Studio** for help.

RESPOND TO THE ESSENTIAL QUESTION

? How do we deal with rejection or isolation?

Gather Information Review your annotations and notes on "Mending Wall." Then, add relevant information to your Response Log. As you determine which information to include, think about:

- why we build "walls" between ourselves and others
- how we deal with feeling rejected or cut off
- how to open a discussion with someone who disagrees with us

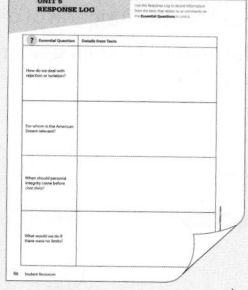

ACADEMIC VOCABULARY

As you write and discuss what you learned from the poem, be sure to use the Academic Vocabulary words. Check off each of the words that you use.

- ❏ **contemporary**
- ❏ **global**
- ❏ **infinite**
- ❏ **simulated**
- ❏ **virtual**

CREATE AND PRESENT

Write a Poem Encourage students to think about the author's message, his use of blank verse, and the imagery he uses before they begin writing their poem. Suggest that students brainstorm a list of things that keep people apart or create a sense of isolation. Then, have them choose one idea or object and create a mind map with words and phrases that describe the idea or object. Have students consider their message, diction, syntax, and use of blank verse. Explain that thinking of these things beforehand will help students incorporate these elements into their poem and maintain consistency while they write it.

When students have finished their first draft, remind them to think again about their goals for the poem. As they edit, have them ask themselves if they accomplished their goals. As a final review, have them read their poem aloud to see if it has the cadence of real speech.

 For **writing support** for students at varying proficiency levels, see the **Text X-Ray** on page 592D.

Present a Poem Presentations should show evidence of practice and an effort to make the poem clear and comprehensible. Students should vary their volume, pitch, and tone to emphasize certain elements, such as word choice, structure, or key ideas.

RESPOND TO THE ESSENTIAL QUESTION

Allow time for students to add details from "Mending Wall" to their Unit 6 Response Logs.

THE CRUCIBLE

Drama by Arthur Miller

GENRE ELEMENTS
DRAMA

A **drama** is a play or presentation intended to be performed in front of an audience. It includes written instructions, or stage directions, that tell the director, cast, and crew how to create the setting and say the lines (or dialogue). Stage directions also explain how characters should act and what the mood of the play is. The mood is the feeling or atmosphere created by the playwright. The playwright uses both dialogue and actions to flesh out the characters. The plot of a play is the series of events that make up the story. Conflict is part of the plot. It is the struggle between opposing forces (often characters) in the story. The conflict or conflicts drive the play's action by creating tension.

LEARNING OBJECTIVES

- Analyze allegory, paradox, figurative language, and irony; analyze the text.
- Research the McCarthy era and its trials.
- Write an evaluation and an analysis; create a multimedia presentation.
- Present your evaluation, multimedia presentation, and analysis.
- Determine the meaning of idioms.
- Identify the function of dialogue.
- **Language** Read dialogue with expression by using stage directions.

TEXT COMPLEXITY

Quantitative Measures	The Crucible	Lexile: N/A
Qualitative Measures	**Ideas Presented** Multiple levels, subtle, implied meanings and purpose. Use of symbolism, irony.	
	Structures Used More complex.	
	Language Used Implied meanings. Figurative language, archaic. Complex sentence structures.	
	Knowledge Required More complexity in theme. Experiences may be less familiar to many. Historical references may make heavier demands.	

RESOURCES

- Unit 6 Response Log
- Selection Audio
- Close Read Screencasts: Modeled Discussion
- Reading Studio: Notice & Note
- Level Up Tutorial: Types of Drama
- Writing Studio: Writing Informative Texts
- Speaking and Listening Studio: Using Media in a Presentation; Participating in Collaborative Discussions
- Vocabulary Studio: Idioms
-  *The Crucible* Selection Test

SUMMARIES

English

The Crucible, one of Arthur Miller's most celebrated plays, is about a witch-hunt in the small town of Salem, Massachusetts, in 1692. Miller wrote it during the "Communist scare," when a witch-hunt of a different sort was being conducted on the floor of the U.S. Congress. From 1950 to 1954, Senator Joseph McCarthy accused people of belonging to the Communist Party, though many accused were innocent. In the same way, several people in the play are accused of witchcraft, though they are innocent. Fear takes over the town.

Spanish

El crisol, una de las obras más célebres de Arthur Miller, trata de una cacería de brujas en el pequeño pueblo de Salem, Massachusetts, en 1692. Miller la escribió durante el "temor rojo", mientras ocurría una cacería de brujas de otro estilo en el Congreso de Estados Unidos. De 1950 a 1954, el senador Joseph McCarthy acusó a gente de pertenecer al partido comunista, aunque muchos de los acusados eran inocentes. De la misma manera, mucha gente en la obra es acusada de brujería, a pesar de su inocencia. El miedo se apodera del pueblo.

SMALL-GROUP OPTIONS

Have students work in small groups and pairs to read and discuss the selection.

Jigsaw with Experts

- Have students count off from 1 to 4. Based on their number, have students review one of the four acts of the play.
- Have students form four groups based on their assigned number and discuss their act, becoming "experts" on it.
- Have students form new groups with one representative from each expert group and then discuss their acts and the play as a whole.

Three Before Me

- After students have created their multimedia presentations, ask them to review and revise the text and images.
- Have each student ask three other students to edit his or her text and provide feedback on the images.
- Have students evaluate the editing and imaging suggestions made by their peers and make appropriate revisions before finalizing their presentations.

Text X-Ray: English Learner Support
for *The Crucible*

Use the Text X-Ray and the supports and scaffolds in the Teacher's Edition to help guide students at different proficiency levels through the selection.

INTRODUCE THE SELECTION
DISCUSS 17TH-CENTURY SALEM

Explain to students that Salem, Massachusetts, was settled by people from England who had come to North America in search of religious freedom. They were a tight-knit group of people who had strong religious beliefs. People in the community disapproved of other religious groups and had many fears, perhaps because they had been persecuted in England for their religious beliefs. They were suspicious of anything that could disrupt their way of life and the freedoms they enjoyed in their community.

Help students gain experience with the terms *suspicious, fearful, persecuted,* and *religious freedom.* Provide sentence frames: *When people are fearful of others, they might _____. When you are suspicious of someone, you _____. If someone is persecuted for their beliefs, they _____. Having religious freedom means _____.*

CULTURAL REFERENCES

The following words or phrases may be unfamiliar to students:

- *heathen* (Act One, paragraph 9): people who are not religious
- *Bible's charitable injunctions* (Act One, paragraph 18): rules such as "love your neighbor," in the Christian holy book, the Bible
- *Lucifer* (Act One, paragraph 18): the devil
- *unnatural causes* (Act One, paragraph 33): things caused by something other than humans or nature, such as the devil
- *a providence* (Act One, paragraph 77): a blessing or a fortunate occurrence
- *mouse* (Act Two, paragraph 45): frightened or meek person
- *charge fraud on Abigail* (Act Two, paragraph 79): say that Abigail is lying

LISTENING

Understand Dialogue

Tell students that dialogue is the words characters speak to each other. Miller uses dialogue that matches the speech patterns of people in the 17th century.

Read aloud paragraphs of the play, and have students reword them in contemporary language. Have students work in small groups. Use the following supports with students at varying proficiency levels:

- Read Act Four, paragraphs 67–68 to students. Have students repeat each sentence after you. Then, read the paragraphs aloud again, using contemporary language. (*I thought about telling you earlier in the week, but—. Why? How long has she been gone?*) Have students repeat after you. **SUBSTANTIAL**
- Work with students in a group. Read aloud Act Four, paragraphs 38–42. Read each line aloud, pause, and have students work in small groups to restate the sentences in more contemporary language before moving on to the next line. **MODERATE**
- Put students in groups of four. Have two students read Act Four, paragraphs 32–41, pausing after every two lines to have the other two students repeat the lines in modern language. **LIGHT**

SPEAKING

Read with Expression

Tell students that one way to improve reading fluency is to learn to read with more expression.

Have students use the stage directions to inform them how characters should sound. Use the following supports with students at varying proficiency levels:

- Read aloud Act Three, paragraphs 248–261. Have students repeat select sentences with expression. **SUBSTANTIAL**
- Have students work in groups of five. Assign roles for Act Three, paragraphs 248–251. Write on the board adjectives that describe each character. Have students discuss how their characters might say their lines and then read the dialogue aloud with expression. **MODERATE**
- Assign roles for Act Three, paragraphs 248–261. Have students think of two adjectives to describe their characters and then read the dialogue aloud with expression. Have students switch roles and repeat the activity. **LIGHT**

READING

Make Predictions

Before students read the play, have them preview part of the text to make predictions about the plot and characters.

Review the conflict introduced in Act One. Then, guide students to use stage directions in Act Four to make predictions about the play. Use the following supports with students at varying proficiency levels:

- Have students read along as you read aloud the stage directions at the beginning of Act Four. Say: *I predict that more people will be executed for witchcraft.* Have students repeat the prediction. **SUBSTANTIAL**
- Have students work in small groups. Ask a volunteer to read aloud the stage directions at the beginning of Act Four. Have students discuss what might happen in this act of the play by completing the following frame: *I know _____, which makes me think _____.* **MODERATE**
- Have students work independently to read the stage directions at the beginning of Act Four silently. Have students discuss: *What might happen in Act Four? How is it connected to Act One?* **LIGHT**

WRITING

Write an Essay

Help students read the writing assignment on page 713.

Allow students to write shorter essays as needed. Use the following supports with students at varying proficiency levels:

- Ask questions to guide students to explain Proctor's decision, such as *How does Proctor feel about lying? How does he feel about telling the truth?* Based on student responses, write a short explanation on the board, and have students copy it into their notebooks. **SUBSTANTIAL**
- Provide sentence frames such as the following that students can use to craft their essays: *At first, Proctor confesses because _____. He changes his mind because _____.* **MODERATE**
- Work with students to add quotations and examples to support their ideas. Provide the following sentence starters: *As Elizabeth says . . . ; Proctor gives his reason when . . . ; Rebecca Nurse reacts to Proctor's confession by . . . .* **LIGHT**

MODERN AMERICAN DRAMA

Have students work in small groups to read through this explanation of modern American drama.

American drama in the 1800s was closely tied to British drama. Well-known British actors played in the United States, and some U.S. actors played in Great Britain. Farces and melodramas were popular in both countries. Both featured stereotyped characters and improbable situations, but farces were intended to be funny, while melodramas played on the audience's emotions.

The realism of American drama in the 1900s was heavily influenced by the ideas of two psychoanalysts—Sigmund Freud and Carl Jung, both of whom explored the effect of the unconscious on human thoughts and behaviors. Like Freud and Jung, modern American dramatists were concerned with people's interior lives.

Today's American theatergoers have a variety of choices. The classics of modern American drama are still performed, and newer playwrights such as August Wilson, Tony Kushner, John Guare, David Mamet, and Ntozake Shange continue to challenge audiences with innovative and thought-provoking works. In addition, Broadway-style musicals with large casts, dancing, and spectacular special effects regularly tour the country.

MODERN AMERICAN DRAMA

The Rise of American Drama Though drama is one of the oldest forms of literature, it was one of the last of the literary genres to develop in the United States. The Puritans in New England regarded theatrical performances as frivolous, so few plays were staged in the 1600s. During the 18th and 19th centuries, drama gradually became an accepted form of entertainment.

The 19th century in particular was a very active period in American theater. Most productions consisted of wildly theatrical spectacles such as simulated chariot races and burning cities, all staged by means of dazzling special effects. Every town of any size had its own theater or "opera house." In spite of all this theatrical activity, not one truly significant American drama was staged during the 1800s, a period that produced Herman Melville, Ralph Waldo Emerson, Walt Whitman, Emily Dickinson, and Mark Twain. Most of the plays performed in the United States were imported from Europe or adapted from novels.

The Trend Toward Realism By the early 20th century, however, American playwrights began to reject the extravagant approach of the commercial theater. Instead, these writers favored realistic settings, characters, actions, and emotions that mirrored ordinary life. As with many artistic revolutions, this movement toward realism began outside the mainstream. By 1916, however, big New York audiences were flocking to small, obscure, off-Broadway theaters to see the works of writers such as Eugene O'Neill (1888–1953). His play *Beyond the Horizon* marked a turning point in presenting true-to-life characters who were struggling to understand their lives. Eventually, mainstream theaters began to showcase realistic plays, too, and realism became established as the dominant mode of American drama.

Building on O'Neill's achievement, American playwrights Thornton Wilder and Lillian Hellman created dramas in the 1930s and 1940s that met with critical and popular success. The post-World War II years also introduced Edward Albee and Lorraine Hansberry, who made significant contributions to the theater. Two of the most notable figures of this time were Tennessee Williams (1911–1983) and Arthur Miller (1915–2005), playwrights who experimented with stagecraft while exploring modern themes and creating works of social relevance.

Themes in Modern American Drama One of the most common themes explored by these playwrights was that of the American dream. Willy Loman, the main character in Miller's *Death of a Salesman*, became the trademark figure of postwar American theater. A lowly salesman who has been discarded by the system to which he has mistakenly devoted his life, Willy Loman proved how the American dream could become twisted and broken. In *The Glass Menagerie* and *A Streetcar*

© Houghton Mifflin Harcourt Publishing Company

WHEN STUDENTS STRUGGLE . . .

Understand Chronological Order Tell students that the numbering of dates and centuries can be confusing. Explain that a century is one hundred years. Then, explain that the years 1900–1999 are not the 19th century, but the 20th century. On the board, make a timeline. Ask students which years are included in the 20th century. *(1900–1999)* Then, ask which years will be included in the 21st century. *(2000–2099)*

 For additional support, go to the **Reading Studio** and assign the following **Level Up Tutorial: Chronological Order**.

Named Desire, southerner Tennessee Williams portrayed characters who, unsuited to modern life, retreat into the fantasy world of an earlier era. In *A Raisin in the Sun*, Lorraine Hansberry (1930–1965) looked at the American dream from the perspective of those who had been excluded. The first major Broadway play by an African-American writer, *A Raisin in the Sun* was hailed by critics as "universal," while also capturing unique aspects of the African-American experience. Politics, too, influenced playwrights. In the 1950s the U.S. government, suspicious of Communist activity in society, held hearings to root out Communist sympathizers. Senator Joseph McCarthy led the effort to identify people with ties to Communism and to pressure them into revealing the names of others who were also supporters of the cause. Arthur Miller's personal experiences with the House Un-American Activities Committee were the creative fodder for his most acclaimed play, *The Crucible,* in which he compared this "Red Scare" to the Salem witch trials.

In contemporary theater, there has been a shift back toward spectacular productions as commercial theater once again relies upon special effects, imaginative settings, and imaginary worlds. Musical theater has become very popular, and many musicals now have touring companies that take productions from Broadway to theaters all over the country. Like any art form, drama undergoes infinite adaptations to reflect the spirit of the times.

Conventions of Drama The two main types of drama are tragedy and comedy. A **tragedy** recounts the downfall of a central character, while a **comedy** is light and humorous in tone and usually ends happily. **Farces** and **melodramas** are exaggerations of these two forms that feature absurd plots, stereotypical characters, humorous dialogue, and over-the-top emotional displays. Most dramas employ many of the narrative techniques seen in fiction, but there are a few elements unique to the genre.

DRAMATIC ELEMENTS	
Script	the text of the play, similar to a book, structured and organized by acts and scenes.
Act	a major unit of action, similar to a chapter in a book. Some plays have as many as five acts.
Scene	a subdivision of an act that often signals a change in time or place.
Dialogue	the conversations characters have with each other. Critical moments in the dialogue can reveal key ideas and themes, character motivations, and conflict.
Actions	movements that correspond to the dialogue, which can help move the plot along or offer insight into emotions and motivations.
Stage Directions	italicized instructions that describe details about characters, such as when they enter and exit, how they look, speak, and react to plot events and other characters. The stage directions also present details about the setting, props, costumes, lighting, and mood of a play.
Exposition	background information that helps the audience understand events happening offstage or prior to other events, or explains the broader cultural, social, and historical context of a play. In Arthur Miller's *The Crucible,* the script relies heavily on exposition to explain the playwright's views on McCarthyism and the parallels he saw between the 1692 Salem witch trials and the 1954 Senate and House hearings on Communist activities.

 ENGLISH LEARNER SUPPORT

Clarify and Reinforce Meaning Before students read Modern American Drama, pre-teach the following vocabulary:

- *drama:* story developed through dialogue and action

- *century:* one hundred years

- *realism:* the accurate and detailed portrayal of real life; literary method developed in the 19th century

- *dialogue:* conversation between two or more people; in drama, the story is told almost exclusively through dialogue

- *act:* subdivision of a play

- *scene:* subdivision of an act; usually establishes a different time or place

- *stage direction:* the playwright's instructions to the director, performer, and crew; usually set in italics; usually tell the setting

- *tragedy:* a drama that presents the downfall of a person who is involved in important events

Write these terms on the board, and read aloud the definitions. Allow students to ask for clarification.

- To practice using these terms, have students point to the beginnings of Act 1, Act 2, Act 3, and Act 4 of the play. Have them point to stage directions. Ask yes/no questions, such as the following: *Is a drama that ends happily a tragedy?* (no) *Would realism include unicorns and dragons?* (no)

- Have partners take turns asking and answering questions using the terms.

Connect to the
ESSENTIAL QUESTION

In *The Crucible*, playwright Arthur Miller creates a cast of characters who have their own personal struggles and crises. But these characters are also embroiled in a civic crisis. The tension between private and public life is heightened when these conflicts collide.

THE CRUCIBLE

Drama by **Arthur Miller**

? ESSENTIAL QUESTION:

When should personal integrity come before civic duty?

602   Unit 6

© Houghton Mifflin Harcourt Publishing Company • Image Credits: © The Geraint Lewis Collection

LEARNING MINDSET

Plan/Predict   Remind students that planning is essential to completing work efficiently and exceptionally. Encourage students to read the introductory materials for this play carefully, then make predictions about the kinds of characters and conflicts they will read about in the play. Have them also look ahead to the Analyze the Text questions and writing assignments that appear after each act. This will help them know what to pay attention to as they read this complex work. Remind students that planning will help them learn discipline and focus, which are important life skills.

QUICK START

How would it feel to be wrongly accused of doing something illegal, immoral, or unethical? Discuss your ideas with a partner.

ANALYZE DRAMATIC ELEMENTS

The **plot** is the series of related events that make up the story of the drama. To understand how Miller structures his plot, look for these elements:

- The **conflict** is a struggle between opposing forces. In Act One, local and personal conflicts escalate into a major, widespread conflict.

- **Complications** are additional problems that make the conflict more difficult to resolve. In Act Two, several events occur that add intensity.

- The **climax** is the point of highest tension or excitement. In Act Three, an event occurs that has the potential to change the outcome of the conflict.

- The **resolution** is the part of the play where conflicts are brought to a close. In Act Four, threads of the plot are tied up and questions are answered.

As you read, notice how dramatic elements such as dialogue, stage directions, and exposition, advance the plot and develop the theme.

ANALYZE CHARACTERS AND MOTIVATIONS

Miller reveals his characters' traits, relationships, and motivations—or reasons for behavior—through direct and indirect characterization. In **direct characterization,** specific details about a character are stated explicitly—often in the stage directions. **Indirect characterization** occurs when readers infer what a character is like based on clues in the text. Stage directions may provide these clues, but you should also look closely at what characters say (their **dialogue**) and how they behave (their **actions**).

In *The Crucible,* Miller incorporates three types of characters. As you read, note which characters fulfill these roles and how their interactions impact events.

- The **protagonist** is the central character of the play. This character is at the center of the conflict and often undergoes radical changes during the course of the play.

- The **antagonist** often opposes the protagonist, giving rise to the central conflict of the play.

- A **foil** is a minor character who provides a striking contrast to another character, thus emphasizing the other character's traits.

Throughout the play, the characters face **moral dilemmas**—situations in which there is a difficult choice between two courses of action. As you read, think about how motivations influence a character's choices when he or she is faced with a moral dilemma. What impact do these choices have on the plot and theme of the play?

GENRE ELEMENTS: DRAMA

- is meant to be performed in front of an audience
- uses stage directions to describe characters, actions, setting, and mood
- uses dialogue to move the plot forward and convey the concerns of characters

The Crucible   603

QUICK START

Have students read the Quick Start activity, then review the terms and brainstorm examples as a class. Then, have students jot down how they would feel and then discuss their ideas. Tell students to keep their lists and compare their feelings to those of the characters in the play.

ANALYZE DRAMATIC ELEMENTS

Help students understand the terms *dialogue, stage directions, conflict,* and *theme,* expanding on the information given as needed. Note that **complications, climax,** and **resolution** all have to do with a **central conflict.** Complications are actions or events that make the conflict harder to solve. The resolution is how it is ultimately solved. Discuss that the nature of drama is that it is intended to be performed for an audience. Most of the plot is developed through spoken words—either interactions between two or more people or when characters speak aloud to themselves. When reading a drama, therefore, explain that readers have to imagine how the characters and settings would appear on stage, using a combination of spoken lines, stage directions, and their own imagination.

ANALYZE CHARACTERS AND MOTIVATIONS

Review the types of characters and **characterizations.** Remind students that **motivations** are the reasons why characters make certain choices or choose to act in certain ways. Because a character's motivations affect his or her actions, they affect the plot and often create complications or additional conflicts. Because motivations affect the plot, understanding character motivations is crucial for understanding the way the plot unfolds and the nature of the central conflict.

Point out that, unlike many plays, Miller has chosen to include long sections of exposition in *The Crucible.* In addition to giving important historical information, plus Miller's analysis of both the Salem witch trials and his own political context, these sections of exposition give a great deal of direct characterization. Preview a few of these sections, pointing out examples.

ANALYZE LITERARY DEVICES

Review the terms *allegory, paradox, dramatic irony,* and *figurative language.* Ask students for examples of other allegories they have read. They might note *The Lord of the Rings, Hunger Games, Animal Farm, Inferno,* or *Pilgrim's Progress.* Discuss the symbolic meaning these novels represent, such as good vs. evil. Then, remind students that figurative language includes **personification, metaphor,** and **simile,** and often gives rise to powerful imagery. Ask students for some examples of figurative language.

LANGUAGE CONVENTIONS

Dialogue Review the information about **dialogue.** Remind students that while dialogue is always important to characterization and plot in any kind of storytelling, in drama it is even more important because the audience does not have a narrator to interpret events and actions. Most of the characterization is developed through dialogue. Explain that playwrights use words and phrases common to the time or place to make their characters seem authentic.

ANNOTATION MODEL

Remind students of the annotation ideas that suggest noticing literary devices, recognizing characters' words and actions that reveal character motivations, and noting how dramatic elements advance the plot and themes. Point out that they may follow the method of marking the text shown in the Annotation Model or use their own system for marking up the selection in their write-in text. They may want to color-code their annotations by using highlighters. Their notes in the margin may include questions about ideas that are unclear or topics they want to learn more about.

 **GET READY**

ANALYZE LITERARY DEVICES

An **allegory** is a work with a literal level of meaning and a symbolic one as well. In such a work, the characters and events represent broader ideas and concepts. The purpose of an allegory may be to convey a general truth about life, to teach a moral lesson, or to criticize a social institution.

On the surface, *The Crucible* is about the Salem witch trials, in which 200 individuals were accused of witchcraft between 1692 and 1693. However, Arthur Miller wrote *The Crucible* in the early 1950s at the height of the Red Scare. With this in mind, the play can be read as an allegory on McCarthyism.

In addition to allegory, Miller employs other literary devices in the play.

- A **paradox** is a statement that seems to contradict itself but may suggest an important truth.

- **Dramatic irony** is a contrast between appearance and reality in which the reader knows more about a situation or character than the characters do.

- **Figurative language** is language that is not literally true.

As you read, note how the various literary devices advance the plot, set a mood, or suggest a theme.

LANGUAGE CONVENTIONS

Dialogue Virtually everything of consequence in a drama—from plot details to character revelations—flows from dialogue, or the conversation between characters. Miller uses dialogue to convey critical information.

> **Uncle, the <u>rumor of witchcraft</u> is all about; I think you'd best go down and deny it yourself.**

In the example, Miller tells you what the main conflict centers around. As you read, note how the playwright advances the plot through dialogue.

ANNOTATION MODEL   **NOTICE & NOTE**

As you read, take notes on details that help you analyze characters, follow the plot, and evaluate literary devices. This excerpt shows one reader's notes on *The Crucible.*

Susanna. (Aye) sir, he have been searchin' his books since he left you, sir. But he (bid) me tell you, that you might look to <u>unnatural things</u> for the cause of it. **Parris** (*his eyes going wide*). No—no. <u>There be no unnatural cause here.</u> Tell him I have sent for Reverend Hale of Beverly, and Mr. Hale will surely confirm that. Let him look to medicine and <u>put out all thought of unnatural causes here.</u> There be none.	*The words "aye" and "bid" show the characters are from the past.* *The reaction of Parris to the idea his daughter is sick by "unnatural causes" shows he is very worried that this was even said.*

BACKGROUND

Arthur Miller (1915–2005) was born in New York City into an upper-middle-class family. His comfortable early life changed when the Great Depression eroded his family's economic circumstances. Miller was unable to go to college until he earned the tuition money by working in a warehouse. Eventually, he attended the University of Michigan. Miller won several awards for his plays during college and chose to pursue a career in the theater. All My Sons and Death of a Salesman, a play that won a Pulitzer Prize in 1949, made Miller a star.

THE CRUCIBLE

Drama by Arthur Miller

Around the same time, hearings were being conducted by Congress to identify suspected Communists. Miller was called to testify before the committee about his association with the American Communist Party. Although he admitted to having attended a few meetings years earlier, he refused to "name names" of other people involved in the meetings. As a result, he was cited for contempt of Congress; this conviction was later overturned. The events of this time period inspired him to write The Crucible, set during the Salem, Massachusetts, witch trials of 1692. He wrote the play to warn against mass hysteria and to plead for freedom and tolerance. In general, Miller's writing explores issues relevant to contemporary readers, such as the complexities of family relationships, personal responsibility, and morality. Many consider him to be the 20th century's greatest American playwright.

BACKGROUND

Have students read the information about the playwright. Tell them that Miller's exploration of, and commitment to, the issues of morality, individual responsibility, family, and the common man have earned him the mantle of the quintessential American playwright of the postwar period. Despite a focus on American life, however, Miller's plays have reached a wide international audience due, in part, to their many stagings and adaptations. Several of Miller's plays have been turned into films, including numerous versions of *Death of a Salesman; All My Sons;* and *The Crucible,* in an all-star, Hollywood remake in 1996.

CLOSE READ SCREENCAST

Modeled Discussion In their eBooks, have students view the Close Read Screencast, in which readers discuss and annotate the following key passages: Parris's daughter is ill (Act One, paragraphs 1–23).

As a class, view and discuss at least one video. Have pairs do a close read of another passage (Act Four, paragraphs 290–294) and record their ideas on the Close Read Practice PDF.

 Close Read Practice PDF

SETTING A PURPOSE

Direct students to use the Setting a Purpose prompt to focus their reading.

ANALYZE CHARACTERS AND MOTIVATIONS

Discuss the opening scene with students. Point out that, as the play opens, Reverend Parris prays near the bed of his daughter. Before any dialogue is spoken, however, the playwright gives some details about Parris. Explain that Miller includes passages of **exposition**—text that explains things to readers—throughout Act One. These passages offer information about the characters, setting, historical context, and the playwright's own perspective on his subject. These notes, of course, are not part of the experience of watching the play. Students should consider how well the play's dialogue conveys the ideas Miller explains in the exposition passages. (**Answer:** *Parris always feels like he is treated unfairly and that is why he will always take "a villainous path." This is an example of direct characterization because the writer directly says that the character is not an admirable or trustworthy person.*)

 For **reading support** for students at varying proficiency levels, see the **Text X-Ray** on page 600D.

 ## ENGLISH LEARNER SUPPORT

Understand Multiple-Meaning Words Explain to students that the word *overture* has more than one meaning. In classical music, an *overture* is music played before the beginning of an opera or musical. The word *overture* can also mean the beginning of or introduction to something. Ask students which meaning fits the use of *overture* in this play. (*the beginning of or introduction to something*) **MODERATE**

 NOTICE & NOTE

Notice & Note

Use the side margins to notice and note signposts in the text.

SETTING A PURPOSE

As you read, consider how dialogue and stage directions reveal characters' motivations and feelings about each other.

CAST OF CHARACTERS
(IN ORDER OF APPEARANCE)

Reverend Samuel Parris	Rebecca Nurse
Betty Parris	Giles Corey
Tituba	Reverend John Hale
Abigail Williams	Francis Nurse
John Proctor	Ezekiel Cheever
Elizabeth Proctor	Marshal Herrick
Susanna Walcott	Judge Hathorne
Mrs. Ann Putnam	Martha Corey
Thomas Putnam	Deputy Governor Danforth
Mercy Lewis	Girls of Salem
Mary Warren	Sarah Good

ACT ONE
An Overture

•

1   (*A small upper bedroom in the home of* Reverend Samuel Parris, *Salem, Massachusetts, in the spring of the year 1692.*

2   *There is a narrow window at the left. Through its leaded panes the morning sunlight streams. A candle still burns near the bed, which is at the right. A chest, a chair, and a small table are the other furnishings. At the back a door opens on the landing of the stairway to the ground floor. The room gives off an air of clean spareness. The roof rafters are exposed, and the wood colors are raw and unmellowed.*

3   *As the curtain rises,* Reverend Parris *is discovered kneeling beside the bed, evidently in prayer. His daughter,* Betty Parris, *aged ten, is lying on the bed, inert.*)

ANALYZE CHARACTERS AND MOTIVATIONS
Annotate: Mark words and phrases in paragraph 4 that describe Parris.

Infer: What impression do you get about Parris from these details? Are these details an example of direct characterization or indirect characterization? Explain.

4   At the time of these events Parris was in his middle forties. In history he cut a villainous path, and there is very little good to be said for him. He believed he was being persecuted wherever he went, despite his best efforts to win people and God to his side. In meeting, he felt insulted if someone rose to shut the door without first asking his permission. He was a widower with no interest in children, or talent with them. He regarded them as young adults, and

until this strange crisis he, like the rest of Salem, never conceived that the children were anything but thankful for being permitted to walk straight, eyes slightly lowered, arms at the sides, and mouths shut until bidden to speak.

5   His house stood in the "town"—but we today would hardly call it a village. The meeting house[1] was nearby, and from this point outward—toward the bay or inland—there were a few small-windowed, dark houses snuggling against the raw Massachusetts winter. Salem had been established hardly forty years before. To the European world the whole province was a barbaric frontier inhabited by a sect of fanatics who, nevertheless, were shipping out products of slowly increasing quantity and value.

6   No one can really know what their lives were like. They had no novelists—and would not have permitted anyone to read a novel if one were handy. Their creed forbade anything resembling a theater or "vain enjoyment." They did not celebrate Christmas, and a holiday from work meant only that they must concentrate even more upon prayer.

7   Which is not to say that nothing broke into this strict and somber way of life. When a new farmhouse was built, friends assembled to "raise the roof," and there would be special foods cooked and probably some potent cider passed around. There was a good supply of ne'er-do-wells in Salem, who dallied at the shovelboard[2] in Bridget Bishop's tavern. Probably more than the creed, hard work kept the morals of the place from spoiling, for the people were forced to fight the land like heroes for every grain of corn, and no man had very much time for fooling around.

8   That there were some jokers, however, is indicated by the practice of appointing a two-man patrol whose duty was to "walk forth in the time of God's worship to take notice of such as either lye about the meeting house, without attending to the word and ordinances, or that lye at home or in the fields without giving good account thereof, and to take the names of such persons, and to present them to the magistrates, whereby they may be accordingly proceeded against." This predilection for minding other people's business was time-honored among the people of Salem, and it undoubtedly created many of the suspicions which were to feed the coming madness. It was also, in my opinion, one of the things that a John Proctor would rebel against, for the time of the armed camp had almost passed, and since the country was reasonably—although not wholly—safe, the old disciplines were beginning to rankle. But, as in all such matters, the issue was not clear-cut, for danger was still a possibility, and in unity still lay the best promise of safety.

9   The edge of the wilderness was close by. The American continent stretched endlessly west, and it was full of mystery for them. It stood,

---

[1] **meeting house:** the most important building in the Puritan community, used both for worship and for meetings.

[2] **shovelboard:** a game in which a coin or disc is shoved across a board by hand.

WHEN STUDENTS STRUGGLE . . .

Understand Setting Explain that the setting affects both the plot and characters of a story. Tell students that the Puritans were a religious group that wanted to reform the Anglican Church in England. The English government retaliated by persecuting Puritans, causing some to immigrate to America. Have students discuss how the setting of a Puritan town might affect the characters and plot. What might life be like in a strict, isolated religious community?

 For additional support, go to the **Reading Studio** and assign the following LEVEL UP **Level Up Tutorial: Setting: Effect on Plot**.

 **NOTICE & NOTE**

dark and threatening, over their shoulders night and day, for out of it Indian tribes marauded from time to time, and Reverend Parris had parishioners who had lost relatives to these heathen.

10 The parochial snobbery of these people was partly responsible for their failure to convert the Indians. Probably they also preferred to take land from heathens rather than from fellow Christians. At any rate, very few Indians were converted, and the Salem folk believed that the virgin forest was the Devil's last preserve, his home base and the citadel of his final stand. To the best of their knowledge the American forest was the last place on earth that was not paying homage to God.

11 For these reasons, among others, they carried about an air of innate resistance, even of persecution. Their fathers had, of course, been persecuted in England. So now they and their church found it necessary to deny any other sect its freedom, lest their New Jerusalem[3] be defiled and corrupted by wrong ways and deceitful ideas.

12 They believed, in short, that they held in their steady hands the candle that would light the world. We have inherited this belief, and it has helped and hurt us. It helped them with the discipline it gave them. They were a dedicated folk, by and large, and they had to be to survive the life they had chosen or been born into in this country.

13 The proof of their belief's value to them may be taken from the opposite character of the first Jamestown settlement, farther south, in Virginia. The Englishmen who landed there were motivated mainly by a hunt for profit. They had thought to pick off the wealth of the new country and then return rich to England. They were a band of individualists, and a much more ingratiating group than the Massachusetts men. But Virginia destroyed them. Massachusetts tried to kill off the Puritans, but they combined; they set up a communal society which, in the beginning, was little more than an armed camp with an autocratic and very devoted leadership. It was, however, an autocracy by consent, for they were united from top to bottom by a commonly held ideology whose perpetuation was the reason and justification for all their sufferings. So their self-denial, their purposefulness, their suspicion of all vain pursuits, their hard-handed justice, were altogether perfect instruments for the conquest of this space so antagonistic to man.

14 But the people of Salem in 1692 were not quite the dedicated folk that arrived on the *Mayflower*. A vast differentiation had taken place, and in their own time a revolution had unseated the royal government and substituted a junta which was at this moment in power.[4] The times, to their eyes, must have been out of joint, and to

---

[3] **New Jerusalem:** in Christianity, a heavenly city and the last resting place of the souls saved by Jesus. It was considered the ideal city, and Puritans modeled their communities after it.

[4] **a junta** (hŏŏn´tə) **. . . power:** Junta is a Spanish term meaning "a small, elite ruling council." The reference here is to the group that led England's Glorious Revolution of 1688–1689.

TO CHALLENGE STUDENTS . . .

Evaluate Author's Purpose Note that Miller's general purpose in the mini-essay is to inform. Then, point out that the purpose of *The Crucible* is not primarily informative. Ask students whether they find this informative passage helpful or counterproductive. Invite suggestions such as these about ways the information could be conveyed to the audience:

- Have an actor play the part of a narrator and present such passages to the audience.
- Print the passages in the play's program.

the common folk must have seemed as insoluble and complicated as do ours today. It is not hard to see how easily many could have been led to believe that the time of confusion had been brought upon them by deep and darkling forces. No hint of such speculation appears on the court record, but social disorder in any age breeds such mystical suspicions, and when, as in Salem, wonders are brought forth from below the social surface, it is too much to expect people to hold back very long from laying on the victims with all the force of their frustrations.

15   The Salem tragedy, which is about to begin in these pages, developed from a paradox. It is a paradox in whose grip we still live, and there is no prospect yet that we will discover its resolution. Simply, it was this: for good purposes, even high purposes, the people of Salem developed a theocracy, a combine of state and religious power whose function was to keep the community together, and to prevent any kind of disunity that might open it to destruction by material or ideological enemies. It was forged for a necessary purpose and accomplished that purpose. But all organization is and must be grounded on the idea of exclusion and prohibition, just as two objects cannot occupy the same space. Evidently the time came in New England when the repressions of order were heavier than seemed warranted by the dangers against which the order was organized. The witch-hunt was a perverse manifestation of the panic which set in among all classes when the balance began to turn toward greater individual freedom.

16   When one rises above the individual villainy displayed, one can only pity them all, just as we shall be pitied someday. It is still impossible for man to organize his social life without repressions, and the balance has yet to be struck between order and freedom.

17   The witch-hunt was not, however, a mere repression. It was also, and as importantly, a long overdue opportunity for everyone so inclined to express publicly his guilt and sins, under the cover of accusations against the victims. It suddenly became possible—and patriotic and holy—for a man to say that Martha Corey had come into his bedroom at night, and that, while his wife was sleeping at his side, Martha laid herself down on his chest and "nearly suffocated him." Of course it was her spirit only, but his satisfaction at confessing himself was no lighter than if it had been Martha herself. One could not ordinarily speak such things in public.

18   Long-held hatreds of neighbors could now be openly expressed, and vengeance taken, despite the Bible's charitable injunctions. Land-lust which had been expressed before by constant bickering over boundaries and deeds, could now be elevated to the arena of morality; one could cry witch against one's neighbor and feel perfectly justified in the bargain. Old scores could be settled on a plane of heavenly combat between Lucifer and the Lord; suspicions and the envy of the miserable toward the happy could and did burst out in the general revenge.

ANALYZE LITERARY DEVICES

Annotate: Mark the paradox that Miller refers to in the final section of the exposition.

Interpret: How does the paradox illuminate the playwright's perspective on his subject?

The Crucible: Act One   609

ANALYZE LITERARY DEVICES

Remind students that the **exposition** expresses Miller's personal perspective on the issues of his play, and that a **paradox** is something that is apparently contradictory. Tell students to focus on the final four paragraphs of this section of the exposition for Miller's explanation of the paradox of Salem society that led to the witch trials. (**Answer:** *Miller highlights the paradox that occurs when a community that is religiously based sets rules to maintain political order: those rules may ultimately lead to repression and disorder. In fact, Miller states that "all organization is and must be grounded on the idea of exclusion and prohibition . . ." Miller feels that the story of Salem is an example of a larger issue that is still with us today: How to maintain a society that is orderly while still protecting the freedom of its citizens.*)

EL ENGLISH LEARNER SUPPORT

Provide Contextual Support Guide students to find the meanings of the listed words and phrases from paragraph 18. Write the first one on the board, and have students underline it in the text. Then, read aloud the sentence, pointing out that the phrase "now be openly expressed" is a clue that clarifies the meaning of *long-held* as "left unexpressed" or "kept secret." Have partners repeat the process with the remaining terms.

- *long-held hatreds:* bitter resentments toward others that people refuse to resolve
- *vengeance:* harmful, punishing action a person takes against someone who has harmed him or her
- *land-lust:* a desire to own a neighbor's land
- *bickering:* arguing about unimportant matters
- *cry witch:* to accuse someone of being a witch
- *envy of the miserable:* the jealousy that unhappy people feel toward happy people **LIGHT**

TEACH

 ANALYZE CHARACTERS AND MOTIVATIONS

Remind students that details about characters are revealed in a play both directly and indirectly. In **direct characterization,** specific details about a character are stated explicitly—often in the **stage directions. Indirect characterization** occurs when readers infer characters' traits from what they say and do. Both stage directions and **dialogue** can provide these clues. (**Answer:** *Having an "endless capacity for dissembling" means she is highly capable of withholding her true feelings and obscuring the truth of a matter. Therefore, what Abigail may say is probably not entirely trustworthy.*)

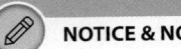
19 (*Reverend Parris is praying now, and, though we cannot hear his words, a sense of his confusion hangs about him. He mumbles, then seems about to weep; then he weeps, then prays again; but his daughter does not stir on the bed.*)

20 *The door opens, and his Negro slave enters.* Tituba *is in her forties.* Parris *brought her with him from Barbados, where he spent some years as a merchant before entering the ministry. She enters as one does who can no longer bear to be barred from the sight of her beloved, but she is also very frightened because her slave sense has warned her that, as always, trouble in this house eventually lands on her back.*)

21 **Tituba** (*already taking a step backward*). My Betty be hearty soon?

22 **Parris.** Out of here!

23 **Tituba** (*backing to the door*). My Betty not goin' die . . .

24 **Parris** (*scrambling to his feet in a fury*). Out of my sight! (*She is gone.*) Out of my—(*He is overcome with sobs. He clamps his teeth against them and closes the door and leans against it, exhausted.*) Oh, my God! God help me! (*Quaking with fear, mumbling to himself through his sobs, he goes to the bed and gently takes* Betty's *hand.*) Betty. Child. Dear child. Will you wake, will you open up your eyes! Betty, little one . . .

25 (*He is bending to kneel again when his niece,* Abigail Williams, *seventeen, enters—a strikingly beautiful girl, an orphan, with an endless capacity for dissembling. Now she is all worry and apprehension and propriety.*)

26 **Abigail.** Uncle? (*He looks to her.*) Susanna Walcott's here from Doctor Griggs.

27 **Parris.** Oh? Let her come, let her come.

28 **Abigail** (*leaning out the door to call to Susanna, who is down the hall a few steps*). Come in, Susanna. (Susanna Walcott, *a little younger than* Abigail, *a nervous, hurried girl, enters.*)

29 **Parris** (*eagerly*). What does the doctor say, child?

30 **Susanna** (*craning around* Parris *to get a look at* Betty). He bid me come and tell you, reverend sir, that he cannot discover no medicine for it in his books.

31 **Parris.** Then he must search on.

32 **Susanna.** Aye, sir, he have been searchin' his books since he left you, sir. But he bid me tell you, that you might look to unnatural things for the cause of it.

33 **Parris** (*his eyes going wide*). No—no. There be no unnatural cause here. Tell him I have sent for Reverend Hale of Beverly, and Mr. Hale will surely confirm that. Let him look to medicine and put out all thought of unnatural causes here. There be none.

ANALYZE CHARACTERS AND MOTIVATIONS

Annotate: Mark the description of Abigail's personality in paragraph 25.

Infer: What does this description suggest about whether Parris should believe what she says?

TO CHALLENGE STUDENTS . . .

Extend Knowledge Tell students that the history of Africans in America goes back to 1619, when 20 African indentured servants came to Virginia. By the 1660s, Africans were being brought to the American colonies in large numbers as both indentured servants and enslaved persons. Have students work in small groups to learn more about slavery in late 17th-century colonial America. The stage directions say Parris brought Tituba from Barbados. Have classmates consult sources to find out about the role Barbados and other islands in the Caribbean played in the slave trade of this period. Be sure students investigate the difference between indentured servants and enslaved persons of the period.

34 **Susanna.** Aye, sir. He bid me tell you. (*She turns to go.*)

35 **Abigail.** Speak nothin' of it in the village, Susanna.

36 **Parris.** Go directly home and speak nothing of unnatural causes.

37 **Susanna.** Aye, sir. I pray for her. (*She goes out.*)

38 **Abigail.** Uncle, the rumor of witchcraft is all about; I think you'd best go down and deny it yourself. The parlor's packed with people, sir. I'll sit with her.

39 **Parris** (*pressed, turns on her*). And what shall I say to them? That my daughter and my niece I discovered dancing like heathen in the forest?

40 **Abigail.** Uncle, we did dance; let you tell them I confessed it—and I'll be whipped if I must be. But they're speakin' of witchcraft. Betty's not witched.

41 **Parris.** Abigail, I cannot go before the congregation when I know you have not opened with me. What did you do with her in the forest?

42 **Abigail.** We did dance, uncle, and when you leaped out of the bush so suddenly, Betty was frightened and then she fainted. And there's the whole of it.

43 **Parris.** Child. Sit you down.

44 **Abigail** (*quavering, as she sits*). I would never hurt Betty. I love her dearly.

45 **Parris.** Now look you, child, your punishment will come in its time. But if you trafficked with⁵ spirits in the forest I must know it now, for surely my enemies will, and they will ruin me with it.

46 **Abigail.** But we never conjured spirits.

47 **Parris.** Then why can she not move herself since midnight? This child is desperate! (Abigail *lowers her eyes.*) It must come out—my enemies will bring it out. Let me know what you done there. Abigail, do you understand that I have many enemies?

48 **Abigail.** I have heard of it, uncle.

49 **Parris.** There is a faction that is sworn to drive me from my pulpit. Do you understand that?

50 **Abigail.** I think so, sir.

51 **Parris.** Now then, in the midst of such disruption, my own household is discovered to be the very center of some obscene practice. Abominations are done in the forest—

52 **Abigail.** It were sport, uncle!

53 **Parris** (*pointing at* Betty). You call this sport? (*She lowers her eyes. He pleads.*) Abigail, if you know something that may help the doctor, for God's sake tell it to me. (*She is silent.*) I saw Tituba waving her arms

---

⁵ **trafficked with:** met with.

The Crucible: Act One   611

© Houghton Mifflin Harcourt Publishing Company

ENGLISH LEARNER SUPPORT

Use Prior Knowledge Have students locate and underline the sentence containing the word *sport*, and ask students what this word means in their everyday lives. Have them give examples of a sport using sentence frames: *An example of a sport is* _____. Then, point out that the word *sport* in paragraph 52 has a similar meaning. Have them discuss what the sentence means. (*"It were sport" means "It was just a game."*)

SUBSTANTIAL/MODERATE

IMPROVE READING FLUENCY

Targeted Passage Explain to students that the characters' lines in a play represent a spoken conversation. Students will likely need practice reading sections of dialogue with variety, intonation, and expression. Tell them that paying attention to punctuation and stage directions will help them in their reading. Have partners read paragraphs 44–58, with each partner reading one character's lines. Model fluent, expressive reading of dialogue with a proficient student first. After students have finished reading in pairs, ask them how the stage directions helped them in their reading.

 Go to the **Reading Studio** for additional support in developing fluency.

over the fire when I came on you. Why was she doing that? And I heard a screeching and gibberish coming from her mouth. She were swaying like a dumb beast over that fire!

54 **Abigail.** She always sings her Barbados songs, and we dance.

55 **Parris.** I cannot blink what I saw, Abigail, for my enemies will not blink it. I saw a dress lying on the grass.

56 **Abigail** (*innocently*). A dress?

57 **Parris** (*It is very hard to say*). Aye, a dress. And I thought I saw—someone naked running through the trees!

58 **Abigail** (*in terror*). No one was naked! You mistake yourself, uncle!

59 **Parris** (*with anger*). I saw it! (*He moves from her. Then, resolved*) Now tell me true, Abigail. And I pray you feel the weight of truth upon you, for now my ministry's at stake, my ministry and perhaps your cousin's life. Whatever abomination you have done, give me all of it now, for I dare not be taken unaware when I go before them down there.

60 **Abigail.** There is nothin' more. I swear it, uncle.

61 **Parris** (*studies her, then nods, half convinced*). Abigail, I have fought here three long years to bend these stiff-necked people to me, and now, just now when some good respect is rising for me in the parish, you compromise my very character. I have given you a home, child, I have put clothes upon your back—now give me upright answer. Your name in the town—it is entirely white, is it not?

62 **Abigail** (*with an edge of resentment*). Why, I am sure it is, sir. There be no blush about my name.[6]

63 **Parris** (*to the point*). Abigail, is there any other cause than you have told me, for your being discharged from Goody[7] Proctor's service? I have heard it said, and I tell you as I heard it, that she comes so rarely to the church this year for she will not sit so close to something soiled. What signified that remark?

64 **Abigail.** She hates me, uncle, she must, for I would not be her slave. It's a bitter woman, a lying, cold, sniveling woman, and I will not work for such a woman!

65 **Parris.** She may be. And yet it has troubled me that you are now seven month out of their house, and in all this time no other family has ever called for your service.

66 **Abigail.** They want slaves, not such as I. Let them send to Barbados for that. I will not black my face for any of them! (*with ill-concealed resentment at him*) Do you begrudge my bed, uncle?

67 **Parris.** No—no.

---

[6] **There be . . . my name:** There is nothing wrong with my reputation.

[7] **Goody:** short for *goodwife*, the Puritan equivalent of *Mrs.*

68 **Abigail** (*in a temper*). My name is good in the village! I will not have it said my name is soiled! Goody Proctor is a gossiping liar!

69 (*Enter* Mrs. Ann Putnam. *She is a twisted soul of forty-five, a death-ridden woman, haunted by dreams.*)

70 **Parris** (*as soon as the door begins to open*). No—no, I cannot have anyone. (*He sees her, and a certain deference springs into him, although his worry remains.*) Why, Goody Putnam, come in.

71 **Mrs. Putnam** (*full of breath, shiny-eyed*). It is a marvel. It is surely a stroke of hell upon you.

72 **Parris.** No, Goody Putnam, it is—

73 **Mrs. Putnam** (*glancing at* Betty). How high did she fly, how high?

74 **Parris.** No, no, she never flew—

75 **Mrs. Putnam** (*very pleased with it*). Why, it's sure she did. Mr. Collins saw her goin' over Ingersoll's barn, and come down light as bird, he says!

76 **Parris.** Now, look you, Goody Putnam, she never— (*Enter* Thomas Putnam, *a well-to-do, hard-handed landowner, near fifty.*) Oh, good morning, Mr. Putnam.

77 **Putnam.** It is a providence the thing is out now! It is a providence. (*He goes directly to the bed.*)

78 **Parris.** What's out, sir, what's—?

79 (Mrs. Putnam *goes to the bed.*)

**CONTRASTS AND
CONTRADICTIONS**

Notice & Note: Mark words in paragraphs 66–68 that show a new side of Abigail.

Cite Text Evidence: What new side of Abigail is revealed in her behavior and the stage directions in these lines?

CONTRASTS AND CONTRADICTIONS

Point out the stage directions in paragraphs 44, 47, 56, and 58, which show Abigail to be terrified of the anger Parris is showing. Note that she is deferential to him, using "sir" to address him and lowering her eyes when confronted. Slowly, a different side of her begins to show. (**Answer:** *Abigail is revealed to be temperamental and headstrong. She speaks to her guardian with "ill-concealed resentment" and "in a temper."*)

NOTICE & NOTE

80 **Putnam** (*looking down at* Betty). Why, *her eyes* is closed! Look you, Ann.

81 **Mrs. Putnam.** Why, that's strange. (*to* Parris) Ours is open.

82 **Parris** (*shocked*). Your Ruth is sick?

83 **Mrs. Putnam** (*with vicious certainty*). I'd not call it sick; the Devil's touch is heavier than sick. It's death, y'know, it's death drivin' into them, forked and hoofed.

84 **Parris.** Oh, pray not! Why, how does Ruth ail?

85 **Mrs. Putnam.** She ails as she must—she never waked this morning, but her eyes open and she walks, and hears naught, sees naught, and cannot eat. Her soul is taken, surely.

86 (Parris *is struck.*)

87 **Putnam** (*as though for further details*). They say you've sent for Reverend Hale of Beverly?

88 **Parris** (*with dwindling conviction now*). A precaution only. He has much experience in all demonic arts, and I—

89 **Mrs. Putnam.** He has indeed; and found a witch in Beverly last year, and let you remember that.

90 **Parris.** Now, Goody Ann, they only thought that were a witch, and I am certain there be no element of witchcraft here.

91 **Putnam.** No witchcraft! Now look you, Mr. Parris—

92 **Parris.** Thomas, Thomas, I pray you, leap not to witchcraft. I know that you—you least of all, Thomas, would ever wish so disastrous a charge laid upon me. We cannot leap to witchcraft. They will howl me out of Salem for such corruption in my house.

93 A word about Thomas Putnam. He was a man with many grievances, at least one of which appears justified. Some time before, his wife's brother-in-law, James Bayley, had been turned down as minister of Salem. Bayley had all the qualifications, and a two-thirds vote into the bargain, but a faction stopped his acceptance, for reasons that are not clear.

94 Thomas Putnam was the eldest son of the richest man in the village. He had fought the Indians at Narragansett,[8] and was deeply interested in parish affairs. He undoubtedly felt it poor payment that the village should so blatantly disregard his candidate for one of its more important offices, especially since he regarded himself as the intellectual superior of most of the people around him.

95 His vindictive nature was demonstrated long before the witchcraft began. Another former Salem minister, George Burroughs, had had to borrow money to pay for his wife's funeral, and, since

---

[8] **fought the Indians at Narragansett:** The Puritans fought a series of battles against the Narragansett Indians over territory that both groups had settled on.

WHEN STUDENTS STRUGGLE . . .

Summarize Have students summarize what the exposition in paragraphs 93–97 tells about the character of Thomas Putnam. (*Putnam is a resentful, vindictive man who feels he has been wronged multiple times in the past by the Salem community. He had a relative who was not promoted to minister of Salem; he persecuted the man who got the job instead of his relative. He also tried to gain more than he was left in his father's will.*)

 For additional support, go to the **Reading Studio** and assign the following ⬛ **Level Up Tutorial: Summarizing**.

the parish was remiss in his salary, he was soon bankrupt. Thomas and his brother John had Burroughs jailed for debts the man did not owe. The incident is important only in that Burroughs succeeded in becoming minister where Bayley, Thomas Putnam's brother-in-law, had been rejected; the motif of resentment is clear here. Thomas Putnam felt that his own name and the honor of his family had been smirched by the village, and he meant to right matters however he could.

96   Another reason to believe him a deeply embittered man was his attempt to break his father's will, which left a disproportionate amount to a stepbrother. As with every other public cause in which he tried to force his way, he failed in this.

97   So it is not surprising to find that so many accusations against people are in the handwriting of Thomas Putnam, or that his name is so often found as a witness corroborating the supernatural testimony, or that his daughter led the crying-out at the most opportune junctures of the trials, especially when—But we'll speak of that when we come to it.

98 **Putnam** (*At the moment he is intent upon getting* Parris, *for whom he has only contempt, to move toward the abyss*). Mr. Parris, I have taken your part in all contention here, and I would continue; but I cannot if you hold back in this. There are hurtful, vengeful spirits layin' hands on these children.

99 **Parris.** But, Thomas, you cannot—

100 **Putnam.** Ann! Tell Mr. Parris what you have done.

101 **Mrs. Putnam.** Reverend Parris, I have laid seven babies unbaptized in the earth. Believe me, sir, you never saw more hearty babies born. And yet, each would wither in my arms the very night of their birth. I have spoke nothin', but my heart has clamored intimations.⁹ And now, this year, my Ruth, my only—I see her turning strange. A secret child she has become this year, and shrivels like a sucking mouth were pullin' on her life too. And so I thought to send her to your Tituba—

102 **Parris.** To Tituba! What may Tituba—?

103 **Mrs. Putnam.** Tituba knows how to speak to the dead, Mr. Parris.

104 **Parris.** Goody Ann, it is a formidable sin to conjure up the dead!

105 **Mrs. Putnam.** I take it on my soul, but who else may surely tell us what person murdered my babies?

106 **Parris** (*horrified*). Woman!

107 **Mrs. Putnam.** They were murdered, Mr. Parris! And mark this proof! Mark it! Last night my Ruth were ever so close to their little spirits; I know it, sir. For how else is she struck dumb now except

---

⁹ **clamored intimations** (klăm´ərd ĭn´tə-mā-shənz): nagging suspicions.

ANALYZE CHARACTERS AND MOTIVATIONS

Annotate: Mark details in paragraph 98 that suggest a threat from Mr. Putnam against Parris.

Analyze: What moral dilemma is evident in the exchange between Putnam and Parris?

ANALYZE CHARACTERS AND MOTIVATIONS

Have students consider the information they learned about Putnam from Miller's exposition. Discuss these questions: Why might Putnam have contempt for Parris? What is his likely motive for trying to cause Parris to "move toward the abyss"? What is the "abyss"? (**Answer:** *Parris faces a choice between losing Mr. Putnam's support if he does not agree that witchcraft is at work, or keeping Putnam's support for saying there is witchcraft.*)

 **ENGLISH LEARNER SUPPORT**

Use Synonyms Help students clarify the meanings of unfamiliar words in paragraphs 98–104 to better understand Mrs. Putnam's perspective and actions. Have them find simpler synonyms for *vengeful, hearty, clamored, intimations, conjure,* and *formidable,* then substitute the synonyms for these terms in the dialogue to better understand it. For example, "I have said nothing, but I have had nagging suspicions," or "Goody Ann, it is a great sin to raise the dead!" **LIGHT**

ENGLISH LEARNER SUPPORT

Analyze Idioms Tell students that an idiom is an expression whose meaning is not obvious from the individual meaning of each word. Point out the idiom "I am undone" in paragraph 111. Discuss the literal meaning of the word *undone*; for example, if the buttons on a shirt are undone, they are not fastened, and the shirt may come apart. Ask questions to lead students to the meaning of the idiom: *What about Parris's situation is coming apart? Why might he feel he is broken or ruined?*

MODERATE/LIGHT

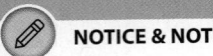

NOTICE & NOTE

some power of darkness would stop her mouth? It is a marvelous sign, Mr. Parris!

108 **Putnam.** Don't you understand it, sir? There is a murdering witch among us, bound to keep herself in the dark. (Parris *turns to* Betty, *a frantic terror rising in him.*) Let your enemies make of it what they will, you cannot blink it more.

109 **Parris** (*to* Abigail). Then you were conjuring spirits last night.

110 **Abigail** (*whispering*). Not I, sir—Tituba and Ruth.

111 **Parris** (*turns now, with new fear, and goes to* Betty, *looks down at her, and then, gazing off*). Oh, Abigail, what proper payment for my charity! Now I am undone.

112 **Putnam.** You are not undone! Let you take hold here. Wait for no one to charge you—declare it yourself. You have discovered witchcraft—

113 **Parris.** In my house? In my house, Thomas? They will topple me with this! They will make of it a—

114 (*Enter* Mercy Lewis, *the Putnams' servant, a fat, sly, merciless girl of eighteen.*)

115 **Mercy.** Your pardons. I only thought to see how Betty is.

116 **Putnam.** Why aren't you home? Who's with Ruth?

117 **Mercy.** Her grandma come. She's improved a little, I think—she give a powerful sneeze before.

118 **Mrs. Putnam.** Ah, there's a sign of life!

119 **Mercy.** I'd fear no more, Goody Putnam. It were a grand sneeze; another like it will shake her wits together, I'm sure. (*She goes to the bed to look.*)

120 **Parris.** Will you leave me now, Thomas? I would pray a while alone.

121 **Abigail.** Uncle, you've prayed since midnight. Why do you not go down and—

122 **Parris.** No—no. (*to* Putnam) I have no answer for that crowd. I'll wait till Mr. Hale arrives. (*to get* Mrs. Putnam *to leave*) If you will, Goody Ann . . .

123 **Putnam.** Now look you, sir. Let you strike out against the Devil, and the village will bless you for it! Come down, speak to them—pray with them. They're thirsting for your word, Mister! Surely you'll pray with them.

124 **Parris** (*swayed*). I'll lead them in a psalm, but let you say nothing of witchcraft yet. I will not discuss it. The cause is yet unknown. I have had enough contention since I came; I want no more.

125 **Mrs. Putnam.** Mercy, you go home to Ruth, d'y'hear?

126 **Mercy.** Aye, mum.

127 (Mrs. Putnam *goes out.*)

128 **Parris** (*to* Abigail). If she starts for the window, cry for me at once.

129 **Abigail.** I will, uncle.

130 **Parris** (*to* Putnam). There is a terrible power in her arms today. (*He goes out with* Putnam.)

131 **Abigail** (*with hushed trepidation*). How is Ruth sick?

132 **Mercy.** It's weirdish, I know not—she seems to walk like a dead one since last night.

133 **Abigail** (*turns at once and goes to* Betty, *and now, with fear in her voice*). Betty? (Betty *doesn't move. She shakes her.*) Now stop this! Betty! Sit up now!

134 (Betty *doesn't stir.* Mercy *comes over.*)

135 **Mercy.** Have you tried beatin' her? I gave Ruth a good one and it waked her for a minute. Here, let me have her.

136 **Abigail** (*holding* Mercy *back*). No, he'll be comin' up. Listen, now; if they be questioning us, tell them we danced—I told him as much already.

137 **Mercy.** Aye. And what more?

138 **Abigail.** He knows Tituba conjured Ruth's sisters to come out of the grave.

139 **Mercy.** And what more?

140 **Abigail.** He saw you naked.

141 **Mercy** (*clapping her hands together with a frightened laugh*). Oh, Jesus!

142 (*Enter* Mary Warren, *breathless. She is seventeen, a subservient, naive, lonely girl.*)

143 **Mary Warren.** What'll we do? The village is out! I just come from the farm; the whole country's talkin' witchcraft! They'll be callin' us witches, Abby!

144 **Mercy** (*pointing and looking at* Mary Warren). She means to tell, I know it.

145 **Mary Warren.** Abby, we've got to tell. Witchery's a hangin' error, a hangin' like they done in Boston two year ago! We must tell the truth, Abby! You'll only be whipped for dancin', and the other things!

146 **Abigail.** Oh, *we'll* be whipped!

147 **Mary Warren.** I never done none of it, Abby. I only looked!

148 **Mercy** (*moving menacingly toward* Mary). Oh, you're a great one for lookin', aren't you, Mary Warren? What a grand peeping courage you have!

149 (Betty, *on the bed, whimpers.* Abigail *turns to her at once.*)

WHEN STUDENTS STRUGGLE . . .

Understand Motivation Explain that paragraphs 143–148 reveal growing speculation and the girls' differing responses to it. Ask the following questions to ensure comprehension:

- According to Mary, who is talking about witchcraft?
- On the basis of Mercy's comment, what do you think the girls had planned to do? Why is that plan not working?
- What does Mary want the girls to do? Why? How will that benefit her?

 For additional support, go to the **Reading Studio** and assign the following [LEVEL UP] **Level Up Tutorial: Character Motivation**.

TEACH

ANALYZE CHARACTERS AND MOTIVATIONS

Tell students that aspects of a character are revealed by that character's **actions** and by other characters' **reactions**. Have the pupils focus on the actions of Abigail as well as her words and the reactions of other characters to Abigail. (**Answer:** *The fact that Abigail is physically rough with Betty [who is just ten years old], and that she threatens to bring a "pointy reckoning" to any girl who talks, reveals that she is hot-tempered, vengeful, and violent. She is motivated to keep the girls quiet to keep herself safe from the accusation of being a witch. Betty's reaction to Abigail is one of terror, as she collapses, cries, and calls for her mother. This also shows that Abigail is frightening to the other girls.*)

ANALYZE CHARACTERS AND MOTIVATIONS

Annotate: Mark details in paragraphs 158–160 that reveal Abigail's relationship to the other girls.

Analyze: What does Abigail's behavior in these lines reveal about her character and motivations?

150 **Abigail.** Betty? (*She goes to* Betty.) Now, Betty, dear, wake up now. It's Abigail. (*She sits* Betty *up and furiously shakes her.*) I'll beat you, Betty! (Betty *whimpers.*) My, you seem improving. I talked to your papa and I told him everything. So there's nothing to—

151 **Betty** (*darts off the bed, frightened of Abigail, and flattens herself against the wall*). I want my mama!

152 **Abigail** (*with alarm, as she cautiously approaches Betty*). What ails you, Betty? Your mama's dead and buried.

153 **Betty.** I'll fly to Mama. Let me fly! (*She raises her arms as though to fly, and streaks for the window, gets one leg out.*)

154 **Abigail** (*pulling her away from the window*). I told him everything; he knows now, he knows everything we—

155 **Betty.** You drank blood, Abby! You didn't tell him that!

156 **Abigail.** Betty, you never say that again! You will never—

157 **Betty.** You did, you did! You drank a charm to kill John Proctor's wife! You drank a charm to kill Goody Proctor!

158 **Abigail** (*smashes her across the face*). Shut it! Now shut it!

159 **Betty** (*collapsing on the bed*). Mama, Mama! (*She dissolves into sobs.*)

160 **Abigail.** Now look you. All of you. We danced. And Tituba conjured Ruth Putnam's dead sisters. And that is all. And mark this. Let either of you breathe a word, or the edge of a word, about the other things, and I will come to you in the black of some terrible night and I will bring a pointy reckoning that will shudder you.[10] And you know I can do it; I saw Indians smash my dear parents' heads on the pillow next to mine, and I have seen some reddish work done at night, and I can make you wish you had never seen the sun go down! (*She goes to* Betty *and roughly sits her up.*) Now, you—sit up and stop this!

161 (*But* Betty *collapses in her hands and lies inert on the bed.*)

162 **Mary Warren** (*with hysterical fright*). What's got her? (Abigail *stares in fright at* Betty.) Abby, she's going to die! It's a sin to conjure, and we—

163 **Abigail** (*starting for* Mary). I say shut it, Mary Warren! (*Enter* John Proctor. *On seeing him,* Mary Warren *leaps in fright.*)

164   Proctor was a farmer in his middle thirties. He need not have been a partisan of any faction in the town, but there is evidence to suggest that he had a sharp and biting way with hypocrites. He was the kind of man—powerful of body, even-tempered, and not easily led—who cannot refuse support to partisans without drawing their deepest resentment. In Proctor's presence a fool felt his foolishness instantly—and a Proctor is always marked for calumny[11] therefore.

---

[10]**bring . . . shudder you:** inflict a terrifying punishment on you.
[11]**marked for calumny** (kăl´əm-nē): singled out to have lies told about him.

165   But as we shall see, the steady manner he displays does not spring from an untroubled soul. He is a sinner, a sinner not only against the moral fashion of the time, but against his own vision of decent conduct. These people had no ritual for the washing away of sins. It is another trait we inherited from them, and it has helped to discipline us as well as to breed hypocrisy among us. Proctor, respected and even feared in Salem, has come to regard himself as a kind of fraud. But no hint of this has yet appeared on the surface, and as he enters from the crowded parlor below it is a man in his prime we see, with a quiet confidence and an unexpressed, hidden force. Mary Warren, his servant, can barely speak for embarrassment and fear.

166   **Mary Warren.** Oh! I'm just going home, Mr. Proctor.

167   **Proctor.** Be you foolish, Mary Warren? Be you deaf? I forbid you leave the house, did I not? Why shall I pay you? I am looking for you more often than my cows!

168   **Mary Warren.** I only come to see the great doings in the world.

169   **Proctor.** I'll show you a great doin' on your arse one of these days. Now get you home; my wife is waitin' with your work! (*Trying to retain a shred of dignity, she goes slowly out.*)

170   **Mercy Lewis** (*both afraid of him and strangely titillated*). I'd best be off. I have my Ruth to watch. Good morning, Mr. Proctor.

171   (Mercy *sidles out. Since* Proctor's *entrance,* Abigail *has stood as though on tiptoe, absorbing his presence, wide-eyed. He glances at her, then goes to* Betty *on the bed.*)

172   **Abigail.** Gah! I'd almost forgot how strong you are, John Proctor!

173   **Proctor** (*looking at* Abigail *now, the faintest suggestion of a knowing smile on his face*). What's this mischief here?

174   **Abigail** (*with a nervous laugh*). Oh, she's only gone silly somehow.

175   **Proctor.** The road past my house is a pilgrimage to Salem all morning. The town's mumbling witchcraft.

176   **Abigail.** Oh, posh! (*Winningly she comes a little closer, with a confidential, wicked air.*) We were dancin' in the woods last night, and my uncle leaped in on us. She took fright, is all.

177   **Proctor** (*his smile widening*). Ah, you're wicked yet, aren't y'! (*A trill of expectant laughter escapes her, and she dares come closer, feverishly looking into his eyes.*) You'll be clapped in the stocks before you're twenty.

178   (*He takes a step to go, and she springs into his path.*)

179   **Abigail.** Give me a word, John. A soft word. (*Her concentrated desire destroys his smile.*)

180   **Proctor.** No, no, Abby. That's done with.

© Houghton Mifflin Harcourt Publishing Company

ENGLISH LEARNER SUPPORT

Use Context to Understand Archaic Language
Point out the archaic phrase "great doings" in paragraph 168, and work with students to infer its meaning. Ask students what Mary is calling "great doings" (*the accusations of witchcraft*). Explain that *great* can mean "big" or "important." Have students work in pairs to come up with a short definition of *great doings* (*for example, "important events"*). Have pairs practice using context to infer meanings of "posh" in paragraph 176 and "sportin' with me" in paragraph 187. (*"posh": nonsense; "sportin' with me": joking*)

MODERATE/LIGHT

ANALYZE DRAMATIC ELEMENTS

Remind students that the **plot** of a play is the series of events that make up the story. The plot revolves around the **conflict,** or the struggle between opposing forces (often characters) in the story. The conflict (or conflicts) of a play drive the play's action by creating tension. In this scene, conflict develops because two people want opposite things. (**Answer:** *Abigail wants to continue the relationship she and Proctor have, but he does not. In fact, Proctor would prefer to act like they never had a relationship. Indeed, Proctor denies that they even touched, which outrages Abigail.*)

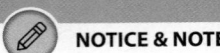
181 **Abigail** (*tauntingly*). You come five mile to see a silly girl fly? I know you better.

182 **Proctor** (*setting her firmly out of his path*). I come to see what mischief your uncle's brewin' now. (*with final emphasis*) Put it out of mind, Abby.

183 **Abigail** (*grasping his hand before he can release her*). John—I am waitin' for you every night.

184 **Proctor.** Abby, I never give you hope to wait for me.

185 **Abigail** (*now beginning to anger—she can't believe it*). I have something better than hope, I think!

186 **Proctor.** Abby, you'll put it out of mind. I'll not be comin' for you more.

187 **Abigail.** You're surely sportin' with me.

188 **Proctor.** You know me better.

189 **Abigail.** I know how you clutched my back behind your house and sweated like a stallion whenever I come near! Or did I dream that? It's she put me out, you cannot pretend it were you. I saw your face when she put me out, and you loved me then and you do now!

190 **Proctor.** Abby, that's a wild thing to say—

191 **Abigail.** A wild thing may say wild things. But not so wild, I think. I have seen you since she put me out; I have seen you nights.

192 **Proctor.** I have hardly stepped off my farm this sevenmonth.

193 **Abigail.** I have a sense for heat, John, and yours has drawn me to my window, and I have seen you looking up, burning in your loneliness. Do you tell me you've never looked up at my window?

194 **Proctor.** I may have looked up.

ANALYZE DRAMATIC ELEMENTS

Annotate: Mark details in paragraph 195 that reveal how Abigail feels about Proctor.

Interpret: What conflict emerges between Abigail and Proctor?

195 **Abigail** (*now softening*). And you must. You are no wintry man. I *know* you, John. I know you. (*She is weeping.*) I cannot sleep for dreamin'; I cannot dream but I wake and walk about the house as though I'd find you comin' through some door. (*She clutches him desperately*).

196 **Proctor** (*gently pressing her from him, with great sympathy but firmly*). Child—

197 **Abigail** (*with a flash of anger*). How do you call me child!

198 **Proctor.** Abby, I may think of you softly from time to time. But I will cut off my hand before I'll ever reach for you again. Wipe it out of mind. We never touched, Abby.

199 **Abigail.** Aye, but we did.

200 **Proctor.** Aye, but we did not.

201 **Abigail** (*with a bitter anger*). Oh, I marvel how such a strong man may let such a sickly wife be—

WHEN STUDENTS STRUGGLE . . .

Analyze Conflict If students have trouble discerning conflict in a scene, encourage them to identify what each character wants or needs. Have them describe some of the other conflicts in the play: (1) Abigail and Mrs. Proctor (*Abigail wants to continue a relationship with her husband; it is assumed Mrs. Proctor does not want this.*) (2) Parris and the Putnams (*Parris wants no mention yet of the possibility of witchcraft; the Putnams want to spread the word of witchcraft in the town.*)

 For additional support, go to the **Reading Studio** and assign the following **Level Up Tutorial: Conflict**.

202 **Proctor** (*angered—at himself as well*). You'll speak nothin' of Elizabeth!

203 **Abigail.** She is blackening my name in the village! She is telling lies about me! She is a cold, sniveling woman, and you bend to her! Let her turn you like a—

204 **Proctor** (*shaking her*). Do you look for whippin'?

205 (*A psalm is heard being sung below.*)

206 **Abigail** (*in tears*). I look for John Proctor that took me from my sleep and put knowledge in my heart! I never knew what pretense Salem was, I never knew the lying lessons I was taught by all these Christian women and their covenanted[12] men! And now you bid me tear the light out of my eyes? I will not, I cannot! You loved me, John Proctor,

---

[12] **covenanted** (kŭv´ə-nən-tĭd): In Puritan religious practice, the men of a congregation would make an agreement, or covenant, to govern the community and abide by its beliefs and practices.

ENGLISH LEARNER SUPPORT

Interpret Stage Directions Remind students that stage directions are shown in italics and parentheses, and that they explain actions the characters take or emotions the characters show as they speak. Have students underline the stage directions in paragraphs 202 and 204. Guide them to understand what these stage directions show about Proctor.

- Have students use gestures or facial expressions to act out each stage direction. **SUBSTANTIAL/MODERATE**

- Have students rewrite the stage directions as complete sentences. (*Proctor speaks while he is shaking Abigail; Proctor is growing unnerved.*) **LIGHT**

and whatever sin it is, you love me yet! (*He turns abruptly to go out. She rushes to him.*) John, pity me, pity me!

207 (*The words "going up to Jesus" are heard in the psalm, and Betty claps her ears suddenly and whines loudly.*)

208 **Abigail.** Betty? (*She hurries to* Betty, *who is now sitting up and screaming.* Proctor *goes to* Betty *as* Abigail *is trying to pull her hands down, calling "*Betty!*"*)

209 **Proctor** (*growing unnerved*). What's she doing? Girl, what ails you? Stop that wailing!

210 (*The singing has stopped in the midst of this, and now* Parris *rushes in.*)

211 **Parris.** What happened? What are you doing to her? Betty! (*He rushes to the bed, crying, "*Betty, Betty!*"* Mrs. Putnam *enters, feverish with curiosity, and with her* Thomas Putnam *and* Mercy Lewis. Parris, *at the bed, keeps lightly slapping* Betty's *face, while she moans and tries to get up.*)

212 **Abigail.** She heard you singin' and suddenly she's up and screamin'.

213 **Mrs. Putnam.** The psalm! The psalm! She cannot bear to hear the Lord's name!

214 **Parris.** No. God forbid. Mercy, run to the doctor! Tell him what's happened here! (Mercy Lewis *rushes out.*)

215 **Mrs. Putnam.** Mark it for a sign, mark it!

216 (Rebecca Nurse, *seventy-two, enters. She is white-haired, leaning upon her walking-stick.*)

217 **Putnam** (*pointing at the whimpering* Betty). That is a notorious sign of witchcraft afoot, Goody Nurse, a prodigious sign!

218 **Mrs. Putnam.** My mother told me that! When they cannot bear to hear the name of—

TO CHALLENGE STUDENTS . . .

Interpret Stage Directions Tell students that the job of a play's director is to collaborate with the actors to make sure they follow the spirit of the playwright's stage directions. Have groups of students choose a scene from this act, such as the one on this page, and perform it. Choose a student to act as the director and other students to act out each of the parts. Give each actor ten minutes to study his or her lines and stage directions. Then have students act out the scene. When they have finished, have the director give each actor feedback on his or her performance based on the stage directions. Then have students perform the scene again.

219 **Parris** (*trembling*). Rebecca, Rebecca, go to her, we're lost. She suddenly cannot bear to hear the Lord's—

220 (*Giles Corey, eighty-three, enters. He is knotted with muscle, canny, inquisitive, and still powerful.*)

221 **Rebecca.** There is hard sickness here, Giles Corey, so please to keep the quiet.

222 **Giles.** I've not said a word. No one here can testify I've said a word. Is she going to fly again? I hear she flies.

223 **Putnam.** Man, be quiet now!

224 (*Everything is quiet. Rebecca walks across the room to the bed. Gentleness exudes from her. Betty is quietly whimpering, eyes shut. Rebecca simply stands over the child, who gradually quiets.*)

225 And while they are so absorbed, we may put a word in for Rebecca. Rebecca was the wife of Francis Nurse, who, from all accounts, was one of those men for whom both sides of the argument had to have respect. He was called upon to arbitrate disputes as though he were an unofficial judge, and Rebecca also enjoyed the high opinion most people had for him. By the time of the delusion,[13] they had three hundred acres, and their children were settled in separate homesteads within the same estate. However, Francis had originally rented the land, and one theory has it that, as he gradually paid for it and raised his social status, there were those who resented his rise.

226 Another suggestion to explain the systematic campaign against Rebecca, and inferentially against Francis, is the land war he fought with his neighbors, one of whom was a Putnam. This squabble grew to the proportions of a battle in the woods between partisans of both sides, and it is said to have lasted for two days. As for Rebecca herself, the general opinion of her character was so high that to explain how anyone dared cry her out for a witch—and more, how adults could bring themselves to lay hands on her—we must look to the fields and boundaries of that time.

227 As we have seen, Thomas Putnam's man for the Salem ministry was Bayley. The Nurse clan had been in the faction that prevented Bayley's taking office. In addition, certain families allied to the Nurses by blood or friendship, and whose farms were contiguous with the Nurse farm or close to it, combined to break away from the Salem town authority and set up Topsfield, a new and independent entity whose existence was resented by old Salemites.

228 That the guiding hand behind the outcry was Putnam's is indicated by the fact that, as soon as it began, this Topsfield-Nurse faction absented themselves from church in protest and disbelief. It was Edward and Jonathan Putnam who signed the first complaint

---

[13] **the time of the delusion:** the era of the witchcraft accusations and trials.

© Houghton Mifflin Harcourt Publishing Company

NOTICE & NOTE

ANALYZE CHARACTERS AND MOTIVATIONS

Explain to students that a playwright will develop and deepen the conflicts between his or her characters as a play goes on, and that conflict arises when characters want different things or react differently to events. Have students consider how Rebecca and Putnam are reacting differently to the events in the play. (**Answer:** *Rebecca does not believe witchcraft is to blame for the girls' illnesses, but Putnam does. Rebecca thinks they should pray and rely on the doctor's skills before rushing into a witch hunt—"seeking loose spirits"—with Reverend Hale.*)

against Rebecca; and Thomas Putnam's little daughter was the one who fell into a fit at the hearing and pointed to Rebecca as her attacker. To top it all, Mrs. Putnam—who is now staring at the bewitched child on the bed—soon accused Rebecca's spirit of "tempting her to iniquity," a charge that had more truth in it than Mrs. Putnam could know.

229 **Mrs. Putnam** (*astonished*). What have you done?

230 (Rebecca, *in thought, now leaves the bedside and sits.*)

231 **Parris** (*wondrous and relieved*). What do you make of it, Rebecca?

232 **Putnam** (*eagerly*). Goody Nurse, will you go to my Ruth and see if you can wake her?

233 **Rebecca** (*sitting*). I think she'll wake in time. Pray calm yourselves. I have eleven children, and I am twenty-six times a grandma, and I have seen them all through their silly seasons, and when it come on them they will run the Devil bowlegged keeping up with their mischief. I think she'll wake when she tires of it. A child's spirit is like a child, you can never catch it by running after it; you must stand still, and, for love, it will soon itself come back.

234 **Proctor.** Aye, that's the truth of it, Rebecca.

235 **Mrs. Putnam.** This is no silly season, Rebecca. My Ruth is bewildered, Rebecca; she cannot eat.

236 **Rebecca.** Perhaps she is not hungered yet. (*to* Parris) I hope you are not decided to go in search of loose spirits, Mr. Parris. I've heard promise of that outside.

237 **Parris.** A wide opinion's running in the parish that the Devil may be among us, and I would satisfy them that they are wrong.

238 **Proctor.** Then let you come out and call them wrong. Did you consult the wardens¹⁴ before you called this minister to look for devils?

239 **Parris.** He is not coming to look for devils!

240 **Proctor.** Then what's he coming for?

241 **Putnam.** There be children dyin' in the village, Mister!

242 **Proctor.** I seen none dyin'. This society will not be a bag to swing around your head, Mr. Putnam. (*to* Parris) Did you call a meeting before you—?

243 **Putnam.** I am sick of meetings; cannot the man turn his head without he have a meeting?

244 **Proctor.** He may turn his head, but not to Hell!

245 **Rebecca.** Pray, John, be calm. (*Pause. He defers to her.*) Mr. Parris, I think you'd best send Reverend Hale back as soon as he come. This

ANALYZE CHARACTERS AND MOTIVATIONS
Annotate: Mark details in paragraph 245 that show Rebecca is religious.

Interpret: How does her faith in God differ from Mr. Putnam's?

---
¹⁴**wardens:** officers appointed to keep order.

WHEN STUDENTS STRUGGLE . . .

Distinguish Characters and Dialogue   Tell students that, when reading a play, they may find it difficult to distinguish among characters. Have students make a chart listing each character and recording details about him or her. Then, have them use their charts to answer this question: Why is Proctor challenging Parris about calling in Reverend Bayley? (*Proctor isn't easily led. Since he hasn't seen children dying, he doesn't think drastic action is needed.*)

For additional support, go to the **Reading Studio** and assign the following **Level Up Tutorials: Character Traits** and **Methods of Characterization**.

will set us all to arguin' again in the society, and we thought to have peace this year. I think <u>we ought rely on the doctor now, and good prayer.</u>

246 **Mrs. Putnam.** Rebecca, the doctor's baffled!

247 **Rebecca.** If so he is, then let us go to God for the cause of it. There is prodigious danger in the seeking of loose spirits. I fear it, I fear it. Let us rather blame ourselves and—

248 **Putnam.** How may we blame ourselves? I am one of nine sons; the Putnam seed have peopled this province. And yet I have but one child left of eight—and now she shrivels!

249 **Rebecca.** I cannot fathom that.

250 **Mrs. Putnam** (*with a growing edge of sarcasm*). But I must! You think it God's work you should never lose a child, nor grandchild either, and I bury all but one? There are wheels within wheels in this village, and fires within fires!

251 **Putnam** (*to* Parris). When Reverend Hale comes, you will proceed to look for signs of witchcraft here.

252 **Proctor** (*to* Putnam). You cannot command Mr. Parris. We vote by name in this society, not by acreage.

253 **Putnam.** I never heard you worried so on this society, Mr. Proctor. I do not think I saw you at Sabbath meeting since snow flew.

254 **Proctor.** I have trouble enough without I come five mile to hear him preach only hellfire and bloody damnation. Take it to heart, Mr. Parris. There are many others who stay away from church these days because you hardly ever mention God any more.

255 **Parris** (*now aroused*). Why, that's a drastic charge!

256 **Rebecca.** It's somewhat true; there are many that quail to bring their children—

257 **Parris.** I do not preach for children, Rebecca. It is not the children who are unmindful of their obligations toward this ministry.

258 **Rebecca.** Are there really those unmindful?

259 **Parris.** I should say the better half of Salem village—

260 **Putnam.** And more than that!

261 **Parris.** Where is my wood? My contract provides I be supplied with all my firewood. I am waiting since November for a stick, and even in November I had to show my frostbitten hands like some London beggar!

262 **Giles.** You are allowed six pound a year to buy your wood, Mr. Parris.

263 **Parris.** I regard that six pound as part of my salary. I am paid little enough without I spend six pound on firewood.

264 **Proctor.** Sixty, plus six for firewood—

 **NOTICE & NOTE**

265 **Parris.** The salary is sixty-six pound, Mr. Proctor! I am not some preaching farmer with a book under my arm; I am a graduate of Harvard College.

266 **Giles.** Aye, and well instructed in arithmetic!

267 **Parris.** Mr. Corey, you will look far for a man of my kind at sixty pound a year! I am not used to this poverty; I left a thrifty business in the Barbados to serve the Lord. I do not fathom it, why am I persecuted here? I cannot offer one proposition but there be a howling riot of argument. I have often wondered if the Devil be in it somewhere; I cannot understand you people otherwise.

268 **Proctor.** Mr. Parris, you are the first minister ever did demand the deed to this house—

269 **Parris.** Man! Don't a minister deserve a house to live in?

270 **Proctor.** To live in, yes. But to ask ownership is like you shall own the meeting house itself; the last meeting I were at you spoke so long on deeds and mortgages I thought it were an auction.

271 **Parris.** I want a mark of confidence, is all! I am your third preacher in seven years. I do not wish to be put out like the cat whenever some majority feels the whim. You people seem not to comprehend that a minister is the Lord's man in the parish; a minister is not to be so lightly crossed and contradicted—

272 **Putnam.** Aye!

273 **Parris.** There is either obedience or the church will burn like Hell is burning!

274 **Proctor.** Can you speak one minute without we land in Hell again? I am sick of Hell!

275 **Parris.** It is not for you to say what is good for you to hear!

276 **Proctor.** I may speak my heart, I think!

277 **Parris** (*in a fury*). What, are we Quakers?[15] We are not Quakers here yet, Mr. Proctor. And you may tell that to your followers!

278 **Proctor.** My followers!

279 **Parris** (*Now he's out with it*). There is a party in this church. I am not blind; there is a faction and a party.

280 **Proctor.** Against you?

281 **Putnam.** Against him and all authority!

282 **Proctor.** Why, then I must find it and join it.

283 (*There is shock among the others.*)

284 **Rebecca.** He does not mean that.

285 **Putnam.** He confessed it now!

---

[15] **Quakers:** an English religious sect—much hated by the Puritans—who often "spoke their heart" during their religious meetings.

286 **Proctor.** I mean it solemnly, Rebecca; I like not the smell of this "authority."

287 **Rebecca.** No, you cannot break charity[16] with your minister. You are another kind, John. Clasp his hand, make your peace.

288 **Proctor.** I have a crop to sow and lumber to drag home. (*He goes angrily to the door and turns to* Corey *with a smile.*) What say you, Giles, let's find the party. He says there's a party.

289 **Giles.** I've changed my opinion of this man, John. Mr. Parris, I beg your pardon. I never thought you had so much iron in you.

290 **Parris** (*surprised*). Why, thank you, Giles!

291 **Giles.** It suggests to the mind what the trouble be among us all these years. (*to all*) Think on it. Wherefore is everybody suing everybody else? Think on it now, it's a deep thing, and dark as a pit. I have been six time in court this year—

292 **Proctor** (*familiarly, with warmth, although he knows he is approaching the edge of* Giles' *tolerance with this*). Is it the Devil's fault that a man cannot say you good morning without you clap him for defamation?[17] You're old, Giles, and you're not hearin' so well as you did.

293 **Giles** (*He cannot be crossed*). John Proctor, I have only last month collected four pound damages for you publicly sayin' I burned the roof off your house, and I—

294 **Proctor** (*laughing*). I never said no such thing, but I've paid you for it, so I hope I can call you deaf without charge. Now come along, Giles, and help me drag my lumber home.

295 **Putnam.** A moment, Mr. Proctor. What lumber is that you're draggin', if I may ask you?

296 **Proctor.** My lumber. From out my forest by the riverside.

297 **Putnam.** Why, we are surely gone wild this year. What anarchy is this? That tract is in my bounds, it's in my bounds, Mr. Proctor.

298 **Proctor.** In your bounds! (*indicating* Rebecca) I bought that tract from Goody Nurse's husband five months ago.

299 **Putnam.** He had no right to sell it. It stands clear in my grandfather's will that all the land between the river and—

300 **Proctor.** Your grandfather had a habit of willing land that never belonged to him, if I may say it plain.

301 **Giles.** That's God's truth; he nearly willed away my north pasture but he knew I'd break his fingers before he'd set his name to it. Let's get your lumber home, John. I feel a sudden will to work coming on.

302 **Putnam.** You load one oak of mine and you'll fight to drag it home!

---

[16]**break charity:** break off; end the relationship.
[17]**clap . . . defamation** (dĕf-ə-mā´shən): imprison him for slander.

ENGLISH LEARNER SUPPORT

Support Comprehension Remind students that a metaphor is a figure of speech that compares two things without using the words *like* or *as*. Have students work in pairs to identify and underline the metaphor in paragraph 289. Ask students what two things are being compared and what the metaphor means. (*Giles compares Parris's will and determination to iron, which is a strong, inflexible metal. The metaphor shows he admires Parris for standing up for himself.*)

LIGHT

303 **Giles.** Aye, and we'll win too, Putnam—this fool and I. Come on! (*He turns to* Proctor *and starts out.*)

304 **Putnam.** I'll have my men on you, Corey! I'll clap a writ on you!

305 (*Enter* Reverend John Hale *of Beverly.*)

306 Mr. Hale is nearing forty, a tight-skinned, eager-eyed intellectual. This is a beloved errand for him; on being called here to ascertain witchcraft he felt the pride of the specialist whose unique knowledge has at last been publicly called for. Like almost all men of learning, he spent a good deal of his time pondering the invisible world, especially since he had himself encountered a witch in his parish not long before. That woman, however, turned into a mere pest under his searching scrutiny, and the child she had allegedly been afflicting recovered her normal behavior after Hale had given her his kindness and a few days of rest in his own house. However, that experience never raised a doubt in his mind as to the reality of the underworld or the existence of Lucifer's many-faced lieutenants. And his belief is not to his discredit. Better minds than Hale's were— and still are—convinced that there is a society of spirits beyond our ken. One cannot help noting that one of his lines has never yet raised a laugh in any audience that has seen this play; it is his assurance that "We cannot look to superstition in this. The Devil is precise." Evidently we are not quite certain even now whether diabolism is holy and not to be scoffed at. And it is no accident that we should be so bemused.

307 Like Reverend Hale and the others on this stage, we conceive the Devil as a necessary part of a respectable view of cosmology.[18] Ours is a divided empire in which certain ideas and emotions and actions are of God, and their opposites are of Lucifer. It is as impossible for most men to conceive of a morality without sin as of an earth without "sky." Since 1692 a great but superficial change has wiped out God's beard and the Devil's horns, but the world is still gripped between two diametrically opposed absolutes. The concept of unity, in which positive and negative are attributes of the same force, in which good and evil are relative, ever-changing, and always joined to the same phenomenon—such a concept is still reserved to the physical sciences and to the few who have grasped the history of ideas. When it is recalled that until the Christian era the underworld was never regarded as a hostile area, that all gods were useful and essentially friendly to man despite occasional lapses; when we see the steady and methodical inculcation into humanity of the idea of man's worthlessness—until redeemed—the necessity of the Devil may become evident as a weapon, a weapon designed and used time and time again in every age to whip men into a surrender to a particular church or church-state.

---

[18] **cosmology** (kŏz-mŏl´ə-jē): a branch of philosophy dealing with the structure of the universe.

308   Our difficulty in believing the—for want of a better word—political inspiration of the Devil is due in great part to the fact that he is called up and damned not only by our social antagonists but by our own side, whatever it may be. The Catholic Church, through its Inquisition,[19] is famous for cultivating Lucifer as the arch-fiend, but the Church's enemies relied no less upon the Old Boy to keep the human mind enthralled. Luther[20] was himself accused of alliance with Hell, and he in turn accused his enemies. To complicate matters further, he believed that he had had contact with the Devil and had argued theology with him. I am not surprised at this, for at my own university a professor of history—a Lutheran, by the way—used to assemble his graduate students, draw the shades, and commune in the classroom with Erasmus.[21] He was never, to my knowledge, officially scoffed at for this, the reason being that the university officials, like most of us, are the children of a history which still sucks at the Devil's teats. At this writing, only England has held back before the temptations of contemporary diabolism. In the countries of the Communist ideology, all resistance of any import is linked to the totally malign capitalist succubi,[22] and in America any man who is not reactionary in his views is open to the charge of alliance with the Red hell. Political opposition, thereby, is given an inhumane overlay which then justifies the abrogation of all normally applied customs of civilized intercourse. A political policy is equated with moral right, and opposition to it with diabolical malevolence. Once such an equation is effectively made, society becomes a congerie of plots and counterplots, and the main role of government changes from that of the arbiter to that of the scourge of God.

309   The results of this process are no different now from what they ever were, except sometimes in the degree of cruelty inflicted, and not always even in that department. Normally the actions and deeds of a man were all that society felt comfortable in judging. The secret intent of an action was left to the ministers, priests, and rabbis to deal with. When diabolism rises, however, actions are the least important manifests of the true nature of a man. The Devil, as Reverend Hale said, is a wily one, and, until an hour before he fell, even God thought him beautiful in Heaven.[23]

310   The analogy, however, seems to falter when one considers that, while there were no witches then, there are Communists and capitalists now, and in each camp there is certain proof that spies of each side are at work undermining the other. But this is a snobbish

---

[19] **Inquisition:** a former tribunal in the Roman Catholic Church dedicated to the discovery and punishment of heresy.

[20] **Luther:** Martin Luther (1483–1546), the German theologian who led the Protestant Reformation.

[21] **Erasmus** (ĭ-răz´məs): Desiderius Erasmus (1466?–1536), a Dutch scholar who sought to restore Christian faith by a study of the Scriptures and classical texts.

[22] **succubi** (sŭk´yə-bī): demons that assume female form. Demons that assume male form are called incubi (ĭn´kyə-bī).

[23] **The Devil . . . beautiful in Heaven:** According to Christian belief, Lucifer was God's favorite angel until the angel rebelled and was cast out of Heaven.

NOTICE & NOTE

ANALYZE LITERARY DEVICES

Annotate: Miller interrupts the action of the play after Mr. Hale enters. Mark lines in this section of exposition that show how Miller draws a comparison between the use of the Devil as a spiritual threat and the fight against Communism in America in the 1950s.

Evaluate: What similarity is the comparison meant to bring out? What is the larger point that Miller is making about "diabolism" in society?

ANALYZE LITERARY DEVICES

Remind students that Arthur Miller wrote *The Crucible* in the early 1950s during the height of the Red Scare. Explain that the Red Scare was a period in American history when the U.S. government, suspicious of Communist activity in various parts of society, held hearings in hopes of rooting out anyone who sympathized with the Communist cause. The Red Scare frightened people into conformity. (**Answer:** *Miller is saying that just as anyone in Salem perceived as disagreeable for any reason was accused of being under the Devil's influence, so too anyone not vigorously and vocally opposed to communism in the 1950s was called a "Red" in America. Miller argues that diabolism is, and always has been, with us—that there is always some set of ideas or part of society that will be associated with "the Devil" for political purposes. He states, "A political policy is equated with moral right, and opposition to it with diabolical malevolence." Miller warns against this tendency, which breeds cruelty and injustice.*)

TO CHALLENGE STUDENTS . . .

Investigate Text References Central to understanding the points Miller raises in the exposition on these pages are the topics of the Spanish Inquisition, Martin Luther, the rise of Russian communism, and 19th-century Victorian morals. Have students work in small groups to investigate one of these topics and prepare a short report in which they connect their findings to Miller's larger point in this exposition. Have students read their finished reports to the class.

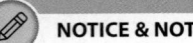

✏ ANALYZE CHARACTERS AND MOTIVATIONS

Point out to students that paragraph 312 provides direct characterization of Reverend Hale. Explain that students can infer Hale's motivation by considering his self image. (**Answer:** *Hale's motivation for coming to Salem is to restore it to a great spiritual state, and he will do anything—even fight the Devil—to succeed in that goal.*)

objection and not at all warranted by the facts. I have no doubt that people *were* communing with, and even worshiping, the Devil in Salem, and if the whole truth could be known in this case, as it is in others, we should discover a regular and conventionalized propitiation of the dark spirit. One certain evidence of this is the confession of Tituba, the slave of Reverend Parris, and another is the behavior of the children who were known to have indulged in sorceries with her.

311   There are accounts of similar *klatches* in Europe, where the daughters of the towns would assemble at night and, sometimes with fetishes, sometimes with a selected young man, give themselves to love, with some bastardly results. The Church, sharp-eyed as it must be when gods long dead are brought to life, condemned these orgies as witchcraft and interpreted them, rightly, as a resurgence of the Dionysiac forces[24] it had crushed long before. Sex, sin, and the Devil were early linked, and so they continued to be in Salem, and are today. From all accounts there are no more puritanical mores in the world than those enforced by the Communists in Russia, where women's fashions, for instance, are as prudent and all-covering as any American Baptist would desire. The divorce laws lay a tremendous responsibility on the father for the care of his children. Even the laxity of divorce regulations in the early years of the revolution was undoubtedly a revulsion from the nineteenth-century Victorian immobility of marriage and the consequent hypocrisy that developed from it. If for no other reasons, a state so powerful, so jealous of the uniformity of its citizens, cannot long tolerate the atomization of the family. And yet, in American eyes at least, there remains the conviction that the Russian attitude toward women is lascivious. It is the Devil working again, just as he is working within the Slav[25] who is shocked at the very idea of a woman's disrobing herself in a burlesque show. Our opposites are always robed in sexual sin, and it is from this unconscious conviction that demonology gains both its attractive sensuality and its capacity to infuriate and frighten.

ANALYZE CHARACTERS AND MOTIVATIONS

Annotate: Mark details in paragraph 312 that tell you how Reverend Hale views himself.

Analyze: What is Hale's motivation for coming to Salem? Cite evidence for the text in your response.

312   Coming into Salem now, Reverend Hale conceives of himself much as a young doctor on his first call. His painfully acquired armory of symptoms, catchwords, and diagnostic procedures are now to be put to use at last. The road from Beverly is unusually busy this morning, and he has passed a hundred rumors that make him smile at the ignorance of the yeomanry in this most precise science. He feels himself allied with the best minds of Europe—kings, philosophers, scientists, and ecclesiasts of all churches. His goal is light, goodness and its preservation, and he knows the exaltation of the blessed whose intelligence, sharpened by minute examinations of enormous tracts, is finally called upon to face what may be a bloody fight with the Fiend himself.

---

[24]**Dionysiac** (dĭ-ə-nĭs´ē-ăk) **forces:** forces associated with Dionysus, the Greek god of wine and ecstasy.

[25]**Slav:** a generic reference to Russians and other Slavic-speaking peoples of Eastern Europe who were under the control of the Soviet Union.

WHEN STUDENTS STRUGGLE . . .

Vocabulary Support Miller becomes increasingly philosophical in his mini-essays, and his diction becomes more difficult. Discuss the meanings of some or all of these terms: *propitiation* (an act that calms or pleases someone); *klatches* (gatherings); *fetishes* (objects believed to have magical powers); *mores* (accepted standards of behavior); *prudent* (careful to avoid danger); *laxity* (looseness); *atomization* (breakup); *yeomanry* (farmers).

 For additional support, go to the **Reading Studio** and assign the following **Level Up Tutorials: Academic Vocabulary** and **Word Knowledge**.

313 (*He appears loaded down with half a dozen heavy books.*)

314 **Hale.** Pray you, someone take these!

315 **Parris** (*delighted*). Mr. Hale! Oh! It's good to see you again! (*taking some books*) My, they're heavy!

316 **Hale** (*setting down his books*). They must be; they are weighted with authority.

317 **Parris** (*a little scared*). Well, you do come prepared!

318 **Hale.** We shall need hard study if it comes to tracking down the Old Boy. (*noticing* Rebecca) You cannot be Rebecca Nurse?

319 **Rebecca.** I am, sir. Do you know me?

320 **Hale.** It's strange how I knew you, but I suppose you look as such a good soul should. We have all heard of your great charities in Beverly.

321 **Parris.** Do you know this gentleman? Mr. Thomas Putnam. And his good wife Ann.

322 **Hale.** Putnam! I had not expected such distinguished company, sir.

323 **Putnam** (*pleased*). It does not seem to help us today, Mr. Hale. We look to you to come to our house and save our child.

324 **Hale.** Your child ails too?

325 **Mrs. Putnam.** Her soul, her soul seems flown away. She sleeps and yet she walks . . .

326 **Putnam.** She cannot eat.

327 **Hale.** Cannot eat! (*Thinks on it. Then, to* Proctor *and* Giles Corey.) Do you men have afflicted children?

328 **Parris.** No, no, these are farmers. John Proctor—

329 **Giles Corey.** He don't believe in witches.

330 **Proctor** (*to* Hale). I never spoke on witches one way or the other. Will you come, Giles?

331 **Giles.** No—no, John, I think not. I have some few queer questions of my own to ask this fellow.

332 **Proctor.** I've heard you to be a sensible man, Mr. Hale. I hope you'll leave some of it in Salem.

333 (Proctor *goes.* Hale *stands embarrassed for an instant.*)

334 **Parris** (*quickly*). Will you look at my daughter, sir? (*leads* Hale *to the bed*) She has tried to leap out the window; we discovered her this morning on the highroad, waving her arms as though she'd fly.

335 **Hale** (*narrowing his eyes*). Tries to fly.

336 **Putnam.** She cannot bear to hear the Lord's name, Mr. Hale; that's a sure sign of witchcraft afloat.

337 **Hale** (*holding up his hands*). No, no. Now let me instruct you. We cannot look to superstition in this. The Devil is precise; the marks of

---

ENGLISH LEARNER SUPPORT

Support Comprehension Remind students that similes are comparisons made using the words *like* or *as*. Have students work in pairs to locate and underline the simile in paragraph 337, which extends to page 632. Have students identify the two things that are being compared in this simile (*marks of the Devil's presence and stone*). Then ask them to interpret what Hale means. (*Hale means that if the Devil is at work it will be obvious— the evidence will be as concrete and solid as a stone.*)
LIGHT

WHEN STUDENTS STRUGGLE . . .

Understand Symbols After students read paragraphs 313–317, in which Hale enters carrying a heavy stack of books, discuss that playwrights sometimes introduce objects that serve as symbols. Ask students to discuss what they think Hale's books symbolize. (*The books are described as "heavy" and "weighted with authority." The books may symbolize scholarly or moral authority.*)

For additional support, go to the **Reading Studio** and assign the following **Level Up Tutorial: Symbols and Allegories.**

ENGLISH LEARNER SUPPORT

Understand Suffixes Point out the word *conviction* in paragraph 358 and write it on the board. Explain that a suffix is added to the end of a base word or word part to create a new word with a different meaning. Circle the word part *convict-* and underline the suffix *-tion*. Explain that the suffix *-tion* changes a verb (convict) to a noun. Other suffixes that are used to create nouns are *-ion*, *-ment*, and *-ity*.

List the following words from page 633: *resentment* (paragraph 360) and *superiority* (paragraph 361). Have students work in pairs to identify the base word and suffix of each, then use a dictionary to find the words' meanings. **MODERATE/LIGHT**

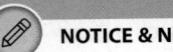

NOTICE & NOTE

his presence are definite as stone, and I must tell you all that I shall not proceed unless you are prepared to believe me if I should find no bruise of hell upon her.

338 **Parris.** It is agreed, sir—it is agreed—we will abide by your judgment.

339 **Hale.** Good then. (*He goes to the bed, looks down at* Betty. *To* Parris.) Now, sir, what were your first warning of this strangeness?

340 **Parris.** Why, sir—I discovered her—(*indicating* Abigail) and my niece and ten or twelve of the other girls, dancing in the forest last night.

341 **Hale** (*surprised*). You permit dancing?

342 **Parris.** No, no, it were secret—

343 **Mrs. Putnam** (*unable to wait*). Mr. Parris's slave has knowledge of conjurin', sir.

344 **Parris** (*to* Mrs. Putnam). We cannot be sure of that, Goody Ann—

345 **Mrs. Putnam** (*frightened, very softly*). I know it, sir. I sent my child—she should learn from Tituba who murdered her sisters.

346 **Rebecca** (*horrified*). Goody Ann! You sent a child to conjure up the dead?

347 **Mrs. Putnam.** Let God blame me, not you, not you, Rebecca! I'll not have you judging me any more! (*to* Hale) Is it a natural work to lose seven children before they live a day?

348 **Parris.** Sssh!

349 (Rebecca, *with great pain, turns her face away. There is a pause.*)

350 **Hale.** Seven dead in childbirth.

351 **Mrs. Putnam** (*softly*). Aye. (*Her voice breaks; she looks up at him. Silence.* Hale *is impressed.* Parris *looks to him. He goes to his books, opens one, turns pages, then reads. All wait, avidly.*)

352 **Parris** (*hushed*). What book is that?

353 **Mrs. Putnam.** What's there, sir?

354 **Hale** (*with a tasty love of intellectual pursuit*). Here is all the invisible world, caught, defined, and calculated. In these books the Devil stands stripped of all his brute disguises. Here are all your familiar spirits—your incubi and succubi; your witches that go by land, by air, and by sea; your wizards of the night and of the day. Have no fear now—we shall find him out if he has come among us, and I mean to crush him utterly if he has shown his face! (*He starts for the bed.*)

355 **Rebecca.** Will it hurt the child, sir?

356 **Hale.** I cannot tell. If she is truly in the Devil's grip we may have to rip and tear to get her free.

357 **Rebecca.** I think I'll go, then. I am too old for this. (*She rises.*)

358 **Parris** (*striving for conviction*). Why, Rebecca, we may open up the boil of all our troubles today!

632 Unit 6

359 **Rebecca.** Let us hope for that. I go to God for you, sir.

360 **Parris** (*with trepidation—and resentment*). I hope you do not mean we go to Satan here! (*slight pause*)

361 **Rebecca.** I wish I knew. (*She goes out; they feel resentful of her note of moral superiority.*)

362 **Putnam** (*abruptly*). Come, Mr. Hale, let's get on. Sit you here.

363 **Giles.** Mr. Hale, I have always wanted to ask a learned man—what signifies the readin' of strange books?

364 **Hale.** What books?

365 **Giles.** I cannot tell; she hides them.

366 **Hale.** Who does this?

367 **Giles.** Martha, my wife. I have waked at night many a time and found her in a corner, readin' of a book. Now what do you make of that?

368 **Hale.** Why, that's not necessarily—

369 **Giles.** It discomfits me! Last night—mark this—I tried and tried and could not say my prayers. And then she close her book and walks out of the house, and suddenly—mark this—I could pray again!

370 Old Giles must be spoken for, if only because his fate was to be so remarkable and so different from that of all the others. He was in his early eighties at this time, and was the most comical hero in the history. No man has ever been blamed for so much. If a cow was missed, the first thought was to look for her around Corey's house; a fire blazing up at night brought suspicion of arson to his door. He didn't give a hoot for public opinion, and only in his last years—after he had married Martha—did he bother much with the church. That she stopped his prayer is very probable, but he forgot to say that he'd only recently learned any prayers and it didn't take much to make him stumble over them. He was a crank and a nuisance, but withal a deeply innocent and brave man. In court once, he was asked if it were true that he had been frightened by the strange behavior of a hog and had then said he knew it to be the Devil in an animal's shape. "What frighted you?" he was asked. He forgot everything but the word "frighted," and instantly replied, "I do not know that I ever spoke that word in my life."

371 **Hale.** Ah! The stoppage of prayer—that is strange. I'll speak further on that with you.

372 **Giles.** I'm not sayin' she's touched the Devil, now, but I'd admire to know what books she reads and why she hides them. She'll not answer me, y' see.

373 **Hale.** Aye, we'll discuss it. (*to all*) Now mark me, if the Devil is in her you will witness some frightful wonders in this room, so please to keep your wits about you. Mr. Putnam, stand close in case she flies.

ANALYZE DRAMATIC ELEMENTS

Annotate: Foreshadowing occurs when a writer provides hints that suggest future events. Mark where Giles' dialogue may foreshadow, or hint at, later events in the play.

Predict: What do you think will happen, based on Giles' story?

 ANALYZE DRAMATIC ELEMENTS

Tell students that **foreshadowing** a future conflict or tragedy adds to the increasing tension, or rising action, of a **plot.** (*Answer: Giles tells a story that his wife reads "strange" books and that, when she reads them, he is unable to pray. Saying this in front of the others may raise suspicion of Giles' wife Martha being possessed by the Devil, a suspicion that may hurt his wife later.*)

The Crucible: Act One   633

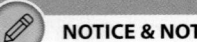 ANALYZE CHARACTERS AND MOTIVATIONS

Remind students that they can infer what is motivating a character's beliefs by studying the character's **dialogue** and **actions.** Point out that Hale is interrogating Abigail in a very threatening way. How does her anxiety over being questioned help explain her bringing someone else into the conversation? (**Answer:** *Abigail probably mentions Tituba for many reasons: She is afraid Betty will die and is genuinely grasping for anything she can think of; Tituba was indeed present in the forest, so it is not a lie to say so; Abigail wants to get the attention—and potential blame—off of herself; Tituba is an easy target because she is a servant from Barbados, a culture that is foreign to the people of Salem, and therefore suspicious to them.*)

Now, Betty, dear, will you sit up? (Putnam *comes in closer, ready-handed. Hale sits Betty up, but she hangs limp in his hands.*) Hmmm. (*He observes her carefully. The others watch breathlessly.*) Can you hear me? I am John Hale, minister of Beverly. I have come to help you, dear. Do you remember my two little girls in Beverly? (*She does not stir in his hands.*)

374 **Parris** (*in fright*). How can it be the Devil? Why would he choose my house to strike? We have all manner of licentious people in the village!

375 **Hale.** What victory would the Devil have to win a soul already bad? It is the best the Devil wants, and who is better than the minister?

376 **Giles.** That's deep, Mr. Parris, deep, deep!

377 **Parris** (*with resolution now*). Betty! Answer Mr. Hale! Betty!

378 **Hale.** Does someone afflict you, child? It need not be a woman, mind you, or a man. Perhaps some bird invisible to others comes to you—perhaps a pig, a mouse, or any beast at all. Is there some figure bids you fly? (*The child remains limp in his hands. In silence he lays her back on the pillow. Now, holding out his hands toward her, he intones.*) In nomine Domini Sabaoth sui filiique ite ad infernos.[26] (*She does not stir. He turns to* Abigail, *his eyes narrowing.*) Abigail, what sort of dancing were you doing with her in the forest?

379 **Abigail.** Why—common dancing is all.

380 **Parris.** I think I ought to say that I—I saw a kettle in the grass where they were dancing.

381 **Abigail.** That were only soup.

382 **Hale.** What sort of soup were in this kettle, Abigail?

383 **Abigail.** Why, it were beans—and lentils, I think, and—

384 **Hale.** Mr. Parris, you did not notice, did you, any living thing in the kettle? A mouse, perhaps, a spider, a frog—?

385 **Parris** (*fearfully*). I—do believe there were some movement—in the soup.

386 **Abigail.** That jumped in, we never put it in!

387 **Hale** (*quickly*). What jumped in?

388 **Abigail.** Why, a very little frog jumped—

389 **Parris.** A frog, Abby!

390 **Hale** (*grasping* Abigail). Abigail, it may be your cousin is dying. Did you call the Devil last night?

391 **Abigail.** I never called him! Tituba, Tituba . . .

392 **Parris** (*blanched*). She called the Devil?

ANALYZE CHARACTERS AND MOTIVATIONS
Annotate: Mark the person who Abigail says called the devil.

Infer: Why does Abigail raise this person's name in her admission? Cite text evidence in your response.

---

[26] **In nomine . . . infernos** *Latin:* "In the name of the Father and Son, get thee back to Hell."

393 **Hale.** I should like to speak with Tituba.

394 **Parris.** Goody Ann, will you bring her up? (Mrs. Putnam *exits.*)

395 **Hale.** How did she call him?

396 **Abigail.** I know not—she spoke Barbados.

397 **Hale.** Did you feel any strangeness when she called him? A sudden cold wind, perhaps? A trembling below the ground?

398 **Abigail.** I didn't see no Devil! (*shaking* Betty) Betty, wake up. Betty! Betty!

399 **Hale.** You cannot evade me, Abigail. Did your cousin drink any of the brew in that kettle?

400 **Abigail.** She never drank it!

401 **Hale.** Did you drink it?

402 **Abigail.** No, sir!

403 **Hale.** Did Tituba ask you to drink it?

404 **Abigail.** She tried, but I refused.

405 **Hale.** Why are you concealing? Have you sold yourself to Lucifer?

406 **Abigail.** I never sold myself! I'm a good girl! I'm a proper girl!

407 (Mrs. Putnam *enters with Tituba, and instantly* Abigail *points at* Tituba.)

408 **Abigail.** She made me do it! She made Betty do it!

409 **Tituba** (*shocked and angry*). Abby!

410 **Abigail.** She makes me drink blood!

411 **Parris.** Blood!!

412 **Mrs. Putnam.** My baby's blood?

413 **Tituba.** No, no, chicken blood. I give she chicken blood!

414 **Hale.** Woman, have you enlisted these children for the Devil?

415 **Tituba.** No, no, sir, I don't truck with no Devil!

416 **Hale.** Why can she not wake? Are you silencing this child?

417 **Tituba.** I love me Betty!

418 **Hale.** You have sent your spirit out upon this child, have you not? Are you gathering souls for the Devil?

419 **Abigail.** She sends her spirit on me in church; she makes me laugh at prayer!

420 **Parris.** She have often laughed at prayer!

421 **Abigail.** She comes to me every night to go and drink blood!

422 **Tituba.** You beg *me* to conjure! She beg *me* make charm—

423 **Abigail.** Don't lie! (*to* Hale) She comes to me while I sleep; she's always making me dream corruptions!

The Crucible: Act One   635

ENGLISH LEARNER SUPPORT

Analyze Language Remind students that synonyms are words that have the same meaning. Have students circle the synonyms in paragraph 406 (*good, proper*). In this example, *proper* is a synonym for *good*. Read aloud the lines, using *good* for both words: "I'm a *good* girl. I'm a *good* girl." Repeat, using *proper* for both words. Then read aloud the lines as written, emphasizing the words *good* and *proper*. Ask students why they think Miller chose to use synonyms instead of repeating the same word. Discuss how using synonyms affects the line.*(It creates emphasis or a pleading tone.)* **LIGHT**

IMPROVE READING FLUENCY

Targeted Passage Give students practice reading dialogue that is heavily punctuated by focusing on paragraphs 393–423. Review the punctuation marks that appear on this page: exclamation mark: *read with excitement*; question mark: *raise intonation at end of question*; em-dash: *pause during reading* or *be interrupted by the next speaker*. Have students work in small groups to practice reading the dialogue aloud. Then, have them discuss how taking note of the punctuation helped improve expression in their reading.

 Go to the **Reading Studio** for additional support in developing fluency.

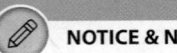

NOTICE & NOTE

424 **Tituba.** Why you say that, Abby?

425 **Abigail.** Sometimes I wake and find myself standing in the open doorway and not a stitch on my body! I always hear her laughing in my sleep. I hear her singing her Barbados songs and tempting me with—

426 **Tituba.** Mister Reverend, I never—

427 **Hale** (*resolved now*). Tituba, I want you to wake this child.

428 **Tituba.** I have no power on this child, sir.

429 **Hale.** You most certainly do, and you will free her from it now! When did you compact with the Devil?

430 **Tituba.** I don't compact with no Devil!

431 **Parris.** You will confess yourself or I will take you out and whip you to your death, Tituba!

432 **Putnam.** This woman must be hanged! She must be taken and hanged!

433 **Tituba** (*terrified, falls to her knees*). No, no, don't hang Tituba! I tell him I don't desire to work for him, sir.

434 **Parris.** The Devil?

435 **Hale.** Then you saw him! (*Tituba weeps.*) Now Tituba, I know that when we bind ourselves to Hell it is very hard to break with it. We are going to help you tear yourself free—

436 **Tituba** (*frightened by the coming process*). Mister Reverend, I do believe somebody else be witchin' these children.

437 **Hale.** Who?

438 **Tituba.** I don't know, sir, but the Devil got him numerous witches.

439 **Hale.** Does he! (*It is a clue.*) Tituba, look into my eyes. Come, look into me. (*She raises her eyes to his fearfully.*) You would be a good Christian woman, would you not, Tituba?

440 **Tituba.** Aye, sir, a good Christian woman.

441 **Hale.** And you love these little children?

442 **Tituba.** Oh, yes, sir, I don't desire to hurt little children.

443 **Hale.** And you love God, Tituba?

444 **Tituba.** I love God with all my bein'.

445 **Hale.** Now, in God's holy name—

446 **Tituba.** Bless Him. Bless Him. (*She is rocking on her knees, sobbing in terror.*)

447 **Hale.** And to His glory—

448 **Tituba.** Eternal glory. Bless Him—bless God . . .

449 **Hale.** Open yourself, Tituba—open yourself and let God's holy light shine on you.

ENGLISH LEARNER SUPPORT

Understand Multiple-Meaning Words Explain to students that the word *resolved* (paragraph 427) has more than one meaning:

- an adjective meaning "feeling strong determination to do something"
- simple past tense of the verb *resolve,* meaning "to settle or solve a problem" or "to make a serious decision to do something"

Have students work with a partner to decide which meaning of *resolved* is used in the text. Have them explain their choice. **MODERATE**

APPLYING ACADEMIC VOCABULARY

☑ **contemporary**   ☑ **global**   ☐ **infinite**   ☐ **simulated**   ☐ **virtual**

Write and Discuss Have students turn to a partner to discuss the following questions. Guide students to include the academic vocabulary words *contemporary* and *global* in their responses. Ask volunteers to share their responses with the class.

- How are the themes of the play—concerning authority, family, morality, and personal responsibility—relevant to **contemporary** American audiences?
- How and why might the play appeal to readers and theater-goers on a **global** scale?

450 Tituba. Oh, bless the Lord.

451 Hale. When the Devil comes to you does he ever come—with another person? (*She stares up into his face.*) Perhaps another person in the village? Someone you know.

452 Parris. Who came with him?

453 Putnam. Sarah Good? Did you ever see Sarah Good with him? Or Osburn?

454 Parris. Was it man or woman came with him?

455 Tituba. Man or woman. Was—was woman.

456 Parris. What woman? A woman, you said. What woman?

457 Tituba. It was black dark, and I—

458 Parris. You could see him, why could you not see her?

459 Tituba. Well, they was always talking; they was always runnin' round and carryin' on—

460 Parris. You mean out of Salem? Salem witches?

461 Tituba. I believe so, yes, sir.

462 (*Now* Hale *takes her hand. She is surprised.*)

463 Hale. Tituba. You must have no fear to tell us who they are, do you understand? We will protect you. The Devil can never overcome a minister. You know that, do you not?

464 Tituba (*kisses Hale's hand*). Aye, sir, oh, I do.

465 Hale. You have confessed yourself to witchcraft, and that speaks a wish to come to Heaven's side. And we will bless you, Tituba.

466 Tituba (*deeply relieved*). Oh, God bless you, Mr. Hale!

467 Hale (*with rising exaltation*). You are God's instrument put in our hands to discover the Devil's agents among us. You are selected, Tituba, you are chosen to help us cleanse our village. So speak utterly, Tituba, turn your back on him and face God—face God, Tituba, and God will protect you.

468 Tituba (*joining with him*). Oh, God, protect Tituba!

469 Hale (*kindly*). Who came to you with the Devil? Two? Three? Four? How many?

470 (*Tituba pants, and begins rocking back and forth again, staring ahead.*)

471 Tituba. There was four. There was four.

472 Parris (*pressing in on her*). Who? Who? Their names, their names!

473 Tituba (*suddenly bursting out*). Oh, how many times he bid me kill you, Mr. Parris!

474 Parris. Kill me!

475 Tituba (*in a fury*). He say Mr. Parris must be kill! Mr. Parris no goodly man, Mr. Parris mean man and no gentle man, and he bid me

© Houghton Mifflin Harcourt Publishing Company

ANALYZE LITERARY DEVICES

Annotate: Dramatic irony occurs when the audience of a drama knows something that some or all of the characters do not know or expect. Find an example of dramatic irony in paragraphs 465–468.

Analyze: Why is this an example of dramatic irony? How does it affect the play?

ANALYZE LITERARY DEVICES

Point out that Tituba is in a difficult position because she has already confessed to contact with the Devil and now must do just as Hale tells her in order to remain on his good side. (**Answer:** *The audience and Tituba understand that, in her prayer, she is asking for protection from Hale and Parris, while Hale and Parris believe she is asking for protection from the Devil. This builds suspense and suggests there will be many more misunderstandings to come.*)

NOTICE & NOTE

rise out of my bed and cut your throat! (*They gasp.*) But I tell him "No! I don't hate that man. I don't want kill that man." But he say, "You work for me, Tituba, and I make you free! I give you pretty dress to wear, and put you way high up in the air, and you gone fly back to Barbados!" And I say, "You lie, Devil, you lie!" And then he come one stormy night to me, and he say, "Look! I have *white* people belong to me." And I look—and there was Goody Good.

476 **Parris.** Sarah Good!

477 **Tituba** (*rocking and weeping*). Aye, sir, and Goody Osburn.

478 **Mrs. Putnam.** I knew it! Goody Osburn were midwife to me three times. I begged you, Thomas, did I not? I begged him not to call Osburn because I feared her. My babies always shriveled in her hands!

479 **Hale.** Take courage, you must give us all their names. How can you bear to see this child suffering? Look at her, Tituba. (*He is indicating* Betty *on the bed.*) Look at her God-given innocence; her soul is so tender; we must protect her, Tituba; the Devil is out and preying on her like a beast upon the flesh of the pure lamb. God will bless you for your help.

480 (Abigail *rises, staring as though inspired, and cries out.*)

481 **Abigail.** I want to open myself! (*They turn to her, startled. She is enraptured, as though in a pearly light.*) I want the light of God, I want the sweet love of Jesus! I danced for the Devil; I saw him; I wrote in his book; I go back to Jesus; I kiss His hand. I saw Sarah Good with the Devil! I saw Goody Osburn with the Devil! I saw Bridget Bishop with the Devil!

482 (*As she is speaking,* Betty *is rising from the bed, a fever in her eyes, and picks up the chant.*)

483 **Betty** (*staring too*). I saw George Jacobs with the Devil! I saw Goody Howe with the Devil!

484 **Parris.** She speaks! (*He rushes to embrace* Betty.) She speaks!

485 **Hale.** Glory to God! It is broken, they are free!

486 **Betty** (*calling out hysterically and with great relief*). I saw Martha Bellows with the Devil!

487 **Abigail.** I saw Goody Sibber with the Devil! (*It is rising to a great glee.*)

488 **Putnam.** The marshal, I'll call the marshal!

489 (Parris *is shouting a prayer of thanksgiving.*)

490 **Betty.** I saw Alice Barrow with the Devil!

© Houghton Mifflin Harcourt Publishing Company

WHEN STUDENTS STRUGGLE . . .

Summarize Plot To ensure students understand the plot so far, draw students' attention to the final two pages of this act. Have them summarize what happens to the characters in these pages. (*Hale compels a terrified Tituba to confess to being possessed by the Devil despite her earlier denials; Parris stands by, fearful and eager to blame Tituba; Abigail and Betty begin naming townspeople they saw with the Devil; Mr. and Mrs. Putnam's suspicions are confirmed when Tituba and Abigail begin naming names.*)

 For additional support, go to the **Reading Studio** and assign the following LEVEL UP **Level Up Tutorial: Plot: Sequence of Events.**

491 (*The curtain begins to fall.*)

492 **Hale** (*as* Putnam *goes out*). Let the marshal bring irons!

493 **Abigail.** I saw Goody Hawkins with the Devil!

494 **Betty.** I saw Goody Bibber with the Devil!

495 **Abigail.** I saw Goody Booth with the Devil!

496 (*On their ecstatic cries, the curtain falls.*)

CHECK YOUR UNDERSTANDING

Answer these questions before moving on to the **Analyze the Text** section on the following page.

1 What is the source of the main conflict in this act of the play?

   A The cause of Betty's strange illness

   B Tituba's presence in the woods

   C Abigail's intimidation of other girls

   D Differences between Parris and Putnam

2 What is Reverend Hale's main qualification for the job of discerning witchcraft?

   F He has already identified many witches.

   G He is recognized everywhere as an expert on witchcraft.

   H He identified a woman as a witch in his own church, and she was shown to be guilty.

   J He identified a woman as a witch in his own church, and she was shown to be not guilty.

3 Why is Mrs. Putnam so passionate in her belief that there is witchcraft afoot?

   A She is secretly in love with Reverend Hale.

   B She witnessed a ritual where witchcraft was done.

   C She has lost seven newborns and believes the cause was supernatural.

   D She believes her opposition to witchcraft will insulate her from accusations.

The Crucible: Act One   639

 ## CHECK YOUR UNDERSTANDING

Have students answer the questions independently.

Answers:

  1. A

  2. J

  3. C

If they answer any questions incorrectly, have them reread the text to confirm their understanding. Then they may proceed to ANALYZE THE TEXT on page 640.

EL ## ENGLISH LEARNER SUPPORT

Oral Assessment Use the following questions to assess students' comprehension and speaking skills.

  1. What problem begins the play? (*Betty's strange illness*)

  2. Do people think Hale is good at finding out about witchcraft? (*Yes. He said a woman at his church was a witch. Later, she was found not guilty of being a witch.*)

  3. Mrs. Putnam has lost seven _____. (*babies*) **SUBSTANTIAL/MODERATE**

ANALYZE THE TEXT

Possible answers:

1. **DOK 4:** *Miller describes 17th-century Salem as a natural breeding ground for feelings of persecution among its people. Theirs was a strict, highly religious society that enforced its own moral code and was prone to seeing enemies everywhere.*

2. **DOK 4:** *When Abigail tells Parris there was ritual dancing the previous evening that entailed "conjuring spirits," this sets in motion the events of the rest of Act One. The characters who were not present at the ritual dance in the woods—or at Abigail's admission in this section—must determine the truth on their own. Readers understand that the girls are frightened and anxious to divert blame.*

3. **DOK 3:** *Reverend Parris is described by Miller as a man who always believed he was being persecuted. Putnam is described as a "man with many grievances" and as having a "vindictive nature." Among Putnam's complaints is his lingering anger that Salem rejected his choice for minister—his brother-in-law. Feeling that his name has been sullied, Putnam becomes a leader in making accusations about others.*

4. **DOK 2:** *Though Miller describes Proctor as a man with little patience for hypocrites, Proctor himself is a sinner—he has had a relationship with Abigail—and so feels a fraud as a prominent member of a society that sees itself as a model of high moral rectitude.*

5. **DOK 4:** *Proctor may be protecting himself against further suspicion by saying earlier he wished to join an anti-religious faction. Yet he said to Hale's face he had not rendered an opinion about witches. Thus, he is in essence covering his bases.*

CREATE AND PRESENT

Write and Share an Evaluation Have students work independently to reread the exposition in Act One and make notes about what it contributes to the play. Then, divide students into small groups to discuss whether the exposition detracts from or enhances the play. Have groups work together to summarize their conclusions. Then, have a whole-class discussion about the effectiveness and necessity of Miller's exposition.

ANALYZE THE TEXT

Support your responses with evidence from the text. NOTEBOOK

1. **Analyze** What does the exposition in the beginning of Act One tell readers about the way they are to perceive the events that follow? Explain.

2. **Analyze** Reread paragraphs 107–127. This part of the play reveals information to readers that the other characters do not have. This is called **dramatic irony.** How does this dramatic irony enable readers to understand the real reasons behind the girls' symptoms and the events that result?

3. **Cite Evidence** What do the stage directions reveal about the motives for the behavior of Thomas Putnam and Reverend Parris? Cite specific details in your response.

4. **Infer** What is meant by the description of Proctor as a man who "has come to regard himself as a kind of fraud" (paragraph 165)? Explain, based on details in this act.

5. **Notice & Note** Early in the play John Proctor says that he is mistrustful of the way Salem uses religion to control others. Then in paragraph 330 he says he "never spoke on witches one way or the other." What is Proctor's motivation for saying this statement? Explain.

CREATE AND PRESENT

Write and Share an Evaluation The passages of exposition are typically not included in the stage production of a play. Based on your reading of the first act, why do you think Miller decided to include them in the text of the play?

❏ Reread the passages in Act One. Write your ideas about what they contribute to the play. Evaluate whether they are necessary and what they add to the play.

❏ Present your insights to a small group.

❏ Summarize the important conclusions that the group reaches. Contribute them to a whole-class discussion.

© Houghton Mifflin Harcourt Publishing Company

LEARNING MINDSET

Problem Solving Remind students that there are many different ways to solve problems. For example, they can ask for help, find a new strategy, or collaborate with others. People solve problems in their own way and each problem might call for a different problem-solving strategy. Remind students that everyone runs into problems when learning something new. This play is complex, with a lot of complications that pile up. Students should be sure to ask for help, change reading strategies, or discuss questions with classmates if they have difficulty comprehending and analyzing the play.

ACT TWO

·

1   (*The common room of* Proctor's *house, eight days later.*

2   *At the right is a door opening on the fields outside. A fireplace is at the left, and behind it a stairway leading upstairs. It is the low, dark, and rather long living room of the time. As the curtain rises, the room is empty. From above,* Elizabeth *is heard softly singing to the children. Presently the door opens and* John Proctor *enters, carrying his gun. He glances about the room as he comes toward the fireplace, then halts for an instant as he hears her singing. He continues on to the fireplace, leans the gun against the wall as he swings a pot out of the fire and smells it. Then he lifts out the ladle and tastes. He is not quite pleased. He reaches to a cupboard, takes a pinch of salt, and drops it into the pot. As he is tasting again, her footsteps are heard on the stair. He swings the pot into the fireplace and goes to a basin and washes his hands and face.* Elizabeth *enters.*)

3 **Elizabeth.** What keeps you so late? It's almost dark.

4 **Proctor.** I were planting far out to the forest edge.

5 **Elizabeth.** Oh, you're done then.

6 **Proctor.** Aye, the farm is seeded. The boys asleep?

7 **Elizabeth.** They will be soon. (*And she goes to the fireplace, proceeds to ladle up stew in a dish.*)

8 **Proctor.** Pray now for a fair summer.

9 **Elizabeth.** Aye.

10 **Proctor.** Are you well today?

11 **Elizabeth.** I am. (*She brings the plate to the table, and, indicating the food.*) It is a rabbit.

12 **Proctor** (*going to the table*). Oh, is it! In Jonathan's trap?

13 **Elizabeth.** No, she walked into the house this afternoon; I found her sittin' in the corner like she come to visit.

14 **Proctor.** Oh, that's a good sign walkin' in.

15 **Elizabeth.** Pray God. It hurt my heart to strip her, poor rabbit. (*She sits and watches him taste it.*)

16 **Proctor.** It's well seasoned.

17 **Elizabeth** (*blushing with pleasure*). I took great care. She's tender?

18 **Proctor.** Aye. (*He eats. She watches him.*) I think we'll see green fields soon. It's warm as blood beneath the clods.

19 **Elizabeth.** That's well.

20 (Proctor *eats, then looks up.*)

TEACH

ENGLISH LEARNER SUPPORT

Acquire Vocabulary Have students circle the word *draught* in the stage directions in paragraph 30. Tell them that the word *draught* is sometimes confused with the similarly spelled word *drought*. Write, spell aloud, and read each word. Have students repeat the words after you. Explain that *draught* means "the amount swallowed at one time." A *drought* is "a period of time, usually long, in which there is little or no rain." Have students use a dictionary to tell you the difference between other easily confused words:

- *pallor* (paragraph 88) and *parlor*
- *crone* (paragraph 121) and *crane*

ALL LEVELS

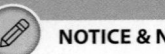

21 **Proctor.** If the crop is good I'll buy George Jacob's heifer. How would that please you?

22 **Elizabeth.** Aye, it would.

23 **Proctor** (*with a grin*). I mean to please you, Elizabeth.

24 **Elizabeth** (*It is hard to say*). I know it, John.

25 (*He gets up, goes to her, kisses her. She receives it. With a certain disappointment, he returns to the table.*)

26 **Proctor** (*as gently as he can*). Cider?

27 **Elizabeth** (*with a sense of reprimanding herself for having forgot*). Aye! (*She gets up and goes and pours a glass for him. He now arches his back.*)

28 **Proctor.** This farm's a continent when you go foot by foot droppin' seeds in it.

29 **Elizabeth** (*coming with the cider*). It must be.

30 **Proctor** (*drinks a long draught, then, putting the glass down*). You ought to bring some flowers in the house.

31 **Elizabeth.** Oh! I forgot! I will tomorrow.

32 **Proctor.** It's winter in here yet. On Sunday let you come with me, and we'll walk the farm together; I never see such a load of flowers on the earth. (*With good feeling he goes and looks up at the sky through the open doorway.*) Lilacs have a purple smell. Lilac is the smell of nightfall, I think. Massachusetts is a beauty in the spring!

33 **Elizabeth.** Aye, it is.

34 (*There is a pause. She is watching him from the table as he stands there absorbing the night. It is as though she would speak but cannot. Instead, now, she takes up his plate and glass and fork and goes with them to the basin. Her back is turned to him. He turns to her and watches her. A sense of their separation rises.*)

35 **Proctor.** I think you're sad again. Are you?

36 **Elizabeth** (*She doesn't want friction, and yet she must*). You come so late I thought you'd gone to Salem this afternoon.

37 **Proctor.** Why? I have no business in Salem.

38 **Elizabeth.** You did speak of going, earlier this week.

39 **Proctor** (*He knows what she means*). I thought better of it since.

40 **Elizabeth.** Mary Warren's there today.

41 **Proctor.** Why'd you let her? You heard me forbid her go to Salem any more!

42 **Elizabeth.** I couldn't stop her.

43 **Proctor** (*holding back a full condemnation of her*). It is a fault, it is a fault, Elizabeth—you're the mistress here, not Mary Warren.

44 **Elizabeth.** She frightened all my strength away.

45 **Proctor.** How may that mouse frighten you, Elizabeth? You—

46 **Elizabeth.** It is a mouse no more. I forbid her go, and she raises up her chin like the daughter of a prince and says to me, "I must go to Salem, Goody Proctor; I am an official of the court!"

47 **Proctor.** Court! What court?

48 **Elizabeth.** Aye, it is a proper court they have now. They've sent four judges out of Boston, she says, weighty magistrates of the General Court, and at the head sits the Deputy Governor of the Province.

49 **Proctor** (*astonished*). Why, she's mad.

50 **Elizabeth.** I would to God she were. There be fourteen people in the jail now, she says. (Proctor *simply looks at her, unable to grasp it.*) And they'll be tried, and the court have power to hang them too, she says.

51 **Proctor** (*scoffing, but without conviction*). Ah, they'd never hang—

52 **Elizabeth.** The Deputy Governor promise hangin' if they'll not confess, John. The town's gone wild, I think. She speak of Abigail, and I thought she were a saint, to hear her. Abigail brings the other girls into the court, and where she walks the crowd will part like the sea for Israel. And folks are brought before them, and if they scream and howl and fall to the floor—the person's clapped in the jail for bewitchin' them.

53 **Proctor** (*wide-eyed*). Oh, it is a black mischief.

54 **Elizabeth.** I think you must go to Salem, John. (*He turns to her.*) I think so. You must tell them it is a fraud.

55 **Proctor** (*thinking beyond this*). Aye, it is, it is surely.

56 **Elizabeth.** Let you go to Ezekiel Cheever—he knows you well. And tell him what she said to you last week in her uncle's house. She said it had naught to do with witchcraft, did she not?

57 **Proctor** (*in thought*). Aye, she did, she did. (*now, a pause*)

58 **Elizabeth** (*quietly, fearing to anger him by prodding*). God forbid you keep that from the court, John. I think they must be told.

59 **Proctor** (*quietly, struggling with his thought*). Aye, they must, they must. It is a wonder they do believe her.

60 **Elizabeth.** I would go to Salem now, John—let you go tonight.

61 **Proctor.** I'll think on it.

62 **Elizabeth** (*with her courage now*). You cannot keep it, John.

63 **Proctor** (*angering*). I know I cannot keep it. I say I will think on it!

64 **Elizabeth** (*hurt, and very coldly*). Good, then, let you think on it. (*She stands and starts to walk out of the room.*)

65 **Proctor.** I am only wondering how I may prove what she told me, Elizabeth. If the girl's a saint now, I think it is not easy to prove she's

ANALYZE DRAMATIC ELEMENTS

Annotate: Mark in paragraph 46 the surprising news Mary Warren shared with Elizabeth.

Analyze: How does this news function as a plot complication? What effect does it have on the play?

ANALYZE CHARACTERS AND MOTIVATIONS

Annotate: Mark a repeated word in the stage directions in paragraphs 58–59.

Analyze: What do the stage directions tell you about the different motivations of the characters?

TEACH

ANALYZE DRAMATIC ELEMENTS

Remind students that a **complication** of the plot is a problem that makes the main conflict more difficult to resolve. (**Answer:** *The main conflict of the play is whether or not there is witchcraft in the town of Salem. Proctor and his wife Elizabeth are already drawn into the conflict because Proctor had a relationship with Abigail and Abigail is at the center of the investigation. Mary works for the Proctors and was present for the dancing in the forest, but claims not to have danced herself. Further, Mary replaced Abigail as the Proctors' maid. So this plot complication draws the Proctors deeper into the conflict and makes it more likely additional bad things will happen.*)

ANALYZE CHARACTERS AND MOTIVATIONS

Explain to students that although two separate **stage directions** may employ the same or similar words, they may suggest very different motivations for the characters. Encourage students to name different reasons people might speak quietly, such as to keep something secret, to avoid being found when hiding, or to avoid waking a sleeping person. (**Answer:** *Elizabeth and Proctor have different motivations to speak quietly in this moment. Elizabeth wants Proctor to go to Salem and dispel any notions of Abigail being a witch. She quietly asks him to do so because she doesn't want to upset him. Proctor agrees with her and speaks quietly, but it is because he is struggling with his thoughts; he feels conflicted in his feelings about getting involved.*)

WHEN STUDENTS STRUGGLE . . .

Interpret Confusing Pronouns   Explain that characters sometimes use pronouns without making their referents clear. Point out that in paragraph 53, *it* refers to Abigail's pretense of saintliness and her judging others, behaviors described in paragraph 52. Have students reread paragraphs 53–65 and use context to identify what *it* refers to in paragraphs 56, 61, and 62. (*the girls' activities in the woods; Proctor going to Salem; his information about Abigail*)

For additional support, go to the **Reading Studio** and assign the following **Level Up Tutorial: Pronouns.**

NOTICE & NOTE

fraud, and the town gone so silly. She told it to me in a room alone—I have no proof for it.

66 **Elizabeth.** You were alone with her?

67 **Proctor** (*stubbornly*). For a moment alone, aye.

68 **Elizabeth.** Why, then, it is not as you told me.

69 **Proctor** (*his anger rising*). For a moment, I say. The others come in soon after.

70 **Elizabeth** (*quietly—she has suddenly lost all faith in him*). Do as you wish, then. (*She starts to turn.*)

71 **Proctor.** Woman. (*She turns to him.*) I'll not have your suspicion any more.

72 **Elizabeth** (*a little loftily*). I have no—

73 **Proctor.** I'll not have it!

74 **Elizabeth.** Then let you not earn it.

75 **Proctor** (*with a violent undertone*). You doubt me yet?

76 **Elizabeth** (*with a smile, to keep her dignity*). John, if it were not Abigail that you must go to hurt, would you falter now? I think not.

77 **Proctor.** Now look you—

78 **Elizabeth.** I see what I see, John.

79 **Proctor** (*with solemn warning*). You will not judge me more, Elizabeth. I have good reason to think before I charge fraud on Abigail, and I will think on it. Let you look to your own improvement before you go to judge your husband any more. I have forgot Abigail, and—

80 **Elizabeth.** And I.

81 **Proctor.** Spare me! You forget nothin' and forgive nothin'. Learn charity, woman. I have gone tiptoe in this house all seven month since she is gone. I have not moved from there to there without I think to please you, and still an everlasting funeral marches round your heart. I cannot speak but I am doubted, every moment judged for lies, as though I come into a court when I come into this house!

82 **Elizabeth.** John, you are not open with me. You saw her with a crowd, you said. Now you—

83 **Proctor.** I'll plead my honesty no more, Elizabeth.

84 **Elizabeth** (*now she would justify herself*). John, I am only—

85 **Proctor.** No more! I should have roared you down when first you told me your suspicion. But I wilted, and, like a Christian, I confessed. Confessed! Some dream I had must have mistaken you for God that day. But you're not, you're not, and let you remember it! Let you look sometimes for the goodness in me, and judge me not.

86 **Elizabeth.** I do not judge you. The magistrate sits in your heart that judges you. I never thought you but a good man, John—(*with a smile*)—only somewhat bewildered.

87 **Proctor** (*laughing bitterly*). Oh, Elizabeth, your justice would freeze beer![1] (*He turns suddenly toward a sound outside. He starts for the door as* Mary Warren *enters. As soon as he sees her, he goes directly to her and grabs her by her cloak, furious.*) How do you go to Salem when I forbid it? Do you mock me? (*shaking her*) I'll whip you if you dare leave this house again! (*Strangely, she doesn't resist him, but hangs limply by his grip.*)

88 **Mary Warren.** I am sick, I am sick, Mr. Proctor. Pray, pray, hurt me not. (*Her strangeness throws him off, and her evident pallor and weakness. He frees her.*) My insides are all shuddery; I am in the proceedings all day, sir.

89 **Proctor** (*with draining anger—his curiosity is draining it*). And what of these proceedings here? When will you proceed to keep this house, as you are paid nine pound a year to do—and my wife not wholly well?

90 (*As though to compensate,* Mary Warren *goes to* Elizabeth *with a small rag doll.*)

---

[1] **your justice . . . beer:** Alcoholic beverages freeze at very low temperatures, so Proctor is sarcastically calling his wife cold-hearted.

The Crucible: Act Two 645

© Houghton Mifflin Harcourt Publishing Company

TO CHALLENGE STUDENTS . . .

Analyze Dialogue Have students discuss Proctor's outburst in paragraph 85. Encourage them to read it aloud a few times to get a feel for the emotions Proctor expresses in these lines. Then, ask students to write a brief essay analyzing the passage in light of these questions:

- How did Elizabeth find out about his affair with Abigail?
- What does Proctor think about himself?
- What are his criticisms of Elizabeth?

As students share their essays, ask how they think the Proctors could resolve their conflict.

ENGLISH LEARNER SUPPORT

Understand Homographs Have students circle the word *compact* in paragraph 106. Explain that this word is a homograph—a word that has the same spelling as another word but a different meaning and pronunciation. Pronounce the word *compact* in this sentence, and have students say it after you. Have pairs work together to find the meaning of the word as it is used. Then, have pairs work together to find the meaning and pronunciation of its homograph, the verb *compact* ("to press something so that it takes up less space"). Have them use both words in sentences.

MODERATE/LIGHT

91 **Mary Warren.** I made a gift for you today, Goody Proctor. I had to sit long hours in a chair, and passed the time with sewing.

92 **Elizabeth** (*perplexed, looking at the doll*). Why, thank you, it's a fair poppet.[2]

93 **Mary Warren** (*with a trembling, decayed voice*). We must all love each other now, Goody Proctor.

94 **Elizabeth** (*amazed at her strangeness*). Aye, indeed we must.

95 **Mary Warren** (*glancing at the room*). I'll get up early in the morning and clean the house. I must sleep now. (*She turns and starts off.*)

96 **Proctor.** Mary. (*She halts.*) Is it true? There be fourteen women arrested?

97 **Mary Warren.** No, sir. There be thirty-nine now—(*She suddenly breaks off and sobs and sits down, exhausted.*)

98 **Elizabeth.** Why, she's weepin'! What ails you, child?

99 **Mary Warren.** Goody Osburn—will hang!

100 (*There is a shocked pause, while she sobs.*)

101 **Proctor.** Hang! (*He calls into her face.*) Hang, y'say?

102 **Mary Warren** (*through her weeping*). Aye.

103 **Proctor.** The Deputy Governor will permit it?

104 **Mary Warren.** He sentenced her. He must. (*to ameliorate it*) But not Sarah Good. For Sarah Good confessed, y'see.

105 **Proctor.** Confessed! To what?

106 **Mary Warren.** That she—(*in horror at the memory*)—she sometimes made a compact with Lucifer, and wrote her name in his black book—with her blood—and bound herself to torment Christians till God's thrown down—and we all must worship Hell forevermore.

107 (*pause*)

108 **Proctor.** But—surely you know what a jabberer she is. Did you tell them that?

109 **Mary Warren.** Mr. Proctor, in open court she near to choked us all to death.

110 **Proctor.** How, choked you?

111 **Mary Warren.** She sent her spirit out.

112 **Elizabeth.** Oh, Mary, Mary, surely you—

113 **Mary Warren** (*with an indignant edge*). She tried to kill me many times, Goody Proctor!

114 **Elizabeth.** Why, I never heard you mention that before.

---

[2] **fair poppet:** pretty doll.

115 **Mary Warren.** I never knew it before. I never knew anything before. When she come into the court I say to myself, I must not accuse this woman, for she sleep in ditches, and so very old and poor. But then—then she sit there, denying and denying, and I feel a misty coldness climbin' up my back, and the skin on my skull begin to creep, and I feel a clamp around my neck and I cannot breathe air; and then (*entranced*) I hear a voice, a screamin' voice, and it were my voice—and all at once I remembered everything she done to me!

116 **Proctor.** Why? What did she do to you?

117 **Mary Warren** (*like one awakened to a marvelous secret insight*). So many time, Mr. Proctor, she come to this very door, beggin' bread and a cup of cider—and mark this: whenever I turned her away empty, she *mumbled*.

118 **Elizabeth.** Mumbled! She may mumble if she's hungry.

119 **Mary Warren.** But *what* does she mumble? You must remember, Goody Proctor. Last month—a Monday, I think—she walked away, and I thought my guts would burst for two days after. Do you remember it?

120 **Elizabeth.** Why—I do, I think, but—

121 **Mary Warren.** And so I told that to Judge Hathorne, and he asks her so. "Sarah Good," says he, "what curse do you mumble that this girl must fall sick after turning you away?" And then she replies (*mimicking an old crone*) "Why, your excellence, no curse at all. I only say my commandments;[3] I hope I may say my commandments," says she!

122 **Elizabeth.** And that's an upright answer.

123 **Mary Warren.** Aye, but then Judge Hathorne say, "Recite for us your commandments!" (*leaning avidly toward them*) and of all the ten she could not say a single one. She never knew no commandments, and they had her in a flat lie!

124 **Proctor.** And so condemned her?

125 **Mary Warren** (*now a little strained, seeing his stubborn doubt*). Why, they must when she condemned herself.

126 **Proctor.** But the proof, the proof!

127 **Mary Warren** (*with greater impatience with him*). I told you the proof. It's hard proof, hard as rock, the judges said.

128 **Proctor** (*pauses an instant, then*). You will not go to court again, Mary Warren.

129 **Mary Warren.** I must tell you, sir, I will be gone every day now. I am amazed you do not see what weighty work we do.

---

[3] **commandments:** the Ten Commandments in the Bible.

© Houghton Mifflin Harcourt Publishing Company

ANALYZE DRAMATIC ELEMENTS

Annotate: Mark phrases in paragraphs 115–117 that express Mary's belief in the witch hunt.

Interpret: What does Mary's dialogue tell you about her character?

ANALYZE DRAMATIC ELEMENTS

Remind students that the **dialogue** is the words that are spoken by a character, but the **stage directions** explain how the words should be spoken. (*Answer: The long story she tells as the scene progresses shows that she is completely taken in by the witch hunt; the stage direction in paragraph 115 describes her as "entranced" as she tells the story. Paragraph 117 also describes her having a "marvelous secret insight." Mary is almost enjoying taking part in the witch hunt; at the very least she loves feeling she is right.*)

130 **Proctor.** What work you do! It's strange work for a Christian girl to hang old women!

131 **Mary Warren.** But, Mr. Proctor, they will not hang them if they confess. Sarah Good will only sit in jail some time (*recalling*) and here's a wonder for you; think on this. Goody Good is pregnant!

132 **Elizabeth.** Pregnant! Are they mad? The woman's near to sixty!

133 **Mary Warren.** They had Doctor Griggs examine her, and she's full to the brim. And smokin' a pipe all these years, and no husband either! But she's safe, thank God, for they'll not hurt the innocent child. But be that not a marvel? You must see it, sir, it's God's work we do. So I'll be gone every day for some time. I'm—I am an official of the court, they say, and I—(*She has been edging toward offstage.*)

134 **Proctor.** I'll official you! (*He strides to the mantel, takes down the whip hanging there.*)

135 **Mary Warren** (*terrified, but coming erect, striving for her authority*). I'll not stand whipping any more!

136 **Elizabeth** (*hurriedly, as Proctor approaches*). Mary, promise now you'll stay at home—

137 **Mary Warren** (*backing from him, but keeping her erect posture, striving, striving for her way*). The Devil's loose in Salem, Mr. Proctor; we must discover where he's hiding!

138 **Proctor.** I'll whip the Devil out of you! (*With whip raised he reaches out for her, and she streaks away and yells.*)

139 **Mary Warren** (*pointing at* Elizabeth). I saved her life today!

140 (*Silence. His whip comes down.*)

141 **Elizabeth** (*softly*). I am accused?

142 **Mary Warren** (*quaking*). Somewhat mentioned. But I said I never see no sign you ever sent your spirit out to hurt no one, and seeing I do live so closely with you, they dismissed it.

143 **Elizabeth.** Who accused me?

144 **Mary Warren.** I am bound by law, I cannot tell it. (*to* Proctor) I only hope you'll not be so sarcastical no more. Four judges and the King's deputy sat to dinner with us but an hour ago. I—I would have you speak civilly to me, from this out.

145 **Proctor** (*in horror, muttering in disgust at her*). Go to bed.

146 **Mary Warren** (*with a stamp of her foot*). I'll not be ordered to bed no more, Mr. Proctor! I am eighteen and a woman, however single!

147 **Proctor.** Do you wish to sit up? Then sit up.

148 **Mary Warren.** I wish to go to bed!

149 **Proctor** (*in anger*). Good night, then!

TO CHALLENGE STUDENTS . . .

Make Inferences Ask students to read paragraphs 144–146 and make inferences about the meaning behind Mary's statements "I only hope you'll not be so sarcastical no more" and "I—I would have you speak civilly to me, from this out." Note that her diction is polite and deferential: "I only hope" and "I would have you." But her meaning is not polite. Have students discuss the way this development affects the level of tension in the play and how it complicates matters for Proctor and Elizabeth.

150 **Mary Warren.** Good night. (*Dissatisfied, uncertain of herself, she goes out. Wide-eyed, both,* Proctor *and* Elizabeth *stand staring.*)

151 **Elizabeth** (*quietly*). Oh, the noose, the noose is up!

152 **Proctor.** There'll be no noose.

153 **Elizabeth.** She wants me dead. I knew all week it would come to this!

154 **Proctor** (*without conviction*). They dismissed it. You heard her say—

155 **Elizabeth.** And what of tomorrow? She will cry me out until they take me!

156 **Proctor.** Sit you down.

157 **Elizabeth.** She wants me dead, John, you know it!

158 **Proctor.** I say sit down! (*She sits, trembling. He speaks quietly, trying to keep his wits.*) Now we must be wise, Elizabeth.

159 **Elizabeth** (*with sarcasm, and a sense of being lost*). Oh, indeed, indeed!

160 **Proctor.** Fear nothing. I'll find Ezekiel Cheever. I'll tell him she said it were all sport.

161 **Elizabeth.** John, with so many in the jail, more than Cheever's help is needed now, I think. Would you favor me with this? Go to Abigail.

162 **Proctor** (*his soul hardening as he senses . . .*). What have I to say to Abigail?

163 **Elizabeth** (*delicately*). John—grant me this. You have a faulty understanding of young girls. There is a promise made in any bed—

164 **Proctor** (*striving against his anger*). What promise!

165 **Elizabeth.** Spoke or silent, a promise is surely made. And she may dote on it now—I am sure she does—and thinks to kill me, then to take my place.

166 (Proctor's *anger is rising; he cannot speak.*)

167 **Elizabeth.** It is her dearest hope, John, I know it. There be a thousand names; why does she call mine? There be a certain danger in calling such a name—I am no Goody Good that sleeps in ditches, nor Osburn, drunk and half-witted. She'd dare not call out such a farmer's wife but there be monstrous profit in it. She thinks to take my place, John.

168 **Proctor.** She cannot think it! (*He knows it is true.*)

169 **Elizabeth** (*"reasonably"*). John, have you ever shown her somewhat of contempt? She cannot pass you in the church but you will blush—

170 **Proctor.** I may blush for my sin.

171 **Elizabeth.** I think she sees another meaning in that blush.

172 **Proctor.** And what see you? What see you, Elizabeth?

ANALYZE CHARACTERS AND MOTIVATIONS

Annotate: Mark stage directions in paragraphs 169–173 that explain the way Elizabeth delivers her statements.

Interpret: Why does Miller set these stage directions in quotation marks? What is revealed about the character of Elizabeth in these moments?

The Crucible: Act Two   649

ANALYZE CHARACTERS AND MOTIVATIONS

Remind students that the atmosphere in this scene is emotionally charged—Elizabeth and Proctor are discussing the affair he has had with Abigail and the consequences of that affair. Proctor is ashamed, and Elizabeth is talking frankly about her husband's relationship with another woman. Yet Elizabeth knows action must be taken, and she must convince her husband to take this action. (**Answer:** *Miller means for Elizabeth's dialogue to be delivered in an insincere way. For example, in paragraph 169, she is not actually "reasoning" with Proctor; rather, she affects a tone of "reasoning," so she might get what she really wants. These stage directions set in quotation marks reveal Elizabeth to be cool-headed and cunning.*)

IMPROVE READING FLUENCY

Targeted Passage   Remind students that the characters' lines in a play represent spoken dialogue between two people, and that the stage directions give information about how the lines should be spoken. Have students read paragraphs 156–175 with a partner. Each student should read one character's lines with variety, intonation, and expression. After students have finished reading, ask them how the stage directions helped them read the lines aloud.

Go to the **Reading Studio** for additional support in developing fluency.

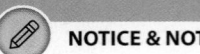
 ENGLISH LEARNER SUPPORT

Understand Figurative Language Have students reread paragraph 185 and underline the example of figurative language. Remind students that figurative language is language that is used in a way that is not literal. Then, have students discuss with partners what Elizabeth means when she says Abigail "has an arrow in" Proctor. *(She means Proctor still cares for Abigail.)* Have students explain how they can tell this meaning. *(Elizabeth and Proctor are discussing Proctor's relationship with Abigail. Elizabeth is pointing out that Proctor seems unwilling to break off the relationship. Being struck by an arrow often symbolizes falling in love.)*

LIGHT

173 **Elizabeth** (*"conceding"*). I think you be somewhat ashamed, for I am there, and she so close.

174 **Proctor.** When will you know me, woman? Were I stone I would have cracked for shame this seven month!

175 **Elizabeth.** Then go and tell her she's a whore. Whatever promise she may sense—break it, John, break it.

176 **Proctor** (*between his teeth*). Good, then. I'll go. (*He starts for his rifle.*)

177 **Elizabeth** (*trembling, fearfully*). Oh, how unwillingly!

178 **Proctor** (*turning on her, rifle in hand*). I will curse her hotter than the oldest cinder in hell. But pray, begrudge me not my anger!

179 **Elizabeth.** Your anger! I only ask you—

180 **Proctor.** Woman, am I so base? Do you truly think me base?

181 **Elizabeth.** I never called you base.

182 **Proctor.** Then how do you charge me with such a promise? The promise that a stallion gives a mare I gave that girl!

183 **Elizabeth.** Then why do you anger with me when I bid you break it?

184 **Proctor.** Because it speaks deceit, and I am honest! But I'll plead no more! I see now your spirit twists around the single error of my life, and I will never tear it free!

185 **Elizabeth** (*crying out*). You'll tear it free—when you come to know that I will be your only wife, or no wife at all! She has an arrow in you yet, John Proctor, and you know it well!

186 (*Quite suddenly, as though from the air, a figure appears in the doorway. They start slightly. It is* Mr. Hale. *He is different now—drawn a little, and there is a quality of deference, even of guilt, about his manner now.*)

187 **Hale.** Good evening.

188 **Proctor** (*still in his shock*). Why, Mr. Hale! Good evening to you, sir. Come in, come in.

189 **Hale** (*to* Elizabeth). I hope I do not startle you.

190 **Elizabeth.** No, no, it's only that I heard no horse—

191 **Hale.** You are Goodwife Proctor.

192 **Proctor.** Aye; Elizabeth.

193 **Hale** (*nods, then*). I hope you're not off to bed yet.

194 **Proctor** (*setting down his gun*). No, no. (Hale *comes further into the room. And* Proctor, *to explain his nervousness.*) We are not used to visitors after dark, but you're welcome here. Will you sit you down, sir?

195 **Hale.** I will. (*He sits.*) Let you sit, Goodwife Proctor.

196   (*She does, never letting him out of her sight. There is a pause as Hale looks about the room.*)

197   **Proctor** (*to break the silence*). Will you drink cider, Mr. Hale?

198   **Hale.** No, it rebels[4] my stomach; I have some further traveling yet tonight. Sit you down, sir. (*Proctor sits.*) I will not keep you long, but I have some business with you.

199   **Proctor.** Business of the court?

200   **Hale.** No—no, I come of my own, without the court's authority. Hear me. (*He wets his lips.*) I know not if you are aware, but your wife's name is—mentioned in the court.

201   **Proctor.** We know it, sir. Our Mary Warren told us. We are entirely amazed.

202   **Hale.** I am a stranger here, as you know. And in my ignorance I find it hard to draw a clear opinion of them that come accused before the court. And so this afternoon, and now tonight, I go from house to house—I come now from Rebecca Nurse's house and—

203   **Elizabeth** (*shocked*). Rebecca's charged!

204   **Hale.** God forbid such a one be charged. She is, however—mentioned somewhat.

205   **Elizabeth** (*with an attempt at a laugh*). You will never believe, I hope, that Rebecca trafficked with the Devil.

206   **Hale.** Woman, it is possible.

207   **Proctor** (*taken aback*). Surely you cannot think so.

208   **Hale.** This is a strange time, Mister. No man may longer doubt the powers of the dark are gathered in monstrous attack upon this village. There is too much evidence now to deny it. You will agree, sir?

209   **Proctor** (*evading*). I—have no knowledge in that line. But it's hard to think so pious a woman be secretly a Devil's bitch after seventy year of such good prayer.

210   **Hale.** Aye. But the Devil is a wily one, you cannot deny it. However, she is far from accused, and I know she will not be. (*pause*) I thought, sir, to put some questions as to the Christian character of this house, if you'll permit me.

211   **Proctor** (*coldly, resentful*). Why, we—have no fear of questions, sir.

212   **Hale.** Good, then. (*He makes himself more comfortable.*) In the book of record that Mr. Parris keeps, I note that you are rarely in the church on Sabbath Day.

213   **Proctor.** No, sir, you are mistaken.

---

[4] **rebels:** upsets.

© Houghton Mifflin Harcourt Publishing Company

ANALYZE CHARACTERS AND MOTIVATIONS

Annotate: Mark the stage direction in paragraph 200 that suggests Hale's feelings.

Infer: What does this stage direction suggest about Hale's emotional state at the moment?

 ANALYZE CHARACTERS AND MOTIVATIONS

Remind students that **stage directions** can reveal characters' feelings and motivations. The stage directions tell the actor to perform an action (wetting his lips), but the actor still needs to decide how to say the line—hesitantly, awkwardly, or some other way. (**Answer:** *Hale wets his lips because he is about to bring up an uncomfortable subject and is apprehensive about doing so.*)

EL **ENGLISH LEARNER SUPPORT**

Understand Stage Directions   Have students locate and underline the stage direction in paragraph 200. Demonstrate what it means to wet one's lips following a pause in speaking, as you read the paragraph aloud. Ask students to explain what wetting one's lips communicates. (*This is something people might do when they are hesitant to speak for some reason.*)

SUBSTANTIAL/MODERATE

TEACH

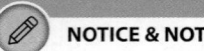

ENGLISH LEARNER SUPPORT

Understand Multiple-Meaning Words Have students locate and circle the word *flushed* in paragraph 227. Explain that this word has more than one meaning. Have pairs work together to explain the meaning of the word *flushed* in this sentence. Then, have them research another meaning of the word by consulting a dictionary and write a sentence using this additional meaning. *(turned red in the face from emotion; cleansed with water; Sam flushed the dust from his eyes.)* **MODERATE**

---

214 **Hale.** Twenty-six time in seventeen month, sir. I must call that rare. Will you tell me why you are so absent?

215 **Proctor.** Mr. Hale, I never knew I must account to that man for I come to church or stay at home. My wife were sick this winter.

216 **Hale.** So I am told. But you, Mister, why could you not come alone?

217 **Proctor.** I surely did come when I could, and when I could not I prayed in this house.

218 **Hale.** Mr. Proctor, your house is not a church; your theology must tell you that.

219 **Proctor.** It does, sir, it does; and it tells me that a minister may pray to God without he have golden candlesticks upon the altar.

220 **Hale.** What golden candlesticks?

221 **Proctor.** Since we built the church there were pewter candlesticks upon the altar; Francis Nurse made them, y'know, and a sweeter hand never touched the metal. But Parris came, and for twenty week he preach nothin' but golden candlesticks until he had them. I labor the earth from dawn of day to blink of night, and I tell you true, when I look to heaven and see my money glaring at his elbows—it hurt my prayer, sir, it hurt my prayer. I think, sometimes, the man dreams cathedrals, not clapboard meetin' houses.

222 **Hale** (*thinks, then*). And yet, Mister, a Christian on Sabbath Day must be in church. (*pause*) Tell me—you have three children?

223 **Proctor.** Aye. Boys.

224 **Hale.** How comes it that only two are baptized?

225 **Proctor** (*starts to speak, then stops, then, as though unable to restrain this*). I like it not that Mr. Parris should lay his hand upon my baby. I see no light of God in that man. I'll not conceal it.

226 **Hale.** I must say it, Mr. Proctor; that is not for you to decide. The man's ordained, therefore the light of God is in him.

227 **Proctor** (*flushed with resentment but trying to smile*). What's your suspicion, Mr. Hale?

228 **Hale.** No, no, I have no—

229 **Proctor.** I nailed the roof upon the church, I hung the door—

230 **Hale.** Oh, did you! That's a good sign, then.

231 **Proctor.** It may be I have been too quick to bring the man to book,[5] but you cannot think we ever desired the destruction of religion. I think that's in your mind, is it not?

232 **Hale** (*not altogether giving way*). I—have—there is a softness in your record, sir, a softness.

---

[5] **bring the man to book:** judge the man.

233 **Elizabeth.** I think, maybe, we have been too hard with Mr. Parris. I think so. But sure we never loved the Devil here.

234 **Hale** (*nods, deliberating this. Then, with the voice of one administering a secret test*). Do you know your Commandments, Elizabeth?

235 **Elizabeth** (*without hesitation, even eagerly*). I surely do. There be no mark of blame upon my life, Mr. Hale. I am a covenanted Christian woman.

236 **Hale.** And you, Mister?

237 **Proctor** (*a trifle unsteadily*). I—am sure I do, sir.

238 **Hale** (*glances at her open face, then at* John, *then*). Let you repeat them, if you will.

239 **Proctor.** The Commandments.

240 **Hale.** Aye.

241 **Proctor** (*looking off, beginning to sweat*). Thou shalt not kill.

242 **Hale.** Aye.

243 **Proctor** (*counting on his fingers*). Thou shalt not steal. Thou shalt not covet thy neighbor's goods, nor make unto thee any graven image. Thou shalt not take the name of the Lord in vain; thou shalt have no other gods before me. (*with some hesitation*) Thou shalt remember the Sabbath Day and keep it holy. (*Pause. Then.*) Thou shalt honor thy father and mother. Thou shalt not bear false witness. (*He is stuck. He counts back on his fingers, knowing one is missing.*) Thou shalt not make unto thee any graven image.

244 **Hale.** You have said that twice, sir.

245 **Proctor** (*lost*). Aye. (*He is flailing for it.*)

246 **Elizabeth** (*delicately*). Adultery, John.

247 **Proctor** (*as though a secret arrow had pained his heart*). Aye. (*trying to grin it away—to* Hale) You see, sir, between the two of us we do know them all. (Hale *only looks at* Proctor, *deep in his attempt to define this man.* Proctor *grows more uneasy.*) I think it be a small fault.

248 **Hale.** Theology, sir, is a fortress; no crack in a fortress may be accounted small. (*He rises; he seems worried now. He paces a little, in deep thought.*)

249 **Proctor.** There be no love for Satan in this house, Mister.

250 **Hale.** I pray it, I pray it dearly. (*He looks to both of them, an attempt at a smile on his face, but his misgivings are clear.*) Well, then—I'll bid you good night.

251 **Elizabeth** (*unable to restrain herself*). Mr. Hale. (*He turns.*) I do think you are suspecting me somewhat? Are you not?

252 **Hale** (*obviously disturbed—and evasive*). Goody Proctor, I do not judge you. My duty is to add what I may to the godly wisdom of the

ANALYZE CHARACTERS
AND MOTIVATIONS
Annotate: Mark stage
directions in paragraphs
247–252 that describe how
Proctor feels.

Evaluate: Is Proctor's weakness
in this scene believable? Why or
why not?

ANALYZE CHARACTERS AND MOTIVATIONS

Explain that these stage directions help the actor decide how to deliver the lines, such as hesitantly, sorrowfully, or anxiously. (**Possible answer:** *Proctor's weakness—that is, his reluctance to give information that might save his wife—is believable.*)

TO CHALLENGE STUDENTS . . .

Analyze Theme Tell students that while Miller's inclusion of the Ten Commandments test may be based on history, it also provides an opportunity for Miller to explore his theme of hypocrisy. Have students work in small groups and discuss the irony of the recitation of the Ten Commandments as a test of purity. (*Residents of Salem must know and live by the Commandments. Some residents who use them as a test of purity have broken Commandments. Putnam has broken the commandment against desiring a neighbor's possessions. Abigail has broken the commandment against adultery. Proctor has also committed adultery, and this is the one commandment he cannot remember.*) When students have finished, ask groups to share their ideas with the class.

court. I pray you both good health and good fortune. (*to* John) Good night, sir. (*He starts out.*)

253 **Elizabeth** (*with a note of desperation*). I think you must tell him, John.

254 **Hale.** What's that?

Elizabeth (*restraining a call*). Will you tell him?

255 (*Slight pause. Hale looks questioningly at* John.)

256 **Proctor** (*with difficulty*). I—I have no witness and cannot prove it, except my word be taken. But I know the children's sickness had naught to do with witchcraft.

257 **Hale** (*stopped, struck*). Naught to do—?

258 **Proctor.** Mr. Parris discovered them sportin' in the woods. They were startled and took sick.

259 (*pause*)

260 **Hale.** Who told you this?

261 **Proctor** (*hesitates, then*). Abigail Williams.

262 **Hale.** Abigail!

263 **Proctor.** Aye.

264 **Hale** (*his eyes wide*). Abigail Williams told you it had naught to do with witchcraft!

265 **Proctor.** She told me the day you came, sir.

266 **Hale** (*suspiciously*). Why—why did you keep this?

267 **Proctor.** I never knew until tonight that the world is gone daft with this nonsense.

268 **Hale.** Nonsense! Mister, I have myself examined Tituba, Sarah Good, and numerous others that have confessed to dealing with the Devil. They have *confessed* it.

269 **Proctor.** And why not, if they must hang for denyin' it? There are them that will swear to anything before they'll hang; have you never thought of that?

270 **Hale.** I have. I—I have indeed. (*It is his own suspicion, but he resists it. He glances at* Elizabeth, *then at* John.) And you—would you testify to this in court?

271 **Proctor.** I—had not reckoned with goin' into court. But if I must I will.

272 **Hale.** Do you falter here?

273 **Proctor.** I falter nothing, but I may wonder if my story will be credited in such a court. I do wonder on it, when such a steady-minded minister as you will suspicion such a woman that never lied,

and cannot, and the world knows she cannot! I may falter somewhat, Mister; I am no fool.

Hale (*quietly—it has impressed him*). Proctor, let you open with me now, for I have a rumor that troubles me. It's said you hold no belief that there may even be witches in the world. Is that true, sir?

Proctor (*He knows this is critical, and is striving against his disgust with* Hale *and with himself for even answering*). I know not what I have said, I may have said it. I have wondered if there be witches in the world—although I cannot believe they come among us now.

Hale. Then you do not believe—

Proctor. I have no knowledge of it; the Bible speaks of witches, and I will not deny them.

Hale. And you, woman?

Elizabeth. I—I cannot believe it.

Hale (*shocked*). You cannot!

Proctor. Elizabeth, you bewilder him!

Elizabeth (*to* Hale). I cannot think the Devil may own a woman's soul, Mr. Hale, when she keeps an upright way, as I have. I am a good woman, I know it; and if you believe I may do only good work in the world, and yet be secretly bound to Satan, then I must tell you, sir, I do not believe it.

Hale. But, woman, you do believe there are witches in—

Elizabeth. If you think that I am one, then I say there are none.

Hale. You surely do not fly against the Gospel, the Gospel—

Proctor. She believe in the Gospel, every word!

Elizabeth. Question Abigail Williams about the Gospel, not myself!

(Hale *stares at her.*)

Proctor. She do not mean to doubt the Gospel, sir, you cannot think it. This be a Christian house, sir, a Christian house.

Hale. God keep you both; let the third child be quickly baptized, and go you without fail each Sunday in to Sabbath prayer; and keep a solemn, quiet way among you. I think—

(Giles Corey *appears in doorway.*)

Giles. John!

Proctor. Giles! What's the matter?

Giles. They take my wife.

(Francis Nurse *enters.*)

Giles. And his Rebecca!

NOTICE & NOTE

ANALYZE DRAMATIC ELEMENTS
Annotate: Mark dialogue in paragraphs 293–303 that tells what happened to the wives of Francis and Giles.

Interpret: Explain whether this event is a plot complication that makes the main conflict more difficult to resolve.

The Crucible: Act Two 655

 ANALYZE DRAMATIC ELEMENTS

ENGLISH LEARNER SUPPORT

Understand Homophones Tell students that homophones are words that sound the same but have different spellings and meanings. Write the word *no* (found in paragraph 274) on the board. Note that it sounds the same as the word *know* (found in paragraph 275). Write the word *know* on the board. Pronounce both words, spell them aloud, and have students repeat after you. Then, have students use each word in a sentence. **MODERATE/LIGHT**

Remind students that **plot complications** are additional problems that make the main conflict more difficult to resolve. They often increase the danger or conflict for the characters. (***Answer:*** *The main conflict of the play is whether or not there is witchcraft at work in Salem. The accusation of two such highly regarded women of the town will make it easier for those who wish to persecute others to throw suspicion on practically anyone they want. This complication does make the main conflict more difficult to resolve because there are many motives people might have for making accusations, making it difficult to sort out the genuine from the false.*)

WHEN STUDENTS STRUGGLE . . .

Summarize Plot Encourage students to think about how the plot of the play develops in this scene. Have students summarize the nature of Hale's suspicions of Proctor and Elizabeth. How are they different? (*Hale goes after Proctor for not going to church enough, and that leads to the Ten Commandments test. Elizabeth comes under his suspicion because she was mentioned by Abigail during Abigail's trial. Compounding Hale's suspicion of Abigail is the fact that Elizabeth does not answer Hale's questions about witches in a way that satisfies him.*)

 For additional support, go to the **Reading Studio** and assign the following **Level Up Tutorial: Summarizing.**

© Houghton Mifflin Harcourt Publishing Company

The Crucible: Act Two **655**

ENGLISH LEARNER SUPPORT

Understand Phrasal Verbs   Write on the board the following: *break in, sleep over, check out*. Tell students that these are phrasal verbs—verbs that are made up of a main verb together with an adverb or preposition or both. Point out that phrasal verbs often require a direct object (someone or something who receives the action), as in *hand something in, go after someone*, or *do something over*. Have students find and circle the phrasal verb in the second sentence of paragraph 311. *(buy ... of)* Then, have them identify the direct object *(a pig)*. To solidify understanding of phrasal verbs, have partners work together to write a sentence using a phrasal verb. *(Example: I will check a book out of the library.)* **LIGHT**

296 **Proctor** (*to* Francis). Rebecca's in the *jail!*

297 **Francis.** Aye, Cheever come and take her in his wagon. We've only now come from the jail, and they'll not even let us in to see them.

298 **Elizabeth.** They've surely gone wild now, Mr. Hale!

299 **Francis** (*going to* Hale). Reverend Hale! Can you not speak to the Deputy Governor? I'm sure he mistakes these people—

300 **Hale.** Pray calm yourself, Mr. Nurse.

301 **Francis.** My wife is the very brick and mortar of the church, Mr. Hale (*indicating* Giles) and Martha Corey, there cannot be a woman closer yet to God than Martha.

302 **Hale.** How is Rebecca charged, Mr. Nurse?

303 **Francis** (*with a mocking, half-hearted laugh*). For murder, she's charged! (*mockingly quoting the warrant*) "For the marvelous and supernatural murder of Goody Putnam's babies." What am I to do, Mr. Hale?

304 **Hale** (*turns from* Francis, *deeply troubled, then*). Believe me, Mr. Nurse, if Rebecca Nurse be tainted, then nothing's left to stop the whole green world from burning. Let you rest upon the justice of the court; the court will send her home, I know it.

305 **Francis.** You cannot mean she will be tried in court!

306 **Hale** (*pleading*). Nurse, though our hearts break, we cannot flinch; these are new times, sir. There is a misty plot afoot so subtle we should be criminal to cling to old respects and ancient friendships. I have seen too many frightful proofs in court—the Devil is alive in Salem, and we dare not quail to follow wherever the accusing finger points!

307 **Proctor** (*angered*). How may such a woman murder children?

308 **Hale** (*in great pain*). Man, remember, until an hour before the Devil fell, God thought him beautiful in Heaven.

309 **Giles.** I never said my wife were a witch, Mr. Hale; I only said she were reading books!

310 **Hale.** Mr. Corey, exactly what complaint were made on your wife?

311 **Giles.** That bloody mongrel Walcott charge her. Y'see, he buy a pig of my wife four or five year ago, and the pig died soon after. So he come dancin' in for his money back. So my Martha, she says to him, "Walcott, if you haven't the wit to feed a pig properly, you'll not live to own many," she says. Now he goes to court and claims that from that day to this he cannot keep a pig alive for more than four weeks because my Martha bewitch them with her books!

312 (*Enter* Ezekiel Cheever. *A shocked silence.*)

313 **Cheever.** Good evening to you, Proctor.

314 **Proctor.** Why, Mr. Cheever. Good evening.

315 **Cheever.** Good evening, all. Good evening, Mr. Hale.

316 **Proctor.** I hope you come not on business of the court.

317 **Cheever.** I do, Proctor, aye. I am clerk of the court now, y'know.

318 (*Enter* Marshal Herrick, *a man in his early thirties, who is somewhat shamefaced at the moment.*)

319 **Giles.** It's a pity, Ezekiel, that an honest tailor might have gone to Heaven must burn in Hell. You'll burn for this, do you know it?

320 **Cheever.** You know yourself I must do as I'm told. You surely know that, Giles. And I'd as lief⁶ you'd not be sending me to Hell. I like not the sound of it, I tell you; I like not the sound of it. (*He fears* Proctor, *but starts to reach inside his coat.*) Now believe me, Proctor, how heavy be the law, all its tonnage I do carry on my back tonight. (*He takes out a warrant.*) I have a warrant for your wife.

321 **Proctor** (*to* Hale). You said she were not charged!

322 **Hale.** I know nothin' of it. (*to* Cheever) When were she charged?

323 **Cheever.** I am given sixteen warrant tonight, sir, and she is one.

324 **Proctor.** Who charged her?

325 **Cheever.** Why, Abigail Williams charge her.

326 **Proctor.** On what proof, what proof?

327 **Cheever** (*looking about the room*). Mr. Proctor, I have little time. The court bid me search your house, but I like not to search a house. So will you hand me any poppets that your wife may keep here?

328 **Proctor.** Poppets?

329 **Elizabeth.** I never kept no poppets, not since I were a girl.

330 **Cheever** (*embarrassed, glancing toward the mantel where sits* Mary Warren's *poppet*). I spy a poppet, Goody Proctor.

331 **Elizabeth.** Oh! (*going for it*) Why, this is Mary's.

332 **Cheever** (*shyly*). Would you please to give it to me?

333 **Elizabeth** (*handing it to him, asks* Hale). Has the court discovered a text in poppets now?

334 **Cheever** (*carefully holding the poppet*). Do you keep any others in this house?

335 **Proctor.** No, nor this one either till tonight. What signifies a poppet?

336 **Cheever.** Why, a poppet—(*He gingerly turns the poppet over.*) a poppet may signify—Now, woman, will you please to come with me?

337 **Proctor.** She will not! (*to* Elizabeth) Fetch Mary here.

---

⁶ **as lief** (lēf): rather.

TO CHALLENGE STUDENTS . . .

Analyze Mood Ask students to reread paragraphs 324–327. Discuss how Proctor's demand for proof in the arrest of his wife goes completely ignored by Cheever, who instead looks for evidence against her (the poppet). Have students write and share a paragraph in which they analyze how Proctor's ineffective cry for proof reflects and furthers the mood of *The Crucible*.

TEACH

ANALYZE LITERARY DEVICES

Review the meaning of **dramatic irony.** Have students think about what they and Proctor know that the other characters don't know. (**Answer:** *Cheever and Hale believe that the needle in the doll was used to harm Abigail, but Proctor and the reader can infer that Abigail has set up Elizabeth by having Mary make the doll and put the needle in it, and then stabbing herself and claiming Elizabeth did it.*)

 NOTICE & NOTE

338 **Cheever** (*ineptly reaching toward* Elizabeth). No, no, I am forbid to leave her from my sight.

339 **Proctor** (*pushing his arm away*). You'll leave her out of sight and out of mind, Mister. Fetch Mary, Elizabeth. (Elizabeth *goes upstairs.*)

340 **Hale.** What signifies a poppet, Mr. Cheever?

341 **Cheever** (*turning the poppet over in his hands*). Why, they say it may signify that she—(*He has lifted the poppet's skirt, and his eyes widen in astonished fear.*) Why, this, this—

342 **Proctor** (*reaching for the poppet*). What's there?

343 **Cheever.** Why (*He draws out a long needle from the poppet.*) it is a needle! Herrick, Herrick, it is a needle!

344 (Herrick *comes toward him.*)

345 **Proctor** (*angrily, bewildered*). And what signifies a needle!

346 **Cheever** (*his hands shaking*). Why, this go hard with her, Proctor, this—I had my doubts, Proctor, I had my doubts, but here's calamity. (*to* Hale, *showing the needle*) You see it, sir, it is a needle!

347 **Hale.** Why? What meanin' has it?

348 **Cheever** (*wide-eyed, trembling*). The girl, the Williams girl, Abigail Williams, sir. She sat to dinner in Reverend Parris's house tonight, and without word nor warnin' she falls to the floor. Like a struck beast, he says, and screamed a scream that a bull would weep to hear. And he goes to save her, and, stuck two inches in the flesh of her belly, he draw a needle out. And demandin' of her how she come to be so stabbed, she (*to* Proctor *now*) testify it were your wife's familiar spirit[7] pushed it in.

349 **Proctor.** Why, she done it herself! (*to* Hale) I hope you're not takin' this for proof, Mister!

350 (Hale, *struck by the proof, is silent.*)

351 **Cheever.** 'Tis hard proof! (*to* Hale) I find here a poppet Goody Proctor keeps. I have found it, sir. And in the belly of the poppet a needle's stuck. I tell you true, Proctor, I never warranted to see such proof of Hell, and I bid you obstruct me not, for I—

352 (*Enter* Elizabeth *with Mary Warren.* Proctor, *seeing* Mary Warren, *draws her by the arm to* Hale.)

353 **Proctor.** Here now! Mary, how did this poppet come into my house?

354 **Mary Warren** (*frightened for herself, her voice very small*). What poppet's that, sir?

355 **Proctor** (*impatiently, pointing at the doll in* Cheever's *hand*). This poppet, this poppet.

ANALYZE LITERARY DEVICES

Annotate: Remember that **dramatic irony** is a contrast between what a character knows and what the reader or audience knows. Mark an example of dramatic irony in the section about the poppet.

Analyze: Why is this an example of dramatic irony?

---

[7] **familiar spirit:** the spirit or demon, most usually in the form of an animal such as a black cat, that was a companion and helper to a witch.

© Houghton Mifflin Harcourt Publishing Company

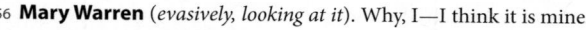
356 **Mary Warren** (*evasively, looking at it*). Why, I—I think it is mine.

357 **Proctor.** It is your poppet, is it not?

358 **Mary Warren** (*not understanding the direction of this*). It—is, sir.

359 **Proctor.** And how did it come into this house?

360 **Mary Warren** (*glancing about at the avid faces*). Why—I made it in the court, sir, and—give it to Goody Proctor tonight.

361 **Proctor** (*to* Hale). Now, sir—do you have it?

362 **Hale.** Mary Warren, a needle have been found inside this poppet.

363 **Mary Warren** (*bewildered*). Why, I meant no harm by it, sir.

364 **Proctor** (*quickly*). You stuck that needle in yourself?

365 **Mary Warren.** I—I believe I did, sir, I—

366 **Proctor** (*to* Hale). What say you now?

367 **Hale** (*watching Mary Warren closely*). Child, you are certain this be your natural memory? May it be, perhaps, that someone conjures you even now to say this?

368 **Mary Warren.** Conjures me? Why, no, sir, I am entirely myself, I think. Let you ask Susanna Walcott—she saw me sewin' it in court. (*or better still*) Ask Abby, Abby sat beside me when I made it.

369 **Proctor** (*to* Hale, *of* Cheever). Bid him begone. Your mind is surely settled now. Bid him out, Mr. Hale.

370 **Elizabeth.** What signifies a needle?

371 **Hale.** Mary—you charge a cold and cruel murder on Abigail.

372 **Mary Warren.** Murder! I charge no—

373 **Hale.** Abigail were stabbed tonight; a needle were found stuck into her belly—

374 **Elizabeth.** And she charges me?

375 **Hale.** Aye.

376 **Elizabeth** (*her breath knocked out*). Why—! The girl is murder! She must be ripped out of the world!

377 **Cheever** (*pointing at* Elizabeth). You've heard that, sir! Ripped out of the world! Herrick, you heard it!

378 **Proctor** (*suddenly snatching the warrant out of* Cheever's *hands*). Out with you.

379 **Cheever.** Proctor, you dare not touch the warrant.

380 **Proctor** (*ripping the warrant*). Out with you!

381 **Cheever.** You've ripped the Deputy Governor's warrant, man!

382 **Proctor.** Damn the Deputy Governor! Out of my house!

WHEN STUDENTS STRUGGLE . . .

Support Comprehension   Have students reread the exchange between Hale and Mary Warren in paragraphs 367–368. Point out that Hale's question, "May it be, perhaps, that someone conjures [bewitches] you even now to say this?" attempts to influence Mary's answer. Discuss with students whom Hale means by "someone"—the Devil? Abigail? Elizabeth?

ENGLISH LEARNER SUPPORT

Understand Figurative Language Focus on paragraph 386 and work with students to interpret its figurative language. Have them locate and underline the phrase "jangling the keys of the kingdom." Tell students this phrase is a biblical allusion—a reference to the statement by Jesus in Matthew 16: "And I tell you that you are Peter, and on this rock I will build my church, and the gates of Hades will not overcome it. I will give you the keys of the kingdom of heaven; whatever you bind on earth will be bound in heaven, and whatever you loose on earth will be loosed in heaven." Have students offer ideas about what this allusion means. (If children are being given the keys of the kingdom, they are being given power only a trusted authority should have.) Then, have students practice interpreting figurative language with a partner:

- "as clean as God's fingers" (*simile*)
- "vengeance is walking Salem" and "vengeance writes the law" (*personification*) **LIGHT**

ANALYZE CHARACTERS AND MOTIVATIONS

Point out that people often avoid eye contact when they feel ashamed. Discuss reasons Proctor might feel ashamed. (**Answer:** *Proctor is probably feeling many things in this moment: fear for his wife's safety; sadness over her being taken away; anger at the situation generally; shame at the role he played in giving Abigail a reason to target Elizabeth; and perhaps shame at not being willing to confess his relationship with Abigail to save his wife and the other accused women.*)

NOTICE & NOTE

383 **Hale.** Now, Proctor, Proctor!

384 **Proctor.** Get y'gone with them! You are a broken minister.

385 **Hale.** Proctor, if she is innocent, the court—

386 **Proctor.** If *she* is innocent! Why do you never wonder if Parris be innocent, or Abigail? Is the accuser always holy now? Were they born this morning as clean as God's fingers? I'll tell you what's walking Salem—vengeance is walking Salem. We are what we always were in Salem, but now the little crazy children are jangling the keys of the kingdom, and common vengeance writes the law! This warrant's vengeance! I'll not give my wife to vengeance!

387 **Elizabeth.** I'll go, John—

388 **Proctor.** You will not go!

389 **Herrick.** I have nine men outside. You cannot keep her. The law binds me, John, I cannot budge.

390 **Proctor** (*to* Hale, *ready to break him*). Will you see her taken?

391 **Hale.** Proctor, the court is just—

392 **Proctor.** Pontius Pilate! God will not let you wash your hands of this![8]

ANALYZE CHARACTERS AND MOTIVATIONS

Annotate: Mark the stage direction in paragraph 393 that describes Proctor's behavior.

Interpret: What is the motivation for this behavior? Cite evidence in your response.

393 **Elizabeth.** John—I think I must go with them. (*He cannot bear to look at her.*) Mary, there is bread enough for the morning; you will bake, in the afternoon. Help Mr. Proctor as you were his daughter—you owe me that, and much more. (*She is fighting her weeping. To* Proctor.) When the children wake, speak nothing of witchcraft—it will frighten them. (*She cannot go on.*)

394 **Proctor.** I will bring you home. I will bring you soon.

395 **Elizabeth.** Oh, John, bring me soon!

396 **Proctor.** I will fall like an ocean on that court! Fear nothing, Elizabeth.

397 **Elizabeth** (*with great fear*). I will fear nothing. (*She looks about the room, as though to fix it in her mind.*) Tell the children I have gone to visit someone sick.

398 (*She walks out the door,* Herrick *and* Cheever *behind her. For a moment,* Proctor *watches from the doorway. The clank of chain is heard.*)

399 **Proctor.** Herrick! Herrick, don't chain her! (*He rushes out the door. From outside.*) Damn you, man, you will not chain her! Off with them! I'll not have it! I will not have her chained!

400 (*There are other men's voices against his.* Hale, *in a fever of guilt and uncertainty, turns from the door to avoid the sight;* Mary Warren *bursts into tears and sits weeping.* Giles Corey *calls to* Hale.)

---

[8] **Pontius Pilate** (pŏn´chəs pī´lət) . . . **hands of this:** the Roman official who presided over the trial and sentencing of Christ. Pilate publicly washed his hands to absolve himself of responsibility for Christ's death.

WHEN STUDENTS STRUGGLE . . .

Understand Metaphors and Similes Remind students that similes compare two things using *like* or *as*, while metaphors compare two things without using these words. Have students reread page 660 and identify a metaphor and a simile, then explain their meanings.

- "You are a broken minister." (*Hale no longer works as a minister should.*)
- "I will fall like an ocean on that court!" (*Proctor will use all his power to defend Elizabeth.*)

For additional support, go to the **Reading Studio** and assign the following **Level Up Tutorial: Figurative Language.**

401 **Giles.** And yet silent, minister? It is fraud, you know it is fraud! What keeps you, man?

402 (Proctor *is half braced, half pushed into the room by two deputies and Herrick.*)

403 **Proctor.** I'll pay you, Herrick, I will surely pay you!

404 **Herrick** (*panting*). In God's name, John, I cannot help myself. I must chain them all. Now let you keep inside this house till I am gone! (*He goes out with his deputies.*)

405 (Proctor *stands there, gulping air. Horses and a wagon creaking are heard.*)

406 **Hale** (*in great uncertainty*). Mr. Proctor—

407 **Proctor.** Out of my sight!

408 **Hale.** Charity, Proctor, charity. What I have heard in her favor, I will not fear to testify in court. God help me, I cannot judge her guilty or innocent—I know not. Only this consider: the world goes mad, and it profit nothing you should lay the cause to the vengeance of a little girl.

ENGLISH LEARNER SUPPORT

Analyze Idioms Remind students that an idiom is an expression whose meaning is not obvious from the individual meaning of each word. Have students read aloud Proctor's dialogue in paragraph 403: "I'll pay you, Herrick, I will surely pay you!" Ask students to define the literal meaning of *pay* (*give money for a product or service*). Then, ask if they think that Proctor is promising to pay Herrick money. (*no*) Ask pairs to work together to infer the meaning of *pay* in paragraph 403. (*In this paragraph, pay means "have revenge on." This usage is related to the idiom "to pay someone back," or "get revenge."*) **ALL LEVELS**

NOTICE & NOTE

409 **Proctor.** You are a coward! Though you be ordained in God's own tears, you are a coward now!

410 **Hale.** Proctor, I cannot think God be provoked so grandly by such a petty cause. The jails are packed— our greatest judges sit in Salem now—and hangin's promised. Man, we must look to cause proportionate. Were there murder done, perhaps, and never brought to light? Abomination? Some secret blasphemy that stinks to Heaven? Think on cause, man, and let you help me to discover it. For there's your way, believe it, there is your only way, when such confusion strikes upon the world. (*He goes to* Giles *and* Francis.) Let you counsel among yourselves; think on your village and what may have drawn from heaven such thundering wrath upon you all. I shall pray God open up our eyes.

411 (Hale *goes out.*)

412 **Francis** (*struck by* Hale's *mood*). I never heard no murder done in Salem.

413 **Proctor** (*He has been reached by* Hale's *words*). Leave me, Francis, leave me.

414 **Giles** (*shaken*). John—tell me, are we lost?

415 **Proctor.** Go home now, Giles. We'll speak on it tomorrow.

416 **Giles.** Let you think on it. We'll come early, eh?

417 **Proctor.** Aye. Go now, Giles.

418 **Giles.** Good night, then.

419 (Giles Corey *goes out. After a moment.*)

420 **Mary Warren** (*in a fearful squeak of a voice*). Mr. Proctor, very likely they'll let her come home once they're given proper evidence.

421 **Proctor.** You're coming to the court with me, Mary. You will tell it in the court.

422 **Mary Warren.** I cannot charge murder on Abigail.

423 **Proctor** (*moving menacingly toward her*). You will tell the court how that poppet come here and who stuck the needle in.

424 **Mary Warren.** She'll kill me for sayin' that! (Proctor *continues toward her.*) Abby'll charge lechery on you, Mr. Proctor!

425 **Proctor** (*halting*). She's told you!

426 **Mary Warren.** I have known it, sir. She'll ruin you with it, I know she will.

427 **Proctor** (*hesitating, and with deep hatred of himself*). Good. Then her saintliness is done with. (Mary *backs from him.*) We will slide together into our pit; you will tell the court what you know.

428 **Mary Warren** (*in terror*). I cannot, they'll turn on me—

WHEN STUDENTS STRUGGLE . . .

Understand Characters Have students reread paragraphs 408–410. Point out that these paragraphs reveal Hale's stubbornness. Ask questions to ensure comprehension:

- Why does Hale say that "a little girl" could not have caused the town frenzy?
- Why does Proctor call Hale a coward?
- Why does Hale think that such terrible events are happening in Salem?

 For additional support, go to the **Reading Studio** and assign the following **Level Up Tutorial: Characters and Conflict.**

429 (Proctor *strides and catches her, and she is repeating, "I cannot, I cannot!"*)

430 **Proctor.** My wife will never die for me! I will bring your guts into your mouth but that goodness will not die for me!

431 **Mary Warren** (*struggling to escape him*). I cannot do it, I cannot!

432 **Proctor** (*grasping her by the throat as though he would strangle her*). Make your peace with it! Now Hell and Heaven grapple on our backs, and all our old pretense is ripped away—make your peace! (*He throws her to the floor, where she sobs, "I cannot, I cannot . . ." And now, half to himself, staring, and turning to the open door.*) Peace. It is a providence, and no great change; we are only what we always were, but naked now. (*He walks as though toward a great horror, facing the open sky.*) Aye, naked! And the wind, God's icy wind, will blow!

433 (*And she is over and over again sobbing, "I cannot, I cannot, I cannot," as the curtain falls.*)

ANALYZE DRAMATIC ELEMENTS

Annotate: Mark striking details in Proctor's speech.

Interpret: What is the meaning of this speech? How does it relate to the central conflict of the play?

CHECK YOUR UNDERSTANDING

Answer these questions before moving on to the **Analyze the Text** section on the following page.

1 Why is Proctor reluctant to testify that Abigail said the dancing was not part of a witches' spell?

A He wants to protect Abigail.

B He wants to protect Elizabeth.

C He wants to hide the fact he was alone with Abigail.

D He wants to make sure people accused of witchcraft are punished.

2 Why does Mary Warren become more demanding of the Proctors?

F Her need for their help has become greater.

G She is being victimized by Abigail and her friends.

H She knows more than they do about how witchcraft works.

J She has more power over them due to her position in the court.

3 Who is the source of conflict between Abigail and Elizabeth?

A Hale

B Parris

C Proctor

D Rebecca

TEACH

 **ANALYZE DRAMATIC ELEMENTS**

Remind students that one of the plot complications is Proctor's affair with Abigail, because keeping this secret interferes with his ability to speak out on other matters—and to shield the innocent from Abigail's malice. Mary's admission that she knows about the affair brings this conflict to an emotional breaking point to end Act Two. (**Answer:** *Proctor is demanding that Mary go with him to court and tell the truth about Abigail seeing her sew the poppet. Proctor knows Mary could decide both their fates—and Elizabeth's and Abigail's—and so "Hell and Heaven grapple" on their backs. He goes on to say they are "naked," meaning the truth is about to be exposed one way or the other—the truth about who is really a witch, in the play's central conflict, and his own truth about his affair with Abigail. "God's icy wind" is the punishment that awaits them all.*)

 CHECK YOUR UNDERSTANDING

Have students answer the questions independently.

Answers:

1. *C*

2. *J*

3. *C*

If they answer any questions incorrectly, have them reread the text to confirm their understanding. Then they may proceed to ANALYZE THE TEXT on page 664.

 ENGLISH LEARNER SUPPORT

Oral Assessment Use the questions to assess students' comprehension and speaking skills.

1. Proctor doesn't want to say Abigail told him the dancing was not a witch's spell. Why? (*He does not want to say he was alone with Abigail.*)

2. Why does Mary Warren become stubborn with the Proctors? (*She has power because she is part of the court.*)

3. Who causes the problems between Abigail and Elizabeth? (*Proctor*)
   MODERATE/LIGHT

ANALYZE THE TEXT

Possible answers:

1. **DOK 3:** *The reader learns that an official court has been convened to hear the charges of witchcraft, and that Mary, the Proctors' servant, has been made an official of the court. Then, the reader learns that Abigail and the other girls who were in the woods are leading the accusations against respectable people. Later, Elizabeth is arrested as a witch. These facts make it clear that to save the lives of innocent people, including his wife, Proctor must testify against Abigail.*

2. **DOK 3:** *Proctor does not accept his wife's suggestion that he go to court and testify that Abigail is lying. He is angry at her for insisting. He is not justified in his attitude because his reluctance stems from pride. He doesn't want to reveal that he spoke alone with Abigail.*

3. **DOK 4:** *When Hale speaks of "secret blasphemy," Proctor thinks of his affair with Abigail. When Proctor tells Mary they will both "slide together" into a pit, he means he and Abigail will have to face the punishment for what they have both done. Proctor will face punishment for adultery, and Abigail will face punishment for adultery and bearing false witness.*

4. **DOK 4:** *Mary shows arrogance ("I am amazed you do not see what weighty work we do") and stubbornness. She refuses to see that Sarah Good's confession is nonsense. Mary also refuses to testify in court against Abigail for fear of what Abigail might do to her. All of this suggests that Mary may not tell the truth.*

5. **DOK 3:** *Mary's stubborn belief in the truth and sincerity of the witch hunt highlights Elizabeth's courage and insight in opposing its unfairness.*

CREATE AND PRESENT

Give a Presentation Have students work with a partner to prepare their presentations. When students have completed a rough outline of their presentations, have them discuss it with another pair of students, pointing out the parallels they have discovered. Have student pairs offer feedback on content and format. Provide time for students to revise and practice their presentations before presenting to the class.

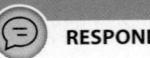 **RESPOND**

ANALYZE THE TEXT

Support your responses with evidence from the text.   NOTEBOOK

1. **Cite Evidence** How do the events in this act affect readers' perception of the moral dilemma in which Proctor and the others find themselves? Cite specific details.

2. **Draw Conclusions** Reread paragraphs 70–87. What do these lines reveal about the character of, and the relationship between, John and Elizabeth Proctor?

3. **Analyze** Why is Proctor struck by Hale's declaration that "some secret blasphemy" has caused all of the confusion? How does Hale's statement relate to Proctor's later words to Mary Warren that he and Abigail will "slide together into our pit; you will tell the court what you know"?

4. **Analyze** What does Mary Warren's behavior in Act Two foreshadow about her testimony in court? Explain.

5. **Draw Conclusions** Often, characters in a drama act as foils for other characters. These characters—often minor ones—contrast strikingly with a main character, clarifying characteristics of the main character. Reread paragraphs 112–123. How could Mary be seen as a foil for Elizabeth?

CREATE AND PRESENT

Give a Presentation With a partner, prepare and share a multimedia presentation on the McCarthy era trials.

❏ Research information using reliable sources that are useful and relevant to the topic. Take notes to document your findings. Identify copyright-free images you might include.

❏ Choose a format to organize the ideas or argument that you want to convey, such as charts, outlines, or slides with facts and illustrations.

❏ Make your presentation to the class and conduct a follow-up discussion about parallels between the McCarthy trials and those depicted in the play.

❏ Speak clearly and use appropriate eye contact and volume.

Go to **Using Media in a Presentation: Types of Media: Audio, Video, and Images** in the **Speaking and Listening Studio** for more help.

ACT THREE

•

1   (*The vestry room of the Salem meeting house, now serving as the anteroom[1] of the General Court.*

2   *As the curtain rises, the room is empty, but for sunlight pouring through two high windows in the back wall. The room is solemn, even forbidding. Heavy beams jut out, boards of random widths make up the walls. At the right are two doors leading into the meeting house proper, where the court is being held. At the left another door leads outside.*

3   *There is a plain bench at the left, and another at the right. In the center a rather long meeting table, with stools and a considerable armchair snugged up to it.*

4   *Through the partitioning wall at the right we hear a prosecutor's voice,* Judge Hathorne's, *asking a question; then a woman's voice,* Martha Corey's, *replying.*)

5 **Hathorne's Voice.** Now, Martha Corey, there is abundant evidence in our hands to show that you have given yourself to the reading of fortunes. Do you deny it?

6 **Martha Corey's Voice.** I am innocent to a witch. I know not what a witch is.

7 **Hathorne's Voice.** How do you know, then, that you are not a witch?

8 **Martha Corey's Voice.** If I were, I would know it.

9 **Hathorne's Voice.** Why do you hurt these children?

10 **Martha Corey's Voice.** I do not hurt them. I scorn it!

11 **Giles' Voice** (*roaring*). I have evidence for the court!

12 (*Voices of townspeople rise in excitement.*)

13 **Danforth's Voice.** You will keep your seat!

14 **Giles' Voice.** <u>Thomas Putnam is reaching out for land!</u>

15 **Danforth's Voice.** Remove that man, Marshal!

16 **Giles' Voice.** You're hearing lies, lies!

17 (*A roaring goes up from the people.*)

18 **Hathorne's Voice.** Arrest him, excellency!

19 **Giles' Voice.** I have evidence. Why will you not hear my evidence?

20 (*The door opens and* Giles *is half carried into the vestry room by* Herrick.)

21 **Giles.** Hands off, damn you, let me go!

22 **Herrick.** Giles, Giles!

---

[1] **vestry room . . . anteroom:** A vestry room is a room in a church used for nonreligious meetings or church business. An anteroom is a waiting room or a room that leads into another.

ANALYZE CHARACTERS AND MOTIVATIONS

Annotate: Mark dialogue that explains what Giles thinks is behind the witch hunt.

Interpret: How does this dialogue suggest a motivation for Putnam's behavior?

ANALYZE CHARACTERS AND MOTIVATIONS.

Tell students to think about the different ways **dialogue** can express character motivations directly or indirectly. In particular, have them consider how a person can say words that reveal his or her own **motivations** as well as how a character can (correctly or incorrectly) identify another character's motivations. (***Answer:*** *Giles believes Putnam is after the land of people in the town, and that is why Putnam wishes to see them accused, jailed, and hanged.*)

ENGLISH LEARNER SUPPORT

Recognize and Use Possessive Nouns Remind students of the rules for showing possession in English:

- For singular nouns not ending in *s*, add an apostrophe + *s*: "Martha Corey's Voice."

- For singular nouns ending in *s*, you may add an apostrophe + *s* or just an apostrophe: "Giles' Voice."

- For plural nouns ending in *s*, add only an apostrophe: "the girls' conviction."

Have students locate and circle the words "Hathorne's Voice." Ask them to identify whether the possessive is singular or plural. (*singular*) Then, have them identify the way this singular noun—Hathorne—forms a possessive (*a singular noun not ending in* s *gets an apostrophe* + s). For additional practice, have students work in pairs to explain how to form a possessive with the following words: *John, the boys, Kansas.*

MODERATE

ENGLISH LEARNER SUPPORT

Understand Language Structures Remind students that the noun a pronoun replaces is called its **antecedent.** Have student identify the antecedents of pronouns in the text:

- Read aloud Giles' dialogue beginning in paragraph 36. Have students circle the pronoun *it* at the end of the sentence. Ask students to underline the antecedent *(question).* Have students circle the pronoun *it* in the phrase "cause of it" in paragraph 44. Have them work in pairs to identify and underline the antecedent *(her interest in books).*

SUBSTANTIAL/MODERATE

- In addition to identifying the examples above, have students circle the pronoun *this* in paragraph 37 and identify its antecedent. *(It refers back to "[causing] a contemptuous riot" or "behaving disrespectfully and outrageously.")* **LIGHT**

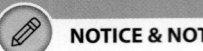

23 **Giles.** Out of my way, Herrick! I bring evidence—

24 **Herrick.** You cannot go in there, Giles; it's a court!

25 (*Enter* Hale *from the court.*)

26 **Hale.** Pray be calm a moment.

27 **Giles.** You, Mr. Hale, go in there and demand I speak.

28 **Hale.** A moment, sir, a moment.

29 **Giles.** They'll be hangin' my wife!

30 (Judge Hathorne *enters. He is in his sixties, a bitter, remorseless Salem judge.*)

31 **Hathorne.** How do you dare come roarin' into this court! Are you gone daft, Corey?

32 **Giles.** You're not a Boston judge yet, Hathorne. You'll not call me daft!

33 (*Enter* Deputy Governor Danforth *and, behind him,* Ezekiel Cheever *and* Parris. *On his appearance, silence falls.* Danforth *is a grave man in his sixties, of some humor and sophistication that does not, however, interfere with an exact loyalty to his position and his cause. He comes down to* Giles, *who awaits his wrath.*)

34 **Danforth** (*looking directly at* Giles). Who is this man?

35 **Parris.** Giles Corey, sir, and a more contentious—

36 **Giles** (*to* Parris). I am asked the question, and I am old enough to answer it! (*to* Danforth, *who impresses him and to whom he smiles through his strain*) My name is Corey, sir, Giles Corey. I have six hundred acres, and timber in addition. It is my wife you be condemning now. (*He indicates the courtroom.*)

37 **Danforth.** And how do you imagine to help her cause with such contemptuous riot?[2] Now be gone. Your old age alone keeps you out of jail for this.

38 **Giles** (*beginning to plead*). They be tellin' lies about my wife, sir, I—

39 **Danforth.** Do you take it upon yourself to determine what this court shall believe and what it shall set aside?

40 **Giles.** Your Excellency, we mean no disrespect for—

41 **Danforth.** Disrespect indeed! It is disruption, Mister. This is the highest court of the supreme government of this province, do you know it?

42 **Giles** (*beginning to weep*). Your Excellency, I only said she were readin' books, sir, and they come and take her out of my house for—

43 **Danforth** (*mystified*). Books! What books?

44 **Giles** (*through helpless sobs*). It is my third wife, sir; I never had no wife that be so taken with books, and I thought to find the cause of it,

---

[2] **contemptuous** (kən-tĕmp´chōō-əs) **riot:** disrespectful, outrageous behavior.

© Houghton Mifflin Harcourt Publishing Company

d'y'see, but it were no witch I blamed her for. (*He is openly weeping.*) I have broke charity with the woman, I have broke charity with her. (*He covers his face, ashamed.* Danforth *is respectfully silent.*)

45 **Hale.** Excellency, he claims hard evidence for his wife's defense. I think that in all justice you must—

46 **Danforth.** Then let him submit his evidence in proper affidavit. You are certainly aware of our procedure here, Mr. Hale. (*to* Herrick) Clear this room.

47 **Herrick.** Come now, Giles. (*He gently pushes* Corey *out.*)

48 **Francis.** We are desperate, sir; we come here three days now and cannot be heard.

49 **Danforth.** Who is this man?

50 **Francis.** Francis Nurse, Your Excellency.

51 **Hale.** His wife's Rebecca that were condemned this morning.

52 **Danforth.** Indeed! I am amazed to find you in such uproar. I have only good report of your character, Mr. Nurse.

53 **Hathorne.** I think they must both be arrested in contempt, sir.

54 **Danforth** (*to* Francis). Let you write your plea, and in due time I will—

55 **Francis.** Excellency, we have proof for your eyes; God forbid you shut them to it. The girls, sir, the girls are frauds.

56 **Danforth.** What's that?

57 **Francis.** We have proof of it, sir. They are all deceiving you.

58 (Danforth *is shocked, but studying* Francis.)

59 **Hathorne.** This is contempt, sir, contempt!

60 **Danforth.** Peace, Judge Hathorne. Do you know who I am, Mr. Nurse?

61 **Francis.** I surely do, sir, and I think you must be a wise judge to be what you are.

62 **Danforth.** And do you know that near to four hundred are in the jails from Marblehead to Lynn,[3] and upon my signature?

63 **Francis.** I—

64 **Danforth.** And seventy-two condemned to hang by that signature?

65 **Francis.** Excellency, I never thought to say it to such a weighty judge, but you are deceived.

66 (*Enter* Giles Corey *from left. All turn to see as he beckons in* Mary Warren *with* Proctor. Mary *is keeping her eyes to the ground;* Proctor *has her elbow as though she were near collapse.*)

---

[3] **Marblehead . . . Lynn:** two coastal towns in Massachusetts, near Salem.

WHEN STUDENTS STRUGGLE . . .

Analyze Characters Help students understand characters' difficulties in making their voices heard. Have small groups reread and discuss paragraphs 45–53:

- How are Hale's attempts to help Giles and Francis hindered?
- Why else might these men be frustrated?
- Will the judges likely be sympathetic to the husbands' efforts to save their wives?

For additional support, go to the **Reading Studio** and assign the following **Level Up Tutorial: Character Motivations.**

ANALYZE CHARACTERS AND MOTIVATIONS

Remind students that the main character around whom most of the action centers is the **protagonist.** The reader often identifies with and feels sympathy for the protagonist. Explain that the character who opposes the protagonist is the **antagonist.** (***Answer:*** *Proctor is the protagonist. The reader sympathizes with his attempt to tell the truth to the court and to free the women who have been wrongfully charged. Parris is the antagonist. He tries to make the court see Proctor as untruthful or nefarious so the women will not be freed.*)

 NOTICE & NOTE

67 **Parris** (*on seeing her, in shock*). Mary Warren! (*He goes directly to bend close to her face.*) What are you about here?

68 **Proctor** (*pressing Parris away from her with a gentle but firm motion of protectiveness*). She would speak with the Deputy Governor.

69 **Danforth** (*shocked by this, turns to* Herrick). Did you not tell me Mary Warren were sick in bed?

70 **Herrick.** She were, Your Honor. When I go to fetch her to the court last week, she said she were sick.

71 **Giles.** She has been strivin' with her soul all week, Your Honor; she comes now to tell the truth of this to you.

72 **Danforth.** Who is this?

73 **Proctor.** John Proctor, sir. Elizabeth Proctor is my wife.

74 **Parris.** Beware this man, Your Excellency, this man is mischief.

75 **Hale** (*excitedly*). I think you must hear the girl, sir, she—

76 **Danforth** (*who has become very interested in* Mary Warren *and only raises a hand toward* Hale). Peace. What would you tell us, Mary Warren?

77 (Proctor *looks at her, but she cannot speak.*)

78 **Proctor.** She never saw no spirits, sir.

79 **Danforth** (*with great alarm and surprise, to* Mary). Never saw no spirits!

80 **Giles** (*eagerly*). Never.

81 **Proctor** (*reaching into his jacket*). She has signed a deposition, sir—

82 **Danforth** (*instantly*). No, no, I accept no depositions. (*He is rapidly calculating this; he turns from her to* Proctor.) Tell me, Mr. Proctor, have you given out this story in the village?

83 **Proctor.** We have not.

84 **Parris.** They've come to overthrow the court, sir! This man is—

85 **Danforth.** I pray you, Mr. Parris. Do you know, Mr. Proctor, that the entire contention of the state in these trials is that the voice of Heaven is speaking through the children?

86 **Proctor.** I know that, sir.

87 **Danforth** (*thinks, staring at* Proctor, *then turns to* Mary Warren). And you, Mary Warren, how came you to cry out people for sending their spirits against you?

88 **Mary Warren.** It were pretense, sir.

89 **Danforth.** I cannot hear you.

90 **Proctor.** It were pretense, she says.

91 **Danforth.** Ah? And the other girls? Susanna Walcott, and—the others? They are also pretending?

ANALYZE CHARACTERS AND MOTIVATIONS
Annotate: Mark phrases in paragraphs 74–84 that show Parris attempting to undermine Proctor.

Analyze: How do these lines help you determine who is the protagonist and who is the antagonist in the play?

WHEN STUDENTS STRUGGLE . . .

Find Meanings of Domain-Specific Terms Explain that **domain-specific terms** are technical terms associated with specialized topics. For example, in paragraphs 53 and 59 students read the term *contempt*—referring to *contempt of court*, from the field of law. Tell students that meaning can often be inferred from context, but if they are unsure, they should consult a dictionary. Have them reread paragraphs 81–82 and use context to define *deposition*. Have students discuss their ideas with a partner and keep a list of legal terms as they read.

For additional support, go to the **Reading Studio** and assign the following [LEVEL] **Level Up Tutorial: Using Context Clues.**

92 **Mary Warren.** Aye, sir.

93 **Danforth** (*wide-eyed*). Indeed. (*Pause. He is baffled by this. He turns to study* Proctor's *face.*)

94 **Parris** (*in a sweat*). Excellency, you surely cannot think to let so vile a lie be spread in open court!

95 **Danforth.** Indeed not, but it strike hard upon me that she will dare come here with such a tale. Now, Mr. Proctor, before I decide whether I shall hear you or not, it is my duty to tell you this. We burn a hot fire here; it melts down all concealment.

96 **Proctor.** I know that, sir.

97 **Danforth.** Let me continue. I understand well, a husband's tenderness may drive him to extravagance in defense of a wife. Are you certain in your conscience, Mister, that your evidence is the truth?

98 **Proctor.** It is. And you will surely know it.

99 **Danforth.** And you thought to declare this revelation in the open court before the public?

100 **Proctor.** I thought I would, aye—with your permission.

101 **Danforth** (*his eyes narrowing*). Now, sir, what is your purpose in so doing?

102 **Proctor.** Why, I—I would free my wife, sir.

103 **Danforth.** There lurks nowhere in your heart, nor hidden in your spirit, any desire to undermine this court?

104 **Proctor** (*with the faintest faltering*). Why, no, sir.

105 **Cheever** (*clears his throat, awakening*). I—Your Excellency.

106 **Danforth.** Mr. Cheever.

107 **Cheever.** I think it be my duty, sir—(*kindly, to* Proctor) You'll not deny it, John. (*to* Danforth) When we come to take his wife, he damned the court and ripped your warrant.

108 **Parris.** Now you have it!

109 **Danforth.** He did that, Mr. Hale?

110 **Hale** (*takes a breath*). Aye, he did.

111 **Proctor.** It were a temper, sir. I knew not what I did.

112 **Danforth** (*studying him*). Mr. Proctor.

113 **Proctor.** Aye, sir.

114 **Danforth** (*straight into his eyes*). Have you ever seen the Devil?

115 **Proctor.** No, sir.

116 **Danforth.** You are in all respects a Gospel Christian?

117 **Proctor.** I am, sir.

The Crucible: Act Three   669

TO CHALLENGE STUDENTS . . .

Analyze Dialogue Direct students' attention to this comment from Judge Danforth: "We burn a hot fire here; it melts down all concealment." (paragraph 95) Have students write and share a statement that explains (1) what the statement means in its immediate contexts and (2) how the statement relates to the title of the play.

ANALYZE CHARACTERS AND MOTIVATIONS

Remind students that a character's **motivations** can often be inferred by combining what readers already know about a character with the character's **dialogue.** Discuss what students already know about Danforth. Have them read paragraph 133 and identify what Danforth "considers," and then infer why he might change the subject. (**Answer:** *Danforth does not want to hear Mary's testimony. By mentioning Elizabeth's claim of pregnancy, he may hope to divert Proctor's attention from his goal of getting Mary to testify.*)

118 **Parris.** Such a Christian that will not come to church but once in a month!

119 **Danforth** (*restrained—he is curious*). Not come to church?

120 **Proctor.** I—I have no love for Mr. Parris. It is no secret. But God I surely love.

121 **Cheever.** He plow on Sunday, sir.

122 **Danforth.** Plow on Sunday!

123 **Cheever** (*apologetically*). I think it be evidence, John. I am an official of the court, I cannot keep it.

124 **Proctor.** I—I have once or twice plowed on Sunday. I have three children, sir, and until last year my land give little.

125 **Giles.** You'll find other Christians that do plow on Sunday if the truth be known.

126 **Hale.** Your Honor, I cannot think you may judge the man on such evidence.

127 **Danforth.** I judge nothing. (*Pause. He keeps watching* Proctor, *who tries to meet his gaze.*) I tell you straight, Mister—I have seen marvels in this court. I have seen people choked before my eyes by spirits; I have seen them stuck by pins and slashed by daggers. I have until this moment not the slightest reason to suspect that the children may be deceiving me. Do you understand my meaning?

128 **Proctor.** Excellency, does it not strike upon you that so many of these women have lived so long with such upright reputation, and—

129 **Parris.** Do you read the Gospel, Mr. Proctor?

130 **Proctor.** I read the Gospel.

131 **Parris.** I think not, or you should surely know that Cain were an upright man, and yet he did kill Abel.[4]

132 **Proctor.** Aye, God tells us that. (*to* Danforth) But who tells us Rebecca Nurse murdered seven babies by sending out her spirit on them? It is the children only, and this one will swear she lied to you.

133 (Danforth *considers, then beckons* Hathorne *to him.* Hathorne *leans in, and he speaks in his ear.* Hathorne *nods.*)

134 **Hathorne.** Aye, she's the one.

135 **Danforth.** Mr. Proctor, this morning, your wife send me a claim in which she states that she is pregnant now.

136 **Proctor.** My wife pregnant!

137 **Danforth.** There be no sign of it—we have examined her body.

138 **Proctor.** But if she say she is pregnant, then she must be! That woman will never lie, Mr. Danforth.

---

[4] **Cain . . . Abel:** According to the book of Genesis in the Bible, Cain and Abel were the sons of Adam and Eve, the first humans.

ANALYZE CHARACTERS AND MOTIVATIONS
Annotate: Mark Danforth's response to Proctor's claim that Mary will admit to lying to the court.

Infer: What is Danforth's reason for telling Proctor that his wife is pregnant?

139 **Danforth.** She will not?

140 **Proctor.** Never, sir, never.

141 **Danforth.** We have thought it too convenient to be credited. However, if I should tell you now that I will let her be kept another month; and if she begin to show her natural signs, you shall have her living yet another year until she is delivered—what say you to that? (John Proctor *is struck silent.*) Come now. You say your only purpose is to save your wife. Good, then, she is saved at least this year, and a year is long. What say you, sir? It is done now. (*In conflict,* Proctor *glances at* Francis *and* Giles.) Will you drop this charge?

142 **Proctor.** I—I think I cannot.

143 **Danforth** (*now an almost imperceptible hardness in his voice*). Then your purpose is somewhat larger.

144 **Parris.** He's come to overthrow this court, Your Honor!

145 **Proctor.** These are my friends. Their wives are also accused—

146 **Danforth** (*with a sudden briskness of manner*). I judge you not, sir. I am ready to hear your evidence.

147 **Proctor.** I come not to hurt the court; I only—

148 **Danforth** (*cutting him off*). Marshal, go into the court and bid Judge Stoughton and Judge Sewall declare recess for one hour. And let them go to the tavern, if they will. All witnesses and prisoners are to be kept in the building.

149 **Herrick.** Aye, sir. (*very deferentially*) If I may say it, sir, I know this man all my life. It is a good man, sir.

150 **Danforth** (*It is the reflection on himself he resents*). I am sure of it, Marshal. (Herrick *nods, then goes out.*) Now, what deposition do you have for us, Mr. Proctor? And I beg you be clear, open as the sky, and honest.

151 **Proctor** (*as he takes out several papers*). I am no lawyer, so I'll—

152 **Danforth.** The pure in heart need no lawyers. Proceed as you will.

153 **Proctor** (*handing* Danforth *a paper*). Will you read this first, sir? It's a sort of testament. The people signing it declare their good opinion of Rebecca, and my wife, and Martha Corey. (Danforth *looks down at the paper.*)

154 **Parris** (*to enlist* Danforth's *sarcasm*). Their good opinion! (*But* Danforth *goes on reading, and* Proctor *is heartened.*)

155 **Proctor.** These are all landholding farmers, members of the church. (*delicately, trying to point out a paragraph*) If you'll notice, sir— they've known the women many years and never saw no sign they had dealings with the Devil.

156 (Parris *nervously moves over and reads over* Danforth's *shoulder.*)

© Houghton Mifflin Harcourt Publishing Company

 ENGLISH LEARNER SUPPORT

Understand Adverbs Remind students that adverbs modify verbs, adjectives, or other adverbs. Often, they end in *-ly*. Provide practice identifying adverbs and words they modify:

- Have students circle the adverb in paragraph 156 (*nervously*). Ask: What did Parris do nervously? (*move*) **SUBSTANTIAL/MODERATE**

- Explain that words like *more, less, often, never,* and *always* are also adverbs. Have students circle the adverbs and identify the actions they modify in paragraphs 155–156. (*delicately: speaks* [*implied*]; *never: saw; nervously: moves*) **LIGHT**

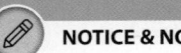

ANALYZE DRAMATIC ELEMENTS

Remind students that a character's **dialogue** can reflect a play's theme. Revisit the last sentence of Miller's opening exposition: "Old scores could be settled on a plane of heavenly combat between Lucifer and the Lord; suspicions and the envy of the miserable toward the happy could and did burst out in the general revenge." Miller notes how people could use the language of virtue and piety as an excuse to air their very human revenges, lusts, and jealousies. In this scene, Danforth uses positive religious language to say something threatening—whether he sees it that way or not. (**Answer:** *Danforth's claim that "the shining sun is up" is unjustified, since the court is being deceived and is actually committing a grave injustice. Danforth's black-and-white thinking and his insistence on his own ability to separate good from evil blind him to reality.*)

NOTICE & NOTE

157 **Danforth** (*glancing down a long list*). How many names are here?

158 **Francis.** Ninety-one, Your Excellency.

159 **Parris** (*sweating*). These people should be summoned. (Danforth *looks up at him questioningly.*) For questioning.

160 **Francis** (*trembling with anger*). Mr. Danforth, I gave them all my word no harm would come to them for signing this.

161 **Parris.** This is a clear attack upon the court!

162 **Hale** (*to Parris, trying to contain himself*). Is every defense an attack upon the court? Can no one—?

163 **Parris.** All innocent and Christian people are happy for the courts in Salem! These people are gloomy for it. (*to Danforth directly*) And I think you will want to know, from each and every one of them, what discontents them with you!

164 **Hathorne.** I think they ought to be examined, sir.

165 **Danforth.** It is not necessarily an attack, I think. Yet—

166 **Francis.** These are all covenanted Christians, sir.

167 **Danforth.** Then I am sure they may have nothing to fear. (*hands* Cheever *the paper*) Mr. Cheever, have warrants drawn for all of these—arrest for examination. (*to Proctor*) Now, Mister, what other information do you have for us? (Francis *is still standing, horrified.*) You may sit, Mr. Nurse.

168 **Francis.** I have brought trouble on these people; I have—

169 **Danforth.** No, old man, you have not hurt these people if they are of good conscience. But you must understand, sir, that a person is either with this court or he must be counted against it, there be no road between. This is a sharp time, now, a precise time—we live no longer in the dusky afternoon when evil mixed itself with good and befuddled the world. Now, by God's grace, the shining sun is up, and them that fear not light will surely praise it. I hope you will be one of those. (Mary Warren *suddenly sobs.*) She's not hearty,[5] I see.

170 **Proctor.** No, she's not, sir. (*to Mary, bending to her, holding her hand, quietly*) Now remember what the angel Raphael said to the boy Tobias.[6] Remember it.

171 **Mary Warren** (*hardly audible*). Aye.

172 **Proctor.** "Do that which is good, and no harm shall come to thee."

173 **Mary Warren.** Aye.

174 **Danforth.** Come, man, we wait you.

175 (Marshal Herrick *returns, and takes his post at the door.*)

176 **Giles.** John, my deposition, give him mine.

ANALYZE DRAMATIC ELEMENTS
Annotate: Mark details that tell you Danforth feels certain he is doing the right thing.

Analyze: Explain whether Danforth is justified in feeling this way.

---
[5] **hearty:** well.
[6] **what the angel said . . . Tobias:** In the Book of Tobit in the Apocrypha, Tobit's son Tobias cured his father's blindness with the help of the angel Raphael.

IMPROVE READING FLUENCY

Targeted Passage Use Danforth's speech in paragraph 169 to help students develop fluency. Remind students what they know of Danforth's character so far: that he is inflexible and has a high opinion of himself. Model reading the speech for students. Have students work in small groups to read the speech aloud. Each student should take a turn reading the entire speech. When students have finished reading, you may wish to invite volunteers to read the speech to the class.

 Go to the **Reading Studio** for additional support in developing fluency.

177 **Proctor.** Aye. (*He hands* Danforth *another paper.*) This is Mr. Corey's deposition.

178 **Danforth.** Oh? (*He looks down at it. Now* Hathorne *comes behind him and reads with him.*)

179 **Hathorne** (*suspiciously*). What lawyer drew this, Corey?

180 **Giles.** You know I never hired a lawyer in my life, Hathorne.

181 **Danforth** (*finishing the reading*). It is very well phrased. My compliments. Mr. Parris, if Mr. Putnam is in the court, will you bring him in? (Hathorne *takes the deposition, and walks to the window with it.* Parris *goes into the court.*) You have no legal training, Mr. Corey?

182 **Giles** (*very pleased*). I have the best, sir—I am thirty-three time in court in my life. And always plaintiff, too.

183 **Danforth.** Oh, then you're much put-upon.

184 **Giles.** I am never put-upon; I know my rights, sir, and I will have them. You know, your father tried a case of mine—might be thirty-five year ago, I think.

185 **Danforth.** Indeed.

186 **Giles.** He never spoke to you of it?

187 **Danforth.** No, I cannot recall it.

188 **Giles.** That's strange, he give me nine pound damages. He were a fair judge, your father. Y'see, I had a white mare that time, and this fellow come to borrow the mare—(*Enter* Parris *with* Thomas Putnam. *When he sees* Putnam, Giles' *ease goes; he is hard.*) Aye, there he is.

189 **Danforth.** Mr. Putnam, I have here an accusation by Mr. Corey against you. He states that you coldly prompted your daughter to cry witchery upon George Jacobs that is now in jail.

190 **Putnam.** It is a lie.

191 **Danforth** (*turning to* Giles). Mr. Putnam states your charge is a lie. What say you to that?

192 **Giles** (*furious, his fists clenched*). A fart on Thomas Putnam, that is what I say to that!

193 **Danforth.** What proof do you submit for your charge, sir?

194 **Giles.** My proof is there! (*pointing to the paper*) If Jacobs hangs for a witch he forfeit up his property—that's law! And there is none but Putnam with the coin to buy so great a piece. This man is killing his neighbors for their land!

195 **Danforth.** But proof, sir, proof.

196 **Giles** (*pointing at his deposition*). The proof is there! I have it from an honest man who heard Putnam say it! The day his daughter cried out on Jacobs, he said she'd given him a fair gift of land.

197 **Hathorne.** And the name of this man?

ENGLISH LEARNER SUPPORT

Understand Suffixes Remind students that a suffix is added to the end of a base word or word part to create a new word with a different meaning. Introduce the suffix *-ery*. Explain that *-ery* is added to words to form nouns of these kinds:

- a craft, trade, or practice, as in *cookery*

- a place, as in *bakery*

- a collection, class, or group, as in *shrubbery*

- a characteristic of something, as in *snobbery*

Have students circle the word *witchery* in paragraph 189 and read the entire sentence aloud. Ask students what the word means (*the practice of witchcraft*). List on the board other nouns from the text ending in *-ery* (*lechery, effrontery, sorcery, adultery*). Have students use a dictionary to define them and then use them orally in sentences that describe events in this act.
MODERATE/LIGHT

198 **Giles** (*taken aback*). What name?

199 **Hathorne.** The man that give you this information.

200 **Giles** (*hesitates, then*). Why, I—I cannot give you his name.

201 **Hathorne.** And why not?

202 **Giles** (*hesitates, then bursts out*). You know well why not! He'll lay in jail if I give his name!

203 **Hathorne.** This is contempt of the court, Mr. Danforth!

204 **Danforth** (*to avoid that*). You will surely tell us the name.

205 **Giles.** I will not give you no name. I mentioned my wife's name once and I'll burn in hell long enough for that. I stand mute.

206 **Danforth.** In that case, I have no choice but to arrest you for contempt of this court, do you know that?

207 **Giles.** This is a hearing; you cannot clap me for contempt of a hearing.

208 **Danforth.** Oh, it is a proper lawyer![7] Do you wish me to declare the court in full session here? Or will you give me good reply?

209 **Giles** (*faltering*). I cannot give you no name, sir, I cannot.

210 **Danforth.** You are a foolish old man. Mr. Cheever, begin the record. The court is now in session. I ask you, Mr. Corey—

211 **Proctor** (*breaking in*). Your Honor—he has the story in confidence, sir, and he—

212 **Parris.** The Devil lives on such confidences! (*to* Danforth) Without confidences there could be no conspiracy, Your Honor!

213 **Hathorne.** I think it must be broken, sir.

214 **Danforth** (*to* Giles). Old man, if your informant tells the truth let him come here openly like a decent man. But if he hide in anonymity I must know why. Now sir, the government and central church demand of you the name of him who reported Mr. Thomas Putnam a common murderer.

215 **Hale.** Excellency—

216 **Danforth.** Mr. Hale.

217 **Hale.** We cannot blink it more. There is a prodigious fear of this court in the country—

218 **Danforth.** Then there is a prodigious guilt in the country. Are *you* afraid to be questioned here?

219 **Hale.** I may only fear the Lord, sir, but there is fear in the country nevertheless.

---

[7] **Oh, . . . lawyer:** Oh, he thinks he is a real lawyer.

TO CHALLENGE STUDENTS . . .

Conduct Research   Discuss with students Miller's unsympathetic portrayal of Judge Danforth. Ask them how much of the portrayal they think is historically accurate and how much is Miller's attempt to convey his theme. Have students conduct research on Thomas Danforth. Then, have students meet in small groups to share their findings. Finally, have the groups meet together to summarize what they have learned.

220 **Danforth** (*angered now*). Reproach me not with the fear in the country; there is fear in the country because there is a moving[8] plot to topple Christ in the country!

221 **Hale.** But it does not follow that everyone accused is part of it.

222 **Danforth.** No uncorrupted man may fear this court, Mr. Hale! None! (*to* Giles) You are under arrest in contempt of this court. Now sit you down and take counsel with yourself, or you will be set in the jail until you decide to answer all questions.

223 (Giles Corey *makes a rush for* Putnam. Proctor *lunges and holds him.*)

224 **Proctor.** No, Giles!

225 **Giles** (*over* Proctor's *shoulder at* Putnam). I'll cut your throat, Putnam, I'll kill you yet!

226 **Proctor** (*forcing him into a chair*). Peace, Giles, peace. (*releasing him*) We'll prove ourselves. Now we will. (*He starts to turn to* Danforth.)

227 **Giles.** Say nothin' more, John. (*pointing at* Danforth) He's only playin' you! He means to hang us all!

228 (Mary Warren *bursts into sobs.*)

229 **Danforth.** This is a court of law, Mister. I'll have no effrontery here!

230 **Proctor.** Forgive him, sir, for his old age. Peace, Giles, we'll prove it all now. (*He lifts up* Mary's *chin.*) You cannot weep, Mary. Remember the angel, what he say to the boy. Hold to it, now; there is your rock. (Mary *quiets. He takes out a paper, and turns to* Danforth.) This is Mary Warren's deposition. I—I would ask you remember, sir, while you read it, that until two week ago she were no different than the other children are today. (*He is speaking reasonably, restraining all his fears, his anger, his anxiety.*) You saw her scream, she howled, she swore familiar spirits choked her; she even testified that Satan, in the form of women now in jail, tried to win her soul away, and then when she refused—

231 **Danforth.** We know all this.

232 **Proctor.** Aye, sir. She swears now that she never saw Satan; nor any spirit, vague or clear, that Satan may have sent to hurt her. And she declares her friends are lying now.

233 (Proctor *starts to hand* Danforth *the deposition, and* Hale *comes up to* Danforth *in a trembling state.*)

234 **Hale.** Excellency, a moment. I think this goes to the heart of the matter.

235 **Danforth** (*with deep misgivings*). It surely does.

236 **Hale.** I cannot say he is an honest man; I know him little. But in all justice, sir, a claim so weighty cannot be argued by a farmer. In God's

---

[8] **moving:** active.

ANALYZE DRAMATIC ELEMENTS

Annotate: Mark the stage directions in paragraphs 223–228.

Analyze: What do the stage directions describe? How do they impact your understanding of events?

ANALYZE DRAMATIC ELEMENTS

Explain to students that when they read detailed stage directions, it is important to visualize what is happening and how it would look on stage. (**Answer:** *The stage directions in this part of the scene are very active; Miller uses words like "rush," "lunge," and "forcing." The scene at this point is charged and exciting as the stage directions describe Giles' attempt to fight Putnam and Proctor's effort to restrain him.*)

■ English Learner Support

Describe Dramatic Elements To help students answer the question, list the following stage directions on the board: *makes a rush, lunges and holds him, starts to turn, pointing at.* Then read the list aloud, instructing students to visualize the action as they listen. Have small groups work together. One student can act out a stage direction from the list while the others guess which one it is. **SUBSTANTIAL/MODERATE**

ANALYZE DRAMATIC ELEMENTS

Tell students that sometimes they will find long **stage directions** that describe multiple events. These stage directions often advance the plot by revealing the characters' feelings and attitudes, even though there is no dialogue. (**Answer:** *Danforth is seriously considering what he has read, because he "moves in thought toward the window" and becomes angry when Parris tries to interrupt his reflections. Proctor is concerned for Mary because he touches her head when she sobs. Francis is hoping fervently that Danforth will believe Mary; he is praying silently. Cheever is uninterested in Mary's testimony: he waits "placidly.")*

EL ENGLISH LEARNER SUPPORT

Understand Idioms Remind students that an idiom is a phrase whose meaning is different from the literal meaning of its words. Have students underline the idiom "the heart of the matter" in paragraph 234. Ask: What is the matter they are speaking about? *(the accusations; whether witchcraft was done)* How is Mary's lying related to the "matter"? *(If she is lying, the case against the accused falls apart.)* Is Mary's deposition of great importance in this matter? *(yes)* Have pairs discuss what they think "the heart of the matter" means. *("The heart of the matter" means the most important part of the business.)* **MODERATE/LIGHT**

name, sir, stop here; send him home and let him come again with a lawyer—

237 **Danforth** (*patiently*). Now look you, Mr. Hale—

238 **Hale.** Excellency, I have signed seventy-two death warrants; I am a minister of the Lord, and I dare not take a life without there be a proof so immaculate no slightest qualm of conscience may doubt it.

239 **Danforth.** Mr. Hale, you surely do not doubt my justice.

240 **Hale.** I have this morning signed away the soul of Rebecca Nurse, Your Honor. I'll not conceal it, my hand shakes yet as with a wound! I pray you, sir, this argument let lawyers present to you.

241 **Danforth.** Mr. Hale, believe me; for a man of such terrible learning you are most bewildered—I hope you will forgive me. I have been thirty-two year at the bar, sir, and I should be confounded were I called upon to defend these people. Let you consider, now—(*to* Proctor *and the others*) And I bid you all do likewise. In an ordinary crime, how does one defend the accused? One calls up witnesses to prove his innocence. But witchcraft is *ipso facto*,[9] on its face and by its nature, an invisible crime, is it not? Therefore, who may possibly be witness to it? The witch and the victim. None other. Now we cannot hope the witch will accuse herself; granted? Therefore, we must rely upon her victims—and they do testify, the children certainly do testify. As for the witches, none will deny that we are most eager for all their confessions. Therefore, what is left for a lawyer to bring out? I think I have made my point. Have I not?

242 **Hale.** But this child claims the girls are not truthful, and if they are not—

243 **Danforth.** That is precisely what I am about to consider, sir. What more may you ask of me? Unless you doubt my probity?[10]

244 **Hale** (*defeated*). I surely do not, sir. Let you consider it, then.

245 **Danforth.** And let you put your heart to rest. Her deposition, Mr. Proctor.

ANALYZE DRAMATIC ELEMENTS

Annotate: Mark the stage directions in paragraphs 246–248.

Analyze: Explain how these stage directions move the plot forward by revealing the feelings and attitudes of the characters. Cite evidence from the text in your response.

246 (Proctor *hands it to him.* Hathorne *rises, goes beside* Danforth, *and starts reading.* Parris *comes to his other side.* Danforth *looks at* John Proctor, *then proceeds to read.* Hale *gets up, finds position near the judge, reads too.* Proctor *glances at* Giles. Francis *prays silently, hands pressed together.* Cheever *waits placidly, the sublime official, dutiful.* Mary Warren *sobs once.* John Proctor *touches her head reassuringly. Presently* Danforth *lifts his eyes, stands up, takes out a kerchief and blows his nose. The others stand aside as he moves in thought toward the window.*)

247 **Parris** (*hardly able to contain his anger and fear*). I should like to question—

---

9 ***ipso facto*** (Latin): by that very fact.
10 **doubt my probity:** question my integrity.

TO CHALLENGE STUDENTS . . .

Direct a Scene What difference does a director make? Ask students to reread paragraph 246. Tell them that although most of this section has no dialogue, it still requires the skill of a director. Have students work in small groups in which one student is the director and the other students are the actors. Have the director direct the scene, telling the actors where and when to position themselves. Also tell them to direct their actors' behavior—what to do and how to do it (quickly, slowly, loudly, softly, and so forth). Showcase the work of all groups and lead a class discussion on how the scenes differed based on the director's interpretation of the text.

248 **Danforth** (*his first real outburst, in which his contempt for* Parris *is clear*). Mr. Parris, I bid you be silent! (*He stands in silence, looking out the window. Now, having established that he will set the gait.*) Mr. Cheever, will you go into the court and bring the children here? (Cheever *gets up and goes out upstage.* Danforth *now turns to* Mary.) Mary Warren, how came you to this turnabout? Has Mr. Proctor threatened you for this deposition?

249 **Mary Warren.** No, sir.

250 **Danforth.** Has he ever threatened you?

251 **Mary Warren** (*weaker*). No, sir.

252 **Danforth** (*sensing a weakening*). Has he threatened you?

253 **Mary Warren.** No, sir.

254 **Danforth.** Then you tell me that you sat in my court, callously lying, when you knew that people would hang by your evidence? (*She does not answer.*) Answer me!

255 **Mary Warren** (*almost inaudibly*). I did, sir.

256 **Danforth.** How were you instructed in your life? Do you not know that God damns all liars? (*She cannot speak.*) Or is it now that you lie?

257 **Mary Warren.** No, sir—I am with God now.

258 **Danforth.** You are with God now.

259 **Mary Warren.** Aye, sir.

260 **Danforth** (*containing himself*). I will tell you this—you are either lying now, or you were lying in the court, and in either case you have committed perjury and you will go to jail for it. You cannot lightly say you lied, Mary. Do you know that?

261 **Mary Warren.** I cannot lie no more. I am with God, I am with God.

262 (*But she breaks into sobs at the thought of it, and the right door opens, and enter* Susanna Walcott, Mercy Lewis, Betty Parris, *and finally* Abigail. Cheever *comes to* Danforth.)

263 **Cheever.** Ruth Putnam's not in the court, sir, nor the other children.

264 **Danforth.** These will be sufficient. Sit you down, children. (*Silently they sit.*) Your friend, Mary Warren, has given us a deposition. In which she swears that she never saw familiar spirits, apparitions, nor any manifest of the Devil. She claims as well that none of you have seen these things either. (*slight pause*) Now, children, this is a court of law. The law, based upon the Bible, and the Bible, writ by Almighty God, forbid the practice of witchcraft, and describe death as the penalty thereof. But likewise, children, the law and Bible damn all bearers of false witness. (*slight pause*) Now then. It does not escape me that this deposition may be devised to blind us; it may well be that Mary Warren has been conquered by Satan, who sends her here to distract our sacred purpose. If so, her neck will break for it. But if she

ENGLISH LEARNER SUPPORT

Recognize Double Negatives Note that Spanish speaking students may not recognize the double negatives used in paragraphs 261, 277, and 280—"I can lie no more," "she never kept no," and "she never saw no poppets"—as being nonstandard English, because double negatives are used in Spanish. Write these double negatives on the board, and work with students to underline the two negatives in each. Model how to correct the double negative by replacing one with "any": *I cannot lie anymore.* Then, give students sentence frames to complete to correct the remaining two: *she never saw _____ poppets; she never kept _____ more.* **SUBSTANTIAL/MODERATE**

For **speaking support** for students at varying proficiency levels, see the **Text X-Ray** on page 600D.

ENGLISH LEARNER SUPPORT

Rephrase Archaic Language Read aloud paragraph 264 and point out that Danforth says, "but if she speak true . . ." Ask students how this phrase could be reworded in modern English. *(but if she speaks the truth)* Write the following archaisms from the text on the board: paragraph 267: "I have naught to change, sir"; paragraph 270: "A poppet were discovered . . .". Have students work with a partner to rewrite them in modern language. *(I have nothing to change, sir. A doll was discovered . . .)* **MODERATE/LIGHT**

speak true, I bid you now drop your guile and confess your pretense, for a quick confession will go easier with you. (*pause*) Abigail Williams, rise. (Abigail *slowly rises.*) Is there any truth in this?

265 **Abigail.** No, sir.

266 **Danforth** (*thinks, glances at Mary, then back to* Abigail). Children, a very auger bit[11] will now be turned into your souls until your honesty is proved. Will either of you change your positions now, or do you force me to hard questioning?

267 **Abigail.** I have naught to change, sir. She lies.

268 **Danforth** (*to Mary*). You would still go on with this?

269 **Mary Warren** (*faintly*). Aye, sir.

270 **Danforth** (*turning to Abigail*). A poppet were discovered in Mr. Proctor's house, stabbed by a needle. Mary Warren claims that you sat beside her in the court when she made it, and that you saw her make it and witnessed how she herself stuck her needle into it for safe-keeping. What say you to that?

271 **Abigail** (*with a slight note of indignation*). It is a lie, sir.

272 **Danforth** (*after a slight pause*). While you worked for Mr. Proctor, did you see poppets in that house?

273 **Abigail.** Goody Proctor always kept poppets.

274 **Proctor.** Your Honor, my wife never kept no poppets. Mary Warren confesses it was her poppet.

275 **Cheever.** Your Excellency.

276 **Danforth.** Mr. Cheever.

277 **Cheever.** When I spoke with Goody Proctor in that house, she said she never kept no poppets. But she said she did keep poppets when she were a girl.

278 **Proctor.** She has not been a girl these fifteen years, Your Honor.

279 **Hathorne.** But a poppet will keep fifteen years, will it not?

280 **Proctor.** It will keep if it is kept, but Mary Warren swears she never saw no poppets in my house, nor anyone else.

281 **Parris.** Why could there not have been poppets hid where no one ever saw them?

282 **Proctor** (*furious*). There might also be a dragon with five legs in my house, but no one has ever seen it.

283 **Parris.** We are here, Your Honor, precisely to discover what no one has ever seen.

284 **Proctor.** Mr. Danforth, what profit this girl to turn herself about? What may Mary Warren gain but hard questioning and worse?

---

[11] **auger** (ô´gər) **bit:** drill.

285 **Danforth.** You are charging Abigail Williams with a marvelous cool plot to murder, do you understand that?

286 **Proctor.** I do, sir. I believe she means to murder.

287 **Danforth** (*pointing at* Abigail, *incredulously*). This child would murder your wife?

288 **Proctor.** It is not a child. Now hear me, sir. In the sight of the congregation she were twice this year put out of this meetin' house for laughter during prayer.

289 **Danforth** (*shocked, turning to* Abigail). What's this? Laughter during—!

290 **Parris.** Excellency, she were under Tituba's power at that time, but she is solemn now.

291 **Giles.** Aye, now she is solemn and goes to hang people!

292 **Danforth.** Quiet, man.

293 **Hathorne.** Surely it have no bearing on the question, sir. He charges contemplation of murder.

294 **Danforth.** Aye. (*He studies* Abigail *for a moment, then.*) Continue, Mr. Proctor.

295 **Proctor.** Mary. Now tell the Governor how you danced in the woods.

296 **Parris** (*instantly*). Excellency, since I come to Salem this man is blackening my name. He—

297 **Danforth.** In a moment, sir. (*to* Mary Warren, *sternly, and surprised*) What is this dancing?

298 **Mary Warren.** I—(*She glances at* Abigail, *who is staring down at her remorselessly. Then, appealing to* Proctor.) Mr. Proctor—

299 **Proctor** (*taking it right up*). Abigail leads the girls to the woods, Your Honor, and they have danced there naked—

300 **Parris.** Your Honor, this—

301 **Proctor** (*at once*). Mr. Parris discovered them himself in the dead of night! There's the "child" she is!

302 **Danforth** (*It is growing into a nightmare, and he turns, astonished, to* Parris). Mr. Parris—

303 **Parris.** I can only say, sir, that I never found any of them naked, and this man is—

304 **Danforth.** But you discovered them dancing in the woods? (*Eyes on* Parris, *he points at* Abigail.) Abigail?

305 **Hale.** Excellency, when I first arrived from Beverly, Mr. Parris told me that.

306 **Danforth.** Do you deny it, Mr. Parris?

307 **Parris.** I do not, sir, but I never saw any of them naked.

LANGUAGE CONVENTIONS

Annotate: Mark words in the dialogue in paragraphs 295–310 that relate to a central problem of the play—whether there was witchcraft done in the forest.

Interpret: How does this dialogue illustrate a complication in the plot?

LANGUAGE CONVENTIONS

Have students summarize what they recall about what happened in the woods and the aspects of what was done that would be associated with witchcraft. Point out that Parris may not want to admit he saw the girls naked to save face in front of the others. (**Answer:** *The central problem of the play is whether or not there was witchcraft present in the woods on the night in question. This section of the scene is full of a lot of "he said/she said" dialogue, which impacts the believability of all the characters—and therefore the truth of what actually happened. For example, Proctor says Parris discovered the girls dancing naked; Parris says he discovered them dancing, but not naked. So both men are speaking some truth, but neither is entirely believable.*)

© Houghton Mifflin Harcourt Publishing Company

ENGLISH LEARNER SUPPORT

Understand and Use Adverbial Phrases Tell students that adverbial phrases are groups of words that function as adverbs and often tell how something is done. Have students underline the adverbial phrase in paragraph 312 that answers the question, "How does Danforth speak?" *(with great worry)*

Have students work in pairs to find an adverbial phrase in paragraph 315 and say what "how" question it answers. *(with a gleam of victory; How does Hathorne speak?)* Then, ask pairs to write questions and answers about how characters speak based on these adverbial phrases. *(How does Hathorne speak? Hawthorne speaks with a gleam of victory in his eyes.)*

MODERATE/LIGHT

ANALYZE DRAMATIC ELEMENTS

Point out to students that this courtroom exchange adds intensity to the plot. (**Answer:** *The method of creating suspense is effective because the reader knows that Mary is an unstable character and may not be confident enough to stand by her confession.*)

308 **Danforth.** But she have *danced*?

309 **Parris** (*unwillingly*). Aye, sir.

310 (Danforth, *as though with new eyes, looks at* Abigail.)

311 **Hathorne.** Excellency, will you permit me? (*He points at* Mary Warren.)

312 **Danforth** (*with great worry*). Pray, proceed.

313 **Hathorne.** You say you never saw no spirits, Mary, were never threatened or afflicted by any manifest of the Devil or the Devil's agents.

314 **Mary Warren** (*very faintly*). No, sir.

315 **Hathorne** (*with a gleam of victory*). And yet, when people accused of witchery confronted you in court, you would faint, saying their spirits came out of their bodies and choked you—

316 **Mary Warren.** That were pretense, sir.

317 **Danforth.** I cannot hear you.

318 **Mary Warren.** Pretense, sir.

319 **Parris.** But you did turn cold, did you not? I myself picked you up many times, and your skin were icy. Mr. Danforth, you—

320 **Danforth.** I saw that many times.

321 **Proctor.** She only pretended to faint, Your Excellency. They're all marvelous pretenders.

322 **Hathorne.** Then can she pretend to faint now?

323 **Proctor.** Now?

324 **Parris.** Why not? Now there are no spirits attacking her, for none in this room is accused of witchcraft. So let her turn herself cold now, let her pretend she is attacked now, let her faint. (*He turns to* Mary Warren.) Faint!

325 **Mary Warren.** Faint?

326 **Parris.** Aye, faint. Prove to us how you pretended in the court so many times.

327 **Mary Warren** (*looking to* Proctor). I—cannot faint now, sir.

328 **Proctor** (*alarmed, quietly*). Can you not pretend it?

329 **Mary Warren.** I—(*She looks about as though searching for the passion to faint.*) I—have no *sense* of it now, I—

330 **Danforth.** Why? What is lacking now?

331 **Mary Warren.** I—cannot tell, sir, I—

332 **Danforth.** Might it be that here we have no afflicting spirit loose, but in the court there were some?

333 **Mary Warren.** I never saw no spirits.

ANALYZE DRAMATIC ELEMENTS

Annotate: Mark what is asked of Mary Warren and how she responds to the request.

Analyze: Consider what you have learned about Mary Warren up to this point. Why is placing great importance upon her testimony an effective way of creating suspense?

334 **Parris.** Then see no spirits now, and prove to us that you can faint by your own will, as you claim.

335 **Mary Warren** (*stares, searching for the emotion of it, and then shakes her head*). I—cannot do it.

336 **Parris.** Then you will confess, will you not? It were attacking spirits made you faint!

337 **Mary Warren.** No, sir, I—

338 **Parris.** Your Excellency, this is a trick to blind the court!

339 **Mary Warren.** It's not a trick! (*She stands.*) I—I used to faint because I—I thought I saw spirits.

340 **Danforth.** *Thought* you saw them!

341 **Mary Warren.** But I did not, Your Honor.

342 **Hathorne.** How could you think you saw them unless you saw them?

343 **Mary Warren.** I—I cannot tell how, but I did. I—I heard the other girls screaming, and you, Your Honor, you seemed to believe them, and I—It were only sport in the beginning, sir, but then the whole world cried spirits, spirits, and I—I promise you, Mr. Danforth, I only thought I saw them but I did not.

ENGLISH LEARNER SUPPORT

Understand Multiple-Meaning Words Have students circle the word *base* in paragraph 347. Explain that *base* is a multiple-meaning word, and a less-familiar meaning is being used here. Ask students to work with partners to list as many meanings of the word *base* as they can think of. *("the part on which something rests," noun; "to set a place as the main place where a business operates," verb)* Point out that after Abigail says they are asking her base questions, she says they "mistrusted" her and then she threatens them. Ask: Are they asking her questions she thinks are good questions, or bad questions? *(bad)* Have students use this context to tell the meaning of the word as used in these lines *("not good," or "of low quality")*. Have them consult a dictionary to check their work. **MODERATE**

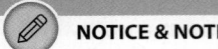

344 (Danforth *peers at her.*)

345 **Parris** (*smiling, but nervous because* Danforth *seems to be struck by* Mary Warren's *story*). Surely Your Excellency is not taken by this simple lie.

346 **Danforth** (*turning worriedly to* Abigail). Abigail. I bid you now search your heart and tell me this—and beware of it, child, to God every soul is precious and His vengeance is terrible on them that take life without cause. Is it possible, child, that the spirits you have seen are illusion only, some deception that may cross your mind when—

347 **Abigail.** Why, this—this—is a base question, sir.

348 **Danforth.** Child, I would have you consider it—

349 **Abigail.** I have been hurt, Mr. Danforth; I have seen my blood runnin' out! I have been near to murdered every day because I done my duty pointing out the Devil's people—and this is my reward? To be mistrusted, denied, questioned like a—

350 **Danforth** (*weakening*). Child, I do not mistrust you—

351 **Abigail** (*in an open threat*). Let *you* beware, Mr. Danforth. Think you to be so mighty that the power of Hell may not turn *your* wits? Beware of it! There is—(*Suddenly, from an accusatory attitude, her face turns, looking into the air above—it is truly frightened.*)

352 **Danforth** (*apprehensively*). What is it, child?

353 **Abigail** (*looking about in the air, clasping her arms about her as though cold*). I—I know not. A wind, a cold wind, has come. (*Her eyes fall on* Mary Warren.)

354 **Mary Warren** (*terrified, pleading*). Abby!

355 **Mercy Lewis** (*shivering*). Your Honor, I freeze!

356 **Proctor.** They're pretending!

357 **Hathorne** (*touching* Abigail's *hand*). She is cold, Your Honor, touch her!

358 **Mercy Lewis** (*through chattering teeth*). Mary, do you send this shadow on me?

359 **Mary Warren.** Lord, save me!

360 **Susanna Walcott.** I freeze, I freeze!

361 **Abigail** (*shivering visibly*). It is a wind, a wind!

362 **Mary Warren.** Abby, don't do that!

363 **Danforth** (*himself engaged and entered by* Abigail). Mary Warren, do you witch her? I say to you, do you send your spirit out?

364 (*With a hysterical cry* Mary Warren *starts to run.* Proctor *catches her.*)

365 **Mary Warren** (*almost collapsing*). Let me go, Mr. Proctor, I cannot, I cannot—

TO CHALLENGE STUDENTS . . .

Analyze Motivation Point out that Abigail dramatically shifts attention away from herself in paragraph 351. Have students discuss these questions:

- What techniques does Abigail use to redirect the attention of the court?
- Why does she deflect interest in herself?

Have students write a brief paragraph analyzing Abigail's motives and share their responses with the class.

366 **Abigail** (*crying to Heaven*). Oh, Heavenly Father, take away this shadow!

367 (*Without warning or hesitation,* Proctor *leaps at* Abigail *and, grabbing her by the hair, pulls her to her feet. She screams in pain.* Danforth, *astonished, cries,* "What are you about?" *and* Hathorne *and* Parris *call,* "Take your hands off her!" *and out of it all comes* Proctor's *roaring voice.*)

368 **Proctor.** How do you call Heaven! Whore! Whore!

369 (Herrick *breaks* Proctor *from her.*)

370 **Herrick.** John!

371 **Danforth.** Man! Man, what do you—

372 **Proctor** (*breathless and in agony*). It is a whore!

373 **Danforth** (*dumbfounded*). You charge—?

374 **Abigail.** Mr. Danforth, he is lying!

375 **Proctor.** Mark her! Now she'll suck a scream to stab me with, but—

376 **Danforth.** You will prove this! This will not pass!

377 **Proctor** (*trembling, his life collapsing about him*). I have known her, sir. I have known her.

378 **Danforth.** You—you are a lecher?

379 **Francis** (*horrified*). John, you cannot say such a—

380 **Proctor.** Oh, Francis, I wish you had some evil in you that you might know me! (*to* Danforth) A man will not cast away his good name. You surely know that.

381 **Danforth** (*dumbfounded*). In—in what time? In what place?

382 **Proctor** (*his voice about to break, and his shame great*). In the proper place—where my beasts are bedded. On the last night of my joy, some eight months past. She used to serve me in my house, sir. (*He has to clamp his jaw to keep from weeping.*) A man may think God sleeps, but God sees everything, I know it now. I beg you, sir, I beg you— see her what she is. My wife, my dear good wife, took this girl soon after, sir, and put her out on the highroad. And being what she is, a lump of vanity, sir—(*He is being overcome.*) Excellency, forgive me, forgive me. (*Angrily against himself, he turns away from the* Governor *for a moment. Then, as though to cry out is his only means of speech left.*) She thinks to dance with me on my wife's grave! And well she might, for I thought of her softly. God help me, I lusted, and there *is* a promise in such sweat. But it is a whore's vengeance, and you must see it; I set myself entirely in your hands. I know you must see it now.

383 **Danforth** (*blanched, in horror, turning to* Abigail). You deny every scrap and tittle[12] of this?

---

[12] **every scrap and tittle:** every tiny bit.

ANALYZE DRAMATIC ELEMENTS

Annotate: Mark the climax of the play.

Predict: How might Proctor's confession change the outcome of the plot?

ANALYZE DRAMATIC ELEMENTS

Remind students that the **climax** of a play is the point of highest tension and excitement. The climax is a turning point in the play—the moment when the ultimate resolution of the play's central conflict is set in motion. (**Answer:** *Proctor's confession might lead the judges to believe that Abigail accused Elizabeth Proctor of witchcraft only because she was out for revenge, and that Abigail has been lying all along.*)

■ English Learner Support

Understand Multiple-Meaning Words Draw students' attention to Proctor's statement "I have known her" in paragraph 377. Remind students that *known* is a form of the verb *know*, and explain that *know* is a multiple-meaning word. Have students look up the word *know*, write three definitions, and decide which one is being used here. Then, ask how the definition of *know* helps students recognize this line as the climax of the play. **MODERATE/LIGHT**

IMPROVE READING FLUENCY

Targeted Passage Tell students that one way to improve reading fluency is to learn to read with more expression. Pages 682–683 of the play have many stage directions that tell the actor to perform the dialogue with a variety of expressions and emotions. Ask students to work in small groups of five or six and take turns reading the roles, paying close attention to the stage directions. Have the rest of the class watch and listen to each group perform. As each group finishes, have the class discuss each group's interpretation.

 Go to the **Reading Studio** for additional support in developing fluency.

ENGLISH LEARNER SUPPORT

Understand Figurative Language Remind students that a metaphor is a figure of speech that compares two things without using comparison words such as *like* or *as*. Have students reread paragraph 390 and ask students if they think Danforth is talking about a literal swamp when he says, "Now we shall touch the bottom of this swamp." *(no)* Ask: What is the swamp he is referring to? *(the entire matter or conflict)* What does this metaphor compare? *(the entire matter and a swamp)* What does this comparison suggest? *(It suggests the entire matter is murky and unpleasant.)*

LIGHT

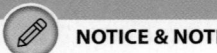

384 **Abigail.** If I must answer that, I will leave and I will not come back again!

385 (Danforth *seems unsteady.*)

386 **Proctor.** I have made a bell of my honor! I have rung the doom of my good name—you will believe me, Mr. Danforth! My wife is innocent, except she knew a whore when she saw one!

387 **Abigail** (*stepping up to* Danforth). What look do you give me? (Danforth *cannot speak.*) I'll not have such looks! (*She turns and starts for the door.*)

388 **Danforth.** You will remain where you are! (Herrick *steps into her path. She comes up short, fire in her eyes.*) Mr. Parris, go into the court and bring Goodwife Proctor out.

389 **Parris** (*objecting*). Your Honor, this is all a—

390 **Danforth** (*sharply to* Parris). Bring her out! And tell her not one word of what's been spoken here. And let you knock before you enter. (Parris *goes out.*) Now we shall touch the bottom of this swamp. (*to* Proctor) Your wife, you say, is an honest woman.

391 **Proctor.** In her life, sir, she have never lied. There are them that cannot sing, and them that cannot weep—my wife cannot lie. I have paid much to learn it, sir.

392 **Danforth.** And when she put this girl out of your house, she put her out for a harlot?[13]

393 **Proctor.** Aye, sir.

394 **Danforth.** And knew her for a harlot?

395 **Proctor.** Aye, sir, she knew her for a harlot.

396 **Danforth.** Good then. (*to* Abigail) And if she tell me, child, it were for harlotry, may God spread His mercy on you! (*There is a knock. He calls to the door.*) Hold! (*to* Abigail) Turn your back. Turn your back. (*to* Proctor) Do likewise. (*Both turn their backs—*Abigail *with indignant slowness.*) Now let neither of you turn to face Goody Proctor. No one in this room is to speak one word, or raise a gesture aye or nay. (*He turns toward the door, calls.*) Enter! (*The door opens.* Elizabeth *enters with* Parris. Parris *leaves her. She stands alone, her eyes looking for* Proctor.) Mr. Cheever, report this testimony in all exactness. Are you ready?

397 **Cheever.** Ready, sir.

398 **Danforth.** Come here, woman. (Elizabeth *comes to him, glancing at* Proctor's *back.*) Look at me only, not at your husband. In my eyes only.

399 **Elizabeth** (*faintly*). Good, sir.

---

[13] **for a harlot:** as a woman of low morals.

400 **Danforth.** We are given to understand that at one time you dismissed your servant, Abigail Williams.

401 **Elizabeth.** That is true, sir.

402 **Danforth.** For what cause did you dismiss her? (*Slight pause. Then* Elizabeth *tries to glance at* Proctor.) You will look in my eyes only and not at your husband. The answer is in your memory and you need no help to give it to me. Why did you dismiss Abigail Williams?

403 **Elizabeth** (*not knowing what to say, sensing a situation, wetting her lips to stall for time*). She—dissatisfied me. (*pause*) And my husband.

404 **Danforth.** In what way dissatisfied you?

405 **Elizabeth.** She were—(*She glances at* Proctor *for a cue.*)

406 **Danforth.** Woman, look at me! (Elizabeth *does.*) Were she slovenly? Lazy? What disturbance did she cause?

407 **Elizabeth.** Your Honor, I—in that time I were sick. And I—My husband is a good and righteous man. He is never drunk as some are, nor wastin' his time at the shovelboard, but always at his work. But in my sickness—you see, sir, I were a long time sick after my last baby, and I thought I saw my husband somewhat turning from me. And this girl—(*She turns to* Abigail.)

408 **Danforth.** Look at me.

409 **Elizabeth.** Aye, sir. Abigail Williams—(*She breaks off.*)

410 **Danforth.** What of Abigail Williams?

411 **Elizabeth.** I came to think he fancied her. And so one night I lost my wits, I think, and put her out on the highroad.

412 **Danforth.** Your husband—did he indeed turn from you?

413 **Elizabeth** (*in agony*). My husband—is a goodly man, sir.

414 **Danforth.** Then he did not turn from you.

415 **Elizabeth** (*starting to glance at* Proctor). He—

416 **Danforth** (*reaches out and holds her face, then*). Look at me! To your own knowledge, has John Proctor ever committed the crime of lechery? (*In a crisis of indecision she cannot speak.*) Answer my question! Is your husband a lecher!

417 **Elizabeth** (*faintly*). No, sir.

418 **Danforth.** Remove her, Marshal.

419 **Proctor.** Elizabeth, tell the truth!

420 **Danforth.** She has spoken. Remove her!

421 **Proctor** (*crying out*). Elizabeth, I have confessed it!

422 **Elizabeth.** Oh, God! (*The door closes behind her.*)

423 **Proctor.** She only thought to save my name!

ANALYZE DRAMATIC ELEMENTS

Annotate: Mark dialogue during Elizabeth's interrogation that tells you she is trying to protect Proctor.

Analyze: Explain how the interrogation of Elizabeth presents a plot complication.

 ANALYZE DRAMATIC ELEMENTS

Remind students that **complications** are events in the play that cause the central conflict to become more difficult to resolve. Remind them that Proctor's attempt to keep his affair secret was a past plot complication, which Elizabeth does not know is now resolved. (**Answer:** *Elizabeth is trying to protect Proctor by not revealing he has been unfaithful to her. She does not know, however, that Proctor has already confessed to adultery and that if she had verified that fact, it actually would have helped both of them. This complicates the central conflict of whether or not the accused women will be convicted of witchcraft.*)

■ **English Learner Support**

Understand Language Conventions Briefly review the uses of em dashes you listed previously. Have students apply their previous learning about em dashes to paragraphs 407–415. Working with partners, have students circle the em dashes and identify the use of each one. Then, ask students to infer why Elizabeth's dialogue includes so many em dashes. (*The em dashes show Elizabeth is hesitating a lot because she is scared, exhausted, or worried about incriminating Proctor.*) **LIGHT**

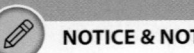

NOTICE & NOTE

424 **Hale.** Excellency, it is a natural lie to tell; I beg you, stop now before another is condemned! I may shut my conscience to it no more—private vengeance is working through this testimony! From the beginning this man has struck me true. By my oath to Heaven, I believe him now, and I pray you call back his wife before we—

425 **Danforth.** She spoke nothing of lechery, and this man has lied!

426 **Hale.** I believe him! (*pointing at* Abigail) This girl has always struck me false! She has—

427 (Abigail, *with a weird, wild, chilling cry, screams up to the ceiling.*)

428 **Abigail.** You will not! Begone! Begone, I say!

429 **Danforth.** What is it, child? (*But* Abigail, *pointing with fear, is now raising up her frightened eyes, her awed face, toward the ceiling—the girls are doing the same—and now* Hathorne, Hale, Putnam, Cheever, Herrick, *and* Danforth *do the same.*) What's there? (*He lowers his eyes from the ceiling, and now he is frightened; there is real tension in his voice.*) Child! (*She is transfixed—with all the girls, she is whimpering open-mouthed, agape at the ceiling.*) Girls! Why do you—?

430 **Mercy Lewis** (*pointing*). It's on the beam! Behind the rafter!

431 **Danforth** (*looking up*). Where!

432 **Abigail.** Why—? (*She gulps.*) Why do you come, yellow bird?

433 **Proctor.** Where's a bird? I see no bird!

434 **Abigail** (*to the ceiling*). My face? My face?

435 **Proctor.** Mr. Hale—

436 **Danforth.** Be quiet!

437 **Proctor** (*to* Hale). Do you see a bird?

438 **Danforth.** Be quiet!!

439 **Abigail** (*to the ceiling, in a genuine conversation with the "bird," as though trying to talk it out of attacking her*). But God made my face; you cannot want to tear my face. Envy is a deadly sin, Mary.

440 **Mary Warren** (*on her feet with a spring, and horrified, pleading*). Abby!

441 **Abigail** (*unperturbed, continuing to the "bird"*). Oh, Mary, this is a black art[14] to change your shape. No, I cannot, I cannot stop my mouth; it's God's work I do.

442 **Mary Warren.** Abby, I'm *here*!

443 **Proctor** (*frantically*). They're pretending, Mr. Danforth!

444 **Abigail** (*Now she takes a backward step, as though in fear the bird will swoop down momentarily*). Oh, please, Mary! Don't come down.

445 **Susanna Walcott.** Her claws, she's stretching her claws!

---

[14] **a black art:** sorcery.

© Houghton Mifflin Harcourt Publishing Company

WHEN STUDENTS STRUGGLE . . .

Understand Plot Structure Point out the transition that occurs immediately after Hale expresses his support of Proctor and his suspicions of Abigail: Abigail screams, "You will not! Be gone! Be gone, I say!" (paragraph 428). Explain that this outburst shifts attention away from the issue of Abigail's honesty. Help students use a storyboard to trace the changing action in the scene.

 For additional support, go to the **Reading Studio** and assign the following [LEVEL UP] **Level Up Tutorial: Plot: Sequence of Events.**

446 **Proctor.** Lies, lies.

447 **Abigail** (*backing further, eyes still fixed above*). Mary, please don't hurt me!

448 **Mary Warren** (*to* Danforth). I'm not hurting her!

449 **Danforth** (*to* Mary Warren). Why does she see this vision?

450 **Mary Warren.** She sees nothin'!

451 **Abigail** (*now staring full front as though hypnotized, and mimicking the exact tone of* Mary Warren's *cry*). She sees nothin'!

452 **Mary Warren** (*pleading*). Abby, you mustn't!

453 **Abigail and All the Girls** (*all transfixed*). Abby, you mustn't!

454 **Mary Warren** (*to all the* Girls). I'm here, I'm here!

455 **Girls.** I'm here, I'm here!

ANALYZE CHARACTERS AND MOTIVATIONS

Annotate: Mark examples of repetition in paragraphs 450–471.

Analyze: Why do the other girls mimic Mary's dialogue?

The Crucible: Act Three   687

✏ ANALYZE CHARACTERS AND MOTIVATIONS

Remind students to consider characters' motivations as they read **dialogue.** Ask students to infer what motivates Abigail to pretend to see the yellow bird. (*After Elizabeth does not verify that Proctor and Abigail had an affair, the judges think Abigail must be possessed. Abigail claims Mary is attacking her in the form of a yellow bird to get the judges to believe in the presence of witchcraft.*) What is the relationship of the other girls to Abigail? (*She is a leader; they are followers.*) (**Answer:** *The other girls mimic Mary's dialogue because they are going along with Abigail's plan to pretend Mary created a yellow bird that is attacking them; mimicking Mary makes it appear Mary is controlling them supernaturally. The escalating repetition creates a sense of hysteria, as if the trial is spiraling out of control.*)

NOTICE & NOTE

456 **Danforth** (*horrified*). Mary Warren! Draw back your spirit out of them!

457 **Mary Warren.** Mr. Danforth!

458 **Girls** (*cutting her off*). Mr. Danforth!

459 **Danforth.** Have you compacted with the Devil? Have you?

460 **Mary Warren.** Never, never!

461 **Girls.** Never, never!

462 **Danforth** (*growing hysterical*). Why can they only repeat you?

463 **Proctor.** Give me a whip—I'll stop it!

464 **Mary Warren.** They're sporting.[15] They—!

465 **Girls.** They're sporting!

466 **Mary Warren** (*turning on them all hysterically and stamping her feet*). Abby, stop it!

467 **Girls** (*stamping their feet*). Abby, stop it!

468 **Mary Warren.** Stop it!

469 **Girls.** Stop it!

470 **Mary Warren** (*screaming it out at the top of her lungs, and raising her fists*). Stop it!!

471 **Girls** (*raising their fists*). Stop it!!

472 (Mary Warren, *utterly confounded, and becoming overwhelmed by Abigail's—and the girls'—utter conviction, starts to whimper, hands half raised, powerless, and all the girls begin whimpering exactly as she does.*)

473 **Danforth.** A little while ago you were afflicted. Now it seems you afflict others; where did you find this power?

474 **Mary Warren** (*staring at* Abigail). I—have no power.

475 **Girls.** I have no power.

476 **Proctor.** They're gulling you,[16] Mister!

477 **Danforth.** Why did you turn about this past two weeks? You have seen the Devil, have you not?

478 **Hale** (*indicating* Abigail *and the girls*). You cannot believe them!

479 **Mary Warren.** I—

480 **Proctor** (*sensing her weakening*). Mary, God damns all liars!

481 **Danforth** (*pounding it into her*). You have seen the Devil, you have made compact with Lucifer, have you not?

482 **Proctor.** God damns liars, Mary!

---

[15] **sporting:** playing a game.
[16] **gulling you:** deceiving you.

© Houghton Mifflin Harcourt Publishing Company

WHEN STUDENTS STRUGGLE . . .

Analyze Characters   Have students reread paragraphs 473–478. Point out that this passage reveals who holds the most power in this court. Have students answer the following questions:

- What does Danforth ask Mary Warren about power? How does Mary respond? Why?
- What do Proctor and Hale tell Danforth?
- Is Hale still a friend of the court? How can you tell?

 For additional support, go to the **Reading Studio** and assign the following LEVEL UP **Level Up Tutorial: Characters and Conflict.**

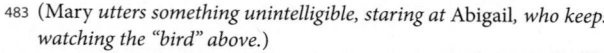
483 (Mary *utters something unintelligible, staring at* Abigail, *who keeps watching the "bird" above.*)

484 **Danforth.** I cannot hear you. What do you say? (Mary *utters again unintelligibly.*) You will confess yourself or you will hang! (*He turns her roughly to face him.*) Do you know who I am? I say you will hang if you do not open with me!

485 **Proctor.** Mary, remember the angel Raphael—do that which is good and—

486 **Abigail** (*pointing upward*). The wings! Her wings are spreading! Mary, please, don't, don't—!

487 **Hale.** I see nothing, Your Honor!

488 **Danforth.** Do you confess this power! (*He is an inch from her face.*) Speak!

489 **Abigail.** She's going to come down! She's walking the beam!

490 **Danforth.** Will you speak!

491 **Mary Warren** (*staring in horror*). I cannot!

492 **Girls.** I cannot!

493 **Parris.** Cast the Devil out! Look him in the face! Trample him! We'll save you, Mary, only stand fast against him and—

494 **Abigail** (*looking up*). Look out! She's coming down!

495 (*She and all the girls run to one wall, shielding their eyes. And now, as though cornered, they let out a gigantic scream, and Mary, as though infected, opens her mouth and screams with them. Gradually Abigail and the girls leave off, until only Mary is left there, staring up at the "bird," screaming madly. All watch her, horrified by this evident fit.* Proctor *strides to her.*)

496 **Proctor.** Mary, tell the Governor what they—(*He has hardly got a word out, when, seeing him coming for her, she rushes out of his reach, screaming in horror.*)

497 **Mary Warren.** Don't touch me—don't touch me! (*At which the girls halt at the door.*)

498 **Proctor** (*astonished*). Mary!

499 **Mary Warren** (*pointing at* Proctor). You're the Devil's man! (*He is stopped in his tracks.*)

500 **Parris.** Praise God!

501 **Girls.** Praise God!

502 **Proctor** (*numbed*). Mary, how—?

503 **Mary Warren.** I'll not hang with you! I love God, I love God.

The Crucible: Act Three   689

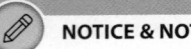 **NOTICE & NOTE**

504 **Danforth** (*to* Mary). He bid you do the Devil's work?

505 **Mary Warren** (*hysterically, indicating* Proctor). He come at me by night and every day to sign, to sign, to—

506 **Danforth.** Sign what?

507 **Parris.** The Devil's book? He come with a book?

508 **Mary Warren** (*hysterically, pointing at* Proctor, *fearful of him*). My name, he want my name. "I'll murder you," he says, "if my wife hangs! We must go and overthrow the court," he says!

509 (Danforth's *head jerks toward* Proctor, *shock and horror in his face.*)

TO CHALLENGE STUDENTS . . .

Research and Contrast Productions Have students work in small groups to locate images from at least one film and one stage production of *The Crucible*. Ask students to compare those representations to the text itself. Challenge students to contrast the strengths and weaknesses in the presentation of setting and characters in all three versions—print, stage, and film.

510 **Proctor** (*turning, appealing to* Hale). Mr. Hale!

511 **Mary Warren** (*her sobs beginning*). He wake me every night, his eyes were like coals and his fingers claw my neck, and I sign, I sign . . .

512 **Hale.** Excellency, this child's gone wild!

513 **Proctor** (*as Danforth's wide eyes pour on him*). Mary, Mary!

514 **Mary Warren** (*screaming at him*). No, I love God; I go your way no more. I love God, I bless God. (*Sobbing, she rushes to* Abigail.) Abby, Abby, I'll never hurt you more! (*They all watch, as* Abigail, <u>*out of her infinite charity, reaches out and draws the sobbing* Mary *to her, and then looks up to* Danforth.</u>)

CONTRASTS AND CONTRADICTIONS

Notice & Note: Mark a surprising detail in paragraph 514 about Abigail's response to Mary Warren's screaming.

Analyze: Explain whether this detail is intended to convey a genuine change in Abigail's behavior.

TEACH

CONTRASTS AND CONTRADICTIONS

Tell students to look for the occasional bit of **verbal irony** in Miller's **stage directions.** Verbal irony is when one uses words that mean the opposite of what one really wants to say. (**Answer:** *Abigail has not demonstrated any charitable or kind characteristics up to this point. Further, Abigail's reason for pulling Mary toward her is because Abigail wants Mary on her side—Abigail needs all the girls who were in the forest to agree that spirits were present. Abigail is not comforting Mary out of charity; it is completely out of self-interest.*)

ENGLISH LEARNER SUPPORT

Understand Multiple-Meaning Words Have students read Proctor's dialogue in paragraph 520 and circle the word *quail*. Ask students to tell the meaning of *quail* with which they are most familiar. *("a small, wild bird")* Ask partners to discuss what Proctor means by "to bring men out of ignorance." *(to tell them the truth)* Then, have partners attempt to determine the meaning of *quail* used here. *("to feel or show fear")*

MODERATE

515 **Danforth** (*to* Proctor). What are you? (Proctor *is beyond speech in his anger.*) You are combined with anti-Christ,[17] are you not? I have seen your power; you will not deny it! What say you, Mister?

516 **Hale.** Excellency—

517 **Danforth.** I will have nothing from you, Mr. Hale! (*to* Proctor) Will you confess yourself befouled with Hell, or do you keep that black allegiance yet? What say you?

518 **Proctor** (*his mind wild, breathless*). I say—I say—God is dead!

519 **Parris.** Hear it, hear it!

520 **Proctor** (*laughs insanely, then*). A fire, a fire is burning! I hear the boot of Lucifer, I see his filthy face! And it is my face, and yours, Danforth! For them that quail to bring men out of ignorance, as I

---

[17] **anti-Christ:** in the New Testament Christ's great enemy, expected to spread evil before Christ conquers him and the world ends (1 John 2:18).

WHEN STUDENTS STRUGGLE . . .

Summarize Plot Make sure students understand how Proctor's attempt to help his wife backfires. Ask them to summarize the events in the courtroom. *(Proctor brings Mary to the court to say she lied. The judge will not believe her unless she can cause herself to faint. Mary cannot. Abigail pretends to be attacked by a spirit. Proctor accuses her of having low morals and confesses his affair with her. Abigail continues pretending to be attacked. Mary, terrified, turns on Proctor.)*

For additional support, go to the **Reading Studio** and assign the following ▣ **Level Up Tutorial: Summarizing.**

have quailed, and as you quail now when you know in all your black hearts that this be fraud—God damns our kind especially, and we will burn, we will burn together!

521 **Danforth.** Marshal! Take him and Corey with him to the jail!

522 **Hale** (*starting across to the door*). I denounce these proceedings!

523 **Proctor.** You are pulling Heaven down and raising up a whore!

524 **Hale.** I denounce these proceedings, I quit this court! (*He slams the door to the outside behind him.*)

525 **Danforth** (*calling to him in a fury*). Mr. Hale! Mr. Hale!

526 (*The curtain falls.*)

CHECK YOUR UNDERSTANDING

Answer these questions before moving on to the **Analyze the Text** section on the following page.

1 What is the setting for this act of the play?

  A A jail

  B A schoolhouse

  C A room in Proctor's home

  D A room in the meeting house

2 What proof does the judge require to show Mary is telling the truth?

  F Mary must faint convincingly.

  G Mary must produce an eyewitness.

  H Mary must give testimony against Abigail.

  J Mary must admit that she herself is a witch.

3 Why does Proctor confess to adultery?

  A To protect himself

  B To protect his wife

  C To protect Abigail

  D To protect his reputation

 CHECK YOUR UNDERSTANDING

Have students answer the questions independently.

Answers:

1. D

2. F

3. B

If they answer any questions incorrectly, have them reread the text to confirm their understanding. Then they may proceed to ANALYZE THE TEXT on page 694.

 ENGLISH LEARNER SUPPORT

Oral Assessment Use the following questions to assess students' comprehension and speaking skills.

1. Where does this part of the play happen? (*a room in the meeting house*)

2. What does the judge say Mary must do to prove she is telling the truth? (*faint*)

3. Why does Proctor confess to his affair with Abigail? (*to protect his wife*)
SUBSTANTIAL/MODERATE

APPLY

ANALYZE THE TEXT

Possible answers:

1. **DOK 4:** *Mary is consistently described in this act as frail, frightened, and weeping, in contrast to Abigail, who stands firm in her deceit. The more Mary seems to lack backbone and waver in her testimony, the stronger Abigail's position appears to be.*

2. **DOK 4:** *When Danforth barely lets Giles make a statement, he reveals himself to be stubborn and unsympathetic. Danforth will be a hard person to sway.*

3. **DOK 4:** *Elizabeth lies about Proctor's adultery because she is trying to save his reputation—she thinks it will harm him to tell the truth that he was unfaithful to her. She is motivated by her love for and loyalty to her husband.*

4. **DOK 2:** *The fact that Proctor has plowed on Sunday is significant because the Puritans believed no work should be done on the Sabbath. The court is trying to determine whether or not Proctor is a religious man whose word can be believed.*

5. **DOK 3:** *In this act, Proctor is much more emotionally involved in trying to challenge and take down the witch hunt. In the beginning of the play, he was more absorbed in resolving the problems in his marriage, and felt the absurdity of the witch hunt would come to light on its own. By the end of Act Three, he is a confessed lecher and a victim of the witch hunt himself. His actions in confessing reveal that he is an honorable and courageous person.*

CREATE AND DISCUSS

Write an Analysis Encourage small groups of students to reread Act Three and consider how the relationship between Proctor and Abigail affects the plot. How might the play have been different if Miller had not included their relationship?

Have a Group Discussion Have students work independently to research historical inaccuracies in the play and to draw conclusions about why Miller may have chosen to change certain details. As students discuss ideas in small groups, remind them to support their opinions with evidence from the play and from their research.

 **RESPOND**

ANALYZE THE TEXT

Support your responses with evidence from the text.   NOTEBOOK

1. **Analyze** Mary Warren might be seen as the foil for Abigail. Explain how she is used to emphasize some of Abigail's traits.

2. **Analyze** What does Danforth's reaction to Giles's outburst at the beginning of the act suggest about his character?

3. **Analyze** Elizabeth faces a moral dilemma regarding her husband's relationship with Abigail. What motivates her decision to lie to Danforth?

4. **Interpret** Why does the court debate whether Proctor plows on Sunday? What is the significance of this debate?

5. **Draw Conclusions** How has Proctor changed from the beginning of the play? What do his actions in this act reveal about his character?

CREATE AND DISCUSS

Go to **Writing Informative Texts: Developing a Topic** in the **Writing Studio** for more help in using evidence.

Write an Analysis The real Abigail Williams was eleven years old in 1692 and had not had an illicit relationship with John Proctor. How would the play be different if Miller had not presented a different version of history? What would be lost? Write an analysis in which you state your response and support it with text evidence.

❑ Identify the ways in which the relationship between Proctor and Abigail affects the development of plot and supports Miller's view about the witch hunts.

❑ Cite details from the play in support of your views.

❑ Write an analysis in which you logically present your ideas based on explicit statements from the text or inferences based on evidence from the text.

 Go to **Participating in Collaborative Discussions** in the **Speaking and Listening Studio** for discussion support.

Have a Group Discussion In a small group, use *The Crucible* as the basis of a discussion on whether writers must be historically accurate in literary works or ought to be permitted to change details when writing about true events in fictional works.

❑ Conduct research to find examples of historical inaccuracies in *The Crucible* in addition to what you learned about the real Abigail Williams.

❑ Think about the impact these departures from history have on your understanding of the play. Consider why Miller chose to change particular details.

❑ State whether you agree with Miller's decision to change details in the play. Cite evidence to support your ideas.

ACT FOUR

1   (*A cell in* Salem *jail, that fall.*

2   *At the back is a high barred window; near it, a great, heavy door. Along the walls are two benches.*

3   *The place is in darkness but for the moonlight seeping through the bars. It appears empty. Presently footsteps are heard coming down a corridor beyond the wall, keys rattle, and the door swings open.* Marshal Herrick *enters with a lantern.*

4   *He is nearly drunk, and heavy-footed. He goes to a bench and nudges a bundle of rags lying on it.*)

5   **Herrick.** Sarah, wake up! Sarah Good! (*He then crosses to the other bench.*)

6   **Sarah Good** (*rising in her rags*). Oh, Majesty! Comin', comin'! Tituba, he's here, His Majesty's come!

7   **Herrick.** Go to the north cell; this place is wanted now.

8   (*He hangs his lantern on the wall.* Tituba *sits up.*)

9   **Tituba.** That don't look to me like His Majesty; look to me like the marshal.

10 **Herrick** (*taking out a flask*). Get along with you now, clear this place. (*He drinks, and* Sarah Good *comes and peers up into his face.*)

11 **Sarah Good.** Oh, is it you, Marshal! I thought sure you be the Devil comin' for us. Could I have a sip of cider for me goin'-away?

12 **Herrick** (*handing her the flask*). And where are you off to, Sarah?

13 **Tituba** (*as Sarah drinks*). We goin' to Barbados, soon the Devil gits here with the feathers and the wings.

14 **Herrick.** Oh? A happy voyage to you.

15 **Sarah Good.** A pair of bluebirds wingin' southerly, the two of us! Oh, it be a grand transformation, Marshal! (*She raises the flask to drink again.*)

16 **Herrick** (*taking the flask from her lips*). You'd best give me that or you'll never rise off the ground. Come along now.

17 **Tituba.** I'll speak to him for you, if you desires to come along, Marshal.

18 **Herrick.** I'd not refuse it, Tituba; it's the proper morning to fly into Hell.

19 **Tituba.** Oh, it be no Hell in Barbados. Devil, him be pleasure-man in Barbados, him be singin' and dancin' in Barbados. It's you folks—you riles him up 'round here; it be too cold 'round here for that Old Boy. He freeze his soul in Massachusetts, but in Barbados he just as sweet and—(*A bellowing cow is heard, and* Tituba *leaps up and calls to the window.*) Aye, sir! That's him, Sarah!

ANALYZE DRAMATIC ELEMENTS
Annotate: Mark details in Miller's stage directions about the setting that affect the mood of the scene.

Analyze: How does the mood reflect recent plot events?

TEACH

 ANALYZE DRAMATIC ELEMENTS

Remind students that stage directions often describe what the set should look like, so they can help set the mood of a scene. Ask students to reread the stage directions that start Act Four and note how Miller describes the jail. Have students consider why he describes the jail this way. (**Answer:** *Miller sets the act in the jail, where there is darkness and very little light. The darkness inside the jail reflects the prisoners' lack of hope as they fall victim to the injustice of the witch hunt. The heavy door indicates how difficult it is to get out of jail; it reinforces the finality and seriousness of the situation.*)

 ENGLISH LEARNER SUPPORT

Understand Multiple-Meaning Words Have students circle the word *great* in the opening stage directions to describe the door to the jail. Tell them that *great* is a word that has more than one meaning. Have students work with a partner to infer the meaning of *great* in this sentence. (*large*) Then, have them check a dictionary to see if they are correct. Have partners list other meanings of the word *great*. (*distinguished, excellent, grand*) **SUBSTANTIAL/MODERATE**

For **reading support** for students at varying proficiency levels, see the **Text X-Ray** on page 600D.

TEACH

ENGLISH LEARNER SUPPORT

Identify Cognates Create and display a word wall with words from Act Four that have Spanish cognates: *materials/materiales* (paragraph 27), *authority/autoridad* (paragraph 35), *continuously/continuamente* (paragraph 47), *providence/providencia* (paragraph 59), *confess/confessor* (paragraph 60), *discover/descubir* (paragraph 73), *innocence/inocencia* (paragraph 88), *opinion/opinion* (paragraph 94), *pardon/perdón* (paragraph 102), *pretense/pretensión* (paragraph 195), *agony/agonia* (paragraph 202), *physical/físico* (202), *mystical/místico* (paragraph 216), *instruction/instrucción* (paragraph 226), *urgently/urgentemente* (paragraph 226).

Tell Spanish-speaking students to highlight these words in their text as they read. Have them use the word wall to help them understand the meaning of each word and the sentence it is in. Encourage students to add other cognates they find to the word wall.

SUBSTANTIAL/MODERATE

For **listening support** for students at varying proficiency levels, see the **Text X-Ray** on page 600C.

 **NOTICE & NOTE**

20 **Sarah Good.** I'm here, Majesty! (*They hurriedly pick up their rags as* Hopkins, *a guard, enters.*)

21 **Hopkins.** The Deputy Governor's arrived.

22 **Herrick** (*grabbing* Tituba). Come along, come along.

23 **Tituba** (*resisting him*). No, he comin' for me. I goin' home!

24 **Herrick** (*pulling her to the door*). That's not Satan, just a poor old cow with a hatful of milk. Come along now, out with you!

25 **Tituba** (*calling to the window*). Take me home, Devil! Take me home!

26 **Sarah Good** (*following the shouting* Tituba *out*). Tell him I'm goin', Tituba! Now you tell him Sarah Good is goin' too!

27 (*In the corridor outside* Tituba *calls on*—"*Take me home, Devil; Devil take me home!*" *and* Hopkins' *voice orders her to move on.* Herrick *returns and begins to push old rags and straw into a corner. Hearing footsteps, he turns, and enter* Danforth *and Judge Hathorne. They are in greatcoats and wear hats against the bitter cold. They are followed in by* Cheever, *who carries a dispatch case[1] and a flat wooden box containing his writing materials.*)

28 **Herrick.** Good morning, Excellency.

29 **Danforth.** Where is Mr. Parris?

30 **Herrick.** I'll fetch him. (*He starts for the door.*)

31 **Danforth.** Marshal. (Herrick *stops.*) When did Reverend Hale arrive?

32 **Herrick.** It were toward midnight, I think.

33 **Danforth** (*suspiciously*). What is he about here?

34 **Herrick.** He goes among them that will hang, sir. And he prays with them. He sits with Goody Nurse now. And Mr. Parris with him.

35 **Danforth.** Indeed. That man have no authority to enter here, Marshal. Why have you let him in?

36 **Herrick.** Why, Mr. Parris command me, sir. I cannot deny him.

37 **Danforth.** Are you drunk, Marshal?

38 **Herrick.** No, sir; it is a bitter night, and I have no fire here.

39 **Danforth** (*containing his anger*). Fetch Mr. Parris.

40 **Herrick.** Aye, sir.

41 **Danforth.** There is a prodigious stench in this place.

42 **Herrick.** I have only now cleared the people out for you.

43 **Danforth.** Beware hard drink, Marshal.

44 **Herrick.** Aye, sir. (*He waits an instant for further orders. But* Danforth, *in dissatisfaction, turns his back on him, and* Herrick *goes out. There is a pause.* Danforth *stands in thought.*)

---

[1] **dispatch case:** a case for carrying documents.

45 **Hathorne.** Let you question Hale, Excellency; I should not be surprised he have been preaching in Andover² lately.

46 **Danforth.** We'll come to that; speak nothing of Andover. <u>Parris prays with him. That's strange.</u> (*He blows on his hands, moves toward the window, and looks out.*)

47 **Hathorne.** Excellency, I wonder if it be wise to let Mr. Parris so continuously with the prisoners. (*Danforth turns to him, interested.*) I think, sometimes, <u>the man has a mad look these days.</u>

48 **Danforth.** Mad?

49 **Hathorne.** I met him yesterday coming out of his house, and I bid him good morning—and he wept and went his way. I think it is not well the village sees him so unsteady.

50 **Danforth.** Perhaps he have some sorrow.

51 **Cheever** (*stamping his feet against the cold*). I think it be the cows, sir.

52 **Danforth.** Cows?

53 **Cheever.** There be so many cows wanderin' the highroads, now their masters are in the jails, and much disagreement who they will belong to now. I know Mr. Parris be arguin' with farmers all yesterday—there is great contention, sir, about the cows. Contention make him weep, sir; it were always a man that weep for contention. (*He turns, as do Hathorne and Danforth, hearing someone coming up the corridor. Danforth raises his head as Parris enters. He is gaunt, frightened, and sweating in his greatcoat.*)

54 **Parris** (*to Danforth, instantly*). Oh, good morning, sir, thank you for coming, I beg your pardon wakin' you so early. Good morning, Judge Hathorne.

55 **Danforth.** Reverend Hale have no right to enter this—

56 **Parris.** Excellency, a moment. (*He hurries back and shuts the door.*)

57 **Hathorne.** Do you leave him alone with the prisoners?

58 **Danforth.** What's his business here?

59 **Parris** (*prayerfully holding up his hands*). Excellency, hear me. It is a providence. Reverend Hale has returned to bring Rebecca Nurse to God.

60 **Danforth** (*surprised*). He bids her confess?

61 **Parris** (*sitting*). Hear me. Rebecca have not given me a word this three month since she came. Now she sits with him, and her sister and Martha Corey and two or three others, and he pleads with them, confess their crimes and save their lives.

62 **Danforth.** Why—this is indeed a providence. And they soften, they soften?

---

² **Andover:** a town in Massachusetts, northwest of Salem.

© Houghton Mifflin Harcourt Publishing Company

ANALYZE CHARACTERS AND MOTIVATIONS

Annotate: Mark words in paragraphs 46–50 that describe Parris.

Analyze: What change in Parris is suggested by these details?

 ANALYZE CHARACTERS AND MOTIVATIONS

Remind students to look for changes in characters over the course of a play. The difference in what a character does and says from the beginning of a play to its ending is called a character's **arc**. The way a character changes often reveals the **theme**, or message. (***Answer:** Parris was greatly in favor of the witch hunt throughout the first three acts. The details that he is praying and crying suggest Parris has had a change of heart and is not as committed to the witch hunt.*)

WHEN STUDENTS STRUGGLE...

Use a Graphic Organizer Draw a T-chart on the board, and label the columns *Problem* and *Solutions*. Have students fill in the *Problem* column with "A faction in Salem does not believe in witchcraft." Then, have them complete the chart with both Danforth's and Parris's solutions. (*Danforth wants to go ahead with the hangings to set an example; Parris wants to postpone the hangings to see if Hale can secure some confessions.*) Discuss the differences between the two solutions and how competing solutions creates additional conflict among the characters.

For additional support, go to the **Reading Studio** and assign the following 🔺 **Level Up Tutorial: Characters and Conflict.**

ENGLISH LEARNER SUPPORT

Use Phrasal Verbs Remind students that phrasal verbs are verbs made up of a main verb together with an adverb or preposition or both, and that phrasal verbs often have a direct object (someone or something), as in *hand something in, go after someone,* or *do something over.*

Have students locate and underline the phrasal verb in paragraph 73 (*is broke into*). Then, ask them to identify the direct object of the verb. (*strongbox*) Have students work with partners to write a sentence using the phrasal verb "broke in" or "break in."

MODERATE/LIGHT

ANALYZE DRAMATIC ELEMENTS

Remind students to look for events that can make the central conflict more difficult to resolve. These events are called plot **complications.** Have students restate the main conflict of the play in their own words. How does what is happening in Andover make resolution more difficult? (***Answer:*** *If residents of Andover—a neighboring town—are resisting and questioning the witch hunt, then perhaps those feelings will migrate to Salem and undermine the judges' case. It makes the central conflict of the play harder to resolve because it shows there is doubt about whether witchcraft is at work.*)

 **NOTICE & NOTE**

63 **Parris.** Not yet, not yet. But I thought to summon you, sir, that we might think on whether it be not wise, to—(*He dares not say it.*) I had thought to put a question, sir, and I hope you will not—

64 **Danforth.** Mr. Parris, be plain, what troubles you?

65 **Parris.** There is news, sir, that the court—the court must reckon with. My niece, sir, my niece—I believe she has vanished.

66 **Danforth.** Vanished!

67 **Parris.** I had thought to advise you of it earlier in the week, but—

68 **Danforth.** Why? How long is she gone?

69 **Parris.** This be the third night. You see, sir, she told me she would stay a night with Mercy Lewis. And next day, when she does not return, I send to Mr. Lewis to inquire. Mercy told him she would sleep in *my* house for a night.

70 **Danforth.** They are both gone?!

71 **Parris** (*in fear of him*). They are, sir.

72 **Danforth** (*alarmed*). I will send a party for them. Where may they be?

73 **Parris.** Excellency, I think they be aboard a ship. (Danforth *stands agape.*) My daughter tells me how she heard them speaking of ships last week, and tonight I discover my—my strongbox is broke into. (*He presses his fingers against his eyes to keep back tears.*)

74 **Hathorne** (*astonished*). She have robbed you?

75 **Parris.** Thirty-one pound is gone. I am penniless. (*He covers his face and sobs.*)

76 **Danforth.** Mr. Parris, you are a brainless man! (*He walks in thought, deeply worried.*)

77 **Parris.** Excellency, it profit nothing you should blame me. I cannot think they would run off except they fear to keep in Salem any more. (*He is pleading.*) Mark it, sir, Abigail had close knowledge of the town, and since the news of Andover has broken here—

78 **Danforth.** Andover is remedied.[3] The court returns there on Friday, and will resume examinations.

79 **Parris.** I am sure of it, sir. But the rumor here speaks rebellion in Andover, and it—

80 **Danforth.** There is no rebellion in Andover!

81 **Parris.** I tell you what is said here, sir. Andover have thrown out the court, they say, and will have no part of witchcraft. There be a faction here, feeding on that news, and I tell you true, sir, I fear there will be riot here.

[3] **remedied:** no longer a problem.

ANALYZE DRAMATIC ELEMENTS
Annotate: Mark details that tell what is happening in Andover.

Interpret: Why might what is happening in Andover be considered a plot complication?

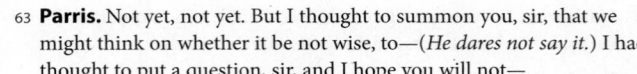

TO CHALLENGE STUDENTS . . .

Research Andover Ask students to find and present a brief introduction to Andover. The introduction might include a map showing the relative locations of Andover and Salem and a brief explanation of Andover's early history, including information about how the community responded to the witchcraft scare that began in Salem.

82 **Hathorne.** Riot! Why at every execution I have seen naught but high satisfaction in the town.

83 **Parris.** Judge Hathorne—it were another sort that hanged till now. Rebecca Nurse is no Bridget that lived three year with Bishop before she married him. John Proctor is not Isaac Ward that drank his family to ruin. (*to* Danforth) I would to God it were not so, Excellency, but these people have great weight yet in the town. Let Rebecca stand upon the gibbet[4] and send up some righteous prayer, and I fear she'll wake a vengeance on you.

84 **Hathorne.** Excellency, she is condemned a witch. The court have—

85 **Danforth** (*in deep concern, raising a hand to* Hathorne). Pray you. (*to* Parris) How do you propose, then?

86 **Parris.** Excellency, I would postpone these hangin's for a time.

87 **Danforth.** There will be no postponement.

88 **Parris.** Now Mr. Hale's returned, there is hope, I think—for if he bring even one of these to God, that confession surely damns the others in the public eye, and none may doubt more that they are all linked to Hell. This way, unconfessed and claiming innocence, doubts are multiplied, many honest people will weep for them, and our good purpose is lost in their tears.

89 **Danforth** (*after thinking a moment, then going to* Cheever). Give me the list.

90 (Cheever *opens the dispatch case, searches.*)

91 **Parris.** It cannot be forgot, sir, that when I summoned the congregation for John Proctor's excommunication[5] there were hardly thirty people come to hear it. That speak a discontent, I think, and—

92 **Danforth** (*studying the list*). There will be no postponement.

93 **Parris.** Excellency—

94 **Danforth.** Now, sir—which of these in your opinion may be brought to God? I will myself strive with him[6] till dawn. (*He hands the list to* Parris, *who merely glances at it.*)

95 **Parris.** There is not sufficient time till dawn.

96 **Danforth.** I shall do my utmost. Which of them do you have hope for?

97 **Parris** (*not even glancing at the list now, and in a quavering voice, quietly*). Excellency—a dagger— (*He chokes up.*)

98 **Danforth.** What do you say?

---
[4] **gibbet** (jĭb´ĭt): gallows.
[5] **excommunication:** banishment from a church. For the Puritans in New England, this punishment resulted in the loss of church privileges.
[6] **strive with him:** struggle with him through prayer.

WHEN STUDENTS STRUGGLE . . .

Summarize Plot Events Ask the following questions about paragraphs 83–104.

- How does Parris feel about Proctor? (*He may not like Proctor but does not think he is evil.*)
- How does Danforth feel about pardoning the convicted? (*Danforth considers it "not just" to offer pardon because other convicted people have already died.*)

 For additional support, go to the **Reading Studio** and assign the following **Level Up Tutorial: Summarizing.**

ENGLISH LEARNER SUPPORT

Understand Metaphors Remind students that a metaphor is a type of figurative language. A metaphor is a direct comparison between two things. Ask students to locate and underline the metaphor in Danforth's speech in paragraph 107 (*an ocean of salt tears*). Have students work with a partner to identify what two things are being compared (*the amount of water in the ocean and the amount of tears*). Then, have them explain what Danforth means by using this metaphor. (*Danforth is saying that even if the people cry out in opposition in great numbers—such that their crying would create as much salt water as in the ocean—he will not back down.*)

MODERATE/LIGHT

99 **Parris.** Tonight, when I open my door to leave my house—a dagger clattered to the ground. (*Silence. Danforth absorbs this. Now Parris cries out.*) You cannot hang this sort. There is danger for me. I dare not step outside at night!

100 (*Reverend Hale enters. They look at him for an instant in silence. He is steeped in sorrow, exhausted, and more direct than he ever was.*)

101 **Danforth.** Accept my congratulations, Reverend Hale; we are gladdened to see you returned to your good work.

102 **Hale** (*coming to* Danforth *now*). You must pardon them. They will not budge.

103 (Herrick *enters, waits.*)

104 **Danforth** (*conciliatory*). You misunderstand, sir; I cannot pardon these when twelve are already hanged for the same crime. It is not just.

105 **Parris** (*with failing heart*). Rebecca will not confess?

106 **Hale.** The sun will rise in a few minutes. Excellency, I must have more time.

107 **Danforth.** Now hear me, and beguile yourselves no more. I will not receive a single plea for pardon or postponement. Them that will not confess will hang. Twelve are already executed; the names of these seven are given out, and the village expects to see them die this morning. Postponement now speaks a floundering on my part; reprieve or pardon must cast doubt upon the guilt of them that died till now. While I speak God's law, I will not crack its voice with whimpering. If retaliation is your fear, know this—I should hang ten thousand that dared to rise against the law, and an ocean of salt tears could not melt the resolution of the statutes. Now draw yourselves up like men and help me, as you are bound by Heaven to do. Have you spoken with them all, Mr. Hale?

108 **Hale.** All but Proctor. He is in the dungeon.

109 **Danforth** (*to* Herrick). What's Proctor's way now?

110 **Herrick.** He sits like some great bird; you'd not know he lived except he will take food from time to time.

111 **Danforth** (*after thinking a moment*). His wife—his wife must be well on with child now.

112 **Herrick.** She is, sir.

113 **Danforth.** What think you, Mr. Parris? You have closer knowledge of this man; might her presence soften him?

114 **Parris.** It is possible, sir. He have not laid eyes on her these three months. I should summon her.

115 **Danforth** (*to* Herrick). Is he yet adamant? Has he struck at you again?

116 **Herrick.** He cannot, sir, he is chained to the wall now.

117 **Danforth** (*after thinking on it*). Fetch Goody Proctor to me. Then let you bring him up.

118 **Herrick.** Aye, sir. (*Herrick goes. There is silence.*)

119 **Hale.** Excellency, if you postpone a week and publish to the town that you are striving for their confessions, that speak mercy on your part, not faltering.

120 **Danforth.** Mr. Hale, as God have not empowered me like Joshua to stop this sun from rising,[7] so I cannot withhold from them the perfection of their punishment.

121 **Hale** (*harder now*). If you think God wills you to raise rebellion, Mr. Danforth, you are mistaken!

122 **Danforth** (*instantly*). You have heard rebellion spoken in the town?

123 **Hale.** Excellency, there are orphans wandering from house to house; abandoned cattle bellow on the highroads, the stink of rotting crops hangs everywhere, and no man knows when the harlots' cry will end his life—and you wonder yet if rebellion's spoke? Better you should marvel how they do not burn your province!

124 **Danforth.** Mr. Hale, have you preached in Andover this month?

125 **Hale.** Thank God they have no need of me in Andover.

126 **Danforth.** You baffle me, sir. Why have you returned here?

127 **Hale.** Why, it is all simple. I come to do the Devil's work. I come to counsel Christians they should belie themselves. (*His sarcasm collapses.*) There is blood on my head! Can you not see the blood on my head!!

128 **Parris.** Hush! (*For he has heard footsteps. They all face the door. Herrick enters with Elizabeth.* <u>Her wrists are linked by heavy chain,</u> *which* Herrick *now removes.* <u>Her clothes are dirty; her face is pale and gaunt.</u> Herrick *goes out.*)

129 **Danforth** (*very politely*). Goody Proctor. (*She is silent.*) I hope you are hearty?

130 **Elizabeth** (*as a warning reminder*). I am yet six month before my time.

131 **Danforth.** Pray be at your ease, we come not for your life. We— (*uncertain how to plead, for he is not accustomed to it.*) Mr. Hale, will you speak with the woman?

132 **Hale.** Goody Proctor, your husband is marked to hang this morning.

(*pause*)

133 **Elizabeth** (*quietly*). I have heard it.

---

[7] **like Joshua . . . rising:** According to the Bible, Joshua became leader of the Israelites after Moses died. He led the people to the Promised Land while the sun stood still.

ANALYZE DRAMATIC ELEMENTS

Annotate: Mark stage directions that show what life has been like for Elizabeth Proctor since she was last seen in Act Three.

Analyze: How does this description help the reader understand her situation?

TEACH

 ANALYZE DRAMATIC ELEMENTS

Remind students that **plot, setting,** and **characters** are all connected. The entrance of the character Elizabeth in this scene contains clues to what is happening to the imprisoned women and the conditions in which they are being held. (**Answer:** *Her situation is dire. The description shows she is being treated very poorly. She has not been eating enough or bathing. She has been in chains.*)

(EL) ENGLISH LEARNER SUPPORT

Understand Suffixes Point out the word *rebellion* in paragraph 121 and write it on the board. Remind students that a suffix is added to the end of a base word or word part to create a new word with a different meaning. Circle the base word *rebel* and underline the suffix *–ion*. Ask students what the base word means (*to rebel is to act against a leader or government*). Then, have them infer what the noun *rebellion* means. (*A "rebellion" is an act or movement of rebelling—an attempt to change a leader or a government.*) For each of the following words, have partners work together to identify the base word and its definition, then infer the meaning of the noun:

- extermination (*getting rid of something; from the verb* exterminate)

- revision (*changing something; from the verb* revise)

MODERATE/LIGHT

NOTICE & NOTE

134 **Hale.** You know, do you not, that I have no connection with the court? (*She seems to doubt it.*) I come of my own, Goody Proctor. I would save your husband's life, for if he is taken I count myself his murderer. Do you understand me?

135 **Elizabeth.** What do you want of me?

136 **Hale.** Goody Proctor, I have gone this three month like our Lord into the wilderness.[8] I have sought a Christian way, for damnation's doubled on a minister who counsels men to lie.

137 **Hathorne.** It is no lie, you cannot speak of lies.

138 **Hale.** It is a lie! They are innocent!

139 **Danforth.** I'll hear no more of that!

140 **Hale** (*continuing to* Elizabeth). Let you not mistake your duty as I mistook my own. I came into this village like a bridegroom to his beloved, bearing gifts of high religion; the very crowns of holy law I brought, and what I touched with my bright confidence, it died; and where I turned the eye of my great faith, blood flowed up. Beware, Goody Proctor—cleave to no faith when faith brings blood. It is mistaken law that leads you to sacrifice. Life, woman, life is God's most precious gift; no principle, however glorious, may justify the taking of it. I beg you, woman, prevail upon your husband to confess. Let him give his lie. Quail not before God's judgment in this, for it may well be God damns a liar less than he that throws his life away for pride. Will you plead with him? I cannot think he will listen to another.

141 **Elizabeth** (*quietly*). I think that be the Devil's argument.

142 **Hale** (*with a climactic desperation*). Woman, before the laws of God we are as swine! We cannot read His will!

143 **Elizabeth.** I cannot dispute with you, sir; I lack learning for it.

144 **Danforth** (*going to her*). Goody Proctor, you are not summoned here for disputation. Be there no wifely tenderness within you? He will die with the sunrise. Your husband. Do you understand it? (*She only looks at him.*) What say you? Will you contend with him? (*She is silent.*) Are you stone? I tell you true, woman, had I no other proof of your unnatural life, your dry eyes now would be sufficient evidence that you delivered up your soul to Hell! A very ape would weep at such calamity! Have the Devil dried up any tear of pity in you? (*She is silent.*) Take her out. It profit nothing she should speak to him!

145 **Elizabeth** (*quietly*). Let me speak with him, Excellency.

146 **Parris** (*with hope*). You'll strive with him? (*She hesitates.*)

147 **Danforth.** Will you plead for his confession or will you not?

148 **Elizabeth.** I promise nothing. Let me speak with him.

---

[8] **like our Lord . . . wilderness:** According to the New Testament, Jesus spent 40 days wandering in the desert while fasting.

WHEN STUDENTS STRUGGLE . . .

Understand Similes Review with students that similes make comparisons using the words *like* or *as*. Ask students to find the two similes on this page and tell how they affect their understanding of the character of Hale. (*paragraph 136: "I have gone this three month like our Lord into the wilderness." Hale is saying he has been spending time alone in thought, as Jesus did in the desert; paragraph 140: "I came into this village like a bridegroom to his beloved, bearing gifts of high religion . . ." Hale is saying he came to Salem with good intentions.*)

For additional support, go to the **Reading Studio** and assign the following **Level Up Tutorial: Figurative Language.**

149 *(A sound—the sibilance of dragging feet on stone. They turn. A pause. Herrick enters with John Proctor. His wrists are chained. He is another man, bearded, filthy, his eyes misty as though webs had overgrown them. He halts inside the doorway, his eye caught by the sight of Elizabeth. The emotion flowing between them prevents anyone from speaking for an instant. Now Hale, visibly affected, goes to Danforth and speaks quietly.)*

150 **Hale.** Pray, leave them, Excellency.

151 **Danforth** *(pressing* Hale *impatiently aside).* Mr. Proctor, you have been notified, have you not? *(Proctor is silent, staring at Elizabeth.)* I see light in the sky, Mister; let you counsel with your wife, and may God help you turn your back on Hell. *(Proctor is silent, staring at Elizabeth.)*

152 **Hale** *(quietly).* Excellency, let—

153 *(Danforth brushes past Hale and walks out. Hale follows. Cheever stands and follows, Hathorne behind. Herrick goes. Parris, from a safe distance, offers.)*

154 **Parris.** If you desire a cup of cider, Mr. Proctor, I am sure I—*(Proctor turns an icy stare at him, and he breaks off.* Parris *raises his palms toward* Proctor.*)* God lead you now. *(Parris goes out.)*

155 *(Alone. Proctor walks to her, halts. It is as though they stood in a spinning world. It is beyond sorrow, above it. He reaches out his hand as though toward an embodiment not quite real, and as he touches her, a strange soft sound, half laughter, half amazement, comes from his throat. He pats her hand. She covers his hand with hers. And then, weak, he sits. Then she sits, facing him.)*

156 **Proctor.** The child?

157 **Elizabeth.** It grows.

158 **Proctor.** There is no word of the boys?

159 **Elizabeth.** They're well. Rebecca's Samuel keeps them.

160 **Proctor.** You have not seen them?

161 **Elizabeth.** I have not. *(She catches a weakening in herself and downs it.)*

162 **Proctor.** You are a—marvel, Elizabeth.

163 **Elizabeth.** You—have been tortured?

164 **Proctor.** Aye. *(Pause. She will not let herself be drowned in the sea that threatens her.)* They come for my life now.

165 **Elizabeth.** I know it.

166 *(pause)*

167 **Proctor.** None—have yet confessed?

168 **Elizabeth.** There be many confessed.

169 **Proctor.** Who are they?

ANALYZE LITERARY DEVICES

Annotate: Mark the figurative language in paragraphs 154 and 164.

Evaluate: How do these figures of speech reveal Proctor and Elizabeth's emotional states?

IMPROVE READING FLUENCY

Targeted Passage Remind students to practice their reading fluency by reading with expression. The scene between Proctor and Elizabeth (beginning in paragraph 155) is rich in emotion. Have students work with a partner and read the scene. Then have them switch roles. After that, have them describe the difference in their experiences reading Proctor's and Elizabeth's parts.

 Go to the **Reading Studio** for additional support in developing fluency.

 ANALYZE LITERARY DEVICES

Remind students that **stage directions** can describe a character's behavior vividly, and **figurative language** is a powerful tool for creating these vivid images. Point out that both examples of figurative language help the reader understand the characters. (**Answer:** *An "icy stare" is an angry, unfriendly look at someone. Proctor gives Parris an icy stare because Proctor, having been through what has happened, is not ready to accept any kindness from Parris at this point. Proctor probably feels that Parris's offering is too little, too late. Support from Parris earlier in the play, when the accusations were being made, would have been helpful; now it is not. The "sea" that threatens to drown Elizabeth is an emotional one. Miller wants to show that she and Proctor refuse to give in to their emotions. Instead of weeping and wailing, they are largely silent and speak with quiet dignity. Both figures of speech show that the two are in control of their own emotions and do not need anything from others.)*

EL ENGLISH LEARNER SUPPORT

Use Contractions Remind students that a contraction joins two words by eliminating one or more letters and using an apostrophe in their place. Help students locate and circle the contractions on pages 703–705. Have partners work together to read each sentence in which a circled contraction appears. One partner reads the sentence aloud as written. The other partner reads the sentence aloud, substituting the two-word form. Have partners alternate roles.

- they're *(they are)*
- they'd *(they would)*
- that's *(that is)*
- nothing's *(nothing is)*
- you've *(you have)*
- I'd *(I would)*
- you'll *(you will)* **SUBSTANTIAL/MODERATE**

NOTICE & NOTE

170 **Elizabeth.** There be a hundred or more, they say. Goody Ballard is one; Isaiah Goodkind is one. There be many.

171 **Proctor.** Rebecca?

172 **Elizabeth.** Not Rebecca. She is one foot in Heaven now; naught may hurt her more.

173 **Proctor.** And Giles?

174 **Elizabeth.** You have not heard of it?

175 **Proctor.** I hear nothin', where I am kept.

176 **Elizabeth.** Giles is dead.

177 (*He looks at her incredulously.*)

178 **Proctor.** When were he hanged?

179 **Elizabeth** (*quietly, factually*). He were not hanged. He would not answer aye or nay to his indictment; for if he denied the charge they'd hang him surely, and auction out his property. So he stand mute, and died Christian under the law. And so his sons will have his farm. It is the law, for he could not be condemned a wizard without he answer the indictment, aye or nay.

180 **Proctor.** Then how does he die?

181 **Elizabeth** (*gently*). They press him, John.

182 **Proctor.** Press?

183 **Elizabeth.** Great stones they lay upon his chest until he plead aye or nay. (*with a tender smile for the old man*) They say he give them but two words. "More weight," he says. And died.

184 **Proctor** (*numbed—a thread to weave into his agony*). "More weight."

185 **Elizabeth.** Aye. It were a fearsome[9] man, Giles Corey.

186 (*pause*)

187 **Proctor** (*with great force of will, but not quite looking at her*). I have been thinking I would confess to them, Elizabeth. (*She shows nothing.*) What say you? If I give them that?

188 **Elizabeth.** I cannot judge you, John.

189 (*pause*)

190 **Proctor** (*simply—a pure question*). What would you have me do?

191 **Elizabeth.** As you will, I would have it. (*slight pause*) I want you living, John. That's sure.

192 **Proctor** (*pauses, then with a flailing of hope*). Giles' wife? Have she confessed?

193 **Elizabeth.** She will not.

194 (*pause*)

---

[9] **fearsome:** courageous.

© Houghton Mifflin Harcourt Publishing Company

WHEN STUDENTS STRUGGLE . . .

Understand Character Motivations Clarify the matter of property law in the account of Giles Corey's death (paragraphs 179–183). If Giles had acknowledged the charges against him, he would have been declared guilty of witchcraft. His land would have been sold at auction. Because Giles refused to acknowledge the charges, he was still executed, but his family could keep his land. Ask students to offer opinions about Giles' decision.

 For additional support, go to the **Reading Studio** and assign the following **LEVEL** **Level Up Tutorial: Character Motivation.**

195 **Proctor.** It is a pretense, Elizabeth.

196 **Elizabeth.** What is?

197 **Proctor.** I cannot mount the gibbet like a saint. It is a fraud. I am not that man. (*She is silent.*) My honesty is broke, Elizabeth; I am no good man. Nothing's spoiled by giving them this lie that were not rotten long before.

198 **Elizabeth.** And yet you've not confessed till now. That speak goodness in you.

199 **Proctor.** Spite only keeps me silent. It is hard to give a lie to dogs. (*Pause. For the first time he turns directly to her.*) I would have your forgiveness, Elizabeth.

200 **Elizabeth.** It is not for me to give, John, I am—

201 **Proctor.** I'd have you see some honesty in it. Let them that never lied die now to keep their souls. It is pretense for me, a vanity that will not blind God nor keep my children out of the wind. (pause) What say you?

202 **Elizabeth** (*upon a heaving sob that always threatens*). John, it come to naught that I should forgive you, if you'll not forgive yourself. (*Now he turns away a little, in great agony.*) It is not my soul, John, it is yours. (*He stands, as though in physical pain, slowly rising to his feet with a great immortal longing to find his answer. It is difficult to say, and she is on the verge of tears.*) Only be sure of this, for I know it now: Whatever you will do, it is a good man does it. (*He turns his doubting, searching gaze upon her.*) I have read my heart this three month, John. (*pause*) I have sins of my own to count. It needs a cold wife to prompt lechery.

203 **Proctor** (*in great pain*). Enough, enough—

204 **Elizabeth** (*now pouring out her heart*). Better you should know me!

205 **Proctor.** I will not hear it! I know you!

206 **Elizabeth.** You take my sins upon you, John—

207 **Proctor** (*in agony*). No, I take my own, my own!

208 **Elizabeth.** John, I counted myself so plain, so poorly made, no honest love could come to me! Suspicion kissed you when I did; I never knew how I should say my love. It were a cold house I kept! (*In fright, she swerves, as* Hathorne *enters.*)

209 **Hathorne.** What say you, Proctor? The sun is soon up.

210 (Proctor, *his chest heaving, stares, turns to* Elizabeth. *She comes to him as though to plead, her voice quaking.*)

211 **Elizabeth.** Do what you will. But let none be your judge. There be no higher judge under Heaven than Proctor is! Forgive me, forgive me, John—I never knew such goodness in the world! (*She covers her face, weeping.*)

The Crucible: Act Four 705

ANALYZE CHARCACTERS AND MOTIVATIONS

Annotate: Mark what Proctor says about his honesty.

Analyze: Why does he feel this way about his honesty?

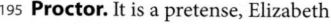 **ANALYZE CHARACTERS AND MOTIVATIONS**

Point out to students that Elizabeth's question prompts Proctor to reveal how he sees himself. (**Answer:** *His honesty has been irreparably broken because he has revealed his liaison to the court and because his relationship with Elizabeth has changed for the worse since then.*)

ANALYZE DRAMATIC ELEMENTS

Review that **conflict** can be external—with a force or another character—or it can be internal. When a character is wrestling with opposing forces within himself or herself—over a certain choice that must be made, for example—he or she is experiencing an internal conflict. A play's **dialogue** and **stage directions** often give clues as to the nature of a character's internal conflict. A moral dilemma, in which a character is not sure which course of action is morally right, is a common type of internal conflict. (**Answer:** *On the one hand, Proctor feels he could live with lying to save his own life, for he is not a saint as Rebecca is, yet he cannot bear to confess to something he did not do, considering it evil. This internal conflict makes the audience question whether Proctor is really going to confess, and if he confesses, if he will really be able to confess thoroughly and convincingly.*)

ANALYZE DRAMATIC ELEMENTS

Annotate: Mark words in paragraphs 217–222 that show Proctor's inner conflict.

Analyze: How do Proctor's thoughts and actions reflect the moral dilemma he faces? How do they affect your understanding of his character?

212 (Proctor *turns from her to* Hathorne; *he is off the earth, his voice hollow.*)

213 **Proctor.** I want my life.

214 **Hathorne** (*electrified, surprised*). You'll confess yourself?

215 **Proctor.** I will have my life.

216 **Hathorne** (*with a mystical tone*). God be praised! It is a providence! (*He rushes out the door, and his voice is heard calling down the corridor.*) He will confess! Proctor will confess!

217 **Proctor** (*with a cry, as he strides to the door*). Why do you cry it? (*In great pain he turns back to her.*) It is evil, is it not? It is evil.

218 **Elizabeth** (*in terror, weeping*). I cannot judge you, John, I cannot!

219 **Proctor.** Then who will judge me? (*suddenly clasping his hands*) <u>God in Heaven, what is John Proctor, what is John Proctor?</u> (*He moves as an animal, and a fury is riding in him, a tantalized search.*) <u>I think it is honest, I think so; I am no saint.</u> (*As though she had denied this he calls angrily at her.*) Let Rebecca go like a saint; for me it is fraud!

220 (*Voices are heard in the hall, speaking together in suppressed excitement.*)

221 **Elizabeth.** I am not your judge, I cannot be. (*as though giving him release*) Do as you will, do as you will!

222 **Proctor.** Would you give them such a lie? Say it. Would you ever give them this? (*She cannot answer.*) You would not; if tongs of fire were singeing you you would not! It is evil. Good, then—it is evil, and I do it!

223 (Hathorne *enters with* Danforth, *and, with them,* Cheever, Parris, *and* Hale. *It is a businesslike, rapid entrance, as though the ice had been broken.*)

224 **Danforth** (*with great relief and gratitude*). Praise to God, man, praise to God; you shall be blessed in Heaven for this. (Cheever *has hurried to the bench with pen, ink, and paper.* Proctor *watches him.*) Now then, let us have it. Are you ready, Mr. Cheever?

225 **Proctor** (*with a cold, cold horror at their efficiency*). Why must it be written?

226 **Danforth.** Why, for the good instruction of the village, Mister; this we shall post upon the church door! (*to* Parris, *urgently*) Where is the marshal?

227 **Parris** (*runs to the door and calls down the corridor*). Marshal! Hurry!

228 **Danforth.** Now, then, Mister, will you speak slowly, and directly to the point, for Mr. Cheever's sake. (*He is on record now, and is really dictating to* Cheever, *who writes.*) Mr. Proctor, have you seen the Devil in your life? (Proctor's *jaws lock.*) Come, man, there is light in the sky; the town waits at the scaffold; I would give out this news. Did you see the Devil?

229 **Proctor.** I did.

230 **Parris.** Praise God!

231 **Danforth.** And when he come to you, what were his demand? (Proctor *is silent.* Danforth *helps.*) Did he bid you to do his work upon the earth?

232 **Proctor.** He did.

233 **Danforth.** And you bound yourself to his service? (Danforth *turns, as* Rebecca Nurse *enters, with* Herrick *helping to support her. She is barely able to walk.*) Come in, come in, woman!

234 **Rebecca** (*brightening as she sees* Proctor). Ah, John! You are well, then, eh?

235 (Proctor *turns his face to the wall.*)

236 **Danforth.** Courage, man, courage—let her witness your good example that she may come to God herself. Now hear it, Goody Nurse! Say on, Mr. Proctor. Did you bind yourself to the Devil's service?

237 **Rebecca** (*astonished*). Why, John!

238 **Proctor** (*through his teeth, his face turned from* Rebecca). I did.

239 **Danforth.** Now, woman, you surely see it profit nothin' to keep this conspiracy any further. Will you confess yourself with him?

240 **Rebecca.** Oh, John—God send his mercy on you!

241 **Danforth.** I say, will you confess yourself, Goody Nurse?

242 **Rebecca.** Why, it is a lie, it is a lie; how may I damn myself? I cannot, I cannot.

243 **Danforth.** Mr. Proctor. When the Devil came to you did you see Rebecca Nurse in his company? (Proctor *is silent.*) Come, man, take courage—did you ever see her with the Devil?

244 **Proctor** (*almost inaudibly*). No.

245 (Danforth, *now sensing trouble, glances at* John *and goes to the table, and picks up a sheet—the list of condemned.*)

246 **Danforth.** Did you ever see her sister, Mary Easty, with the Devil?

247 **Proctor.** No, I did not.

248 **Danforth** (*his eyes narrow on* Proctor). Did you ever see Martha Corey with the Devil?

249 **Proctor.** I did not.

250 **Danforth** (*realizing, slowly putting the sheet down*). Did you ever see anyone with the Devil?

251 **Proctor.** I did not.

252 **Danforth.** Proctor, you mistake me. I am not empowered to trade your life for a lie. You have most certainly seen some person with the

© Houghton Mifflin Harcourt Publishing Company

CONTRASTS AND CONTRADICTIONS

Notice & Note: Mark words that show a contrast between Rebecca and Proctor.

Analyze: How is Rebecca a foil for Proctor? Which of Proctor's traits are highlighted in comparison to Rebecca?

The Crucible: Act Four   707

CONTRASTS AND CONTRADICTIONS

Remind students that a character who is a **foil** highlights the traits of another character through their differences. (**Answer:** *Rebecca is standing her ground even after having been imprisoned; she is refusing to confess to being a witch even though she knows it will result in her death. This highlights the inner conflict of Proctor, who cannot decide whether to lie and live or tell the truth and die.*)

WHEN STUDENTS STRUGGLE . . .

Understand Conflict Help students understand the conflict by having small groups list what each character wants. (*Danforth wants Proctor to confess and to name other accused people; Rebecca wants Proctor to tell the truth; Proctor wants to save his life by confessing, but not by naming others; Hale and Parris want Danforth to accept Proctor's confession and spare his life.*)

For additional support, go to the **Reading Studio** and assign the following **Level Up Tutorial: Character Motivation.**

Devil. (Proctor *is silent.*) Mr. Proctor, a score of people have already testified they saw this woman with the Devil.

253 **Proctor.** Then it is proved. Why must I say it?

254 **Danforth.** Why "must" you say it! Why, you should rejoice to say it if your soul is truly purged of any love for Hell!

255 **Proctor.** They think to go like saints. I like not to spoil their names.

256 **Danforth** (*inquiring, incredulous*). Mr. Proctor, do you think they go like saints?

257 **Proctor** (*evading*). This woman never thought she done the Devil's work.

258 **Danforth.** Look you, sir. I think you mistake your duty here. It matters nothing what she thought—she is convicted of the unnatural murder of children, and you for sending your spirit out upon Mary Warren. Your soul alone is the issue here, Mister, and you will prove its whiteness or you cannot live in a Christian country. Will you tell me now what persons conspired with you in the Devil's company? (Proctor *is silent.*) To your knowledge was Rebecca Nurse ever—

259 **Proctor.** I speak my own sins; I cannot judge another. (*crying out, with hatred*) I have no tongue for it.

260 **Hale** (*quickly to* Danforth). Excellency, it is enough he confess himself. Let him sign it, let him sign it.

261 **Parris** (*feverishly*). It is a great service, sir. It is a weighty name; it will strike the village that Proctor confess. I beg you, let him sign it. The sun is up, Excellency!

262 **Danforth** (*considers; then with dissatisfaction*). Come, then, sign your testimony. (*to* Cheever) Give it to him. (Cheever *goes to* Proctor, *the confession and a pen in hand.* Proctor *does not look at it.*) Come, man, sign it.

263 **Proctor** (*after glancing at the confession*). You have all witnessed it—it is enough.

264 **Danforth.** You will not sign it?

265 **Proctor.** You have all witnessed it; what more is needed?

266 **Danforth.** Do you sport with me? You will sign your name or it is no confession, Mister! (*His breast heaving with agonized breathing,* Proctor *now lays the paper down and signs his name.*)

267 **Parris.** Praise be to the Lord!

268 (Proctor *has just finished signing when* Danforth *reaches for the paper. But* Proctor *snatches it up, and now a wild terror is rising in him, and a boundless anger.*)

269 **Danforth** (*perplexed, but politely extending his hand*). If you please, sir.

270 **Proctor.** No.

271 **Danforth** (*as though* Proctor *did not understand*). Mr. Proctor, I must have—

272 **Proctor.** No, no. I have signed it. You have seen me. It is done! You have no need for this.

273 **Parris.** Proctor, the village must have proof that—

274 **Proctor.** Damn the village! I confess to God, and God has seen my name on this! It is enough!

275 **Danforth.** No, sir, it is—

276 **Proctor.** You came to save my soul, did you not? Here! I have confessed myself; it is enough!

277 **Danforth.** You have not con—

278 **Proctor.** I have confessed myself! Is there no good penitence but it be public? God does not need my name nailed upon the church! God sees my name; God knows how black my sins are! It is enough!

279 **Danforth.** Mr. Proctor—

280 **Proctor.** You will not use me! I am no Sarah Good or Tituba, I am John Proctor! You will not use me! It is no part of salvation that you should use me!

281 **Danforth.** I do not wish to—

282 **Proctor.** I have three children—how may I teach them to walk like men in the world, and I sold my friends?

283 **Danforth.** You have not sold your friends—

284 **Proctor.** Beguile me not! I blacken all of them when this is nailed to the church the very day they hang for silence!

285 **Danforth.** Mr. Proctor, I must have good and legal proof that you—

286 **Proctor.** You are the high court, your word is good enough! Tell them I confessed myself; say Proctor broke his knees and wept like a woman; say what you will, but my name cannot—

287 **Danforth** (*with suspicion*). It is the same, is it not? If I report it or you sign to it?

288 **Proctor** (*He knows it is insane*). No, it is not the same! What others say and what I sign to is not the same!

289 **Danforth.** Why? Do you mean to deny this confession when you are free?

290 **Proctor.** I mean to deny nothing!

291 **Danforth.** Then explain to me, Mr. Proctor, why you will not let—

292 **Proctor** (*with a cry of his whole soul*). Because it is my name! Because I cannot have another in my life! Because I lie and sign myself to lies! Because I am not worth the dust on the feet of them that hang! How may I live without my name? I have given you my soul; leave me my name!

ANALYZE LITERARY DEVICES

Annotate: Mark examples of repetition in paragraphs 273–284.

Analyze: What does this repetition tell the audience about Proctor?

The Crucible: Act Four 709

 **ANALYZE LITERARY DEVICES**

Remind students that authors often use **repetition** to emphasize an idea or feeling. When students see lines that are repeated by characters, these lines are likely to be important lines that highlight a key moment of the plot. To help interpret what Proctor means here and what his state of mind is, note that he also repeats "You will not use me!" in paragraph 280. (**Answer:** *His insistence that his confession is enough is increasingly desperate and shows he is not fully convinced confessing is the right thing to do. Signing a confession is another step and could have repercussions beyond his own death, since it would stand as documented proof of his wickedness that could be used against his family at some later time.*)

TO CHALLENGE STUDENTS . . .

Evaluate Resolution Ask students to work with a partner to dig deeper into the play's ending. Have them discuss whether they were surprised by the ending of the play and how the conflict was resolved. Have them think about the climax (*Proctor's admission of adultery in Act Three*) and evaluate whether it ultimately changes the outcome of the play's conflict. (**Possible answers:** *The outcome of the play is not really affected by Proctor's admission of adultery. He confessed only to expose Abigail's reasons for accusing him—she wanted revenge on Proctor and Elizabeth. In the end, Abigail gets away with her accusation and Proctor is hanged because he ultimately chooses not to confess. The ending of the play is more tragic because Proctor admits adultery and still meets a tragic end.*)

ANALYZE LITERARY DEVICES

(**Answer:** *The pronouncement is ironic because Danforth's court and its judgments are based on lies—the lies of Abigail, the other girls, and adults who are emotionally overwrought or who use the situation to take advantage of their neighbors.*)

 **NOTICE & NOTE**

ANALYZE LITERARY DEVICES

Annotate: Mark what Danforth says about himself in paragraph 293.

Analyze: What is ironic about Danforth's statements?

293 **Danforth** (*pointing at the confession in* Proctor's *hand*). Is that document a lie? If it is a lie I will not accept it! What say you? I will not deal in lies, Mister! (Proctor *is motionless.*) You will give me your honest confession in my hand, or I cannot keep you from the rope. (Proctor *does not reply.*) Which way do you go, Mister?

294 (*His breast heaving, his eyes staring,* Proctor *tears the paper and crumples it, and he is weeping in fury, but erect.*)

295 **Danforth.** Marshal!

296 **Parris** (*hysterically, as though the tearing paper were his life*). Proctor, Proctor!

297 **Hale.** Man, you will hang! You cannot!

298 **Proctor** (*his eyes full of tears*). I can. And there's your first marvel, that I can. You have made your magic now, for now I do think I see some shred of goodness in John Proctor. Not enough to weave a banner with, but white enough to keep it from such dogs. (Elizabeth, *in a burst of terror, rushes to him and weeps against his hand.*) Give them no tear! Tears pleasure them! Show honor now, show a stony heart and sink them with it! (*He has lifted her, and kisses her now with great passion.*)

299 **Rebecca.** Let you fear nothing! Another judgment waits us all!

300 **Danforth.** Hang them high over the town! Who weeps for these, weeps for corruption! (*He sweeps out past them.* Herrick *starts to lead* Rebecca, *who almost collapses, but* Proctor *catches her, and she glances up at him apologetically.*)

301 **Rebecca.** I've had no breakfast.

302 **Herrick.** Come, man.

303 (Herrick *escorts them out,* Hathorne *and* Cheever *behind them.* Elizabeth *stands staring at the empty doorway.*)

TO CHALLENGE STUDENTS . . .

Analyze Genre Did you laugh or did you cry? Review with students the two traditional genres of drama: comedy and tragedy. Have students work in pairs to research the characteristics of tragedy and tragic heroes. Then, have students discuss what makes *The Crucible* a tragedy. (*Tragedies dramatize sad or horrible events experienced by a single individual. The individual is usually heroic, and often it is his or her own tragic flaw that brings about the tragic events. The Crucible is a tragedy not only because of its horrible events, but because Proctor's affair with Abigail [his flaw] causes Abigail to want to take revenge and initiate the witch hunt, which is the central conflict of the play.*)

304 **Parris** (*in deadly fear, to* Elizabeth). Go to him, Goody Proctor! There is yet time!

305 (*From outside a drumroll strikes the air.* Parris *is startled.* Elizabeth *jerks about toward the window.*)

306 **Parris.** Go to him! (*He rushes out the door, as though to hold back his fate.*) Proctor! Proctor! (*again, a short burst of drums*)

307 **Hale.** Woman, plead with him! (*He starts to rush out the door, and then goes back to her.*) Woman! It is pride, it is vanity. (*She avoids his eyes, and moves to the window. He drops to his knees.*) Be his helper!— What profit him to bleed? Shall the dust praise him? Shall the worms declare his truth? Go to him, take his shame away!

308 **Elizabeth** (*supporting herself against collapse, grips the bars of the window, and with a cry*). He have his goodness now. God forbid I take it from him!

309 (*The final drumroll crashes, then heightens violently.* Hale *weeps in frantic prayer, and the new sun is pouring in upon her face, and the drums rattle like bones in the morning air. The curtain falls.*)

CHECK YOUR UNDERSTANDING

Answer these questions before moving on to the **Analyze the Text** section on the following page.

1 What is one effect of the witch hunt on people's everyday lives?

A Crops cannot be harvested.

B People are losing their jobs.

C There are more robberies being committed.

D The bank is repossessing many people's homes.

2 About how many people total stand accused of witchcraft?

F About 30

G About 50

H About 80

J About 100

3 How does the play end?

A Abigail is sentenced to death.

B Elizabeth is sentenced to death.

C Rebecca and Proctor are sentenced to death.

D Elizabeth and Proctor are sentenced to death.

The Crucible: Act Four   711

 CHECK YOUR UNDERSTANDING

Have students answer the questions independently.

Answers:

1. *A*

2. *J*

3. *C*

If they answer any questions incorrectly, have them reread the text to confirm their understanding. Then they may proceed to ANALYZE THE TEXT on page 712.

ENGLISH LEARNER SUPPORT

Oral Assessment   Use the following questions to assess students' comprehension and speaking skills.

1. How does the witch hunt affect the townspeople? (*Crops cannot be harvested.*)

2. About how many people are accused of witchcraft? (*about 100 people*)

3. What happens at the end of the play? (*Proctor and Rebecca are sentenced to death.*)
SUBSTANTIAL/MODERATE

APPLY

ANALYZE THE TEXT

Possible answers:

1. **DOK 3:** *Danforth wants Proctor to save his own soul: ". . . may God help you turn your back on Hell." Parris fears a revolt in Salem if Proctor is hanged: "I fear there will be riot here." Hale believes life is sacred: ". . . life is God's most precious gift; no principle, however glorious, may justify the taking of it." He also feels guilty for not having fought harder to establish Proctor's innocence: "if he is taken I count myself his murderer."*

2. **DOK 4:** *Proctor resolves his dilemma by refusing to admit to a lie and by submitting to the punishment of hanging. This reflects one of Miller's themes—protecting one's name. In the beginning, Proctor is worried about testifying against Abigail because the truth of their affair might ruin his reputation. At the end of the play, however, Proctor refuses to lie to protect his name and dies because of it.*

3. **DOK 2:** *The Crucible symbolizes a spiritual trial in which characters are "refined" and emerge stronger and better than before. It suggests the theme of people being able to redeem themselves.*

4. **DOK 4:** *Each of these scenes reveals the paradox that the accusers are automatically believed and the accused are automatically disbelieved. The accusers are favored because their accusations align with the fears and prejudices of the judges. Miller is conveying that these kinds of witch hunts cannot result in justice.*

5. **DOK 4:** *Characters such as Hale and Parris, who were in favor of the witch hunts, turn against them. There are signs that other people in Salem are turning against them as well, suggesting the trials will come to an end.*

RESEARCH

Remind students that *The Crucible* serves as a critique of the United States government's pursuit of Communist subversion in American society during the 1950s. This period of anti-Communist "witch hunting" is known as the Red Scare.

Extend Have students work in small groups to discuss how researching McCarthy helps illuminate what they read in *The Crucible*.

RESPOND

ANALYZE THE TEXT

Support your responses with evidence from the text. 📓 NOTEBOOK

1. **Cite Evidence** Explain why each of the following characters wants Proctor and the other prisoners to confess: Danforth, Parris, and Hale. Cite evidence in support of your response.

2. **Analyze** Explain how Miller conveys a major theme of the play through the resolution of Proctor's moral dilemma about whether to confess.

3. **Interpret** A crucible is a severe test or trial. It is also a vessel in which materials are melted at high temperatures to produce a more refined substance. What does a crucible symbolize in this drama? How does this symbol suggest a theme?

4. **Analyze** Reread the passages identified in the list. What is the central paradox, or contradiction, of the trials? What truth is Miller hoping to reveal about these kinds of witch hunts by discussing this paradox?
   • Act Two, paragraph 386
   • Act Three, paragraph 169
   • Act Three, paragraph 241

5. **Notice & Note** Over the course of the play, characters change in surprising ways. What do these changes suggest about the future of the Salem witch trials?

RESEARCH TIP
When researching a controversial figure such as Joseph McCarthy, use reliable sites such as those run by museums, government historical agencies, and educational institutions. Well-known encyclopedias can give you basic biographical information.

RESEARCH

Miller's *The Crucible* is a commentary on the human failures that brought about McCarthyism. Who was Joseph McCarthy and what did he believe? Research the period of history, which was known as the Red Scare, and the role of Senator Joseph McCarthy. Look for answers to the questions in the chart and complete it with your answers.

QUESTION	ANSWER
What was the House Committee on Un-American Activities?	*a committee of the US House of Representatives; investigated accusations of disloyalty to the nation*
What was McCarthy's initial claim about the State Department?	*He claimed he had a list of 205 members of the Communist Party who had infiltrated the State Department.*
How and when was McCarthy finally stopped?	*during the Army-McCarthy hearings, people did not like how McCarthy treated witnesses; his reputation was ruined*

Extend What do McCarthy's actions have in common with the perpetrators of the witch hunt in *The Crucible*? With a group, discuss what you learned about McCarthy and whether it helped you see both a literal and symbolic meaning in the play. Is *The Crucible* an effective allegory?

WHEN STUDENTS STRUGGLE . . .

Reteaching: Analyze Dramatic Elements Remind students that characters can be described through **direct** and **indirect characterization.** Have students reread paragraph 218 in Act One. Ask: What do you learn about Giles directly? *(He is 83, muscular, canny, and inquisitive.)* Have students reread paragraphs 196–227 in Act Three and tell what they learn about Giles indirectly. *(Giles shows integrity in refusing to name the man who can provide proof.)*

 For additional support, go to the **Reading Studio** and assign the following **Level Up Tutorial: Elements of Drama.**

CREATE AND DISCUSS

Write an Essay Why does John Proctor change his mind and tear up the confession even though this virtually condemns him to die? In four or five paragraphs, discuss Proctor's perception of a morally righteous person and how that perception affects his decision. Think about Rebecca Nurse's reaction to his confession and Elizabeth's assertion that "there be no higher judge under Heaven than Proctor is!"

- ❏ Explain the choices Proctor must make to arrive at his decision.
- ❏ Clarify how Proctor's idea of morality differs from that of the judges.
- ❏ Use quotations and examples from the play to support key points.

Have a Discussion Share your essay with a small group.

- ❏ Share your essay. Listen as others share.
- ❏ Discuss John Proctor's decision, and say whether you agree or disagree with it. What other choices could he have made? How would these reflect on his character?
- ❏ Note the most important points of agreement and disagreement among group members. Share these with the class.

RESPOND TO THE ESSENTIAL QUESTION

 ? When should personal integrity come before civic duty?

Gather Information Review your annotations and notes on *The Crucible*. Then, add relevant information to your Response Log. As you determine which information to include, think about:

- the inner conflict John Proctor faces
- the motivations behind characters' actions
- whether characters believed they were performing a civic duty

 Go to **Writing Informative Texts: Overview** in the **Writing Studio** for help.

Go to **Participating in Collaborative Discussions** in the **Speaking and Listening Studio** for help.

ACADEMIC VOCABULARY
As you write and discuss what you learned from *The Crucible*, be sure to use the Academic Vocabulary words. Check off each of the words that you use.

- ❏ **contemporary**
- ❏ **global**
- ❏ **infinite**
- ❏ **simulated**
- ❏ **virtual**

APPLY

CREATE AND DISCUSS

Write an Essay Have students analyze the role Proctor's ideas about moral righteousness play in his decision to tear up his confession. Encourage them to reread Act Four and trace the evolution of Proctor's decision, including Rebecca Nurse's initial reaction. When students have finished writing, have them exchange essays with a partner and offer constructive feedback. After students have made revisions, ask volunteers to read their essays to the class.

For **writing support** for students at varying proficiency levels, see the **Text X-Ray** on page 600D.

Have a Discussion As students form small groups, have them choose one or two people to take notes about their discussion and decide how they will present the group's ideas to the class. Have students share their essays and their opinions of John Proctor's decision while others listen and ask clarifying questions. When students have finished their discussions, call the class back together to share and discuss the main points of agreement and disagreement of each group.

RESPOND TO THE ESSENTIAL QUESTION

Allow time for students to add details from *The Crucible* to their Unit 6 Response Logs.

© Houghton Mifflin Harcourt Publishing Company

APPLY

VOCABULARY STRATEGY:
Determine the Meaning of Idioms

Read through the examples with students. Have them
work in pairs to locate and interpret idioms from the text.
Suggest different pairs focus on different acts. Then, share all
examples in a class discussion.

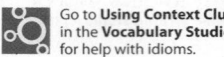 **RESPOND**

 Go to **Using Context Clues**
in the **Vocabulary Studio**
for help with idioms.

VOCABULARY STRATEGY: Determine the Meaning of Idioms

An **idiom** is a type of figurative language whose meaning is different from
the literal meaning of its words. Idioms are common figures of speech and are
often associated with certain time periods and locations.

IDIOM	MEANING
Now I am undone. (Act One, paragraph 111)	This idiom means something similar to "I am ruined!"
I'll pay you, Herrick, I will surely pay you! (Act Two, paragraph 403)	This idiom is similar to the idiom "getting payback." It means something like "I will have revenge!"
Take it to heart, Mr. Parris. (Act One, paragraph 254)	This idiom is related to the heart being central and vital. It means something like "Consider it very important."
I think this goes to the heart of the matter. (Act Three, paragraph 234)	This idiom is also related to the heart being central and vital. It means something like "the most important part of the business."

Practice and Apply Find two idioms in the text. Read the idiom in context
and infer its meaning. Then, check their meanings using an online idiom
dictionary. Share your idioms, their context clues, and their meanings with the
class.

IDIOM	INFERRED MEANING	RESEARCHED MEANING
"Your name in the town—it is entirely white, is it not?" (Act 1, paragraph 61)	There is no wrongdoing in your reputation.	You have a purely good reputation.
"stiff-necked people" (Act 1, paragraph 61)	people who are slow to change	stubborn people

© Houghton Mifflin Harcourt Publishing Company

EL ENGLISH LEARNER SUPPORT

Vocabulary Strategy Remind students that an idiom is an expression whose meaning is not
obvious from the individual meaning of each word. Help them practice understanding idioms:

- Read aloud Act 3, paragraph 380. Help students find the idiom "good name." Ask if they
  think this describes a person's actual name. Guide them to infer that Proctor's good
  name is his good reputation. **SUBSTANTIAL/MODERATE**
- Provide students with a list of idioms: "good name" (Act 3, paragraph 380); "breathe
  a word" (Act 1, paragraph 160); "blood on my head" (Act 4, paragraph 127). Have
  partners read each idiom in context and infer its meaning.
  LIGHT

LANGUAGE CONVENTIONS: Dialogue

Dialogue is the foundation of drama. It can reveal a variety of character traits and motivations. In addition, it performs other important functions.

Dialogue moves the plot forward. Through characters' speech, readers learn about plot developments and gain a greater understanding of the central conflict and its impact. For example, consider how Danforth's update on the witch trials in Act Four conveys important information about current events:

> Twelve are already executed; the names of these seven are given out, and the village expects to see them die this morning.

Dialogue conveys theme. Characters' speeches often state important ideas that help readers recognize the playwright's underlying message. In Act Four, when Proctor refuses to sign his name to a written confession, he cries out,

> Because it is my name! Because I cannot have another in my life! Because I lie and sign myself to lies!

This articulates an important message of the play: One's personal integrity is too high a price to pay for life. One's name—symbolically one's reputation and honor—cannot be sacrificed, not even to preserve life.

Dialogue conveys setting and character. How characters speak can bring authenticity to a historical setting. In *The Crucible*, Miller carefully constructs his dialogue to match the historical time period in which he sets his play. His word choice and use of inverted sentences reflect the speech of 17th-century Salem, adding to the authenticity of his setting and realistic depiction of his characters. Consider these examples from the play:

> Aye, sir, he have been searchin' his books since he left you, sir. But he bid me tell you, that you might look to unnatural things for the cause of it. *(Act One, paragraph 32)*

> Let him look to medicine and put out all thought of unnatural causes here. There be none. *(Act One, paragraph 33)*

Here, instead of *yes*, Miller uses the word *aye*, a word that was commonplace in the 1600s but is rarely used today. He uses *be* rather than *are*, the verb form we use in this context today.

Practice and Apply Read the following examples of dialogue from Act Four. Complete the chart by identifying whether each example advances the plot, helps create setting, or conveys theme.

DIALOGUE	FUNCTION
Aye. It were a fearsome man, Giles Corey.	*evoke setting*
Would you give them such a lie? . . . You would not; . . . It is evil.	*convey theme*
Danforth. They are both gone? **Parris** (*in fear of him*). They are, sir.	*develop plot*

LANGUAGE CONVENTIONS: Dialogue

Remind students that plays are meant to be watched, therefore dialogue has several functions because there is no narrator explaining characters' thoughts or feelings. When reading a play, it is important to think about how the characters would deliver a line and what information is revealed through dialogue.

Review each function of dialogue and the examples that follow. Then, discuss how Miller's diction (word choice) and syntax (word order in sentences) reflect the contemporary speech of 17th-century Salem, adding to the authenticity of his setting and the realistic depiction of his characters. Work with students to reword each example on the page in modern diction and syntax and discuss how Miller's choices add to the setting and atmosphere of the play.

Practice and Apply Have students work with partners to complete the chart.

ENGLISH LEARNER SUPPORT

Revise Archaic Language in Dialogue Display these lines from the play: "Great stones they lay upon his chest until he plead aye or nay." (Act Four, paragraph 183)
"What profit him to bleed?" (Act Four, paragraph 307)

- Read aloud the lines and have students repeat them as written. Then, write and read aloud the lines in modern language: *They placed large stones on his chest until he said yes or no. Does it help him to be hurt?* Have students repeat after you. **SUBSTANTIAL**

- Provide sentence frames for students to help them revise the lines in modern English: *They placed large _____ on his chest until he said _____. Does it _____ to _____?* Have students share their completed sentences aloud. **MODERATE**

- Have students work in pairs to rewrite the sentences in modern English. Then, have partners compare sentences and discuss any variations. Ask: Why did Miller choose to write dialogue as it would have been spoken in the 17th century? **LIGHT**

THE CRUCIBLE

Production Images by Walter Kerr Theatre, New York

GENRE ELEMENTS
MEDIA

Media is very similar to written text. It conveys an author's message, targets a specific audience, and is created for a specific purpose. It does so, however, through visual images rather than words. These images may complement a written work or take the place of one. Examples include videos, television broadcasts, and photos. Other media includes both text and visuals. Examples are websites on the Internet, magazines, and newspapers.

LEARNING OBJECTIVES

- Analyze visuals.
- Research a stage or film production.
- Create a multimodal version of a play scene.
- Present your multimodal production.
- Use academic vocabulary.
- **Language** Discuss images using the key word *visualize*.

TEXT COMPLEXITY

Quantitative Measures	The Crucible Production Images	Lexile: N/A
Qualitative Measures	**Ideas Presented** Literal, explicit, and direct.	
	Structures Used N/A	
	Language Used N/A	
	Knowledge Required Experiences may be less familiar to many; cultural or historical references may make heavier demands.	

Online Ed

RESOURCES

- Unit 6 Response Log

- Reading Studio:
  Notice & Note

- Level Up Tutorial: Analyzing Visuals;
  Elements of Drama

- Speaking and Listening Studio:
  Using Media in a Presentation

- *The Crucible* Production Images
  Selection Test

SUMMARIES

English

Four photographs show images from the 2016 Broadway production of *The Crucible*, directed by Ivo van Hove. The production followed Miller's script but did not always follow his stage directions.

Spanish

Cuatro fotografías muestran imágenes de la producción de Broadway de 2016 de *El crisol*, dirigida por Ivo van Hove. La producción siguió el guión de Miller, pero no siguió completamente las acotaciones.

 ## SMALL-GROUP OPTIONS

Have students work in small groups and pairs to read and discuss the selection.

Think-Pair-Share-Write

- Use this activity as a planning strategy for creating a multimodal version of the story.

- Have students select a scene and excerpt to use for their creations.

- Ask: *What are two mediums you might want to use to interpret the excerpt? What are the advantages and disadvantages of each?*

- Have students partner with another student to listen, discuss, and share their ideas.

- Tell students to write a paragraph describing their plan for this assignment.

Numbered Heads Together

- Use this activity during a discussion of the production images.

- Have students form into groups of four and then number off 1-2-3-4 within the group.

- Ask: *Why might the play's director have chosen the actresses he did to play the roles of Abigail and Betty?*

- Have students discuss their responses in their groups.

- Call a number from 1 to 4. That "numbered" student then responds for the group.

Text X-Ray: English Learner Support
for *The Crucible* Production Images

Use the Text X-Ray and the supports and scaffolds in the Teacher's Edition to help guide students at different proficiency levels through the selection.

INTRODUCE THE SELECTION
DISCUSS PLAY AND SCREENPLAY ADAPTATIONS

Tell students that Arthur Miller wrote *The Crucible,* which premiered in 1953 on Broadway. Yet although Miller wrote the screenplay, the play's director, lighting designer, and costume designer brought their own interpretations to the production. The photos in this selection are from a 2016 Broadway production directed by Ivo van Hove. He used a new approach with how he staged the play. His lighting and set decorator borrowed elements from horror movies. He also portrayed the characters as timeless characters rather than as characters in a specific historical period.

Discuss plays or movies students have seen and the decisions involved in bringing them from a written script to a finished film or theatrical production. Provide the following sentence frames:

- *The actors decide how to _____.*
- *The costume designer makes decisions about _____.*
- *The director's role is to _____.*

CULTURAL REFERENCES

The following words or phrases may be unfamiliar to students:

- *testifies* (page 721 caption): makes a statement in court or to a person in authority
- *confess* (page 722 caption): admit wrongdoing
- *recants* (page 723 caption): changes what one has said earlier

---

LISTENING

Analyze Set Design, Lighting, Costumes, and Blocking

Review the following terms: *set design, lighting, costumes, blocking.*

Use the following supports with students at varying proficiency levels:

- Read aloud the captions and have students identify the associated images. Then ask yes/no questions about the set design, lighting, and costumes of each production image. **SUBSTANTIAL**
- Have students work in pairs. One partner selects a production image and uses the term *set design, lighting, costumes,* or *blocking* to complete the frame: *This production should get an award for _____.* The partner reuses the term and completes the frame: *It should get an award for _____ because _____.* **MODERATE**
- Have students work in small groups. One person expresses his or her opinion about a production image's lighting, set design, costumes, or blocking. The next person states agreement or disagreement with the statement and says why and then makes a new statement. Have students continue the process until they have expressed their opinions twice. **LIGHT**

SPEAKING

Analyze Effectiveness of a Multimodal Text

Have students discuss the effectiveness of the stage production based on the production images.

Use the following supports with students at varying proficiency levels:

- Ask students one-word questions to elicit their responses to the stage production. **SUBSTANTIAL**
- Have students discuss in small groups by completing the following frames: *The stage production looks _____ because _____. I would [not] like to see the stage production because _____.* **MODERATE**
- Have students discuss in small groups. Ask: *Did the stage production match the way you visualized the play? Why or why not? Would you like to see it? Why or why not?* **LIGHT**

READING

Analyze Production Images

Have students look at the first image and read the caption. Tell them to compare the actress portraying Abigail to the play's description of the character (Act One, paragraph 23).

Read aloud the stage direction in Act One, paragraph 23. Use the following supports with students at varying proficiency levels:

- Ask students in a small group yes/no questions about Abigail's age and appearance. **SUBSTANTIAL**
- Have students work in pairs. Have them complete the following sentence frames: *The stage direction says Abigail is _____. In the photograph, she looks _____.* **MODERATE**
- Have students work in pairs. Have them create a T-chart. Label the left column "Similar" and the right column "Different." Have them list ways the actress portraying Abigail matches the screenplay's description and the ways she is different. **LIGHT**

WRITING

Write a Treatment

Work with students to read the writing assignment on page 725.

Use the following supports with students at varying proficiency levels:

- Work with a group of students to choose a scene. Then, draw a T-chart on the board and have students list the setting, characters, events, medium, and other elements of the original play. **SUBSTANTIAL**
- Provide sentence frames such as the following that students can use to craft their treatments: *The medium I chose is _____. In this scene, the characters _____. Events that happen in this scene are _____. The setting is _____. My interpretation will show _____.* **MODERATE**
- Remind students that their treatment should be a vivid description. Have them visualize their multimodal version of their chosen scene, then brainstorm descriptive words and phrases. Help students list these for use in their treatments. **LIGHT**

Connect to the
ESSENTIAL QUESTION

In Arthur Miller's *The Crucible*, characters face both external conflicts as well as internal conflicts. These internal conflicts often emerge from a character's difficulty deciding which of two unpleasant choices is morally right. The way a play is staged can emphasize these internal conflicts through lighting, set design, and the way characters appear on the stage.

MEDIA

THE CRUCIBLE

Production Images by
Walter Kerr Theatre, New York

? ESSENTIAL QUESTION:

When should personal integrity come before civic duty?

716   Unit 6

© Houghton Mifflin Harcourt Publishing Company • Image Credits: © Sara Krulwich/The New York Times/Redux Pictures

QUICK START

You have read Arthur Miller's *The Crucible*. Think about the lengthy explanations Miller included in the text. How might some of those ideas be presented in a staged version? Jot down your ideas and then discuss them with a partner.

MAKE CONNECTIONS

When you see a play, your unique experiences will influence your perception of what is happening. If you have read the **script,** or written version of the play, you may already have ideas about its characters and themes. You may have seen other stage or film versions that would inform your evaluation of the performance. In addition, you bring your own memories, personal experiences, and relationships, as well as any prior knowledge about the play's historical and social context. As the drama unfolds, you connect all these elements with what you see and hear from the stage.

As you view the production images, think about the scenes they correspond with in *The Crucible* script. Make notes about your thoughts, experiences with the play, or prior knowledge of the historical context that relate to what you see in the images. Describe the connections you make in the chart.

IMAGE	CONNECTIONS
Act One, Reverend Parris's home.	
Act Three, courtroom.	
Act Four, prison.	
Act Four, prison.	

QUICK START

Have students read the Quick Start activity and review Miller's explanations. Invite volunteers to summarize or point out the most important facts from the expositions. Then, have students think about ways this information could be conveyed on the stage. Have students discuss their ideas with a partner.

MAKE CONNECTIONS

Ask students if they have ever seen a movie based on a book they read. How did the movie differ from the mental picture students formed while reading the book? Have students share their experiences and why watching the movie was different than reading the book.

Remind students that since they just read the script of *The Crucible,* they have already formed some ideas about what it would look like on stage. They have seen some photographs and have formed mental pictures of its settings, characters, and events. Now they will see more photos of someone else's vision of the play. Tell students to look for ways the photos in this section are similar and different from the mental picture they have already formed from reading the script.

TEACH

ANALYZE EFFECTIVENESS OF MULTIMODAL TEXT

Review the aspects of a dramatic production in the chart and discuss how people other than actors affect each aspect of a production. For example, casting involves the actors who audition as well as the director, assistant director, casting director, and various people who help to organize the auditions. The playwright's stage directions may provide some clues as to how the writer envisions the cast. Stage directions will also guide costume and set designers, as well as lighting and sound.

Then, point out that by the time the audience sees a play, hundreds of hours of preparation have already gone into bringing the story to life. The design process starts months in advance of the performances. Director, designers, and producer meet to discuss the set, costumes, props, sound, and lighting that will be used. Auditions are held, a cast is chosen, and rehearsals begin. Once the rehearsal period is complete, the cast rehearses with all technical elements in place in a series of "tech" and dress rehearsals.

Tell students that as they look at the photos, they should consider that each one shows the work of many people with different areas of expertise.

 **GET READY**

GENRE ELEMENTS: PRODUCTION IMAGES

- are used to promote a film or performance of a play
- may convey key ideas about the work to an audience
- include captions that describe the scene

ANALYZE EFFECTIVENESS OF MULTIMODAL TEXT

The script of a play can be read and analyzed, but plays are meant to be performed. A stage production involves a director, actors, set designers, lighting designers, a stage manager, and other people who collaborate to bring the story to life. An effective presentation should convey the central message of the play to the audience. Images from a stage production should give the public a general idea of the set and cast, as well as some insight into the director's vision for his or her retelling. As you view the photo stills of this stage production of *The Crucible*, keep in mind the following aspects of a dramatic production:

ASPECTS OF A DRAMATIC PRODUCTION	
Casting	The actors' physical characteristics and acting styles have a significant impact on the audience's perception of characters and plot. Use your knowledge of Miller's stage directions to evaluate how closely the director's choices align with the way Miller saw his characters.
Blocking	Actors' positions, movements, and gestures affect the impact of a scene. Note how the relationships between the characters, as well as their emotions, are revealed through their posture, gestures, and positions relative to other characters.
Lighting	Lighting is used to create mood, emphasize characters' reactions, build suspense, and draw the audience into the action. Consider what the lighting emphasizes in each scene and from where on the set the light originates. How does the lighting help the audience understand what characters are experiencing? How does it create a mood?
Set Design and Costuming	Sets and costumes create a sense of when and where the action takes place. Think about how quickly you form an impression of the play's time and place from the set and the actors' costumes. Notice details of these elements to determine whether the director has closely followed the playwright's vision or has made creative changes to them to achieve his or her own purpose.

In addition to providing a snapshot of how a particular drama is staged, production images are often used to promote a play or film to a wider audience. They are usually accompanied by a caption that provides additional information, including the names of characters and other information about the scene. As you view the photo stills of this stage production of *The Crucible*, evaluate them not only on how well they represent the director's vision, but also on how well they might serve as marketing or promotional items.

BACKGROUND

There are several written versions of The Crucible, *all of which Arthur Miller authored or co-authored. He wrote the play,* The Crucible, *which premiered in 1953 on Broadway and has been presented countless times since then. Miller's play was later adapted for opera in 1961, and Miller wrote the screenplay for the film in 1996. The photos in this lesson are from the 2016 Broadway production starring Ben Whishaw and Saoirse Ronan. Ivo van Hove is the Belgian director of the Toneelgroep Amsterdam theater company, but is renowned on Broadway for his critically acclaimed avant garde interpretations of well-known plays. This production of* The Crucible *furthered his acclaim.*

THE CRUCIBLE

Production Images by
Walter Kerr Theatre, New York

The characters and story follow the script, but these images reveal a fresh approach to set design, costumes, and lighting that do not strictly follow Miller's stage directions. In addition, the cast is a group of international actors. The play's essence, however, remains the same—a tale of mass hysteria and the fears and rationalizations of the people who succumb to it.

CAST OF CHARACTERS
(IN ORDER OF APPEARANCE)

Reverend Samuel Parris	Rebecca Nurse
Betty Parris	Giles Corey
Tituba	Reverend John Hale
Abigail Williams	Francis Nurse
John Proctor	Ezekiel Cheever
Elizabeth Proctor	Marshal Herrick
Susanna Walcott	Judge Hathorne
Mrs. Ann Putnam	Martha Corey
Thomas Putnam	Deputy Governor Danforth
Mercy Lewis	Girls of Salem
Mary Warren	Sarah Good

BACKGROUND

After students read the Background note, explain that directors make alterations to the setting, casting, and costuming of a play that introduce anachronisms—elements that seem to be out of their proper time or from contrasting time periods. For example, a director may set Shakespeare's *Hamlet* in a modern mansion and give Hamlet a smart phone, yet leave the text unchanged. Students should look for anachronisms in Ivo van Hove's version of *The Crucible*. They should think about how the casting, setting, or costuming does not reflect Puritan culture and consider what these changes are intended to say about the play's themes.

WHEN STUDENTS STRUGGLE . . .

Use a Graphic Organizer Have individuals or partners use a chart to analyze the effect of the aspects of each photo. Have students discuss their ideas with a partner.

	Casting	Blocking	Lighting	Set Design	Costumes
Description					
Effect					

 For additional support, go to the **Reading Studio** and assign the following ![LEVEL] **Level Up Tutorial: Analyzing Visuals.**

SETTING A PURPOSE

Direct students to use the Setting a Purpose prompt to focus their reading.

 MAKE CONNECTIONS

Have students review the corresponding dialogue and stage directions from *The Crucible* beginning in Act One, paragraph 477, and describe what is happening in the photo. Encourage students to describe how they had envisioned this scene previously and how the photo compares to their mental picture. (**Answers: Annotate:** *The set design is very different—instead of a house in Puritan Salem, it's a modern school room. The scene is lit from a spotlight to the left and above the actors, so that it highlights the girls but casts shadows in the background.* **Connect:** *The lighting gives an eerie glow to the scene and enhances the horror of the girls' accusations. The modern set design gives the impression that the scene could take place in any time or place.*)

■ **English Learner Support**

Understand Multiple-Meaning Words Before students answer the Make Connections questions, provide the meanings for the word *set* below. Have student pairs choose the definition that fits in the context of a play. Then, have partners work together to describe the set using this sentence frame: *The _____ is part of the set.*

- To put in a certain place
- A group of things that belong together
- To arrange a table for a meal
- The scenery built for a theater performance
- A group of games that form part of a match
- A group of persons who share an interest
  SUBSTANTIAL/MODERATE

 For **listening, speaking,** and **reading support** for students at varying proficiency levels, see the **Text X-Ray** on pages 716C–716D.

SETTING A PURPOSE

As you view the photos, consider how a staged production of a play differs from the written script.

MAKE CONNECTIONS
Annotate: How do the set design and lighting in this photo conform to, or break with, the setting Miller describes in the script of Act One?

Connect: How do the lighting and set design affect the audience's perception of the scene?

Act One, Reverend Parris's home. Abigail and Betty begin to accuse their neighbors of witchcraft, as Reverend Parris looks on.

Act Three, courtroom. John Proctor, Deputy Governor Danforth, Reverend Parris, Marshall Herrick, Judge Hathorne, and Ezekiel Cheever listen as Mary Warren testifies against Abigail.

MAKE CONNECTIONS

Annotate: In this image, what observations can you make about the casting, set design, and costumes?

Connect: How are these aspects similar to and different from those in the written play?

✏ MAKE CONNECTIONS

Have students describe the costumes and design of the room (chairs, flooring, etc.). Ask them to identify elements that seem most out of place considering the original setting of the play, such as Mary's hooded sweatshirt. (***Answers:*** ***Annotate:*** *The cast is multiethnic. The set looks like a classroom but not a traditional one. The costumes are modern clothing, and the girls wear school uniforms.* **Connect:** *Miller wanted to portray a particular historical context and community. The casting, set, and costumes in this production take the play completely out of the historical context and evoke nothing of Puritan Salem.*)

TO CHALLENGE STUDENTS . . .

Research Ivo van Hove Challenge students to research online interviews with Ivo van Hove and find insight into his purpose for setting *The Crucible* in more modern times with a diverse cast. Have them choose three quotations from van Hove that reflect his purpose and explain how the quotations illuminate the design and casting decisions. Ask students to present their findings and ideas to the class.

ANALYZE EFFECTIVENESS OF MULTIMODAL TEXT

Remind students that **blocking** is the placement and movement of actors on the stage. Are characters close together, or far apart? What feelings does their body language express? How is the relationship of the characters reflected in these choices? (**Answers: Annotate:** *The setting is stark and industrial. The stacked chairs against the windows suggest bars that block escape. The characters are separated by distance and look like they might be arguing. The clothes are drab and plain.* **Analyze:** *The harsh setting emphasizes the difficult ordeal the characters have endured, and the difficult choices they contemplate. The blocking suggests the tension and emotional distrust they still feel with each other. It doesn't convey the mutual understanding they come to at the end of this scene. The costumes enhance gloomy prison effects and the difficulty the characters still have in forgiving each other.*)

NOTICE & NOTE

ANALYZE EFFECTIVENESS OF MULTIMODAL TEXT

Annotate: Mark the most important information in the caption. Describe the set, costumes, and the blocking of this scene.

Analyze: Explain whether the image matches the description in the caption. How effectively do the setting, costumes, and actors communicate the events and characters' emotions in this scene?

Act Four, prison. John and Elizabeth Proctor discuss whether John should confess or not.

APPLYING ACADEMIC VOCABULARY

☑ **contemporary**   ☑ **global**   ❏ **infinite**   ❏ **simulated**   ❏ **virtual**

Write and Discuss Have students turn to a partner to discuss the questions below. Guide students to include the Academic Vocabulary words *contemporary* and *global* in their responses. Ask volunteers to share their responses with the class.

- How are the actors' costumes **contemporary** with the setting design?
- How does the casting and design choices reflect the play's **global** themes?

Act Four, prison. John Proctor recants his confession.

ANALYZE EFFECTIVENESS OF MULTIMODAL TEXT

Annotate: Describe the lighting in relation to the actor's gestures and position on stage.

Interpret: What emotions do you think the actor is trying to portray? What does the lighting contribute to the scene?

ANALYZE EFFECTIVENESS OF MULTIMODAL TEXT

Point out the strong religious image (crucifixion of Jesus) this photo evokes and discuss why the director might have chosen to characterize Proctor this way in this lighting at this particular moment of the play. (**Answers: Annotate:** *The actor is lit by a strong spotlight that illuminates his profile. He stands as if he's facing the sun, with his arms outstretched.* **Interpret:** *The actor is showing his relief at having recanted his confession and refusing to compromise his personal integrity. The lighting suggests he has found redemption, even though his actions will lead to his death. The audience might feel admiration and happiness for him.*)

■ English Learner Support

Analyze Images To help students understand how the photo reflects this scene in the play, have them meet in small groups and discuss the following questions:

- Read the caption, then reread Act Four of *The Crucible,* pages 708–710, lines 259–302. Which lines correspond to the photo? Why do you think so?
- What is Proctor feeling in this photo? Does this reflect the stage directions in the script? Why do you think so? **LIGHT**

ANALYZE MEDIA

Possible answers:

1. **DOK 2:** *The set is a school room, not a Puritan community, and it looks like it stays the same except for the props, which move around. The lighting is stark and dramatic, casting shadows to create mood and highlighting certain characters to emphasize their emotions or actions. The costumes are modern, plain, and dark, and make the characters look more like a contemporary audience. The actors are more ethnically diverse, which takes the action out of Puritan Salem and brings it into the present globalized society.*

2. **DOK 4:** *The photos reveal that the director wanted to break with traditional interpretations of the play and bring the action into a modern setting. He may have wanted to stress the relevance of the play in the current moment. The photos imply that the theme still comes through, although some viewers might not like the modern interpretation. Others may find it makes more sense to them because it looks like something they know.*

3. **DOK 4:** *In the stills, John Proctor seems to be angry with Abigail, which is consistent with the script. He also seems tense with Elizabeth, which is partially consistent. The stills do not convey the complexity of their relationship and how it evolves over time.*

4. **DOK 4:** *The captions contain information about the moment captured in the image—what is happening in the play, what the characters are doing, and how they are responding to events. Including captions makes the images more effective because they connect the viewer to the play's story, theme, and action. Without captions, viewers would only be guessing at what the images represent.*

5. **DOK 4:** *A still for an ad might draw people in because it intrigues them or they find it dramatic. The effect of that same still used in a review might be enhanced or diluted, depending on the reviewer's opinion of the production. The reviewer may also explain more about what the audience is looking at, so the still is less open to interpretation.*

RESEARCH

An Internet search using "The Crucible play review" will generate plenty of options for students.

Extend Have students show examples of the playbills and posters they found and suggest whether or not they found them effective. Ask students how they might have advertised the play.

⊜ **RESPOND**

ANALYZE MEDIA

Support your responses with evidence from the images. ⊟ NOTEBOOK

1. **Compare** In what ways do the production images depart from the play as it is written? Consider details in the photos related to set, lighting, costuming, and casting in your response.

2. **Analyze** What do the differences between the script and the images reveal about the director's purpose? How effectively do the images convey the play's message about persecution and hysteria?

3. **Analyze** How do the images portray John Proctor's relationship with Abigail and Elizabeth? What aspects of each relationship are missing?

4. **Evaluate** What information do the captions contain? Explain whether the inclusion of captions contributes to the effectiveness of the images.

5. **Synthesize** Production images are often used in advertising campaigns to promote theatrical productions or films. Several of these images appeared in a *New York Times* critical review of the play. How might the message and impact of the photos change when used in a review as opposed to an advertisement?

RESEARCH TIP
When seeking out information on performances, keep in mind that established news outlets, such as the *New York Times*, are considered to be reliable sources. On the other hand, information from social media sites or lesser known sources may lack credibility. These sources are more likely to include faulty reasoning. For example, they may make a false assumption about why a play was well-received that is not based on fact.

RESEARCH

Today, *The Crucible* is considered Arthur Miller's masterpiece and is staged all over the globe in theatrical productions large and small. Research information or reviews about a stage or film version of this play. Complete the chart with the information you find.

PRODUCTION DETAILS	SUMMARY OF REVIEW	
Who directed the performance and what was his or her vision for the story?		
Who portrayed the main characters and what was noteworthy about their performance?		
How was the overall performance received by the public?		

Extend Find a playbill or a poster that advertises the production you researched. Consider the production elements you learned about in this lesson and the information you gathered in your research. Is the playbill or poster an effective marketing tool for this production? Why or why not?

WHEN STUDENTS STRUGGLE . . .

Reteach: Analyze Effectiveness of Multimodal Text For additional practice in interpreting and evaluating the photos, have students work with a partner to discuss how the actors portray the characters' feelings for each other in these photographs. How do the facial expressions, body postures, and gestures reflect anguish, anger, stubbornness, fear, or other feelings? How effective are the actors in the photos conveying these emotions? How does the lighting help communicate these feelings? Have students share their conclusions with the class.

 For additional support, go to the **Reading Studio** and assign the following ⟦LEVEL UP⟧ **Level Up Tutorials: Elements of Drama** and **Analyzing Visuals**.

CREATE AND PRESENT

Write a Treatment Create a multimodal version of the story.

❏ Choose a scene from the play you find compelling or interesting.

❏ Find an excerpt that has an identifiable beginning, middle, and end.

❏ Reread the scene and decide which medium you will use to interpret it—such as a comic book, song, or newspaper article.

❏ Consider how your interpretation will be similar to and different from the original. Will it have the same setting, characters, and events? Alternately, will you set the story in an unusual setting or create a modern version?

❏ Draft a "treatment" of the scene. A treatment is a short prose piece that vividly describes the major elements of the drama. Describe which medium you will use and how you will interpret the characters, setting, and events. What message will you convey? If you are creating an alternate stage or film version, include details about casting, costume and set design, lighting, and blocking.

Present Your Ideas Finish your treatment, and then share it with the class. In a class discussion, evaluate the various interpretations and media.

❏ Which medium seemed the most effective for traditional interpretations of the story? Why?

❏ Which interpretations were most creative and original?

❏ Did any of the interpretations lead you to see *The Crucible* in a new way? If so, explain.

Go to **Using Media in a Presentation** in the **Speaking and Listening Studio** for help.

CREATE AND PRESENT

Write a Treatment Emphasize that when directors choose to change the setting of a drama—by setting it in a different time period, for example—they make this change with a purpose in mind. The purpose is often to bring out parallels between the original time period and the new time period. Students should make any changes intentionally and be prepared to give a reason that connects to the characters, events, or themes of the play.

For **writing support** for students at varying proficiency levels, see the **Text X-Ray** on page 716D.

Present Your Ideas Have each student present their treatments and encourage the class to ask questions about the purpose of choices the "director" made.

RESPOND TO THE ESSENTIAL QUESTION

Allow time for students to add details from *The Crucible* Production Images to their Unit 6 Response Logs.

RESPOND TO THE ESSENTIAL QUESTION

? When should personal integrity come before civic duty?

Gather Information Review your notes on *The Crucible* production photos. Then, add relevant information to your Response Log. As you determine which information to include, think about:

• the message conveyed by the images
• whether the images added insight into the conflict between personal integrity and society's expectations

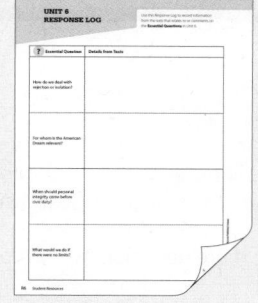

ACADEMIC VOCABULARY

As you write and discuss what you learned from the production images, be sure to use the Academic Vocabulary words. Check off each of the words that you use.

❏ **contemporary**
❏ **global**
❏ **infinite**
❏ **simulated**
❏ **virtual**

MY DUNGEON SHOOK

Open Letter by James Baldwin

GENRE ELEMENTS
OPEN LETTER

An **open letter** is similar to a personal letter, such as one written to a friend, but it is intended to be read by a wider audience. It often includes an appeal to that larger audience, such as a request to do something or to consider an idea or new way of thinking about something. Open letters often communicate a social or political message and are used to protest an issue.

LEARNING OBJECTIVES

- Analyze audience, message, and rhetorical devices.
- Research federal legislation of the 1960s and make connections to the selection.
- Write an open letter.
- Present your letter to a group.
- Determine denotations and connotations.
- Write sentences of varying structure.
- **Language** Discuss the author's message using the key term *integration*.

TEXT COMPLEXITY

Quantitative Measures	My Dungeon Shook	Lexile: 1040L
Qualitative Measures	**Ideas Presented** Multiple levels, implied meanings; abstract, difficult ideas; use of symbolism.	
	Structures Used More complex; narrow perspective; more deviation from chronological order.	
	Language Used More inference is demanded.	
	Knowledge Required More complexity in theme; experiences may be less familiar to many; cultural and historical references may make heavier demands.	

RESOURCES

- Unit 6 Response Log
- 🔊 Selection Audio
- 📖 Reading Studio: Notice & Note
- Level Up Tutorial: Author's Purpose
- Writing Studio: Writing as a Process
- 💬 Speaking and Listening Studio: Giving a Presentation
- Vocabulary Studio: Denotation and Connotation
- ❗ Grammar Studio: Sentence Structure
- ✅ "My Dungeon Shook" Selection Test

SUMMARIES

English

Baldwin's letter to his nephew and namesake urges him to define himself in his own terms and not in the white world's terms. Baldwin writes that white Americans have needed to make black people believe they are inferior to whites, and that until white Americans understand the cruelty in their own history, they cannot be freed from it. He extols his nephew for not succumbing to white people's definition of him. He encourages him to help white Americans see their true selves, because until they do, African Americans will never be free.

Spanish

La carta de Baldwin a su sobrino y homónimo le ruega a definirse a sí mismo en sus propios términos y no en los términos del mundo blanco. Baldwin escribe que los blancos americanos han necesitado hacerles creer a la gente negra que son inferiores y que hasta que los blancos americanos no entiendan la crueldad en su propia historia, no podrán liberarse de ella. Encomia a su sobrino por no sucumbir ante la definición que la gente blanca tiene de él. Lo anima a ayudar a los blancos americanos a ver su realidad, porque mientras no lo hagan, los afroamericanos jamás serán libres.

SMALL-GROUP OPTIONS

Have students work in small groups and pairs to read and discuss the selection.

Pinwheel Discussion

- After students have read the letter, have them discuss the five guided reading questions on Student Edition pages 729–733.
- Have students form groups of ten. Five students in each group stand in the center facing out. The other five stand facing in, each paired with a student facing out.
- Read the first question and have each pair discuss their answers.
- Have the outer group of students rotate to form new pairs. These pairs then discuss the second question. Repeat until all questions have been discussed.

Double-Entry Journal

- Have each student draw a line down the middle of a paper, making two columns. Title the columns *Quotes from the Text* and *My Notes*.
- As students read the selection, have them record significant or confusing text in the left column.
- In the right column, students should write questions, interpretations, or other notes.
- After they read, have students meet in small groups to discuss their notes and ask questions about confusing text.

Text X-Ray: English Learner Support
for "My Dungeon Shook: Letter to My Nephew"

Use the Text X-Ray and the supports and scaffolds in the Teacher's Edition to help guide students at different proficiency levels through the selection.

INTRODUCE THE SELECTION
DISCUSS THE EMANCIPATION PROCLAMATION AND FREEDOM

Tell students that in 1863, Abraham Lincoln's Emancipation Proclamation freed the slaves in the Confederate States of America. This is the "One Hundredth Anniversary" to which Baldwin refers. He is writing this letter to his nephew approximately one hundred years after the proclamation, explaining that he thinks African Americans are not really free yet.

Ask students what rights, liberties, or opportunities people need to truly be free. Provide sentence frames, such as: *People need the right to _____ in order to be free. When people are free, they have opportunities to _____.*

CULTURAL REFERENCES

The following words or phrases may be unfamiliar to students:

- *era* (paragraph 1): a time period
- *the Negro* (paragraph 1): African Americans
- *ghetto* (paragraph 5): a poor, crowded neighborhood
- *the heart of the matter* (paragraph 5): the main idea or most important point
- *Harlem* (paragraph 5): a neighborhood in New York City that became the center of African American culture in the early 1900s

LISTENING

Identify Supporting Details

Draw students' attention to the sentence in paragraph 1 that describes how James's grandfather had a terrible life because he believed what white Americans said about him ("Well, he is dead . . . said about him."). Explain that this statement refers to white Americans' treatment of black Americans in general.

Have students listen as you read aloud paragraph 1. Tell them to jot down words and phrases to support Baldwin's statement. Use the following supports with students at varying proficiency levels:

- Repeat words and phrases from the paragraph, such as: *you are tough, dark, vulnerable, moody.* Have students raise their hands if Baldwin is describing how white Americans viewed black Americans. **SUBSTANTIAL**
- Have students meet with a partner and discuss the words and phrases they jotted down. Ask: *What was life like for James's grandfather?* **MODERATE**
- Have students discuss with a partner the words and phrases they jotted down. Have students complete the following sentence: *James's grandfather believed he _____ because _____.* **LIGHT**

SPEAKING

Analyze Author's Message

Read aloud paragraph 6 and briefly discuss Baldwin's attitudes about acceptance and integration. Reread this sentence: "And if the word integration means anything, this is what it means: that we, with love, shall force our brothers to see themselves as they are, to cease fleeing from reality and begin to change it."

Have students work in small groups to discuss the quotation. Use the following supports with students at varying proficiency levels:

- Ask yes/no questions about the quotation to elicit understanding of Baldwin's meaning of the word *integration* and what African Americans could do to promote change. Include questions such as: *Does Baldwin want African Americans to change?* (yes) *Can change happen?* (yes) *Does Baldwin want his nephew to be strong?* (yes) *Should his nephew flee from reality?* (no) **SUBSTANTIAL**

- Have students complete the following sentence frames and discuss their ideas: *Baldwin wants African Americans to _____ because _____. Change will come if _____. The change that is needed is _____.* **MODERATE**

- Ask: *Do you agree or disagree with Baldwin's statement? Why?* Have students discuss their opinions. **LIGHT**

READING

Draw Conclusions

Tell students that when they draw conclusions, they are making a judgment based on evidence from the text. Drawing conclusions can help students better understand the text.

Use the following supports with students at varying proficiency levels:

- Have students echo read the first sentence in paragraph 3. Point out the footnote. Then, ask students guiding questions to draw a conclusion about what Baldwin means: *Does Baldwin think that black people are treated fairly?* (no) **SUBSTANTIAL**

- Have pairs read paragraph 3 aloud. Then, have students draw a conclusion about how Baldwin felt. Provide a sentence frame: *He thinks black people are _____.* **MODERATE**

- Have pairs read paragraph 3 and then discuss how they think Baldwin feels. Ask: *Why does he make this comparison? How does he feel? What does he tell his nephew?* **LIGHT**

WRITING

Use Repetition

Work with students to read the writing assignment on Student Edition page 735. Review repetition, the use of the same word more than once for effect. Model a sentence with repetition and then ask for examples.

Use the following supports with students at varying proficiency levels:

- Give students verbs, such as *like*. Have them complete a sentence with this format: *I [verb] ___ and I [verb] ___.* Encourage students to add adverb or noun phrases to complete their sentences. **SUBSTANTIAL**

- Have each student write a sentence and then switch sentences with a partner. Ask each student to write a new, related sentence that repeats a word from their partner's sentence. **MODERATE**

- Have students work in groups. Tell them to each write a word on a slip of paper, collect the slips, and then each draw a slip from the pile. Students can then write a sentence using their word twice in a sentence. **LIGHT**

Connect to the
ESSENTIAL QUESTION

James Baldwin questions whether African Americans are being included in the American dream. He discusses how many African Americans have been harmed by exclusion from the dream.

ANALYZE & APPLY

MY DUNGEON SHOOK:

Letter to My Nephew on the One Hundredth Anniversary of the Emancipation

Open Letter by **James Baldwin**

? *ESSENTIAL QUESTION:*

For whom is the American Dream relevant?

726   Unit 6

QUICK START

Part of growing up is envisioning who you want to be and making your vision become a reality. What gives you confidence to pursue your vision? What are some things that can get in your way? Discuss your ideas with your group.

ANALYZE RHETORICAL DEVICES

Authors use **rhetorical devices** to convey meaning or achieve a purpose. When used effectively, they capture attention, evoke emotion, or ignite critical thinking on the part of the reader or audience. Below are three types of rhetorical devices you will encounter as you read.

- **Paradox**—a statement that appears contradictory or absurd, but when thought through, can be considered a possible truth. Baldwin uses this device to get his reader to think deeply about familiar ideas.

  It is the innocence which constitutes the crime.

- **Repetition**—the use of the same word, phrase, or sentence more than once for effect. Baldwin uses repetition to express deep emotion.

  You must accept them and accept them with love.

- **Allusion**—an indirect reference to a person, place, event, or literary work that the author believes readers will know and understand.

  . . . your countrymen, have caused you to be born under conditions not very far removed from those described for us by Charles Dickens in the London of more than a hundred years ago.

As you read, notice how the author uses rhetorical devices to craft his message and shape your perceptions.

ANALYZE AUDIENCE AND MESSAGE

The **audience** for a literary piece is the person or persons the author expects to read his or her work. James Baldwin addressed this letter to his nephew, but also published it in his groundbreaking essay collection, *The Fire Next Time*. As you read, think about the information Baldwin includes. Which details are intended for his nephew? Which are directed to a wider audience?

The author's **message** is the most important idea he or she tries to convey to the audience. Baldwin uses language with specific connotations to convey his message. **Connotation** refers to the emotional response evoked by a particular word. For example, there is a positive connotation when someone is described as "determined." However, describing that person as "stubborn" carries a negative connotation. Notice when Baldwin employs language to elicit an emotional response from the audience. How does his use of language shape your understanding of his message?

GENRE ELEMENTS: OPEN LETTER

- addressed to a specific person but published for a wider readership
- generally written to present an idea, protest, or appeal
- conveys a message to its intended audience

QUICK START

After students have discussed the Quick Start questions in their groups, ask volunteers to share with the class their experiences of pursuing a goal or project. How did they overcome obstacles? Encourage students to think about how to address anticipated problems instead of treating them as impassable roadblocks.

ANALYZE RHETORICAL DEVICES

Help students understand that repetition is not only used to emphasize a concept and add emotion. For example, Baldwin uses repetition to make his readers question their original understanding of the word being repeated. In the example quoted, he is implying that our original understanding of acceptance might not include the concept of accepting with love.

ANALYZE AUDIENCE AND MESSAGE

Tell students that as they read they should think about why Baldwin published this letter for the rest of the world to read, as well as sending it to his nephew. As they read, encourage them to compare and contrast what the audiences of "the world" and "Baldwin's nephew" will likely understand. Will all of the world understand the same things from the letter?

CRITICAL VOCABULARY

Encourage students to read all the sentences before deciding which word or words best completes each one. Remind students to look for context clues that match the precise meaning of each word. Once they have chosen words to complete each sentence, suggest that they reread the sentences to make sure the words they selected make sense.

Answers:

1. *truculent, impertinent*

2. *inhumanity*

3. *unassailable, strive*

4. *fixed, constitute*

■ English Learner Support

Use Cognates Tell students that the Critical Vocabulary word *constitute* has a Spanish cognate, *constituir*. Similarly, *humanity*, the opposite of *inhumanity*, is *humanidad* in Spanish. **ALL LEVELS**

LANGUAGE CONVENTIONS

Sentence Structure As they read, encourage students to analyze the syntax Baldwin uses. Why does he use short sentences in some places and longer ones in others?

 ANNOTATION MODEL

Remind students that they may annotate the text by underlining or circling it, or they may use their own system for marking up the selection in their write-in text. They may want to color-code their annotations by using highlighters. Their notes in the margin may be about rhetorical devices they find and how they relate to the author's message or about the author's use of sentence structure.

 **GET READY**

CRITICAL VOCABULARY

truculent	constitute	impertinent	unassailable
strive	inhumanity	fixed	

See how many Critical Vocabulary words you already know by completing the following sentences.

1. Egged on by their leader's angry, _____ speech, the mob stormed the city square, many chanting rude, _____ slogans.

2. The Holocaust is considered the most extreme act of _____ in modern history.

3. The Constitution of the United States outlines _____ rights and guides citizens to _____ for fairness and equal opportunity.

4. Having unchanging, _____ beliefs gives a person stability, even though it may _____ an attitude of closed-mindedness.

LANGUAGE CONVENTIONS

Sentence Structure In order to make writing appeal to readers, authors use a variety of sentence structures. Some of the techniques authors use include alternating long and short sentences to produce rhythm, using short sentences to emphasize a point, and using a variety of sentence structures to prevent monotony. As you read, notice the different sentence structures that Baldwin employs and the impact it has on your understanding.

ANNOTATION MODEL   **NOTICE & NOTE**

As you read, notice how Baldwin conveys his message to his audience. Note how he uses rhetorical devices to convey his message. In the model, you can see one reader's notes about the text.

Dear James,

I have begun this letter <u>five times</u> and <u>torn it up five times</u>. I keep seeing your face, which is also the face of your father and my brother. Like him, you are <u>tough, dark, vulnerable, moody</u>—with a very definite tendency to sound truculent because you want <u>no one to think you are soft</u>. You may be <u>like your grandfather</u> in this. I don't know, but certainly both <u>you and your father resemble him</u> very much physically.

repetition; wants message to be clear

complex description of James

The writer's message might relate to how things change or stay the same over time.

BACKGROUND

James Baldwin *(1924–1987) During the racial and social unrest that characterized the 1950s and 60s, James Baldwin profoundly influenced the ways in which both black and white people perceived the plight of African Americans. He bluntly described the personal torments black people endured, thus compelling black people to overcome, and white people to acknowledge, the physical and psychological damage racism inflicts on individuals and on society.*

MY DUNGEON SHOOK:

Letter to My Nephew on the One Hundredth Anniversary of the Emancipation

Open Letter by James Baldwin

SETTING A PURPOSE

As you read, see if you can identify the rhetorical devices Baldwin uses to convince his nephew to believe in himself.

1 Dear James:
I have begun this letter five times and torn it up five times. I keep seeing your face, which is also the face of your father and my brother. Like him, you are tough, dark, vulnerable, moody—with a very definite tendency to sound **truculent** because you want no one to think you are soft. You may be like your grandfather in this, I don't know, but certainly both you and your father resemble him very much physically. Well, he is dead, he never saw you, and he had a terrible life; believed what white people said about him. This is one of the reasons that he became so holy.[1] I am sure that your father has told you something about all that. Neither you nor your father exhibit any tendency towards holiness: you really *are* of another era, part of what happened when the Negro left the land and came into what the

---
[1] **so holy:** Baldwin's stepfather was a minister who raised his children in a strict, conservative, religious environment.

Notice & Note

Use the side margins to notice and note signposts in the text.

---

truculent
(trŭk´yə-lənt) *adj.* eager for a fight; fierce.

ANALYZE AUDIENCE AND MESSAGE

Annotate: In paragraph 1, mark phrases that convey up Baldwin's message to his nephew.

Analyze: Why might information about the grandfather be of interest to Baldwin's nephew?

My Dungeon Shook: Letter to My Nephew 729

BACKGROUND

After students read about Baldwin's work, have them think about what the information says about Baldwin as a person. For example, have them consider what it means that Baldwin cared strongly about helping other people and felt their pain and not just his own. Discuss how a writer's observation and communication skills would help him bear witness to what he and others have experienced.

SETTING A PURPOSE

Direct students to use the Setting a Purpose prompt to focus their reading.

ANALYZE AUDIENCE AND MESSAGE

Tell students that by discussing his nephew's elders such as his grandfather and father, Baldwin begins this essay talking about the culture and family that gave birth to his nephew, James. Baldwin is not pretending it is all a happy history; he warns his nephew not to make his grandfather's mistakes. (**Answer:** *By describing the grandfather he never knew, Baldwin gives James an example of how believing what others say could destroy his future. Baldwin wants James to understand that he should not let societal attitudes and beliefs define who he is as a man, especially those based on the color of his skin. James should learn from the history of his people to help him cope with prejudice.*)

For **listening support** for students at varying proficiency levels, see the **Text X-Ray** on page 726C.

CRITICAL VOCABULARY

truculent: Baldwin says his nephew sounds tough and ready to fight so others won't think he is weak.

ASK STUDENTS why Baldwin thinks being truculent is not a good choice. (*Baldwin thinks it shows that his truculent nephew is too concerned with what others think of him, an attitude Baldwin believes is destructive.*)

TEACH

 ## ANALYZE RHETORICAL DEVICES

Discuss with students why Baldwin uses paradox to focus on this particular concept. Lead them to understand that people (then and now) tend to believe that not knowing about a problem makes you innocent. Baldwin wants his audience to think about the problem and educate themselves. (***Answer:*** *For years, white people have been ignorant of or ignored the conditions in which black Americans live and the suffering that results. Baldwin argues that by choosing not to understand the ramifications of racism, white Americans can have a false sense of innocence. For Baldwin, their complicity is a crime.*)

EL ## ENGLISH LEARNER SUPPORT

Word Definitions In paragraph 2, point out the phrase "those tears he sheds invisibly" and explain that *shed tears* means "produce and release tears." Explain that "shedding invisible tears" means that a person is carrying a sadness inside that is not obvious to those around him or her. **MODERATE**

EXTREME OR ABSOLUTE LANGUAGE

Have students think about the connotations of certainty. In addition to what he's implying to his nephew, Baldwin is telling the rest of his audience that he is someone who knows his truth and he is not adjusting his opinion to make it more appealing to them. (***Answer:*** *By expressing extreme certainty and an uncompromising position, Baldwin is establishing his role as a teacher and mentor. He wants to convince James—and the public—that his experience as a black man gives him firsthand knowledge of the issue.*)

CRITICAL VOCABULARY

strive: Baldwin knows that James will need to struggle to become tough and wise in the face of destruction.

ASK STUDENTS what Baldwin is striving for in this essay. *(He wants to teach his nephew to strive to become strong and gain understanding.)*

constitute: Baldwin believes that innocence amounts to a crime.

ASK STUDENTS what constitutes Baldwin's opinion on ignorance of racism. *(It is no excuse.)*

730   Unit 6

ANALYZE RHETORICAL DEVICES

Annotate: In the last sentence of paragraph 2, mark the two contradictory words that make this sentence a paradox.

Interpret: Based on Baldwin's logic, how can this statement be a possible truth?

strive
(strīv) *v.* to struggle or fight forcefully; contend.

constitute
(kŏn´stĭ-tōot) *v.* to amount to; equal.

EXTREME OR ABSOLUTE LANGUAGE

Notice and Note: In paragraph 3, mark the phrases where Baldwin expresses extreme certainty or an uncompromising position.

Infer: What is Baldwin's purpose for using such language?

---

late E. Franklin Frazier[2] called "the cities of destruction." You can only be destroyed by believing that you really are what the white world calls a *nigger*. I tell you this because I love you, and please don't you ever forget it.

2   I have known both of you all your lives, have carried your Daddy in my arms and on my shoulders, kissed and spanked him and watched him learn to walk. I don't know if you've known anybody from that far back; if you've loved anybody that long, first as an infant, then as a child, then as a man, you gain a strange perspective on time and human pain and effort. Other people cannot see what I see whenever I look into your father's face, for behind your father's face as it is today are all those other faces which were his. Let him laugh and I see a cellar your father does not remember and a house he does not remember and I hear in his present laughter his laughter as a child. Let him curse and I remember him falling down the cellar steps, and howling, and I remember, with pain, his tears, which my hand or your grandmother's so easily wiped away. But no one's hand can wipe away those tears he sheds invisibly today, which one hears in his laughter and in his speech and in his songs. I know what the world has done to my brother and how narrowly he has survived it. And I know, which is much worse, and this is the crime of which I accuse my country and my countrymen, and for which neither I nor time nor history will ever forgive them, that they have destroyed and are destroying hundreds of thousands of lives and do not know it and do not want to know it. One can be, indeed one must **strive** to become, tough and philosophical concerning destruction and death, for this is what most of mankind has been best at since we have heard of man. (But remember: *most* of mankind is not all of mankind.) But it is not permissible that the authors of devastation should also be innocent. It is the innocence which **constitutes** the crime.

3   Now, my dear namesake, these innocent and well-meaning people, your countrymen, have caused you to be born under conditions not very far removed from those described for us by Charles Dickens[3] in the London of more than a hundred years ago. (I hear the chorus of the innocents screaming, "No! This is not true! How *bitter* you are!"—but I am writing this letter to *you*, to try to tell you something about how to handle *them*, for most of them do not yet really know that you exist. I *know* the conditions under which you were born, for I was there. Your countrymen were *not* there, and haven't made it yet. Your grandmother was also there, and no one has ever accused her of being bitter. I suggest that the innocents check

---

[2] **E. Franklin Frazier:** African American sociologist (1894–1962) who studied the structure of black communities.

[3] **described . . . by Charles Dickens:** Dickens (1812–1870) was a British novelist whose works frequently described the hardships suffered by the poor in London.

with her. She isn't hard to find. Your countrymen don't know that *she* exists, either, though she has been working for them all their lives.)

4   Well, you were born, here you came, something like fifteen years ago; and though your father and mother and grandmother, looking about the streets through which they were carrying you, staring at the walls into which they brought you, had every reason to be heavyhearted, yet they were not. For here you were, Big James, named for me—you were a big baby, I was not—here you were: to be loved. To be loved, baby, hard, at once, and forever, to strengthen you against the loveless world. Remember that: I know how black it looks today, for you. It looked bad that day, too, yes, we were trembling. We have not stopped trembling yet, but if we had not loved each other none of us would have survived. And now you must survive because we love you, and for the sake of your children and your children's children.

5   This innocent country set you down in a ghetto in which, in fact, it intended that you should perish. Let me spell out precisely what I mean by that, for the heart of the matter is here, and the root of my dispute with my country. You were born where you were born and faced the future that you faced because you were black and *for no other reason*. The limits of your ambition were, thus, expected to be set forever. You were born into a society which spelled out with brutal clarity, and in as many ways as possible, that you were a worthless human being. You were not expected to aspire to excellence: you were expected to make peace with mediocrity. Wherever you have turned, James, in your short time on this earth, you have been told where you could go and what you could do (and *how* you could do it) and where you could live and whom you could marry. I know your countrymen do not agree with me about this, and I hear them saying, "You exaggerate." They do not know Harlem, and I do. So do you. Take no one's word for anything, including mine—but trust your experience.

6   Know whence you came. If you know whence you came, there is really no limit to where you can go. The details and symbols of your life have been deliberately constructed to make you believe what white people say about you. Please try to remember that what they believe, as well as what they do and cause you to endure, does not testify to your inferiority but to their **inhumanity** and fear. Please try to be clear, dear James, through the storm which rages about your youthful head today, about the reality which lies behind the words *acceptance* and *integration*. There is no reason for you to try to become like white people and there is no basis whatever for their **impertinent** assumption that *they* must accept *you*. The really terrible thing, old buddy, is that *you* must accept *them*. And I mean that very seriously. You must accept them and accept them with love. For these innocent people have no other hope. They are, in effect, still trapped in a history which they do not understand; and until they understand

---

NOTICE & NOTE

ANALYZE RHETORICAL DEVICES

Annotate: In paragraph 4, mark words that are repeated at least twice.

Analyze: What effect does the use of repeated words have on the message?

LANGUAGE CONVENTIONS

Annotate: Mark the sentences in paragraph 5 that are a different length than the others.

Evaluate: This paragraph is composed of long sentences with dependent clauses that are typical of speech patterns. What effect do the shorter sentences have on Baldwin's message?

inhumanity
(ĭn-hyōō-măn´ĭ-tē) *n.* lack of pity or compassion.

impertinent
(ĭm-pûr´tn-ənt) *adj.* rude; ill-mannered.

WHEN STUDENTS STRUGGLE . . .

Author's Purpose   Have individuals or partners use a chart to help them understand the two purposes Baldwin has. Students should list what he is saying to his two audiences.

What James Should Do	What Americans Should Do

 For additional support, go to the **Reading Studio** and assign the following [LEVEL] **Level Up Tutorial: Author's Purpose.**

ANALYZE RHETORICAL DEVICES

Discuss with students the emotional effects of repeating *loved* and *trembling*. Baldwin says repeatedly that they are trembling and not just a little bit, but that they are loved. He thinks they must pass on that love to the next generation. (**Answer:** *It creates a rhythmic flow and emphasizes the idea that love supports African Americans and helps them get through difficulties. It also indicates that James is loved and because of that he can survive for the sake of future generations. He must carry on.*)

LANGUAGE CONVENTIONS

Tell students that shorter sentences are often used for emphasis, especially when used in a text that has mostly longer sentences. Shorter sentences stand out among longer sentences. The shorter sentences can be understood quickly and can convey a sense of urgency. (**Answer:** *The longer sentences connect many interrelated ideas, such as the complicated, problematic nature of racism, its many facets, and the consequences for the black man. The shorter sentences are specific, direct, and simple to understand. Baldwin is distilling the problem into a piece of advice: James needs to trust his own experience of living in Harlem and let it guide his future actions.*)

 For **speaking** and **reading support** for students at varying proficiency levels, see the **Text X-Ray** on page 726D.

CRITICAL VOCABULARY

inhumanity: Racism shows the lack of compassion of the racist.

ASK STUDENTS why Baldwin would consider ignoring another person's problems as an example of inhumanity. (*It is considered part of human nature to one another, so not doing that shows inhumanity.*)

impertinent: Baldwin says white people are rudely assuming that they must accept African Americans.

ASK STUDENTS how the patronizing ignorance of the white people Baldwin describes is impertinent. (*The white people are impertinent to assume that they are the ones to accept African Americans and not vice versa.*)

ANALYZE AUDIENCE AND MESSAGE

Point out to students that when Baldwin's uses the word *you*—as in "intended that you should perish"—it makes the message apply more broadly. The *you* could be read as being directed at James, but it also could be read as addressing all African Americans. (**Answer:** *The phrases emphasize how terrible the problem of racism is, but they also emphasize how Baldwin has not given up on the power of African Americans to use love to heal white America.*)

EL

ENGLISH LEARNER SUPPORT

Synonyms Explain that Baldwin uses the synonyms *fixed* and *immovable* to emphasize how most white Americans have viewed African Americans in only one way. African Americans have had a permanent inferior position in their minds, and to change white Americans' thinking, African Americans would have to alter how they see themselves. Have students suggest other synonyms and discuss the differences in connotation.

LIGHT

CRITICAL VOCABULARY

fixed: African Americans have had a steady and immovable place in society.

ASK STUDENTS why Baldwin objects to African Americans being fixed in society. (*He wants African Americans to be free to be whoever they want to be.*)

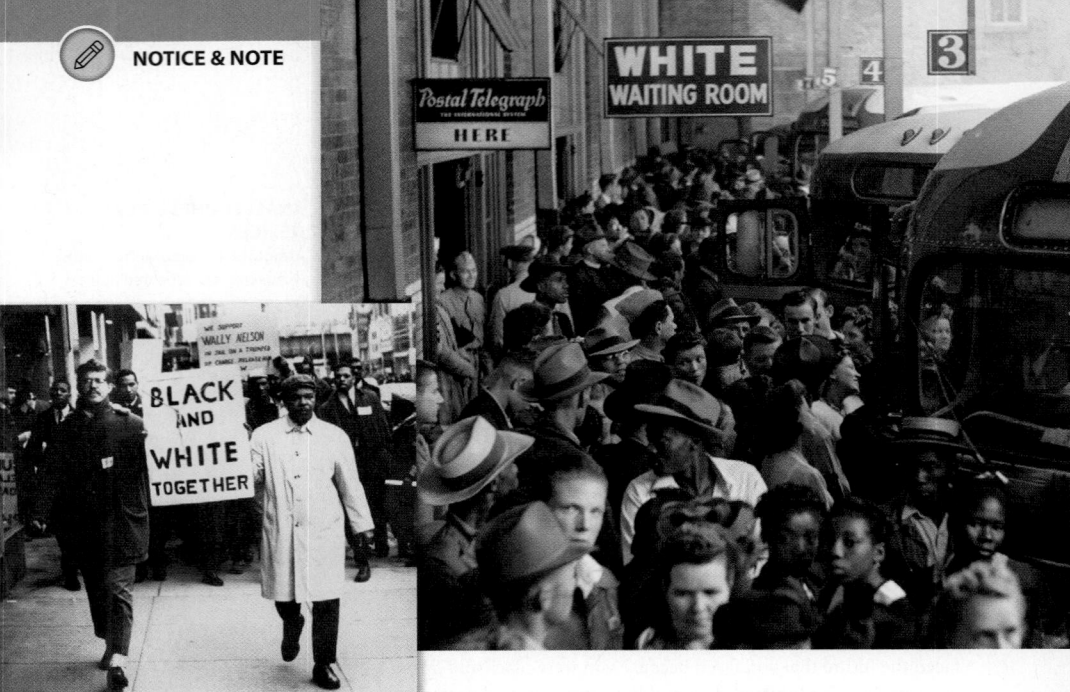

NOTICE & NOTE

ANALYZE AUDIENCE AND MESSAGE

Annotate: Mark two examples of details in paragraph 6 that evoke an emotional response from the audience.

Analyze: What impact do these phrases have on the message the writer conveys?

fixed
(fĭkst) *adj.* firmly in position; stationary.

it, they cannot be released from it. They have had to believe for many years, and for innumerable reasons, that black men are inferior to white men. Many of them, indeed, know better, but, as you will discover, people find it very difficult to act on what they know. To act is to be committed, and to be committed is to be in danger. In this case, the danger, in the minds of most white Americans, is the loss of their identity. Try to imagine how you would feel if you woke up one morning to find the sun shining and all the stars aflame. You would be frightened because it is out of the order of nature. Any upheaval in the universe is terrifying because it so profoundly attacks one's sense of one's own reality. Well, the black man has functioned in the white man's world as a **fixed** star, as an immovable pillar: and as he moves out of his place, heaven and earth are shaken to their foundations. You, don't be afraid. I said that it was intended that you should perish in the ghetto, perish by never being allowed to go behind the white man's definitions, by never being allowed to spell your proper name. You have, and many of us have, defeated this intention; and, by a terrible law, a terrible paradox, those innocents who believed that your imprisonment made them safe are losing their grasp of reality. But these men are your brothers —your lost, younger brothers. And if the word *integration* means anything, this is what it means: that we, with love, shall force our brothers to see themselves as they are, to cease fleeing from reality and begin to change it. For this is your home, my friend, do not be driven from it; great men have done great things here, and will again, and we can make America what America

---

APPLYING ACADEMIC VOCABULARY

☐ **contemporary**   ☐ **global**   ☑ **infinite**   ☑ **simulated**   ☐ **virtual**

Write and Discuss Have partners discuss the following questions. Guide students to include the academic vocabulary words *infinite* and *simulated* in their responses.

- Do you think James Baldwin considers people's capacity for change as **infinite**? Why or why not?
- Would Baldwin have accepted **simulated** fairness from white Americans until he could get true fairness? Support your answer with evidence from the text.

must become. It will be hard, James, but you come from sturdy, peasant stock, men who picked cotton and dammed rivers and built railroads, and, in the teeth of⁴ the most terrifying odds, achieved an **unassailable** and monumental dignity. You come from a long line of great poets, some of the greatest poets since Homer. One of them said, *The very time I thought I was lost, My dungeon shook and my chains fell off.*⁵

7   You know, and I know, that the country is celebrating one hundred years of freedom one hundred years too soon. We cannot be free until they are free. God bless you, James, and Godspeed.

Your uncle,
James

---
⁴ **in the teeth of:** in spite of.
⁵ ***The very time . . . fell off:*** a quotation from the traditional spiritual "My Dungeon Shook." It alludes to the biblical story of Paul and Silas (Acts 16), who were freed from an unjust imprisonment by the action of an earthquake.

CHECK YOUR UNDERSTANDING

Answer these questions before moving on to the **Analyze the Text** section on the following page.

1 According to Baldwin, why did James' grandfather have a terrible life?

A White people in the community ignored him.

B He was unable to complete his education.

C White business owners would not employ him.

D He believed what white people said about him.

2 Baldwin says that James was born into a society that viewed him as —

F a bitter man

G a powerful survivor

H a worthless human being

J an ambitious student

3 What is Baldwin's advice to James about how to treat white people?

A Accept them and accept them with love.

B Feel sorry for them because of their ignorance.

C Teach them that they are enslaved by their beliefs.

D Convince them to accept African Americans.

My Dungeon Shook: Letter to My Nephew   733

unassailable
(ŭn-ə-sāʹlə-bəl) *adj.* undeniable.

ANALYZE RHETORICAL DEVICES

Annotate: Recall that a **paradox** is a statement that appears contradictory but presents a possible truth. Mark two paradoxes in paragraph 7.

Interpret: How are these statements paradoxical? What insights on race in America do these two statements convey?

ANALYZE RHETORICAL DEVICES

Discuss with students why Baldwin uses paradox. (*to capture attention and evoke emotion*) Point out that using paradox at the end of the letter leaves a strong impression with the reader. (**Possible answer:** *The statements reveal the paradox that for 100 years the nation has assumed slavery was over, and that all citizens were free. Baldwin points out that neither black nor white Americans are free because they are both constrained by narrow definitions of race and privilege. These paradoxes sum up his arguments concisely.*)

EL ENGLISH LEARNER SUPPORT

Multiple-Meaning Words Help students use context to clarify the meaning of these words and phrases as used in the selection: *stock* meaning "ancestry," *dammed* meaning "blocked by a dam," *monumental* meaning "great," and *line* meaning "a series of persons." **MODERATE/LIGHT**

CHECK YOUR UNDERSTANDING

Have students answer the questions independently.

Answers:

1. *D*

2. *H*

3. *A*

If they answer any questions incorrectly, have them reread the text to confirm their understanding. Then they may proceed to ANALYZE THE TEXT on page 734.

EL ENGLISH LEARNER SUPPORT

Oral Assessment Use the following questions to assess students' comprehension and speaking skills:

1. Did James' grandfather believe what white people said about him? (*yes*)

2. Do some people think James is a worthless human being? (*yes*)

3. Baldwin thinks that James should _____ white people with love. (*accept*)

SUBSTANTIAL/MODERATE

CRITICAL VOCABULARY

unassailable: James' ancestors know that they are undeniably worthy of respect as people.

ASK STUDENTS whether Baldwin thought the capacity of African Americans for great achievements was unassailable. (*Yes, because history shows unassailable examples of what they were able to do against terrible odds.*)

ANALYZE THE TEXT

Possible answers:

1. **DOK 2:** *While innocence usually carries a positive connotation, the word has a negative connotation as used by Baldwin. Instead of conveying a lack of guilt, "innocence" to Baldwin suggests a lack of understanding, as when he suggests that innocence is a crime.*

2. **DOK 4:** *Nephew: personal memories of the boy's father; "dear namesake;" "how to handle them;" don't try to be like white people, but accept them with love; don't allow yourself to feel inferior because white people fear losing their identity. Wider audience: White Americans need to take responsibility for their inadvertent support for inequality. If white Americans understand Baldwin's message to James, then they should cease fearing they will lose their own identity as they allow black Americans to shape their own.*

3. **DOK 4:** *Baldwin's appeal to his nephew to allow no one else to define him is clear. His argument to his nephew is stated in concrete terms and supported with examples that young James can understand. The argument made to the wider public is passionately stated. Baldwin offers rebuttals to expected criticism, but there aren't as many examples of white cruelty to support some of the claims, nor is there a direct call to action.*

4. **DOK 4:** *The composers of the spiritual were the poets of the enslaved, and the biblical reference was meant to give enslaved people hope. Baldwin uses the reference to give his nephew hope and to tie James' fight for dignity to that of his ancestors. White Americans might read the allusion and think that Baldwin was calling black Americans to fight for equality, which may have alarmed some of them.*

5. **DOK 4:** *The uncompromising language conveys his certainty and courage, thereby adding power and emphasis to his message. It encourages his audience to take his message seriously and to draw on their own strength and courage.*

RESEARCH

Remind students that certain sources from the time will be quite subjective, so they should look for a variety of sources and be alert for bias.

Extend While they are researching discrimination, encourage students to form a researched opinion on how various measures of racial disparity have changed since Baldwin's time.

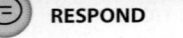 **RESPOND**

ANALYZE THE TEXT

Support your responses with evidence from the text. 📓 NOTEBOOK

1. **Interpret** Baldwin refers to innocence throughout the text. As Baldwin uses the word, does it carry a positive or negative connotation? Cite specific examples in your response.

2. **Analyze** In the letter, which details are directed to his nephew, and which to a wider audience? Look specifically at paragraphs 2, 3, and 6.

3. **Evaluate** What is Baldwin's overall message? Explain whether Baldwin conveys his message effectively to both his nephew and to the wider audience. Cite text evidence in your response.

4. **Analyze** The title of this letter, "My Dungeon Shook," is an allusion to a popular spiritual, which in turn alludes to a biblical story. How does this allusion support Baldwin's claim that his nephew is worthy in his own right? How might it resonate with white Americans reading this letter?

5. **Notice & Note** Baldwin uses uncompromising language to support his message about race in America. How does this kind of language add strength to his argument? What impact does it have on his audience?

RESEARCH

RESEARCH TIP
As you search for reputable sites, be sure you check for credibility, bias, and accuracy. Use more than one source and compare their information. Check for bias by noting opinions and slanted language.

Baldwin wrote this letter during the 1960s, a time of deep racial prejudice and social unrest. Research some of the federal legislation that was passed during that period to address the political, social, and economic problems caused by racism. Then, decide what impact the legislation had on the issues Baldwin discusses.

LEGISLATION	MAIN FOCUS	IMPACT ON ISSUES MENTIONED BY BALDWIN
Civil Rights Act of 1964	*banned discrimination; equal access to public places and jobs; desegregated schools*	
Voting Rights Act of 1965	*outlawed discriminatory voting practices such as literacy tests*	
Fair Housing Act of 1968	*banned discrimination in sale, rental, and financing of housing*	

Extend With a partner, discuss other groups that may face discrimination today, such as people with disabilities. What kinds of legislation would you propose to resolve those difficulties?

WHEN STUDENTS STRUGGLE . . .

Reteach: Author's Purpose Have students use the messages they charted as showing author's purpose and put them together. Taken altogether, what do they suggest James Baldwin's purpose is? Have pairs of students discuss, each citing their evidence.

 For additional support, go to the **Reading Studio** and assign the following LEVEL UP **Level Up Tutorial: Author's Purpose.**

CREATE AND PRESENT

Write an Open Letter Over 60 years have passed since Baldwin wrote his letter to his 15-year-old nephew. Since that time civil rights were granted protection by law and racial equality improved to the point that Americans elected an African American president. However, there are still advances in this area to be made. Write an open letter to a friend or family member with your message about civil rights and racial equality. Remember, this will be an open letter, so your audience will include the public.

- ❏ Review historic or current events to decide on a topic.
- ❏ Determine your message. You may emphasize the progress that has been made or discuss advances that are still to come.
- ❏ Decide on how you will support your message.
- ❏ Write a rough draft of your letter. Confirm that you have a clear thesis statement, adequate support, and compelling word choice.
- ❏ Revise as needed, adding relevant details and rhetorical devices for clarification and emphasis.

Present Your Letter Read your letter to your group. Remember, you can use verbal and nonverbal techniques as you read to convey your meaning and the importance of your message.

- ❏ Determine where you might raise or lower your voice. Select words and phrases to emphasize.
- ❏ Decide when to make eye contact with your audience.
- ❏ Vary your reading speed, and remember to pause for effect.

 Go to **Writing as a Process** in the **Writing Studio** for help with the writing process.

 Go to **Giving a Presentation: Delivering Your Presentation** in the **Speaking and Listening Studio** for help with verbal and nonverbal delivery techniques.

RESPOND TO THE ESSENTIAL QUESTION

 For whom is the American Dream relevant?

Gather Information Review your annotations and notes on "My Dungeon Shook: Letter to My Nephew." Then, add relevant information to your Response Log. As you determine which information to include, think about:

- what life is like in America according to Baldwin
- whether the concept of the American Dream has changed
- the difference in meaning between *fair* and *equal*

UNIT 6
RESPONSE LOG

ACADEMIC VOCABULARY
As you write and discuss what you learned from "My Dungeon Shook: Letter to My Nephew," be sure to use the Academic Vocabulary words. Check off each of the words that you use.

- ❏ **contemporary**
- ❏ **global**
- ❏ **infinite**
- ❏ **simulated**
- ❏ **virtual**

CREATE AND PRESENT

Write an Open Letter Encourage students to plan their letters before they start writing. Students should write reasons that support their messages and perhaps write ways our country has and has not progressed since the time of Baldwin's letter.

For **writing support** for students at varying proficiency levels, see the **Text X-Ray** on page 726D.

Present Your Letter Have students practice reading their letters by reading to a partner. Remind partners about giving specific constructive advice, such as "it would help if you enunciated more" instead of just "I couldn't understand you."

RESPOND TO THE ESSENTIAL QUESTION

Allow time for students to add details from "My Dungeon Shook: Letter to My Nephew" to their Unit 6 Response Logs.

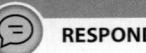

APPLY

CRITICAL VOCABULARY

Answers:

1. *insolent*

2. *indisputable*

3. *belligerent*

4. *compose*

5. *rigid*

6. *attempt*

7. *cruelty*

VOCABULARY STRATEGY:

Analyze Denotation and Connotation

Answers:

DENOTATION	CONNOTATION
disposed to or eager to fight; belligerent	outraged, frustrated
to struggle, fight forcefully; try	determined
to be the elements or parts of; compose	signify formally
lack of pity or compassion	insensitivity, cruelty
firmly in position; stationary	rigid, stubborn
impossible to dispute or disprove; undeniable	cannot be taken away

 RESPOND

WORD BANK

truculent   impertinent

strive   fixed

constitute   unassailable

inhumanity

Go to **Denotation and Connotation** in the **Vocabulary Studio** for help.

CRITICAL VOCABULARY

Practice and Apply Choose the word that is closest in meaning to the Critical Vocabulary word.

1. impertinent: (a) insolent (b) impossible (c) unfriendly

2. unassailable: (a) unproven (b) indisputable (c) weakened

3. truculent: (a) belligerent (b) rude (c) civilized

4. constitute: (a) restrict (b) measure (c) compose

5. fixed: (a) broken (b) rigid (c) resilient

6. strive: (a) attempt (b) retreat (c) wallow

7. inhumanity: (a) kindness (b) intolerance (c) cruelty

VOCABULARY STRATEGY: Analyze Denotation and Connotation

Words often have nuances of meaning. The literal meaning of a word, or **denotation,** is determined by consulting a dictionary. A word also has a **connotation,** or an emotional response that is evoked when the word is used. Understanding word connotations helps the reader to more effectively identify and analyze the author's message.

In Baldwin's letter, he uses the word *unassailable* to describe "dignity." The denotation of *unassailable* is "impossible to dispute or disprove; undeniable." Baldwin did not use the word *undeniable* because people can attempt to deny or dispute someone's dignity. Instead, Baldwin deliberately chose a more intense word to indicate that dignity cannot successfully be taken away. If you consider the connotation of *unassailable,* you understand that it means "unquestionable, untouchable, cannot be revoked."

Practice and Apply Complete the table by first writing the word's denotation. Then, identify the connotation associated with the word as it is used in the text. Consider the emotion each word makes you feel.

VOCABULARY WORD	DENOTATION	CONNOTATION
unassailable	undeniable	positive, intense
truculent		
strive		
constitute		
inhumanity		
fixed		
impertinent		

© Houghton Mifflin Harcourt Publishing Company

736   Unit 6

EL ENGLISH LEARNER SUPPORT

Sound Transfer Note that the short *i* as in *inhumanity, constitute,* and *fixed* may be a difficult sound for speakers of Spanish, Hmong, Cantonese, Haitian Creole, and Korean, as the sound either does not exist in the language, does exist but is pronounced somewhat differently, or is likely to be confused with another sound. Be sure to pronounce such words for students while they can see the letters. Then, have them repeat chorally. **SUBSTANTIAL/MODERATE**

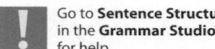

LANGUAGE CONVENTIONS:
Varied Sentence Structure

An essential part of a writer's style is **syntax,** or how the writer arranges words to construct phrases, clauses, and sentences. Effective writers employ varied sentence structure and length to create an engaging rhythm that holds the reader's interest.

There are many ways to vary sentence structure.

- Alternate long and short sentences to avoid monotony and produce rhythm.

> **I suggest that the innocents check with her. She isn't hard to find.**

- Use short sentences to emphasize a point.

> **They do not know Harlem, and I do. So do you.**

- Alternate subject-verb order with other introductory phrases or clauses.

> **Wherever you have turned, James, in your short time on this earth, you have been told where you could go. . . .**

- Combine sentences into compound or complex sentences.

> **I tell you this because I love you, and please don't you ever forget it.**

Practice and Apply Review the letter that you wrote for your Create and Present activity to look for an opportunity to vary sentence structure. Write your revision below. When you have finished, share your sentences with a partner and compare your use of varied sentence structure.

> [!] Go to **Sentence Structure** in the **Grammar Studio** for help.

LANGUAGE CONVENTIONS:
Varied Sentence Structure

Have students rewrite the sample sentences so both are long or short. Then, have them discuss with a partner how the change in syntax affects the readers' interest and changes the effect of the sentences. Encourage students to realize that the urgency of short sentences is ideal when the writer intends emphasis but that it can be rather intense if there are too many. Similarly, the mental challenge of an exceedingly long sentence means it should be used sparingly and with intention.

Practice and Apply Have students review the sentence structures in their paragraphs for good usage and balance, first on their own and then with a partner.

My Dungeon Shook: Letter to My Nephew   737

 ENGLISH LEARNER SUPPORT

Language Conventions Use the following supports with students at varying proficiency levels:

- Have students find and mark three short sentences and three long sentences in the selection. **SUBSTANTIAL**
- Have students pick a short sentence and a long sentence in the selection and then discuss with a partner why they think the length of each is effective. **MODERATE**
- Have students pick a short sentence and a long sentence in the selection and rewrite them with a different length. Have them discuss with a partner how the sentences changed. **LIGHT**

SPEECH ON THE VIETNAM WAR, 1967

Speech by Martin Luther King Jr.

GENRE ELEMENTS
SPEECH

A **speech** is a formal communication to an audience, made for the purpose of presenting evidence that supports a specific position on an issue. In an effective speech, the speaker anticipates and addresses counterarguments that might be made against his or her position and uses rhetorical devices to emphasize ideas represented in the speech.

LEARNING OBJECTIVES

- Identify the structural elements of a speech.
- Conduct research on legislation from government sites.
- Write an article.
- Participate in a group discussion.
- Use suffixes to understand meaning.
- Identify imperative mood.
- **Language** Discuss rhetorical devices using the key term *metaphor*.

TEXT COMPLEXITY

Quantitative Measures	SPEECH ON THE VIETNAM WAR, 1967	Lexile: 1290L
Qualitative Measures	**Ideas Presented** Multiple levels of meaning, some difficult ideas.	
	Structures Used Complex, deviates from chronological.	
	Language Used Complex sentence structures, some figurative language.	
	Knowledge Required More complexity in theme. Experiences may be less familiar to many. Cultural or historical references may make heavier demands.	

Online Ed

RESOURCES

- Unit 6 Response Log

- 🔊 Selection Audio

- 📖 Reading Studio:
  Setting a Purpose

- LEVELUP Level Up Tutorial: Analyzing
  Arguments

- Writing Studio:
  Writing Arguments

- 💬 Speaking and Listening Studio:
  Analyzing and Evaluating
  Presentations

- 🔵 Vocabulary Studio: Common Roots,
  Prefixes, and Suffixes

- ❗ Grammar Studio:
  Correct Use of Verbs

- ✓ "Speech on the Vietnam War, 1967"
  Selection Test

SUMMARIES

English

Martin Luther King Jr. gave this speech three years after he received the Nobel Peace Prize, and two years after the first U.S. troops were sent to fight in the Vietnam War. Although he knew his opposition to this war angered many politicians whose agendas benefitted from the war, King felt he could not remain silent because he felt that the war was "destroying the soul of our nation." King saw a destructive connection between poverty, racism, and the war. In this speech, King, a preacher, uses rhetorical devices to draw the connection between peace, civil rights, and the "soul" of all of America.

Spanish

Martin Luther King Jr. dio este discurso tres años antes de recibir el Premio Nobel de la Paz y dos años después de que las primeras tropas americanas fuesen enviadas a luchar en la Guerra de Vietnam. A pesar de que sabía que su oposición a la guerra enojaba a muchos políticos cuyas campañas se beneficiaban por la guerra, King sentía que no podía quedarse callado porque la guerra estaba "destruyendo el corazón de la nación". King vio una conexión destructiva entre el racismo y la guerra. En este discurso, King, que era predicador, usa recursos retóricos para crear una conexión entre la paz, los derechos civiles y el "alma" de los Estados Unidos.

SMALL-GROUP OPTIONS

Have students work in small groups and pairs to read and discuss the selection.

Think-Pair-Share

- Have students pair up and assign each pair one of these passages: paragraphs 2–3, paragraphs 7–8, paragraph 10, or paragraph 20.

- Instruct students to first individually determine what point or position their passage supports.

- Have students discuss with their partners to create a shared response, and then have each pair share their response with the class.

Three Before Me

- After students have finished composing their articles for the writing activity on Student Edition page 757, ask them to review and revise the text.

- Have each student ask three other students to edit his or her text.

- Have students evaluate the editing suggestions made by their peers and make appropriate revisions before writing the final draft to be turned in.

Text X-Ray: English Learner Support
for "Speech on the Vietnam War, 1967"

Use the Text X-Ray and the supports and scaffolds in the Teacher's Edition to help guide students at different proficiency levels through the selection.

INTRODUCE THE SELECTION
DISCUSS THE MILITARY DRAFT

Explain that the military draft is a procedure in which selected people are required to serve in the military. Tell students that while the draft can help add to military strength in times of conflict, it also has disadvantages. Some American soldiers drafted to fight in Vietnam objected to the war. Additionally, poor Americans were more likely to be drafted, since many wealthier families used money or influence to prevent their sons from having to serve.

Ask students to discuss the pros and cons of using a military draft, as opposed to relying only on those who volunteer to serve. Offer the following sentence frames:

- *The benefits of using a military draft include _____.*
- *The problems with a military draft include _____.*
- *One advantage/disadvantage of a draft is _____.*

CULTURAL REFERENCES

The following words or phrases may be unfamiliar to students:

- *gone mad* (paragraph 2): showing signs of mental instability or acting in a wild, uncontrolled way
- *civil rights* (paragraph 5): the rights for people to have full legal, social, and economic equality, regardless of race
- *bard* (paragraph 5): wise poet or storyteller
- *incandescently clear* (paragraph 7): completely obvious
- *the brotherhood of man* (paragraph 8): the idea that people are all connected and should depend on each other
- *cherished institutions* (paragraph 18): important traditions or customs
- *lay hand on the world order* (paragraph 44): change the way things often happen in the world

LISTENING

Understand Rhetorical Devices

Read aloud paragraph 51 of King's speech. Instruct students to listen for metaphors and other rhetorical devices.

Use the following supports with students at varying proficiency levels:

- Explain that when speakers use figurative language, they use words to mean something other than their precise, literal meanings. Repeat several phrases from the paragraph, such as *the god of hate, the oceans of history,* and *nations and individuals*. Ask yes/no questions to help students identify which phrases are examples of figurative language. **SUBSTANTIAL**
- Point out that the phrase "the god of hate" is a metaphor that shows the power that this emotion has over people. Say: *Based on this metaphor, identify other metaphors in this paragraph*. Have students write down the metaphors as they listen to the paragraph. **MODERATE**
- As students listen to the paragraph, instruct pairs to make a two-column chart to record the two things being compared in each metaphor. Then, have pairs review the chart together and discuss how the metaphors are related. **LIGHT**

SPEAKING

Use the Imperative Mood

Assist students to rewrite the paragraph in the imperative mood as instructed on Student Edition page 759. Then, have them read the revised paragraph aloud.

Write the following helping verbs on the board: *could, should, would*. Use the following supports with students at varying proficiency levels:

- Read two to three of the sentences in the paragraph aloud, and have students repeat them after you. Identify for them the subject and the helping verbs. Direct students to remove subjects and helping verbs and read back the resulting imperative sentence. **SUBSTANTIAL**

- Have students read each sentence aloud. Assist them as each sentence is read to identify the subject and the helping verbs. Then, help them determine how to change one sentence to the imperative mood. Have students read the resulting sentence aloud. **MODERATE**

- Have partners take turns reading each sentence aloud to each other. The partners can work together to identify the subject and helping verb in each sentence and change appropriate sentences to the imperative mood. Have pairs read their new imperative sentences aloud to each other. **LIGHT**

READING

Understand Repetition

Help students understand King's use of the parallelism (repetition) and its purpose in paragraph 18. Assist them in identifying the repeated words (*We have*) and the effects of the repetition.

Use the following supports with students at varying proficiency levels:

- Define *parallelism* to students and help them identify that "We have" is repeated. Have students circle "We have" wherever it appears in the paragraph. **SUBSTANTIAL**

- Have partners identify the repetition in this passage ("We have") and determine the meaning of the main verbs. Then ask: *Who is "we"? Who is the subject, or victim, of these actions?* **MODERATE**

- Instruct students to work in pairs to identify the parallelism in this paragraph, the repetition of the phrase "We have." Have the pairs discuss what the paragraph is about and why King uses repetition. *(to emphasize U.S. responsibility for the suffering of Vietnamese people)* **LIGHT**

WRITING

Vary Verbs

Work with students to read and prepare for the writing assignment on Student Edition page 757. Explain that they can use a variety of verbs to explain and respond to King's argument.

Use the following supports with students at varying proficiency levels:

- Review the meaning of the verbs that begin each bullet point: *Identify, Evaluate, Include, Support*. Display and read aloud a sample sentence for each of the bulleted instructions (for example, a sentence that identifies King's purpose, and a sentence that evaluates his evidence). Have students copy the sample sentences into their notebooks. **SUBSTANTIAL**

- Provide students with a list of verbs to use to describe and respond to King's ideas, such as *claims, describes, explains, opposes,* and *supports*. Supply sentence frames that students can use to explain King's claims and evidence, such as: *King claims _____ because _____.* **MODERATE**

- Have students work with a partner to create a list of verbs to describe and respond to King's argument. Encourage them to consult the list as they write their articles. **LIGHT**

SPEECH ON THE VIETNAM WAR, 1967

Speech by **Martin Luther King Jr.**

738   Unit 6

Connect to the ESSENTIAL QUESTION

As a minister, Martin Luther King Jr. would know well the instruction in the Bible to obey the government except when what the government is doing is in direct opposition to what God commands. His struggle was deciding where the line was drawn and what form his disagreement with the government would take. He chose a path that matched his beliefs, which was to show love where hate exists and to peacefully oppose the wrongdoing that he saw. This is a question that many have struggled with throughout history: how to fight evil without becoming evil.

ESSENTIAL QUESTION:

When should personal integrity come before civic duty?

© Houghton Mifflin Harcourt Publishing Company • Image Credits: © Bettmann/Getty Images

LEARNING MINDSET

Persistence Ask students to think of great athletes, inventors, or others with whom they are familiar, who have impressive careers or accomplishments. Discuss what would have happened if these people had ever given up trying, practicing, and working past difficulties. Relate that learning is very much like any other endeavor—there will be challenges and difficulties, but with persistence, the challenges will be overcome and, like a top athlete, the student gets to a higher level of "performance." Encourage students to keep persistence in mind, and suggest they keep telling themselves, "I can do this. I just have to stick with it."

QUICK START

You are probably familiar with Dr. Martin Luther King Jr.'s accomplishments related to civil rights. However, he also addressed the issue of the Vietnam War. Generate three questions you have about King and the Vietnam War.

ANALYZE AND EVALUATE ARGUMENTS

An **argument** is speech or writing that expresses a position on an issue or problem and supports it with reasons and evidence. As you read, notice the following characteristics of King's argument.

Structure Arguments usually begin with a thesis statement followed by reasons and evidence that support the thesis. King structures this argument differently. First, he presents reasons and evidence that lead to his conclusion about the war in Vietnam. He then elaborates on that conclusion; that conclusion becomes support for a second argument and leads to a call to action. As you read, trace the structural elements of King's argument.

Evidence Evaluate the evidence that King provides. Does he include facts that are accurate and verifiable? Has he been thorough in supporting his points? Does the evidence flow logically from point to point?

Counterarguments An argument often takes into account other points of view, anticipating counterarguments that opponents of the position might raise. A writer might respond to a counterargument by acknowledging that it is sensible with a concession or demonstrating why it is incorrect with a rebuttal. It may even be noted that the opposing argument is presenting a **logical fallacy,** or error in reasoning, and is therefore invalid. Note instances when King acknowledges counterarguments and how he addresses them.

ANALYZE AND EVALUATE RHETORICAL DEVICES

A **rhetorical device** uses language to directly affect an audience in a specific way. In an argument, rhetorical devices might serve to emphasize a point or to make parts of an argument memorable. Rhetorical devices include:

- **Allusion:** reference to a well-known person, place, event, or literary work
- **Direct Quotation:** statement from another person on the topic
- **Metaphor:** figure of speech that directly compares two things
- **Simile:** figure of speech that compares two things using *like* or *as*
- **Parallelism:** use of similar language constructions to express related ideas
- **Repetition:** use of a repeated word or phrase to emphasize ideas
- **Rhetorical Question:** question posed without the expectation of a reply because the writer views the answer as obvious

As you read, look for the ways King uses rhetorical devices. Consider whether they are effective and if they strengthen his argument.

GENRE ELEMENTS: SPEECH
- presents evidence to support a position on an issue
- anticipates and addresses counterarguments
- includes rhetorical devices to emphasize ideas

Speech on the Vietnam War, 1967   739

QUICK START

To help students think of questions, depending on their familiarity with the conflict in Vietnam, you might want to share some information such as the dates the United States was involved, which presidents were serving for getting us involved and escalating the war, and the fact that it was never officially declared a war. Also remind students that Martin Luther King Jr. believed in achieving his goals through peaceful means.

ANALYZE AND EVALUATE ARGUMENTS

Explain that, while the structure of King's speech offers a thesis and evidence, it can also be described as a problem-solution argument. King identifies two major problems that concern him and then offers the solution for each. The first problem he identifies is that the United States is fighting in Vietnam. The second and larger problem is that, in his view, society values money and things more than it values people. Tell students to look for the answers to these questions as they analyze the arguments offered in the speech. Make sure students understand that what the author presents as evidence in an argument may be opinion or a single point of view. Being an argument, it will by definition never be unbiased. That does not mean it is not true, just that there may be other opinions.

ANALYZE AND EVALUATE RHETORICAL DEVICES

Relate to students that rhetoric is the art of using language effectively and persuasively in speaking or writing. Rhetoric was once a separate subject in formal education across Europe and in the U.S., as it was thought that it was a vital skill for citizens of free countries. Rhetorical devices are ways that writers use words to convey a certain meaning or to convince their audience of their point of view. There are many types of rhetorical devices, including figures of speech and allusions. Writers choose the devices or phrasing that will send the message they intend. Rhetorical devices help connect what is being said to things the listener or reader already knows.

CRITICAL VOCABULARY

Suggest that students scan the list of words to see if any look familiar and then look for sentences that work with the words they already know. Then they can look for context clues in the remaining sentences to choose the correct words.

Answers:

1. *indigenous/recalcitrant*

2. *extortionist/eviscerate*

3. *reparations/insurgency*

4. *facile/adamant*

■ English Learner Support

Use Cognates Tell students that three of the Critical Vocabulary Words have Spanish cognates: *indigenous/ indígena, reparation/reparación,* and *facile/fácil.*
ALL LEVELS

LANGUAGE CONVENTIONS

Imperative Mood Point out that, in the imperative mood, the verb generally comes in a phrase or clause. For example, in the speech, King says, "Take immediate steps . . ." However, it may come after an adverb, such as "Realistically accept the fact . . . ." This is not the only construction where verbs lead (they do in questions, as well), but if students see a verb beginning a sentence, they can check to see if it is imperative mood.

ANNOTATION MODEL

Remind students that annotating the text as they read, such as underlining important details and circling key words that support the argument, can help them connect better with what they are reading. Point out in this sample that underlined words are vivid rhetorical devices that appeal strongly to the emotions. Explain that this is just an example, and students can use it as a guideline or create their own systems of annotating text. They may want to color-code their annotations using highlighters. Their notes in the margins may include observations, items that need clarification, words or events to look up, or issues that they'd like to research further.

 **GET READY**

CRITICAL VOCABULARY

facile	indigenous	insurgency	recalcitrant
eviscerate	extortionist	reparations	adamant

To see which Critical Vocabulary words you already know, fill in the blanks.

1. The _____ population was _____ in lending support to the cause, but the leader's bold stance encouraged their participation.

2. The _____ will _____ the fund with his demands for money.

3. _____ were made to the citizens to make up for the destruction caused during the attempted _____ against the king.

4. The man's _____ manner was contrary to how _____ he was about protecting those he believed could not protect themselves.

LANGUAGE CONVENTIONS

Imperative Mood The mood of a verb shows the way in which a thought or idea is expressed. Verbs in the **imperative mood** can give an order, make a request, or offer a word of advice. In the imperative mood, the subject is not typically stated but is understood.

> **Come** here right now!
> **Arrive** early to get the best seat.

As you read King's speech, note his use of the imperative mood and the effect it has on the mood and tone of his argument.

ANNOTATION MODEL   NOTICE & NOTE

As you read, note the author's use of language and structure to support his argument. Notice the use of rhetorical devices and the impact they have. In the model, you can see one reader's notes about the speech.

It seemed as if there was a real promise of hope for the poor, both black and white, through the poverty program. There were experiments, hopes, new beginnings. Then came the buildup in Vietnam, and I watched this program broken and eviscerated as if it were some idle political plaything of a society gone mad on war. And I knew that America would never invest the necessary funds or energies in rehabilitation of its poor so long as adventures like Vietnam continued to draw men and skills and money like some demonic, destructive suction tube.

"idle political plaything" is a powerful way to denounce ending help for the poor

Simile presents war as extremely evil and costly.

BACKGROUND

Martin Luther King Jr. *(1929–1968), a preacher and social activist, was the most prominent leader of the civil rights movement from the mid-1950s until his assassination in 1968. Committed to nonviolent protests, his efforts aided in the passage of the Civil Rights Act of 1964 and the Voting Rights Act of 1965. He became concerned about U.S. involvement in the Vietnam War, and gave this speech on April 4, 1967, at the Riverside Church in New York City.*

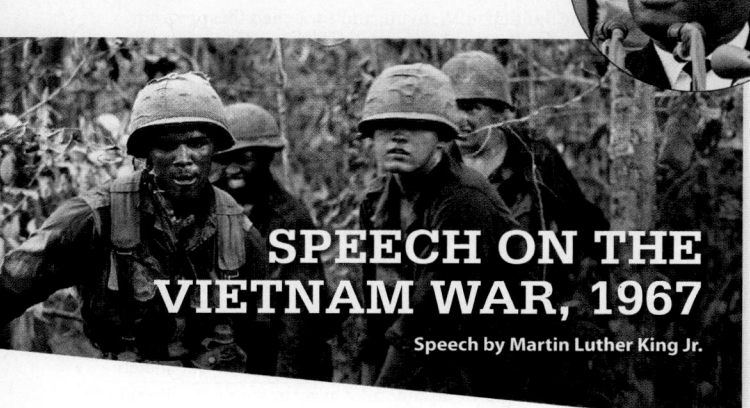

SPEECH ON THE VIETNAM WAR, 1967

Speech by Martin Luther King Jr.

SETTING A PURPOSE

As you read, look for connections between King's opposition to the war and his civil rights work. Note any questions you have as you read.

1   I come to this platform tonight to make a passionate plea to my beloved nation. This speech is not addressed to Hanoi or to the National Liberation Front.[1] It is not addressed to China or to Russia. Nor is it an attempt to overlook the ambiguity of the total situation and the need for a collective solution to the tragedy of Vietnam. Neither is it an attempt to make North Vietnam or the National Liberation Front paragons of virtue, nor to overlook the role they must play in the successful resolution of the problem. While they both may have justifiable reasons to be suspicious of the good faith of the United States, life and history give eloquent testimony to the fact that conflicts are never resolved without trustful give and take on both sides. Tonight, however, I wish not to speak with Hanoi and the National Liberation Front, but rather to my fellow Americans.

---

[1] **National Liberation Front:** also known as the Vietcong, revolutionary fighters in South Vietnam.

Notice & Note

Use the side margins to notice and note signposts in the text.

ANALYZE AND EVALUATE ARGUMENTS

Annotate: Mark the two sentences in paragraph 1 that identify the audience for King's speech.

Infer: What does King's identification of his audience suggest about the purpose of his speech?

BACKGROUND

Have students read the biographical information on Martin Luther King Jr. Explain that in 1967, opposition to the war in Vietnam was just beginning. U.S. involvement was escalating; the first combat troops had been sent over in 1965 to support the government of South Vietnam against the communist North Vietnam and its allies in the south, the Viet Cong. Criticism of the U.S. government's policy by such a leading figure was not welcome. Martin Luther King Jr.'s stance antagonized the White House and made some of the other leaders of the civil rights movement concerned that he might be jeopardizing support for their agenda.

SETTING A PURPOSE

Direct students to use the Setting a Purpose prompt to focus their reading.

✎ ANALYZE AND EVALUATE ARGUMENTS

Point out to students that King mentions most of the parties involved in the conflict, but he states that he is not addressing everyone involved. His argument will be focused. (**Answer:** *He isn't going to tell the enemy what they should do; rather, he wants to focus on what he believes Americans should do. Since Americans are his audience, he is directly addressing them and intends to give them a course of action to follow.*)

ANALYZE AND EVALUATE ARGUMENTS

Tell students to look for specific details about the poor and how the war in Vietnam affects them. (**Answer:** *These details underscore the fact that higher proportions of the poor are being asked to fight—and often die—in Vietnam for the purpose of ensuring rights for the Vietnamese that the African American soldiers don't have at home.*)

CRITICAL VOCABULARY

facile: King points out that the connection between the conflict in Vietnam and the conflict at home might seem easy to make. A key to understanding this word is "It seemed," because *facile* implies that the easy answer ignores how complicated things really are.

ASK STUDENTS what referring to the connection between civil rights and the war in Vietnam as facile suggests about King's view of the conflict. (*The relationship is more complicated than it seems at first.*)

eviscerate: Explain that *viscera* refers to internal organs, so *eviscerate* can literally mean to remove one's organs.

ASK STUDENTS what King says has been eviscerated and what that means. (*The poverty program was eviscerated, meaning that the most important parts were taken away.*)

 NOTICE & NOTE

facile
(făs´əl) *adj.* achieved with little effort or difficulty.

eviscerate
(ĭ-vĭs´ə-rāt) *v.* to take away a vital or essential part of

ANALYZE AND EVALUATE ARGUMENTS

Annotate: Mark phrases in paragraph 3 that describe what life is like for the poor in the United States.

Evaluate: How do these details about life in the United States relate to the Vietnam War?

2   Since I am a preacher by calling, I suppose it is not surprising that I have seven major reasons for bringing Vietnam into the field of my moral vision. There is at the outset a very obvious and almost **facile** connection between the war in Vietnam and the struggle I and others have been waging in America. A few years ago there was a shining moment in that struggle. It seemed as if there was a real promise of hope for the poor, both black and white, through the poverty program.[2] There were experiments, hopes, new beginnings. Then came the buildup in Vietnam, and I watched this program broken and **eviscerated** as if it were some idle political plaything of a society gone mad on war. And I knew that America would never invest the necessary funds or energies in rehabilitation of its poor so long as adventures like Vietnam continued to draw men and skills and money like some demonic, destructive suction tube. So I was increasingly compelled to see the war as an enemy of the poor and to attack it as such.

3   Perhaps a more tragic recognition of reality took place when it became clear to me that the war was doing far more than devastating the hopes of the poor at home. It was sending their sons and their brothers and their husbands to fight and to die in extraordinarily high proportions relative to the rest of the population. We were taking the black young men who had been crippled by our society and sending them eight thousand miles away to guarantee liberties in Southeast Asia which they had not found in southwest Georgia and East Harlem. So we have been repeatedly faced with the cruel irony of watching Negro and white boys on TV screens as they kill and die together for a nation that has been unable to seat them together in the same schools. So we watch them in brutal solidarity burning the huts of a poor village, but we realize that they would hardly live on the same block in Chicago. I could not be silent in the face of such cruel manipulation of the poor.

4   My third reason moves to an even deeper level of awareness, for it grows out of my experience in the ghettos of the North over the last three years, especially the last three summers. As I have walked among the desperate, rejected, and angry young men, I have told them that Molotov cocktails[3] and rifles would not solve their problems. I have tried to offer them my deepest compassion while maintaining my conviction that social change comes most meaningfully through nonviolent action. But they asked, and rightly so, "What about Vietnam?" They asked if our own nation wasn't using massive doses of violence to solve its problems, to bring about

---

[2] **poverty program:** legislation, often called the "War on Poverty," enacted in 1964 during Lyndon Johnson's administration.
[3] **Molotov cocktails:** homemade incendiary weapons made by filling breakable bottles with a flammable liquid, attaching and lighting wicks, and throwing them at a target.

EL ## ENGLISH LEARNER SUPPORT

Preteach Vocabulary   There are several words in this speech that may be unfamiliar to English learners. On page 741, words such as *ambiguity, collective, resolution,* and *justifiable* might need to be explained. On this page, key words that may need explaining include *rehabilitation, demonic, compelled, proportions, solidarity,* and *manipulation.* Moving through the speech, allow students time to identify unfamiliar words before the story is read and discuss them again as the words are encountered in context. **ALL LEVELS**

the changes it wanted. Their questions hit home, and I knew that I could never again raise my voice against the violence of the oppressed in the ghettos without having first spoken clearly to the greatest purveyor of violence in the world today: my own government. For the sake of those boys, for the sake of this government, for the sake of the hundreds of thousands trembling under our violence, I cannot be silent.

5   For those who ask the question, "Aren't you a civil rights leader?" and thereby mean to exclude me from the movement for peace, I have this further answer. In 1957, when a group of us formed the Southern Christian Leadership Conference, we chose as our motto: "To save the soul of America." We were convinced that we could not limit our vision to certain rights for black people, but instead affirmed the conviction that America would never be free or saved from itself until the descendants of its slaves were loosed completely from the shackles they still wear. In a way we were agreeing with Langston Hughes, that black bard of Harlem, who had written earlier:

6   O, yes, I say it plain,
        America never was America to me,
        And yet I swear this oath—
        America will be!

7   Now it should be incandescently clear that no one who has any concern for the integrity and life of America today can ignore the present war. If America's soul becomes totally poisoned, part of the autopsy must read "Vietnam." It can never be saved so long as it destroys the deepest hopes of men the world over. So it is that those of us who are yet determined that "America will be" are led down the path of protest and dissent, working for the health of our land.

ANALYZE AND EVALUATE ARGUMENTS

Annotate: Mark the sentence in paragraph 5 that states a counterargument against King.

Analyze: What rebuttal does King offer to the counterargument?

Speech on the Vietnam War, 1967   743

ANALYZE AND EVALUATE ARGUMENTS

Remind students that answering arguments that might be made against the points made by the author is a classic element of a persuasive speech. (**Answer:** *King points out that his vision has been ensuring rights for all Americans, not just certain rights for African Americans.*)

ANALYZE AND EVALUATE ARGUMENTS

Remind students that a logical fallacy is an error in reasoning. King is speaking at a church, so he knows his audience will understand that peace is a key aspect of the teachings of Jesus. He uses this common understanding to point out that ignoring this important belief would be an error. (**Answer:** *King uses rhetorical questions to point out what he believes to be the error of the logical fallacy. This technique is effective since the answers to the rhetorical questions are understood and reasonable.*)

NOTICE & NOTE

ANALYZE AND EVALUATE ARGUMENTS

Annotate: Mark the logical fallacy in paragraph 9.

Draw Conclusions: How does King address the logical fallacy put forth by those who ask why he is speaking out? Evaluate the effectiveness of this technique.

8 As if the weight of such a commitment to the life and health of America were not enough, another burden of responsibility was placed upon me in 1964. And I cannot forget that the Nobel Peace Prize[4] was also a commission, a commission to work harder than I had ever worked before for the brotherhood of man. This is a calling that takes me beyond national allegiances.

9 But even if it were not present, I would yet have to live with the meaning of my commitment to the ministry of Jesus Christ. To me, the relationship of this ministry to the making of peace is so obvious that I sometimes marvel at those who ask me why I am speaking against the war. Could it be that they do not know that the Good News[5] was meant for all men—for communist and capitalist, for their children and ours, for black and for white, for revolutionary and conservative? Have they forgotten that my ministry is in obedience to the one who loved his enemies so fully that he died for them? What then can I say to the Vietcong[6] or to Castro or to Mao as a faithful minister of this one? Can I threaten them with death or must I not share with them my life?

10 Finally, as I try to explain for you and for myself the road that leads from Montgomery[7] to this place, I would have offered all that was most valid if I simply said that I must be true to my conviction that I share with all men the calling to be a son of the living God. Beyond the calling of race or nation or creed is this vocation of sonship and brotherhood. Because I believe that the Father is deeply concerned, especially for His suffering and helpless and outcast children, I come tonight to speak for them. This I believe to be the privilege and the burden of all of us who deem ourselves bound by allegiances and loyalties which are broader and deeper than nationalism and which go beyond our nation's self-defined goals and positions. We are called to speak for the weak, for the voiceless, for the victims of our nation, for those it calls "enemy," for no document from human hands can make these humans any less our brothers.

11 And as I ponder the madness of Vietnam and search within myself for ways to understand and respond in compassion, my mind goes constantly to the people of that peninsula. I speak now not of the soldiers of each side, not of the ideologies of the Liberation Front, not of the junta in Saigon, but simply of the people who have been living under the curse of war for almost three continuous decades now. I think of them, too, because it is clear to me that there will be no

---

[4] **Nobel Peace Prize:** an annual award given to an individual who best promotes international friendship, reduces military forces, and fosters peaceful relations. King won the prize in 1964.

[5] **Good News:** the Gospels, or the written accounts of Jesus and his teachings.

[6] **Vietcong:** the National Liberation Front, South Vietnamese revolutionaries.

[7] **Montgomery:** Alabama city and site of the 1955 bus boycott, a civil rights protest that brought King to national prominence.

APPLYING ACADEMIC VOCABULARY

☑ **contemporary**   ☑ **global**   ☐ **infinite**   ☐ **simulated**   ☐ **virtual**

Write and Discuss Have students turn to a partner to discuss the following questions. Guide students to include the academic vocabulary words *contemporary* and *global* in their responses. Ask volunteers to share their responses with the class.

- How did Dr. King's speech address **contemporary** issues of injustice?
- What was the **global** impact of American fears about the spread of communism?

meaningful solution there until some attempt is made to know them and hear their broken cries.

12   They must see Americans as strange liberators. The Vietnamese people proclaimed their own independence in 1954—in 1945 rather—after a combined French and Japanese occupation and before the communist revolution in China. They were led by Ho Chi Minh. Even though they quoted the American Declaration of Independence in their own document of freedom, we refused to recognize them. Instead, we decided to support France in its reconquest of her former colony. Our government felt then that the Vietnamese people were not ready for independence, and we again fell victim to the deadly Western arrogance that has poisoned the international atmosphere for so long. With that tragic decision we rejected a revolutionary government seeking self-determination and a government that had been established not by China—for whom the Vietnamese have no great love—but by clearly **indigenous** forces that included some communists. For the peasants this new government meant real land reform, one of the most important needs in their lives.

13   For nine years following 1945 we denied the people of Vietnam the right of independence. For nine years we vigorously supported the French in their abortive effort to recolonize Vietnam. Before the end of the war we were meeting 80 percent of the French war costs. Even before the French were defeated at Dien Bien Phu, they began to despair of their reckless action, but we did not. We encouraged them with our huge financial and military supplies to continue the war even after they had lost the will. Soon we would be paying almost the full costs of this tragic attempt at recolonization.

14   After the French were defeated, it looked as if independence and land reform would come again through the Geneva Agreement. But instead there came the United States, determined that Ho should not unify the temporarily divided nation, and the peasants watched again as we supported one of the most vicious modern dictators, our chosen man, Premier Diem.[8] The peasants watched and cringed as Diem ruthlessly rooted out all opposition, supported their **extortionist** landlords, and refused even to discuss reunification with the North. The peasants watched as all of this was presided over by United States influence and then by increasing numbers of United States troops who came to help quell the **insurgency** that Diem's methods had aroused. When Diem was overthrown they may have been happy, but the long line of military dictators seemed to offer no real change, especially in terms of their need for land and peace.

15   The only change came from America as we increased our troop commitments in support of governments which were singularly

---

[8] **Premier Diem** (dē-ĕm´): Ngo Dinh Diem (1901–1963), the first president of South Vietnam in 1955, who was later killed in a military coup.

Speech on the Vietnam War, 1967   745

indigenous
(ĭn-dĭj´ə-nəs) *adj.* native to a land.

NUMBERS AND STATS

Notice & Note: In paragraph 13, mark the statistic King cites that explains how America supported the French against Vietnam.

Evaluate: How is this statistic relevant to King's argument?

extortionist
(ĭk-stôr´shən-ĭst) *n.* one who obtains something by force or threat.

insurgency
(ĭn-sûr´jən-sē) *n.* rebellion or revolt.

NUMBERS AND STATS

Remind students that a successful argument offers evidence to support opinions. Each time King makes a statement, he shares what he considers the best evidence in support that statement. It is also worth remembering that King presents only one side of the argument. (**Answer:** *King presents details about North Vietnam's struggle for independence and says the United States "denied the people of Vietnam the right of independence." The statistic is relevant because it shows how committed the United States was to this position.*)

CRITICAL VOCABULARY

indigenous: The rebel forces, while at least in part made up of Communists, were native Vietnamese.

ASK STUDENTS why King might think indigenous forces should have been supported, rather than opposed. (*Other countries, such as China, had not yet become involved in the conflict. This was a fight started by indigenous Vietnamese. Clearly, King sees that as giving their cause greater legitimacy.*)

extortionist: According to King, the first president of South Vietnam supported landlords who were extortionists who mistreated their tenants, demanding more than the peasants could afford.

ASK STUDENTS how the United States reacted to the extortionist landlords and what impact that might have on the Vietnamese rebels. (*The peasants noticed that the United States supported the president who was supporting the extortionist landlords. This would have to make the rebels consider the United States an enemy.*)

insurgency: The insurgency was a rebellion started by Vietnamese who had been trained in North Vietnam, and its goal was the overthrow of Diem and his government.

ASK STUDENTS what happened in response to the insurgency. (*The United States sent more troops to help stop the insurgency.*)

WHEN STUDENTS STRUGGLE . . .

Analyze Chronology In paragraphs 12–14, King uses chronological order. Remind students that *then, following, before,* and *after* signal the time relationship between events.

Have students create a simple timeline with the information included in this part of the text. Have them compare their timelines with a partner. Then ask students how King views U.S. actions in Vietnam before the war. Why does he include this information in his speech?

For additional support, go to the **Reading Studio** and assign the following LEVEL UP **Level Up Tutorial: Analyzing Arguments.**

© Houghton Mifflin Harcourt Publishing Company

ANALYZE AND EVALUATE RHETORICAL DEVICES

Remind students that parallelism is a rhetorical advice that uses repetition to connect ideas. (**Answer:** *When King uses these phrases, he focuses attention on what the United States has done to the Vietnamese. These phrases show that King holds the United States responsible for events that have hurt the Vietnamese.*)

For **reading support** for students at varying proficiency levels, see the **Text X-Ray** on page 738D.

corrupt, inept, and without popular support. All the while the people read our leaflets and received the regular promises of peace and democracy and land reform. Now they languish under our bombs and consider us, not their fellow Vietnamese, the real enemy. They move sadly and apathetically as we herd them off the land of their fathers into concentration camps where minimal social needs are rarely met. They know they must move on or be destroyed by our bombs.

16   So they go, primarily women and children and the aged. They watch as we poison their water, as we kill a million acres of their crops. They must weep as the bulldozers roar through their areas preparing to destroy the precious trees. They wander into the hospitals with at least twenty casualties from American firepower for one Vietcong inflicted injury. So far we may have killed a million of them, mostly children. They wander into the towns and see thousands of the children, homeless, without clothes, running in packs on the streets like animals. They see the children degraded by our soldiers as they beg for food. They see the children selling their sisters to our soldiers, soliciting for their mothers.

17   What do the peasants think as we ally ourselves with the landlords and as we refuse to put any action into our many words concerning land reform? What do they think as we test out our latest weapons on them, just as the Germans tested out new medicine and new tortures in the concentration camps of Europe? Where are the roots of the independent Vietnam we claim to be building? Is it among these voiceless ones?

ANALYZE AND EVALUATE RHETORICAL DEVICES

Annotate: Mark examples of parallelism in paragraph 18.

Evaluate: What behavior does this use of parallelism emphasize?

18   We have destroyed their two most cherished institutions: the family and the village. We have destroyed their land and their crops. We have cooperated in the crushing of the nation's only noncommunist revolutionary political force, the unified Buddhist Church. We have supported the enemies of the peasants of Saigon. We have corrupted their women and children and killed their men.

19   Now there is little left to build on, save bitterness. Soon the only solid physical foundations remaining will be found at our military bases and in the concrete of the concentration camps we call "fortified hamlets." The peasants may well wonder if we plan to build our new Vietnam on such grounds as these. Could we blame them for such thoughts? We must speak for them and raise the questions they cannot raise. These, too, are our brothers.

20   Perhaps a more difficult but no less necessary task is to speak for those who have been designated as our enemies. What of the National Liberation Front, that strangely anonymous group we call "VC" or "communists"? What must they think of the United States of America when they realize that we permitted the repression and cruelty of Diem, which helped to bring them into being as a resistance group in the South? What do they think of our condoning the violence

(EL) ENGLISH LEARNER SUPPORT

Master the Terms The analysis of the arguments in this selection requires an understanding of the word *parallelism* as used in the margin note. Explain to students that one meaning of *parallel* is "having comparable parts or similarities." Help students find examples of parallelism, or similar phrases, in the text. Discuss what makes them parallel, even though they are not identical.

Make sure students know they can request assistance if any of the terms used to describe rhetorical devices are unclear, or in explaining how the devices are used (for example, many allusions may be unfamiliar).   **MODERATE**

which led to their own taking up of arms? How can they believe in our integrity when now we speak of "aggression from the North" as if there were nothing more essential to the war? How can they trust us when now we charge them with violence after the murderous reign of Diem and charge them with violence while we pour every new weapon of death into their land? Surely we must understand their feelings, even if we do not condone their actions. Surely we must see that the men we supported pressed them to their violence. Surely we must see that our own computerized plans of destruction simply dwarf their greatest acts.

21 How do they judge us when our officials know that their membership is less than 25 percent communist, and yet insist on giving them the blanket name? What must they be thinking when they know that we are aware of their control of major sections of Vietnam, and yet we appear ready to allow national elections in which this highly organized political parallel government will not have a part? They ask how we can speak of free elections when the Saigon press is censored and controlled by the military junta. And they are surely right to wonder what kind of new government we plan to help form without them, the only party in real touch with the peasants. They question our political goals and they deny the reality of a peace settlement from which they will be excluded. Their questions are frighteningly relevant. Is our nation planning to build on political myth again, and then shore it up upon the power of a new violence?

22 Here is the true meaning and value of compassion and nonviolence, when it helps us to see the enemy's point of view, to hear his questions, to know his assessment of ourselves. For from his view we may indeed see the basic weaknesses of our own condition, and if we are mature, we may learn and grow and profit from the wisdom of the brothers who are called the opposition.

23 So, too, with Hanoi. In the North, where our bombs now pummel the land, and our mines endanger the waterways, we are met by a deep but understandable mistrust. To speak for them is to explain this lack of confidence in Western words, and especially their distrust of American intentions now. In Hanoi are the men who led the nation to independence against the Japanese and the French, the men who sought membership in the French Commonwealth and were betrayed by the weakness of Paris and the willfulness of the colonial armies. It was they who led a second struggle against French domination at tremendous costs, and then were persuaded to give up the land they controlled between the thirteenth and seventeenth parallel as a temporary measure at Geneva. After 1954 they watched us conspire with Diem to prevent elections which could have surely brought Ho Chi Minh to power over a united Vietnam, and they realized they had

ANALYZE AND EVALUATE ARGUMENTS

Annotate: Mark the sentence in paragraph 23 that summarizes why Vietnam and the United States cannot negotiate terms of peace.

Analyze: What counterargument and rebuttal are presented in this paragraph?

ANALYZE AND EVALUATE ARGUMENTS

Point out to students that paragraph 23 runs onto the next page, so students will need to continue reading to find the summary sentence. Explain that the entire paragraph should be considered when analyzing the argument offered here. (**Answer:** *King proposes the counterargument that it is the North Vietnamese who are prolonging the war by their refusal to negotiate. Then, to rebut that counterargument, King lists times the political efforts of North Vietnam were sabotaged by the French and Americans, to show why the North Vietnamese would be unlikely to trust the United States.*)

ENGLISH LEARNER SUPPORT

Recognize Affixes Write these suffixes and their meanings on the board: *-al* (of or relating to); *-ful* (full of); *-less* (not having); *-ize* (cause to conform to or become like); and *-ion* (state or condition). Point out to students that these suffixes appear in the following words found on page 748. You may wish to write these on the board as well.

traditional

powerful

voiceless

brutalize

corruption

Help students work through how the suffix creates the meaning for each word. (For example, discuss *tradition*, and then point out that *-al* makes it "of or relating to tradition.") **MODERATE**

QUOTED WORDS

Point out to students that this quotation is from a Buddhist leader in Vietnam. Tell students that peace is one of the basic teachings of the Buddha. (**Answer:** *This quotation from an indigenous speaker underscores what King had been saying about the negative impact of the way the United States handled the conflict. It would also help King's audience understand why the Vietnamese people had a negative view of the U.S. actions.*)

---

been betrayed again. <u>When we ask why they do not leap to negotiate, these things must be remembered.</u>

24   Also, it must be clear that the leaders of Hanoi considered the presence of American troops in support of the Diem regime to have been the initial military breach of the Geneva Agreement concerning foreign troops. They remind us that they did not begin to send troops in large numbers and even supplies into the South until American forces had moved into the tens of thousands.

25   Hanoi remembers how our leaders refused to tell us the truth about the earlier North Vietnamese overtures for peace, how the president claimed that none existed when they had clearly been made. Ho Chi Minh has watched as America has spoken of peace and built up its forces, and now he has surely heard the increasing international rumors of American plans for an invasion of the North. He knows the bombing and shelling and mining we are doing are part of traditional pre-invasion strategy. Perhaps only his sense of humor and of irony can save him when he hears the most powerful nation of the world speaking of aggression as it drops thousands of bombs on a poor, weak nation more than eight hundred, or rather, eight thousand miles away from its shores.

26   At this point I should make it clear that while I have tried in these last few minutes to give a voice to the voiceless in Vietnam and to understand the arguments of those who are called "enemy," I am as deeply concerned about our own troops there as anything else. For it occurs to me that what we are submitting them to in Vietnam is not simply the brutalizing process that goes on in any war where armies face each other and seek to destroy. We are adding cynicism to the process of death, for they must know after a short period there that none of the things we claim to be fighting for are really involved. Before long they must know that their government has sent them into a struggle among Vietnamese, and the more sophisticated surely realize that we are on the side of the wealthy, and the secure, while we create a hell for the poor.

27   Somehow this madness must cease. We must stop now. I speak as a child of God and brother to the suffering poor of Vietnam. I speak for those whose land is being laid waste, whose homes are being destroyed, whose culture is being subverted. I speak for the poor of America who are paying the double price of smashed hopes at home, and dealt death and corruption in Vietnam. I speak as a citizen of the world, for the world as it stands aghast at the path we have taken. I speak as one who loves America, to the leaders of our own nation: The great initiative in this war is ours; the initiative to stop it must be ours.

28   This is the message of the great Buddhist leaders of Vietnam. Recently one of them wrote these words, and I quote:

QUOTED WORDS

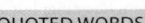

Notice & Note: In paragraph 28, mark details in the quotation from the Buddhist leader that describe the effects of the Americans' behavior on the Vietnamese.

Draw Conclusions: How is the quotation relevant to King's argument?

Each day the war goes on the hatred increases in the heart of the Vietnamese and in the hearts of those of humanitarian instinct. The Americans are forcing even their friends into becoming their enemies. It is curious that the Americans, who calculate so carefully on the possibilities of military victory, do not realize that in the process they are incurring deep psychological and political defeat. The image of America will never again be the image of revolution, freedom, and democracy, but the image of violence and militarism.

Unquote.

29   If we continue, there will be no doubt in my mind and in the mind of the world that we have no honorable intentions in Vietnam. If we do not stop our war against the people of Vietnam immediately, the world will be left with no other alternative than to see this as some horrible, clumsy, and deadly game we have decided to play. The world now demands a maturity of America that we may not be able to achieve. It demands that we admit that we have been wrong from the beginning of our adventure in Vietnam, that we have been detrimental to the life of the Vietnamese people. The situation is one in which we must be ready to turn sharply from our present ways. In order to atone for our sins and errors in Vietnam, we should take the initiative in bringing a halt to this tragic war.

30   I would like to suggest five concrete things that our government should do immediately to begin the long and difficult process of extricating ourselves from this nightmarish conflict:

31   Number one: End all bombing in North and South Vietnam.

32   Number two: Declare a unilateral cease-fire in the hope that such action will create the atmosphere for negotiation.

33   Three: Take immediate steps to prevent other battlegrounds in Southeast Asia by curtailing our military buildup in Thailand and our interference in Laos.

34   Four: Realistically accept the fact that the National Liberation Front has substantial support in South Vietnam and must thereby play a role in any meaningful negotiations and any future Vietnam government.

35   Five: Set a date that we will remove all foreign troops from Vietnam in accordance with the 1954 Geneva Agreement. [*Sustained applause*]

36   Part of our ongoing [*Applause continues*], part of our ongoing commitment might well express itself in an offer to grant asylum to any Vietnamese who fears for his life under a new regime which included the Liberation Front. Then we must make what **reparations** we can for the damage we have done. We must provide the medical aid that is badly needed, making it available in this country if necessary. Meanwhile [*Applause*], meanwhile, we in the churches and

ANALYZE AND EVALUATE ARGUMENTS
Annotate: In paragraph 29, mark the conclusion King reaches regarding the Vietnam War.

Draw Conclusions: How do King's proposals in paragraphs 31–35 affect his conclusion?

LANGUAGE CONVENTIONS
Annotate: In paragraphs 31–35, mark the words King uses to tell the government what to do.

Evaluate: Is King's use of mood appropriate to his purpose at this point in the speech? How would using different verb phrases alter his message?

reparations
(rĕp-ə-rā´shəns) *n.* compensation or payment from a nation for damage or injury during a war.

Speech on the Vietnam War, 1967   749

ANALYZE AND EVALUATE ARGUMENTS

Explain to students that, after stating what he thinks should happen, King outlines how he thinks it should be done. (**Answer:** *The proposals listed are concrete steps King believes the United States should take. They show that King has thought about how his conclusion can be implemented. While this does not strengthen his point, it makes his suggestion of ending the war seem more plausible.*)

LANGUAGE CONVENTIONS

Point out to students that the imperative mood is used in King's list of steps to be taken: *end, declare, take, accept, set.* Ask students what the impact is of using the imperative mood in giving these recommendations. (**Answer:** *The imperative mood adds emphasis, which is appropriate.*)

WHEN STUDENTS STRUGGLE...

Analyze the Argument Have students use a chart like the one below to follow the steps of King's argument. Have them go through the speech and find things that King condemns and things he recommends. Then, discuss how the two columns are related.

U.S. should NOT Do	U.S. SHOULD do
Send more troops	Set a date for removing troops

 For additional support, go to the **Reading Studio** and assign the following ⬛ **Level Up Tutorial: Analyzing Arguments.**

CRITICAL VOCABULARY

reparations: King recommends reparations to compensate, or pay, Vietnam for the damage done by the war.

ASK STUDENTS what they have read in King's speech so far that makes it seem natural for him to suggest reparations. (*He spoke earlier about demonstrating God's love, so making reparations to people who have been hurt would seem natural for him.*)

ANALYZE AND EVALUATE ARGUMENTS

Remind students that King is concerned not only with Vietnam. You might direct students back to the opening of the speech (especially paragraphs 2–3), where King mentions that the poor, including African Americans, are sent overseas in disproportionately large numbers, and discuss the impact of that on the opinions expressed here. (**Answer:** *According to King, the war in Vietnam is a symptom of a problem in American society. War should not be America's solution to protecting their interests overseas; otherwise, there will be a series of Vietnams. In the next paragraph, he mentions a list of countries where political problems have led to the United States' sending advisors or troops to try to keep governments from being overthrown.*)

ANALYZE AND EVALUATE ARGUMENTS

Annotate: Identify the phrase in paragraph 39 that states the next part of the focus of King's speech.

Analyze: How does the argument about ending the war in Vietnam relate to this idea? What evidence does King offer to support his assertion?

synagogues have a continuing task while we urge our government to disengage itself from a disgraceful commitment. We must continue to raise our voices and our lives if our nation persists in its perverse ways in Vietnam. We must be prepared to match actions with words by seeking out every creative method of protest possible.

37   As we counsel young men concerning military service, we must clarify for them our nation's role in Vietnam and challenge them with the alternative of conscientious objection.[9] [*Sustained applause*] I am pleased to say that this is a path now chosen by more than seventy students at my own alma mater, Morehouse College, and I recommend it to all who find the American course in Vietnam a dishonorable and unjust one. [*Applause*] Moreover, I would encourage all ministers of draft age to give up their ministerial exemptions and seek status as conscientious objectors. [*Applause*] These are the times for real choices and not false ones. We are at the moment when our lives must be placed on the line if our nation is to survive its own folly. Every man of humane convictions must decide on the protest that best suits his convictions, but we must all protest.

38   Now there is something seductively tempting about stopping there and sending us all off on what in some circles has become a popular crusade against the war in Vietnam. I say we must enter that struggle, but I wish to go on now to say something even more disturbing.

39   The war in Vietnam is but a symptom of a far deeper malady within the American spirit, and if we ignore this sobering reality [*Applause*], and if we ignore this sobering reality, we will find ourselves organizing "clergy and laymen concerned" committees for the next generation. They will be concerned about Guatemala and Peru. They will be concerned about Thailand and Cambodia. They will be concerned about Mozambique and South Africa. We will be marching for these and a dozen other names and attending rallies without end unless there is a significant and profound change in American life and policy. [*Sustained applause*] So such thoughts take us beyond Vietnam, but not beyond our calling as sons of the living God.

40   In 1957 a sensitive American official overseas said that it seemed to him that our nation was on the wrong side of a world revolution. During the past ten years we have seen emerge a pattern of suppression which has now justified the presence of U.S. military advisors in Venezuela. This need to maintain social stability for our investments accounts for the counter-revolutionary action of American forces in Guatemala. It tells why American helicopters are being used against guerrillas in Cambodia and why American napalm[10]

---

[9] **conscientious objection:** the refusal to participate in military actions because of moral or religious beliefs.
[10] **napalm:** an incendiary fuel used in U.S. bombs to burn Vietnamese opponents.

and Green Beret forces have already been active against rebels in Peru.

41   It is with such activity in mind that the words of the late John F. Kennedy come back to haunt us. Five years ago he said, "Those who make peaceful revolution impossible will make violent revolution inevitable." [*Applause*] Increasingly, by choice or by accident, this is the role our nation has taken, the role of those who make peaceful revolution impossible by refusing to give up the privileges and the pleasures that come from the immense profits of overseas investments. I am convinced that if we are to get on the right side of the world revolution, we as a nation must undergo a radical revolution of values. We must rapidly begin [*Applause*], we must rapidly begin the shift from a thing-oriented society to a person-oriented society. When machines and computers, profit motives and property rights, are considered more important than people, the giant triplets of racism, extreme materialism, and militarism are incapable of being conquered.

42   A true revolution of values will soon cause us to question the fairness and justice of many of our past and present policies. On the one hand we are called to play the Good Samaritan on life's roadside, but that will be only an initial act. One day we must come to see that the whole Jericho Road[11] must be transformed so that men and women will not be constantly beaten and robbed as they make their journey on life's highway. True compassion is more than flinging a coin to a beggar. It comes to see that an edifice which produces beggars needs restructuring. [*Applause*]

43   A true revolution of values will soon look uneasily on the glaring contrast of poverty and wealth. With righteous indignation, it will look across the seas and see individual capitalists of the West investing huge sums of money in Asia, Africa, and South America, only to take the profits out with no concern for the social betterment of the countries, and say, "This is not just." It will look at our alliance with the landed gentry of South America and say, "This is not just." The Western arrogance of feeling that it has everything to teach others and nothing to learn from them is not just.

44   A true revolution of values will lay hand on the world order and say of war, "This way of settling differences is not just." This business of burning human beings with napalm, of filling our nation's homes with orphans and widows, of injecting poisonous drugs of hate into the veins of peoples normally humane, of sending men home from dark and bloody battlefields physically handicapped and psychologically deranged, cannot be reconciled with wisdom,

---

[11] **Jericho Road:** an ancient route between Jerusalem and Jericho. In the New Testament, the Good Samaritan stops on this road to help an injured robbery victim.

ANALYZE AND EVALUATE RHETORICAL DEVICES

Annotate: Mark the allusion King includes in paragraph 42.

Analyze: What does King hope to achieve by using this rhetorical device?

 ANALYZE AND EVALUATE RHETORICAL DEVICES

Find out how much students know about the story of the Good Samaritan from the Bible. You might want to mention that this was a corollary to the command Jesus had just given to "Love your neighbor as yourself." It was a way of defining who a neighbor was—in this case, someone who needed help. (**Answer:** *With this device, King is suggesting that it is not enough to simply help the person you see who is in need. He wants to see a world in which there is no danger.*)

ENGLISH LEARNER SUPPORT

Confirm Understanding of Rhetorical Devices   The use of quotation marks on this page might cause some confusion for students. At the top of this page, King includes a quotation from John F. Kennedy. However, in paragraphs 43–44, the "quotations" are not in fact quotations from anyone, but a personification of revolution—the revolution will say. Help students identify when King is actually quoting people and when he is simply stating his own ideas as a way of bringing to life his goals. **MODERATE**

TEACH

ANALYZE AND EVALUATE RHETORICAL DEVICES

Point out to students that in looking for the word *revolution*, they should look for it in multiple forms, including *revolutionary* and *antirevolutionaries*. You may wish to point out that the line about "the people who sat in darkness have seen a great light" is an allusion to the prophecy in the book of Isaiah from the Bible that a Messiah would come. So King is making this not merely a political issue, but also a religious issue. (**Answer:** *To King, revolution is change. He reassures his listeners, however, that communism and Marxism are not the only options for change. King suggests recapturing the revolutionary spirit that drove American colonists to fight for their own freedom and using that spirit to help others fight for theirs.*)

justice, and love. A nation that continues year after year to spend more money on military defense than on programs of social uplift is approaching spiritual death. [*Sustained applause*]

45   America, the richest and most powerful nation in the world, can well lead the way in this revolution of values. There is nothing except a tragic death wish to prevent us from reordering our priorities so that the pursuit of peace will take precedence over the pursuit of war. There is nothing to keep us from molding a **recalcitrant** status quo with bruised hands until we have fashioned it into a brotherhood.

recalcitrant
(rĭ-kăl′sĭ-trənt) *adj.* stubbornly resistant to and defiant of authority.

46   This kind of positive revolution of values is our best defense against communism. [*Applause*] War is not the answer. Communism will never be defeated by the use of atomic bombs or nuclear weapons. Let us not join those who shout war and, through their misguided passions, urge the United States to relinquish its participation in the United Nations. These are days which demand wise restraint and calm reasonableness. We must not engage in a negative anticommunism, but rather in a positive thrust for democracy [*Applause*], realizing that our greatest defense against communism is to take offensive action in behalf of justice. We must with positive action seek to remove those conditions of poverty, insecurity, and injustice, which are the fertile soil in which the seed of communism grows and develops.

ANALYZE AND EVALUATE RHETORICAL DEVICES

Annotate: Mark the repeated word *revolution* in paragraphs 47 and 48.

Analyze: What does King mean by this term? What effect does the repetition have on his argument?

47   These are revolutionary times. All over the globe men are revolting against old systems of exploitation and oppression, and out of the wounds of a frail world, new systems of justice and equality are being born. The shirtless and barefoot people of the land are rising up as never before. The people who sat in darkness have seen a great light. We in the West must support these revolutions.

48   It is a sad fact that because of comfort, complacency, a morbid fear of communism, and our proneness to adjust to injustice, the Western nations that initiated so much of the revolutionary spirit of the modern world have now become the arch antirevolutionaries. This has driven many to feel that only Marxism has a revolutionary spirit. Therefore, communism is a judgment against our failure to make democracy real and follow through on the revolutions that we initiated. Our only hope today lies in our ability to recapture the revolutionary spirit and go out into a sometimes hostile world declaring eternal hostility to poverty, racism, and militarism. With this powerful commitment we shall boldly challenge the status quo and unjust mores, and thereby speed the day when every valley shall be exalted, and every mountain and hill shall be made low [*Audience:*] (*Yes*); the crooked shall be made straight, and the rough places plain.[12]

---

[12] **every valley shall be . . . plain:** biblical quote from the Old Testament Book of Isaiah describing the arrival of the Messiah.

CRITICAL VOCABULARY

recalcitrant: King points out that it is hard to get people to give up the status quo—things as they have always been used to having, so they are *recalcitrant*.

ASK STUDENTS why they think people are recalcitrant when asked to change the way they live. (*Possible answer: most people like the familiar and change can be difficult; it is hard to convince people to be a brotherhood if they focus on differences, such as race and economic status.*)

49   A genuine revolution of values means in the final analysis that our loyalties must become ecumenical rather than sectional. Every nation must now develop an overriding loyalty to mankind as a whole in order to preserve the best in their individual societies.

50   This call for a worldwide fellowship that lifts neighborly concern beyond one's tribe, race, class, and nation is in reality a call for an all-embracing and unconditional love for all mankind. This oft misunderstood, this oft misinterpreted concept, so readily dismissed by the Nietzsches[13] of the world as a weak and cowardly force, has now become an absolute necessity for the survival of man. When I speak of love I am not speaking of some sentimental and weak response. I'm not speaking of that force which is just emotional bosh. I am speaking of that force which all of the great religions have seen as the supreme unifying principle of life. Love is somehow the key that unlocks the door which leads to ultimate reality. This Hindu-Muslim-Christian-Jewish-Buddhist belief about ultimate reality is beautifully summed up in the first epistle of Saint John: "Let us love one another (*Yes*), for love is God. (*Yes*) And every one that loveth is born of God and knoweth God. He that loveth not knoweth not God, for God is love. . . . If we love one another, God dwelleth in us and his love is perfected in us." Let us hope that this spirit will become the order of the day.

51   We can no longer afford to worship the god of hate or bow before the altar of retaliation. The oceans of history are made turbulent by the ever-rising tides of hate. History is cluttered with the wreckage of nations and individuals that pursued this self-defeating path of hate. As Arnold Toynbee says: "Love is the ultimate force that makes for the saving choice of life and good against the damning choice of death and evil. Therefore the first hope in our inventory must be the hope that love is going to have the last word." Unquote.

52   We are now faced with the fact, my friends, that tomorrow is today. We are confronted with the fierce urgency of now. In this unfolding conundrum of life and history, there is such a thing as being too late. Procrastination is still the thief of time. Life often leaves us standing bare, naked, and dejected with a lost opportunity. The tide in the affairs of men does not remain at flood—it ebbs. We may cry out desperately for time to pause in her passage, but time is **adamant** to every plea and rushes on. Over the bleached bones and jumbled residues of numerous civilizations are written the pathetic words, "Too late." There is an invisible book of life that faithfully records our vigilance or our neglect. Omar Khayyam[14] is right: "The moving finger writes, and having writ moves on."

---

[13] **Nietzsches** (nē´chəz): a reference to the German philosopher Friedrich Nietzsche (1844–1900), who rejected Christianity and its associated morality.
[14] **Omar Khayyam:** (1048–c. 1132) influential Persian poet and scholar.

ANALYZE AND EVALUATE RHETORICAL DEVICES

Annotate: Mark the metaphors in paragraph 51.

Analyze: Explain how the use of metaphors supports King's message.

adamant
(ăd´ə-mənt) *adj.* inflexible and insistent, unchanging.

 ANALYZE AND EVALUATE RHETORICAL DEVICES

Remind students that a metaphor compares two unlike things to help make something abstract seem more understandable. Discuss each metaphor, and then point out that King contrasts the negative metaphors with love, which he sees as stronger. (**Answer:** *By telling people who believe in God—the people at the church where he is speaking—that hate has been made a god would certainly get their attention. Retaliation is how the god of hate is worshiped, and rising hatred stirs up history, like a tidal wave in the ocean.*)

For **listening support** for students at varying proficiency levels, see the **Text X-Ray** on page 738C.

TO CHALLENGE STUDENTS . . .

Analyze Allusions   In paragraph 52, there are two important allusions. "The tide in the affairs of men" is from Shakespeare's *Julius Caesar*, Act IV, scene 3. "The moving finger" is quoted from Omar Khayyam, but the quotation is itself an allusion to the famous handwriting on the wall at Belshazzar's feast, recorded in the Bible (Daniel 5:5, 24–26). Have students select one of these allusions, research what it means in its original context, and what King likely hopes his audience will understand from his use of the allusion. Ask students to write a few sentences detailing what they discover and, if possible, share it with a partner who picked the other allusion.

CRITICAL VOCABULARY

adamant: King notes that time is inflexible and insistent, or adamant—it does not change its mind or go in any direction except forward.

ASK STUDENTS why King would describe time as being adamant to people whose minds he is trying to change. (*He might be trying to show them that, since time is adamant and won't change its mind, the only way things will improve is if they do.*)

ANALYZE AND EVALUATE ARGUMENTS

Remind students that the whole point of persuasive rhetoric is the eventual call to action. King has finally arrived at the place where he tells his listeners what he wants them to do in response to his argument. (**Answer:** *By saying that it is a beautiful struggle that lies ahead, even if it is long and bitter, he conveys just how important he thinks this is.*)

NOTICE & NOTE

A man visits the Vietnam War Memorial in Washington, DC.

53   We still have a choice today: nonviolent coexistence or violent coannihilation. We must move past indecision to action. We must find new ways to speak for peace in Vietnam and justice throughout the developing world, a world that borders on our doors. If we do not act, we shall surely be dragged down the long, dark, and shameful corridors of time reserved for those who possess power without compassion, might without morality, and strength without sight.

54   Now let us begin. Now let us rededicate ourselves to the long and bitter, but beautiful, struggle for a new world. This is the calling of the sons of God, and our brothers wait eagerly for our response. Shall we say the odds are too great? Shall we tell them the struggle is too hard? Will our message be that the forces of American life militate against their arrival as full men, and we send our deepest regrets? Or will there be another message—of longing, of hope, of solidarity with their yearnings, of commitment to their cause, whatever the cost? The choice is ours, and though we might prefer it otherwise, we must choose in this crucial moment of human history.

55   As that noble bard of yesterday James Russell Lowell eloquently stated:

> Once to every man and nation comes a moment to decide,
> In the strife of Truth and Falsehood, for the good or evil side;
> Some great cause, God's new Messiah offering each the bloom or
>   blight,
> And the choice goes by forever 'twixt that darkness and that light.
> Though the cause of evil prosper, yet 'tis truth alone is strong
> Though her portions be the scaffold, and upon the throne be
>   wrong

ANALYZE AND EVALUATE ARGUMENTS

Annotate: Mark the call to action in paragraph 54.

Evaluate: Explain whether King effectively conveys the importance of taking action.

© Houghton Mifflin Harcourt Publishing Company • Image Credits: © Bettmann/Getty Images

IMPROVE READING FLUENCY

Targeted Passage   Use paragraph 54 to model how to read a persuasive speech. Have students follow along as you read the text with appropriate phrasing and emphasis. Then, have students work with partners to read paragraphs 45–48. Partners should take turns reading aloud the paragraphs in this section. Encourage students to provide feedback and support for pronouncing difficult words. Remind students that this was a speech, so they should think about the pace of their reading, making sure the audience has time to let the ideas sink in.

   Go to the **Reading Studio** for additional support in developing fluency.

Yet that scaffold sways the future, and behind the dim unknown
Standeth God within the shadow, keeping watch above his own.

56   And if we will only make the right choice, we will be able
to transform this pending cosmic elegy into a creative psalm of
peace. If we will make the right choice, we will be able to transform
the jangling discords of our world into a beautiful symphony of
brotherhood. If we will but make the right choice, we will be able
to speed up the day, all over America and all over the world, when
justice will roll down like waters, and righteousness like a mighty
stream. [*Sustained applause*]

**ANALYZE AND EVALUATE
RHETORICAL DEVICES**

Annotate: What phrase is
repeated in paragraph 56?

Analyze: How does this
repetition add strength to the
conclusion of King's argument?

CHECK YOUR UNDERSTANDING

Answer these questions before moving on to the **Analyze the Text** section on
the following page.

1 What does King describe as a "real promise of hope for the poor"?

  A The rehabilitation of the poor

  B The buildup in Vietnam

  C The War on Poverty

  D The National Liberation Front

2 What is the main focus of King's thoughts as he considers the "madness of
Vietnam"?

  F The people of Vietnam

  G The government in Saigon

  H The soldiers on each side

  J The Liberation Front

3 King says he is convinced that we as a nation must undergo a radical
revolution of —

  A materialism

  B technology

  C capitalism

  D values

Speech on the Vietnam War, 1967   **755**

 ## ANALYZE AND
EVALUATE RHETORICAL
DEVICES

Ask students why they think parallelism is a popular
technique with those who give persuasive speeches.
(**Answer:** *King is ending his argument with a strong call to
action. By repeating this phrase, he is emphasizing the need for
a revolution of values and for transforming conflict into peace
and brotherhood.*)

CHECK YOUR
UNDERSTANDING

Have students answer the questions independently.

Answers:

  1. *C*

  2. *F*

  3. *D*

If they answer any questions incorrectly, have them reread
the text to confirm their understanding. Then they may
proceed to ANALYZE THE TEXT on page 756.

 ## ENGLISH LEARNER SUPPORT

Oral Assessment Use the following questions to assess students' comprehension and
speaking skills.

1. King said the War on _____ gave hope to the poor. (*Poverty*)

2. Did King say the United States should end all bombing in Vietnam? (*yes*)

3. Does King think Americans should change their values? (*yes*)
    SUBSTANTIAL

ANALYZE THE TEXT

Possible answers:

1. **DOK 4:** *King's seven reasons provide a clear context for his controversial position. They help justify his stand against the war by linking it with the Civil Rights Movement and with his status as a Nobel Prize recipient and clergyman.*

2. **DOK 4:** *It is unlikely a student would choose to challenge King based on paragraph 12, except possibly noting "Our government felt that the Vietnamese people were not ready for independence." However, a student interested in the topic might offer a challenge. Most students will respond that the textual evidence in this paragraph indicates that the United States simply acted to keep Vietnam controlled by France.*

3. **DOK 4:** *In paragraph 17, King's questions focus attention on violence and suggest that the United States is destroying, not rebuilding, Vietnam. The questions in paragraph 20 invite listeners to acknowledge the grievances and motivations of the National Liberation Front.*

4. **DOK 4:** *The conclusion does logically follow the evidence. If, as he says, the war is motivated by people trying to maintain the status quo, rather than to liberate people, then it follows that what people value needs to change. They must care more about people than about "business as usual."*

5. **DOK 4:** *Kennedy contrasts peaceful revolution and violent revolution. King hopes that the feelings of respect people generally had for Kennedy would lend legitimacy to his argument.*

RESEARCH

Point out the research tip to students. Note that there are also many excellent history sites that cover the Civil Rights Movement that could be good sources of information on these laws.

Extend Encourage students to think about the positive gains and what it took to achieve them, as well as the remaining negatives. They may also want to think about how laws work: they affect the legal system but do not change attitudes. What might be done to change attitudes?

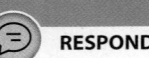

RESPOND

ANALYZE THE TEXT

Support your responses with evidence from the text. ☷ NOTEBOOK

1. **Analyze** How does King's explanation for speaking out against the war at the beginning of his speech lend authority to his argument?

2. **Evaluate** In paragraph 12, King suggests that the United States is not really acting to liberate the Vietnamese people. Defend or challenge King's claim, citing evidence from the text in your response.

3. **Analyze** King poses several rhetorical questions during the course of his speech. Explain the effect of this rhetorical device in paragraph 17 and at the beginning of paragraph 20.

4. **Evaluate** King concludes that the United States should take part in a "positive revolution of values." Does this conclusion logically follow from the evidence he has presented? Why or why not?

5. **Notice & Note** What two things are contrasted in the quotation from John F. Kennedy in paragraph 41? What effect does he hope it will have on his audience?

RESEARCH TIP
When researching a specific law, select primary sources from government websites that include the actual law and possible explanations. Websites of other organizations may have a biased viewpoint on the legislation.

RESEARCH

In paragraph 3 of King's speech, he refers to the hardships suffered by African Americans both at home in America and away in Vietnam. He refers to the generations of African Americans being denied equal opportunities, and refers to the lack of political power and representation seen by that community. Research the two major laws that were passed to address these issues, and answer the following questions.

QUESTION	ANSWER
How did the Civil Rights Act of 1964 end legal discrimination and segregation?	*This act banned segregation in public places, such as schools, theaters, restaurants, and hotels. It banned employment discrimination on the basis of race, color, religion, sex, or national origin.*
What were the issues preventing black Americans from voting prior to the Voting Act of 1965?	*African Americans were given wrong information for elections; they were told they were not sufficiently literate; they were told they did not fill out forms correctly; they were asked to recite the Constitution; they were threatened and assaulted.*

Extend Did the passage of the Civil Rights Act of 1964 and the Voting Act of 1965 fully resolve the issues they intended to address? Write a paragraph in which you discuss the effectiveness of the laws.

LEARNING MINDSET

Problem Solving Remind students that, just as different people have different problems, so too there are different ways of solving problems. Each person has to find the solution or group of solutions that works best for him or her. Explain that identifying a variety of strategies makes it possible to change strategies when one isn't working. Being patient and rereading might work for some. Looking up words, quotations, or additional background information might help get others through a road block. Talking with a partner or asking someone, such as a teacher or someone who has already taken the class, could make something clear. Every time you solve a problem, you get better at solving problems, and that is one of the keys to getting smarter.

CREATE AND DISCUSS

Write an Article Pretend you are a journalist living in 1967. Review your notes. Then write an article that either supports or opposes King's claims.

❏ Identify the purpose of King's argument and his major claims.

❏ Evaluate the evidence presented and the logic of King's conclusions.

❏ Include discussion of King's style and the devices that he uses to command attention.

❏ Support your position with textual evidence.

Have a Group Discussion With a group, discuss the effectiveness of King's speech.

❏ Discuss King's main points and how the evidence supports his points.

❏ Present examples of King's rhetorical devices and how they enhance his argument.

❏ Listen carefully to the contributions of your classmates and adjust your view of King's speech as needed.

❏ Evaluate King's conclusions on the Vietnam War.

 Go to **Writing Arguments** in the **Writing Studio** for help.

 Go to **Analyzing and Evaluating Presentations** in the **Speaking and Listening Studio** for help.

RESPOND TO THE ESSENTIAL QUESTION

 ? When should personal integrity come before civic duty?

Gather Information Review your annotations and notes on King's speech. Then, add relevant information to your Response Log. As you determine which information to include, think about:

• ways that King demonstrates personal integrity

• passages that suggest King's view of civic duty

• whether personal integrity and civic duty must be opposed

• other convictions or obligations that drive King's beliefs and actions

UNIT 6
RESPONSE LOG

ACADEMIC VOCABULARY

As you write and discuss what you learned from the speech, be sure to use the Academic Vocabulary words. Check off each of the words that you use.

❏ **contemporary**

❏ **global**

❏ **infinite**

❏ **simulated**

❏ **virtual**

Speech on the Vietnam War, 1967   757

CREATE AND DISCUSS

Write an Article Let students know that being "divided" is an option—they may support some aspects of the speech and not others. The point of the article is to evaluate the evidence offered in the speech—what works and what doesn't. Encourage students to look up articles written in 1967, both for and against the war, or possibly with mixed opinions. This will enable them to have a context in which to evaluate the speech.

 For **writing support** for students at varying proficiency levels, see the **Text X-Ray** on page 738D.

Have a Group Discussion Instruct students to listen attentively, so that their comments are based on what is being said, not on their having missed a point. Suggest they listen primarily for whether the examples given are appropriate for what the speaker is saying.

RESPOND TO THE ESSENTIAL QUESTION

Allow time for students to add details from "Speech on the Vietnam War, 1967" to their Unit 6 Response Logs.

CRITICAL VOCABULARY

Answers:

1. *more likely*

2. *hurting*

3. *more likely*

4. *unhappy*

VOCABULARY STRATEGY:

Suffixes

Answers:

Correct base words, definitions, and possible sentences are given at right. You might want to encourage students to define other words that end with *-ation*, *-ism*, or *-ence*, such as *elimination, communism,* or *affluence*.

RESPOND

WORD BANK

facile	insurgency
eviscerate	reparations
indigenous	recalcitrant
extortionist	adamant

Go to **Common Roots, Prefixes and Suffixes** in the **Vocabulary Studio** for help with suffixes.

CRITICAL VOCABULARY

Practice and Apply Use your understanding of the Critical Vocabulary words to answer each question.

1. If you're an **extortionist** who is **adamant** about payment, are you less or more likely to get your money?

2. If you **eviscerate** an **insurgency,** are you helping or hurting the rebels?

3. If making **reparations** is a **facile** move for a government, will they be less or more likely to go through with the payments?

4. If the **indigenous** population is **recalcitrant** about allowing corporations to harvest their natural resources, are they happy or unhappy about gaining corporate partners?

VOCABULARY STRATEGY: Suffixes

Several Critical Vocabulary words derive their meaning from the addition of suffixes. For example, the suffix *-ous* means "relating to or having the quality of." This suffix forms an adjective, such as *continuous*. Other suffixes form nouns. Knowing some common suffixes and the part of speech they form will help you define unfamiliar terms.

Noun Suffixes:
-ation, *-tion* = action, resulting state
-ism = belief or doctrine
-ence = action or process, quality or state

Practice and Apply For each word below, identify the suffix and the base word. Break down each word into its parts to clarify the meaning.

- Identify the base, or main word, without the suffix.
- Define the base word.
- Write a sentence using the nouns formed by each suffix.

WORD / BASE WORD	DEFINITION OF BASE WORD	SENTENCE
Word: domination Suffix: *-tion* Base word: dominate	to control, govern, or rule by superior authority	The emperor was amassing an army to achieve his goal of world domination.
Word: cynicism Suffix: *-ism* Base word: *cynic*	*someone who thinks everyone is motivated by self-interest*	*His cynicism made it hard for him to trust his fellow workers.*
Word: interference Suffix: *-ence* Base word: *interfere*	*to be or create a hindrance or obstacle*	*One person's interference can hold up an entire project.*

EL ENGLISH LEARNER SUPPORT

Vocabulary Strategy Give students additional practice in determining the meanings of words with suffixes. Point out, for example, the suffix *-ist* in the vocabulary word *extortionist*. This is generally related to the suffix *-ism*. Someone who follows a doctrine, or *-ism*, will be identified as an *-ist*. For example, a follower of Buddhism is a Buddhist. Note that the suffixes *-ism* and *-ist* can also relate to practice, such as extorting. Point out that in the speech, *agreement, government,* and *commitment* share the *-ment* suffix, meaning an action or result. Discuss how this ending affects the verbs *agree, govern,* and *commit*. **ALL LEVELS**

LANGUAGE CONVENTIONS:
Imperative Mood

The **mood** of a verb shows the way in which a thought or idea is expressed. The **imperative mood** is used to give orders, make requests, or issue advice. In the imperative mood, the subject is not typically stated but is understood. For comparison, this chart shows examples expressed in both the imperative mood and the indicative mood. A verb in the **indicative mood** expresses a fact or asks a question. Verbs in most sentences are in the indicative mood.

INDICATIVE MOOD	IMPERATIVE MOOD
We must stop attacking the countryside.	Stop attacking the countryside.
We urge the government to sign the peace treaty.	Sign the peace treaty.
Returning soldiers should be given jobs.	Give jobs to returning soldiers.

Read this sentence from the speech.

End all bombing in North and South Vietnam.

Martin Luther King Jr. could have said the sentence in this way instead.

The government should end all bombing in North and South Vietnam.

In the second sentence, notice that by adding a subject and a helping verb the mood changes from imperative to indicative. In the indicative sentence, the emphasis on the verb, or the action, is diluted. As a result, the intensity of the original version is lost, making the sentence less effective in conveying urgency, emotion, and meaning.

Practice and Apply Rewrite the following paragraph, changing some of the sentences to the imperative mood.

These are tips that I have found helpful for successful speech-giving. First, it is important to make sure you have prepared a set of speaking notes. Your main ideas and most important details should be written on large index cards. You should be able to see your notes at a glance. Second, you should practice in front of a mirror by yourself, incorporating gestures and working on eye contact. Third, it is a good idea to ask a friend or family member to listen to your speech. Finally, you should get a good night's sleep before the big day. If you are well rested, you will be able to do your best.

Go to **Correct Use of Verbs** in the **Grammar Studio** for help.

LANGUAGE CONVENTIONS:
Imperative Mood

Explain that the imperative mood will not always be the most appropriate way to make a request. Students should consider when the extra emphasis is needed. For example, it can be when there is a degree of urgency: "Run for home base," "Throw the ball," "Give her a turn." Generally, a less emphatic, less urgent mood should be used. But when a point needs to be made, or when someone needs to act *now*, the imperative mood is effective.

Practice and Apply Students' rewrites should show an understanding of the imperative mood. (***Possible rewrite:*** *These are tips that I have found helpful for successful speech-giving. Prepare a set of speaking notes. Write your main ideas and key details on large index cards. You should be able to see your notes at a glance. Practice in front of a mirror by yourself. Incorporate gestures. Work on eye contact. Get a good night's sleep before the big day. If you are well rested, you will be able to do your best.*)

For **speaking support** for students at varying proficiency levels, see **Text X-Ray** page 738D.

 ENGLISH LEARNER SUPPORT

Language Conventions Note that all languages have a way of communicating orders or instructions, though some approaches are less direct than others. You might want to ask students to share how orders are given or requests are made in their native languages. Explain that in English, the imperative mood offers the most direct way of giving an instruction or order. Direct students to page 749, and help them identify the imperative mood in this part of King's speech. Discuss how different this passage would be if the imperative were not used.
SUBSTANTIAL

© Houghton Mifflin Harcourt Publishing Company

AMBUSH
Short Story by Tim O'Brien

GENRE ELEMENTS
SHORT STORY

A **short story** is a fictional work that often centers on a single idea and is driven by one main conflict. This conflict can be either external, involving a dispute or problem between characters, or internal, involving a main character's struggle with his or her own desires or feelings. In this selection, the author uses a **frame story,** which is a story told within a story, as a way to set the stage for an internal conflict.

LEARNING OBJECTIVES

- Analyze internal conflict, characterization, and structure.
- Conduct research on the natural environment of Vietnam.
- Write a personal narrative using a story frame.
- Discuss a personal narrative.
- Distinguish between connotation and denotation.
- Use transitions to signal shifts in time or topic.
- **Language** Discuss past and present events in a story, using appropriate verb tense and chronological words.

TEXT COMPLEXITY

Quantitative Measures	Ambush	Lexile: 950L
Qualitative Measures	**Ideas Presented** Multiple levels of meaning; use of symbolism; some ambiguity; greater demand for inference.	
	Structures Used Clear, mostly chronological with some flashbacks.	
	Language Used Mostly explicit; some figurative language, imagery.	
	Knowledge Required More complexity in theme; experiences may be less familiar to many; cultural or historical references may make heavier demands.	

RESOURCES

- Unit 6 Response Log

- 🔊 Selection Audio

- Level Up Tutorial:
  Setting

- Reading Studio:
  Notice & Note

- Writing Studio:
  Writing Narratives

- Speaking and Listening Studio:
  The Content of Your Presentation:
  Narrative

- Vocabulary Studio:
  Connotation and Denotation

- ☑ "Ambush" Selection Test

SUMMARIES

English

This story is a narrative about the author's experience as a soldier in the Vietnam War. This war was considered by many to be an unwarranted act of American aggression. Despite this controversy, the Americans who fought and died there were brave men and women who returned to a country that did not necessarily embrace them as heroes. This narrative is a frame story—a story told within a story—and is written from the author's perspective as he recalls a memory to tell his young daughter. In it, he details the conflicting feelings he felt during the war, and continues to feel throughout his life.

Spanish

Esta historia es una narración de la experiencia del autor como soldado en la Guerra de Vietnam. La guerra comenzó en 1955 y no concluyó hasta 1975; se considera por muchos como un acto de agresión americana injustificado. A pesar de la controversia, los americanos que lucharon y murieron en la guerra eran hombres y mujeres valientes, quienes regresaron a un país que no necesariamente los recibió como héroes. Es una narración enmarcada (una historia dentro de una historia) y está escrita desde la perspectiva del autor mientras recuerda una historia para contarle a su hija. En ella, detalla sus sentimientos contradictorios durante la guerra, que continuó teniendo por el resto de su vida.

 ## SMALL-GROUP OPTIONS

Have students work in small groups and pairs to read and discuss the selection.

Double-Entry Journal

- Have students draw a line down the center of a sheet of paper.
- Ask students to title the left column *Quotes from "Ambush"* and the right column *My Notes*.
- Have students record interesting, confusing, or surprising text passages in the left column.
- Then, beside each passage, have them write their own interpretation, paraphrase, or question in the right column.

Three Before Me

- After students have finished composing their frame stories, ask them to review and revise the text.
- Have each student ask three other students to edit his or her text.
- Have each student evaluate the editing suggestions made by their peers and make appropriate revisions before writing the final draft to be turned in.

Text X-Ray: English Learner Support
for "Ambush"

Use the Text X-Ray and the supports and scaffolds in the Teacher's Edition to help guide students at different proficiency levels through the selection.

INTRODUCE THE SELECTION
DISCUSS THE VIETNAM WAR

In this lesson, students will need to know about the Vietnam War. Explain that Americans were sent to Vietnam to support South Vietnamese forces in their fight against the Communist-supported North Vietnamese. Vietnam had once been a French colony, and the North Vietnamese believed that they were fighting for their freedom to rule themselves. For this reason, people in the United States were divided. Were American forces fighting communism, or were they fighting against another country's freedom?

Instruct students to discuss the following question in small groups: *If you were a soldier sent to fight in a foreign war, what conflicting feelings might you have?*

Explain that when people feel *conflicted* or have *conflicting feelings*, they are confused or think that both sides of an argument could be right. Supply sentence frames to aid in the discussion, such as the following: *I would feel both _____ and _____. My emotions would be _____ and _____.*

CULTURAL REFERENCES

The following words or phrases may be unfamiliar to students:

- *ambush* (title; paragraph 4): the act of lying in wait to attack by surprise
- *grenade* (paragraph 2): a small bomb or explosive missile that is detonated by a fuse and thrown by hand or shot from a launcher. In this story, the fuse is started by removing a pin.
- *switching off* (paragraph 4): trading places or roles
- *sorting it out* (paragraph 8): making a decision; deciding how one feels about something
- *dwell on* (paragraph 8): continue thinking about

LISTENING

Understand Characterization

Help students grasp characterization through the main character's thoughts, actions, and words.

Have students listen as you read aloud the first paragraph of the story. Use the following supports with students at varying proficiency levels:

- Review the use of quotation marks to show when someone is speaking. As you read the paragraph aloud, have students follow along in the text. Ask them to circle what the narrator says and underline what the narrator thinks. Review the details that students circled and underlined. Help students recognize the difference between what the narrator says (he did not kill anyone) and what he thinks (he did kill someone, but does not want to tell his daughter about it). **SUBSTANTIAL**

- As you read the paragraph, have students note what the narrator says and what the narrator thinks. Ask them to discuss this question with a partner, using their notes: *What is the difference between what the narrator says and what the narrator thinks?* **MODERATE**

- Have students discuss the "difficult moment" described in the paragraph with a partner or in a small group. Ask the following questions: *Why does the narrator think the moment was difficult? What did he decide? Why do you think he made the decision?* **LIGHT**

SPEAKING

Discuss the Development of a Narrative

Have students discuss the connection between the narrator's memories of the past and his thoughts during the present. Guide them to use present- and past-tense verbs and other clues to determine when the events in the story take place.

Use the following supports with students at varying proficiency levels:

- Review the concept of past-tense and present-tense verbs with students. Guide students to use verbs in the first two paragraphs of the story to determine which events are occurring in the present and which occurred in the past. Say several of the verbs aloud, such as *hope, asked,* and *passed.* Have students repeat each verb and say "Present" or "Past." **SUBSTANTIAL**
- Have partners read paragraphs 1 and 2 aloud to each other. Ask them to discuss clues about when events in the story happen, such as verb tenses and words that refer to time. **MODERATE**
- Have students work with a partner to paraphrase what happens in the first two paragraphs. Ask them to discuss which events happened in the past and why the narrator is remembering them. Remind them to use appropriate past and present verb tenses in their discussion. **LIGHT**

READING

Make Inferences

Help students make inferences about the main character's feelings of regret, based on details in the text.

Use the following supports with students at varying proficiency levels:

- Review the meaning of the words *regret* and *peril* with students. Then, read paragraph 5 aloud in phrases or short sentences and have students echo read. Help students identify words and phrases in the text that show why the narrator regrets killing the young man (for example, "I was in no real peril"). **SUBSTANTIAL**
- Have students reread paragraphs 5–7 and discuss them in a small group. Guide students to identify how the narrator's choice makes him feel regret. Provide the following sentence frame: *When _____ made the choice to _____, I understood that the character felt _____.* **MODERATE**
- Ask students: *Does the narrator regret killing the young man?* Have them discuss the question with a partner and use evidence from paragraphs 5–8 to support their answer. **LIGHT**

WRITING

Write a Frame Story

Help students structure and write the frame story for the assignment on Student Edition page 769.

Use the following supports with students at varying proficiency levels:

- Have students draw a series of pictures to tell their frame story. Ask them to write one or two sentences to accompany the pictures. Allow them to use words from their native language. **SUBSTANTIAL**
- Have students brainstorm by listing a few regrets they have had. Ask them to write one sentence about each, using a sentence frame: *I chose to _____ but I could have chosen to _____ instead.* **MODERATE**
- Remind students that they can tell their readers more about their frame story by explaining the choices they could have made when they faced a conflict. Have them plan the frame story by outlining the conflict and the choices they could have made, then use the outline to write the story. **LIGHT**

AMBUSH

Short Story by **Tim O'Brien**

? Connect to the
ESSENTIAL QUESTION

The narrator of "Ambush" feels isolated and likely to be rejected by what he has done as a soldier. While he was an isolated soldier, the narrator killed a man in a decision he still questions.

? ***ESSENTIAL QUESTION:***

How do we deal with rejection and isolation?

760   Unit 6

QUICK START

Think of an important decision you made that you regretted or second-guessed later. Freewrite about what happened and how it feels when you look back on what happened.

ANALYZE CHARACTERIZATION

Characterization refers to the techniques a writer uses to develop characters. There are four basic methods of characterization:

- A writer may use physical description.
- The character's own actions, words, thoughts, and feelings might be presented.
- The actions, words, thoughts, and feelings of other characters provide another means of developing a character.
- The narrator's own direct comments also serve to develop a character.

A story's plot and theme are shaped by its characters' behaviors and underlying motivations, which often contribute to **moral dilemmas,** a form of **internal conflict.**

ANALYZE TEXT STRUCTURE

A story's **structure** is the way that it is put together—the arrangement of its parts. Tim O'Brien's short story "Ambush" includes a **frame story,** a device in which one story is told inside another story. The story opens with a frame—the narrator describes a time when his daughter asked him about the war. In a flashback, he then recounts an experience he'd had earlier, as a soldier in war. Use a graphic like the one below to keep track of the events in the outer and inner story.

STORY 1	STORY 2
Beginning:	
	Beginning:
	Middle:
	End:
End:	

As you read, pay attention to the structure of the story and think about how the author uses structure to achieve his purpose and convey the theme.

GENRE ELEMENTS: SHORT STORY

- usually centers on one main conflict
- may use several techniques to portray characters
- may use a frame story in which a story in the past is told within a second story

QUICK START

After students read the Quick Start, invite them to share why they second-guessed themselves. What was the basis for those feelings? How did they end up resolving or coping with those feelings?

ANALYZE CHARACTERIZATION

Remind students that internal conflict happens in a text when a problem—often the main problem—is inside a character's mind. Often the problem cannot be easily solved by anyone else, although other characters can and usually do give advice.

ANALYZE TEXT STRUCTURE

Tell students that authors use a frame story if the main plot of the story takes place mostly in one time frame but the plot needs the context of a different time. Frame stories do not have to be time-based but are often a way to jump backward to a different time in the context of the present.

Ambush   761

TEACH

CRITICAL VOCABULARY

Remind students to think of a synonym or a definition before choosing which word to use to fill in the blank. After they've chosen words to fill in each blank, encourage them to look at whichever blanks they filled in last to make sure those definitions or synonyms make sense for that word.

Answers:

1. *ponder*

2. *gape*

3. *platoon*

4. *sliver*

5. *peril*

6. *grope*

■ English Learner Support

Use Cognates Tell students that the Critical Vocabulary word *peril* has a Spanish cognate in the word *peligro*.
ALL LEVELS

LANGUAGE CONVENTIONS

Transitions Tell students to think about what transitions tell the reader and how they give a hint about what to expect. For instance, in the quoted example, the transition tells us that the narrator only had half an hour where nothing happened. After that, something happened.

ANNOTATION MODEL

Encourage students to also look for instances of characterization and for how the author adds in descriptions of the main character while describing other things.

CRITICAL VOCABULARY

| platoon | grope | sliver | ponder | peril | gape |

Find out how many Critical Vocabulary words you already know by writing the correct word next to the prompt.

1. Synonym for *think*

2. A way of looking

3. A group of soldiers

4. A thin piece

5. Synonym for *danger*

6. Feel about blindly

LANGUAGE CONVENTIONS

Transitions Words and phrases that show how ideas are related to one another are called **transitions.** Using transitions effectively helps an author create coherence so that all sentences are related to one another and ideas flow in a logical manner. Transitions can communicate time or sequence, spatial relationships, degree of importance, compare-and-contrast relationships, or cause and effect. Notice the time transition in the second sentence.

> I reached out and found three grenades and lined them up in front of me; the pins had already been straightened for quick throwing. And <u>then</u> for maybe half an hour I kneeled there and waited.

ANNOTATION MODEL   NOTICE & NOTE

As you read, look for any internal conflicts, such as a moral dilemma, that a character experiences. The model shows one reader's notes about "Ambush."

> When she was nine, <u>my daughter Kathleen asked if I had ever killed anyone</u>. She knew about the war; she knew I'd been a soldier. "You keep writing these war stories," she said, "so I guess you must've killed somebody." <u>It was a difficult moment, but I did what seemed right</u>, which was to say, <u>"Of course not,"</u> and then to take her onto my lap and hold her for a while. Someday, I hope, she'll ask again.

The narrator has to make a choice.

He is conflicted. His answer reflects his concern for her rather than the truth.

BACKGROUND

Tim O'Brien (b. 1946) *served in Vietnam, and his military experience provides much of the material for his fiction and personal narratives. In 1990 O'Brien published* The Things They Carried, *a remarkable fictional memoir about the Vietnam War and its human effects. The book is made up of interconnected stories narrated by a character named Tim O'Brien, who, the author says, is not himself. "Ambush" comes from that collection.*

AMBUSH

Short Story by Tim O'Brien

SETTING A PURPOSE

As you read, look for how O'Brien uses the narrator's internal conflict to shape the plot and theme of "Ambush."

1 When she was nine, my daughter Kathleen asked if I had ever killed anyone. She knew about the war; she knew I'd been a soldier. "You keep writing these war stories," she said, "so I guess you must've killed somebody." It was a difficult moment, but I did what seemed right, which was to say, "Of course not," and then to take her onto my lap and hold her for a while. Someday, I hope, she'll ask again. But here I want to pretend she's a grown-up. I want to tell her exactly what happened, or what I remember happening, and then I want to say to her that as a little girl she was absolutely right. <u>This is why I keep writing war stories:</u>

2 He was a short, slender young man of about twenty. I was afraid of him—afraid of something—and as he passed me on the trail I threw a grenade that exploded at his feet and killed him.

3 Or to go back:

4 Shortly after midnight we moved into the ambush site outside My Khe. The whole **platoon** was there, spread out in the dense brush along the trail, and for five hours nothing at

Notice & Note

Use the side margins to notice and note signposts in the text.

LANGUAGE CONVENTIONS
Annotate: In paragraph 1, mark the sentence that signals a transition.

Analyze: What is the shift in setting that is being indicated with this sentence?

platoon
(plə-to͞on´) *n.* a subdivision of a company of troops consisting of two or more squads or sections and usually commanded by a lieutenant.

Ambush 763

BACKGROUND

Explain to students that much of this story is set in Vietnam, which was a difficult war for the United States. The reasons for fighting in the war were unpopular with U.S. citizens back home. The war also had many casualties. Introduce the story by pointing out the ambiguity at its core: as with the rest of the stories in *The Things They Carried*, the main character is Tim O'Brien, who fought in Vietnam like the author did. In the story, the main character writes about the war years later—just like the author does in real life. Emphasize that although the story is fictional, it is driven by some of the author's own real-life experiences.

SETTING A PURPOSE

Direct students to use the Setting a Purpose prompt to focus their reading.

LANGUAGE CONVENTIONS

Discuss with students what the "This" in the last sentence of paragraph 1 refers to. The author is essentially saying: This thing I am about to tell you is why I keep writing war stories. (**Answer:** *The story shifts from his home in the present to Vietnam during the Vietnam War.*)

For **listening** and **speaking support** for students at varying proficiency levels, see the **Text X-Ray** on pages 760C–760D.

TO CHALLENGE STUDENTS . . .

Compare to History Have students research what it was like to be a soldier in the Vietnam War. Discuss how that sort of lifestyle would affect a person over the long term. How would it affect one's decision-making skills?

CRITICAL VOCABULARY

platoon: The squads of troops were waiting along the trail.

ASK STUDENTS whether they would expect to be scared of a single person when surrounded by a platoon of friendly people. (*generally not, because it would be one man against the whole platoon*)

grope
(grōp) *v.* to reach about uncertainly; feel one's way.

sliver
(slĭv´ər) *n.* a small narrow piece, portion, or plot.

all happened. We were working in two-man teams—one man on guard while the other slept, switching off every two hours—and I remember it was still dark when Kiowa shook me awake for the final watch. The night was foggy and hot. For the first few moments I felt lost, not sure about directions, **groping** for my helmet and weapon. I reached out and found three grenades and lined them up in front of me; the pins had already been straightened for quick throwing. And then for maybe half an hour I kneeled there and waited. Very gradually, in tiny **slivers**, dawn began to break through the fog, and, from my position in the brush I could see ten or fifteen meters up the trail. The mosquitoes were fierce. I remember slapping at them, wondering if I should wake up Kiowa and ask for some repellent, then thinking it was a bad idea, then looking up and seeing the young man come out of the fog. He wore black clothing and rubber sandals and a gray ammunition belt. His shoulders were slightly stooped, his head cocked to the side as if listening for something. He seemed at ease. He carried his weapon in one hand, muzzle down, moving without any hurry up the center of the trail. There was no sound at all—none that I can remember. In a way, it seemed, he was part of the morning fog, or my own imagination, but there was also the reality

CRITICAL VOCABULARY

grope: O'Brien reached for his helmet and weapon.

ASK STUDENTS why O'Brien groped for his weapon but neatly arranged his grenades. *(because the grenades had to be neatly set up and straightened to be useful)*

sliver: Little bits of dawn were visible through the fog.

ASK STUDENTS why only slivers of dawn were visible. *(The fog was extremely heavy.)*

WHEN STUDENTS STRUGGLE . . .

Setting Have students read this page and look for details that describe the setting. Discuss why the setting matters, not just in the sense that if it were not a war zone it would be a different story, but how the setting matters to the character. It's almost dawn and he's been sleeping in two-hour shifts, so he's tired. Also, the fog makes it harder to see.

 For additional support, go to the **Reading Studio** and assign the following **Level Up Tutorial: Setting.**

of what was happening in my stomach. I had already pulled the pin on a grenade. I had come up to a crouch. It was entirely automatic. I did not hate the young man; I did not see him as the enemy; I did not **ponder** issues of morality or politics or military duty. I crouched and kept my head low. I tried to swallow whatever was rising from my stomach, which tasted like lemonade, something fruity and sour. I was terrified. There were no thoughts about killing. The grenade was to make him go away—just evaporate—and I leaned back and felt my head go empty and then felt it fill up again. I had already thrown the grenade before telling myself to throw it. The brush was thick and I had to lob it high, not aiming, and I remember the grenade seeming to freeze above me for an instant, as if a camera had clicked, and I remember ducking down and holding my breath and seeing little wisps of fog rise from the earth. The grenade bounced once and rolled across the trail. I did not hear it, but there must have been a sound, because the young man dropped his weapon and began to run, just two or three quick steps, then he hesitated, swiveling to his right, and he glanced down at the grenade and tried to cover his head but never did. It occurred to me then that he was about to die. I wanted to warn him. The grenade made a popping noise—not soft

ponder
(pŏn´dər) *tr. v.* to think about (something) with thoroughness and care.

ANALYZE CHARACTERIZATION
Annotate: In paragraph 4, mark the narrator's thoughts and feelings about killing the young man.

Draw Conclusions: What do these details tell you about the narrator's motivation for throwing the grenade?

Ambush 765

ANALYZE CHARACTERIZATION

Encourage students to notice the author's use of characterization here to convey the character's feelings rather than directly saying O'Brien felt that it was complicated because he didn't want to kill the young man. Instead, the author shows us how the character O'Brien felt by telling us what he was and was not thinking. (**Answer:** *He is motivated by deep fear, not by hate or a sense of duty.*)

■ English Learner Support

Homonyms Tell students that the verb *duck* has nothing to do with waterbirds. Ask students to infer the meaning from the context. They should gather that ducking down must mean "lowering your head to avoid being seen or hit by something." **SUBSTANTIAL/MODERATE**

CRITICAL VOCABULARY

ponder: O'Brien was not carefully thinking through issues of morality, politics, or duty.

ASK STUDENTS when O'Brien began to ponder issues of morality, politics, or duty. (*He started pondering them once the event had already happened.*)

WORDS OF THE WISER

Tell students that the narrator's initial discussion with Kiowa mirrors his self-analysis since then. He was troubled and brought it up immediately, but he is still discussing it and still not sure whether he was right. (**Answer:** *Kiowa assures him that he did the right thing and should not be upset or try to second-guess his actions. The narrator was upset and expressed regret about killing the young man.*)

 For **reading support** for students at varying proficiency levels, see the **Test X-Ray** on page 760D.

CRITICAL VOCABULARY

peril: O'Brien was not in any danger.

ASK STUDENTS why O'Brien was scared if he was not in peril. *(because he had just seen an enemy combatant while everyone else was asleep; it was a high-stress situation)*

766 Unit 6

---

but not loud either—not what I'd expected—and there was a puff of dust and smoke—a small white puff—and the young man seemed to jerk upward as if pulled by invisible wires. He fell on his back. His rubber sandals had been blown off. He lay at the center of the trail, his right leg beneath him, his one eye shut, his other eye a huge star-shaped hole.

peril
(pĕr´əl) *n.* imminent danger.

5   For me, it was not a matter of live or die. I was in no real **peril**. Almost certainly the young man would have passed me by. And it will always be that way.

6   Later, I remember Kiowa tried to tell me that the man would've died anyway. He told me that it was a good kill, that I was a soldier and this was a war, that I should shape up and stop staring and ask myself what the dead man would've done if things were reversed.

WORDS OF THE WISER

Notice & Note: In paragraph 6, what does Kiowa tell the narrator about his actions?

Infer: What do Kiowa's words tell us about the narrator's immediate reaction to killing the young man?

© Houghton Mifflin Harcourt Publishing Company • Image Credits: © Keystone Pictures USA/Alamy

766   Unit 6

APPLYING ACADEMIC VOCABULARY

☑ **contemporary**   ☐ **global**   ☐ **infinite**   ☑ **simulated**   ☐ **virtual**

Write and Discuss Have students turn to a partner to discuss the following questions. Guide students to include the Academic Vocabulary words *contemporary* and *simulated* in their responses. Ask volunteers to share their responses with the class.

- In what ways are moral dilemmas like O'Brien's dilemmas a **contemporary** issue?
- Do you think O'Brien's ethical concerns are **simulated** for the sake of his daughter from the frame story?

7   None of it mattered. The words seemed far too complicated. All I could do was **gape** at the fact of the young man's body.

8   Even now I haven't finished sorting it out. Sometimes I forgive myself, other times I don't. In the ordinary hours of life I try not to dwell on it, but now and then, when I'm reading a newspaper or just sitting alone in a room, I'll look up and see the young man step out of the morning fog. I'll watch him walk toward me, his shoulders slightly stooped, his head cocked to the side, and he'll pass within a few yards of me and suddenly smile at some secret thought and then continue up the trail to where it bends back into the fog.

gape
(gāp, găp) *intr.v.* to stare wonderingly or stupidly, often with the mouth open.

ANALYZE TEXT STRUCTURE
Annotate: In paragraph 8, mark the story the narrator tells about the young man.

Analyze: Is this part of the main story or the frame story? Explain.

CHECK YOUR UNDERSTANDING

Answer these questions before moving on to the **Analyze the Text** section on the following page.

1 What is the lie that the narrator tells his daughter?

   A That he did not fight in the war

   B That he killed someone because he was in danger

   C That he didn't kill anyone in the war

   D That he doesn't remember what happened

2 What was the narrator doing on the night he threw the grenade?

   F Moving along the trail with his whole platoon

   G Clearing dense brush in a two-man team

   H Straightening the pins on three grenades

   J Standing guard for the final watch of the night

3 Why does Kiowa think that the narrator did the right thing?

   A The young man would have died anyway.

   B The young man was there as a spy.

   C The young man was a threat.

   D The platoon was in peril.

 ENGLISH LEARNER SUPPORT

Oral Assessment Use the following questions to assess students' comprehension and speaking skills.

1. Did the main character tell his daughter the truth about killing anyone? *(no)*

2. What was the main character on guard duty? *(yes, for the last time that night)*

3. Did Kiowa say it was right to kill the man? *(yes, because the man would have died anyway)*
   SUBSTANTIAL/MODERATE

TEACH

ANALYZE TEXT STRUCTURE

Have students discuss what this ending says about the narrator's decision about killing the man. Encourage them to realize that despite Kiowa's assurances and his attempts to agree, in the end, he wishes he'd let the man walk away. (**Answer:** *This story is part of the frame story. It is what the author imagines in the present time and wishes had happened.*)

CHECK YOUR UNDERSTANDING

Have students answer the questions independently.

Answers:

   1. *C*

   2. *J*

   3. *A*

If they answer any questions incorrectly, have them reread the text to confirm their understanding. Then they may proceed to ANALYZE THE TEXT on page 768.

CRITICAL VOCABULARY

gape: All he could do is stare at the man's body wonderingly.

ASK STUDENTS whether they think O'Brien would gape if the man had been uninjured by the grenade. (*No, he would not gape then. O'Brien gaped at the man because he was dead.*)

APPLY

ANALYZE THE TEXT

Possible answers:

1. **DOK 2:** *The narrator kills a young man in Vietnam. The narrator is upset about killing the man because the narrator is not sure he did the right thing. Many years later, his young daughter asks him if he killed anyone and he tells her he didn't. The narrator often imagines a scenario in which he did not kill the young man.*

2. **DOK 2:** *The narrator knows that the possibility that the young man would have just kept walking will never be realized because the choice he made never allowed for a different outcome.*

3. **DOK 4:** *The story in the last paragraph is what the narrator imagines as a way of comforting himself. It tells us that the narrator deals with regret in life by imagining events the way he thinks they should have happened. This helps develop the theme about regrets from the past influencing the present.*

4. **DOK 4:** *The frame shows that many years after the war, the narrator continues to struggle with the same moral dilemma. The fact that he lied to his daughter when she was young but wants to tell her the truth highlights the complexity of the issue for him. Without the frame, one might imagine that the young American soldier accepted the outcome as his friend Kiowa told him he should.*

5. **DOK 4:** *Students' answers will vary, but they should recognize that the narrator continues to struggle with the killing many years later. They may indicate that Kiowa's words bring him some comfort when he thinks about the incident or that the moral ambiguity of the phrase "a good kill" is the source of the young soldier's internal conflict.*

RESEARCH

Tell students that besides firsthand accounts of the physical setting of Vietnam, sources about the country of Vietnam and its environment may also be useful.

Connect Students may note that the fog, heat, humidity, and massive plant growth would have been hindrances that were hard to adjust to.

ANALYZE THE TEXT

Support your responses with evidence from the text. ▤ NOTEBOOK

1. **Interpret** How does the narrator's behavior in the past create a moral dilemma when he is speaking with his daughter? Is this dilemma adequately addressed in the story? Explain.

2. **Interpret** What does the narrator mean when he says in paragraph 5 that "it will always be that way"?

3. **Analyze** In paragraph 8, what does the story about the young man tell the reader about the narrator's character? How does this help develop the theme?

4. **Evaluate** How does the frame contribute to the impact of the story? Consider what would be lost without the first and last paragraphs.

5. **Notice & Note** Kiowa tells his comrade that "it was a good kill." How effective are Kiowa's words in helping the narrator overcome his internal conflict?

RESEARCH

RESEARCH TIP
While it is best to rely on sources written by historians, you may find useful information in firsthand accounts by people involved in historical events such as the Vietnam War.

A major part of the challenge for soldiers in the Vietnam War was the natural environment in which they fought. Do some research to find out more about the weather and the terrain that American soldiers endured.

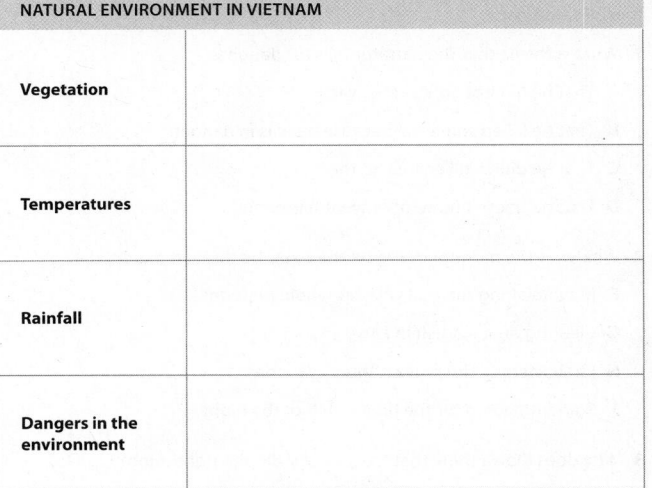

NATURAL ENVIRONMENT IN VIETNAM	
Vegetation	
Temperatures	
Rainfall	
Dangers in the environment	

Connect Based on the details the author gives in "Ambush," what are the dangers the narrator faced from the natural environment?

WHEN STUDENTS STRUGGLE . . .

Reteach: Setting Have students look for places in the story where the setting is mentioned indirectly. For instance "spread out in the dense brush along the trail" implies that there was dense brush that they made a trail through. Discuss the advantages of this way of laying out the setting instead of just saying "There was a lot of dense brush, and we spread out along it."

 For additional support, go to the **Reading Studio** and assign the following [LEVEL UP] **Level Up Tutorial: Setting.**

CREATE AND DISCUSS

Use a Frame Story Think of a moment in your life that you regret. Then, write a personal narrative about it using a frame story. Think about what purpose the frame story might serve in conveying meaning or adding impact.

❑ Make sure the frame story and main story relate to each other in a meaningful way.

❑ Be creative in how you shift between settings.

❑ Use transitions to signal shifts in time or setting.

Discuss Your Story With a partner, take turns sharing your personal narratives.

❑ Talk about how your frame adds meaning to the story or what other purpose it serves.

❑ Give each other feedback on how effective your narratives are and what changes you might make.

 Go to **Writing Narratives** in the **Writing Studio** for help.

 Go to **The Content of Your Presentation: Narrative** in the **Speaking and Listening Studio** for help.

RESPOND TO THE ESSENTIAL QUESTION

? How do we deal with rejection and isolation?

Gather Information Review your annotations and notes on "Ambush." Then, add relevant information to your Response Log. As you determine which information to include, think about:

• why soldiers might feel rejected or isolated
• how rejection affects our emotions
• why isolation is so difficult
• how rejection and isolation might be good for us

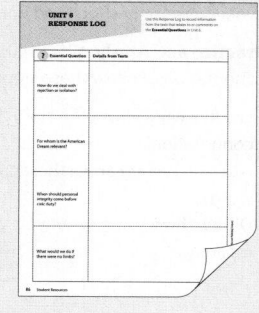

ACADEMIC VOCABULARY

As you write and discuss what you learned from "Ambush," be sure to use the Academic Vocabulary words. Check off each of the words that you use.

❑ **contemporary**
❑ **global**
❑ **infinite**
❑ **simulated**
❑ **virtual**

CREATE AND DISCUSS

Use a Story Frame Discuss with students how many possibilities there are. For example, a story frame can be used to show ramifications as well as the main character's own regrets. The main character would not even need to be in the frame story.

Discuss Your Story Encourage students to approach their partner's story like a piece of literature and analyze the frame story from that point of view.

 For **writing support** for students at varying proficiency levels, see the **Text X-Ray** on page 760D.

RESPOND TO THE ESSENTIAL QUESTION

Allow time for students to add details from "Ambush" to their Unit 6 Response Logs.

CRITICAL VOCABULARY

Answers:

1. *sliver*

2. *gape*

3. *platoon*

4. *peril*

5. *ponder*

6. *grope*

VOCABULARY STRATEGY:
Connotation and Denotation

Answers:

Answers will vary.

 RESPOND

WORD BANK
platoon
grope
sliver
ponder
peril
gape

Go to **Denotation and Connotation** in the **Vocabulary Studio** for help.

CRITICAL VOCABULARY

Practice and Apply Complete the sentences with one of the Critical Vocabulary words.

1. She was disappointed to find only a small _____ of cheese.

2. After the accident, all I could do was _____ at the smashed-up car.

3. After the war, my grandfather corresponded with a man who had been in his _____.

4. They seemed at ease, unaware of the _____ they were really in.

5. Before falling asleep, I lie in bed and _____ the events of the day.

6. When the power went out, I had to _____ for the flashlight.

VOCABULARY STRATEGY:
Connotation and Denotation

A word's dictionary meaning is called its **denotation**. The images or feelings you connect to a word add a finer shade of meaning, called **connotation**. The connotation of a word goes beyond the word's basic dictionary definition. Writers use connotations of words to communicate positive or negative feelings. Make sure you understand the denotation and connotation of a word when you read it or use it in your writing.

> **None of it mattered. The words seemed far too complicated. All I could do was <u>gape</u> at the fact of the young man's body.**

The word *gape* means the same thing as *stare*, but this particular usage evokes a sense of shock and horror.

Practice and Apply Work with a partner to explore words with different connotations. Follow these steps:

- List five words from the story that have a strongly positive or negative connotation.
- Use a dictionary and a thesaurus to find definitions and synonyms of the words.
- Discuss how using synonyms with different connotations would affect meaning.

EL ENGLISH LEARNER SUPPORT

Connotation and Denotation Tell students that they should watch for words that have slightly different connotations. Write the following words on the board: *gape, look at*. Discuss that the two words have slightly different connotations because *gape* has a more intense meaning. Encourage students to look back at the definition of *ponder* on page 765. Ask if they think *ponder* has a different connotation than *consider*. *(yes, because to ponder something means to consider [or think about] it with thoroughness and care)* **MODERATE**

LANGUAGE CONVENTIONS: Transitions

Authors use **transitions** to signal shifts to the reader. These transitions are like road signs that tell the reader where they are going, such as another time, location, or point of view. Transitions help a reader follow a story, especially when the narrative moves around in time rather than progressing in a strictly linear fashion, which occurs when authors use structural devices such as flashbacks and frame stories. Transitions can be in the form of time and place phrases, punctuation, formatting, section breaks, and chapter breaks.

In "Ambush," Tim O'Brien uses transitions to guide the reader through the story frame structure.

> **But here I want to pretend she's a grown-up. I want to tell her exactly what happened, or what I remember happening, and then I want to say to her that as a little girl she was absolutely right. <u>This is why I keep writing war stories:</u>**

> **He was a short, slender young man of about twenty. I was afraid of him—afraid of something—and as he passed me on the trail I threw a grenade that exploded at his feet and killed him.**

The colon (:) at the end of the first paragraph signals a shift to a war story from the past.

From paragraph 7 to paragraph 8, the author shifts from the past time of the flashback to present time.

> **None of it mattered. The words seemed far too complicated. All I could do was gape at the fact of the young man's body.**

> **<u>Even now</u> I haven't finished sorting it out. Sometimes I forgive myself, other times I don't.**

The phrase *even now* signals to the reader that the story is shifting back to present time from the flashback.

Practice and Apply Go back to the personal narrative you wrote using a frame story. Read it carefully to be sure that the reader knows when you shift between the frame story and the main story. If necessary, revise it by using transitions that signal shifts in time and place to the reader.

LANGUAGE CONVENTIONS: Transitions

Tell students that a good transition will tell readers not just that they are going somewhere but exactly where they should expect to be. For instance, in the first example, we are told to expect a war story. In the second example, we are told that we are returning to the present time. Explain that when they are writing their own transitions, they should think about what context they are transitioning from and what context they are transitioning to. Explain that their transitions can set the mood for the reader. For example, have them discuss what their expectations would be if the transition were "Then the door slowly squeaked open" compared to "Unfortunately, the door opened!"

Practice and Apply Have students review the transitions in their frame stories alone and then with their partners.

 ENGLISH LEARNER SUPPORT

Language Conventions Use the following supports with students at varying proficiency levels:

- Pair students and have the partners make a list of transitions. **SUBSTANTIAL**

- Have students find other places that use transitions and discuss them with a partner. **MODERATE**

- Have students take a couple of transitions—either the example transitions, transitions from their story, or a partner's transitions—and change the transitions to signal something completely different. **LIGHT**

THE UNIVERSE AS PRIMAL SCREAM

Poem by Tracy K. Smith

GENRE ELEMENTS
POETRY

Poetry is text presented in lines and stanzas. These lines and stanzas, as well as sound devices like alliteration and rhythm, help express the poem's mood and enhance the poem's meaning. Often, poems condense meaning in fewer words than literary works in other genres. Poets use allusions, personification, and sensory images to express meaning.

LEARNING OBJECTIVES

- Analyze poetic elements and literary devices.
- Research Tracy K. Smith's poetry.
- Write a literary analysis.
- Discuss literary elements in a poem.
- **Language** Recognize sound devices when a poem is read aloud.

TEXT COMPLEXITY

Quantitative Measures	The Universe as Primal Scream	Lexile: N/A
Qualitative Measures	**Ideas Presented** Multiple levels, subtle, implied meanings; abstract, difficult ideas; use of symbolism.	
	Structures Used Complex, perhaps parallel plot lines; deviates from chronological or sequential.	
	Language Used Implied meanings; alliterative, figurative language; complex sentence structures.	
	Knowledge Required Explores complex ideas; refers to ideas that may be beyond students' experiences.	

RESOURCES

Online Ed

- Unit 6 Response Log
- 🔊 Selection Audio
- 📖 Reading Studio: Notice & Note
- Level Up Tutorial: Elements of Poetry; Imagery
- 💬 Speaking and Listening Studio: Participating in Collaborative Discussions
- ✔ "The Universe as Primal Scream" Selection Test

SUMMARIES

English

In "The Universe as Primal Scream," Smith compares the universe to twin babies who scream loudly and strongly. She imagines they scream so fiercely that the building they are in lifts up and flies into space. Smith then explores concepts of the afterlife, eternity, the heavens, God, and the universe, and how they would respond to the humans' cries.

Spanish

En "El universo como grito primordial", Smith compara al universo con gemelos bebés, quienes gritan fuertemente. Se imagina que gritan tan ferozmente que el edificio en el que están se levanta y vuela al espacio. Smith explora los conceptos de la vida después de la muerte, la eternidad, el cielo, Dios y el universo y cómo responderían a los llantos humanos.

 SMALL-GROUP OPTIONS

Have students work in small groups and pairs to read and discuss the selection.

Double-Entry Journal

- Tell students to use a notebook or journal to record double-entry journal notes as they read.
- Have each student draw a line from top to bottom in the middle of a page to create two columns. Have students title the left column *Imagery* and the right column *My Notes*.
- Tell students to use the left column to jot down words and phrases of the poem that contain imagery.
- Have students write notes, interpretations, or questions in the right column.

Three Before Me

- After students have written their literary reviews, have them ask three other students to edit their writing.
- Students can ask peers to evaluate the clarity of their ideas or edit their writing for spelling, capitalization, and grammar.
- Have students evaluate their peers' writing based on their requests and make suggestions for revisions.
- Have students revise their literary reviews based on peer feedback.

Text X-Ray: English Learner Support
for "The Universe as Primal Scream"

Use the Text X-Ray and the supports and scaffolds in the Teacher's Edition to help guide students at different proficiency levels through the selection.

INTRODUCE THE SELECTION
DISCUSS THE POEM'S TITLE

Tell students the title of the poem is a simile comparing the universe to a primal scream. Explain that a primal scream is a release of raw, or intense, emotion. It can express intense feelings of pain, anger, sadness, or uncertainty.

Ask students to give examples of when a person might give a primal scream. Then, ask them for examples of why a baby might give a primal scream. Supply the following sentence frames:

- A primal scream might express feelings of ____.
- A person giving a primal scream might have deep feelings of ____.
- A baby might give a primal scream because ____.

CULTURAL REFERENCES

The following words or phrases may be unfamiliar to students:

- *on the nose* (line 1): at the exact time
- *let loose* (line 4): do freely
- *decibel* (line 13): a measure of the loudness or intensity of a sound
- *Old Testament* (line 19): the first portion of the Christian Bible
- *on shuffle* (line 28): playing songs in a random order
- *still at it* (line 31): still engaged in the same activity (of screaming)

LISTENING

Identify Sound Devices

Explain that poetry is intended to be read aloud. Review sound devices, such as line breaks, alliteration, and rhythm.

Find a video or audio recording of the poet reading the poem aloud. Use the following supports with students at varying proficiency levels:

- Play the recording through line 9 of the poem. Have students raise their hands when the poet pauses while reading. Then, review with students the places where the poet paused and have them circle the relevant parts of the text. Explain how line breaks and punctuation are associated with pauses or breaks in the poem. **SUBSTANTIAL**
- After students listen to the poem read aloud, have them discuss what they heard with a partner. Ask: *Was it easier or harder to understand the poem when it was read aloud? Why?* **MODERATE**
- Have students silently read the poem as they listen to the poet read the poem aloud. Tell them to mark places in the text where the poet pauses or emphasizes words. Then, have them review what they marked with a partner. Encourage students to discuss how the poet's reading contributes to the meaning of the poem. **LIGHT**

SPEAKING

Analyze a Poem

Explain that in the first stanza, the poet is describing noise in an apartment building. Ask: *What are possible meanings of the noise?*

Read aloud the first stanza. Use the following supports with students at varying proficiency levels:

- Tell students to think about why the babies are crying. Ask questions to elicit the concept that the babies want to be heard and have their needs met. **SUBSTANTIAL**
- Have students work in pairs and use the following sentence frames to discuss the question: *The babies are _____ because _____. The neighbor is _____ because _____.* **MODERATE**
- Have students work in small groups. Have them discuss the meaning of the noise from the perspective of the babies and from the perspective of the person listening to their cries. **LIGHT**

READING

Cite Text Evidence

Circulate throughout the room and offer support as needed and check for comprehension.

Use the following supports with students at varying proficiency levels:

- Read aloud lines 1–9, pausing after short sentences or phrases to have students echo read. Then, ask questions about the lines you read and have students identify the phrases or words that answer the questions. **SUBSTANTIAL**
- Have students work in small groups. Tell them to skim the poem and jot down words and phrases that describe the universe. Then, have them discuss what the poem says about the universe, citing text evidence. **MODERATE**
- Have students work in pairs, with each student generating a question about the poem and giving it to his or her partner. Have students write responses using text evidence and share their responses aloud. **LIGHT**

WRITING

Write Imagery

Tell students to use the poem as a model for writing their own imagery. Model by reading aloud the sentence started in line 10. Use that sentence's structure and meaning to create a new sentence: *Maybe the dance teacher is proud of the two wobbly legs she trained to perfection.*

Use the following supports with students at varying proficiency levels:

- Read aloud lines 20–23. Ask: *What image do you see? Is it like a father or a furnace? Are you ready to meet it?* Have students draw a picture of the image they see in their mind's eye. Help them write a brief caption for it. **SUBSTANTIAL**
- Read aloud lines 28–30. Explain how they provide images of ordinary life. Have students use the second and third sentences as models to describe an image of an ordinary scene in their homes. **MODERATE**
- Have students identify a line or lines of the poem that contain an image of personal power. Have them use those lines as a model to write sentences that contain imagery about their own personal power. **LIGHT**

Connect to the
ESSENTIAL QUESTION

We all face limits—time, strength, rules, the law of gravity. The ultimate limit identified in Smith's poem is death— the thing that "refuses to let us keep anything for long." However, another limit mentioned in the poem is at the opposite end of life: the limited mobility and comprehension of an infant. So all our lives are lived with limits, and we can only imagine what life would be like if infants could talk and no one ever died.

THE UNIVERSE AS PRIMAL SCREAM

Poem by **Tracy K. Smith**

? ESSENTIAL QUESTION:

What would we do if there were no limits?

772 · Unit 6

QUICK START

Each of us has a family, whether it is biological, adopted, or a group of friends we consider family. Make some notes about your family. How is family a part of the cycle of life? How do families change over time?

MY FAMILY	CHANGES OVER TIME

ANALYZE POETRY

The line is a core unit of a poem, and line length is an essential element of the poem's meaning and rhythm. A **line break,** or where a line of poetry ends, may occur at the end of a sentence. It may also occur in the middle of a sentence, creating a pause or emphasis. Smith even uses a line break to lead into a new stanza.

Poems also communicate ideas through sound devices like alliteration. **Alliteration** is the repetition of consonant sounds at the beginnings of words. Poets use alliteration to impart a musical quality to their poems, to create mood, to reinforce meaning, to emphasize particular words, and to unify lines or stanzas.

Poets use a variety of poetic elements to convey meaning. As you read the poem, use a chart like this to help you analyze these poetic elements and their effects.

ELEMENT OF POETRY	EFFECTS

GENRE ELEMENTS: POETRY
- consists of lines and stanzas
- may be rhymed or unrhymed depending on style
- includes literary devices such as allusions, personification, and images that appeal to the senses

TEACH

QUICK START

Have students read the Quick Start and then discuss some of the changes that take place related to the life cycle, such as adding a new member of the family, losing a grandparent, or growing up ourselves. Encourage students to list on the left of the chart the individuals who make up their families. Then, have students mention how those individuals have changed during the students' lifetimes. Tell students they should include themselves in the list of family members because they, too, are changing and are part of the cycle of life.

ANALYZE POETRY

Remind students that sound elements are a major part of what makes poetry different from prose. In Smith's writing, line breaks contribute to the rhythm as well as to the drama. Sensory language sometimes focuses on sound in this poem—from screaming children to chopping onions to breaking glass. Alliteration adds to the music, as does a bit of internal rhyme. Relate that alliteration does not have to be the same consonant letter, but rather the same consonant sounds, as with *come* and *kids* in line 31. Encourage students to read the poem aloud to get a sense of the poem's music.

ANALYZE AND EVALUATE LITERARY DEVICES

Review with students each of the literary devices listed on the student page, and tell them that Smith's work makes extensive use of each of these. The tone's poem is informal, so idioms flow into lines that are otherwise weighty with meaning. In addition to "on the nose," look for "let loose" and "still at it."

■ English Learner Support

Understand Idioms Other expressions Smith employs may not be familiar to some students. Explain what they mean: *roll out* ("flow out quickly"), *knock . . . to the floor* ("destroy"), *sweep . . . clean* ("clear away forcefully"). Allow students to discuss the expressions with someone who speaks their native language to connect the expressions with words from their own language that might parallel the ones in the poem. **SUBSTANTIAL**

✐ ANNOTATION MODEL

Remind students that annotating the text, identifying important points, and making notes in the margins as they read can help them connect better with what they are reading. Point out in this sample that margin notes describe the line break and the imagery. Explain that these are just suggestions, and students can use these as guidelines or create their own systems. They may want to color-code their annotations using highlighters. Their notes in the margin may include comments about ideas that stand out, images that are particularly effective, questions about passages that are unclear or allusions they want to learn more about.

◎ GET READY

ANALYZE AND EVALUATE LITERARY DEVICES

To understand the message of "The Universe as Primal Scream," it is important to analyze the language the author has used. The author's word choices help to build the poem's meaning by setting the tone and mood, by revealing key information about the speaker, and by triggering associations in the mind of the reader or listener. Use this chart to analyze the literary devices Smith uses in "The Universe as Primal Scream."

LANGUAGE CHOICES	ANALYZING MEANING
An **idiom** is an informal expression that means something other than the literal meaning of its individual words. Line 1: "5pm <u>on the nose</u>"	What does the use of idioms suggest about the speaker? What image does the idiom convey? How does this affect the tone and mood?
Imagery is the use of words that appeal to the senses. Line 2: a sound that is "high, shrill and metallic"	What **connotations,** or emotional associations, do these words convey? What sound, or what mental picture, does the description create in the reader's imagination?
An **allusion** is a brief reference to a historic, literary, popular, or mythical person, place, or event. Lines 14–15: "we'll ride to glory / Like Elijah."	Consider what this allusion reveals about the speaker's state of mind, frame of reference, thoughts, or mood. How does the allusion connect to the global subject of the poem?
Personification is a type of figurative language that gives human traits to objects, animals, or abstract ideas. Line 18: "Let the heaven we inherit approach."	What picture does this create in the reader's mind? What does this comparison to a person reveal about the speaker's attitude toward the infinite and unknowable?

ANNOTATION MODEL

NOTICE & NOTE

As you read the poem, notice allusions, imagery, and other literary devices you find. Note the meaning and effect of the poetic elements in the poem. In the model, you can see one reader's notes about the poem.

> 5pm on the nose. They open their mouths
> And it rolls out: <u>high, shrill and metallic.</u>

line break occurs mid-sentence

imagery appeals to sense of sound

BACKGROUND

Tracy K. Smith *(b. 1972) was born in Falmouth, Massachusetts. This poem is from her collection* Life on Mars, *for which she won the 2012 Pulitzer Prize. In her poems, Smith delves into ideas about the universe and the future. Her influences include science fiction, movies (such as* 2001: A Space Odyssey*), and even music (the collection's title is borrowed from a David Bowie song). She describes the book as an elegy for her late father, who was an engineer for the Hubble Telescope, and spent many years exploring the mysteries of the universe.*

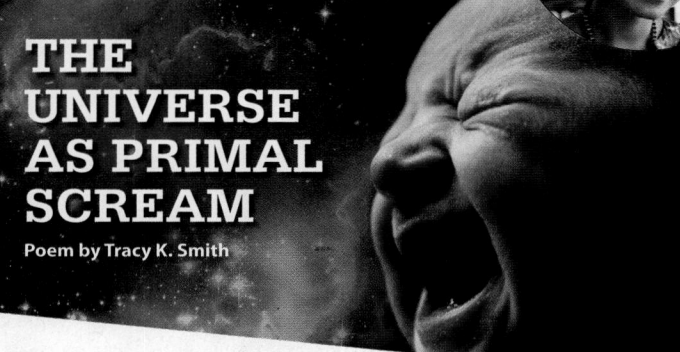

THE UNIVERSE AS PRIMAL SCREAM

Poem by Tracy K. Smith

SETTING A PURPOSE

As you read, notice how one idea leads to another as the speaker builds to speculations about life and death. Write down any questions that you generate as you read.

5pm on the <u>nose</u>. They open their mouths
And it rolls out: high, shrill and <u>metallic</u>.
First the boy, then his <u>sister</u>. Occasionally,
They both let loose at once, and I think
5 Of putting on my shoes to go up and see
Whether it is merely an experiment
Their parents have been conducting
Upon the good crystal, which must surely
Lie shattered to dust on the <u>floor</u>.

Notice & Note

Use the side margins to notice and note signposts in the text.

ANALYZE POETRY
Annotate: Mark where sentences end in the first stanza.

Analyze: What is surprising about where the sentences end in relation to the line breaks? Why might the poet have chosen to break the lines as she did?

BACKGROUND

Tracy K. Smith received her BA at Harvard University and earned a Master of Fine Arts in creative writing at Columbia University. Her first published poetry collection, *The Body's Question*, won the Cave Canem prize for the best first book by an African American poet. Each subsequent book has won critical acclaim and awards, with her 2011 book, *Life on Mars* (which includes the poem here) winning the Pulitzer Prize for Poetry. In 2017 Smith was named poet laureate for the United States. The collection *Wade in the Water*, published in 2018, is the first collection published since Smith became poet laureate. Smith teaches creative writing at Princeton University.

SETTING A PURPOSE

Direct students to use the Setting a Purpose prompt to focus their reading.

 ## ANALYZE POETRY

Remind students the use of line breaks is one of the ways a poet can add rhythm or drama to a poem. *(**Answer:** The breaks tend to fall in the middle of sentences. Only in one instance—if you don't count the end of the stanza—does a break come at the end of a sentence. The poet might have wanted to create a pause to emphasize the images she's creating or to establish a rhythm that leads the reader onward.)*

For **listening**, **speaking**, and **reading support** for students at varying proficiency levels, see the **Text X-Ray** on pages 772C–772D.

 ## ENGLISH LEARNER SUPPORT

Preteach Vocabulary There are several words in this poem that may be unfamiliar to English learners. On page 775, *universe*, *primal*, and *shrill* might need to be explained—though ask students if there are others they do not know. On page 776, define *inherit*, and on page 777, *hiccough*. Allow students time to learn unfamiliar words before the poem is read and discuss them again as the words are encountered in context. **ALL LEVELS**

ANALYZE AND EVALUATE LITERARY DEVICES

Remind students that personification is attributing human characteristics to nonhuman things, such as objects or abstract ideas. (**Answers:** *God, death, the universe, heaven, fate*)

For **writing support** for students at varying proficiency levels, see the **Text X-Ray** on page 772D.

10 Maybe the mother is still proud
    Of the four pink lungs she nursed
    To such might. Perhaps, if they hit
    The magic decibel, the whole building
    Will lift-off, and we'll ride to glory
15 Like Elijah.[1] If this is it—if this is what
    Their cries are cocked toward—let the sky
    Pass from blue, to red, to molten gold,
    To black. Let the heaven we inherit approach.

    Whether it is our dead in Old Testament robes,
20 Or a door opening onto the roiling infinity of space.
    Whether it will bend down to greet us like a father,
    Or swallow us like a furnace. I'm ready
    To meet what refuses to let us keep anything
    For long. What teases us with blessings,

ANALYZE AND EVALUATE LITERARY DEVICES

Annotate: Mark examples of personification in lines 21–26.

Analyze: What is being personified in these lines?

---

[1] **Elijah** (ĭ-lī´jə): biblical prophet who ascended to Heaven in a burning chariot.

WHEN STUDENTS STRUGGLE . . .

Develop Reading Fluency Use lines 19–34 to give students practice in reading poetry. Remind them that poetry must be read with attention to rhythm and punctuation. Before they read, walk them through the images and allusions so they read with understanding, as well as fluency. Have student pairs practice reading the lines aloud. Ask them if they better understand the devices used to create rhythm and meaning.

For additional support, go to the **Reading Studio** and assign the following **Level Up Tutorial: Elements of Poetry.**

25 Bends us with grief, Wizard thief, the great
Wind rushing to knock our mirrors to the floor,
To sweep our short lives clean. How mean²

Our racket seems beside it. My stereo on shuffle.
The neighbor chopping onions through a wall.
30 All of it just a hiccough against what may never
Come for us. And the kids upstairs still at it,
Screaming like the Dawn of Man,³ as if something
They have no name for has begun to insist
Upon being born.

_____

² **mean:** inferior or shabby.
³ **Screaming like the Dawn of Man:** an allusion to the opening segment of the 1968 film *2001: A Space Odyssey*, which features shouting, ape-like creatures.

ANALYZE POETRY

Annotate: Mark the instances of alliteration in lines 25 and 26.

Analyze: What are the effects of this alliteration?

ANALYZE AND EVALUATE LITERARY DEVICES

Annotate: Mark the allusion in the last stanza. Read the footnote at the end of the selection if you need help.

Evaluate: Why do you think the poet includes an allusion to this work? How does the allusion relate to the title of the poem?

CHECK YOUR UNDERSTANDING

Answer these questions before moving on to the **Analyze the Text** section on the following page.

1 In the first stanza, why did the crystal break?

  A The volume of the children's crying shattered it.

  B The children threw the crystal to the floor.

  C The crystal broke on its own.

  D The parents dropped the crystal.

2 What is described in the third stanza?

  F Stormy weather

  G Space flight

  H The afterlife

  J Time travel

3 What noises in the last stanza are made by the kids upstairs?

  A Hiccoughing

  B Screaming

  C Chopping onions

  D Sweeping

The Universe as Primal Scream 777

ANALYZE POETRY

Point out that, in addition to the alliteration in these lines, there is also an internal rhyme of *grief* and *thief* in line 25. There is another internal rhyme in line 27 as well: *clean* and *mean*. The alliteration and the rhymes contribute to the sound. (**Answer:** *It adds a musical quality to the lines. It helps underscore that most of the poem is talking about sound, so the poet would want to use sound as part of the poem.*)

Once students have identified the alliteration in lines 25 and 26, you may want to point out "seems/stereo/shuffle" in line 28, and discuss how that helps underscore the "mean racket."

ANALYZE AND EVALUATE LITERARY DEVICES

Remind students that an **allusion** is a reference to another work, with the hope that the meaning of the item alluded to will contribute to the reader's understanding of the writer's ideas. Explain that the word *primal*, which appears in the title, refers to things that are "original, primitive, of or relating to the earliest forms of something." (**Answer:** *Smith's poem uses images from science, the Bible, space, and science fiction to explore ideas about the universe and eternity. The allusion refers to apes in the movie screaming, while the title compares the universe to a primal, or primitive, scream.*)

CHECK YOUR UNDERSTANDING

Have students answer the questions independently.

Answers:

1. *A*

2. *H*

3. *B*

If they answer any questions incorrectly, have them reread the text to confirm their understanding. Then they may proceed to ANALYZE THE TEXT on page 778.

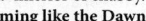 **ENGLISH LEARNER SUPPORT**

Oral Assessment Use the following questions to assess students' comprehension and speaking skills.

1. The speaker wants to see if the children's screaming caused crystal to _____. (*break*)

2. Does the speaker think about going up to the children's home? (*yes*)

3. In the last stanza, the children are _____. (*screaming*)
   SUBSTANTIAL

ANALYZE THE TEXT

Possible answers:

1. **DOK 2:** *Smith likely chose 5 p.m. because that is the traditional end of the workday and beginning of the evening, which will fade into night. This twilight time may connect to her theme of the beginning and end of life. (Students may also note that the end of day idea is also found in lines 16–18, where sunset is described, passing from blue, to red, to molten gold, to the black of night.)*

2. **DOK 4:** *Smith's diction suggests that she views life clinically or scientifically.*

3. **DOK 3:** *The biblical story of Elijah, like the poem, is about life ending, but ending with a heavenly goal. The "ride to glory" in line 14 is a common metaphor for going to heaven, and heaven is mentioned in line 18. The "molten gold" of the sunset parallels the flaming chariot of Elijah. So like the poem, the allusion is about death and what happens afterwards.*

4. **DOK 4:** *The list reveals that, while the speaker is certain that death will come, she does not know what follows death. She is hoping death will be kind, like a good father, but worries that it will be like a furnace.*

5. **DOK 2:** *She wants to link the concepts in the two stanzas, creating a contrast between the vast and important issues of death and a possible afterlife and the mundane activities of everyday life that consume so much of our attention.*

RESEARCH

Organizations that focus on poetry, such as the Poetry Foundation and the Academy of American Poets, have websites that are good sources of information. In addition, websites for booksellers will list her works and offer insight into their contents. Furthermore, because she was named poet laureate of the United States in 2017, the Library of Congress offers information.

Connect Because much of the poem is about life and death and includes the idea of how the mundane crowds out more important thoughts, you might want to ask students what distractors keep them from "big ideas," and what they think about when they do consider limits.

RESPOND

ANALYZE THE TEXT

Support your responses with evidence from the text. 🗒 NOTEBOOK

1. **Infer** Why did Smith choose "5pm" as the time for the events of this poem? What might be the connection between this time and her theme?

2. **Analyze** Consider Smith's **diction,** or word choice, in the first stanza. What do the words *metallic, experiment,* and *conducting* suggest about the speaker?

3. **Draw Conclusions** Reread lines 10–18 and the accompanying footnote describing the biblical prophet Elijah. How does the allusion to Elijah relate to the subject of the poem?

4. **Analyze** What is the speaker hoping for in the third stanza (lines 19–27)? What does the careful list of possible scenarios reveal about the speaker's doubts and anxieties?

5. **Infer** Why does the poet break the sentence in lines 27–28 across two stanzas? What function does this line break serve?

RESEARCH TIP
When reading a source, you might find new keywords you can use to continue your research. Note these words so you don't forget them.

RESEARCH

Smith won a Pulitzer Prize for her collection of poems, *Life on Mars*. Do some research online to learn more about her body of work and the common themes in her poems. *Answers will vary. One example is given.*

WORK	THEMES
Life on Mars	*Themes include grief, death, and people's place in the universe.*

Connect Think about the activities you engage in and the various roles you play in your daily life. How do these help you determine your place in your family, your community, the world, and maybe even the universe? Take some time to freewrite about these ideas.

WHEN STUDENTS STRUGGLE . . .

Reteach: Imagery Explain that poets use imagery to help make ideas clear and to appeal to the senses. Saying that the screams of babies could have shattered crystal creates an image of a sound that is piercing and extremely loud, or shattering. Guide students through the poem, hunting for other examples of imagery and asking what senses they appeal to. (Examples include the "four pink lungs" in line 11 or the changing colors of sunset in lines 16–18.)

 For additional support, go to the **Reading Studio** and assign the following ᴸᴱⱽᴱᴸ **Level Up Tutorial: Imagery.**

CREATE AND DISCUSS

Write a Literary Analysis Evaluate how the author's use of sound imagery helps to reveal the meaning of the poem.

❏ Make a list of the sounds that the author describes throughout the poem.

❏ Note the connotative meanings associated with the sound images.

❏ Write an analysis of the poem's sound imagery. Include evidence from the text and use the conventions of Standard English.

Discuss the Poem Review the notes you took as you read "The Universe as Primal Scream." Discuss the literary elements in the poem and your interpretation of its meaning with a small group.

❏ Make your interpretation of the poem clear and specific.

❏ Include your analysis of the literary elements in the poem. Refer to your essay for an explanation of the sound devices.

❏ Be open and respectful to any questions and observations on your interpretation.

❏ Ask relevant and insightful questions about the interpretations of other members of the group.

Go to **Participating in Collaborative Discussions** in the **Speaking and Listening Studio** for help.

RESPOND TO THE ESSENTIAL QUESTION

? What would we do if there were no limits?

Gather Information Review your annotations and notes on the poem. Then, add relevant information to your Response Log. As you determine which information to include, think about:

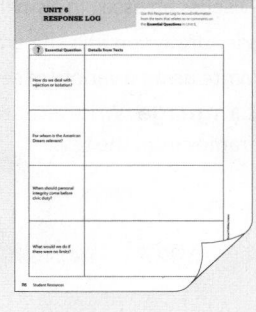

• constraints that limit human behavior and creativity
• the view expressed in the poem about the limitations on our lives
• whether limitations can have a positive effect

ACADEMIC VOCABULARY
As you write and discuss what you learned from the poem, be sure to use the Academic Vocabulary words. Check off each of the words that you use.

❏ **contemporary**
❏ **global**
❏ **infinite**
❏ **simulated**
❏ **virtual**

CREATE AND DISCUSS

Write a Literary Analysis Encourage students to turn back to pages 773 and 774 to review the instructions on analyzing poetry and literary devices, as well as the definitions of the various devices. Students should also review their margin notes and responses to the analysis questions. They can use these plus the suggestions listed on this page to evaluate how the author uses literary elements, especially sound imagery, to build meaning.

Discuss the Poem Remind students to think about what they want to say and state it as clearly as possible. They should then listen carefully to what others have to say and then react based on the merits of the comments and their understanding of the poem. Their reactions may be a question for further information or insight, affirmation, or disagreement—but they should only disagree if they are prepared to offer evidence of a different interpretation. Encourage them to review the instructions on this page to make sure they stay on topic.

RESPOND TO THE ESSENTIAL QUESTION

Allow time for students to add details from "The Universe as Primal Scream" to their Unit 6 Response Logs.

MENTOR TEXT

HOW IT FEELS TO BE COLORED ME

Essay by Zora Neale Hurston

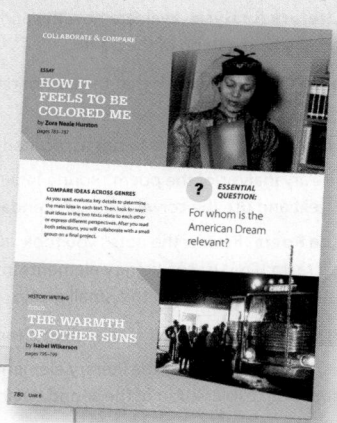

This essay serves as a **mentor text**, a model for students to follow when they come to the Unit 6 Writing Task: Writing a Personal Essay.

GENRE ELEMENTS
ESSAY

An **essay** focuses on a single subject. It can be an informative text, an argumentative text, or an autobiographical text. Hurston's essay is both an argumentative text and an autobiographical text. It focuses on her own life and expresses a claim about her experiences. This is the main idea, or the most important point she wants to make. Rather than stating the main idea directly, she reveals it through details and evidence. She expresses her attitude, or tone, through her use of diction, imagery, and figurative language.

LEARNING OBJECTIVES

- Analyze tone and development of ideas.
- Research race relations to find evidence to support or refute Hurston's claims about race.
- Write an argumentative essay.
- Discuss an essay in a small group.
- Identify synonyms and antonyms.
- Write using a variety of sentence lengths.
- **Language** Write an autobiographical paragraph using sentence frames from the text.

TEXT COMPLEXITY

Quantitative Measures	How It Feels to Be Colored Me	Lexile: 950L
Qualitative Measures	**Ideas Presented** Multiple levels, use of symbolism and irony; greater demand for inference.	
	Structures Used Primarily explicit; largely conventional.	
	Language Mostly explicit; some unconventional language.	
	Knowledge Required More complexity to theme; experiences may be less familiar to many; cultural or historical references may make heavier demands.	

RESOURCES

- Unit 6 Response Log
- 🔊 Selection Audio
- 📖 Reading Studio:
  Notice & Note
- Level Up Tutorial: Main Idea and
  Supporting Details; Reading for
  Details
- Writing Studio:
  Writing Arguments
- 💬 Speaking and Listening Studio:
  Participating in Collaborative
  Discussions
- Vocabulary Studio:
  Synonyms and Antonyms
- ❗ Grammar Studio:
  Sentence Structure
- ✅ "How It Feels to Be Colored Me"/*The
  Warmth of Other Suns*

SUMMARIES

English

Hurston describes herself as a little girl growing up in the African American community of Eatonville, Florida, where she boldly interacted with white tourists, much to her family's chagrin. At the age of 13, Hurston went to Jacksonville to attend school, where she discovered that she is a colored girl. Hurston discusses the impact of this lesson on her adult personality and her worldview, explaining that she finds race both important and irrelevant to her identity.

Spanish

Hurston se describe a sí misma como una niñita creciendo en la comunidad afroamericana de Eatonville, Florida, donde interactuaba audazmente con turistas blancos, para el disgusto de su familia. A los 13 años, Hurston fue a estudiar en una escuela de Jacksonville, donde descubrió que era una niña de color. Hurston discute el impacto que esta lección tuvo en su personalidad adulta y en su cosmovisión, explica que la raza le parece tanto importante como irrelevante para su identidad.

 ## SMALL-GROUP OPTIONS

Have students work in small groups and pairs to read and discuss the selection.

Reciprocal Teaching

- Have students read the essay. Then, provide the following question stems: How did the author _____? Why did _____? What might have happened if _____?
- Tell students to use the stems to write three to five questions.
- Have students form groups of three.
- Have each student ask their group at least two of their questions. Have groups discuss each answer until they reach a consensus.

Sticky Note Peer Review

- After students have finished writing their essays, ask them to review their peers' writing and provide constructive feedback.
- Have students work in small groups and take turns reading their papers aloud.
- As one student reads, have listeners write the following on sticky notes:
  1. positive comments, such as words they liked
  2. suggestions to improve the essay
  3. questions they have about the essay
- Listeners should then initial their sticky notes and give them to the writer.

Text X-Ray: English Learner Support
for "How It Feels to Be Colored Me"

Use the Text X-Ray and the supports and scaffolds in the Teacher's Edition to help guide students at different proficiency levels through the selection.

INTRODUCE THE SELECTION
DISCUSS THE AUTHOR

Raised in the all-black town of Eatonville, Florida, Zora Neale Hurston followed her mother's advice to "jump at de sun"—to follow her dreams—no matter how impossible they seemed. When she was 13 years old, her mother died and her father remarried. She was sent to school in Jacksonville, Florida, a city with both white and black students. Life was very different in Jacksonville, and Hurston learned what it meant to be African American.

Discuss the concept of *culture shock*, or the way people can be startled by the experience of moving to or visiting an unfamiliar place. Ask students to share personal experiences with culture shock. Supply the following sentence frames: *When I encountered ____, I felt ____. I was surprised to learn that ____.*

CULTURAL REFERENCES

The following words or phrases may be unfamiliar to students:

- *the town* (paragraph 2): the actual town, or the people of the town
- *cane chewing* (paragraph 2): chewing sugarcane
- *sobbing school* (paragraph 6): self-pity, or feeling sorry for oneself
- *helter-skelter* (paragraph 6): disorderly
- *at my elbow* (paragraph 7): nearby

LISTENING

Identify Character Traits

Explain that a character's actions, thoughts, words, and feelings all give the reader insight into the character traits, or characteristics, of a person.

Have students listen as you read aloud selected sentences or paragraphs. Use the following supports with students at varying proficiency levels:

- Read aloud this sentence from paragraph 11: "I dance wildly inside myself." Ask: *Is she happy or sad? (happy) Is she strong or weak? (strong)* Provide a sentence frame to help students answer: She is ___. Then, display the answers in a list of the author's character traits. Repeat with other sentences. **SUBSTANTIAL**
- Read paragraph 3 aloud to students in a small group. Ask questions such as *Is she friendly or unfriendly?* to help students identify the following traits: happy, friendly, curious, joyful. Display traits in a list. **MODERATE**
- Have students work in small groups. Ask a volunteer in each group to read aloud paragraph 3. For every sentence that illustrates a character trait, have students raise their hands and name the trait. Ask another volunteer to write it on the board in a list. **LIGHT**

SPEAKING

Discuss Key Ideas and Details

Remind students that identifying key ideas and details will help them better understand the text and theme. One main idea of this text is how Hurston felt about being colored.

Use the following supports with students at varying proficiency levels:

- Have students choral read the first sentence of paragraph 16 of the selection. Ask students: *Did Hurston feel angry about being colored? (no) Does she feel like it is her country? (yes)* **SUBSTANTIAL**
- Ask a volunteer to read aloud paragraph 16. Then pair students and have them reread the paragraph and discuss how Hurston felt about being colored. **MODERATE**
- Have student pairs take turns reading aloud paragraphs 15 and 16. Then have students use a Think-Pair-Share activity to discuss how Hurston felt about being colored. **LIGHT**

READING

Connect Idioms to Text

Introduce and explain the meaning of the following two idioms: *pity party* (an example or instance of self-pity) and *move on* (to continue living without letting a bad experience bother you). Tell students that they will connect the idioms to paragraphs 6 and 7 of the essay.

Use the following supports with students at varying proficiency levels:

- Read aloud paragraphs 6 and 7. Pause as you read to ask questions: *Is there sadness in her soul? (no) Does she belong to the crying "school of Negrohood"? (no) Does the world belong to the strong or the weak? (strong)* Display the phrases to help students understand the meaning of the two idioms: *no sorrow in her soul, doesn't belong to the sobbing school, the world belongs to the strong.* Then, ask: *Is she having a pity party? (no) Why not? (She is not crying.) Is she moving on? (yes)* **SUBSTANTIAL**
- Provide a list of idioms from paragraphs 6 and 7, including *sobbing school, low-down dirty deal*, and *weep at the world.* Have a student read aloud paragraphs 6 and 7 to a small group. Have students interrupt the reading when each idiom is illustrated and discuss it. Ask them to determine which of Hurston's idioms have similar meanings to *pity party* and *move on.* **MODERATE**
- Have students read paragraphs 6 and 7 silently and note words or phrases that have the same meaning as the idioms. Examples: *sobbing school* means "pity party"; *I am busy sharpening my oyster knife* means "I am moving on." Ask them to discuss their words and phrases in a small group. **LIGHT**

WRITING

Write an Autobiographical Paragraph

Read aloud paragraph 5. Have students use the paragraph to write their own autobiographical paragraphs describing a move or another change in their lives.

Use the following supports with students at varying proficiency levels:

- Help students complete the frames: *I lived in ___ until I was ___. Then I moved to ___. I remember ___.* Then, have them draw a picture describing how they felt in their new place. **SUBSTANTIAL**
- Have students complete frames: *I lived in ___ until I was ___. Then I moved to ___. My new home was ___. I felt ___ because ___. My new home is ___ than my old home because ___.* **MODERATE**
- Have students work in small groups to create sentence frames based on paragraph 5. Then, have them write their paragraphs using those frames. **LIGHT**

Connect to the
ESSENTIAL QUESTION

"How It Feels to Be Colored Me" offers a personal take on racial differences as they existed half a century after the Civil War ended slavery. Hurston's narration will provide students with additional context for examining the roles of race, gender, and geography as they move on to compare the two texts in this section.

COMPARE IDEAS ACROSS GENRES

Discuss with students that both of these selections examine how African Americans have been treated in the past in the south. They also look at African Americans' responses to this treatment. Encourage students to keep track of the differences and similarities in how the selections present this topic.

MENTOR TEXT

At the end of the unit, students will be asked to write a personal essay. "How It Feels to Be Colored Me" provides a model for how a writer can express ideas about a personal experience in society.

COLLABORATE & COMPARE

ESSAY

HOW IT FEELS TO BE COLORED ME

by **Zora Neale Hurston**
pages 783–787

COMPARE IDEAS ACROSS GENRES

As you read, evaluate key details to determine the main idea in each text. Then, look for ways that ideas in the two texts relate to each other or express different perspectives. After you read both selections, you will collaborate with a small group on a final project.

ESSENTIAL QUESTION:

For whom is the American Dream relevant?

HISTORY WRITING

from

THE WARMTH OF OTHER SUNS

by **Isabel Wilkerson**
pages 795–799

How It Feels to Be Colored Me

QUICK START

How do you approach a new or unfamiliar situation? With a partner, discuss ways of dealing with these situations.

ANALYZE DEVELOPMENT OF IDEAS

An **essay** is a short work of nonfiction about a single subject. Hurston's essay is about discovering her identity and self-pride. It is autobiographical because it focuses on aspects of Hurston's life. Generally, writers of autobiographical essays use the first-person point of view, combining objective description with the expression of subjective feelings.

In an essay, the **main idea** is the most important point a writer wants to make about a topic. The main idea can be **explicit,** or stated outright; more often, the main idea is indirectly stated, or **implicit.** The reader must infer the writer's main idea from key details in the selection. The essay's organizational structure may suggest the main idea. For example, is the writer presenting two opposing views on a topic or arguing a specific viewpoint? As you read, note important details and what they suggest about the writer's main idea.

ANALYZE TONE

Tone is the attitude a writer expresses toward a subject. The tone of a text may be described as intimate or distant, serious or humorous, ironic or earnest. In informational texts such as an essay, tone is often developed through **diction,** or word choice. The details a writer includes may also contribute to tone. Hurston employs diction, imagery, and figurative language to take the reader on this journey.

LITERARY ELEMENT	EXAMPLE FROM TEXT	TONE
Diction	There is no great sorrow dammed up in my soul, nor lurking behind my eyes.	By taking a firm stance against "great sorrow," Hurston strikes a resilient tone.
Imagery	The native whites rode dusty horses, the Northern tourists chugged down the sandy village road in automobiles.	The vivid description contributes to a thoughtful tone.
Figurative language	Among the thousand white persons, I am a dark rock surged upon, overswept by a creamy sea.	The metaphors convey a tone of both isolation and strength.

As you read "How It Feels to Be Colored Me," analyze and evaluate Hurston's tone. What is the overall tone, and how does it shape your perception of events?

GENRE ELEMENTS: AUTOBIOGRAPHICAL ESSAY

- usually focuses on a single subject
- reveals the main idea through explanations, personal examples, and anecdotes
- uses diction, imagery, and figurative language to reveal tone

---

TEACH

QUICK START

After students read the Quick Start, invite them to share their thoughts with the class. Guide students to think about how their own life experiences have provided them with strategies for approaching unfamiliar situations. What personal qualities or resources do students rely on when faced with something new and unexpected?

ANALYZE DEVELOPMENT OF IDEAS

Remind students that authors of autobiographical essays often combine objective descriptions with the expression of subjective feelings. Review the differences between implicit and explicit presentation of the main idea of a text and help students produce a graphic organizer that aids them in interpreting the relationship between specific details and the main idea of the text. Students should write the main idea of the paragraph in one column and record implicit and explicit details that lead them to conclude that this is the main idea. For example, a student interpreting the first paragraph might write as the main idea, "The narrator is not ashamed of her race," with the statement that she "offers no extenuating circumstances" as support for this.

ANALYZE TONE

Direct students to consider the relationship between the author's tone and the impression the text leaves on the reader, noting specific details such as the author's use of imagery and repetition. How do these aspects of the author's tone help the reader understand her purpose in writing? Define for students another feature of Hurston's writing that develops the tone of this piece, parallel structure. **Parallel structure** involves the use of similar grammatical constructions to express ideas that are related or equal in importance.

TEACH

CRITICAL VOCABULARY

Encourage students to use prior knowledge and to look for clues in each word to determine the correct answers.

Answers:

1. *a*

2. *b*

3. *a*

4. *b*

5. *b*

6. *a*

7. *b*

8. *a*

■ English Learner Support

Use Cognates Spanish cognates include: *tímido/timid; exclusive/exclusive; espectro/specter; narcótico/narcotic;* and *pigmento/pigment.* **ALL LEVELS**

LANGUAGE CONVENTIONS

Sentence Variety Review with students practices for combining sentences and how these affect the pacing of a text. Discuss using semicolons, converting a sentence into a subordinate clause, and using dashes to set off information. Tell students that in addition to these accepted, formal means of combining information, Hurston's text also employs sentence fragments. Direct students to pay attention to the effect Hurston's use of sentence fragments has on the pacing of the text and to consider reading passages aloud to better understand this effect.

ANNOTATION MODEL

Remind students of annotation strategies such as underlining important details and circling words that signal how the text is organized. Point out that they may follow these suggestions or use their own system for marking up the selection in their write-in text. They may want to color-code their annotations by using highlighters. Their notes in the margin may include questions about ideas that are unclear or topics they want to learn more about.

 **GET READY**

© Houghton Mifflin Harcourt Publishing Company

CRITICAL VOCABULARY

extenuating	timid	specter	narcotic
exclusive	pigmentation	circumlocution	miscellany

Choose the word that is most closely related to the Critical Vocabulary word.

1. **miscellany**   a. collection   **b.** displacement

2. **pigmentation**   a. obscure   **b.** coloration

3. **timid**   a. shy   **b.** brash

4. **extenuating**   a. inexcusable   **b.** justifiable

5. **specter**   a. temptation   **b.** phantom

6. **narcotic**   a. numbing   **b.** gratuitous

7. **circumlocution**   a. restatement   **b.** evasion

8. **exclusive**   a. select   **b.** comprehensive

LANGUAGE CONVENTIONS

Sentence Variety Adding sentence variety can bring an essay to life. Using too many sentences with the same structure and length can make a text feel monotonous. Varying sentence style and structure can also add emphasis, improve clarity, and enhance the text's flow. Long sentences can incorporate a lot of information, and short sentences can emphasize key points. The right variety and combination of sentences enhance the tone and mood of text.

As you read "How It Feels to Be Colored Me," notice how Hurston varies her sentences to keep the reader engaged.

ANNOTATION MODEL

NOTICE & NOTE

As you read the selection, notice the details that develop the writer's main ideas. This model shows one reader's notes about an excerpt from the essay.

<u>The front porch might seem a daring place for the rest of the town, but it was a gallery seat to me.</u> My favorite place was atop the gate-post. Proscenium box for a born first-nighter. Not only did I enjoy the show, but I didn't mind the actors knowing that I liked it. I actually <u>spoke to them in passing. I'd wave at them and when they returned my salute,</u> I would say something like this: "Howdy-do-well-I-thank-you-where-you-goin'?" <u>Usually automobile or the horse paused at this,</u> and after a queer exchange of compliments, I would probably "go a piece of the way" with them, as we say in farthest Florida.

Calling the front porch a "gallery seat" is an interesting choice of words. Why is it a "gallery seat"?

Details reveal what she enjoyed about being on the front porch.

BACKGROUND

Zora Neale Hurston *(1891–1960) grew up in the all-black town of Eatonville, Florida. In 1925 she moved to New York City to study anthropology. After World War I, a huge migration north brought African Americans to the New York City neighborhood called Harlem. Hurston joined other black artists, writers, and musicians who became part of a great cultural movement known as the Harlem Renaissance. She returned to the South to collect African American folklore, which she published in the collection* Mules and Men. *Sadly, her work fell out of favor in the 1940s, and Hurston died poor and nearly forgotten.*

HOW IT FEELS TO BE COLORED ME

Essay by Zora Neale Hurston

PREPARE TO COMPARE

As you read, make note of how Hurston conveys the way she felt about events at the time. This information will help you compare the essay with the excerpt from The Warmth of Other Suns *that follows it.*

1 I am colored but I offer nothing in the way of **extenuating** circumstances except the fact that I am the only Negro in the United States whose grandfather on the mother's side was *not* an Indian chief.

2 I remember the very day that I became colored. Up to my thirteenth year I lived in the little Negro town of Eatonville, Florida. It is **exclusively** a colored town. The only white people I knew passed through the town going to or coming from Orlando. The native whites rode dusty horses, the Northern tourists chugged down the sandy village road in automobiles. The town knew the Southerners and never stopped cane chewing when they passed. But the Northerners were something else again. They were peered at cautiously from behind curtains by the **timid**. The more venturesome would come out on the porch to watch them go past and got just as much pleasure out of the tourists as the tourists got out of the village.

Notice & Note

Use the side margins to notice and note signposts in the text.

---

extenuating
(ĭk-stĕn´yōō-ā´ting) *adj.* lessening the severity of a fault, partially excusing.

exclusive
(ĭk-sklōō´sĭv) *adj.* not allowing something else.

timid
(tĭm´ĭd) *adj.* lacking self-confidence; shy.

How It Feels to Be Colored Me   783

BACKGROUND

After students have read the background information, provide them with the following additional context for Hurston's work and its mixed reception by critics. Between 1865 and 1900, more than 100 independent towns were founded by African Americans trying to escape racial prejudice. Eatonville, Florida was the oldest of these self-governing black communities. Growing up in Eatonville, Hurston was sheltered from the experiences of exclusion and contempt that shaped the lives of many African Americans, which shaped her opinions on race. Hurston often came under fire by African American writers who felt she minimized the seriousness of racial prejudice.

PREPARE TO COMPARE

Direct students to use the Prepare to Compare prompt to focus their reading.

CRITICAL VOCABULARY

extenuating: Hurston is unapologetic about her racial identity and refuses to embellish her identity with circumstances that would make her race less prominent.

ASK STUDENTS what extenuating circumstances others might offer and which Hurston parodies in her refusal. *(Hurston implies that other African Americans claim Native American ancestry to minimize their racial identity.)*

exclusive: Eatonville was not home to any white residents; it was exclusively populated by African Americans.

ASK STUDENTS how this exclusivity conditions the way Eatonville citizens respond to whites passing through their town. *(They are curious about northern whites but also cautious.)*

timid: Timid Eatonville residents did not dare to come out on the porch; they would satisfy their curiosity about visitors by peeking from behind the curtains.

ASK STUDENTS how residents who were not timid responded to visitors. *(They would watch from the porch, and Zora would greet strangers on the road.)*

LANGUAGE CONVENTIONS

Ask a student volunteer to read the passage aloud so that students can better appreciate the effect of these shorter sentences on the pacing of the text. How does this use of pacing reinforce your perception of the author's purpose? Her audience? (**Answer:** *Each of them is between longer compound sentences. They break up the series of longer sentences, which contributes to a conversational style. The paragraph flows smoothly because of the sentence variety.*)

ANALYZE DEVELOPMENT OF IDEAS

Remind students of the critical reception of Hurston's work by other African American writers. How does her personal treatment of race fit with other stories they know from the same period? (**Possible answer:** *Details such as "I am too busy sharpening my oyster knife" suggest that, even though Hurston realizes she is a colored girl, she does not believe in holding herself back from achieving her goals, or in defining herself as "tragically colored."*)

■ English Learner Support

Identify Important Details Ask students to orally paraphrase the first sentence of paragraph 6, using this frame: *The author does not _____ that it is _____ to be black.* Then, have partners focus on "There is no great sorrow . . . hurt about it." Have pairs describe the author's reaction against the feeling of "tragically colored." (*"the world is to the strong despite a little pigmentation more or less"*)

MODERATE

For **reading** and **writing support** for students at varying proficiency levels, see the **Text X-Ray** on page 780D.

CRITICAL VOCABULARY

pigmentation: Hurston compares her race to the pigmentation of a fabric that will not rub or wash out.

ASK STUDENTS what other words and images Hurston uses to describe her pigmentation. (*a fabric that will "neither rub nor run," "colored," "a fast brown"*)

LANGUAGE CONVENTIONS
Annotate: Mark the short simple sentences in paragraph 3.

Evaluate: How do these sentences add variety to the paragraph? How do they contribute to the style of the text?

ANALYZE DEVELOPMENT OF IDEAS
Annotate: Mark the sentence that expresses the main idea of paragraph 6.

Infer: How do the details support the main idea?

pigmentation
(pĭg-mən-tā´shən) *n.* coloration of tissues by pigment.

3   The front porch might seem a daring place for the rest of the town, but it was a gallery seat to me. My favorite place was atop the gate-post. Proscenium box for a born first-nighter.[1] Not only did I enjoy the show, but I didn't mind the actors knowing that I liked it. I actually spoke to them in passing. I'd wave at them and when they returned my salute, I would say something like this: "Howdy-do-well-I-thank-you-where-you-goin'?" Usually automobile or the horse paused at this, and after a queer exchange of compliments, I would probably "go a piece of the way" with them, as we say in farthest Florida. If one of my family happened to come to the front in time to see me, of course negotiations would be rudely broken off. But even so, it is clear that I was the first "welcome-to-our-state" Floridian, and I hope the Miami Chamber of Commerce will please take notice.

4   During this period, white people differed from colored to me only in that they rode through town and never lived there. They liked to hear me "speak pieces" and sing and wanted to see me dance the parse-me-la,[2] and gave me generously of their small silver for doing these things, which seemed strange to me for I wanted to do them so much that I needed bribing to stop. Only they didn't know it. The colored people gave no dimes. They deplored any joyful tendencies in me, but I was their Zora nevertheless. I belonged to them, to the nearby hotels, to the county—everybody's Zora.

5   But changes came in the family when I was thirteen, and I was sent to school in Jacksonville. I left Eatonville, the town of the oleanders,[3] as Zora. When I disembarked from the riverboat at Jacksonville, she was no more. It seemed that I had suffered a sea change.[4] I was not Zora of Orange County any more, I was now a little colored girl. I found it out in certain ways. In my heart as well as in the mirror, I became a fast brown—warranted not to rub nor run.

6   But I am not tragically colored. There is no great sorrow dammed up in my soul, nor lurking behind my eyes. I do not mind at all. I do not belong to the sobbing school of Negrohood who hold that nature somehow has given them a low-down dirty deal and whose feelings are all hurt about it. Even in the helter-skelter skirmish that is my life, I have seen that the world is to the strong regardless of a little **pigmentation** more or less. No, I do not weep at the world—I am too busy sharpening my oyster knife.[5]

7   Someone is always at my elbow reminding me that I am the granddaughter of slaves. It fails to register depression with me. Slavery is sixty years in the past. The operation was successful and the patient is doing well, thank you. The terrible struggle that made

---

[1] **Proscenium . . . first-nighter:** A proscenium box is a box near the stage. A first-nighter is a person who attends the opening night of a performance.
[2] **parse-me-la:** a dance movement popular with Southern African Americans of the period.
[3] **oleanders:** evergreen shrubs with fragrant flowers.
[4] **sea change:** a complete transformation.
[5] **oyster knife:** a reference to the saying "The world is my oyster," implying that the world contains treasure waiting to be taken, like the pearl in an oyster.

TO CHALLENGE STUDENTS . . .

Create Tone Ask students to describe the tone of paragraph 3 and identify words or phrases that help create the tone. Students might notice the combination of rich, complex vocabulary together with some short sentences and casual oral language. They might also point out Hurston's use of quotations to highlight regional language and ideas. Then, have students work in pairs to unpack the tone in another paragraph of their choosing. After discussion, challenge students to write a short autobiographical text imitating Hurston's tone.

me an American out of a potential slave said "On the line!" The Reconstruction said "Get set!"; and the generation before said "Go!" I am off to a flying start and I must not halt in the stretch to look behind and weep. Slavery is the price I paid for civilization, and the choice was not with me. It is a bully adventure and worth all that I have paid through my ancestors for it. No one on earth ever had a greater chance for glory. The world to be won and nothing to be lost. It is thrilling to think—to know that for any act of mine, I shall get twice as much praise or twice as much blame. It is quite exciting to hold the center of the national stage, with the spectators not knowing whether to laugh or to weep.

8   The position of my white neighbor is much more difficult. No brown **specter** pulls up a chair beside me when I sit down to eat. No dark ghost thrusts its leg against mine in bed. The game of keeping what one has is never so exciting as the game of getting.

9   I do not always feel colored. <u>Even now</u> I often <u>achieve the unconscious Zora of Eatonville</u> before the Hegira.[6] I feel most colored when I am <u>thrown against a sharp white background</u>.

10   <u>For instance at Barnard</u>. "Beside the waters of the Hudson"[7] I feel my race. Among the thousand white persons, <u>I am a dark rock surged upon, overswept by a creamy sea. I am surged upon and overswept,</u> but through it all, I remain myself. When covered by the waters, I am; and the ebb but reveals me again.

11   Sometimes it is the other way around. A white person is set down in our midst, but the contrast is just as sharp for me. For instance, when I sit in the drafty basement that is The New World Cabaret with a white person, my color comes. We enter chatting about any little nothing that we have in common and are seated by the jazz waiters. In the abrupt way that jazz orchestras have, this one plunges into a number. It loses no time in **circumlocutions**, but gets right down to business. It constricts the thorax and splits the heart with its tempo and **narcotic** harmonies. This orchestra grows rambunctious, rears on its hind legs and attacks the tonal veil with primitive fury, rending it, clawing it until it breaks through to the jungle beyond. I follow those heathen—follow them exultingly. I dance wildly inside myself; I yell within, I whoop; I shake my assegai[8] above my head, I hurl it true to the mark *yeeeeooww*! I am in the jungle and living in the jungle way. My face is painted red and yellow, and my body is painted blue. My pulse is throbbing like a war drum. I want to slaughter something—give pain, give death to what, I do not know. But the piece ends. The men of the orchestra wipe their lips and rest their fingers. I creep back slowly to the veneer we call civilization with

---

[6] **Hegira:** journey (from the name given to Muhammad's journey from Mecca to Medina in 622).
[7] **Barnard . . . Hudson:** Barnard is the college in New York City from which Hurston graduated in 1928. "Beside the water . . . " is a reference to the first line of the college song. The college is located near the Hudson River.
[8] **assegai:** a type of light spear used in southern Africa.

© Houghton Mifflin Harcourt Publishing Company

NOTICE & NOTE

specter
(spĕkˊtər) *n.* a ghostly apparition; a phantom.

ANALYZE TONE
Annotate: Mark details in paragraphs 9–10 that contribute to the author's overall tone.
Summarize: How would you describe Hurston's tone in these paragraphs?

circumlocution
(sûr-kəm-lō-kyoōˊshən) *n.* the use of unnecessarily wordy language, especially in being vague or evasive.

narcotic
(när-kŏtˊĭk) *adj.* inducing sleep or stupor; causing narcosis.

ANALYZE TONE

Guide students to focus on how Hurston's use of images conveys the ideas of strength and persistence. How does the author's tone help the reader navigate the frequent changes of imagery she uses to describe herself? (**Answer:** *Her tone is one of pride—she knows who she is, so, in spite of the obstacles she encounters, she remains true to herself.*)

■ English Learner Support

Listen for Key Words Read paragraph 10 aloud, asking students to listen for the dominant image in the passage. (*water*) Ask students which details help them identify the image. Then, challenge them to guess at the meaning of unknown words such as *ebb* and *reveal*.   **LIGHT**

For **listening support** for students at varying proficiency levels, see the **Text X-Ray** on page 780C.

CRITICAL VOCABULARY

specter: Hurston imagines whites to be haunted by their slave-owning past.

ASK STUDENTS why and how Hurston says these specters appear to whites of her generation. (*In another time, these whites would have had slaves at their kitchen tables and making their beds.*)

circumlocution: If jazz music were a conversation, no time would be wasted—it would go straight to the point.

ASK STUDENTS what other words Hurston uses to describe the lack of circumlocution in jazz music. (*abrupt, down to business*)

narcotic: Like a drug, jazz music affects the listener in her body.

ASK STUDENTS how the image of jazz as narcotic is resumed at the end of the passage. (*Hurston describes herself as awakening from a vision, "creeping back to civilization" at the end of the song.*)

WHEN STUDENTS STRUGGLE . . .

Understand Ideas Students may struggle with the frequent changes of imagery, particularly as images change within the same paragraph. To help students keep track of the main idea, remind them to annotate their text so that the main theme of each paragraph is highlighted. Then, ask them how a given detail relates to this theme. For example, paragraph 11 contains many details and changes of imagery, but the topic sentence cues students to focus on the contrast between Hurston's response and that of her white companion.

 For additional support, go to the **Reading Studio** and assign the following **Level Up Tutorial: Main Idea and Supporting Details.**

ENGLISH LEARNER SUPPORT

Understand Italics Explain to students that less formal texts may use italics to indicate that a reader should emphasize a particular word. Read the end of paragraph 13 and the beginning of 14 aloud twice, with and without the intended emphasis of the italics, and ask students to describe the difference.
MODERATE

ANALYZE DEVELOPMENT OF IDEAS

Remind students of the genre characteristics of the autobiographical essay and ask them what key words or other cues help them separate objective from subjective descriptions. How do subjective details support the implicit main idea in this contrast? (**Answer:** *Hurston conveys a strong emotional connection to the music, while the white man's compliment does not suggest the same type of connection.*)

 For **speaking support** for students at varying proficiency levels, see the **Text X-Ray** on page 780D.

 NOTICE & NOTE

ANALYZE DEVELOPMENT OF IDEAS

Annotate: Mark the details in paragraphs 12–13 that suggest a contrast.

Analyze: What difference between Hurston and the white man do these details suggest?

the last tone and find the white friend sitting motionless in his seat, smoking calmly.

12   "Good music they have here," he remarks, drumming the table with his fingertips.

13   Music! The great blobs of purple and red emotion have not touched him. He has only heard what I felt. He is far away and I see him but dimly across the ocean and the continent that have fallen between us. He is so pale with his whiteness then and I am *so* colored.

14   At certain times I have no race, I am *me*. When I set my hat at a certain angle and saunter down Seventh Avenue, Harlem City, feeling as snooty as the lions in front of the Forty-Second Street Library, for instance. So far as my feelings are concerned, Peggy Hopkins Joyce on the Boule Mich[9] with her gorgeous raiment, stately carriage, knees knocking together in a most aristocratic manner, has nothing on me. The cosmic Zora emerges. I belong to no race nor time, I am the eternal feminine with its string of beads.

15   I have no separate feeling about being an American citizen and colored. I am merely a fragment of the Great Soul that surges within the boundaries. My country, right or wrong.

16   Sometimes, I feel discriminated against, but it does not make me angry. It merely astonishes me. How *can* any deny themselves the pleasure of my company! It's beyond me.

---

[9] **Peggy . . . Boule Mich:** a wealthy woman of Hurston's day, walking along the Boulevard Saint-Michel in Paris.

APPLYING ACADEMIC VOCABULARY

❑ **global**   ☑ **simulated**   ❑ **contemporary**   ☑ **infinite**   ☑ **virtual**

Write and Discuss Have student pairs discuss the following questions and include the words *simulated, virtual,* and *infinite* in their responses. **1.** What makes Hurston's enjoyment of jazz more real than the **simulated** enjoyment of her white companion? **2.** How does Hurston manage the transition from the entirely African American town of Eatonville to the **virtually** all white college she attends? **3.** Why does Hurston use images of the **infinite** to describe herself, such as the ocean, the cosmos, or a rock that cannot be swept away?

17   But in the main, I feel like a brown bag of **miscellany** propped against a wall. Against a wall in company with other bags, white, red, and yellow. Pour out the contents, and there is discovered a jumble of small things priceless and worthless. A first-water[10] diamond, an empty spool, bits of broken glass, lengths of string, a key to a door long since crumbled away, a rusty knife-blade, old shoes saved for a road that never was and never will be, a nail bent under the weight of things too heavy for any nail, a dried flower or two, still a little fragrant. In your hand is the brown bag. On the ground before you is the jumble it held—so much like the jumble in the bags, could they be emptied, that all might be dumped in a single heap and the bags refilled without altering the content of any greatly. A bit of colored glass more or less would not matter. Perhaps that is how the Great Stuffer of Bags filled them in the first place—who knows?

---

[10]**first-water:** of the highest quality or purity.

NOTICE & NOTE

miscellany
(mĭs´ə-lā-nē) *n.* a collection of various items, parts, or ingredients, especially one composed of diverse literary works.

ANALYZE TONE

Annotate: Mark the simile in paragraph 17 that explains how Hurston feels.

Evaluate: Hurston extends the comparison to conclude the essay. How does she develop her conclusion and what tone does it express?

CHECK YOUR UNDERSTANDING

Answer these questions before moving on to the **Analyze the Text** section on the following page.

1 When does Hurston first realize she is a colored girl?

   A When she attends Barnard

   B When she moves to Jacksonville

   C When she performs for the Northerners

   D When she goes to the jazz club in New York

2 What metaphor does Hurston use to convey she does not accept the self-pitying role of a victim?

   F *My favorite place was atop the gate-post.*

   G *It is a bully adventure and worth all that I have paid . . .*

   H *No, I do not weep at the world—I am too busy sharpening my oyster knife.*

   J *They liked to hear me "speak pieces" and sing and wanted to see me dance . . .*

3 What does Hurston think of herself in comparison to Joyce?

   A She feels bad for herself.

   B She feels an air of superiority.

   C She aspires to be more like Joyce.

   D She thinks that she and Joyce are similar.

 ANALYZE TONE

Direct students to compare this final image with some of the previous images Hurston has used to describe race in this essay. Why does she end the essay with this image? What conclusion does it provide the reader? (***Answer:*** *Hurston feels like a "brown bag of miscellany" and then mentions that there are other bags of different colors and describes numerous small items contained in them, some valuable, some worthless. She thinks if they were emptied into a heap and refilled, their contents would not differ much. Hurston uses the comparison to express the conclusion that all people have much in common. In describing the "jumble" that people are made of, her tone seems a bit subdued, almost melancholy.*)

CHECK YOUR UNDERSTANDING

Have students answer the questions independently.

Answers:

1. *B*

2. *H*

3. *B*

If they answer any questions incorrectly, have them reread the text to confirm their understanding. Then, they may proceed to ANALYZE THE TEXT on page 788.

ENGLISH LEARNER SUPPORT

Oral Assessment Use the following questions to assess students' comprehension and speaking skills.

1. When Hurston moves to Jacksonville, she learns she is a _____. (*colored girl*)

2. Does Hurston pity herself for being treated as a colored girl? (*No, I do not weep at the world—I am too busy sharpening my oyster knife.*)

3. Does Hurston think Joyce is as good as she, Hurston, is? (*No, she feels superior.*)

SUBSTANTIAL/MODERATE

CRITICAL VOCABULARY

miscellany: Hurston compares people to bags filled with diverse objects ranging from junk to treasure.

ASK STUDENTS how we know these bags of miscellany are metaphors for human beings. (*Hurston begins by describing herself as one bag among many bags of different colors, and the items inside relate to a person's journey through life.*)

ANALYZE THE TEXT

Possible answers:

1. **DOK 4:** *In paragraph 4, Hurston builds on her main idea, which is that she didn't know she was black until she left Eatonville. She explains that the only difference she saw between whites and blacks was that blacks stayed in Eatonville, and whites only passed through the town. She says, "They liked to hear me 'speak pieces' and sing and wanted to see me dance the parse-me-la, and gave me generously of their small silver for doing these things, which seemed strange to me for I wanted to do them so much that I needed bribing to stop." This suggests that the whites who passed through didn't treat her negatively.*

2. **DOK 2:** *Hurston repeats "slave" and "slavery" in paragraph 7. This repetition contributes to her determined and confident tone.*

3. **DOK 2:** *The author doesn't feel badly for herself. She takes a sympathetic tone towards her white counterparts and says, "No brown specter pulls up a chair beside me when I sit down to eat. No dark ghost thrusts its leg against mine in bed."*

4. **DOK 2:** *In paragraph 16, she says, "How can any deny themselves the pleasure of my company! It's beyond me." The author expresses pride in herself.*

5. **DOK 3:** *The author expresses that she feels proud and confident being an African American. She understands that she is different from white people, but it does not bother her. As she states, "I am not tragically colored. There is no great sorrow dammed up in my soul." The main idea is conveyed implicitly through details, thoughts, and descriptions of her life.*

RESEARCH

Remind students to confirm controversial information with multiple sources whenever possible and to use the proper citation format when crediting sources.

Extend As students share their findings and ideas with a partner, instruct them to practice active listening by taking notes and invite them to summarize their partner's research for the class.

RESPOND

ANALYZE THE TEXT

Support your responses with evidence from the text. NOTEBOOK

1. **Evaluate** What is the most important idea Hurston expresses in paragraph 4? What details in the paragraph support this idea?

2. **Infer** What important word does Hurston repeat in paragraph 7? What key idea does this repetition convey?

3. **Interpret** In paragraph 8, the author says, "The position of my white neighbor is much more difficult." What tone, or attitude, is expressed through this description of her circumstances?

4. **Interpret** What do the details in paragraph 16 suggest about the author's view of herself? Cite text evidence in your response.

5. **Draw Conclusions** What is the main idea of the selection? Is it explicitly or implicitly stated? Cite details that support this idea in your response.

RESEARCH TIP
Be sure to use credible and accurate sources when conducting research. Websites with URLs that end in .edu or .gov are often good sources of information on academic subjects.

RESEARCH

"How It Feels to Be Colored Me" was published in 1928. Around this time, other texts were published about race relations in the United States and its impact on African Americans. With a partner, identify two texts on this topic, and compare their main points with Hurston's ideas about race in her essay. Be sure to cite evidence from the texts to support your comparison. Share your findings with the class.

AUTHOR AND TITLE	MAIN IDEA	COMPARISON WITH HURSTON'S IDEAS

Extend Research another informational or fictional text by Zora Neale Hurston. How does she address the topic of race in this text? Compare and contrast this text with "How It Feels to Be Colored Me" and share your findings with a partner.

© Houghton Mifflin Harcourt Publishing Company

WHEN STUDENTS STRUGGLE . . .

Reteach: Analyze Ideas and Details Note that the text is autobiographical in nature. Remind students of the difference between the concepts of *subjective* and *objective*, *implicit* and *explicit*. Ask them to consider how these concepts can help them to identify the main idea in each paragraph as well as in the essay as a whole. Direct them to choose one image from the text and note the details connected to it. Then, have students describe its relationship to the main idea and whether that image is of a subjective feeling or an objective event.

 For additional support, go to the **Reading Studio** and assign the following Level Up Tutorial: Reading for Details.

CREATE AND DISCUSS

Write an Argumentative Essay Using relevant text evidence, write an essay in which you defend or challenge Hurston's claims about race.

❏ Develop a clear thesis that is supported by specific examples and engaging details.

❏ You may also draw evidence from meaningful personal experiences or any reading you have done on the topic.

❏ What background knowledge or details from personal experiences will you use to support your main ideas? What evidence from the selection clearly and effectively supports your thesis? Which of Hurston's claims might you challenge?

❏ Vary your sentences to ensure clarity and flow.

Discuss Other Perspectives In a small group, discuss your essays and how they relate to Hurston's essay. Take turns explaining the viewpoints in your essays and whether or not they align with the ideas and tone in "How It Feels to Be Colored Me."

❏ Take turns sharing your thoughts.

❏ Support your opinions with evidence and examples from the text.

❏ Be respectful when addressing ideas you may not agree with.

RESPOND TO THE ESSENTIAL QUESTION

 For whom is the American Dream relevant?

Gather Information Review your annotations and notes on "How It Feels to Be Colored Me." Then, add relevant details to your Response Log. As you determine which information to include, think about:

• the important experiences that impact Hurston's sense of identity

• how Hurston's perspective on race changes over the course of the text

• the tone, or attitude, that Hurston conveys in the text

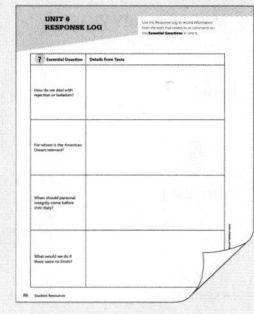

 RESPOND

Go to **Writing Arguments** in the **Writing Studio** for help.

 Go to **Participating in Collaborative Discussions** in the **Speaking and Listening Studio** for help.

ACADEMIC VOCABULARY

As you write and discuss what you learned from the essay, be sure to use the Academic Vocabulary words. Check off each of the words that you use.

❏ **contemporary**
❏ **global**
❏ **infinite**
❏ **simulated**
❏ **virtual**

CREATE AND DISCUSS

Write an Argumentative Essay Help students prioritize the information they obtain by first brainstorming ideas about where to look for evidence that supports or contrasts with Hurston's view of race. Remind students that critical arguments should make concessions to the opposing viewpoint, identifying ideas they hold in common before focusing on differences.

Discuss Other Perspectives Remind students to practice active listening with their partners, particularly when they are in disagreement. Review strategies for respectfully disagreeing with a partner and how to show respect when listening to another's description of his or her life experiences. Encourage students to discuss and debate, noting that it is important that participants in a discussion challenge and question one another. Model for students how they might bring up ideas or counterarguments. Note that even if they agree on a point, they can help others refine their ideas by asking questions or bringing up other points.

RESPOND TO THE ESSENTIAL QUESTION

Allow time for students to add details from "How It Feels to Be Colored Me" to their Unit 6 Response Logs.

CRITICAL VOCABULARY

Answers:

1. *exclusive, pigmentation*

2. *specter, narcotic*

3. *circumlocution, extenuating*

4. *miscellany, timid*

VOCABULARY STRATEGY:
Synonyms and Antonyms

Have the class brainstorm a list of prefixes and their meanings. To help students find *attenuate*, be sure to cover the prefix *ad-*, meaning "toward" and note that it can indicate direction or addition. Note that *ad-* sometimes becomes *at-* in English.

Answers:

• *impel: synonym—compel; antonym—expel*

• *extenuate: synonym—attenuate*

• *essential: antonym—nonessential*

• *extrinsic: antonym—intrinsic*

WORD BANK
extenuating
exclusive
timid
pigmentation
specter
circumlocution
narcotic
miscellany

 Go to **Synonyms and Antonyms** in the **Vocabulary Studio** for help.

CRITICAL VOCABULARY

Practice and Apply Fill in the blanks with the Critical Vocabulary words. Each sentence uses two words.

1. The dancer uses an _____ line of makeup for professional artists to cover the area with different skin _____.

2. When Isabel recounted her dream of a _____ haunting the house, her sister said it was caused by the _____ effects of eating too much pizza.

3. Rather than use _____ to explain his absence, James used the _____ circumstances surrounding his illness as an excuse.

4. When Emy's grandpa hoarded a _____ of junk, she was too _____ to ask him to discard it, even though she hated the clutter.

VOCABULARY STRATEGY:
Synonyms and Antonyms

To understand the meaning of a word, you sometimes need to understand its **antonym,** or opposite, or its **synonym,** a word with a similar meaning. It is possible to create synonyms or antonyms by adding or changing prefixes. In the selection, the word *exclusive*, which means "with limited access," can be changed to its antonym *inclusive*, which means "to include all," by replacing the prefix *ex-* with *in-*. If you add the prefix *non-* to *narcotic*, the result is its antonym, *non-narcotic*. Consulting a dictionary will help you verify the meaning of words you change.

Practice and Apply For each of the following vocabulary words, identify a synonym or antonym by adding or changing a prefix.

VOCABULARY WORD	SYNONYM OR ANTONYM
impel	*compel; expel*
extenuate	*attenuate*
essential	*non-essential*
extrinsic	*intrinsic*

EL ENGLISH LEARNER SUPPORT

Understand Prefixes Give students additional practice in identifying key prefixes that can help them guess the meaning of a word. Explain prefixes *in-*, *ex-*, and *non-* and have students write them down. Then, have them add *anti-*, *mis-*, and *un-*. Explain that these can reverse the meaning of a word. Direct students to use a dictionary to find two examples of each prefix that alters the meaning of a word they already understand. Note that it is difficult to guess which prefix is used to negate a particular word and that not all words beginning with these letters are using them as a prefix (for example, *misunderstand* versus *missile*).

MODERATE/LIGHT

LANGUAGE CONVENTIONS:
Sentence Variety

You have seen that diction and **syntax** help a writer develop a distinctive tone. In "How It Feels to Be Colored Me." Hurston varies sentence length and structure to create an informal, conversational style that hums with energy. To do so, she combines **simple** and **compound** sentences, as well as fragments. She also uses **parallelism,** similar grammatical structures, to express ideas of similar meaning or importance. Here is an example from the selection.

> It is exclusively a colored town. The only white people I knew passed through the town going to or coming from Orlando. The native whites rode dusty horses, the Northern tourists chugged down the sandy village road in automobiles. The town knew the Southerners and never stopped cane chewing when they passed. But the Northerners were something else again.

The first sentence is a short, simple sentence that emphasizes its content. In the sentences that follow, Hurston uses parallel structure by starting each thought with the word *The*. This repetition helps tie together the separate sentences about the different people who passed through and the town's residents. If you look at the syntax, there is a simple sentence with added descriptive phrases, a compound sentence, and another simple sentence with a compound predicate. The final sentence is a short fragment, which grabs the reader's attention by emphasizing the residents' opinion of Northerners. The sentence variety allows the text to flow smoothly and keeps the reader engaged.

Practice and Apply Write a short paragraph summarizing your opinion of Hurston's style in "How It Feels to Be Colored Me." Use a variety of sentences of different lengths to achieve fluency and clarity.

! Go to **Sentence Structure** in the **Grammar Studio** for help.

LANGUAGE CONVENTIONS:
Sentence Variety

Divide students into mixed ability groups and instruct each group to search the text for the following: sentence fragments, repetition, parallelism, and combined sentences (using punctuation or conjunctions). Once each group has an example from the text, invite them to lead a discussion on the effect of this structure on the rest of the paragraph in which it appears.

Practice and Apply After students have completed the exercise, divide them into pairs to peer edit their summary paragraphs. Instruct students to pay attention to sentence structure and variety while editing and to try reading their partner's summary aloud to test the effect of different sentence structures.

 ENGLISH LEARNER SUPPORT

Sentence Structure Use the following supports with students at varying proficiency levels to help in understanding sentence structure:

- Review subjects and verbs. Have student pairs identify the subjects and verbs in each sentence in the example. **MODERATE**

- Review subjects and verbs. Point out the third sentence "The native whites . . . in automobiles" in the example. Note the use of two subjects and two verbs. Ask for volunteers to identify this sentence's subjects and its verbs. **SUBSTANTIAL**

- Challenge students to include sentences with one and two subjects and one and two verbs in their paragraphs for Practice and Apply. Encourage them to focus on varying the length of their sentences. **LIGHT**

from THE WARMTH OF OTHER SUNS

History Writing by Isabel Wilkerson

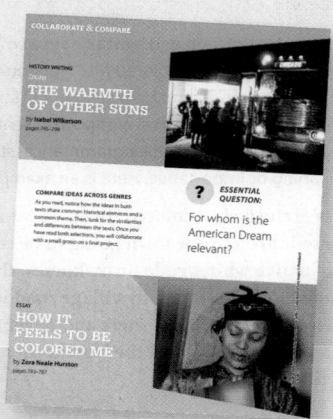

GENRE ELEMENTS
HISTORY WRITING

History writing includes informational text that covers a specific period of time (such as the Cold War) or a historical issue (such as the history of popular music in the United States). History writing discusses key people and events related to the time period or topic. The purpose of history writing usually relates to a specific aspect of the historical period, such as a cultural or social issue. The author may develop that aspect through a cause-effect, compare-contrast, or problem-solution organization.

LEARNING OBJECTIVES

- Determine author's message and audience.
- Research the book the excerpt is from.
- Write a historical essay.
- Discuss the historical essay in a group.
- Determine words' letter patterns.
- Use correct spelling for plural nouns and words ending in a consonant.
- **Language** Discuss the author's message using Academic Vocabulary.

TEXT COMPLEXITY

Quantitative Measures	*from* **The Warmth of Other Suns**	Lexile: 1240L
Qualitative Measures	**Ideas Presented** Multiple levels, use of irony and satire; greater demand for inference.	
	Structures Used More complex; more deviation from chronological or sequential order.	
	Language Used Implied meanings; complex sentence structures.	
	Knowledge Required More complexity to theme; experiences may be less familiar to many; cultural or historical references may make heavier demands.	

RESOURCES

- Unit 6 Response Log
- Selection Audio
- Reading Studio: Notice & Note
- Level Up Tutorial: Evidence; Audience; Comparison-Contrast Organization
- Writing Studio: Conducting Research
- Speaking and Listening Studio: Participating in Collaborative Discussions
- Vocabulary Studio: Analyzing Word Structure
- Grammar Studio: Spelling
- "How It Feels to Be Colored Me"/*The Warmth of Other Suns*

SUMMARIES

English

The author compares how whites and African Americans in the South lived during the late 1800s and early 1900s. She provides examples of the different laws and social customs in various locations of the United States.

Spanish

El autor compara cómo los blancos y afroamericanos vivían en el Sur durante el final del siglo XIX y el principio del siglo XX. Da ejemplos de distintas leyes y costumbres sociales en varios sitios de los Estados Unidos.

SMALL-GROUP OPTIONS

Have students work in small groups and pairs to read and discuss the selection.

Gallery Walk

- Tape large sheets of paper on the walls and write a question or topic addressed in the selection (for example, the Great Migration).
- Form students into small groups or pairs in front of each sheet. Have them discuss the topic or question and write their ideas on the sheet.
- After all groups have had a chance to note something, signal groups to move to the next sheet and repeat the activity. Continue until all students have responded to all topics or questions.
- As a class, discuss students' ideas.

Sticky Note Peer Review

- After students have finished writing their historical essays, ask them to review their peers' writing and provide constructive feedback.
- Have students work in small groups and take turns reading their papers aloud.
- As one student reads, have listeners write the following on sticky notes:
  1. positive comments, such as words they liked
  2. suggestions to improve the essay
  3. questions they have about the essay
- Listeners then initial their sticky notes and give them to the writer.

Text X-Ray: English Learner Support
for *The Warmth of Other Suns*

Use the Text X-Ray and the supports and scaffolds in the Teacher's Edition to help guide students at different proficiency levels through the selection.

INTRODUCE THE SELECTION
DISCUSS RACIAL SEGREGATION

To discuss the selection, students will need to understand the history of racial segregation in the United States. Explain that after slavery ended, African Americans still faced discrimination. Particularly in the South, laws in the early-to-mid-20th century restricted where they could work, live, and attend school. In certain states, laws required businesses to provide separate water fountains, bathrooms, and other facilities for African Americans and whites.

Explain that the term *racial segregation* describes the practice of separating people into groups based on their race or ethnic background. Have students use this term in a sentence, such as *Racial segregation was unjust because* _____ and *Racial segregation limited where people could* _____.

CULTURAL REFERENCES

The following words or phrases may be unfamiliar to students:

- *colored* (paragraph 1): African American
- *Jim Crow* (paragraph 1): laws that limited African Americans' rights
- *slaveholding ancestors* (paragraph 1): previous generations of whites who owned slaves
- *ride of 36 hours* (paragraph 3): the approximate time it took to travel from the South to the North
- *lest the races brush elbows* (paragraph 7): to prevent people from different races from having physical contact with each other
- *rules of the road* (paragraph 9): rules people obey when driving a car

LISTENING

Generate Questions

Read aloud paragraphs 1–4. Tell students to reflect on the author's message and write a question about something they do not understand or want to know more about.

Use the following supports with students at varying proficiency levels:

- Ask students guided questions to help them generate questions about the passage, such as: *Do you understand what Jim Crow laws are? Do you want to know more about how African Americans were treated?* Help students turn these questions into their own questions. Write their questions on the board. **SUBSTANTIAL**
- Have students read their questions aloud in a small group. After all questions have been read aloud, have students discuss which question was most interesting to them and explain why. **MODERATE**
- Have students work in groups of three and number off 1, 2, and 3. Student 1 asks a question. Student 2 answers it. Student 3 adds to Student 2's response. Have the students switch roles and repeat the process until all students have shared their questions. **LIGHT**

SPEAKING

Use Academic Vocabulary

Review the word *subservience* and its definition. Ask: *How did the new generation of whites expect African Americans to be subservient?*

Use the following supports with students at varying proficiency levels:

- Choral read paragraph 9. Pause after each sentence to help students understand unknown words and phrases. Provide sentence frames to help students answer the question: *African Americans could not ___ a white driver on the road. African Americans were not allowed to _____.* **SUBSTANTIAL**
- Have students review paragraphs 9 and 10 from the selection in a small group. Students can work together to complete the following frame: *Whites expected African Americans to be subservient by _____.* **MODERATE**
- Have students meet in small groups to discuss the question. Have them use evidence from the selection to support their responses. **LIGHT**

READING

Paraphrase Text

Have students show comprehension by paraphrasing an excerpt of the selection.

Use the following supports with students at varying proficiency levels:

- Choral read the first sentence of paragraph 6. Provide sentence frames to help students paraphrase the sentence: *African Americans could only go to _____ on certain days. Sometimes they were not ____ at all.* **SUBSTANTIAL**
- Have one student read aloud a sentence from paragraphs 6–10. The partner then paraphrases it. Have students take turns with additional sentences. **MODERATE**
- Have students work independently and write a paraphrase of a sentence from paragraphs 6–8. Then, have them share their paraphrases in a group. Ask the other group members to identify the sentence in the text that was paraphrased. **LIGHT**

WRITING

Identify Details

Tell students to skim the selection and jot down examples of rules and practices of racial segregation.

Use the following supports with students at varying proficiency levels:

- Have students create a web diagram showing how African Americans and whites were segregated during the text's time period. Have students write the date in the center circle. Students can draw pictures or write phrases that express how African Americans were treated. **SUBSTANTIAL**
- Have students use their notes to complete the following sentence frames: *African Americans in the early 1900s could not _____. White Americans in the early 1900s could _____.* Tell students to share their sentences with a partner. **MODERATE**
- Have students work with a partner and use their notes to make a list of the rules for African Americans in the early 1900s. Then, ask the partners to work together to write a paragraph describing how the rules would make life difficult for African Americans. **LIGHT**

TEACH

Connect to the
ESSENTIAL QUESTION

This excerpt from Isabel Wilkerson's historical text highlights the extreme practices of segregation in the Jim Crow South that motivated many African Americans who participated in the Great Migration. This excerpt will help students think critically about the role of race and geography in determining who really has access to the American Dream.

COMPARE IDEAS ACROSS GENRES

Remind students both texts fall under the category of "informative texts" and both writers are motivated by their personal experience. Ask students to consider the role of formal and informal language in these texts from different genres and direct them to consider how the use of personal experience in each text determines their response.

HISTORY WRITING

from

THE WARMTH OF OTHER SUNS

by **Isabel Wilkerson**
pages 795–799

COMPARE IDEAS ACROSS GENRES

As you read, notice how the ideas in both texts share common historical elements and a common theme. Then, look for the similarities and differences between the texts. Once you have read both selections, you will collaborate with a small group on a final project.

ESSENTIAL QUESTION:

For whom is the American Dream relevant?

ESSAY

HOW IT FEELS TO BE COLORED ME

by **Zora Neale Hurston**
pages 783–787

792　Unit 6

GET READY

TEACH

from **The Warmth of Other Suns**

QUICK START

Think about reasons why you like where you live. What would have to change for you to want to move away? Share your ideas with a partner.

ANALYZE INFORMATIONAL TEXTS

History writing is a kind of informational text that deals with events in the past. Historical narratives cover a specific time period, event, or person in history, and usually include authentic references and details on what life was like at the time. As with many informational texts, authors support their ideas with evidence, examples, and their own commentary.

History writing will usually feature a clear **organizational design,** such as cause and effect or compare and contrast. Writers choose the organizational design that best supports their purpose. For example, a writer who wants to explain how to solve a problem might use a "how-to" organizational design. As you read, think about the important ideas in the text and how the organizational design supports those ideas.

DETERMINE AUTHOR'S MESSAGE AND AUDIENCE

The **author's message** is the main idea expressed in the text. To determine the main idea of a passage, read it carefully and identify the most important details. Authors may emphasize particular ideas depending on their intended **audience.** You can infer who the intended audience is once the message is identified or through careful study of the details the author includes.

As you read, consider the way the author uses language and how that informs and shapes the perception of readers. For example, when the writer says that "a generation came into the world unlike any other in the South," that is a clue for readers to note details that make the particular generation unique. Record the writer's important ideas and supporting details in the chart below.

IMPORTANT IDEA	SUPPORTING DETAILS
A generation came into the world unlike any other in the South	*no personal recollection of slavery; free, but not free; Jim Crow; not subservient; no contrived intimacy with whites*
Possible answer: new generation began looking for a way out	*possible to escape their severe limitation in the South*
Possible answer: segregation and different sets of rules in all areas of life	*Possible answers: elevators; ambulances; waiting rooms; curfews; rules of the road*

© Houghton Mifflin Harcourt Publishing Company

GENRE ELEMENTS: HISTORY WRITING

- discusses significant individuals or events that occurred in the past
- features an organizational design that supports the writer's purpose
- supports important ideas with carefully selected details

QUICK START

As students complete the Quick Start assignment, ask for a show of hands of students who have previously moved and invite those students to share their reasons for moving with the class. After students have discussed their views with a partner, invite partners to summarize the similarities and differences in their views and share a key comparison with the class.

ANALYZE INFORMATIONAL TEXTS

Review with students the features common to informational texts in general and history writing in particular. Because this excerpt starts and ends mid-chapter, it may be difficult to tease out a clear thesis statement and conclusion. Mention that good informational texts have these elements, as well as supporting evidence and pertinent examples. Direct students to pay attention to the author's organizational structure and purpose at the paragraph level, noting that topic sentences may act as a sort of thesis for the paragraph in question. How does the author use contrast to help the reader assimilate the large quantity of detailed information provided in each paragraph? In the excerpt as a whole?

DETERMINE AUTHOR'S MESSAGE AND AUDIENCE

Review with students common purposes authors have for writing: to inform, to persuade, and to entertain. How do these purposes help the student identify the target audience? As students review the relationship between main ideas and supporting details, direct them to think about how the author's choice of which details to include can reveal both the author's purpose and the intended audience. Ask students to consider what kinds of details would change if the audience for the piece or the author's purpose were different. For example, if the author were attempting to persuade the reader that segregation was harmful, what does this indicate about the reader's beliefs and what details would most strongly aid the author in this purpose?

TEACH

CRITICAL VOCABULARY

Encourage students to read all the sentences before deciding which word best completes each one. Remind them to look for context clues that match the precise meaning of each word.

Answers:

1. *segregated, conventional*

2. *conceivable, infraction*

3. *sentiment, ferry*

4. *subservience, contrived*

■ English Learner Support

Use Cognates Inform Spanish speakers of the following cognates in the Critical Vocabulary words: *sentiment/ sentimiento, conventional/convencional.* **ALL LEVELS**

LANGUAGE CONVENTIONS

Spelling Ask students if they can think of any other spelling rules for changing a word's part of speech, such as *-tion, -able, -al,* etc. Have them work in groups to list as many forms of one of the Critical Vocabulary words as they can, noting any questions about spelling they come across. Remind students of other tricky spelling variations, such as *-ible/-able, in-/un-,* etc., and suggest that they look up these words in a dictionary or make flashcards to help with memorizing spelling.

ANNOTATION MODEL

Remind students of annotation strategies such as underlining important details and circling words that signal how the text is organized. Point out that they may follow this suggestion or use their own system for marking up the selection in their write-in text. They may want to color-code their annotations by using highlighters. Their notes in the margin may include questions about ideas that are unclear or topics they want to learn more about.

 **GET READY**

CRITICAL VOCABULARY

subservience	sentiment	ferry	segregated
contrived	infraction	conceivable	conventional

To determine how many Critical Vocabulary words you already know, fill in the blanks.

1. The teacher explained that it was unjust to keep students _____ as was done in the past and that the _____ school practice of learning all together was fairest for everyone.

2. I tried every _____ thing I could think of to get myself out of trouble for my _____ of the club rules.

3. I had a positive _____ toward charity, and I demonstrated it by offering to _____ people in need around town on errands.

4. The employee's low bow demonstrated _____ toward the boss, but those who saw his smirk knew it was _____.

LANGUAGE CONVENTIONS

Spelling Using proper spelling is important when communicating your ideas formally in writing. Knowing basic spelling rules and using a dictionary to double check your work will help you spell words you may not use frequently.

For example, the adjective *subservient* can be changed to a noun by adding the correct suffix. Is the correct spelling of the noun form *subservience* or *subserviance*? You can be sure of the correct spelling by knowing that the suffix *-ence* is added to adjectives and the suffix *-ance* is added to verbs.

As you read the excerpt from *The Warmth of Other Suns*, note the correct spelling of all Critical Vocabulary words, as well as any other words with which you aren't familiar.

ANNOTATION MODEL

NOTICE & NOTE

As you read, mark details that hint at the author's message. Notice details that suggest the organizational design of the text. In the model, you can see one reader's notes about the excerpt from *The Warmth of Other Suns*.

> "In the years leading up to and immediately following the turn of the twentieth century, a generation came into the world unlike any other in the South. It was made up of young people with no personal recollection of slavery— they were two generations removed from it.

This sounds like a hint of the author's message—something about this new generation.

This detail tells me how this generation is different.

BACKGROUND

"The Great Migration" was the term given to the mass exodus of over 6 million African Americans from the southern states during the period from 1916 to 1970. **Isabel Wilkerson** *(b. 1961) was born in Washington, DC, to parents who had participated in the Great Migration, moving north during the civil rights era. Their journey would later inspire her award-winning historical epic story of the Great Migration, The Warmth of Other Suns. Wilkerson has spoken and taught at universities across the United States.*

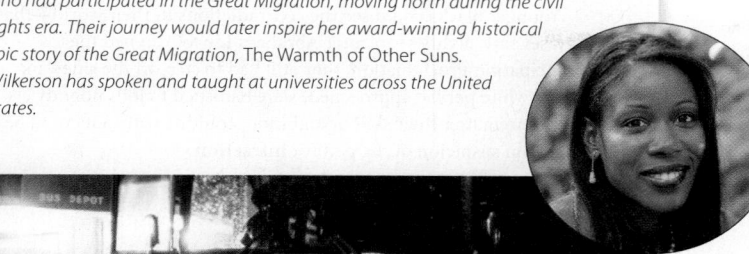

from
THE WARMTH OF OTHER SUNS
History Writing by Isabel Wilkerson

PREPARE TO COMPARE

As you read, notice the way Wilkerson illustrates the differences in the way whites and African Americans lived.

1 In the years leading up to and immediately following the turn of the twentieth century, a generation came into the world unlike any other in the South. It was made up of young people with no personal recollection of slavery—they were two generations removed from it. The colored members of this generation were free but not free, chafing under Jim Crow and resisting the studied **subservience** of their slave parents and grandparents. They had grown up without the **contrived** intimacy that once bound the two races. And it appeared that young whites, weaned on a formal kind of supremacy, had grown more hostile to blacks than even their slaveholding ancestors had been.

2 "The **sentiment** is altogether different now," William C. Oates, the old-guard former governor of Alabama, said in 1901 of the newer generation of white southerners. "When the Negro is doing no harm, why, the people want to kill him and wipe him from the face of the earth."

3 The colored people of this generation began looking for a way out. "It is too much to expect that Negroes will indefinitely

NOTICE & NOTE ✎

Notice & Note

Use the side margins to notice and note signposts in the text.

subservience
(səb-sûr´vē-əns) *n.* the condition of being subordinate in capacity or function.

contrived
(kən-trīvd´) *adj.* obviously planned or calculated; not spontaneous or natural.

sentiment
(sĕn´tə-mənt) *n.* a thought, view, or attitude, especially one based mainly on emotion instead of reason.

The Warmth of Other Suns 795

Magnum... Harcourt Publishing Company • Image Credits: © Collins Massey... © 2004 I I E S, Inc. Reality © Corbis Historical/Getty Images

---

TEACH

BACKGROUND

After students have read the background information, provide them with the following contextual information about Wilkerson and her book. Wilkerson was the first African American woman to win a Pulitzer Prize. While this portion of the book focuses on the evils of the Jim Crow South, later sections complicate the notion that the North was free from such prejudice, describing the new lives and hardships of African Americans upon relocating to the urban North. The title of the book comes from Richard Wright's 1945 autobiography *Black Boy*, in which he reflects on his decision to leave the South during the Great Migration:

> I was leaving the South to fling myself into the unknown. . . .

> . . . I was taking a part of the South to transplant in alien soil, to see if it could grow differently, if it could drink of new and cool rains, bend in strange winds, respond to the warmth of other suns and, perhaps, to bloom. . . .

PREPARE TO COMPARE

Direct students to use the Prepare to Compare prompt to focus their reading.

CRITICAL VOCABULARY

subservience: Former slaves had been expected to show subservience, behaving deferentially towards whites.

ASK STUDENTS to give examples of ways of behaving subserviently in conversation. (*not making eye contact, not speaking until spoken to, not talking back*)

contrived: The intimacy between slaves and their owners was forced and contrived, caused by the legal status of the slaves rather than authentic feelings towards whites.

ASK STUDENTS how contrived intimacy might appear different than authentic intimacy. (*forced politeness, coldness, lack of spontaneous physical contact*)

sentiment: Oates describes the hostile sentiment and irrational anger towards African Americans held by white southerners long after the abolition of slavery.

ASK STUDENTS to give examples that reflected public sentiment on the part of white southerners towards African Americans at this time. (*African Americans were not allowed to use the same facilities as whites and could be harshly punished or killed for minor offenses.*)

DETERMINE AUTHOR'S MESSAGE AND AUDIENCE

Guide students to notice the relationship between themes in the topic sentence and the presentation of data such as statistics and years. How does having the topic sentence help them contextualize this information and determine which aspects are most important? (**Answer:** *The quotation from the U.S. Labor Department states that African Americans can get out of the South in only 36 hours, so African Americans won't put up with the same conditions that existed after the Civil War.*)

 ENGLISH LEARNER SUPPORT

Recognize Dated Language Direct students' attention to the different labels used to characterize race throughout the text. Inform students that "colored" is employed here as it was used at the time, but that this adjective is no longer appropriate as a racial description. **ALL LEVELS**

For **listening support** for students at varying proficiency levels, see the **Text X-Ray** on page 792C.

CRITICAL VOCABULARY

infraction: Under Jim Crow, African Americans could be harshly punished or executed for any type of infraction, including breaking unwritten rules for interacting with whites.

ASK STUDENTS what normal behaviors would have constituted infractions in the South at this time. (*not stepping off the sidewalk when a white person passed, initiating a handshake with a white person, using the white bathrooms in a public restaurant*)

 NOTICE & NOTE

DETERMINE AUTHOR'S MESSAGE AND AUDIENCE

Annotate: Mark the sentence in paragraph 3 that expresses its main idea.

Analyze: What supporting evidence for this idea does the paragraph contain?

infraction
(ĭn-frăk´shən) *n.* the act or instance of infringing, as of a law or rule; a violation.

endure their severe limitations in the South when they can escape most of them in a ride of 36 hours," the Labor Department warned. "Fifty years after the Civil War, they should not be expected to be content with the same conditions which existed at the close of the war."

4 Younger blacks could see the contradictions in their world—that, sixty, seventy, eighty years after Abraham Lincoln signed the Emancipation Proclamation, they still had to step off the sidewalk when a white person approached, were banished to jobs nobody else wanted no matter their skill or ambition, couldn't vote, but could be hanged on suspicion of the pettiest **infraction**.

 ENGLISH LEARNER SUPPORT

Pronounce Stressed Syllables For native Spanish speakers, the pronunciation of nominalizations ending in *-tion*, *-tional*, and *-able* may be difficult as the stress is placed on the ultimate or penultimate (respectively) syllables in the Spanish equivalents. Practice the Critical Vocabulary words with correct stress in English and allow students to repeat your pronunciation. **SUBSTANTIAL/MODERATE**

5 *These were the facts of their lives:*

6 There were days when whites could go to the amusement park and a day when blacks could go, if they were permitted at all. There were white elevators and colored elevators (meaning the freight elevators in back); white train platforms and colored train platforms. There were white ambulances and colored ambulances to **ferry** the sick, and white hearses and colored hearses for those who didn't survive whatever was wrong with them.

7 There were white waiting rooms and colored waiting rooms in any **conceivable** place where a person might have to wait for something, from the bus depot to the doctor's office. A total of

ANALYZE INFORMATIONAL TEXTS

Annotate: Mark the phrases in paragraph 6 that describe how African Americans and whites lived during this time.

Infer: What is the author's purpose for comparing the ways whites and African Americans lived?

ferry
(fĕr´ē) *v.* to transport (people or goods) by vehicle.

conceivable
(kən-sēv´ə-bəl) *adj.* formed or developed in the mind.

© Houghton Mifflin Harcourt Publishing Company

WHEN STUDENTS STRUGGLE . . .

Identify Evidence Have students make a T-chart to note differences between African Americans and whites that the author details. Then, have students work with a partner to write 2-3 sentences summarizing the kinds of differences and what they show about how African Americans were treated by whites and by the law.

 For additional support, go to the **Reading Studio** and assign the following **Level Up Tutorial: Evidence.**

TEACH

ANALYZE INFORMATIONAL TEXTS

Remind students of the different purposes that can motivate an author's writing. How does the use of contrast as a structure for presenting information help guide the reader's understanding? (**Answer:** *The author is providing facts, so the reader can recognize the differences in the way whites and African Americans lived and realize how difficult this period was for African Americans. The author's purpose is to inform readers about what life was like and to explain that African Americans would not tolerate this for long.*)

EL ENGLISH LEARNER SUPPORT

Use Context Clues Direct students to the final sentence of paragraph 6 and have them discuss how they might use the general idea of the sentence and the connotations of surrounding words to understand the meaning of the words *ambulance*, *ferry*, and *hearse*. **LIGHT**

 For **reading support** for students at varying proficiency levels, see the **Text X-Ray** on page 792D.

CRITICAL VOCABULARY

ferry: Using separate ambulances to ferry patients to the hospital is one example of segregation.

ASK STUDENTS what other vehicles ferry passengers in this paragraph. (*trains, hearses, elevators*)

conceivable: Any public place you could think of was required to separate whites from African Americans.

ASK STUDENTS what other conceivable shared spaces were affected by segregation, besides those the author cites here. (*water fountains, lunch counters*)

■ English Learner Support

Assimilate Cultural Knowledge Direct students to consider again the Essential Question guiding this lesson. What do they already know about "the American Dream"? What context clues in the text help them create a picture of the ideal of the American Dream as it is contrasted with the reality of African Americans at this time? **LIGHT**

BIG QUESTIONS

Discuss with students how Wilkerson contrasts interactions between white people and interactions between a white person and an African American. Direct students to focus on how this text challenged, changed, or confirmed their prior knowledge and opinions about life in the South after the Civil War. Remind them that it is acceptable and even desirable to change or modify opinions based on new information and ask them to reflect on how this text alters their understanding of this period. (*Answer: The writer includes this detail as an example of the grossly unfair treatment African Americans endured.*)

 ANALYZE INFORMATIONAL TEXTS

Instruct students to reflect on what they know about the author's purpose and audience as they consider the effect of repetition in this passage. How does the author's compare-contrast structure help them think about the role repetition plays here? (*Answer: Wilkerson is trying to demonstrate how everything was segregated between the two races. By repeating the contrasting words over and over, she demonstrates that different people lived in two distinct worlds.*)

CRITICAL VOCABULARY

segregated: Despite the extra cost, owners were required to provide separated bathrooms and other facilities.

ASK STUDENTS what things in a theater might have been segregated at this time. (*bathrooms, water fountains, entrances, seating areas, ticket counters*)

conventional: Segregation even impacted conventional driving rules, creating a separate set of rules for African Americans to follow that differed from the norm.

ASK STUDENTS what the unintended consequences of such *unconventional* traffic rules might be. (*accidents if drivers weren't aware of the other driver's race*)

 **NOTICE & NOTE**

segregated
(sĕg´rĭ-gāt-ĕd) *adj.* separated; isolated.

conventional
(kən-vĕn´shə-nəl) *adj.* based on or in accordance with general agreement, use, or practice; customary.

BIG QUESTIONS

Notice & Note: Mark the historical event described in paragraph 9.

Infer: Does this change or confirm what you know about life for African Americans at the time? Explain.

ANALYZE INFORMATIONAL TEXTS

Notice: In paragraph 10, mark each instance of the words *white* and *colored*.

Analyze: Why does Wilkerson repeat these two contrasting words? What effect does this have on her writing?

---

four restrooms had to be constructed and maintained at significant expense in any public establishment that bothered to provide any for colored people: one for white men, one for white women, one for colored men, and one for colored women. In 1958, a new bus station went up in Jacksonville, Florida, with two of everything, including two segregated cocktail lounges, "lest the races brush elbows over a martini," *The Wall Street Journal* reported. The president of Southeastern Greyhound told the *Journal*, "It frequently costs fifty percent more to build a terminal with **segregated** facilities." But most southern businessmen didn't dare complain about the extra cost. "That question is dynamite," the president of a southern theater chain told the *Journal*. "Don't even say what state I'm in."

8   There was a colored window at the post office in Pensacola, Florida, and there were white and colored telephone booths in Oklahoma. White and colored went to separate windows to get their license plates in Indianola, Mississippi, and to separate tellers to make their deposits at the First National Bank of Atlanta. There were taxicabs for colored people and taxicabs for white people in Jacksonville, Birmingham, Atlanta, and the entire state of Mississippi. Colored people had to be off the streets and out of the city limits by 8 P.M. in Palm Beach and Miami Beach.

9   Throughout the South, the **conventional** rules of the road did not apply when a colored motorist was behind the wheel. If he reached an intersection first, he had to let the white motorist go ahead of him. He could not pass a white motorist on the road no matter how slowly the white motorist was going and had to take extreme caution to avoid an accident because he would likely be blamed no matter who was at fault. In everyday interactions, a black person could not contradict a white person or speak unless spoken to first. A black person could not be the first to offer to shake a white person's hand. A handshake could occur only if a white person so gestured, leaving many people having never shaken hands with a person of the other race. The consequences for the slightest misstep were swift and brutal. Two whites beat a black tenant farmer in Louise, Mississippi, in 1948, wrote the historian James C. Cobb, because the man "asked for a receipt after paying his water bill."

10   It was against the law for a colored person and a white person to play checkers together in Birmingham. White and colored gamblers had to place their bets at separate windows and sit in separate aisles at racetracks in Arkansas. At saloons in Atlanta, the bars were segregated: Whites drank on stools at one end of the bar and blacks on stools at the other end, until the city outlawed even that, resulting in white-only and colored-only saloons. There were white parking spaces and colored parking spaces in the town square in Calhoun City, Mississippi. In one North Carolina courthouse, there was a white Bible and a black Bible to swear to tell the truth on.

APPLYING ACADEMIC VOCABULARY

☐ **infinite**   ☑ **contemporary**   ☐ **simulated**   ☐ **virtual**   ☑ **global**

Write and Discuss Have students turn to a partner to discuss the following questions. Guide students to include the academic vocabulary words *contemporary* and *global* in their responses. Ask volunteers to share their responses with the class.

- How has your understanding of **contemporary** racial justice issues changed?
- How does your knowledge of history help you put this information in a **global** context?

CHECK YOUR UNDERSTANDING

Answer these questions before moving on to the **Analyze the Text** section on the following page.

1 How had the lives of African Americans in the South changed since the signing of the Emancipation Proclamation?

A They were able to vote.

B They saved money in a new bank.

C They used the same waiting rooms as whites.

D They were no longer held as slaves.

2 An African American could visit an amusement park —

F only on even days of the week

G only on odd days of the week

H on days reserved for African Americans only

J on days reserved by whites

3 According to the author, what would happen if an African American motorist and a white motorist got into a car accident in the South?

A The African American had to accept the blame for the accident.

B The new laws protected anyone who got into an accident.

C The motorists reported the accident to different police officers.

D The African American could only drive on certain roads.

 For **speaking support** for students at varying proficiency levels, see the **Text X-Ray** on page 792D.

CHECK YOUR UNDERSTANDING

Have students answer the questions independently.

Answers:

1. *D*

2. *H*

3. *A*

If they answer any questions incorrectly, have them reread the text to confirm their understanding. Then, they may proceed to ANALYZE THE TEXT on page 800.

ⓔⓛ ENGLISH LEARNER SUPPORT

Oral Assessment Use the following questions to assess students' comprehension and speaking skills.

1. The Emancipation Proclamation _____ slaves. *(freed)*

2. When could African Americans visit amusement parks? *(on days set aside for them)*

3. African Americans were _____ if they got into an accident with a white driver. *(to blame)*
MODERATE

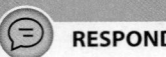

APPLY

ANALYZE THE TEXT

Possible answers:

1. **DOK 4:** *Wilkerson examines the differences between the way African Americans and whites lived. Throughout the text, Wilkerson presents examples of how African Americans were treated unfairly in comparison to whites. This supports her purpose of informing readers about the injustice and explaining why African Americans wished to move elsewhere.*

2. **DOK 4:** *Most students will say that the writer supports this idea adequately because she includes numerous examples of mistreatment at the hands of whites. Some students may say that though there are numerous examples, she does not present a comparison to the mistreatment of African Americans when they were enslaved.*

3. **DOK 2:** *Even though the facilities were more expensive, businessmen felt they had to maintain segregation where they were. Throughout the text, the writer presents evidence that although African Americans were no longer held in slavery, society wanted to maintain separation between African Americans and whites.*

4. **DOK 3:** *Wilkerson's message is to show that the treatment of African Americans was unjust. Details such as "the conventional rules of the road did not apply when a colored motorist was behind the wheel" and "a black person could not contradict a white person" are intended to make the mistreatment of African Americans clear.*

5. **DOK 4:** *Wilkerson's message is that African Americans wished to leave the South because of the harsh treatment they endured. The author supports this message by including examples of harsh treatment, including policies of segregation.*

RESEARCH

Review with students what constitutes an acceptable, credible source. Remind students to confirm controversial information with multiple sources whenever possible and to use the correct citation format when crediting sources.

Extend Before students begin research, direct them to think about strategies for organizing their information and for determining which information is the most important to present. Guide students to use the questions provided to direct their research and help them use that information to turn the question into a thesis statement or topic sentence for their presentation of information.

RESPOND

ANALYZE THE TEXT

Support your responses with evidence from the text. 📓 NOTEBOOK

1. **Analyze** Wilkerson uses a compare-and-contrast organizational design. Why is this organizational design an appropriate choice for her subject? How does it support her purpose?

2. **Evaluate** The writer comments in paragraph 1 that "young whites . . . had grown more hostile to blacks than even their slaveholding ancestors had been." Explain whether the writer adequately supports this idea. Cite evidence and examples from the text in your response.

3. **Infer** In paragraph 7, the author states that though building segregated facilities was more expensive, "southern businessmen didn't dare complain about the extra cost." Why did the businessmen keep quiet on this issue? Cite text evidence in your response.

4. **Draw Conclusions** What is the author's message? What details support this message?

5. **Notice & Note** How does Wilkerson's use of language impact the way you perceive the treatment of African Americans? Cite text evidence in your response.

RESEARCH TIP
When researching authors and their works, some sources such as Wikipedia are unreliable because they can be edited by anyone with a computer. The author's and publisher's websites are more authoritative sources.

RESEARCH

Do some research on *The Warmth of Other Suns*, the book that this excerpt comes from. Answer the questions in the chart.

QUESTION	ANSWER
How many years did Isabel Wilkerson take to write the book?	*15 years*
How many interviews did Wilkerson conduct as she was writing the book?	*More than 1200 interviews*
Where does the title of the book come from?	*A book by Richard Wright*

Extend With a partner, research the Great Migration. Why did so many African Americans move from southern to northern states during this time? How did this mass migration affect American culture? Did the lives of the people who migrated improve substantially? Present your results to the class.

WHEN STUDENTS STRUGGLE . . .

Reteach: Determine Author's Message and Audience Direct students to highlight the sentence in paragraph 1 that best tells them what to expect about the author's purpose. Using this sentence as a guide, ask students to consider how the specific details presented in the concluding paragraph clarify the intended audience for the text. Encourage them to think of counter examples to help clarify this notion of audience—what might Wilkerson have included if she were writing to lawmakers at the time of the Great Migration, for instance?

 For additional support, go to the **Reading Studio** and assign the following [LEVEL] **Level Up Tutorial: Audience.**

CREATE AND DISCUSS

Write a Historical Essay Consider an event from American history related to a political or social injustice. Conduct some research and write a brief essay in which you describe the event's historical significance.

❏ Identify the historical event in your opening paragraph.

❏ Describe the details of what happened. You may provide an example of mistreatment or discuss how the injustice was overcome.

❏ Explain why the event is important in your conclusion.

Discuss Your Essay Now that you've written your essay, share it with the group.

❏ Read your essay to the group. Be sure to explain why the event you are discussing is significant.

❏ Ask if your classmates are familiar with the event and invite them to share their views.

❏ Listen respectfully for different thoughts on why the event is significant.

 Go to **Conducting Research** in the **Writing Studio** for help.

 Go to **Participating in Collaborative Discussions** in the **Speaking and Listening Studio** for help.

RESPOND TO THE ESSENTIAL QUESTION

? For whom is the American Dream relevant?

Gather Information Review your annotations and notes from *The Warmth of Other Suns*. Then, add relevant details to your Response Log. As you determine which information to include, think about:

• how an individual's experience may shape his or her priorities

• why one person's dream may be different from another person's

• whether different opportunities are available to different people

UNIT 6 RESPONSE LOG

ACADEMIC VOCABULARY

As you write and discuss what you learned from the text, be sure to use the Academic Vocabulary words. Check off each of the words that you use.

❏ **contemporary**

❏ **global**

❏ **infinite**

❏ **simulated**

❏ **virtual**

CREATE AND DISCUSS

Write a Historical Essay Once students have chosen an event to write about, direct them to use the question "Why was this event important?" to guide their organization of information. Once they have organized their research into several categories, help them develop these categories into topic sentences and then to use those themes to craft a more specific thesis as to why the event is important to understand.

 For **writing support** for students at varying proficiency levels, see the **Text X-Ray** on page 792D

Discuss Your Essay Separate students into mixed-ability groups to peer edit each other's essays and work together to summarize the main ideas for discussion. Guide students to brainstorm possible questions their presentations may raise and to practice responding to comments and questions from the class.

RESPOND TO THE ESSENTIAL QUESTION

Allow time for students to add details from *The Warmth of Other Suns* to their Unit 6 Response Logs.

APPLY

CRITICAL VOCABULARY

Answers:

1. *subservience, segregated*

2. *conventional, infraction*

3. *contrived, sentiment, conceivable*

4. *ferry*

VOCABULARY STRATEGY:
Word Families

Have students work in pairs to complete the Practice and Apply activity. If students are having difficulty, help them identify the prefixes of each word and review the prefix meanings. After students complete the activity, call on volunteers to share answers. List the related words students generate on the board.

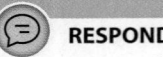 **RESPOND**

Go to **Analyzing Word Structure** in the **Vocabulary Studio** for help.

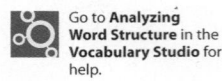

WORD BANK
subservience
contrived
sentiment
infraction
ferry
conceivable
segregated
conventional

CRITICAL VOCABULARY

Practice and Apply With a partner, discuss and write an answer to each of the following questions. Then, work together to write a sentence for each vocabulary word.

1. Which two words are related to separateness?

2. Which two words are related to customary practices or violating them?

3. Which three words are related to mental and emotional thinking?

4. Which word is related to motion?

VOCABULARY STRATEGY:
Word Families

A **word family** is a set of words that all descend from the same word root. The Critical Vocabulary word *segregated* is part of the word family based on the Latin root *greg* meaning "group" or "herd." The word is formed by adding the prefix *se-* meaning "apart" and the suffix *-ate* meaning "state or quality of" so that *segregated* means "separated" or "isolated."

The meanings of words in word families are influenced by their prefixes and suffixes. For example, the word *aggregate* is in the same word family *segregate*. However, their meanings are very different because the prefix *a-*, a variant of the prefix *ad-*, means toward. Thus, *aggregate* means "to bring together."

Learning about word families can help you understand unfamiliar words that have the same root. Identifying the common prefixes and suffixes applied to those roots can help you determine the meanings of unfamiliar words.

Practice and Apply Determine the root of each Critical Vocabulary word, as well as the prefix and suffix attached to it. Then, identify two more words that share the same root. Use a dictionary or online reference tool to check your work.

WORD	ROOT	PREFIX AND SUFFIX	RELATED WORDS
subservience	*serv*	*prefix: sub* *suffix: ience*	*service, conservation*
infraction	*fract*	*prefix: in* *suffix: tion*	*fracture, refract*
conceivable	*ceiv*	*prefix: con* *suffix: able*	*preconceived, receivable*

 ENGLISH LEARNER SUPPORT

Use Context Clues Direct students to use context clues to determine the connotations of words with the given prefix, suffix, or base letter combination. To determine the meaning of the prefix *con-*, first help students brainstorm a list of words using this prefix (such as *construct, convention, conversation, consult*). Then, have them think about what these words have in common—the idea of coming or bringing together. Guide students to use dictionaries and other support materials to aid in their vocabulary acquisition. **LIGHT**

LANGUAGE CONVENTIONS: Spelling

It is important to spell all words correctly when you communicate your ideas in writing. Learning basic spelling rules and checking your spelling in a dictionary will help you spell words that you may not use frequently.

Some spelling rules are for words ending in a consonant or for forming plural nouns.

Spelling Rule: In words of more than one syllable, double the final consonant when (1) the word ends with one consonant preceded by one vowel and (2) the word is accented on the last syllable.

      Example: be-gin' + ing = be-gin'ning

Spelling Rule: When a singular noun ends in *y* with a consonant before it, change the *y* to *i* and add *-es*.

      Example: army = armies

Being familiar with the basic rules of spelling will help you learn to spell unknown words. Remember that the best way to check your spelling is by using a print or online dictionary.

Practice and Apply Draft a paragraph in which you express your opinion on the excerpt from *The Warmth of Other Suns*. Use as many of the Critical Vocabulary words as possible. Check your paragraph for spelling, and use a dictionary to look up the spelling of any words you are unsure of. Then, exchange your paragraph with a partner. Edit each other's paragraphs, correcting any spelling errors.

Go to **Spelling** in the **Grammar Studio** for help.

LANGUAGE CONVENTIONS: Spelling

Using the Word Families exercise on page 802, divide students into mixed-ability groups and assign each group a word base, prefix, or suffix. Direct groups to brainstorm and attempt to spell as many related words as they can in a timed period and have groups exchange lists to check for spelling errors and review any applicable spelling rules.

Practice and Apply As students peer edit, ask them to identify at least one instance where a spelling rule helps them assess the spelling of a particular word.

The Warmth of Other Suns   803

EL ENGLISH LEARNER SUPPORT

Use Spelling Strategies Use the following supports with Spanish speakers at varying proficiency levels to improve spelling:

- Have Spanish speakers memorize common spelling differences in cognates between the two languages, such as *-tion/-cion* and *-able/-ible*. As a group, have students come up with several examples of these spelling differences. **SUBSTANTIAL**

- Have students work in pairs to create a table listing common spelling differences in Spanish and English cognates. **MODERATE**

- Have students work in pairs to search the selection for English words that have Spanish cognates. Based on these words, encourage them to make generalizations about spelling differences. **LIGHT**

COMPARE IDEAS ACROSS GENRES

Before students begin working on the diagram, review the specialized terms used to discuss genre in each category and write these terms on the board: *implicit, explicit, subjective, objective, first-person, third-person*, etc. Brainstorm other key terms students have used to talk about tone, diction, rhetorical devices, and structures for these selections. Guide students to look for more subtle comparisons between the texts, such as the role of geographical location, as well as more obvious structural comparisons.

ANALYZE THE TEXTS

Possible answers:

1. **DOK 2:** *Wilkerson outlines how life was segregated in the South for people of color by noting what was legal or illegal as well as the consequences of breaking those written (or unwritten) rules. She offers a quote from a former Alabama governor detailing the murderous intent many white southerners had for blacks despite them having done nothing wrong. Hurston's description is less about how life was in the South and more about her reaction (or non-reaction) to it. She admits that she sees that separation exists but chooses not to acknowledge it.*

2. **DOK 4:** *Although both texts would provide a useful perspective, the piece by Wilkerson provides more details and more information that could be used to develop a strong argument toward proving how unjust the treatment was.*

3. **DOK 4:** *Hurston chose to represent the difficulties of southern life for blacks and their unequal treatment through the details of her personal experiences. Wilkerson relies on factual information and examples to convey difficulties that seem more severe than anything Hurston was dealing with.*

4. **DOK 3:** *The man in Wilkerson's essay was badly beaten simply for asking for something to which he was entitled because his request broke the unwritten rule that black people were not allowed to question whites. In Hurston's essay, she brazenly approaches white visitors to her town, seemingly without expecting to be rebuked for her unabashed actions. Each passage is a good illustration of what the authors intended to communicate.*

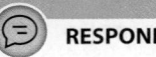 **RESPOND**

Collaborate & Compare

HOW IT FEELS TO BE COLORED ME
Essay by Zora Neale Hurston

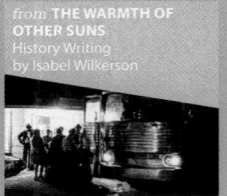
from **THE WARMTH OF OTHER SUNS**
History Writing
by Isabel Wilkerson

COMPARE IDEAS ACROSS GENRES

In "How It Feels to Be Colored Me," Hurston presents her unique perspective on facing the social and racial restrictions imposed on African American individuals in the 1920s. In the excerpt from *The Warmth of Other Suns*, contemporary journalist Wilkerson details the circumstances African Americans faced that led to the Great Migration.

Historical writing and autobiographical essays are types of informational texts that use different elements of style and present information to the audience in a distinct way. However, both texts feature similarities as well. For example, both types of writing are based on facts.

In a small group, complete the Venn diagram with similarities and differences between the selections.

"How It Feels to Be   Both   from *The Warmth*
Colored Me"   *of Other Suns*

ANALYZE THE TEXTS

Discuss these questions in your group.

1. **Compare** What are the differences between Wilkerson's and Hurston's descriptions of life in the South for African Americans? What ideas are emphasized in each text?

2. **Evaluate** Which of these texts would be more effective at convincing people that the treatment of African Americans during this time period was unacceptable? Explain your answer.

3. **Analyze** How do the Hurston essay and the excerpt from *The Warmth of Other Suns* address the difficulties of life for African Americans?

4. **Contrast** Contrast the experience of the man who asked for the receipt in paragraph 9 from *The Warmth of Other Suns* to Hurston's experience with town passersby in paragraphs 2–3 of "How It Feels to Be Colored Me." How do these passages relate to the message of each text?

 ENGLISH LEARNER SUPPORT

Compare Texts Ask students simple questions to guide them to briefly state what the texts are about, and the focus and purpose of each text. Then, have partners work to complete these frames: *Both writers _____ living in the South. Hurston emphasizes _____. Wilkerson focuses on _____. Hurston's purpose is to _____. Wilkerson's purpose is to _____. One criticism of Hurston's text is _____. Wilkerson's text helps to show _____.* **MODERATE**

COLLABORATE AND DEBATE

Now with your group, continue exploring the differences between history writing and autobiographical essays. Follow these steps:

1. **Review the first selection.** Reread "How It Feels to Be Colored Me" and determine the main idea and author's purpose for writing.

2. **Review the second selection.** Reread the excerpt from *The Warmth of Other Suns* and determine the main idea and author's purpose. Use a chart to record and synthesize the information from each selection.

SELECTION	MAIN IDEA	AUTHOR'S PURPOSE
from *The Warmth of Other Suns*	During the period of the Great Migration, people of color living in the South had to deal with a wide variety of unfair, unequal, and unethical practices just because of the color of their skin.	to outline the types of segregation seen at this time, in order to demonstrate how wrong the treatment was
"How It Feels to Be Colored Me"	No matter the hardships that life throws at her, Hurston will rise above it and follow her dreams to success.	to demonstrate that nothing can hold you back but yourself

3. **Evaluate each author's effectiveness** Determine which author was most effective at meeting her intended purpose. Consider organizational design, key ideas, and use of language in your evaluation.

4. **Debate within your group.** Split into two smaller groups, each defending one author's effectiveness. Listen actively to members of your group and ask them to clarify points you do not understand. Use logical, text-based evidence to rebut their claims and to support your own.

RESPOND

Go to **Preparing for Discussion** in the **Speaking and Listening Studio** for help.

COLLABORATE AND DEBATE

Divide students into mixed-ability groups and review strategies for sharing work and participating equally during collaborative sharing. Invite students to begin their discussions by sharing how they relate personally to the texts and guide them to take into account the differences in their experiences when debating ideas.

1. **Review the first selection.** Remind students of the annotation strategies they used earlier to determine the main idea and analyze the role of different images used to support this idea.

2. **Review the second selection.** Guide students in developing the graphic organizer to compare information from the two texts, including considerations of genre as well as subject.

3. **Evaluate each author's effectiveness.** Help students develop criteria for comparing the two authors, including how well their tone supported their purpose and the effect of the piece on the audience. Direct students to then rate each selection on these aspects and total the scores.

4. **Debate within your group.** In addition to reviewing the strategies for respecting the opinions of others, ask listening students to take notes on the views and points made by their classmates. Invite a representative from each group to share the results of the debate with the class.

WHEN STUDENTS STRUGGLE. . .

Practice Close Reading Help students identify a key passage from each text to compare directly, choosing passages that are in similar locations (introductions, conclusions) or that address similar subjects. Have students make a list of the textual features of each passage, such as narration style, tone, imagery, and topic. Ask students to choose the strongest feature of each passage and to explain their choices. Have them use these opinions to develop a thesis comparing the two writers.

 For additional support, go to the **Reading Studio** and assign the following **Level Up Tutorial: Comparison-Contrast Organization.**

© Houghton Mifflin Harcourt Publishing Company

POETRY
Poem by Marianne Moore

THE LATIN DELI
Poem by Judith Ortiz Cofer

GENRE ELEMENTS
ARS POETICA

The first **ars poetica**, or poem analyzing the nature of poetry, was written by the Latin poet Horace in the first century BCE. An *ars poetica* follows in the tradition of Horace, explaining or defining "the art of poetry." It expresses the poet's ideas about poetry while using forms and techniques salient to traditional and contemporary poems.

LEARNING OBJECTIVES

- Evaluate the use of sensory details.
- Research past versions of a poem.
- Write a compare and contrast essay about the definition of poetry.
- Present a definition of poetry with a group.
- Identify how figurative language develops theme.
- **Language** Discuss poems, using connecting words.

TEXT COMPLEXITY

Quantitative Measures	Poetry/The Latin Deli	Lexile: N/A
Qualitative Measures	**Ideas Presented** Poetry works on multiple levels with greater ambiguity and implemented meaning; some abstract ideas and demand for inferences.	
	Structures Used More complex language and poetic structure.	
	Language Used Implied meaning, allusive and figurative language along with complex sentence structures.	
	Knowledge Required Explores complex ideas with cultural and historical references that may make heavy demands.	

RESOURCES

- Unit 6 Response Log
- 🔊 Selection Audio
- 📖 Reading Studio: Notice & Note
- Level Up Tutorial: Theme; Imagery
- Writing Studio: Writing Informative Texts
- Speaking and Listening Studio: Participating in Collaborative Discussions
- ☑ "Poetry"/"The Latin Deli" Selection Test

SUMMARIES

English

"Poetry": In this poem, the speaker begins by saying that like others, she dislikes poetry, calling it "all this fiddle." Later, she also gives reasons to like poetry for its genuineness, imaginativeness, and sense of reality.

"The Latin Deli": The speaker begins by presenting a woman she calls the "Patroness of Exiles" "presiding" over a deli and all those who come there seeking some part of a home far away. It is through her, the deli, and its items (which are read from a list "like poetry") that people from Latin-American and Caribbean countries can remember the places they left.

Spanish

"Poesía": en este poema, la narradora comienza al decir que, igual que a otros, no le gusta la poesía, llamándola "todo este chanchullo". Luego, da razones para apreciar la poesía debido a su autenticidad, imaginación y sentido de la realidad. "La charcutería latina": la narradora comienza al presentar a una mujer a la que llama la "patrona de los exiliados" que "preside" sobre una charcutería y todos sus clientes, quienes buscan ahí un pedazo de su lejano hogar. A través de ella, la charcutería y sus artículos (que son leídos de una lista "como poesía") los latinoamericanos y caribeños pueden recordar los lugares que dejaron.

 ## SMALL-GROUP OPTIONS

Have students work in small groups and pairs to read and discuss the selection.

Send a Problem

- After reading both poems aloud with students, pose this question: *How can you describe the worlds within each poem?*
- Call on a student. Wait up to 11 seconds.
- If the student has no response, direct him or her to call one another student by name to answer that same question.
- Have students continue asking each other for assistance as needed. Monitor responses and ask more questions as appropriate.

Numbered Heads Together

- Break students into groups of four and assign each student a number 1-2-3-4 within that group.
- Pose the following question: *How does each poet define poetry? Which definition do you enjoy more and why?*
- Have students discuss their responses in their groups.
- Call a number 1 through 4. Those "numbered" students then respond aloud to the class.

Text X-Ray: English Learner Support
for "Poetry" by Marianne Moore and "The Latin Deli" by Judith Ortiz Cofer

Use the Text X-Ray and the supports and scaffolds in the Teacher's Edition to help guide students at different proficiency levels through the selections.

INTRODUCE THE SELECTION
DISCUSS FIGURATIVE LANGUAGE

Remind students that poems often contain figurative language, in which words are used to mean something other than their common or literal meanings. Review common types of figurative language, such as simile and metaphor, which compare two seemingly different things that are connected in some way. Provide the following sentence frame to clarify understanding:

The color of the sky is like _____.

Ask students: *What else is blue?* Have students use the sentence frame to create a simile.

Consider using visual aids of the sky and other blue items (ex: blueberries, ocean, etc.).

CULTURAL REFERENCES

The following words or phrases may be unfamiliar to students:

- *high-sounding interpretation can be put upon them* (Moore, line 7): they can be interpreted in a sophisticated way
- *raw material* (Moore, line 29): the basic substances used to make a product
- *plastic Mother and Child* (Cofer, line 2): plastic figurines representing Mary and Jesus, used to symbolize a person's Christian faith
- *Patroness of Exiles* (Cofer, line 7): a woman who supports those who have left their homelands; the phrase makes her sound like a religious figure
- *the A&P* (Cofer, line 32): a chain grocery store that used to have locations throughout the United States

LISTENING

Identify Sensory Details

Explain to students that sensory details create **imagery** in a poem. These images work to transmit the meaning of the poem. Use gestures to indicate the five senses as you read.

Reread lines 18–38 from "The Latin Deli" aloud to students. Use the following supports with students at varying proficiency levels:

- Reread lines 18–24 to students. Tell them you will ask some questions about the character depicted in the poem. Model that they should give a thumbs up if the answer is *yes* or a thumbs down for *no*. For example, ask: *Does the woman speak Spanish?* (yes) *Does she ignore her customers?* (no) **SUBSTANTIAL**
- Have students note details about the woman and the deli as you read the lines aloud. Then, have students compare notes with partners. Ask them to identify details in their notes that contain sensory imagery. **MODERATE**
- Ask students to note sensory details about the woman and the deli as you read the lines aloud. Then, have students describe their details to partners, using their own words. **LIGHT**

SPEAKING

Discuss Sensory Details

Have students discuss the concrete, sensory details in both poems. Circulate around the room to make sure students are using correct pronunciation and understand the meaning of the new vocabulary.

Use the following supports with students of varying proficiency levels:

- Display and read aloud the following sentences: *Two images in "The Latin Deli" that I can see are "ancient register" and "formica counter." Two images in "Poetry" that I can see are "elephants" and "a wild horse."* Have students repeat the sentences back to you. Clarify pronunciation. **SUBSTANTIAL**
- Instruct students to complete sentence frames to discuss the details that stand out to them. Example frame: *The images in _____ (name of poem) that I can _____ (sense) are _____ (textual evidence).* **MODERATE**
- Ask students to find imagery in each poem that addresses a sense other than sight. Have students discuss these images in pairs. **LIGHT**

READING

Identify Figurative Language

Explain to students that they will look for examples of figurative language in both poems and try to figure out what message each poet is trying to convey.

Use the following support for varying proficiency levels:

- Have students read lines 11–15 in "Poetry" and lines 34–35 in "The Latin Deli." Ask students to identify figurative language in those lines. **SUBSTANTIAL**
- Direct students to make their own Figurative Language Posters to illustrate the literal and figurative meaning of sayings in the poems. Give examples of figurative language from the poems for students to visualize. **MODERATE**
- Have students create four-column figurative language logs with the following heads: Textual Example, Literal Meaning, Intended Meaning, Connection to Real Life. Instruct students to fill in the logs as they reread the poems in pairs. **LIGHT**

WRITING

Compare and Contrast Two Poems

Work with students to read the writing assignment on Student Edition page 817.

Use the following supports with students at varying proficiency levels:

- Provide a word bank of compare/contrast connecting words and phrases, such as *likewise*, *in the same way*, *however*, and *on the other hand.* Display simple sentences and have students choose a word to complete the sentence. For example: *"Poetry" is about poems, _____ "Latin Deli" is about a person.* **SUBSTANTIAL**
- Provide sentence frames that students can use to craft their essays. For example: *Moore says that poetry is like _____, while Cofer relates poetry to _____. The images in Moore's poem are _____. However, in Cofer's poem, the images are _____.* **MODERATE**
- Work with students to create a word bank of compare/contrast connecting words and phrases. Have students refer to the word bank as they write to transition between ideas. **LIGHT**

? Connect to the ESSENTIAL QUESTION

Ask students to think about what kinds of things they consider "limits" on themselves. Encourage students to examine different types of limits—mental, social, physical, and so on. Then, ask the students if limits are necessarily negative. Have the class try and come up with a few limits that might be helpful or positive.

COMPARE THEMES

Encourage students to look for words or images that are similar or overlap between both poems. Explain that even though the poems may seem to be about different subjects, there are points of commonality between both pieces.

POEM

POETRY

by **Marianne Moore**
pages 809–811

COMPARE THEMES

As you read, notice key details and language choices that indicate each poem's theme. Consider how the poets use figurative language to develop the themes and how the themes are related to each other. After you read both poems, you will collaborate with a small group on a final project.

 ESSENTIAL QUESTION:

What would we do if there were no limits?

POEM

THE LATIN DELI: AN ARS POETICA

by **Judith Ortiz Cofer**
pages 812–815

806   Unit 6

QUICK START

What poems have you read or heard that stand out in your memory? What do you enjoy about them? Are there poems you recall that you dislike? What does poetry mean to you? Make notes in the chart below. Then, discuss your responses with a partner.

A poem I liked:	Why I liked it:
A poem I disliked:	Why I disliked it:
My definition of poetry:	

DETERMINE THEME

The two poems you will read in this section are **ars poetica,** or poems analyzing the nature of poetry. *Ars poetica* is a Latin phrase meaning "the art of poetry." The Latin poet Horace wrote a poem titled "Ars Poetica" in the first century BCE. In it, he outlined standards for poetry and the criticism of poetry. Since then, many other poets have written *ars poetica*. Understanding this unique subgenre of poetry will help you determine the **theme,** or central idea, that each poet wants to convey.

Themes are not usually stated directly, but they can be inferred from clues or evidence in the text. Evidence for a theme can include:

- words, phrases, or concepts that are repeated
- powerful images and figurative language
- the historical and/or cultural context of the poem

As you read "Poetry" and "The Latin Deli," pay attention to the ideas each poet develops over the course of her poem and how those ideas build on each other, contributing to an overall theme. Consider how each poet defines poetry.

GENRE ELEMENTS: ARS POETICA
- explains or defines the "art of poetry"
- expresses the poet's ideas about poetry
- follows the tradition of Horace's original "Ars Poetica"
- uses the forms and techniques of poetry

QUICK START

Remind students that poems are not limited to patterns of rhyming at the end of each line. Note that sound is often an important part of poetry, and that rhyming and similar sounds within lines can create a pleasing effect. Ask students to choose parts of the poem with interesting sounds. Have them look deeper into what sounds are used in these parts and discuss what effects are created by these sounds.

DETERMINE THEME

As students read for clues about theme, remind them that repetition is an important part of poetry—repetition of sounds, words, images, and even whole lines are used to create different effects. Remind students as they read to keep their eyes open for repetition on the micro level (sounds) on up to the larger conceptual level (ideas and images).

TEACH

EVALUATE FIGURATIVE LANGUAGE

Review the definitions and examples for each of the types of figurative language. Then, work together as a class to create new examples of each type of figurative language. Discuss how each example might affect the mood and tone of text. If time permits, have students work on their own to choose a single image and try to use it in each type of figurative language. For instance, a student might choose the image of the moon as a starting point for each of his or her examples.

ANNOTATION MODEL

Explain to students that in situations like the opening lines of Marianne Moore's poem, one of the things that can be confusing is determining the subject. Moore uses the pronoun "it" to refer to poetry. Although "Poetry" is the title of the poem she doesn't refer to it specifically in the initial lines of her poem. Encourage students to stop and investigate any part of the poems where the subject becomes unclear. Instruct them to look to the title and surrounding lines as clues.

GET READY

EVALUATE FIGURATIVE LANGUAGE

Poets frequently use figurative language and imagery to communicate meaning. **Figurative language** is language that has meaning beyond the literal meaning of the words. It often finds a point of similarity between two things that might at first seem completely unlike each other. If the comparison is direct, using words such as *like* or *as*, it is a **simile.** If the comparison is indirect or implied, not using *like* or *as*, it is a **metaphor.**

Imagery is language that appeals to the senses. Poets use imagery to help readers experience sights, sounds, tastes, smells, and textures so they can understand a place or an event in a vivid, sensory way. The chart shows an example of each type of figurative language from "The Latin Deli."

FIGURATIVE LANGUAGE	EXAMPLE FROM "THE LATIN DELI"
Simile: a comparison using *like* or *as*	. . . the green plantains hanging in stalks like votive offerings (lines 5–6)
Metaphor: a comparison that does not use *like* or *as*	who spends her days selling canned memories (line 9)
Imagery: words and phrases that appeal to the senses	the heady mix of smells from the open bins of dried codfish (lines 4–5)

As you read "Poetry" and "The Latin Deli," look for instances of figurative language. Consider how the poets' use of this type of language contributes to the meaning of the poem.

ANNOTATION MODEL

NOTICE & NOTE

As you read, notice details that will help you determine the theme. Note examples of figurative language that are striking to you. In the model, you can see one reader's notes about the opening lines of "Poetry."

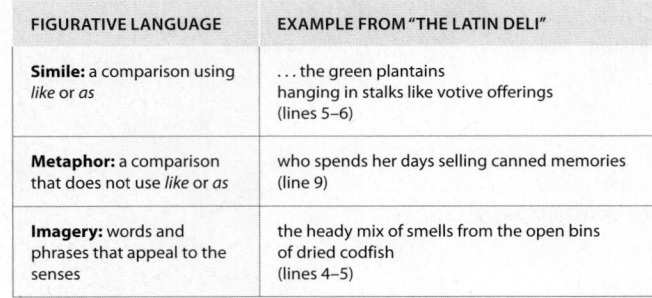

I, too, dislike it: there are things that are important beyond all this fiddle.
Reading it, however, with a perfect contempt for it, one discovers in
it after all, a place for the genuine.

> People dislike poetry because it can seem like nonsense. But poetry can express things that are genuine.

808   Unit 6

© Houghton Mifflin Harcourt Publishing Company

BACKGROUND

Marianne Moore *(1887–1972) was a true original, known for having diverse interests and an eccentric appearance when in public. In 1918 she moved to New York City where she associated with other writers, served as editor of a prestigious literary journal, and wrote poetry. A highly innovative poet, she mixed direct observation with quoted material and experimented with stanza forms and line lengths. She was awarded a Pulitzer Prize for her complex, meticulously crafted poems and was esteemed by her peers in the poetry community.*

POETRY
Poem by Marianne Moore

PREPARE TO COMPARE

As you read, pay attention to details and language that tell you how the writer would define poetry. Think about how this is related to the theme of the poem.

I, too, dislike it: there are things that are important beyond all this fiddle.[1]
    Reading it, however, with a perfect contempt for it, one discovers in
    it after all, a place for the genuine.
        Hands that can grasp, eyes
5   that can dilate, hair that can rise
            if it must, these things are important not because a

high-sounding interpretation can be put upon them but because they are
    useful. When they become so derivative[2] as to become unintelligible,
    the same thing may be said for all of us, that we
10   do not admire what
    we cannot understand: the bat
        holding on upside down or in quest of something to

---
[1] **fiddle:** *n.* slang for "nonsense."
[2] **derivative:** *adj.* copied or adapted from others.

Notice & Note

Use the side margins to notice and note signposts in the text.

DETERMINE THEME
Annotate: Mark the places in the first two stanzas where the poet states her general ideas about poetry.

Interpret: According to Moore, what makes poetry good or bad?

BACKGROUND

Marianne Moore's interests ranged from baseball to Muhammad Ali to exotic animals, which she scrutinized during her frequent trips to the zoo. Gifted with an eye for detail, she wrote precise, witty descriptions of these and other subjects. Moore was known for her unusual style of dressing, often sporting a three-cornered hat and a black cape. She was admired by many prominent imagist and Modernist poets, including T.S. Eliot.

PREPARE TO COMPARE

Direct students to use the Prepare to Compare prompt to focus their reading.

🖉 DETERMINE THEME

Encourage students to look for pronouns such as "I," "one," "these," and so on, as clues about the author's feelings and thoughts. (*Examples might include: "I, too, dislike it"; "all this fiddle"; "one discovers . . . the genuine"; "these things . . . useful"; "they become . . . unintelligible"; "we do not admire . . . cannot understand."*)

Explain that Moore uses adjectives to describe good and bad poetry. Have students note the adjectives from the first two stanzas to get a better idea of her opinions. (***Answer:*** *Good poetry is "genuine" and "useful." It describes things in a way that people understand and can relate to. Bad poetry is unoriginal and relies on people making complicated interpretations of it. It is supposed to be deep, but instead is trivial and fake because no one can really understand what it is saying.*)

TO CHALLENGE STUDENTS . . .

Evaluate Form Explain that "Poetry" is written in syllabic verse. This form appears at first glance to be free verse, but in fact is not. To explore the form, have students begin by counting the syllables in the first and last lines of each stanza. They will find 19 syllables in the first lines and 13 syllables in the last lines. Moore plays with form by varying line lengths and syllable counts in the remaining lines. Tell students that critical opinion on syllabic verse is divided and invite them to contribute to the debate by responding to these questions: *Is syllable count too arbitrary to hinge a poem upon? Can syllable count create rhythm, or does rhythm arise from other aspects of the poem?* Invite students to explain the poem's syllabic structure and their conclusions to the class.

For **speaking** and **reading support** for students at varying proficiency levels, see the **Text X-Ray** on page 806D.

NOTICE & NOTE

eat, elephants pushing, a wild horse taking a roll, a tireless wolf under
a tree, the immovable critic twitching his skin like a horse that feels a flea,
15   the baseball fan, the statistician—
          nor is it valid
              to discriminate against "business documents and

school-books"; all these phenomena are important. One must make a
20   distinction
          however: when dragged into prominence by half poets, the result is not
                                                                        poetry,

WHEN STUDENTS STRUGGLE . . .

Understand Theme Have students focus on the theme of poetry in the last stanza. Help them determine Moore's ideas about poetry. Guide students to identify and restate the two elements she says reflect an interest in poetry and connect them to her final lines:

- "the raw material of poetry" (line 29): ideas and images that produce an emotional response
- "that which . . . genuine" (lines 31–32): ideas that are clearly stated and useful

 For additional support, go to the **Reading Studio** and assign the following ᴸᴱⱽᴱᴸᵁᴾ **Level Up Tutorial: Theme.**

nor till the poets among us can be
    "literalists[3] of
25   the imagination"—above
       insolence and triviality and can present

for inspection, "imaginary gardens with real toads in them," shall we have
    it. In the meantime, if you demand on the one hand,
    the raw material of poetry in
30   all its rawness and
    that which is on the other hand
       genuine, then you are interested in poetry.

---

[3] **literalists:** *n.* people who adhere to the explicit sense of a given text or doctrine.

EVALUATE FIGURATIVE LANGUAGE

Annotate: Mark the metaphor in the last stanza.

Cite Evidence: What is the meaning of the metaphor? Explain your answer using textual evidence.

CHECK YOUR UNDERSTANDING

Answer these questions about "Poetry" before moving on to the next selection.

1 According to Moore, good poetry —

  A is genuine

  B uses complex symbols

  C is more important than other kinds of documents

  D describes trivial things in an imaginative way

2 Moore uses "a wild horse taking a roll" (line 13) as an example of —

  F a subject described as "all this fiddle" (line 1)

  G something with a "high-sounding interpretation" (line 7)

  H something that people "cannot understand" (line 11)

  J the "raw material of poetry" (line 29)

3 "Half poets" (line 21) produce work that is —

  A discriminated against by true poets

  B trivial and unimaginative

  C too raw and demanding for readers

  D less important than other types of documents

 © Houghton Mifflin Harcourt Publishing Company

EVALUATE FIGURATIVE LANGUAGE

After students have pointed out the metaphor, ask them what two contrasting ideas the metaphor is introducing. Encourage students to think about why Moore has chosen a metaphor that uses the contradictory ideas of "imaginative" and "real" to describe poetry. (**Answer:** *"Imaginary gardens with real toads in them" are poems that are imaginative but also have genuine substance. Moore contrasts these types of poems with works of "half poetry" that she views as trivial. She wants poets to be "literalists of the imagination" and describe things that are real and meaningful in imaginative ways, instead of recycling ideas and images that are hard to understand and have little real meaning.*)

■ English Learner Support

Explain Metaphors Have students list adjectives they associate with gardens and toads (examples for gardens: *beautiful, fragrant, colorful;* examples for toads: *ugly, slimy, gray*). Then, have them explain the contrast evoked by the metaphor. Encourage them to use words that highlight contrasts, such as *although, whereas, but, on the other hand.* (For example: *Gardens are beautiful, but toads are ugly. A poet should describe the beautiful and the ugly just as one should describe the imaginary and the real.*) **MODERATE**

CHECK YOUR UNDERSTANDING

Have students answer the questions independently.

Answers:

  1. *A*

  2. *H*

  3. *B*

If they answer any questions incorrectly, have them reread the text to confirm their understanding. Then they may proceed to the next selection.

 ENGLISH LEARNER SUPPORT

Oral Assessment Use the following questions to assess students' comprehension and speaking skills.

1. In Moore's opinion, what word describes good poetry? *(genuine)*

2. Is the line "a wild horse taking a roll" an example of something we *can* understand, or *cannot* understand? *(cannot understand)*

3. What is a word that Moore use to describe bad poetry? *(trivial, unimaginative)* **SUBSTANTIAL**

BACKGROUND

As students read Cofer's biography, ask them to think about the ideas of identity and background. Explain that while Marianne Moore incorporated her opinion into her poem on poetry, Cofer uses actual personal experience and details from her life as an entry point to poetry. Encourage students to think about their own backgrounds and how certain elements might be used as a starting point for a poem.

PREPARE TO COMPARE

Direct students to use the Prepare to Compare prompt to focus their reading.

✏️ EVALUATE FIGURATIVE LANGUAGE

Remind students that when they begin an essay, it is often helpful to use some sort of detail or interesting information to "hook" the reader. Students should keep this in mind as they read the opening lines to Cofer's poem. (**Answer:** *The use of rich imagery sets the mood for the entire poem. It helps readers visualize the setting and the main character and put themselves "in" the poem. By using religious imagery to describe the displays and the storekeeper, the poet establishes a reverent tone.*)

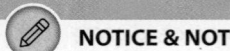

✏️ NOTICE & NOTE

BACKGROUND

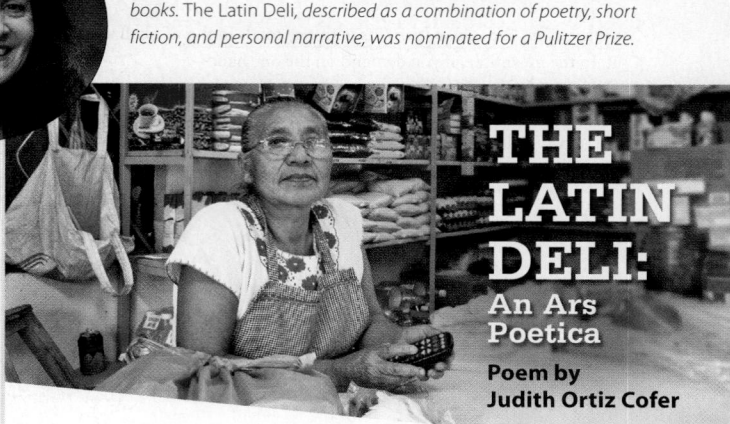

Judith Ortiz Cofer *(1952–2016) was born in Puerto Rico but moved to New Jersey at a young age. During her childhood, she traveled between Puerto Rico and the United States, and themes related to her Puerto Rican and American identities appear in her work. She wrote across multiple genres, including poetry, fiction, creative nonfiction, and children's books. The Latin Deli, described as a combination of poetry, short fiction, and personal narrative, was nominated for a Pulitzer Prize.*

THE LATIN DELI:
An Ars Poetica

Poem by Judith Ortiz Cofer

Notice & Note

Use the side margins to notice and note signposts in the text.

EVALUATE FIGURATIVE LANGUAGE

Annotate: Mark sensory details in lines 1–9.

Analyze: Why do you think the author uses rich imagery in the opening lines of the poem?

PREPARE TO COMPARE

As you read, note Cofer's use of rich imagery and figurative language. Consider why she describes the piece as an ars poetica.

Presiding over a formica counter,
plastic Mother and Child magnetized
to the top of an ancient register,
the heady mix of smells from the open bins
5 of dried codfish, the green plantains[1]
hanging in stalks like votive offerings,[2]
she is the Patroness of Exiles,
a woman of no-age who was never pretty,
who spends her days selling canned memories
10 while listening to the Puerto Ricans complain
that it would be cheaper to fly to San Juan
than to buy a pound of Bustelo coffee here,
and to Cubans perfecting their speech
of a "glorious return" to Havana—where no one
15 has been allowed to die and nothing to change until then;
to Mexicans who pass through, talking lyrically[3]
of *dólares* to be made in El Norte—

---

[1] **plantains:** type of banana.
[2] **votive offerings:** sacrifices made to fulfill a vow or offered in devotion.
[3] **lyrically:** highly enthusiastically.

WHEN STUDENTS STRUGGLE . . .

Understand Imagery To help students evaluate figurative language, note Cofer's use of imagery. Explain that her imagery is centered around specific cultural and historical references. This gives her poem a strong sense of place and background. Point out the strong imagery in the first stanza of "The Latin Deli," and show students how Cofer uses specific sensory detail to paint an image. Ask for volunteers to point out other instances of imagery in the following lines and discuss as a class what senses are being used to create that imagery.

 For additional support, go to the **Reading Studio** and assign the following 🔼 **Level Up Tutorial: Imagery.**

                    all wanting the comfort
of spoken Spanish, to gaze upon the family portrait
20 of her plain wide face, her ample bosom
    resting on her plump arms, her look of maternal interest
    as they speak to her and each other
    of their dreams and their disillusions—
    how she smiles understanding,
25 when they walk down the narrow aisles of her store
    reading the labels of packages aloud, as if
    they were the names of lost lovers: *Suspiros*,[4]

_____
[4] *suspiros* (soõs-pĕ´rōs): type of small sponge cake.

For **listening support** for students at varying proficiency levels, see the **Text X-Ray** on page 806C.

IMPROVE READING FLUENCY

Targeted Passage Read lines 1-17 of the poem aloud as a model for the students, showing how line breaks and punctuation work to create pauses in the poem. Discuss as a class the different tools used to create pauses and rhythm in the poem. Then, have students work in pairs, taking turns to read lines 18-28 aloud. Encourage students to read slowly and evenly, thinking about how the poet encourages the reader to pause or to emphasize certain words or ideas.

 Go to the **Reading Studio** for additional support in developing fluency.

DETERMINE THEME

Explain to the students that many poets believe that the mundanities of normal life can be poetic. Encourage students to zoom out from the poetic nature of the last stanza and look at the scene that is unfolding, reflecting on the motivations and desires of the customers and the woman working at the deli. (**Possible answers:** *It is important to hold on to one's culture as a part of personal identity. Shared culture is a unifying force. The beauty of everyday life can be a kind of poetry.*)

■ English Learner Support

Understand Theme Ask students to discuss "would not satisfy . . . old man." Have them identify what would not satisfy the man's hunger. Then, ask them to explain what he is really hungry for. After discussion, have students complete the frame: _____ *would not satisfy the man's hunger because he is really hungry for* _____. **MODERATE**

NOTICE & NOTE

DETERMINE THEME

Annotate: Underline words and phrases in lines 29–38 that indicate the importance of the Latin deli to its customers.

Infer: What theme or themes can you infer from these words and phrases?

Merengues,[5] the stale candy of everyone's childhood.
          She spends her days
30 slicing *jamón y queso*[6] and wrapping it in wax paper
tied with string: plain ham and cheese
that would cost less at the A&P, but it would not satisfy
the hunger of the fragile old man lost in the folds
of his winter coat, who brings her lists of items
35 that he reads to her like poetry, or the others,
whose needs she must divine, conjuring up products
from places that now exist only in their hearts—
closed ports she must trade with.

---

[5] *merengues* (mä-rän´gäs): candy made of meringue (mixture of egg whites and sugar).

[6] *jamón y queso* (khä-mōn ēkä´sō): Spanish for "ham and cheese."

© Houghton Mifflin Harcourt Publishing Company

CHECK YOUR UNDERSTANDING

Answer these questions before moving on to the **Analyze the Texts** section on the following page.

1 Who is the "Patroness of Exiles" (line 7)?

  A The poet

  B The plastic figurine on the register

  C The woman who runs the deli

  D One of the deli customers

2 How does the store owner respond to her customers' conversations?

  F By busying herself wrapping ham and cheese

  G With maternal interest and understanding

  H By gathering items on people's grocery lists

  J With disillusion and disinterest

3 Why do customers come to the Latin Deli?

  A The store owner is known for her fast service.

  B The Latin Deli has lower prices than the other stores.

  C The store owner knows the latest news from their home countries.

  D The Latin Deli has products that remind them of their childhood and homeland.

✎ CHECK YOUR UNDERSTANDING

Have students answer the questions independently.

Answers:

 1. *C*

 2. *F*

 3. *D*

If they answer any questions incorrectly, have them reread the text to confirm their understanding. Then they may proceed to ANALYZE THE TEXT on page 816.

ENGLISH LEARNER SUPPORT

Oral Assessment Use the following questions to assess students' comprehension and speaking skills.

 1. Who listens to the people from other countries and helps them (line 7)? *(the woman who runs the deli)*

 2. Does the store owner keep busy while her customers talk? *(Yes. She keeps busy wrapping ham and cheese.)*

 3. The Latin Deli has products that remind people of _____ . *(their homelands when they were children)* **SUBSTANTIAL**

ANALYZE THE TEXT

Possible answers:

1. **DOK 2:** *The speaker, like the reader, sometimes dislikes poetry but can also discover "the genuine" in poetry. Poetry can sometimes capture in an image something profoundly true and useful. "Hands that can grasp, eyes / that can dilate," and "hair that can rise" are important, not when they are used as symbols of the incomprehensible, but when they express real emotion.*

2. **DOK 4:** *Moore makes the statement as one of her lines of evidence for why people—herself included—do not always like poetry. She is implying that for poetry to be "good" and "genuine" and "useful," it must be understandable. She backs up her argument by providing a list of animals and people that are supposedly not understandable and therefore not to be admired.*

3. **DOK 4:** *The indents break the flow of the poem just enough to signal the content. The first 17 lines of the poem set the environment, the tone, and the mood. They describe the store, its owner, and patrons in rich but general terms. Beginning at line 18, the poet describes the customers and owner in more detail, indicating a common bond they share, no matter what country they are from. At line 29, the poet focuses specifically on the store owner, her actions, and her unique role in the community.*

4. **DOK 3:** *The poet calls a detailed description of an everyday scene an ars poetica. Even though she does not directly analyze poetry, the poem's subject is presented with rich imagery that evokes a response in the reader, just as poetry does. The reader can infer that the poet sees poetry as something that goes beyond words on a page and includes real-life and "ordinary" experiences that engage the senses and trigger thoughts and memories.*

5. **DOK 3:** *The voice in "The Latin Deli" is that of an insightful observer. Students' choices of similes and metaphors will vary, but their answers should explain how each simile or metaphor contributes to the poem's meaning.*

RESEARCH

Remind students to use quotation marks and try different wording combinations to help search for specific information as they research.

Extend Guide students to discuss what is lost and/or gained in the longer and shorter versions of Moore's poem. Encourage them to keep this discussion in mind as they develop their answers about Cofer's poem.

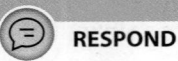 **RESPOND**

ANALYZE THE TEXTS

Support your responses with evidence from the text. NOTEBOOK

1. **Summarize** Reread and summarize lines 1–11 of "Poetry." What is important about "Hands that can grasp, eyes / that can dilate, hair that can rise"?

2. **Critique** Why does Moore make the statement "we do not admire what we cannot understand?" Explain whether the statement effectively supports her theme.

3. **Analyze** Note extremely indented lines 18 and 29 of "The Latin Deli." How do these oddities of form help to organize the ideas in the poem? Explain.

4. **Draw Conclusions** "The Latin Deli" is subtitled "An Ars Poetica," but poetry itself is only mentioned once and the poem does not directly analyze poetry as a form of writing. How might the subject of the poem be related to poetry? Does the author effectively express an idea about poetry in the poem? Explain.

5. **Evaluate** In addition to rich imagery, "The Latin Deli" contains several similes and metaphors. Choose one simile or metaphor, and discuss how it contributes to the meaning of the poem.

RESEARCH

RESEARCH TIP
When searching for very specific information, consider using more specific search terms. For this research project, a search term such as "Marianne Moore poetry" may not yield the most relevant results. Include more detailed descriptors such as "final version" to yield better results.

The version of Marianne Moore's "Poetry" you read in this section was not her final version of the poem. Over the course of several decades, Moore revised and re-revised the poem. The shortest version she ever published was only three lines long; it was published alongside the longer version you read here. Complete the chart with details about "Poetry."

QUESTION	ANSWER
When were the 29-line and 3-line versions of "Poetry" published?	*29-line version: 1924* *3-line version: 1967*
Besides length, what were the primary differences in content between the two versions?	*does not contain all imagery and metaphors; only the first 3 lines of the longer version*
What do the differences between the 29-line poem and the final 3-line version tell you about Moore's theme and purpose for writing?	*theme and purpose did not change; 3 lines explicitly state her main point; poetry should be genuine and truthful, not lost in interpretations*

Extend Moore was heavily criticized for having altered "Poetry" so drastically. Nonetheless, she successfully condensed the main theme in the shortened form. Could the same be done with "The Latin Deli"? Consider the theme(s) presented by Cofer and the way in which she develops the theme(s). Explain why you do or do not believe that Cofer's poem could be shortened while still keeping its meaning. If you believe it can be shortened, describe how.

WHEN STUDENTS STRUGGLE . . .

Reteach: Figurative Language Remind students that **imagery** is when language is used to evoke the reader's senses. For example, in "The Latin Deli," the narrator paints a vivid picture of the deli and its customers by using visual, auditory, and taste related descriptions.

To reinforce the students' understanding of imagery, guide them in finding other examples in "Poetry" and "The Latin Deli." Then, discuss with students the senses used and whether the descriptions are effective in conveying strong images to the reader.

For additional support, go to the **Reading Studio** and assign the following [LEVEL] **Level Up Tutorial: Imagery.**

CREATE AND DISCUSS

Write a Compare-and-Contrast Essay Compose a three- to five-paragraph essay comparing and contrasting the definitions of poetry presented in "Poetry" and "The Latin Deli."

❏ Think about each poem's primary theme and any secondary themes you may have identified.

❏ Consider why both poems are considered *ars poetica*. How does each poet incorporate the elements of that particular subgenre of poetry?

❏ Analyze how each poet's use of figurative language and/or line breaks and poem structure contributes to their definitions.

Discuss Your Findings With a small group, discuss your conclusions about the themes of the poems.

❏ Allow group members to present key similarities and/or differences they noted in their essays.

❏ Ask group members to clarify any key points from their essays that you do not understand and to cite evidence explaining their positions.

❏ Determine as a group whether you believe that the definitions/ explanations of poetry offered by the two poets are in agreement or not.

 Go to **Writing Informative Texts: Organizing Ideas** in the **Writing Studio** for help with comparison-contrast writing.

 Go to **Participating in Collaborative Discussions** in the **Speaking and Listening Studio** for help.

RESPOND TO THE ESSENTIAL QUESTION

? What would we do if there were no limits?

Gather Information Review your annotations and notes on "Poetry" and "The Latin Deli." Then, add relevant information to your Response Log. As you determine which information to include, think about:

• What are the limits of, or criteria for, poetry?

• In what ways do the two poems "push the limits" of poetry?

• How important are rules, or limits, to poetry as a genre?

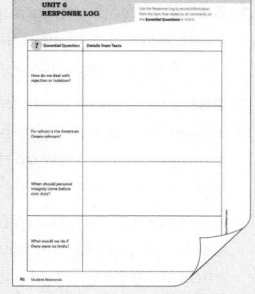

ACADEMIC VOCABULARY
As you write and discuss what you learned from the poems, be sure to use the Academic Vocabulary words. Check off each of the words that you use.

❏ **contemporary**
❏ **global**
❏ **infinite**
❏ **simulated**
❏ **virtual**

CREATE AND DISCUSS

Write a Compare-and-Contrast Essay Encourage students to plan the topics of each paragraph before they begin writing the main drafts of their essays. Remind them that each paragraph should focus on one particular topic, and that topic should be clearly detailed in the first sentence or two of the paragraph. Explain that the instructions ask for three main points to be hit, but those points could be broken down into smaller pieces (i.e. students might choose to focus two paragraphs on figurative language: one on imagery, and one on simile/metaphor).

 For **writing support** for students at varying proficiency levels, see the **Text X-Ray** on page 806D.

Discuss Your Findings As they discuss, encourage students to share their thoughts on the poets' definitions of poetry, and to add their own opinions about what else may or may not be used to define poetry. Have students try and go deeper into the authors' definitions, examining what ideas this brings up in their own thoughts about poetry.

RESPOND TO THE ESSENTIAL QUESTION

Allow time for students to add details from "Poetry" and "The Latin Deli" to their Unit 6 Response Logs.

COMPARE THEMES

As students fill out their charts, encourage them to brainstorm a list of repeated or connected images in each of the poems. Remind students that images might have certain things in common that are not necessarily obvious, and that looking for the connections between images in a poem can help highlight the themes.

ANALYZE THE TEXTS

Possible answers:

1. **DOK 3:** *Cofer uses memorable images much more than important statements. Her poetry is less concise and the themes are not as apparent, but she creates a scene that the reader can become part of. Moore tends to make important statements more often. She then supports or explains the important statements with memorable images.*

2. **DOK 4:** *Moore's use of role of critic gives a sense of authority to her poetic voice. She develops her theme directly, stating a critical position that may at first seem surprising coming from a poet. She is able to use the dual role of poet and critic to give added support to her main points about the value of poetry as a genre. Cofer draws on her cultural heritage, using rich descriptions of a scene and characters that she has observed to develop her theme of the poetry in everyday life.*

3. **DOK 4:** *Moore and Cofer do not offer traditional definitions of poetry as a genre of strict forms, rhyme schemes, and elevated language and symbolism. They manipulate line lengths and stanzas to suit their messages and use language and images that are not intended to be difficult to understand, supporting Moore's definition of poetry as the expression of genuine concepts in an imaginative way and Cofer's definition of poetry as something intangible that is revealed in daily life and ordinary people.*

4. **DOK 3:** *Moore's interpretation is more effective because it is stated directly. Cofer's interpretation of poetry is more difficult to understand because it is not directly stated and is one of several themes that she develops at the same time.*

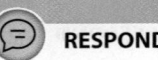
RESPOND

Collaborate & Compare

POETRY
Poem by
Marianne Moore

**THE LATIN DELI:
AN ARS POETICA**
Poem by Judith Ortiz Cofer

COMPARE THEMES

Both "Poetry" and "The Latin Deli" are *ars poetica*. Even though both poems explore the nature of poetry, they may express different themes, or central messages. Sometimes a poem may express more than one theme.

Poets usually do not state themes directly, but you can infer the theme by analyzing key details. Key details include important statements and memorable images that appear in the poem. With your group, complete the chart with key details from both poems. Identify at least two of each type of key detail.

	"POETRY"	"THE LATIN DELI"
Important Statements	*[Poetry] is a place for the genuine.*	*would not satisfy the hunger of . . . old man*
	we do not admire what we cannot understand	*they speak of . . . dreams and their disillusions*
Memorable Images	*a wild horse taking a roll*	*heady mix of smells from open bins*
	a tireless wolf under a tree	*the stale candy of everyone's childhood*

ANALYZE THE TEXTS

Discuss these questions in your group.

1. **Compare** With your group, review the key details you cited in your chart. How are the ways the poets use important statements and memorable images the same? How are they different?

2. **Analyze** Moore speaks from the perspective of a literary critic, and Cofer speaks from the perspective of someone with more than one ethnic and cultural identity. How does the social context of each poet affect their poetic voices and the way they develop their themes?

3. **Connect** How are the definitions of poetry offered by Moore and Cofer similar to or different from other definitions of poetry you have encountered?

4. **Evaluate** Either directly or indirectly, both poets express their ideas about how poetry is, or should be, defined. Which poet's interpretation of poetry is more effective or meaningful?

ENGLISH LEARNER SUPPORT

Analyze Poetry Have students work in pairs, using the following questions to help analyze and interpret the two selections. First, have students discuss the questions orally. Then, have each pair work together to write a short paragraph answering the questions. Review students' writing with them, offering suggestions for varied vocabulary and sentence structure.

1. What is a major theme in each of the two poems? What images can you point to that support this theme?

2. What are some ways that these two poems are similar? How do they differ? **LIGHT**

COLLABORATE AND PRESENT

In your group, continue to explore the ideas in the poems by comparing their themes to enhance your understanding of the definition of poetry. Follow these steps:

1. **Determine relevant themes.** With your group, review your chart and responses to the analysis questions to identify themes from each poem that help define poetry. You may also include each group members' ideas from the compare and contrast essays you completed individually. Identify themes you agree on as a group.

2. **Compare and contrast ideas about poetry.** Using the themes you identified as a guide, compare and contrast the poets' definitions of and ideas about poetry. Remember that you used key details to infer the themes. You can use a chart to organize your ideas.

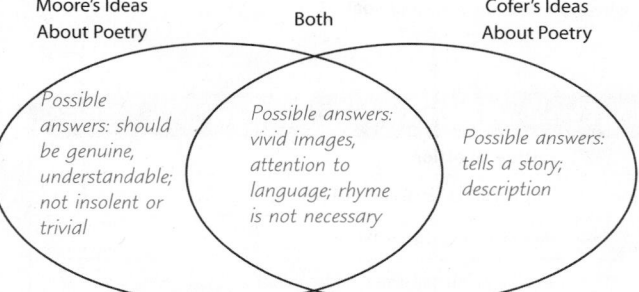

Moore's Ideas About Poetry

Both

Cofer's Ideas About Poetry

Possible answers: should be genuine, understandable; not insolent or trivial

Possible answers: vivid images, attention to language; rhyme is not necessary

Possible answers: tells a story; description

3. **Create a definition.** In your group, discuss the similarities and differences between Moore's and Cofer's ideas as identified in your chart. Decide whether you agree with their definitions or parts of their definitions. Consider, too, whether their definitions are complete or whether you would include other elements in a definition of poetry based on your experiences with the genre. As a group, craft a working definition of poetry.

4. **Present to the class.** Present your group's definition of poetry to the class. Be sure to discuss the definitions of Moore and Cofer and how the themes introduced in their poems contributed to your group's understanding and definition of poetry. You may choose to create a visual aid to convey your definition to the class.

Go to **Delivering Your Presentation** in the **Speaking and Listening Studio** for help.

COLLABORATE AND PRESENT

Remind students that poetic themes are not always obvious, and that there is some room for interpretation. Encourage students to look beyond the surface of the poems and explore the figurative language and underlying ideas that each author deals with.

1. **Determine relevant themes.** Encourage students to let each group member speak. Have students engage in active discussion, supporting their choices of themes and working together to choose which themes to include in the chart.

2. **Compare and contrast ideas about poetry.** As students fill out their diagrams, remind them to consider and discuss the details of each similarity and difference to dig deeper into the nuances of the poems.

3. **Create a definition.** Urge students to brainstorm their own ideas about poetry and what defines it on paper before creating a group definition. As students consider the elements of the authors' definitions, encourage them to add their own details and ideas about what makes something a poem or not.

4. **Present to the class.** Remind students to give each person in the group a chance to engage in the presentation, whether through giving the audience information or providing support for visual aids.

WHEN STUDENTS STRUGGLE . . .

Reteach: Analyze Theme Students may struggle with the concept of theme. Explain that a theme is an underlying idea, image, or message in a piece of writing. Give examples of themes from some popular works, such as the themes of family and sacrifice in the Harry Potter books. Then, ask students to name themes in books or films, and discuss them as a class. Finally, ask students what ideas they get from reading the two poems. Help students connect specific passages and ideas, such as cultural identity, present in each of the poems.

For additional support, go to the **Reading Studio** and assign the following **Level Up Tutorial: Theme.**

INDEPENDENT READING

READER'S CHOICE

Setting a Purpose Have students review their Unit 6 Response Logs and think about what they've already learned about the connections, spaces, and walls between people in a society. As they choose their Independent Reading selections, encourage them to consider what more they want to know.

NOTICE & NOTE

Explain that some selections may contain multiple signposts; others may contain only one. And the same type of signpost can occur many times in the same text.

LEARNING MINDSET

Grit Encourage students to adopt flexible thinking patterns. Tell them flexible people don't see problems; they see opportunities. Offer praise for students' efforts or strategies, not for getting something right.

INDEPENDENT READING

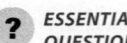 **ESSENTIAL QUESTIONS**

Review the four Essential Questions for this unit on page 569.

Reader's Choice

Setting a Purpose Select one or more of these options from your eBook to continue your exploration of the Essential Questions.

- Read the descriptions to see which text grabs your interest.
- Think about which genres you enjoy reading.

NOTICE & NOTE

In this unit, you practiced noticing and noting the signposts and asking big questions about nonfiction. As you read independently, these signposts and others will aid your understanding. Below are the anchor questions to ask when you read literature and nonfiction.

Reading Literature: Stories, Poems, and Plays	
Signpost	**Anchor Question**
Contrasts and Contradictions	Why did the character act that way?
Aha Moment	How might this change things?
Tough Questions	What does this make me wonder about?
Words of the Wiser	What's the lesson for the character?
Again and Again	Why might the author keep bringing this up?
Memory Moment	Why is this memory important?

Reading Nonfiction: Essays, Articles, and Arguments	
Signpost	**Anchor Question(s)**
Big Questions	What surprised me? What did the author think I already knew? What challenged, changed, or confirmed what I already knew?
Contrasts and Contradictions	What is the difference, and why does it matter?
Extreme or Absolute Language	Why did the author use this language?
Numbers and Stats	Why did the author use these numbers or amounts?
Quoted Words	Why was this person quoted or cited, and what did this add?
Word Gaps	Do I know this word from someplace else? Does it seem like technical talk for this topic? Do clues in the sentence help me understand the word?

 ENGLISH LEARNER SUPPORT

Develop Fluency Select a passage from the text that matches students' reading abilities. Read the passage aloud while students follow along silently.

- Have students go through the passage and underline words that are similar to words in their native languages and circle words they do not know. Then, have them use a bilingual dictionary to look up the marked words before reading the passage on their own. Check their comprehension by asking yes/no questions about the passage.
SUBSTANTIAL

- Have student pairs go through the passage and mark words they do not know, then look them up. Then, have them take turns explaining the meanings of new words to each other before reading the passage. Check their comprehension by asking questions about the passage.
MODERATE

- Allow more fluent readers to select their own texts. Set a specific time for them to read silently, such as 30 minutes. To check their comprehension, have them write a summary of what they have read.
LIGHT

You can preview these texts in Unit 6 of your eBook.

Then, check off the text or texts that you select to read on your own.

POEMS

**Poems of the
Harlem Renaissance**
Langston Hughes, Jean Toomer,
Countee Cullen, and Arna Bontemps

*What concerned the writers
of the Harlem Renaissance?
Read poems by four of its
prominent members.*

ESSAY

**Martin Luther King Jr.:
He Showed Us the Way**
César Chávez

*Find out why César Chávez
believes that King's form of
protest is the only way to
achieve meaningful change.*

ESSAY

Mother Tongue
Amy Tan

*Discover how a best-selling
novelist learned to appreciate
the expressiveness of her
mother's imperfect English.*

SHORT STORY

Reality Check
David Brin

*Explore the ways humans
may continue to evolve when
all concrete possibilities have
been exhausted.*

ARTICLE

**YouTube Stars Stress Out, Just
Like the Rest of Us**
Neda Ulaby

*Discover why life as a
YouTube celebrity is not all it's
cracked up to be.*

Collaborate and Share With a partner discuss what you learned from at least
one of your independent readings.

- Give a brief synopsis or summary of the text.
- Describe any signposts that you noticed in the text and explain what they revealed to you.
- Describe what you most enjoyed or found most challenging about the text. Give specific examples.
- Decide if you would recommend the text to others. Why or why not?

 Go to the **Reading Studio**
for more resources on
Notice & Note.

WHEN STUDENTS STRUGGLE . . .

Keep a Reading Log As students read their selected texts, have them keep a reading log for
each selection to note signposts and their thoughts about them. Use their logs to assess how
well they are noticing and reflecting on elements of their texts.

Reading Log for (title)		
Location	**Signpost I Noticed**	**My Notes about It**

MATCHING STUDENTS TO TEXTS

Use the following information to guide students in choosing
their texts.

**Poems of the Harlem
Renaissance**
    Genre: poems
    Overall Rating: Accessible

**Martin Luther King Jr:
He Showed Us the Way**   **Lexile: 1120L**
    Genre: essay
    Overall Rating: Accessible

Mother Tongue   **Lexile: 1120L**
    Genre: essay
    Overall Rating: Accessible

Reality Check   **Lexile: 920L**
    Genre: short story
    Overall Rating: Accessible

**YouTube Stars Stress Out,
Just Like the Rest of Us**   **Lexile: 1160L**
    Genre: Article
    Overall Rating: Accessible

Collaborate and Share To assess how well students
read the selections, walk around the room and listen to
their conversations. Encourage students to be focused and
specific in their comments.

Online
 Ed **for Assessment**

- Independent Reading Selection Tests

 Encourage students to visit the **Reading Studio** to
download a handy bookmark of **NOTICE & NOTE**
signposts.

UNIT 6 Task

• WRITE A PERSONAL ESSAY

MENTOR TEXT

HOW IT FEELS TO BE COLORED ME

Essay by Zora Neale Hurston

LEARNING OBJECTIVES

Writing Task

- Write a personal essay that answers an Essential Question.
- Synthesize information from one or more texts.
- Interact with textual evidence to express personal experience in society.
- Develop a clear thesis.
- Use personal experiences to explain textual evidence.
- Write using Standard English grammar and punctuation.
- Plan, draft, revise, and edit an essay.
- Use sensory language to help the reader visualize.
- **Language** Write an engaging introduction.

Assign the Writing Task in *Ed.*

Online

RESOURCES

- Unit 6 Response Log
- Writing Studio: Writing Informative Texts
- Reading Studio: Revising to Add Supporting Details
- Grammar Studio: Commas with Introductory Elements

Language X-Ray: English Learner Support

Use the instruction below and the supports and scaffolds in the Teacher's Edition to help you guide students at different proficiency levels.

INTRODUCE THE WRITING TASK

Reread the writing task with students. Explain that students must respond to both a quotation from a text *and* an Essential Question, using personal examples.

Provide students with a bank of quotations from various texts in the unit that relate to the Essential Questions. Use a Think-Pair-Share

and ask students: *What do these quotations mean to you?* Then, ask students to connect each quotation from the quotation bank to one of the four Essential Questions of the unit.

WRITING

Create an Engaging Introduction

Remind students that an effective personal essay can engage readers by presenting a conflict, situation, or observation. Explain to students that an introduction should both interest readers in the topic and preview what the essay will be about.

Use the following supports with students at varying proficiency levels:

- Have students think of personal stories that might include some conflict or that involve an interesting situation. Then, have each student create a set of labeled pictures that tell his or her personal story. **SUBSTANTIAL**
- Provide the following paragraph outline to help students craft their introductions:
  I. Hook: personal experience (2–3 sentences)
  II. Respond to Essential Question (1 sentence)
  III Introduce textual quotation (1 sentence)
  IV. Thesis or main idea of essay (1 sentence) **MODERATE**
- Instruct students to revise their introductions to include imagery that engages the reader. Have students find three places in their introductions where they can add sensory details. **LIGHT**

WRITING

WRITE A PERSONAL ESSAY

Introduce students to the Writing Task by reading the introductory paragraph with them. Remind students to refer to the notes they recorded in their Unit 6 Response Logs as they plan and draft their personal essays. The Response Logs should address the connections, spaces, and walls between people in a society. Drawing on their personal experiences will make their own writing more interesting and well informed.

 For **writing support** for students at varying proficiency levels, see the **Language X-Ray** on page 822B.

USE THE MENTOR TEXT

Point out that students' personal essays will be similar to the essay "How It Feels to Be Colored Me" in that they will relate something about their own personal experiences in society. However, their essays will be shorter than Hurston's and will address one or more of the Essential Questions from their own perspectives.

WRITING PROMPT

Review the prompt with students. Encourage them to ask questions about any part of the assignment that is unclear. Make sure they understand that the purpose of their personal essays is to explore one or more of the Essential Questions from their own perspectives.

■ English Learner Support

Learn New Expressions Point out to students that the topic in the Writing Prompt uses architectural terms in a figurative way. Here, the verb *bridge* means "to connect" or "to reduce the distance between." And the phrase *break down walls* as used in the Writing Prompt means "to improve understanding between people with different opinions." Restate the Writing Prompt in a simpler way, such as "Telling your personal story can help you make connections and improve how people understand each other or have different opinions." **ALL LEVELS**

 WRITING TASK

Write a Personal Essay

Go to **Writing as a Process** in the **Writing Studio** for help writing a personal essay.

This unit focuses on the connections, spaces, and walls between people in a society. Many of the selections are personal in nature because each person makes different connections, explores or avoids certain spaces, and builds or tears down walls between themselves and others, depending on their place in society. For this writing task, you will write a personal essay that synthesizes information from one or more of the texts and is connected to one of the Unit Essential Questions. For an example of a well-written personal essay you can use as a mentor text, review Zora Neale Hurston's personal essay "How It Feels to Be Colored Me."

As you write your essay, use the notes from your Response Log.

Writing Prompt

Read the information in the box below.

This is the topic or context for your personal essay.

> Telling your personal story is a way to make new connections, bridge spaces, and break down walls.

Think about how the writers in this unit explored the Essential Questions.

How do your own experiences and the unit selections give you insight into these Essential Questions?

> How do we deal with rejection or isolation?
> For whom is the American Dream relevant?
> When should personal integrity come before civic duty?
> What would we do if there were no limits?

How can you use a personal essay to explore how a quotation has deep meaning for you?

Did a particular author write something that made you think more deeply about your own sense of self? **Write** a personal essay in which you interact with a quotation from one of the selections. Explain how this quotation helps you express something true about your own experience in a society.

Be sure to—

Review these points as you write and again when you finish. Make any needed changes.

- ❏ Introduce the thesis of your personal essay by quoting the writer.
- ❏ Use examples and personal experiences to explain and elaborate on the quotation and what it means to you.
- ❏ Use transitions so your readers can follow your train of thought.
- ❏ Conclude by summing up your overall message and offering final insight.

 LEARNING MINDSET

Asking for Help Encourage students to ask their peers, teachers, or parents for help when they need it. Explain that asking for help from others can help them get "unstuck" and move forward. Rather than equaling failure, seeking help is a way of "trying smarter."

1 Plan

Before you start writing, you need to plan your essay. First, review your notes from the unit's selections. Discuss with a partner the following questions:

- Which authors did you feel "spoke" to you? What specific ideas and words stayed in your mind?
- Which quotations from the unit seem to have significance for you or relate to your own experience?

Now choose a quotation. Write the quotation in the top row of the chart. Add the source information. Use the blank space to do a freewriting exercise called a "mind map." Begin with a key word (or a few) from the quotation. Write the key word in the center of the space below and circle it. Take 15 minutes or so to add additional words and phrases, extending from this one word. These can be images, moments of significance in your life, and other experiences that you associate with the key word.

Personal Essay Mind Map

Quotation:

Source of Quotation:

WRITING TASK

Go to **Writing as a Process: Planning and Drafting** for more help.

Notice & Note

From Reading to Writing

As you plan your personal essay, apply what you've learned about signposts to your own writing. Remember that writers use common features, called signposts, to help convey their message to readers.

Think how you can incorporate **Signposts** into your essay.

Go to the **Reading Studio** for more resources on **Notice & Note**.

Use the notes from your Response Log as you plan your personal essay.

UNIT 6
RESPONSE LOG

1 PLAN

Allow time for students to review the selections in Unit 6 and compile lists of interesting quotations that might serve as springboards for their essays. Suggest students use graphic organizers, such as charts, to record the quotations that speak to them. Next, have them consider the relevance of each quotation to the Essential Questions and to their own experiences and choose the ones that they think will best suit their purposes.

NOTICE & NOTE

From Reading to Writing

Remind students to think about how they can use signposts in their personal essays. One of the signposts they will use is **Quoted Words**, since quotations will serve as the springboards for their essays. Students can also use Quoted Words to provide support for points they are trying to make. Remind students to format their direct quotations correctly and to give credit to the sources.

Background Reading As they plan their essays, remind students to refer to the notes they took in the Response Log. They may also review the selections to find additional facts and examples to support ideas they want to include in their writing.

TO CHALLENGE STUDENTS . . .

Connect Art to Theme Challenge each student to find an image—either a photograph, painting, drawing, or other visual representation—that reflects the theme of his or her essay. Encourage students to look at their own photographs or artwork they have created, or to look through museum websites and online photo archives. For example, the work of such artists as Picasso, Escher, or Goya includes images that support a theme about the individual in society. After students have chosen and obtained prints of their images, form small groups to discuss the relationships between the images and the narratives. Suggest that each student cite text evidence from the narrative to help explain why the image represents the theme.

WRITING

Organize Your Ideas Remind students that the introductions to their personal essays should begin with an interesting anecdote or quotation that leads into the thesis statement. The thesis statement should indicate how the quotation relates to their main ideas. To help students organize their ideas, suggest that they review the Essential Questions and their Response Logs. By thinking about the details and examples they have gathered, students can select the best way to organize them clearly and logically. They may devote several paragraphs to a main idea and supporting examples or experiences, but they should remember to start a new paragraph for each main idea. The conclusion should follow logically from the thesis and should convey a reflection on the experiences students have described in their essays.

② DEVELOP A DRAFT

Remind students to follow their graphic organizers as they draft their essays, but point out that they can still make changes to their writing plan during this stage. As they write, they may discover they need a different example to support an idea or that a particular detail belongs in a different paragraph. They may also find they need to revise their thesis statement or develop a stronger conclusion.

■ English Learner Support

Express Ideas To help students learn to express themselves more fluently, suggest that English learners use words or phrases from their home language when they cannot think of the correct words or phrases in English. **SUBSTANTIAL**

 **WRITING TASK**

 Go to **Writing Informative Texts: Organizing Ideas** for more help.

Organize Your Ideas Look at your mind map and find ideas and experiences that come through strongly. You will use these for your personal essay, but you must organize them in a way that will help you draft the essay. First, develop a strong thesis statement. Clearly state the message you want your personal essay to convey, and explain how this connects to your selected quotation. Next, list main ideas that relate to and explain your message, along with supporting examples and experiences. Then, list some ideas for your concluding section. You can use the chart below to map out the organizational structure of your essay.

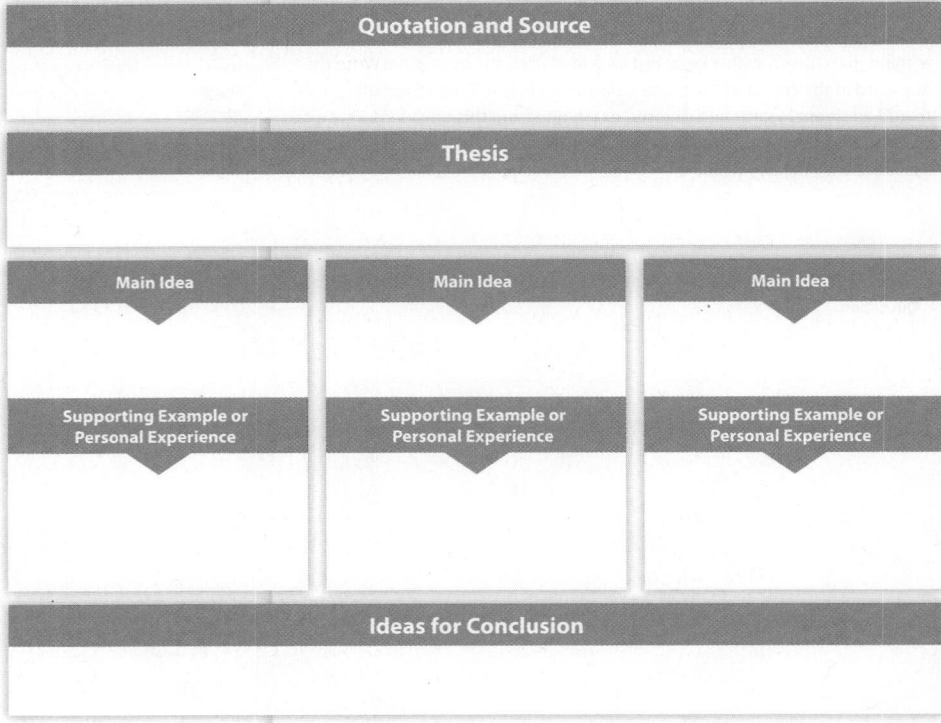

② Develop a Draft

 You might prefer to draft your essay online.

Once you have completed your planning activities, you will be ready to begin drafting your personal essay. Refer to your graphic organizers as well as any notes you took as you studied the texts in this unit. These will provide a kind of map for you to follow as you write. Using a word processor or online writing application makes it easier to make changes or move sentences around later when you are ready to revise your first draft.

WHEN STUDENTS STRUGGLE . . .

Develop a Draft Use the following ideas to help struggling writers develop their drafts: Suggest visual learners draw memories of the experiences they will discuss. Remind students to write in languages that reflect their own voices. Suggest that students have peers read their drafts. Encourage students to add sensory details when revising. Remind students to include their thoughts, feelings, and observations.

 For additional support, go to the **Reading Studio** and assign the following **LEVEL Up Tutorial: Revising to Add Supporting Details.**

Use the Mentor Text

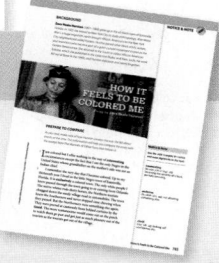

WRITING TASK

Essay Structure

A personal essay reflects the author's mind and outlook and often has a unique structure as a result. One essay may be tightly focused; another may meander. But every detail is relevant, whether the writer uses narrative, compare and contrast, chronology, or a combination. Notice how Hurston uses various structures to express her perspective on the world.

> No one on earth ever had a greater chance for glory. The world to be won and nothing to be lost. . . .
>
> The position of my white neighbor is much more difficult. . . . The game of keeping what one has is never so exciting as the game of getting.

Hurston shows her sense of self as someone who has nothing to lose, in contrast to those who have much and so always fear losing it.

Apply What You've Learned Consider how you could use comparisons to strengthen your main ideas. Can you contrast being alone to being part of a group, or being in a natural setting to being in a city? What contrasts might help you address the important distinctions between the self, society, and nature?

Style and Voice

One purpose of a personal essay is to let the writer's unique perspective shine. An author's writing style is the vehicle for his or her voice, or writing personality. Notice how Zora Neale Hurston lets her own voice come through loud and clear.

> Sometimes, I feel discriminated against, but it does not make me angry. It merely astonishes me. How can any deny themselves the pleasure of my company! It's beyond me.

Hurston's short sentences and informal language let her personality come through.

Apply What You've Learned How can you let your personality shine through in your writing? Think of how you naturally talk. Consider your unique personality traits. Now read through your essay and find places you can insert a little spark of yourself. Note this in your graphic organizer.

WHY THIS MENTOR TEXT?

"How It Feels to Be Colored Me" provides a strong example of a personal essay. Use the instructions below to help students use the mentor text as a model for writing personal essays from their own unique perspectives and in their own voices.

USE THE MENTOR TEXT

Essay Structure Ask a volunteer to read aloud paragraphs 1 and 2 of Hurston's essay on page 783. Then, guide the class in analyzing the structure of Hurston's essay using the following questions:

- How does the first paragraph help set the tone?
- What is the basic structure of the essay?
- What is Hurston's thesis?
- What are her main ideas, and how do they relate to her thesis? How does she support those ideas?
- How does Hurston use literary devices, such as figurative language, to express her thoughts or ideas?

Tell students to use what they learned from this activity as they write and revise their own essays.

Style and Voice Point out that **style** is the distinctive way in which something is written. Style refers not so much to what is said but how it is said. Unlike other types of essays with which students may be more familiar, a personal essay is meant to be informal and to convey the writer's unique voice. The term **voice** refers to a writer's unique use of language that allows a reader to "hear" his or her personality. The elements of style that determine a writer's voice include sentence structure, diction, and tone. Personal essays, like Hurston's, are often written in the first person, helping give readers the impression that the writer is speaking to them. Reread the example and ask students what makes Hurston's style or voice unique. What do they "hear"?

© Houghton Mifflin Harcourt Publishing Company

 ENGLISH LEARNER SUPPORT

Understand Academic Language To help students understand the instructions for this writing activity, introduce the following vocabulary:

- *insight:* ideas that make a topic clearer
- *narrative:* writing that tells of a personal event or a series of events
- *chronological:* the order in which events occur

- *structure:* the way a literary work is put together
- *perspective:* a particular point of view or way of looking at things
- *transition:* a word or phrase that helps make a logical connection between sentences or paragraphs   **ALL LEVELS**

WRITING

3 REVISE

Project a draft essay and model how to use the questions, tips, and revision strategies suggested in the chart to evaluate and revise. Then, have students answer each question in the chart to determine how they can improve their drafts.

With a Partner Have students ask peer reviewers to evaluate their personal essays by answering the following questions:

- Does my quotation tie in with my thesis?
- Do all of my main points support my thesis?
- Are all of my main points well supported by examples or personal experiences?
- Are there any examples or personal experiences that don't seem to fit?
- Does the essay seem as though it could have been written by anyone, or does it reflect my personality?

Remind students that in peer reviews they should offer positive, constructive responses to each other's writing. Students should use the reviewers' feedback to help them revise their essays.

 WRITING TASK

 Go to **Writing as a Process: Revising and Editing** for help making your personal essay stronger.

3 Revise

On Your Own Once you have written your draft, you'll want to go back and look for ways to improve your personal essay. As you reread and revise, think about whether you have achieved your purpose. The Revision Guide will help you focus on specific elements to make your writing stronger.

Revision Guide

Ask Yourself	Tips	Revision Techniques
1. Does my introduction engage the reader and establish a clear connection between the chosen quotation and my own experience?	**Highlight** sentences that get the audience interested. **Underline** the connection between your experience and the chosen quotation.	**Add** vivid language and details to interest the reader. **Reword** your introduction to **clarify** the connection.
2. Do I present relevant details and examples to support my central idea(s) and make my message understood?	**Highlight** each central idea. **Underline** examples and details that support each idea and **note** any ideas that seem unsupported.	**Add** examples and explanations for any idea that is not strongly supported. **Delete** ideas and examples that are not relevant to your main points.
3. Is my essay logically organized with smooth transitions linking ideas and evidence?	**Note** major sections that reflect your organization. **Underline** each transitional word or phrase.	**Reorder** paragraphs if needed. **Add** transitions to **clarify** relationships between ideas.
4. Do I use language that is appropriate to the purpose and audience?	**Highlight** language that seems out of place—either too formal or too informal for the purpose and audience.	**Reword** text for a more consistent style.
5. Does my conclusion follow logically from the ideas I present?	**Note** where the conclusion summarizes your ideas and drives home your message.	**Add or reword** your conclusion if needed to sum up your essay's main message.

ACADEMIC VOCABULARY
As you conduct your **peer review,** be sure to use these words.
- ❏ contemporary
- ❏ global
- ❏ infinite
- ❏ simulated
- ❏ virtual

With a Partner Once you and your partner have worked through the Revision Guide on your own, exchange personal essays and evaluate each other's draft in a **peer review.** Focus on providing revision suggestions for at least three of the items mentioned in the chart. Explain why you think your partner's draft should be revised and what your specific suggestions are.

When receiving feedback from your partner, listen attentively and ask questions to make sure you fully understand the revision suggestions.

© Houghton Mifflin Harcourt Publishing Company

 ## ENGLISH LEARNER SUPPORT

Understand Personal Essays and Pronouns Explain to students that personal essays differ from other kinds of informative or persuasive essays. In a personal essay, writers usually address their own experiences, thoughts, and feelings, often using the first-person voice and less formal language. In other kinds of essays, such as persuasive essays, writers try to convince readers to adopt a certain view. In informative essays, writers inform readers about a topic. Review first-person pronouns (*I, my, mine*) and how to use them. Give examples of your thoughts or experiences to model how to use first-person pronouns in a personal essay.
ALL LEVELS

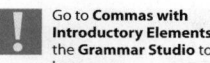

4 Edit

Once you have addressed the organization, development, and flow of ideas in your personal essay, you can look to improve the finer points of your draft. Edit for the proper use of standard English conventions, and make sure to correct any misspellings or grammatical errors.

> ! Go to **Commas with Introductory Elements** in the **Grammar Studio** to learn more.

Language Conventions

Sensory Language Sensory language appeals to the five senses and helps the reader visualize what the writer describes. Using sensory language is an effective way of communicating your unique perspective because you can help the reader see things though your eyes and share your experiences in powerful ways.

EXAMPLES FROM TEXT	EFFECT OF SENSORY LANGUAGE
The native whites <u>rode dusty horses,</u> the Northern tourists <u>chugged down the sandy village road</u> in automobiles.	The sensory language emphasizes the contrast between the native whites and the Northern tourists as they move down the road.
For instance, when I sit in the <u>drafty basement</u> that is The New World Cabaret with a white person, my color comes.	The sensory language helps readers feel what it is like to sit and watch The New World Cabaret.
It <u>constricts the thorax and splits the heart</u> with its tempo and narcotic harmonies. This orchestra grows rambunctious, <u>rears on its hind legs</u> and attacks the tonal veil with primitive fury, <u>rending it, clawing it</u> until it breaks through to the jungle beyond.	The sensory language in this section helps readers feel the euphoria of the music and its effect on the writer. The reader can more fully enter the experience of the author when she describes it in such vivid ways.

5 Publish

Finalize your personal essay and choose a way to share it with your audience. Consider these options:

- Present your essay as a speech or video recording.
- Post your essay as a blog on a classroom or school website.

WHEN STUDENTS STRUGGLE . . .

Use Sensory Language To help students recognize sensory language, suggest they go through *How It Feels to Be Colored Me* and mark all of the examples of sensory language they find. Then, have them identify which sense each example appeals to. When they finish, ask volunteers to share their examples with the class. Then, have students work together to review their essays and find places where they can add sensory language.

 For additional support, go to the **Reading Studio** and assign the following [LEVEL UP] **Level Up Tutorial: Revising to Add Supporting Details.**

---

4 EDIT

Suggest that students read their drafts aloud to assess how clearly and vividly they have presented their ideas. Tell them to look for places where they can use sensory language to help create images in their readers' minds.

LANGUAGE CONVENTIONS

Sensory Language Point out that sensory language appeals to the senses of sight, sound, touch, smell, or taste. Adding adjectives and using concrete nouns can help readers imagine what something looks like, sounds like, feels like, smells like, or tastes like. Writers can also use figurative language, such as similes and metaphors to make comparisons between ideas. When Hurston tells us that the orchestra "rears on its hind legs," she is using a metaphor to compare it to a jungle animal. This metaphor continues to the end of the sentence. Review the examples in the chart. Elicit other examples from students.

■ English Learner Support

Use Sensory Language To help students recognize sensory language, give them ten minutes to list as many adjectives for each of the five senses as they can think of. Students can also draw pictures and write phrases that describe the pictures. Provide the following examples to start with:

    sight—radiant, foamy

    sound—clinking, wheezing

    feeling—bumpy, oily

    smell—earthy, pungent

    taste—sweet, bitter **MODERATE/LIGHT**

5 PUBLISH

Provide students with other options for presenting their narratives. Encourage them to submit their stories to an online literary journal or to collect the narratives and publish a class book of essays on the topic of the individual and society.

WRITING

USE THE SCORING GUIDE

Allow students time to read the scoring guide and to ask questions about any words, phrases, or ideas that are unclear. Then have partners exchange final drafts of their personal essays. Ask them to score their partner's essay using the scoring guide. Each student should write a paragraph explaining the reasons for the score he or she awarded in each category.

Use the scoring guide to evaluate your personal essay.

Writing Task Scoring Guide: Personal Essay			
	Organization/Progression	**Development of Ideas**	**Use of Language and Conventions**
4	• The organization is effective and logical throughout the essay. • Transition words and phrases effectively link related ideas and examples.	• The introduction engages the reader's attention and includes a thesis statement that clearly identifies the connection between the writer and a quotation. • The topic is strongly developed with relevant ideas, details, and examples from experience. • The concluding section supports the ideas presented.	• The writing reflects a consistent style. • Language is vivid and precise. • Sentence structures vary and have a rhythmic flow. • Spelling, capitalization, and punctuation are correct. • Grammar and usage are correct.
3	• The organization is confusing in a few places. • Transitions are needed in a few places to link related ideas and examples.	• The introduction could do more to arouse the reader's curiosity; the thesis statement identifies the connection between the writer and a quotation from the unit. • One or two key points could use additional support in the form of relevant ideas, vivid details, and examples from experience. • The concluding section mostly supports the ideas presented.	• The style is inconsistent in a few places. • Vague language is used in a few places. • Sentence structures vary somewhat. • Some spelling, capitalization, and punctuation mistakes occur. • Some grammatical and usage errors are repeated in the essay.
2	• The organization is confusing in some places and often doesn't follow a pattern. • More transition words and phrases are needed throughout to link ideas and examples.	• The introduction provides some information about a topic but does not include a clear connection between the writer and a quotation from the unit. • Most key points need additional support in the form of relevant ideas, vivid details, and examples from the writer's own experience. • The concluding section is confusing and does not follow from the ideas presented.	• The style is often inconsistent. • Vague, general language is used in many places. • Sentence structures barely vary, and some fragments or run-on sentences are present. • Spelling, capitalization, and punctuation are often incorrect but do not make reading difficult. • Grammar and usage are incorrect in many places, but the writer's ideas are still clear.
1	• A logical organization is not used; information is presented randomly. • Transitions are not used, making the essay difficult to understand.	• The appropriate elements of an introduction are missing. • Relevant ideas, vivid details, and examples from the writer's own experience are missing. • The essay lacks an identifiable concluding section.	• The style and tone are inappropriate for the essay. • Language is too vague or general to convey the information. • Repetitive sentence structure, fragments, and run-on sentences make the writing difficult to follow. • Spelling, capitalization, and punctuation are incorrect throughout. • Many grammatical and usage errors change the meaning.

Reflect on the Unit

By completing your personal essay, you have created a writing product that pulls together and expresses your thoughts about the reading you have done in this unit. Now is a good time to reflect on what you have learned.

Reflect on the Essential Questions

- Review the four Essential Questions on page 569. How have your answers to these questions changed in response to the texts you've read in this unit?

- Which selections showed how people deal with rejection or isolation?

- Where is the balance between personal integrity and civic duty?

- Which selection had the most insightful perspective on the American Dream?

Reflect on Your Reading

- Which selections were the most interesting or surprising to you?

- What are some examples from the texts you've read that show connections between people? Spaces between people? Walls between people?

Reflect on the Writing Task

- What difficulties did you encounter while working on your personal essay? How might you avoid them next time?

- What part of the personal essay was the easiest and hardest to write? Why?

- What improvements did you make to your personal essay as you were revising?

UNIT 6 SELECTIONS
- "A Rose for Emily"
- "Mending Wall"
- *The Crucible*
- The Crucible Production Images
- "My Dungeon Shook: Letter to My Nephew"
- Speech on the Vietnam War, 1967
- "Ambush"
- "The Universe as Primal Scream"
- "How It Feels to Be Colored Me"
- from *The Warmth of Other Suns*
- "Poetry"
- "The Latin Deli: An Ars Poetica"

Reflect on the Unit   829

REFLECT ON THE UNIT

Have students reflect on the questions independently and write some notes in response to each one. Then, have students meet with partners or in small groups to discuss their reflections. Circulate during these discussions to identify the questions that are generating the liveliest conversations. Wrap up with a whole-class discussion focused on these questions.

LEARNING MINDSET

Self-Reflection Explain to students that an important part of developing a learning mindset is the ability to recognize strengths and weaknesses. As students reflect on the unit, encourage them to ask themselves these questions: *Did I ask questions if I needed help? Did I review my work for possible errors? Am I proud of the work I turned in?*

HMH |

Student Resources

Response Logs R1

Using a Glossary R7

Pronunciation Key R7

Glossary of Academic Vocabulary R8

Glossary of Critical Vocabulary R9

Index of Skills R14

Index of Titles and Authors R22

Acknowledgments R23

 **HMH** *Into Literature* **Studios**

For more instruction and practice,
visit the HMH *Into Literature* Studios.

 Reading Studio

 Writing Studio

 Speaking & Listening Studio

 Grammar Studio

 Vocabulary Studio

UNIT 1
RESPONSE LOG

Use this Response Log to record information from the texts that relates to or comments on the **Essential Questions** in Unit 1.

? Essential Question	Details from Texts
Why are we bound to certain places?	
What motivates people to explore the unknown?	
What does it mean to be a stranger in a strange land?	
What happens when cultures collide?	

UNIT 2
RESPONSE LOG

Use this Response Log to record information from the texts that relates to or comments on the **Essential Questions** in Unit 2.

? Essential Question	Details from Texts
What does oppression look like?	
How do we gain our freedom?	
How can we share power and build alliances?	
How do we transform our lives?	

© Houghton Mifflin Harcourt Publishing Company

R2   Student Resources

R2   Student Resources

UNIT 3
RESPONSE LOG

Use this Response Log to record information from the texts that relates to or comments on the **Essential Questions** in Unit 3.

? Essential Question	Details from Texts
In what ways do we seek to remain true to ourselves?	
How do we relate to the world around us?	
What do we secretly fear?	
When should we stop and reflect on our lives?	

UNIT 4
RESPONSE LOG

Use this Response Log to record information from the texts that relates to or comments on the **Essential Questions** in Unit 4.

? **Essential Question**	**Details from Texts**
When is self-determination possible?	
What divides us as human beings?	
How do we face defeat?	
What is the price of progress?	

UNIT 5
RESPONSE LOG

Use this Response Log to record information from the texts that relates to or comments on the **Essential Questions** in Unit 5.

? Essential Question	Details from Texts
To what degree do we control our lives?	
Why do humans cause harm?	
What are the consequences of change?	
What makes a place unique?	

© Houghton Mifflin Harcourt Publishing Company

UNIT 6
RESPONSE LOG

Use this Response Log to record information from the texts that relates to or comments on the **Essential Questions** in Unit 6.

? Essential Question	Details from Texts
How do we deal with rejection or isolation?	
For whom is the American Dream relevant?	
When should personal integrity come before civic duty?	
What would we do if there were no limits?	

Using a Glossary

A glossary is an alphabetical list of vocabulary words. Use a glossary just as you would a dictionary—to determine the meanings, parts of speech, pronunciation, and syllabification of words. (Some technical, foreign, and more obscure words in this book are defined for you in the footnotes that accompany many of the selections.)

Many words in the English language have more than one meaning. This glossary gives the meanings that apply to the words as they are used in the selections in this book.

The following abbreviations are used to identify parts of speech of words:

adj. adjective   *adv.* adverb   *n.* noun   *v.* verb

Each word's pronunciation is given in parentheses. A guide to the pronunciation symbols appears in the Pronunciation Key below. The stress marks in the Pronunciation Key are used to indicate the force given to each syllable in a word. They can also help you determine where words are divided into syllables.

For more information about the words in this glossary or for information about words not listed here, consult a dictionary.

Pronunciation Key

Symbol	Examples	Symbol	Examples	Symbol	Examples
ă	pat	m	mum	ûr	urge, term, firm, word, heard
ā	pay	n	no, sudden* (sŭd´n)	v	valve
ä	father	ng	thing	w	with
âr	care	ŏ	pot	y	yes
b	bib	ō	toe	z	zebra, xylem
ch	church	ô	caught, paw	zh	vision, pleasure, garage
d	deed, milled	oi	noise	ə	about, item, edible, gallop, circus
ĕ	pet	ŏŏ	took		
ē	bee	ōō	boot	ər	butter
f	fife, phase, rough	ŏŏr	lure		
g	gag	ôr	core	**Sounds in Foreign Words**	
h	hat	ou	out		
hw	which	p	pop	KH	*German* ich, ach; *Scottish* loch
ĭ	pit	r	roar	N	*French,* bon (bôn)
ī	pie, by	s	sauce	œ	*French* feu, œuf; *German* schön
îr	pier	sh	ship, dish		
j	judge	t	tight, stopped	ü	*French* tu; *German* über
k	kick, cat, pique	th	thin		
l	lid, needle* (nēd´l)	*th*	this		
		ŭ	cut		

*In English the consonants *l* and *n* often constitute complete syllables by themselves.

Stress Marks

The relative emphasis with which the syllables of a word or phrase are spoken, called stress, is indicated in three different ways. The strongest, or primary, stress is marked with a bold mark (´). An intermediate, or secondary, level of stress is marked with a similar but lighter mark (´). The weakest stress is unmarked. Words of one syllable show no stress mark.

GLOSSARY OF ACADEMIC VOCABULARY

adapt (ə-dăpt´) *v.* to make something suitable for a particular situation; to adjust to an environment.

ambiguous (ăm-bĭg´yōō-əs) *adj.* open to more than one interpretation.

analogy (ə-năl´ə-jē) *n.* a similarity in some respects between things that are otherwise dissimilar or a comparison based on such similarity.

clarify (klăr´ə-fī) *v. tr.* to make clear or easier to understand.

coherent (kō-hîr´ənt) *adj.* holding together in an orderly, logical, or consistent way.

confirm (kən-fôrm´) *v.* to support or establish the certainty or validity of; verify.

contemporary (kən-tĕm´pə-rĕr-ē) *adj.* belonging to the same period of time; of about the same age; current or modern.

contrary (kŏn´trĕr-ē) *adj.* opposite or opposed in character or purpose.

definitely (dĕf´ə-nĭt-lē) *adv.* in a clearly defined manner; explicitly precisely; decidedly.

denote (dĭ-nōt´) *tr. v.* to mark; indicate; to serve as a symbol or name for the meaning of; signify.

deny (dĭ-nī´) *tr. v.* to declare untrue; assert to be false; to refuse to believe.

device (dĭ-vīs´) *n.* something made for a specific purpose; a literary technique used to achieve a certain effect.

displace (dĭs-plās´) *v.* to move or force from one place or position to another.

dynamic (dī-năm´ĭk) *adj.* characterized by change, movement, or activity.

format (fôr´măt) *n.* a plan for the organization and arrangement of a specified production.

founder (foun´dər) *n.* someone who sets up, establishes, or provides the basis for something.

global (glō´bəl) *adj.* spherical in shape; worldwide; total.

ideological (ī-dē-ə-lŏj´ĭ-kəl) *adj.* based on ideas, beliefs, or doctrines.

implicit (ĭm-plĭs´ĭt) *adj.* implied or understood though not directly expressed.

infinite (ĭn´fə-nĭt) *adj.* having no boundaries or limits; immeasurably great or large.

publication (pŭb-lĭ-kā´shən) *n.* the act of making public in printed or electronic form; the product of this act.

quote (kwōt) *v.* to repeat or copy words from a source such as a book usually with an acknowledgment of the source; to give a quotation; *n.* a quotation.

revise (rĭ-vīz´) *v. intr.* to alter or edit; to reconsider and change or modify.

revolution (rĕv-ə-lōō´shən) *n.* the overthrow and replacement of a government, often through violent means.

simulated (sĭm´yə-lā-tĭd) *adj.* made in resemblance of or as a substitute for another; performed or staged in imitation of a real event or activity.

somewhat (sŭm´wŏt, -hwŏt, -wŭt, -hwŭt) *adv.* to some extent or degree.

topic (tŏp´ĭk) *n.* the subject of a speech, essay, discussion, or conversation.

unify (yōō´nə-fī) *v.* to make into or become a unit; consolidate.

unique (yōō-nēk´) *adj.* being the only one of its kind; remarkable or extraordinary.

virtual (vûr´chōō-əl) *adj.* existing or resulting in essence or effect though not in actual form; existing in the mind.

GLOSSARY OF CRITICAL VOCABULARY

abandonment (ə-băn´dən-měnt) *n.* a lack of restraint or inhibition.

abdicate (ăb´dĭ-kāt) *v.* to relinquish or cede responsibility for.

abhor (ăb-hôr´) *v.* to regard with horror or loathing; detest.

abject (ăb´jĕkt) *adj.* miserable and submissive.

abstraction (ăb-străk´shən) *n.* something that is not part of the concrete, material world.

acrid (ăk´rĭd) *adj.* unpleasantly sharp, pungent, or bitter to the taste or smell.

adamant (ăd´ə-mənt) *adj.* inflexible and insistent, unchanging.

affect (ə-fĕkt´) *v.* to cause or influence.

affluence (ăf´lōō-əns) *n.* wealth.

anomalous (ə-nŏm´ə-ləs) *adj.* unusual.

apprehension (ăp-rĭ-hĕn´shən) *n.* fear or anxiety; dread.

archaic (är-kā´ĭk) *adj.* relating to, being, or characteristic of a much earlier period.

artifice (är´tə-fĭs) *n.* a clever means to an end.

atrocious (ə-trō´shəs) *adj.* evil or brutal.

augment (ôg-mĕnt´) *v.* to make (something already developed or well underway) greater, as in size, extent, or quantity.

automation (ô-tə-mā´shən) *n.* the automatic operation or control of equipment, a process, or a system.

avert (ə-vûrt´) *v.* to turn away.

belatedly (bĭ-lā´tĭd-lē) *adv.* done too late or overdue.

bravado (brə-vä´dō) *n.* a show of bravery or defiance, often in order to make a false impression or mislead someone.

cabal (kə-băl´) *n.* a group united in a secret plot.

calamity (kə-lăm´ĭ-tē) *n.* an event that brings terrible loss or lasting distress.

caliber (kăl´ə-bər) *n.* level of ability.

capacity (kə-păs´ĭ-tē) *n.* ability to hold or have something; function or role.

cardinal (kär´dn-əl) *adj.* most important; prime.

catalyst (kăt´l-ĭst) *n.* a substance, usually used in small amounts relative to the reactants, that modifies and increases the rate of a reaction without being consumed in the process.

cede (sēd) *v.* to yield or give away.

circumlocution (sûr-kəm-lō-kyōō´shən) *n.* the use of unnecessarily wordy language.

circumvent (sûr´kəm-vənt) *v.* to avoid or get around by artful maneuvering.

clave (klāv) *v. Archaic* past tense of *cleave:* to cling; to adhere.

codify (kŏd´ĭ-fī) *v.* to arrange or systematize.

compelled (kəm-pĕld´) *v.* forced (a person) to do something; drove or constrained.

composed (kəm-pōzd´) *adj.* self-possessed; calm.

conceivable (kən-sēv´ə-bəl) *adj.* formed or developed in the mind.

configuration (kən-fĭg-yə-rā´shən) *n.* arrangement of parts or elements.

conjure (kŏn´jər) *v.* to influence or effect by or as if by magic.

conquistador (kŏng-kē´stə-dôr, kŏn-kwĭs´tə-dôr) *n.* a 16th-century Spanish soldier-explorer who took part in the defeat of the Indian civilizations of Mexico, Central America, or Peru.

consolation (kŏn´sə-lā´shən) *n.* act of giving comfort.

constitute (kŏn´stĭ-tōot) *v.* to amount to; equal.

GLOSSARY OF CRITICAL VOCABULARY

contrive (kən-trīv´) *v.* to plan skillfully; to design.

contrived (kən-trīvd´) *adj.* obviously planned or calculated; not spontaneous or natural.

conventional (kən-vĕn´shə-nəl) *adj.* based on or in accordance with general agreement, use, or practice; customary.

copious (kō´pē-əs) *adj.* extensive.

defection (dē-fĕkt´shŭn) *n.* the abandonment of one social or political group in favor of another.

delicacy (dĕl´ĭ-kə-sē) *n.* something pleasing and appealing, especially a choice food.

delinquency (dĭ-lĭng´kwən-sē) *n.* shortcoming or misbehavior.

delinquent (dĭ-lĭng´kwənt) *adj.* failing to do what law or duty requires.

demurred (dĭ-mûrd´) *v.* disagreed politely or politely refused to accept a request or suggestion.

deprecate (dĕp´rĭ-kāt) *v.* to express disapproval.

deprive (dĭ-prīv´) *v.* to keep from possessing or enjoying; deny.

diligence (dĭl´ə-jəns) *n.* consistent, thorough effort and dedication.

discord (dĭs´kôrd) *n.* disagreement or conflict.

disposed (dĭ-spōzd´) *adj.* having a preference, disposition, or tendency.

disposition (dĭs-pə-zĭsh´ən) *n.* character or temperament.

distinction (dĭ-stĭngk´shən) *n.* difference in quality.

divers (dī´vərz) *adj.* various; several.

efface (ĭ-fās´) *tr. v.* to rub or wipe out; erase.

elusive (ĭ-loo´sĭv) *adj.* difficult to define.

emblem (ĕm´bləm) *n.* an identifying mark or symbol.

engross (ĕn-grōs´) *v.* to completely engage the attention or interest.

eradicate (ĭ-răd´ĭ-kāt) *v.* tear up by the roots; eliminate.

establish (ĭ-stăb´lĭsh) *v.* to formally set up; institute.

estrangement (ĭ-strănj´mənt) *n.* the condition of being detached or withdrawn; alienation.

evince (ĭ-vĭns´) *v.* to reveal or give evidence of.

eviscerate (ĭ-vĭs´ə-rāt) *v.* to remove the necessary or important parts of.

exclusive (ĭk-skloo´sĭv) *adj.* not allowing something else.

expedience (ĭk-spē´dē-əns) *n.* a self-interested means to an end.

expedition (ĕk-spĭ-dĭsh´ən) *n.* a journey, especially a difficult or hazardous one, undertaken after extensive planning and with a definite objective in mind.

extenuating (ĭk-stĕn´yoo-ā-tĭng) *adj.* serving to make a fault or an offense seem less serious.

extortionist (ĭk-stôr´shən-ĭst) *n.* one who obtains something by force or threat.

extremity (ĭk-strĕm´ĭ-tē) *n.* the outermost or farthest point or portion; the hand or foot.

façade (fə-säd´) *n.* false or misleading appearance.

facile (făs´əl) *adj.* easy to make or understand.

felicity (fĭ-lĭs´ĭ-tē) *n.* great happiness.

ferry (fĕr´ē) *v.* to transport (people or goods) by vehicle.

fixed (fĭkst) *adj.* firmly in position; stationary.

flotilla (flō-tĭl´ə) *n.* a fleet of small water craft.

formidable (fôr´mĭ-də-bəl) *adj.* difficult and intimidating.

frantically (frăn´tĭ-kəl-lē) *adv.* excitedly, with strong emotion or frustration.

gape (gāp, găp) *intr. v.* to stare wonderingly or stupidly, often with the mouth open.

grope (grōp) *v.* to reach about uncertainly; feel one's way.

illumination (ĭ-loo-mə-nā´shən) *n.* awareness or enlightenment.

imperative (ĭm-pĕr´ə-tĭv) *adj.* of great importance; essential.

GLOSSARY OF CRITICAL VOCABULARY

impertinent (ĭm-pûr´tn-ənt) *adj.* rude; ill-mannered.

impunity (ĭm-pyōō´nĭ-tē) *n.* exemption from punishment, penalty, or harm.

inclination (ĭn-klə-nā´shən) *n.* a characteristic disposition or tendency to act in a certain way; a propensity.

incorrigible (ĭn-kôr´ĭ-jə-bəl) *adj.* incapable of being reformed or corrected.

indeterminate (ĭn-dĭ-tûr´mə-nĭt) *adj.* not precisely known.

indigenous (ĭn-dĭj´ə-nəs) *adj.* native to a land.

induced (ĭn-dyōōst´) *v.* led or moved, as to a course of action, by influence or persuasion.

ineffable (ĭn-ĕf´ə-bəl) *adj.* beyond description; inexpressible.

infinitesimal (ĭn-fĭn-ĭ-tĕs´ə-məl) *adj.* immeasurably or incalculably minute.

infraction (ĭn-frăk´shən) *n.* the act or instance of infringing, as of a law or rule; a violation.

ingenious (ĭn-jēn´yəs) *adj.* having great inventive skill and imagination.

inhumanity (ĭn-hyōō-măn´ĭ-tē) *n.* lack of pity or compassion.

insuperable (ĭn-sōō´pər-ə-bəl) *adj.* impossible to overcome.

insurgency (ĭn-sûr´jən-sē) *n.* rebellion or revolt.

intangible (ĭn-tăn´jə-bəl) *adj.* unable to be defined or understood.

interminable (ĭn-tûr´mə-nə-bəl) *adj.* seemingly endless.

internalize (ĭn-tûr´nə-līz) *v.* to take in and make an integral part of one's attitudes or beliefs.

invest (ĭn-vĕst´) *v.* to grant or endow.

lucid (lōō´sĭd) *adj.* easily understood.

malign (mə-līn´) *tr. v.* to make evil, harmful, and often untrue statements about (someone).

metaphysical (mĕt-ə-fĭz´ĭ-kəl) *adj.* based on speculative or abstract reasoning.

miscellany (mĭs´ə-lā-nē) *n.* a collection of various items, parts, or ingredients, especially one composed of diverse literary works.

mitigate (mĭt´ĭ-gāt) *v.* to lessen.

narcotic (när-kŏt´ĭk) *adj.* inducing sleep or stupor; causing narcosis.

noblesse oblige (nō-blĕs´ ō-blēzh´) *n.* the responsibility of people in a high social position to behave in a noble fashion.

oblige (ə-blīj´) *v.* to compel or require (someone) to do something.

obstinacy (ŏb´stə-nə-sē) *n.* stubbornness.

ostensibly (ŏ-stĕn´sə-blē) *adv.* apparently.

ostentatious (ŏs-tĕn-tā´shəs) *adj.* conspicuous and vulgar.

panic (păn´ĭk) *n.* sudden, overpowering feeling of fear.

parity (păr´ĭ-tē) *n.* equality, being equivalent.

patent (păt´nt) *n.* an official document granting ownership.

pathos (pā´thŏs) *n.* something that evokes pity or sympathy.

peril (pĕr´əl) *n.* imminent danger.

pertinacity (pûr-tn-ăs´ĭ-tē) *n.* firm, unyielding intent.

perturbation (pûr-tər-bā´shən) *n.* disturbance or agitation.

pigmentation (pĭg-mən-tā´shən) *n.* coloration of tissues by pigment.

platoon (plə-tōōn´) *n.* a subdivision of a company of troops consisting of two or more squads or sections and usually commanded by a lieutenant.

plausibility (plô-zə-bəl´ĭ-tē) *n.* likelihood; believability.

pliable (plī´ə-bəl) *adj.* easily bent or shaped; easily influenced, persuaded, or controlled.

poignant (poin´yənt) *adj.* physically or mentally painful.

GLOSSARY OF CRITICAL VOCABULARY

polarity (pō-lăr´ĭ-tē) *n.* separation to opposite sides.

ponder (pŏn´dər) *tr. v.* to think about (something) with thoroughness and care.

posse (pŏs´ē) *n.* a group of civilians temporarily authorized by officials to assist in pursuing fugitives.

postulate (pŏs´chə-lāt) *v.* to assume or assert the truth, reality, or necessity of, especially as a basis of an argument.

presaging (prĕs´ĭj-ĭng) *adj.* predicting.

pristine (prĭs´tēn) *adj.* pure or unspoiled.

project (prə-jĕkt´) *v.* to communicate or put forth.

proposition (prŏp-ə-zĭ´shən) *n.* a plan suggested for acceptance; a proposal.

prostrate (prŏs´trāt) *adj.* lying down with the head facing downward.

protrude (prō-trōōd´) *v.* to stick out or bulge.

provision (prə-vĭzh´ən) *n.* food supply.

provocation (prŏv-ə-kā´shən) *n.* the act of provoking or inciting.

recalcitrant (rĭ-kăl´sĭ-trənt) *adj.* uncooperative and resistant of authority.

reckless (rĕk´lĭs) *adj.* acting or done with a lack of care or caution.

reckoning (rĕk´ə-nĭng) *n.* a settlement of accounts.

recompense (rĕk´əm-pĕns) *n.* payment in return for something, such as a service.

regenerate (rĭ-jĕn´ə-rāt) *v.* to form, construct, or create anew.

regimen (rĕj´ə-mən) *n.* a system or organized routine of behavior.

remunerative (rĭ-myōō´nər-ə-tĭv) *adj.* bringing in money or profit.

reparations (rĕp-ə-rā´shəns) *n.* compensation or payment from a nation for damage or injury during a war.

rudiment (rōō´də-mənt) *n.* basic form.

sceptical (skĕp´tĭ-kəl) *adj.* marked by or given to doubt; questioning.

segregated (sĕg´rĭ-gāt-əd) *adj.* separated; isolated.

sentiment (sĕn´tə-mənt) *n.* a thought, view, or attitude, especially one based mainly on emotion instead of reason.

settlement (sĕt´l-mənt) *n.* a small community in a sparsely populated area.

sliver (slĭv´ər) *n.* a small narrow piece, portion, or plot.

specter (spĕk´tər) *n.* a ghostly apparition; a phantom.

stem (stĕm) *intr. v.* to have or take origin or descent.

stoically (stō´ĭk-lē) *adv.* without showing emotion or feeling.

straits (strāts) *adj.* a position of difficulty, distress, or extreme need.

strive (strīv) *v.* to struggle or fight forcefully; contend.

subservience (səb-sûr´vē-əns) *n.* the condition of being subordinate in capacity or function.

summarily (sə-mĕr´ə-lē) *adv.* quickly and without ceremony.

sundry (sŭn´drē) *adj.* various or assorted.

superfluous (sōō-pûr´flōō-əs) *adj.* unnecessary.

supplant (sə-plănt´) *v.* to take the place of.

supposition (sŭp-ə-zĭsh´ən) *n.* the act of supposing; a belief or assumption.

systematize (sĭs´tə-mə-tīz) *v.* to form something into an organized plan or scheme.

tableau (tăb´lō) *n.* a dramatic scene or picture.

tepid (tĕp´ĭd) *adj.* lukewarm; indifferent.

tidings (tī´dĭngs) *pl. n.* information or news.

timid (tĭm´ĭd) *adj.* lacking self-confidence; shy.

transient (trăn´zē-ənt) *adj.* temporary; short-term.

transition (trăn-zĭsh´ən) *n.* process of change.

trifling (trī´flĭng) *adj.* frivolous; inconsequential.

GLOSSARY OF CRITICAL VOCABULARY

truculent (trŭk´yə-lənt) *adj.* eager for a fight; fierce.

tumultuous (to͞o-mŭl´cho͞o-əs) *adj.* stormy, intense.

tyrannical (tĭ-răn´ĭ-kəl) *adj.* characteristic of a tyrant or tyranny; despotic and oppressive.

unalienable (ŭn-āl´yə-nə-bəl) *adj.* impossible to be taken away.

unassailable (ŭn-ə-sā´lə-bəl) *adj.* undeniable.

undulation (ŭn-jə-lə´shən, ŭn-dyə-, -də-) *n.* a regular rising and falling or movement to alternating sides; movement in waves.

unfathomed (ŭn-făth´əmd) *adj.* located at the deepest place.

unimpeded (ŭn-ĭm-pēd´əd) *adj.* not delayed or obstructed in its progress.

unremitting (ŭn-rĭ-mĭt´ĭng) *adj.* constant; never stopping.

vacant (vā´kənt) *adj.* blank, expressionless.

vanquish (văng´kwĭsh) *v.* to defeat in a contest or conflict.

venture (věn´chər) *v.* to risk or dare.

vindicate (vĭn´dĭ-kāt) *v.* to demonstrate or prove the validity of; justify.

virtuous (vûr´cho͞o-əs) *adj.* having or showing virtue, especially moral excellence.

virulent (vîr´yə-lənt) *adj.* extremely hostile or malicious.

volatile (vŏl´ə-tl) *adj.* evaporating readily at normal temperatures and pressures.

watershed (wô´tər-shěd) *n.* a turning point, a crucial dividing line.

wring (rĭng) *v.* to obtain through force or pressure.

Index of Skills

Key

Teacher's Edition subject entries and page references are printed in **boldface** type. Subject entries and page references that apply to both the Student Edition and the Teacher's Edition appear in lightface type.

A

absurdity, 483
academic citations, 122, 200
Academic Vocabulary, 5, 17, 31, 53, 63, 77, 88, 99, 109, 123, 129, 139, 153, 165, 175, 187, 198, 209, 221, 229, 241, 249, 263, 287, 309, 320, 329, 337, 347, 359, 375, 393, 409, 423, 435, 446, 457, 479, 493, 503, 515, 525, 535, 553, 564, 573, 589, 599, 713, 725, 735, 757, 769, 779, 789, 801, 817, 826
act, 601
actions, 601, 603
active voice, 56, 60, 65, 89, 565
adaptation
    present, 309
    write, 309
addressee, 341
Again and Again (Notice & Note), 597
agreement, subject-verb, 132, 141
Aha Moment (Notice & Note), 586
allegory, 604
alliteration, 158, 243, 773
allusion, 48, 50, 55, 331, 397, 411, 480, 727, 739, 774
    analyze, 416, 418
ambiguity, 131, 269, 594
analysis, Create and Present, 423, 694
analyze
    allusion, 416, 418
    Analyze Media, 128, 358, 724
    Analyze the Text, 16, 30, 52, 62, 76, 80, 108, 122, 138, 152, 164, 174, 186, 190, 220, 228, 240, 248, 262, 266, 286, 308, 312, 336, 346, 374, 392, 408, 412, 422, 434, 438, 478, 492, 502, 514, 524, 534, 552, 556, 588, 598, 640, 664, 694, 712, 734, 756, 768, 778, 788, 800, 804, 816, 818
    argumentative texts, 101, 103, 107, 331, 335
    arguments, 397, 400, 402, 405, 739, 741, 742, 743, 744, 745, 747, 749, 750, 754
    audience, 727, 729, 732
    author's craft, 251, 254, 259
    author's message, 594, 596
    author's purpose, 55, 58, 169, 173, 179, 182, 184, 185, 331, 334, 379, 382, 383, 384, 386, 387, 388, 390, 397, 399, 403, 404, 406, 483, 485, 487, 489, 490, 527, 529, 532, 533, 539, 542, 547

author's use of language, 67, 71, 75
character, 459, 462, 463, 464, 467, 469, 474, 477, 603, 606, 610, 615, 618, 625, 634, 643, 649, 651, 660, 665, 668, 670, 687, 697, 701
characterization, 476, 575, 577, 578, 579, 585, 760, 765
development of key ideas, 223, 227
diction, 520, 521, 593, 595
digital text, 126
dramatic elements, 603, 620, 633, 643, 647, 655, 663, 672, 675, 676, 683, 685, 695, 698, 706
essays, 223, 225
evidence, 35, 38
figurative language, 233, 236, 237, 239
folk literature, 7, 10, 12, 14
idea development, 781, 784, 786
idiom meanings, 188
imagery, 245
informational text, 35, 41, 113, 115, 117, 119, 379, 381, 383, 385, 389, 390, 793, 797, 798
language, 55, 59, 61, 169, 179, 416, 418, 425, 431
letters, 341, 345
lines and stanzas, 243, 246
literary devices, 136, 604, 609, 628, 637, 658, 703, 709, 710, 774, 776, 777
literary elements, 131, 134, 269, 272, 275, 279, 281, 284, 285, 361, 363, 364, 365, 370, 371, 425, 428, 429, 575, 577, 578, 579, 585
media, 128
media effectiveness, 352, 354, 357
message, 727, 729, 732
mood, 291, 294, 295, 297, 300, 306
motivations, 603, 606, 610, 615, 618, 625, 634, 643, 649, 651, 660, 665, 668, 670, 687, 697, 701
multimodal text, 718, 722, 723
plot, 131, 133, 135, 137
plot structure, 21, 27, 28, 291, 293, 296, 300, 303, 305
poetry, 211, 214, 217, 593, 595, 773, 775, 777
point of view, 507, 509, 510, 513
rhetorical devices, 727, 730, 739, 746, 751, 753, 755
satire, 483, 485, 487, 489, 490
selections, 81

setting, 459, 462, 464, 468, 471, 473, 476, 575, 577, 579, 579, 585
sound devices, 158, 160, 162, 234, 236, 243, 246, 415, 417, 420
speaker, 157, 415, 418
structure, 113, 116, 212, 214, 215, 216, 218, 233, 237, 238, 269, 271, 272, 277, 278, 280, 298, 361, 365, 366, 369, 373
syntax, 520, 521, 593, 595
text structure, 101, 104, 106, 761, 766
thematic development, 21, 23, 29
theme, 157, 160, 163, 212, 214, 215, 216, 218, 233, 237, 238
tone, 169, 179, 183, 341, 344, 483, 488, 490, 781, 785, 787
voice, 47, 49, 51, 158, 160, 162, 169, 179, 181, 184, 415, 418
anaphora, 495
annotate. *See also* Annotation Model
Annotation Model, 8, 22, 36, 48, 56, 68, 102, 114, 132, 144, 158, 170, 180, 212, 224, 234, 244, 252, 270, 292, 332, 342, 362, 380, 398, 416, 426, 460, 484, 498, 508, 520, 530, 540, 576, 594, 604, 728, 740, 762, 774, 782, 794, 808
antagonist, 603
antonym, 5, 790
appeals, 101, 331, 412
    emotional, 412
    ethical, 336
    logical, 108, 412
Applying Academic Vocabulary, 12, 26, 40, 60, 72, 106, 118, 134, 148, 216, 226, 236, 284, 306, 343, 371, 382, 401, 406, 418, 464, 488, 512, 525, 532, 544, 549, 580, 636, 722, 732, 744, 766, 786, 798
appositive, 270, 283, 289
appositive phrase, 270, 283, 289
archaic vocabulary, 64
archetypes, 7, 10
argument, 397
    adapt for debate, 449
    analyze, 397, 400, 402, 405, 739, 741, 742, 743, 744, 745, 747, 749, 750, 754
    compare, 396, 412
    evaluate, 397, 400, 402, 405, 739, 741, 742, 743, 744, 745, 747, 749, 750, 754
    genre characteristics, 445
    genre elements, 397

presenting, 109, 503
reading, 314
writing, 77, 109, 221, 503
argument, write an
    author's craft, 445
    background reading, 443
    edit draft, 447
    mentor text use, 445
    organize ideas, 444
    plan for writing, 443
    publish, 447
    revise draft, 446
    Scoring Guide, 448
    writing prompt, 442
argumentative essay, 139, 789
argumentative texts, analyze, 101, 103, 107, 331, 335
ars poetica, 807
articles, reading, 314
ask questions, 143
assonance, 243
audience, 55, 179, 527, 539, 727, 793
    analyze, 727, 729, 732
    determine, 793, 796
author's craft
    analyze, 251, 254
    argument, 445
    elements of, 251
    mentor text, 197
    dramatic irony, 563
author's message, 21, 23, 30, 55, 85, 793
    analyze, 594, 596
    determine, 793, 796
author's purpose, 169, 179, 331, 379, 483, 527, 539
    analyze, 55, 58, 169, 179, 182, 184, 185, 331, 334, 379, 382, 383, 384, 386, 387, 388, 390, 397, 399, 403, 404, 406, 527, 529, 532, 533, 539, 542, 547
    compare, 80, 526, 538, 556–557
    determine, 126
    evaluate, 67, 70, 71, 72
autobiographical essay, 781
autobiographical sketch, create, 435
autobiography, 153
    genre elements, 425

B

background knowledge, 143
background reading
    argument, 443

explanatory essay, 318
    literary analysis, 85
    personal essay, 823
    research report, 195
    short story, 562
balanced sentences, 332, 334, 339
behavior, 459
bias, 30, 76, 194, 336, 734, 756
Big Questions (Notice & Note), 798
biographical essay, 347
blank verse, 593
blocking, 718
body
    article, 113
    letter, 341
brainstorm, 483

C

call to action, 101, 331, 412, 445
capitalization, 498, 505
casting, 718
cause and effect, 392, 502
characteristics of poetry. *See also* line
    breaks; poetry; stanzas
    line breaks, 519, 522
    stanzas, 519, 522
characterization, 12, 13, 15, 425, 761
    analyze, 476, 575, 577, 578, 579, 585,
      761, 765
    direct, 425, 603
    indirect, 425, 603
character motivation, 31, 269. *See also*
    motivation, character
characters
    analyze, 459, 462, 463, 464, 467, 469,
      474, 477, 603, 606, 610, 615, 618,
      625, 634, 643, 649, 651, 660, 665,
      668, 670, 687, 697, 701
    dialogue and, 716
    share and discuss, 435
    thematic development and, 21
chronological order, 113, 379
cite evidence, 62
    Analyze the Text, 122, 138, 174, 312,
      438, 478, 556, 588, 640, 664, 712
claim, 87, 331, 397, 408, 412
clauses, 79
clauses, noun, 342, 344, 349
climax, 603
Close Read Screencast, 57, 213, 333,
    462, 605
closing, letter, 341
clues, context, 264, 310, 504
coherence, 287, 762
Collaborate & Compare, 80–81, 166–167,
    190–191, 266–267, 312–313, 412–
    413, 438–439, 556–557, 804–805,
    818–819

collaborative discussion, 2, 96, 206, 326,
    454, 570
collective noun, 141
comedies, 601
compare
    across genres, 54, 66, 414, 424, 780,
      792, 804
    Analyze Media, 358, 724
    Analyze the Text, 190, 220, 266, 336,
      412, 552, 556, 804, 818
    arguments, 77, 396, 412
    author's purpose, 80, 526, 538, 556–557
    genres, 80
    main ideas, 250, 266, 267
    prepare to, 57, 69, 160, 162, 171, 181,
      253, 258, 271, 293, 399, 404, 417,
      427, 529, 541, 783, 795, 809, 812
    themes, 156, 166, 268, 290, 312, 313,
      806, 818
    types of sources, 81
    voice and tone, 168, 178, 190
    writer's voice, 438
comparison and contrast, 113
    essay, 409, 817
complex sentence, 155
complications, 603
compose. *See* develop draft
composition, photographs, 352
compound sentence, 155, 791
comprehension, monitor, 143, 150
concession, 497
conclusion, 101
    article, 113
    draw. *See* draw conclusions
    present, 91
    revise, 88
confirm predictions, 507, 511, 575, 581,
    582, 584, 586, 587
    Analyze the Text, 514
conflict, 603
    external, 425
    internal, 425
conjunction, subordinating, 79
connect
    Analyze Media, 358
    Analyze the Text, 16, 164, 186, 248,
      514, 523, 818
    research, 52, 138, 434, 478, 778
connections, make, 351, 355, 356, 717,
    720, 721
connotations, 67, 176, 288, 727, 736,
    770, 774
    negative, 72
connotative meaning, 436
consistent tone, 460
consonance, 243
contested usage, 180, 189
context, historical, 131

context clues, 32, 264, 310, 394, 504
contradictions. *See* Contrasts and
    Contradictions (Notice & Note)
contrasts, Analyze the Text, 80, 164, 166,
    438, 804
Contrasts and Contradictions (Notice &
    Note), 24, 121, 274, 389, 612, 691,
    707
conventions, 155
costuming, 718
counterarguments, 101, 739
    argumentative essay, 139
    Collaborate & Compare, 109
    evaluate, 497, 500, 501
Create and Debate
    argument, 77, 221
    didactic placard, 359
    essay, 187
Create and Discuss
    analysis, 423
    article, 757
    autobiographical sketch, 435
    autobiographies, 153
    compare and contrast essay, 409, 817
    dramatic reading, 409
    essay, 153, 229, 287, 713
    historical essay, 801
    historical report, 393
    letter, 175, 337
    literary analysis, 589, 779
    poem, 53, 241
    short story, 515
    small group discussion, 175, 229
    speech, 337
    story frame, 769
Create and Present
    adaptation, 309
    analysis, 694
    argument, 109, 503
    argumentative essay, 139, 789
    biographical essay, 347
    dramatic monologue, 31
    essay, 123, 129, 263
    evaluation of a play, 640
    informational text, 63
    multimedia presentation, 664
    myth, 17
    narrative, 553
    open letter, 735
    poem, 249, 525, 599
    prose adaptation, 165
    review, 479
    satire, 493
    short story, 375
    speech, 535
    theme board, 165
    treatment, 725
creation myth, 7

Critical Vocabulary, 8, 18, 22, 32, 36, 56,
    64, 68, 78, 102, 110, 114, 124, 132,
    140, 144, 154, 170, 176, 180, 188,
    224, 230, 252, 264, 270, 288, 292,
    310, 332, 338, 342, 348, 362, 376,
    380, 394, 398, 410, 426, 436, 460,
    480, 484, 494, 498, 504, 508, 516,
    530, 536, 540, 554, 576, 590, 728,
    736, 740, 758, 762, 770, 782, 790,
    794, 802
critics, opinions of, 514
critique
    Analyze Media, 358
    Analyze the Text, 816

D

Dark Romantics, 269
dashes, 199, 517, 555
    use in poetry, 233
date, on letter, 341
debate, 77, 139, 187, 221, 359
    adapt argument for, 449
    collaborate and, 805
    hold, 450
    practice for, 450
defend or challenge author's claims,
    109
denotation, 288, 736, 770
denotative meaning, 436
dependent clause, 68, 73, 79, 289
descriptions, annotate, 23
details
    evaluate, 7, 12, 35, 76, 103, 157, 166,
      167
    offer, from text, 87
    sensory, 517
develop a draft
    argument, 444
    explanatory essay, 318
    literary analysis, 86
    personal essay, 824
    report, 196
    short story, 563
develop key ideas, 223, 227
development of ideas, analyze, 781, 784,
    786
dialect, 426, 433, 437, 425
dialogue, 603, 604, 679
    create effective, 679
diction, 47, 55, 113, 169, 177, 179, 331,
    346, 425, 483, 520, 781
    analyze, 520, 521, 593, 595
dictionary, 124
didactic placard, 359
digital text, analyze, 126
direct characterization, 425, 603
direct quotation, 739
direct statements, in poetry, 212

discussion. *See* collaborative discussion; Create and Discuss; group discussion; panel discussion; small group discussion

domain-specific words, 111

draft writing. *See* develop a draft

drama
conventions of, 601
genre elements of, 603

dramatic elements, 603, 620, 633, 643, 647, 655, 663, 672, 675, 676, 683, 685, 695, 698, 706

dramatic irony, 563, 604, 637, 640

dramatic monologue, 31

dramatic production, aspects of, 718

dramatic reading, 409
present, 423, 525

draw conclusions
Analyze the Text, 16, 52, 76, 108, 138, 152, 174, 186, 408, 534, 552, 664, 694, 778, 788, 800, 816
word meanings, 264

E

edit draft
argument, 447
explanatory essay, 321
literary analysis, 89
personal essay, 827
report, 199
short story, 565

em dash, 199

emotional appeals, 412

end rhyme, 158

English
formal, 170, 177
Standard, 144, 155

English Learner Support, 1, 2, 8, 9, 10, 11, 12, 13, 15, 18, 19, 22, 23, 24, 25, 27, 29, 32, 33, 36, 38, 40, 41, 44, 45, 50, 51, 56, 58, 59, 60, 61, 64, 65, 68, 71, 75, 78, 79, 80, 82, 85, 86, 87, 88, 89, 91, 94, 96, 102, 104, 107, 110, 111, 114, 116, 117, 118, 120, 121, 124, 125, 126, 128, 132, 133, 134, 135, 136, 137, 140, 141, 144, 145, 146, 149, 151, 154, 155, 158, 159, 160, 161, 163, 170, 172, 173, 176, 177, 180, 183, 185, 188, 189, 190, 192, 195, 196, 197, 198, 199, 201, 204, 206, 207, 208, 212, 214, 216, 219, 224, 227, 230, 231, 235, 238, 239, 246, 247, 252, 254, 255, 257, 260, 261, 264, 266, 272, 274, 281, 285, 288, 289, 292, 293, 296, 301, 306, 307, 310, 311, 312, 314, 317, 319, 320, 321, 324, 326, 328, 333, 335, 338, 339, 342, 344, 345, 348, 349, 352, 357, 358, 360, 362, 365, 366, 368, 370, 371, 373, 376, 377, 380, 381, 384, 385, 387, 389, 391, 395, 398, 399, 402, 403, 404, 406, 407, 410, 411, 412, 417, 419, 421, 426, 432, 433, 436, 438, 440, 443, 444, 445, 446, 447, 449, 452, 454, 455, 460, 461, 463, 465, 466, 467, 471, 472, 474, 475, 477, 480, 481, 484, 486, 487, 491, 494, 495, 498, 500, 501, 504, 505, 508, 510, 512, 513, 516, 517, 522, 523, 528, 530, 531, 532, 533, 536, 537, 543, 545, 549, 551, 554, 555, 556, 558, 561, 562, 563, 564, 565, 568, 570, 572, 576, 577, 580, 581, 587, 590, 591, 594, 595, 597, 601, 606, 609, 610, 611, 615, 616, 619, 621, 623, 627, 631, 632, 635, 636, 639, 641, 642, 646, 650, 651, 652, 655, 656, 660, 661, 663, 665, 666, 670, 671, 673, 675, 676, 677, 678, 680, 682, 683, 684, 685, 692, 693, 695, 696, 698, 700, 701, 703, 711, 714, 715, 720, 723, 728, 730, 732, 733, 736, 737, 740, 742, 746, 748, 751, 755, 758, 759, 762, 765, 767, 770, 771, 774, 775, 777, 782, 784, 785, 786, 787, 790, 791, 794, 796, 797, 798, 799, 802, 803, 804, 811, 814, 815, 818, 820, 822, 824, 825, 826, 827

enunciation, 202

essay, 781
analyze, 223, 225
argumentative, 139
autobiographical, 781
biographical, 347
compare and contrast, 409, 817
Create and Discuss, 713
genre elements, 179
historical, 801
presenting, 12, 263
reading, 314
structure of, 825
writing, 123, 129, 153, 187, 229, 263, 287

essential appositive, 289

Essential Question, 1, 5, 6, 17, 20, 31, 34, 42, 53, 54, 63, 66, 77, 82, 84, 85, 92, 95, 99, 100, 109, 112, 123, 126, 129, 130, 139, 142, 153, 165, 168, 175, 178, 187, 192, 205, 210, 222, 232, 242, 250, 268, 290, 312, 325, 330, 340, 350, 360, 378, 396, 414, 424, 440, 453, 458, 482, 496, 506, 518, 538, 558, 560, 561, 569, 574, 592, 602, 716, 726, 738, 760, 772, 780, 792, 806, 820
reflect on, 93, 203, 323, 451, 567, 829

respond to, 5, 17, 31, 53, 63, 77, 99, 109, 123, 129, 139, 153, 165, 175, 187, 209, 221, 229, 241, 249, 263, 287, 309, 329, 337, 347, 359, 375, 393, 409, 423, 435, 457, 479, 493, 503, 515, 525, 526, 535, 553, 573, 589, 599, 713, 725, 735, 757, 769, 779, 789, 801, 817

establish a purpose. *See* Setting a Purpose

ethical appeal, 336

etymology, 111, 376

evaluate
Analyze Media, 128, 358
Analyze the Text, 62, 76, 80, 108, 122, 152, 166, 174, 186, 190, 228, 240, 248, 262, 266, 286, 336, 374, 392, 412, 434, 438
arguments, 397, 400, 402, 405, 739, 741, 742, 743, 744, 745, 747, 749, 750, 754
author's purpose, 67, 70, 71, 72
counterarguments, 497, 500, 501
details, 7, 12, 35, 76, 103, 157, 166, 167
evidence, 35
figurative language, 808, 811, 812
graphic features, 497, 500
literary devices, 774, 776, 777
nuances in meaning, 176
plot, 131, 133, 135, 137
print and graphic features, 143, 146, 147, 149
rhetorical devices, 739, 746, 751, 752, 753, 755
speech, 337

evaluation, write and share, 640

evidence, 101, 331, 397, 412. *See also* cite evidence
analyze, 35, 38
arguments, 739
cite, 122, 138, 174, 478, 556
evaluate, 35, 38
offer, from text, 87

exaggeration, 483

exclamations, 517

explanatory essay, writing, 316–322
background reading, 317
draft development, 318
edit draft, 321
mentor text, 319
organize ideas, 318
plan for writing, 317–318
publish, 321
revise draft, 320
Scoring Guide, 322
writing prompt, 316

explicit idea, 781

exposition, 601

extended metaphor, 240

external conflict, 425

Extreme or Absolute Language (Notice & Note), 148, 730

eye contact, 202

F

facial expression, 202

farces, 601

figurative language, 67, 233, 236, 237, 239, 563, 604, 781
evaluate, 808, 811, 812

figures of speech, 251
in poetry, 212

first-person point of view, 131, 361, 425

flashback, 21, 27

flash forward, 21

foil, 603

folk literature, 7
analyze, 10, 12, 14

foot, 234

foreign words and phrases, 74, 78, 590

foreshadowing, 28, 633

formal English, 170, 177

formal language, 231

fragments, 791

frame story, 761

free verse, 211, 212, 519

freewriting, 47

From Reading to Writing (Notice & Note), 85, 317, 443, 561, 823

G

gather information, 17, 31, 53, 63, 77, 109, 123, 129, 139, 153, 165, 175, 187, 221, 229, 241, 249, 263, 287, 309, 337, 347, 359, 375, 393, 409, 423, 435, 479, 493, 503, 515, 525, 535, 553, 589, 599, 713, 725, 735, 757, 769, 779, 789, 801, 817

genre, 55, 804
characteristics, 197
compare across, 414, 424, 780

Genre Elements
argument, 397
ars poetica, 807
autobiographical essay, 781
autobiography, 143, 425
blank verse, 593
drama, 603
essay, 179, 223, 251
free verse, 211, 243, 519
historical narrative, 55
history writing, 113, 379, 793
informational text, 35, 251
investigative journalism, 539
letter, 169, 341
multimodal text, 497
novel, 527
open letter, 727
photojournalism, 351

poetry, 47, 157, 233, 415, 773
production images, 717
public document, 101
satire, 482
short story, 21, 131, 269, 291, 361, 459, 507, 575, 761
speech, 331, 739
video, 126
gestures, 202
graphic features, 143
evaluate, 143, 146, 147, 149, 497, 500
informational video, 126
group discussion, 63, 241, 337, 393, 413, 435, 515, 757

H

historical context, 131
historical essay, 801
historical narrative, 55, 379
historical report, 393
history writing, 113, 379, 793
humor, 483
hyperbole, 251
hyphenation, 114, 125

I

idea development, analyze, 781, 784, 786
ideas
develop key, 223, 227
explicit or implicit, 781
organize for writing, 86, 196, 318, 444, 562, 824
present, 129, 725
ideas, main, 781
compare, 250, 266–267
compare across genres, 792, 804
support, 319
identify, Analyze the Text, 422
idiom, 188, 426, 428, 437, 774
determine meaning of, 714
illustrate, 129
imagery, 17, 67, 76, 212, 244, 774, 781, 808
images, production, 717
imperative mood, 740, 759
implicit idea, 781
Improve Reading Fluency, 14, 27, 39, 69, 120, 149, 184, 255, 281, 299, 363, 386, 429, 466, 470, 475, 582, 611, 635, 649, 672, 683, 703, 754, 813
independent clause, 68
Independent Reading, 82–83, 192–193, 314–315, 440–441, 558–559, 820–821
indirect characterization, 425, 603
infer, 7
Analyze the Text, 16, 52, 80, 152, 166, 190, 220, 228, 248, 266, 308, 346,

374, 392, 492, 514, 534, 588, 598, 640, 734, 778, 788, 800
author's purpose, 67
beliefs and customs, 7, 11, 13, 15
poem's theme, 157
infinitive phrases, 36, 39
infinitives, 36, 39
informal style, 224, 226, 231
information
present, 201
synthesize, 527, 530, 539, 543, 546, 548, 550
informational text, 35, 113
analyze, 35, 41, 113, 115, 117, 119, 793, 797, 798
Create and Present, 63
information gathering. *See* gather information
Instructional Overview and Resources, 1A–1D, 94A–94F, 204A–204D, 324A–324F, 452A–452D, 568A–568H
internal conflict, 425, 761
internal rhyme, 158, 166
interpret, Analyze the Text, 30, 52, 138, 164, 166, 186, 220, 228, 240, 248, 262, 286, 379, 381, 383, 385, 389, 390, 408, 412, 422, 434, 523, 598, 694, 712, 768, 788
interview, present, 553
inverted syntax, 47, 50
investigative journalism, genre elements, 539
irony, 113, 251, 483, 514
verbal, 341

K

key ideas, summarize to identify, 22, 251

L

language
analyze, 55, 59, 61, 169, 179, 416, 418, 425, 431
author's use of, 67, 71, 75
Extreme or Absolute (Notice & Note), 148
figurative, 67, 233, 236, 237, 239, 563, 604, 781, 808
formal vs. informal, 231
sensory, 362, 368, 377, 827
Language Conventions
active and passive voice, 56, 60, 65, 89, 565
anaphora, 484, 486, 495
appositives and appositive phrases, 270, 283, 289
balanced sentences, 332, 334, 339
capitalization, 498, 499, 505
clauses, 68, 78

consistent tone, 481
contested usage, 180, 182, 189
dashes, 199, 540, 545, 555
dependent clauses, 73, 79
dialect, 426, 433, 437
dialogue, 604, 679, 715
effective sentences, 508, 511, 517
formal English, 170, 177
hyphenation, 114, 120, 125
idioms, 426, 428, 437
imperative mood, 740, 759
infinitives and infinitive phrases, 36, 39
informal style, 224, 226, 231
misplaced modifiers, 380, 387, 395
parallelism, 484, 495
parallel structure, 102, 105, 111
point of view, 576, 583, 591
prepositions and prepositional phrases, 530, 532, 537
reflexive pronouns, 8, 11, 19
rhetorical devices, 398, 400, 411
rhetorical questions, 251, 252, 255, 265
semicolons, 292, 302, 311, 321
sensory language, 362, 368, 377, 827
sentence structure, 728, 731, 737
sentence variety, 150, 782, 784, 791
spelling, 794, 803
Standard English, 144, 155
subject–verb agreement, 132, 134, 141
subordinate clauses, 73, 79
tone, 460, 470
transitions, 762, 763, 771
verb tenses, 22, 25, 33, 447
word choice and tone, 172
Language X-Ray: English Learner Support, 84B, 194B, 316B, 442B, 560B, 822B
Latin roots, 154
Learning Mindset, 1, 34, 42, 54, 62, 82, 84, 93, 94, 112, 122, 130, 138, 192, 194, 202, 204, 232, 240, 260, 314, 316, 323, 324, 330, 336, 414, 422, 440, 442, 451, 452, 458, 478, 526, 534, 558, 560, 567, 568, 602, 640, 738, 756, 820, 822, 829
letter
analyze, 341, 345
genre elements, 169, 341
open, 727, 735
writing, 175, 337
lighting, 718
limited point of view, 507
line breaks, 234, 243, 519, 522, 773
lines of poetry, analyze, 243, 246
literary analysis
Create and Discuss, 589
write, 779
literary analysis, writing a, 84–89
background reading, 85

claim or thesis statement, 87
details and evidence, 87
develop draft, 86–87
edit draft, 89
language conventions, 89
organize ideas, 86
plan for writing, 85–86
publish, 89
revise draft, 88
writing prompt, 84
literary devices, 251
analyze, 136, 604, 609, 628, 637, 658, 703, 709, 710, 774, 776, 777
literary elements, 21, 53
analyze, 131, 134, 269, 272, 275, 279, 281, 284, 285, 361, 363, 364, 365, 370, 371, 425, 428, 429
characterization, 575, 577, 578, 579, 585
setting, 575, 577, 579, 585
literature
folk, 7
reading, signposts/anchor questions for, 82, 192, 314, 440, 558, 820
logical appeal, 108, 412
logical fallacy, 739

M

main ideas, 781
compare, 250, 266, 267
supporting, 319
make and confirm predictions, 507, 511, 575, 581, 582, 584, 586, 587
make connections, 351, 355, 356, 717, 720, 721. *See also* connect
make inferences, 7, 11, 13, 15, 169. *See also* infer
make predictions. *See* make and confirm predictions; predict
meaning
connotative, 436
denotative, 436
draw conclusions about, 264
idioms, 188
multiple-meaning words, 18, 124
nuances in, 176, 288, 494
media, analyze, 128, 352, 354, 357, 358
melodramas, 601
Memory Moment (Notice & Note), 366
mental image, 17
create, 519, 523
Mentor Text, 34A, 34, 84, 87, 112A, 112, 194, 197, 250A, 250, 316, 319, 396A, 396, 442, 445, 506A, 506, 560, 563, 780A, 780, 822, 825
mentor text use, for writing
argument, 445
explanatory essay, 319
literary analysis, 87

personal essay, 825
research report, 197
short story, 562
message, 55, 179, 527, 539, 727
analyze, 727, 729, 732
metaphor, 52, 251, 739, 808
extended, 240
meter, 158, 234
misplaced modifiers, 380, 387, 395
modern American drama, 600–601
conventions of drama, 601
rise of American drama, 600
themes in, 600
trend toward realism, 600
modifiers, misplaced, 380, 387, 395
monitor comprehension, 143, 150
monologue, dramatic, 31
mood, 21, 33, 520, 593, 759. *See also* tone
analyze, 291, 294, 295, 297, 298
imperative, 740, 759
moral dilemmas, 603, 761
motivation, character, 31, 269, 459
analyze, 603, 606, 610, 615, 618, 625,
634, 643, 649, 651, 660, 665, 668,
670, 687, 697, 701
multimedia presentation, 664
multimodal text
analyze, 718, 722, 723
genre elements, 497
multiple-meaning words, 18, 124, 516
myth, 7, 17

N

narrative
historical, 55, 379
write, 553
narrative techniques, 21
narrator, 361
naturalism, 459
negative connotations, 72
nonessential appositive, 289
nonfiction, signposts/anchor questions
for reading, 82, 192, 314, 440, 558,
820
nonverbal techniques, 202, 450
Notice & Note
Again and Again, 597
Aha Moment, 586
Big Questions, 798
Contrasts and Contradictions, 24, 121,
274, 389, 612, 691, 707
Extreme or Absolute Language, 148,
730
From Reading to Writing, 85, 195, 317,
443, 561, 823
Memory Moment, 366
Quoted Words, 40, 172, 226, 335, 749
Tough Questions, 431
Word Gaps, 74, 549

Words of the Wiser, 467, 766
noun, collective, 141
noun clauses, 342, 344, 349
novel, genre elements, 527
nuances in word meaning, 176, 494

O

omniscient narrator, 507
open letter
genre elements, 727
write, 735
organizational design, 793
outside source, 143

P

panel discussion, 92. *See also* Participate
in a Panel Discussion
paradox, 240, 604, 727
parallel construction, 495. *See also*
parallelism
parallelism, 102, 111, 331, 397, 411, 495,
739, 791
parallel structure, 102. *See also*
parallelism
paraphrase, 47
Analyze the Text, 52
inverted syntax, 47, 50
poetry, 52
parenthetical element, 555
Participate in a Panel Discussion, 91–92
passive voice, 56, 60, 65, 89, 565
past tense, 22
peer review, 198, 320, 446, 564, 826
persona, poem's speaker, 157
personal essay
develop a draft, 824
edit draft, 827
mentor text use, 825
organize ideas, 824
plan for writing, 823
publish, 827
revise draft, 826
Scoring Guide, 828
writing prompt, 822
personal narrative, 769
personification, 251, 774
photojournalism, 352
genre elements, 351
phrases
appositive, 270
precise, 517
pitch, 202
plan for writing
argument, 443
explanatory essay, 318
literary analysis, 85,
personal essay, 823
report, 195
short story, 562

plays, reading, 314
plot, 131, 603
analyze, 131, 133, 135, 137
dialogue and, 716
evaluate, 131, 133, 135, 137
thematic development and, 21
plot structure, analyze, 21, 27, 28
poems/poetry
analyze, 211, 214, 217, 593, 595, 773,
775, 777
characteristics of, 519, 522
compare and contrast ideas about, 819
Create and Present, 599
discuss, 53, 241
discuss literary elements in, 779
genre elements, 35, 157, 415, 773
paraphrase, 52
present, 249
reading, 314
write, 525, 53, 241, 249
point of view, 131, 361, 507, 576
analyze, 507, 509, 510, 513
choose effective, 591
first-person, 361, 425
third-person limited, 361
third-person omniscient, 361
Practice and Apply
critical vocabulary, 18, 32, 64, 78, 110,
124, 140, 154, 176, 188, 230, 264,
288, 310, 338, 348, 376, 394, 410,
436, 480, 494, 504, 516, 536, 554,
590, 736, 758, 770, 790, 802
language conventions, 19, 33, 65, 79,
111, 125, 141, 155, 177, 189, 231,
265, 289, 311, 339, 349, 377, 395,
411, 437, 481, 495, 505, 517, 537,
555, 591, 715, 737, 759, 771, 791, 803
vocabulary strategy, 18, 32, 64, 78, 111,
124, 140, 154, 176, 188, 230, 264,
288, 310, 338, 348, 376, 394, 410,
436, 480, 494, 504, 516, 536, 554,
590, 714, 736, 758, 770, 790, 802
precise words and phrases, 517
predict, 12, 75, 182, 251, 253, 278, 305
predictions, make and confirm, 507, 511,
514, 575, 581, 582, 584, 586, 587
prefixes, 140
prepositional phrase, 530, 537
prepositions, 530, 537
present. *See also* Create and Present;
presentation
argument, 503
biographical essay, 347
collaborate and, 313
dramatic reading, 423, 525
ideas, 267, 725
interview, 553
letter, 735
literary analysis, 91–92

poem, 599
research report, 201–202
review, 479
satire, 493
speech, 535
presentation
deliver, 92, 202
practice, 202
multimedia, 664
present tense, 22
Present Your Ideas, 81
primary source, 35, 38, 54, 55, 80, 81, 194
print and digital resources, vocabulary
strategy, 230
print features, 143
evaluate, 143, 146, 147, 149
production images, genre elements, 717
pronouns, reflexive, 8, 11, 19
pronunciation, 338
prose adaptation, writing, 165
protagonist, 603
public document, genre elements, 101
publish
argument, 447
explanatory essay, 321
literary analysis, 89
report, 199
short story, 565
punctuation, poetry, 234
purpose. *See also* author's purpose
analyze author's, 55, 58, 67, 70, 71,
72, 80
determine author's, 126
mentor text and, 319
purpose for reading. *See* Setting a
Purpose

Q

questions
anchor, 314
ask, 143
rhetorical, 251
quotation, direct, 739
Quoted Words (Notice & Note), 40, 172,
226, 335, 749

R

reading, dramatic, 409
realism, 459
rise of, 328
trend toward, 600
reasons, 101, 397
rebuttal, 497
Reflect on the Unit, 93, 203, 323, 451,
567, 829
reflexive pronouns, 8, 11, 19
relevant sources, 194, 195
repetition, 55, 158, 234, 251, 397, 411,
517, 727, 739

reread, 143
research, 3, 16, 30, 52, 62, 76, 97, 108, 122, 128, 138, 152, 164, 174, 186, 207, 220, 228, 240, 248, 262, 286, 308, 455, 478, 492, 502, 514, 524, 534, 552, 557, 571, 588, 598, 712, 724, 734, 756, 768, 778, 788, 800, 816
research report, writing, 194–203
　adapt for presentation, 201–202
　author's craft, 197
　background reading, 195
　develop draft, 196
　edit draft, 199
　genre characteristics, 197
　language conventions, 199
　mentor text use, 197
　organize ideas, 196
　plan for writing, 195–196
　publish, 199
　revise draft, 198
　scoring guide, 200
　thesis, 196
　writing prompt, 194
resolution, 603
resources, print and digital, 230
Response Logs, 5, R1–R6
review
　peer, 198
　present, 479
　write, 479
revise draft
　argument, 446
　explanatory essay, 320
　literary analysis, 88
　personal essay, 826
　report, 198
　short story, 564
rhetorical devices, 55, 331, 397, 398, 400, 411, 727. See also entries for specific devices
　analyze, 727, 730, 739, 751, 752, 753, 755
　evaluate, 739, 746, 751, 752, 753, 755
rhetorical question, 251, 252, 255, 265, 739
rhyme, 158
rhyme scheme, 233, 234
rhythm, poetry, 158, 211, 234, 415
root word, 154
　Latin, 154

S

salutation, 341
satire, 483
　analyze author's purpose, 483, 485, 487, 489, 490
　genre elements, 483
　present, 493
　write, 493

scene, 601
Scoring Guide
　argument, 448
　explanatory essay, 322
　literary analysis, 90
　personal essay, 828
　research report, 200
　short story, 566
script, 601, 717
secondary source, 54, 80, 81, 194
second-person point of view, 131
selections, analyze, 81
semantic map, 110
semicolons, 292, 302, 311, 321
sensory details, 517
sensory language, 362, 368, 377, 827
sentences
　compound, 791
　effective, 508, 517
　simple, 791
　types of, 155
sentence structure, 728
　balanced, 332, 334, 339
　determine word meanings through, 348
　varied, 737
sentence variety, 782, 784, 791
set design, 718
setting, 131, 459, 575
　analyze, 459, 462, 464, 468, 471, 473, 476, 575, 577, 579
　dialogue and, 716
　thematic development and, 21
Setting a Purpose, 9, 23, 37, 49, 82, 103, 115, 127, 133, 145, 192, 214, 225, 236, 245, 314, 333, 343, 354, 363, 381, 440, 461, 485, 499, 509, 521, 558, 577, 595, 606, 719, 729, 741, 763, 775, 820
short story
　Create and Present, 375
　discuss, 515
　genre elements, 21, 131, 361, 575, 459, 507, 761
　write, 515
short story, write a
　author's craft, 563
　background reading, 562
　develop a draft, 563
　edit draft, 565
　mentor text use, 563
　organize ideas, 563
　plan for writing, 561
　publish, 565
　revise draft, 564
　Scoring Guide, 566
　writing prompt, 560
signature, 341
signpost, 85
simile, 67, 251, 739, 808

simple sentence, 155, 791
slant rhyme, 234
small group discussion, 175, 229, 287, 393, 515, 589, 713, 817
sound devices, 158
　analyze, 158, 160, 162, 415, 417, 420
　poetry, 234, 236, 243, 246
sound elements, informational video, 126
source
　biased, 76
　compare types of, 81
　objective, 76
　outside, 143
　primary, 55, 80, 81, 194
　relevant, 194, 195
　secondary, 80, 81, 194
speaker, 415
　analyze, 415
　poem's, 157, 211
speaking rate, 202
specialized vocabulary, 78
speech
　evaluate, 337
　genre elements, 331, 739
　present, 535
　write, 535
spelling, 791, 803
stage directions, 601
Standard English, 144, 155
stanza, 47, 51, 233, 519, 522
　analyze, 243, 246
stories, reading, 314
story frame, 769
structure, 47, 101. See also text structure
　analyze, 113, 116, 212, 214, 215, 216, 218, 233, 237, 238, 269, 271, 272, 277, 278, 280, 298, 361, 365, 366, 369, 373
　arguments, 739
　mentor text and, 319
　personal essay, 825
　plot, 291, 293, 296, 300, 303, 305
　poetry, 212, 214, 215, 216, 218, 233, 237, 238
　sentence, 728, 731, 737
　story, 269, 271, 277, 278, 280, 761
style
　informal, 224, 226, 231
　personal essay, 825
　writer's, 292
style guides, 155
subjects, photographic, 352
subject–verb agreement, 132, 141
subordinate clause, 68, 73, 79. See also dependent clause
subordinating conjunction, 79
suffixes, 140, 410, 758
summarize, 30, 63, 77, 88, 92, 251, 253, 256, 258, 260, 261

Analyze Media, 128
Analyze the Text, 174, 186, 262, 434, 816
support, 397
suspense, 131, 269, 425
symbol, 269
　in poetry, 212
synonym, 5, 56, 436, 790
syntax, 79, 101, 113, 169, 177, 179, 425, 483, 508, 517, 520, 737, 791
　analyze, 520, 521, 593, 595
synthesize information, 527, 530, 539, 543, 546, 548, 550
Analyze Media, 724
Analyze the Text, 62, 76, 190, 286, 308, 312, 346, 422, 502, 534, 552, 556, 588
　collaborate to, 312
　information, 267

T

technical terms, 67, 554
text. See also Analyze the Text
　argumentative, 101, 103, 107
　informational, 35, 41, 113, 115, 117, 119
Text Complexity, 6A, 20A, 34A, 46A, 54A, 66A, 100A, 112A, 126A, 130A, 142A, 156A, 168A, 178A, 210A, 222A, 232A, 242A, 250A, 268A, 290A, 330A, 340A, 350A, 360A, 378A, 396A, 414A, 424A, 458A, 482A, 496A, 506A, 518A, 526A, 538A, 574A, 592A, 600A, 716A, 726A, 738A, 760A, 772A, 780A, 792A, 806A
text evidence. See evidence
text structure, 101, 104, 106. See also structure
　analyze, 761, 766
Text X-Ray: English Learner Support, 6C–6D, 20C–20D, 34C–34D, 46C–46D, 54C–54D, 66C–66D, 100C–100D, 112C–112D, 126C–126D, 130C–130D, 142C–142D, 156C–156D, 168C–168D, 178C–178D, 210C–210D, 222C–222D, 232C–232D, 242C–242D, 250C–250D, 268C–268D, 290C–290D, 330C–330D, 340C–340D, 350C–350D, 360C–360D, 378C–378D, 396C–396D, 414C–414D, 424C–424D, 458C–458D, 482C–482D, 496C–496D, 506C–506D, 518C–518D, 526C–526D, 538C–538D, 574C–574D, 592C–592D, 600C–600D, 716C–716D,

726C–726D, 738C–738D,
760C–760D, 772C–772D,
780C–780D, 792C–792D,
806C–806D
thematic development, analyze, 21, 23, 29
theme, 21, 271, 807
analyze, 157, 160, 163
compare, 156, 166, 268, 290, 312, 313,
806, 818
determine, 807, 809, 812
dialogue and, 716
modern American drama, 600
poetry, 157, 212, 214, 215, 216, 218,
233, 237, 238, 244
point of view and, 361
theme board, presenting, 165
theme statement, create, 313
thesaurus, 124
thesis, 101, 331
article, 113
thesis statement, 87, 223
third-person point of view, 131, 507
limited, 361
omniscient, 361
**To Challenge Students, 12, 25, 59, 81,
85, 119, 150, 171, 181, 195, 217,
262, 269, 280, 298, 304, 317, 364,
369, 384, 388, 390, 405, 413, 430,
443, 465, 469, 473, 489, 503, 521,
545, 547, 550, 561, 579, 586, 596,
608, 610, 622, 629, 645, 648, 653,
657, 669, 674, 676, 682, 690, 698,
709, 710, 721, 753, 763, 784, 809,
823**
tone, 47, 55, 67, 169, 179, 341, 379, 392,
460, 481, 483, 520, 593, 781
analyze, 169, 179, 183, 341, 344, 483,
488, 490, 781, 785, 787
compare voice and, 168, 178, 190
consistent, 481
Tough Questions (Notice & Note), 431
tragedy, 601
transitions, 762, 763, 771
treatment, write, 725

U

understatement, 341
universal characters, 7. *See also*
archetypes
usage, contested, 180, 189

V

verbal irony, 251, 341
verbal techniques, 202, 450
verb tenses, 22, 25, 33, 447
vocabulary
Academic Vocabulary, 5, 17, 31, 53, 63,
77, 88, 99, 109, 123, 129, 139, 153,
165, 175, 187, 198, 209, 221, 229,
241, 249, 263, 287, 309, 320, 329,
337, 347, 359, 375, 393, 409, 423,
435, 446, 457, 479, 493, 503, 515,
525, 535, 553, 564, 573, 589, 599,
713, 725, 735, 757, 769, 779, 789,
801, 817, 826
archaic vocabulary, 64
Critical Vocabulary, 8, 18, 22, 32, 36,
56, 64, 68, 78, 102, 110, 114, 124,
132, 140, 144, 154, 170, 176, 180,
188, 224, 230, 252, 264, 270, 288,
292, 310, 332, 338, 342, 348, 362,
376, 380, 394, 398, 410, 426, 436,
460, 480, 484, 494, 498, 504, 508,
516, 530, 536, 540, 554, 576, 590,
728, 736, 740, 758, 762, 770, 782,
790, 794, 802
specialized vocabulary, 78
Vocabulary Strategy
allusions, 480
antonyms, 790
archaic vocabulary, 64
connotation, 770
context clues, 32, 310, 394, 504
denotation, 770
domain-specific words, 111
etymology, 376
foreign words and phrases, 590
idioms, 188, 714
Latin roots, 154
multiple-meaning words, 18, 516
nuances in meaning, 176, 288, 494
precise meaning of words, 736
prefixes and suffixes, 140
print and digital resources, 124, 230
pronunciation, 338
suffixes, 410, 758
synonyms, 436, 790
technical terms, 554
word families, 536, 802
word meanings, 264, 348
word origins, 480

voice, 65, 169, 179, 415, 593
active and passive, 65
analyze, 47, 49, 51, 158, 160, 162, 169,
179, 181, 184, 415
compare tone and, 168, 178, 190
compare writer's, 438
personal essay, 825
poem, 158
voice modulation, 202
volume, 202

W

**When Students Struggle, 3, 11, 16, 24,
28, 30, 37, 49, 52, 56, 76, 83, 86, 92,
97, 105, 108, 115, 127, 135, 146,
152, 162, 164, 167, 169, 174, 186,
191, 193, 196, 199, 202, 207, 215,
220, 225, 228, 237, 245, 248, 256,
258, 275, 286, 295, 297, 302, 308,
313, 315, 318, 321, 327, 334, 344,
346, 355, 365, 366, 372, 374, 383,
392, 400, 404, 408, 420, 423, 431,
434, 439, 441, 444, 447, 450, 456,
463, 468, 472, 476, 487, 492, 502,
511, 514, 522, 524, 531, 542, 546,
552, 557, 559, 562, 565, 571, 578,
583, 585, 588, 598, 600, 607, 614,
617, 620, 624, 630, 631, 638, 643,
655, 659, 660, 662, 667, 668, 686,
688, 692, 697, 699, 702, 704, 707,
712, 719, 724, 731, 734, 745, 749,
764, 768, 776, 778, 785, 788, 797,
800, 805, 810, 812, 816, 819, 821,
824, 827**
word choice, 67. *See also* diction
word families, 154, 536, 802
Word Gaps (Notice & Note), 74, 544, 549
word meanings. *See also* meaning
draw conclusions about, 264
nuances in, 288
sentence structure to determine, 348
Word Network, 5, 99, 209, 329, 457, 573
word origins, 480
word root, 5
words
context clues for, 32
denotation of, 176
determine precise meaning of, 736
domain-specific, 111
multiple-meaning, 18, 124, 516
precise, 517

quoted, 40
Words of the Wiser (Notice & Note),
467, 766
write
analysis, 423
argument, 503
autobiographical sketch, 435
biographical essay, 347
compare and contrast essay, 817
essay, 713
historical essay, 801
historical report, 393
history, 379, 793
literary analysis, 589
narrative, 553
poetry, 525, 599
prompt, 316
review, 479
satire, 493
short story, 375, 515
speech, 535
writer's style. *See* style
writing process
develop draft, 86, 196, 318, 444, 563,
824
edit draft, 89, 199, 321, 447, 565, 827
plan for writing, 85, 195, 318, 443,
562, 823
publish, 89, 199, 321, 447, 565, 827
revise draft, 88, 198, 320, 446, 564, 826
writing prompt
explanatory essay, 316
literary analysis, 84
report, 194
argument, 442
personal essay, 822
short story, 560

INDEX OF TITLES AND AUTHORS

A

Acosta, Teresa Palomo, 245
Adams, Abigail, 171
Ambush, 763
Anderson, Jourdon, 343
Autobiography, The (excerpt), 145

B

Balboa, 23
Baldwin, James, 729
Because I could not stop for Death, 237
Bierce, Ambrose, 363
Bradford, William, 57
Bradstreet, Anne, 49
Brady, Matthew, 353
Building the Transcontinental Railroad
   (excerpt from *The Chinese in
   America*), 381

C

Chang, Iris, 381
Chernow, Ron, 115
Chicago, 521
Chopin, Kate, 509
Civil War Photographs, 353
Cofer, Judith Ortiz, 812
Coming of Age in the Dawnland (excerpt
   from *1491*), 69
Crucible, The, 605, 719
Declaration of Independence, The, 103
Declaration of Sentiments, 399
Desperate Trek Across America, A, 37

D

Dickinson, Emily, 235
Dunbar, Paul Laurence, 162

F

Faulkner, William, 577
Food Product Design (excerpt from *Fast
   Food Nation*), 541
Franklin, Benjamin, 145
Frost, Robert, 595

G

Gardner, Alexander, 353

H

Hawthorne, Nathaniel, 271
Hayden, Robert, 417
*Here Follow Some Verses Upon the Burning
   of Our House, July 10th, 1666*, 49
How It Feels to be Colored Me, 783

Hurston, Zora Neale, 783

I

In the Season of Change, 245
Incidents in the Life of a Slave Girl
   (excerpt), 427
Iroquois storytellers, 9

J

Jacobs, Harriet, 427
Jefferson, Thomas, 103
Johnson, Charles, 133
Jungle, The (excerpt), 529

K

King, Martin Luther, Jr., 741

L

Last Child in the Woods (excerpt), 258
Latin Deli, The: An Ars Poetica, 812
Lean In (excerpt), 181
Letter to John Adams, 171
Lincoln, Abraham, 333
London, Jack, 461
Louv, Richard, 258
Lowest Animal, The, 485

M

Mann, Charles C., 69
Marr, Bernard, 499
Mending Wall, 595
Miller, Arthur, 605
Minister's Black Veil, The, 271
Moore, Marianne, 809
Much Madness is divinest Sense, 238
Murray, Sabina, 23
*My Dungeon Shook: Letter to My
   Nephew*, 729
My Friend Walt Whitman, 225

O

O'Brien, Tim, 763
Occurrence at Owl Creek Bridge, An, 363
Of Plymouth Plantation (excerpt), 57
Oliver, Mary, 225
On Being Brought from Africa to America,
   159

P

Pit and the Pendulum, The, 293
Poe, Edgar Allan, 293
Poetry, 809

R

Reséndez, Andrés, 37
Rose for Emily, A, 577
Runagate Runagate, 417
Russell, Andrew J., 353

S

Sandberg, Sheryl, 181
Sandburg, Carl, 521
Schlosser, Eric, 541
Second Inaugural Address, 333
Sinclair, Upton, 529
Smith, Tracy K., 775
Soldier for the Crown, A, 133
Song of Myself (excerpt), 213
Soul selects her own Society, The, 236
Speech on the Vietnam War, 1967, 741
*Speech to the American Equal Rights
   Association*, 404
Stanton, Elizabeth Cady, 399
Story of an Hour, The, 509
Sympathy, 162

T

Tell all the Truth but tell it slant, 239
Thomas Jefferson: The Best of Enemies, 115
Thoreau, Henry David, 253
To Build a Fire, 461
To My Old Master, 343
Truth, Sojourner, 404
Twain, Mark, 485

U

Universe as Primal Scream, The, 775

W

Walden (excerpt), 253
Walt Whitman, 213
Warmth of Other Suns, The (excerpt), 795
Wheatley, Phillis, 159
*Why Everyone Must Get Ready for the
   Fourth Industrial Revolution*, 499
Wilkerson, Isabel, 795
World on the Turtle's Back, The, 9

ACKNOWLEDGMENTS

"Ambush" from *The Things They Carried* by Tim O'Brien. Text copyright © 1990 by Tim O'Brien. Audio copyright © 1990 by Tim O'Brien. Reprinted by permission of Houghton Mifflin Harcourt Publishing Company, Tim O'Brien, HarperCollins Publishers Ltd., and Janklow and Nesbit Associates.

"Balboa" from *Tales of the New World* by Sabina Murray. Text copyright © 2011 by Sabina Murray. Reprinted by permission of Grove/Atlantic, Inc. Any third-party use of this material, outside of this publication, is prohibited.

"Because I could not stop for Death," "Much madness is divinest Sense," "The Soul selects her own Society," and "Tell all the truth but tell it slant" from *The Poems of Emily Dickinson* edited by Thomas H. Johnson. Text copyright © 1951, 1955, renewed 1979, 1983 by the President and Fellows of Harvard College. Text copyright © 1914, 1918, 1919, 1924, 1929, 1930, 1932, 1935, 1937, 1942 by Martha Dickinson Bianchi. Text copyright © 1952, 1957, 1958, 1963, 1965 by Mary L. Hampson. Reprinted by permission of The Belknap Press of Harvard University Press, Cambridge, Mass.

"Building the Transcontinental Railroad" from *The Chinese in America: A Narrative History* by Iris Chang. Text copyright © 2003 by Iris Chang. Reprinted by permission of Viking Books, an imprint of Penguin Publishing Group, a division of Penguin Random House LLC. All rights reserved. Any third-party use of this material, outside of this publication, is prohibited. Interested parties must apply directly to Penguin Random House LLC for permission.

The Crucible by Arthur Miller. Text copyright 1952, 1953, 1954, renewed © 1980, 1981, 1982 by Arthur Miller. Reprinted by permission of Viking Books, an imprint of Penguin Publishing Group, a division of Penguin Random House LLC, and The Wylie Agency LLC. All rights reserved. Any third-party use of this material, outside of this publication, is prohibited. Interested parties must apply directly to Penguin Random House LLC for permission.

"A Desperate Trek Across America" by Andrés Reséndez from *American Heritage*, Fall 2008, Vol. 58, Issue 5. Text copyright © 2008 by American Heritage Publishing. Reprinted by permission of American Heritage Publishing via Copyright Clearance Center.

Excerpt from *Fast Food Nation: The Dark Side of the All-American Meal* by Eric Schlosser. Text copyright © 2001 by Eric Schlosser. Any third party use of this material, outside of this publication, is prohibited. Interested parties must apply directly to Penguin Random House, Inc. for permission. Reprinted by permission of Houghton Mifflin Harcourt, Penguin Books Ltd., Random House Audio Publishing Group, a division of Penguin Random House LLC, and the author. All rights reserved.

Excerpt from *1491: New Revelations of the Americas Before Columbus* by Charles C. Mann, map by Nick Springer and Tracy Pollack of Springer Cartographics LLC. Text and illustration copyright © 2005 by Charles C. Mann. Any third party use of this material, outside of this publication, is prohibited. Interested parties must apply directly to Penguin Random House LLC for permission. Reprinted by permission of Alfred A. Knopf, an imprint of the Knopf Doubleday Publishing Group, a division of Penguin Random House LLC, Granta Publications, and Roam Agency on behalf of Charles C. Mann. All rights reserved.

"The World on the Turtle's Back" from *The Great Tree and the Longhouse: The Culture of the Iroquois* by Hazel W. Hertzberg. Text copyright © 1966 by American Anthropological Association. Not for sale or further reproduction. Reprinted by permission of American Anthropological Association.

"In the Season of Change" by Teresa Palomo Acosta. Text copyright © 1994 by Teresa Palomo Acosta. Reprinted by permission of the author.

From *Last Child in the Woods* (Introduction) by Richard Louv. Text copyright © 2005 by Richard Louv. Reprinted by permission of Algonquin Books of Chapel Hill. All rights reserved.

"The Latin Deli: An Ars Poetica" by Judith Ortiz Cofer from *The Americas Review*, Vol. 19, No. 1. Text copyright © 1991 by Arte Público Press - University of Houston. Reprinted by permission of Arte Público Press - University of Houston.

Excerpt from *Lean In: Women, Work, and the Will to Lead* by Sheryl Sandberg. Text copyright © 2013 by Lean In Foundation. Reprinted by permission of Alfred A. Knopf, an imprint of the Knopf Doubleday Publishing Group, a division of Penguin Random House LLC and William Morris Endeavor Entertainment, LLC. All rights reserved. Any third-party use of this material, outside of this publication, is prohibited. Interested parties must apply directly to Penguin Random House LLC for permission.

"The Lowest Animal" from *Letters from the Earth* by Mark Twain, edited by Bernard DeVoto. Text copyright © 1938, 1944, 1946, 1959, 1962 by The Mark Twain Company. Text copyright 1942 by The President and Fellows of Harvard College. Reprinted by permission of HarperCollins Publishers.

"My Dungeon Shook: Letter to My Nephew on this One Hundredth Anniversary of the Emancipation" by James Baldwin. Text copyright © 1962, 1963 by James Baldwin. Copyright renewed. Originally published in *The Progressive*. Collected in *The Fire Next Time*, published by Vintage Books. Reprinted by arrangement with the James Baldwin Estate.

"My Friend Walt Whitman" from *Blue Pastures* by Mary Oliver. Text copyright © 1995 by Mary Oliver. Reprinted by permission of Houghton Mifflin Harcourt Publishing Company.

"Poetry" from *The Collected Poems of Marianne Moore* by Marianne Moore. Text copyright © 1935, renewed 1963 by Marianne Moore. Reprinted with the permission of Scribner, a Division of Simon & Schuster, Inc., and Literary Estate of Marianne Moore, David M. Moore, Executor.

"A Rose for Emily" from *Collected Stories of William Faulkner* by William Faulkner. Text copyright 1930, renewed 1958 by William Faulkner. All rights reserved. Any third party use of this material, outside of this publication, is prohibited. Interested parties must apply directly to Random House LLC for permission. Reprinted by permission of Random House, an imprint and division of Penguin Random House LLC, W. W. Norton & Company, Inc., and Curtis Brown Group Ltd, London on behalf of The Estate of William Faulkner. All rights reserved.

ACKNOWLEDGMENTS

"Runagate Runagate" from *Collected Poems of Robert Hayden* by Robert Hayden, edited by Frederick Glaysher. Text copyright © 1966 by Robert Hayden. Reprinted by permission of Liveright Publishing Corporation.

"A Soldier for the Crown" from *Soulcatcher and Other Stories* by Charles Johnson. Text copyright © 1998 by Charles Johnson. Reprinted by permission of the WGBH Educational Foundation.

Excerpt from "Speech on the Vietnam War, New York City, April 4, 1967" by Martin Luther King, Jr. Text copyright © 1967 by Dr. Martin Luther King, Jr., renewed 1991 by Coretta Scott King. Reprinted by permission of Writers House on behalf of the Heirs of the Estate of Martin Luther King, Jr.

"Thomas Jefferson: The Best of Enemies" by Ron Chernow from *Time Magazine*, July 5, 2004. Text copyright © 2004 by Time, Inc. Reprinted by permission of Time, Inc. All rights reserved.

"The Universe as Primal Scream" from *Life on Mars* by Tracy K. Smith. Text copyright © 2011 by Tracy K. Smith. Reprinted by permission of The Permissions Company, Inc., on behalf of Graywolf Press, Minneapolis, Minnesota. www.graywolfpress.org

Excerpt from *The Warmth of Other Suns: The Epic Story of America's Great Migration* by Isabel Wilkerson. Text copyright © 2010 by Isabel Wilkerson. Any third party use of this material, outside of this publication, is prohibited. Interested parties must apply directly to Penguin Random House LLC for permission. Used by permission of Random House, an imprint and division of Penguin Random House LLC and ICM Partners. All rights reserved.

"Why Everyone Must Get Ready For the 4th Industrial Revolution" by Bernard Marr from Forbes.com, April 5, 2016. Text copyright © 2016 by Bernard Marr. Reprinted by permission of Bernard Marr.